A Companion to Shakespeare and Performance

Blackwell Companions to Literature and Culture

This series offers comprehensive, newly written surveys of key periods and movements and certain major authors, in English literary culture and history. Extensive volumes provide new perspectives and positions on contexts and on canonical and post-canonical texts, orientating the beginning student in new fields of study and providing the experienced undergraduate and new graduate with current and new directions, as pioneered and developed by leading scholars in the field.

Recently Published

For a full list of titles available in the Blackwell *Companions to Literature and Culture* series, please visit www.blackwellpublishing.com/literature

A COMPANION TO

SHAKESPEARE
AND
PERFORMANCE

EDITED BY **BARBARA HODGDON**
AND **W. B. WORTHEN**

WILEY-BLACKWELL
A John Wiley & Sons, Ltd., Publication

Library of Congress Cataloging-in-Publication Data

A companion to Shakespeare and performance / edited by Barbara Hodgdon and W.B. Worthen.
p. cm.—(Blackwell companions to literature and culture)
Includes bibliographical references and index.
ISBN 978-1-4051-1104-1 (hard cover : alk. paper)—ISBN 978-1-4051-8821-0 (pbk)
1. Shakespeare, William, 1564–1616—Dramatic production—Handbooks, manuals, etc.
2. Shakespeare, William, 1564–1616—Film and video adaptations—Handbooks, manuals, etc.
I. Hodgdon, Barbara, 1932– II. Worthen, William B., 1955– III. Series.

PR3091.C64 2005
822.3'3—dc22
2005006322

A catalogue record for this book is available from the British Library.

Set in 11/13pt Garamond 3 by SPi Publisher Services, Pondicherry, India
Printed and bound in Malaysia by KHL Printing Co Sdn Bhd

1   2008

Contents

Illustrations

Notes on Contributors

Susan Bennett is University Professor and Professor of English at the University of Calgary. Her book *Performing Nostalgia: Shifting Shakespeare and the Contemporary Past* (1996) looked at the ideological investments of contemporary performances of Shakespeare's plays in both traditional and non-traditional theatre settings. "Shakespeare on Vacation" is one of a series of essays she has written on the subject of theatre and tourism.

James C. Bulman is Henry B. and Patricia Bush Tippie Chair of English at Allegheny College. General Editor of the *Shakespeare in Performance* Series for Manchester University Press, he has published a stage history of *The Merchant of Venice* (1991) and the anthologies *Shakespeare, Theory, and Performance* (1996) and *Shakespeare on Television* (1998). He currently is editing *Henry IV, Part Two* for the Arden Shakespeare.

Richard Burt is Professor of English and Film and Media Studies at the University of Florida. He is the author of *Medieval and Early Modern Film and Media* (2008), *Unspeakable ShaXXXspeares: Queer Theory and American Kiddie Culture* (1998), and *Licensed by Authority: Ben Jonson and the Discourses of Censorship* (1993). He has published numerous articles on Shakespeare, censorship, and medieval film and is the editor of six books, including the two-volume *Shakespeares After Shakespeare: An Encyclopedia of the Bard in Mass Culture and Popular Culture* (2006) and *Shakespeare After Mass Media* (2001).

Michael Cordner is Ken Dixon Professor of Drama in the Department of Theatre, Film and Television at the University of York, England. He is General Editor of Oxford English Drama for Oxford University Press and has published editions of plays by Farquhar, Etherege, Vanbrugh, Otway, Lee, Dryden, Southerne, and Sheridan. He is writing monographs on the relationships between Shakespearean editing and performance and on the Restoration comedy of marriage, 1660–1688. He also regularly directs early modern plays – most recently, James Shirley's *Hyde Park* and John Marston's *The Malcontent*.

Anthony B. Dawson is Professor of English emeritus at the University of British Columbia and a former President of the Shakespeare Association of America. His books include *Indirections: Shakespeare and the Art of Illusion* (1978), *Watching Shakespeare* (1988), *Hamlet* (Shakespeare in Performance series, 1995), and, with Paul Yachnin, *The Culture of Playgoing in Shakespeare's England* (2001). He has recently published an edition of *Troilus* *and Cressida* for the New Cambridge Shakespeare series (2003), and, with Gretchen Minton, is currently editing *Timon of Athens* for the Arden Shakespeare.

Elizabeth A. Deitchman received her PhD from the University of California, Davis. Her chapter in this volume is drawn from her doctoral dissertation entitled "Shakespeare's American Dreams: Movies and Millennial Culture." She is now working as a professional actor in the San Francisco Bay Area.

Peter S. Donaldson is Professor of Literature and Director of the Shakespeare Electronic Archive at MIT. He is the author of *Machiavelli and Mystery of State* (1988) and of *Shakespearean Films/Shakespearean Directors* (1990) and of many articles on Shakespeare on Film and on digital media. Currently he is working on XMAS, a cross media annotation system to support the creation and remote sharing of multimedia essays using DVDs, and on a book on Shakespeare media crossings.

Miriam Gilbert is Professor of English at the University of Iowa. Her work in performance criticism includes studies of *Love's Labour's Lost* (1993) and *The Merchant of Venice* (The Arden Shakespeare, 2002), as well as essays on teaching Shakespeare through performance.

John Gillies teaches at the University of Essex. In addition to various articles and book chapters, he is the author of *Shakespeare and the Geography of Difference* (1994), co-editor (with Virginia Mason Vaughan) of *Playing the Globe: Genre and Geography in English Renaissance Drama* (1998); and co-editor (with Ryuta Minami and Ian Carruthers), of *Performing Shakespeare in Japan* (2001). He also has co-authored two multimedia packages: "Shakespeare in Japan: Deguchi Norio," and "Performing Shakespeare in China, 1980–90."

Stuart Hampton-Reeves is Professor of English and Drama at the University of Central Lancashire, where he has developed programs in Drama, Theatre Studies and e-learning. His research interests include Shakespeare in performance, the history plays, and the study of performance cultures. He is a founder member of the British Shakespeare Association and the performance editor of the journal *Shakespeare*.

Diana E. Henderson is Associate Professor of Literature at the Massachusetts Institute of Technology, where she also teaches in the Comparative Media Studies and Women's Studies Programs. Her publications include *Passion Made Public: Elizabethan Lyric, Gender, and Performance* (1995), numerous articles on early modern poetry and drama, and the forthcoming *Shake-shifters: The Art of Collaborating with Shakespeare Across Time and Media*. She is editing Blackwell's *Concise Companion to Shakespeare on Screen*.

Margo Hendricks is Associate Professor of Literature at University of California, Santa Cruz. Co-editor of *Women, Race, and Writing in the Early Modern Period* (1994), she has published on Marlowe, Shakespeare, race and Renaissance culture, and Aphra Behn and has recently completed a study of race, color passing, and early modern English literature. Her current research explores race and Shakespeare; a future project will examine African women in Renaissance English culture.

Barbara Hodgdon is Professor of English at the University of Michigan and Ellis and Nelle Levitt Distinguished Professor Emerita at Drake University. Her books include: *The Shakespeare Trade: Performances and Appropriations* (1998), *Henry IV, Part One: Texts and Contexts* (1997), *Henry IV, Part Two*, Shakespeare in Performance Series (1993), and *The End Crowns All: Closure and Contradiction in Shakespeare's History* (1991). She was guest editor of a special issue of *Shakespeare Quarterly* (Summer 2002) on Shakespeare films; she is currently editing *The Taming of the Shrew* for the Arden 3 Shakespeare series.

Peter Holland is McMeel Family Professor in Shakespeare Studies and Department Chair of the Department of Film, Television, and Theatre at the University of Notre Dame, Indiana. Previously he was Director of the Shakespeare Institute of the University of Birmingham at Stratford-upon-Avon. His publications include the Oxford edition of *A Midsummer Night's Dream* (1994) and *English Shakespeares: Shakespeare on the English Stage in the 1990s* (1997). He is editor of *Shakespeare Survey*.

Margaret Jane Kidnie is Associate Professor of English at the University of Western Ontario. She has published on textual studies, performance, and adaptation, edited *Ben Jonson: The Devil is an Ass and Other Plays* (2000), and co-edited with Lukas Erne *Textual Performances: The Modern Reproduction of Shakespeare's Drama* (2004). Her *Philip Stubbes: The Anatomie of Abuses* (2002) was awarded Honorable Mention by the MLA Committee on Scholarly Editions. She is currently editing *A Woman Killed with Kindness*, preparing a *Handbook to The Taming of the Shrew*, and writing a monograph on Shakespearean performance and adaptation.

Ric Knowles is Professor of Theatre Studies at the University of Guelph, and Member of the Graduate Faculty at the University of Toronto. He is editor of the periodicals *Modern Drama* and *Canadian Theatre Review*, and author of the award-winning *The Theatre of Form and the Production of Meaning* (1999), *Shakespeare and Canada* (2004), and *Reading the Material Theatre* (2004). He is also editor of *Theatre in Atlantic Canada* (1985) and co-editor of *Modern Drama: Defining the Field* (2003) and *Staging Coyote's Dream: An Anthology of First Nations Drama in English* (2003). He is general editor of the Playwrights Canada series, *Critical Perspectives on Canadian Theatre*.

Douglas Lanier is Associate Professor of English at the University of New Hampshire. He has written a number of studies of Shakespeare and popular adaptation, as well as articles on Jonson, Milton, the Jacobean masque, and literature pedagogy. His book, *Shakespeare and Modern Popular Culture* was published in 2002. He is currently working on a bibliography of popular film adaptations for *Shakespeare Alive!*, ed. Richard Burt (2005) as well as a book project concerning cultural stratification and the early modern British stage.

Courtney Lehmann is Professor of English and Film Studies and Director of the Humanities Center at the University of the Pacific. She is an award-winning teacher, author of *Shakespeare Remains: Theater to Film, Early Modern to Postmodern* (2002), and co-editor, with Lisa S. Starks, of *Spectacular Shakespeare* and *The Reel Shakespeare* (both 2002). She is currently completing a book on Shakespeare, film, and feminism.

Peter Lichtenfels is Professor of Theatre at University of California, Davis, where he teaches acting and directing. He is presently co-editing *Romeo and Juliet*, and *The Fifth Wall* with Lynette Hunter for Arden. He has been Artistic Director of the Traverse Theatre, Edinburgh, The Leicester Haymarket Theatre and directs worldwide. Most recently he has directed Sartre's *The Flies* for The Stratford Festival of Canada.

James N. Loehlin is Director of the Shakespeare at Winedale Program and Regents Professor of English at the University of Texas, Austin. He has published works on the performance dimensions of *Henry V* (1996), *Romeo and Juliet* (2002) and *Henry IV, Parts I and II* (2008), as well as Chekhov's *The Cherry Orchard* (2006). He has written articles on

Shakespearean film, performance and pedagogy, and has directed more than 30 productions of Shakespeare's plays.

Ania Loomba is Catherine Bryson Professor of English at the University of Pennsylvania. She is author of *Gender, Race, Renaissance Drama* (1988), *Colonialism/Postcolonialism* (1998) and *Shakespeare, Race and Colonialism* (2002).

Kathleen McLuskie is Director of the Shakespeare Institute at Stratford-upon-Avon. Her published work includes an edition of *Plays on Women* (2000), a collection of essays on Shakespeare and Modernism (2001) and essays on the feminist and economic implications of early modern theatre. Her current research explores "Selling Shakespeare," a study of aesthetic resistance to consumerism from early modern times to the present day.

Laurie E. Osborne is the Chair and Professor of English at Colby College. She has published *The Trick of Singularity: Twelfth Night and the Performance Editions* (1996) as well as several essays on Renaissance audiences and Shakespeare in film and popular culture. Her most recent work includes "Clip Art: Theorizing the Shakespearean Film Clip" in *Shakespeare Quarterly* 54 (2002), "Cutting Up Characters in Trevor Nunn's *Twelfth Night*" in *Spectacular Shakespeare: Critical Theory and Popular Cinema* (2002) and an in-progress essay entitled "Narrating the Stage/Staging Narrative."

Simon Palfrey grew up in Australia and was a Rhodes Scholar at Oxford. His publications include *Late Shakespeare: A New World of Words* (1997), *Doing Shakespeare* (The Arden Shakespeare, 2004), "Macbeth and Kierkegaard," *Shakespeare Survey* 57 (2004), and (with Tiffany Stern) *Shakespeare in Parts* (2005). He currently teaches at the University of Liverpool.

Peggy Phelan is the Ann O'Day Maples Chair in the Arts and Professor of Drama, Stanford University, California. She is the author of the Survey essays for *Art and Feminism* ed. by Helena Reckitt (2001) and *Pipilotti Rist* (2001). She is also the author of *Mourning Sex: Performing Public Memories* (1997) and *Unmarked: The Politics of Performance* (1993). She co-edited *The Ends of Performance* (1997) with Jill Lane, and with the late Lynda Hart, she co-edited *Acting Out: Feminist Performances* (1993). Currently she is writing a book entitled *Twentieth Century Performance*.

Paul Prescott is Assistant Professor of English at the University of Warwick, and has acted and taught Shakespeare in the UK, the USA, and Japan. His publications include *Richard III* (Palgrave Shakespeare Handbooks), introductions to *Coriolanus* and *Hamlet* (New Penguin Shakespeare), and 'Declan Donnellan and Cheek by Jowl' (*Routledge Companion to Directors' Shakespeare*). His current projects include *Shakespeare and the Director* (with Dennis Kennedy, Oxford Shakespeare Topics).

Carol Chillington Rutter is Professor of English at the University of Warwick and Director of the CAPITAL Centre, a government-funded Centre of Excellence in Teaching and Learning. Her books include *Clamorous Voices: Shakespeare's Women Today* (1988), *The Documents of the Rose Playhouse* (1984, 1999), *Enter the Body: Women and Representation on Shakespeare's Stage* (2001), and, with Stuart Hampton-Reeves, *Henry VI in Performance* (2006). Her most recent book is *Shakespeare and Child's Play: Performing Lost Boys on Stage and Screen* (2007). She holds a Warwick Award for Teaching Excellence.

Richard Schoch is Professor of Drama at Queen Mary, University of London. He is the author of *Shakespeare's Victorian Stage* (1998), *Not Shakespeare* (2002), and *Queen Victoria and* *the Theatre of her Age* (2004) and the recipient of fellowships from the Folger Shakespeare Library, the Leverhulme Trust, and the Stanford Humanities Center.

G. B. Shand is Professor of English and Drama Studies at York University's Glendon College in Toronto, Canada. He has published widely on text and performance in early modern drama, and has assisted on numerous stage productions in Canada and England.

Robert Shaughnessy is Professor of Theatre at the University of Kent. His publications include *Representing Shakespeare: England, History and the RSC* (1994) and *The Shakespeare Effect: A History of Twentieth-Century Performance* (2002), and, as editor, *The Cambridge Companion to Shakespeare and Popular Culture* (2007).

Bruce R. Smith, College Distinguished Professor of English at the University of Southern California, is the author of *The Key of Green: Passion and Perception in Renaissance Culture* (2008), *Shakespeare and Masculinity* (2000), *The Acoustic World of Early Modern England* (1999), *Homosexual Desire in Shakespeare's England* (1991), and *Ancient Scripts and Modern Experience on the English Stage 1500–1700* (1988). In addition to other fellowships, he has held an International Globe Fellowship at Shakespeare's Globe in London.

Tiffany Stern is author of *Rehearsal from Shakespeare to Sheridan* (2000) and *Making Shakespeare* (2004) and editor of the anonymous *King Leir* (2000) and Sheridan's *The Rivals* (2004). She is currently completing one book that she is co-writing with Simon Palfrey, *Shakespeare in Parts*, and writing another entitled *The Fragmented Playtext*.

Joanne Tompkins teaches at the University of Queensland, Australia. She researches in the area of postcolonial, multicultural, and intercultural theatre, and is the co-author of *Post-Colonial Drama* (with Helen Gilbert, 1996) and *Women's Intercultural Performance* (with Julie Holledge, 2000). A co-editor of *Modern Drama*, she is currently investigating spatiality in theatre, including the use of virtual reality to assist in the analysis of space.

Wendy Wall is Professor of English at Northwestern University, Illinois, with a specialization in early modern literature and culture. She is author of *The Imprint of Gender: Authorship and Publication in the English Renaissance* (1993) and *Staging Domesticity: Household Work and English Identity in Early Modern Drama* (2002), as well as co-editor for *Renaissance Drama*. She is currently at work on a book entitled *Reading Food: A Culinary History from Shakespeare to Martha Stewart*.

W. B. Worthen is Professor and Chair of the Department of Theatre at Barnard College. He is the author of *The Idea of the Actor* (1984), *Modern Drama and the Rhetoric of Theater* (1992), *Shakespeare and the Authority of Performance* (1997), *Shakespeare and the Force of Modern Performance* (2003), and *Print and the Poetics of Modern Drama* (2006). He is also the editor of several volumes, including the *Wadsworth Anthology of Drama*.

Yong Li Lan is Associate Professor at the National University of Singapore, where she teaches theatre history and intercultural theatre; she also is head of the Theatre Studies Programme. She is co-editor, with Dennis Kennedy, of *Foreign Shakespeare 2: Performance in the New Asias* (forthcoming) and the author of essays on intercultural and internet Shakespeare.

Acknowledgments

Like a theatrical performance, a collection such as this one depends on those behind the scenes, on collaborative labor which brings critical performances into view as a book. Here, Emma Bennett played a starring role: her invitation to frame this project as well as her enthusiastic support and guidance have been crucial at every stage of the process. The entire Blackwell team has provided generous and gracious help, and we would like in particular to mention production editors Karen Wilson and Anna Oxbury, Susan Dunsmore, whose meticulous attention to contributors' essays has helped to shape the manuscript's final stages, Marie Lorimer, and Ann Dean. Credits for photographs and images appear in captions, but the following individuals and archives have been especially helpful: John Bunting, Jeremy Butler, The Guildhall Library, Metro Imaging, Pentagram, Photofest Inc., Photomosaic, Robert Silvers, The Shakespeare Birthplace Trust, and The Stratford Festival Archives. Special thanks also to Susie Evans at Shakespeare's Globe, Helen Hargest at The Shakespeare Centre Library, David Howells, Curator of the Royal Shakespeare Company Collection, and Mark Slaughter at Cheek by Jowl.

To all, our deep thanks.
Barbara Hodgdon
W. B. Worthen

Introduction: A Kind Of History

Barbara Hodgdon

Prologue

Just as James C. Bulman's *Shakespeare, Theory, and Performance* (1996) identified itself as "taking arms against the theoretical presuppositions of the previous generation of performance critics," this *Companion to Shakespeare and Performance* brings together a group of critics who are in the process of reconfiguring the intricate instabilities and contingencies that emerge in conversations "about" and "between" Shakespeare and performance. Certainly, the present climate of disciplinary shifts and cross-disciplinary allegiances constitutes an ideal moment to reassess past critical strategies and to experiment with or reinvent new ones. Mining work of the recent past, the chapters in this collection move to explore the fictions and frictions that currently weave through, collide with, and (re)mark its two central terms or keywords (Williams 1985) – "Shakespeare" and "performance" – at this moment in time. The voices represented here constitute a "beginning *again*" – a double witnessing that, while courting continuities between past and present, seeks to reshape critical practices, critical re-performances.

Act 1

It has become *de rigueur* in reconceptualizing critical projects to search for foundational moments. How did the study of Shakespearean performances engage with the enthusiastic exploration of a performance past, traditionally the province of theatre history? The path that project follows does not take form as a linear narrative but instead twists and turns and is bound to a current consciousness of "history" and historical representation in general, complicated by what Vivian Sobchack (2000) calls "our own historically-altered sense of what 'being-in-time' in relation to 'the past' feels like." The work that framed, sustained, and provoked an earlier generation of writing to and writing back from performance can be represented by a (no means complete) catalogue of players: Bernard Beckerman (*Shakespeare at the Globe*, 1962), John Russell Brown (*Shakespeare's Plays in Performance*, 1966), Michael Goldman (*Shakespeare and the Energies of Drama*, 1972), and J. L. Styan, whose *The Shakespeare Revolution* (1977) forged links between theatre history and the imaginative recreation of dramatic texts to proclaim "a new role for stage-centered criticism" (Bulman 1996: 1). Although it risks oversimplification, for these critics, "Shakespeare" represented "an ever-fixed mark," the pole star governing both performance and critical practice (Shakespeare, Sonnet 116). Just as any performance began with (or from) Shakespeare, critical performances measured distances to and from authorial origin and agency, marked out reading strategies that, however derivative of literary methodologies – especially New Criticism – also took account of what Philip C. McGuire called the plays' "theatrical dimension" (1979). The (unspoken) ideal (it was not, as yet, an ideology) of this stage-centered critical practice had to do with attempting to discern Shakespeare's "intentions," with revealing the theatrical strategies traced out on the printed page. Despite Peter Brook's dictum that if a play is permitted to speak for itself, it may not make a sound (Brook 1968: 38), the implicit notion was that it could do so.

By the early 1980s, the idea that the *place* to study the plays was the theatre – whether that meant actual performance spaces, classroom theatres, or theatres of the mind's eye – had taken hold. Given a name – "performance criticism" – it also had become (at least partially) institutionalized. Yet the very act of naming reveals the extent to which the study of Shakespeare as a performed event existed on the margins of Shakespeare studies. Even at the time but certainly at this distance, "performance criticism" sounds uncomfortably oxymoronic: a label in which "criticism" gives legitimacy to the messy, contradictory, slightly suspect materiality of theatrical culture. Generically open, performance criticism encompassed an eclectic mix of critical styles and practices: reviews, from thumbnail notices in various journals (notably *Shakespeare Quarterly* or *The Shakespeare Newsletter*) to longer accounts of productions and actors' performances, primarily of major British or Canadian theatrical companies' seasons, such as those published annually in *Shakespeare Survey*; essays praising or finding fault with revivals, monitoring Shakespeare's presence or conducting mourning rites over his absence; and, less often, the theoretically-inflected essay attempting to chart the "gap" between text and performance, literature and theatre, the absent agency of the text and the present agency of the actor. Around mid-decade, that move achieved stasis, became stalled into repetitions of the same. Somewhat curiously, this resting point is where those who still respond adversely to the linkages joining Shakespeare and performance imagine the project still is. And as the term performance has gained increasing currency in the precincts of literary studies, responsive and responsible critics have indeed come to make ritual gestures toward "performance," mentioning it in footnotes or bringing it forward to illustrate an otherwise literary, text- or context-based argument. Significantly, that essentially marginal activity marks the very difficulty of mobilizing performance to address text.

Act 2

Meanwhile, methodologies and vocabularies from adjacent fields – anthropology, sociology, semiotics – burred onto writing of and about performance. Following Victor Turner and Clifford Geertz, whose work already had been mined by Stephen Greenblatt's "cultural poetics" (Turner 1982, Geertz, 1973, Greenblatt 1988), stage-centered critics took an ethnographic turn, wrote "thick descriptions" of Shakespeare performance events, usually (though not always) from a (potentially colonizing) literary perspective outside "native" theatrical culture. In addition, work by Patrice Pavis (1982; see also Barthes 1972, Elam 1980) brought vocabularies of semiotics to bear on the project. In many ways, though, it was Derrida's critique of *writing*, which paradoxically located the text as prior to *speech*, that made the greatest impact on performance theory's encounter with the drama in the 1980s and 1990s (Derrida 1974). On the one hand, of course, it enabled a wide range of theorists, notably Herbert Blau (1982), to undo the supplementary character of the concept of perform-ance in traditional dramatic criticism. At the same time, though, while one might take the Derridean critique precisely to deconstruct the opposition between writing and speech, to many critics, Derrida's undoing of the traditional priority seemed merely to restore the priority of the text. In an odd sense, this notion of the text pervades the more disheveled practices of the New Historicism, for while the New History was able to find textuality – and, of course, subversion – everywhere, the one place where the profoundly ambivalent metaphoricity of "thickly" textualized social practice was not often found was the stage. In a related way, even those critics committed to reading bodies onstage found it useful – both critically and discipli-narily – to adopt the tools of the mastering discourse of literature: what once had been called Shakespeare's play-in-performance or a "playtext" (McGuire 1985) now ac-quired a borrowed alias: "performance text."

Retrospectively, that phrase marked the initial sign of what became a gradual shift toward "performance studies," the field then on the way to becoming institutionalized as a discipline by Richard Schechner and others (Schechner 1985, Phelan 1997). At such a moment of "high textuality," conceptualizing a performance as a text, thereby affirming that it could be *read like a text*, constituted a powerful if limited move. And again, that move followed a direction already taken by film studies, where the formal analysis of film texts had been instrumental in legitimizing and institutionalizing film as a disciplinary area of study. However, one effect of that naming was to shape resistance into what became a long-standing controversy, formalized as a "text vs. performance" debate – in Harry Berger, Jr.'s phrase, between the "Slit-eyed Analyst" and the "Wide-eyed Playgoer" (Berger 1989) – over reading, hearing, and viewing practices. Staged, the text was perceived as finite: given a local habitation and requiring attention to the obduracy of actors' bodies and voices and their potential to displace and intrude between Shakespeare and the critic, performance was perceived as a consumable "product" of text to which the deconstructive reader had no key, a detriment or impasse which blocked the potentially infinite variety and mobility that could be achieved through detailed, moment-to-moment engagement with Shakespeare's book. Of course, one might think that in comparison to the mute inscriptions of the page, the delicate nuances of an actor's simplest gesture are nearly infinite in their signifying potentiality, so that a moment-to-moment engagement with performance might well lead to a sense of the many unexplored journeys, alternate interpretations, signaled by a given production. But the notion of the multiplicity of the stage's signification has been radically restrained by the sense that it's the page that permits the reader's freedom.

Simultaneously, Shakespeare studies, that narrowly expansive (another oxymoron) branch or offshoot of early modern studies (Jacob Burckhardt's "Renaissance" had by this time been debunked by Michel Foucault), consolidated into an historical discipline. Situating Shakespeare's texts within historical contexts as well as exploring their textual histories became required protocol, "always historicize" the rule for the new age of historiography. And the historical narratives being told were inflected (some would say infected) and managed not only by Foucault, Fredric Jameson and others (Foucault 1971, Jameson 1981) but also by further developments within literary theory. Ideology was on everyone's lips; postmodernism, postcolonial theory, feminist theory, queer theory, cultural studies, and film studies were colonizing, or being colonized by, Shakespeare studies. How might Shakespearean performance move toward theory? How might theory move toward Shakespearean performances? As though addressing these questions, the title of Bulman's landmark collection put theory smack between "Shakespeare" and "performance." The project formerly called "performance criticism" now had a middle term.

Act 3

To the extent that *Shakespeare, Theory, and Performance* set out to re-map the territory, part of what made that possible had to do with developments at another front, at sites of performance itself. Not only were more exciting performances being staged (Peter Brook's "Deadly Theatre" had given way, at least in some quarters, to something like "Immediate Theatre" [Brook 1968]), but cross-disciplinary allegiances with cultural studies and film studies also had generated a quickened awareness of media other than theatre. Television, video-cassette recorders, DVD technology, and computers broadened considerably the sense of what performance is, what it does, and what it might be made to do. And just as theatrical performance itself opened up to technology, so too did pedagogical practice: the film clip played beside the text; entire courses were devoted to Shakespeare films; with increasing frequency, classrooms became laboratories for exploring the plays in rehearsal, as process.

Certainly by now most had tacitly affirmed that plays (or playtexts) were not repositories of unitary meaning but were open sites of negotiation among text, performers, and audiences where textual obligation met performative option head on. By the mid-1990s, as fantasy histories of early modern theatre practice gave way to present-day histories, it became possible to include as part of the project stagings directed by Ariane Mnouchkine, Peter Sellars or Yukio Ninagawa; films by Peter Greenaway or Derek Jarman; or even Fred Curchack's one-man *What Fools These Mortals Be*. Whether drawing from Brecht, Beckett, Noh, Kabuki or kathakali, Shakespearean performances increasingly and freely borrowed, assimilated or reworked theatrical traditions, forms and styles in order to keep going, but where did alterity see its own reflection in such criss-crossing networks of cultural exchange? Although the push to configure such performances in terms of "old" textual paradigms and formalist theory remains, these as well as others that raided non-Shakespearean sources and "foreign" cultures themselves push against those paradigms: rather than conforming to the previous ideal of merely interpreting Shakespeare, such performances make their own meanings and so invite, even demand, different ways of seeing, of saying – and of writing.

Also figuring in the mix were popular films, especially those which, tracking away from "Shakespeare's text" *qua* text (Baz Luhrmann's *Romeo + Juliet* 1996; Richard Loncraine's *Richard III* 1997; Michael Almereyda's *Hamlet* 2000) moved fluently between high and low culture, one moment voicing "Shakespeare," the next registering resistance (Hall 1981). What did it mean to find a "popular" Shakespeare, one embedded in a culture of mass-mediation? Or to come to terms with the somewhat uneasy co-existence of Shakespeare in relation to a fluid, omnipresent panorama of other performances – advertising, comic books, music, video games, digital media? "Shakespeare +," one might say. Yet despite easy talk of adaptations, appropriations, off-shoots, spin-offs, and crossing boundaries and borders, the relationship of such performances "to" Shakespeare has as yet no adequate term, and has received only limited theorization: existing vocabularies either have seemed inefficient or have collapsed in on themselves (see Massai 2005).

Act 4

Concomitantly, several other developments contributed to a shift in the Shakespeare–performance dyad. Following the death of the author (and the subject) and the waning of grand narratives as explanatory devices for both historians and critics, Richard Schechner (1992) proclaimed the death of dramatic theatre, calling it "the string quartet of the 21st century: a beloved but extremely limited genre, a subdivision of performance." There was, of course, a visible agenda: Schechner was claiming ground for his own discipline, currently a field of studies that officially disclaims drama, especially written drama and especially Shakespeare (unless it involves intercultural performances), devoting its major energies to performance art. Toward the end of the decade, W. B. Worthen's *Shakespeare and the Authority of Performance* (1997) focused incisively on how fidelity to a textual Shakespeare, as exhibited in directing, acting, and scholarship, constrains the work of performance. By deconstructing the still prevalent notion that the performance, as a "reading" of the text, is always-already oriented toward an absent, determining, authorizing entity, and that the more emphatically it signals that reading relationship, the more it advertises itself as *not*-performance, Worthen's intervention decentered performance criticism as well as the latent assumption that performance is simply another term for interpretation and repositioned the project of studying Shakespearean performance within the wider discourse of performance studies, carving out a space that Schechner had ignored – and changing dramatically the "force" and importance of performance within Shakespeare studies.

If Schechner's agenda aimed at marginalizing (if not closing down altogether) theatre as a form of performance, that lying behind Worthen's influential historiography leads to a Janus-faced question. What kinds of Shakespeare performance does the theatre need? What kinds of theatres does Shakespeare need? As Worthen's book went to press, the resurfacing of Shakespeare's Globe on London's Bankside, near its original site, seemed poised to offer at least a partial answer. Whereas much critical energy once had been spent on imaginative conjectures of a theatre of origins for Shakespeare, now that it had appeared, it was not entirely sure what that might mean: did the Bankside space actually represent a simulacrum of "the real thing?" Whether one sides with those who view the space more as theme park or historical re-enactment than theatre and see "original practices" productions as more invested in theatre archaeology than in doing innovative work, the new Globe has been responsible for a renewed attention to actors' bodies and voices and, perhaps most significantly, to how close encounters between onstage and offstage performers and performances, blurring boundaries between stage and world, affirmed the relationship of actor to audience as central to the theatrical experience (Kiernan 1999, Escolme 2005). Yet, however "true" to the historical circumstances of the early modern theatre, re-creating such a dynamic can neither reify the past, which is always lost, nor recover the historicity of Shakespearean drama, for audiences bring to performance events – even Globe performances – assumptions derived from present-day cultural imaginaries (Worthen 2003).

Act 5

Titling this collection Shakespeare *and* Performance rather than Shakespeare *in* Performance makes an important distinction; significantly, the focus here is as much on how performance occurs "in between" these two terms as on how it might be located in one or the other. Implicitly, this work also seeks to further decenter and denaturalize the complex link between "Shakespeare" and "performance" – to solidify a move already in process to replace the "vs." of the text vs. performance debate as well as the idea of Shakespeare "in" performance and to reframe both categories of cultural production and the relations between them. Yet that does not entail erasing or entirely forgetting past critical history. How, after all, could a field of study so predicated on restaging, re-presenting, and playing back performance's disappearances become amnesiac about its heritage? The cover image for this volume traces one part of that heritage, remembers two of its predecessors: Styan's *Shakespeare Revolution*, the cover of which printed a production still from Peter Brook's 1970 *Midsummer Night's Dream*, and Bulman's *Shakespeare, Theory, and Performance*, which reproduced the poster image for Robert Lepage's 1992 *Dream* on its cover. Here, Sally Jacobs's sketch for Brook's famous touchstone for a "revolutionary" theatrical Shakespeare marks a moment when performance itself was still a dream, existed only as a childlike drawing or map. Hardly a *tabula rasa* (or even an "empty space"), it gestures away from Shakespeare's text toward performance as labor, work, play – as a provisional process.

Outsides and insides. The essays collected here decisively mark a move from the essentializing orthodoxy of performance criticism to the theoretical heterodoxy of Shakespeare performance studies, a more encompassing, expansive, expressive, and relational arena for rethinking performance. Although it would be possible to see that re-naming, like performance criticism, as yet another attempt to end legitimacy for the study of performance by a self-reflective conquest of a disciplinary territory with a rapid growth curve, it is equally clear that the critical project of studying Shakespeare performances has come of age. What, then, are the concerns, narratives, and theoretical paradigms that shape this inquiry? The Part titles in the Contents – "Terms of Performance," "Materialities: Writing and Performance," "Histories," "Performance Technologies, Cultural Technologies," "Identities of Performance," and "Performing Pedagogies" – suggest some local as well as more global categories. Yet the voices represented here do not confine themselves to or within those areas but constitute contributions to an ongoing conversation. Whether sampling, scrolling, covering or reframing past conversations, shifting vocabularies and paradigms, reframing the weight of operative traditions, or exploring key issues animating the field, these contributors bring a freshened awareness of the processes of writing and representing critical history. Acknowledging their intimate relation to performance as a subject of study (see Nora 1989), they make it a means of understanding. "What is Shakespeare performance studies?" This collection offers a time-bound answer – one that awaits the next (critical) performance.

Epilogue

What does the future of such a project look like? It is difficult to imagine, because one's investment lies always in the moment, in "being there" – even if that location changes every time the house lights go down (or stay lit) and another performance begins. Writes Peggy Phelan:

> Shakespeare matters because he predicted the muddle we are currently in: "All the world's a stage" and we are caught in the endless performance of our own self-conceptions as "players" (or "playa's," as the rap songs sing). We need the play because

it might retrospectively, retroactively, give us access to the non-play, the one we missed when we were memorizing our lines. We still believe in the distinction between the "authentic" non-playing world, but we simply cannot locate it anywhere at all, except perhaps in the vast archive we call "the history of Shakespeare's plays as performance" – a weird but compelling idea of the authentic as the lost archive of the performances we also missed. It is the mutuality of missing the past and missing the present that might give us some kind of consolation, if not anything more generative than that. (Phelan 2005)

As this book goes out into the world, who, one might ask, is that "we" of whom Phelan speaks? For the most part, critics have responded to the loss or disappearance of performance by attempting to preserve it, by documenting, recording, and recoding it. It is, warns Phelan, a desire to resist, "for what one otherwise preserves is an illustrated corpse" (Phelan 1997: 3). Is that, perhaps, the challenge that waits in the wings?

References and Further Reading

Barthes, Roland (1972). *Critical Essays*. Trans. Richard Howard. Evanston, IL: Northwestern University Press.

Beckerman, Bernard (1962). *Shakespeare at the Globe 1599–1609*. New York: Macmillan.

Berger, Harry, Jr. (1989). *Imaginary Audition: Shakespeare on Stage and Page*. Berkeley, CA: University of California Press.

Blau, Herbert (1982). *Take up the Bodies: Theater at the Vanishing Point*. Urbana, IL: University of Illinois Press.

Bristol, Michael & McLuskie, Kathleen (eds.) (2001). *Shakespeare and Modern Theatre: the Performance of Modernity*. London and New York: Routledge.

Brook, Peter (1968). *The Empty Space*. Harmondsworth: Penguin Books.

Brown, John Russell (1966). *Shakespeare's Plays in Performance*. London: Edward Arnold.

Bulman, James C. (ed.) (1996). *Shakespeare, Theory and Performance*. London and New York: Routledge.

Carlson, Marvin (1990). *Theatre Semiotics: Signs of Life*. Bloomington, IN: Indiana University Press.

Derrida, Jacques (1974). *Of Grammatology*. Trans. Gayatri Chakravorty Spivak. Baltimore, MD: Johns Hopkins University Press.

Elam, Keir (1980). *The Semiotics of Theatre and Drama*. London and New York: Methuen.

Escolme, Bridget (2005). *Talking to the Audience: Shakespeare, Performance, Self*. London and New York: Routledge.

Fischer-Lichte, Erika (1997). *The Show and the Gaze of Theatre: A European Perspective*. Iowa City: University of Iowa Press.

Foucault, Michel ([1966] 1971). *The Order of Things: An Archaeology of the Human Sciences*. New York: Pantheon Books.

Geertz, Clifford (1973). *The Interpretation of Cultures*. New York: Basic Books.

Goldman, Michael (1972). *Shakespeare and the Energies of Drama*. Princeton, NJ: Princeton University Press.

Goldman, Michael (1985). *Acting and Action in Shakespearean Tragedy*. Princeton, NJ: Princeton University Press.

Greenblatt, Stephen (1988). *Shakespearean Negotiations: The Circulation of Social Energy in Renaissance England*. Berkeley, CA: University of California Press.

Hall, Stuart (1981). "Notes on Deconstructing 'The Popular'." In Raphael Samuel (ed.) *People's History and Socialist Theory*. Boston, MA: Routledge and Kegan Paul, pp. 227–40.

Hodgdon, Barbara (1998). *The Shakespeare Trade: Performances and Appropriations*. Philadelphia, PA: University of Pennsylvania Press.

Jameson, Fredric (1981). *The Political Unconscious: Narrative as a Socially Symbolic Act*. Ithaca, NY: Cornell University Press.

Kiernan, Pauline (1999). *Staging Shakespeare at the New Globe*. London and New York: Macmillan/St. Martin's.

Massai, Sonia (ed.) (2005). *World Wide Shakespeares: Local Appropriations in Film and Performance*. London and New York: Routledge.

McGuire, Philip (1985). *Speechless Dialect: Shakespeare's Open Silences*. Berkeley, CA: University of California Press.

McGuire, Philip C. &. Samuelson, David A (eds.) (1979). *Shakespeare: The Theatrical Dimension*. New York: AMS Press.

Nora, Pierre (1989). "Between Memory and History: *Les Lieux de mémoire*." Trans. Marc Roudebush. *Representations* 26: 7–25.

Pavis, Patrice (1982). *Languages of the Stage: Essays in the Semiology of Theatre*. Trans. Susan Melrose. New York: Performing Arts Journal Publications.

Phelan, Peggy (1997). *Mourning Sex: Performing Public Memories*. London and New York: Routledge.

Phelan, Peggy (2005). Personal communication, 3 April.

Phelan, Peggy & Lane, Jill (eds.) (1998). *The Ends of Performance*. New York: New York University Press.

Schechner, Richard (1985). *Between Theater and Anthropology*. New York: Performing Arts Journal Publications.

Schechner, Richard (1992). "A New Paradigm for Theatre in the Academy." *The Drama Review: The Journal of Performance Studies* 36.4: 7–10.

Smith, Paul (1993). *Clint Eastwood: A Cultural Production*. Minneapolis and London: University of Minnesota Press.

Sobchack, Vivian (2000). "What Is Film History?, or, the Riddle of the Sphinxes." In Christine Gledhill & Linda Williams (eds.) *Reinventing Film Studies*. New York: Oxford University Press, pp. 300–15.

Styan, John L. (1977). *The Shakespeare Revolution*. Cambridge: Cambridge University Press.

Turner, Victor (1982). *From Ritual to Theatre: The Human Seriousness of Play*. New York: Performing Arts Journal Press.

Turner, Victor (1986). *The Anthropology of Performance*. New York: PAJ Publications.

Williams, Raymond (1985). *Keywords: A Vocabulary of Culture and Society*. New York: Oxford University Press.

Worthen, W.B. (1997). *Shakespeare and the Authority of Performance*. Cambridge: Cambridge University Press.

Worthen, W. B. (2003). *Shakespeare and the Force of Modern Performance*. Cambridge: Cambridge University Press.

PART I
Overviews
Terms of Performance

1

Reconstructing Love: *King Lear* and Theatre Architecture

Peggy Phelan

Open to the sky, enveloped by wooden arms, the new Globe theatre emerges from London's Bankside like one of Prospero's sleepers, awakened from the grave by some black magic. Set atop wooden pegs, the Globe has been reconstructed with unseasoned oak timbers, while "its roof is made with water-reed thatch, and its three hundred feet of wall is plastered with lime and goats' hair by means of a technique that goes back to the year 2400 B.C." (Kiernan 1999: 3). The Globe is provocatively historical, perhaps even archaic, in its architecture, and at the same time, absolutely up to date about tourism, marketing, and theatre scholarship. The reconstructed Globe incarnates the best speculations about the house Shakespeare wrote for — speculations supported by archaeological research, visual interpretation of drawings, historical and cultural scholarship, and a nexus of beliefs and assumptions about the project of reconstruction more generally (see Orrell 1992, Blatherwick & Gurr, 1992, Mulryne & Shewring 1997, for information about the Globe's history and archeological findings; and Worthen 2003, for a discussion of the Globe's performativity).

But the performances of the plays, texts deduced from four centuries of fascinatingly obsessive editorial intervention, take place in a city full of strange noises that now include airplane engines, car horns, and cell phones. To hear Richard III's famous wail "My kingdom for a horse," swallowed by the grinding gears of a London cab is to think of Richard's transportation problem in an entirely new way. The audience for these performances, many of them schoolchildren and tourists burdened with cameras and umbrellas, clad in Nikes and Gore-Tex, musters the occasional heckle and jeer. But mainly the audience seems, like many of the actors and directors interviewed by Pauline Kiernan about their experience working at the new Globe, awe-struck (Kiernan 1999: 129–57). There is something curiously reverential about most people's encounter with the reconstructed Globe, even when that encounter is framed through the comedies, or the sometimes dreary measurements common to theatre history. This reverence stems from something more than the now habitual genuflection over Shakespeare's astonishing genius, an obeisance I gladly and frequently perform; it is supplemented by the sense that there is something wondrous about living history itself. Straddling two historical moments, the reconstructed Globe seems in this sense a vividly theatrical space, a place that relies on a double sense of ground. The ground of the material stage and the ground reserved for the spectatorial "groundlings" invoke the earlier grounds of the historical Globe. This sense of being in two different historical places at once is part of the compelling allure of the new Globe.

The reconstructed Globe officially opened in 1997. Sam Wanamaker, a Texan character actor, first had the desire to rebuild the Globe in 1949. Assuming that someone from England would take charge, Wanamaker did not formally pursue the project until 1970, when he established the Globe Playhouse Trust. The story of how Wanamaker put together a team of academics, archaeologists, celebrities and wealthy patrons of the arts to realize his dream of reconstructing the Globe has been told frequently (Mulryne & Shewring 1997; Covington 1997 are among the best). Marjorie Garber reads Wanamaker's desire psychoanalytically: "Naturally it would be an American who longs for this, who makes it his dream; [Wanamaker wants to] rebuild not just a building but Shakespeare himself.... This plan longs for origins, for the moment when the dream began, for the navel of the dream" (1990: 246). Garber is alluding here to Freud's *Interpretation of Dreams*, and more particularly to Freud's own dream of finding the navel of the unconscious in dreams themselves. Freud concluded that dreams are expressions of wish fulfillments, and that the unconscious creates dreams to dramatize the consequences of these wishes and their repressions, these wishes and their realizations. Freud locates the navel of the collective unconscious in the drama of Oedipus. While theatre and psychoanalysis are deeply interwoven, thus far, the immense literature devoted to these affinities has been dedicated to describing the drama of the unconscious and the psychoanalytic situation of characters and plots. Here, I would like to build on the affinities between psychoanalysis and theatre to suggest something about the uncanny dimensions of theatrical architecture.

The Globe and the Theatre

Stephen Orgel's 1975 formulation puts the advent of Elizabethan theatre architecture concisely:

> All at once theatre was an institution, a property, a corporation. For the first time in more than a thousand years it had the sort of reality that meant most to Renaissance society: it was *real* in the way "real estate" is real; it was a location, a building, a possession – an established and visible part of society. (1975: 2)

But as Orgel well knows, such an enormous transformation does not happen "all at once." Nor is it easy to become a "visible part of society" when one's art rests on deception and disguise, when one has to seek licenses and find a paying audience. Inscribed within the architecture of both the original and reconstructed Globe is a profound ambivalence about the enclosures produced by theatrical architecture itself.

Architecture attempts to fix space, to arrange material so that a particular place gains form, and from that form, meaning and aesthetic or utilitarian purpose. But at its best, theatre aspires to expose the formlessness lurking within and beyond the temporary contingencies of physical form – architectural, theatrical, and mortal. Reconstructing theatrical architecture necessarily underlines the loss of the original version. In this underlining, theatrical architecture registers, in its very boards, a return to form that also announces its own temporary nature. Theatrical architecture, as a servant of both arts, tries to please architecture's aspiration to hold itself together, to be "a given," and theatre's aspiration to take nothing as given, especially nothing in the field of the visible.

Theatrical architecture answers an oscillating desire to be at once located and to be free of location's fixed points. It makes a place for an experience that aims to remove the viewer from a singular sense of fixed space and time. The conflict between the desire to be still and the desire to move and to be moved is inscribed quite literally in theatre architecture. This two-sidedness continues to animate the particular geography of the Globe's multiple spatial and temporal locations.

Architecture is always in excess of "building"; it combines that term as both noun and verb. The origin of architecture is not known; debates suggest it might have been a tomb, a home, or a temple (Hollier 1989: 6–10). The ancient Roman Vitruvius's *Ten Books of Architecture* distinguishes "architecture" from "shelters." Shelters, always material constructs, exist prior to architecture and are assembled from nature's raw materials, while architecture, often theoretical and not necessarily embodied in the physical world, is assembled from insights drawn from mathematics, history, philosophy, music, medicine, astronomy and law. Architecture is deliberate and rehearsed, while shelters are improvised and spontaneous. Or to put it slightly differently, architecture participates in representational economies, while shelter participates in the rhetorical economy of the real. In a prescient remark, Vitruvius states: "In all things but especially in architecture, there are two inherent categories: the signified and the signifier" (1999: 34). The distinction between the signifier and the signified results in an excess, something (some *thing*) that cannot be fully contained, even by architecture's enthusiastic embrace of containment. Just as an architect builds on (and builds up) the pre-architectural shelter, architecture both reflects and extends something other than itself. Denis Hollier claims that architecture "always represents something other than itself from the moment that it becomes distinguished from mere building" (1989: 31–2).

As a signifier, architecture exceeds the thing it signifies. A tomb is not merely a place for the dead; it is a statement about the distinction between life and death. It reflects a need to mark death, to set a place for it within life, but also to locate that place at a distance from the hurly-burly of life's (market) place. Hence, the silence and stillness and indeed the stony-ness of the cemetery (Phelan 1997, Hollier 1989).

If architecture seeks to establish location and address, theatre architecture stages the paradoxical desire to set aside a space to explore being out of place, to inhabit, however fleetingly, a kind of no-place. In this desire, theatre shares aspirations with utopia, the fantasy of an ideal no-place, an idealization made possible by its lack of specific location.

The sixteenth-century Globe itself was created as a kind of architectural dare. Andrew Gurr tells the complicated story of the old Globe's construction with admirable brio: "it was built in a feverish and illegal last-minute gamble by a playing company desperately short of money and desperate to secure any sort of playhouse for itself" (1988: 3). The story, as dramatic as most Renaissance plots, goes like this: James Burbage had leased land from Giles Allen for 21 years beginning in 1576. That site was the home of the Theatre. But legally, Allen owned the building built on his site and he declined to renew Burbage's request to extend the lease. (He claimed he wanted to use the timbers for a "better purpose.") Therefore, at the end of the lease in April 1597, Burbage would have been without land or architecture. Burbage died in February of that year and he passed the contested lease onto his two sons, Richard and Cuthbert. They negotiated with Giles during 1597–98, but failed to come to terms. According to Gurr, "On 28 December [1598] the two Burbages, a friend, the builder Peter Steete and 12 workmen assembled at the Theatre to pull it down and transport its 'woode and tymber' across the river to make a framework for the Globe. Giles Allen promptly sued" (1988: 8). Shakespeare, who "contributed 10% of the cost of pulling down the Theatre and using its timbers for the Globe, knew the operation was illegal" (1988: 3). This act of theft, and the daring involved in going outside the law, may have played a role in Shakespeare's fascination with illegitimacy throughout his playwriting career.

Theatre architecture seeks to "give a local habituation and a name" to the quest to be without habitation and name. Renaissance theatre architecture creates dwellings for experiences that are about the defiant or sad loss of identity. And insofar as identity is itself a form of property, as law so often asserts, theatre architecture is a kind of laboratory for investigations not only into the loss of identity but also into the condition of being without property. The anxiety often occasioned by such dissolution is handled by the creation of "property masters" and "house managers," stalwarts against the disappearance of the theatrical enterprise itself. Theatre architecture is fixed and "real" in the sense that Orgel meant, but it houses characters and situations intent on experiencing a dissolution into some "other" space, indeed, sometimes into a kind of no-space. Prospero's final speech in *The Tempest*:

> Our revels now are ended. These our actors,
> As I foretold you, were all spirits and
> Are melted into air, into thin air:
> And, like the baseless fabric of this vision,
> The cloud-capp'd towers, the gorgeous palaces,

> The solemn temples, the great globe itself,
> Yea, all which it inherit, shall dissolve
> And, like this insubstantial pageant faded,
> Leave not a rack behind.

Usually taken as Shakespeare's own farewell to theatre, these lines are about a certain will to architectural dissolution as well – they express a desire to be free of the constraints of architectural fixedness (and the nettlesome complexities it raises for inheritance). And perhaps too they express Shakespeare's retrospective acknowledgment of his own complicity in the dismantling of the Theatre; for Shakespeare was one of those who paid to have the architecture of the Theatre transformed into a faded, insubstantial pageant on December 28, 1598. The Theatre was dead and gone but its timbers were recycled to build the Globe.

Building the first Globe, then, like reconstructing the new old Globe, was an activity of reconstruction. Not only did its architecture revise the tradition of the itinerant actor and enable actors to become Gentlemen, the King's Servants or the Queen's Men, as Orgel points out, but it also initiated a particular kind of reconstruction. Between 1567 and 1614, some 11 or 12 amphitheatres were built in or just outside London. Some were converted from inn-yards (the Boar's Head and the Red Bull); some were radically revised soon after opening (the Rose expanded audience capacity by about 400 between its opening in 1587 and its renovation in 1592); and the Theatre was dismantled and moved south of the river to Bankside, where, under the name the Globe, it joined the Rose and the Swan. All these theatres, although differing in size and location, were based on remarkably similar designs and architectural plans. In both a material and a conceptual sense, the architectural enterprise of constructing Elizabethan theatres was steeped in reconstructing them. Moreover, the design of these houses was based on an understanding of the spatial requirements of previous plays. Thus, Elizabethan playhouses looked back to past houses and previous plays, while erecting structures that would help ensure a future of the same. The building of the original Globe was based on a return to the very timbers of a previous house, and when it burned down during a performance of *Henry VIII* in 1613, it was rebuilt on the same foundation in 1614, where it remained until 1644, when it was pulled apart to make tenements, smaller and multiple houses from the large but then outlawed playhouse (Blatherwick & Gurr 1992, Orrell 1992). In the early 1800s, a new foundation was established for the site now known as 1/15 Anchor Terrace. The style of that foundation was "pioneered by Sir Robert Smirke when he was appointed to strengthen the sinking foundations at Millbank Penitentiary in the early 1800s" (Blatherwick & Gurr 1992: 323).

Thus the "original" Globe both stemmed from and launched a series of repetitions and returns that make the 1997 incarnation of the Globe the most recent version of an ongoing project of reconstruction. While the term reconstruction posits a conception of a singular original, in the case of the Globe, the original building seems never to have been actually new, and never entirely "itself."

The reconstructed Globe of 1997 emerges, then, as a complicated negotiation between architecture-as-return and architecture-as-new-form. The footings of the original Globe were excavated in London in 1989 and 1991, but it was impossible to discern which of the remains came from the first Globe, the one erected from the oaks and scaffolds of Burbage's Theatre in 1598, and which remains were from the reconstruction on the same foundation in 1614. The excavations did show that the playhouse must have been a 20-sided polygonal structure of 100 feet, a much larger space than originally anticipated. But because of complications with the location of the foundation's footings, the reconstruction was moved to a slightly different location, approximately 200 yards from the original site. Thus, the reconstruction is based on true findings, but these truths undergo displacement before reconstruction begins – or perhaps more accurately, before reconstruction continues. This continuation repeats the history of the original Globe as a mobile and evolving architectural form.

Repetition and the Life Drive

In his remarkable 1920 essay, *Beyond the Pleasure Principle*, Freud argues that stillness and death are central to life's animation and vitality. Speculating that the life drive emerges from a kind of splitting of "the germ cells," in which one part of the organism dies while another part returns to an earlier condition to "repeat the performance" of development, Freud suggests that this splitting governs the drive toward death and life:

> The whole path of development to natural death is not trodden by all the elementary entities which compose the complicated body of one of the higher organisms. Some of them, the germ cells, probably retain the original structure of living matter and, after a certain time . . . separate themselves from the organism as a whole. Under favourable conditions, they begin to develop – that is, to repeat the performance [*das Spiel wiederholen*] to which they owe their existence; and in the end once again one portion of their substance pursues its development to a finish, while another portion harks back once again as a fresh residual germ to the beginning of the process of development . . . They are the true life drives. (vol. 18: 38–9)

This "harkening back" is the creative act that constitutes the life drive for Freud. The "elementary entities" upon which the architects and scholars responsible for the reconstructed Globe frame the performance by which they negotiate the new existence of built space are the germ cells that link the two buildings, the rebuilt original and the new reconstruction. To offer a repetition of my own: as with the life drive, this performance involves a complicated negotiation between architecture-as-return and architecture-as-new-form.

Freud's essay helps suggest that this negotiation between the past and the present, between the act of harkening back and beginning anew, is expressed in all living history, but perhaps appropriately, the theatrical architecture of the Globe makes these negotiations especially dramatic. The reconstructed Globe exposes the ways in which buildings contain the complex histories of their own development – from inspiration, to sketch, to model, to blueprint, to building – and how reconstructions of those inspirations in turn rely on sketches, close reading of stage directions, survey maps, and extant city cartography to confirm the "original" form. Each version of the building's composition repeats an earlier conception and transforms it. Thus, at the core of both architecture and Freud's conception of the life and death drives is an extraordinarily challenging negotiation with re-animation, reconstruction, and repetition (Phelan 2002).

To focus on these concepts, rather than on linear historical development, allows us to intervene in the teleological narrative of the reconstruction of the Globe as the fruition of Wanamaker's idea. Such an intervention is needed because the teleological narrative no longer suffices as a description of the complex blend of accident, speculation, politics, tourism, finance, myth, and accuracy that the reconstructed Globe embodies. Freud's emphasis on "repeating the performance" necessary for development (in both senses) allows us a tantalizing glimpse of another notion of the life and death drives, one that suggests that living history is a repetitive oscillation between animation and stillness. To consider the life and death drives in relation to theatre architecture, then, one must first move away from the reification of the realized building as architecture's singular end-point. While it is easy enough to acknowledge the multiple origins of buildings, it is more difficult to see that such multiplicity logically entails multiple endings.

Architecture tends to be seen as a fixed object, indeed, as a given, and it is this fixity that links it to the permanent stillness we associate, perhaps incorrectly, with singular death. What little we know about death suggests that it might be a more mutative state than we generally suppose. Theatrical architecture resists fixity and provides another vantage point from which to consider our relationship to "the promised end."

Architecture as Discovery

The living history of the reconstructed Globe reminds us that buildings contain histories of other lost buildings and unseen forms within them. Additionally, theatrical architecture repeats elements of other buildings within its own history. Take, for example, the common blurring of the terms theatre and house; a theatre is a playhouse and it often stages plays about houses and families, exposing their mutual fascination with secrets. The through-the-looking-glass quality of theatre's domestic interventions often seems to embody the lyrical speculations of the French philosopher Gaston Bachelard. In *The Poetics of Space*, Bachelard brilliantly illuminates the ways in which domestic architecture responded to the human desire for pockets, hideaways, and unseen interiors by creating elaborate closets, doors, attics, and ornate doorknobs. Houses and theatres share an obsession with visual secrets: "Wardrobes with their shelves, desks with their drawers and chests with their false bottoms are veritable organs of the secret psychological life. Indeed, without these . . . our intimate life would lack a model of intimacy" (Bachelard 1969: 78).

Perhaps without theatre architecture, drama itself would lack a model of intimacy. When Hamlet ushers in the emotional atlas of the well-chambered play that bears his name by saying: "I have that within which passeth show," his statement is both a reference to the scene in which he plays the grieving son, and a reference to the pockets of the house he will soon turn inside out. Those who seek to hide in the folds of the dark court's intimate curtains, such as Polonius, will be discovered within; those who seek to escape the confines of the playhouse entirely – Ophelia, Rosencrantz and Guildenstern – will die as well: from exposure. For Shakespeare, the enclosure offered by architecture was only rarely a benign sheltering. The playhouse was a drama of entrances and exits, a technology for exposing the elaborate ways in which we expose and hide ourselves, both from the audience we can see and the audience we call our intimates, ourselves. The tragi-comedy that houses our most intimate dramas must, perforce, contain things hidden from sight. This is the design principle that organizes the structure of the Elizabethan playhouses, from the tiring rooms to the inner closets, and this is also the structural principle of the unconscious. Sometimes we learn that there are secrets too intimate to share with our intimates, even with ourselves.

Part of theatrical architecture's contribution to "the secret psychological life" has to do with the way it returns us to the same set/ting, even while it shows us different scenes in the same space. (It was Laplanche and Pontalis who emphasized this important feature of the unconscious when they wrote: "Fantasy is not the object of desire, but its setting," 1986: 26.) Thus, both the expansive exhilaration and hideous confinement of the erotic rhythm of Antony and Cleopatra is expressed by a kind of simple cross-cutting – Egypt in one scene, Rome the next, Return. Aware all the while that one is an audience member standing or sitting in London, one moves back and forth and up and down with the actors as they circle the 20-sided polygonal structure and "the globe." The theatre places the bedroom and the battlefield between the same two poles. The stage becomes a church, a court, a forest, a ship's wet deck. The audience slips between knowing and dreaming, between motion and stillness, and we return again, and again, to sort those measures out. We return because the play does not end. Shakespeare repeated himself; four centuries of actors and spectators have recited his repetitions.

For contemporary actors encountering the new old Globe, the specific force of the architecture has been surprising, offering both new limitations and new possibilities for staging the plays. Many of these surprises have to do with the discovery space, the partially hidden and partially open stage space so crucial for Shakespeare's plots. Pauline Kiernan describes the situation this way:

> [T]he fixed physical structure and architectural characteristics of the stage . . . present limitations to staging and blocking, but also offer effective dramaturgical possibilities. A central opening, flanked by two entry doors, demands to be used not only for exit and entrance, but for concealment of eavesdropping and for discovery. Not everyone in the

audience can see what is being staged within the discovery spaces, but if characters on stage are describing what they are seeing there, the whole house can listen and find out. (1999: 7)

No doubt Kiernan is right to point out the importance of listening to a Shakespeare play. But her assumption that the architectural structure is a kind of limitation that needs to be augmented by sound overlooks the possibility that not all scenes are meant to be equally accessible to all viewers. This limitation of sight fuels much of the fun of the plays' plots through disguise and misrecognition. While the capacity for disguise can be celebrated or lamented as a symptom of self-fashioning, these disguises also expose the limits of a visual-centric world-view (Greenblatt 1980). Indeed, in many of Shakespeare's plays it is the gap between what one sees and one what cannot see that drives the drama. Visual evidence is not a guarantee of much at all in Shakespeare's plays. In *Othello*, "the ocular proof" of Desdemona's infidelity is the handkerchief so skillfully manipulated by Iago; while in *King Lear*, blind Gloucester sees more than he saw when his eyes were functioning. The architecture of the discovery space, the blind spot within the physical space, frames the epistemological undertaking of the plays themselves: how to live with the relationship between what Bachelard calls "secret psychological life" and the pressures and joys of public performance. In this, the theatrical blind spot represented by the discovery space is the objective correlative for the tragicomedy of Renaissance drama generally.

Stephen Greenblatt (1980) has persuasively demonstrated Renaissance drama's characteristic interest in self-fashioning, but an equally persistent, if harder to see and grasp, interest in self-erasure drives these plays as well. Shakespeare's genius was to make a link between a character's sense of psychological and architectural confinement in a theatre space that oscillates between claustrophobic imprisonment and radical, if always uncertain, freedom (Moretti 1982).

Building *King Lear*

It is fruitful to think for a moment of play texts as modes of architecture. Thus, within the structure called *King Lear,* specific arrangements of words create a platform for action, motion, and performing. The text provides a basic design plan and specific choices determine how well or ill particular ensembles build the play. The metaphor becomes richer when one thinks about two quite different extant texts of *Lear*, the Pied Bull's Quarto of 1608 and the 1623 Folio (Weis 1993, Taylor & Warren 1983). Perhaps our contemporary interest in questions such as "Which version came first?" and "What suggests performance information and what suggests foul papers?" might be offset by a broader understanding of the role of repetition and variants, the contingencies of perspective and the mutative distortions of collective memory, changing casts, and the shifting demands of architectural space in thinking about textual issues. We know that the play was performed at the Globe and at Blackfriars, and for King James on St Stephen's Day in 1606. These differing contexts and settings (to say nothing of the various motives that actors, printers, and others might have in producing a text) are likely to produce multiple texts and variant histories to go with their mutative circumstances. While archeologists cannot discern which of the two foundations for the Globe they found in the late 1980s, neither can we discern which of the surviving texts of *King Lear* is the "original." In this particular play, because it is so concerned with division, multiplication, and repetition, these several origins take on an uncanny force.

Philip Armstrong usefully reminds us: "Discussions of *King Lear* always begin again. For the text in question is irreconcilably double: there are two plays, a Folio and a Quarto, and each has an equal claim to 'authenticity' " (1994: 414). Discussions of "good" and "bad" Folios and Quartos have more than a little in common with the question of paternal and maternal legacy in *King Lear*, as well. Both plots in the play are structured around absent mothers: Gloucester has both a legitimate and a bastard son, and Lear, at one point, raises a question about Regan's paternity, "if thou shouldst not be glad / I would divorce me from thy mother's tomb / Sepulchring an adultress" (2. 4. 127–9) and calls Goneril "a degenerate bastard," although he later claims she is his rightful daughter, "for Gloucester's bastard son / Was kinder to his father than my daughters / Got 'tween the lawful sheets" (4. 6. 114–16).[1] This anxiety about legitimate transmission works to inform current textual debates about the two versions of *Lear*. Stanley Wells concludes his argument in favor of differentiating the Folio and Quarto versions of the play with this remarkable claim: "To split asunder the two texts of *King Lear* is a work of restoration, not of destruction. We shall lose by it no more than a wraith born of an unholy union: we shall gain a pair of legitimate – though not identical – twins" (1983: 20). In this, Wells is a bit like Lear who wants to divide his kingdom to consolidate his empire and to avoid strife after his death. But the love test Lear devises produces an unexpected need to reclaim his power. In trying to create a space for his own self-erasure, Lear unwittingly sets out on a different kind of discovery altogether.

The Love Test

Lear's decision to divide his kingdom is a piece of political theatre, a ceremony of division that comes after the decisions have been already made (Asher 2000). Before the ceremony begins, Kent and Gloucester have begun to interpret Lear's choices, to read back into his divisions a set of preferences. Kent begins the play with this observation to Gloucester:

> KENT: I thought the King had more affected the Duke of Albany than Cornwall.
> GLOUCESTER: It did always seem so to us; but now in the division of the kingdom it
>   appears not which of the Dukes he values most, for equalities are so
>   weight'd that curiosity in neither can make choice of either's moiety.
>
>   (1.1.1–6)[2]

Kent's belief that Lear "affected" Albany more than Cornwall is a smart assessment on Lear's part, as subsequent events will make clear. But the King seems genuinely undecided about who should be Cordelia's husband, and therefore, about her inheritance. Thus, Cordelia has the most at stake in the love test Lear launches.

As a piece of theatre set within the play, the love test functions as an examination of what, if anything, distinguishes performance from the real. In this sense, the love test is meta-theatrical and operates in much the same way as The Mouse Trap in *Hamlet*. Shakespeare suggests that piling representation upon representation will paradoxically fortify the real, and this reinforced outline of the real will provide a resistant force against which performance can be measured. In staging plays within plays, Shakespeare sets his now clichéd proposition that "All the world's a stage" against something that might disprove it. This something would have to have an enigmatic and deeply surprising nature about it – perhaps loyalty, a true heart, courage, guilt, or a still-functioning conscience. Qualities of feeling are the core of Shakespeare's sense of character. His plays are fascinated by whether or not these virtues can be feigned or if they have a foundation, a robust architecture if you will, that will outlast the insubstantial pageants of theatricality *tout court*. In this sense, Shakespeare's plays are absorbed by the limits of theatricality, an absorption that exploits theatricality in order to defeat it.

In Shakespeare's plays, conscience is buffeted by the temptations of theatre, especially when a certain relation to power is at stake. Claudius wants to consolidate his power while Lear claims to want to relinquish his. But this claim, like so much else in the first act of the tragedy, sets off a reversal; for rather than abandoning his will-to-power as he had planned, Lear exerts it with swift authority. In addition to disinheriting his favorite daughter, Lear also goes for his sword to strike Kent. Banishing Cordelia and Kent fast upon the heels of his announced wish to be done with the cares of state, Lear sets off a play that proceeds in a kind of reverse order; the old king becomes a child, and Cordelia, the youngest, becomes a military leader and ruler before her untimely death.

Stanley Cavell (1969) argues that Lear is motivated to stage the love test because he wants to avoid love, thinking himself unworthy of it. Cavell suggests that by using his property to pay for the public exclamation of how much he is loved, Lear thinks that he has been spared the obligation of returning the (false) love announced so lavishly by Goneril and Regan:

> Cordelia is alarming precisely because he knows she is offering the real thing, something a more opulent third of his kingdom cannot, must not, repay; putting a claim on him he cannot face. She threatens to expose both his plan for returning false love with no love, and expose the necessity of that plan – his terror of being loved, of needing love. (1969: 290)

But what exactly is love and how does the theatre of *King Lear* dismantle, discover, and reconstruct it?

Whatever Lear's exact psychological or moral motivations, he begins the play in the grip of the death drive:

> ... Know that we have divided
> In three our kingdom; and 'tis our fast intent
> To shake all cares and business from our age,
> Conferring them on younger strengths, while we
> Unburden'd crawl toward death.
>
> (1.1.36–40)

Lear's desire for self-erasure expresses itself as a desire to shake off the cares and obligations he has to both his kingdom and his kin. His first two daughters, who are already married and have already received their inheritance, respond to Lear's empty ceremony by stuffing that emptiness with words, elaborate promises, and other highly inflated rhetoric. Much of their rhetoric recalls the kind of language Queen Elizabeth perfected, a language that joins the personal and the political. In her "Golden Speech" of 30 November 1601, Elizabeth proclaimed:

> There is no jewel, be it of never so rich a price, which I set before this jewel; I mean your love... Yea, my own properties I count yours, and to be expended for your good. Therefore, render unto them from me, I beseech you, Mr. Speaker, such thanks as you imagine my heart yieldeth, but my tongue cannot express. (quoted in Dodd 1999: 482)

Taking a page from Elizabeth and employing elaborate rhetoric in service of claiming her incapacity to find the words to express her love, Goneril replies to Lear's demand for love with similarly theatrical words:

> Sir, I love you more than word can wield the matter
> Dearer than eye-sight, space and liberty;
> Beyond what can be valued rich or rare; ...
> A love that makes breath poor and speech unable;
> Beyond all manner of so much I love you.
>
> (1.1.54–7, 59–60)

Goneril touches here on the entwined relationship between space, liberty, and vision central to the drama of love that the rest of the play examines. She links her love to something "beyond" value, a beyond that Freud associated with repetition and the death drive. As Regan repeats her sister's speech and sentiment, "I am made of that self metal as my sister / And prize me at her worth. In my true heart / I find she names my very deed of love," they set off a process of merging that makes it increasingly difficult to differentiate them by the end of the play when, desiring the same man, they die together in suicidal pursuit of him. But here in Act 1, the play pursues the exhaustion of language and subject caused by the incessant call of the "beyond" Goneril's rhetoric sets in motion.

While we quite easily now say that "the personal is the political," *King Lear* exposes the difficulties of the effort to conjoin these two realms. Richard Halpern, reading the play as a kind of allegory for James I's concept of absolutist rule, argues that the play reflects James' attempt to turn "kingship from a political into a property relation" (1991: 221). While there is much of value in Halpern's argument, it overlooks the psychological force of the play. In *Lear*, the conjunctions and disjunctions of the political and the personal are part of what give the play its enduring interest.

This conjoining of the personal and the political risks misfiring, as it eventually did for Elizabeth, because it blurs the different kinds of power wielded by the crown and the heart. The blurring also creates a certain kind of confusion or mixture of genre that makes the literary texture of the play hard to settle. There are elements of history, tragedy, romance, myth, fairytale, and allegory in *Lear* (Halio 1992 untangles each of these elements). As Halpern argues, "By so clearly violating the political rationality of the history plays and by incorporating so many mythic or folkloric elements, the division of the kingdom signals the play's generic allegiance to the 'timeless' realm of romance – an allegiance suggested as well by the setting, at once medieval and pre-Roman and indeterminately 'long ago' " (1991: 218–19). The difficulty of locating the play's genre is reflected in the differing titles of the Quarto and the Folio. In the Quarto, the title page reads, *True Chronicle Historie of the life and death of King Lear . . .* , while the Folio names it *The Tragedie of King Lear,* and places the play between *Hamlet* and *Othello.* The two titles reflect the resistance to fixed place that the play as a whole examines.

The divided play begins with the ceremony of division. Goneril and Regan play Lear's game and speak the language of public love modeled by Queen Elizabeth. But Cordelia, who is suffering a similar exhaustion as Lear's, insofar as she has spent her life listening to her older, tediously verbal sisters and has spent her most recent days listening to two suitors "long in our court" woo her, answers Lear's empty ceremony with an emptiness of her own. Cordelia's statements in the love test begin as asides. Sensing that she has failed before she has begun, Cordelia's first lines are, "What shall Cordelia speak? Love, and be silent." This posture of silence, a role she has been playing with her suitors, her sisters, and her father, is exhausting because it requires that she defer to the words and wills of others. Listening is often a tutelage in repression, and as the youngest, "our last, and least," Cordelia has become familiar with silence and knows its secret alcoves and austere shelters. And she also knows that Lear will not accept her silence in this scene. This is why Cordelia begins the play as wearily and as warily as anyone on stage. Because she loves Lear, Cordelia wants to please him, but what he asks betrays her feeling and so she cannot please him by giving him what he thinks he wants. Rather, she exposes the utter emptiness of his ceremony and his demand for love when she mouths her deceptively simple "nothing":

LEAR: Now, our joy,
           Although our last and least; to whose young love
           The vines of France and milk of Burgundy

     Strive to be intress'd; what can you say to draw
     A third more opulent than your sisters? Speak.
CORDELIA: Nothing, my Lord.
LEAR: Nothing?
CORDELIA: Nothing.

           (1.1.81–8)

In going out to shelter Lear's emptiness with her own, Cordelia discovers her "secret psychological life." Cordelia's response ushers in her transition from childhood to adulthood, with much more upheaval than wedding vows would have wrought. For in refusing to play Lear's game, Cordelia sees that she is capable of wounding someone she loves. Surprised by her own cleaving of her former relation to her self and to her father, Cordelia emphasizes her awakening in a series of asides in which she names herself as if to create a separate space from which to observe her newly revealed self. Standing "aside," indeed beside herself, Cordelia watches and listens to the theatricality of her sisters' speeches and her father's demand. Trying to soften the blow she knows she has inflicted, Cordelia tries to find comfort in the righteousness of mathematics: "I love your Majesty / According to my bond; no more nor less." And when this will not staunch the blood she has drawn, she swings at her sisters as well:

     Why have my sisters husbands if they say
     They love you all? Happily, when I shall wed,
     That lord whose hand must take my plight shall carry
     Half my love with him, half my love and duty:
     Sure I shall never marry like my sisters,
     To love my father all.

          (1.1.98–103)

Cordelia's math attempts to bring them all back to the ground of reason. She asserts her "bond," to move the family back from the precipice of Goneril's "beyond." She feels love happening to her, which is different from feeling herself to be a loving daughter and sister, as she (and everyone else) assumed she was. This emotional tumult shocks everyone on stage, with the possible exception of France. It causes an especially brutal response from Lear. Love happens to Lear as well, but not in the first act. Here he only grasps that Cordelia's answer unsettles his plan for the future and also calls into question his own judgment and sanity. For how could he have favored the daughter who hurts him most? "I lov'd her most, and thought to set my rest / On her kind nursery" (1.1.122–3). Cordelia's double/d nothing deprives him of both a secure future and a known past.

  Scrambling to make new plans, Lear decides he will divide his time, kill his time even, between the homes of his two older daughters, but not before he answers Cordelia's wound to him by inflicting a greater wound on her. Lear answers Cordelia's "nothing" in terms of the economy of property and dowry. He disowns and disinherits her in one blow. Refusing Cordelia's metaphysical calculations, Lear answers her "nothing" in bluntly literal terms. Kent tries to plead for her, and Cordelia, who is not interested in becoming a sacrificial victim or a suicidal madwoman, also tries to defend herself. But Lear exiles them both in response to what he believes to be Cordelia's displacement of him from her heart. Thus, the play begins in the grip of anguished homelessness.

Cordelia tries to answer the emptiness within Lear's theatre of love with her own emptiness. But in answering his emptiness with her own, she animates a love that is hard to house.[3] This is the heart's essential homelessness: it beats because it cannot settle into a grammar of possession; it cannot be housed within the architecture of property. It flings itself against the wall of its confinement – architectural, theatrical, and mortal. In the grip of his own mortality, Lear imagines himself as a loving warden, benignly regarding the docile Cordelia. When he fantasizes his last days, he imagines he will step down from his position of guard and join her in her cell. This is the fantasy that sustains him throughout the course of the play: "Come, let's away to prison." But whereas he sees himself as a loving warden going through the paces of a love test, Cordelia experiences the test itself as a demand that costs more than she is willing to pay – her freedom to speak "as she feels" rather than mouthing what she "ought to say." Lear's shock at Cordelia's response comes both because he believed her to be essentially accommodating (in all senses) and because he thought her incapable of addressing him with anything but passive obedience. (This is how she got to be the favorite.) Thus, his wound comes from seeing that his sense of their intimacy has been based on a blind spot; he has seen his plan but he has not seen her. And this blindness lets him see for the first time that his intimate fantasy of their past and future might well have been a secret even to himself. The love test examines Lear's own secrets in the realm of love, cells of fantasy he has locked off even from himself. As this secret is exposed, Cordelia sees her own power to hurt and her own interest in overlooking Lear's startling caprice. The thematic links between blindness, the unforeseen, and the overlooked are worked out with an often cruel literalness as the play continues.

Cordelia's "nothing" flattens the structure of the family, and since this is a political family, the subsequent upheaval disrupts the political and geographical boundaries of England (Gillies 2001, Brayton 2003). This is another way of saying that love, and its inevitable misfires, have large consequences. Lear's loss is France's gain: "Thy dowerless daughter, King, thrown to my chance / Is Queen of us, of ours, and our fair France" (1.1.255–6) and it is from France that Cordelia finds a different perspective on the divisions within her father's kingdom. The voluminous, although not entirely convincing, critical literature that reads *King Lear* as a comment on the Unionist doctrine of James I traces the over-determined similarities between James and Lear (Halpern 1991, Dodd 1999, Holbrook 2000), but it seems to me nonetheless that *Lear* is primarily a play about collapsing too swiftly the distinctive economies of love and property. Love and property prompt a certain kind of acquisitiveness, but the nature of love prohibits us from owning it. Love happens in a way that cannot be predicted, held, or bartered. *King Lear* is concerned with the unforeseen consequences of love happening, and those consequences range from bastard children to grief-stricken dukes and kings. In both the political economy of the family and the state, a similar blind spot occurs. Lear's night in the storm causes him to revise his "reason not the need" speech, and he comes to see that he has taken "too little care" not only of his youngest daughter, but also of the disenfranchised and impoverished subjects in his realm.

Lear begins the play too concerned about his own future and overlooks the consequences of his actions on the social order and on those closest to him. Lear also is blind to the differences in his daughters. Cordelia is not the same as her older sisters, who are also not the same person, although they become less distinct as the play continues (for a good discussion of doubling and rhyming in relation to Goneril and Regan, see Booth 1983, especially pp. 43–57). Differentiation does not necessarily mean diminishment, a lesson Cordelia could not teach very well in the first act, judging from the mathematical calculations she offers Lear before her marriage. Kent's cry, "I'll teach you differences," to Oswald promises to keep the distinct positions between King and servant clear. But this pedagogy will not take once the King is intent on abdicating his throne, while keeping the ceremonies of kingship.

Cordelia's difference from her sisters and from Lear is not only due to her age and her unmarried status, although these two facts play a part in her separateness. Her difference comes from that "something" that exceeds performance and in that excess touches the real. The love that happens to Cordelia in the love test is one that resists its own location, that cannot settle its own address. Cordelia is as distressed by what she says as Lear is, and she chooses to say it only because the alternatives have been exhausted by her sisters. Her impossible position locates her in a no-place; thus she answers Lear's property auction with her "nothing." The no-place, the place of negation and the place of exile to which Cordelia is banished, also exposes the utopia and blind idealism that she and Lear share. He has an ideal fantasy of a future without strife; she harbors a vision of love that exceeds the heart her father has, at least in the beginning of the play. Cordelia's "no place" sends both of them to undiscovered places within their "secret psychological lives" until they are reunited just before "the promised end." At the beginning of the play, Lear cannot follow Cordelia into the radical emptiness (the "nothing" and no space) she offers. In exiling her, Lear loses his own compass and orientation, her "still soliciting eye." Without the structural organization of family and kingship, Lear lacks an answering and responsive voice. (The Fool and Kent do their best, but Lear is looking for Cordelia's love.) Lear, having lost Cordelia, becomes unmoored from the psychological and political coherence that social and linguistic address offers.

Love's essential grammar is "I love you"; this grammar implies both a location and a direction, a passage, from me here to you there. But theatre continually puts pressure on both location and subjects. The subject who speaks in the theatre is always displaced.[4] This is why J. L. Austin famously excluded theatre from his analysis of the speech act; for in theatre, the speech act is already a performative act undertaken by the actor who attempts to become the character (Austin 1962). In the love test, the theatre within the theatre, the love at issue is marked by a repeated emphasis on love as a saying, rather than love as a doing. Lear: "Which of us shall *we say* does love us most?" (1.1.50). Here, the saying of love produces property and power, but it destroys love's superfluous force, its unique and distinguishing excess. To be loved by Cordelia is a different experience than being loved by Goneril. The dissolution of love's specificity comes back to haunt Lear when Goneril and Regan strip him of his retinue. They say there is no need to have separate attendants, for their servants will serve the King as well. Lear's impassioned "Reason not the need" rejoinder expresses his grief and rage over the economy he himself set in motion with the love test. It is here that the axis of the play tilts, and Lear begins to feel the insistent beating of his own breaking heart. As with Cordelia, he attempts to placate this breaking wound with the comforts of counting:

> You think I'll weep;
> No, I'll not weep:
> I have full cause of weeping; but this heart
> Shall break into a hundred thousand flaws,
> Or ere I'll weep. O fool, I shall go mad!
> (2.4.281–5)

Lear manages to forestall this break but his effort threatens to fracture his reason. He, like Cordelia, begins to stand outside, or beside, himself and in this departure from his singular location and sense of self he begins his trajectory toward an absolute exposure, a radical property-lessness. Standing beside himself, Lear demonstrates the doubling at work in speech acts that occur (if never quite take place) in the theatre; for in each speech act the actor works to cohabit the line with the character he or she portrays. This accounts for the peculiar intimacy of theatre; in the effort to cohabit the enunciation the character and the actor provide a model for the couple more broadly. Moreover, this model emphasizes that such an aspiration to be (with) the other rests on an imaginary leap, a fantasy that cannot ever be fully controlled or scripted in advance. To love is to yield to a happening that is "beyond" the known location of the one who solicits and the one who responds. Theatre creates a fantastic and fantasmatic dwelling that is commodious enough for spectators to enter, to find a place within, and intimate enough to illuminate the precarious and fragile performance that allows that cohabitation to be embodied on stage, however fleetingly.

But the actor who plays Cordelia cannot bring this cohabitation into being. She continually names herself Cordelia, as if she is a third person. While the first use of her own name ("What shall Cordelia speak?") might be explained as a theatrical device to identify herself to the audience, her return to third person address three times in the scene emphasizes her awakening to a self she had not yet known. Her sisters do not use this form of speech. It is as if Cordelia *feels* Lear's dividing of his kingdom (and thus of her home) as a radical self-division; she sees herself playing a part in a script she cannot alter, even while she stands apart from that role, watching it divide and destroy both the kingdom and her kin. Cordelia's self-division in Act 1 presages the divisions to follow, divisions that result in her death and the death of her family.

Dividing the Mortal Body

The excess cruelty of *King Lear* suggests a kind of will to divide that begins with Lear's division of his kingdom, but extends across a great number of divisions by the play's end. The line between mind and body is stretched and pressured most acutely in Lear's exposure to the storm, "when the mind's free / the body's delicate" (3.4.11–12). The storm is the logical end-point of the play's incessant division between architecture and shelter, between representation and the real. Outside the hovel, the pre-architectural space that represents the opposite end-point of the play's palaces and castles, Lear hears his heart; the surprise within its sound leads him to think it is breaking:

> KENT: Good my Lord, enter here.
> LEAR: Will it break my heart?

This hovel marks the "no place" and emptiness toward which Cordelia's "nothing" beckoned him. Abjuring "all roofs," Lear discovers nature's own discovery space. Yielding to the fool's discomfort before his own, Lear describes the space he long avoided: "In boy, go first. You houseless poverty... How shall your houseless heads and unfed sides / Your loop'd and window'd raggedness, defend you from seasons such as these? O! I have ta'en / Too little care of this!" (3.4.26, 30–2). In pausing before the emptiness Cordelia first offered him, Lear for the first time sees the condition of someone else before his own. This is where love happens to Lear.

The hovel itself is a piece of theatre, a place within a theatre; therefore it is not entirely empty. Tom O'Bedlam, a character composed from bits and pieces by a desperate Edgar, inhabits it. Staging a piece of theatre within the theatre and repeating the love test from the position of propertylessness, the play now pits Edgar's fake madness against Lear's real disintegration. As the storm rages inside and out, the line between reason and insanity becomes increasingly muddied. The failure to maintain this line retrospectively blurs some of Lear's earlier attempts to divide the female body into two, demarcating what is "below" as monstrous. The erosion of the line between reason and madness also anticipates the fragility of the line between life and death.

Shakespeare writes two different versions of the "promised end." One is an "image of that horror" that exists as image and end-point of a certain kind of theatricality, one represented within theatre architecture as a set, and therefore as mutative and freeing. The other version undoes the redemption in the first, suggesting that in the end theatre will always fade before the real force of the mortal line that divides us both from our dreams of love and from ourselves.

The first version, "the image" of the promised end appears when the suicidal Gloucester attempts to hurl himself from the cliff at Dover. Led to it by Edgar/Tom, blind Gloucester believes himself to be hovering in the hand of a stranger at the end of land, the limit of property as such. Edgar/Tom describes an immaterial landscape with the vividness of a really good art historian in front of a landscape painting:

> Come on sir; here's the place: stand still. How fearful
> And dizzy 'tis to cast one's eyes so low!
> The crows and choughs that wing the midway air
> Show scarce so gross as beetles; half way down
> Hangs one that gathers samphire, dreadful trade!
> Methinks he seems no bigger than his head.
> The fishermen that walk along the beach
> Appear like mice, and yond tall anchoring bark
> Diminish'd to her cock, her cock a buoy
> Almost too small for sight. The murmuring surge,
> That on th'unnumbered idle pebble chafes,
> Cannot be heard so high. I'll look no more,
> Lest my brain turn, and the deficient sight
> Topple down headlong.
>
> (4.6.11–24)

Edgar's opening command, "stand still," recalls the confinement of Kent in the stocks and anticipates the imprisoned stillness of Lear and Cordelia in the next act. Here, before the stillness promised by the death drive, Edgar/Tom paints a scene, "an insubstantial pageant," for his despairing father. Gloucester has lost his access to external sight; all he can see is his inward vision. Poised on a cliff made of words and theatrical timber, Gloucester's pause before committing himself to self-erasure, revises the trajectory of architectural spaces that *Lear* has traversed.

While the play basically pursues a kind of descending route from interior, built space to the natural hovel of the outside shelter, much along the model described by Vitruvius, there are complications. One of the most crucial scenes in the play occurs when Lear discovers Kent in the stocks. The stocks are a kind of architectural outline of the prison (or the Tower). As a trace, they outline a more foreboding architecture of confinement. But in their starkness, they represent the capricious power of law. As the stocks are wheeled onstage at Cornwall's command, their very mobility suggests the transforming trajectory of power. Kent's confinement is a still-point that allows Lear to recognize what he did when he sought to divide his kingdom and "retain / The name and all th' addition to a king" (1.1.134–5). Lear's initial desire was to become living history. He wanted to retain the name and allowance of King but nothing else. It is Gloucester who is the first to recognize that Lear's mixed motives "prescrib'd his power / Confined to exhibition" (1.2.24–5). The hollowness of that spectacle renders Lear "an O without a figure," an outline of a man who cannot feel or hear his heart. The stocks, an architectural device that outlines the representational economy of the prison, emphasizes the killing force of the law. Lear's death drive and the stocks conjoin to suggest that the stillness promised by death renders the mortal body a kind of prison. This is what Lear wants to flee in Act 1.

Edgar/Tom's command to Gloucester to "stand still" while he paints a portrait of a landscape that is entirely fantasmatic, introduces another kind of perspective, another level of illusion, into the play. Gloucester serves as a foil for Lear throughout the play and his own death drive comes to the fore after his eyes have been individually plucked out in an excessively violent, deeply physical way. The disgorging of the first eye, an image of absolute horror that prompts the audience to look away, is repeated a moment later with the second eye. Gloucester's blinding emphatically insists that even the old and withered are confined to bodies with organs, and it is precisely this interiority that makes the body a prison we must suffer.

In his desire for self-erasure, Gloucester repeats Lear's death drive. But unlike the king, Gloucester "needs" to be led by his son, however unknowingly. At the lip of what he believes to be his death, Gloucester pauses. Then he falls. His life is spared, however, by the reassertion of theatre's ground. He crashes through the structure of landscape that relies on the illusion of perspective so ably described by Edgar/Tom and finds another level of the real. After being spared from this death, he sees Edgar beneath the façade of his performance as Tom. When Edgar relates the true picture of the landscape Gloucester has traversed, Gloucester repeats the death he just missed, and this time the stillness holds. Or seems to. In this play, each performance is overlaid on another. Beneath Edgar's exposed performance as Tom lies the actor's performance of Edgar. Just as Gloucester has to endure two separate acts of blinding, so too must he endure two kinds of death at the end of the play. Although Gloucester's second seeing cost him his heart, his death has a kind of happiness that Lear's and Cordelia's lack. Gloucester and Edgar's journey paints an image of the promised end and then displaces it, momentarily reuniting the father and son, if only for the blink of an eye.

Lear and Cordelia, however, discover another ending. Like Edgar and Gloucester, Lear and Cordelia are reunited and at last Lear can invite Cordelia to his fantasmatic space: "Come, let's away to prison; / We two alone will sing like birds in the cage" (5.3.8–9). As the image of a promised end, Lear's prison represents a kind of freedom. Relieved of the need to create borders and divisions, Lear's fantasized prison will also relieve him of his loneliness; this relief in turn will revive his life drive. He and Cordelia will inhabit a mutual emptiness that fills itself with gossip and carelessness. Cordelia, not surprisingly, neither endorses nor rejects Lear's fantasy. She will soon embody a different order of confinement.

Edmund's note writes her death sentence and when Lear returns to the stage with her dead body in his arms in a kind of fallen Pietà, he enters something more than the image of the promised end. He feels his heart as still as her own and as he begs her to breathe, his own breath diminishes:

> No, no, no life!
> Why should a dog, a horse, a rat, have life,

> And thou no breath at all? Thou'lt come no more,
> Never, never, never, never, never!
>
> (5.3.304–7)

Choking his own life drive, Lear dies in the echoing howl of his repeating nothing. Entering the borderless place of death, he awakens to the emptiness of his beating heart. Hearing his heart beat, he lets it break and joins Cordelia in the radical no-place of death, the ground that stages the "no" foretold in her initial "nothing."

Coda

If theatrical architecture creates an archive of spaces that exist in order to stage their own disappearance, it gives testimony as well to those who find themselves in the midst of having lost their place, their space in the social relation. What remains radical about the dialogue initiated by Cordelia is her willingness to accept the exile brought about by her refusal to pretend that love can be scripted and staged, that it can arrive in the location it seeks. Cordelia remains true to the essential aspiration of love itself, even while it means she wounds the one she loves. The essential aspiration of her love is to be with her beloved, to follow him into the homelessness of his own heart, to be with him even when she is prohibited by him from sharing the same location with him. Trying to keep her faith with love's aspiration leads to her death, but not before she illuminates for Lear that they are bonded and bound by love's beating heart. This illumination comes in time to break his heart.

Lear tries to roar over his heart's persistent beat. The silence and nothing that Cordelia offers Lear remain for us a vivid (and awe-full) testament to our own self-dividing relationship to a love that empties us out and in that self-erasing sustains us, allowing us, sometimes, to become an "us." Such a love requires that we recognize our own aspiration toward self-erasure, what Freud called the death drive, and our desire to resist getting lost, to be grounded within a space we might call home.

But perhaps most remarkably of all, Cordelia's attempt to follow Lear into his own emptiness does not make us love her more than we love Lear. As a catalyst for our own awakening to love's radical demand for freedom, Cordelia serves to allow Lear's more faltering heart to combust with our own. Lear's question, "Who is it that can tell me who I am?" is theatre's, and our own, most intimate question. Without a fixed boundary in time or space, theatre strips us of our location and gives us a taste of a property-less being. Exposed with Lear to the elemental force of the need for love, the audience of *King Lear* also loses the sheltering consolations of architectural form. The discovery space that theatre opens onto exposes us to an "identification of anxiety, the final revelation of *you are this — you are this, which is so far from you, this which is the ultimate formlessness*" (Lacan 1988: 155). Theatre architecture offers us a glimpse of this formlessness and its reconstructions expose the effort we make to keep from discovering it.

NOTES

1 The discussion of women in *Lear* is among the
most illuminating in the critical literature,
especially in terms of psychoanalytic interpretations of the play. See Kahn (1986) for the
beginning point. See also Thompson (1991)
and Adelman (1992) for excellent discussions
of the maternal, femininity, and sexual difference in the play.
2 All quotes taken from Kenneth Muir's Arden
edition (1972).
3 For the centrality of the heartbeat see Nancy
(1991). His essay and a subsequent conversation he had with Avital Ronell and Wolfgang
Schirmacher in August 2001 have influenced
my sense of *Lear's* many heartbreaks.
4 Kristeva (1997) traces the logical end-point of
this breakdown. She argues:

To say that theater does not take place implies first that the speaking animal has
reached a point in its experience which signifies that its only inhabitable place – locus
– is language (*le langage*). Since no set or
interplay of sets is able to hold up any longer
faced with the crisis of state, religion, and
family, it is impossible to prefer a discourse
– to play out a discourse – on the basis of a
scene, sign of recognition, which would
provide for the actor's and the audience's
recognition of themselves in the same
Author. (1997: 277)

I am suggesting that this loss of habitable place in
the theatre is already underway in *King Lear*.

REFERENCES AND FURTHER READING

Adelman, Janet (1992). "Suffocating Mothers in
King Lear." In *Suffocating Mothers: Fantasies of Ma-
ternal Origin in Shakespeare's Plays, "Hamlet" to "The
Tempest.*" New York: Routledge, pp. 103–29.

Armstrong, Philip (1994). "Uncanny Spectacles:
Psychoanalysis and the Texts of *King Lear,*"
Textual Practice 8, 3: 414–34.

Asher, Lyell (2000). "Lateness in *King Lear.*" The
Yale Journal of Criticism 13, 2: 209–28.

Austin, J. L. (1962). *How to Do Things with
Words*, ed. J. O. Urmson & Marina Sbisá.
Cambridge, MA: Harvard University Press.

Bachelard, Gaston (1969). *The Poetics of Space*,
trans. Maria Jolas. Boston: Beacon Press.

Blatherwick, Simon & Gurr, Andrew (1992).
"Shakespeare's Factory: Archaeological Evaluations on the Site of the Globe Theatre at
1/15 Anchor Terrace, Southwark Bridge Road,
Southwark." *Antiquity* 66: 315–29.

Booth, Stephen (1983). *"King Lear," "Macbeth,"
Indefinition, and Tragedy*. New Haven, CT: Yale
University Press.

Brayton, Dan (2003). "Angling in the Lake of
Darkness: Possession, Dispossession, and the

Politics of Discovery in *King Lear.*" *ELH* 70:
399–426.

Cavell, Stanley (1969). "The Avoidance of Love:
A Reading of *King Lear.*" In *Must We Mean
What We Say?: A Book of Essays*. New York:
Charles Scribner's Sons, pp. 267–353.

Covington, Richard (1997). "The Rebirth of Shakespeare's Globe." *Smithsonian Features* 28 (November 8): 64–75.

Dodd, William (1999). "Impossible Worlds:
What Happens in *King Lear*, Act 1, Scene 1?"
Shakespeare Quarterly 50, 4: 477–507.

Freud, Sigmund ([1922] 1953–1974). "Beyond the
Pleasure Principle." In *The Standard Edition of
the Complete Psychological Works of Sigmund Freud*,
ed. James Strachey, vol. 18. London: Hogarth
Press.

Garber, Marjorie (1990). "Shakespeare as Fetish."
Shakespeare Quarterly 41: 242–50.

Gillies, John (2001). "The Scene of Cartography
in *King Lear.*" In Andrew Gordon & Bernhard
Klein (eds.) *Literature, Mapping, and the Politics
of Space in Early Modern Britain*. Cambridge:
Cambridge University Press, pp. 109–37.

Greenblatt, Stephen (1980). *Renaissance Self-Fashioning: From More to Shakespeare*. Chicago: University of Chicago Press.

Gurr, Andrew (1988). "Money or Audiences: The Impact of Shakespeare's Globe." *Theatre Notebook* 42: 3–14.

Halio, Jay (ed.) (1992). *The Tragedy of King Lear*. Cambridge: Cambridge University Press.

Halpern, Richard (1991). "*Historica Passio*: King *Lear*'s Fall into Feudalism." In *The Poetics of Primitive Accumulation: English Renaissance Culture and the Genealogy of Capital*. Ithaca, NY: Cornell University Press, pp. 215–69.

Holbrook, Peter (2000). "The Left and *King Lear*." *Textual Practice* 14, 2: 343–62.

Hollier, Denis (1989). *Against Architecture: The Writings of Georges Bataille*, trans. Betsy Wing. Cambridge, MA: MIT Press.

Kahn, Coppelia (1986). "The Absent Mother in *King Lear*." In Margaret W. Ferguson, Maureen Quilligan, & Nancy Vickers (eds.) *Rewriting the Renaissance: The Discourses of Sexual Difference in Early Modern Europe*. Chicago: University of Chicago Press, pp. 33–49.

Kiernan, Pauline (1999). *Staging Shakespeare at the New Globe*. London: Macmillan Press and St Martin's Press.

Kristeva, Julia (1997). "Modern Theater Does Not Take (a) Place." In Timothy Murray (ed.) *Mimesis, Masochism, and Mime: The Politics of Theatricality in Contemporary French Thought*. Ann Arbor: University of Michigan Press, pp. 277–81.

Lacan, Jacques (1988). *The Seminar of Jacques Lacan*, book II: *The Ego in Freud's Theory and in the Technique of Psychoanalysis*, ed. Jacques-Alain Miller. New York: W. W. Norton and Co.

Laplanche, Jean & Pontalis, J. B. (1986). "Fantasy and the Origins of Sexuality." In Victor Burgin, James Donald, & Cora Kaplan (eds.) *Formations of Fantasy*. London: Methuen, pp. 5–34.

Moretti, Franco (1982). " 'A Huge Eclipse': Tragic Form and the Deconsecration of Sovereignty." In Stephen Greenblatt (ed.) *The Power of Forms in the English Renaissance*. Norman, OK: Pilgrim Books, pp. 7–36.

Muir, Kenneth (ed.) (1972). *The Arden Edition of the Works of William Shakespeare*: "*King Lear*." London: Methuen.

Mulryne, J. R. & Shewring, Margaret (eds.) (1997). *Shakespeare's Globe Rebuilt*. Cambridge: Cambridge University Press.

Nancy, Jean-Luc (1991). "Shattered Love." In Peter Connor (ed.) *The Inoperative Community*. Minneapolis: University of Minnesota Press, pp. 82–109.

Nancy, Jean-Luc (2001). "In Conversation with Avital Ronell and Wolfgang Schirmacher." Available at: www.egs.edu.

Orgel, Stephen (1975). *The Illusion of Power: Political Theater in the English Renaissance*. Berkeley, CA: University of California Press.

Orrell, John (1983). *The Quest for Shakespeare's Globe*. Cambridge: Cambridge University Press.

Orrell, John (1992). "Spanning the Globe." *Antiquity* 66: 329–33.

Phelan, Peggy (1997). "Uncovered Rectums: Disinterring the Rose Theatre." In *Mourning Sex: Performing Public Memories*. London: Routledge, pp. 73–94.

Phelan, Peggy (2002). "Architecture and the Life Drive." In Philip Ursprung (ed.) *Herzog and de Meuron: Natural History*. Montreal: CCA Press.

Rudnytsky, Peter L. (1999). " 'The Darke and Vicious Place': The Dread of the Vagina in *King Lear*." *Modern Philology* 96, 3: 291–311.

Taylor, Gary & Warren, Michael (eds.) (1983). *The Division of the Kingdoms: Shakespeare's Two Versions of "King Lear."* Oxford: Clarendon Press.

Thompson, Ann (1991). "Are There Any Women in *King Lear*?" In Valerie Wayne (ed.) *The Matter of Difference: Materialist Feminist Criticism of Shakespeare*. New York: Harvester Wheatsheaf, pp. 117–28.

Vitruvius (1999). *Ten Books of Architecture*, trans. Ingrid D. Rowland. Cambridge: Cambridge University Press.

Weis, Rene (1993). *"King Lear": A Parallel Text Edition*. London: Longman.

Wells, Stanley (1983). "The Once and Future *King Lear*." In Gary Taylor & Michael Warren (eds.) *The Division of the Kingdoms: Shakespeare's Two Versions of "King Lear."* Oxford: Oxford University Press, pp. 1–22.

Worthen, W. B. (2003). "Globe Performativity." In W. B. Worthen *Shakespeare and the Force of Performance*. Cambridge: Cambridge University Press, pp. 79–116.

2

Shakespeare's Two Bodies

Peter Holland

Staging the Monograph

In 1957 the great medieval historian Ernst Kantorowicz published *The King's Two Bodies*. For nearly half a century now, applying his outline of the concept of the King's two bodies to Shakespeare's histories has been an orthodoxy of Shakespearean criticism. Few notions derived from early modern and earlier cultural contexts have proved so durable in their unquestioning acceptance by Shakespeare scholars. Though David Norbrook, in a brilliant cultural reading of Kantorowicz himself as well as mid-seventeenth-century political usage of the terminology, has questioned just how pervasive the idea was, the presence of the doctrine is still repeated as early modern cultural fact. Kantorowicz traced, in enormous detail and with immense authority, the long history of the concept, dominant in the Middle Ages and equally in the early modern period, that the king was possessed of two bodies, a body natural and a body politic. While the former was subject to the vagaries of mortality, the latter was eternal, literally embodying the nation and the authority of sovereignty, for, as an Elizabethan jurist described it, "his Body politic is a Body that cannot be seen and handled, consisting of Policy and Government, and constituted for the Direction of the People, and the Management of the public weal" (Kantorowicz 1957: 7). Kantorowicz demonstrated how the theory was vestigially but still powerfully present in a variety of apparent paradoxes: the slogan of the parliamentarians in the English Civil War, "Fighting the king to defend the King" (1957: 23), makes sense only if they were for the concept of kingship, the nation-state that might contain all the king's subjects and still be the body politic of the king, while vigorously opposing the application of kingship in the particular body natural of King Charles I, the arbitrary ruler.

Exploring the implications of the theory for Shakespeare's *Richard II*, Kantorowicz demonstrated that Richard's tragedy could be seen as the inadequate linkage of the two bodies, the failure perfectly to blend into a coherent whole the two forms of existence: the natural body on the one hand, fallible, individualistic and fatal; the body politic on the other, flawless, abstract and divine. As the two bodies separate in the political chaos of Bolingbroke's usurpation, Richard's deposition and eventual murder, so Bolingbroke faced a subsequent problem of a different inadequacy of unity, a failure of legitimacy that could only be resolved by his son, Henry V. Kantorowicz's revelation of the presence of a historicized political theory in the play's material form, something that, for instance, articulated the distinction of the bodies at every step of the play's trajectory in Richard's uses of pronouns, the "I" of the single body versus the "we" of the king's double corporeality, passed into critical orthodoxy, an accepted fundamental part of the play's means to mean.

Kantorowicz's work also made the comparatively rare transition from academy to theatre, the only comparable example probably being Peter Brook's use of Jan Kott's writing for his production of *King Lear* (Royal Shakespeare Company, 1962). In one of the finest of all British Shakespeare productions, John Barton, influenced by the work of his wife, the Shakespeare scholar Anne Barton, applied Kantorowicz's thinking about *Richard II* to his 1973 Royal Shakespeare Company production. Ian Richardson and Richard Pasco were cast as both Richard and Bolingbroke: at the production's start each night a figure looking like Shakespeare offered the two actors, each wearing rehearsal clothes (or at least a carefully chosen representation of such clothing), a crown and a mask which they held between them, "Shakespeare" nodded at one and he played Richard that night while the other played Bolingbroke. Of course the event was only apparently aleatory: the performance schedule announced which way round it was to be that night so that playgoers could choose which Richard to see or catch the reverse casting. But the inscription of the reading across the leading actors' bodies as well as both the characters' produced a physicalization of meaning in the process of performance that was remarkable and unusual in the practice of Shakespearean performance. Seen at the time by Stanley Wells as "in some respects the most strongly interpretative production of a Shakespeare play that I have ever seen" (1977: 65) – itself, I take it, a mark of the lack of such kinds of productions 30 years ago – and, over a longer perspective, as a production in which "[p]robably never has the connection between the academic and theatrical Shakespeare establishments been closer" (Kennedy 2001: 241–2), Barton's *Richard II* was remarkably prepared to make the anterior process of production into a visible event, re-casting the leads in play each night, rebalancing the relationship of two roles (so that, for once, Bolingbroke was no longer subordinate to the star role of Richard) as an articulation of scholastic reading.

The theory and production serve as a kind of prologue to my argument, marking a movement in mainstream classical theatre that linked a specifically academic reading of text to the theatricalization of that reading which allowed meaning to be, in its turn, read as positioned in the foregrounding of the apparent arbitrariness of the choice of the performer's body, casting as performance. Unlike in stage presence (Pasco taller and heavier, committed and emotional, the tragedian by stage presence; Richardson light and sardonic, the balancing comedian), the actors were offered as similar by haircut and matching beards, hair defining their emblematic connected-ness, however marked the difference in performance of each role would be.

I want this justifiably famous moment of problematized connections within mainstream Shakespeare production – actor and character, body and meaning, aca-demic and theatre – to stand as the start for a repositioning of the theory of the king's two bodies in relation to Shakespearean performance. More specifically, I will work with the dichotomous potential of the ancient terms of Kantorowicz's presentation to produce another tension: not body natural and body politic but body natural and body corporate. For the single largest recent growth area of Shakespeare publication and a remarkable application of a theory of Shakespeare to a practice lie well outside the conventions of the academic literature, drama and theatre departments where we usually expect to find Shakespeare; it is instead the application of Shakespeare to corporate management practice.

If buried within the concept of the business corporation is still the audible presence of the body as *corpus*, Shakespeare has become a resource through whose work, reified as lessons in management theory, the abstract bodies of the business structure and the human bodies that work within that structure can be manipulated. My approach, then, will need to explore what goes on in such writing, adumbrated in books with titles like *Shakespeare in Charge: The Bard's Guide to Leading and Succeeding on the Business Stage* or *Shakespeare on Management: Leadership Lessons for Today's Managers* or, most recently and startlingly for its extraordinary patterns of connections, a book on *Inspirational Leadership: Henry V and the Muse of Fire*, with the subtitle-cum-tagline "Timeless insights from Shakespeare's greatest leader," written not by an ex-business-man but a theatre director, Richard Olivier, son of Laurence Olivier and director of a group called Olivier Mythodrama Associates, which runs courses for one of the UK's major business schools, Cranfield School of Management, at the repro Globe in London where Richard Olivier directed the theatre's opening production of *Henry V* in 1997.[1] It needs no Freud to see the anxiety about the father that that text manifests, with its grainy still of Henry V from the father's 1944 film as the image on the cover.

"Shakespeare and management" is a place where the voicing of different early twenty-first-century concepts of the body can be tracked far beyond the human, the conventional limits of the theatrical body, allowing for a reconceptualization of Shakespeare (seen through the lens of a predictably but terrifyingly conservative business ethic) equally as radical as anything achieved by conventional literary or theatrical scholarship. What this kind of theory voices as a desirable practice for the bodies it defines (workers and corporations) is a consequence of its redefinition of the space of Shakespearean performance. The theatre of Shakespearean drama shifts from conventional theatre spaces to offices and boardrooms, not exactly street theatre but unquestionably a shifting away from where theatre is traditionally made. The theatre of performance, in such institutions, is revisualized as a space where performance is differently measured, not by the acclaim of critics but in balance-sheet, share-price, stock options and the income of the individual CEO.

Finally, I will move on to explore how the Royal Shakespeare Company as a corporate body, the largest institution devoted to Shakespeare performance in the world, functions in relation to its bodies natural, not least those of its actors and other employees, what happens, in effect, when the kinds of texts that occur on its stages are transferred into the practice of its corporate identity, the world of logos and branding, franchising and globalization, to which it has recently aspired, redefining as it does so what a theatre company is and how it sees itself when it seeks to align its form, its sense of company, less with other theatre companies than with corporations with similar multi-million pound turnovers and when it develops a belief in certain functions of the market economy which, sooner or later, have to be translated into the inconveniences of people. For however much the RSC may have chosen for a while to be selling a concept of "Shakespeare," a cultural brand with a remarkable market potential, it can finally only do so through a product which is human, which depends on bodies. In the context of early twenty-first-century cultural practice as much as in early modern London, theatre is made by companies whose institutional existences, unseen by audiences who consume only their visible cultural product, define modes of existence as bodies, as corporations and as companies of human bodies. In the negotiations between these different concepts of the word "company" lie the cultural purposes to which Shakespeare productions are put.

Bodies and Voices

Within the cultural forms taken by theatre companies are manifest forms of the tension caused by being trapped between the corporate and the collegial: on the one side, the theatre board of directors and, on the other, a version of the "band of brothers" myth (the theatre company as strolling players or invading army). These twin models offer polar variations of the placing of authority – one vested in the directors' and performers' sense of the aims of their practice and the other based in the accountability of directors (in the business sense) to the company's shareholders. In the practice of theatre, however, there is a further aspect of such modeling of the relationship of individual to company: the relationship of individual to text (or play-script or other demarcation of the pre-existing object of performance). This function-ing of authority, the authority of Shakespeare over the actor, has been superbly charted by W. B. Worthen. One area in which this process is especially manifest and which Worthen did not explore is the range of texts designed to train the actor to speak Shakespeare. I will establish the connection between voice-training and management practice later. I want first, though, to explore the perhaps overly familiar tension between body and voice, articulated this time as a contrast between the actor's necessary body and the training of the voice.

It's time for the reader to do some work.

If you turn to the long line of books on the Shakespeare shelves of almost any bookshop that are designed to help the would-be Shakespeare actor, you will find that, according to my check of a large sample of currently available books, they are overwhelmingly concerned with Shakespeare and voice. If the body figures at all – and often it does not rate even a passing mention – it is usually conceived as the necessary physiological concomitant of voice production. Shakespeare, from this perspective, is spoken text, and the plays might as easily be performed on radio as in the theatre. Just as performances, at Stratford and elsewhere, often offer supplemental transpositions – audio-described performances for the blind, signed or surtitled performances for the deaf – which define the possibility of completing that which cannot be seen/heard and hence indicate the incompleteness of the unseen or unheard, so I am suggesting a tension within the conceptualization of the completeness of the text in the contrast between actor-training and audience-memory – or, more accurately, spectator-memory.

But that clearly is not the job that the authors of manuals for actors have set themselves. Obviously, a popular book called *How to Speak Shakespeare* might quite reasonably be expected not to concentrate on the body, but Cal Pritner and Louis Colaianni's guide offers only four pages that explore the translation of line into movement, as they find the "implied stage directions" in the first meeting of Romeo and Juliet (2001: 94–8). Even at the point where they move from, in their words, "the technical aspects of Shakespeare's text" to "acting the text" (2001: 119), their analysis of the body in motion is restricted only to noting that at some point in the balcony scene Juliet comes on stage. One might have expected something more aware of the body in Madd Harold's *The Actor's Guide to Performing Shakespeare for Film, Television and Theatre* (2002), but I could not find a single passage which was not actually describing the technique necessary solely for audio work.

Body for Harold equals lungs and larynx, a fragmentation of the physical that is here internalized, the unseen of voice production. In the production of *Julius Caesar* by Romeo Castellucci for the Socíetas Raffaello Sanzio in 1997, the unseen became seen as the production made visible its investigation of the physiology of voice production as part of an astonishing study of the politics of rhetoric. When a character in the opening scene placed a laryngoscope down his throat so that his delivery of some of the play's opening scene was accompanied by the sight of his larynx hugely magnified, projected onto a screen upstage, when the actor playing Brutus delivered his forum speech in bursts punctuated by inhaling from a helium canister so that he sounded like Donald Duck, or when the actor playing Antony, who had had a laryngectomy so that he had no vocal chords, spoke by inhaling gulps of air and using a throat mike, the activity of speaking became visibly as well as audibly corporealized, the body's activity of voicing painful, constricted, a visual agony (Kennedy 2001: 352–5). The physiology of speech here becomes more than a necessary concomitant to the projection of Shakespeare's verse; instead it can become quite literally projected, a visible manifestation of the interior of the body, that which makes speech possible at all. Through his deliberate and extraordinary fragmentation of the body, Castellucci denies the denial of body, the ways in which the high cultural values ascribed to the Shakespearean voice are themselves a spurning of the body or rather, perhaps, a denial of the body's functionality, its fleshiness – as in the value accorded to the languorous, the elongated balletic body of, say, the young John Gielgud.

There are similar tropes of a denial of the body at work in classic late twentieth-century texts on speaking Shakespeare like Cicely Berry's immensely influential *Voice and the Actor* (1973) or, for the USA, Kristin Linklater's *Freeing Shakespeare's Voice* (1992). Linklater, Berry, who ran the RSC's Voice Department, and Patsy Rodenburg, long-time Director of Voice at the Royal National Theatre, are superb voice coaches who have achieved outstanding success countering the flow of actor-training which prepares actors to work with contemporary texts in theatre spaces small enough to be analogous to television, not to speak complex early modern verse on large stages to a thousand listeners. It is not my intention to disparage or mock their substantial achievements (see Knowles 1996, Werner 2001: 21–30). Rather, I want to see how the dominance of voice over body is also part of a particular re-structuring of dominance of the Shakespeare text over the actor in which the actor as vehicle through which the text is sounded has only to listen accurately to the text in order to make apparent the unitary meaning that the text is believed to have.

The actor's task is to get it right, not to make choices, to do what Shakespeare requires, not what the social and historical conditions of performance demand. One extreme of this theory is the assumption, increasingly prevalent among actors, that the 1623 First Folio carries a set of secret codes, apparently placed there by Heminges and Condell, to which the actor must attend. Terminal *e* and doubled *l*, for example, are thus deliberate signs of emphasis (with "arme" more emphatic than "arm" or "maiesticall" than "maiestical") while initial capitalization of nouns in mid-line is supposed to contain similar potent information.[2] That such encoding, another manifestation of the modern obsession with versions of conspiracy theory, flies in the face of everything textual bibliographers have established about the nature both of copy and of compositorial practice for the printing of that volume is, of course, no bar, for these accounts depend on the assumption that actors speak across the centuries to actors (not the readers whom Heminges and Condell actually addressed in their prefatory epistle) so that later generations "yet unborn" can accurately speak Shakespeare and present their master's voice.

Patsy Rodenburg's *Speaking Shakespeare* (2002), the most recent work by one of the major figures in voice-training, stands apart from what it is tempting to see as a kind of lunatic fringe of F1-fanatics. It is a clear and effective statement of where such voice work leads and is at least aware of the necessity of rethinking the body. Unusually for such books, a very early section is devoted to the body, with these explicit aims:

- to open the body and free it of any tensions that could restrict the breath, voice and speech muscles, and to be centred, alert and aware;
- to clear the body to allow the text to pass through unimpeded – the actor is like a vessel for the text;
- to eliminate any tensions that block flexibility and hamper the audience's connection to feeling;

- to achieve the state of readiness: the fully engaged mental and physical presence required in order to survive in heightened existence.

(Rodenburg 2002: 15)

Rodenburg is of course describing an anterior readiness to the presence of the body on stage; this preparedness of the body "should be the starting point of all rehearsal" (2002: 15). Her ideal body is neither the inert body that lacks exercise nor the body sculpted by too much time in the gym: "Neither state allows any physical flexibility, grace or passage of emotions." Both make it difficult to "engage and energise the power of the verse and language" (2002: 15).

For Rodenburg, the actor must rediscover the early modern body. Her historicized body is unlike the kind of body that recent fine work on the early modern conception of the body has generated. What Keir Elam has mockingly and unfairly called a "body boom" in the development of "Shakespeare Corp" (1996: 142) has been marked by an uncovering of the early modern body in new lights. Gail Kern Paster's (1993) investigation of the Foucauldian discipline of shame in the early modern body, Jonathan Goldberg (1992) on the sodomized body, Peter Stallybrass (1986) on the enclosed body, Laura Levine (1994) on the effeminization of the masculine body, Jonathan Sawday (1995) on the dissected body, and the essays on individual organs and body parts in David Hillman's and Carla Mazzio's (1997) collection have all been part of a remapping of the body, ultimately, of course, in the light of Mary Douglas, as a complex culturalized object. But Rodenburg's early modern body is different. It is defined by living in a dangerous world "where men openly carried weapons," where "people not only walked vast distances, but did so on rough ground which automatically centers the body and keeps you alert," where lifting a heavy sword "require[d] the body being centred," where "[s]louching ... in front of a monarch ... was not an option" (2002: 16). A public world but "[e]ven his intimate and private scenes are all about potent events and problems ... These are not relaxed scenes. Nothing in his plays is either casual or informal" (2002: 17). This banal account of how the early modern body differs is comically inadequate to such research. It is instead a vision of the body dependent on costume-drama, the body in costume, the kind of assumption that has led productions at Shakespeare's Globe in London to trumpet their recreation of Elizabethan costume through the use of the right dyes, including urine, and their use of early modern underwear, which the actors reported as transforming their bodies into the right walk for Shakespeare but which we could see as an invisible fetishization of the newly marketable commodity of the early modern authentic as a liberation for their bodies.

Rodenburg sees the modern "cool" style as impossible for Shakespeare, the "swaying, hip-hop walk" that is the "perfect indication of urban physicality ... confusing, if not ridiculous" when "[w]earing a period costume" (2002: 17). Note, of course, that Rodenburg seems here to assume period costume as the requirement for Shakespearean performance, so that the body is locked back into time. Rodenburg's antagonism to the cool walk makes rigid assumptions about the forms of connection between voice and body, assuming that you cannot talk the talk unless you walk the walk. Eventually, the failure of the cool is seen as a form of denial, so that the search is for a physical state that will respond to the heightened nature of the language by its alertness and consequently by its engagement with the structured otherness of Shakespearean language.

But she is equally fierce on the opposite of this cool denial:

> the *bluff* . . . [that] imposes a fake sense of power on the body and voice. Here the chest is heaved up, the back of the rib cage locked, the shoulders pulled back and the chin thrust forward. The shell of the body has been braced to appear strong and grand . . . The text gets covered with a generalized varnish of power, which wipes out the subtleties of the language. (2002: 18)

For Rodenburg, the test of the bluff state is the same set of assumptions about the physical world: "try fighting, walking on rough ground or riding like this and you will quickly realize how inefficient and unreal it is" (2002: 18).

Rodenburg's approach to the body is a prelude to the hard work on the voice and brain that occupies most of the book. Much of her analysis is brilliant, the result of fine close reading, sustained attention to the details of complex language. But Rodenburg connects the kinds of Shakespearean language to which she gives this attention with the forms of focus, what she describes as the circles, in which performance is manifest. In a section on "Focus and Energy" Rodenburg outlines a set of foci for voice energy that are designed to counteract the twin threats of denial and bluff, summed up here as "[o]ne translates broadly into devoicing and mumbling; the other into pushing and shouting" (2002: 217). The foci are defined as "three circles of concentration," a term that obviously, though here silently, derives from the circles of attention in traditional Stanislavskian actor-training. Significantly, as I have argued, Stanislavskian theatre is fundamentally incompatible with the forms of Shakespearean theatre because of its assumptions about the nature of realist character, the forms of psychologism within which the self resides, forms opposed to the nature of early modern subjectivity out of which Shakespearean theatre emerges (see Holland 1989).

Here are Rodenburg's three circles:

> The *First Circle* is where you engage with yourself. Here you speak, listen and use language from and for yourself. You have no need to communicate to the world. The First Circle relates to the energy of denial. When an actor lives here, the audience can seem irrelevant . . .
>
> The *Third Circle* is someone talking to the whole world – not to individuals, but in a general sweep to everyone. It relates to the energy of bluff. It's an attempt to connect outwardly. It can be a place of shouting, pushing, aggression, over-heartiness and general eye-contact . . .
>
> The *Second Circle* . . . is to do with connecting, listening and speaking to individuals. It translates into the state of readiness . . . The Second Circle is center, is open, is strong,

is vulnerable; it is not random. In the Second Circle we speak to connect. (2002: 217–18)

Revealingly, one of the exercises that Rodenburg prescribes for understanding the circles is to sit in front of a mirror:

- In the First Circle you will see yourself with a surrounding smear.
- In the Third Circle you will see a mask of yourself.
- In the Second Circle you will begin really to see yourself in the mirror, clear and *present*.

(2002: 219)

There is nothing much surprising here until Rodenburg begins to apply this methodology, for the language used to describe the circles is so loaded with value indicators, placing a premium on the second circle and displaying deep dissatisfaction with the other two, a strategy apparent in the refusal of numerical sequence in the outlining above, that it would appear that only the Second Circle is desirable – and we might remember that the second circle of Dante's *Inferno* is reserved for the lustful. But, as she explores a series of speeches in the last third of the book, the description of the actor's work can often sound like a set of instructions for a learner driver grappling with a stick-shift: for Edgar's speech in *King Lear* that marks his translation to Poor Tom, she recommends "Try starting in First, moving through Second into Third and then back to First on the final line" (2002: 265); for the duologue between the Macbeths after the murder of Duncan, "Experiment with Lady Macbeth staying in Second on Macbeth, but with Macbeth connected somewhere else in First, Second or Third" (2002: 313). It need not sound quite so ridiculous: for Shylock's "Hath not a Jew eyes?": "At first this seems straightforward: Salerio and Salanio, having pestered Shylock, are receiving an answer delivered in the Second Circle. However, if you assume that Shylock is surrounded by Christians – including the audience – then your options are open to move into Third. You can then take us all in" (2002: 284). By which, I take it, she does not mean that Shylock can trick us all.

The Circles are not, then, devised as a schema in which everything tends towards the Second. But there is little indication that Rodenburg conceives of a form of Shakespearean speech in which one might actively aim to achieve the reflection with the surrounding smear or even that some characters' language is sustainedly invested with the characteristics of the Third Circle's reflection of the mask. Richard II might, for instance, represent a character whose attempts to remove the mask, to move towards Second or First, become a major motor of the play while Bolingbroke assumes the mask of kingship without being able ever to lose the smear. Writing of *King Lear*, Grigori Kozintsev, the great Russian theatre and film director, argued that "In the first scene Lear's face must not be visible; only the mask of power... There is no hint of the real suffering and then the thoughtful eyes which appear later, when the mask has disappeared. I repeat: at first it is a mask of power rather than regal serenity"

(1977: 47). But Rodenburg has no space for the retention of the mask and the significance of its removal.

Rodenburg's exploration of language, then, assumes that the dominant form of linguistic interaction recognizes forms of contact even though there may be moments at which the character is invested in or modulates towards the private First Circle or the global, highly theatricalized audience-awareness of the Third. The Circles, that is, do not sit comfortably, conform effectively, either with Rodenburg's value-systems or with the nature of many characters' discourse – or, rather, they can conform with the range of Shakespearean characterization only by ignoring the value-systems that Rodenburg offers.

But, in any case, the kinds of language that Rodenburg chooses for her exercises are fascinatingly selected for their indications of her views of Shakespearean interaction. The majority are soliloquies or quasi-soliloquies (e.g., Antony to Caesar's corpse or Anne to the body of Henry VI). Those cases that are duologues are analyzed as if essentially non-interactive. Only rarely do Shakespearean characters in Rodenburg's selection engage with others – most markedly in the two substantial scenes she chooses (the Macbeths after Duncan's murder, Viola's and Olivia's first meeting). Characters present on stage, bodies existing in the physical space of performance, evanesce into nothingness, ignored by Rodenburg. Mass scenes, climactic moments which involve complex distributions of voices in the aural patterning of the play, hierarchies of the sounding of the text, and which also necessitate multiple perspectives, simultaneity of physical as well as aural event, vanish. Shakespeare becomes an assemblage of individuals talking, arrogantly and often solipsistically, character as bodies in action totally replaced by voices in a world dominated by the rights of speech (no wonder that Rodenburg's first textbook was called *The Right to Speak*). Community, the social, that sheer complexity of the societal which Shakespeare charts in the group scenes that mark the possible impossibilities of endings and climax, all such concerns vanish into a world of making by individuals with disregard for those other bodies with whom they share theatrical and social space.

But even in those cases where interaction is noticed, where the presence of others is more than an acknowledgement of the text's noticing of their presence (and Rodenburg's method leaves no space to notice those presences the text does not voice), here too Rodenburg's definition of the social is dominated by an evaporation of the specific. There is barely any recognition, even here, that dialogue is driven by social, political, cultural and, above all, deeply specific historical constructs. She is still essentially working with an essentialist view of the Shakespearean self, a transcendent universalism of individual identity, alienated from history, divorced from social meaning, separated from the exactness of registers in which early modern English constructs contact. Rhetorics, the devices of structured formal speech, pass almost unnoticed and instead there is that same quest for an inner emotional truth which Richard Knowles and Sarah Werner found in earlier voice training manuals. The truth of the actor's performance is then to be achieved through a connection between self and voice which is the actor's, not the character's, for, in Rodenbeurg's vocal world, there is no unlikeness that needs to be demonstrated, no distance that must be signaled.

If Rodenburg's work, like that of Berry and Linklater, voices a markedly archaic Shakespeare, a disembodied voice speaking across centuries the timeless truths about humanity, an origin of moral statement and emotional veracity that have no physicality, only feeling and thought and the power of speech – and I keep hearing the comment of H. M. Warner of Warner Brothers in 1927, "Who the hell wants to hear actors talk?" (quoted in *The Week*, January 11, 2003: 10) – its denial of the social in its choice of material and its way of treating that material creates a kind of desire for the First Circle, for the malleability of the world that is defined by that degree of interiority, and an equal desire for the Third Circle's performativity, its globalization, its sheer assuredness that evades the emotional Second Circle.

The Company Voice

The forms of understanding, the forms of limitation, the forms of denial of history, the forms of rejection of what is specific to Shakespeare as an early modern writer who uses voice and body in a theatrical space, all these modes of creating a particular kind of Shakespeare for the actor's voice that underpin Rodenburg's work are identical to those underpinning the uses to which Shakespeare is put for corporate management study. In both multiplicity, possibility and ambiguity are denied in the search for a meaning that is unambiguously true, essentialist, applicable, relevant, moral, trustworthy and, above all, effective. Studies of Shakespeare and corporate management investigate characters. Moreover, these studies are entirely dominated by the belief that Shakespeare can be construed as the action of a few individuals divorced from that complex of early modern cultural meaning which academics have worked so hard to recreate and understand for its otherness, for the extent to which the plays are, as Brecht said, *zeitgebunden*, tied to their times (Heinemann 1985: 216). Such characters are praised for the extent to which they are voices who make their speech and, through their speech, their worlds; voice, not the body, is the unequivocal sign of the presence of the character. If, in one sense, the applicability to management practices of Shakespeare is the consequence of a readerly vision of Shakespeare, a Shakespeare performed only inside the head of the reader and then transferred to the office and boardroom, then such an approach to Shakespeare as a collection of disembodied voices, each solipsistically constructing a world that can be made into their image, is strikingly similar to the version of Shakespearean drama that emerges from actor voice-training guides. In both, the privileging of the individual over the social, of success for the one over the values of (the) company are being strenuously advanced. Isolation, manifested most particularly as soliloquy (which is assumed to mean talking to oneself rather than talking to/with the spectators), is privileged. The silent presence of a character transmuting or commenting on the action (as, for instance, a Celia can comment on what a Rosalind/Ganymede is doing with Orlando) is rendered invisible as well as inaudible. In such a structure bodies are devalued – actors' bodies in particular – so that voices, the voices of the powerful can dominate.

But in such contexts and within such assumptions, the possibilities of language to have multiple and variant discordant meanings are suppressed. Language, in such readings, has only unitary value, value which has no connection to the forms of theatre voicings. One example of the genre must stand for many. *Power Plays*, subtitled *Shakespeare's Lessons in Leadership and Management*, is, perhaps even more than Richard Olivier's book on *Henry V*, an odd collaboration. The exact shares of authorship are difficult to determine but much of the book is written by John Whitney, director of a Center for Quality Management and a professor at Columbia Business School. Whitney has also been a CEO, COO, director of several companies, the man recruited from his position as Associate Dean at Harvard Business School to rescue the Pathmark supermarket chain; he subsequently spent many years specializing in "corporate turnarounds" (i.e., various other restructurings and reorganizations that rescue ailing companies) as well as other kinds of consultancy work (Whitney 2000: 14). The other author is "the founder and CEO of Shakespeare & Company," not the ultimate integration of Shakespeare into the corporate structure but a theatre company which has been performing in Lenox, Massachusetts, since 1978 and is currently engaged in trying to reconstruct the Rose Theatre there. Packer and Whitney have taught management skills together for some time, including "a course called 'In Search of the Perfect Prince' on Shakespeare and Leadership at Columbia Business School" (2000: 15).

In the chapter of *Power Plays* concerned with "Women and Power," a chapter written by Packer, she turns from consideration of Rosalind – "Rosalind organizes the country folk, arranges four marriages, makes everyone think the way she thinks, is witty, intelligent, and forceful. Could Rosalind become a CEO? I think so" (2002: 125), and a comparison of Rosalind with Anita Roddick, founder of Body Shop (comparing a character in a play with an individual in the business world is a recurrent method throughout this book and others in the genre), to making a point about women in power through a consideration of Gertrude, who "watches Ophelia drown without sending for help or trying to help her herself":

> Why would one woman watch a younger woman drown? ... Shakespeare only hints at the reason for her callousness: Gertrude serves the crown. Her power is derived from being married to a king ... Like Nancy Reagan or Princess Diana or Clare Boothe Luce, she must always acknowledge the primacy of this married relationship as the source of her power ... Otherwise it's trouble. And Ophelia ... is trouble. Ophelia is dangerous. She's telling the truth and rocking the boat. And it's the boat Gertrude is sailing in that she's rocking. (2000: 125–6)

If we leave to one side for a moment the astonishingly clichéd language of the piece, there is a striking lack, a suppression here, of a whole series of problems. There seems to be no sign of moral condemnation, apart from that passing mention of Gertrude's "callousness," itself a surprisingly weak term. Packer is curious about Gertrude's behavior but does not decry it. Morality is not a feature of this analysis, simply efficacy, the anxiety about the position within a company of Gertrude defined as "an obvious example of a woman who has power by proxy," someone who, "like... countless CEOs' second wives... are trophy wives" (2000: 126).

But equally there is nothing whatsoever in *Hamlet* that indicates that Gertrude observed the events she describes in the speech narrating Ophelia's drowning. Gertrude could have been told all this by someone else and been the bearer, but not the observer, of bad tidings. The speech becomes, for Packer, simply and unquestioningly a statement of complicit guilt – insofar, that is, that Packer sees it as being terribly guilty. There is no possibility here of the speech existing as a rhetorical construct, an example of the long line of messengers' accounts in which speech is dissociated from speaker. It is, obviously, possible to play the speech as an expression of conspiratorial responsibility – though I have never seen (heard?) it done – but it is only one narrow reading out of the possibilities of the text. The speech is brutalized – and the nature of Gertrude along with it – in the interest of serving an analytic end, one which is part of the book's continual use of Shakespeare to justify, never to question or subvert, the forms of corporate capitalism's management structures. Less Shakespeare and company than Shakespeare co-opted, *Power Plays* is a pristine example of Shakespearean appropriation, one that, though co-authored by someone who is "[a]rguably the most prolific female director of Shakespeare's plays in the world" (www.shakespeare.org/home/company.html), is unarguably blind to bodies and voices in theatrical space, to the openness of interpretation, to the ways in which language may be presented as meaning by the performers and received as meaning by the playgoers.

We could, of course, construct a reading of Packer's reading, a way in which Packer acts as Whitney's trophy wife (a Shakespeare theatre director and a woman) for the writing of his text, one which is dominated by him and in which he generously allows Packer's voice occasional audibility. Even the chapter on "Women and Power" is controlled by his permission of her voicing. It opens with an epigram taken from the French Queen in the last scene of *Henry V*, "Haply a woman's voice may do some good," a moment where a woman's voice does no good at all in the offstage negotiations over the peace treaty, for "When articles too nicely urged be stood upon" – and the article that her husband stands upon is the clause that disinherits her son, the Dauphin – he is forced to consent, while onstage a woman's body, "our capital demand, comprised / Within the fore-rank of our articles," is the visible subject of Henry's endless voicing of desire for possession: "I love France so well that I will not part with a village of it, I will have it all mine" (5.2.93–4, 96–7, 173–4). Whitney's voice follows: "Tina Packer does not think the issue of women's equality with men in business is resolved yet. In this chapter – in Tina's own words – she gives us her views on the subject" (2000: 117). Packer's voice is constricted here by Whitney as completely as she in turn constricts Gertrude's: her views are apparently not his in this formulation and the intimate "Tina" controls her as completely as Henry V's possessive anglicizing of Katherine of France into Kate. As David Brent,

Ricky Gervais's wonderful creation, says, in BBC Television's brilliant television series *The Office*, "You have to be 100% behind someone before you can stab them in the back" (quoted in *The Week*, January 25, 2003: 10).

It is, of course, the case that the action of a Shakespeare play can be appropriated to diverse uses. It may make sense to some to suggest that Petruchio's actions on the road back to Padua, the sun/moon scene, show how he, "ever the good executive, test markets his new approach as he proceeds" (Augustine & Adelman 1999: 52) and that his "method of handling change in a creative and determined manner furnishes six critical lessons on seizing opportunities, grasping future potential, staying in familiar territory, forcing change, moving fast, and becoming nimble" – or rather it will only make sense if you are sure, as the authors of *The Bard in Charge* are (but I am not) that "Kate and Petruchio become the most compatible couple in all Shakespeare [because] change has enabled them to live together, happily ever after" (1999: 54). I don't find it impossible to read the play this way, only that its action is not necessarily so much of a fairy tale. But then the teaching of management skills and leadership methods seems not to involve the possibility of multiple incompatible readings of events. Outcome is all in these corporate raidings of Shakespeare's assets, stripped out for use as "lessons in leadership and management," "leadership lessons," and a "guide to leading and succeeding on the business stage." But outcome for a company is less clear than outcome for a character locked into the narrative closure of a play, as repeated comments on case-studies draw breath to wonder what will happen to a company in the throes of reorganization and upheaval at the time of writing.

The Company's Bodies

These texts on Shakespeare and corporate success constitute a corpus (of course) of theory of an interconnection of the individual to the company, none of which seems relevant to the interconnection more normally observed within the practices of Shakespeare in performance, that between actor and ensemble. The actor's body is effectively aligned within such conceptualization of business behavior with the expendable worker, hirelings in the corporate structure in which, unlike the Lord Chamberlain's Men, no actor is sharer. The unvoiced doubt or subversive possibility is suppressed within a power structure in which, with the actor voicing the supposedly unequivocal meaning of the Shakespeare play, s/he has no freedom within the role s/he plays in the institution's practice. Powerless yet visible, the actor is the visible sign of the Shakespearean corporation in practice, ostensibly feted but contractually vulnerable, desired and yet controlled.

I want therefore to move finally from my appalled fascination with the closed readings that generate these studies to a brief case-study of my own, the corporate changes at the Royal Shakespeare Company since 2000, an example, within a theatre company, of applying the kinds of skills that the Shakespeare and management guides are designed to instill. The company's recent painful corporate writhings reflect on the institutions which make performance possible and the bodies and voices that are heard and suppressed, seen but unvoiced in the actions of such a company, a company in which the word used to stand for ensemble company, the collaboration of performance, but, for a time, seemed nearer to the corporate than in any other analogous institution for the making of theatre. By trying to turn theatre company into theatre corporation, the RSC's then leaders believed they were being visionary, realist, prudent and efficient. They proved to be perfect exemplars of bad managers, convincing proof that, as self-appointed guardians of a Shakespearean heritage, they were blissfully unable to learn from, as it were, *The Bard's Guide to Leading and Succeeding on the Business Stage*. As the title of the last chapter of Colin Chambers' excellent account of the RSC phrases it, "Company or Corporation?"[3]

The RSC is the world's largest theatre company. At many moments in its recent history it has had nearly 200 actors on the payroll, playing in as many as seven theatre spaces at the same time in Stratford, in London and on tour. Controlled by the terms of its Royal Charter, subsidized substantially, though inadequately, by grants from the Arts Council, the UK's public body for dispensing government arts funding, as well as by corporate sponsorship (including, in its long-term link with Allied Domecq, the largest sponsorship deal in UK arts history), the company took on its effectively normative form when in 1960 Peter Hall turned the old-style Stratford company into one with a new, twin-based existence, playing in Stratford and London. In the intervening years it grew and grew: adding two more theatres in Stratford, the Other Place and the Swan, to its mainstage home, the Royal Shakespeare Theatre, finally establishing a permanent purpose-built London base at the Barbican Theatre (with its small stage, the Pit) inside the City of London, touring regularly to Newcastle after the close of the Stratford season, and deriving significant income from the continued success of shows that had originated in its seasons, most especially the musical *Les Misérables*, every production of which worldwide paid some royalties back to the RSC.

In May 2001 the Royal Shakespeare Company, embodied for the purpose by its Artistic Director, Adrian Noble, announced a radical shake-up, the most substantial redefinition of the company's work since Hall created the RSC. The company would move out of its permanent residency at the Barbican complex; it would consider the demolition of the Royal Shakespeare Theatre, its main auditorium in Stratford-upon-Avon; it would no longer create seasons of productions through the work of a single large company of actors, assembled for a contract period of up to two years, playing a season in Stratford and then, after visiting Newcastle, taking their work to London; it would form companies for individual projects, playing wherever appropriate; the RSC would tour more widely in the UK and, especially, in the US; and it would create an Academy to train actors for the professional stage. Identified as "Project Fleet" (as in fleet of foot, not, as Michael Dobson once suggested, by analogy with the stench of the Fleet Ditch in Shakespeare's London), the new working model was announced in the press with the approval of the RSC's Board.

The RSC's corporate structure had just been overhauled. Now power was vested in a Board of about 16 governors, the remainder, nearly 40 in number, playing no part in decision-making. The corporate body was now as much a denial of ensemble and interconnectedness as Project Fleet's abandonment of the RSC as ensemble company, creating franchises and fragmentation in place of the networks that defined the practice of ensemble. Indeed, the majority of governors were informed about these radical changes in the RSC's operating model by being sent the press release, received by them the day after the news broke. The new model may have streamlined the operation of the company's corporate format but it also aligned it more strongly with a business enterprise. In a tellingly corporate move, the renaming of the old Council as a Board suggested as much. But the Board had no responsibilities to shareholders and was not subject to the Governors' censure. Instead it could do as it pleased, within the constraints of its charter and as long as it appeased its funders. The assumption of the Board's power was combined with a far more vulnerable assumption that the RSC's power in the marketplace was close to invulnerable; it was assumed, for instance, that there would be a long queue of London theatres lining up to take the RSC's shows as and when the RSC chose to play in London, a hypothesis totally at odds with the facts of London theatres where there is always more product lining up to find a vacant theatre to play in than empty theatres looking for mainstream classical Shakespeare productions to fill them.

Buried in the announcement of Project Fleet were further hopes and changes. The new shorter contracts were intended to enable major stars and others who were less than willing to commit themselves to long repertory seasons to come to or return to the RSC. There was much bruiting of names from the world of film: Morgan Freeman as Othello, for instance. The RSC's third theatre in Stratford, The Other Place, a small auditorium seating up to 170, the usual home for the RSC's new play commissions, would close, breaking the Hall belief that new drama, world drama and Shakespearean drama should weave together in the RSC to the benefit both of the actors' development and the audience's interests. The last performances there before this closure in December 2001, were of *Cymbeline* by the New York company, Theatre for a New Audience, whose directorate were amazed and appalled that such a magnificent venue was to be mothballed. Most disturbingly, there were to be a number of redundancies. Bodies were dispensable. There was no space in the new model for discussion, debate or representations, let alone compromise, and there was a widespread belief, never contradicted, that the redundancies had been rushed through to avoid being subject to the national implementation of a European Union directive on redundancy consultations. The technicians' union came within a few days of a balloted strike. Management played tough, hiring one of Margaret Thatcher's ex-assistants in developing anti-union legislation, and thereby offering a model for leadership that immediately lost the confidence of much of the workforce. The response in the British press moved towards increased hostility at the break-up of the ensemble model, the company as a company of actors rather than as a business machine, which Project Fleet was adumbrating. But the RSC's actors, frightened of being blacklisted by management and thereby unable to secure future contracts with the company, were forced to remain publicly silent.

As the RSC searched for new sources of funding, especially the US campus dollar, through expensive residencies in Michigan, at Davidson College, at Columbia and, if possible, Stanford, helped by the backing of the President of the University of Michigan whose move to Columbia cemented the RSC's ties there, so plans became ever wilder. Predicating Project Fleet on the need to find the right venue for a production rather than fitting it to existing theatre spaces, the RSC announced a season of late Shakespeare plays at the Roundhouse in London, an erstwhile locomotive turntable house which had been the graveyard of numerous theatre and other arts projects since the 1960s. Since promenade productions would not transfer to Stratford, plans were seriously investigated either to close the main theatre and play the late plays in a tent on the banks of the Avon or to floor over the auditorium of the RST to allow an onstage audience to encircle the playing-space. Such plans might have made sense with limitless funding, but in an era of financial austerity they proved impracticable, and the first fruits of Project Fleet's commitment to finding the right space for the show rather than fitting the show to the space was to have the productions restaged to fit behind the Royal Shakespeare Theatre's proscenium arch. Audiences at the Roundhouse were, as many had predicted, extremely low, both in percentage and in box-office terms. This move by the RSC, north from the center of London, was fuelled by an anxiety bordering on panic among the main British theatre companies that the core audience for theatre was old and aging. But if younger people came to the Roundhouse older people did not and the younger audience is not a basis for an economically viable operation without heavy subsidy (of the kind the National Theatre would shortly secure for its own seasons which enabled them to price hundreds of seats at £10).

In May 2002 Adrian Noble abruptly announced his resignation, an embarrassingly few days after the reviews of his stage production of the film *Chitty Chitty Bang Bang* guaranteed his income for the next few years. His successor, Michael Boyd, has reneged on most of what Project Fleet was ostensibly about and has, after an initial flurry of bizarre plans, including, most memorably, the idea of turning the Royal Shakespeare Theatre into a sound-stage for filming RSC shows, returned to the ensemble model of company with a long-term plan of a permanent grouping that raised the stakes to something that smacks even more of the Comédie Française or the Moscow Art Theatre than Hall's RSC (based on the Berliner Ensemble), with all the risks of fossilized, dull styles that characterize those fabled companies. Redundancies proved not to be at the level initially announced, but some employees were sacked and legal actions against the RSC for unfair dismissal continued. Even more disturbingly, in the aftermath of Project Fleet's losses, Boyd too purged staff, dismissing, among others, the heads of design and voice, both of whom had opposed Noble's plans but were swept out by the new broom.

What has been the net result? Some have lost jobs and careers. Those governors outside the Board who protested the decision either publicly or privately were rapped over the knuckles by the Board's chairman for disloyalty and found themselves retired from their connection with the company. The company was saddled with a massive deficit, not least from the ill-fated Roundhouse project, with severe consequences for the nature of its operations in years to come. It has a new – and good – Artistic Director in Michael Boyd. Project Fleet conspicuously failed to attract the major stars or other returnees to its ranks that were hoped for: the production of *Antony and Cleopatra* in the Royal Shakespeare Theatre in the summer of 2002, for instance, did finally, after much searching, cast an Antony in Stuart Wilson, but his return to the stage after a long absence showed why he is a good film actor who had realized that was where his future lay; otherwise, the cast looked much like before, though even more undercast than usual. Nonetheless, the RSC had fine productions during the corporate convulsions, though most of those were by Gregory Doran, Boyd not having directed a show for the company for over two years. It lost much support, suffers from low workplace morale, and has, for now at least, lost the respect of and the cash from audiences in London. Its recent infrequent visits to the capital were conspicuous financial failures – with seasons closing early, much of the 2003 Stratford season was not brought to London for the first time in decades (not least because no venue was available) – until the sell-out success in London's West End of *All's Well that Ends Well*, perhaps a prescient title, a success predicated neither on the RSC's company name nor on its being an ensemble company but on the urgent wish of crowds to see Judi Dench in probably her last Shakespeare role on stage. The RSC in London has lost out to the tourist attraction of the Globe and the exhilarating popularity of the brilliance of the National Theatre under Nicholas Hytner. Employees are disaffected; the theatre community is suspicious; and the Chairman, Lord Alexander, finally resigned, to be replaced by Sir Christopher Bland, whose surname sounds worryingly like a character in a play by Ben Jonson. The elaborate plans to demolish the Royal Shakespeare Theatre have been effectively abandoned and the appointment for the project of a radical Dutch architect, Erick van Egeraat, with no experience of building theatres, terminated.

For some future author of another book on Shakespeare and corporate management, the failure of the Board and the company's management team to learn from Shakespeare would be an interesting topic. But what would they have learned? From the kinds of books that have appeared so far, perhaps only that a certain ruthlessness in the workplace is desirable. Shakespeare's theatre company, the Lord Chamberlain's/King's Men, lasted for more than 50 years, by far the longest-lived early modern company. It was owned by the actor-sharers who hired others to complete the cast. As a mythic model for a body corporate one could do much worse, for there is no evidence that the actual experience of an actor-sharer, hireling or boy working for the company was as ideal as the force of the myth might lead one to wish. As Colin Chambers rightly emphasizes, the earlier forms of the RSC were structures in which actors had remarkably little power and were often alienated from the administration and in which the equally potent myth of the company as family has to be seen against a reality in which the family "was also primarily patriarchal, heterosexual and white" (2004: 187).

In his closing sentence Chambers shows that the RSC's confusion over its identity as company, what kind of a body it is, is one that is hardly unique to its status, its size or its concerns as a producer of theatre: "Whether or not the RSC can regenerate again

as an innovative company at the centre of theatrical creativity or becomes an institution enslaved to corporate demands is a question as critical for an increasingly
uncertain Britain as it is for the company itself" (2004: 191). In the opposition
that Kantorowicz made us understand, the body politic was by definition unnatural.
Perhaps Shakespearean companies like the RSC – though by no means solely the RSC
– even while they need to reinvestigate what kinds of bodies they contain, what sort of
institutions they are and what it means to be a company, are inevitably constricted by
the models of operation that the forms of the modern state enshrine, the twenty-first-
century version of the king's two bodies. *The Oxford English Dictionary* in part defines
company as "A body of persons combined or incorporated for some common object, or
for the joint execution or performance of anything" (*n.* 6.a), something that might as
aptly describe a theatre company as the *OED*'s example, "*esp.* a mediæval trade guild."
The ensemble model for the RSC was more than a practice for making theatre that
enabled the interconnectedness of ten or more plays through the cross-casting of most,
though not all, the actors; it was also a sign of the recognition of theatre as a
collaborative project not amenable to corporate management practice derived from
systems devoted to profit as the greatest mark of successful performance.

Where studies of Shakespeare and leadership see his plays as the place in which the
power and prerogative of the powerful individual are examined, we might see the
plays as potentially also exploring structures of containment of individualism in favor
of different notions of the shared, the communal, the social. The problem is not
whether Adrian Noble or Lord Alexander proved to be more or less Coriolanus or
Henry V or Iago in the processes of corporate change, in the way that the alignment of
corporate individual to Shakespeare character is modeled in the studies of Shakespeare
and business. Rather, it was the failure to see the collectivity of bodies in the theatre
company, a grouping in which many voices need to be heard, by offering instead a
model that rejected discussion, debate and those connections between Rodenburg's
three circles that alone seem desirable, for rule by fiat, locating power as a silencing,
something which Shakespeare drama often charts but of which it rarely if ever
approves. For the disjunction between body natural and body corporate in this
performance institution was as complete as the problem for Richard II that Kantorowicz charted in 1957, convincing proof of the wholeness of the bodies that make up
both the company and its corporate identity. It was a reversal of Sir Edmund
Plowden's statement in the late sixteenth century that "what the King does in his
Body politic, cannot be invalidated or frustrated by any Disability on his natural
Body" (Kantorowicz 1957: 7), for the results of what many saw as Adrian Noble's
mid-life crisis undoubtedly affected the workings of this body corporate. The collectivity of theatre bodies, reconnected to their voices, redefines the institutions within
which Shakespeare performance takes place, in ways that makes Henry V's call to his
"band of brothers" much more than the rhetoric of inspirational leadership.

Notes

1 In a slightly different but intimately intercon-
nected vein, see Leech (2001): the lengthy
subtitle tells the purchaser that the book will
teach "How to give a speech like Hamlet,
persuade like Henry V, and other secrets
from the world's greatest communicator,"
while the bullet-points on the jacket announce
that "You'll discover how to jump-start your
career through inspiration and vivid anecdotes." A puff on the jacket from "Walt
Robertson, the president of the System Division of Maxwell Technologies," praises Leech's
book as "A great management tool. Take this
book off the shelf and say to a colleague, 'Let's
see how Shakespeare would handle this communication problem!' "

2 The high priest of this particular religion or
master cryptographer at deciphering this code
is Neil Freeman (see Freeman 2001, and its
subsequent versions as editions of individual
plays). For the transposition into performance
of this fetishizing of F1 as explanation of all
difficulties, combined with an unconvincing
reconstruction of what is assumed to be early

modern performance practice, see the work of
Patrick Tucker and the Original Shakespeare
Company, in part recounted by Tucker. No
Shakespearean textual scholar has thought it
worthwhile to publish a rebuttal of the bizarre
assumptions in Freeman's work but as the
work becomes ever more influential in drama
training, it is high time to do so.

3 Chambers' excellent book appeared after this
chapter was written and we proved to have
been thinking about the RSC's history in
strikingly similar ways; I have been able to
incorporate only a little of his fine thinking.
For a longer and earlier but still very helpful
view of the RSC's history, see Beauman
(1982). For a more celebratory view of the
institution at work, including some useful
discussion with people in, for instance, the
RSC's administration and finance departments, see Adler (2001). On the upheavals of
Project Fleet, see the opposing articles by
Gilbert and Wells (2002), with their titles
setting John of Gaunt excoriating Richard II
against Paulina encouraging Leontes.

References and Further Reading

Adler, Steven (2001). *Rough Magic: Making Theatre
at the Royal Shakespeare Company*. Carbondale, IL:
Southern Illinois University Press.

Augustine, Norman & Adelman, Kenneth (1999).
*Shakespeare in Charge: The Bard's Guide to Lead-
ing and Succeeding on the Business Stage*. New
York: Talk Miramax Books.

Beauman, Sally (1982). *The Royal Shakespeare Company: A History of Ten Decades*. Oxford: Oxford
University Press.

Berry, Cicely (1973). *Voice and the Actor*. London:
Harrap.

Berry, Cicely (1987). *The Actor and His Text*. London: Harrap.

Berry, Cicely (2001). *Text in Action*. London: Virgin Publishing.

Brine, Adrian & York, Michael (2000). *A Shakespearean Actor Prepares*. Lyme, NH: Smith and Kraus.

Chambers, Colin (2004). *Inside the Royal Shakespeare Company: Creativity and the Institution*.
London: Routledge.

Corrigan, Paul (1999). *Shakespeare on Management:
Leadership Lessons for Today's Managers*. London:
Kogan Page Ltd.

Elam, Keir (1996). " 'In What Chapter of His
Bosom?': Reading Shakespeare's Bodies." In
Terence Hawkes (ed.) *Alternative Shakespeares* 2.
London: Routledge, pp. 140–63.

Freeman, Neil (ed.) (2001). *First Folio of Shakespeare in Modern Type*. New York: Applause
Books.

Gilbert, Miriam (2002). "The Leasing-Out
of the RSC." *Shakespeare Quarterly* 53: 512–
24.

Goldberg, Jonathan (1992). *Sodometries*. Stanford,
CA: Stanford University Press.

Harold, Madd (2002). *The Actor's Guide to Performing Shakespeare for Film, Television and Theatre.* Hollywood, CA: Lone Eagle Publishing Co.

Heinemann, Margot (1985). "How Brecht Read Shakespeare." In Jonathan Dollimore & Alan Sinfield (eds.) *Political Shakespeare.* Manchester: Manchester University Press, pp. 202–30.

Hillman, David & Mazzio, Carla (eds.) (1997). *The Body in Parts.* London: Routledge.

Holland, Peter (1989). "Stanislavskii i problema Iago [Stanislavsky and the Problem of Iago]." *Sovremennaya Dramaturgia* 6: 184–8.

Kaiser, Scott (2004). *Mastering Shakespeare.* New York: Allworth Press.

Kantorowicz, Ernst (1957). *The King's Two Bodies: A Study in Mediaeval Political Theology.* Princeton, NJ: Princeton University Press.

Kennedy, Dennis (2001). *Looking at Shakespeare,* 2nd edn. Cambridge: Cambridge University Press.

Knowles, Richard Paul (1996). "Shakespeare, Voice, and Ideology." In James C.Bulman (ed.) *Shakespeare, Theory, and Performance.* London: Routledge, pp. 90–112.

Kozintsev, Grigori (1977). *King Lear: The Space of Tragedy.* London: Heinemann.

Leech, Thomas (2001). *Say It Like Shakespeare.* New York: McGraw-Hill.

Levine, Laura (1994). *Men in Women's Clothing.* Cambridge: Cambridge University Press.

Linklater, Kristin (1992). *Freeing Shakespeare's Voice.* New York: Theatre Communications Group.

Martin, Jacqueline (1991). *Voice in Modern Theatre.* London: Routledge.

Norbrook, David (1996). "The Emperor's New Body? Richard II, Ernst Kantorowicz, and the politics of Shakespeare criticism." *Textual Practice* 10: 329–57.

O'Brien, Timothy (1974). "Designing a Shakespeare Play: *Richard II.*" *Shakespeare Jahrbuch (Bochum)* 110: 111–20.

Olivier, Richard (2002). *Inspirational Leadership: Henry V and the Muse of Fire.* London: Spiro Press.

Paster, Gail Kern (1993). *The Body Embarrassed.* Ithaca, NY: Cornell University Press.

Pritner, Cal & Colaianni, Louis (2001). *How to Speak Shakespeare.* Santa Monica, CA: Santa Monica Press.

Rodenburg, Patsy (1992). *The Right to Speak.* London: Methuen Drama.

Rodenburg, Patsy (2002). *Speaking Shakespeare.* New York: Palgrave Macmillan.

Sawday, Jonathan (1995). *The Body Emblazoned.* London: Routledge.

Shafritz, Jay M. (1999). *Shakespeare on Management: Wise Business Counsel from the Bard.* New York: HarperBusiness.

Stallybrass, Peter (1986). "Patriarchal Territories: The Body Enclosed." In Margaret Ferguson et al. (eds.) *Rewriting the Renaissance.* Chicago: University of Chicago Press.

Tassel, Wesley Van (2000). *Clues to Acting Shakespeare.* New York: Allworth Press.

Tucker, Patrick (2001). *Secrets of Acting Shakespeare: The Original Approach.* London: Routledge.

Wells, Stanley (1977). *Royal Shakespeare.* Manchester: Manchester University Press.

Wells, Stanley (2002). "Awaking your Faith." *Shakespeare Quarterly* 53: 525–35.

Werner, Sarah (2001). *Shakespeare and Feminist Performance.* London: Routledge.

Whitney, John O. & Packer, Tina (2000). *Power Plays.* New York: Simon and Schuster, Inc.

Worthen, W. B. (1997). *Shakespeare and the Authority of Performance.* Cambridge: Cambridge University Press.

3
Ragging *Twelfth Night*: 1602, 1996, 2002–3

Bruce R. Smith

> But
> O O O O that Shakespeherian Rag—
> It's so elegant
> So intelligent ...
> > T.S. Eliot, *The Waste Land*

When John Manningham sat down to record the performance of *Twelfth Night* that he heard and saw at the Middle Temple on 2 February 1602, he suffered a slip of the pen. "At our feast wee had a play called '~~Mid-~~ Twelve night, or what you will' " (1976: 48, 312). In that "~~Mid-~~" Manningham's modern editor has seen a testimonial to the fame of *A Midsummer Night's Dream*, which some scholars persist in associating with an elite private occasion like the gathering of law students, masters, and guests in the great hall of the Middle Temple at Candlemas 1602 (1976: 312). What was on Manningham's mind more likely, though, was midnight. "Not to be abed after midnight is to be up betimes," Sir Toby quips to Sir Andrew in the first lines of *Twelfth Night* 2.2. The eating and drinking that have taken place before midnight give way to the raucous joking and singing after midnight that rouse Malvolio from his bed. "My masters, are you mad? Or what are you?" Malvolio fumes. "Have you no wit, manners, nor honesty, but to gabble like tinkers at this time of night? ... Is there no respect of place, persons, nor time in you?" (2.3.83–5, 88–9, in Shakespeare 1987: 699). Eating, drinking, and carousing were, of course, just what John Manningham and his peers were doing the night they enjoyed *Twelfth Night*.

The lateness of the merry-making is one of the things that the students of Grey's Inn flaunted in the souvenir pamphlet recording their 1594 Christmas revels. On the first "grand night" of the festival the student lord of misrule and his court danced the galliard and other dances "until it was very late" (Bland 1968: 28). On the second grand night, it was "about Nine of the Clock at night" (1968: 29) when the Grey's Inn revelers received a retinue of their counterparts from the Temple. What ensued, after general confusion caused by the press of guests in the hall, was "dancing and Revelling with Gentlewomen; and after such Sports, a Comedy of Errors (like to Plautus his Menechmus)" – proceedings that would have prolonged the sports well past midnight. In his diary Manningham might, then, have been conflating two different frames of time: diurnal time in the fictional narrative of *Twelfth Night* and performance time in the physical space of Middle Temple Hall. To judge from the Grey's Inn pamphlet, the fictional time in 2.2 and the clock time in Middle Temple Hall on 2.2.02 may in fact have been one and the same. Understandably, then, Manningham might have fused the midnight revels of Sir Toby, Sir Andrew, Feste, and Maria with the midnight revels he and his fellow students were enjoying. If so, it was a third frame of time, festive time, that invited that fusion.

Diurnal time, performance time, and festive time hardly exhaust the multiple ways in which time is experienced in performances of *Twelfth Night*. By my reckoning, at least 14 frames of time are brought into play in any *Twelfth Night* production. Here they are, in ranked order from the shortest to the longest:

1   speech rhythm
2   musical rhythm
3   asides
4   beats, completions of motives within scenes
5   scenes
6   stage time, varying shares of lines among the persons of the play
7   duration of the entire performance
8   diurnal time
9   festive time
10 seasons
11 time presumed to have lapsed within the fiction
12 back stories
13 generational time
14 cultural time.

With a script other than *Twelfth Night* minor adjustments might be necessary toward the middle of the list – classical precept held, for example, that duration of performance, diurnal time, and time presumed to have lapsed in the fiction ought to be one and the same, and *The Tempest* honors that rule – but the beginning and the end of the list would hold true for any of Shakespeare's plays.

To designate these ways of experiencing of time I have chosen the word "frame" rather than "measure." With respect to time, "measure" is a concept grounded in physics. It entails objective calibration. Thus speech rhythm can be measured in iambs, musical rhythm in time signatures, asides in seconds, beats in minutes, and so on. The word "frame" is grounded in phenomenology, specifically in the concept of epoché, whereby a thinker brackets a certain experience and considers just how he or she comes to know that experience. The word "frame" catches the intentionality in the act of bracketing and sets off the subjectivity of the knowledge gained thereby (Moran 2000, 146–52). Thus speech rhythm can be calibrated in iambs – x / x / x / x / x / – but it is experienced as a series of "up beats" – ta-dum ta-dum ta-dum ta-dum ta-dum – that has an onward drive heard in the ear and felt in the gut. Each of the 14 frames of time in *Twelfth Night* can be understood in two ways, objectively and subjectively, as a calibration of time and as an experience of time. Through measure we mark time; through frames we remark time.

At a given moment all 14 frames of time are available for remarking. What the audience is scripted to hear first in *Twelfth Night* is musical rhythm. Then comes speech rhythm: "If music be the food of love, play on" (1.1.1). Orsino's speech begins a beat that dramatizes the mood of the duke's melancholy love-longing, a beat that continues without the "stop time" of an aside and reaches its end at line 22, when Valentine enters with the news that Orsino's latest appeal to Olivia has been rebuffed – a message that commences a new beat that concludes the scene 18 lines later. Using Andrew Gurr's estimate of the 2.4 seconds per line it would take to turn *Romeo and Juliet*'s 3,000 lines into two hours' traffic on the stage, beat one in *Twelfth Night* lasts about 1 minute 13 seconds, beat two about 44 seconds, the whole scene about 2 minutes 17 seconds (Gurr 1996: 81–2). Orsino is scripted to speak 30 of the scene's 40 lines, giving him the largest share of stage time. To this point, performance time and the time presumed to have elapsed in the fiction are the same. Curio's question, "Will you go hunt, my lord?" (1.1.16) provides the scene's only clue to diurnal time, just before dawn or else full day. If Valentine's reference to Olivia's prolonged mourning (1.1.25–31) counts as festive time – after all, funeral rites and mourning were as much a rite of passage in early modern life as celebrations of the twelfth night of Christmas – the description of her veiled sequestration sorts oddly with the May-Day suggestiveness of Orsino's "bank of violets, / Stealing and giving odour" (1.1.6–7). Seasonal time is not easy to sense at this juncture. The back story, too, remains pretty vague. Olivia's father, the Captain tells Viola, "died some twelvemonth since" (1.2.33), her brother "shortly" thereafter (1.2.35). How long has Orsino been courting Olivia? Months? Years? Since before her father and brother died? Or only afterwards? The script never answers such questions. Other elements in the back story, those pertaining to Viola and Sebastian, emerge as more important. Of the four ages of generational time invoked in Feste's final song, Orsino would seem to occupy a place toward the youthful end of "man's estate" (5.1.389). Cultural time, finally, is only just becoming apparent in Scene 1, before the romance world of shipwrecks, rescues, and reunions – vaguely distant in time as well as space – is called into being in Scene 2. Clearly enough, not all of the 14 frames of time are equally important in *Twelfth Night* 1.1. All 14 frames are established, but they emerge and recede as the play progresses. They ask to be remarked in different ways at different times. Beneath it all there is one constant: speech rhythms, often in the form of iambic pentameter.

To think about time in *Twelfth Night* productions we need, then, to think about multiple frames of time, all available for remarking at any one moment, deployed in counterpoint to the omnipresent pulse of speech rhythms, but brought into play with constantly varying emphases. The acoustic equivalent, in historical terms, might seem to be found in polyphony, in the multiple melodic lines of, say, a motet by William Byrd as those lines move over a sustained bass that grounds the rhythm and often enough establishes harmonic progressions as well. The melodic lines in a Byrd motet move in an analogical relationship to one another, a motif in the cantus part inspiring a repetition or variation in the tenor part and so forth. Not for nothing has Foucault isolated analogy as one of four structural principles of similitude in Renaissance thinking (1970: 21). The parallel between polyphonic music and the dramatic experience of time breaks down, however, when we consider how loosely coordinated the 14 frames of time can be. In Act 1, Scene 4, roughly 15 minutes into the play, Valentine congratulates Viola/Cesario on having won Orsino's favor in just three days (1.4.3); by Act 5, two hours or so later in performance time, the three days of back story and the events of the day-night-day that the audience has witnessed thereafter turn into three months (5.1.91, 96). How long, then, have Orsino and Viola/Cesario known one another? Five days? Three months? Three hours? Or all of the above? Differences in how frames of time can be related to one another vary not only within the confines of a single production but from one production to another. Cultural time in the Middle Temple *Twelfth Night* is not at all the same thing as cultural time in Trevor Nunn's 1996 film of the play, which finds a Victorian midpoint between our own historical moment and Shakespeare's, or in the period costumes and all-male casting of Tim Carroll's production, mounted in 2002 to mark the four-hundredth anniversary of *Twelfth Night*'s first recorded performance. At the opposite extreme, even the smallest frame of time, speech rhythm, can vary, as directors and actors choose to emphasize verse rhythms or to downplay them in favor of prosier delivery.

A truer model of how time varies from one *Twelfth Night* performance to another is (thank you, T. S. Eliot) ragtime. Ragtime music depends on a regular musical rhythm, but what happens above that bass rhythm is open to all sorts of syncopations, all sorts of variations. Ragtime is ragged time, in the sense of "a rough, irregular, or straggling form; having a broken jagged outline or surface; full of rough or sharp projections" (*OED*, "ragged" 2). That sense of irregularity-within-regularity, I believe, is just how the 14 frames of time are experienced as listener-spectators move from "If music be the food of love" to "The rain it raineth every day." With apologies to Eliot, I would suggest that every performance of a Shakespeare play is ragtime. The original February 1602 *Twelfth Night* at Middle Temple Hall, Trevor Nunn's 1996 film, and Tim Carroll's commemorative 2002 production allow us to experience ragtime in three quite distinct renditions.

Experiencing Time

Before turning to these three productions, we should first do our own bracketing of time and consider just what we mean when we talk about time in the theatre. Most scholarship on time in Shakespeare's plays is really not about time itself but about ideas about time. Thus, Frederick Turner distinguishes nine "aspects" of time that modern readers and audiences share with Shakespeare and his contemporaries: time as an objective historical fact, as personal experience, as agent, as realm or sphere, as a phenomenon in nature, as a medium of cause and effect, as particular moments or periods, as revealer or unfolder, as rhythm (1971: 3–5). David Kastan contrasts medieval certainties about time as evidence of God's providence with Renaissance anxieties about time as a force of change and dissolution (1982: 7–8). Time in Kastan's analysis is a function of dramatic genres, which "shape" time in distinctive ways. My interest here is the phenomenon that precedes the ideas that Turner and Kastan so usefully catalog and explore. What is time? Try defining it without using the words "time" or "temporal." You'll likely find yourself invoking space in one form or another, defining time in terms of intervals, spans, periods, points. Space is, indeed, at the root of the word "time." Tîmon in Old Teutonic combines tî- (to stretch, to extend) with -mon or -man (a suffix that turns the concrete into the abstract) (*OED*, "time" etymology). Hence the definition in the *Oxford English Dictionary* with the longest span of citations, extending back to the ninth century: "a limited stretch or space of continued existence" (*OED*, "time" I.1.a). Space is no less present in the *OED*'s two other basic definitions: "time when, a point of time, a space of time treated without reference to its duration" (II) and "time as the abstract entity within which particular stretches or points take place" (III).

Performances of *Twelfth Night* embrace all three of these basic senses of time. Events unfold in seconds, minutes, and hours that are experienced, within the fiction, as days, weeks, and months (*OED* I). The letter-trick that Maria, Sir Toby, Sir Andrew, and Fabian pull on Malvolio comes to fruition in a precise, much anticipated moment: "Enter Malvolio, cross-gartered and wearing yellow stockings, with Maria" (3.4.16 SD). Here is fit revenge on "a time-pleaser" (2.3.142), someone who is always *au point* (*OED* II). It is, finally, a larger entity, something subsuming these spans and points, that Viola/Cesario grasps for when he/she/he exclaims, "O time, thou must untangle this, not I" (2.2.40) (*OED* III). Even in this abstract invocation, time is a matter of space. If Viola/Cesario and the other protagonists uncoil strands of string as they walk the stage from moment to moment, the entity that makes sense of it all is a pair of hands with nimbly moving fingers.

It's the movement in those fingers that lets us hear ragtime. Even the most scientific, precisely calibrated measures of time, George Lakoff and Mark Johnson demonstrate, ultimately make reference to the human body, specifically the human body in motion. Time, they insist, does not exist apart from human knowing; rather, "time is something 'created' via our bodies and brains" (Lakoff & Johnson 1999: 167). All our ways of knowing time are functions of three basic elements: space, motion, and the events that occur as a result of motion in space:

> Every day we take part in "motion-situations" – that is, we move relative to others and others move relative to us. We automatically correlate that motion (whether by us or by others) with those events that provide us with our sense of time, what we will call "time-

defining events": our bodily rhythms, the movements of clocks, and so on. In short, we
correlate time-defining events with motion, either by us or by others. (1999: 151)

To co-relate is to "with-connect." The "with" in that connection happens via metonymy and metaphor. To the degree that we ourselves create events by moving in space
or witness events as people and objects move toward us, we conceptualize time in
terms of metonymy. "But at my back I always hear / Time's wingèd chariot hurrying
near": Andrew Marvell's sense of the future approaching him from behind finds
counterparts in other languages besides early modern English (2003: 82, Lakoff &
Johnson 1999: 141). To the degree that we project our experience of movement onto
other objects, we conceptualize time in terms of metaphor. "The clock upbraids me
with the waste of time" (3.1.129): when Olivia uses that phrase to dismiss Viola/
Cesario, she implicitly compares time to money, to coins that can be dropped or
thrown away in just the way Malvolio has tossed Olivia's ring at Viola/Cesario's feet.
Metonymy or metaphor: either way, time is knowable only in terms of "motion-
situations," the movement of bodies and objects in space to produce events. Time
is directional and irreversible because events are directional and irreversible. Time is
continuous because events are continuous. Time is segmentable because events have
beginnings and endings. Time can be measured because events can be counted (Lakoff
& Johnson 1999: 138).

     In the theatre this concatenation of space–motion–event suggests that time percep-
tion is not only a function of direct textual references but the effect of bodies moving in
space in certain ways. Or, on occasion, of bodies not moving in space. Time in *Twelfth
Night*'s first scene is framed by music with "a dying fall" (1.1.4), by allusion to things
falling into "abatement and low price/ Even in a minute" (1.1.13), by the main speaker's
being hunt*ed* rather than hunt*ing* (1.1.16–22), by his receiving a messenger rather than
sending one (1.1.22 ff), by future prospects of Olivia's walking a chamber round for
seven years (1.1.25–9). The first three minutes of *Twelfth Night* ask audiences to
experience time in slow motion, virtually in a state of suspension. Cues to the ways
time can be framed may be present in the script, but ultimately it is production choices
that create time. "Motion-situations" do the main work of framing. Framing doesn't
stop at the apron's edge. To the degree they share the same physical space, audiences,
too, are part of the space–motion event. Time at 120 feet in the Olivier Theatre on
London's South Bank is not the same as time at 50 feet in the reconstructed Globe down
the river. Different still is the audience's experience of time in a sequence of moving
images projected on a screen. The intrusion of a moving object not present in
Shakespeare's script – a camera – matters in every sense of the word.

Middle Temple, 1602

As evidence for the timing of *Twelfth Night* in its first recorded performance we
possess two documents: the script as printed in the 1623 First Folio and the entry in

John Manningham's diary, probably recorded soon after the February 1602 event. With respect to timing, we should think of the printed script as a musical score. Certain events are scheduled to happen in a certain order, for relatively shorter or longer durations. At the same time, we should not confuse the score with the performance. As with a musical score, the printed text sets certain parameters within which performance choices can be made. Taking a cue from Pierre Bourdieu, we might think of the script as an instance of *habitus*, a predetermined range of possibilities out of which choices are made, "a system of lasting, transposable dispositions which, integrating past experiences, functions at every moment as a *matrix of perceptions, appreciations, and actions*" (Bourdieu 1977: 82–3; emphasis in original). No less important than not confusing the score for the performance is not confusing the performance for the effect. Manningham's diary entry activates frames of time that seem quite specific to one particular performance on 2 February 1602.

The situation of freedom-within-limits characterizes even the smallest unit of time, verse rhythm. As a director, Peter Hall is famous for his insistence that timing is coded in the text: "Shakespeare tells you when to go fast, when to go slow, when to pause, when to come in on cue, which words to emphasize; he doesn't tell you why, that's the actor's choice. But the score is very, very detailed indeed" (Crowdus 1998: 49). With varying degrees of specificity each of the other 13 frames of time are also set in place by the printed text. References to music in the spoken text ("play on," 1.1.1), fragments of songs ("Hold thy peace, thou knave," 2.3.63), full texts of songs ("O mistress mine," 2.3.38 ff), and stage directions ("*Music,*" SD before 2.4.50) introduce musical rhythm at fixed points in the proceedings. Asides, though seldom used in this play and never marked explicitly in the printed text, call now and again for time out from the I speak/you speak rhythm of dialogue. Within scenes, beats are often indicated by entrances and exits. The play's 17 scenes are set to follow one another in an established rhythm: short (1.1), moderate (1.2), moderate (1.3), moderate (1.4), long (1.5), moderate (2.1), long (2.3), moderate (2.4.), moderate (2.5), moderate (3.1), moderate (3.2), moderate (3.3), long (3.4), moderate (4.1), moderate (4.2), short (4.3), long (5.1). Notably, the long scenes (1.5, 2.3, 3.4, 5.1) all involve the supposed subplot. Who has the largest share of the play's lines and hence the most stage time? Not Viola, but Sir Toby. Feste comes in third (Shakespeare 1969: 31). Michael Pennington comments on the sudden slowing of time when Sir Toby, Maria, and their cronies appear for the first time in 1.5: "Every time the play starts to move forward, it seems to pause and spread like water" (2000: 56). The actual duration of performance of the entire play depends, of course, on how rapidly the actors deliver their lines, not to mention blocking considerations, but the parameters of choice are determined by the printed text. In outdoor performances at the Globe, as Pennington observes, diurnal time was always a factor: the company "had to have an eye on the arrival of dusk" (2000: 181). Diurnal time in *Twelfth Night*'s printed text is marked most prominently by night, by the midnight revels of 2.3; all the other scenes take place at an unspecified anytime. The revelers of 2.3 are responsible for shifting the frame of festive time from mourning ("What a plague means my niece to take the death of her brother thus?" 1.3.1–2) to the holiday spirit suggested by the play's title. With respect to seasonal time, the wintry penumbra of *Twelfth Night*, January 6, is continued in the rain of Feste's last song.

When it comes to fictional time – time imagined as elapsing – Shakespeare pulls his frequent trick of establishing two frames. (*Othello* provides another well-known instance.) As we have observed already, some textual references suggest that four days elapse between 1.1 and 5.1; other references suggest three months (Osborne 1996: 1–14). A 1990 symposium of directors, all of whom had produced *Twelfth Night*, reached a rare consensus on the unimportance of the script's contradictions with respect to lapsed time. "The trouble is that the technical label 'double time' creates rather than defines problems," John Barton argues, "because it's in most of Shakespeare, and in many other Elizabethan and Jacobean plays. They didn't think twice about it, they didn't need to label it, and nobody raised any questions" (in Billington 1990: 6). Sir Philip Sidney, for one, did think twice when he famously derided disrespect for time in English plays, but that didn't stop most professional playwrights from doing exactly what Barton describes. Pennington catches the likely effect of such schemes when he comments on Valentine's precise indication of lapsed time in 1.4 – after just one scene has intervened since the shipwreck of 1.2: "To sneak in a narrative gap now – that Viola has been with Orsino for three days – gives the characters a more spacious history: we seem to have lived with them that bit longer, even as the action rockets along" (Pennington 2000: 53).

Until moving to Los Angeles, I had rarely encountered the term "back story" in print, much less heard someone say it. Suddenly there the word was, almost everyday, in the *Los Angeles Times* (political events have back stories in Los Angeles, not backgrounds) and in the comments of my students at the University of Southern California. Viola, so a cinema student informed me, has the longest back story of any character in *Twelfth Night*. And so she does. That story surfaces at crucial moments, when Olivia asks, "What is your parentage?" (1.5.267), when Viola/Cesario tells Orsino, "My father had a daughter loved a man" (2.4.107), when Sebastian asks, "What countryman? What name? What parentage?" (5.1.229) and Viola replies, "Of Messaline. Sebastian was my father. / Such a Sebastian was my brother, too" (5.1.230). Viola's story, we can assume, goes back at least 12 years, since as a female she would need to be that age to marry in early modern England (Wrightson 1982: 67). She shares her back story with Sebastian, but he gets much less stage time in which to command our attention. In specifying a date *ante quem* for Viola's story we are not asking, "How many children had Lady Macbeth?" (Knights 1979: 270–306), as if we were psychoanalysts or method actors. Rather, we are attending to just what the script tells us about the character's past, no more than that, but no less either. Compared with Viola, *Twelfth Night's* other characters are very much denizens of the here-and-now. Antonio has a back story that extends to wars at some unspecified time in the past, as does Orsino. Olivia's story goes back no further than her brother's death. Sir Andrew blurts out, "I was adored once, too" (2.3.175). Just when remains uncertain. How long has Maria fancied Sir Toby? We never really know. References to wars, to a brother's death, to being adored once are momentary flashes that light up vague, undefined reaches of the past. To judge simply by the number of references in the printed text, the primary back story in *Twelfth Night* is Viola's. Aside from the androgynous youthfulness that makes Viola and Sebastian so attractive, the script provides very few clues to generational time. How old are Orsino and Olivia? Sir Andrew and Fabian? Sir Toby and Maria? Malvolio? Modern productions often make the characters in the subplot noticeably older than the characters in the main plot, but the script provides no solid justification for that choice. Feste, in his final song if not in his sagacity throughout, embraces four generations: "tiny boy," "man's estate," the married man, the old man going to bed (5.1.385, 389, 393, 397). Cultural time, finally, seems from the printed script to be the present, if not a vague romantic past where shipwrecks, miraculous rescues, and unexpected reunions were common. Illyria may be distant in geographical space, but nothing in the script invests it with the chronological distance of the Ephesus of *The Comedy of Errors*, the Rome of *Titus Andronicus*, the Athens of *A Midsummer Night's Dream*, the Agincourt of *Henry V*, the Britain of *King Lear*, or the Tyre of *Pericles*.

The attention that John Manningham gives to particular frames of time seems partly to be a function of the occasion, the celebration of a major feast day in the yearly round of social life at the inns of court, and partly a function of cues in the script. Manningham's entry is worth quoting in full:

> At our feast wee had a play called "~~Mid~~- Twelve night, or what you will"; much like the commedy of errores, or Menechmi in Plautus, but most like and neere to that in Italian called Inganni.
>
> A good practise in it to make the steward beleeve his Lady widowe was in Love with him, by counterfayting a letter, as from his Lady, in generall termes, telling him what shee liked best in him, and prescribing his gesture in smiling, his apparaile, &c., and then when he came to practise, making him beleeve they tooke him to be mad. (1976: 48)

More than half of what Manningham writes down concerns the subplot, a response that the length of the relevant scenes (1.5, 2.3, 3.4, 5.1) actively encourages. What Manningham remembers specifically about these scenes involves movement: counterfeiting the letter, prescribing gesture, coming to practice. The likely conflation of diurnal time and festive time in Manningham's cancelled "~~Mid~~-" we have noticed already. When Manningham misremembers Olivia's status – in the printed text she is a sister in mourning, not a lady-widow ripe for another husband – he may be introducing a generational time frame. A rich widow would have offered a ticket to financial security for someone like Manningham, precisely at the age (late twenties) when most men in early modern England got married (Wrightson 1982: 68). The comparisons that Manningham makes with "The Comedy of Errors," "Menaechmi," and "Inganni" set in place a frame of cultural time that seems specific to Manningham's personal circumstances. "A comedy of errors (like to Plautus his Menaechmus)" had been performed at another legal household, Grey's Inn, at Christmas eight years before (Bland 1968: 32); Plautus provides the kind of classical reference that a law student like Manningham had been educated to make at school and at Magdalene College, Cambridge; reference to the Italian comedy *Gli'Ingannati* (printed without attribution in 1537) displays Manningham's acquaintance with a cultural scene outside England. For Manningham the most prominent frames of time in *Twelfth Night* seem to have been, in this order, diurnal time, festive time, cultural time, generational time, and scenes. Those, at least, are the frames of time that he explicitly remarks.

Putting what Manningham has to say side by side with the printed script serves as a reminder that performance history is always a matter of potentialities, a matter of performance choices on the part of actors and interpretative choices on the part of listener/spectators. Taken together, however, these two documents do suggest certain distinctive patterns in the ragtime of *Twelfth Night* 1602. Among the 14 frames of time some receive greater emphasis in the printed text than others. Frequent shifts between verse and prose and lengthy stretches of prose call attention to speech rhythms. Aside from *Merry Wives*, only *Much Ado* is prosier than *Twelfth Night* (Shakespeare 1969: 31). Musical rhythms are played out against speech rhythms from the beginning of the play to the end. More music is called for in *Twelfth Night* than in any other of Shakespeare's comedies. Scenes involving the subplot go on at greater length. Diurnal time (night) and festive time (carousing) are conflated. Less important are asides (only 3.4, the scene when Sir Andrew and Viola are tricked into fighting one another, invites a sustained sequence of asides), actors' stage time (speaking parts are fairly evenly distributed, with no character assigned more than 500 lines), lapsed time in the fiction (four days? three months? who cares?), back stories (most characters live in the present, even Viola's back story is not very detailed), generational time (the only ages we can begin to guess are Viola's and Sebastian's), and cultural time (nothing specific implies that events are happening anytime other than now). Manningham hears many of these distinctive rhythms (diurnal time, festive time, scenes) even as he supplies rhythms of his own (generational time, cultural time).

Trevor Nunn's Film, 1996

1.   EXT. NIGHT. SEA.
The sea, surging and angry, ceaselessly rolling, mounting and crashing, is almost obscured by slanting rain.
2.   INT. NIGHT. SHIP.
A steamer, big enough to carry fifty passengers, with some cabins and deck areas, lurches through the spray.
3.   INT. NIGHT. SHIP.
Some thirty or so passengers are sitting in a saloon, thick with smoke, being entertained by two girls, one at a piano, the other with a concertina, singing a music hall song that has the audience convulsed. The song is called "O mistress mine."

Nunn, (1996: 3)

The opening sequence of Trevor Nunn's *Twelfth Night* establishes the seven frames of time that are most emphatically remarked through the whole film: musical rhythm, scenes, actors' stage time, diurnal time, seasonal time, back story, and cultural time. With its quick cuts and extreme shifts in location – from panorama of the sea to detail of the ship, from exterior to interior – the sequence also shows off the material means that makes these remarkings of time possible: the camera. In an interview with François Laroque, Nunn expresses keen consciousness of his medium and of the changes that film not only makes possible but positively demands:

> This time I recognized that I was doing Shakespeare on film, and even though the budget was really quite small it seemed to me it was very important that I made a movie rather [than] a filmed play, so I did much more adaptation of the text than I ever would have done if I'd been doing "the play" for television. I made an adaptation of the text which included changing its chronology, reducing it considerably, cross-cutting between incidents to increase both contrast and meaning and, of course, making shorter, more charged scenes. (Laroque 1997: 89)

The result of those changes is a heightening of some time frames and a suppressing of others.

The song being sung in the ship's saloon establishes musical rhythm as a time frame even more important in the film than in the printed text of the play. It is, in fact, Feste's voice, singing the first stanza of "When that I was and a little tiny boy," that begins the film's final cut. After test-screenings Nunn was forced to add Feste as a story teller to explain in voice-over verses what the opening dumb show presents to the viewer's eye (Nunn 1996: "Introduction" (n.p.)). Nunn's most immediate route to *Twelfth Night* was via a series of musicals: *Cats, Les Misérables, Starlight Express, Sunset Boulevard* (Crowl 2003: 80, Nunn 1996: n.p.) – and it shows. In the printed script of 1623 Feste's songs are set-pieces designed to show off the singing ability of Robert Armin, the comedian-singer who had joined the company in 1599 or 1600 (Wiles 1987: 144–58). In Nunn's film Feste's performance of "O mistress mine" (scene 64) becomes a piquant reprise of the song Viola and Sebastian used to entertain the ship's passengers (scene 3). Cuts between several spaces carry the song to Olivia's bedroom (scene 65) and to Orsino's castle (scene 66) before returning to the kitchen where Feste is singing (scene 67). The camera's focus during Feste's second song, "Come away death" (scene 96), insinuates the lyrics into the subjective experience of Orsino and Viola/Cesario, echoing Orsino's preference for music with "a dying fall" (scene 30) and Viola/Cesario's sadness that she cannot confess to Orsino the true object of her love (scene 68). Nunn's highly sophisticated manipulations of musical rhythm contrast with the spontaneity – or the illusion of spontaneity – that he coached from his actors. Nunn observes:

> The camera is associated with eavesdropping on the real event. Consequently, what is said in front of the camera needs to convey to the cinema audience the sense that it has not been written, that the language of the screen is being invented by the character in

the situation spontaneously at that moment. We must not be aware of the writer. (Crowdus 1998: 50)

That is to say, we must not anticipate the speech rhythms. Iambic pentameter the speeches may be, but they must sound like uncalculated utterances.

The quick cuts in the opening sequence set up a rhythm of short scenes that is altogether characteristic of film as a medium. The printed script's 17 scenes become 140 in Nunn's screen play. Once again, it is the camera that facilitates this fundamental change in the play's rhythms. In the transcript of Gary Crowdus's interviews with directors of 1990s' Shakespeare films, Nunn agrees with Baz Luhrmann that

> a cinematic rendering of Shakespeare requires, first of all, a great deal of highly developed visual imagination and inventiveness, often beyond anything that Shakespeare delineated in the text, such as changing location, breaking scenes into smaller units, or setting them in unusual places that allow for some sort of heightened perception. I think this is very important and unquestionably this is the business of cinema. (Crowdus 1998: 51)

As H. R. Coursen notes, once Shakespeare has got his characters on stage, he tends to keep them there for a while (1999: 206). Except for battle scenes, two minutes seems to be the minimum. In effect, the characters live their lives in increments of two to ten minutes, and mostly if not exclusively in the company of other people. In film, by contrast, characters live their lives in increments of seconds, but they also enjoy moments of complete privacy – complete, that is, except for the camera and the spectator. If nothing is unusual about the shortness of Nunn's scenes – they simply replicate the rhythm of most contemporary films – his penchant for cross-cutting between scenes has caught the attention of several reviewers and critics (Coursen 1999: 207–8, Osborne 2002: 89–109, Crowl 2003: 79–90). In film, as in the theatre, time is experienced through movement. Here it is the camera, not the actors, that is doing most of the moving. One sequence in particular stands out. The scenes numbered 55–75 in the filmscript interpolate into the midnight revels of Shakespeare's 2.3 a series of private scenes centered on Maria, Olivia, Malvolio, Orsino, and Viola/Cesario via quick cuts between and among the smoking room in Orsino's castle, Olivia's garden, Maria's bedroom, the kitchen of Olivia's house, the drawing room in Orsino's castle, Olivia's bedroom, Malvolio's bedroom, the music room of Olivia's house, the stairs in Olivia's house, and Viola/Cesario's attic room. What gives this movement/time continuity is, in part, Feste's singing "O mistress mine" (scenes 63–9). Another factor is the intimacy of the bedroom scenes (58, 61, 65, 71, 74, 75), an intimacy that extends to Orsino's smoking room and drawing room when he and Viola/Cesario are left alone (scenes 55, 63, 66, 68). More fundamental still is the fact that all these scenes take place over a single night, and seem to be taking place simultaneously.

As Nunn observes in his introduction to the screenplay, the specificity of what the camera catches in light and in landscape makes it impossible to tolerate the double time scheme of the printed script: "On film such essentially poetic contradictions or vagaries work less well, because scenes are being photographed in a real climate, against real cloudscapes, during a real season, so it becomes much more necessary to be finite about the passage of time" (Nunn 1996: n.p.). And so he does – to a degree. Two emphatically remarked frames of diurnal time are set in place in the film's two night sequences (scenes 55–75 and 93–8). In effect, Nunn invents a second night where the printed script specifies only one, and he uses that second night to heighten the building intimacy between Orsino and Viola/Cesario, who, alone with Feste in a barn, almost kiss while Feste sings "Come away death" (scene 96). The sequence ends on cliffs above the crashing sea, as Orsino drowns his desire by sending Viola/Cesario on another mission to Olivia (scene 98). There may be two nights in the film, but how many days? The beaching of the shipwreck survivors as "the sun is coming up" (scene 16) finds its complement toward the end in a sequence of cross-cut scenes at "evening" as first Feste, then Sir Andrew, then Antonio, then Sir Toby and Maria, then Malvolio take their leave from Olivia's estate (scenes 134–8). Metaphorically at least, only one day seems to have passed. With respect to diurnal time, Nunn manages to satisfy cinema's need for specificity at the same time that he maintains the printed script's suggestive vagueness.

I am not the only viewer who has noted in the leave-taking sequence how distinctly wintry the light looks and how few leaves remain on the trees lining Olivia's drive. Where Nunn's screenplay specifies evening I and other viewers have seen winter. The autumnal landscape of the outdoor scenes render the frame of seasonal time perhaps the most obvious of all. "Together we made . . . a film, an autumnal film," Nunn says at the close of his introduction to the screenplay (Nunn 1996: n.p.). H. R. Coursen associates the film with "early autumn, the time of Keats's 'mist and mellow fruitfulness'" (1999: 204); Samuel Crowl finds the inspiration for Nunn's "bittersweet, autumnal approach" in Mozart and Chekhov (2003: 79). If Nunn's film casts long shadows, it is because he has made the frames of back story and actors' stage/ screen time so full of movement. In his screenplay Nunn may have retained, as he proudly claims, 65 percent of the original printed script (Crowdus 1998: 49), but some characters have benefited from these retentions more than others. It is not Sir Toby who has the largest share of time before the spectator/listeners in Nunn's film but Viola. Rearrangement of the play's chronology, beginning not with Orsino in a mood of love-longing but with Viola and her brother entertaining the ship's passengers, suffering shipwreck, attempting to save each other, washing up in separate places on the beach, receiving help from separate rescuers, finding separate ways of negotiating the strange world of Illyria, has the effect of making the whole story very much Viola's story. The 12 years of back story in the original script have been telescoped into a single incident, but that single incident endows Viola with a history that the spectators have actually witnessed, not just heard about in passing references.

Nunn makes sure that Viola/Cesario never loses her kinetic dominance over screen time: he invents multiple journeys for her between Orsino's castle and Olivia's house where the original script specifies only two (1996: n.p.), cross-cuts never leave her out of the camera's range for long, frequent close-ups set up a physical intimacy between viewer and actor that, according to some film theorists, slows down the viewer's sense of passing time. All the protagonists benefit, at one moment or another, from the camera's quick and sudden scrutiny of their faces. What is going on behind those eyes? By implication all the protagonists have back stories of their own. Even Malvolio, the spoilsport, the butt of practical jokes, becomes in Nunn's handling a man with a history. Once again, the moving camera is responsible for that transformation. In Nunn's words,

> The scale of the house, the number of servants, and the workforce needed to keep the place running, somehow gave extraordinary authority and credibility to Malvolio. So there's a whole set of circumstances which can be presented only because of cinematic verisimilitude that provides layers of, first of all, credibility and, finally, of tragic meaning to Malvolio's story. (Crowdus 1998: 52)

Mention of the physical and social layout of Olivia's house points up the final frame that Nunn has emphasized, cultural time. According to the screenplay's introduction, it was gender considerations, Viola's need to become her brother, that prompted Nunn's choice of a nineteenth-century setting:

> I wanted this story to happen in a society where the differences between men and women were at their greatest, when men were clothed to reveal their shape in trousers and boots and close-fitting waistcoats and jackets; and when conversely women were considered delicate, sensitive and decorative creatures, wearing clothing to hide and disguise them, and were reliant upon male strength and decorum to defend them. (Nunn 1996: n.p.)

Hence the scenes (26 and 76) in which spectator/listeners see and hear the physical discomfort Viola feels when she shears off her hair and binds up her breasts. To judge from Merchant-Ivory films of classic novels and any number of BBC and PBS dramatizations, not to mention Kenneth Branagh's films of *Much Ado About Nothing* (1993) and *Hamlet* (1996), the nineteenth century has become the default choice for a setting that seems historically past yet comfortably familiar. Middle-class spectator/listeners can imagine themselves living in the nineteenth century, especially in one of those tasteful houses with servants, in a way they cannot imagine themselves living in the eighteenth century, much less the seventeenth or the sixteenth. To its credit, cultural time in Nunn's *Twelfth Night* is more complicated than that. Katherine Eggert has detected two frames of cultural time in the film, one centered on the "Upstairs Downstairs" domestic household of the 1890s and one on the pre-Raphaelite décor and costuming of the 1840s (2003: 85). Nunn himself has called attention to the fact that Llanhydrock, the estate in Cornwall that became Olivia's house, combines an exterior façade from the time of Shakespeare's play with nineteenth-century interior décor (Laroque 1997: 94). The mid-point between 1602 and 1996 is actually 1799, but Nunn finds a frame of cultural time that allows his spectator/listeners and Shakespeare's characters to meet in the middle distance. The nineteenth century turns out to be a suggestive space/time in more ways than one. Each historical period, Nunn observes with an unacknowledged nudge from Bakhtin, has its "going form." In the seventeenth century, it was drama; in the nineteenth century, the novel. "There's obviously a sense in which the cinema is now the going form" (Crowdus 1998: 54, Bakhtin 1981: 3–40). *Twelfth Night* in the nineteenth century, on film, becomes a way of both novelizing the original script and making it current in the 1990s. The Shakespeherian rag of 1996 is played in seven distinctive rhythms, in three historical styles. It is the motion-picture camera, always itself in motion, that makes that performance possible.

Middle Temple, Shakespeare's Globe, and the American Tour, 2002–3

To some ears at least, Mark Rylance's delivery of Olivia's lines in the Middle Temple's great hall in February 2002 sounded like jazz. Paul Taylor, writing on February 2 – the very day *Twelfth Night* had been performed in the great hall four hundred years before – described Rylance's vocal virtuosity this way:

> Technically, he can riff on the iambic pentameter of Jacobean verse like a great jazz musician descanting on the melodic line of a Gershwin standard. Fundamentally, he's that very rare bird – someone who can use his uncloyingly sweet, innocent demeanour and phenomenal talent for varying the speed and timbre of verse as the stalking horse from behind which all manner of seditious things may dart at his will. (Taylor 2002: 2)

What Taylor describes here is ragtime: against the regular beat of iambs Rylance can play out all sorts of rhythmic variations. "Iambic pentameter doesn't have to be unnatural to be beautiful," Rylance remarked in an interview. "It has a wide range of expression, which includes very mundane, rather secular conversational things: 'Who's there?' You don't need to say, 'Whooose they-ah?'" (Hohenadel 2003: 3). When the commemorative production at the Middle Temple transferred to Shakespeare's Globe, speech rhythms continued to be remarked by reviewers. The *Observer*'s Susannah Clapp celebrated the way Rylance's Olivia "melts into naturalness in a second, breaking his lines with a stammer at moments of high emotion, while holding the beat of the verse" (2002: 700). Brian Logan found lightness and flexibility in all the actors' delivery: "Hardly a line trips by without comic or dramatic effect. No one drones on – the verse is brought to life by skilled performers and likeable comic choreography" (2002: 697). The result of such stylized timing for Ben Brantley, writing in the *New York Times*, was a paradoxical naturalness. Virginia Woolf, Brantley recalls, thought the language of the English Renaissance was incapable of talking about ordinary things.

> Most contemporary productions of Shakespeare try to ignore this anti-naturalism, steering actors into conversational line readings that go against the grain of the

language. Mr. Rylance and company take the opposite route, acknowledging, embracing and even heightening the exaggerations and distortions of style. It is a glorious paradox – and one peculiar to the theater – that this leads them and us to what a character in "Twelfth Night" describes as "a natural perspective that is and is not." (2003: 3)

Nothing could be further from the seemingly spontaneous timing that Nunn coached from his actors in the 1996 film. To be fair, not every reviewer of the Globe *Twelfth Night* could feel the rhythm that Taylor, Logan, and Brantley professed to hear. Nicholas de Jongh thought that Rylance's "cool, upper-crust voice is caught in a mournful rut that not even love changes" (2002: 696), Rhoda Koenig complained that the verse-speaking sounded "a bit prosy at times and occasionally careless" (2002: 699), while Katherine Duncan-Jones found the vocal work generally to be weak (2004: 2).

Such punctilious attention to the shortest frame of time, speech rhythm, was part and parcel of the largest frame, in every sense of the word: cultural time. Four hundred years later to the day Carroll and his troupe mounted *Twelfth Night* in the space where it had received its first recorded performance, and to mark the occasion they turned to what press releases, program notes, and interviews call "original practices." None of the documents that I have seen makes the connection explicit, but the term "original practices" seems to be inspired by the fashion, since the 1970s, for performing sixteenth-, seventeenth-, eighteenth-, and early nineteenth-century music on "original instruments." The balance between voice and accompaniment is undeniably different when Dowland's songs are sung to a lute, not to a guitar or a piano. Beethoven's keyboard sonatas, so the logic goes, were designed to exploit the dry, percussive qualities of the fortepiano, not the metal-harp-enhanced sonorities of the modern pianoforte. So, by analogy, were Shakespeare's plays designed to exploit certain types of music, certain physical spaces, certain types of human bodies.

As for the music, no details of period correctness were overlooked in Carroll's *Twelfth Night*. A consort of musicians, visually present throughout, played on recorders, hautboys, sackbuts, rauschpfiefes, and other replicas of early modern instruments as the audience assembled, just as a consort played before performances by the King's Men at the Blackfriars Theatre (Smith 1999: 221–2). The cast's spirited singing of William Cornish's "Hey, Robin," extrapolated from 4.2.72–9, set the story off on its musical way. The "dying strain" that captivated Orsino in 1.1 was John Dowland's "Lachrymae." "O mistress mine" was sung by Feste in Thomas Morley's setting of 1599. "When that I was and a little tiny boy" used the earliest tune associated with these words in manuscript sources. The catches brawled out by Sir Toby and friends had been meticulously researched (Walker 1994: 222–36). As for space, what could have been truer to the period than the very room in which the play was first performed? Candles provided part of the illumination. The shape of the playing place changed when the production transferred to Shakespeare's Globe in May 2002, but candlelight and the aura of period specificity moved across the river with the players. For the American tour in Autumn 2003 an approximation of the Middle Temple configuration was constructed: a hall screen with two doors and a musicians' gallery above anchored a long rectangular playing space with the audience ranged on three sides. All in all the effect was not unlike the Swan Theatre in Stratford-upon-Avon. It was "period" bodies, however, that most excited the imaginations of publicists, interviewers, audiences, and reviewers. Carroll's *Twelfth Night* featured an all-male cast.

In interviews and in articles he has written himself, Mark Rylance, artistic director at Shakespeare's Globe, has taken pains to distinguish "original practices" from "authenticity." "I never call this work authentic," Rylance wrote:

> It isn't. We choose the known practices that may be helpful to the modern relationship between actor and audience. Hand-made clothing, live music and dance of the period, not to mention single-gender casting, have created worlds close to the worlds of the building and the original writing. These practices may not be too familiar to modern audiences, yet our audience's enthusiasm for such productions has inspired us to develop our understanding and skills. (2003: 1)

Taylor remarks how often the word "now" crops up in Rylance's interviews (2003: 3). Be that as it may, authenticity is just what most reviewers of Carroll's *Twelfth Night* told themselves they were experiencing. Walking past the actors as they trussed themselves in period costumes and applied period-recipe make-up amid the glow of candlelight – that is how most patrons entered the Middle Temple's great hall and the mock-up of that space on the American tour – inevitably encouraged the illusion of a journey back in time (Figure 3.1). Candlelight, a conspicuous element at the Middle Temple, the Globe, and the American performances alike, made night the one and only diurnal time frame of the production and encouraged spectators to see the performance as an illusion or a dream, a pre-post-modern piece of virtual reality in which candle flames were doing the work of digitalization.

The Globe's "most doggedly authentic Elizabethan production so far" (Michael Coveney, *Daily Mail*), "an authentic Elizabethan experience" (Dominic Cavendish, *Daily Telegraph*), "the Globe's most historically authentic to date … turning the clock back 400 years" (Maddy Costa, *Guardian*), "comes closest to fulfilling what must surely be one of the theatre's principal aims – giving audiences some idea of what a performance at the original Globe would have been like" (John Gross, *Sunday Telegraph*): effusions like these from British critics were hyped even more in America. So authentic, so Elizabethan, was the staging that the Chicago *Windy City Times*'s reviewer imagined that the guarantor of that authenticity had been present at the play's first performance: "Handmade costumes, a sextet of Elizabethan musicians, and an all-male cast of 13 hearken back to its original production before Queen Elizabeth I at the Middle Temple Hall in 1602." (In fact, no document survives that connects the queen with the 1602 Middle Temple revels.) In sum, "a time machine couldn't transport you better back to Elizabethan days" (Reed 2003: 2).

FIGURE 3.1   Mark Rylance as Olivia; backstage at *Twelfth Night*, Middle Temple (2002)
Photograph MTH Photos by John Tramper. Reproduced with permission of Shakespeare's Globe.

So overwhelming was the frame of cultural time in Carroll's *Twelfth Night* that audiences and reviewers were apt to miss the production's subtler rhythms. From my own experience (I caught up with the production at the University of California at Los Angeles on October 30, 2003), I can attest that beats, completions of motives within scenes, were articulated with remarkable clarity. Scene after scene unfolded with an exquisite sense of timing. Partly that was a function of the physical configuration of hall screen, actors, and audience. Lois Potter, reviewing the Middle Temple performance for the house organ of Shakespeare's Globe, commented on how the long, narrow acting space "introduced a division into the acting areas and a divided focus, as when, after the interrupted duel, Viola soliloquized at one end and Sir Toby and Fabian conversed at the other" (Potter 2002: 2). (A similar separation of the stage into two distinct worlds happened when the conspirators watched Malvolio pick up the forged letter and when Feste taunted Malvolio in prison.) In the printed text of 3.4 Viola's speeches are, in effect, asides, time out from the on-going action. Ian Johns seconded Potter in observing how seldom the actors in Carroll's production even glanced toward the audience (Potter 2002: 2, Johns 2002: 698). The wide expanse of the Globe's stage, no less than the long, narrow playing spaces of the Middle Temple performances and the American tour, necessitated attention-getting movement that translated for spectator/listeners into a heightened awareness of time. Reviewers could not avoid remarking that Rylance's Olivia seemed to glide across the stage as if on casters: "Clenched into his corset, Rylance sweeps round the stage with the kinetic constipation (at once terribly funny and touching) of a Japanese actor in kabuki" (Taylor 2002: 2). Kabuki theater, which began in Japan at about the same time Shakespeare was writing his scripts halfway around the world, is just where Rylance says he began his glissando trajectory out of the hall screen's doors and onto the stage of the Globe: "I use onnagata tecnhique [*sic*] in terms of making smaller movements with the feet and pulling my arms in to make them seem shorter and more delicate" (Rosenthal 2002: 2). A reviewer in Pittsburgh noted the way Rylance favored "taking a longer, circuitous route to whatever point on the stage he is headed for" (Miner 2003: 2).

The result, for most spectators, was a palpable slowing down of time that seemed altogether appropriate for the journey they imagined themselves to be taking to an historical time when experiential time moved more slowly than it does today. The slow timing of several beats in particular caught the attention of reviewers: the "priceless, slow-burning scene" when Orsino and Viola/Cesario almost kissed while Feste sang "Come away, death" (Bassett 2002: 698) and "the daringly slow timing" in the duel scene when Olivia forgot herself and manfully wrested the sword out of Sir Andrew's hands (Koenig 2002: 699). The final effect of Rylance's slow kabuki-like movement was to expand Olivia's share of stage time, in subjective impression more than in measurable minutes. If the printed text suggests ensemble balance among the actors, if Nunn's film belongs to Viola, Carroll's *Twelfth Night* was very much about Rylance's Olivia. For many people, including most reviewers and academic critics of Shakespeare in performance, the 2002–3 production remains "Mark Rylance's *Twelfth Night*," not Tim Carroll's. In an interview published during the American tour, Rylance called attention to the cast's attempts to speed up as well as slow down:

> "It depends on us telling the story well," Rylance says, "knowing when we're going around a corner or through some woods in the story, and we need to slow down because the people following may get lost. But when we come to a clear place, where they can see ahead, we need to really speed up, or they'll get bored and start to look around and feel their legs." (Hohenadel 2003: 3)

Quickened moments there may have been, but most audience members experienced Rylance's performance, and the show as a whole, as an arresting instance of slow motion within a cultural time frame that encouraged that effect.

The heightening of speech rhythm, musical rhythm, diurnal time, beats, stage time, and cultural time served to suppress any awareness of other time frames in the play, most notably generational time. Katherine Duncan-Jones is particularly insistent on this point. The female roles in this "original practices" production were played, not by pre-pubescent boys, but by adult men. Rylance was 42 years old when he played Olivia (Peter 2002: 698) – at the upper limits of life expectancy in 1600 (Sharpe 1997: 38). Duncan-Jones is surely right that a truly authentic production of *Twelfth Night* in 2002–3 would have invited the attention of the vice squad: "'Original practice' would have shown us grown men flirting with and sometimes kissing children, and, almost more offensively, in the Viola–Orsino plot, a child falling passionately in love with a mature male. Clearly, this would be wholly unacceptable in today's culture" (2004: 1). As original a practice as all-male casting may have been, the focus in the performances of Rylance and other transvestite members of the cast was on gender, not on generations, not even on sexuality. More than one reviewer faulted the production for avoiding any suggestion that Antonio might have been erotically interested in Sebastian (de Jongh 2002: 696). With respect to sexuality, this *Twelfth Night* was distinctly out of period. In the last analysis, the truly insurmountable barrier to a genuinely "authentic" production is the very time frame that loomed largest in the quadricentennial *Twelfth Night*: cultural time. John Peter catches the fundamental irony. Even if the play's story was imagined by the original audience to have taken place at a romantic distance, at some unspecified time in the past, they would still have expected to see it in contemporary costume, not in historically accurate garments that took up to 200 working hours each to produce (Taylor 2002: 2). Peter's observation is on the mark: "We have very different expectations from the Elizabethans. They were content to see almost everything in contemporary clothes, just as most early Italian Renaissance painting seems to be set in contemporary Tuscany. It was a psychological-didactic device: it told you that the present could see itself in the past" (2002: 697–8). In his public statements about Shakespeare's Globe in general and about this production in particular, Rylance has stressed the give-and-take between past and present, the "radically alternative way of engaging with the present" that past practices inspire (Taylor 2002: 3). To judge from the reviews, however, most spectator/listeners found the accentuation of cultural time in the 2002–3 *Twelfth Night* so insistent that they could hardly hear or see anything else.

With respect to time, two things are remarkable about ragtime: the way it accommodates multiple rhythms at the same time and the way it encourages the performance to go on and on, as the rhythms shift from one iteration of the theme to another. That Shakespeherian rag: when will we hear the last cadence? Not as long as there are new productions to configure and reconfigure the 14 frames of time that shape experience in the theatre.

ACKNOWLEDGEMENTS

I would like to thank the students in my undergraduate Shakespeare course at the University of Southern California in spring 2004 for their energetic and imaginative collaboration in isolating the frames of time in *Twelfth Night*. This chapter began in our discussions of the play. For logistical support in locating reviews and other elusive texts, I am grateful to Barbara Hodgdon, Elisabeth McKetta, Lois Potter, Nathan Stogdill, and Patricia Tatspaugh.

References and Further Reading

Bakhtin, Mikhail (1981). "Epic and Novel." In *The Dialogic Imagination*, trans. Caryl Emerson & Michael Holquist. Austin, TX: University of Texas Press.

Bassett, Kate (2002). Review of *Twelfth Night*. *Independent on Sunday*, May 26. Rpt. *Theatre Record* 22, 11: 698.

Billington, Michael (ed.) (1990). *Directors' Shakespeare: Approaches to Twelfth Night*. London: Nick Hern.

Bland, Desmond (ed.) (1968). *Gesta Grayorum, or The History of the High and Mighty Prince Henry, Prince of Purpoole, Anno Domini 1594*. Liverpool: Liverpool University Press.

Bourdieu, Pierre (1977). *Outline of a Theory of Practice*, trans. Richard Nice. Cambridge: Cambridge University Press.

Brantley, Ben (2003). "The Male 'Twelfth Night' Is a True Masquerade." *New York Times*, October 19. Available at: www.nytimes.com (accessed April 3, 2004).

Cavendish, Dominic (2002). Review of *Twelfth Night*. Rpt. *Theatre Record* 22, 11: 697.

Clapp, Susannah (2002). Review of *Twelfth Night*. *Observer*, June 16. Rpt. *Theatre Record* 22, 11: 699–700.

Costa, Maddy (2002). Review of *Twelfth Night*. *Guardian*, May 24. Rpt. *Theatre Record* 22, 11: 697.

Coursen, H. R. (1999). *Shakespeare: The Two Traditions*. Madison, NJ: Fairleigh Dickinson University Press, London: Associated University Presses.

Coveney, Michael (2002). Review of *Twelfth Night*. Rpt. *Theatre Record* 22, 11. 696–7.

Crowdus, Gary (1998). "Shakespeare in the Cinema: A Film Directors' Symposium." *Cineaste* 24, 1: 48–55.

Crowl, Samuel (2003). *Shakespeare at the Cineplex*. Athens, OH: Ohio University Press.

de Jongh, Nicholas (2002). Review of *Twelfth Night*. *Evening Standard*, 23 May. Rpt. *Theatre Record* 22, 11: 696.

Duncan-Jones, Katherine (2004). "Displays Sublime but Inauthentic." *Times Literary Supplement* April 6. Available at: www.thetls.co.uk/archive/story.aspx?story_id=2077829 (accessed April 5, 2004).

Eggert, Katherine (2003). "Sure Can Sing and Dance: Minstrelsy, the Star System, and the Post-Postcoloniality of Kenneth Branagh's *Love's Labour's Lost* and Trevor Nunn's *Twelfth Night*." In Richard Burt & Lynda E. Boose (eds.) *Shakespeare the Movie II*. London: Routledge.

Gross, John (2002). Review of *Twelfth Night*. *Sunday Telegraph*, June 2. Rpt. *Theatre Record* 22, 11: 699.

Gurr, Andrew (1996). *The Shakespearian Playing Companies*. Oxford: Clarendon Press.

Eliot, T. S. (1991). *Collected Poems, 1909–1962*. New York: Harcourt Brace.

Foucault, Michel (1970). *The Order of Things: An Archeology of Human Sciences*. New York: Random House.

Hohenadel, Kristin (2003). "Relax, Folks, It's Just Shakespeare." *Los Angeles Times*, October 21. Available at: www.shaksper.net/archives/2003/2045.html (accessed April 3, 2004).

Johns, Ian (2002). Review of *Twelfth Night*. *The Times*, May 5. Rpt. *Theatre Record*, 22, 11: 698.

Kastan, David (1982). *Shakespeare and the Shapes of Time*. Hanover, NH: University Press of New England.

Koenig, Rhoda (2002). Review of *Twelfth Night*. Rpt. *Theatre Record* 22.11: 699.

Knights, L. C. (1979). *"Hamlet" and Other Shakespearean Essays*. Cambridge: Cambridge University Press.

Lakoff, George & Johnson, Mark (1999). *Philosophy in the Flesh: The Embodied Mind and Its Challenge to Western Thought*. New York: Basic Books.

Laroque, François (1997). Interview given by Trevor Nunn, director of the film *Twelfth Night*, to François Laroque. *Cahiers élisabéthains* 52: 89–96.

Logan, Brian (2002). Review of *Twelfth Night*. *Time Out*, May 29. Rpt. *Theatre Record* 22,11: 697.

Manningham, John (1976). *The Diary of John Manningham of the Middle Temple, 1602–1603*, ed. Robert Parker Sorlien. Hanover, NH: University Press of New England.

Marvell, Andrew (2003). *The Poems of Andrew Marvell*, ed. Nigel Smith. London: Longman.

Miner, Ann (2003). "Shakespeare's Globe Theatre in *Twelfth Night*." Available at: www.talkinbroadway.com/regional/pitt/p77.html (accessed April 3, 2004).

Moran, Dermot (2000). *Introduction to Phenomenology*. London: Routledge.

Nunn, Trevor (1996). *William Shakespeare's Twelfth Night: A Screenplay*. London: Methuen.

Osborne, Laurie (2002). "Cutting Up Characters: The Erotic Politics of Trevor Nunn's *Twelfth Night*." In Courtney Lehmann & Lisa S. Starks (eds.) *Spectacular Shakespeare: Critical Theory and Popular Cinema*. Madison, NJ: Farleigh Dickinson University Press.

Osborne, Laurie (1996). *The Trick of Singularity: Twelfth Night and the Performance Editions*. Iowa City: University of Iowa Press.

Pennington, Michael (2000). *Twelfth Night: A User's Guide*. New York: Limelight.

Peter, John (2002). Review of *Twelfth Night*. *Sunday Times*, June 2. Rpt. *Theatre Record* 22,11: 697–8.

Potter, Lois (2002). "Showing Some Respect." *Around the Globe* 21 (Summer): 2–3.

Reed, Rick (2003). Review of *Twelfth Night*. *Windy City Times*, December 3. Available at: www.windycitymediagroup.com/article=36335 .html (accessed April 3, 2004).

Rosenthal, Daniel (2002). "Treading the Broads," *Independent*, 22 May. Available at: http://enjoyment.independent.co.uk/theatre/features/story. jsp?story=297701 (accessed April 3, 2004).

Rylance, Mark (2003). "Unsex me here," *Guardian*, May 7. Available at: www.guardian.co.uk/ arts/features/story/0,11710,950564,00.html (accessed April 3, 2004).

Shakespeare, William (1969). *The Complete Works*, ed. Alfred Harbage. Baltimore, MD: Penguin.

Shakespeare, William (1988). *The Complete Works*, ed. Stanley Wells & Gary Taylor. Oxford: Clarendon Press.

Sharpe, J. A. (1997). *Early Modern England: A Social History 1550–1760*, 2nd edn. London: Arnold.

Smith, Bruce R. (1999). *The Acoustic World of Early Modern England: Attending to the O-Factor*. Chicago: University of Chicago Press.

Taylor, Paul (2002). "A *Twelfth Night* to Remember." *Independent*, February 2. Available at: www.enjoyment.independent.co.uk/theatre/ interviews/story.jsp?story=117831 (accessed April 3, 2004).

Turner, Frederick (1971). *Shakespeare and the Nature of Time*. Oxford: Clarendon Press.

Walker, James (1994). "Appendix: The Music." In Roger Warren & Stanley Wells (eds.) *William Shakespeare: Twelfth Night*. Oxford: Oxford University Press.

Wiles, David (1987). *Shakespeare's Clown: Actor and Text in the Elizabethan Playhouse*. Cambridge: Cambridge University Press.

Wrightson, Keith (1982). *English Society 1580–1680*. New Brunswick, NJ: Rutgers University Press.

4

On Location

Robert Shaughnessy

Between January and December 2003 there were more than 60 professional Shakespearean productions in England, Scotland, Wales and Northern Ireland. This total included a half-dozen productions each of *Twelfth Night*, *A Midsummer Night's Dream*, *Hamlet*, and *As You Like It*, large-, medium- and small scale shows traveling between the playhouses of major conurbations and small-town sports centers, productions at the Royal National Theatre, Shakespeare's Globe and Stratford-upon-Avon, a summer season in the grounds of the Botanic Gardens, Glasgow, and stagings of *The Merchant of Venice* and *The Winter's Tale* amidst the ruins of Ludlow Castle. For the historian of contemporary Shakespearean performance cultures, the geographical range and diversity of setting provoke consideration of the ways in which current practices of Shakespearean production are regionally inflected, and, moreover, shaped and conditioned by the built – and sometimes natural – environments in which they occur. Here, I want to address the environmental and discursive contexts of the two most prominent, and most obviously contrasting, places in which theatrical Shakespeares are made, nodal points on the contemporary theatrical map: the theatres of Stratford-upon-Avon, and Shakespeare's Globe in London. In their own distinctive ways, these offer clearly contrasting rhetorics, suggesting alternative versions of geographically-grounded authenticity (birthplace, workplace); contrasting architectural styles (a hybrid of the residual Victorian and the modernist in Stratford; the postmodern archaeological facsimile on Bankside) and functions in the local, the global and the national cultural economies: the heavily state-subsidized, internationally profiled arts organization operating from a regional base, private enterprise operating within the heart of the capital. My concern is with how these spaces and places mean, and also with how their users – performers, audiences – negotiate these meanings; as we shall see, this entails different styles of writing, different avenues of approach. In the first instance, though, it is necessary to consider the question of point of view.

Looking Down

"Walking in the City" is one of the key chapters in Michel de Certeau's (1984) classic work of cultural analysis, *The Practice of Everyday Life*. It begins with an investigation of a form of behavior most of us engage in when visiting an unfamiliar city, in the form of a densely lyrical account of an excursion to the rooftop of what was at the time of writing one of Manhattan's tallest buildings, to take in the view of the city spread out below. From the observation platform, de Certeau writes, the city can be surveyed in all of its spectacular diversity: "extremes of ambition and degradation, brutal oppositions of races and styles, contrasts between yesterday's buildings, already transformed into trashcans, and today's urban irruptions that block out space." As vision and spectacle, New York City is, from this privileged vantage point, both a text to be read, and a space in which meaning and knowledge become performable: "a stage of concrete, steel and glass" upon which "the tallest letters in the world compose a gigantic rhetoric of excess in both expenditure and production" (1984: 91). Extreme in the claims of its architecture, New York is, nonetheless, exemplary: the archetype of modern urban organization and experience, speaking a chaotic, polyglot vernacular that the bird's-eye view marshals into order, coherence and legibility, allowing the multiplicity of everyday practices that constitute daily life in the metropolis to be overseen, known and understood as "the clear text of the planned and readable city" (1984: 93). Moreover, de Certeau emphasizes, the habit of surveying the city from a position far removed from street level, and thus "totalizing the most immoderate of human texts," is driven by desire and infused with pleasure: the "erotics of knowledge" which inform such an "ecstasy of reading" conveying a vision of transcendence that comes from being "lifted out of the city's grasp . . . no longer possessed, whether as player or played, by the rumble of so many differences." Separated from the crowd, distanced, individuated and transfigured into a "voyeur," the rooftop spectator becomes "a solar Eye, looking down like a god," experiencing the sublime "exaltation of a scopic and gnostic drive: the fiction of knowledge is related to this lust to be a viewpoint and nothing more" (1984: 92).

For the theatre historian interested in locating Shakespearean performance spaces and performances in both the early modern and postmodern city, de Certeau's account of the interplay between viewing, knowledge and location is extremely apposite, and not just for its use of theatrical metaphors. I shall be concerned in the first part of this chapter with the contemporary Shakespeare's Globe, but I start with the grounds of its historical antecedent in order to map the terrain – cultural and conceptual, as well as material – upon which it has been built; to locate it not only as an object of surveillance but a product of it. The readable urban space evoked by de Certeau is a historical phenomenon; and what is imagined here as the perfection of a visionary project realizes a fantasy which informs the very emergence of the modern city. "The desire to see the city," de Certeau points out, "preceded the means of satisfying it"; medieval and early Renaissance artists "represented the city as seen from a perspective that no eye had yet enjoyed" (1984: 92). Whether imagined, narrated or pictorially documented, the overview of the city scene developed in the early modern period as a crucial means of classifying, ordering and regulating the daily life of the metropolis; for de Certeau, the historical development of the visual conventions and apparatuses of representation that have defined and regulated the city as systematically viewable have been instrumental to the formation of modern civic economic and political identity. The view of Bankside featured in the 1572 *Civitas Londini,* John Norden's 1593 *Map of London*, the 1599 *View of the Cittye of London from the North Towards the Sowth*, J. C. Visscher's *London*, printed in 1616 (Figure 4.1): theatre historians have long been aware that these visions of London, which at best provide partial, conflicting and ambiguous evidence of the exterior configuration of the playhouses they incorporate, are texts of desire rather than photographically reliable documents. As I. A. Shapiro demonstrated more than half a century ago, Visscher's much-reproduced octagonal Globe was the work of an artist who had most likely never visited London, and who had probably assembled the image from already published sources. Unlike Hollar, whose Long View has been subjected, by John Orrell, to precise geometric scrutiny which confirms its accuracy to within 2 percent (Orrell 1983, Mulryne & Shewring 1997: 50–65), Visscher did

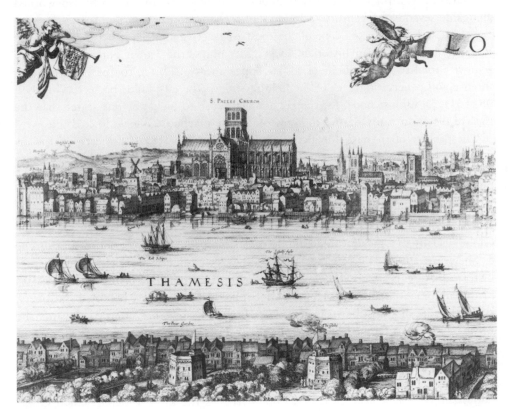

FIGURE 4.1   Claes Van Visscher's engraving of London, 1616
Reproduced with permission of the Guildhall Library.

not climb the stone steps of the tower of St Saviour's to sketch the city; as Shapiro and Orrell respectively conclude, his Globe consequently has "no independent authority," being "something of a shambles, and certainly not based on an independent and accurate survey" (1948: 31, 1983: 38).

We might, however, pause to wonder whether both the authentic eyewitness record of the view and the fabrication of it – and the willingness of contemporary and subsequent viewers to entertain the fraudulent alongside the genuine – can be read, via de Certeau, as an articulation of a desire to see the city that exceeds considerations of documentary fact; a desire, moreover, that is implicated within a developing visual culture of surveillance and control, and that is far from neutral in intent and application. "Perspective vision and prospective vision," de Certeau writes, "constitute the twofold projection of an opaque past and an uncertain future onto a surface that can be dealt with." The geometrical principles of linear perspective which Hollar employs to such persuasive effect in the Long View "inaugurate . . . the transformation of the urban *fact* into the *concept* of city" (1984: 93–4). As the cultural geographer Denis Cosgrove points out, this geometry, while "at one level a very practical affair," served "a society and an economy exercising new degrees of material and cultural control over its environment" (1988: 262), and as such also worked alongside seventeenth-century techniques of accountancy, navigation, surveying, cartography and artillery. As "one of the most distinctive and popular products of the Renaissance," the urban historian Lucia Nuti notes, the "town portrait" works to achieve "totality in the field of visual appearances"; subject to the "located, but intense and penetrating eye" of the draughtsman, "the city holds no secrets" (1999: 98–101). Or almost none: for the panoramas refuse to yield the one secret that the theatre historian really desires to know: what the playhouse *interior* looked like.

The probity of the visual evidence has particularly mattered to theatre historians not only because the continued reproduction of the images within scholarly, pedagogic and theatrical domains sustains perceptions of the early modern theatrical scene but also because they have been used as the basis for modern reconstructions. Visscher's discredited Globe nonetheless "ruled thinking about the design for several more decades," complains Andrew Gurr, recurring "as the standard image of the Globe, usually in a nicely-coloured nineteenth-century redrawing" (Gurr, in Mulryne & Shewring 1997: 31). Much as we would wish to doubt Visscher's reliability as historical evidence, however, we should not be too quick to dismiss its appeal as historical romance. Although Hollar's Globe, hedged with neatly trimmed shrubbery, is firmly part of the suburban scene, Visscher's is a structure oriented towards the world of pastoral, flanked by trees and set in open ground on the city's semi-rural edge. Moreover, Visscher humanizes his imagined landscape, incorporating a knot of delinquent pedestrians, spectators queuing as if to peer, surreptitiously, into a peepshow; viewers of a playhouse interior that remains for us a scene of desire, tantalizingly beyond the reach of vision. If this is the kind of detail which Orrell calls "seductive" (Mulryne & Shewring 1997: 52), its effect is complicated by the relationship between the human figures and the building. The proportions are patently absurd: allowing for the 10 percent difference between the height of the average Elizabethan and the modern Westerner, and therefore assuming that the tallest figure in the composition stands at 1.6 meters, Visscher's playhouse can be roughly calculated as 10 meters in height and 12 meters across. Taking into account the galleries and outer walls, this yields us an inner yard approximately 6 meters in diameter: a cockpit indeed. The point is not that viewers fail to register the disparity of scale but that the absurdity of the dimensions simply adds to the allure of a nutshell bounding infinite dramaturgical space.

For all the inaccuracies of the Visscher depiction, the aesthetic of the Globe as doll's house or prototype toy theatre plays an important part of the twentieth-century history of Globe reconstruction. Assessing this twentieth-century tradition, Gabriel Egan notes that the Globe "occupies special places in the collective conscious and unconscious of Shakespeare studies," adding that "the act of making a physical reconstruction focuses the minds of supporters and objectors in a way that no hypothetical model can" (1999: 1); this is evident even when the model is, literally, just that. Size matters: Orrell's work in designing the Bankside Globe was initially informed by an interrogation of a scale model built in the 1970s by Roy Waterson (and based upon the conjectures of Richard Southern and C. Walter Hodges). A quarter of a century earlier, John Cranford Adams manufactured the model playhouse which not only featured in his 1942 book, *The Globe Playhouse*, but extensively reproduced and circulated in editions and other educational materials in the decades that followed; a version of it, seen from the air, naturally, and soundtracked by swelling brass and strings and celestial choir, features in the opening sequence of Olivier's 1944 film of *Henry V*. The Merrie Englande, model village character of these timber-and-thatch constructs is obvious; what interests me more is not only that, as an artefact which can be measured, minutely scrutinized and photographed, the Globe-as-dollhouse presents itself as a powerful empirical corroboration of Adams's hypothetical reconstruction of the playhouse, but that the relation between the observer and the object observed encodes a particular "erotics of knowledge" in its configuration of scholarship, performance and architecture. Observing that the miniature "is a cultural product, the product of an eye performing certain operations, manipulating, and attending in certain ways to, the physical world," Susan Stewart proposes that the dollhouse, "the most consummate of miniatures," occupies the "space within enclosed space," its "aptest analogy" being "the locket or the secret recesses of the heart: center within center, within within within" (2001: 55, 61). Peering down into the tiny world of the Globe, we are looking with the eye of nostalgia, as "the miniature, linked to nostalgic versions of childhood and history, presents a diminutive, and thereby manipulatable, version of experience, a version which is domesticated and protected from contamination" (2001: 69). This is brought home forcefully, if unwittingly, in the iconic image of Adams proudly displaying his creation, as shown on the website of Hofstra University (of which Adams became president): like Gulliver in a Tudorbethan Lilliput, or King Kong in Manhattan, he looks down with the eye of an urban god, looming over an ordered, pristine and uninhabited environment which can be manipulated and inspected from every angle, but which demands, in particular, to be seen from above. The relationship between past, present and future Globes that is defined by this image, is, in more senses than one, a model one. Perhaps to really get (to) the Globe, imaginatively, we need ourselves to miniaturize, to disembody and then rematerialize as homunculi, inserted into the inert spaces of two-dimensional cityscape and three-dimensional model.

New Globe Walk

Although some constituents of the Bankside Globe experience suggest a continuity with this way of seeing the early modern theatre in urban space, other aspects of its architectural form and context suggest other trajectories of access, other angles of approach. As far as the Globe's architect, Theo Crosby, was concerned, the project operated from the outset within the context of a postmodern reclamation of the city-text that envisioned "an attitude to architecture which sees it as a kind of language – that is, as a set of meanings, stories, directions which make the forms expressive" (Day 1996: 128–9) (Figure 4.2). The Globe, in other words, would be defined through the multiple uses – and not only performance-centered uses – to which it would be put. This suggests another way of getting to grips with Globe performativity on the ground, and that involves descending to street level, to engage with the figure that de Certeau diametrically opposes to the solitary and aloof scopophile: the pedestrian. Just as surveillance is understood by de Certeau as both a practice and a metaphor for forms of knowing, relations to knowledge, and one's imaginary place in the civic order, so, too, the act of walking in the city is designated both an everyday function and a burden of signification. Engaged in the "murky intertwining daily behaviours" that elude the gaze of the rooftop onlooker, de Certeau writes of how the "ordinary practitioners of the city" wander through "an urban 'text' they write without being able to read it"; tracing pathways that are "unrecognized poems in which each body is an element signed by many others" (1984: 93). Pedestrianism is an example of everyday practice as "making do," or "tactic," by which, as Marvin Carlson summarizes, "specific instances of behaviour improvised by individuals according to the perceived demands of the moment and unknowable in advance" work to resist, interrogate and re-appropriate the "strategies" of power, the "institutionalized frameworks, scripts, or patterns of action that serve as general guides to behaviour" (2004: 44–5). Walking is an amateur art of performance conducted in the interstices of the rational city's grid; acts of walking (ambling, strolling, striding) here rather than there, this route rather than that, comprise a multiplicity of negotiations with, and reinventions of, the spatial order, whereby "the act of walking is to the urban system what the speech act is to language" (1984: 97); that is, a unique, contingent and potentially resistant use of that system.

   If, as I have suggested, de Certeau's account of the relations between epistemology and perspective offers a way of positioning what W. B. Worthen (2003) calls Globe

FIGURE 4.2   Theo Crosby, architect of Shakespeare's Globe
Photograph reproduced with permission of Pentagram.

performativity, the ethics and aesthetics of pedestrianism (and, more generally, of tactics and use) open up a number of new routes for performance analysis. Such is the path trodden by Alan Read in *Theatre and Everyday Life*, which proposes an "ethics of performance" engaged with de Certeau's concern with "the use that is made of representations," and rooted in "a poetics of the image in theatre which does not wish to exclude the political context of its creation nor the ethical dimension of its relations with an 'other' in the audience" (1993: 133). Read's primary focus of investigation is the interface between the avant-garde and what he terms the "lay" theatre in the realms of everyday life, represented, for instance, by the "topographical practices" of "the operations of theatre in and on neighbourhoods, in site-specific events and in the streets of the city"; what is of particular relevance here is the recognition that "these are not necessarily large-scale events but often micro-movements, pedestrian activity barely discernible from the everyday" (1993: 138). But the theoretical model has a more general application. Specifically, I wish to draw upon Read's sense of the porosity and the ambiguity of the boundaries between theatre and the everyday in order to suggest some of the varieties of use that are available to the spectator-pedestrian in the context of Globe performativity's official narratives, systems and structures. There has, of course, been much critical discussion of the legitimacy of its mobilization of a rhetoric of "authenticity" around its architectural form and theatrical practice, and upon the ways in which this mandate informs the competing, possibly contradictory, claims to func-tion as working theatre, scholarly resource, tourist attraction, London landmark, theme park and ersatz heritage site. W. B. Worthen, in particular, makes the point that the Globe experience evades an overly narrow remit of theatrical performance, in that it participates in the practices of "living history" re-enactment and of the theme park, manifesting "the spectacle of the past before us, allowing us to engage it only in its own 'reconstructed' accent," but also covertly signalling an anxiety "not so much about the power of theatre or of Shakespeare . . . but about the ability of theatre, Shakespearean theatre, to occupy a distinctive place in modern life" (2003: 114–16).

In a number of obvious and important ways the Globe facilitates and even privileges walking as a mode of performative interaction. It is, of course, one of the key features of the Globe theatrical experience that the standing participant scores the double advan-tage of relatively inexpensive entry (tickets are £5, compared to £13 for the poorest of the gallery seats) and freedom of movement. The solidarity of the standing crowd, its proximity to the stage and visibility to the performers, are the pre-requisites of the participatory, directly communicative aspect of Globe performance, and have been much remarked upon; what has been less noticed is that the yard, especially for spectators of less than average height, may be an ideal place to listen to the spoken word but is hardly conducive to the comfortable viewing of stage action or *mise en scène*. Globe theorists and practitioners (the more adept of whom, such as Mark Rylance, treat the yard as a conversational space) have repeatedly stressed the primacy of audition over vision in both early modern performance and the reconstruction, and in this respect echo the emphases (although not – yet – the theoretical and cultural implications) of Bruce Smith's recent, brilliant investigation of playhouse speech and sound, *The Acoustic World of Early Modern England*, which argues that, as an "extraordinarily efficient" instrument for "propagating sound" the 1599 Globe was also an apparatus for the vocal and aural production of subjectivity: "the subject . . . finds its identity through the multiple 'speech communities' to which it happens to belong" (1999: 208, 244). Most modern theatregoers, imagining identity as primarily constituted by seeing rather than speech, nonetheless stubbornly persist in acting as spectators first and audiences second. The standee's facility to trade places, to view the stage from a range of angles, goes some way towards restoring the satisfactions of scopophilia within acoustic space; it also allows a mitigation of the effects of one of the most intractable, and hotly disputed, aspects of the playhouse's architectural authenticity, the stage posts, by allowing the walker to follow the performers as they move around the platform, and to keep them in view. If there were a pedestrian style most appropriate to Globe performance, it would be stalking; ideally, it should complement the footwork of the performers (which may incorporate incursions in the yard itself) who, for their part, too, have been directed to alleviate the blocking effect of the posts by keeping on the move. But being fully attentive to Globe performance is, by the nature of the building and the theatregoing experience it stages, a heroically doomed labor: one's eye is drawn relentlessly away from onstage action and towards fellow audience members, towards the assertively modern neighboring build-ings which interrupt the prospect of sky through the open roof; while the anomaly of open-air performance perceptually amplifies the ambient sound of the city, the noise of the everyday no longer the muffled background to stage speech but its equal and partner.

Afforded certain hard privileges which force a rethinking of conventional configurations of ticket pricing, physical comfort, and quality of view, the Globe pedestrian may also be thought of as occupying the space between two disciplinary paradigms: that is, between a semiotics of theatre, on the one hand, and a phenomenology of performance, on the other. Unwittingly, but potentially productively, the maneuvers that are compelled by the Globe stage's "authentic" disruptions of the visual field indicate that the student of Globe performativity might be advised to re-orient and multiply the positioning of her gaze, envisaging its meaning-making activities as a complex, ragged network of encounters, negotiations and transactions spun around the stage rather than centered upon it. As Worthen observes, the movements of the inhabitants of the yard to inspect the structure or to regard the event from different perspectives mark out multiple trails of living history which supplement and sometimes, perhaps, contradict the intent of the performance work itself: "to the degree that the Globe shares the performative horizon of theme parks and living-history re-enactments, the stage performance must fail wholly to govern the force of Globe performativity" (2003: 109–10). The scope for ambulatory improvisation is not confined to the yard and auditorium. One of the key characteristics of the Globe space is its permeability, in that the freedom of the spectator to come and go during performances suspends certain of the key protocols of audience entrance and exit, as well as facilitating a range of styles, intensities, and durations of engagement with either the architecture or the performance (or both). Again, pedestrianism is institutionally legitimated and regulated in the form of half-hourly walking tours, which formalize the experience within the official narrative, but which also draw attention to the existence of multiple thresholds, demarcating the various pedestrian zones of the Globe site.[1] Here, the domain of the ticketholder begins not at the doors to the auditorium but at the glass boundary of the stone piazza that surrounds the building-within-a-building of a Globe that is already theatricalized. An indeterminate space for strolling, loitering, meeting and departure, this area is a place of intersection and convergence, site of an expanding anthology of what de Certeau describes as "spatial stories," the pedestrian narratives that have been individually and collectively composed in the form of the journeys taken to the theatre, and retraced, differently, when the performance ends. Located, presciently, in a street recently re-named New Globe Walk, it is well within London's congestion charge zone (which at an entry cost of £8 exceeds the cost of a £5 standing ticket); blocks away from on- or off-street parking, and at least ten minutes' walk away from its nearest tube stations, the Globe is, pre-eminently, a place to be walked to as well as walked through.

Westward Ho

Shakespeare's Globe in Southwark is a structure which invites potential visitors to think of it, at least in the first instance, from above, but the theatres of Stratford-upon-Avon (and the Royal Shakespeare Theatre (RST) in particular) are, by contrast, customarily envisaged and imaged from a point of view located at ground level. If the postcard racks in the theatre bookshops, newsagents and souvenir emporiums of Stratford are any guide, the standard commemorative image of the RST is the long-shot view of the 1930s' brick building seen from the opposite (south-east) bank of the Avon; in the foreground, invariably, is the waterway, suggestive by association of the Thames and hence the original Globe, upon which swans and barges placidly glide, and in which the reflected image of the theatre building suggests a precise, balanced symmetry of nature and culture. In some ways, though, the RST's appeal as a cultural landmark is counter-intuitive: unlike the other Shakespearean Stratford sites, it is not old – or, at least, not old enough. As at the Globe, the relation between profile and function is complex: the RST does not, on the face of it, manifest the interior dynamics of the performance space on its outside, and from the moment the recon-structed theatre opened in 1932, commentators have been struck by the disparity between what was famously likened to a Soviet barracks, a crematorium, a power station, corporate headquarters, and a jam factory, and its practical and institutional identity as a space to house Shakespeare. In part, of course, the affirmative modernity of the building was a reaction against the extreme Victorianism of its predecessor, a "frankly fantastical" assembly of neo-Elizabethanism and contemporary Gothic, per-ilously reliant upon asbestos-coated timber, and "built of red brick with dressings of stone . . . incorporating Tudor gabling, Elizabethan chimneys, Gothic turrets, and minarets," and housing a 700-seat auditorium with "an oddly ecclesiastical appear-ance, emphasized by a high pointed roof, and Gothic arches which flanked the gallery" (Beaumann 1982: 12). Although its founders claimed prior to its 1879 opening that the theatre would be "one which will harmonise with the rustic character of its surroundings without loss of dignity or picturesque effect," it would later be derided as "an ogre's castle escaped from some German fairy tale" and "a cross between a German helmet and a bride's cake" (quoted in Bott 1974: n.p.); and as George Bernard Shaw observed in 1925, the year before it mysteriously burned down (prompting him to send a congratulatory telegram), it was "an admirable building, adapted for every conceivable purpose – except that of a theatre" (Beaumann 1982: 92). Read less as a folly than as a monument, however, it seems that the old Shakespeare Memorial Theatre *was* suited, both externally and internally, to the purpose of the particular practices of commemorative theatricality that it was built to house. Peggy Phelan has suggested that "theater architecture . . . is doubly mi-metic," that is, "constructed around an image of the bodies to be staged in its building" (1997: 81), and the Shakespeare Memorial Theatre's etymological and architectural affinity with Victorian funerary monuments points towards a close, if unconscious connection between bardolatry (also a form of mourning) and a festival mode of performance understood as ritual disinterment or resurrection. By contrast, as it was conceived by its architect, Elisabeth Scott, the 1932 rebuild reflected a new secularism and egalitarianism, manifested in the interior by the abolition of the conventional Victorian horseshoe-shaped circle and its replacement with a "circle'" that runs laterally across the auditorium, thereby eradicating the patterns of seeing and being seen that characterized society theatre-going up to the 1930s; from now on, spectators would be trained, as in a cinema, to focus their attention on the stage rather than each other (the gulf between circle and stage would subsequently be bridged, in 1950, by the addition of side balconies). The theatre's drawbacks were obvious from the start, and have been extensively documented (and partially alleviated by periodic attempts to extend the stage into the auditorium), but Baliol Holloway's complaint (in 1934) that performing in the space "is like acting to Calais from the cliffs of Dover" (Beaumann 1982: 113) continues to resonate; worse still, to contemporary eyes, the auditorium blatantly emphasizes the economic and class divisions that it was intended to surmount.

Trapped *in situ*, more or less silent and immobile, looking one way for the duration of the performance, possibly with a restricted view; it will already be apparent that the scope of negotiation available to the Stratford spectator, certainly as compared to the peregrinations available to the pedestrian at Shakespeare's Globe, is extremely limited. It is, of course, a hardly untypical experience of mainstream Shakespearean theatregoing that extends well beyond Stratford, and of a theatre structure which, as Baz Kershaw puts it, primarily works as a *"disciplinary system"* by physically "ensnaring every kind of audience in a web of mostly unacknowledged values, tacit commitments to forces that are beyond their control, and mechanisms of exclusion that ensure that most people stay away" (1999: 31). It is a static version of the benevolent incarceration that de Certeau finds in railway travel, whereby the equally immobilized spectator is "pigeonholed, numbered, and regulated in the grid of the railway car, which is a perfect actualization of the rational utopia," and where "rest and dreams reign supreme" (1984: 111). Just as the act of walking, for de Certeau, is simultaneously an everyday practice, a way of knowing, or epistemology, and a political metaphor, so the repose of the rail traveler functions here in more than a literal sense; atomized in transit through a landscape which is contemplated rather than encountered, the passenger is the polar opposite of the pedestrian, a passive consumer rather than an active negotiator, a viewer rather than a participant. Applied to the experience of the average Stratford theatregoer, it seems an apt enough analogy. But the vehicular frame of reference has further resonances.

Michael Adler observes that "the décor of the auditorium calls to mind that of a 1930s luxury ocean liner" (2001: 23); it seems an entirely appropriate association for an enterprise that was facilitated by the rapid expansion of the international transport infrastructure, and financed primarily by trans-Atlantic capital, and to a building whose prow is formed by the shell of the old theatre, its bows by the auditorium, and its stern by the foyer and box office, and which is moored on the banks of the Avon, poised as if to set sail majestically westwards, nostalgically into the future. Less reminiscent of the Victorian theatre it annexes than of the 1930s' picture palaces whose classically inflected Art Deco dreamed of the new world from where the visions they housed originated, the SMT's hybrid architecture articulates a more fundamental, although not consciously acknowledged, sense of dislocation that has been endemic to theatre at Stratford from the outset, and which successive attempts to modernize the building and its activities have simply exacerbated (it is a rupture which is also exposed in the tellingly territorial imagery employed by Baliol Hollo-way, imaging the actor standing at the threshold of England, vainly projecting towards a distant, alien shore). Despite appearances, theatre does not occupy a natural place in the landscape of Shakespearean Stratford; as Barbara Hodgdon notes, it is symptomatic that the itinerary of the annual Birthday procession on 23 April conspicuously avoids any encounter with "the sites where Shakespeare – through his texts and the actors who interpret them – becomes (re)embodied... the Royal Shakespeare Theatre, the Swan, and The Other Place...; the institutional spaces so central to marketing his theatrical reputation are situated... at the margins, falling outside the traffic pattern of the ceremonial pilgrimage" (1998: 193–4). For most historians, the efforts of the Flower family as governors, of Bridges-Adams, Jackson, Quayle and Hall as artistic directors, and of the Royal Shakespeare Company as an institution, to establish Stratford as the world center of Shakespearean theatre can be endorsed not only as heroic, but, in a more crucial sense, as entirely legitimate, and even necessary. Whether it is Charles Flower confronting the bourgeois philistinism of Victorian Stratford to upgrade its memorial from a piece of statuary to a working theatre, William Bridges-Adams struggling with the prejudices of metropolitan critics during the 1930s to position the SMT as a national rather than provincial presence, Peter Hall securing subsidy in the 1960s in order to extend the company's remit from the national to the international, or Adrian Noble steering the embattled organization through a period of marketization, mediatization and entrenchment in which live theatre has been increasingly relegated to the margins of culture, the assumption has been that it is both right and appropriate, and somehow *natural* that Stratford should be the place of Shakespearean theatrical commemoration and cele-bration. Theatre history is usually written by the apologists for its victors, and this impression makes sense today because it is how it is; but it need not have been, and a different reading of history shows that it was only made so by a great deal of concerted work against the grain of regional culture and demography.

The precariousness of performance in Stratford can be traced as far back as the very beginnings of the Stratford cult, in David Garrick's notorious Shakespeare Jubilee of 1769, which, over three days, featured recitals, costume masquerades, dinners and breakfasts, and a firework display but not a production of a Shakespeare play; rather than seeing this as a perverse and faintly scandalous omission, as many subsequent commentators have done, we might consider it an astutely pragmatic response to local circumstances. A century later, the recent extension of the railway to Stratford, which was already facilitating the development of touristic pilgrimage (increasingly, Beau-mann notes, "the visitors' book at the Birthplace included American names" [1982: 4]) made the 1864 Shakespeare Tercentenary, centered on a festival of six plays in a purpose-built pavilion, a viable proposition; even then, the event ran at a loss which could only be recouped through the demolition of the pavilion and auctioning of its fittings. The fiasco was ridiculed in *The Times* as a misguided instance of provincial "hero-worship"; the newspaper went on to observe that even among those "zealous believers" in Shakespeare "who go from time to time, out of pure love, to see them acted in London, not one in ten thousand would go out of his way to see them acted in Stratford." Quoting this comment, Beamann chafes at its "mandarin confidence in the innate superiority of the capital" (1982: 6) and records that the "deep and absolute" divide between the provincial and the metropolitan would impact upon theatre in Stratford for at least half a century; but the basic point that, for the metropolitan audiences upon which the festivals would become dependent, Stratford lay at the end of a considerable detour, was – and remains – a valid one. The objections resurfaced a decade later, when the plans for the first Memorial Theatre were announced: the sense was that "if there had to be a theatre" (and this was not generally agreed), Beaumann writes, "then obviously the West End, not Warwickshire, was the place for it" (1982: 13). In effect, Charles Flower and his followers wished to engineer a reversal of the historic trajectory of theatregoing, orienting it away from, rather than towards, the city; and this during a period which not only saw the pace and scale of urbanization increase, but also, reflecting this, an increased clustering of the theatrical trade in the metropolitan center. That the SMT, sailing against the tide of history, managed to build an audience is testament to the persistence of an emergent practice of Shakespearean cultural consumption that began to work a limited engagement with performance into the itinerary of the Stratford pilgrim (for the first half-century this was barely sufficient to sustain summer festivals of a few weeks); and it was utterly dependent upon (and, more importantly, produced by) the development of a road, rail and air transport network that represented the modernity that the Stratford experience, in other respects, was imagined to resist. By the 1920s, the expansion of both motor transport and air travel, and the careful co-ordination of the repertory with the needs of the local hospitality industry, had established a national and, increasingly, international audience base that seemed largely indifferent to the questions of theatrical vitality, aesthetic quality and innovation that exercised the Memorial's artistic director and his national critics. The sources of the theatre's loyalties were revealed when the issue arose of funding the rebuilding of the theatre after the 1926 fire: it rapidly became apparent that the nation's desire to invest emotionally and ideologically in Shakespeare was not matched in financial terms. After a year of appeals backed by the media, political, and some elements of the theatrical, establishment, just over one-tenth of the £250,000 required had been raised in the UK. The Chair of the Governors, Archie Flower, travelled to the United States, initiating the inauguration of the American Shakespeare Foundation in 1927, which, in a space of months, had promised £160,000. The project of rebuilding an English home for Shakespeare performance was, evidently, perceived as more urgent abroad than domestically;[2] Stratford's dependency upon, primarily, American capital in order to sustain its version of deep Englishness could not be more apparent.

It is a fair guess that Archie Flower sold the idea of the SMT to moneyed American Shakespeareans less on its aspirations to be a beacon of theatrical innovation and experiment than on the promise of authentic heritage that could be all the more effectively sentimentalized at a distance. Yet, whatever the ambiguous benefits of trading upon associations with place, the history of production at Stratford has been more decisively shaped by resistance, rather than accommodation, to the pressures of locale and tradition. This has been particularly marked during the modern period that was inaugurated by Peter Hall's reinvention of the festival system into the Royal Shakespeare Company in the early 1960s. For the theatre workers and critics who descended on Stratford in the post-war years, the SMT was a byword for the parochial, the retrograde and the second-rate: Peter Brook recalled that in Stratford – before he arrived – "every conceivable value was buried in deadly sentimentality and complacent worthiness – a traditionalism approved largely by town, scholar and Press" (1972: 51). The immediate consequence of Peter Hall's appointment as Artistic Director was an end to Stratford's isolationism, and an emphatic repositioning of the work as metropolitan by affiliation, and international in style and scope. Hall's policy in the early years was founded upon the new relationship between Stratford and London; in particular, it was hoped that the RSC would eventually acquire a base on the South Bank, as part of the projected National Theatre. The importance Hall attached to the London operation was underlined in 1966: urged to economize by the RSC governors, he reversed expectations by cutting back the Shakespeare work at Stratford rather than in the contemporary repertoire in the capital (Adler 2001: 56–7). In the first seasons, Hall led a stylistic drive to sever the links both with the theatre's own past and, by extension, with the mythological landscape of Stratford itself, in which the fabric, canvas and timber of recycled stock sets and costumes were as homely and familiar as the interiors of half-timbered teashops. It did not happen all at once: reviewing John Barton's 1960 *Shrew,* played within the localized, lovingly crafted setting of a War-wickshire alehouse, Robert Speaight relished "an older and almost forgotten England relived before one's eyes . . . the Shrew that Shakespeare drew, tracing its pedigree right down from Chaucer and Langland, and from the carvings that a curious eye may discover on the choir-stalls of an English, or a French, cathedral" (1960: 446–7). More prescient was the same season's *Troilus and Cressida,* which featured a permanent sandpit set which seemed "the wasteland at the outskirts of empire" (Alan Brien, *Spectator*, July 29, 1960), and which suggested a rather different conception of the relation between theatrical space and dramatic world, between the locale of perform-ance and the kind of cultural space the company was attempting to fashion for itself. Every effort was made in the early years to establish Stratford as a European theatre, with Brecht and Beckett providing the most obvious reference points, although the Orientalist strain which would be most fully realized in Brook's 1970 *Dream* was already evident in his 1962 *King Lear* ("flat white setting, combining Brecht and Oriental theatre," wrote Kenneth Tynan in the *Observer* [November 11, 1962]). The sense of geographical and cultural displacement was palpable; in this instance, in a production apparently positioned on the wrong side of the Cold War, which was admired, according to Speaight, "by everyone who likes to take their Shakespearian interpretations from East Berlin" (1963: 419). Yet the avant-garde metropolitan internationalism embraced by the 1960s' RSC operated within a uniquely complex, and volatile context of reception. That the singularity of its location might be a crucial element of Stratford performance was generally, tactfully ignored by commentators, but for the *Shakespeare Survey* reviewer, Gareth Lloyd Evans, writing in 1969, the anomaly of the theatre's Stratford location could no longer be avoided; in that it manifested itself in a bafflingly heterogeneous audience, and in an accordingly fragmented theatrical experience: luring "the curious and the envious, the theatregoer and the non-theatregoer," and thereby annihilating "the customary and sharp distinctions between the knowledgeable theatregoer, the occasional theatregoer, and the positively anti-theatregoer," Stratford creates "the most unpredictable audience in the world" (1969: 135–6). One of the company's ways of addressing the varying levels of cultural competence within both its domestic and international audiences, Lloyd Evans noted, was a visual aesthetic similar to that of "foreign circuses whose acts are obviously designed to be filmed and sold on the international market" (1969: 137); already, whether at home or tour, the company was already conversant with what Alan Read has called the international '"Esperanto' of the image" (1993: 101). It was Peter Brook, again, who supplied both the definitive version of this method and the theatrical agenda for the 1970s' English Shakespearean theatre, in the legendary production of *Dream* which framed impeccable speech within a white box, and which included "among its repertory of signifying surfaces" a non-English, "Eastern" idiom of "orientalist performance techniques, costumes based on those worn by Chinese acrobats, Indian raga, and Asian incantations" (Hodgdon 1998: 187). Brook's determination to annex the Stratford stage as a white empty space certainly eradicated the traces of Mendelssohn and Reinhardt, woodland and gossamer fairies (as well as geography, history, and cultural memory); more than that, it successfully disengaged the show from its Stratford moorings and set it on an international trail that definitely established its style as both directorial signature and global brand.

Much discussed and much imitated, the production defined the template for at least a decade of work which would be further shaped by the black-box studio theatre movement and the oil-driven economic downturn that both enforced scenic austerity and made travel to Stratford even more of a test than ever. In 1972, the organisation abandoned the contractual arrangements initiated by Hall at the start of the previous decade, whereby actors had committed to the company for a period of three years, for single-season contracts; and along with them, the hope that performers might, at least nominally, become members of a community rather than resentful boarders. Thus far I have been sketching a relationship between theatrical event, vocabulary, site and context that is apparently antithetical to that of the Globe: whereas, at Bankside, performance is relentlessly overdetermined by its setting, performance at Stratford has been predominantly marked by the tactics of disaffiliation. But the early 1970s also saw the emergence of attempts to connect the work of the organization with the locality; particularly on what many would regard as the fringes of the company's work (especially its Shakespeare work), in its educational outreach and community-based activities. In 1974, the opening show at The Other Place (which was then envisaged by its director, Buzz Goodbody, as an "alternative" to main house cultural and theatrical values), a truncated version of *King Lear*, was pointedly "aimed at Midlands school students rather than the arts page readers of the daily papers" (Chambers 1980: 7); the national critics were not invited. This isolationism did not last, of course; the following year saw national reviewers acclaiming Goodbody's *Hamlet* as a landmark production; importantly, however, for Peter Thomson, it was a production character- ized by an absolute contiguity of event, text, place and space, which was emphatically *not* "transferable": "it belonged to the physical conditions in which it had been rehearsed . . . we were silent participants in a series of events whose intense logic required that they take place here and nowhere else" (1976: 151). This was not the case with Trevor Nunn's *Macbeth* in the following year, which transferred effortlessly to the Royal Shakespeare Theatre, to the newly-opened Warehouse in London in 1977, and subsequently to TV; as Brook had done for the main stage six years before, Nunn in this production codified the rapprochement of the environmental and the televisual, black-box Shakespeare that would continue up to and beyond the closure of the first Other Place (marked by his *Othello*, in which McKellen played Iago) in 1989. It was in the non-Shakespearean work at The Other Place and the Swan that the company most directly engaged with its own context: in the mixed-media satire on the Stratford tourist trade, *I Was Shakespeare's Double* (1974), in its revival of Edward Bond's drama of Shakespeare's last days, *Bingo* (1976; the play was revived again at the Swan in 1995), and in Peter Barnes's Garrick satire *Jubilee* (2001).

In 1983, The Other Place made its most significant attempt to date to realize Goodbody's hope of staging "work with a specifically local character," which might cultivate "an audience who hitherto thought the RSC were out of touch" (Chambers 1980: 40), by mounting Barry Kyle's adaptation of *The Dillen,* the memoir of a local itinerant worker, George Hewins; devised as a collaboration between theatre profes- sionals and Stratford amateurs, this was a promenade production that took its performers and audiences out into the streets and fields around the town. A widely used device in community performance, the promenade, Baz Kershaw notes, is "designed to make the performances more accessible, by blurring the distinction between 'reality' and 'play', so that the transition into performance consciousness is modulated by conventions drawn from non-theatrical, social occasions" (1992: 192). In this instance, the pedestrian activities which the authors of a recent article on the production have identified as "key motifs" disruptively shadowed the itineraries of the walking tours which define Shakespearean Stratford, rewriting its official narrative as comfortably bourgeois, heritage site, and offering, as Kyle put it, "a voice to another storyteller that wasn't Shakespeare . . . Stratford's proletarian Falstaff" (Prentice & Leongamornlert 2002: 50). The format of *The Dillen* was itself elegiac, a retrieval of a tradition of community-based theatrical celebration that was disappearing into history, "nostalgic less for the Victorian past than for the engaged theatre of the previous twenty years" (2002: 48). Nonetheless, the aspiration towards communality it harbored, and the pedestrian aesthetic that it adopted, lingered on, albeit in a more attenuated and, paradoxically, unlocalized form. Pedestrianism surfaced again, just over a decade later, in David Thacker's production of *Julius Caesar*, which was seen briefly at The Other Place before being taken on tour: set in a mediatized, fictive Baltic state, the production cast the spectators as witnesses and extras, carefully worked by the performers to flesh out the crowd scenes. Kershaw suggests that, in the circumstances of promenade community performance, "our role as audience is made ambiguous: we are both a part of, and apart from, the action" (1992: 192); in this instance, however, the ambiguity was defined by what Russell Jackson records as "customary English disengagement," wryly confessing that "we were a half-hearted, sheepish lot even before the Tribunes started to work on us" (1994: 339). As Jackson observes, the occasion allowed for a multiplication of pedestrian encounters and viewpoints, as "each member of the crowd saw things differently" (1994: 339); those who wished to, nonetheless, could opt for the security of a gallery seat, above the action and looking down on it.

Community participation of another kind was attempted, again in *Julius Caesar,* on the main stage during the 1995 season, in a production directed by Peter Hall which repeated a trick used in his 1984 National Theatre *Coriolanus*: drawing upon a local corps of supernumeraries, the crowd was represented by an awkward-looking group, Peter Holland reported, "rhubarbing away, mouthing comments to each other . . . and then allow[ing] a few professional actors, career plebeians as it were, to dominate them" (1997: 233). The device had been more successfully used a year before, in a *Measure for Measure* in which the "citizens of Vienna" were represented by a neighborhood watch of "citizens of Stratford," described by Holland as "dozens of middle-aged men, clad in gowns, wigs and mortar-boards" (1997: 209). The local was manifested even more cosily, and self-referentially, in the same season's *Twelfth Night,* which was explicitly set in Stratford itself, with, Russell Jackson records, "toy-theater drops and sliding flats against a background of miniaturized Stratford architecture" (1994: 353); thus rendering "the play's events an episode in the history of the town where the audience was watching the production" (Holland 1997: 191). Needless to say, the miniature topography of this Stratford included New Place, Hall's Croft and Holy Trinity Church, but not, say, the municipal car park and the McDonald's — let alone the town's most prominent building, the Royal Shakespeare Theatre itself. In a way, although unsurprising, the omission indicates a telling blind spot, given that the clearest sense of local allegiance, and the strongest manifestations of the awareness of immediate environment, have been found in those main-stage productions which have engaged with the enclosed legacy of the theatre building, and its architecture, and with the echoes of the work it has housed. The most extreme instance of this self-referentiality was the 1989 *As You Like It*, directed by John Caird and designed by Ultz, which essayed a Pirandellian doubling of stage and auditorium spaces, with a set that "reproduced the thirties décor of the public areas of the theatre itself, the art deco marquetry panelling, chaises longues, and lamps of the dress circle bar, the huge silver-figured clock of the foyer showing the correct time and dominating the stage," with actors who "entered the stage from the auditorium and continued to move freely between the two spaces," and dancers "in the uniforms of ushers and usherettes" (Smallwood 1990: 491). Since the 1980s, RSC self-reflexive-ness has figured within a characteristically postmodern visual idiom which treats cultural, theatrical and media history as an undifferentiated, anachronistic source of referents and images; the strongest sense of a relationship to its own context and history has been in the form of allusion, quotation, parody and homage to previous productions, nowhere more strongly (and predictably) than in its stagings of *Dream*, which, even in the early 2000s, 30 years and a dozen productions on from Brook's, remain locked in inter-textual combat with it. This tradition reached a bitter culmination in the production of *Dream* which, unseasonably opening in the winter months of 2002, seemed to mark the end of an era for the RSC at Stratford, and which to many onlookers epitomized the company's chronic artistic and organizational problems. Critics heralded the show, previewed at Stratford before a national tour, as an unmitigated disaster, an overly conceptualized, undercast, perverse and humor-less monochrome vision, which, like Robert Lepage's notorious Royal National Theatre version of 1992, "engaged Brook's production through a process of negative quotation" (Hodgdon 1998: 176), presenting the play in a black box haunted by horror-movie iconography, half-human trees, giant insects and Complicite-style fair-ies, and in which the mechanics ("a grey-garbed, preposterously hatted blend of Soviet convicts and British hikers" [*The Times*, February 21, 2002]) swayed through their first meeting, in a whimsically appropriate metaphor for the RSC's current situation, in a third-class railway carriage, "with telegraph poles whizzing by on an inset screen" (*Observer*, February 21, 2002).

For many, the production's failures were eloquent of the company's larger difficulties: as the first RSC production of the 2002 season, it inaugurated the new system brought in under the company reorganization, led by Artistic Director Adrian Noble and managing director Chris Foy, and code-named Project Fleet, whereby discrete, balkanized cells within the company were to mount work in a range of venues in Stratford and London, around the country and internationally, operating independently of each other under the company umbrella. Gone was the principle of cross-fertilization between classic and contemporary work that had been one of the RSC's founding principles for a quarter of a century, and with it, moreover, the ensemble system and long-term contracts that tied actors to the company and to Stratford; at the same time, Noble abandoned the company's long-standing claim upon the Barbican as its London base, embarking on a high-risk policy of staging work in the capital's commercial theatre districts. In 2002 this resulted in a season of Elizabethan and Jacobean rarities at the Swan (*Edward III*, *Eastward Ho!*, *The Roman Actor*, *The Malcontent*, *The Island Princess*) which subsequently transferred to London's Gielgud Theatre, and a late plays season at the Roundhouse (*The Winter's Tale*, *The Tempest*, *Pericles*), which, as promenade productions, were notable in the context of the current discussion for their adoption of an aesthetics of pedestrianism, and perhaps indicated that someone, somewhere was keeping an eye on what was afoot at Shakespeare's Globe.

That Noble's plans for the RSC (and the manner in which he attempted to drive them through) should have generated controversy, and provoked widespread criticism and opposition should come as no surprise. Once again, however, it needs to be recognized that the company's location in Stratford remains a core issue. Since the mid-1990s, the RSC's increasingly peripatetic identity as a national touring company (supported by a sophisticated educational and outreach system) has been partially defined through a combined discourse of enterprise, access and inclusivity, and as such has been congenial to the political culture of Blairism, and – relatively – uncontroversial in application. Indeed, it is now this aspect of the RSC's activities, rather than its role as active custodian of Shakespeare's theatrical reputation in Stratford, that is stressed as its primary mission; as the programmes for the 2004 season insist "we tour RSC productions throughout the UK and abroad . . . we want to give as many people as possible, from all walks of life, the chance to find out more about the company and our work." But this national commitment had also been driven by the pressing need to cultivate an audience constituency to balance the long-term decline of its regional base, and it was the more drastic aspects of Project Fleet's response to this that fuelled the most vociferous and deeply felt opposition to the plan. Believing that some of the RSC's biggest problems lay in its theatrical architecture, Noble incorporated into Project Fleet proposals to demolish the RST (a building he described, using the familial vocabulary which has long been used by the RSC in reference to itself, as "dysfunctional") and, with the aid of £50 million of National Lottery funding (which the RSC would need to match) to build a new theatre on the site. What form this would take remained imprecise, although it was hoped that it would be a place of utopian flexibility: ideally, it would be

> like an airport hangar or a shed, a really big space which could shutter off, curtain off; very flexible, with movable seating units. You could do something promenade, in the round, big space, small space, that allows with ease a director or designer to go in and completely redefine it. You dictate the space, rather than the other way round. (Adler 2001: 249)

Predictably enough, the vision of a new theatre aroused both enthusiastic support and passionate opposition at a national level, with Prince Charles, on the one hand, continuing his campaign against modern architecture by warning against the prospect of a "modern and horrible" building and the chair of the Commons Media and Culture Select Committee, on the other, referring to the "neanderthal conditions" of the existing structure (*Guardian*, March 27, 2002). The terms of the debate indicated that the theatre was a highly-charged symbolic battleground, with what had in the 1930s been intended as a monument to classlessness now perpetuating social hierarchy and exclusivity: as Sinead Cusack put it, the configuration promoted a "them and us" mentality, divided between the "the rich in the expensive seats and the poor devils at the back who can hardly hear" (*Guardian*, January 9, 2002). For Noble, the exclusionary qualities of the theatre intersected significantly with audience demographics: "Over a quarter of our audience are under 25 . . . at the moment many young people sit a long way from the stage and can feel like second class citizens" (*Guardian*, October 18, 2001).

At the local level, however, objections to Noble's plans focused very specifically upon what was widely perceived not only as the destruction of a valued local amenity, but also, associated with this, an unauthorized act of municipal redevelopment that was tantamount to an act of cultural colonialism. For, as part of a design for the Stratford site that sought, more ambitiously, to re-engineer the cultural infrastructure of the town and change both the context and the nature of the theatregoing experience, Noble proposed to *pedestrianize* the area around the theatre, creating a "theatre village" in which the performance venue lay at the center of a set of edutainment and lifestyle amenities, whereby Shakespeare could be experienced holistically, as part of a day-long package of diversions: "people could arrive in the morning, take part in an education programme, have lunch in a fantastic restaurant, visit a costume exhibition, join a fight or voice workshop, and then in the evening see a show" (*Guardian*, October 18, 2001). A settlement within the existing municipal economy, a phantom double which was perhaps akin to the theatricalized and miniaturized Stratford of the 1994 *Twelfth Night,* Noble's planned "theatre village" was immediately derided as a kind of Disneyfied Shakespeareland (and was subsequently abandoned). Opposition, as coordinated by a local campaign group HOOT (Hands Off Our Theatre), and as voiced in the local press, was vigorous: a succession of enraged correspondents to the *Stratford-upon-Avon Herald* accused the RSC of reneging upon long-standing commitments to maintain the grounds around the theatres, of attempting to lure tourist business away from the town, of planning to build a footbridge across the Avon which "will successfully spoil the view to the church which is known all over the world" (letter to the *Herald*, February 2), of wanton vandalism in the proposal to demolish the Grade II-listed RST, and of generally acting with arrogant disregard of the views of the townspeople. Perhaps what most strikes the outsider about the temper of the debate is that local anger at Noble's plans generally paid less heed either to the quality of the RSC's current or recent work or to the practical merits of reconfiguring the RST's interior (the key points of debate at national level) than to their likely impact upon local infrastructure: the leisure and hospitality economies of Stratford, but also, more intangibly, the allegedly communal grounds around the building whose rights of use had been bequeathed by immemorial custom and sustained through practice.

The perception, both within the company and without, that Noble was acting as a kind of absentee landlord during the crucial period in which Project Fleet was conceived, half-implemented, and then put on hold was reinforced by the fact that during 2001–2 he was enjoying what was termed a "sabbatical" from the RSC, in which he was released to direct the West End musical spectacular of *Chitty Chitty Bang Bang.* As the critics pointed out, Noble stood to gain a substantial sum from the show's success; sure enough, the opening was followed by Noble's announcement of his resignation on 24 April, and, after some months of maneuvering, the appointment of Michael Boyd as his successor in July. At the time of writing, it remains to be seen whether the demolition and reconstruction work inflicted on the RST in the wake of Project Fleet will alleviate the long-term problems inherent in the Stratford location. For the present, and for the purposes of this chapter, it is apt enough to note that the man who sought to transform the Stratford experience into a zone for walkers should have made his exit from the place at the wheel of a show about, of all things, a flying car.

London Bankside and Stratford offer sharply contrasting configurations of spectatorship and audience-performance interaction which, between them, represent the most visible, if not the most typical, manifestation of twenty-first-century English theatrical Shakespeare. At one extreme, there is a seemingly monolithic historical pastiche which, even as it attempts to constrain theatrical practice within the mandate of authenticity, allows for practices of pedestrian circulation that, at the least, complicate and compromise the project. At the other, we have a regime of production, and institutional style which, even as it is defined by determinedly unlocalized, relentlessly peripatetic mobility, nonetheless continues to harbor dreams of belonging, of inhabiting a neighborhood, of being at home.

NOTES

1 The 1999 Globe season included a programme of educational events (repeated in 2000) that went under the banner headline of "In Shakespeare's Shoes," which included readings of *The Cobbler's Prophecy* and *The Shoemakers Holiday*, and which prompted Patrick Spottiswood to quip in the promotional literature that it was merely coincidental that the International Shakespeare Globe Fellow that season was the Arden Third Series general editor and Professor of Shakespeare Studies at King's, Richard Proudfoot.

2 The original SMT, similarly, was more popular in the United States than in the UK: "Virtually the only major support came from America" (Beaumann 1982: 18). The building of The Swan, similarly, happened as a result of an extraordinary act of individual generosity on the part of the American oil magnate Frederick Koch. It has been well documented that it was largely American money, and the energies of an American theatrical entrepreneur, Sam Wanamaker, that made possible the construction of Shakespeare's Globe.

REFERENCES AND FURTHER READING

Adler, Michael (2001). *Rough Magic: Making Theatre at the Royal Shakespeare Company*. Carbondale, IL: Southern Illinois University Press.

Beaumann, Sally (1982). *The Royal Shakespeare Company: A History of Ten Decades*. Oxford: Oxford University Press.

Bott, John (1974). *The Figure of the House: The Remarkable Story of the Building of Stratford's Royal Shakespeare Theatre*. Stratford-upon-Avon: Royal Shakespeare Company.

Brook, Peter (1972). *The Empty Space*. Harmondsworth: Penguin.

Carlson, Marvin (2004). *Performance: A Critical Introduction*, 2nd edn. London: Routledge.

Chambers, Colin (1980). *Other Spaces: New Theatre and the RSC*. London: Eyre Methuen.

Cosgrove, Denis (1988). "The Geometry of Landscape: Practical and Speculative Arts in the Sixteenth-Century Land Territories." In Denis Cosgrove & Stephen Daniels (eds.) *The Iconography of Landscape: Essays on the Symbolic Representation, Design and Use of Past Environments*. Cambridge: Cambridge University Press, pp. 254–76.

Day, Barry (1996). *This Wooden "O": Shakespeare's Globe Reborn*. London: Oberon Books.

de Certeau, Michel (1984). *The Practice of Everyday Life*, trans. Steven Rendall. Berkeley, CA: University of California Press.

Egan, Gabriel (1999). "Reconstructions of the Globe: A Retrospective." *Shakespeare Survey* 52: 1–16.

Hodgdon, Barbara (1998). *The Shakespeare Trade: Performances and Appropriations.* Philadelphia, PA: University of Pennsylvania Press.

Holland, Peter (1997). *English Shakespeares: Shakespeare on the English Stage in the 1990s.* Cambridge: Cambridge University Press.

Jackson, Russell (1994). "Shakespeare at Stratford-upon-Avon, 1994–95." *Shakespeare Quarterly* 46: 340–57.

Kershaw, Baz (1992). *The Politics of Performance: Radical Theatre as Cultural Intervention.* London: Routledge.

Kershaw, Baz (1999). *The Radical in Performance: Between Brecht and Baudrillard.* London: Routledge.

Lloyd Evans, Gareth (1969). "The Reason Why: The Royal Shakespeare Season 1968 Reviewed." *Shakespeare Survey* 22: 135–44.

Mullaney, Steven (1988). *The Place of the Stage: License, Play and Power in Renaissance England.* Chicago: University of Chicago Press.

Mulryne J. R. & Shewring, Margaret (eds.) (1997). *Shakespeare's Globe Rebuilt.* Cambridge: Cambridge University Press.

Nuti, Lucia (1999). "Mapping Places: Chorography and Vision in the Renaissance." In Denis Cosgrove (ed.) *Mappings.* London: Reaktion.

Orrell, John (1983). *The Quest for Shakespeare's Globe.* Cambridge: Cambridge University Press.

Phelan, Peggy (1997). *Mourning Sex: Performing Public Memories.* London: Routledge.

Prentice, Catherine & Leongamornlert, Helena (2002). "The RSC Goes Walkabout: *The Dillen* in Stratford, 1983." *New Theatre Quarterly* 69: 47–58.

Read, Alan (1993). *Theatre and Everyday Life: An Ethics of Performance.* London: Routledge.

Shapiro, I. A. (1948). "The Bankside Theatres: Early Engravings." *Shakespeare Survey* 1: 25–37.

Smallwood, Robert (1990). "Shakespeare at Stratford-upon-Avon, 1989 (Part II)." *Shakespeare Quarterly* 41: 491–9.

Smith, Bruce R. (1999). *The Acoustic World of Early Modern England: Attending to the O-Factor.* Chicago: University of Chicago Press.

Speaight, Robert (1960). "The 1960 Season at Stratford-upon-Avon." *Shakespeare Quarterly* 11: 446–7.

Speaight, Robert (1963). "Shakespeare in Britain." *Shakespeare Quarterly* 14: 419–32.

Stewart, Susan (2001). *On Longing: Narratives of the Miniature, the Gigantic, the Souvenir, the Collection.* Durham, NC: Duke University Press.

Thomson, Peter (1976). "Towards a Poor Shakespeare: The Royal Shakespeare Company at Stratford in 1975." *Shakespeare Survey* 29: 151–6.

Worthen, W. B. (2003). *Shakespeare and the Force of Modern Performance.* Cambridge: Cambridge University Press.

5

Where Is *Hamlet*? Text, Performance, and Adaptation

Margaret Jane Kidnie

> But in general, the answer to the old question – "If the *Mona Lisa* is in the Louvre in Paris, where is *Hamlet*?" – has been unvarying. There is only one *Mona Lisa*, and, yes, it is in the Louvre; as for *Hamlet* . . . it too has a restricted documentable existence as the text of the play in the First Folio, the good Second Quarto, the bad First Quarto, or some ideal combination of these sources.
>
> Stillinger Review: *Textualterity: Art, Theory, and Textual Criticism*

Jack Stillinger's answer to James McLaverty's well-known ontological riddle interests me precisely because it seems so self-evidently true.[1] Stillinger presents as commonplace the attitude that *Hamlet* resides, ultimately, in its earliest documentary witnesses. If one desires to "look at" *Hamlet* (and so approximate the manner in which one might "look at" the *Mona Lisa* in the Louvre), one turns to the three editions printed between 1603 and 1623. Each copy, even within a single edition, may vary in its bibliographical details as a result of stop-press correction in the early modern printing house, but this additional level of instability to a three-text play seems not to affect an ability to identify the thing we call *Hamlet*. So little does textual variation among the documents hinder recognition, the play can even be found in "some ideal combination of these sources." We locate *Hamlet*, therefore, not just in a variety of non-identical rare books, but in an unspecified range of editorially-mediated modern versions of those books. To put this a different way, the ontological anxiety generated by the riddle is quelled (or to use Stillinger's phrasing, Shakespeare's play achieves a "restricted documentable existence") by calling a play a text, where "text" is understood to refer to certain print exemplars. Other forms of reproduction set in opposition to *Hamlet*-as-text are copies that by definition have only a derivative existence. Stillinger only gestures at these forms, but the context of his reflections on art and space – a review of Joseph Grigely's *Textualterity*, a monograph that advocates a type of radical textual democracy – implies that the category might include, for instance, graphic novels, portraits and cartoons, and performance. I'm not citing Stillinger at such length in order to take issue with him. On the contrary, his account is almost certainly – "in general" – the "unvarying" answer to the riddle. And yet his comments are provocative in the way they expose so vividly how our conception of Shakespeare's plays continues to be dominated by an ideology of print.

Grigely argues that the idea that text exists as an object, and specifically as a literary object, is one legacy of the Anglo-American textual tradition as it was established in the early twentieth century by such scholars as W. W. Greg and R. B. McKerrow (1995: 91). We might, he suggests, instead examine how an artwork functions in practice and in history, not as an object, but as a cultural process, and so conceive of it as "an ongoing – and infinite – manifestation of textual appearances, whether those texts are authorized or not" (1995: 99). His position that individual texts can never be repeated nor works of literature finally completed, a view that builds on Nelson Goodman's philosophical treatment of the ontology of works of art in *Languages of Art*, leads him controversially to conclude – in a striking reworking of Greg's comment that "Authority is never absolute, but only relative" (1950–51: 19) – that texts in a historical sequence (the work's discrete instantiations) cannot be assigned even relative authority:

> [I]nstead of viewing literature, or artworks, as finished productions, we might instead view them as works of fluxion that experience stasis or duration in a particular edition or a particular exhibition space. Yet, what is particular about a particular edition or a particular exhibition space is ultimately undermined by its instability: it is particular primarily in our conceptualization of it as such, not by virtue of its implied or physical context…If two texts are different, they are essentially equal in their differences because those differences – and the interpretations we bring to bear upon them – are individual in their context: one text cannot be more individual than another. (Grigely 1995: 95–6)

Whether one is speaking of *Hamlet* or the *Mona Lisa*, the work, then, is less a thing or object, than it is an unbounded diachronic series of events. Grigely's argument is a strong expression of textuality as experienced cultural history that refuses to prioritize one moment of inscription over another: the Q1 *Hamlet* of 1603 is no less or more significant to one's idea of the "work" than the Folio *Hamlet* of 1623, Thomas Bowdler's edition of 1807, or the Wells–Taylor edition of 1986.

After including texts as varied as comic books and Charles Knight's pictorial edition as equally legitimate expressions of Shakespeare's work, Grigely pursues his argument a step further:

> Nor is it necessary to exclude performances from this formulation. Where a series of performances is based on a specific text (what Goodman might call a score), and given
> $$W[ork] \rightarrow T[ext]_1, T_2, T_3, \ldots T_N$$
> then we might say that
> $$T[ext]_x \rightarrow P[erformance]_1, P_2, P_3, \ldots P_N. \text{ (1995: 100)}$$

Even performance might be included. What is remarkable about this formulation is not its novelty, but the way Grigely is able so readily to assume a second-order status for performance within a theory that seeks to remind us that "we do not normally conceive a book in terms of itself as a work, but in terms of its texts, or in any case the specific texts with which we have had encounters" (1995: 100). What we encounter through performance, evidently, is not a performance, but a score, another print or (potentially) manuscript text. Stillinger's and Grigely's formulations of the work – the one conventional, the other radical – interest me precisely for the similarity, rather than difference, between them. At the heart of both theoretical analyses is a profound, and all the more profound because unexamined, anti-theatrical bias that seeks to cordon off *Hamlet* from performance.

The ideology of print is so powerful that to define a Shakespeare play in terms of anything but some combination of extant print, or hypothesized manuscript, documents seems almost inconceivable. Like all powerful ideologies, it seems natural, commonsense even, that the "real" *Hamlet* is always, in the last analysis, found in a book. The pervasiveness of such an attitude, despite a now established body of theory and research on Shakespeare and performance, can be readily perceived, even in books and articles devoted to performance. Michael Bristol and Kathleen McLuskie, for instance, celebrate Shakespeare's "valued works" while holding at arm's length the "outlandish liberties" modern theatre takes with those works (2001: 1). Alan C. Dessen, approaching theatre from a very different theoretical perspective, unpacks a critique of late twentieth-century performance through an extended comparison of the spoken and printed word. A rhetoric of origins – "substantial differences from the original"; "the original signals and strategies"; "only the rare scholarly voice will lament the loss of the original continuity or counterpoint" – locates authority exclusively with the early Octavo, Quartos, and Folio, and so brings into question the "price tags" and "trade offs" occasioned by performance (2002: 3, 37, 108). An emphasis on origins is framed in a slightly different manner by Michael D. Friedman who offers a strong statement of what I am calling an ideology of print. Arguing that performance is derived from text, he writes:

> In the realm of performance choices, a production approaches authenticity to the degree that it abides by what the text demands or encourages and avoids what the text discourages or forbids. Conversely, the more a production ignores what the text demands or encourages and employs choices that the text discourages or forbids, the further it moves toward an adaptation. (2002: 50)

What is authentic is the text – in Shakespeare's case, by necessity some form of printed text. The performance, by comparison, is authentic insofar as it can reproduce the text, but the necessary distance between one and its other, a source and that which "really proceed[s] from its reputed source" (2002: 34), implies that performance has at best a precarious claim to authenticity. Indeed, Friedman goes on to clarify that "Since all performances must 'adapt' the printed text to the idiom of the stage...all productions, in this sense are adaptations" (2002: 50). Authenticity, in other words, always already present in the text, inevitably eludes performance; performance is measured in relation to the text in degrees of *in*fidelity and *in*authenticity.

My purpose is not to argue that it is in the theatre where one encounters, like the *Mona Lisa* in the Louvre, *Hamlet*. Richard Levin brought to our attention long ago the interpretive tangle that attends on enthusiastic claims that a play "really exists only in performance":

> This would mean that any alterations made in the text during any performance, even including actors' errors, would become parts of the "real" play. Then there would be no "real" play, but only the aggregate of all the different performances, which would all be equally legitimate, since the author's text, and hence his meaning, could no longer be relevant . . . But it then would make no sense to say that a play can be really understood only in performance, because there would be no independent "reality" apart from the performance that could be understood. (1986: 548)

To seek simply to set on its head the binary relation of text and performance by asserting the priority of performance over text, as Levin demonstrates by pushing us inexorably towards his position that the play resides in the author's text, is not a critical strategy able to resist a dominant ideology of print. So long as Shakespeare's play is theorized, implicitly or explicitly, as a thing or object, the "real" play, logically, must always be located with the text (whether or not one seeks to align that text with an author). To identify the play-as-object with performance, as Levin's reasoning makes clear, would be either to shatter that object into an infinite number of performances, or to make it self-identical with an individual performance.

"Text," as currently understood within a dominant ideology of print, is indifferent to, even antithetical to, performance: a performance is "of" the text; the text stands alone. Performance cannot be seen to form a component part of the "play," because performance is already constructed in language as a non-essential embellishment of, or deviation from, the play-as-text. This distinction, in turn, enables yet another pairing that still further confirms performance's second-order status: performance and adaptation. At what point does a performance take so many liberties with the text that it gets down-graded to the status of adaptation? Isn't *every* performance, as Friedman asks, an adaptation? Such questions, sometimes framed so as to seem to free performance from the tyranny of text, in practice perpetuate an anti-theatrical bias. They implicitly affirm that there is always something – some *thing* – anterior to performance, against which performance can be measured on a sliding scale of (il)legitimate interpretation. So marginalized, performance is relegated to a second-order status, at least in academic discourse, by acculturated reading strategies founded on an idea of text as literary object.

What place can exist for performance in such an ontology? A performance (as distinct from a production) can neither be repeated in time or space, nor transported out of its own time and space. Unlike books, that we can hold, look at, inherit, edit, and sell, again and again, performance survives, if it survives at all, as memory, traces in the archive, and a sensation of loss or desire. For Peggy Phelan, "Performance's only life is in the present": "To the degree that performance attempts to enter the economy of reproduction it betrays and lessens the promise of its own ontology. Performance's being...becomes itself through disappearance" (1993: 146). If one understands Shakespearean performance in terms of its near-complete immersion within a circulation of capital, a relation that has been operational since Shakespeare's plays came into their earliest existence on the stage, then it emerges as an almost entirely consumable commodity – not a good, but a service. But one might insist on the distinction, easily elided, between "a performance" as a one-off experience (an experience for which one, usually, pays money), and "performance" as a term able to frame any number of such unique experiences as generically related in terms of the physical activity and audience-actor dynamic to which they give rise.[2] The distance between these two definitions is successfully bridged by thinking of (a) performance as *eventual* – as having the status of an event (bounded in time and space), and as always coming into being. "Performance," we might say, thus slips between an irrecoverable present moment, and an irrecoverable, because indeterminate, future.

Precisely because it is eventual, in this dual sense, (a) performance is inimical to a dominant ideology of print. The formulation of play as text as literary object constructs – through material presences, *not* through irrecoverable absences – an idea of a Shakespearean play as foundational, as the "source" against which we are then able to measure, for instance, performance. One of the things that interests me most about the phrase "text and performance" is the extent to which it sustains, even generates, a perception of textual stability – and this despite a growing theoretical and pragmatic renunciation of an earlier generation's desire finally to recover the "original manuscript" by stripping away "the veil of print" (Bowers 1959: 81).[3] The equal and opposite tension established by "and" has a curious polarizing effect, making text seem fixed, outside of history, to the same extent that performance, pulling in the opposite direction, comes to seem provisional, irremediably contaminated by, or lost to, history.

To what extent, then, can one argue that there is (a) performance in a text? On a purely linguistic level, if performance is "of" the text, then how can it also be "in" the text? A prepositional shift from "of" to "in" would presumably return us of necessity to the sort of logical inconsistency outlined by Levin. Even to argue the more limited position that the text contains, if not performance, then cues to performance, instructions or guidelines that should or must be followed, seems to me problematic. Desdemona protests her innocence in *Othello*:

> O God, Iago,
> What shall I do to win my lord again?
> Good friend, go to him; for by this light of heaven,
> I know not how I lost him. Here I kneel.
> If e're my will did trespass 'gainst his love,

> Either in discourse of thought or actual deed,
> Or that mine eyes, mine ears, or any sense
> Delighted them in any other form,
> Or that I do not yet, and ever did,
> And ever will – though he do shake me off
> To beggarly divorcement – love him dearly,
> Comfort forswear me. Unkindness may do much,
> And his unkindness may defeat my life,
> But never taint my love. I cannot say "whore".
> It does abhor me now I speak the word.
> To do the act that might the addition earn,
> Not the world's mass of vanity could make me.[4]
>
> (4.2.152–68)

In *Studying Plays*, Mick Wallis and Simon Shepherd draw readers' attention to the interpretive significance of the stage image created by the intra-dialogic direction in the fourth line cueing the actor playing Desdemona to kneel:

> [I]f we also note that she is kneeling, we start to see that Shakespeare is here constructing a formal picture, an emblem, rather like that in a stained-glass window...But let us look a little more widely. Also on stage are Desdemona's servant Emilia, and her husband Iago, Othello's right-hand man, who has deceived his master into suspecting Desdemona...
>
> What we have, then, are two pictures, one inside the other. Inside is the emblematic Desdemona, pure and innocent. But the total stage picture is of Iago manipulating Desdemona into her posture of defeat, and revelling in it. Surrounding the emblem of innocence is the emblem of villainy and deception. This double emblem is part of the way in which this scene produces meaning for an audience. (1998: 4)

"Here I kneel." An embedded cue for action could probably be no more unambiguous than this, and Wallis and Shepherd, assuming that the cue will be taken up by performers, offer a perceptive reading of the text. But instructions for performance work at one remove (at least) from performance. The passage from *Othello* creates an imagined environment and visual images of characters in physical proximity to one another; specifically, we understand that Desdemona's character (note: character, not actor) is in dialogue with two others, Emilia and Iago. The text tells a story, in other words, but as a form of *literary* narrative, not performance. This form of storytelling is not entirely unrelated to dialogue passages in a narrative poem or even in some novels, and the interpretations Wallis and Shepherd tease out of the passage grow out of familiar New Critical practices of close reading.

Does Desdemona kneel? In the *book*, she does. If we consider the stage, however, the most we can say is that she might. Perhaps the actor playing the part bows his or her head and spreads open his or her arms, but does not actually kneel. Perhaps the text is modified so that the lines from "Here I kneel" to the end of the speech are cut, thus eliding the intra-dialogic cue. Before dismissing this possibility as overly inventive, as an option that loses sight of the "real" play, we might recall that this is exactly how her speech appears in the 1622 Quarto (Shakespeare 1622: sig. L1). Or perhaps these same lines are cut, *and yet* the actor playing Desdemona chooses to kneel. All of these possibilities, whether focusing on enacted behavior or the lines as spoken on stage, show how the "double emblem" that Wallis and Shepherd identify as central to how Desdemona's speech "produces meaning for an audience" may, or may not, shape "the total stage picture". The double emblem can only be located with any security for a reading audience of (a version of) the Folio text.

Apart from issues of ontology, what separates (a) performance from the text as literary object is the labor of theatrical agents of production.[5] Such creativity both is imminent, always potentially coming into being, and cannot survive the moment of performance. (A) performance is related to text, but not in any way that we can predict with certainty. This is why a supposed performance "in" the text frequently cannot be traced in actual theatre productions – it was never there in the first place. For example, Edward Gero, playing Worcester in Bill Alexander's production of *Henry IV, Part 1* at Washington, DC's Shakespeare Theatre (2004), did not exit when told to "get thee gone" by the King (1.3.14). Instead, Gero walked upstage left to stand at a distance from the others until his "re-entry" after the King's departure. Greg Hicks, playing Coriolanus with the Royal Shakespeare Company (2002–3), likewise reinterpreted an exit during the capitol scene – one cued by a Folio stage direction. Instead of leaving the stage, Hicks retired upstage to sit cross-legged on a low chair, his back to the audience, after delivering a curt reply to Menenius' request to "Pray now, sit down" (2.2.76). In this staging, whether the character of Coriolanus could "hear" his "nothings monstered" remained an open question.

Even intra-dialogic instructions for performance as apparently self-evident as "Get . . . into the box-tree" (*Twelfth Night,* 2.5.14) may end up remaining a feature of the text's, and not the performance's, narrative. In Aaron Posner's Folger Theatre production of *Twelfth Night* (2003), the lights came up on Malvolio (Rick Foucheux) holding a seated frieze downstage right. The actors playing Sir Toby, Sir Andrew, Feste, and Maria entered noisily stage left, assembled themselves on a set of stairs facing Malvolio, and then pushed a button on a remote control to start the "video" of Malvolio's gulling in the garden. When Malvolio, deep in daydream, begs "Cousin Toby" to "give [him] this prerogative" (2.5.68–9), Toby's "What, what!" cued Maria to "rewind" the video, causing Foucheux to speak and act the line backwards before delivering it a second time. It was a superb and brilliantly executed theatrical moment. By seeming to introduce a multi-media component (recorded video) into the live stage production without actually doing so, Posner provoked not just a heightened recognition of actorly technique, but a sudden sensation of longing and desire. The repetition viewers witnessed was no repetition at all, but merely an *effect* of repetition created within live performance: there was no way for a theatre spectator to experience that repetition again. One's household familiarity with the video medium, the everyday assumption that one can always "play it again," was summoned up, only to be implicitly denied. Spectators were thus tantalized by the very impossibility of repetition. In short, the delight occasioned by Foucheux's virtuoso performance, as the "video" was rewound, repeated, and fast forwarded, was sharpened by the way the remote control, paradoxically, became symptomatic of all that can never be preserved from live performance or found in a printed text – performance itself.

Performance is an activity, creative labor that operates at a necessary distance from the text as literary object. One might question, however, whether Shakespeare's texts are marked not by performance, but by *a* performance, specifically, an early modern performance. Might the text preserve the history of those earliest stagings? To ask this question is to consider whether the earliest printed texts function in relation to the earliest performances after the manner of modern promptbooks. In order to supplement my memory of the Posner staging of the box-tree scene, I drew on the production's unique promptbook in the Folger Shakespeare Library archives. A promptbook, of course, is not performance – it is yet another book. However, it is one of the traces that permits studying a performance after it has disappeared. One of my students once likened theatre archives to a bombsite, an apt comparison that clarifies the relationship of a promptbook to performance. The bomb, like the performance, is gone, entirely consumed by the moment of its detonation, but its explosive impact and the traces it leaves behind are sometimes sufficient to let us think deeply both about the bomb and the moment of its explosion. Is it possible to draw in a similar manner on the printed texts of Shakespeare's plays?

The problem here is not just theoretical, but also methodological: the Octavo, Quartos, and Folio, simply put, are not theatrical playbooks (the early modern manuscript documents that most closely resemble modern promptbooks), nor can their origins in playbooks be traced with any certainty.[6] Another, even more pressing, objection is that if one does choose to regard them as playbooks, despite objections of provenance, study of the 16 manuscript playbooks surviving from Shakespeare's time indicates that these documents never achieved the standards of consistency we today look for in a promptbook. A playbook, in other words, is not identical to a promptbook. As William B. Long observes:

> These manuscript plays are by no means invariably neat and orderly; authorial stage-directions are very seldom changed in the theater; speech-heads are not regularized; copious markings do not appear to handle properties, entrances, and music. Regularization and completeness simply were not factors in theatrical marking of an author's papers. Theatrical personnel seem to have marked the book only in response to problems. (1985: 123)

The players, Long concludes, "did not possess or desire to possess books in which all problems had been solved and all ambiguities worked out" (1985: 135). Only if one indulges two highly speculative premises – that these early printed texts function like playbooks, and that playbooks, without falling into errors of anachronism, may be regarded as promptbooks – neither of which is supported by textual scholarship, can one argue that the dialogue and stage directions offer evidence of a (but which?) early modern performance.

Our desire to recover these performances is powerful and seductive. However, to conclude that there is performance "in" these early printed texts is not just to mistake text for performance, but to confuse dramatic literature and scripts, and so fall prey to the same sorts of problem identified in Wallis's and Shepherd's close reading of *Othello*. Such a confusion erases from view, in particular, a process of cuts and rearrangements that typically, at least today, precedes performance. As ever, there is little hard evidence that this sort of creative activity, potentially executed anew as many times as a play was revived or staged in a different space or for a different audience, was prevalent in Shakespeare's time. Nor, however, is there strong evidence that it did not happen. Roslyn L. Knutson argues from the evidence of Henslowe's *Diary* that theatrical companies did not usually incur the added expense of commissioning textual revisions since revivals of old plays were often profitable to the players without such changes. What Knutson's research does not indicate, however, is how much of the *existing* playbook was actually used on any given occasion. The stationer Humphrey Moseley tells us in his prefatory letter to the Beaumont and Fletcher Folio of 1647 that

> When these *Comedies* and *Tragedies* were presented on the Stage, the *Actours* omitted some *Scenes* and Passages (with the *Authour's* consent) as occasion led them; and when private friends desir'd a Copy, they then (and justly too) transcribed what they *Acted*. But now you have both All that was *Acted*, and all that was not; even the perfect full Originalls without the least mutilation. (Greg 1957: 1233–4)

Given Moseley's letter, we might do well to remember even just a few of the unresolved mysteries that continue to haunt textual studies: the long and short versions of Desdemona's "Here I kneel" speech; the rearranged sequence of action around the "nunnery scene" found in the 1603 Quarto of *Hamlet*; the remarkable, because unusual, brevity of the sole surviving text of *Macbeth*. Without arguing the case more forcefully than the evidence will permit, one might consider that these anomalies mark the gap between dramatic literature and scripts.

Precisely this distance is brought to our attention in the letter "To the Reader" printed in Davenant's abridgement of *Hamlet* (1676): "This Play being too long to be conveniently Acted, such places as might be least prejudicial to the Plot or Sense, are left out upon the Stage: but that we may no way wrong the incomparable Author, are here inserted according to the Original Copy with this Mark ["] " (sig. [A]2a). As Peter Holland comments, this letter "marks one step in the opening of an explicit gap between text and performance in the representation of the text" (1997: 16). However, we should be careful to recognize, with Lukas Erne, that this is specifically "a bibliographical and not... a theatrical milestone" (2003: 167). Erne persuasively argues that 12 of Shakespeare's surviving plays – all tragedies and histories – are too long for performance, and that Shakespeare wrote them knowing that they would be substantially cut for performance. According to Erne, Shakespeare wrote more than was strictly necessary for the stage in order to accommodate the perceived tastes of an intended readership, and so to build for himself a specifically literary reputation (2003: 172–4). If, then, one chooses to ignore the theoretical, textual, and ontological complexities surrounding text and performance, if one insists that it is possible to find performance "in" a text, one still comes up against the possibility that, at least in the case of Shakespeare, at least one-third of the texts that have survived, including *King Lear*, *Cymbeline*, and *Richard III*, seem not to record even the dialogue spoken on stage.

This is not to imply that these extant texts are of no evidentiary value to theatre historians. As a historical resource, they suggest the conventions and habits of patterning within which early modern agents of production (a group that might include playwrights, scribes, compositors, censors, printers, and actors) composed and circulated dramatic literature. It seems compelling to argue, for example, that the prevalence of a cue such as "above" or "aloft" indicates that there tended to be a useable space in the playhouses that in some way signalled relative elevation among actors (Dessen and Thomson 1999). Likewise, it seems probable that certain properties mentioned recurrently in the texts functioned as a form of theatrical shorthand – boots and sickchairs, for instance, variously suggesting travel and illness (Dessen 1995: 39–63, 109–26). To discern theatrical conventions, however, is not to recover a performance. There remains a gap between what a passage of text instructs, and how it was actually – even ever – performed. An acting company might have fully grasped the implications of a textual instruction to "enter above" or "enter sick," and for any number of reasons the cued actor may, or may not, have entered above or in a sickchair. Once again, (a) performance, "authentic" or otherwise, cannot be located in these texts.

But doesn't firmly emphasizing the distinction between text and performance ultimately promote less, rather than more, interest in theatre, and herald a return to the bad old days of reading Shakespeare's plays as poems (Styan 1977: 170–4)? I don't think so. On the contrary, to insist that printed words are not the same as live theatre, to recognize that there is no performance "in" a text, is to expose a prevailing ideology of print that serves to support a peculiar form of institutional anti-theatricality. Performance continues to elude, in particular, the editing of Shakespeare's plays, despite efforts to identify one printed text as lying closer to the playhouse, or to devote pages of marginal commentary to stage history.[7] Its absence is sensed as one reads (ever more) print texts that locate *Hamlet* in "the First Folio, the good Second Quarto, the bad First Quarto, or some ideal combination of these sources." Performance comes back to haunt our studies, precisely because books cannot contain it. Perhaps it is because this drama so obviously has a life and a history on the stage that to ignore performance altogether has not proven to be a sustainable critical method. And yet to regard performance as integral to a "Shakespeare play" is precluded by an ideology of print. Performance is thus constructed as at once derivative of, *and* located in, the text. The position is illogical, but it remains largely unquestioned since it is the only way to accommodate performance within an understanding of play as text as literary object.

So long as Shakespeare's plays are conceived of as texts, foundational and tangible, performance will continue to occupy a precarious place within the academy and the classroom. "Performance-sensitive" readings of dramatic literature that fail to account for an ideology of print are for this reason deceptive, because they allow one to assume that Shakespeare studies has achieved a critical openness to performance without, however, disturbing the priority implicitly afforded text. Paradoxically, it is by insisting on difference – by reinforcing rather than eliding the boundary that separates text from performance – that one might resist assigning a subsidiary status to performance. This strategy cannot correct an anti-theatrical bias, but at least it allows one to stand at a distance from it, and so interrogate it.

How then, if one does not assume (a) performance is already in the text, might one prepare theatrically-aware editions? What might commentaries attuned to a play's other life in the theatre look like? What is an appropriate editorial method in relation to stage directions and speech prefixes, those elements of dramatic literature emended and supplemented as a matter of course by Shakespeare's editors? To approach the last question first, it is perhaps useful to consider that such labor is undertaken on behalf of readers of literature who would otherwise find it difficult to infer stage business (Wells 1984: 66). Editorial directions and speech prefixes shape a sense of action, and so draw out for readers a particular story: Romeo and Juliet kiss here and not there; the First Citizen, or the Second Citizen, is the "big toe" of Menenius's parable; Calchas is present among the Greeks (or he is not) when Cressida is kissed "in general."[8] These and other such interventions are the subject of critical debate, and scholars continue to argue whether other, and better, editorial decisions might be made.[9] The curious conundrum that confronts the editor of early modern drama is the rule of thumb that directions should be introduced cautiously, and only to clarify business already in the text, but that an editorial direction is redundant if the action can be inferred with ease from the dialogue. Editors, it would seem as a matter of praxis, add directions at precisely those points in the text where the action is most open to (variable) interpretation.

Editorial conventions guiding the preparation of early modern drama have tended towards making firm decisions on the reader's behalf, building certainty, rather than uncertainty, into the text. If it seems ambiguous where a character enters, then an editor, sometimes with great misgivings, has to make a choice. Discussing Ferdinand's entrance into his sister's closet in *The Duchess of Malfi*, Antony Hammond describes both the arbitrariness of such decisions and the anxiety they engender: "If I were staging this, I would have Ferdinand enter unseen. (It does not much matter where; one of the curses of editing is that you have to *choose*, when choice is impossible: our note reads, 'the timing of this entry is not self-evident, nor does it need to be precisely determined...' Still, you have to print it somewhere!)" (1992: 95). Increasingly, however, editors are asking whether a better strategy might be to present readers with ambiguity and uncertainty; to give readers, in other words, not answers to indeterminate textual problems, but a sense of where there is interpretive work left to be done and insights into how to construct their own answers (Cox 2004, Hodgdon 2004, Hunter & Lichtenfels 2002, Kidnie 2000, 2004). Alternatively, if one agrees with the view that the editor's function is to edit, and that this procedure includes sorting out perceived tangles in the action that might seem to make the drama inaccessible, especially to a first-time reader, then editors might approach that task by arriving at perhaps unexpected decisions that prompt readers to ask questions. Barbara Hodgdon, for example, in her forthcoming Arden 3 edition of *Taming of the Shrew*, cues Petruchio to exit the final scene alone. The reader is given guidance, but by resisting the usual editorial emendation of the Folio stage directions which sees Katherine exit with her husband, Hodgdon foregrounds that guidance itself as a potential critical discussion point (2002: 102–6).

Commentary raises slightly different problems. In effect, the issue is how one might write about performance in relation to a printed text that cannot contain it. One option, already a familiar one, is to focus on the interpretive choices made by actual (past) productions. Many single-volume editions offer overviews of stage history, and the form is pursued more expansively in, for instance, the Text in Performance series published by Manchester University Press and Cambridge University Press's Shakespeare in Performance series. However, one might reasonably wish to know more about, not what *has* been done, but what *might* be done. Hodgdon explains that what is at stake here is the creation of "forms of annotation and presentation that might position readers, not as passive external witnesses to either an editorial imaginary or an already existing performance 'product' but as active participants in the processes of making their own imagined performance(s)":

> Perhaps the most useful distinction to make between "old" and "new" protocols is between "the work performed" and "the work as something which is 'coming-into-performance'": the first emphasizes arriving at a form as instantiation and enactment (the province of specific details drawn from stage history, which is not the same as performance), the second concerns thinking with means that are always coming into form through processes of material theatre, through visualizing and hearing bodies in space. (2004: 212, 220)

This is increasingly the sort of engagement with Shakespeare's plays instructors are attempting to support in the classroom. The theoretical waters, however, are treacherous. If one neglects the "processes of material theatre," text could potentially resurface within an unexamined practice as the legitimizing or authenticating source of performance.

A new series of *Shakespeare Handbooks*, forthcoming from Palgrave Macmillan under the general editorship of John Russell Brown, sets out "to help a reader come to an individual and well-informed assessment of the text and what it can become in the theatre" (Brown n.d.: 1). Volumes in the series seek to "encourage an imaginative engagement with [a particular] play's action" by indicating to readers both "how the play can be staged" and "the opportunities and problems that actors face as they develop their performances" (Brown n.d.: 1). How can a play be staged? As Hodgdon puts it, "translating contingency into manageable print form resembles attempting to pin down Cleopatra's 'infinite variety'" (2004: 212). What is *not* possible in the theatre? It is all, at base, potential, and the challenge facing the *Shakespeare Handbooks* series is to consider how "infinite variety" might best be encompassed by a book. I have started preliminary work on *Taming of the Shrew*, and what strikes me immediately is how this sort of performance-oriented exploration of the text is conducive to a peculiar form of close analysis and literary inventiveness. One looks for patterns, and teases out possible meanings. In short, one seeks to *notice* things, such as an apparent glitch in the plot – Petruchio's and Hortensio's knowledge of Lucentio's marriage to Bianca (4.5) – or a potential non-speaking role for "cousin Ferdinand" in (4.1). This may well be one way to enter into the very labor that separates text from performance, and it comes as no real surprise to learn that a silent cousin Ferdinand (Scott A. Hurst) appeared on stage in Richard Monette's staging at the Stratford Festival of Canada (1988). The danger, however, is the very familiarity of such practices of close reading. They draw on formalist skills honed by New Criticism, an association indicative of the ease with which one might slide back into assuming that one is "teasing out" an actual performance "found" in the text. The *Shakespeare Handbooks* series, however, might sail between the Scylla of an imagined editorial staging and the Charybdis of a performance "in" the text by considering that such a project is not best served by attempts to provide readers with a body of knowledge (this is what happens/happened, or this is what the text instructs). Rather, this sort of performance-oriented criticism might train readers in a *process* of creative and imaginative thought, a process that includes close textual analysis but also, for example (the list is not comprehensive), considerations of stage business, casting, theatre space, acting style, costuming, music cues, and the shaping of a script through cuts and rearrangements. By necessity, one will not be able to anticipate where such an investigation might lead each reader, but surely it is precisely a similar combination of uncertainty and originality that prompts one to pay money to see any Shakespearean play in performance.

Text and performance are linked by assumptions, conventions, and conditions of theatre that a reader brings to, rather than finds "in", a text. These contingencies are part of the bridge that allows theatre practitioners to move from text to performance, yet they equally forcefully separate text from performance as distinct media. I have been at pains to show how an ideology of print that lies behind the familiar construction of "text and performance" privileges text over performance, assigning to performance a second-order status. Is there a way, however, to elude or reconfigure altogether, rather than just to invert, this binarism? In other words, how might one theorize "Shakespeare's play" differently, in such a way as to include performance? Is such a thing possible? Where could we locate *Hamlet* with any security, if not exclusively in its print manifestations? How would we teach it – or market it – to undergraduates? What would "it" *be*? Such questions perhaps seem less strange if one remembers that these plays achieved their first publication in performance in the playhouses, only subsequently, and by no means inevitably, taking on markedly altered existences as books in Octavo, Quarto, and Folio format. E. A. J. Honigmann has suggested that far from seeing the play as a text, "frozen in time," "Shakespeare's colleagues thought of it as a time-traveller, a living organism which adjusts to changing circumstances yet remains, essentially, the same play...: how can we come to terms with this sameness and plurality?" (2004: 86). Where would an early modern audience have located the "real" *Hamlet*? In one or more non-identical performances, or in one or more non-identical books? Or in some combination of these different media? Or perhaps editions and performances reached different constituencies, different "audiences"?

A firm answer is almost certainly not available, partly because of the historical distance that prevents one from polling those long-gone customers at the theatres and bookstalls, but also because the question itself – requiring a choice between text and performance – speaks to a particular way of thinking about drama that inadequately accounts for the complex ways in which, even now, one experiences a play. Grigely explains how the word "text" conveniently points to everything and anything: "almost without fail [it] sounds right, supplanting a vague uncertainty with a certain vagueness" (1995: 89). The word "play," I would argue, is even more slippery. It sidesteps entirely recent debates in textual studies about versions and works, it can embrace either edition(s) or performance(s), or both, and most importantly, unlike "text," it does not have to sound particularly theorized, yet remains a term used by theoreticians of all stripes. This commonplace term, by its very ordinariness, allows us to assume that we all know what we mean when we use it, without requiring us ever to ask what it means, or how we use it. But consider how it turns up in everyday spoken English. "Did you see the play last night?," "Have you read the play?" (sometimes followed by, "No, and I bet she gives us a quiz on it.") "I'm going to Stratford tomorrow to see the play." Or substitute the title – *Twelfth Night, Othello* – for "the play." Even the possessive construction – "I saw a performance of the play years ago" – avoids anything like specificity. What is it that she saw a performance of? *King Lear, Richard II, Cymbeline* – simply, "the play." When one tries to theorize (a) performance "of" a text, one too easily assumes that "what she saw" years ago, what she is trying to describe, is "a performance of [the text of] the play." This is neither what the phrase expresses, nor, I think, what it means. The same, but less easily discerned, slippage occurs in discussions of the reading experience where "the play" refers not in any precise way to "the First Folio, the good Second Quarto, the bad First Quarto, or some ideal combination of these sources," but rather to the play as found on one's bookshelf, or assigned for classroom study. She saw the play, he read the play, but what is identified as "the play" in such instances is more nebulous and far-reaching than a term such as "text" seems to suggest.

An ideology of print that constructs play as text conceals the extent to which one already knows that Shakespeare's plays are not found in texts, at least not texts in the sense of one or more supposedly authentic, originary, printed objects. What seems incontestable is that (a) performance is always in danger of marginalization in academic study, precisely because it leaves so few traces, and those few highly unstable and difficult to recover. It does not follow, however, that performance has no ontological significance within a theorized conception of "the play." Where is *Hamlet*? To return one last time to McLaverty's riddle, *Hamlet*, I would argue, exists in a shared cultural and lived space that embraces and ranges across both performance(s) and text(s). It emerges, in other words, out of the tension that exists at any one historical moment between a particular construction of performance and a particular construction of text, a network of relations to which W. B. Worthen (2003) has given the name "dramatic performativity." The ontology of "the play" consists of a peculiar and ever-changing *dynamic* that enables one through time to assign (fairly) precise boundaries to both text and performance. Performance is therefore never incidental to an idea of *Hamlet* – it is not an embellishment of, or deviation from, the "real" thing. It is a basic part of the way the next synchronic point (and the next, and the next) are constructed in a diachronic process called "Shakespeare's play," thereby creating and thus perpetuating an illusion of relative canonical stability. Shakespeare's plays change over time, and in a particular time, under the ongoing pressure of cultural and creative processes. It is in part through performance, above all through the ways performance is brought into a relational tension with text, that one can arrive at all at a provisional and subjective knowledge of the "real" thing.

When is it no longer possible to recognize a textual or theatrical performance as "the play"? Where does one locate the boundary limits of play-as-process? The question is easiest to pin down in terms of performance: how far can theatrical practitioners engage in what I have called the creative labor of performance – cuts, rearrangements, perhaps even insertions of new dialogue – before a spectator will no longer accept that this is Shakespeare's play? How might one distinguish between Shakespeare and not-Shakespeare, authentic play and travesty? What happens if Romeo and Juliet survive? If the bed-trick is stripped from *Measure for Measure*, or the Bianca–Lucentio subplot from *Taming of the Shrew*? If the lovers of *A Midsummer Night's Dream* never return to the court (or get out of the box)? If Shakespeare's verse is transformed into rap?[10] Where exactly does one want to draw the line separating performance from adaptation? Do such performances "really" constitute Shakespeare's plays?

To start with the last question, the bald answer is that it all depends. The fortunes of Shakespeare's plays over the past four hundred years suggest that their ontological boundaries, in terms both of text and performance, are as elastic as critical opinion and popular estimation will allow. *King Lear* can have a happy ending (Tate 1681), Miranda can have a sister (Dryden and Davenant 1670), Gary Taylor can insert his own verse into a modern-spelling reconstructed edition of *Pericles* (Wells and Taylor 1986), and none of these alterations impede an audience's ability to recognize "Shakespeare's play." This is by no means to imply that the audiences for these particular texts and performances have been conned, or fobbed off with a fake. My point, on the contrary, one supported by Orgel (2002: 234), is that "authentic" and "inauthentic" are terms that have no transhistorical or absolute meaning. We lack a measuring yard – or perhaps it is more accurate to say that the measuring yard we use shrinks and extends over time. Shakespeare's play is whatever a dominant consensus of voices agrees to recognise as Shakespeare's play. Nor should one assume that this is a historical practice that no longer operates in more recent, more textually and theatrically informed, times. With the publication of the Oxford Shakespeare, "Shakespeare's play" became "Shakespeare's plays" with the celebrated two-text *King Lear* (Wells and Taylor 1986: xxxvii). The challenge then for university instructors, in particular, was to consider how one could teach *King Lear* as plays instead of play within the time pressures imposed by a one-term or two-term curriculum. The inclusion in the Norton Shakespeare of 1997 of a conflated text of *King Lear* alongside the *History* and the *Tragedy* functioned like a flag, or perhaps the next milestone, indicating how a textual conception of the play(s) had been modified in just over ten years by the Oxford editors, but not entirely.

It is precisely because Shakespeare's plays are mutable that borders have to be patrolled: if they were no longer policed, they would disappear. Every time an editor learns that he or she should choose the Folio over the Quarto as copy-text (or the other way around) because that is what Shakespeare's play has always been; every time an editor is advised to add, omit, reword, or reposition a stage direction because that is the "proper" decision; every time a reviewer comments that "the director is imposing a private agenda on the play rather than exploring and resolving its difficulties – which is much harder work," or a critic seeks to "free Shakespeare" by restricting the limits within which the plays are legitimately performed; at each of these moments a conception of "Shakespeare's play" is being brought into existence, performatively, in language.[11] It is only by patrolling the borders – by identifying and naming the "outlandish liberties" – that we can come to know what *Hamlet* is, and where we can find it.

This is not to imply, however, that there is ever complete agreement about what counts, or should count, as Shakespeare's play. To look more closely at the Anglo-North American situation at the turn of the twenty-first century, there are probably many texts and performances that the vast majority of people would immediately agree constitute Shakespeare's plays. Greg Doran's 2003–4 Royal Shakespeare Company production of *All's Well that Ends Well* starring Judi Dench might offer one example, Charles Forker's Arden 3 edition of *Richard II* another. Equally, some texts and performances clearly have connections to the canon but nonetheless are identified by a majority as something other than Shakespeare's plays. One thinks here, perhaps, of the Reduced Shakespeare Co.'s long-running London production of *The Compleat Works of Wllm Shkspr (Abridged)*, or Djanet Sears's *Harlem Duet*. However, there is always a liminal, gray area that resists clear categorization. Whereas some would call the texts and performances falling into this area "Shakespeare," others will reject that possibility utterly: in such instances, the "majority" tend not to lend their voices one way or another, and so the debate of what should "count," what is "legitimate," continues. This marginal area is neither wholly within what is easily accepted as Shakespeare's play, nor is it wholly without it. Texts and performances that fall into this category at the time of this writing (Spring 2004) might include *Textarc*, an on-line electronic textual performance / concordance of *Hamlet* devised and designed by W. Bradford Paley (www.textarc.org), or *Elsinore*, Robert Lepage's one-man produc-tion of *Hamlet*. Such examples, and the hype that often surrounds them, are crucial to study because they mark, in practice, the politics of where and how an ever-shifting boundary between "Shakespeare's play" and "adaptation" is currently being negotiated and renegotiated.[12]

Paradoxically, then, I find myself in agreement with Friedman's "In Defense of Authenticity," but for different reasons than the ones he cites. Yes, there are authentic performances (and texts), and yes, there are adaptations. And there always will be. However, what one chooses to locate as either "authentic" or "adaptation," which performances and texts are included as "Shakespeare" or banished as "not Shakespeare," will alter, sometimes imperceptibly, sometimes suddenly, over time. Shakespeare's play, or rather, what can feasibly be called Shakespeare's play, emerges into view through an ongoing activity of patrolling or policing that is more, or less, responsive to shifting politics and criticism. It is therefore crucial to mark, and intervene in, the critical energy that is expended to assert particular attitudes towards authority, because it is only within history and culture that the term "Shakespeare's play" can find meaning. The present anxieties around authentic text and inauthentic performance are not about deciding once and for all issues of authenticity, but about the exertion of power, specifically, the power to say what Shakespeare's play will be, by seeming to discern, but in fact negotiating, the line between performance and adaptation. The very activity of documenting how the texts are betrayed by the stage temporarily erases a radically unstable textual condition, and so allows one – in a quite remarkable sleight of hand – to locate the "real" thing within "the text itself." In sum, an anti-theatrical opposition between text and performance is asserted in order to avoid the realization that in terms of ontology one can never say, in an absolute sense, what *Hamlet* is, or where one can find it: there is no *thing* that will always, forever, be *Hamlet*. This is quite different from saying there is no *Hamlet*. There is always a *Hamlet*. And most readers and spectators have a sense of what it looks like, because it is only by means of the agreement (or failure of agreement) prompted by varied and competing responses to a range of texts and performances that it is continually brought into being. The challenge facing textual scholars and performance critics who wish to bring these two disciplines into closer dialogue is to investigate further how a theoretical conception of the play as temporal and cultural process might reconfigure an understanding of both textual and theatrical Shake-speare, and thereby counter an existing anti-theatrical bias supported by a dominant ideology of print.

NOTES

1   McLaverty's question was prompted by Bateson's comparison of the ontological status of *Hamlet* to the *Mona Lisa*.

2   Performance is a contested theoretical term, particularly as it relates (or not) to the theatre, and I use it here to distinguish a complex of past, present, and future forms of activity on a stage from the specific theatrical event (which I describe, instead, as "a performance"). Bulman captures the limitations of universalist and essentialist treatments of performance contingencies.

3   Mowat usefully notes that our experience of interpreting surviving early modern manuscripts should suggest that even the recovery of Shakespeare's holograph copies would by no means resolve the editorial problem and so allow us to "fix" (in both senses of the word) the text (1998: 134).

4   All quotations of Shakespeare are from Wells and Taylor (1986), unless otherwise indicated. I have omitted the editorial stage directions.

5   W. B. Worthen frames a similar point, arguing that performances of all sorts – reading and criticism, as well as acting – are "dialectically related" to text "through the labor of enactment" (1989: 452). On reading and criticism as interpretive modes related to theatrical performance, see also Hodgdon (1985: 57–65).

6   Efforts to establish the provenance of Shakespeare's early printed texts have bedevilled textual scholarship throughout the twentieth, and now into the twenty-first, century. See Werstine (1997: 481–97).

7   The Oxford editors, perhaps most famously and controversially, distinguish between "editions based upon foul papers" as the "individual, private form" of a play, and "editions based upon prompt-books" as the "socialized" theatrical form, deliberately choosing, where there is a choice to be made, the latter as copy-text (Wells and Taylor 1997: 15).

8   No kiss is cued during the shared sonnet at the Capulet ball in the First Quarto of 1597, the Second Quarto of 1599, or the Folio, and so editors insert one or more directions to kiss; the Folio speech prefixes cue the Second Citizen (and not, as most editors indicate, the First Citizen) to enter into dialogue with Menenius in the opening scene of *Coriolanus*; finally, although Calchas is included in both the Quarto and Folio entry directions to *Troilus and Cressida*, 4.6, editors tend to erase him from this scene as a "ghost" on the grounds that he never speaks.

9   On the staging of these moments, see Williams (1994, 2002), Bevington (1998: 367–8), Kidnie (2004), and Warren (2004). Dessen provides numerous examples where editorial directions offer not the only, nor even arguably the best, staging available (2002: 209–34).

10 These possible scenarios allude, in turn, to MacDonald (1990), Marowitz (1978), Garrick (1756), *The Donkey Show*, created and directed by Randy Weiner and Diane Paulus, *A Midsummer Night's Dream*, directed by Peter Brook (Royal Shakespeare Company, 1970), and *The Bomb-itty of Errors*, written by Jordan Allen-Dutton, Jason Catalano, GQ, and Erik Weiner.

11 George Walton Williams discerns a "proper" placement of a cue to kiss during the shared sonnet in *Romeo and Juliet* (2002: 120); the reviewer is John Peter for *The Sunday Times* (May 10, 1998) as quoted in Dessen (2002: 91); and "Free Shakespeare" is the title of a seminal article in which John Russell Brown argues that theatre practitioners should "find a way of presenting Shakespeare freely," in such a way as to "bring Shakespearian qualities to the theatre, and allow audiences to respond in ways that are generally recognised as appropriate to Shakespeare's genius" (1971: 134).

12 Issues of anonymity and early modern collaboration are not irrelevant to this analysis of what we accept, or not, as Shakespeare's play. *Edward III*, for example, excluded from the Oxford *Complete Works* in 1986 but included in the revised edition projected to appear in the summer of 2005, might be seen to

occupy a liminal position not entirely dissimilar to, say, Lepage's *Elsinore*. An instance such as *Edward III*, however, brings into focus the evolving shape of Shakespeare's canon, whereas my focus here is specifically the recognizable shape of the single *play* and how it changes over time.

REFERENCES AND FURTHER READING

Bateson, F. W. (1961). "Modern Bibliography and the Literary Artifact." In G. A. Bonnard (ed.) *English Studies Today*, 2nd series. Bern: Francke Verlag, pp. 67–77.

Bevington, D. (ed.) (1998). *Troilus and Cressida*. London: Thomson Learning.

Bowers, Fredson (1959). *Textual and Literary Criticism*. Cambridge: Cambridge University Press.

Bristol, M. & McLuskie, Kathleen (eds.) (2001). *Shakespeare and Modern Theatre: The Performance of Modernity*. London: Routledge.

Brown, J. R. (1971). "Free Shakespeare." *Shakespeare Survey* 24: 127–35.

Brown, J. R. (n.d.). *Shakespeare Handbooks*, unpublished series guidelines.

Bulman, J. C. (1996). "Introduction: Shakespeare and Performance Theory." In J. C. Bulman (ed.). *Shakespeare, Theory, and Performance*. London: Routledge, pp. 1–11.

Cox, J. D. (2004). "Open Stage, Open Page? Editing Stage Directions in Early Dramatic Texts." In L. Erne & M. J. Kidnie (eds.) *Textual Performances: The Modern Reproduction of Shakespeare's Drama*. Cambridge: Cambridge University Press, pp. 178–93.

Davenant, William (1676). *Hamlet*. London: n.p.

Dessen, A. C. (1995). *Recovering Shakespeare's Theatrical Vocabulary*. Cambridge: Cambridge University Press.

Dessen, A. C. (2002). *Rescripting Shakespeare: The Text, the Director, and Modern Productions*. Cambridge: Cambridge University Press.

Dessen, A. C. & Thomson, L. (1999). *A Dictionary of Stage Directions in English Drama, 1580–1642*. Cambridge: Cambridge University Press.

Dryden, J. & Davenant, W. (1670). *The Tempest, or the Enchanted Island*. London, n.p.

Erne, Lukas (2003). *Shakespeare as Literary Dramatist*. Cambridge: Cambridge University Press.

Erne, Lukas & Kidnie, Margaret Jane (eds.) (2004). *Textual Performances: The Modern Reproduction of Shakespeare's Drama*. Cambridge: Cambridge University Press.

Forker, C. R. (ed.) (2002). *King Richard II*. London: Thomson Learning.

Friedman, M. D. (2002). "In Defense of Authenticity." *Studies in Philology* 99: 33–56.

Garrick, David (1756). *Catharine and Petruchio*. London: n.p.

Greg, W. W. (1950–1). "The Rationale of Copy-Text." *Studies in Bibliography* 3: 19–36.

Greg, W. W. (1957). *A Bibliography of the English Printed Drama to the Restoration*, 4 vols. London: The Bibliographical Society.

Grigely, J. (1995). *Textualterity: Art, Theory, and Textual Criticism*. Ann Arbor, MI: University of Michigan Press.

Hammond, A. (1992). "Encounters of the Third Kind in Stage-Directions in Elizabethan and Jacobean Drama." *Studies in Philology* 89: 71–99.

Hodgdon, Barbara (1985). "Parallel Practices, or the Un-Necessary Difference." *The Kenyon Review* 7: 57–65.

Hodgdon, Barbara (2002). "Who Is Performing 'in' These Text(s)?; or, *Shrew*-ing Around." In A. Thompson & G. McMullan (eds.) *In Arden: Editing Shakespeare*. London: Thomson Learning, pp. 95–108.

Hodgdon, Barbara (2004). "New Collaborations with Old Plays: The (Textual) Politics of Performance Commentary." In L. Erne & M. J. Kidnie (eds.) *Textual Performances: The Modern Reproduction of Shakespeare's Drama*. Cambridge: Cambridge University Press, pp. 210–23.

Holland, Peter (1997). *English Shakespeares: Shakespeare on the English Stage in the 1990s*. Cambridge: Cambridge University Press.

Honigmann, E. A. J. (2004). "The New Bibliography and its Critics." In L. Erne & M. J. Kidnie (eds.) *Textual Performances: The Modern Reproduction of Shakespeare's Drama*. Cambridge: Cambridge University Press, pp. 77–93.

Hunter, L. & Lichtenfels, P. (2002). "Reading in the Moment: Theatre Practice as a Guide to Textual Editing." In A. Thompson & G. McMullan (eds.) *In Arden: Editing Shakespeare.* London: Thomson Learning, pp. 138–56.

Kidnie, Margaret Jane (2000). "Text, Performance, and the Editors: Staging Shakespeare's Drama." *Shakespeare Quarterly* 51: 456–73.

Kidnie, Margaret Jane (2004). "The Staging of Shakespeare's Drama in Print Editions." In L. Erne & M. J. Kidnie (eds.) *Textual Performances: The Modern Reproduction of Shakespeare's Drama.* Cambridge: Cambridge University Press, pp. 158–77.

Knutson, R. L. (1985). "*Henslowe's Diary* and the Economics of Play Revision for Revival, 1592–1603." *Theatre Research International*, 10: 1–18.

Levin, R. (1986). "Performance-Critics *vs* Close Readers in the Study of English Renaissance Drama." *Modern Language Review* 81: 545–59.

Long, W. B. (1985). "Stage-Directions: A Misinterpreted Factor in Determining Textual Provenance." *Text* 2: 121–37.

MacDonald, A.-M. (1990). *Goodnight Desdemona (Good Morning Juliet).* Toronto: Playwrights Canada Press.

Marowitz, C. (1978). "*Measure for Measure.*" In *The Marowitz Shakespeare.* New York: Marion Boyars, pp. 181–225.

McLaverty, J. (1984). "The Mode of Existence of Literary Works of Art: The Case of the *Dunciad Variorum.*" *Studies in Bibliography* 37: 82–105.

Mowat, B. (1998). "The Problem of Shakespeare's Text(s)." In L. E. Maguire & T. L. Berger (eds). *Textual Formations and Reformations.* Newark: University of Delaware Press, pp. 131–48.

Orgel, S. (2002). *The Authentic Shakespeare.* London: Routledge.

Phelan, Peggy (1993). *Unmarked: The Politics of Performance.* London: Routledge.

Sears, D. (1997). *Harlem Duet.* Winnipeg: Scirocco Drama.

Shakespeare, William (1622). *The Tragedy of Othello, the Moore of Venice.* London: n.p.

Stillinger, J. (1998). Review: *Textualterity: Art, Theory, and Textual Criticism. Text* 11: 383–6.

Styan, J. L. (1977). *The Shakespeare Revolution: Criticism and Performance in the Twentieth Century.* Cambridge: Cambridge University Press.

Tate, N. (1681). *The History of King Lear.* London: n.p.

Thompson, A. & McMullan, G. (eds.) (2002). *In Arden: Editing Shakespeare.* London: Thomson Learning.

Wallis, M. & Shepherd, S. (1998). *Studying Plays.* London: Arnold.

Warren, Michael (2004). "The Perception of Error: The Editing and the Performance of the Opening of 'Coriolanus'." In Lukas Erne & Margaret Jane Kidnie (eds.) *Textual Performances: The Modern Reproduction of Shakespeare's Drama.* Cambridge: Cambridge University Press, pp. 127–42.

Wells, Stanley (1984). *Re-Editing Shakespeare for the Modern Reader.* Oxford: Clarendon Press.

Wells, Stanley & Taylor, Gary with Jowett, J. & Montgomery, W. (eds.) (1986). *William Shakespeare: The Complete Works.* Oxford: Oxford University Press.

Wells, Stanley & Taylor, Gary with Jowett, J. & Montgomery, W. (1997). *William Shakespeare: A Textual Companion.* New York: W. W. Norton and Company.

Werstine, Paul (1997). "Plays in Manuscript." In J. D. Cox & D. S. Kastan (eds.) *A New History of Early English Drama.* New York: Columbia University Press, pp. 481–97.

Williams, G. W. (1994). "The Entrance of Calchas and the Exit of Cressida." *The Shakespeare Newsletter* 44, 5: 18.

Williams, G. W. (2002). "To Edit? To Direct? – Ay, There's the Rub." In A. Thompson & G. McMullan (eds.) *In Arden: Editing Shakespeare.* London: Thomson Learning, pp. 111–24.

Worthen, W. B. (1989). "Deeper Meanings and Theatrical Technique: The Rhetoric of Performance Criticism." *Shakespeare Quarterly* 40: 441–55.

Worthen, W. B. (2003). *Shakespeare and the Force of Modern Performance.* Cambridge: Cambridge University Press.

6
Shakespeare and the Possibilities of Postcolonial Performance
Ania Loomba

Shakespeare is everywhere in a nation such as India, in the very language of political debate and public utterance, of Bombay cinema, of signs on the road, in names of prize-winning varieties of mangoes, in reflections upon the past, or in pronouncements about current affairs. Let me quote from a letter to the editor published in *The Hindu*, a leading English-language daily:

> I wonder whether water or blood is flowing in the veins of those who support the diabolic carnage being perpetrated by the US in Afghanistan. Not only Shylock but also Iago is dwelling in the hearts of the US, which is massacring several lives all over the world and pretends to be above aboard. Hence, he can by no means be blamed who thinks Iago would have been a mere fictitious character without "life and blood" in it, thus Shakespeare's *Othello* becoming an artistic failure, had America not been. (Faisal 2001)

It was my son who helped me figure this letter out. Recent US actions in Afghanistan, says the writer, are as evil as Shylock and Iago's deeds were; such actions prove that Shakespeare had got it right, that he had his finger on the pulse of social evil. Thus, the US invasion of Afghanistan has proved that *Othello* is not an artistic failure. The author, incidentally, is a Member of Parliament from Kerala.

Has he read Shakespeare or thought about *Othello*? Does that matter? In this letter, Shakespeare merely provides the language in which anti-imperialist sentiments can be expressed. Of course, not so long ago the language of imperialism was widely used to praise Shakespeare: "the England of trade, commerce, imperialism and the penal code has not endured," wrote a well-known Indian academic, "but the imperishable Empire of Shakespeare will always be with us. And that is something to be grateful for" (Narasimhaiah 1964: v). The Universal Bard who once facilitated transmission of English Culture to colonized cultures subsequently became a spokesman *for* these cultures – one of those rare literary voices who, it seems, could convey the compulsions of Prospero as well as the agonies of Caliban. And make money in the process. But if we once had sharply polarized versions of the Bard that contested each other – an imperialist Shakespeare versus a revolutionary Third World-ist one – in our postcolonial/or neo-colonial world, where both colonialism and revolution have become unfashionable terms, it sometimes seems that a neo-imperial Shakespeare and a postcolonial one can be collapsed into a single highly marketable Shakespeare who *simultaneously* represents both once-colonized and once-colonizing cultures. The tension between the two seems to melt in the face of new "hybrid" or "cross-cultural" Shakespeares that now play to an increasingly "global" market.

In this chapter, I want to discuss a range of Shakespearean performances that use India, as well as Indian performances that use Shakespeare. The intricate pattern of borrowing and difference that characterizes the performative spaces in which Shakespeare meets India, I will suggest, can move us beyond the formulaic ways in which the terms "empire" and "postcoloniality" are often invoked in analyses of Shakespeare productions in the once-colonized world, and help us think about the multiple and shifting meanings of the terms "local" and "global." Even more important, they demonstrate how theatre enriches and complicates our sense of the political, often by appearing to be at odds with received wisdom about the postcolonial condition. Finally, if as Raymond Williams suggests, "the most fundamental cultural history is always a history of forms," then the *form* of these performances indexes some of the nuances of their interactions with both Shakespeare and Indian theatre and society (1989: 83).

In most parts of the world, Rustom Bharucha reminds us, "exposure to 'other' cultures has not always been a matter of choice" (1990: 1). It was colonialism that willy-nilly fostered a long tradition of intercultural performances in once-colonized countries. There, the transmission of the Shakespearean play among the natives depended upon its being reproduced in "inauthentic" circumstances, and upon its being imitated by those who were deemed simultaneously in need of and incapable of receiving it. Such a process resulted not only in "hybridizing" Shakespeare but also in creating new forms of theatre: in fact, it would not be an exaggeration to claim that Shakespeare was one of the many midwives who assisted in the birth of the modern public theatre in India. Western-style public theatres were established in Calcutta, Bombay, and Madras partly on the strength of their adaptations and translations of Shakespeare's plays. It is true that in the big cities such performances took place on Western-style proscenium stages, and their stars were named after famous English theatre personalities – thus, Ganpatrao Joshi, famous for his performances as Macbeth, was called the Garrick of Maharashtra; the manager K. P. Khatau was known as the Irving of India, and Aga Hashr Kashmiri, the most prolific adapter of Shakespeare in Urdu, was nicknamed "Shakespeare-e-Hind" (Shakespeare of India). But the performances themselves drew heavily upon local and indigenous theatrical traditions, and the borrowings from the Bard were not evident to the audiences, most of whom were unfamiliar with Shakespeare (see Loomba 1997).

Although enormously popular, these performances were not taken seriously as *Shakespearean* theatre, although many years ago the English critic C. J. Sisson did make the case that in fact they came closer to the form and spirit of the original performances of Shakespeare than any production on the English or Westernized Indian stages of his day (Sisson 1926). Among those Indians who had been schooled to think of Shakespeare as a mark of high culture, more conventional college productions that were properly respectful of the Bard found greater favor, as did Western theatre companies. Hence English director Geoffrey Kendal's traveling troupe, "Shakespeareana," that toured India extensively from the 1940s to the early 1960s, playing in palaces, public theatres, clubs, schools and colleges, catered to an Indian desire to get to an "authentic" Shakespeare which was necessarily an imported commodity. Thus, a critic wrote in *The Statesman* that the presence of the Kendals in Calcutta "has raised the cultural level of the city, and could they be persuaded to make it their home, at least during every winter, Calcutta would be less cut off from the rest of the world" (Kendal 1986: 99). Kendal himself claimed not only that Indians were their most discerning audience – "they really are the best in the world. Nothing escapes their attention" – but also that the troupe was *avant garde* in its approach:

> we were ahead of our time . . . we would use local musicians and the songs of Elizabethan England seemed to harmonize perfectly with an Indian flute or sitar. I costumed some of the productions in local dress, which had the effect of bringing the two cultures together. And from this a wonderful understanding between actor and audience developed. (1986: 77, 122–3)

But Kendal, despite thinking of his company as an integral "part of the Indian scene" even after Independence, and of Shakespeare as their "password" to it, conceived of his theatre as existing at a remove from Indian politics, and particularly from the enormous nationalist upheavals of the country: "armed with Shakespeare, whose plays were so much appreciated in India, we felt we could ignore the warnings about nationalistic movement and possible troubles. India was moving towards independence, but we did not see that it might affect us" (1986: 85). Thus, India could provide some local color – native music or costumes – that could be incorporated into Shakespearean performances, but these performances themselves did not have to engage with Indian society or theatre in any more fundamental way. The real performative and interpretative meanings of Shakespeare were still made "at home."

Has that situation changed today? In fact, does the idea of "authentic" or "inauthentic" Shakespeare have any meaning in a world where the entire Shakespeare trade is fueled by a frank acknowledgement of the legitimacy of inauthenticity? For even the New Globe is, as Dennis Kennedy has put it, "a form of staged authenticity," combining aspects of the shrine with those of the amusement park (1998: 181, 188). In this situation, the inauthenticity of the "foreign" or indeed any other devotee should matter less than it once did, just as the authenticity of Shakespeare himself is less important to both audiences and vendors. The non-Western craving for "authentic" Shakespeare seems now to be matched with a Western craving for "foreign Shakespeare." As a result, the global traffic in

Shakespeare, and the traffic in global Shakespeare both come together to market a newly "intercultural" Shakespeare that combines, promotes, and yet, at the same time, often ignores or diminishes both Shakespeare and the "postcolonial" culture being marketed.

Rustom Bharucha rightly points out that some of the most outstanding figures in Euro-American theatre today have turned to "India" for theatrical inspiration and experimentation, but

> What has happened to the Indian theatre since Independence, or for that matter, since Herasim Lebedeff, a Russian adventurer, initiated the "modern Indian theatre" with two Bengali adaptations of European farces in the late eighteenth century, seems to be of no interest to interculturalists. Nor are they concerned with the assimilation of colonial models like the proscenium theatre, which have been totally transformed in the company-theatre tradition that flourished in all parts of India...It is our "tradition," our much glorified "past," to which they have turned to find revelations (if they happen to be mystical), or to extract material (like the *Bhagvad Gita*, which served as the libretto for Philip Glass's *Satyagraha*, not to mention the *Mahabharata*, which provided Brook with a "story"). Last but not the least, India has provided interculturalists with a wide range of techniques, including Yoga, the *mudras* and eye-exercises of Kathakali, and more recently, the martial arts techniques of *Kalaripayettu*. (1990: 4)

"Hybrid" or "cross-cultural" productions, dominantly understood as Western theatre that has absorbed elements of non-Western technique and form, are today touted as the way to reach the real heart of theatre itself.

They are also seen as the most effective means to uncover the real Shakespeare. According to Ariane Mnouchkine: "We have taken Asian forms of theatre as a base to work from because the very origin of theatrical form is there...Shakespeare's text is itself masked in any case: it is not a conversation in a sitting room or a café. It is not realism but poetry" (1996: 97). An organic fit between Shakespeare and something called "Asian forms" is indicated here, and increasingly, Shakespeare has become the means of marketing an exoticized Third World, Orient, or Africa to the West. The import of foreign-language productions of Shakespeare to English-speaking countries, it has been suggested, depends upon a post-modern economy which detaches form from its social origins, and makes it available in a cultural supermarket, so that "ethnic theatres" are available for random sampling pretty much like Indian samosas or African masks. Dennis Kennedy argues that Shakespearean Orientalism has become a global product, and the selling power of Ariane Mnouchkine's use of Kathakali or Kabuki relies on "substituting an aesthetic experience for a social one" (1995: 58–9). In her analysis of *Umabatha*, the long-running production of *Macbeth* in Zulu, Kate McLuskie points out that when cosmopolitan directors like Brook and Mnouchkine integrate the Shakespeare text with African or Indian performance styles "they release the arts of colonial cultures from their originating relationship to the cultures which produced them and reinvest them with both the symbolic value and the exchange value of the metropolis" (1999: 162). John Russell Brown has also called this "theatrical pillage"; Mnouchkine and Brook are, he says, "raiders across a frontier" who "bring back strange clothes as their loot and try to wear them as if to the manner born" (1998: 9).

But "multicultural" productions reproduce some of the dynamics of a colonial economy not only by taking the raw material from the so-called postcolonial world to fashion new products for a Western market, but also by re-exporting these finished products back to the *postcolonial* market. The British company Footsbarn recently toured India with its *A Winter's Tale*, and in interviews given to the press there, members of the company claimed that their "feelings are similar to what Geoffrey and Laura Kendal felt when they began to tour India with Shakespeareana 50 years ago." Their *A Winter's Tale* had the Oracle of Delphi intoning Malayalam chants, one of the company "affectionately" calling the choreographer from Kerala "curried Guinness." Another confessed "We hate cultural colonialisation (*sic*), where you can just buy others' cultures. We integrate various cultural elements into our plays because we are from different cultures. We're family" (Shedde 1999). The Kendals, it should be remembered, were also an international Shakespearean family; their company trained Indian actors including the cinema stars Utpal Dutt and Shashi Kapoor, and their daughter Jennifer even married the latter. But despite their deep roots in India, the troupe counted upon a colonial mentality in India which would make audiences flock to an authentically English performance. Footsbarn (or Steven Berkoff, or indeed the RSC who have also toured India recently) benefit from the persistence of such a mentality today, even as they cater to not just a Western but also a new *Indian* urban market for "ethnicity." Thus, a Western production that includes some Indian touches caters to an Indian upper-class desire to be simultaneously very Western and very Indian, a subject to which I will later return.

The global market in postcolonial Shakespeares is now dependent upon a simultaneous attention to, and erasure of, the local. Under the banner, "Globe to Globe," the reconstructed Globe theatre now regularly showcases "international" Shakespeares such as *Umbatha* and a production of *King Lear* in Kathakali style, directed by Annette Leday and David McRuvie. An earlier version of this production had premiered in 1989 in Kerala, India, the home of Kathakali, and then subsequently traveled to Italy, the Netherlands, France and Spain, Singapore and Edinburgh. Quoting a British reviewer, the Globe's web page promised that this "Intense, hypnotic and spectacularly beautiful . . . *Lear* . . . will linger in the memory when more conventional productions have been forgotten." But apart from its borrowings from Kathakali, what exactly was unconventional about this *Lear*? When it played in Kerala, what was controversial, apart from the fact that it was a story drawn from outside Kathakali's usual repertoire of tales from the Hindu epics *Mahabharata* and *Ramayana*, was that its King appeared bare-headed and without make-up. Kathakali, which is a highly formal style of theatre that evolved at about the same time as Shakespearean drama, depends upon elaborate and heavy costumes, mask-like make-up and over 500 eye, hand and face gestures or *mudras* through which actors "speak" to the audience (see Zarrilli 1984). The costume and make-up of characters reflect not just their exterior form but also the interior being of a character. Hence for a noble figure to appear without make-up does not signify a social or emotional disturbance so much as a loss of all personality (Zarrilli 1992, Awasthi 1993). For Lear to appear without his head-dress signifies not a loss of *social* status or a disturbance of his emotional being, but an erosion of his entire selfhood. Thus, in Kathakali, a make-up-less figure is simply sound and fury, signifying nothing. Therefore, for many viewers in India Annette Leday's and David McRuvie's production of *Lear* marked an unsuccessful fusion of forms. Pointing out that this *Lear* insults Kathakali viewers by flouting every one of its deeply thought-out practices, the Indian critic Suresh Awasthi concludes that it is not "aesthetically possible to attempt new stories in Kathakali nor will any such attempts result in a meaningful experience" (1993: 177). A similar argument informs John Russell Brown's critique of the "theatrical pillage" of Asia by Western impresarios – Theyyam and Kathakali, he argues, are designed to be performed in the "presence of gods," i.e. in a religious context alone (1998: 11).

In both these critiques, it is the authenticity of Indian tradition rather than of Shakespeare that is at stake. As Bharucha cautions, however, the point is not to resurrect national or cultural barriers, but to question the terms on which any inter-cultural borrowings or collaborations take place. Similar debates about the extent to which modern theatre can appropriate traditional or pre-modern theatrical forms have marked theatrical experimentation elsewhere in Asia, especially Sri Lanka (see Gunawardena 1997). I cannot agree with the suggestion that Kathakali can only be performed in its "traditional" contexts, that the answer to cultural plunder is a return to some notion of cultural purity, either of Shakespeare or of these forms. In a rapidly changing India, forms like Kathakali are hardly performed only in the "presence of gods"; they are developing in new ways, and to the extent that many of India's older theatrical traditions were rooted in intense hierarchies, some of these changes are necessary for their survival and health. So, for example, women have begun to perform these once all-male arts, and performances have begun to move out of temples and homes into more diverse venues, acquiring new audiences, new meanings and new dynamism in the process. Ironically, it is precisely the notion of a cultural essence that is at the heart of the new markets for Kathakali, which has become an especially popular medium for showcasing not only what Dennis Kennedy calls Shakespeare without Shakespeare, but also what we may call India without India. Kathakali is spectacular and flamboyant, while being especially difficult for the non-initiated spectator, whether Indian or Western, to decode. As such, it has become an increasingly touristy form both within the country and abroad: if Shakespeare was, and still is, widely regarded as embodying the essence of Western culture, Kathakali is vulnerable to being read as an easy symbol of authentic India. Together they make a potent commodity for the new global market.

If the idea of an "authentic" Shakespeare was invoked during the colonial and some postcolonial years to secure the hegemony of either the English elite or the English-speaking native elite in India, Africa and other parts of the colonized world, today the authenticity of some mythic Indian culture is used to establish a different hierarchy. If one was Anglophilic and colonial, the other is nativist and only *rhetorically* anti-colonial. Let me briefly clarify. During the colonial period and even after Independence, a colonial literary canon (whose apex was Shakespeare) kept indigenous texts out of the schoolroom; moreover, feminist, anti-colonial or indeed other contextual readings of any of the "great" masterpieces of English literature were disallowed. Thus, not many interesting interpretations of Shakespeare emerged from the Indian academy, especially any which might explicitly engage with both Shakespeare and Indian society. In the 1980s some Indian literary critics (and other intellectuals) started to focus on the way in which English studies (and formal education in general) were the product of colonial rule. They drew attention to Thomas Babington Macaulay and his infamous "Minute on Indian Education" to demonstrate the invidious colonial provenance of the discipline, and of English-language education in general. Macaulay had, as is by now well known, argued that British colonialism needed to ensure that Indians were "ruled by their own kings, but wearing our broadcloth, and working with our cutlery"; this could be done by educating a small section of Indians so that they would be "Indian in blood and color, but English in taste, in opinions, in morals, and in intellect" (Macaulay 1957: 729, 716).

Now, in an interesting irony, the same colonial origins of education in English have been increasingly invoked by the ideologues of the ruling Bhartiya Janata Party, which along with its neo-fascist allies or "family" as they are known in India (the Shiv Sena, the Bajrang Dal, and the Vishwa Hindu Parishad), has been aggressively assaulting multiculturalism, religious minorities, women and lower castes, all in the name of a true "Indian" culture and tradition, defined as Hindu in sensibility and ancient in provenance. This Hindu Right uses the rhetoric of colonialism to suggest that all Indian Muslims and Christians are as foreign to India as the British were, and that defenders of multicultural and secular India are all children of Macaulay, Marx and the *madrasas* (or Muslim schools) (see Elliott 2001, Delhi Historians Group 2004, Taneja 2004). But as Mridula Mukherjee and Aditya Mukherjee (2004) point out:

> In fact, one of the ironies of the situation is that despite all the talk of Bhartiyakaran or Indianization, the historiography that the RSS ideologues and followers espouse is essentially colonial. And though they like to call others the children of Macaulay, they are the direct descendants of James Mill, who first divided the history of India into Hindu period, Muslim period and British period. The notion that Hindus in the medieval period were suffering under Muslim tyranny is also a colonial construct, as the British rule could then be projected as having freed the Hindus from this tyranny. Further, depicting the Hindus and Muslims as warring communities created the justification for the British presence in India, and also prevented them from uniting against the British. The communal interpretation of Indian history is based on the colonial interpretation; it merely adds a few more elements to it.

Erstwhile champions of the Western canon have now become aggressive defenders of "Indian culture," "indigenous" literary traditions and critical methods, all of which are defined by their distance from a real or imagined "West."

These are not just seminar room or newspaper debates. In the past few years, the Hindu Right has been increasingly aggressive in policing artistic and cultural activity in India. Not only has it engineered attacks on non-Hindu citizens and property (the demolition of the Babri mosque in 1992, the anti-Muslim riots in Bombay in 1993 and the genocide of Muslims in Gujarat in February 2002 are the best-known instances) and championed the creation of a "Hindu" nuclear bomb, but it has also destroyed art exhibitions, burnt books and cinema halls, roughed up film-makers and artists, intimidated historians who offer a different version of India's past, rewritten school textbooks, and vandalized pitches to prevent Pakistani (and therefore Muslim) cricketers from playing in India. To set right our colonial ills, the ideologues of the ruling party have proposed that school students must sing hymns to the Hindu goddess Saraswati, that girls should be taught home-making, and that "moral studies" and "Vedic mathematics" should be part of the school curriculum.

The study of Shakespeare, once upheld by a Westernized elite as the necessary core of postcolonial education, is now denounced as evidence of the "inauthenticity" of some Indians. Indeed, in one instance a performance of *Romeo and Juliet* was attacked and disrupted by the self-appointed champions of Indian culture. Despite this declared incompatibility between an authentic Shakespeare and an authentic "Hindu" India, in practice, champions of both have shared many assumptions about caste, class, gender, and even the new global order. Historically, they have even shared attitudes to Shakespeare – the Bard, it was once claimed, confirmed the insights of classical Sanskrit dramatist Kalidasa, and both upheld a conservative social order and suggested that the masses were stupid, women should be obedient to their fathers and husbands, and so on. But, and that is the point I am interested in pursuing here, such a binary also fails to capture the dynamic of hundreds of Shakespeare performances in India which, even in colonial times, were equally unconcerned with the authenticity or purity of either Shakespeare or Indian culture. These productions were rooted in Indian performance traditions, but they simultaneously reached out to and experimented with Shakespeare – both were vocabularies they needed in order to express themselves. Of course, most of these performances were not in English – the English language theatre in India remained meekly imitative of conservative British performances.

I am not suggesting that cultural or economic differences simply dissolve when it comes to Shakespeare. Although, as Dennis Kennedy points out, Anglophone critics "have tended to look upon Shakespeare's popularity in other countries as an example of his comprehensive appeal," in fact, cross-cultural performances illuminate both dialogues and national or global asymmetries but the latter are quite different from those imagined by colonialists and nativists (1993: 2). For example, in 1996, a Delhi-based dancer-director Sadanam Balakrishnan designed a production of *Othello* in Kathakali that has been playing in India in different and constantly revised versions. For Balakrishnan, the daring and innovation lay in stretching, playing upon the rules of Kathakali, rather than in simply ignoring them to produce a spectacular version of *Othello* (see Loomba 1998). This production was also criticized for stepping out of the traditional repertoire of Kathakali stories, but it differed enormously from the Annette Leday and David McRuvie's Kathakali *Lear* in that it primarily sought to expand the vocabulary of Kathakali. It also addressed itself to Indian audiences with their double-consciousness (however imperfect) of both Shakespeare and Kathakali. The Leday–McRuvie *King Lear*, on the other hand, was entirely oriented towards the western market, and to audiences who knew nothing about Kathakali, although it made the gesture of opening in India.

These are not differences of form alone. If, for the global *Lear*, it was more important to stage a new and marketable Shakespeare rather than to speak a new language of Kathakali, for the local *Othello*, Shakespeare was flattened in being appropriated. For example, the production almost entirely erased Othello's difference, whether we understand that as a difference of race or caste or religion. Othello's hands were painted black and the narration which accompanies the dancing identifies him as "malechh," a term that means outcaste, polluted or dirty. But his green make-up identified him as an entirely heroic and morally superior being, and he was indistinguishable as a type from Desdemona's father, or Cassio. Iago, on the other hand, was placed within the group of "black beard" characters who are, in the world of Kathakali, vile schemers. Thus, the binaries of good and evil that Kathakali inherits from older religious theatres were mapped onto Shakespeare's play, ironically white-washing Othello into a white man.

As I have suggested elsewhere, Balakrishnan's *Othello* was not interested in Shakespeare at all, except as a suitably weighty means through which it could experiment with its own performative lineage (Loomba 1998). Thus, it challenged both those who think that Kathakali should not venture outside its own traditional narratives, and those for whom the authenticity of Shakespeare is compromised by an alien form. As a result, this production annoys Indian patrons for whom Shakespeare is inappropriate for a Kathakali production, and it is too tedious and inaccessible for the Western market for which Kathakali is just a style. Arjun Raina (who played the Duke in the original production and has also functioned as an informal impresario for the production) suggests that "Shakespeare is like a magic icon on a computer screen, click on it and new worlds open up for you" (Raina, 1999). But these new worlds are different for the Indian producer and the Western one – Balakrishnan's actors struggle to make a living, and spectacular as the Kathakali *Othello* is, unless it finds foreign funding, it will reach a very limited audience compared to the Leday–McRuvie *Lear*. It will probably also remain invisible to the same Western critics who might analyze the inter-culturalism of *Lear* or of the Shakespeare plays produced by Peter Brook and others. As Raina also admits, "real immersion in form means you don't travel well," so this Kathakali Shakespeare doesn't quite work either for the Kathakali trade or for the international Shakespearian market, although it briefly captivated a niche market of those Indians who can straddle both those worlds.

In flattening Shakespeare, the Kathakali *Othello* also disengages from its own complex context. Kerala, where Kathakali was born and is still rooted, has an almost equal mix of Christians, Hindus, and Muslims, and elaborate caste differences further bifurcate each of these groups. To the extent that Kathakali is traditionally an upper-caste Hindu form, it would be far more radical for it to deal with these differences than it is for it to enact a story from Shakespeare. Thus, it is not accidental that the production ignores the question of Othello's difference. In marked contrast is a recent Indian film in Malayalam called *Kaliyattam* which is also made and set in Kerala and declares itself to be an "adaptation" of *Othello* (Surya Cine Arts, 1997, English title: *The Play of God*). In this film, director Jayaraj places the story of *Othello* in the context of Theyyam, a religious dance theatre of north Kerala. The word "Theyyam" is a corrupt form of "Devyam" or God, while "attam" means dance – thus "Theyaa-attam" or Theyyam means the God's Dance. "Kaliyattam" refers to both an annual festival at which Theyyam is performed as well as the aboriginal dance form from which Theyyam evolved. Theyyam itself draws upon earlier tribal dances which were domesticated by the Brahmins or upper castes after the region was conquered by the Aryans from the North. In the film, Theyyam does not provide the medium of the performance itself. Rather the politics and dynamics of Theyyam provide the connection to Shakespeare's play. Othello and Iago are both players of a Theyyam troupe, and Othello is its lead dancer.

This is a brilliant move, juxtaposing the contradiction that lies at the heart of Theyyam with that which lies at the heart of *Othello*. For in the Theyyam tradition, the main dancer or "kolam," who plays and personifies the deity, mythological character or spirit being worshipped, is drawn from one of several lower castes of Kerala, but during the dance, he becomes "possessed" by the divine spirit and thus becomes a manifestation of divinity. While thus possessed and embodying the divine spirit, he is worshipped by the upper castes, who, in the normal course of events would not allow even his shadow to cross their paths. By allowing the lower castes to perform divinity, upper-caste culture allowed a limited space for the expression of lower-caste/tribal discontent – thus, Theyyam performances, during which the performers can and do often highlight the injustices of caste society, can be seen as safety valves that ultimately serve to contain the discontent of the marginalized. To cast Othello as a Theyyam dancer is thus to capture his double status as outsider and insider, as well as to offer a perceptive commentary on the contradictions of caste politics and theatre in Kerala. Othello is both necessary for white Venetian security and a threat to its identity; the kolam is also simultaneously central to and marginalized by upper class society. Othello/Kannan Perumalayan is divine as long as he is in costume. Desdemona/Thamara is an upper-caste lady also captivated by Othello's performances, which, for Brabantio are the equivalent of "black magic." Othello performs heroic deeds in his ritual roles as the performer of Theyyam, and the roots of Iago's jealousy lie in the fact that he, being the clown of the company, is not allowed to perform them. Also Cassio's punishment for his drunken brawl is that he is forbidden from performing Theyyam, and Desdemona pleads with her husband to allow Cassio back on the stage.

In the film, Theyyam also provides the vocabulary for expressing moments of heightened emotion. Thamara and Perumalayan make love by playing with make-up colors and ingredients, marking each other's bodies; thus their transgressive love also appropriates the rules and tools of the sacred dance. During Perumalayan's fits of jealousy, the spirits of Theyyam emerge from the Kerala landscape and through their dancing embody his doubts and fears. But his inner turmoil also means that Per- umalayan cannot actually perform – without Desdemona, Othello's occupation is gone. The Theyyam also becomes the medium of Othello's suicide – in the last scene, after killing Iago, Perumalayan enters the sacred fire to kill himself. If, in the original play, Othello impales himself on the sword which has been his means of his perform- ance as a warrior, in this film he dies in the theatrical fire of Theyyam, which is also his performative medium. Despite this, Theyyam remains the context for, rather than the medium of, the film. But although it seems that director Jayaraj wants to use both Shakespeare and Theyyam not to reflect upon either of them so much as upon the question of caste in Kerala, in this respect the film is ultimately disappointing, for it doesn't do anything with its explosive ingredients and with the astute positioning of Othello as a Theyyam "kolam." The film has been accused of nostalgia, of picturing a modern-day Kerala which seems devoid of any signs of modernity or urbanity. While Theyyam has been the medium of social protest in Kerala, in this film the question of caste difference vanishes, and is not articulated alongside the theme of jealousy. Thus the Theyyam element, so powerfully evocative of the tension at the heart of the play, ultimately dissolves into little more than a period setting.

Despite the fact that this film won the award for the best feature film in India's annual Film Awards, as well as several awards in European film festivals, neither *Kaliyattam* nor the Kathakali *Othello* are even mentioned by a recent story in the glossy Indian news magazine *Outlook* entitled "Shakespeare Masala Mix" which is only interested in the fact that "Shakespeare, shaken and stirred, seems to be the favorite cocktail in Delhi's *English* theatre circuit" (Joshi 2000: 70, emphasis added). Delhi has been home to innovative theatre largely because it houses the National School of Drama, whose repertory and alumni have created some of India's most innovative productions in a variety of Indian languages, including performances of Shakespeare (see, for example, the description of a *King Lear* performance in Gargi 1991). But the city's English language plays by and large mimic successful and mainstream British productions, and this remains true even of many of the current "experiments" with Shakespeare. Thus, for example, despite claims about its daring and irreverence, the Indian version of *The Complete Works of William Shakespeare* is a faithful copy of the original by the Reduced Shakespeare Company in England. Theatre directors have now learnt to mouth comparisons between Shakespeare and the enormous film industry of Bombay (increasingly referred to as Bollywood). There is also a shrewd economic calculation at play – most theatrical groups in India are either amateur, or even if professional, dependent upon corporate sponsorship. Shakespeare is one reliable way of ensuring survival. The opportunities Shakespeare brings for Indian producers of Shakespeare and the Western Shakespeareans who use "India" are not identical, as I have already noted, but there are also significant differences within the Indian spectrum where an English-language Shakespeare will circulate far more widely than a "regional" one.

But let me turn to another English-language production which is included in the *Outlook* essay but which departs from the norm; indeed, according to the Delhi theatre critic Keval Arora, this production has "re-written the rules by which Shakespeare is produced in India" (Arora 1999). United Players' Guild's *Othello: A Play in Black and White* (1999), after a huge success in Delhi, went on to win a Fringe First award at the Edinburgh Theatre Festival in 1999, packing in audiences there as well as in other cities in India and abroad. Director Roysten Abel says he was inspired by Carlos Saura's film *Carmen* as well as Sadanam Balakrishnan's Kathakali *Othello*. This is not the first time that a local Indian production has had international success, but what is different here is that *Othello: A Play in Black and White* is not a packaging of authentic India via Shakespeare but an *exposé* of Indian racism and elitism through Shakespeare. The Kathakali *Othello*, I have suggested, uses color extravagantly, and yet it renders both Shakespeare and India monochromatic. *Othello: A Play in Black and White* is literally mounted in two colors – the cast wears all black jeans or simple skirts and it deliberately mimics the bare minimalism of some Western theatres – yet it pays attention to the complex shadings within Shakespeare as well as its own social context (Abel, 1999). Recently the production has been turned into a film called *In Othello* (2004) which I do not discuss in this chapter.

The play's opening line is "Why the fuck do we have to do this play in Kathakali?" A Delhi-based group of actors, much like United Players' Guild, the group that performed the play, has assembled to rehearse *Othello*. The director of the play within the play is an Italian woman, Daniella, who has decided to stage the play in Kathakali precisely in order to exploit that Western market for which India is "the Mystic and the Ethnic"; Kathakali, she reckons, fits into both categories. Thus, the play takes a dig at the Shakespearean Orientalism of Western productions. As an outsider, however, the Italian director can disregard the hierarchies of Delhi's English language theatre. She casts Adil, a small-town young actor from the Eastern Indian state of Assam, as Othello, bypassing Barry, an older experienced English-born actor who, as one of the best-established names on the Delhi stage, had fully expected that he would get the leading role.

The characters' names and social situations are taken from their real lives – thus the Adil (Othello) of the play is really Adil Hussain, a relatively unknown actor from Assam, a part of India that (like Mizoram) the Indian mainstream regards with its own brand of Orientalism, as racially "other," "tribal," unsophisticated, lacking depth and maturity. Barry (cast as Iago in the play within the play) is in real life Barry John, an Englishman who is one of the best-known directors and actors of the English-language stage in India. Thus, Iago's malignity is thus understood as an English-speaking established actor's hostility to the less sophisticated newcomer, or the Westernized establishment's hostility to social change in India. But director Roysten Abel is not interested in a simple binary opposition between the center and the periphery. In interviews he confesses that the idea of this play came to him when his wife, an Assamese, was not cast in a play because the director felt that she didn't look like an Indian. He was also shaped by his own experience as a non-Hindi-speaking

South Indian in the National School of Drama in Delhi (NSD) where plum roles went to those who could speak Hindi. Adil Hussain also testifies to a similar experience at NSD which made him turn to Kathakali in search of a performative language which would overcome the linguistic hierarchies of India (see Handique 1999). While at an obvious level Barry/Iago represents the English-speaking elite, he can also be read as the right-wing Hindu Mafia which increasingly controls official structures of patronage, and claims to represent "Indian culture." That's why, Abel says, Iago is cast as an old man, who tells the young Othello: "These robes have been earned dearly and they will not be handed over so easily. The obsession for youth must end here, NOW." And the young Othello is not just from India's geographical margins but he is a Muslim too. Because the Hindu Right in India today is relentlessly anti-tribal as well as anti-Muslim, the play brilliantly brings together the exclusions of the older Westernized elite, as well as the newly powerful Hindu nationalists. By making Adil not Hindi but Assamese-speaking, and by choosing to mount his political satire through an English-language production of Shakespeare, Abel manages to widen his political critique and not play into a simple Indian/ Western opposition. Like the Mizo performances of *Hamlet*, which I have discussed elsewhere, we are here made aware of the multiple layers, the many hybridities within postcolonial society, but whereas the Mizo *Hamlet* plays to the politically marginalized sections of India, Abel's *Othello* speaks directly to the elites it critiques (Loomba 1993).

Adil/Othello grapples unsuccessfully with Shakespeare's English lines, breaking out now and again into his native tongue, Assamese. In that language Shakespeare is familiar to him, and he is able to play the role with passionate abandon. Thus, the play comments on the question of translation – whereas Shakespeare purists might argue that his plays lose something in translation, *Othello: A Play in Black and White* suggests that for Adil, the *English* Shakespeare is a painful translation of the Assamese original he knows and loves. Lushin, the actress who plays Desdemona, coaches him and in the process they fall in love. As a lover too, Adil is hesitant in English, but powerfully confident in Assamese, which is an alien tongue both for Lushin/ Desdemona and for the audiences who watched the play in Delhi or in Edinburgh. Thus *Othello* turns into a tragedy of Indian class and regionalism, both heightened by neo-colonialism.

For Abel, the need to appropriate the play to address Indian "racism" also impels him to locate it in its originating context: thus, there is a scene where three choral figures read aloud seventeenth-century writings about racial difference taken from Hakluyt's *Principall Navigations*. If the Kathakali *Othello* turns away from the question of Othello's difference in both Shakespeare's text and contemporary India, Abel's production searches for every possible language in which to hammer the point home. At one point, Othello croons to Desdemona a well-known song in which Krishna, the dark-skinned God of Hindu mythology asks his mother Yashoda why his lover Radha is so fair while he himself is dark: "Yashodha mayya se bole Nanadalala, Radha kyon gori, mein kyon kala?" Of course, Krishna's divine status mediates his skin color, which can no longer be read as a marker of an inferior class, caste or tribe as it often is in everyday life in India. Thus, the vocabulary of Hindu mythology, early modern Christianity, European travel writing, as well as contemporary Indian society is appropriated here to question the status quo. For Abel, the "truth" about contemporary India is at stake, rather than the authenticity of Indian theatrical forms or of the Western text. As with Shakespeare's original play, one of the disturbing features of this production is the fact that Othello does begin to conform to some of the stereotypes of the "tribal" boy. Abel changes the ending of the play, and his Othello ends up nearly strangling Desdemona on stage, but pulling back at the end. Like any other postcolonial Shakespeare, Abel's play is dependent upon once-colonial structures of patronage such as the British Council, American patrons of the Third World such as the Ford Foundation, and to a lesser extent, local Indian companies.

In conclusion, I want to turn to another Shakespeare-inspired performance in India which is complexly connected to the ones I have been discussing. *The Magic Hour* is produced and enacted by Arjun Raina, whom I have earlier mentioned as playing the Duke in Sadanam Balakrishnan's Kathakali *Othello*. Raina is a London-trained Shakespearean who started learning Kathakali on his return to India. Recently, he has adapted Kathakali into a new kind of form altogether. He calls this "khelkali" (in Hindi "khel" means "to play") in which the classical form of Kathakali is spliced with Indian folk dance and song, slides, street magic, stand-up comedy routine as well as bits of Shakespeare's English text. Elaborate Kathakali headdresses are discarded although facial make-up is retained, and Sanskrit and Malayalam are also dropped in favor of English or Hindi. Thus self-consciously hybrid form is designed to "play" with classical theatre as well as with more contemporary artistic forms as well as politics.

In *The Magic Hour*, Raina plays with both Kathakali and Shakespeare's *A Midsummer Night's Dream*. He invokes the little Indian boy over whom Oberon and Titania quarrel, as well as the forest in which they do so, to ask his audience to consider what is happening in the Narmada Valley in western India. In this valley large multinational corporations and the Indian government are locked in conflict with millions of villagers over the building of huge dams across the River Narmada: the government contends this will alleviate droughts and famines in the region while the activists point out that huge dams the world over have failed to do so. In this case, the price will be that hundreds of villages will be submerged, millions of people will be displaced, and both the environment and old tribal cultures will be damaged irreparably. Thus, Raina uses both Shakespeare and Kathakali to question not so much India's colonial heritage as what some describe as a neo-colonial situation that lingers today. In order to do so, Raina dances key lines from Shakespeare in the style of Kathakali, but he mouths the English text as he does so, or sometimes asks someone else to read in English as he dances in Kathakali. Thus, unlike the Kathakali version of *Othello*, the fusion of Indian form and English words is immediately accessible to the audience. These excerpts from Shakespeare (although he does not announce when they come, and so the audience's knowledge of the original shapes their awareness of his use of Shakespeare) are interspersed with his own stand-up routine – speaking in a thick Malayali accent, he asks his audience not to laugh at his accent for after all, he says, he is using it to enact the great Shakespeare, and he is also using the great classical form of Kathakali. Thus, he invokes the cultural authority of both the classical forms that he actually appropriates.

Raina performs this play in different contexts – he has played it as part of rallies and demonstrations in the Narmada Valley itself, as well as in different venues in India and the US. Predictably, it is college campuses in the US that have given the play its widest exposure abroad. In an early performance of the show in New Delhi, he addressed an official of the British Council who was sitting in the audience, and threatened that if his show was not sent to the Edinburgh Festival, he would seek the patronage of the Ford Foundation. Thus, he alluded both to Roysten Abel's *Othello* which *was* sent to Edinburgh by the British Council, and more generally to the role of foreign cultural/aid agencies that are fundamental to the structures of patronage that operate in a country like India. In the US he speaks a different language, drawing attention to his own difference from the audience, but also startling them with his use of American colloquialisms. In this production then, the deliberately playful use of Kathakali deromanticizes and politicizes India as a performative space, calling attention to the multiple contexts in which a postcolonial Shakespeare circulates and is open for adaptation and hybridization today:

> Raina equates Shakespeare to a plane you would grab to hijack attention. He's also the icon of the White culture, of colonial authority. "Something gets released when you exercise your power over this icon. The idea is to deform this play, not into something ugly but to give it your own beauty and shape," he says. For him, reinventing Shakespeare is a political act, a reason, perhaps, why it appeals to a political city like Delhi. (Joshi 2000: 71)

Like Abel, Raina is acutely aware that intercultural forms change in performance and depend acutely on context. As he told me:

> When I perform this show in the United States, I tell people, that just like the little Indian boy in *A Midsummer Night's Dream*, whom the Fairy King Oberon wants for his henchman, we Indians were once henchmen to the British but we have now grown up. But in India, I use the play to tell people that we are still henchmen to other masters, and I will tell them to grow up.

In a recent book, Rustom Bharucha (2001) argues that, despite the fact that so many "intercultural" performances simply reproduce the economic and cultural dynamics and inequities of globalization, we must remain open to the possibilities of truly intercultural work. While Third World artists cannot be exempt from being part of, or even exploiting, the global market's hunger for the exotic, Balakrishnan's *Othello*, Jayaraj's *Kaliyattam*, Abel's *Othello: A Play in Black and White* and Raina's *A Magic Hour* all indicate a wide range of dialogues which are possible between Shakespeare and India. Dennis Kennedy suggests that the best "intercultural" performances "are not about culture and they are not about Shakespeare: they are about Shakespeare *in* culture" (1995: 63). These performances I have discussed indicate a variety of ways in which Shakespeare remains "in" Indian theatre and culture, and continues to be a medium for facilitating new kinds of Indian performances. They also indicate that authenticity, both of Shakespeare and India, is often a stumbling block towards genuine experimentation. From them we learn that ironically, it may be the least "authentically Indian" theatrical form that comes closest to allowing a genuine dialogue with both Shakespeare and the conditions of its own performance, both locally and within the international market.

ACKNOWLEDGEMENTS

This chapter could not have been written without the help of many people. I would like to thank Roysten Abel and Sadanam Balakrishnan for discussing their work with me, and Arjun Raina for generously sharing his work and ideas. Also Keval Arora for making his writings on *Othello: A Play in Black and White* available to me, for conducting an interview with Roysten Abel on my behalf, and also for filming the production for me. I am grateful to Sanjay Kak for filming the Kathakali *Othello* and for locating a DVD of *Kaliyattam*, to Dennis Kennedy and William Worthen for opportunities to present earlier versions of this chapter, and to Barbara Hodgdon for her encouragement and advice.

REFERENCES AND FURTHER READING

Arora, Keval (1999). "Shakespeare Revisited." *First City* December 22.

Awasthi, Suresh (1993). "The Intercultural Experience and the Kathakali *King Lear*." *New Theatre Quarterly* 9, 33: 172–8.

Bharucha, Rustom (1990). *Theatre and the World, Performance and the Politics of Culture*. London: Routledge.

Bharucha, Rustom (2001). *The Politics of Cultural Practice: Thinking through Theatre in an Age of Globalization*. New Delhi: Oxford University Press.

Brown, John Russell (1998). "Theatrical Pillage in Asia: Redirecting the Intercultural Traffic." *New Theatre Quarterly* 14, 53: 9–19.

Delhi Historians' Group (2004). "The Communalization of Education: The History Textbooks Controversy." September 8. Available at: http://cyber_bangla0.tripod.com/Delhi_Historian.html

Elliott, John (2001). "India Moves to 'Talibanise' History: Children Will Learn that the Chinese Are Descended from Hindu Warriors if Indian Ministers Have Their Way with the School Curriculum." *New Statesman* December 17.

Faisal, Mohammed (2001). "American Hegemony." Letters to the Editor, *The Hindu* October 16.

Gargi, Balwant (1991). "Staging King Lear in India." *TDR: The Drama Review* 15, 3: 93–100.

Gunawardena, A. J. (1997). "Is It the End of History for Asia's Modern Theatres?" *Theatre Research International* 22, 1: 73–80.

Handique, Maitreyee (1999). "The Dark Side of Theatre." *Business Standard* March 27–8.

Joshi, Namrata (2000). "Shakespeare Masala Mix." *Outlook* May 1: 70–1.

Kendal, Geoffrey, with Colvin, Claire (1986). *The Shakespeare Wallah*. London: Sidgwick and Jackson.

Kennedy, Dennis (1993). "Introduction: Shakespeare Without his Language." In Dennis Kennedy (ed.) *Foreign Shakespeare, Contemporary Performance*. Cambridge: Cambridge University Press, pp. 1–18.

Kennedy, Dennis (1995). "Shakespeare and the Global Spectator." *Shakespeare Jahrbuch* 131: 50–64.

Kennedy, Dennis (1998). "Shakespeare and Cultural Tourism." *Theatre Journal* 50: 175–88.

Loomba, A. (1993). "Hamlet in Mizoram." In Marianne Novy (ed.) *Cross-Cultural Performances: More Women's Re-Visions of Shakespeare*. Urbana-Champaign, IL: University of Illinois Press, pp. 227–50.

Loomba, A. (1997). "Shakespearian Transformations." In John J. Joughin (ed.) *Shakespeare and National Culture*. Manchester: Manchester University Press, pp. 109–41.

Loomba, A. (1998). "'Local-Manufacture Made-in-India Othello Fellows': Issues of Race, Hybridity and Location in Postcolonial Shakespeares." In Ania Loomba & Martin Orkin (eds.) *Postcolonial Shakespeares*. London: Routledge, pp. 143–63.

Macaulay, Thomas Babington (1957). "Minute of 2 February 1835 on Indian Education" and "Speech in Parliament on the Government of India Bill, 10 July 1833." In G. M. Young (ed.) *Macaulay, Prose and Poetry*. Cambridge, MA: Harvard University Press, pp. 729, 716.

McLuskie, Kate (1999). "*Macbeth/Umabatha*: Global Shakespeare in a Post-Colonial Market." *Shakespeare Survey* 52: 154–65.

Mnouchkine, Ariane (1996). "The Theatre is Oriental." In Patrice Pavis (ed.) *The Intercultural Performance Reader*. London: Routledge, pp. 93–6.

Mukherjee, Mridula & Mukherjee, Aditya (2004). "Communalism of Education: The History Textbook Controversy – An Overview." March 8. Available at: http://www.sacw.net/HateEducation/MridulaAditya122001.html

Narasimhaiah, C. D. (ed.) (1964). *Shakespeare Came to India*. Bombay: Popular Prakashan.

Raina, Arjun (1999). Personal communication, November 21.

Taneja, Nalini (2004). "BJP's Assault on Education and Educational Institutions." March 8. Available at: http://www.ercwilcom.net/indo-window/sad/article.php?child=29&article=27

Shedde, Meenakshi (1999). "How Now, Will Shakespeare, Methinks You Sound Good in Malayalam." *The Times of India*, Bombay, December 26.

Sisson, C. J. (1926). *Shakespeare in India: Popular Adaptations on the Bombay Stage*. London: The Shakespeare Association.

Williams, Raymond (1989). *The Politics of Modernism*. London: Verso.

Zarrilli, Phillip B. (1984). *The Kathakali Complex*. New Delhi: Abhinav.

Zarrilli, Phillip B. (1992). "'For Whom Is the King a King?' Issues of Intercultural Production, Perception, and Reception in a *Kathakali King Lear*." In Janelle G. Reinelt & Joseph Roach (eds.) *Critical Theory and Performance*. Ann Arbor, MI: University of Michigan Press, pp. 16–40.

FILMOGRAPHY

In Othello (2004). Director Roysten Abel. ANB Motion Pictures.

PART II
Materialities
Writing and Performance

7

The Imaginary Text, or the Curse of the Folio

Anthony B. Dawson

Reality is an activity of the most august imagination.
Wallace Stevens

Imagining the Text

Texts have changed their status over the past 20 years or so. And along with those changes has come a shift in the way we look at the relation between text and performance. Not so long ago, a Shakespeare text was a relatively stable object, difficult to pin down in every detail but nevertheless knowable and dependable. Curiously and even paradoxically, it was not really an object in a material sense, but rather an immaterial entity whose various materializations emerged from, and at the same time pointed back to, its non-physical source. Its relation to performance was certainly various, but not vexed by the kinds of discontinuities that are assumed and asserted today.

Textual scholars used to set as their goal the re-constitution of texts that, in their material form – i.e. they way they have come down to us – were seen to be imperfect and partial. In Fredson Bowers' classic formulation, the task of the textual editor was to see past the "veil of print," i.e., strictly speaking to *imagine* an ideal text, what the author wrote, or perhaps more accurately, what the author would have written had he had all his wits about him – a situation that could never quite be achieved in real life. Now, this act of imagination was not what it has sometimes been portrayed as by the critics of the "New" (now old) Bibliography; that is to say, it was not simply a pipe dream or a cat chasing its tail. Based on extremely careful analysis of material facts, it was a disciplined form of imaginative reconstruction – the imagination, that is, was deployed in the service of a hermeneutic process of producing knowledge. It was, in the full sense of the term, an *historical* endeavor. In other words, if what such a bibliographer sought was in some sense "imaginary," that does not mean it was fanciful or irrational.

Today, the idea of something immaterial standing behind and aloof from its material manifestations is viewed with suspicion or even incredulity. The New Bibliographers have become what E. M. W. Tillyard's work was to new historicists in the 1980s, the favorite whipping boy of those who would forge a different path, an alien Other who, unlike all those other Others who have been eagerly embraced in recent critical work, can still be demonized without fear of reprisal. While it is not my purpose here to rehabilitate their work – it would be impertinent to imply that they need such a defense – I am interested in the forms of imagination they employed and the distrust of their imaginative energy current in the ineluctably materialist textual world we now inhabit. And I want to consider how conceptions of performance are grounded in ways of imagining text and vice versa. More particularly, I aim to show that today's textual criticism and the oddly parallel movement to concentrate on the Folio in modern rehearsal halls are related in their tendency to erase the very history that they claim to credit.

In the middle of Shakespeare's *Troilus and Cressida*, the eponymous hero/lover, who has been mooning about the seemingly inaccessible Cressida since the beginning of the play, finally gets his chance to meet her face to face, and his thoughts rush passionately ahead as he imagines the coming assignation. "Th'imaginary relish is so sweet," he says, that it enchants him, haunting his senses and driving him to wonder "What will it be / When that the wat'ry palate tastes indeed / Love's thrice-repurèd nectar?" (3.2.16–19).[1] We are accustomed to reading Troilus' ecstatic immersion in the imaginary as a sign of his sensuous self-involvement, his immature tendency to live inside his own head; such failures, it is often said, keep him from being able to see what's in front of his eyes – most especially Cressida. He worries about losing "distinction" in his joys (l. 24) when faced with the "real" thing – the clarity of his imaginative apprehension will be lost in the hurly burly of material existence. He wants to maintain a sense of what Ulysses earlier called "degree" (i.e., order and priority), applied now to sexual rather than political relations, and to the captains within his own mind rather than to those on the battlefield. As I suggested, critics are often impatient with Troilus' dreaminess, but perhaps, instead of scolding him, we could extend some sympathy to the dilemma he faces. Imaginative life, after all, is something we all claim to value; it is even a form of knowledge. Material life is messy – so why not enjoy the imaginary relish? Without it, sex, like so much else, would be rather a flat affair. More to my purpose here, however, what (if anything) might Troilus' dilemma tell us about our relations to the text? In that it pinpoints a stand-off between the imaginary and the material, drawing comfort from the joys of the former while fearing the muddle of the latter, it nicely epitomizes the conflict between older and newer ways of understanding texts.

What I mean by this is that the opposition between imaginative perception and immersion in the real which Troilus is experiencing is replayed in recent scholarly debates about what constitutes the "text." A certain impatience with imaginative apprehension along with a privileging of material reality and a clear-eyed, even microscopic, scanning of what is actually there is the standard attitude adopted by textual critics these days. But, for all their insistence on the materiality of the text, there is a metaphysical residue in their belief in a kind of purity and integrity to each and every document. While such critics emphasize the collaborative nature of particular texts, they eschew any kind of connection *between* texts, regarding each individual manifestation of a "work" as complete and whole. Textual miscegenation, in this rhetoric, breeds contamination. In what follows, I want to stake a claim for the textual imaginary and for what might be called "métis" texts.[2] My purpose is to set the extraordinary work that has been done on the material text in the past two decades in a wider context, focusing on its implicit and explicit historical claims about theatrical provenance and value, on the relation between "versions" and "original," and on the influence recent textual work has had on contemporary performance.

With regard to Shakespeare, the attack on the idealized text and the kinds of textual conflation and eclecticism that typically went along with idealization began in earnest in the late 1970s and early 1980s. One sign of the shift was the publication, in 1983, of *The Division of the Kingdoms*, a book that, carrying on previous work (Warren 1978, Taylor 1980, Urkowitz 1980, Blayney 1982), declared the independence and integrity of the two early texts of *King Lear*, Q1 and F. The very title was a call to arms: the plural "kingdoms" was adopted from the opening lines of the 1608 Quarto version of the play (the Folio reading is singular), and the insistence on plurality of texts was one of the grand messages.[3] The implication was that these tough-minded scholars were mounting an assault on the kingdom that was Shakespeare; the further possible implication, made fairly clear in the play itself – that dividing a kingdom isn't always the most enlightened policy – was ignored. To be fair, the only "authority" targeted directly by the volume's editors was the "spuriously joined" conflation of Q and F; they sought a "textual devolution" (Taylor & Warren 1983, vi–vii) not a full-scale revolution. But to some extent they initiated a movement which has led to the undermining even of the principles by which they themselves worked. They weren't yet thinking about pluralizing "Shakespeare," though that in effect is what has happened. From now on, "Shakespeare" would be "Shakespeares"; alternate early texts would be treated less as evidence upon which to reconstruct a version as close as possible to what the prefatory epistle to *Troilus and Cressida* calls "the birth of [Shakespeare's] brain," and more as entirely distinct "versions" – fraternal twins, we might say, to continue the epistle-writer's metaphor. This was the view taken by Michael Warren in a ground-breaking early article that to some extent set the stage for the later division. In that essay, Warren argued that the differences between the Q1 and F versions were not simply random, nor merely the result of playhouse interference, but added up to systematic evidence for authorial revision; he based much of his analysis on theatrical considerations, noting the changes in Albany's and Edgar's roles as well as smaller instances of "theatrical proportion" visible in each of the texts but lost when the two are conflated. Each text was integral in itself and to conflate them was to obscure that integrity. He concluded with a strong statement, one that also came to underpin much of the subsequent textual work not only on *King Lear* but also on several other multi-text plays: "Conflated texts such as are commonly printed are invalid, and should not be used either for production or for interpretation" (Warren 1978: 98, 105).

This view has now taken hold with a vengeance, and has become an orthodoxy, despite substantial critique from a variety of eminent scholars (see Edwards 1982, Muir 1983, Knowles 1997); I want here to re-visit it from a slightly different angle. What does it actually mean to say that, for example, Q and F are "separate versions of *King Lear*" (Warren 1978: 105)? What is this *King Lear* of which they are versions? Attempts to answer that question have led to the view, as suggested by W. B. Worthen many years later, that "Hamlet" is nothing but the sum-total of all the Hamlet texts that have been produced and all the performances that have been mounted since it first burst upon the world some time around 1601 (1997: 14–19). R. A. Foakes, in his recent Arden 3 edition of *King Lear*, takes a different position; while accepting Warren's idea of separate versions, he regards them, rather in the manner of the *Troilus and Cressida* epistle writer, as pointing back to an identifiable, if not precisely material, original, which he (perhaps following Thomas Tanselle) calls the "work" (Foakes 1997). For him, although he does not put it in these terms, the imagined existence of such an original justifies his own eclectic and conflated text, even though he still feels obliged, given the current climate, to provide an elaborate mark-up system to indicate the differences between Q1 and F. Despite such concessions, the clear implication is that the "original" remains more or less intact even though it can produce different versions of itself; revision, that is, does not dislodge the idea of an original. Just so – if I or my editor decide at a late stage in the process of writing this chapter, while, perhaps, working on the page proofs, to introduce a few changes (get a fact right, eliminate stylistic infelicities, highlight a new idea), the chapter remains for all intents and purposes the same; if it is published in slightly different forms in two places, it would be wrong for me to pad my CV by claiming two different papers. So in this sense, it seems to me that, as Knowles and others have suggested, Shakespeare wrote only one *King Lear*, not two.

What is at stake here are different ideas of the relation between a version and its original, a relation that is complicated by the addition of performance. Let me offer an example from outside the immediate field – the case of Billie Holiday or Nina Simone singing "Strange Fruit" (not to mention more recent versions by Shirley Verrett and Sting). The song was written by a white New York school-teacher named Abel Meeropol (who used the pseudonym Lewis Allen) in the mid-1930s, and first published as "Bitter Fruit" in a 1937 issue of the *New York Teacher* (Daniels 2002). As a text printed on various websites, it is clearly unstable – in a ten-minute search, I was able to find four different versions of the lyrics, two representing Holiday's supposed rendition and two Simone's, none identical.[4] No doubt, too, when Holiday sang it, the lyrics shifted to match the occasion, all the more so as the politics associated with the song, very much part of the Communist Meeropol's original intention, began to catch fire (at first Holiday seemed either unaware of or unimpressed by the political resonances [Daniels 2002]). Simone brought a different talent and a more firmly committed political position to her rendition. (Her apparent change of the first word from "Southern" to "Seven" multiplies the political and racial oppression and moves it from a strictly regional into an unlocalized national space.) In the words of critic Mark Richardson (2003): "Where Holiday delivered the disturbing imagery from the remove of a ghost (a choice which played to her strengths), Simone sounds like a witness to the scene made deranged by the brutal spectacle." But for all this instability those of us familiar with and moved by the song, know what it is and recognize it in its different raiments. How we do so, I'm suggesting, is by triggering a recognition of an imaginary, or imagined, object.

I am not about to attempt it here, but it would be possible to analyze the versions of "Strange Fruit" in the ways that recent critics have discussed not only the Shakespearean text but literary texts more generally – i.e., by hunting down the earliest printing and any manuscript versions that might have survived, following through the various versions recorded by Holiday, studying reports of unrecorded performances, checking out changes in the text from one performer to another, and so on. All this would confirm both the instability and the collaborative nature of the text. But it would also confirm, I think, that there is something separable from the different material manifestations of the song which goes under the name "Strange Fruit," and which originated with the songwriter. Incidental differences, no matter how numerous, don't erase the fundamental identity of the various versions. There are, of course, hard cases – if the song is sung in German to a different tune, is it still the same song? Is Kurosawa's film, *Ran* (1985), a "version" of *King Lear*? But these hard cases seem to me not to scuttle the case for identity, but clinch it; they are "hard" just because most cases are relatively easy. We can only make the judgment whether a given example is hard or not because we recognize that the imagined text has a real existence. Its precise relation to each succeeding version is a matter that can be sorted out through specific, focused analysis of the particular instance.

What I have been saying is not directly inconsistent with Warren's position on *King Lear*. He simply does not take up the question of what Q and F are versions *of*. He does, however, regard the performance of a conflated text as inadmissible, since he sees each material version as integral and unassailable. Foakes, on the other hand, regards performance based on a conflated text as perfectly fine, though he annotates his text in such a way that it is fairly easy, after one gets the hang of it, to sort out most of the differences between the two texts, thus leaving, as he says, the final molding of textual details in the hands of the performer/interpreter (1997: 119). Let's look at an example. Warren cites the following two passages from Q1 and F respectively, corresponding to 2.4.12–23 in most modern editions (though some recent editors, such as Foakes, revert to Q/F and treat 2.2, 2.3 and 2.4 as a single scene):

Quarto

LEAR:	Whats he, that hath so much thy place mistooke to set thee here?	
KENT:	It is both he and shee, your sonne & daugter.	
LEAR:	No.	KENT: Yes.
LEAR:	No I say,	KENT: I say yea.
LEAR:	No no, they would not.	KENT: Yes they haue.

LEAR: By *Iupiter* I sweare no, they durst not do't,
        They would not, could not do't, . . .

                                  (E3)

Folio

LEAR: What's he,
        That hath so much thy place mistooke
        To set thee heere?
KENT: It is both he and she,
        Your Son, and Daughter.
LEAR: No.
KENT: Yes.
LEAR: No I say.
KENT: I say yea.
LEAR: By *Iupiter* I sweare no.
KENT: By *Iuno*, I sweare I.
LEAR: They durst not do't:
        They could not, would not do't: . . .

               (TLN 1286–98)

Modern texts typically conflate these two passages; here is Foakes's version, complete with annotative apparatus (the passages surrounded by the superscript Q or F indicate bits found only in those texts):

LEAR: [*to Kent*] What's he, that hath so much thy place mistook
        To set thee here?
KENT: It is both he and she,
          Your son and daughter.
LEAR: No.
KENT: Yes.
LEAR: No, I say.
KENT: I say, yea.
[Q]LEAR: No, no, they would not.
KENT: Yes, they have.[Q]
LEAR: By Jupiter, I swear no.
[F]KENT: By Juno, I swear ay.
LEAR[F]:   They durst not do't:
        They could not, would not do't, . . .

               (2.2.202–13)

Warren's argument is that conflating the two passages produces a version which "has *no* authority" and which obscures the fact that in each of the early texts there are three exchanges between Lear and Kent, each leading to a "powerful climax." Producing four exchanges through conflation thus fails to respect the "theatrical proportions of the play" (1978: 98). One thing that Warren does not note, however, is that the exchange in Q is not exactly symmetrical – the climax comes *after* the completion of the third exchange, as part of a fourth, uncompleted exchange, on "By *Iupiter* I sweare no." (It is possible that Warren's very adroit analysis has fallen prey to the metaphysical allure of the number three.) Conflating the texts completes the symmetry and provides the climax by adding the F only line, "By *Iuno,* I sweare I." At the same time, the conflated version ignores the Q emphasis, which assigns Lear the climactic line in the exchange, instead following F, which gives it to Kent.

If we look beyond the immediate context, we might be able to find good performative reasons for giving Kent the climactic phrase – as in F – and even for allowing a quadruple, rather than a triple exchange. Two scenes earlier Kent was placed in the stocks, creating a conflict between the powerful Duke of Cornwall and Gloucester, whose castle, much against his will, has become a site of abuse of the King's messenger. Kent remains onstage during the intervening scene (Act 2 Scene 3 in most texts, though the action is continuous) in which Edgar announces his decision to become a Bedlam beggar: "Edgar I nothing am." The emblematic staging, in which Kent's descent from nobleman to servant and now to common criminal is figured by his onstage presence in the stocks, frames Edgar's parallel degradation. When Lear enters at the beginning of Act 2 Scene 4, with Kent once again the silent onstage watcher, we are prepared for further degradation. Kent hails the diminished King, perhaps with a hint of triumphant irony, as if to prove that he was right in Act 1 when he warned Lear of the folly of his actions. The quoted exchange follows. The last time we saw Lear before this entrance, he appeared almost helpless ("O, let me not be mad, not mad, sweet heavens"), and his attempt to recapture his authority here is likewise futile. Kent has the dramatic advantage in that the correctness of his moral vision, in the topsy-turvy world of the play, is ironically assured by his confinement to the stocks. His slightly sarcastic hailing of his master and the way he subtly corrects Lear ("It is both he and she...") suggest his moral advantage. Hence it seems appropriate to give him the climactic word in the little set of exchanges – "By *Iuno,* I sweare I." Q therefore seems to miss a nuance, while F's version is more alert to the dramatic complexity of the moment. But of course this does not in itself justify adding the little Q only exchange ("No no, they would not... Yes they haue.") in a conflated version with "*no* authority," as Warren puts it. However, one could reasonably surmise that Q accidentally omitted the final climactic line (and hence in an edited version of Q such as the Oxford, the editor might justifiably complete the exchange by adding the line from F), but one has to face the fact that F, perhaps deliberately, omits the third pair of lines.[5] Foakes argues that the "changes in F... strengthen [the] exchange" (2.2.209–12n), though he doesn't say why. But I would argue that, in performance, a four-stage exchange, capped by Kent, could be just as dramatically interesting as a three-stage one, perhaps more so. One of Shakespeare's most powerful such interchanges, between Othello and Emilia in the final scene of *Othello*, has five stages – or perhaps four or six, depending on how one counts them; earlier in *King Lear*, in the exchanges with Cordelia ("Nothing, my lord"), there are two sets of two. The point is simply that three is not a magic number nor one that automatically confers dramatic superiority.

Since definitive arguments about the precise relation of each text to the imaginary original are impossible, a certain eclecticism seems not only admissible but desirable. It might, indeed, be a more "historical" way of proceeding since it acknowledges the necessary element of interpretation in all historical work. My purpose is not to suggest that Warren's astute analysis is wrong, only that one can find plausible arguments for a different interpretation of the textual remnants that have come down to us, one that grants more "authority" to an imagined, but nonetheless powerfully present, entity – the idea of the play – and less to the discrete bits of data that have come down to us. And I would argue that doing so recognizes more fully the historical dimension of our work. Conflation, that is, acknowledges the complexity of historical relations between texts, including what I am calling their imaginary component, more fully than textual purity.

Folio Fixations

One unforeseen consequence of the shift in our understanding of the nature of texts has been, in performance circles, a valorization of what is seen as the "original." This is clearly paradoxical because recent textual criticism has worked hard to undermine the very concept of the original, instead drawing attention to the contingent nature of all texts. But theatrically-focused enthusiasts such as Neil Freeman and Patrick Tucker have seized on the material features of the Folio text as uniquely significant and have advocated detailed attention to them as a key to successful performance (Freeman 2000a, 2000b, 2001, Tucker 2002). The influence of this movement has been such that, in rehearsal rooms across North America and the UK, it is now commonplace for actors to be seen struggling with original spelling and searching for the hidden meaning of capitalized words, errant colons and split lines. Important figures in American and British Shakespeare performance, such as renowned voice teacher Kristin Linklater, and Shakespeare's Globe Artistic Director Mark Rylance have endorsed the practice of working with the "original" text. Meanwhile, business enterprises, such as Applause Books, whose Shakespeare editions quote Linklater and Rylance on their covers, have been quick to cash in on the fetishization of the Folio, marketing books which some readers see as analogous to musical scores. (While Freeman, the editor of the Applause series, now advocates a more exploratory approach than he did in earlier interventions, nevertheless when he discusses punctuation and sentence form, he indicates quite clearly that he sees such matters as strong, and implicitly authorial, indications of how characters should be understood and performed [see especially 2000: xvii–xx].) Such books can certainly be a helpful prop for an insecure actor, since they give a sense of being in direct communication with some quasi-mystical and deeply authoritative voice from the past, indeed with Shakespeare himself; but it completely misses the complex, and deeply vexed nature of the relationship between the material texts and what I called above the "imaginary" text. Here indeed we confront a much more suspect kind of idealization, since modern producers and actors are being told that a set of "imaginary" relations (in the pejorative sense) are actually real.

Of course, there is nothing wrong with taking a good hard look at the Folio and other early texts in order to exploit any cues that one might be able to glean from them. Indeed, to do so can undoubtedly be a fruitful and sometimes wonderfully revealing process. But at the same time I remain skeptical – partly because of the bandwagon effect, with its almost religious air of "true belief," and even more because Folio-worship suggests to the unwary that the work of "modern texts," the demonized Other in this discourse, is misleading and even dangerous. When approaching Shakespeare, actors often do feel intimidated, and they can feel even more so when faced with the daunting array of footnotes and scholarly commentary in, say, an Arden edition. Hence, for them, a potent appeal of relying on the "original" is the sense that to do so offers a simple and free access to a kind of truth, hidden perhaps but open to discovery, available in and through the accidental difficulties but essential simplicity of F; and the fact that it *is* hidden tends to augment its sacred character.

One of the most common justifications for working with the "original" text, besides the appeal to authenticity, is simply that it works. In his recent book, Patrick Tucker, Director of London's Original Shakespeare Company and a member of the Board of the Globe Theatre, describes in impressive detail his adoption of early modern acting practices in his work with modern actors. He not only relies exclusively on the Folio text, but he also makes extensive use of actors' "parts" or cue scripts, and backstage "plots" or "plats", similar to those used in the Elizabethan theatre, where actors learned their parts from scripts which contained only their own lines plus the two or three words that formed their cue; they could consult a backstage "plot" in order to get a sense of the overall narrative, the order of the scenes, what happened and who appeared in each, and the like (see Greg 1931, and Stern 2000). The book is laced with the testimony of actors as well as Tucker's own claims that actors he has worked with have had no difficulty dealing with various Folio readings which have puzzled editors and often been changed by them. It is, of course, the actor's job to try to act what he or she is given to act, and it is certainly possible to give a plausible reading of lines that editors and scholars might find unlikely or wrong. In his revealingly titled chapter, "The Folio Secrets," Tucker gives the following example from Enobarbus's colorful description of Cleopatra in *Antony and Cleopatra*:

> The Poope was beaten Gold,
> Purple the Sailes: and so perfumed that
> The Windes were Loue-sicke.
> With them the Owers were Siluer,
> Which to the tune of Flutes kept stroke...
> (TLN 903–7)

Noting that modern editions inevitably "remove the half-lines by pushing two lines together," he claims that "for an actor it is much better to play the speech as it appears in the Folio", meaning that Enobarbus "ends the thought on . . . *Love-sicke*" (Tucker 2002: 237; his italics and regularized orthography).[6] Now an actor certainly could play the speech that way, linking the prepositional phrase "With them" to the following clause about the "Owers," but to do so would be banal and flat. So punctuated, "With them" is simply a filler, meaning something like "along with that": as well, the phrase raises the question of what "them" could refer to – the "Windes"? But what could it mean to say that the oars were silver with the winds? Or the "Sailes"? – the oars, along with the sails, were silver? But the sails are purple. It seems much more likely that what Shakespeare had in mind is that the winds had fallen in love with the perfumed sails, and hence editorial emendation, putting the period after "them" instead of "sicke" (first done in the eighteenth century), and perhaps adjusting the lineation to match, makes excellent sense.

Still Tucker is driven to the position he adopts on meaning and punctuation out of his reverence for the Folio and his belief that its half-lines have a hidden performative meaning: "in the pause" after "Loue-sicke," he writes, Enobarbus "realizes that the others listening to him are spellbound – and so he starts afresh . . . All the actors I have worked with on these passages prefer the Folio text as an acting guide" (2002: 237). There are several claims and assumptions here that are typical of the sorts of reverence I want to question. First, note that Tucker's main argument rests on the existence of two half-lines in succession; for him, as for John Barton a generation ago and for acting teachers everywhere by now, a half-line is a probable indication of a pause. So Tucker assumes a pause after "sicke," and this takes precedence over the way stopping the sentence there clouds and flattens the meaning. He not only assumes a pause but fills it with a gratuitous character note, that Enobarbus only now "realizes" the effect he is having on his hearers, an unlikely possibility since Enobarbus is such a canny and self-aware character.

Like Warren and the "new textualists" generally, Tucker regards conflated texts as having "*no* authority." To demonstrate the illegitimacy of conflation, he cites facsimile versions of the same passage in Q1, Q2 and F of *Romeo and Juliet*, alongside their modern equivalent. (Tucker inadvertently mis-labels his facsimiles; what he cites as Q2 is actually F and vice versa. In my transcription, I correct the error, which doesn't materially affect his argument though it does make a difference to mine.) Here are the passages:

Pardon me Sir, that am the Messenger of such bad tidings.
ROM: Is it euen so? Then I defie my Starres.
(Q1 1597)

O pardon me for bringing these ill newes,
Since you did leaue it for my office sir.
ROM: Is it in so? Then I denie you starres.
(Q2 1599)

O pardon me for bringing these ill newes,
Since you did leaue it for my office Sir.

ROM: Is it euen so?
Then I denie you Starres.
　　　　(F 1623)

In modern editions, Romeo's speech is typically printed as follows:

Is it e'en so? Then I defy you, stars!
(5.1.24; final punctuation varies between period and exclamation)

Tucker comments that this produces "a line that there is not a scintilla of evidence that Shakespeare ever wrote" (2002: 277). I would argue in contrast that there is plenty such evidence and it is right there in the texts. Evidence is distinct from data; it forms part of an interpretive process of making sense of the given material – here the three different versions of the passage. Evidence, that is, only becomes evidence when we adduce it as part of an argument (Dawson 2004). And, in this instance, we can produce good evidence for the conflated reading of *Romeo and Juliet*. We can, that is, reconstruct the imaginary text, the "birth of his brain," and that is exactly what most editors have done. For starters, the "in" in Q2 (universally regarded among scholars as the most authoritative text, though its relation to Q1 is ambiguous and complex), makes no sense and is clearly incorrect, while "euen" no doubt carries the right meaning ("in" then is probably a compositorial error or perhaps reflects haste or a lapse of attention on Shakespeare's part in the writing of his draft). But "in," since it fits metrically, also strongly suggests that "euen" in Q1 and F should be monosyllabic (thus modern "e'en"). As for the rest of the line, Q1, the so-called "bad" text, provides the other significant variants: "defie" for "denie," and "my" for "you." Starting with the first of these, it's hard to figure out exactly what, if we follow Q2, it might mean to "deny" the stars – that they exist is undeniable, and denying their *influence* is precisely what Romeo is *not* doing. So the evidence provided by Q1 allows us, even obliges us, to imagine that Shakespeare meant "defy" and might indeed have written "defy" but that somehow the word got lost on the journey into print. As for Q1's "my," it could no doubt be defended, but since Romeo is saying that he will take fate into his own hands, it seems confusing and even contradictory to declare that the stars are somehow his.[7] Hence there is good evidence, as part of a process of literary and critical judgment, to support conflating the texts. Indeed, to refuse conflation in this instance would be to contribute to intellectual muddle and hence also to aesthetic impoverishment.

One of the things about fetishization, in the Marxist sense, is that it occludes the real history, the actual relations of production. This is a potential problem with overstressing the Folio as a sign system for directing performance. Processes of transmission are left out of the equation and thus the thoughts and intentions of a number of different subjects, all of whom have had an effect on the final material product, are obscured. Something similar happens when the "new textualists" downplay the process of transmission (which inevitably leads back, however tentatively, to the brain of the author), in favor of a concentration on the isolated and self-contained material object/text. Paradoxically, while both critics and performers lay claim to a focused historicism, they ignore a crucial, diachronic and intention-intensive element of what it means to do history.

Tucker's work with "cue scripts," despite the obvious *élan* with which he pursues his goal, illustrates the bind. He gives his actors only their own "parts," comprising their lines and cues, so that they have little idea of who is onstage with them or what the overall rhythm of the scene might be, and then brings them together to act and discover. Since this approximates what we know about the way Elizabethan actors worked, the idea is to get closer to original practices. It's an intriguing idea that can produce vibrant results, but it ends up erasing the history it seeks to re-create. That is because the parts it relies on are themselves derived from F, the printed text which has already been granted a kind of primacy. In the actual Elizabethan theatre, actors would have been given their handwritten parts, prepared by a scribe from a manu-script copied directly or indirectly from an authorial draft; if the one surviving example is at all typical, the "parts" show quite different orthographic and punctu-ation features from printed texts. There are, for example, few capitalized letters and short lines; periods are extremely scarce, even at the end of speeches, and there are only sporadic commas, often seemingly misplaced (see Greg 1931). This means that the actual script actors worked with did not look all that much like F; when translated to modern performance, this difference disappears since the "parts" are produced directly from F, and this in itself undermines the claim that F's cues for the actor provide a way of accessing original practices. In the historical circumstances of Shakespeare's theatre, that is, cues for the actors did not arise from print and its conventions, whereas in Tucker's modern experiments, they (necessarily) do. Also changing the historical landscape is the fact that for an Elizabethan actor, the cue script or "part" represented standard practice, and was thus familiar to him. For the modern actor the situation is precisely the opposite – i.e., it is emphatically *de-familiarizing*; indeed, this is one of the prime advantages of experimenting with early texts and techniques. Thus claims about returning to an origin encounter difficulties not only because of the theoretical problems associated with the very idea of an original, but also because trying to erase historical difference never quite works in practice.

I'm afraid I've been providing a rather jaundiced and one-sided view of Tucker's friendly and enthusiastic book; he has a lively and unpretentious style and is well informed about Elizabethan stage practices. I've focused on what I see as its short-comings because they seem to me symptomatic of attitudes prevalent in performance circles today – most especially the tendency to fetishize the Folio as an "origin," thus obscuring its historical situatedness, and following from that an undue reliance on its accidental features as signs for the actor.

The general situation as I have outlined it is thus paradoxical: textual scholars began by questioning eclecticism and conflation in bibliography, emphasizing the independence of different material texts and their consequent instability and contin-gency; but when such ideas spread to performance circles, they ended up having the opposite effect. Performers who seized on the increased interest in looking closely at old texts have absorbed the lesson of textual uniqueness but have deployed it in ways that can make textual scholars wince – in the theatre, the unique early text has increasingly become a point of origin, a series of almost infallible signs of either Shakespeare's intentions or those of the collectivity of early modern performers. Ironically, however, both groups narrow the range of what counts as "history" even as they emphasize the historical nature of their undertakings. Put another way, modern textual scholars tend to refuse the idea of an imaginary text, which, as I have been arguing, is a necessary component of the interpretive process we call history. They regard each material version as separate and isolated, with no privileged access to an imagined origin and without decisive relations to any other version. By contrast, performance people who privilege what they see as the original entertain an idea of the imaginary text, but they identify it directly with a specific material manifestation in the Folio; perhaps too much influenced by Heminge and Condell, who in the volume's Preface (designed to encourage readers to "buy") claim that Shakespeare's "mind and hand went together," they see no significant difference between Shakespeare's intentions and what appears in print in F.

One reason that this kind of misreading arises is that readers of plays today have become used to print formats and conventions that are a kind of blueprint for performance. As W. B. Worthen (2003) has persuasively shown, contemporary playwrights frequently seek to determine the details of performance through punctuation, designation of places to pause, breaking up of the dialogue in various ways, and so on. These are features of *textual* production, influenced by other movements in modern writing such as the formatting of poetry, which writers use to try to control the unruly world of the stage. But this was emphatically not the case in Shakespeare's day, where the very idea of printing plays was itself new, and there were no typographic elements familiarly associated with performance practices. Indeed, as Lukas Erne (2003) has recently argued, Elizabethan playwrights may have regarded theatrical scripts and readerly texts, designed for the stage and the printer/reader respectively, as sharply distinct. Beyond that, actors, of course, did not work from printed texts, but rather from hand-written "parts" and "plots" and probably some kind of "playbook" – a hand-written version of the complete play with some playhouse annotation (often surprisingly little from a modern point of view). Hence the idea of reading the Folio, or even the Quarto texts, as though they were designed with performance clues in mind, is to miss a fundamental distinction between the conventions of print in the period and those of performance.

The Applause editions offer an interesting case in point. While generally following the Folio very closely, these editions make one key change in formatting. After every period, they drop a line to "help" the reader "quickly spot the new steppingstone in an argument" and thus, if the reader is an actor, enable him/her to mark a "point of transition" (Freeman 2000b: xvii). This of course assumes that there *is* a point of transition, that the character *is* undergoing a change in "thought pattern." Furthermore, it's an attempt to use modern typographic signs to highlight what is claimed to be an implicit typographic code in F. This strikes me as misleading. In the *Antony and Cleopatra* example above, the new sentence seems to miss Enobarbus's "thought pattern"; nevertheless, Applause prints it thus:

> . . . and so perfumed that
> The Windes were Love-sicke. →
>
> With them the Owers were Silver . . .

The arrow represents the fact that F sets two short lines while most modern texts join them, and the extra space between the lines indicates a supposed break in thought. (A footnote explains that the break "allow[s] Enobarbus a moment of personal recollection before continuing the new sentence" [Freeman 2000b: 36] and notes that most modern texts remove the period and re-line.) My point here is not so much that this misrepresents what Enobarbus apparently means, though I think it does; rather, I want to underline the irony that in seeking to emphasize the performative, these editions rely on the practices of print and the ideological formations that underpin print culture in general. This is true not only in cases like the one quoted, but in every single instance. Whenever there's a period, the printed line drops down (if this occurs mid-line, the second half of the line is dropped and indented; end-line periods are followed by a blank line); but where F prints a colon with virtually the same effect as a period, there is no line drop. This implies again that the typography has a performative significance (i.e., a period has a different meaning for the character and for the actor than a colon), even though it's easy to find instances where there *is* a shift of thought after a colon. Take Gloucester's speech to Edgar in *King Lear* 4.1:

> Here take this purse, ÿ whom the heau'ns plagues
> Haue humbled to all strokes: that I am wretched
> Makes thee the happier: Heauens deal so still:
> Let the superfluous, and Lust-dieted man . . .
> (F version, TLN 2249–52)

Three colons, each with a slightly different register. Whatever we make of them, it's clear that there is a change after "happier:," since Gloucester moves from directly addressing Edgar to addressing the heavens and calling for a more equal distribution of goods in the world at large. But because a colon rather than a period follows "happier," Applause offers no typographical indication of the shift since it operates on the assumption that print-forms have fixed performative value, a conviction ironically derived from the habit of reading *modern* plays in modern printed editions. The Applause editions use the look of the work on the page as a guide to performance, even as they critique printed editions since the eighteenth century for falling prey to similar ideological formations (grammar over rhetoric, regularization over variety, order over messiness, and so on). In such a context, "performance" loses some of its freedom and becomes subject to different but equally sharp regulation.

Coming at similar issues from a different angle, Edward Pechter (2003) has recently shown that scholarly openness to material texts long considered inferior is frequently defended on theatrical grounds, and in ways that suggest an overall abatement of aesthetic value; qualities such as speed, drive, or elimination of moments that do not advance the plot, are tagged as paramount, and vague phrases such as "performable and lively" or "accomplished theatricality"[8] appear in defenses of texts formerly known as "bad quartos." Downgraded are more complex pleasures such as "prolongation and dilation," lateral movements of thought and/or sympathy, or subtle reflection on the action. Citing William Carroll (1988), Pechter suggests that, by privileging simple virtues, "Shakespeareans are investing themselves in a drastically diminished concept of theatrical value." Clearly defined action is no doubt a good thing, but "to claim that brevity and straight-ahead simplicity constitute in all cases the essence or totality of theatrical value seems...at best to mistake a particular means for a general end" (2003: 514). While it is possible, even likely, that certain early texts do arise out of specifically theatrical circumstances, "to assert theatrical origin is not to identify theatrical value" (2003: 511). The same point could be extended to today's performers who claim a peculiarly theatrical origin for their work with the early texts. Not as inclined to accept all texts as "equal" in the manner of the "new textualists," they nevertheless fasten on the specifically theatrical value of textual features regardless of the consequent aesthetic loss – as in the *Antony and Cleopatra* and *Romeo and Juliet* examples discussed above.

Timon's Farewell

Near the end of *Timon of Athens* there appears a sequence that presents a challenge to editors and producers alike since, among other things, it indicates the unfinished nature of the text as we have it. Editors have long been aware of the rough uncertainties of the Folio version of the play, the fact that it seems to have been rushed into print to fill a gap left open by the decision, later reversed, to omit *Troilus and Cressida*. *Timon*, that is to say, was brought in to replace *Troilus*, and the manuscript available to the volume's editors appears to have been seriously deficient. There is a whole raft of inconsistencies, from the names of characters to gaping holes in the plot, but I only want to focus on one of these here.

Shakespeare's tragedies typically end on an elegiac note, a retrospective glance at the pain and heroism of the central figure(s), often with a tinge of irony mixed with the quieting sadness; after the carnage comes a moment of reflection when the survivors recoup, or try to, the losses that they and the dead have suffered. *Timon*, while in many ways atypical, ends on a similar note, with an announcement of Timon's death and the reading of an epitaph – or, to be exact, two epitaphs which contradict each other. Therein lies the problem. Shakespeare seems to have copied both epitaphs more or less verbatim from Plutarch's *Lives*, the book he relied on for some aspects of the story. (Plutarch's tale of Timon is a short digression in his history of Mark Antony, which Shakespeare used extensively for *Antony and Cleopatra* as well as for *Julius Caesar*.) If we try to imagine the process that led to the textual situation we are now faced with, we can construct a scenario something like the following: uncertain as to which epitaph to use in the final version, Shakespeare copied out both versions from Plutarch, changing them only minimally, with the apparent intention of coming to a final decision later on. Since *Timon of Athens* is almost certainly a collaboratively written play, it is of course possible that Thomas Middleton, the main collaborator, had something to do with the choice of epitaphs; but Shakespeare, around the time he was working on *Timon*, was writing *Antony and Cleopatra* with Plutarch's book open in front of him, so it is likely that he is the one responsible.[9] What the collaboratively composed manuscript actually looked like, we can only speculate, but, judging by the printed text in F, it may well have been messy and hard to read, spotted with marginal insertions and changes. The evidence of the double epitaph strongly suggests that it was a working manuscript rather than a theatrical one, though the distinction between the two is at best blurred and may even be non-existent (Long 1985, Werstine 1990). This means that the compositors probably had a difficult time making their way through the task of setting the text and it means as well that there is more leeway than in some less problematic texts for editors to re-think certain passages – such as the one under discussion.

Here are the epitaphs as they appear in F:

> *Alcibiades reades the Epitaph.*
> *Heere lies a wretched Coarse, of wretched Soule bereft,*
> *Seek not my name: A Plague consume you, wicked Caitifs left:*
> *Heere lye I Timon, who aliue, all liuing men did hate,*
> *Passe by, and curse thy fill, but passe and stay not here thy gate.*

To my knowledge, only one editor, C. J. Sisson, has actually cut one of these (the first), though most comment on the inconsistency between "Seek not my name" and "Heere lye I Timon" in successive lines. Complicating the picture is the fact that in the previous scene, a short one involving a new character called, simply, Soldier, we seem to have yet another epitaph:

> *Enter a Souldier in the Woods, seeking Timon.*
> SOL: By all description this should be the place.
> Whose heere? Speake hoa. No answer? What is this?
> *Tymon is dead, who hath out-stretcht his span,*
> *Some Beast reade this; There do's not liue a Man.*
> Dead sure, and this his Graue, what's on this Tomb,
> I cannot read: the Charracter Ile take with wax,
> Our Captaine hath in euery Figure skill;
> An ag'd Interpreter, though yong in dayes . . .
> (TLN 2496–504)

"What is this?" The question implies that the Soldier comes across something and is momentarily uncertain. Following that, we have two rhymed lines, cryptic and indeterminate, lines that have elicited many pages of puzzled critical commentary. The lines could be a third epitaph – but then why does the soldier go on to speak of taking the character in wax to present to his interpretively skilled Captain (Alcibiades)? One suggestion has been that here too there are two epitaphs, one in English easily read by the literate but under-educated soldier, the other in Latin or Greek and thus proving too much for him. In the Applause version there's a revealing footnote: "since Ff do not italicise the lines it would suggest that the text is intended to be heard as the Soldier's comment" (93 n2). Once again the power of typography dictates the performative understanding. But all the lack of italics tells us is that the compositor probably did not regard the two lines as part of a written text being read onstage by the speaker.

What these passages need is a considered act of historical interpretation – a way of making sense, based on a reconstruction of probable intention. If we try to imagine performance, it's clear that the Soldier has to find or pick up something ("What is this?"), and we can imagine further that the following two lines are a response to what he has discovered – this supposition derives from the grammar of performance not from the modalities of print. How is it that the soldier pronounces Timon dead – has he come across the corpse? Possible but very unlikely: there's no indication that he carries off a corpse when he exits, and given the exigencies of Elizabethan staging (think, for example, of Hamlet lugging Polonius's guts into the neighbor room), he would have to do so before Alcibiades enters a moment later with "his powers before Athens." So, no corpse. Perhaps the Soldier is simply guessing, but more likely he is reading something, a message from Timon perhaps, announcing his own death and reiterating in his usual misanthropic way that only beasts could read his epitaph since men do not exist – they are all, that is, beasts. So, a kind of pre-epitaph perhaps, a message from beyond the grave directing those who come later how to read the actual epitaph, itself still unspoken and unreadable to our soldier, who thus determines to copy the figure in wax. At the end of the next, and final, scene, he again appears (or so it seems – he is now called Messenger) presenting the wax tablet to Alcibiades, who reads – both or one of the two epitaphs printed in F? My guess, given the evidence of the soldier's speech, is that it's only one, and it's the second one. If, that is, we take the rhymed lines in the Soldier's speech as something written and declaring that "Tymon is dead," then it seems reasonable to deduce that the first of the two formal epitaphs, which refuses to name the grave's occupant, doesn't belong. So I think Sisson is right to cut it.

Such a decision is unlikely to please those textual scholars who attach themselves to the materiality of the text, the uniqueness of what is printed and its only oblique relation to the work of which, one might claim, it is a version. Nor will it please those who are wedded to the idea that the Folio text is a set of signs for performance. Performance certainly does not have to care about the supposed intentions of the author. But if it claims to do so, then it can't rely simply on typographic or printed "evidence," since the data provided by early printed texts need to be interpreted and made sense of. And that process is always in some ways aesthetic, an act of critical judgment. That is, it always draws on criteria and principles about what constitutes value. It seems to me that making sense is one of those values; in Shakespeare at least, coherence is a kind of baseline, a foundation upon which other more complex values may be said to rest. Of course, lively interpretive energy is often required to find or make coherence, but the energy we expend in so doing is based on the assumption that there *is* coherence; and when it comes to stage action, clarity about what is required in order to make sense is normally quite easy to establish. That is precisely why *Timon of Athens* is so puzzling and why so many readers have seen it as unfinished and partially incoherent; Shakespeare doesn't usually leave crucial incidents, such as the possible discovery of the tragic hero's corpse, uncertain. It is noteworthy that in Plutarch, the two epitaphs are clearly distinguished, the first said to be Timon's own, the second the work of the poet Callimachus (the incident with the soldier is not in Plutarch). So the text as we have it muddies what is clear in the source to no discernible aesthetic purpose.

What *is* going on in these final moments? Why does the soldier make his anonymous, uncertain entry, looking for Timon? If we invoke a wider Shakespearean context, we can recognize him as that ordinary Shakespearean observer entering the play near the end whose sympathy adds dimension to the plight of the hero – the Groom of the stable in *Richard II*, Kent returning in *King Lear*, the anonymous guards in *Antony and Cleopatra,* but in this play he is denied direct connection, emphasizing the absolute isolation of Shakespeare's loneliest hero. The soldier finds not the living man but only an ambiguously written message. Like the audience, the soldier is thwarted in his quest, never allowed the intimacy he, or we, might desire. A. D. Nuttall comments that in this play "Shakespeare is essaying the almost impossible task of dramatising negation itself" (1989: 141); in such circumstances, Shakespeare's apparent hesitation over the epitaphs is understandable and might even be seen as a sign of the dramaturgical difficulty. Still, we might speculate that the play is moving toward the slightly softer, less directly abrasive tone of the second: "*Heere lye I Timon, who aliue, all liuing men did hate,/ Passe by, and curse thy fill, but passe and stay not here thy gate.*" The invective is replaced by a concern with those who remain; if we want, we are free to curse, but more compellingly, we are invited simply (like Yeats's "Horseman") to pass by, to forget what in fact refuses to be put to rest. The epitaph undermines itself, since in telling us to forget it inevitably reminds us of what has taken place. In doing so it speaks of Timon's own impossible project of forgetting mankind. Perhaps too, if we widen the context of historical interpretation even more, we can see an echo here of all those other voices of the dead that sound through not only Shakespeare's tragedies but the annals of sixteenth-century history, voices choked but not quite silenced by the many attempts by reformers to separate the community of the living from that of the dead – see Duffy (1992), Diehl (1997), Neill (1997), and Wood-bridge (2003). Thus, the presence of the unknown soldier figures both a desire to do more than pass by and a baffling of that very hope. Another way of saying this would be to suggest that, as the play reflects on Timon's fate, it begins to shift away from his headlong misanthropy into a subtler configuration: Timon's hatred of mankind is put into dialogue with our own feelings of displacement, our inability directly to speak to or hear from the dead, a dilemma that was especially pronounced in the later sixteenth and early seventeenth centuries. We are left with our sense of loss – cursing is painful and useless, passing by our only alternative. But for something like this to register we need first to make sense of the action itself before we can appreciate, or even see, what else is going on. Retaining both epitaphs highlights the muddle; printing or performing only the second facilitates meditations that, while not directly theatrical in the simple sense that Pechter rightly rejects, have an aesthetic register, an aura we might say, that is certainly amenable to performance. That aesthetic has little to do with character, at least in the narrow sense favored by those who would read textual signs primarily as character notes. If we pay too much attention to the motives, drives and intentions of characters, and not enough to elements that both subtend and over-arch the action, we miss the resonance associated in this instance with loss, and thus diminish the overall aesthetic experience.

The final moments of *Timon of Athens* pose textual and aesthetic challenges that can, I think, be best negotiated if we hold on to some idea of what I have been calling the imaginary text as part of a process of producing historical knowledge. Those challenges obviously won't be easily overcome, but insistence on some of the widely accepted views about how to deal with early texts in both scholarly and theatrical circles is likely to produce more distortion and take us farther from the complex aesthetic pleasures that imaginative editing and reading can uncover. The end of the play produces, at Timon's grave site and in the retrospective reading of his epitaphs, a "strange and bitter crop," to cite the final line of "Strange Fruit" – or should that be " . . . bitter cry"– as one record of Holiday's version claims? For Timon as for us, the crop *is* the cry and the only way we can know that is by an imaginative and aesthetically nuanced interpretive act.

Notes

1 References to *Troilus and Cressida* are from my edition, Cambridge Shakespeare (2003). Other references to Shakespeare are taken from the Riverside Shakespeare unless otherwise stated.

2 In Canada, the word "métis" refers to a person of mixed French and Amerindian ancestry. Formerly used in pejorative ways, it is now a mark of a particular and valued heritage. I adopt it here in the same spirit.

3 Citations to the quarto version refer to the first quarto, 1608, not the second, issued by Jaggard in 1619, with a false date of 1608.

4 Available at www.wsws.org/articles/2002/feb2002/frut-f08.shtml; www.sing365.com/music/lyric.nsf/SongUnid/0FD7F982CC9A2BB3482569A10026F46D; and www.lyricsfreak.com/n/nina-simone/100706.html. The first line(s) of the four versions run as follows: "Southern trees bear a strange fruit"; "Southern trees bear strange fruit"; Southern trees / Bear strange fruit"; and "Seven trees / Bearin' strange fruit."

5 Neither the 1986 Complete Oxford nor the recent single volume (Wells 2000) adds the F line. Needless to say, I am skirting some large

issues here – most importantly that of how the two early texts are related – itself an historical question. Editorial decisions will naturally be affected depending on whether we regard F as strictly a *revision* of Q, or whether we regard the relationship of the two texts as more mixed and uncertain.

6 It is odd that throughout the book early modern "u" for modern "v" is silently regularized [as is "i" for "j"], without explanation that I could find; Freeman's Applause texts (2000a, 2000b, 2001) do the same, but carefully note the fact in the Introduction.

7 Note also that Romeo's reply is printed as two short lines in F and one regular iambic line in Q2; this might lead astray those performers who rely heavily on F since they would be inclined to mandate a pause after "euen so"

despite the fact that Q2, the text presumably closest to Shakespeare's own draft, gives no such indication.

8 Scott McMillin, in the Introduction to his edition (Cambridge, 2001) of Q1 of *Othello*, 14, and G. B. Shand in *Shakespearean Illuminations: Essays in Honor of Marvin Rosenberg*, eds. Jay Halio & Hugh Richmond (Newark and London, 1998), 34; both quoted in Pechter (2003: 507, 512).

9 The whole business of collaboration complicates the issue of the imaginary text as I am developing it, but also makes it that much more imperative, since it is impossible to conceive of collaborative results without some kind of determinative idea shared among the collaborators.

References and Further Reading

Blayney, Peter (1982). *The Texts of King Lear and Their Origins*, vol. I: *Nicholas Okes and the First Quarto*. Cambridge: Cambridge University Press.

Bowers, Fredson (1959). *Textual and Literary Criticism*. Cambridge: Cambridge University Press.

Carroll, William C. (1988). "New Plays vs. Old Readings: *The Division of the Kingdoms* and Folio Deletions in *King Lear.*" *Studies in Philology* 85, 2: 225–44.

Daniels, Peter (2002). *World Socialist Website*. Available at: www.wsws.org/articles/2002/feb2002/frut-f08.shtml

Dawson, Anthony B. (ed.) (2003). *Troilus and Cressida*. Cambridge: Cambridge University Press.

Dawson, Anthony B. (2004). "Staging Evidence." In Peter Holland & Stephen Orgel (eds.) *From Script to Stage in Early Modern England*. Basingstoke and New York: Palgrave Macmillan, pp. 89–110.

Diehl, Huston (1997). *Staging Reform: Reforming the Stage: Protestantism and Popular Theater in Early Modern England*. Ithaca, NY: Cornell University Press.

Duffy, Eamon (1992). *The Stripping of the Altars: Traditional Religion in England, 1400–1580*. New Haven, CT: Yale University Press.

Edwards, Philip (1982). Review of Urkowitz (1980) and P. W. K. Stone *The Textual History of King Lear. Modern Language Review* 77, 3: 694–8.

Erne, Lukas (2003). *Shakespeare as Literary Dramatist*. Cambridge: Cambridge University Press.

Foakes, R. A. (ed.) (1997). *King Lear*. The Arden Shakespeare, 3rd series. London: Methuen.

Freeman, Neil (ed.) (2000a). *The Tragedie of King Lear*. New York: Applause.

Freeman, Neil (ed.) (2000b). *The Tragedie of Anthonie and Cleopatra*. New York: Applause.

Freeman, Neil (ed.) (2001). *The Life of Tymon of Athens*. New York: Applause.

Greg, W. W. (1931). *Dramatic Documents from the Elizabethan Playhouses*, 2 vols. Oxford: Clarendon Press.

Knowles, Richard (1997). "Two *Lears*? By Shakespeare?" In James Ogden & Arthur H. Scouten (eds.) *Lear from Study to Stage: Essays in Criticism*. London: Associated University Presses, pp. 57–78.

Long, William (1985). "Stage-Directions: A Misinterpreted Factor in Determining Textual Provenance." *Text* 2: 121–36.

McMillin, Scott (ed.) (2001). "Introduction." In William Shakespeare *The First Quarto of Othello*. Cambridge: Cambridge University Press.

Muir, Kenneth (1983). "The Texts of *King Lear*: An Interim Assessment of the Controversy." *The Aligarth Journal of English Studies* 8, 2: 99–113.

Neill, Michael (1997). *Issues of Death: Mortality and Identity in English Renaissance Tragedy*. Oxford: Oxford University Press.

Nuttall, A. D. (1989). *Timon of Athens*. New York: Harvester Wheatsheaf.

Pechter, Edward (2003). "What's Wrong with Literature?" *Textual Practice* 17, 3: 505–25.

Richardson, Mark (2003). "Nina Simone: One Woman, Twelve Songs." *Pitchfork Media*. Available at: www.pitchforkmedia.com/watw/03-04/nina-simone.shtml

Shand, G. B. (1998) in Jay Halio & Hugh Richmond (eds.) *Shakespearean Illuminations: Essays in Honor of Marvin Rosenberg*. Newark and London: University of Delaware Press.

Sisson, C. J. (ed.) (1954). *The Complete Works*. London: Odhams.

Stern, Tiffany (2000). *Rehearsal from Shakespeare to Sheridan*. Oxford: Oxford University Press.

Tanselle, G. Thomas (1989). *The Rationale of Textual Criticism*. Philadelphia, PA: Pennsylvania Press.

Taylor, Gary (1980). "The War in *King Lear*." *Shakespeare Survey* 33: 27–34.

Taylor, Gary & Warren, Michael (eds.) (1983). *The Division of the Kingdoms: Shakespeare's Two Versions of King Lear*. Oxford: Clarendon Press.

Tucker, Patrick (2002). *Secrets of Acting Shakespeare: The Original Approach*. New York: Routledge.

Urkowitz, Steven (1980). *Shakespeare's Revision of King Lear*. Princeton, NJ: Princeton University Press.

Warren, Michael (1978). "Quarto and Folio *King Lear* and the Interpretation of Albany and Edgar." In David Bevington & Jay L. Halio (eds.) *Shakespeare, Pattern of Excelling Nature*. Newark: University of Delaware Press, pp. 95–107.

Wells, Stanley. (ed.) (2000). *King Lear*. Oxford: Oxford University Press.

Wells, Stanley & Taylor, Gary (eds.) (1986). *William Shakespeare: The Complete Works*. Oxford: Oxford University Press.

Werstine, Paul (1990). "Narratives about Printed Shakespeare Texts: 'Foul Papers' and 'Bad' Quartos." *Shakespeare Quarterly* 41, 1: 65–86.

Woodbridge, Linda (2003). "Afterword: Speaking with the Dead." *PMLA* 118, 3: 597–603.

Worthen, W. B. (1997). *Shakespeare and the Authority of Performance*. Cambridge: Cambridge University Press.

Worthen, W. B. (2003). "The Imprint of Performance." In W. B. Worthen & Peter Holland (eds.) *Theorizing Practice: Redefining Theatre History*. New York: Palgrave, pp. 213–34.

8

Shakespearean Screen/Play

Laurie E. Osborne

The term "screenplay" neatly, and perhaps oxymoronically, combines film and stage while eliding the crucial component of print. The term apparently doubles the performative at the expense of the textual, unless we take "play" to refer to text rather than performance. Simultaneous with these connotations of performance, the term carries a double denotative meaning: "screenplay" signifies not only the shooting script but also the subsequently published text. Recent critical disputes underscore the conflict between these modes of the work's identity. William Horne argues that the shooting script (which he calls the screenplay) merits its own position as an aesthetic object related to film (1992: 53). He distinguishes this object from the published form in that "the work can only be a true screenplay if it exists prior to the film" (1992: 52) and asserts that screenplay-as-shooting-script participates in the creative process of film production. Others, notably Katherine and Richard Morsberger, have argued not only that the printed screenplay should include representative features of both the finished film and process of filmmaking but also that such published texts are invaluable in anchoring the academic study of film (Morsberger & Morsberger 1975: 50–1). Horne regards these arguments as flawed in misidentifying what he thinks should be the true aesthetic object of study: the actual shooting script. However, I argue that the published screenplay is itself an aesthetic object worthy of analysis.

This chapter distinguishes between the shooting script and the published screenplay or the screenplay edition. Published screenplays, like those of the prominent Shakespearean films I address here, may build on the working script of a film, but they are produced afterwards; they are not the dog-eared typed scripts used during the production but the glossy, textually-produced artifacts that *follow* the film. Unlike a script for performance or shooting script, the screenplay edition typically presents itself as a retrospective creation while it promises insight into performance as a process.

In analyzing this paradox, I argue that the published screenplay's functions and its potential audiences usefully contextualize and qualify the materials that it offers and that we often use in our scholarship and teaching. More important, the published screenplay participates in a print–performance cycle that has both a lengthy history and a complex future. In the case of Shakespearean film, the published screenplay follows a long history of performance editions and moves towards the construction of the latest performances, now rendered on DVD. As such, printed screenplays have wider influence and significance than their relatively small print runs and audiences imply.

Although Shakespearean critics of film use these resources frequently, few have stopped to consider their position as "Shakespearean" texts or their function in relation to film or indeed to the stage-to-page Shakespeare which used to corner the market on such books. Published Shakespearean screenplays emerge in the twentieth century as the latest of Shakespeare's performance editions, those texts that are based in and on performance. The eighteenth- and nineteenth-century counterparts to the screenplay edition are typically neglected by textual critics and most often lumped with promptbooks by performance critics (Osborne 1996: 14–29). Shakespearean screenplays, in contrast, have a higher academic recognition factor because they serve as scholarly sources for work on Shakespearean film. In effect, this newest variation on the performance edition acquires credibility through the textual inter-pellation of several audiences and through their self-conscious explorations of rela-tionship between textuality and performance. The films' investment in Shakespearean popular and academic appeal permeates the screenplay edition. As a result, Shake-speare, "as seen on TV and film," enters an ongoing cycle of performance and print that illuminates their mutual influence.

Play by William Shakespeare, Screenplay by –

Shakespearean film performance currently generates the complex blend of produced artifacts: soundtracks, movie posters, promotional/study packets, websites, and – most important – screenplay editions. This proliferation of objects seems to disperse Shakespearean cultural authority. However, the most elaborate of these objects, the screenplay (and recently the DVD) editions, work to recuperate status, often para-doxically through recourse to print-based structures.

The screenplay edition addresses four target audiences – academics (both students and professors), film critics, fans, and general filmgoers. Their material richness and diverse formats, designed to appeal to these audiences, reveal an array of overlapping purposes. This analysis therefore benefits from Jerome McGann's arguments that we must attend to the materials beyond the words of the literary work, including not only the paratexts – introductions, appendixes, figures, indexes, table of contents, and so on – but also the bibliographic codes, such features as typeface, paper quality, inking, and other material elements of the book (1991:13). Such choices of material form are not value-neutral; in fact, they derive from – and therefore expose – interpretive assumptions about the status and meaning of the work. As McGann argues of literary texts, "every part of the productive process is meaning-constitutive" (1991: 33). My discussion of published Shakespearean screenplay draws on their paratexts and bibliographic coding in order to argue that these texts function as more than the Shakespearean equivalent of *Little Women, Based on the Film with Winona Ryder*. They register a highly complex relationship between text and performance; they negotiate between published performances and performed texts.

Shakespearean screenplays imperfectly disguise their own influential textuality as they supplement and celebrate the film production. Still more important, their textual and bibliographic strategies reappear as elements of performance now reproduced on DVD. This merging or blurring of textual forms and performance has the important consequence of underscoring the materiality that text shares with performance, especially in terms of marketability. Screenplay editions thus undercut the mystique that has so often set performance in contrast to text.

The first and most overt purpose of these texts is promotional. Screenplays function similarly, though not identically, to the merchandising efforts that accompany many films. Like such spin-off merchandise, the promotional impetus and potential gain work as a two-way street. The latest Pixar film promotes interest in McDonald's Happy Meals that contain related toys which in turn promote the film to Happy-Meal-eaters who have not yet seen the movie or who have and may cajole their parents into taking them again or buying the video. This promotion becomes cyclical: releasing more toys advertises the sequel whose success creates spin-off toys which in turn may inspire a video game or cartoon series, and so forth, until economic exhaustion or household overflow stems the cycle. A text is not a toy, or even a soundtrack which is the more marketable promotional tie-in that arises from Shakespearean films; however, the promotional – or interest-generating – model is clearly relevant. For evidence, we need only look to the array of Shakespeare's plays published with cover art taken from films, even if the texts within have no hint of the screenplay about them. Consider, for example, the Bantam edition of *Much Ado about Nothing*, edited by David Bevington (1993) which has Branagh's cast on the cover and a smattering of photos inserted but no other reference that I can find to the film. The full-fledged screenplay edition elaborates this promotional function with more features related to film production (Branagh 1993).

All of the screenplay textual materials can constitute promotion and draw different audiences. The normative introductions, screenplay "stage directions" and text formatting lure both academics and film buffs, giving information about the process of mounting the film and often about the director's intent behind casting choices, cuts and camera moves. Some screenplay editions expand this appeal to cinematically or academically sophisticated readers with features that specifically invoke textual forms: Russell Jackson's "Film Diary" for Kenneth Branagh's *Hamlet* (1996), Peter Greenaway's display of the array of books he conceived as *Prospero's Books* (1991), and Ian McKellen's parallel text of facing pages of images and commentary opposite the screenplay of *Richard III* (1996). The diary, the book, and academic-style side-by-side formatting draw on familiar, conventional text and formatting to offer the

academic reader (potentially) new information about the film performances and –
equally important – a resource for quoted evidence. The screenplay edition presents
the student or critic of film with the production details and camera directions from
behind the scenes, while drawing on the verbal paratexts of academic or semi-
academic writing.

These same textual features can also intrigue fans of particular performers, directors, designers, or even the playwright. However, fan audiences may have greater
appreciation for visual appeal of these texts. Glossy paper, lavishly illustrated covers
and pictures of Calista Flockhart or Michelle Pfeiffer in *déshabillé* may be of limited
use to academics or film buffs analyzing Michael Hoffman's *A Midsummer Night's
Dream*, but such images definitely "sell" the book (and by extension the film) to fans
of particular actors, actresses, or directors. Full double-page reproductions of the set's
floor plans and overlaid designs for Prospero's books record the visual process of Peter
Greenaway's filmmaking, providing a direct appeal to would-be film makers and to
Greenaway fans. In these cases, bibliographic codes involving typeface and pictorial
elements draw one kind of readership while paratexts, with their invocation of
conventional forms taken from book publishing, draw others. The boundaries are
not, however, so distinct, as even some of the pseudo-academic features in *Dream*, in
particular the sidebar commentary from the actors, seem fan-directed. Flockhart's
"annotations" illustrate such fan appeal –"As long as people are being born and having
children, and falling in love and getting married, and dying, then Shakespeare is
relevant" (Hoffman 1999: 45). Despite the academic format, these comments in the
margins are star blurbs rather than annotations of interest to scholars or film critics.

Screenplay editions stage the film for the reader's gaze, most obviously in the more
heavily visual screenplay editions, like *MND*, *Prospero's Books*, and Taymor's coffee-
table book, *Titus*. In these books, the glossy paper and non-standard size of the pages
are bibliographic elements of the text that signal the predominantly pictorial appeal
of these screenplays. However, even those screenplay editions which stage themselves
as more explicitly academic – say, Trevor Nunn's *Twelfth Night: A Screenplay*, published by Methuen or W. W. Norton's many Branagh screenplays – typically include
images; however, often those pictures do less to display the action in the film than to
offer the iconic images of the actors involved. The Norton screenplay for *Much Ado
about Nothing* even includes a section of such shots as its cast list. These "headshots"
are quite similar to those on theatrical playbills, another under-examined printform
that can enrich our understanding of the interactions between author/auteur, text, and
performance. As a result, the Shakespearean screenplay edition, whether inclined
toward an academic readership or not, is an insistently hybrid form; it combines, at
the very least, language and image. These texts always prove McGann's contention
that "all texts, like all other things human, are embodied phenomena, and the body of
the text is not exclusively linguistic" (1991: 13).

Promotion to the general audience, listed so casually above, in fact interpellates the
presumptive average filmgoer into one of the positions enumerated above: as academic, film buff or fan. However, what exactly the text promotes beyond itself is not

entirely self-evident. Although such editions are typically in the works or planned during film production, they rarely if ever appear before the film. As a result, since they are published with or after the film's release, the film would seem to generate consumption of the text rather than the other way around. Printed screenplays thus occupy the opposite position from the shooting script which the screenwriter produces before filming and may revise during production. To put it another way, an interest in Julie Taymor's, or Kenneth Branagh's, or Ian McKellen's Shakespearean film drives the purchase of the screenplay editions.

Elaborate screenplays like Taymor's hardcover, oversized, and extravagantly illustrated *Titus* or, more modestly, Hoffman's *Dream* can serve as a kind of postproduction promotion of a film whose box office takings fell short of expectation (see Burt 2001). Nonetheless, using the screenplay to promote the film seems to be the exception rather than the rule. Instead, filmgoers in the several different audiences purchase the screenplay because they want to work with, analyze or re-experience a certain film in a different form or because they are or have become fans of a particular cinematic artist.

Very early screenplay editions of Shakespeare are particularly interesting in this regard since the films themselves were not so readily available to audiences after the film's initial release as they now are on video and DVD. These texts, like the later counterparts, often reveal as much about the contemporaneous conditions of stage and film as about the actual productions. George Cukor's (1936) film of *Romeo and Juliet* produced a screenplay edition as well: *Romeo and Juliet by William Shakespeare: A Motion Picture Edition, Illustrated with Photographs*. This text claims Cukor's film as "the first serious attempt to give, with all the scenic, histrionic, and artistic resources of Hollywood a cinematic version of one of Shakespeare's great tragedies" (*Romeo and Juliet* 1936: 271). The elaborate and highly textual structure of the "motion picture edition" lives up to this announced seriousness in the film.

In addition to a smattering of still photographs from the film (a very early version of the visual cast list), this screenplay edition includes both "Romeo and Juliet, by William Shakespeare" and "Romeo and Juliet: The Scenario Version." The three major actors get their say in chapters about the characters they play as do the director, the "screen playwright," the art director, and both "fashion designers" who worked on the film. The table of contents for the screenplay in effect mirrors the cast and production list, with each "chapter" falling somewhere between two and four pages. This grand tour of possible perspectives on the film production follows the doubled text of the tragedy and precedes the closing chapter of the book, intriguingly and oddly titled "A Preliminary Guide to the Study and Appreciation of the Screen Version of Shakespeare's *Romeo and Juliet*."

This "motion picture edition" concludes so paradoxically because it incorporates, as its publishers note, the "study guide, of which some half-million copies will be distributed in secondary schools throughout the country ... included here to demonstrate to the reader the efforts that major motion picture companies are expending to stress the educational features of their products" (*Romeo and Juliet* 1936: 270). While this publisher's note praises the included study guide, Max J. Herzberg's

Foreword to the study guide also lauds the "beautiful edition of both play and photoplay issued by Random House" and identifies its and the screenplay edition's audience as "students of the screen" (*Romeo and Juliet* 1936: 272). The study guide itself oscillates back and forth between academic materials (Shakespeare's sources, the theatrical history of the play and Shakespearean language) and film features (photoplay and sound). Clearly, creating study guides for Shakespearean films is neither a recent website phenomenon – exemplified in New Line's *Twelfth Night* site (www.flf.com/twelfth/index.html) or the site for *Looking for Richard* (www.r3.org/pacino/lesson1.html) – nor merely a contemporary promotional technique for drawing academic attention to Shakespearean cartoons or TNT special films like *The King of Texas*. This blend in such a very early Shakespearean screenplay edition demonstrates the consistently mixed form and multiple audiences addressed by the screenplay edition while also revealing that the academic audience has been key from the beginning.

Despite these continuities, screenplay editions, including the earliest, emerge from particular moments in the history of film production/reproduction and in the history of publishing. The relatively recent access to film performance on demand serves as an important context for late twentieth- and twenty-first-century screenplay editions. Now, with the ascendance of film as an art form, possibilities for purchase, private viewing and even piracy constitute the potential and the hazards of the film performance industry. Now that it is as easy to buy the DVD as to buy the screenplay, what does the text have to offer that is distinct from (re)viewing the film? This particular kind of promotion in print exposes an evolving relationship between Shakespearean texts, film and their audiences.

Shakespeare, Now a Major Motion Picture

The screenplay editions' complex paratextual and bibliographic features reveal two significant purposes related to the promotional cycle I have already outlined here: full material use (and reuse), and creation of an historical record. The first may seem less important, but its effects are provocative because of the ways these materials are represented as text. Current Shakespearean screenplay editions typically make as full use as possible of all the work that went into the film production, the seven-tenths of the iceberg that is not discernible as separate efforts in the film as released. For example, Hoffman's *Dream* screenplay offers "Readers . . . the rare opportunity to see production designers' drawings of sets and costumes and to peruse art by Moreau, Waterhouse, the Pre-Raphaelites, and the ancient Etruscans alongside shots from the film that these pieces inspired. Scores of sumptuous photographs accompany the text" (www.amazon.com/exec/obidos/ASIN/0061073563/qid=979916268/sr=1-3/ref=sc_b_3/107-0166163-1723735) (Figure 8.1).

Hoffman's set images, artistic inspirations, costume designs and so forth provide the backdrop to the elaborate typeface of the published script and thus position the

FIGURE 8.1   Michael Hoffman, screenplay for *William Shakespeare's A Midsummer Night's Dream*, 1999
Screenplay reprinted with permission of HarperCollins. *The Evening Star* (top right) by Edward Burne-Jones, 1870 (gouache), private collection / www.bridgeman.co.uk

language of the play, visually decorative in its own right, superimposed on the film's visual choices. Similarly, Greenaway's screenplay edition of *Prospero's Books* includes descriptions, design and images from all of the 24 books seen so swiftly in the film as well as story boards of the film's narrative, but these design features stand on their own in the book. In a screenplay edition, the actors' literal words from the production most often appear in the context of editorial decisions about including or excluding images, choices that signal on the page the relative significance of the verbal text of Shakespeare's play.

At the same time, almost all screenplays offer a typeset version of the working typed screenplay with filming directions, often with formatting on the page that announces the text's relationship to film. Even the screenplay edition of the BBC *Twelfth Night* warns the reader that "these texts with theatrical divisions into scenes and acts are supplemented with their television equivalents. In other words, we are also publishing the television scripts on which the production was based" (*Twelfth Night* 1980: 9). The introductions recount the labors and vicissitudes of financing and moments of creative inspiration for filming. Both the hidden work and, in many cases, the not-so-visible participants in construction are unveiled in the most thorough screenplays. Published screenplays thus implicitly often critique the auteur/actor promotion they seem at the same time to embrace.

While the communal efforts of film definitely receive acknowledgement, more cynical readers might find that the occasionally self-laudatory tone in these editions reads like self-promotion. This observation helps to explain the screenplay edition's position in the promotional cycle, late enough only to be promoted by the film or possibly to inspire video purchase. For, while the screenplay appears too late to sell the film, they nonetheless serve as an interest-generating mechanism for the performers and directors; consequently, screenplays reanimate the merchandising cycle and create interest in the directors and performers, future productions and even future Shakespearean performances.

Certainly Branagh's array of screenplay editions, with their ever more elaborate packaging and contents, promote the subsequent Branagh Shakespearean films *and* screenplay editions. Branagh's growing stature as a Shakespearean film director both generates and justifies the increasingly complex and expensive screenplay texts. The screenplay edition of Branagh's *Henry V*, first published in 1989 by Renaissance Films and later republished and possibly augmented with extensive photographs by Norton in the first American edition in 1997, includes only a brief introduction and scattered images from the film. His text for *Much Ado About Nothing*, subtitled *The Screenplay, Introduction, and Notes on the Making of the Movie*, also offers a synopsis of the plot and two pictorial "essays" on "The Film" (in color) and "The Shoot" (in black and white). Branagh's *Hamlet*, published as a glossy illustrated hardcover (no dust jacket), includes the *very* long text as well as the introduction, cast list, brief explanation of "The Choice of Text" (Branagh 1996: 174), the "Film Diary" and quite an elaborate photo-essay on the film. Branagh's screenplay editions alone demonstrate a competitive marketing acceleration of including extra materials in ways that recall the performance editions of the nineteenth century, with their ever-more-complex use of textual materials to invoke the proximity between the edition and the production (Osborne 1996: 32–42). However, the materials available from film productions currently as well as the publishers' capabilities to include these materials test the apparent boundaries between print and performance. In fact, the potential for the texts to be more than typographical is significantly expanding.

Such recycling of performance materials broadens the appeal of the screenplay itself to its component audiences by making use of the ancillary products of film and wresting financial support from those products (however slight might be the monetary rewards of these publications). In this recycling, screenplays differ dramatically from other promotional merchandising. Toys based on children's films are frequently new products, created in relationship with the films/cartoons. While this kind of promotion recycles only the image and some plot elements, screenplay editions re-structure the shooting script through typesetting, superimposed images, and so forth, as they also reuse and make visible the film's means of production. As a result, their production as *texts* becomes the crucial factor in defining the cultural work done by these books. The relative invisibility of the screenplay edition for film theory and criticism derives from its insistent textuality, in the same way that Horne (1992) argues that the shooting script suffers obscurity because of an ingrained assumption that film utterly supersedes text to the extent that pre-existing writings for the film are irrelevant.

The screenplay editions have the unintended effect of showing just how much of the creative process of film performance occurs on paper. The oral description of the books Greenaway wants for his film must take the form of drawn designs before they can be realized on film; the ideas McKellen discusses with Loncraine and others about how to open the film must appear in the shooting script before they can be translated into images and into the screenplay edition. Letters, contracts, and shooting script revisions are all obvious written components of film performance; the collaborative, even "oral" nature of film production requires a textual record. Screenplay editions also insist that the visual components necessary to create a film performance are also textual; this is the cumulative effect of set designs, production stills, story boards and the compiled images, or photo-essays, that the screenplay edition incorporates. The text, to be blunt, is not just "words, words, words" but the material form those words take, the visual images incorporated therein, and in fact any feature related to the performance that can be committed to a flat, reproducible surface.

In fact, the "photo-essays" are often just as interpretive as the introductions in presenting carefully chosen visual moments that invoke the kinetic movement of performance. In Branagh's *Hamlet*, for example, like the other Norton texts, inset images represent the intent of the cross-cut reaction shots in the film performance. Thus the picture of *The Mousetrap* includes Hamlet and Ophelia, Rosencrantz and Guildenstern's glance back at Hamlet, and in the crucial layout space of the upper right corner, the largest inset image – Claudius's look of shock and guilt. This image demonstrates that the screenplay edition reuses visual materials as carefully as it reconstructs the written materials.

As McGann has suggested, every text records editorial choices that arise from interpretive assumptions; we must recognize this fact and attend to these interpretations, registered especially in the screenplay editions' bibliographic codes. Ultimately, the printed text itself is a material, historically positioned *event* rather than the supposedly transparent rendering of "the poem," "the play," or, in the case of the screenplay, "the film." In this view of the published screenplay, text resembles performance more than differing from it. The screenplay edition establishes itself as an event, a material performance which occurs within a particular context of available production modes and offers both repeated experiences and, paradoxically, limited availability due to small print runs.

Notes on the Making of the Movie

This understanding of the text as event becomes still more complex, oddly enough, in the most critically (and high-mindedly) important purpose the authors claim for these texts: to record and justify both the textual and the cinematic choices in filming. This historical function seems to insist on performance and text as distinct entities. The text we now hold in our hands can offer, as Ian McKellen's Introduction does, several revisions of the film opening in one place. Kenneth Branagh can explain the history of his involvement with *Hamlet* that led to his particular choice to film the "entire" text. His screenplay edition can augment the "history" offered in the introduction with a Film Diary, recorded by Russell Jackson and thus authorized as grist for the academic mill.

Two crucial features emerge from this self-conscious production of history. The first is an almost unconscious appeal to text as a way of constructing and stabilizing the authority of a given film performance, especially by supplying academic paratextual materials. The screenplay is often presented as a blueprint, rounded out with entertainment value. As Peter Greenaway notes of his screenplay edition, "The film-script is very detailed. Its ambition is to inform everyone who has to use it – from those raising money to finance the film, to actors and extras, camera crew, costume designers, picture-researchers, painters, carpenters, set dressers ... Since the reading of scripts can be tedious, there is some evidence it is written to be entertaining" (1991: 12). The information offered extends well beyond anything actually realized in the film, including descriptions of smells as well as visual inspirations. On the other hand, the more materials these published screenplays introduce to recuperate and invoke performance, the more likely that those materials will be subsumed into established textual and even academic forms. The annotated screenplays as diverse as those by McKellen and Hoffman use a classically academic split page to annotate the text with fan detail and film facts.

The screenplay edition's textual self-consciousness leads to a second, more interesting result: Shakespearean screenplay editions frequently struggle with the relationship between Shakespeare as text, filmed Shakespeare, and Shakespeare in stage performance (especially in the cases where the film was inspired by a stage production). In his screenplay edition of *Twelfth Night*, Trevor Nunn uses his introduction to explain that, "as a direct result of the test-screening process ... I was asked to provide a form of voice over introduction or explanation to ease the audience more comfortably into the story" (1996: xv), and then to reveal his reluctance to ventriloquize Shakespeare in offering the prologue speech. The closing of his introduction makes explicit the self-exculpatory mode: "so, this concludes my confession; I resisted; I wept; I tampered" (1996: xvi). In its historical mode, the screenplay edition directly engages crucial relationships and tensions between stage and film, performance and print, screenwriters and "the playwright."

Ian McKellen records similar anxieties about cutting and amending *Richard III*: "Not having him [Shakespeare] present to consult, I think of his having just left the rehearsal-room, soon to return with the gentle query I've sometimes heard from living playwrights: 'What the hell do you think you are doing to my play?'" (1996: 15). The screenplay edition even closes with a visual reminder of this issue in the line-drawn cartoon of Shakespeare, using McKellen's imagined question as the caption. In the course of his Introduction, McKellen has also justified his changes by reminding us that all stage productions alter Shakespeare's texts and always have. His Introduction and, indeed, the text as a whole invokes a stage history of cutting and changing *Richard III*. As McKellen points out, directors always rework a printed version in performance, but, as the published screenplays demonstrate, the reworking occurs both in performance and on the page.

Frequently, where a director or actor uses both stage and film in performing Shakespeare, print (in the form of the screenplay edition) becomes a crucial locus for defining the relationship between live and recorded performance. Ian McKellen's Introduction sets up this function when he discusses his reasons for working toward a film production, founded in his desire for a production of *Richard III* that would endure beyond "the fading memories of those who were there in person"(1996: 7). As he explores the options, he clearly distinguishes between an academic record and a performance:

> The most obvious way of preserving a live performance is the least satisfactory. Our Richard III had already been fixed for posterity on 26 May 1992, when three cameras were let into the Lyttleton Theatre, as part of the British Museum's experiment in saving plays for the future, by recording them during a scheduled public performance. It was agreed that the three separate videotapes would never be edited and could only ever be viewed simultaneously by a visitor to the Museum in Covent Garden. The adjacent screens show the full stage, the principals in each scene, and a close-up of whoever is speaking, so that the viewer, rather like a theatre audience, can "edit" the production, by switching attention between the three images. This triple record may be adequate for academic study, visually augmenting the stage-manager's prompt-book that tabulates the actors' moves. It does not, unfortunately, capture much of the impact of the original occasion. (McKellen 1996: 7–8)

The films of his RNT *Richard III* available at the Theatre Museum are, in a sense, the recording of theatrical performance for academic purposes; the film, *Richard III*, stands as an independent artistic product, a performance in its own right that, while in no way reproducing the stage production, nonetheless claims to capture its "performance" in more vital ways.

His commentary reveals several interesting assumptions. First, the impulse to capture a performance recalls Richard Burton's rather bored account of the revolutionary technique of "Electronovision" that will make live performances, like his 1964

Hamlet, available as events for a more general audience. His interview and promotional TV spot for the technique are included in the newly released DVD of this production, now indeed "fixed for posterity," or so it seems. The "electronovision" *Hamlet* recorded the stage performance and sought to reinstate the performance as a limited access event – a sort of early pay-per-view – but it has now become a film record of the performance, despite Burton's objections. In contrast, the decision to create the multiple archived videotapes of McKellen's *Richard III* embraces the principle of a film record; its material strategies seek to reproduce the choice of perspective that a live theatre audience apparently has and film audiences implicitly do not. Both McKellen's Introduction and the Burton DVD announce their efforts to wrestle with the problem of "fixing" live performance so that its peculiar features are still accessible even though now recorded.

Second, McKellen's Introduction explicitly engages (and dismisses) academic interest in performance. Such study is relegated to the multi-video experience of a scholar who must visit Covent Garden and watch unedited videotapes. That experience, with the appropriate documentation of the prompt-book, serves well enough for the academic but cannot supply the "impact of the original occasion." What supposedly *can* supply that impact is the carefully cut and spliced film production, supplemented by this screenplay. Note that in both cases filmed performance unites with text, even though the scholar watching the videotapes and reading the promptbook seems to have direct access to the "raw data" and simultaneously, apparently as a result, to miss the "impact."

Third, half-hidden in this account are the structures of textuality that seem inevitably to accrue not only to the screenplay edition, but also to the filmed performance. The three videotapes are "unedited" by those taping the live performance, but the viewer, always offered all three at once, must "edit" as the theatre audience does. In the context of the videos McKellen discusses and dismisses here, the "editing" could equally well invoke film editing; indeed it models the spectator's theatrical attention on film editing, as though watching a play involved the selection of perspectives, of different camera shots. Though McKellen brackets academic interest and doesn't even mention the written text as a possible mode for preserving the "impact of the original," his Introduction and his screenplay edition cannot avoid their implication in printed text and even in academic editing, particularly since his text is "annotated." Moreover, his account of creating the film is a history of writing, revision, and editing.

This self-conscious history-production serves as the most useful feature of the screenplay editions for Shakespearean critics of film, yet we often assume that screenplays and their introductions offer transparent access to film performance. Russell Jackson's promisingly titled essay, "From Play-script to Screenplay," does not actually address either the shooting script or the screenplay edition; his argument examines how the play-script evolves in its reincarnation into film performance (Jackson 2000). In "From Shakespeare's Text to Branagh's Script" (2000: 92–115), Sarah Hatchuel analyzes the nuances of Branagh's development of Shakespearean film scripts by consistently citing the subsequently published screenplay editions. The convenience of these editions, which offer useful page references and commentary, outweighs the fact that the published editions are not the same as the scripts used and revised in the course of filming. McKellen's descriptions of the three alternate openings he wrote for *Richard III* or a cursory comparison of the typed first draft of the screenplay for Hoffman's *Dream* with the published texts clearly indicate the distance between the working script under development and the screenplay as finally published. The screenplay edition is neither a fixed map for performance nor a complete record – it does both more and less.

At the same time that the screenplay edition includes the excess of film production and supplements the film with commentary and script alternatives, it necessarily offers a less-than-complete account of the filming itself. For example, when Ian McKellen reveals that he finished the manuscript for the screenplay edition on the same day that Loncraine completed editing of the film, this coincidence effectively insures that the text cannot be a fully accurate representation of the actual film production, since it cannot include crucial final film editing. Nor can it represent the screenplay in use, since that text has now been refashioned.

All screenplay editions, in fact, must misrepresent the film production process because they supply their versions of the shooting script in an order allied to the film's final edited version. As critics like early Walter Benjamin have pointed out, the actual performance/production of film scenes rarely matches the sequence in the final cut of the film (Benjamin 1992). Branagh's screenplay edition of *Hamlet* exposes but does not fully represent this disparity by including Jackson's "Film Diary." The screenplay text of *Hamlet* more or less matches up with the film itself, not including final edits, but Jackson's account of the production makes it very obvious that the process of filming occurred out of sequence.

At the same time, screenplay editions can simply omit interesting or significant production features. While working on Trevor Nunn's *Twelfth Night*, I went to the film repeatedly and, at the third viewing, noticed that Imogen Stubbs appeared as Sebastian arguing with Feste in a long shot. After viewing the film again to look for such substitutions, I discovered several and wrote Trevor Nunn to inquire about the strategy. He acknowledged the twin exchanges I had noticed and added that, "There were several more … but they would take a research grant and more time than I can afford to discover them" (Nunn, personal communication, May 8, 1997). Nunn cannot give details in the screenplay edition that he does not have. However, the text does not even mention the doubling at all, so that it simply does not record the director's strategy of implanting "swift physical images on the collective retina of the audience so that the final moment of reunion would be credible and moving" (Nunn, personal communication, May 8, 1997).

Though screenplay editions offer a version of production history, now augmented and represented visually on DVD screenplays, those versions emerge through the director's or screenwriter's perspective. When a published screenplay does present alternate viewpoints, as in Branagh's *Hamlet* where his introduction and Russell

Jackson's "Film Diary" offer different accounts of the film, the relative authority of the various voices inevitably prioritizes those accounts. When readers/reviewers praise McKellen's breezy, welcoming style, they also inadvertently point out that his style and chosen anecdotes bias the history he provides. To the extent that the actor, director, or screenplay author has unusual access to the detail of production, his or her perspective proves extremely valuable. To the extent that the screenplay functions as self-promotion, the author may consciously or unconsciously limit the information he or she shares. Even more significant, developing the screenplay edition while producing the film creates its own biases. Russell Jackson, for example, served as both the literary consultant and the "film diarist" for Branagh's *Hamlet*. The more detailed the planning for the text, the more likely its anticipated publication could influence the production in process in complex ways.

I would not argue that Shakespearean film scholars rely too much on published screenplays. However, these texts do bear a complex relationship to film performance that we must acknowledge and contextualize whether we are examining the record of the history of the filming or tracing the creative process of transforming Shakespeare's plays into film scripts. The published screenplay cannot serve merely as the established history of the performance, a straightforward record of the creative process or even, as Olivier's screenplay edition of *Henry V* suggests, "a model of how to adapt a classic stage play to the needs of cinema" (Olivier 1945: iii).The dual filters of material access and invested perspective determine what is available in the published screenplay.

Moreover, as limitations on reproducibility diminish, underlying interpretive assumptions become still more important. For example, although lyrics, language and musical scores can appear in the screenplay, sound itself does not as yet. Although some film tie-in texts for children's cartoon features employ microchips and speakers so that their readers can press a section of the page and hear snippets of the productions' soundtrack, such books are considered "toys" and their mechanisms (and complicated production) place them outside the screenplay's current publication features. As a result, including the aural components of performance takes a backseat to the visual in current screenplay editions, but those circumstances could easily change.

The screenplay edition is grounded in its temporally-bounded materiality, limited and enabled by the technologies of production which allow it to occur at a specific time and in a particular form. However, its re-iterability, replication and seeming permanence distinguish it from performance less and less. In defense of this rather odd assertion, I would point out that the two features that performance claims over text – immediacy of presence and visual, kinetic appeal – are aspects which textual production, and its digital analog, the DVD, are now testing to the limit. The immediacy of the actors' auras has been supplanted by the production of the star, an arguably illusory or hollow version of presence that replaces the immediate presence of the actor and his/her aura (Dyer 1986). On DVD, the print annotations to the screenplay become filmed interviews and excess performances available in the film of trailers, outtakes, and so forth. Even as the limits set by available methods of production become more and more permeable, perspective and vested interest will remain an issue.

Now Available on DVD

As DVD films begin to incorporate textual features as well as sectioning the film into scenes (and sometimes even chapters!), they begin to subsume the screenplay features and "re-textualize" film performance. DVD Shakespearean performances potentially offer a new version of the published screenplay, one that includes both performance and commentary as performance. This important shift has already occurred in the case of Kenneth Branagh's films: his recent film of *Love's Labour's Lost* is his first Shakespearean production to generate a DVD edition but no published screenplay.

Widespread current access to the digital technology of reproduction, coupled with the available extra space available for recording materials on the DVDs, has encouraged producers to enhance their DVD versions of Shakespearean and other productions with added materials not available on the older-format versions on videotape. In this way, DVD designers draw audiences by providing outtakes, theatrical trailers and cut scenes like those on Branagh's *Love's Labour's Lost*, a film class with Julie Taymor on the DVD *Titus*, interviews and commercials by Richard Burton extolling "electronovision" with his *Hamlet*, interviews with actors and directors, and theatrical trailers. These added materials, presented in the form of performance, nonetheless draw on and extend the promotional strategies and, more important, the textual structures I have been exploring in the published screenplays. These filmed introductions and annotations remain closely linked to their print counterparts and consequently draw attention to the close relationship between print and filmed performance. In effect, the paratextual (a.k.a. verbal) additions to the screenplay edition blend into bibliographic coding of the visual reproduction, the extra-linguistic features of such editions.

The most overt signal of this relationship lies in the Menus included in every DVD to allow the viewer to start watching the film *in medias res*. Unlike videotape, DVD allows the viewer to open up the production at any point. This ability, invaluable to teachers trying to show an illustrative scene or scholars working with sections of performance, generates a restructuring of what film performance can be. As we have all no doubt noticed, DVDs are cued so they can start at any of a series of scenes, or even more revealingly, chapters. Whichever term a Shakespearean DVD uses, the scene/chapters are most often textually-based; on Shakespearean DVDs, these sections often have illustrative and sometimes distinctively un-Shakespearean titles. Furthermore, they functionally fragment a continuous performance to offer an alternative print-style way to "read" a film. In effect, DVD chapters imply page numbers as they point explicitly to their alliance with printed texts, to book-like features including chapter titles and tables of contents.

This segmenting is not new to film performance which has always consisted of potentially countable frames. However, the DVD format records the film performance, as most texts are recorded now, in digital form; even more important, that underlying common register of data results in a textualization of performance, or more accurately the revelation that film has always already been a text, so long as we accept McGann's assertion that text has always been more than linguistic. At the same time, this digital commonality enables the cinematic reworking of textual forms, like annotation. In many recent DVD editions, including the *Macbeth* adaptation, *Scotland, PA*, the DVD edition offers viewers the opportunity to watch the film but hear an alternate soundtrack – the director's or actor's commentary about the ongoing action and production choices. This strategy translates the type of ongoing commentary Ian McKellen registers in side-by-side print form into a disjunction of sound and image in performance. In this annotative format, the commentary aligns with the visual enactment, not the language of the production, a particularly interesting situation for Shakespearean films since Shakespeare's verbal text could disappear entirely. These moves to DVD, with its combination of paratextual and bibliographic codes, drive home the point that the film terms like "editing" and "print" have always made, slyly undercutting the opposition between print and film performance.

Like any edition, the DVD proceeds from editorial and material choices that arise from an invested point of view, at the least, and an underlying interpretation at most. The added material may serve as post-production aggrandizement and marketing, as Richard Burt suggests of the *Titus* DVD (Burt 2001), or it may offer to make performance permanent or to provide access to genuine orality, as Richard Burton's commentary on *Hamlet* seems to promise. Still more interesting in the ontological status of performance are the inclusions of cut scenes, like those that Branagh's *Love's Labour's Lost* supplies on DVD. Those scenes are clearly both part of the envisioned film and integral to the actors' experience of performing Shakespeare's comedy: the meeting with the Muscovites, the courting of the woman with the wrong token, and the Pageant of the nine Worthies, complete with the announcement of Jacquenetta's pregnancy contribute to overall characterization and plot even when they do not appear in the final version of the film. These scenes are simultaneously part of the DVD *Love's Labour's Lost* and excluded from the film performance. Their presence on the DVD both underscores and undoes the power of editing in creating film performance.

We need to examine the "editorial" choices of DVD Shakespeares in light of the arguments I have been advancing about the published screenplay. By exploring the interactions of print and performance, between screenplay edition and DVD, we can appreciate both the persistence of print forms and the shifting contexts for both performance and text. We can more accurately assess and use both film reproductions and screenplay editions. Just as important, we can rethink the pervasiveness McGann attributes to the textual condition. The evolution of screenplay editions and their emergence into new digital formats require that we explore what we might call the cine-textual condition.

References and Further Reading

Benjamin, Walter (1992). "Art in the Age of Mechanical Reproduction." In G. Mast et al. (eds.) *Film Theory and Criticism: Introductory Readings*. New York: Oxford University Press.

Bevington, David (ed.) (1993). *Much Ado about Nothing, Now a Major Motion Picture by Kenneth Branagh*. New York: Bantam Books.

Branagh, Kenneth ([1989] 1997). *William Shakespeare's Henry V: Screenplay and Introduction by Kenneth Branagh*. New York: W.W. Norton, Inc. (1997 reprint of 1989 Renaissance Film Company edn.).

Branagh, Kenneth (1993). *Much Ado About Nothing, by William Shakespeare: Screenplay, Introduction, and Notes on the Making of the Movie by Kenneth Branagh*. New York: W. W. Norton.

Branagh, Kenneth (1996). *Hamlet, by William Shakespeare: Screenplay, Introduction, and Film Diary*. New York: W. W. Norton.

Burt, Richard (2001). "Shakespeare and the Holocaust: Julie Taymor's *Titus* is Beautiful, or Shaksploi Meets (the) Camp." *Colby Quarterly* 37: 78–106.

Dyer, Richard (1986). *Heavenly Bodies: Film Stars and Society*. New York: St Martin's Press.

Greenaway, Peter (1991). *Prospero's Books: A Film of Shakespeare's The Tempest*. New York: Four Walls Eight Windows.

Hatchuel, S. (2000). *A Companion to the Films of Kenneth Branagh*. Winnipeg: Blizzard Publishing.

Hoffman, Michael (1999). *William Shakespeare's A Midsummer Night's Dream: Adapted for the Screen and Directed by Michael Hoffman*. New York: HarperEntertainment.

Horne, W. (1992). "See Shooting Script: Reflections on the Ontology of the Screenplay." *Literature/Film Quarterly* 20, 1: 48–54.

Jackson, Russell (ed.) (2000). *The Cambridge Companion to Shakespeare on Film*. Cambridge: Cambridge University Press.

King of Texas. Press materials. TNT productions.

McGann, Jerome (1991). *The Textual Condition*. Princeton, NJ: Princeton University Press.

McKellen, Ian (1996). *William Shakespeare's Richard III*. New York: Overlook Press.

Morsberger, Richard E. & Morsberger, Katherine M. (1975). "Screenplays as Literature: Bibliography and Criticism." *Literature/Film Quarterly* 3, 1: 49–55.

Nunn, Trevor (1996). *William Shakespeare's Twelfth Night: A Screenplay*. London: Methuen.

Olivier, Laurence (1945). *Henry V (Classic Film Scripts)*. London: Lorimer Publishing.

Osborne, Laurie (1996). *The Trick of Singularity: Twelfth Night and the Performance Editions*. Iowa City: University of Iowa Press.

Romeo and Juliet, by William Shakespeare: A Motion Picture Edition, Illustrated with Photographs (1936). New York: Random House.

Taymor, Julie (2000). *Titus: The Illustrated Screenplay*. New York: Newmarket Press.

Twelfth Night: The BBC Shakespeare (1980). London: BBC Inc.

Filmography

King of Texas (2002). Directed by Uli Edel. TNT/Hallmark production, May 2002 airdate.

Love's Labour's Lost (2000). Directed by Kenneth Branagh. Miramax Films, DVD.

Richard Burton's Hamlet (1995). Image Entertainment (Atlantic Programmes, 1964), DVD.

Scotland, PA (2002). Directed by Billy Morrisette. Sundance: Channel Home Entertainment.

Titus: Special Edition (2000). Directed by Julie Taymor. Fox Searchlight Films, DVD.

9
What Does the Cued Part Cue?
Parts and Cues in *Romeo and Juliet*
Simon Palfrey and Tiffany Stern

The Part

When Viola cannot immediately answer a question because it is "out of [her] part," when Flute speaks "all [his] part at once, cues and all," parts are being casually referred to by Shakespeare as the unit of performance. But "part" was not, in the early modern period, simply the role the actor would play. It was the written paper on which the words to be spoken were transcribed. That scribal "part" contained on it everything the actor was going to say, topped and tailed by cues of one to three words from the immediately preceding speech. The actor was to study the cues with the same measure of care – or, as we shall see, perhaps even more – that he bestowed upon his own speeches.

For a number of reasons, actors in the early modern theatre never received the complete text of the play in which they were to perform. It was in no one's interest to write out the entire play time after time: paper was scarce, and producing endless handwritten copies would be laborious, expensive, and unnecessary. Moreover, it would be positively unhelpful to have more copies of a full text in existence than were essential: the more copies in circulation, the more likely that one would fall into the hands of a rival company – or a printer. Yet when printing became faster and cheaper and laws of copyright evolved to protect intellectual property more securely, this same system of transcribing and disseminating parts remained. Even by the eighteenth century, when most plays were published in cheap, accessible editions, actors continued to be given parts (then called "lengths" or "sides"), sometimes cross-referenced to a printed text. The conclusion is irresistible: there was thought to be a virtue in this primitive technology. For both actor and playwright the hand-written part offered possibilities – a practical facility, a communicative economy – that the full text simply did not.

Whether or not Shakespeare was keen to print his plays, he certainly intended to publish (in its sense of "broadcast") his texts in part form. Importantly, the part was the first, and perhaps the only, unit of text Shakespeare actively designed to be examined, meditated upon, enacted – and interpreted. Sustained evidence of the primacy of the part as a mediator of performance comes from play revisions. Often, as in *Hamlet*, revisions occur within a speech so that the cues can be left intact and will not have to be relearned (see Stern 2004: 135–6). Authors revised and restructured along part lines: more significantly, they wrote plays with parts and cues firmly in mind. But we also need to recognize just how intense was an actor's relationship to his part. The actor's part was learned and memorized in private, away from other parts, away from the full text, often in the actor's home at night or early in the morning. "The Player so beateth his parte too him selfe at home, that hee gives it right gesture when he comes to the scaffolde," writes Gosson; Dekker draws an analogy in which the chief actor goes "into his bed-chamber, where he [is] fast enough lockt all night, to rehearse his parts by himselfe" (Gosson 1579, K2; Dekker 1963, II, 345). In Shakespeare's period and beyond, chief actors, having fully learned or "conned" their own parts, seem often to have taken pride in disdaining all else; there are many stories of their refusal to attend group rehearsal, condemning them to know little of the plays they acted in beyond their own texts (see Stern 2000 *passim*). For the actor, the part was everything. If we want a historically and materially sensitive feel for the production of a Shakespeare play, then we need to recover its generation through these fractured texts and solitary practices.

Contrary to widespread assumptions, plenty of actors' parts survive intact. There are 40-odd British professional theatrical parts from the eighteenth century, one Restoration part, four university parts (bound together) from the early seventeenth century, an amateur and a professional part from the sixteenth century, three parts (bound together) from the fifteenth century, three from the fourteenth – and fragments of parts are attached to plays in manuscript. Furthermore, there are abundant extant parts from the continent. Examining these parts collectively reveals that they share an abiding consistency of form, exemplified in the most famous early modern English part, that of "Orlando" in Robert Greene's *Orlando Furioso* (Dulwich MS, see Greg 1922). Owned by the actor Edward Alleyn, this part differs from surviving amateur and university parts of the same period, in which cues are long and the cue-speaker is named. But it is, in look and nature, similar both to later professional parts and to continental professional parts of a comparable date.

In the center of the manuscript part of "Orlando" is the "body" of the text: all the speeches the actor had to learn. Flanking his speeches are the cues – sometimes the words of other characters, sometimes stage directions – with long "tails" extending back into the space occupied by the speeches. The cue-words are aligned to the right of the manuscript, so that the cue-tail and the directions visibly cut across and through the actor's speeches. In professional parts these cues were from one to three words in length, as seen in this excerpt from Alleyn's part, where the cues are "Lords of India" and "to doe":

Twelue peres of fraunce, twelue divylles, whats y^t
what J haue spoke, ther J pawne my sword

to seale it, on the helme, of him that dare
Malgrado of his hono^r combatt me

                                        of
_____Lords Jndi<a
You that so proudly bid him fight
out wth your blade, fo^r why your turne is next
tis not this champion, can discorage me
_____pugnant N. victus
You sir that braued your <c>hevaldry
wher is the honor of the howse of fraunce
_____to doe
ffaire princesse what J may belonges to the
wittnes J well haue hanseled yet my sword
now sir you that will chastyce when you meet
bestirr you french man fo^r Jle taske you hard
_____Oliuer victus
Provide you lordes, determyne who is next
pick out the stoutes champion of you all
they wer but striplinges, call you these y^e pe^rs
hold madam, and yf my life but last it out
Jle gard your person wth the peires of fraunce

Almost as important as what the part includes is what it excludes. Here the "Orlando" part contains a complex fight scene. However, though Alleyn knows who to fight and who will win, he is not told to whom he is speaking, nor who will speak the cues, nor how long he will have to wait to hear them. In the absence of such contextual certainty, the cue assumes enormous significance. It is to this that we now turn.

The Cue

It is difficult to over-estimate the importance of the cue. For the actor, attentive listening on stage was crucial: to miss or mistake a cue was to stop the play:

BOY[ET]:   Why that contempt will kill the keepers heart,
            And quite divorce his memory from his part.
QUEE[N]:   Therefore I doe it, and I make no doubt,
            The rest will [n]ere come in, if he be out.
            (*Love's Labour's Lost*; Hinman 1968: TLN 2041–4; using
            act/scene/line references from Evans 1997: 5.2.149–52)

Such study is still more imperative when rehearsal worked as it did in the early modern theatre: at best one reading of the whole play to some of the company, and then each actor left to learn his part on his own or with limited help. Group rehearsal, when it took place, happened after all the parts had been committed to memory (see Stern 2000: 61–72). A major actor will have picked up the basic story he was in and, knowing which role or roles were his, had a sense of the relationship his part had with others. But, such broad knowledge once granted, it is unlikely that even a run-through would have done much more than whet the curiosity, or provoke the kinds of questions that only subsequent studying of the cued part could help to answer.

However, the cue's importance is far from limited to its practical efficiency. No other bit of the actor's part carries quite the same concentration of information. This might seem unlikely. After all, a cue is severed and brief, shorn of context, and attributed to no one: floating thus in space and time, a cue may well appear to be a thoroughly unhelpful guide to anything. But the cued part lasted for so many years in the form it did because of its omissions and ellipses. Being co-owned by two actors (the one who speaks the cue and the one who hears it), the cue is the hinge between addressor and addressee: though belonging to both, it can be possessed absolutely by neither. Consequently, the cue can uniquely concentrate and animate what is at stake in a specific dramatic moment. It is the cue that grants the part-text its potential to develop a narrative line that is at once simultaneous with and different from that of the play-text.

Moreover, given the way cues were not attributed in the professional theatre, the right-hand "cue-text" had, visually, a unity of its own: it did not seem to be a collection of words spoken by different and separate people (although, of course, it often was in reality). But, though not clearly emanating from anyone, the cue nevertheless has the same range of addressing options as any other dialogical act: it can be interrogatory, provoking, counterpointing, argumentative. Like many other instances of dense wordplay, Shakespeare's more loaded cues not only comment upon their situation but project into future ones, often pointing toward consequences or judgments that are otherwise not yet in play. Cues, then, have to be studied – by us as by the actors – just as carefully as the supposedly less fractured speech-acts that they cue.

As far as the actor is concerned, the cued character (and hence the actor himself) is always at the core. Hence the part can tell the actor – deliberately or by chance – a story that is not quite the same as the story told by the full text: a story that is about him. If we add to this the fact that different cued parts are telling their different stories at the same time, then we might be getting closer to the ways in which the supposedly basic technology of the part helped to facilitate plays of such complex and multiple perspectives. Although a play is a performed event, it is equally a meeting of numerous independent and interlocking parts.

The actors for whom Shakespeare wrote were trained to identify, in the cue, a large matrix of relations and relationships. Again and again, Shakespeare's cues predict or pun upon the speaker or the spoken moment, and resonate with information, instructions, and irony. A part's cues will always, of course, cumulatively give the actor information about his part and its contexts. But some cues do a great deal more.

In particular, cues are likely to be most pregnant with meaning in three situations: in scenes where a character is being introduced; in scenes where a character undergoes radical change; and at moments when the cues are spoken, more than once, in quick succession. Here, we look briefly at instances of all three, limiting our exploration to some parts from *Romeo and Juliet*.

Early Cues

A part's early cues are scripted so as to be interpreted by the actor in simultaneously different ways. They always provide information about the immediate locality of any dialogue and the particular stimulus into speech. Equally, they offer clear guidance concerning characterization, often encapsulating the mode and orientation of a particular role. Huddling slightly aside from the actor's speaking text, such cues offer their own mini-narratives, bearing potentially telling relationships – oblique, critical, contradictory – to the larger narrative of full scene or play.

Romeo's opening speeches leave little doubt about the kind of persona he is to adopt upon entering: languishing in love, he is uninterested in the world outside himself. Since the length and insistent self-reference of Romeo's speeches establish that his dialogue dominates his first scene, in full text it will be clear that Romeo's interlocutor, Benvolio, offers little more than an inquisitive sounding-board for the hero's exultant love-melancholy. A good example is Romeo's manipulation of conceits about time:

BEN[VOLIO]:	Good morrow Cousin.
ROM[EO]:	Is the day so young?
BEN[VOLIO]:	But new strooke nine.
ROM[EO]:	Aye me, sad houres seeme long:
	Was that my Father that went hence so fast?
BEN[VOLIO]:	It was: what sadnes lengthens Romeo's houres?

(TLN 163–9; 1.1.160–3)

Read in part-form, however, and allowing a maximum length of three words to cue phrases, it becomes much more doubtful how securely time is Romeo's servant:

_____Good morrow Cousin.

Is the day so young?

_____new strooke nine.

Aye me, sad houres seeme long: Was that my Father that went hence so fast?

_____lengthens Romeo's houres?

Not having that, which having, makes them short

_____In love.

Out.

_____Of love.
Out of her favour where I am in love.

(TLN 163–73;1.1.159–68)

The cues here establish a series of alternative frames in which to place Romeo's affliction: Romeo's is neither the only timeframe nor the only perspective. The first three cue-phrases propose a subtle movement between three models of temporality ("Good morrow Cousin" / "new strooke nine"/ "lengthens Romeo's houres"). In the first cue, Romeo and the "morrow" arrive together, as though sun and hero are interlinked (by the end of the play "The Sunne for sorrow will not shew his head" TLN 3181; 5.3.306). The second ("new strooke nine"), although pragmatic and situational, establishes the government of clocks as beyond the hero's control. The threat to Romeo's freedom here intimated is then taken up by the third cue ("lengthens Romeo's houres"): Romeo's body cannot control time; instead, it will control him. The differences between cue-text and play-text illuminate one of the play's themes: the clash between rival claims to generic control. The romantic affects of Romeo will be pitted against the tragic effects of star-crossed destiny. Romeo is thus already written as the unwitting victim of time – it will change him, torture him (it "lengthens" him, as though on a rack), and, very soon, kill him.

    The early cues given to Romeo continue in similar counterpointing fashion: here is this "right-hand" cue-text in sequence, shorn of Romeo's speeches, and, again, assuming three-word cues:

_____In love.
_____Of love.
_____rough in proofe.
_____I rather weepe.
_____good hearts oppression.
_____do me wrong.
_____that you love?
_____tell me who.
_____suppos'd you lov'd
_____is soonest hit.
_____still live chast?
_____thinke of her.
_____Examine other beauties[.]

(TLN 170–236; 1.1.65–228)

The chain of cues offers a quizzical and angular corrective to the hero's solipsistic world. These inceptive or initiatory cues – early cues that remarkably often provide the seeds for the character's subsequent development – move from acknowledging that Romeo is "in love" to a brisk, even cynical, narration of the possibilities "of love." If you love – and, assuming a three-word cue, the sceptical "if" is a real presence in cues such as "suppos'd you lov'd" – then make it count, that is, make her have sex with you. Failing this, move on: "thinke of her" – who exactly? – and "Examine other beauties." The effect of the cues is double. First, they succinctly express the prevailing sexual ethos of Verona's young men. Of course in full text this is already apparent: the cues here ensure that the Romeo-actor knows the world he is entering. Second, they hint at what the Romeo-actor may not know: that the love he will not name is indeed a love he can learn to "forget." The cues look ahead to "her" usurpation by some other beauty. This introduction to the Romeo-part is typical: in a part's first scene, cues consistently work to place, furnish, and frame the character.

Transitional Cues

Another important function of cues is to signal transitions in a character's disposition or destiny. Consider Romeo's entrance with Benvolio, Mercutio, and five or six other maskers. His cues (bridging two scenes, again without his text) are:

_____to happy daies.

Enter Romeo

_____and be gone.

_____have you dance.

_____a common bound.

_____a tender thing.

_____to his legs.

(TLN 452–87; 1.3.105–14.1.34)

The cues provide the basic picture: broadly choric, they build up the sense that the masked ball will indeed propel Romeo into some unforeseen "bound" or "dance," egged into action by his friends. But this focus shifts when he refuses to dance, saying "Ile be a Candle-holder and looke on, / The game was nere so faire, and I am done" (TLN 491–2; 1.4.38–9). From this point onwards the cues Romeo receives cease to have him as their clear focus:

_____burne day-light ho.

_____our fine wits.

_____may one aske?

_____and so did I.

_____dreamers often lye.

_____This is she.

_____come too late.

(TLN 496–556; 1.4.43–105)

The Romeo-actor receives a series of instrumental cues, doing little more than oiling the brisk conversation. But, on a deeper level, the phrases also signify that Romeo will no longer be "cued" by his friends. This is signaled, in particular, by a cue that is, again, more striking out of its immediate dialogical context than it is within it: "This is she." For whereas the previous six cues have been traded line-by-line, the Romeo-actor will have to wait for about 40 lines before hearing this cue. Yet the actor does not have in his script either the long wait or the reason for it – that Mercutio is delivering his Queen Mab *tour de force*. Mercutio possesses the stage during his "Mab" fantasy, but, as the cues show, he has emphatically not possessed the hero. Whereas everyone else may be watching Mercutio in astonished awe, the Romeo-actor has to retreat into a lengthy, suspended, and uncertain silence, waiting for the words "this is she." Furthermore, although "this is she" actually refers to Mab, for the Romeo-actor "she" may well set up an expectation that some woman – perhaps the long-awaited Juliet? – is going to enter the scene. Yet Juliet does not appear. Instead, "she" turns out to be his friend's grandstanding flight of fancy. Consequently, Romeo's irritation at Mercutio's endless speech – "Peace, peace, Mercutio, peace," and, tellingly, "Thou talk'st of nothing" – can be all the more pressingly felt by the actor. The part encourages the actor to respond with appropriately urgent exasperation – though not necessarily for the appropriate reason. In turn, because the "she" of Romeo's returning cue is not present on stage, it allows the very next cue he receives, "come too late," similarly to invoke his absent other half. It is precisely because the cues are not satisfied entirely by immediacies that they gather this predictive capability. The cue-text and full-text are working in a subtly distinctive contrapuntal fashion. The effect is to point – for the actor, for the audience – Romeo's decisive entrance into destiny: one that "is she" will also, fatally, come "too late."

Whereas this scene gives transitional cues for the Romeo-part, it gives the first cues for the Mercutio-part. Here too the early cues encapsulate the basic character:

> _____beare the light.
> Nay gentle Romeo we must have you dance.
> _____I cannot move.
> You are a Lover, borrow Cupids wings,
> And soare with them above a common bound.
> _____pricks like thorne.
> If love be rough with you, be rough with love,
> Pricke love for pricking, and you beat love downe,
> Give me a Case to put my visage in,
> A Visor for a Visor, what care I
> What curious eye doth quote deformities:
> Here are the Beetle-browes shall blush for me.
> _____I am done.
> Tut, duns the Mouse, the Constables owne word,
> If thou art dun, weele draw thee from the mire.
> Or save your reverence love, wherein thou stickest
> Up to the eares, come we burne day-light ho.

_____that's not so.

I meane sir I delay,
We wast our lights in vaine, lights, lights, by day;
Take our good meaning, for our Judgement sits
Five times in that, ere once in our fine wits.

_____wit to go.

Why may one aske?

_____dreame to night.

And so did I.

_____what was yours?

That dreamers often lye.

_____dreame things true.

O then I see Queene Mab hath beene with you.
... This is she

_____talk'st of nothing.

True, I talke of dreames ...

(TLN 465–547; 1.4.12–96)

Once again, the cue-phrases give the information "Mercutio" needs to place his part. The cues the actor receives divide broadly into three types: comments from Mercutio's addressor about himself ("I cannot move" and "I am done"); direct questions or responses to Mercutio ("that's not so," "what was yours," "talk'st of nothing"); and statements that offer a more general picture or proposition whose provenance and trajectory is unclear ("beare the light," "pricks like thorne," "wit to go," "dreame to night," "dreame things true"). All three work very precisely toward focusing the Mercutio-part. This is true even of those cues that are self-evidently about his addressor (in both cases, Romeo). For these two early cues set up Mercutio as their counter and opposite: if the interlocutor (Romeo) is "done," Mercutio has barely begun; if he "cannot move," Mercutio will be all animation, hence his impatient responses to Romeo's abject cues: both times he refuses Romeo's sense, transforming the lover's somnolence into category-defying activity (a flying body, a burning daylight) in which sexual abandon (flying Cupid, love sticking up to the ears/arse) is overwhelmed by imaginative intensity. But we should also see how the supposedly neutral (context-free) cues themselves establish Mercutio's antagonistic relationship with others. All of these describe or comment upon Mercutio, even when their function within the full speech has nothing to do with him: "bear the light," "prick like thorn," "wit to go," "dream tonight." Although none of these cues in fact talk "about" Mercutio, they nonetheless place him: he brings to the group light, prickliness, wit, and dream—together, a briskly cumulative "cue" for the part.

However, though in part-terms the cues are all about Mercutio, in full-play terms they are all about Romeo, as the hero bemoans the pain of love. The disjunction between part-text and play-text establishes the terms of Mercutio's jealous role. He will be jealous of his own possession (of wit, applause, eyes, voice); jealous about

Romeo's obsession; anxious to heal both rifts by pushing himself all the more dazzlingly into view – but unable to confess to any of it other than in impossibly masked conceits. The distribution of cues helps place Mercutio's paradigmatic Queen Mab fantasy in an appropriately taut, contested, and needy psychological context. It is therefore interesting that in Q1 Benvolio cues Mercutio's Queen Mab speech with his simple question, "Queene Mab what's she?" In Q2 and F, however, Benvolio's line is absent. Perhaps this is a scribal error: but in the supposedly authoritative text(s), Mercutio's self-fantasy is cued by no one at all – or by no one but Mercutio himself. Indeed, the early cues help to mark the character's defining public aggression and private neediness.

Such careful scripting of cross-purposes has suggestive implications for characterization. The technology used for writing and learning the cued part harnesses and produces the actor's identification with his role. This is not to propose any straightforward line between the actor's ego and emotions and that of the character. Nevertheless, in the disjunctions between play-text and part-text, in the false starts and mistaken attributions that ensue, Shakespeare is often scripting a battle for understanding. If in some sense the actor has to fight for his presence, for integrity, coherence, or acknowledgment, then it is likely that the "character" thereby embodied will give off the sparks of such a struggle. The fact of each role's isolation – that the part is written, transcribed, learnt, and acted as a separate unit – helps to ensure the character's claims to independence. But more than that, it helps to ensure the freestanding status of character itself: in other words, the part makes a claim to its own ontological integrity. This apparently primitive manner of textual circulation becomes a crucial motor of the affective power, integrity, and sophistication of Shakespeare's plays.

Repeated Cues

By "repeated cues" we mean a cue-phrase that is said more than once within a short space of time – usually, though not necessarily, within a single speech. If we take the function of cues very literally, as an actor might who speaks his part absolutely on cue, oblivious to anything else, then the repeated cue means that one speaker will interrupt or talk over another speaker. And what then? The play becomes a shambles, its players at incoherent cross-purposes, unsure who goes first or what comes next? Surely, then, playwrights, particularly playwrights who are also actors, would repeat cues at their peril. But this is not the case. Shakespeare does not often repeat cues, but when he does so the repetition is pointed and plotted. Once noticed by the actor, the repeated or premature cue becomes an instruction – an invitation – all its own.

To illustrate, consider a simple passage that contains repeated cues. We will look at it, first in full, then broken down into the relevant parts. It starts at the midpoint of one of the garrulous Nurse's lengthy speeches. As presented on Folio's printed page it looks like this, save that we have highlighted several moments when the Nurse sends out her cue early:

NURSE:	...the day before she broke her brow, and then my husband, God be with his soule, a was a merrie man, tooke up the child, yea quoth he, doest thou fall upon thy face? thou wilt fall backward when thou hast more wit, wilt thou not Jule? And by my holydam, the pretie wretch left crying, **and said I**: to see now how a jeast shall come about: I warrant, and I should live a thousand yeares, I never should forget it: wilt thou not Jule quoth he? and pretie foole it stinted, **and said I**.
OLD LA[DY]:	Inough of this, I pray thee hold thy peace.
NURSE:	Yes Madam, yet I can not chuse but laugh, to thinke it should leave crying, **and say I**: and yet I warrant it had upon it brow, a bump as big as a young Cockrels stone: a perillous knock, and it cryed bitterly. Yea quoth my husband, fallst upon thy face, thou wilt fall backward when thou commest to age: wilt thou not Jule? It stinted, **and said I**.
JULI[ET]:	And stint thou too, I pray thee Nurse, say I.

(TLN 388–405; 1.3.38–58)

But when we consider the parts of the Old Lady (Juliet's mother) and Juliet we find something rather interesting. Old Lady's part might have looked like this:

_____[and] said I.
Inough of this, I pray thee hold thy peace.

Juliet's part like this:

_____[and] said I.
And stint thou too, I pray thee Nurse, say I.

Both Juliet and her mother have a cue that will lead them to interrupt the Nurse— not separately, as the text suggests, but in unison, and more than once. The only way of preventing this from happening would be to give the two women longer cues. Elongating the cues to "stinted and said I" could prevent mid-speech interruption (where the words are "crying, and said I") but will not prevent the two women from responding at the same time: both share the longer cue, "It stinted, and said I." Indeed, stretch the cues out still longer, creating a six-word cue (thus far exceeding any on record in a professional part), and even that is not much help: "Old Lady" has "foole it stinted ...," Juliet has "Jule? it stinted ...." The rhyme is almost guaranteed to confuse the two actors: it seems near impossible to prevent Juliet and her mother from speaking together. Indeed, given the normality of cues of three or fewer words, the mid-speech interruptions seem similarly plotted. The only other alternative would be to provide the Old Lady and Juliet with indications that they must hear the cue more than once and remain silent before the "actual" cue. That would necessitate adding to their parts something along these lines:

OLD LADY: _____and said I (× 2)
             Inough of this, I pray thee hold thy peace.
JULIET: _____and said I (× 3 and 1/2)
          And stint thou too, I pray thee Nurse, say I.

Any such device requires the writer of the actors' parts (the prompter) first to notice that the cue is repeated in the Nurse's part, then to count up how many times, and finally to mark up the two parts, "Old Lady" and "Juliet," with the extra information: all very troublesome in the hectic theatre of the time. It requires, too, Shakespeare the writer-actor repeating a cue thoughtlessly, oblivious to the difficulties to which it will give rise. This is yet more unlikely. But the strongest argument in favor of the intended repeated cue is that the sense of the play at this point can only be enhanced by interruption. This occurs in two basic ways. First, if it is the Nurse who is interrupted, then the scene's humor is emphasized. She is recalling a story that she has told many times before; indeed, she repeats a familiar cycle of re-telling the story even within her two consecutive speeches. She is thus seen comically to tire one or both of her addressees. No one hears her gleeful reminiscence without escalating exasperation – "inough of this," "stint thou!" Everyone wants the Nurse to shut up. Second, it might be that the two instantaneously "cued" respondents interrupt not only the Nurse, but also each other. Alongside the garrulous humor are terse disagreement, familial tension, and a divisive past and future in miniature.

Let us consider the first option, and assume that the interruption is scripted. We now have actors with very different kinds of information about the scene. The Nurse-actor will see at once that s/he gives out repeated cues, thereby being invited to play with his fellow actors. Perhaps s/he pauses as the first "cue-like" speech is given, letting the other actors begin their interruption before riding over their speeches with her continued text – "to see now how a jeast shall come about," "and yet I warrant . . ." Perhaps s/he lets the actors speak their entire lines before going on to give them the cue again – forcing the entire text once more – and once more still. Repetition enhances both comedy and bathos. In turn, once the Old Lady and Juliet recognize what is happening, they too can "play" the moment. When the Old Lady, for instance, hears her cue, she begins to speak her cued line. What happens when she then hears her cue once more? She has three options. She can stop speaking, wait until the cue has been finished, and start her own cued line again from the beginning. She can simply keep on speaking so that the cueing and cued voices speak over one another. Or she can continue from where she left off, "drip-feeding" her lines every time she hears the cue until the cueing actor indicates to her that she can see her line through. And she can vary one against the other on different days of performance.

Depending on how the actors play one another, the text might go something like:

NURSE:	and said I [pause] –
OLD LADY:	Inough of this, – [JULIET and OLD LADY exchange glances]
JULIET:	And stint thou –
	– to see now how a jeast shall come about: I warrant, and I should live a thousand yeares, I never should forget it: wilt thou not Jule quoth he? and pretie foole it stinted, and said I. [long pause]
OLD LADY:	[pause] Inough of this, I pray thee hold thy peace.
JULIET:	[pause] And stint thou too, I pray thee Nurse, say I.
NURSE:	Yes Madam, yet I can not chuse but laugh, to thinke it should leave crying, and say I [raises warning finger] – and yet I warrant it had upon it brow, a bump as big as a young Cockrels stone: a perillous knock, and it cryed bitterly. Yea quoth my husband, fallst upon thy face, thou wilt fall backward when thou commest to age: wilt thou not Jule? It stinted, and said I.
OLD LADY:	[shouts] Inough of this, I pray thee hold thy peace.
JULIET:	[wearily] And stint thou too, I pray thee Nurse, say I.

Or like this:

NURSE:	and said I [pause] –
OLD LADY:	Inough of this, – [JULIET and OLD LADY exchange glances]
JULIET:	And stint thou –
	– to see now how a jeast shall come about: I warrant, and I should live a thousand yeares, I never should forget it: wilt thou not Jule quoth he? and pretie foole it stinted, and said I. [long pause]
OLD LADY:	[hesitant] – I pray thee … [JULIET and OLD LADY exchange glances]
JULIET:	[hesitant] – I pray thee …
NURSE:	Yes Madam, yet I can not chuse but laugh, to thinke it should leave crying, and say I – [mischievous slight pause]
OLD LADY:	– hold …
JULIET:	– Nurse …
	– and yet I warrant it had upon it brow, a bump as big as a young Cockrels stone: a perillous knock, and it cryed bitterly. Yea quoth my husband, fallst upon thy face, thou wilt fall backward when thou commest to age: wilt thou not Jule? It stinted, and said I. [pause]
OLD LADY:	[long pause] thy peace! Inough of this, I pray thee hold thy peace.
JULIET:	[long pause] say I! And stint thou too, I pray thee Nurse, say I.

The second possibility – that the scene might be setting up Juliet and her mother to be talking to each other as much as to the Nurse – becomes all the more likely once we grant to the players a certain performance-attentive liberty. The moment might even play like this:

NURSE:	… said I –
OLD LADY:	[to Nurse] Inough of this.
JULIET:	[to her mother] And stint thou too.

OLD LADY: [to Juliet] I pray thee hold thy peace.
JULIET: [to Nurse] I pray thee Nurse, say I.

In this scenario, the Nurse's double-cue – to mother and daughter simultaneously – invites their simmering tensions suddenly to boil over. After all, the context of the scene is the mother preparing to tell her unwilling 13-year-old child to "thinke of marriage now." And there is a subdued but uncertain rivalry between the mother and her surrogate, the Nurse ("Nurse give leave awhile … Nurse come backe againe") who has such an easy and affectionate relationship with Juliet. Indeed, the Nurse's reminiscence might have been designed to irritate and rebuke a semi-absent parent. For this reason, many theatre productions choose to play the mother as a nervous and fidgety matriarch, herself abandoned to the altar when a child, at odds with her adolescent daughter and obscurely jealous both of her and of her Nurse.

The opportunities for the Juliet-actor in this scene are still more acute. The cue-effect can give to the player a certain tense alertness to context: s/he knows the role is premised upon filial rebellion as much as love at first sight, and here is her mother, in her very first scene, interrupting a joyous recounting of her past. Looked at in this way, the cue-effect comically foreshadows much greater "extemporizing" – Juliet's disobedience toward the "cues" of her parents – to come. So, Juliet's "Nurse, say I" can be understood as a defiant return of the cue to the Nurse: as though to say "ignore my resentful mother; tell me more of me, but remember that I am no longer the child you speak of." And as she gives the stage back to her Nurse, Juliet's interruption of her mother becomes a preparation to do and be without either of them. For, as we have seen, Juliet could be interrupting the Nurse just as much as her mother is. The Nurse's words are hardly less provoking to the adolescent than to the mother. She repeats the same joke twice, quoting her merry husband to the effect that Juliet will "fall backeward" when she has more wit and comes to age; this when the toddler Juliet has a bump on her brow "as big as a young Cockrels stone." The tone is genially bawdy, but there is at the same time something mercilessly pre-determining about the whole anecdote. For Juliet, her sex is her own to withhold or to give; for the Nurse, it is always, somehow, public. Whichever way we see the Juliet-actor using this gift of a free-floating cued response – as a rebuke to her mother, or to her nurse, or to both – it is Juliet who in every sense possesses the cue-space.

To summarize: there are a number of possible ways of acting, or responding to, a repeated cue. There are always at least two players to take into account: the one giving the repeated cue, and the one (or ones) being cued to speak. Their respective relations to the repeated cue are quite different from one another. Importantly, the cue is always co-owned. Because the actor throwing out the repeated cue will know that he is scripted to do so, he can choose to do so in various ways. He can "play" the moment; he can equally "play" the actor that he is cueing: the repeating cues might be fired out like shots, sudden and stunning; they might be delayed, floating, teasing. It is crucial to any reading of cued parts, and repeated cues within them, that this "foreknowledge" of the actor giving the cues be factored in to possible reconstructions of the dramatic moment.

Linked to this is the fact that the same actor might at one point be the speaker of a repeated cue, and at another point its receiver (perhaps not in the same play, but indubitably in a repertory season). This reinforces the likelihood that, once he hears a cue being repeated, the actor receiving the now "premature" cue will instinctively draw upon the stock of options that experience has taught him. It is difficult to think of a technique more likely to harness the kinds of attention, tension, and responsiveness to nuance that such dramatic moments require. Actors famously need to be "in" their moments, as though surprised by them, to give the play a compelling charge: repeated cues, representing both a practiced array of techniques and an abrupt, serendipitous, or mischievous interruption to expectations, help to make this happen.

Almost always the repeated cue signifies one of a few things: the early delineation of a garrulous, embarrassed or isolated character (usually a fusty or superannuated type); the creation of a "self-speaking" moment, where the actor exists in his own existential bubble and the repeated cue is effectively a self-cue; the pointing of intense conflict between one figure and another; and the "operatic" technique of ascending, usually tragic, climax.

It is in *Romeo and Juliet* that Shakespeare first attempts such tragic effects – indeed affects – through repeated cues: in the scene of mistaken mourning for the presumed-dead Juliet. Of course, this is tragedy with a twist. The heroine is not dead; everyone watching knows it; and so the extravagant mourning is mercilessly ironized. In the "bad" Q1 text, 4.5 is written like this, with repeated cues and communal speaking highlighted in bold:

NURSE:	. . . ah mee, alack the day, some Aqua vitae hoe.
	Enter Mother.
MOTH[ER]:	How now what's the matter?
NUR[SE]:	Alack the day, **shees dead, shees dead, shees dead**.
MOTH[ER]:	Accurst, unhappy, miserable time.
	Enter Oldeman.
CAP[ULET]:	Come, come, make hast, wheres my daughter?
MOTH[ER]:	Ah **shees dead, shees dead**.
CAP[ULET]:	Stay, let me see, all pale and wan.
	Accursed time, unfortunate olde man . . .
	O heere she lies that was our hope, our joy,
	And being dead, dead sorrow nips us all.
	All at once cry out and wring their hands.
ALL CRY:	**And all our joy, and all our hope is dead,**
	Dead, lost, undone, absented, wholy fled.
CAP[ULET]:	**Cruel, unjust, impartiall destinies**
	Why to this day have you preserv'd my life?
	To see my hope, my stay, my joy, my life,
	Deprivde of sence, of life, of all by death,
	Cruell, unjust, impartial destinies.

CAP[sic. Paris?]:	O sad fac'd sorrow map of misery,
	Why this sad time have I desird to see.
	This day, this unjust, this impartiall day
	Wherein I hop'd to see my comfort full,
	To be deprived by suddaine destinie.
MOTH[ER]:	O woe, alacke, distrest, why should I live?
	To see this day, this miserable day.
	Alacke the time that ever I was borne,
	To be partaker of this destinie.
	Alacke the day, alacke and welladay.
FR[IAR]:	O peace for shame, if not for charity ...

It is clear from the Q1 transcription that the scene, as remembered or recorded, involved a variety of cross- and communal-outcries: "*All at once cry out and wring their hands.*" The text even gives two lines that "All cry," perhaps indicating that all the mourners are to intone the words as one; perhaps indicating that each actor is to choose a word or phrase to make his own. But what is abundantly clear is the connection between criss-crossing voices and scripted repeated cues. If the recorder recalls or requires a scene rife with echo and interruption, then he also knows exactly how the parts must be – or must have been – written.

The script of Q2 and F differs in various details, but there the use of repeated cues is even greater:

MO[THER]:	O me, O me, my Child, my onely life:
	Revive, looke up, or I will die with thee:
	Helpe, helpe, call helpe.
	Enter Father.
FA[THER]:	For shame bring Juliet forth, her Lord is come.
NUR[SE]	Shee's dead: deceast, **shee's dead**: alacke the day.
MO[THER]:	Alacke the day, **shee's dead, shee's dead, shee's dead.**
FA[THER]:	Ha? Let me see her: out alas shee's cold,
	Her blood is setled and joynts are stiffe:
	Life and these lips have long bene separated:
	Death lies on her like an untimely frost
	Upon the sweetest flower of all the field.
	(TLN 2596–607; 4.5.19–29)

The words differ from Q1, but the effect is identical. The cue for Capulet to speak, "shee's dead," comes early; it is the Nurse's very first expostulation after his entrance. Consequently, Capulet can be cued to begin his five-line speech the moment that the Nurse begins her speech; Lady Capulet's thrice-spoken "shee's dead" would therefore be not so much Capulet's cue as her echo of the Nurse's early cue. The effect could then be to free both the Nurse-actor and Mother-actor to speak their brief sighs of grief – "she's dead," "alack the day," "deceased," "she's dead" – at any propitious moment during the father's expatiation over the corpse:

> Shee's dead.
> Ha?
> – deceast –
> Let me see her:
> – shee's dead.
> – out alas shee's cold,
> Her blood is setled and joynts are stiffe:
> – alacke the day.
> Life and these lips have long bene separated:
> – alacke the day.
> Death lies on her –
> – shee's dead –
> like an untimely frost –
> – shee's dead
> Upon the sweetest flower of all the field.
> – shee's dead

Of course all sorts of variations are possible: the two women might time their interventions to "answer" Capulet's gradually horrified recognitions; or they might dole them out as though oblivious to his awakening, suspended instead in their own private horror. Either way the cue-effect works to punctuate and counterpoint the father's otherwise potentially stilted and rather academic apostrophizing.

Unique to the Q2/F script is the role of the Nurse in escalating the scale of mourning. She is given a very early cue phrase, thus inviting the subsequent two speakers to join her in a round-robin of woe:

> O wo, O wofull, wofull, **wofull day**,
> Most lamentable day, most **wofull day**,
> That ever, ever, I did yet behold.
> O day, O day, O day, O hatefull day,
> Never was seene so blacke a day as this:
> **O wofull day, O wofull day**.
>   (TLN 2629 34; 4.5.49–54)

As in Q1, the speech that follows is set up with innumerable potential pauses, ripe for interruption.

The distinctive speaking style used by Shakespeare throughout this scene – monotonous, list-like, heavily repetitive – makes much more sense once we identify the cue-technique. And an alternative explanation offers itself as to how Q1's "*All at once cry out* " scene might be intended to be acted/have been acted. For the first of the three individual speeches of misery, Capulet's, is in fact topped and tailed by the same line: "Cruell, unjust, impartiall destinies." In other words, the speech begins with the cue that also marks its end: as soon as Capulet has spoken his first line, the next speaker has been cued. Capulet's five lines might then be interspersed with

Paris's answering – or echoing – five lines. (In turn, the mother's cue, "suddaine destinie," is itself suggested by the final phrase of Capulet's repeated cue, "impartiall destinies." Perhaps she too is cued to chime in simultaneously with her "O woe . . . .")

Played in this fashion, and in either text, the scene is no less ritualized, no less formulaic and ceremonial than a "linear" performance in which actors speak one after another. But it is almost certainly more dramatic, allowing for a mixture of communal ritual and, in its gift to the actor of choice, spontaneity, and improvisation, something closer to the recklessness of grief. The repeated cue-effect can help the actors achieve a scene that is precariously balanced between competing affects – between sincerity and irony, communality and individuality, tragedy and its subversion. The element of hysteria in the mourning keeps us aloof from it; the palpably bad verse can seem to be a marker of blame and even insincerity. But just as the grief is misplaced and embarrassing, it is also genuine and prophetic: Juliet will very soon be dead. To the extent that the misplaced mourning is a burlesque, then it is the violent, carnival-esque precursor to the "gloomie peace" in store. The mingled messages sent out by the cues are the very emotional effects that Shakespeare is orchestrating.

Given this expressive potential, it is unsurprising that Shakespeare uses the material limits of the part not just as a technical challenge, but as a creative catalyst. An actor as well as an author, Shakespeare not only made parts. He was also made by them.

REFERENCES AND FURTHER READING

Allen, Michael J. B. & Muir, Kenneth (eds.) (1981). *Shakespeare's Plays in Quarto: A Facsimile Edition of Copies Primarily from the Henry E. Huntington Library*. Berkeley, CA: University of California Press.

Dekker, Thomas (1963). *The Non-Dramatic Works of Thomas Dekker*, 5 vols, ed. Alexander B. Grosart (1884). New York: Russell and Russell.

Evans, G. Blakemore et al. (1997). *The Riverside Shakespeare*. Boston: Houghton Mifflin Company.

Gosson, Stephen (1579). *The Ephemerides of Phialo*. London.

Greg, W. W. (ed.) (1922). *Two Elizabethan Stage Abridgements: "The Battle of Alcazar" and "Orlando Furioso."* Oxford: Malone Society.

Greg, W. W. (ed.) (1931). *Dramatic Documents from the Elizabethan Playhouses*, 2 vols. Oxford: Clarendon Press.

Hinman, Charlton (1968). *Mr. William Shakespeare's Comedies, Histories, & Tragedies (The First Folio)*. New York: Norton.

Stern, Tiffany (2000). *Rehearsal from Shakespeare to Sheridan*. Oxford: Clarendon Press.

Stern, Tiffany (2004). *Making Shakespeare*. London: Routledge.

Wells, Stanley & Taylor, Gary (eds.) (1987). *William Shakespeare: A Textual Companion*. Oxford: Clarendon Press.

10

Editors in Love? Performing Desire in *Romeo and Juliet*

Wendy Wall

When questions about Shakespeare's text – or texts – become questions about the manuscript – or manuscripts – behind them, we pass, inevitably, into the sphere of desire, the desire for the missing object, which, in certain post-Freudian accounts, defines the nature of desire.

> Goldberg, " 'What? In a Name That Which We Call a Rose' "

"What's in a Name?"

If you open a standard edition of *Romeo and Juliet* and read the ending, what do you find? After a dramatic scene in a dark tomb in which Romeo rashly kills Paris and drinks poison, after Juliet awakes in the arms of her dead lover and stabs herself, and after the Friar scurries away in fright – we find a calm conclusion presided over by the highest state authority. As if ushering in the light of reason, Prince Escalus calls for witnesses, evaluates testimony, announces the truth of the matter, and then declares that punishments will be meted out judiciously. The two noble households reconcile, as Capulet and Montague retrospectively sanction the marriage and agree to build statues memorializing their children. Together the fathers and ruler script a narrative making sense of the violence that has occurred, identifying the deaths of Romeo and Juliet as a familial sacrifice and mythologizing the lovers into a "tale of woe." What we witness is the collective social processing of unruly personal desires, now replaced by a communal desire for a more flexible order orchestrated by powerful men.

But when we turn to the two most popular versions of this story in the twentieth century, films by Franco Zeffirelli (1968) and Baz Luhrmann (1996), we discover quite different endings. In neither is Paris even present at the end, nor is there a clear reconciliation of families or much confidence in the process by which Verona will be restored to order. There is no assessment of evidence, review of testimony, or juridical findings. Instead Zeffirelli substitutes ritual for the unveiling of truth; he shows the families marching two by two into the church at a joint funeral for Romeo and Juliet, hinting through this visual symmetry at a tentative future peace. The parents are prominent in this mournful ritual; Lady Montague is notably *not* dead in the film. Luhrmann, by contrast, focuses on visual excess and irony. His Juliet awakens in the spectacularly candlelit church where she had been married just in time to glimpse Romeo alive. After she shoots herself, Luhrmann monumentalizes the lovers' transcendent passion through flashbacks to previous film moments in which they are vibrant and amorous. The film ends with ironizing television news footage of body bags and police helicopters amid a riotous urban scene. Following a brief emotional venting by Captain Prince ("All are punished!"), an anchorwoman assumes the prince's final choric lines, rendering them as a flat sound bite. The last image is of a television set bleakly losing its signal.

Luhrmann's stylistic choices suggest that his film indicts an ongoing chaotic urban anomie for fracturing the world into consumable and deadly postmodern spectacle, while Zeffirelli accentuates the communal atonement necessary when exuberant youth culture is quashed by rigid social structures (which nevertheless are reasserted in milder form by the funeral procession). Both versions, as Barbara Hodgdon observes of Zeffirelli's film and Peter Hall's stage performances, construct a "sense of ending from textual absence" (1989: 348); that is, both depart from the verbal text, as they frame desire, and its relationship to family and state, differently. Audiences might well ask: Is either version more faithful to the text? Is either authentic? Or are they creative interpretations of a text that needs to be updated over time?

In order to answer such questions, we must first locate *the* text to which later versions can be compared. Where exactly is the text to which performances and films should be faithful or not? When we search for the author's text to serve as our bedrock, we find instead two distinct "originals": the 1597 Quarto and the 1599 Quarto (quartos were cheap – and cheaply-published – books). Neither of the title pages to these early editions bears the name of Shakespeare. Instead, each boasts the book's affiliation to a live performance and to a particular theatre company. Subsequent editions – quartos printed in 1609, 1622, and the version published in the First Folio (1623) – all "descend" from the 1599 quarto (Q2), so there are in fact two early texts that possess "independent authority"(Hoppe 1948: 57). Modern editions of the play, such as the Norton, Riverside, or Arden, all use the second quarto (Q2) as their base text, but even so these editions vary among themselves, each conflating parts of other texts and making emendations differently. Today we commonly think of performances as mutating, while the text remains stable. But is this, in fact, true?

Editors reassure readers that there is really only one legitimate version of *Romeo and Juliet:* the second quarto. Nonetheless, over the centuries editors have failed to offer a consistent story to account for the second quarto's legitimacy. In the nineteenth century, Alexander Pope suggested that the early Quartos were drafts that Shakespeare wrote and later revised (Pope 1821: 7). It follows then that later editions represent the "final intentions" of the playwright, which changed over time (though Pope omitted the parts of even the final version that seemed to him so improper that they must have been added by actors or printers). When editors, in the 1760s, began to question whether the First Folio was based on authorial papers, they ushered in a shift in editorial policy that remained until the early twentieth century. Such skepticism left editors with a desire for a phantasmatic original that they felt could not be retrieved. Their response? They emended at will to clarify and improve the plays for readers.

Nineteenth-century editors hinted that the origins of the first quartos were more scandalous than the theory of authorial revision suggests. The conjecture that Quartos were first attempts by a novice playwright began to take a back seat to the more sensational story of stolen, pirated, or corrupted scripts. Those telling this story usually noted that the First Quarto (Q1) was not entered into the Stationers' Register, the log in which plays were supposed to be recorded. Editors also complained that the halting meter, abrupt dialogue, and abbreviated speeches of Q1 made it too inferior to be even the draft of a great playwright: it simply had to have been doctored, or more likely, misremembered by someone else. These piecemeal ideas came to fruition as a coherent theory in the work of the "New Bibliographers" of the early twentieth century, who argued for a scientific and systematic method for explaining textual variation – one that would look to the practices of Renaissance printers and compositors in order to re-compose a single, coherent, authorial source play.

Brian Gibbons gives the standard line in his Introduction to the Arden edition: "*Romeo and Juliet* Q1 is a Bad Quarto, piratical and dependent on an especially unreliable means of transmission" (2000: 1). Q2, he explains, was based on "foul papers" (a now-lost copy marked up with revisions by the author) and therefore derives from the most authentic source. The earlier Quarto turns out in fact to be a later "pirated" text produced by an actor, a group of actors, or a promptbook keeper who attempted to recreate the script for nefarious purposes. This text is doubly "bad": it is both memorially reconstructed and purposely shortened for touring. Signs of its badness include "anticipations, recollections, transpositions, paraphrases, summaries, repetitions, and omissions" (Gibbons 2000: 2). Q1 is truncated and jumbled because of the faulty memory of actors; a corrupting stage milieu thus has caused the textual dilemma.

W. W. Greg first developed the theory of memorial reconstruction through an analysis of *The Merry Wives of Windsor*, where he elaborated and tested Alfred Pollard's general hypothesis of "bad quartos." Harry Hoppe then offered a book-length argument, in 1948, for how this account specifically applied to *Romeo and Juliet*. In many ways, this was a *tour-de-force* argument, for it sets up an airtight, if circular, set of claims and evidence. Since the text considered to be superior in quality, Q2, is said to derive from Shakespeare's manuscript, all its repetitions and inconsistencies (which in some cases look *exactly* like the problems blamed on faulty memory) are held, counter-intuitively enough, to be proof of an authorial presence. Mistakes in Q1 prove that it is illegitimate; mistakes in Q2 prove that it is authentic. As such, the New Bibliographers are able to preserve the Bard from the apparent evidence of his own texts. The editorial dream of a lost original manuscript is the key phantasmatic linchpin for this theory, for that mythic origin – which we can never access – stabilizes the chaos of texts in their multiple incarnations. There may well never have been a single Shakespearean manuscript version of *Romeo and Juliet*; but if there is to be one, true, Shakespearean text, its absence dictates that editors be creative in reconstructing it.

Recently, scholars have questioned the theory of memorial reconstruction on many fronts. They point out that many texts deemed legitimate weren't listed in the Stationers' Register, so this omission doesn't support a case of piracy. Paul Werstine points to other historical and logical problems, namely that: (1) there is no evidence of actors ever reconstructing scripts in England; (2) the supposed actor-reporters oddly fail to get all of their own lines correctly while they do cite other actors' lines verbatim; and (3) this theory doesn't account for why all editors draw from the "bad" Quarto (the Arden, for instance, uses over 100 variants from the Quarto it denounces as corrupt). Other scholars turn to historical evidence of early modern "habits of thought." The notion of memory routinely assumed by editors is at odds with Renaissance theories of cognition and mnemonic practices. Laurie Maguire points out that Renaissance memory was largely the organized recollection of general events (commemoration) rather than memorization, the literal remembering of exact words; for this was a residually oral culture (1996: 113–46). W. B. Worthen notes the theory's bias against performance as well as its reductive idea of memory:

> In a theatre in which literacy must have been variable (it is not certain, for example, that all of the actors could read their parts, or that they needed to read to learn them), the notion that "memorial reconstruction" is a corrupting influence, rather than the dominant, appropriate, intrinsic means of communication, may be something of an anachronism. (2003: 42)

Both the "good" and "bad" Quartos of *Romeo and Juliet* seem saturated in the oral transmission that New Bibliographers assumed differentiated them.

What we discover when we survey the history of playscripts are editors blinded by a fantasy of textual production based on modern ideas of memory, copyright, intellectual property, and authorship. The drive to establish integrity and singularity – a text anchored through a reconstructed single line of transmission from the writer – is a goal at odds with the realities of theatrical practice in the Renaissance. Modern editors seek to isolate the authorial hand from other influences, but by and large, playwrights in the period did not, and did not care to work in such pristine isolation from their theatrical colleagues. Instead, as Stephen Orgel persuasively argues, a playwright never imagined his script as a finished product but saw it as a working copy to be shaped by numerous hands: the prompter, actors, publisher, censor, later revival actors, and compositors. Instead of corrupting forces obscuring "what Shakespeare wrote," these influences were the expected collaborative steps that enabled a text to take proper form. As Orgel puts it, "The autograph manuscript was where Shakespeare started, not where he ended – the first step, not the final version" (1988: 6). It's not that we can't find the missing original, then; it's that no original truly existed in the way that modern readers expect. Playwriting in the early modern period instead embraced variation, change, and evolution; it often shows a profound lack of concern for intellectual property, fixed origins, or authorial control. In love with a familiar and beloved literary figure, modern editors dream of a definitive *Ur-text*. How could the greatest playwright in English *not* control his own texts? How might he retain his stature if we can't identify any single text to attribute absolutely to him? How could there be two *authentic originals*?

Such questions have not historically bothered directors and performers. That is, theatrical producers have not, on the whole, felt burdened by a need to preserve an original *Romeo and Juliet*. Plays produced shortly after Shakespeare's death, when the theatres reopened after the Civil War in 1660, were extensively rewritten and adapted to suit the tastes and desires of contemporary audiences. In James Howard's 1660s' production of *Romeo and Juliet*, both lovers survive to be reunited. This adaptation was played in repertory along with the tragic version so that audiences could see the lovers live happily ever after one night, and die the next (Loehlin 2002: 7). In 1679 Thomas Otway melded about 750 lines from the 1685 Folio of *Romeo and Juliet* into a Roman political tragedy, *The History and Fall of Caius Marius*, creating a play so hugely popular that it typically displaced "Shakespeare's" version from the stage for 150 years. One of Otway's more durable revisions was the addition of a conversation in the tomb between the lovers. Having Juliet wake up before Romeo dies became standard theatrical practice (audiences shocked by Luhrmann's "innovation" of the ending might be surprised to find that he was repeating a well-worn theatrical convention). In the next century, Theophilus Cibber combined Shakespeare's and Otway's versions with *The Two Gentlemen of Verona*. And the most significant eighteenth-century adaptation, by David Garrick, stripped away much of the play's rhyme, increased its spectacle, and elaborated Otway's added scene in the tomb. Tinkering with the text was standard practice on the stage for over two centuries.

Performances also freely employed stage techniques that flaunted their active reconstruction of the play rather than their faithfulness to an "original" (Loehlin 2002: 7–85). In the nineteenth century, Romeo was more often played by an actress than by an actor, thus inflecting the tale of mythic passion – one of the West's greatest love stories – with homoeroticism. Several prominent performances also used family members in the lead roles. Cibber's decision to play Romeo to his 14-year-old daughter's Juliet added an incestuous tinge to the ill-fated love portrayed in his 1744 production, an inflection evident as well when Sarah Siddons played Juliet in the provinces opposite her brother, John Philip Kemble, later that century. Though Charlotte Cushman restored the seventeenth-century text for her 1845 production, she did so in a performance in which she cross-dressed as Romeo to her sister's rendering of Juliet. The "authenticity" of the "original" text was restored in the same moment that the performance foregrounded Cushman's incestuous cross-gendering of the lead actors. Shifting the template for the family romance and calling attention to the text's malleability was the performance norm for centuries. It is only recently that the "authenticity" of the verbal text (the practice of using scholarly editions based on an original and not adding lines) has become a sacred performance goal, with setting, costume, editing of text, and acting style enabling interpretative freedom.

Recognizing the text's instability is not usually an editorial priority for modern editions. The standard editorial line today – that the earliest though necessarily corrupted copy based on the "original" *must* be identified and preserved – is in fact a relatively recent idea. Earlier editors, throwing up their hands at the mystery of a Renaissance playtext's origin, conceded the necessity of altering the plays for modern publication. But the New Bibliographers of the twentieth century had more faith in scientific method, and, as such, they sought to correct what they saw as previous editors' shocking disregard for proper origins. In doing so, they strikingly echoed the impulses aired in the conclusions of *Romeo and Juliet*. Here Capulet and Montague seek to tidy up social chaos by sanctioning the marriage of dead children after the fact. Penitent and grieving, they attempt to reconstruct the legitimacy of the family as a viable social institution in Verona. The father's permission for marriage must be granted retrospectively and the family must control the legend.

When editors seek to construct proper genealogies for texts, they often deploy the vocabulary of familial relationships to bring the multiple versions of the plays into order. In seeking the provenance for each text, editors establish lines of proper "filiation." R. B. McKerrow, for instance, observed that eighteenth-century editors primarily went wrong in not understanding the importance of suitable textual "lines of descent" (1933: 106). When editors relied on recent editions or indiscriminately collated all early texts, they displayed a lack of regard for proper genealogy. McKerrow writes:

> [I]f we want Shakespeare's original text the only place where we have any chance of finding it is in a quarto or folio which is at the head of a line of descent, and ... if descendants of such a quarto or folio have different readings from their ancestor, those readings must be either accidental corruptions or deliberate alterations by compositors or proof-readers, and can in no case have an authority superior to, or even as great as, the readings of the text from which they differ. (1933: 107)

Bad editions are characterized as rebellious heirs who don't respect the mark of their legitimate "ancestor," while good editions rely on works that "descend" faithfully from a proper progenitor. Only a systematic rather than eclectic comparison of early texts can illuminate the lines of family descent that travel back to the author-forbearer.

McKerrow's language is not exceptional; that is, New Bibliographers often frame their work as restoring family resemblances and identities, the very structures that offspring like Romeo and Juliet specifically attempted to escape. Throughout the playtexts, lovers disavow an identity grounded in familial origin. "Deny thy father and refuse thy name; / Or if thou wilt not, be but sworn my love, /and I'll no longer be a Capulet," croons Juliet in the balcony scene (Shakespeare 2000: Q2 2.1.77–9; Q1

2.1.74–6). Romeo later thinks of radically amputating his ancestral tie: "O tell me, Friar, tell me, / In what vile part of this anatomy /Doth my name lodge? Tell me, that I may sack / The hateful mansion" (Q2 3.3.104–7; Q1 3.3.95–8). Annihilating the family name and remaking one's self *sui genesis* is the utopian fantasy that the lovers share. Noting that editions tend to "degenerate with each reprint" (McKerrow 1933: 115), editors strive to correct generational alterations bibliographically, retrospectively endowing the family with the authority that it has lost – in the fictional world of Verona, the theatrical milieu of Renaissance England, and the landscape of editorial history. Crying "A plague on both your (play)houses," twentieth-century editors sometimes theorize away textual differences, eliminate stage variation, and sort relationships into a stable kinship system; that is, they reenact Escalus's and the patriarch's final gestures as they constitute orderly texts to be read.

Two Plays Alike in Dignity: Reading "Troublesome Doubles"

So why are there two versions of *Romeo and Juliet*? When we broach this question, we begin to reconceptualize the traditional relationship of text to performance. Jonathan Goldberg's work on *Romeo and Juliet* is instructive for this task, for he asks what its printed texs are, if not traces of – but also unfinished material for – performance. Patiently unraveling the logic used by editors to distinguish the two texts and to account for their origins, Goldberg argues that Q1 is a printed materialization of a particular performance, while Q2 is a conflated set of script options and revisions that don't make sense unless edited or altered. Q2, he states, is derived from a manuscript that "offers an anthology of possible performances of the play, one of which is captured by Q1" (1994: 186; but see Dillon 1994 and Jowett 1998, who point out problems in seeing the text as a record of performance). As an alternative to collecting performance possibilities, Q2 can also be understood, Goldberg notes, to record a set of temporally spaced revisions over time, changes prompted by the circumstances of theatrical production. Goldberg's formulation interestingly puts *performance* at the center of a story of textual origins.

Building on work by Stephen Orgel, Goldberg strikingly arranges text and performance in an unstable chronological order, with one text preceding performance and one produced after it. Q1, he argues, is a practical model for editors, for someone has pared material to create an abbreviated version. Q2 exists as a compilation of options, second thoughts, revisions, and movable parts. Because scripts were not imagined to be finished products, performances and revivals shaped a text over time, activating different parts of the script. As Goldberg puts it, "There never was a final *Romeo and Juliet*, a single authoritative or authorial version of the play. There were only versions, from the start. Scripts to be acted, they presumed multiplicities and contingencies, the conditions of theater" (1994: 265). Orgel writes:

> The point is that the acting text of a play always was different from the written text –
> this means not simply that it was different from the printed text, though it certainly

means that, but that it was different from the script, what the author wrote … [I]t implies as well that Shakespeare habitually began with more than he needed, that his scripts offered the company a range of possibilities, and that the process of production was a collaborative one of selection as well as of realization and interpretation. (1988: 28)

The Q2 for *Romeo and Juliet* demonstrates that a text might contain more material than any one performance could ever use, and that the text might also accrete new elements over time. In Goldberg's account, our "original" *Romeo and Juliet* was as mercurially unstable as its title characters or its subsequent performances.

Common sense may say that early printed versions represent some authorial hand *underlying* the performance (that is, the *true* text precedes performance), but this is precisely a claim that the title pages to the first two quartos avoid. Q1 *Romeo and Juliet* boasts that it captures the play "as it hath been often (with great applause) plaid publiquely." Q2 offers a text "newly corrected, augmented, and amended: As it hath been sundry times publiquely acted." These printed originals vest authority not primarily in the author but in performance, materializing that event in ways that shape its meaning (the published text includes descriptive speech tags, adds ornamental borders, and dictates meter through line breaks). The title pages purport to offer a trace of *something* in writing, corrected or not (by whom? from what?), which records a live event. The written text thus belatedly takes its meaning from theatre. Since the text is *of* a performance (rather than the other way around), the simple question "is a modern performance faithful to *the* text?" appears to be inadequate at best, and more likely anachronistic.

As a way to alert Shakespeare's modern readers to the very different understanding of *writing, authorship,* and *drama* that prevailed in his theatre, it might be fruitful to let readers see interesting variations *within* early texts, which are characterized by Jill Levenson as a "field of energy." She writes, "When there are multiple versions of the same play, the relationship between them establishes a field of energy for the viewer's imagination and perhaps an analogue for the play's origins in changing theatrical or other socio-economic factors" (2000: 106). The two quartos of *Romeo and Juliet* do, in fact, register striking differences in linguistic texture and some plot differences (in Q1 Benvolio, not Mercutio, gives the famed Queen Mab speech, for instance, and later dies). Critics routinely note that Q2, 20 percent longer than Q1, includes more figurative language, longer speeches, and fewer descriptive stage directions. The quartos also characterize individuals and relationships differently. To take one example: Q2 Lady Capulet asks her daughter near the beginning of the play, "How stands your disposition to be married?" to which Juliet gives an evasive answer, "It is an honour that I dream not of." Her mother's reply? "Well, think of marriage now" (1.3.67–8; 71). Don't dream, she orders, consider my wishes. In Q1, however, Lady Capulet responds to her daughter with information that Juliet is, in fact, desirable, "Well, girl, the noble Count Paris seeks thee for his wife." Rather than a parental dictate, this quarto has a mother flatter her daughter (Basile 2000). Similarly in Q2,

Lord Capulet issues a marital "decree" to his daughter (Q2 3.5.137), while in Q1 he inquires about Juliet's opinion (Q1 3.5.102–3). Though the plot remains consistent, Q2 presents a rigid familial hierarchy strongly challenged by rebellious daughters and kin; it stages the family as an institution internally in crisis.

The endings also represent the family differently. I began this chapter by describing the play's concluding events. In both versions, surviving families and state authority work to translate events into a socially meaningful "story of woe." Both endings rest on commemoration and anticipation; that is, both look backwards to tragic loss and forward to future representations of that loss. But is the family "name" rehabilitated as a viable institution in Verona, emerging from its pathological tie to fated death? Or does the oddly crass language used by both fathers suggest the feudal family's limited role as a player in society? Such questions, as asked, prove elusive, since they take subtly different forms in the earliest texts.

First, the prince is positioned in relation to his ruled subjects differently in the quartos. Declaring everyone chastised, Q2 Prince includes himself in those suffering a divine retribution for the feud: "See what a scourge is laid upon your hate," he proclaims, "That heaven finds means to kill your joys with love; / And I, for winking at your discords, too, / Have lost a brace of kinsmen. All are punished" (Q2 5.1.292–5). "Eskales" (as he is called) then watches the fathers make a claim to establish value by joining hands and promising collaborative building. He responds by reminding them of the "glooming peace" at hand and then by separating himself from those he governs: "Go hence to have more talk of these sad things; Some shall be pardoned and some punishéd" (Q2 5.1.307–9). The effect is to have the city-state emerge forcefully from Verona's competitive political scene. The prince emphasizes his juridical role in assigning blame, while directing the fathers to leave and converse further. Capulet's and Montague's agreement, he implies, is not tantamount to a final closure, nor do family heads have the right to oversee a legend of this magnitude. They need to reconsider their positions and await further command.

The Q1 Prince, on the other hand, draws the families into a collaborative conversation, even in his lecture to them. He almost invites family heads to pitch in and make sense of baffling matters: "Come, Capulet, and come, old Montague. / Where are these enemies? See what hate hath done" (Q1 5.1.204–5). The Prince's directive, "Come," is echoed (dare I say "appropriated") by Capulet, who then feels empowered to forge a single family out of two. "Come, brother Montague, give me thy hand" (Q1.5.1.206), he commands, replicating the Prince's verb in his marriage-like proposal. This repetition aligns state and domestic authorities rhetorically, an effect enhanced by the Prince's closing response to the fathers: "Come, let us hence to have more talk of these sad things; / Some shall be pardoned and some punished" (Q1 5.1.217–18). Through this formulation, the Prince incorporates the families into the juridical process rather than issuing a directive to his subjects. The effect is a mutual joining of authorities rather than a reprimand through which the state elevates itself. Q1 audiences witness a weak, harmonious social group, a bit unsure as to how to establish peace after this tragedy.

Taking into account multiple playtexts complicates critics' readings of *the* play that tease out its representation of state, family, and desire. For instance, Dympna Callaghan maintains that *Romeo and Juliet* enacts an emergent ideology of romantic love that transfers power from feudal family to centralized state. In her reading, the play lauds the seemingly individualized and universalizing eroticism that, in fact, fits the needs of a powerful state and nuclear family (one that slots women into subordinate roles in oppressive social structures). Escalus's control of the story, his issuing of punishments, and his appropriation of power from friar and father require a new mode of desire severed from the confines of the feudal family. Callaghan's argument, however, only truly pertains to Q2. Since Q1 shows the Prince's *weak* power and doesn't stage a conflict between family and state, *the* play can't be used as synecdochal evidence of an historical shift in ideology in the period generally. In fact, choosing Q2 as the basis for an edition unwittingly commits an editor (or critic) to a text embedded more fully in the ideology that Callaghan articulates. Reading Q1 along with Q2 fractures this critical narrative and instead allows us to see the multiple political and dramatic options available at the time, options that frame desire within different social configurations.

These variants are striking not only because they reveal possible cues for performance (or records of performance options) but also because they seem to anticipate issues that critics and editors later face. That is, while the characters in the play struggle to create order in the aftermath of tragedy, the very fact of multiple playtext versions implicitly raises the issue of how events endure in time. Does there need to be one stable "legend" or "text" that survives? In both quartos, the fathers create statues that commemorate the lovers and forge a kinship bond, but what these monuments symbolize *precisely* is indeterminate. Is it the enduring love and power of the family, a sign of the power and authority of the statues' creators? Or the sign of their inevitable weakness, something that the state needs to bolster? If the story of Romeo and Juliet is legendary and perdurable (as the Prince's catchy rhymed couplet signifies), it's a legend with an unstable meaning. And the play itself, in all its manifestations, is part of that fluctuating legend. Both playtexts thus strikingly end with a provocative call for the audience to think of events as necessarily caught in a constant process of construction and reconstruction. Do the two endings offer fantasy-laden representations of how the meaning of spectacle, statue or play can be monumental but also up for grabs at the same time? It seems so. For the play's famous and relentless "self remarking textuality" (Goldberg 1994: 191) reflects its awareness of the fact that it retells a famous legend that everyone knows (Lehmann 2001). While the prologue leaps ahead in time to anticipate a tragic ending prescribed in the past as a "star-cross'd" force, the ending looks forward to a future commemoration of the recent deaths. The result is a self-conscious story, aware of the oddity of being unstable, predetermined, and un-nameable all at the same time.

The ending that I described in the opening to this chapter is more complicated than I first acknowledged, for there are multiple representations of family, social order, state, and desire even in the original texts of the play. Luhrmann's decision to erase the family reconciliation in his film is not a defiant rejection of *the* text, but instead might be seen as continuing the process of revising the story, a process that might well have occurred on the stage in Shakespeare's day, and one that is perhaps recorded in the variants of Q1 and Q2. Zeffirelli's concluding image loosely echoes Q2's attention to the family's role in forging social order. Neither film grants government much authority, since both relegate the Prince's choric lines to other characters: Zeffirelli has the friar offer a voice-over giving the concluding lines, while Luhrmann grants them to a television broadcaster. The films are not "faithful" or "unfaithful" to a single text (obviously, since there isn't only one); instead they replay the constellation of issues configured in the earliest texts, where the ending was game for alteration. Modern editions inevitably weigh in about such matters as well. When editors argue that Q2 is the single "ancestor" for *Romeo and Juliet*, they implicitly use the language of family relations to create a stable vertical structure that can make sense of the plurality of texts. But, as we have seen, the plays themselves aren't quite as confident about that structure. As Leah Marcus (1996) argues, unearthing and reading multiple texts can allow critics to release early modern plays from the ideological pressures that have been brought to bear on them editorially.

This is precisely what Jill Levenson seeks to do in the recent Oxford *Romeo and Juliet*. By introducing Q2 and Q1 between the same covers as equal, "mobile" variants (rather than offering a composite text), Levenson attempts to reflect the uncertain textual terrain every editor faces. She suggests that these versions represent "two different and legitimate kinds of witnesses to two different stages of an ongoing theatrical event" (2000: 127). But is their distinctiveness sustained? For Levenson, in several places, emends Q2 in ways that look peculiarly like Q1, omitting, for example, the repetition of lines assigned in Q2 to both Romeo and Friar Laurence (Q2 2.1–2.2; see also Q2 3.3.38). At first glance, such corrections appear necessary, since it would be confusing for readers to encounter repeated lines. But in using Q1 to alter Q2, Levenson in essence cross-breeds the very texts that she sets out to distinguish. In doing so, she refuses Randall McLeod's (aka Random Cloud's) exhortation that editors leave repeated lines intact so as to document "options" given to actors, options that readers access only through such messy material traces (Cloud 1982: 424–7). Cloud argues for an "infinitive text" that would register plural possibilities (1982: 422). Even Levenson's "mobile text" edition, by contrast, finds it necessary to erase such troubling nomadism *within* a given text, conflating two "legitimate" but disorderly options into a singular passage. Two variants "alike in dignity" slide into one kinship system in this moment, despite the fact that the edition's goal is to let the texts stand as what Marcus calls "troublesome doubles" (1996: 129). In some instances, Q1 offers a "solution" for Q2's quandaries; thus they must share an ancestor. Though Levenson's edition as a whole works against the model of a family textual lineage, the familiar editorial desire for a unifying integrity surfaces in the actual practices of emendation.

Shared phantasmatic desires, it seems, drive the fictional characters, editors, and directors of *Romeo and Juliet*. Though directors have historically sought to *innovate* the text, and editors to *recover* it, both grapple in practice with its fluctuations. Directors often describe performances as *of a* text, but the very existence of multiple film and stage versions hints at the textual fluidity that Renaissance theatre conditioned and that editors are slow in recognizing. As characters in *Romeo and Juliet* worry about whether identity inheres firmly in the word or is variable ("What's in a name?"), they are themselves the products of texts dogged by these issues.

Who's in Love? Performing the Text

I conclude with the most popular account, in the late twentieth century, of origins and *Romeo and Juliet*. The Academy Award-winning film *Shakespeare in Love* (dir. John Madden 1998) offers a compelling if anachronistic view of dramatic production in the Renaissance, along with a fictional account of the "real" story reputedly fueling the play. In this film, Shakespeare is a fledgling playwright hampered by his financial woes and by the banal conventions of stagecraft. The film fictionalizes his escape from this predicament by having him fall in love and translate his experience into a new and "authentic" play form. Breathtakingly erasing the fact that the story of Romeo and Juliet was a well-known legend in the Renaissance, writers Tom Stoppard and Marc Norman celebrate the play as the outpouring of a tormented soul barred from true love. In this *Bildungsroman*, young Will matures from an impotent writer into a master craftsman appreciated even by Queen Elizabeth. In this representation, however, patriarchal authority overrides the forceful passion of the lovers. Will is unable to cross class barriers to wed aristocratic Viola de Lessup centrally because her father and the queen uphold a social code allowing parental control of marriage; that is, the film weighs in decidedly to settle the questions raised by *Romeo and Juliet*'s ambiguous closure. The success of the staged play in the film suggests that art is the idealized, transformative, and compensatory product for failed love. As such, *Shakespeare in Love* offers another new ending to the story.

The film goes out of its way to show the economic realities of Renaissance theatre, as rival companies vie for scripts, sex controls stage licensing, actors' egos dictate the plot, and money rules the industry. But out of this crass matrix, Will writes a play that is truly singular because indebted to "life." Such a scenario gives cinematic form to the desires fueling editorial work: the craving for a viable integral playscript firmly tied to the author's presence. *Shakespeare in Love* indulges this fantasy by dwelling on the image of the playwright's ink-stained hands, as he writes alone in his study, usually with soaring accompanying music. Readers are privy to the "true" text of *Romeo and Juliet* (it's Q2 not Q1! the product of Shakespeare's own hand! there's no textual problem!). *Shakespeare in Love* thus validates the now-traditional modern-editorial account of the play's origins, privileging the written text as paramount over any particular stage version. It then goes further in authorizing the story as not only the property of the author but as a transcription of his actual feeling.

Even this immensely nostalgic view of theatrical production, however, includes moments that trouble the conventional understanding of the relationship between writing and performance. In the middle of the film, Will (Joseph Fiennes) is in bed with Viola (Gwynneth Paltrow), the elite woman who has cross-dressed as a boy to perform in his play (*Romeo and Ethel the Pirate's Daughter*). During their ardent love making, they rehearse scenes from his script based on their own romance.

The complication here is that Madden cross-cuts this sex scene with a dress rehearsal of the same scene in the Rose theatre. This juxtaposition is striking for several reasons, the first being that Viola plays two distinct genders and parts. While originally the model for Juliet, she plays Romeo on stage to a cross-dressed boy Juliet. Yet she rehearses as the female Viola in bed with the author, who himself reads the part of Juliet. In the bedroom, as Will and Viola use the lines of the play to express passion, the cross-cutting interestingly disturbs the gendered identities of "Romeo" and "Juliet," the fictional characters who are to repeat, in artistic form, the passion of Viola and Will (Juliet witnesses her "part" as split and embodied by two males). The multiplication of gender roles creates a free play of erotics, one fueled simultaneously by the thrill of being released from fixed identities and by the sheer excitement of acting; that is, the flexibility of identity is registered in terms of both gender and theatricality.

The lovers can indulge in illicit passion and illicit acting because they are briefly freed from who they are. Performing the script becomes an aphrodisiac, as *acting* signifies the release from the identities that bar the lovers from each other. After all, Viola has fallen in love not with Will but with her ideal of the great author; in turn, Will falls in love with both a boy actor who is an ardent fan of his, and an abstract idealized woman. Viola's desires are parodied in the balcony scene, where she calls out dreamily "Romeo, Romeo" (instead of "Will, Will"), and then continues, "a comedy by William Shakespeare." What she craves is clearly theatre. Acting then appropriately enables their passion as well as allowing them to express it (though the film disavows this later when they "mature" and proclaim to love the "true" person). The bedroom/stage rehearsal scene intensifies the collision between acting and eros established elsewhere in the film by inserting acting directly into sexuality. At one point, Will and Viola speak the same sentence in unison and then compete playfully for ownership of it. "That's my line!" says Viola, while Will arches his back and whispers in the throes of passion, "Oh, but it is mine too." Sharing lines, they seem to reflect on the generative confusion of parts they enact ("the more I give to thee / The more I have . . ."). Such collaboration merges performance, playwriting, and sex. Here the playscript isn't a belated and secondary record of love but instead constitutes the passion that is supposed to precede the script. Showing the play to produce the desire it supposedly documents, the film collapses the temporal logic that upholds its theory of authorship.

This collapse has implications for the text as well. In the middle of the scene, when the Nurse calls out to the boy Juliet on stage, Madden cuts to the bedroom where a naked Viola and Will are similarly interrupted by the cries of the "actual" Nurse. At this confusing moment, there is a stark collision of the "real" and "fictional," an epistemological time warp much like that in *A Midsummer Night's Dream* when the audience is invited to snicker at Bottom's hopeless pretensions for playing Pyramus when he is "really" just Bottom. In both instances, this play within the text constructs a fictional "real." Logically, *Shakespeare in Love* should have Will and Viola read the Nurse's interruption from the script; instead it *happens at the very moment that they rehearse.* How can this be, if the script is already written? In *Shakespeare in Love*, the play is insistently legitimated as the translation of "real life," but this rehearsal momentarily calls into question the clear before-and-after of writing and acting. The result is a tiny fracturing of the ordered chronology that the film requires: author loves, then writes, then play is performed. Instead the text seems to follow performance; and writing and performance seem to saturate "life." Though the film goes on to straighten out the queerness of this scene – the disordering of performance and script, and its scrambling of gendered positions – it allows the audience a glance at the pleasures of a more wayward textual and sexual logic; that is, the scene unmoors the fantasy of textual priority and authority on which the film rests.

From editors in love with a fantasy of the author and his orderly family of texts, we move to a fictional fantasy of the Great Author so in love that he can write for the first time. Though the film shows Family decidedly prevailing in the "outer" story with the Author decidedly prevailing in the theatre, its bedroom rehearsal scene hints at the disorderly structures that revisionary editorial theory and *Romeo and Juliet* take up. In both quartos, the characters' final speeches dwell on past events, their reconstruction as present stories, and their mobile repetition in the future – as a "story of woe." In recent accounts of Renaissance playwriting and textual production, texts also sometimes seem to *follow* performance, so that the author is seen as part of a collaborative process in which he is not always at the center. In creating *Shakespeare in Love,* writers silently employed this flexible chronology: they generated the "life" story of Will Shakespeare precisely by working backwards from *Romeo and Juliet*, creating a "real" personal author from the evidence of a fiction. Unwittingly amplifying the editorial quest for textual origins, the film lodged the answer in a powerful fantasy that put the text, state, and family back in perfect order: it all depends on an author in love with an actor in love with a writer – a circuit of desire that audiences, it seems, loved.

REFERENCES AND FURTHER READING

Basile, Michael (2000). "Teaching Mothers in *Romeo and Juliet*: Lady Capulet, from Brooke to Luhrmann." In Maurice Hunt (ed.) *Approaches to Teaching Shakespeare's "Romeo and Juliet."* New York: The Modern Language Association of America, pp. 125–30.

Callaghan, Dympna C. (1994). "The Ideology of Romantic Love: The Case of *Romeo and Juliet*." In, Dympna C., Lorraine Helms & Jyotsna Singh (eds.) *The Weyward Sisters: Shakespeare and Feminist Politics.* Cambridge, MA: Blackwell, pp. 59–101.

Cloud, Random (1982). "The Marriage of Good and Bad Quartos." *Shakespeare Quarterly* 33: 421–31.

Dillon, Janette (1994). "Is There a Performance in this Text?" *Shakespeare Quarterly* 45: 74–86.

Gibbons, Brian (ed.) ([1980] 2000) "Introduction." In William Shakespeare *Romeo and Juliet*, Arden edn. London: Methuen.

Goldberg, Jonathan (1994). " 'What? In a Name That Which We Call a Rose': The Desired Texts of *Romeo and Juliet*." In Randall McLeod (ed.) *Crisis in Editing: Texts of the English Renaissance*. New York: AMS Press, pp. 173–201.

Greg, W. W. (ed.) (1910). William Shakespeare *The Merry Wives of Windsor, 1602*. Oxford: Clarendon Press.

Hodgdon, Barbara (1989). "Absent Bodies, Present Voices: Performance Work and the Close of *Romeo and Juliet*'s Golden Story." *Theatre Journal* 41: 341–59.

Hoppe, Harry (1948). *The Bad Quarto of "Romeo and Juliet."* Ithaca, NY: Cornell University Press.

Jowett, John (1998). "Henry Chettle and the First Quarto of *Romeo and Juliet*." *Papers of the Bibliographical Society of America* 92: 53–74.

Lehmann, Courtney (2001). "Strictly Shakespeare? Dead Letters, Ghostly Fathers, and the Cultural Pathology of Authorship in Baz Luhrmann's *William Shakespeare's Romeo + Juliet*." *Shakespeare Quarterly* 52: 189–221.

Levenson, Jill (ed.) (2000). "Introduction." In William Shakespeare *Romeo and Juliet*. Oxford: Oxford University Press.

Loehlin, James N. (ed.) (2002). "Introduction." In William Shakespeare *Romeo and Juliet*. Cambridge: Cambridge University Press.

Maguire, Laurie (1996). *Shakespearean Suspect Texts: The Bad Quartos and their Contexts*. Cambridge: Cambridge University Press.

Marcus, Leah (1996). *Unediting the Renaissance: Shakespeare, Marlowe, Milton*. New York: Routledge.

McKerrow, Ronald B. (1933). "The Treatment of Shakespeare's Text by his Earlier Editors, 1709–1768." *Proceedings of the British Academy* 19: 89–122.

Orgel, Stephen (1988). "The Authentic Shakespeare." *Representations* 21: 1–25.

Pollard, Alfred (1909). *Shakespeare's Folios and Quartos*. London: Methuen.

Pope, Alexander (1821). "Preface." In *The Plays and Poems of William Shakespeare*. London: n.p.

Shakespeare, William (2000). *Romeo and Juliet*, ed. Jill Levenson. Oxford: Oxford University Press.

Werstine, Paul (1999). "A Century of 'Bad' Shakespeare Quartos." *Shakespeare Quarterly* 50, 3: 310–33.

Worthen, W. B. (2003). *Shakespeare and the Force of Modern Performance*. Cambridge: Cambridge University Press.

FILMOGRAPHY

Romeo and Juliet (1980). Directed by Franco Zeffirelli. Paramount Pictures/Home Video.

Shakespeare in Love (1998). Directed by John Madden. Written by Marc Norman & Tom Stoppard. Miramax Home Entertainment.

William Shakespeare's Romeo + Juliet (1997). Directed by Baz Luhrmann. Twentieth Century Fox Home Entertainment.

11

Prefixing the Author: Print, Plays, and Performance

W. B. Worthen

After four centuries of dramatic publishing, we are now familiar – perhaps too familiar – with the appearance of plays in print. Yet in Shakespeare's era, putting plays into books was not yet habitual; the elements of the play that point off the page, toward performance – act and scene divisions, speech prefixes, stage directions, punctuation – seem to have been especially troublesome. Modern editors, given the task of producing legible texts of the plays for modern readers, have had to confront these factors, typically regularizing such idiosyncrasies to the norms of modern dramatic publishing. Yet while early modern drama does present a range of specific problems arising from the ways the texts have been transmitted, modern drama often betrays similar irregularities in the ways the play takes the page. That is, while modern plays are printed much more systematically, the disposition of the dialogue, the location of speech prefixes, the use of white space on the page are far from conventional; indeed, many playwrights appear to see these accidentals as ways to make a substantial intervention in the shaping of performance. These elements of early modern plays in print witness the complexity of the modern editor's task, the challenges of tracing the texts of the play from the playwright(s), through the various copyists and revisers of the playhouse, to the still-emerging practices of the print shop. Here, though, I would like to consider them from a slightly eccentric angle, asking not what their treatment by editorial practice and theory might say directly about Shakespeare, but what they might suggest about a persistent problem, a problem still very much with us: the troubled interface between writing, print, and performance.

We might take our bearings on the (modern) form of Shakespeare's printed plays by thinking for a moment about David Antin's "talk poems." Antin's poetry is improvised in performance, and so deploys its own idiosyncrasies on the page – almost no punctuation, unjustified left and right margins, gaps of five or six spaces between phrases – to assert the printed page's dependence on the oral origin of the poem. The page makes complex claims about the poem's identity as writing and as performance, though, for the page is neither a record of an actual performance (Antin closely edits the appearance of the page when he decides to print the poem, usually long after its initial performance), nor is it exactly a prescription for future performances (Antin gave up "reading" already-written poems because it felt too much like "acting"). Antin's work raises important questions for the printform of plays and other performance works – including Shakespeare's plays – which seem to use the design of the page to record, instigate, and/or represent performance. How does the book teach us to unfreeze its talking? How do we regard the printform of plays as a means of encoding the drama, of representing its molten performance, theatrical *play*?

The page makes complex claims about the poem's identity as writing and performance, even if we understand that the play is neither a record of actual performance nor an exact prescription or scoring for future performance. How does the book encode the drama, and teach us to decode print as theatrical *play*? The question of how to represent plays in print is the presiding question of the editing of early modern drama, and much of the most significant practical and theoretical work on this problem has been sustained by the task of editing Shakespeare's plays for modern readers. In the past century, Shakespeare studies has seen two revolutions in editorial practice and textual theory, revolutions in how we understand the relationship between writing, print, and performance in Shakespeare's era, and in how best to represent – or perform – that relationship in modern editions of the plays (editions, in other words, that encode the identity of "drama" in ways recognizable to us). The intensive, even "scientific" study of Shakespeare's printed drama in the first half of the twentieth century – the New Bibliography associated with W. W. Greg, A. W. Pollard, R. B. McKerrow, Fredson Bowers and others – integrated a Romantic concern for the authentic transmission of Shakespeare's writing from the (now lost) manuscripts to print with an inevitable attention to the use and function of writing in the theatre. Many of the practices and judgments of the New Bibliography have been reinterpreted, revised, or rejected in the New-New wave of textual scholarship begun in the 1970s, epitomized by the 1986 Oxford Shakespeare, and expanded in other editions and in a brilliant efflorescence of textual criticism and theory since. These two moments of controversy in the history of Shakespearean editing represent a searching and pragmatic encounter with the conceptualization of drama in print and its production for modern readers. More important, we can also understand this engagement with the printform of Shakespeare's plays as an index of a typically modern desire to render the anomalies of drama coherent within the regime of a dominant print culture. Changes in editorial practice enact a changing valuation of dramatic writing: while these values typically take the form of historical discovery, discovery about the past, they usually participate in the values of contemporary culture – and, I would argue, in contemporary attitudes toward dramatic writing and theatrical performance. The outline of the shift from the New to the New-New Bibliography in Shakespeare studies is generally familiar – the multiplication of texts, decentering of the author, revaluation of the "theatrical" elements in the textual transmission process; this shift also articulates with a changing valuation of the relationship between writing and performance in the identity of drama. Rather than tracing a history of modern Shakespeare editing, I want look in a slightly different direction, to see how one or two problems posed by dramatic writing in the first age of print, far from being mere eccentricities thankfully resolved by print's growing sophistication, point to ongoing instabilities in the working of printed drama and its changing relationship to the institutions of performance.

In his foundational book, *On Editing Shakespeare and the Elizabethan Dramatists* (1955), Fredson Bowers frames a series of questions that all editors of Shakespeare's plays must face as they work, in his now infamous phrase, to "strip the veil of print" (1955: 87) from the early books that construct and conceal Shakespeare's plays: "What was the nature of the lost manuscript which served as printer's copy?," "What was the nature of the printing process itself, and what can be gathered from this to shed light on the transmission of the text from the lost manuscript to the derived printed document with which the editor must work?," and "What is the relation between all preserved examples of the text, in printed or in manuscript form, and what are the degrees of authority, both specific and general, in these examples?" (1955: 8). Print is intricate, not to say seductive, in the ways it veils the author's hand, but Bowers works to lay out the various possible states of copy-text, "of every conceivable variety," which nonetheless fall "into the following major classes, some of them speculative":

(1) author's foul papers; (2) authorial or scribal fair copies not intended for direct theatrical use; (3) foul papers or fair copies partially marked by the prompter as a preliminary for transcription into prompt; (4) scribal transcripts made for private individuals and not for theatrical purposes, the source being foul papers, fair copy, or theatrical promptbook; (5) a manuscript promptbook itself; (6) a scribal transcript of a promptbook; (7) an unrevised copy of an earlier printed edition; (8) an unauthoritatively revised copy of an earlier printed edition, the revisions presumably originating with the publisher or his agent; (9) an authoritatively revised copy of an earlier edition marked by the author; (10) a copy of an earlier printed edition annotated by comparison with some manuscript, usually assumed to be authorial or prompt, preserved in the theatre's archives; (11) a subdivision of the above, consisting of an earlier printed edition marked and used by the theatre company as a promptbook, or another copy of an edition marked for the printer to conform to such a printed promptbook; (12) another possible subdivision of the above, a new and as yet untested theory, which conjectures a scribal transcript made for the printer of such a marked printed prompt-book, or else a manuscript made up for the printer by an independent act of conflating a printed edition with a manuscript preserved in the theatre; (13) the "foul papers," fair copy, promptbook, or transcript of a promptbook of a memorial reconstruction of the text without direct transcriptional link with any manuscript derived from author's autograph, in other words, the copy for a so-called "bad quarto." (Bowers 1955: 11–12)

None of the actual copy texts used in the printing, and none of the manuscripts, fair or foul, of Shakespeare's plays have survived (*Sir Thomas More* may be partly an exception), though manuscript plays by other playwrights do remain. Perhaps not surprisingly, then, the veils multiply. Bowers continues:

Many of these classes may be mixed by introducing additional manuscript material, as a new scene, of different textual history from that of the main copy; or, in reverse, of introducing leaves from a printed edition to fill out gaps in a manuscript or to obviate transcription in part; or the patching of printed copy by leaves from a different edition.

For many early modern plays the genetic record is very shallow (one, occasionally two relevant print editions) and often confused: working to provide an authoritative modern edition, the editor typically tracks the ghostly hand of the author through the scattering of signs on the surface of a single printed page. These signs may stem from a number of agents – the writer, various playhouse copyists, the compositors setting the type – and the ideological character of the editor's work is perhaps most readily visible in the ways those signs are made to register changing conceptions of authorship. Bowers admits the "speculative" character of some of his thinking, and the main lines of contemporary textual critique begin precisely from that point of speculation, or by noting how the ideological character of the New Bibliography's understanding of authorship in fact determines the evidentiary status of the print record, and of the various texts hypothesized behind it. Even when it recognized (as Greg, Bowers, and others often did) the challenges posed by early modern theatre practice to a Romantic sense of individual authorship, the New Bibliography tended to see the impact of theatre, as it remains in the signs and signals scattered on the page, as a distraction from, and corruption of, the authorial work. Greg, for instance, was well aware of the bearing of theatre practice on Shakespeare's writing: in Shakespeare's theatre, "the author may never have produced a definitive text for us to recover" (Greg, "Preface to the First Edition," 1951: ix). "[I]n his earlier days particularly it is the conditions of the theatre" that "appear to have determined the manner of his composition," a "carelessness" in managing the details of "action and of language [that] were apt to be left standing with the knowledge that they could be trusted to straighten themselves out in rehearsal," a carelessness that seems "to have remained generally unaltered so long as he continued to be actively connected with the stage." Nonetheless, the value of Shakespearean writing, and the practice of editing, arise from its symmetry with more individualized modes of composition: "I do not think that Shakespeare, in his later days at least, wrote for the stage only: the length of some of his pieces, which must always have rendered their complete performance difficult, suggest that he had some sort of publication in mind" (1951: viii).

Greg's sense of Shakespeare's understanding of print as the medium of drama is arresting. Despite his unrivalled familiarity with early modern dramatic manuscripts – which clearly violate many of the claims made for the hypothesized relationship between the "foul papers," "fair copy," and "prompt copy" of Shakespeare's plays – Greg represents an author writing for posterity in print, producing an ideal and complete dramatic script that he knew could not be fully realized onstage, transmitting that manuscript (with the errors and inconsistencies characteristic of a writer working with a standing company) to the theatre where it would necessarily be altered for performance and by performance, and – through more indirect and multiple channels – finally make its way into print. Print at once creates the possibility of a dramatic *author* in the modern sense (a writer whose designs transcend their merely momentary and functional use on the stage) and also records that fundamentally literary notion of playwriting, provided we can read through the superficial inconsistencies of the printed page to perceive the authorial designs beneath. This playwright sounds, perhaps, a bit more like Jonson than Shakespeare, but if we are thinking of the proportion of nontheatrical, "literary" matter to stageable dialogue and business as an index to the ways print can establish a pretension to authorship, the playwright who comes most to mind is Greg's older contemporary Bernard Shaw, whose prefaces rival the length of some of his plays and fulfill Greg's sense of the modern playwright as a writer of *books* (W. W. Greg, 1875–1959; G. B. Shaw, 1856–1950).

Contemporary textual theory stands on the shoulders of Greg, McKerrow, and Bowers, while sometimes trying to cut them off at the knees. The materialist rethinking of the condition of Shakespeare's writing, of its implication in the early modern theatre and the interpretive challenge posed to editors by the print record also models alternative ways of imagining the relationship between dramatic writing, print, and performance. The Shakespeare that emerges here was neither unconcerned by nor obsessed by print. Instead, Shakespearean writing is conceived as fully collaborative with the process of stage production, a process that undermines (or at least alters) the presumptive authority of "foul papers," that may place a new and higher value on transcripts made for various (legal, theatrical, patronage) purposes, and that often requires revision and so tends to produce multiple copies of the same playtext with different and incommensurable claims to authority. The multiple agency of theatrical writing may well remain in the printed play, traced in the "accidental" or "inconsistent" features of the *mise-en-page* that nonetheless speak to the play's material origins: habits of punctuation, varying speech prefixes, the use of actors' names in place of characters' names, and so on. Much as the New New Shakespeare is a creature of the collaborative work of the theatre, the plays are also creatures of the early modern print shop, where compositors worked to produce plays as printed books, struggling with unfamiliar and irregular conventions for printing drama, with their own education and work habits, with the technological limits of the press and the practices of printing and proofing, and inevitably with the legibility of the copy texts they were supplied. The kerning of letterforms, the distribution of type, the casting off of the text and laying out of the formes, even the composition of the ink itself all bear on the process that brought Shakespeare's plays into bookish form. The New Bibliography – epitomized in this case by Charlton Hinman's magisterial edition of and commentary on the *The First Folio of Shakespeare* – at once invented and refined the study of print shop practice and its bearing on the process and product of Shakespeare's plays in print, and regarded the print shop (much as it regarded the theatre) as throwing a veil of corruption between the author and the modern reader. Again, from the more materialist perspective of recent editing and textual theory, these features register a kind of cultural authorship, the collaboration of the plays' printers in bringing the plays into this form and moment of their historical being.

The tension between a Romantic and a materialist Shakespeare has been enacted in visible form, by the Oxford Shakespeare and its Norton successor, and by new editions of the Riverside, Cambridge, Folger, and Arden texts. The new Shakespeare edition is unmistakable: it typically contains both a quarto- and a folio-based version of *King Lear* (sometimes with a third, conflated text); alters familiar names (no "Falstaff" in the Oxford *1 Henry IV*, and no "Puck" either) and renames plays, too (the Oxford editors believe *Henry VIII* was popularly known as *All Is True*, so that's the title they use); it may even include some plays (*Edward III* in the Riverside second edition) or parts of plays (*Sir Thomas More*) in which Shakespeare is thought (though not universally) to have had a hand. The consequences of this new attitude toward "The Materiality of the Shakespearean Text," to recall the provocative essay by Margreta de Grazia and Peter Stallybrass, have become an increasingly prominent element in pedagogy as well. the "old typefaces and spellings, irregular line and scene divisions, title pages and other paratextual matter," the irregularities of stage-directions, and speech-prefixes and other "character" designations, "remain obstinately on the pages of the early texts, insisting upon being looked *at*, not seen *through*" (1993: 256–7), and modern editions have worked recently to retain elements of this complexity. To the extent that modern editions also insist on "being looked *at* rather than seen *through*" they draw our attention back to the conceptual problems posed by printed drama. How *do* we read a play in print? Textual multiplicity and materiality draw attention away from the notion of the perdurable work identical in all its manifestations and toward a sense of writing changing and being changed by the circumstances of its use: a sense, in other words, of the fungibility of the text that's intrinsic to the history of (early and late) modern theatre.

In many respects, in the sixteenth and seventeenth centuries the reciprocal identities of printed and performed drama were weighted differently than they are today, after the rise of print culture. With a very few, notable exceptions, print played little role in the theatre, as plays were submitted, copied, distributed into parts, and learned from manuscript. It's perhaps not surprising that the dual identity of drama is persistently registered in the printform of plays. If we regard the naming of the "author" as one sign of the emerging character of dramatic writing as print *literature*, then many early modern printed plays seem to represent *performance* as the defining condition of the drama's identity, and the printed book as a kind of memorial record of that event. The title pages of many quarto editions of plays either locate the author as a kind of afterthought to the play's performed identity – "The Tragedy of Othello | The Moor of Venice | As it hath been diverse times acted at the | Globe, and at the Black-Friars, by | his Majesty's Servants | Written by William Shakespeare" (McMillin 2001) – or merely seem unconcerned or uninterested in the category of authorship as a way to mark the play's identity or even its marketability; for many printed plays, such as the first quarto of Shakespeare's *Titus Andronicus*, the identity of drama seems to lie in how "it was Plaide."

At the same time, as Jonson and Middleton make clear (to say nothing of Heminge and Condell), some writers (and actors) not only saw the written text as independent from production, but also put considerable effort into making fair copy manuscripts for presentation, overseeing the details of print (Jonson revised plays for inclusion in his 1616 *Works*). Arguing that Shakespeare may have understood himself both as a writer of scripts for theatrical use and as a "literary dramatist," Lukas Erne reminds us that Heminge and Condell advertised the 1623 folio of Shakespeare's plays as "cur'd, and perfect of their limbes; and all the rest, absolute in their numbers, as he conceived them," distinguishing their edition from the "diuerse stolne, and surreptitious copies" previously in circulation. And this convention was echoed in the 1647 folio edition of Beaumont and Fletcher's *Comedies and Tragedies*, which notes that "When these *Comedies* and *Tragedies* were presented on the Stage, the *Actours* omitted some *Scenes* and Passages (with the *Authour's* consent) as occasion led them; and when private friends desir'd a Copy, they then (and justly too) transcribed what they *Acted*. But now you have both All that was *Acted*, and all that was not; even the perfect full Originalls without the least mutilation" (Erne 2003: 149). These claims at once witness a "literary" desire to register the entire, original, authorial composition in print as "the work of drama," and the emerging marketability of such a notion of the play's identity. Indeed, Lukas Erne has recently developed Greg's sense of Shakespeare writing for print posterity to argue that the unplayable length of many of Shakespeare's printed plays records the drama's dual identity: while plays were necessarily cut and reshaped for performance, the length of many of Shakespeare's plays suggests that they were not "meant for performance before undergoing abridgement and adaptation for the stage" (2003: 219). That is, rather than seeing – as many editors, including those of the Oxford edition have done – the longer and shorter versions of some of Shakespeare's plays as representing a literary original and a subsequent theatrical version of "the play," Erne argues that Shakespeare, as the Lord Chamberlain's/King's Men house playwright, did not have to churn out plays to spec (as a sharer in the company, he was not under the economic pressure felt by other playwrights to write only as much as could and would be performed, in order to get another play written for sale to a company; and, of course, he was unusually intimate with how, and by whom, his plays would be remade for and in performance). For this and other reasons (the pretensions to a "literary" career registered throughout the sonnets, and in a sense documented in the relatively widespread appropriation of Shakespeare's writing in various popular miscellanies), Shakespeare may well have supplied his company with "much material that was never, nor was ever intended to be, performed" (2003: 136). Whether or not excessive "material" of Shakespeare's too-long plays signals the rise of the "literary dramatist," or perhaps witnesses other alternatives is not at issue here. (Is it at all plausible that as house playwright, Shakespeare might well have had the incentive and the freedom to write extra "material" not for print posterity but to provide a wider range of options and opportunities for his company to think through the play's performance potentialities? Did Shakespeare provide not a full and organic text to be cut down for performance, but a kind of dramatic miscellany of "material" to be shaped, selectively, into performance?) What is important is that Erne's challenging and sophisticated reading of the state of Shakespeare's printed plays enacts the ongoing problem of plays in print, the ways that print reshapes and rearticulates the dual identity of drama. Print invites us to locate the possibility of writing as a "literary dramatist" at the origin of print publishing.

Whether or not we take Shakespeare to have written his plays with a print posterity in mind, the possibility of a "literary" drama is cognate with the rise of print, witnessed not only by the Jonson, Shakespeare, and Beaumont and Fletcher folios, but also by Molière's close supervision of the printing of his plays (apparently insisting on a rhetorical pattern of punctuation that would be undone by later editors; see Chartier 1999: 18–19), and by Congreve's attention both to layout and design elements (sending his publisher Jacob Tonson to the Netherlands to purchase special type founts, so that he could differentiate between *i* and *j* and between *u* and *v*; see Peters 2000: 58). The rise of standard, literary editions of Shakespeare in the eighteenth and nineteenth centuries also opened the possibility of rival "theatrical" editions, a genre that has persisted not only in the "acting editions" of plays addressed specifically to the institutions and practices of professional stage production, but is also embodied in the screenplays of various film productions (the Craig Pearce and Baz Luhrmann script for *William Shakespeare's Romeo + Juliet* comes to mind). To say nothing of performance practice, the history of drama in print points to the difficulty of essentializing the relationship between writing and performance, a relationship that has changed in dynamic ways with the development of the institutions of literary publishing, theatrical publishing, copyright, and theatrical performance. And while it's commonplace today to take this relationship as fixed by its late-nineteenth-century form, typified by the novelization of printed drama characteristic of Ibsen and Shaw, the relationship between performance and print has remained fluid.

Attention to Shakespeare's texts, an effort to think about the relationship between dramatic writing and stage production in sixteenth- and seventeenth-century London, and a revaluation of the meaning of printed texts has, in this sense, enabled a rethinking of the purpose and function not only of texts in print culture generally, but of the slippery relationship between dramatic writing, print culture, and the pervasively oral culture of the theatre. This strikes me as the burden of the most surprising element of the revolution in editorial practice: the changing value of theatrical orality. From the outset, orality was linked to "badness," largely through Greg's sense that the badness of the "bad quartos" conceived by A. W. Pollard in 1909 could be explained as the result of the "memorial reconstruction" of the texts, by actors, by other playhouse personnel, or even by scribes in the audience (we might remember that compositors, too, need to remember what they've seen long enough to set the words in type). Despite the fact that in oral culture oral means ("reporting") may well be valued as more complete, more accurate than written means of recording communications, the New Bibliography evoked its modernity by relying on writing as the guarantor of authenticity, asserting a homology between the function of writing in Shakespeare's theatre and on the print-oriented modern stage:

> it is safer to base the selection of the folio in preference to the quarto text of *Richard II* and *King Lear* upon a recognition of the fact that in both the quarto shows evidence of reporting, whereas the folio seems to derive its general character from manuscript tradition, rather than upon any literary judgment of textual probability, will hardly be questioned. (Greg 1951: xxiii, xxxii)

Yet "memorial reconstruction"– or, more fairly, the transmission of "texts" by non-textual means – is not only an essential element of theatre, but a multiple and variable one, intrinsic to a theatre and a culture on the border between orality and literacy, and still intrinsic to an institution fundamentally reliant on oral means of production. Despite the pervasive consequences of the rise of print on the practice of theatre, and on our understanding of theatre relative to literature, the stage remains a venue where texts are written and rewritten on the basis of what makes sense as speech and action; where writing is transformed into and communicated by behavior, not as writing; where skills are taught and transmitted not through reading and writing but through personal training; and where the vagaries of memory – vagaries, it should be noted, only from the perspective of print – are essential to the practices of live performance (much more so than in film or television, too).

The problems posed by early texts are distinctive; can we see them, nonetheless, as also representative of longer-term slippages between print and performance? Stage directions and speech prefixes are important because they are where the authorial meets the theatrical, where the writing meets the performer, where the poetics of the drama meet the conventions of the stage. Editors of Shakespeare's plays are faced with a baffling set of textual events, at least from a modern point of view. In many of the plays, a given role will be indicated by several different speech prefixes, sometimes in the same scene (as when the character "Lady Capulet" is variously indicated by "Wife" or "Lady," among others); sometimes the name of an actor will replace the prefix or the character's name in a stage direction (as when "Will Kemp" enters, rather than "Peter" in Q2 *Romeo and Juliet*, or "Kemp" and "Cowley" replace "Dogberry" and "Verges" in *Much Ado About Nothing*). Since the prefixes are abbreviated in the early texts, it's even occasionally difficult to know which role the abbreviated prefix may be for: Coriolanus or Cominius in *Coriolanus*, for instance. Characters are frequently listed as entering a scene in which they have no lines; in some cases, characters who have no lines in the entire play haunt stage directions; at other times, characters are told to *exit* the page when they still have matter to speak onstage. Granted, these problems arose in the first era of dramatic publishing, when the textual status of the play's agents – actors or characters – had yet to be decided (if it has been decided), or at least regularized. Is it possible, though, to see these inconsistencies as only cosmetically resolved in modern editions, as pointing to a tension in the relationship between print and performance that still exists today? And can we see both the "Romantic" and the "materialist" resolution of these problems as part of the history of modern drama in the age of print?

All editions are acts of interpretation, but they interpret considerably more than the words on the page. Particularly in the case of drama, an interpretation of the purpose of the text tends to guide the representation of the "accidentals" of design, typography, orthography, and punctuation, its "accessories" – following R. B. McKerrow's loaded distinction "between the actual text of the plays, in the sense of the matter which is intended to be spoken by the characters, and such accessories as act and scene headings, the speakers' names, and to some extent also the stage directions" (1939: 19). McKerrow's distinction between the authorial (the *characters'* speech) and the conventional (everything else) not only reflects the typical critical understanding of the authorial warrant of dramatic writing (it's about the *characters* created by an *author*) but the conventions of modern publishing and theatre practice as well, which tend to regard everything outside the dialogue as non-dramatic and non-authorial, having different properties and propriety, and different status as property. The play depends on the sign of the Author: yet authority is variably registered in different zones of the book, even in different zones of a given page. The widespread practice of lifting stage design and even some actors' business from the premiere production and silently incorporating them as stage directions merely substantiates the notion that while the author's creation may end with the dialogue, his property may extend considerably farther on the page. As recent litigation suggests, this appropriation absorbs the designers' and the stage manager's work into the apparently "authorial" text, work which receives no credit or payment, despite the fact that it can now be copied in subsequent productions licensed by the author and his or her agents, and is generally understood to be part of the author's writing (see Lyman 2002).

Oddly enough, then, dealing with speech prefixes becomes a way of tracking one element of the conception of printed drama: how the printform of the play relates to an understanding of the interface between authorial writing and stage practice. McKerrow's insistence on "character" persists in more recent editions. Involved in the most radical revision of editorial practices in recent memory, the Oxford Shakespeare, Stanley Wells provides a useful summary of the ways some of the inconsistencies of early modern printed plays may reflect the business of theatre: "Shakespeare wrote, not as a dramatist whose work would be completed at the moment that he delivered script to the company for which it was written, but as one who knew that he would be involved in the production process," with the result that "there is frequently little attempt in the [printed] scripts that survive to objectify many aspects of the imagined performance which would nevertheless have had to be communicated to the performers before the play could exist on the stage"; in this case, failing to "objectify" them by naming them consistently in the speech prefixes (1984: 57) . The various inconsistencies in the attribution of roles and the direction of stage business can be smoothed over (and so be smoothed away) only by regarding them to be both ancillary to the author's work – the dialogue – and as so fully overdetermined by the authorial dialogue as the defining essence of dramatic composition as to be fully derivable from it. Shakespeare was, in this view:

> so overridingly preoccupied by thoughts of what the characters should say that he could content himself with the sketchiest of stage directions, sometimes even omitting to

indicate that a character should be present, frequently omitting to indicate when he should leave, sometimes not even bothering too much about who should speak particular lines or about providing dialogue to cover necessary action. (Wells 1984: 58)

Shakespeare was providing dialogue to be copied into parts; the various headings – Kemp or Dogberry, Cowley or Verges, in *Much Ado* – would be clear enough to allow the distribution of sides to the actors, who might even conceivably be helped in learning their lines by the switching from characters' names to their apparent function (as in the slippage between "Armado" and "Braggart" in *Love's Labour's Lost*), or even in the slippage between the character's various social functions in the drama – Lady or Old Woman in *Romeo and Juliet* (see Long 1997: 26). It is, finally, the principle that what dramatic authors create is *character* that enables us to regularize these theatrical expediencies in dramatic, literary form, as though the purpose of the script is to "objectify" the play's performance for consumption by readers, rather than to provide the performers with the raw material for their performance.

What's striking here is the surprising persistence of Greg's sense of a writer writing for print posterity, even in the more assertively "theatrical" conception of Shakespeare rightfully claimed by the innovative Oxford text. Although Wells's Shakespeare is no longer a Romantic poet hoping to transcend the evanescent business of the stage through print, he is a fabricator of characters whose literary identity (their words *as* characters) is hedged off from contamination by the merely theatrical accessories that surround them, the speech prefixes and the actors who use them. Given the modern relationship between conventions of printed drama and conventions of "character," and the edition's scrupulous attention to the needs of modern readers, it's hard to imagine a different, more workable compromise than the one the Oxford edition achieves. Thinking of "characters" rather than "roles" leads to the choice of "Dogberry" over "Kemp." When the edition departs from tradition and allows prefixes to change – typically to indicate a change in social and political status – it regularizes this variability to an objective view of the dramatic action: "Princess" becomes "Queen" at the appropriate moment in the last act of *Love's Labour's Lost* (though the editors note that the First Quarto alternates these prefixes throughout); "Bolingbroke" becomes "King Henry" after his accession to the throne (again noting and regularizing the First Quarto practice, which changes the prefix later in the play) (Wells 1984: 64–5; see also Wells et al. 1997, commentaries on *Love's Labour's Lost, Richard II*). Stephen Orgel remarks that "If the play is a book, it's not a play": true enough (1999: 23). Yet what does it mean for a play to be represented in a book, and what does the shape of that book do? Must we understand print's purpose as "objectifying" the play – an understanding of print that sounds considerably more Shavian than Shakespearean? As a document that both *records* and *instigates* performance, how does the book *represent* (or *objectify*) performance? Are there alternatives to the way performance might be objectified on the page? Is the play merely a fossil frozen in book form, or does the book provide a means – for readers, for actors – to thaw it out?

McKerrow arrestingly refers to these elements as *names*, "the names by which the characters are indicated" (1997: 2). The debate about prefixes points to a question in the matter of printed drama itself: are the "accessories" meant to register in the fictive plane of dramatic representation (as names, in other words) or on the functional plane of theatrical presentation (as directions)? The Oxford edition's invented prefix "King Claudius" marks this tension, a desire to have it both ways – the prefix as name (Claudius) and as social, dramatic, and even theatrical direction (play the king). This tension cannot be resolved because the rise of print ensures that texts can be, will be, read in both ways by different readers with different purposes, and sometimes by the same reader with different purposes, and sometimes by the same reader with different purposes at the same time. One way to understand the materiality of early modern texts is to take this fact of their (dis)organization seriously, as opening onto an ongoing problem in the "identities" of printed drama, rather than as a simple failure yet to understand or imagine how plays must and should be represented on the page, in print. De Grazia and Stallybrass, for instance, suggest that the variability of prefixes in printed drama implies the possibility that "character is posterior to speech," rather than a coherent entity that dictates a consistent label (1993: 268). And Randall McLeod notes that the erasure of these differences – which are also mainly erased from editions like the Oxford, which choose different prefixes (Oxford uses "Robin" in place of the conventional "Puck," but uses it consistently throughout; the Folio uses these prefixes interchangeably) – actually makes it rather difficult to know what impact they might have on our reading or performing practices, and so on our sense of the drama itself: the plays "abound in these polynomials, but as the editors have hidden all trace of them, the Newton of their calculation has yet to appear" (1982: 49, 50). We are all, in this sense, still in the Bradleyan orbit of "character" criticism, not so much because we want to know the number of Lady Macbeth's children as because our understanding of the materiality of the text, our discrimination of its signifying features, continues to locate the trace of the author in discriminate places in the text, here in the logic of "character" which should be represented with a singular, individualized *name*, rather than by a changing (functional?) set of designations. As McLeod suggests, concealing the inconsistencies of the text, foisting "single names on characters to whom Shakespeare responded, while creating them, with many names, is to impose retrospective understanding on the text, to seek artofficial [*sic*] rather than real creating," a tradition he terms "obliterature" (1982: 84). This reading of prefixes goes considerably beyond the fact that early modern texts tend to be irregular in announcing the entrance or exit of characters in the proper locations in the text: the text itself provides ambiguous information about who the characters are, who is speaking, precisely (it might be thought) by refusing to name the roles *as* characters in the modern sense.

Prefixes may, now, be so fully laminated to modern notions of character – as *names* – as to be impossible to leverage away, even despite the Oxford edition's considerable effort in this direction. And yet there's an important sense in which early modern prefixes register a reality of theatre: onstage, "character" is not something you are, it's something – as perhaps it was in the early modern theatre – you *do*. Thinking about speech prefixes as "names" is a decisively literary notion, as though "character" is something prior to its enactment. It is also, in theatrical terms, a decisively modern notion. Given the composition of Shakespeare's and of other early modern companies, and what we know of the distribution of parts, the pace of the repertory, and what we can hypothesize about rehearsal, it seems more than apparent that a given actor would deploy a given line of business as his performance *métier*. In this sense, playing a part like Bottom or Hamlet involves not so much finding the character's original "name," but in creatively assimilating the language and action given in the text to the paradigmatic theatrical business that is the actor's particular professional competence – what audiences come to see, what he has to sell, his *stuff*. Bottom's "lover or a tyrant" parodies this notion of theatre, but of course the success of *A Midsummer Night's Dream* depends on it. The play requires a good physical comic, an irascible old man, winsome and winning lovers, and perhaps just a touch of melancholy, unpredictable violence in Theseus and Oberon. In Shakespeare's theatre, the role precedes its "name"; the "name" individuates and specifies the role, and in Shakespeare's practice significantly deepens and expands its potentiality, but it does not give to airy nothing a local habitation, quite the reverse. Shakespeare's names name something that's already there.

Much as Greg's – and now Erne's – sense of the theatrically excessive printed text as a sign of authorial pretension evokes a rather Shavian Shakespeare, so too the notion of the text's implication in realistic mimesis – as an objectification of the dramatic world rather than as a set of signals to theatrical practice – may owe more to the 1890s than to the 1590s. The multiple designation "Armado"/"Braggart" (or "Dogberry"/ "Kemp") implies an attitude toward the script distinct from the "novelized" writing of Ibsen or Shaw or O'Neill, and perhaps also points to the sense in which thinking of speech prefixes as "names" is distinctive of a certain, historically-bound sense of drama and the dramatic – the "objectivity" of modern realism. Indeed, Erne presents a fascinating update of this hypothesis, suggesting that, in some texts at least, the presence of stage directions does not mark the text's *theatrical* provenance but instead traces its *literary* identity, the playwright's effort to objectify the play for an audience of readers. For instance, in the second quarto *Romeo and Juliet*, when Juliet is told by her father that she will marry Paris the following Thursday, she says, "Good Father, I beseech you on my knees"; in the First Quarto version, we find the line, "Good father, heare me speake?" followed by the stage direction *"She kneeles downe"* (Erne 2003: 223). Here, and elsewhere, Erne argues that stage directions speak not to the text as a record of performance, but instead to a desire to use the text to "allow a reader to imagine a point of stage business that could otherwise only be conveyed in performance" (2003: 222). Alternatively, the famous Chorus speeches of *Henry V* may not have been performed onstage, creating the possibility that "Writing longer plays for readers than his company needed for the theatre, Shakespeare encourages and enables his readers to use their 'imaginary forces' to construct in their mind's eye the 'wooden O' ": the text, in this sense, records the "literary dramatist's" efforts not to enable readers to imagine the fictive scene of the drama but the theatrical immediacy of performance (2003: 225). Yet while Erne takes the stage directions as the sign of the "literary dramatist's" effort to objectify the play, he also wants to refuse McKerrow's distinction between the play and its accessories: Juliet's *kneeles* is not the sign of theatrical intervention, but the trace of authorial intent, of Shakespeare's desire to address a reading public.

This functional-and-fictive understanding of prefixes characteristic of the New-New editorial work also resonates with contemporary writing for the stage, suggesting that there may well be more pervasive shifts in our understanding of writing and performance taking place. The vivacity of this tension remains – or has recently returned to view – not only in texts of performance art where the slippage between writer/performer/character may be in part what the work is about, but also in more formal plays, which have frequently sought to use the design of the speech prefix – critical on the page, irrelevant in performance – to trouble an easy assimilation of the role both to the standing conventions of realistic acting, and to the standing conventions of consistent literary "character": Suzan-Lori Parks's BLACK MAN WITH WATERMELON, and LOTS OF GREASE AND LOTS OF PORK; Adrienne Kennedy's SHE WHO IS CLARA PASSMORE WHO IS THE VIRGIN MARY WHO IS THE BASTARD WHO IS THE OWL; or Samuel Beckett's MOUTH, AUDITOR, or W2, to name only a few of the more interesting designations of the past forty years or so (and to set aside plays, such as Heiner Müller's *Hamletmachine*, which dispense with prefixes altogether). One of the most widely-staged plays of recent years, *The Laramie Project*, is notable here, too, for the overlapping between author, character, and prefix designations, for the kinds of (mis)information these names provide about the writing and performance of the play, and, finally for the ways naming marks our own hesitations about the identities of drama on page and stage. The name "Moisés Kaufman" shares the authorial by-line of *The Laramie Project* ("by Moisés Kaufman and members of Tectonic Theater Project"), alone holds the copyright accreditation, stands as the sole author of the volume's Introduction, is listed among the play's Characters, and appears as a speech-prefix for a role in the play (though in both the Denver and New York openings, the role was played by John McAdams, a member of Tectonic Theater Project listed on the title page as a dramaturg). Several of the play's "Associate Writers" – Stephen Belber and Greg Pierotti – are also listed as "Characters," and also appear as speech-prefixes; these two roles were also played in Denver and New York by actors named Stephen Belber and Greg Pierotti, though – like all the roles in the play – they have been played by many other actors since. While performer and character, role and name, theatrical writer and dramatic author are all rationalized on the page, the tensions marked in different ways by the irruption of Kemp and Cowley into the drama, or by Puck's inability to keep his name straight have not been entirely resolved by modern dramatic publishing (Kaufman 2001).

We have been and remain of several minds about the status of printed drama, a confusion that lies at the heart of dramatic publishing: if a play as a book is not a play, then how does the book represent the play? Discussing the editing of Shakespeare as a kind of adaptation, Jonathan Bate and Sonia Massai take a standard position:

> Within the realm of fiction, drama is the textually least stable genre: play writing does not derive from a solitary act of creation but is, instead, the result of a collaborative effort between the playwright and his company, which reaches its natural completion only through performance. The fruition of a playtext takes place through an endless process of rewriting, revision, and adaptation, carried out by editors, adaptors, and directors. (1997: 130)

Sensitive though they are to the ongoing work on dramatic texts, Bate and Massai nonetheless seem to set dramatic texts in an odd relationship to cultural production, as though the work of other kinds of writing was indeed fixed by its first manifestation in print, at least to the extent that this manifestation reflected the isolated inspiration of the author. What is further troubling about these remarks is the teleology applied to dramatic writing, the sense that it receives its "natural completion only through performance." While creating and specifying a significant value for dramatic performance, this phrasing (passing over the question of whether there is any "natural" way theatre should use texts) locates the theatre's proper function as finally dependent on the designs of the author, or of the text. But how is that "natural completion" achieved? It may be fairer to suggest that different eras have naturalized that relationship in different ways. Particularly now, in the late age of print, it seems no longer the case that other kinds of fiction are protected from theatrical representation (Mary Zimmerman's adaptations of Leonardo da Vinci's notebooks, of Ovid's *Metamorphoses*; Frank Galati's adaptation of *The Grapes of Wrath*); they are certainly amenable to translation into film. So, too it may appear that a range of print effects inherent in dramatic publishing may or may not have a direct "completability" on the stage.

Surely much of the inconsistency of printed drama in Shakespeare's era has to do with the absence of strict conventions of dramatic publishing, conventions that would emerge fitfully over the next two hundred years and that remain significantly less consistent than the conventions of published fiction today. The variability of printed drama in Shakespeare's era, though, may also point to a different understanding of the ontology or value of writing, in which it is less the function of theatre to complete and so reify the author's work, than to use it, to see it as material for use. Perhaps not surprisingly, insofar as dramatic writing had seemed at one time a special case, in the revolution of textual theory it has come in an odd way to seem the central, representative case. Where once plays were seen as tangential and troublesome elements in the history of print, texts whose collaborative or communal character intrudes a sense of accidental and irregular inconsistency into the reiterative mode privileged as print's proper history, it's now the case that insofar as "playtexts ... are designed to change as the conditions of performance change," they are exemplary of the condition of print, in which (recalling the influence of theorists like D. F. McKenzie, Jerome

McGann, Peter Shillingsburg and others), texts cannot be seen as "independent of [their] material embodiment," an embodiment which is at once the record of their individual and cultural fashioning, a semantically rich context of signification, the moment and mode of their irruption into history (Orgel 1999: 117, 118). The language of performance – or "embodiment" – suffuses editorial theory today, perhaps best summarized by Peter L. Shillingsburg: "one could say that every new embodiment of a literary work of art is a new, additional, and altered embodiment. That is important because a reader approaching a new text, particularly a reader alert to what is being read, cannot help being influenced in certain ways by the object that 'contains' the literary work" (1993: 33). If dramatic writing in its collaborative dimension troubles the category of print authorship, dramatic production – the multiplication of different texts for a single stage production *and* the sense of difference that emerges between different stage productions – troubles the "reiterative" logic of print.

What would it mean to an understanding of modern dramatic performance to attend to the printed form of plays, Shakespearean and otherwise (Shakespeare is, it should be remembered, the most often performed *and* printed of modern playwrights)? In the course of the long twentieth century the publishing of drama has undergone a number of changes and innovations, many of them sponsored by playwrights, some of them having more to do with the practices – innovative enough in many cases – of publishers. The revolution in the understanding of the text enables us to look anew at the pages of plays, not so much to determine authorial intention as to begin to make a clearer and more interesting demarcation between the spheres of drama, the page and the stage, and the ways that the materiality of each sphere impinges on the other. Contemporary textual theory and editorial practice have obviously felt the effects of Barthes and Foucault, and of the rise of a materialist criticism explicitly grounded in cultural studies. It's also true that digital technology has provided both the means of new editorial work – enabling the duplication, collocation, scanning, and comparison of texts in ways unimaginable to the generation of Greg or of Hinman. Moreover, the fluidity of texts in digital media, their identity as digitalized bits and bytes with other forms of digital representation (sound, imagery), and indeed the representational structure of hypermedia and interface design have radically changed our understanding of "texts" in ways we are all still working to comprehend. Perhaps, as Margreta de Grazia suggests, it's not only the historicity of Shakespeare's texts but the historicity of the interface between writing and performance that "eludes the binary logic of the One and the Many, as well as the two reproductive technologies of staticizing print and generative images" (1995: 251). But the movement to a more materialist textual theory and editorial practice in Shakespeare studies can also be seen both as a symptom of a shifting understanding of print and performance, and also of changing ways of *making* performance and of *using* writing in the theatre. These changes are immediately visible in performance art, in the emphasis on "performance" in certain aspects of contemporary poetry and poetics, even perhaps in the rise of a markedly anti-literary field of "performance studies." If Shakespearean editing takes place less in the world of Okes and Jaggard than of Michael Best and (inevitably) of Steve Jobs and Bill Gates, so too it also takes place less in the world of the Burbages, Heminge and Condell, and Marlowe and Jonson than the world of Baz Luhrmann and Michael Almereyda, of Declan Donnellan and Anne Bogart, of Samuel Beckett and Suzan-Lori Parks and Caryl Churchill. Contemporary performance culture – a term I mean here to embrace writing, publishing, and performing practices across a range of media, including the theatre – isn't what it was in 1600 or in 1900.

Our own performance culture is part of the context of modern Shakespeare on the stage and on the page. Emerging textual theory and editorial practices reflect the discovery of new information about Shakespeare and his theatre, as well as changing ways of interpreting that past. Yet while our interrogation of early texts enacts a principally historical concern, a concern actively to represent the pastness of the plays in our editions of them, we enact this concern on the horizon of contemporary writing, contemporary publishing, contemporary performance. Like a performance on the stage, an edition marks its historicity most clearly in its ways of imagining the relationship between the past of the text and the present moment of its production. Editing Shakespeare, committing any play to print, necessarily marks performance on the page, reflecting the work we want to enable the writing to *do*. Much like Dogberry and Kemp, the differences between O'Neill's Emperor Jones and Parks's Black Man With Watermelon can't be attributed solely to the traces of ink on the page, even the traces recognized as "dialogue." Yet these accidents of the page record the narrative of the changing interface between writing and performance, a history that took a new shape in Shakespeare's day with the rise of print, and is undergoing a second transformation with the impact of digital textualities. The materiality of writing exerts a palpable, if accessory, influence on our imagination of the stage.

REFERENCES AND FURTHER READING

Bate, Jonathan & Massai, Sonia (1997). "Adaptation as Edition." In D. C. Greetham (ed.) *The Margins of the Text*. Ann Arbor, MI: University of Michigan Press, pp. 129–49.

Beckett, Samuel (1990). *The Complete Dramatic Works*. London: Faber and Faber.

Bowers, Fredson (1955). *On Editing Shakespeare and the Elizabethan Dramatists*. Philadelphia, PA: University of Pennsylvania Library, for the Philip H. and A. S. W. Rosenbach Foundation.

Chartier, Roger (1999). *Publishing Drama in Early Modern Europe*. London: British Library.

de Grazia, Margreta (1995). "The Question of the One and the Many: The Globe Shakespeare, The *Complete King Lear*, and The New Folger Library Shakespeare." *Shakespeare Quarterly* 46: 245–51.

de Grazia, Margreta & Stallybrass, Peter (1993). "The Materiality of the Shakespearean Text." *Shakespeare Quarterly* 44: 255–83.

Erne, Lukas (2003). *Shakespeare as Literary Dramatist*. Cambridge: Cambridge University Press.

Greg, W. W. (1951). *The Editorial Problem in Shakespeare: A Survey of the Foundations of the Text*, 2nd edn. Oxford: Clarendon Press.

Greg. W. W. (1955). *The Shakespeare First Folio: Its Bibliographical and Textual History*. Oxford: Clarendon Press.

Hinman, Charlton (1963). *The Printing and Proof-Reading of the First Folio of Shakespeare*, 2 vols. Oxford: Clarendon Press.

Hinman, Charlton (1996). *The First Folio of Shakespeare*, introduction by Peter W. M. Blayney. New York: W. W. Norton.

Kaufman, Moisés & the members of Tectonic Theater Project (2001). *The Laramie Project*. New York: Vintage Books.

Kennedy, Adrienne (1988). *The Owl Answers*. In *In One Act*. Minneapolis: University of Minnesota Press, pp. 25–45.

Long, William B. (1997). "A Perspective on Provenance: The Context of Varying Speech-Heads." In George Walton Williams (ed.) *Shakespeare's Speech-Headings: Speaking the Speech in Shakespeare's Plays* (Papers of the Seminar in Textual Studies, Shakespeare Association of America, March 29, 1986, Montreal). Newark: University of Delaware Press, pp. 21–44.

Lyman, Elizabeth Dyrud (2002). "The Page Refigured: The Verbal and Visual Language of Suzan-Lori Parks." *Performance Research* 7, 1: 90–100.

Maguire, Laurie E. (1996). *Shakespearean Suspect Texts: The "Bad" Quartos and Their Contexts*. Cambridge: Cambridge University Press.

McGann, Jerome (1991). *The Textual Condition*. Princeton, NJ: Princeton University Press.

McKerrow, R. B. ([1935] 1997). "A Suggestion Regarding Shakespeare's Manuscripts." *Review of English Studies* 11: 459–65. Reprinted in George Walton Williams (ed.) *Shakespeare's Speech-Headings: Speaking the Speech in Shakespeare's Plays* (Papers of the Seminar in Textual Studies, Shakespeare Association of America, March 29, 1986, Montreal). Newark: University of Delaware Press, pp. 1–9.

McKerrow, R. B. (1939). *Prolegomena for the Oxford Shakespeare*. Oxford: Clarendon Press.

McLeod, Randall ([1982] 1999). "UN *Editing* Shak-speare." *Sub-Stance* 33: 26–55. Reprinted in Stephen Orgel & Sean Keilen (eds.) *Shakespeare and the Editorial Tradition*. New York: Garland, pp. 60–89.

McLeod, Randall (1997). "What's the Bastard's Name? Random Cloud." Reprinted in George Walton Williams (ed.) *Shakespeare's Speech-Headings: Speaking the Speech in Shakespeare's Plays* (Papers of the Seminar in Textual Studies, Sha-

kespeare Association of America, March 29, 1986, Montreal). Newark: University of Delaware Press, pp. 133–209.

McMillin, Scott (ed.) (2001). William Shakespeare *The First Quarto of Othello*. Cambridge: Cambridge University Press.

Müller, Heiner (1984). *Hamletmachine and Other Texts for the Stage*, ed. and trans. Carl Weber. New York: Performing Arts Journal Publications.

Ong, Walter J. (1982). *Orality and Literacy: The Technologizing of the Word*. London: Routledge.

Orgel, Stephen ([1996] 1999). "What is an Editor?" *Shakespeare Studies* 24: 23–9. Reprinted in Stephen Orgel & Sean Keilen (eds.) *Shakespeare and the Editorial Tradition*. New York: Garland, pp. 117–23.

Parks, Suzan-Lori (1995). *The America Play and Other Works*. New York: Theatre Communications Group.

Pearce, Craig & Luhrmann, Baz (1996). *William Shakespeare's Romeo and Juliet: The Contemporary Film, the Classic Play*. Screenplay by Craig Pearce & Baz Luhrmann, play by William Shakespeare. New York: Bantam Doubleday.

Peters, Julie Stone (2000). *Theatre of the Book 1480–1880: Print, Text, and Performance in Europe*. Oxford: Oxford University Press.

Shakespeare, William (1936). *Shakespeare's Titus Andronicus: The First Quarto 1594*. New York: Charles Scribner's Sons.

Shakespeare, William (1986). *William Shakespeare: The Complete Works, Original-Spelling Edition*, ed. Stanley Wells & Gary Taylor. Oxford: Clarendon Press.

Shakespeare, William (1997). *The Riverside Shakespeare*, gen. ed. G. Blakemore Evans, 2nd edn. Boston: Houghton Mifflin.

Shillingsburg, Peter L. (1993). "Polymorphic, Polysemic, Protean, Reliable, Electronic Texts." In George Bornstein & Ralph G. Williams (eds.) *Palimpsest: Editorial Theory in the Humanities*. Ann Arbor, MI: University of Michigan Press, pp. 29-43.

Wells, Stanley (1984). *Re-Editing Shakespeare for the Modern Reader, Based on Lectures given at the Folger Shakespeare Library, Washington, DC*. Oxford: Clarendon Press.

Wells, Stanley & Taylor, Gary, with Jowett, John & Montgomery, William (1997). *William Sha-*

kespeare: A Textual Companion, reprinted with corrections. New York: W. W. Norton.

Werstine, Paul (1986). "McKerrow's 'Suggestion' and Twentieth-Century Shakespeare Textual Criticism." *Renaissance Drama* 19: 149–73. Reprinted in Stephen Orgel & Sean Keilen (eds.) *Shakespeare and the Editorial Tradition*. New York: Garland, pp. 153–77.

Werstine, Paul (1998). "Hypertext and Editorial Myth." *Early Modern Literary Studies* 33, January (special issue). Available at: http://purl.ocl-c.org/emls/03-3/wersshak.html (accessed August 20, 2002).

PART III
Histories

12

Shakespeare the Victorian

Richard W. Schoch

My subject is the historiography of Shakespeare in performance during the Victorian era – that is, I will be analyzing the methods and materials used by historians to describe, contextualize, and interpret those performances. Yet, although I refer to the production and reception of individual Shakespearean dramas, my primary interest is metacritical. How, I want to ask, can scholarship on a particular drama shed light on larger interpretive questions? In order to situate those issues, a brief overview of the dominant characteristics of Victorian Shakespeare seems in order. Several aspects of nineteenth-century theatre have been central to recent histories of Shakespeare in performance: pictorialism, historical consciousness, "rational amusement," respect-ability, nationalism, and imperialism. I am mindful, of course, that theatre historians (myself included) subjectively construct – as opposed to objectively detect – patterns of significance in past performances.

Let me begin, then, in a traditionally empirical mode, with performance style. Pictorialism, although it featured in the full range of nineteenth-century theatrical productions from melodrama to pantomime, was especially identified with Shakespeare revivals. The actor-managers who dominated London's leading theatres during these years – W. C. Macready (Covent Garden 1837–39, Drury Lane 1841–43), Samuel Phelps (Sadler's Wells 1844–62), Charles Kean (Princess's 1851–59), Henry Irving (Lyceum 1878–1902), and Herbert Beerbohm Tree (Her/His Majesty's 1897–1917) – were all committed to pictorial *mise en scène*. This kind of staging entailed not only highly elaborate scenery, but also detailed costumes and properties, spectacular scenic and lighting effects, and the frequent use of *tableaux vivants*. Pictorialism was not *what* actor-managers thought about when they staged their productions; it was *how* they thought. It was all but inconceivable to imagine a Victorian production of Shakespeare as anything other than an animated painting, as the critic E. S. Dallas suggested when he labelled Charles Kean's antiquarian revivals of Shakespeare a brand of "pre-Raphaelitism" (Dallas 1856: 219).

This union of theatrical and visual culture made historical subjects particularly attractive. Performance was a powerful agent of historical consciousness in the nineteenth century because it realized the past with an immediacy greater than that of literature, painting, or even photography. Indeed, the theatre's commitment to historical accuracy was the very sign of its modernity. To prefer anachronistic performances of Shakespeare, as Charles Dunphy of *The Morning Post* argued, was to prefer "the semaphore to the electric telegraph" or "the stage-coach to the locomotive" (Dunphy 1857). The measure of success for Shakespearean revivals became their ability to surpass the vivacity and precision of history novels, genre paintings, museum collections, and architectural restorations.

Archaeological eclecticism flourished throughout the century, which saw a lively range of historical places, personages, and events recreated for eager and expanding audiences. While Shakespeare's English and Roman chronicle plays were obvious choices, his tragedies, comedies, and romances were all treated as opportunities for historical instruction. In the early 1840s Macready commissioned the antiquarian Charles Hamilton Smith to provide sketches of medieval and Renaissance costumes for possible productions of *The Merchant of Venice, Romeo and Juliet,* and *The Two Gentlemen of Verona* (Downer 1966: 235). Kean, in 1857, played Prospero as a "Polish necromancer of the 17th century" in a long black gown adorned with cabalistic characters (Smith 1857). And the Renaissance costumes for Irving's *The Merchant of Venice* (1879) were inspired by the paintings of Titian and Veronese.

For all its sensual delights, Victorian theatrical historicism was intimately tied to the middle-class obsession with rational amusement: the education and instruction of mass audiences through popular culture. Far from sharing the critic G. H. Lewes's lament that a "didactic mania" to "teach, teach, teach" had overtaken the stage, actor-managers confidently asserted that the theatre was an "engine for the direction of the public mind" (Lewes 1842, Kean 1856). In an 1881 lecture delivered at the Edinburgh Philosophical Institution, Irving declared that "the stage is, intellectually and morally ... the source of some of the finest and best influences" (Richards 1994: 188). Utilitarian views of performance became a commonplace in Victorian popular culture, justifying everything from "temperance" melodramas to pedantic playbill essays on *Macbeth* and *Henry VIII*. Like many commonplaces, it sometimes seemed less than truthful. And thus William Bodham Donne, the long-serving Examiner of Plays, observed that the maxim "the stage is a great moral engine for the education of the people" was nothing but an empty platitude (1851: 512).

Whether a tiresome cliché or a principled stance, the reformist agenda appealed strongly to actor-managers who mythologized themselves as gentlemanly proprietors of reputable places of amusement. Lavish revivals of Shakespeare were central to this self-promoting mythology. Through such productions, theatres could educate a mass, metropolitan audience and thus acquire respectability for themselves – and for their long-maligned profession – as agents of moral and social improvement. This aspirational zeal was exemplified, above all, by the careers of Kean and Irving. So high-minded had the theatre become by the 1850s that Gladstone, who only 20 years earlier had condemned the stage as sinful, unashamedly enjoyed Kean's antiquarian revival of *Richard II* (1857) and spent an afternoon touring the Princess's Theatre, where he engaged Kean in a "long conversation on the question of Government subvention to the Drama" (Matthew 1978: 222). And in 1895 the theatrical profession received the ultimate seal of approval when Queen Victoria made Irving the first actor-knight.

Despite the Lord Chamberlain's insistence that direct references to political events be removed from playscripts, Victorian critics and audiences found no difficulty in recognizing – indeed, advocating – the political utility of Shakespeare in performance. As we might expect, those performances served the interests of both nationalism and imperialism. It would be mistaken, however, to suppose that Shakespearean performances only registered changes in identity that occurred in some zone of "reality" from which the theatre was excluded. Rather, theatrical performance was one site where collective national and international identities were produced, negotiated, and distributed. Victorian Shakespeare did not so much project a single, coherent theory of identity as it became the playing field, the active occasion, for the constitution of various historicist and nationalist perspectives by ideologically conscious spectators. The political efficacy of nineteenth-century Shakespeare rested, moreover, upon the large and socially diverse audience which Shakespearean revivals attracted. Indeed, what qualified the Victorian theatre as a significant site of national debate was its *lack* of social uniformity. Quite apart, then, from the kinds of plays it produced, the theatre was important to the development of nationalism because it offered one of the few unregulated opportunities where "a variety of social orders could learn together how to be English" (Baer 1992: 195).

Performance Documentation and Evidence

Thus far I have preferred analysis to citation, argument to factual narrative in order to explain the cultural significance of a century-long performance tradition and to identify what I see as the principal patterns and themes emerging from myriad factual detail. Whatever one might call this process – inductive reasoning, narratological emplotment, or just plain research – it counts synthesis as a virtue. But there is a more pressing reason why I have *not* told the story of Victorian Shakespeare through a chronological, factual narrative drawn from "authoritative" primary sources that I have consulted. That reason is my desire to analyze the role that documentation and evidence play in performance historiography, most especially that of Shakespearean performance. Having mapped some dominant themes in recent scholarship on Victorian Shakespeare, I now want to examine the historiographical shifts that have made current research possible.

I start with the epistemological status of historians. Very few scholars today would argue, as nineteenth-century positivists did, that historians must be – or even could be – impartial. Most of us would accept that the kind of history we write depends upon our own theoretical premises – that history comes from somewhere. Scholars construct histories of "subjectively chosen" objects, Erika Fischer-Lichte observes, by asking "subjectively chosen" questions (1997: 342). Yet "subjective" does not mean "personal"; rather, it means the structuring forces of cognition that, while neither natural nor essential, cannot be reduced to individual taste or preference. Consider one obvious, yet frequently ignored, example. In most histories of Shakespeare in performance the structuring mechanisms are periodization and plays: this is *how* we think about such performances, how they organize themselves in our consciousness. Thus, we are accustomed to reading (and writing) books with such titles as *Restoration Shakespeare* and *Hamlet through the Ages*. But we are not so accustomed to thinking about how these structures – these ideational "givens" – actually create their own object of study. It is possible to imagine performance histories of Shakespeare that do not cling to periodization and do not regard performances as performances *of plays*. Yet it is difficult to write such histories, primarily because of the normative force of institutional practices and conceptual biases.

In turning to the actualities of writing history, we must dispense with the facile notion that doing performance history in the aftermath of theory means no longer having to spend time in archives. Nothing could be less true. Yet in recognizing that the need for the sheer hard work of archival research remains undiminished, let us recognize that the findings of such research are not transparent to their own meaning. Let us also remain aware that the archive is not a neutral or disinterested place. It is always, as Jacques Derrida observes in *Archive Fever* (1998), a site of authority. To organize disparate historical materials into a "collection" is already to interpret the past. Moreover, the very notion of a "collection" participates in an (all too seductive) epistemology of presence. Michel de Certeau, in *The Writing of History* (1988), explains that the archival collection presumes the totality of the past events that it documents. Putting the matter bluntly, an archive produces history just as much as it records and preserves history.

In articulating how historiographical operations are inevitably conditioned and constrained, we must not assume that the raw materials of history exist in a pre-archival "state of nature." Far from being neutral, the primary materials out of which archives are constituted are themselves inevitably biased because they are inevitably the result of organizing concepts and theoretical frameworks. Every piece of evidence is always already an interpretation, always already a claim upon the meaning of the event it imperfectly documents. Even so-called "undiscovered" evidence necessarily bears – by virtue of its very existence – the imprint of interpretation. Evidence, in other words, doesn't just happen.

In today's post-positivist moment, we understand that evidence, far from being value-neutral, is actually saturated with value. But this does not mean that we can discount evidence. Indeed, it is precisely the interpretive saturation – the *discursive* truth of evidence – that compels our continuing interest in it. Just as cultural meanings are made in a performance, such meanings are made in the evidence that not merely survives, but retrospectively creates the performance. By this I mean what

Shannon Jackson calls a "performative understanding" of historical materials: that "letters, autobiographies, speeches, legal documents, and essays are situated speech acts reflecting the contingencies of certain contexts and employing familiar tropes to reach specific audiences" (1998: 261). Performativity is not a trait that historical materials acquire only after they are placed in an archive. Rather, performativity is a constitutive dimension of historical materials.

Jackson's emphasis on the inherent materiality of historical research is a salutary reminder that the tools of the trade for theoretically-minded performance historians have not really changed. Even when repudiating the assumptions and aspirations of positivism, performance historians today must rely upon the same sources that the discipline of theatre studies traditionally has valued: promptbooks, scenic designs, costume sketches, illustrations, photographs, playbills, financial records, diaries, correspondence, and newspaper and periodical reviews. The difference lies in how these documentary sources are understood and used. Our task no longer can be to reconstruct performances, to issue aesthetic judgments about them, or even just to place them in their social context. Rather, our task must be to explore the broad discursive activity of theatrical events. In short, we must try to assess the efficacy of past performances by focusing on the "cultural work" that they accomplished – both in their own historical moment and, now, for us. In making such an assessment, we must be mindful of the ways in which institutional practices, scholarly predispositions, and the performative nature of evidence not only enable certain questions to be asked, but also condition what the answers will be. (To put the matter in the graceless jargon of management consultants, inputs determine outputs.)

Writing about Shakespeare on the Victorian Stage

Remaining within this historiographical framework, I now want to adopt a more specific focus by looking at some of the ways "old" evidence about Shakespeare on the stage can be put to "new" uses. I concentrate on four broad but, at times, overlapping, types of evidence: primary, secondary, marginal, and collateral. The case studies that I have chosen – all from the nineteenth century – should tell us something about the cultural vitality of Shakespearean performance. When, in my discussion, I refer to the work of other scholars, I do so not to criticize their findings but to explain how those findings represent a particular moment in performance historiography, a particular instance of disciplinary norms. I hasten to add that this perspective must equally apply to my own work, including the history you are now reading.

Let us start with the promptbook, the example *par excellence* of authoritative primary evidence. It is not difficult to see why the promptbook – the annotated script that details, among other aspects of performance, the running time, actors' entrances and exits, scene changes, music, and lighting cues – has been a vital documentary source for theatre historians. This artifact "prompts" the recovery of the original performance by indicating (although not always fully or accurately) what was seen and heard upon the stage. Invariably, however, the promptbook textualizes performance. That is, it necessarily privileges those dimensions of a performance event that can be textually encoded or, more broadly, that enact textual functions. Here, for example, is the so-called closet scene from Henry Irving's *Hamlet* (Lyceum 1878).

Like his predecessors, Irving had to decide how to represent the portraits of old Hamlet and Claudius, the "counterfeit presentment of two brothers." In 1709, Nicholas Rowe's illustrated edition of Shakespeare provided an early example. Two full-length portraits hang on the upstage wall of Gertrude's bedroom. Possibly inspired by Thomas Betterton's Restoration staging of Shakespeare's tragedy, this illustration was generally disregarded by subsequent generations of actor-managers. After all, it was rarely possible for the actors playing Claudius and old Hamlet to resemble portraits which were most likely taken from property-room stock: a more pragmatic approach, which became dominant in the eighteenth century, was for Hamlet to carry two medallion portraits. In the nineteenth-century theatre, practice varied. Macready transformed the Queen's closet into "a Royal Picture Gallery" that included portraits not only of Claudius and old Hamlet, but also of Gertrude and Hamlet himself (Sprague 1945: 168). And, in an image worthy of Gothic fiction, the Ghost emerged from within – and retreated back into – his own portrait. In Charles Fechter's production (Princess's Theatre 1861) Gertrude wore the miniature of Claudius around her neck so that Hamlet could tear it off and furiously throw it on the floor. Edwin Booth, toward the end of his career, split the difference: Gertrude wore a miniature of Claudius and Hamlet pointed to a full-length wall portrait of his late father.

Irving disregarded all these precedents. He gestured toward the audience, as if the portraits hung on the stage's imaginary "fourth wall." Through this innovative staging Irving made the scene deliberately ambiguous: the portraits were either part of the illusory theatrical world or hallucinations in Hamlet's tortured mind. Yet whichever option a spectator chose, the scene still made sense. No doubt this was because both options demanded that the audience remain conscious of the performance *as* a performance. In the first scenario, the audience is invited to obey the rules of theatrical illusionism. If Hamlet sees something, then it must be there. We imagine that the portraits are hung on the invisible fourth wall. In the second scenario, the audience is privy to the distorted reality of the character Hamlet. The portraits may be hallucinations, but the character is genuinely hallucinating. We imagine that the portraits are visible to Hamlet.

Yet this scene, for all its obvious theatricality, has also been regarded as a disavowal of stage action. Louis Barbato, among others, has argued that Irving's decision to dispense with actual portraits was anti-theatrical and that he had kept the Lyceum stage free of unnecessary scenery and properties for the sake of textual purity. The absence of the portraits, Barbato writes, demonstrated Irving's "devotion to the play's poetry" (1985: 156). Since Barbato's claims are based on promptbook analysis, we can hardly find them surprising. After all, he cannot see what his selected evidence does not preserve. The promptbook cannot document the purported absence of *mise en scène*.

It cannot register the negative capability, as it were, of the absent portraits. It can only register a normative textual presence.

Words, Words, Words

But let us look at the scene in light of other evidence. Everything we know about the monumentality of Irving's Shakespearean revivals – from the massive flight of steps leading down to Juliet's tomb in *Romeo and Juliet* (1882) to the 30-foot high church columns in *Much Ado about Nothing* (1882) – tells us that his pictorial aesthetic was even more spectacular than that of Kean and Macready. Irving never presupposed the centrality of texts. If anything, he presupposed the malleability of texts: that they are necessarily conditioned by the material exigencies of performance. As the actor-manager himself explained in *The Nineteenth Century*, his decision to use "imaginary" portraits in *Hamlet* was based upon a desire not to preserve the integrity of Shakespeare's tragedy but to capture his audience's imagination. He believed that spectators would reject both full-length pictures and medallions as mere "mechanical device[s]." If "practical difficulties" made "literal conformity with the text" impossible, Irving argued, then he had "complete justification" for departing from the text. "It is not a question of violating the poet's ideal," he elaborated, "but of choosing from amongst certain effects those which will create the most vivid impression" (Irving 1879: 262).

For Irving, then, the text is a function of its possibilities in performance. The "counterfeit presentments" remained an ekphrasis – a word-picture – not because Irving was committed to the inviolability of Shakespeare's words (he was not) but because he was committed to the inviolability of theatrical "effect." His decision not to visualize the text was the result of a prior decision that, in this instance, pictorial effects would be unacceptable to his audience. Yet, by strictly adhering to prompt-book analysis, we might fail to recognize how spectatorial experience of this production of *Hamlet* actually dictates the production's textual parameters. And we might also fail to recognize that the intelligibility of the scene requires that the audience think, not in a literary mode, but in a theatrical one.

Having seen that primary sources encode norms about how to look at the events which they document, let us now move on to consider how secondary sources also perform an evaluative, and not merely descriptive, function. For historians of nine-teenth-century culture, no secondary sources have been more plentiful than news-papers and periodicals. But the way historians treat these sources has been subject to scrutiny. "[P]eriodicals can no longer be regarded," Lyn Pykett explains, as "trans-parent records which give access to, and provide the means of recovering, the culture which they mirror" (1990: 7). For theatre historians, this shift in perception means that secondary accounts of performance are discursive formations in their own right and not (at least not principally) confirmations of presumably authoritative primary sources. Because journalistic reviews are readings – and not iterations – of a perform-ance, they do not express anterior assumptions about theatrical culture so much as they constitute those very assumptions. The review is, consequently, no less real and no less significative than the event which it might be presumed only to recount. To get a sense of how performance historians might re-evaluate their use of newspaper and periodical reviews, consider the Haymarket Theatre's production of *The Taming of the Shrew* (1844, 1847).

For two centuries, Shakespeare's play survived in the theatre only through adaptation and alteration, from John Lacy's *Sauny the Scot* (1667) to David Garrick's *Catharine and Petruchio* (1756). Indeed, the latter play held the stage for nearly one hundred years: Macready, forsaking his own commitment to textual restoration, even produced an altered version of Garrick's text in 1842. In 1844, however, *The Taming of the Shrew* was acted on a British stage for the first time since before the Restoration. The immediate reason for the revival was the chance to cast Louisa Nisbett (then Lady Boothby) in the role of Kate: recently widowed, the comic actress had returned to the stage to earn her living. The dramatist and antiquarian J. R. Planché, who oversaw the production, wanted to restore Shakespeare's original Folio text – including the Induction – and to stage the play in an Elizabethan style. With the consent of Benjamin Webster, the Haymarket's manager, the production opened on March 16, 1844 and was revived for a brief run three years later.

When theatre managers of the 1840s presented historical dramas they usually commissioned (or recycled) painted wing-and-drop scenery that depicted, with ever-increasing precision, the interior and exterior settings appropriate to the play's action – that is, modern staging techniques were used to represent historical settings. Yet Planché had something else in mind. He wanted to use original – that is, Elizabethan – staging techniques for *The Taming of the Shrew*. Having read J. P. Collier's *English Dramatic Poetry* (1831), he believed that public playhouses in Shakespeare's day consisted of a bare stage, curtains hung against the back wall, and screens and curtains placed on the sides of the acting area (Macdonald 1971: 159). This, then, was what he wanted to show on the Haymarket stage.

In the eventual production, Planché and Webster used only two painted backdrops: the outside of an alehouse (for the first Induction scene) and the inside of a nobleman's bedroom (for the second Induction scene and the play proper). The theatre's drop curtain was used only at the end of the entire performance. The tale of Katherine and Petruchio was thus presented as the play performed in the Lord's bedchamber by the strolling actors. The Lord and his servants assembled downstage left, while Christopher Sly and his party sat downstage right. The location of scenes – "a room in Baptista's house" or "in a public place in Padua" – was indicated by placards fastened to the curtains and (possibly) by rearranging the curtains and screens (Planché 1872: II, 83–6). In keeping with the historical precision of the scenic apparatus, the characters were dressed as Elizabethans. Sly remained onstage throughout, including the intervals between the acts, drinking wine and eating refreshments. During the fifth act, after having fallen into a drunken stupor, he was carried offstage by servants as the final curtain was brought down. Planché was immensely pleased with his own work: "The revival was eminently successful, incontestably proving that a good play, well acted, will carry the audience along with it, unassisted by scenery" (Planché 1872: II, 85).

Other appraisals were mixed. Some critics welcomed the simplicity of the *mise en scène* as a needed corrective to the vogue for spectacular sets, costumes, and properties. According to the *Dramatic Mirror* (November 3, 1847), the absence of heavy and intricate scenic devices "permitted the undivided attention of the audience to the business of the drama." *The Illustrated London News* (March 23, 1844) argued that the Haymarket production amply demonstrated that "mere gew-gaw accessories of the stage are not necessary." In a more spirited indictment of theatrical upholstery – and this a full decade before Kean's extravagant productions – *Bentley's Miscellany* (April 1844) declared that "[h]ere at one blow by the substitution of a contrivance beautiful in its simplicity, the whole army of scene-painters, carpenters, and shifters are ingeniously swamped." The *Athenaeum* (March 23, 1844), however, regretted that the "pedantic affectation of accuracy" hitherto associated with "scenic art" was not renounced, but simply transferred to the text. Instead of "faithfully represent[ing] the localities of [the] drama," the production faithfully represented the period when the drama was written. The problem, so the *Athenaeum* claimed, was that the original text did not warrant such scrupulous preservation. In a more strident account, *The Morning Post* (March 18, 1844) declared its preference for the "pleasant abridgement" of Garrick's *Catharine and Petruchio* to Shakespeare's "long, wearisome, and yet unfinished comedy of five acts."

In analyzing this production, theatre historians have been stymied by the lack of primary sources, for neither the promptbook nor the original set design has survived. There are, however, a good number of secondary sources, including Planché's memoirs and journalistic reviews, some of which I have cited above. Jan Macdonald relies upon these as well as other sources to reconstruct the production's scenery and staging – inferring, as it were, the substance of the promptbook *manqué*. For example, one of the main issues she seeks to resolve is whether the "side curtains" between the wings and the pilasters were "practicable" (Macdonald 1971: 161). Weighing up the available evidence, Macdonald decides that the curtains were probably just decorative. She drifts into an interpretation of the performance that she has been trying to rebuild, but she does not acknowledge that her interpretation is activated – indeed, determined – by the very archaeological procedures that she has followed.

Since Macdonald's primary goal is to explain how the pseudo-Elizabethan scenery worked, she naturally regards *mise en scène* as the key that unlocks the performance's concealed meaning. Thus, she interprets the Haymarket's production of *Shrew* as a backlash against the increasingly dominant convention of historically accurate staging. "[I]t is possible," she asserts, that "nineteenth-century critics were able to see [in the production] acting untrammelled by complicating setting and costumes" (1971: 162). The production's virtue, then, was to banish "setting and costumes" so that "acting" could emerge free and clear upon the now uncluttered Haymarket stage. This salvific interpretation – the performance is "saved" from the deformations wrought by spectacle – is presented as the logical conclusion to be drawn from an impartial analysis of evidence. And, as we have seen, this view was indeed articulated by some contemporary critics. Yet it seems more the case that the evidence – and the historian's prior decision to focus on that evidence – have already dictated the interpretive strategies for which it will be deployed. In reconstructing the Haymarket *Shrew*, Macdonald has constructed the object of her own inquiry.

To be sure, this is the frustrating condition of all historical study: that the past only ever appears to us through the mediation of contemporary concerns. Yet what is missing from Macdonald's account is self-reflexivity, the awareness that performance is never an innocent object simply waiting to be unveiled and interpreted. She rightly directs attention to the production's pseudo-Elizabethan *mise en scène* but then draws the wrong conclusion from it – wrong in the sense not of being untruthful, but of possessing no explanatory value. If, as Macdonald claims, the Haymarket revival of *Shrew* was an effective reproach to antiquarian spectacle, then why was the experiment not repeated at other theatres and with other Shakespearean plays? Why, moreover, did historically accurate *mise en scène* become even more dominant in the 1850s? Simply to label the production a "novelty" (Macdonald 1971: 169) is to ignore its own perspective on historical accuracy.

If we really want to examine the Haymarket *Shrew* in light of Victorian debates on stage spectacle, then we must approach the evidence from another angle. Let us return, then, to the newspaper and periodical reviews and try to read them not as confirmations of (absent) primary sources but as interpretive acts in their own right. From this perspective we will want to focus, most especially, on evidence that does more than describe the scenery. Consider, once again, the *Athenaeum*'s shrewd insight that the production, far from disavowing the "pedantic affectation of [historical] accuracy," displaced that "affectation" onto the text itself. Here is testimony that the production was committed to historical accuracy all along. The history that mattered, however, was the history of the dramatist and not the history of his characters. We now have further insight into why the Haymarket advertised its use of the "original text" as "acted divers times at the Globe and Blackfriars, Playhouses, 1606" (Playbill, Haymarket Theatre, March 16, 1844). That claim was possible because the entire production – including the structure of the playing spaces – was a period piece. Indeed, so self-consciously Elizabethan was this *Taming of the Shrew* that one of Hollar's "views" of London was painted on the act drop and Webster's costume (as Sly) made him look like Shakespeare. Moreover, the restoration of the Induction goes well beyond notions of textual integrity. There is a historicist function also at play here, since the scene is the only one in the Shakespearean canon that is indisputably set in Shakespeare's time.

All this marked a departure from the dominant convention of historicizing the *action* of a Shakespearean play. Indeed, that convention became established with Planché's famed antiquarian revival of *King John* (Covent Garden 1823). But Planché did not abandon his historicist principles when he staged *The Taming of the Shrew*. Rather, he engaged in a different mode of historicism. The production authenticated itself as Elizabethan through both *what* it represented and *how* it represented. It failed to meet expectations not because it lacked history, but because it emphasized the wrong history. The irony of the Haymarket *Shrew* was that it recreated the one historical moment least identified with Shakespeare: his own.

In examining Irving's *Hamlet* and the Planché–Webster *Shrew*, I have been looking at different ways of reading more or less the same evidence about a particular Shakespearean performance. I now want to consider how anterior decisions about what "counts" as evidence – the initial setting aside of material deemed to be of greatest relevance – inevitably circumscribe hermeneutic activities. My example is a production that is generally considered of marginal importance in the history of nineteenth-century Shakespeare: Squire and Marie Bancroft's revival of *The Merchant of Venice* (Prince of Wales's Theatre 1875).

Although a critical and commercial failure (it was withdrawn from the repertoire after 36 performances, having lost £3,000), the Bancrofts' production is remembered for Ellen Terry's accomplished portrayal of Portia four years before she played the role opposite Irving at the Lyceum. For my purposes, however, the most striking feature of *The Merchant of Venice* was its antiquarian and picturesque scenery. In the summer of 1874, Bancroft and his scene-painter, George Gordon, traveled to Venice to sketch San Marco, the Rialto, and the Grand Canal. E. W. Godwin (Terry's husband and father of the three-year-old Edward Gordon Craig), who had come to the Bancrofts' attention through his articles on "The Architecture and Costume of Shakespeare's Plays," served as the production's archaeological advisor. One strategy the Bancrofts learned from Godwin was to adapt Shakespeare's text so that a single "set scene" could be used for the duration of each act. For example, Shylock's trial and the "ring" scene could both be set in the Doge's Palace. This was a pragmatic necessity in a theatre as small as the Prince of Wales's, where the proscenium opening was only 20 feet by 20 feet. *The Merchant of Venice* was performed as a series of seven "scenes" or tableaux; only five backdrops were required since two of them – Portia's mansion in Belmont and the exterior of Shylock's house – were each used twice. "It all looked so unlike a theatre," Bancroft approvingly recalled, "and so much more like old Italian pictures" (Bancroft & Bancroft 1911: 229).

Yet it was precisely because of this unwavering commitment to looking like "old Italian pictures" that *The Merchant of Venice* failed at the box office. In adopting a richly pictorial aesthetic, the Bancrofts embarked upon a production that conflicted with the intimate, drawing-room atmosphere of their hugely successful stagings of T. W. Robertson's "cup and saucer" comedies, such as *Society* (1865) and *Caste* (1867). So ill-equipped for lavish scenic effects was the small theatre on Tottenham Street that part of a wall had to be removed to accommodate the massive columns faithfully reproduced from the Doge's Palace. Although the scene-painters dealt with the comparatively low proscenium opening by reducing the scale of the buildings depicted on the painted backdrops, an unfortunate consequence was that the actors appeared to be giants whenever they stood near the perspective scenery.

Moreover, the Bancrofts confounded the expectations of their audience, which associated pictorial Shakespeare with larger West End theatres. At the Prince of

Wales's Theatre they expected domestic interiors and "bric à brac" stage properties, not "[t]he gay, idle, *insouciante*, and withal mysterious life of the Queen of the Adriatic" (*Athenaeum* April 24, 1875). The "public" that patronized this theatre, as James Spedding observed in *Fraser's Magazine*, was not predisposed to find Shakespeare "attractive" (1875: 68). This disjunction between audience expectation and performance reality explains why customarily well-behaved spectators interrupted the opening performance with "outbursts of ribaldry" aimed chiefly at actors wearing picturesque fifteenth-century costumes. In short, the Bancrofts championed a production style that was wrong for their theatre and wrong for their audience.

But does this make the Bancrofts' production the "wrong" sort of evidence to document the Victorian obsession with theatrical historicism? Is this production a "weak" instance of the phenomenon? Many scholars have dismissed their *Merchant* as an example of pictorial Shakespeare in its detriment. But surely it is an example of pictorial Shakespeare in its perverse exaltation: an against-all-odds effort to make theatrical historicism succeed in the place where it was likeliest to fail. Indeed, I would argue that the Bancrofts' revival of *Merchant of Venice* is *more* significant than the revivals staged by Kean (1856) and Irving (1879) because it betrays the pressure actor-managers felt to perform Shakespeare as an animated history painting. So intense was this pressure that the Bancrofts adopted a *mise en scène* entirely unsuited to their theatre, their audience, and their own managerial experience. Yet, at least for the Bancrofts, there was no alternative. What, then, can we learn by analyzing a "failed" instance of pictorial Shakespeare? How does this deepen our understanding of Victorian theatrical practice? Significantly, failure is not the negation of meaning but the ground upon which meaning can be constructed. From a broader historiographical perspective, we can see that the "wrong" sort of evidence can sometimes be the most illuminating because it forces us to question our – often unacknowledged – standards of correctness.

Thus far, I have looked at documentation of such traditional aspects of stage history as *mise en scène*, dramaturgy, acting, and theatre management. Let me now, in some final examples, widen my focus to examine the relationship between performance and the society that creates it. Such an examination entails working with collateral evidence: that is, the records, artifacts, and materials that build up around a performance event. Collateral evidence does not document the formal aspects of a given performance so much as what might be called the surrounding "culture of performance." In some respects this is the most crucial form of evidence because it enables present-day historians to assess a performance's efficacy. Here, I have chosen examples of collateral evidence that document Shakespeare's place in nineteenth-century cultural nationalism. The first is about royal patronage of Shakespearean drama; the second concerns the campaign to allow London's minor theatres to perform Shakespeare.

Although Queen Victoria was the most prominent patron of Charles Kean's antiquarian revivals of Shakespeare at the Princess's Theatre in the 1850s, she was roundly censured in the early years of her reign for failing to promote the "national drama" and for preferring French plays and foreign opera. "If our [theatre] managers would only perform Shakspeare in French," *Punch* tartly proposed in 1844, "there might be a chance of the national drama being patronised by royalty" (*Punch* 1847: 144). Victoria's indifference to Shakespeare – that is, her failure to be sufficiently "English" in her cultural tastes – came under harsh scrutiny in 1847 when the poet's birthplace in Stratford-upon-Avon was auctioned. Shamefully, the government had refused to purchase the building. Private philanthropists organized fundraising events throughout the country to prevent the house in Henley Street from falling into the hands of commercial speculators. (One of the potential buyers was the showman P. T. Barnum, who no doubt would have created the first Shakespeare "theme park.") In the end, the house was privately purchased on behalf of the British public. But when more money was needed to keep the property open, the theatrical community did its best to make Shakespeare's birthplace a national monument by staging a benefit performance at Covent Garden.

That performance – which consisted of scenes from Shakespeare's most popular plays – offered theatregoers an extraordinary opportunity to witness the best actors of the day: Macready as Henry IV, Phelps as Prospero, Frances ("Fanny") Kemble as Queen Katharine, Helen Faucit as Juliet, and Mrs. Warner as Hermione. Undeterred by astoundingly high ticket prices, the capacity audience at Covent Garden must have been at least partly attracted by the promised appearance of Queen Victoria and Prince Albert. The *Athenaeum* (November 20, 1847), whose editor, Hepworth Dixon, had led the campaign to save Shakespeare's birthplace, boasted that "the patronage of Her Majesty and the Prince Consort has been obtained" for the "Shakspeare Night." Yet, although Dixon rejoiced at the prospect of the "queen drinking enjoyment at the sweet Shakspeare fountain," he rejoiced in vain, for the royal box remained empty that night.

Why, on the evening of December 7, did the Queen stay at Osborne House on the Isle of Wight when she had agreed to attend the "Shakspeare Night" in London? She says nothing about the missed performance in her journal. *Punch* (July–December 1847: 221), however, solved the mystery of the Queen's failure "to do reverence to the Genius of England – the Master Poet of Humanity." The stoker of the Royal train, so Mr. Punch claimed, had stayed at home with his sick wife and child. Under this unfortunate circumstance –"*the* favourite stoker being absent" – Victoria and Albert could not possibly travel to London. The story was fanciful, of course. But its criticism was just.

The *Athenaeum* (December 11, 1847), extreme in its earlier praise, took a similarly dim view of royal absenteeism:

> In a house thus crowded to an excess ... there was something most remarkable in the appearance of an empty box. The missing parties were those who are habitually absent from the Shakspeare banquet – the Royal patrons of the night made it their distinction to stay away. There was something painful in the sight of their vacant box. It was more than empty – it looked *foreign*. We had our eye much upon it; and wherever our contemporary saw Shakspeare, we are certain he was not sitting in that box.

In contrast to the otherwise crowded pit, boxes, and gallery, the unoccupied royal box symbolized not cultural nationalism but cultural defection. In the *Athenaeum's* pointed phrase, there was something distinctly *"foreign"* about Victoria's absence from the "Shakspeare banquet." How could the nation embrace the "old English drama" when the "sovereign" herself applauded only "French trash" (*Theatrical Journal*, September 21, 1853)? The Queen's "habitual" failure to patronize Shakespeare was, from the public's perspective, a failure to provide cultural governance.

The story of Victoria's absence from the "Shakspeare Night" is a story about the monarch's unwillingness to meet her responsibilities. As her critics complained, she did not prize Shakespeare highly enough. In a contrasting case, managers of London's minor theatres in the 1830s and early 1840s prized Shakespeare too highly. This was apparent most of all in their fight to abolish the patent system that prevented them from producing scripted drama. In this protracted struggle for theatrical emancipation, Shakespeare's ideological vitality was a central and recurring theme.

On May 31, 1832, Parliament named Edward Bulwer-Lytton, the playwright and politician, chairman of its Select Committee on Dramatic Literature and charged him with the task of examining the chaotic state of theatrical licensing and censorship. That Parliament convened a committee on theatrical licensing and passed the Great Reform Bill in the same year is hardly a coincidence, for the campaign to end the monopoly of the patent theatres turned on the same rhetoric of property and ownership as the concurrent campaign for nationwide electoral reform. In the political sphere, the issue was whether the property and privilege of the landed gentry – the traditional basis of aristocratic government and Georgian constitutional monarchy – could be safely replaced by expanded suffrage and direct political representation. Equivalent issues were debated in the theatrical world: was the national drama better served by the longstanding aristocratic stewardship of the royal patents or by market forces? For the sake of political economy – free trade and individual self-interest – Shakespeare ought to be deregulated. Culture, as well as politics, needed to be reformed. But for the sake of moral economy – the expression of national identity through the national drama – Shakespeare ought to be protected. Britain's greatest poet must be insulated from the dangers of the marketplace. (In the history of Shakespeare's afterlife, the need to protect the Bard from the evils of mass culture has been a recurring trope.)

In the slow transition from theatrical oligarchy to theatrical democracy, Shakespeare was the cultural equivalent of the franchise – the ticket of admission to nationhood itself. In Thomas Carlyle's famous tribute, "Shakespeare is ours; we produced him, we speak and think by him; we are of one blood and kind with him" (1841: 130–1). Anticipating, as it were, the conviction that Britons "speak and think" by Shakespeare, Bulwer-Lytton focused his inquiry not on infringements of the royal patents but on the oppression of the minor theatres. More specifically, he investigated prohibitions against performing Shakespeare. Although the Committee failed to persuade Parliament to emancipate the minor theatres, Bulwer-Lytton and his colleagues defined emancipation in terms of access to Shakespeare – whether that access be desired, denied, or even compelled.

Coda

Where, then, does the project of theatre historiography stand? When theatre historians write about Shakespeare and performance – or, for that matter, about any kind of performance – they inevitably write a double narrative: the narrative of the performances themselves and the meta-narrative of how they understand those performances. This double narrative, for all its constructedness, is not fictive. Indeed, following Hayden White, we can see that the historiographical double narrative transforms the "real" (something that happened) into the "true" (something that has meaning). Facts appear – that is, they are apprehended by our consciousness – only in light of the narrative structures that make their appearance possible. Moreover, those narrative structures are never constant. This is why the *truth* about past performances of Shakespeare will always change even though the *reality* of those performances may not. We will always tell different stories through accounts of Shakespeare's theatrical afterlife. We will always find new truths in old realities. Which is another way of saying – although for a radically different set of reasons than Ben Jonson had in 1623 when the First Folio was published – that Shakespeare is, indeed, "for all time."

REFERENCES AND FURTHER READING

Baer, Marc (1992). *Theatre and Disorder in Late Georgian London*. Oxford: Clarendon Press.

Bancroft, Marie & Bancroft, Squire (1911). *The Bancrofts: Recollections of Sixty Years*. London: Thomas Nelson and Sons.

Barbato, Louis R. (1985). "*Hamlet* on the Nineteenth-Century London Stage." *Shakespeare Jahrbuch* 121: 151–9.

Carlyle, Thomas (1841). *On Heroes, Hero-Worship, and the Heroic in History*. London: Ginn and Company.

Dallas, E. S. (1856). "The Drama." *Blackwood's Magazine* 79: 210–29.

de Certeau, Michel (1988). *The Writing of History*. Trans. Tom Conley. New York: Columbia University Press.

Derrida, Jacques (1998). *Archive Fever*. Trans. Eric Prenowitz. Chicago: University of Chicago Press.

Donne, W. B. (1851). "Poets and Players." *Fraser's Magazine* 44: 500–19.

Downer, Alan S. (1966). *The Eminent Tragedian: William Charles Macready*. Cambridge, MA: Harvard University Press.

Dunphy, Charles (1857). Letter to Charles Kean, Y.c. 830 (2). Folger Shakespeare Library, Washington, DC.

Fischer-Lichte, Erika (1997). *The Show and Gaze of Theatre: A European Perspective*. Iowa City. University of Iowa Press.

Fontane, Theodor (1999). *Shakespeare in the London Theatre 1855–58.*, ed. and trans. Russell Jackson. London: Society for Theatre Research.

Foulkes, Richard (2002). *Performing Shakespeare in the Age of Empire*. Cambridge: Cambridge University Press.

Irving, Henry (1879). "An Actor's Notes on Shakespeare, No. 3: 'Look here, upon this picture, and on this.'" *The Nineteenth Century* 5 (February): 260–3.

Jackson, Shannon (1998). "Performance at Hull-House." In Della Pollock (ed.) *Exceptional Spaces:*

Essays in Performance and History. Chapel Hill, NC: University of North Carolina Press, pp. 261–93.

Kean, Charles (1856). Letter to Sir William Snow Harris, Y.c. 393 (247). Folger Shakespeare Library, Washington, DC.

Lewes, G. H. (1842). *Westminster Review* 37: 78.

Macdonald, Jan (1971). *"The Taming of the Shrew* at the Haymarket Theatre, 1844 and 1847." In Kenneth Richard & Peter Thompson (eds.) *Nineteenth-Century British Theatre*. London: Methuen, pp. 157–70.

Marshall, Gail & Poole, Adrian (eds.) (2003). *Victorian Shakespeare*, 2 vols. Basingstoke: Palgrave Macmillan.

Matthew, H. C. G. (ed.) (1978). *The Gladstone Diaries*, vol. V (1855–60). Oxford: Clarendon Press.

Moody, Jane (2000). *Illegitimate Theatre*. Cambridge: Cambridge University Press.

Planché, J. R. (1872). *Recollections and Reflections*, 2 vols. London: Tinsley Brothers.

Punch (1847). "Monsieur Shakspeare." *Punch* 12: 144.

Pykett, Lyn (1990). "Reading the Periodical Press: Text and Context." In Laurel Brake, Aled Jones, & Lionel Madded (eds.) *Investigating Victorian Journalism*. Basingstoke: Macmillan, pp. 1–15.

Report from the Select Committee on Dramatic Literature, with Minutes of Evidence (1832). London: House of Commons.

Richards, Jeffrey (ed.) (1994). *Sir Henry Irving: Theatre, Culture, and Society*. Keele: Keele University Press.

Schoch, Richard (1998). *Shakespeare's Victorian Stage: Performing History in the Theatre of Charles Kean*. Cambridge: Cambridge University Press.

Schoch, Richard (2002). *Not Shakespeare: Bardolatry and Burlesque in the Nineteenth Century*. Cambridge: Cambridge University Press.

Schoch, Richard (2004). *Queen Victoria and the Theatre of her Age*. Basingstoke: Palgrave Macmillan.

Smith, Emma Hamilton (1857). Letter to Ellen Kean, Art vol. d4. Folger Shakespeare Library, Washington, DC.

Sprague, A. C. (1945). *Shakespeare and the Actors*. Cambridge, MA: Harvard University Press.

Spedding, James (1875). *The Merchant of Venice* at the Prince of Wales's Theatre. *Fraser's Magazine* July: 64–8.

13

Shakespeare Goes Slumming: Harlem '37 and Birmingham '97

Kathleen McLuskie

Show and Tell

"I expect it would be better if you saw it." The student, frustrated by the imaginative labor of turning words on the page of Shakespeare text into the discourse of criticism, shifts the ground to a discussion of performance. By invoking the authority of performance, she no longer has to think through the varieties of tone of voice in which a line can be said ("Give me the daggers," *Macbeth*, 2.2) or how the reactions of those silent on stage and absent from the script (when *does* the doctor enter in Macbeth 4.3?) will make up the theatrical dynamic of a scene. The minor characters (Lennox, Macdonald, A Lord, Seyton) are easily distinguished by costumes and beards, height and girth and the locations of the action are clear or irrelevant, uncomplicated by pedantic strictures about editorial stage directions. All the work of casting and costuming, set design and lighting, rehearsals, marketing and front of house are hidden; the product, a Shakespeare play, is made immediately accessible and available for judgment.

The appeal of the approach through theatre is that it offers an immediacy of experience. The real-time simultaneity of the action, the co-location of actors and audience in the same space, creates an effect that is not reproduced in any other literary form. Nonetheless that immediacy, that sense of a total experience of the play, by making certain choices and avoiding others, occludes other dimensions of the play's potential. As W. B. Worthen puts it: "Performance signifies an absence, the precise fashioning of the material text's absence, at the same time that it appears to summon the work into being, to produce it as performance … summons one state of the work while it obviates others" (1997: 17).

Theatre history and its analysis have as their aim to recapture the whole of a text's potential by working through as many of the recorded performances as possible. However, in doing so, those activities compromise the immediacy of performance by turning event back into discourse. The "two hours passage" of the stage and the pleasures it provides are located in a continuum of history or aesthetics that only exist after the event and can often be judged or disputed by those who need not even have been present at the show (see Worthen 1997: 6–7).

The creative tension between the present moment of the theatre-event and the discourses of analysis had its origins in the debates over theatre in the early modern period. Alongside the anxieties over the social implications of the new entertainment – the fear of crowds, the logistics of traffic control, the concerns for public health or opportunities for sexual misconduct – there emerged a polarization between the values of language and the more immediate pleasures of the event shared between players and audience.

When Hamlet advised, "let those that play your clowns speak no more than is set down for them," he deplored the collusive enjoyment of those "that will themselves laugh to set on some quantity of barren spectators to laugh too." He separates the understanding of "necessary questions of the play" (3.2.34–8), the play's discursive significance, from the localized pleasures of a particular performance. Prospero puts the case more elegiacally. He reminds the lovers in *The Tempest* that the masque of reapers is an "insubstantial pageant." The elegiac tone comes from Prospero's discursive slide from the insubstantiality of the masquing pageant to the elusive other world of dreams and then to life itself:

> We are such stuff
> As dreams are made on, and our little life
> Is rounded with a sleep.
>   (4.1.155–8)

The long philosophical and religious tradition that separated the world of the senses from the higher world of intellectual and spiritual truth gave particular force to the opposition between momentary theatrical pleasure and the "necessary questions" of written drama. Early modern articulations of these oppositions also mapped onto and helped to formalize conceptions of social status. Hamlet is clear that those who appreciate the physical theatre are the groundlings "who for the most part are capable of nothing but inexplicable dumb-shows and noise" (3.2. 10-11). The simple alignment of high thinking with high social status was to some extent challenged by contemporary playwrights. Dekker used the printed version of his "Magnificent Entertainment" for James's royal entry into London to mock poets who "make a false flourish with the borrowed weapons of all the old Maisters of the noble science of Poesie" since he was aware that "The multitude is now to be our Audience" (Dekker 1955: 65). However, for the most part the division between show and intellectual substance was that articulated by Heywood when he included a show that "consisteth of Anticke gesticulations and other Mimicke postures, devised onely for the vulgar, who are better delighted with that which pleaseth the eye, than contenteth the eare" (Heywood 1637).

This separation of physical performance from other pleasures of theatre was reinforced by commercial and regulatory distinction. When the revived boy player companies opened new theatre spaces in the halls of the religious houses, they differentiated their offerings in terms of the exclusivity of their respective audiences. However, that distinction also came to be mapped onto different theatrical styles. The "drum and trumpet" that came to be a synecdoche for boisterous performance pleasure was placed in opposition to a theatre of language and ideas that also laid claims to greater verisimilitude. These oppositions were articulated by many of the dramatists of the early modern theatre but perhaps most eloquently and consistently in the repeated apologias of Ben Jonson's prologues. He insisted on his solution to the way that

> ... other plays should be
> Where neither Chorus wafts you o'er the seas,
> Nor creaking thrones come down, the boys to please
> Nor nimble squib is seen, to make afear'd
> The gentlewomen, nor rolled bullet heard
> To say, it thunders, nor tempestuous drum
> Rumbles to tell you when a storm doth come;
> But deeds and language such as men do use
> And persons such as Comedy would choose
> When she would show an image of the times,
> And sport with human follies, not with crimes.
> (14–24; Jonson 1972: 5)

In this, now famous, prologue, Jonson carefully constructs his ideal audience by explicitly excluding the supposed tastes of children and women, in favour of "deeds and language such as men do use." He also may have explicitly been contrasting his work with Shakespeare's in his references to the descending throne (seen in *Cymbeline*) and the Chorus such as the ones in *Henry V* that took the audience, with all due apology for theatrical inadequacy, to the "vasty fields of France" (Prologue, line 12). Shakespeare was also, more evidently, cited in *Bartholomew Fair*'s reference to the "Tales, Tempests, and such like drolleries" of the rejected theatre of the past age (Jonson 1995: 332). It is important to remember, however, that this prologue appears only in the Folio version of the play, written some 18 years after the first performance of the play. It represents less an attack on a fellow playwright than an emerging discourse of modernity used to insist on the value both of new plays and of particular revivals.

These efforts to construct and then control the discourses of theatrical value may also have had a special purchase in the context of an emerging competitive commercial theatre. The written dramatic texts of the secular theatre had a particular value: they could be repeated and revived or published in other forms; they were not tied exclusively to the repeated narratives and particular occasions of the church year or the festive cycle of the court. As such, they seem to have required frequent discursive elaboration that produced and re-produced a number of settled cognate differentiations: between commerce and art, between ideas and action, between language and sensory experience and between new and old-fashioned styles of performance.

Since these are contested discursive distinctions, there are dangers in mapping them onto the history of performed drama. The tension between descriptive aim of mapping and the inevitably tendentious nature of history has been evident in most attempts to do so. The critical conflict over the nature of the early modern audience (Cook 1981, Butler 1984) and evaluations of Henslowe's role in the development of commercial theatre (Knutson 1991: 15–20, Rogers 2002) all reveal the persistence of these terms of value into the twentieth century as much as they resolve the question of their impact on the development of early modern theatre. These terms of value are particularly loaded in the twentieth century because of their intersection with the cultural value assigned to Shakespeare. As we have seen, Shakespeare is, if anything, consigned in the early modern debate to the negative pole of the oppositions of value. However, by the twentieth century, his work had been resituated at their fulcrum. As Rosalind Knutson states, Shakespeare's plays have become the reason for further study of his period and his contemporaries: "Because one of these members (of the Chamberlain's and the Kings Men) was William Shakespeare, ... theatre historians have treated every scrap of information as priceless treasure" (1991: 2).

The story of Shakespeare's accumulation of cultural capital has often been told (Taylor 1991, Bristol 1996). However, the particular cultural capital involved in the relationship between ideas and performance mediates that process and inflects the terms of that accumulation.

Interpretation and Meaning

At this stage in the early twenty-first century the early modern opposition between physical styles of performance and ideas seems to have lost its purchase in the cultural valuation of Shakespeare. The Shakespeare revolution (Styan 1977) that brought performance to the center of Shakespeare studies in the mid-twentieth century is complete and the technologies of film and video make Shakespeare performance available to all but the most cash-strapped college and secondary school classroom. Nonetheless, debates over the significance of Shakespeare continue and the role of performance in the articulation of those debates will bear further scrutiny.

In his critique of the "dogmatic, self-defeating functionalism" of anti-essentialist accounts of Shakespeare's cultural significance, Michael Bristol asserts that "any theory that attempted to account for a work's particular shape based only on its social afterlife would lack even a minimal descriptive and explanatory competence" (1996: 25). In this statement, Bristol shifts the ground from the cultural reception of Shakespeare to the immanent significance of the work, presumed to reside in its "particular shape." In doing so, he occludes performance completely: in performance, the "work's particular shape," its multi-dimensional existence in time and space and sound, is precisely what is changed. Even when the lines and speeches are taken directly from a currently authorized text, their relationship to spoken speech is continually at issue in performance and opens the question of the precise nature of the cultural object that is being transmitted in the name of Shakespeare.

Interviewed about her experience of playing Lady Macbeth, Sinead Cusack expressed her admiration for the emotional power, precisely, of a particular line in the play. Describing Macbeth and his lady meeting after she has received his account of the witches' prophecy, she notes: "And then Lady Macbeth says 'He that's coming / Must be provided for.' It's an amazing line. She's going to play hostess to Duncan at Dunsinane, and 'provide' is what gracious hostesses always do. It a wonder of a line to play because the reverberations do the acting for you, make the audience go 'Aaaagh!'" (Rutter 1988: 62).

Cusack's account suggests a synergy between the line of text, the actor's performance and the audience's physical reaction. The source of that reaction is, however, based on a purely textual effect. The line gains its effect of irony and double entendre because of its position in a narrative that sets up its own expectation of action: the suspense-filled question of how those narrative expectations will be fulfilled. The narrative of *Macbeth* is formally constructed to produce those effects of suspense, through the double movement of the fulfilment of two sets of prophecies and the secondary narrative of revenge for the murder of Macduff's children (McLuskie 2003: 393–7). Turning the *effect* of suspense into the *affect* of reaction to the line requires an imaginative engagement with the fate of the characters that can equally easily come from a narrative read or heard. We should be clear that this imaginative engagement is an effect that is learned through a process that combines socialization and education (O'Dair 2000), a process that is reproduced in the socialization of every individual but is also a product of particular historical circumstances.

The place of *Macbeth* in the English education system had ensured that both Cusack and her audience had received that socialization. Elsewhere in her interview, she provides a moment-by-moment account of the interpretative sub-text that had informed her performance, loading even its physical dimension with critical meaning. Describing her change of role into Queen of Scotland in the second part of the play, she says:

> The next time we see her she has been crowned and she is dressed in full regalia, in a black velvet dress, tightly corseted, a Tudor cape up to her ears, a ruff that came right up to her chin, and the crown on top. When I had to put on those huge heavy robes I thought I'd never be able to bear the weight – it was amazing to stand there bowed down by those clothes. It was a great design point. It's a play that's constantly talking about borrowed robes. (Rutter 1988: 66)

Cusack's description of the significance of her costume moves from the physical effect of heavy clothing to its symbolic function in communicating a change that had overtaken her character after Duncan's murder. The relationship between the performance effect and its meaning is facilitated by her reference to Cleanth Brooks's famous essay: "The Naked Babe and the Cloak of Manliness" (1959), in which he effectively links the image strands of clothing and of children into a closely woven account of the organic nature of the play's underlying thought patterns.

Brooks's essay, with its intense focus on teasing out the multiple ambiguities and resonances of the play's language might seem to be the antithesis of performance criticism. However, its assimilation as an intellectual justification of the design ideas in a production marks a telling effect in the role of performance in the transmission of Shakespeare. Cusack was performing in the late 1980s in the most prestigious Shakespeare company in the UK (if not in the world), a company that frequently worked with academics and whose entire purpose was to explicate Shakespeare to the population as a whole. Its assimilation of academic criticism into performance was, however, the product of a process that had begun at a much earlier stage. From the eighteenth century on, the reproduction of the play in both texts and performances had been accompanied by critical writing that had the effect of turning the play into a moral fable, illustrating the effects of poetic justice and considering the ethical and psychic nature of the characters' motivation.

What became available for transmission was interpretation. The ethical emphasis of criticism gave the characters a life that extended beyond the stage and turned them into exemplary figures illustrating the nature of ethical choice and the action of moral judgment. This essentially literary approach also informed performance as actors described the effects they sought in ethical terms. Describing her preparation for the performance of Lady Macbeth, Adelaide Ristori begins with the character's motivation. However, the information that she uses to develop the character comes not from the text but from her sense of the psychic and ethical dimensions of a relationship between Macbeth and his lady that is read off and through the text into the narrative situation: "I saw in Lady Macbeth, not merely a woman actuated by low passions and vulgar instincts, but rather a gigantic conception of perfidy, dissimulation and hypocrisy." Ristori moves from this preconception of the Lady's character to a description of the mechanics of performance. However the language of her description corroborates the initial judgment: "I uttered the first words of this monologue ('come ye spirits') in a hollow voice, with bloodthirsty eyes, and with the accent of a spirit speaking from out of some abyss, and as I continued, my voice grew louder and more resonant, until it changed into an exaggerated cry of joy at the sight of my husband" (Ristori 1888, in Thompson and Roberts 1997: 204–5).

There is, of course, a fundamental gap between the description and the experience of a performance. There can be no guarantee that the meaning that Ristori attributes to her "bloodthirsty eyes" or her "exaggerated cry of joy" would necessarily be communicated to her audience. Nor would an audience necessarily have grasped the symbolic significance of Sinead Cusack's change of clothes. In theatre history, analysis stands in for experience.

The effect of this dominance of interpretation was to normalize the play's narrative by abstracting it into the recognizable behavior of men and women, in spite of the extremity of their circumstances. The relationship between the experience of performance and ethical judgment of the characters became conflated in the methodologies of criticism. In the early twentieth century, some of these interpretations were codifed by A.C. Bradley in a series of notes to the Lectures that made up his influential book, *Shakespearean Tragedy*. His long note asking "Did Lady Macbeth really faint?" (Bradley 1969: 417–19) illustrates the point. He addresses Lady Macbeth's single-line call for help in the midst of the "scene of confusion where Duncan's murder is discovered" and enquires, "Does Lady Macbeth really turn faint or does she pretend?" The revealing word in his question is "really." In one sense there is no "really": we are witnessing a play, not a narrative of events which did occur at some other time; the text provides no evidence one way or the other; nothing in the narrative or progression of the action hangs on it. Nevertheless Bradley was able to draw on other critics who had argued the case and turned it into a key question for Lady Macbeth's character.

The process of Bradley's argument is more interesting than the question he begins with since it provides a paradigm for interpretative criticism. He takes other episodes from the play – Lady Macbeth's return to the scene of the murder, her emotional collapse in Act 3 and suicide in Act 4 – as illustrative of an essential personality. He also canvasses reasons why she might have pretended to faint – to deflect attention from her husband's false reaction to the news of the murder – and he provides additional stage business for an ideal performance suggesting that even though she has no additional lines, the interval between the first and second call to attend to the lady is "occupied in desperate efforts on her part to prevent herself from giving way, as she sees for the first time something of the truth to which she was formerly so blind, and which will destroy her in the end" (Bradley 1969: 418–19).

His conclusion is particularly telling: "Shakespeare, of course, knew whether he meant the faint to be real: but I am not aware if an actor of the part could show the audience whether it was real or pretended. If he could, he would doubtless receive instructions from the author" (1969: 419). Bradley tries to place the ultimate authority for the text's meaning in the intentions of its author. However, he also recognizes that the text provides no clue to those intentions. As a result, the play's meaning must rest in interpretation of its unspoken truth, informed by assumptions about human nature. It assumes a consistency between character and action and locates personality in conventional assumptions about a gendered morality assumed to lie behind the text.

The gendering of morality also lies behind the authorities he cites in support for the different views about the meaning of the action. The commentary in the Variorum edition of the play includes extensive notes on particular performances as well as bibliographical and linguistic notes, and it echoes Bradley's preoccupation with the faint. The controversy is rehearsed in a long note on her line that turns on the credibility of Lady Macbeth's character. As one of the commentators put it:

Call her a Fiend – she was a woman. Down stairs she comes – and stands among them all, at first like one alarmed only – astounded by what she hears – and striving to simulate the ignorance of the innocent – "What in our house?" "Too cruel anywhere!" What she must have suffered then Shakespeare lets us conceive for ourselves. (Furness 1915: 162)

The Variorum commentator's note extends the audience's engagement with the play by allowing for the possibility of its sympathy for Lady Macbeth's suffering. The lines of the play provide a conduit into an emotional arena far more extensive than their immediate referents. The exercise of criticism was designed to create an audience that would respond not merely to the play's narratives and their pleasures of suspense and the fulfilment of prophecy but also to the sense that the moment-by-moment experience of the play would offer an intensity of ethical and psychic awareness. In the process, the gap between ideas and performance that had exercised anti-theatrical commentators from early modern period times was bridged by critical analysis that explained and charted an appropriate response to the action of the play.

This effort of interpretative criticism was in part made necessary precisely because of intractable elements in the performance of the play's narrative. At the play's heart there lay a significant barrier to this emotional and ethical engagement: the fact that the whole action was initiated and progressed by supernatural agents: the witches, the dagger and the ghost. Various devices were employed from Davenant's late seventeenth-century adaptation onwards, to deal with these supernatural forces in the play. Davenant moved the locus of motivation away from the witches to an interiorized ethical abstraction adding speeches about "Ambition" and in so doing provided the basis for subsequent moral readings of the action (McLuskie 2003). Dr. Johnson historicized the witches, turning their impact from an incredulous disincentive to engagement to a mark of historical authenticity, based on James VI and I's supposed interest in witchcraft. In the theatre, the physical presence of the witches could be turned to a different advantage. John Downes, who worked with Davenant, reported that this version of *Macbeth,* for all its moral coherence, was especially admired for "all its Finery, as new Cloath's, new Scenes, Machines (as flyings for the Witches), with all the Singing and Dancing in it" (Downes 1987: 33). Later nineteenth-century productions further elaborated the witches with the addition of choruses of singing witches and set-piece tableaux of witch effects, often played by comic character actors (see Trewin 1971).

The trend of interpretative performance, on the other hand, was to turn the supernatural into abstraction or to remove it altogether. In 1794, for example, the actor John Philip Kemble chose to ignore the stage instruction "Enter ghost" throughout the banquet scene (Donohue 1971: 24). His Macbeth ranted and recoiled from an empty space, allowing the theatre audience to share the courtiers' astonishment that he "looked but on a stool." Kemble was able to make this change since he could assume that his audience would know the play well enough to remember that a ghost appears at this stage. The effect, often repeated in subsequent performances, is to place the audience outside Macbeth, denying them a shared experience of the horror at the gory locks and the 20 trenched gashes on the figure who could appear on stage. The connection between performance and audience is through Macbeth's interior struggle rather than the events to which he responds. The effect was to secure an emphasis entirely on the interiority of the performance, returning it to the shared ethical and psychic sensibilities celebrated by Ristori and Cusack.

This normalization even of the play's supernatural action extended beyond the romantic tradition to inform twentieth-century productions that were, in other respects, self-consciously avant-garde. When Komisarjevsky produced *Macbeth* at the Shakespeare Memorial Theatre in 1933, his constructivist aluminium set and transhistorical mix of mediaeval and modern weaponry proclaimed a break from the traditions of romantic Shakespeare. As the reviewer of the *Sheffield Daily Telegraph* enthused, "Komisarjevsky has eliminated time and, so far as the text allows, has eliminated space; he has made the tragedy universal" (Berry 1983: 75, Kennedy 1993: 129).

The universality achieved, however, was recognized by other reviewers as a device to ensure the now primary theatrical pleasure of recognition, the sense that the characters and events of the play inhabit the same world as the audience. One of the most memorable innovations of Komisarjevsky's production was to remove the magical elements of the witches. They open the play as "three old hags, robbing a dead soldier" (*Birmingham Post*, April 19, 1933, in Berry 1983: 75). The act of battlefield looting emphasizes their evil in completely rational terms that place the play in a world of violence and horror but one that could easily be transposed to a modern context. The production was described as "an attempt to relate Shakespeare to an age dominated by psychological conceptions, rationalising the play's magic and witchcraft and making Banquo's ghost a mere figment of the imagination" (*The Times*, April 19, 1933, in Berry 1983: 76). The theatre lighting, moreover, was used to give a symbolic meaning to the action: the ghost was not merely absent but created by "a gigantic shadow of Macbeth himself thrown against his castle walls." Banquo's ghost, the witches, the Scottish setting and the seventeenth-century political implications of regicide and national conflict had become mere particulars able to be brought up or played down as a vehicle for the essential drama of the human psyche.

Slumming with Shakespeare

The combination of effective technical devices and high production values in the twentieth century allowed the development of a theatre experience that offered autonomous aesthetic satisfaction. The connection to Shakespeare gave that experience an ethical and psychic dimension, carried over from earlier interpretation, that transformed the text into abstracted cultural value that assured its constant reproduction. The remaining question for the cultural brokers charged with this reproduction was how to ensure a sufficiently extended audience for the product.

The changing economic base of theatre production in the early years of the twentieth century made an extension to the mass audience a pressing necessity. As Rena Fraden (1996: 32) notes, the costs of materials used in American productions between 1913 and 1928 rose 200 percent, and wages increased as much as 522 percent. One response to this economic pressure was a theatre movement that valorized simplicity of setting and a directness of approach to its audience, often invoking a similar simplicity in the plays' original conditions of production (Kennedy 1993: 34–43). Economic necessity was accompanied by cultural anxiety that the extended audience might not be able to respond to the valued complexity of Shakespeare. The solution lay both in an energetic program of education, and a discursive insistence on the significance of innovative performance as the route into the heart of Shakespeare.

These discussions drew on the polarization of spectacle and language that had emerged in the early modern commercial theatre. They had a similar function in creating a rhetoric of innovation but they reversed the poles of value, insisting on the vitality and accessibility of spectacle as opposed to the dead and exclusive nature of "Establishment" Shakespeare (Marowitz 1991: 15, Worthen 1997: 71).

The polarization of tradition and innovation was, of course, a discursive overlay onto the processes of reproduction. As we have seen, criticism and performance co-existed and informed one another throughout Shakespeare's afterlife. Nevertheless, particular productions can reveal the transforming effect of that process on both the written text and the nature of performed Shakespeare. The productions chosen are in no way paradigmatic. The sheer number and eclecticism of productions of Shakespeare defy comprehensive synthesis. However, by addressing both a canonical and an uncanonical production, it is possible to identify some of the terms of engagement with Shakespeare that characterize the contemporary cultural moment.

In 1997, an educational television production of *Macbeth* addressed the problematic of popularization both by using the dominant medium of mass communication and by locating the play in the self-consciously working-class world of a Birmingham council-housing estate. The style of the production used the familiar signifiers of urban realism, old cars, rundown flats and the windswept corners and angles of 1960s' public housing. The performance opened with a narrative of a localized situation in which the Scottish play was reconfigured through the power conflict of local gangs. The narrative echoed contemporary criticism of the play by demystifying Duncan's regal authority, presenting him as an ageing punk gang-leader whose power was in decline. Malcolm and Macbeth presented the gang's violent and competitive younger generation, shown raiding flats, dealing drugs and beating up their rivals with baseball bats; the witches were children scurrying threateningly along the balconies and through the boarded-up flats, their cavern part children's den, part magic hideout. Cawdor's execution was in a car soused with petrol and the interior settings of the public scenes were either in Macbeth's flat or in a pub where the men were shown drinking and gambling. These images of working-class life, however, were drawn as much from the television realism of police procedurals as from actual working-class existence. The debt to a catalogue of popular culture was especially evident in the scene of Duncan's funeral that evoked the rainy weather, the solemn procession of people and funeral cars and the numinous graveside encounter of countless mafia movies.

More important than these changes of setting or transpositions of lines is the change in the point of view from which the scenes are shot. The demands of television naturalism turn the play inside out, shifting the audience's attention from the text's intense focus on the figure of Macbeth, reacting to events off stage – the welcome feast for Duncan; the scene of the murder, the death of his Lady; the approach of Birnam Wood. The television conventions of frequent changes of shot and reassertions of location produce a quite different interaction between Macbeth and the world of the gang. Duncan's welcome feast is seen through an open door. Duncan and his gang are sprawled, drinking beer, across the domestic living room. Lady Macbeth is centre screen, seated, smoking, isolated from the party. She joins Macbeth in the bedroom and the dialogue of persuasion and resolution paces and punctuates a literal sexual action. Even the murder of Duncan, kept off stage in the play, is enacted in the television version. Macbeth does not bring a weapon with him but has to extract a knife from the pocket of a sleeping bodyguard. The scene's emotional tension comes from localized suspense over whether Macbeth can do the deed without waking others in the room. Lines from Macbeth's and his Lady's panic-stricken colloquy about the murder are retained in the following sequence, but their reference point is an act that has been seen, not one that is being created for the audience in the murderer's fractured recollections.

It is this shift of audience point of view, as much as the flat English Midlands accents or the modern setting, which defines the style of the television version. The cutting ensures that attention is tied to the human interaction between Macbeth and his lady. Lady Macbeth's sleepwalking is transposed to the kitchen where she is seen washing her hands at the sink. She is then shown on the roof of the high-rise flats, looking out over the city and the camera cuts to a shot of her falling body. "Tomorrow and tomorrow" is spoken over her body, lying on the pavement, surrounded by the witch-children and the neighbors, their impassive faces framed in close-ups.

This attention to working-class naturalism ensures that the play's historical problems of magic and the supernatural are completely removed from the action. A solemn, older, Black-British woman is given the lines from 2.4, in which the Old Man recounts the portents that surrounded Duncan's murder. She speaks the lines directly to Macbeth, a tendentious, but not supernatural, reminder of the precariousness of his new position. Macbeth speaks the address to the magic dagger sitting at his kitchen table. In keeping with modern convention, the dagger is invisible, "a false creation/Proceeding from the heat-oppressed brain" (2.1. 36–7). The ghost of Banquo does appear but he is only glimpsed as the camera whirls around the room following Macbeth's gyrations in a hectic drinking-game.

Yet in spite of this conscious elimination or naturalization of the historical play, the production cannot do without its residual claims to Shakespearean significance. After the action has ended, Malcolm has resumed his father's power – and his position at the pub's bar. The camera shifts to the empty urban wasteland in which Macduff stands alone, with the high-rise flats in long shot beyond him. He speaks Ross's lines from the scene in England: "Alas poor country, / Almost afraid to know itself" (4.3. 166–7). This portentous extrapolation of the action attempts to turn the production, at its close, into a statement about the condition of England. The role of "Shakespeare" in providing added significance to the everyday is too precious to lose.

The production's dependence on the cultural capital of "Shakespeare" is even more evident in the treatment of Macbeth's Lady. She is played as an ordinary working-class woman, a friend of Lady Macduff, affectionate and helpful with her children and shown carrying the children across a street, or comforting them when they are frightened by the explosions of casual violence in the feast scene. After she has heard the news of Macbeth's encounter with the witches (delivered on a telephone answering-machine), she enters a child's bedroom, furnished with a musical mobile above the tiny cot. Her invocation of the "spirits that tend on mortal thoughts" is there set against the tinkle of the mobile's music and an unexplained connection is made between the plan to murder Duncan and the absence of her child. In the scene where she urges Macbeth to the murder, critical commonplaces about the sexual undercurrent of that dialogue are literalized into action. Its deeper psychic motivation is also underscored. When Macbeth cries "Bring forth men children only," his lady is astride him. The camera cuts to a bedside photograph of a small child: Lady Macbeth's hand comes into shot and turns the photo face down as she reminds Macbeth that their power will silence suspicion. Her longing for children is given a particularly literal representation after the death of Banquo. In bed after the exhaustion of the feast and the ghost's appearance, she suddenly gets up and goes to the bathroom cabinet, reaching down a pack of tampons. Then in silent and unarticulated rage, she breaks up a different packet, presumably a pregnancy-testing kit.

This rendering of Lady Macbeth's motivation via unspoken visual signifiers gives it particular power as the sub-text to the play's action. However, it too is normalized in the suggestion of Duncan's sexual power over her. Before the welcome feast, his greeting is sexually aggressive. The extra-textual gesture once again opens up the range of meaning, allowing for motivation based on sexual jealousy, or resentment at sexual exploitation to replace those of dynastic ambition and the lust for royal power.

Late twentieth-century ideas about competitive masculinity and inner-city violence informed this production and signalled its explicit separation from "Establishment" Shakespeare but the treatment of Lady Macbeth ties it firmly back to the reproduction of Shakespeare in literary criticism. Feminist criticism (Adelman 1992: 130–64) in the late twentieth century had used psychoanalysis to return an interest in the play to Lady Macbeth. In doing so, these echoed Freud's own essay on the subject (Freud 1985) and provided a robust response to the critical tradition that mockingly dismissed the question of Lady Macbeth's children. L. C. Knights's famous essay, "How Many Children Had Lady Macbeth?" was a rejection of "all the irrelevant moral and realistic canons that have been applied to Shakespeare's plays, for the sentimentalising of his heroes ... and his heroines" (1991: 129). He proposed instead to deal with "Shakespeare primarily as a poet" (1991: 129), arguing that the only way to deal with the particular power of the play was "to allow full weight to each word, exploring its tentacular roots, and to determine how it controls and is controlled by the rhythmic movement of the passage in which it occurs (1991: 130). The resulting analysis has proved enormously influential, highlighting passages which it is now impossible for any critic to ignore: the passages dealing with confusion created by paradox (1.1.10–11; 1.2.7–9), the passages which identify the ambiguous gender of the witches (1.3.43–4), and above all the passages which speak of a concern with the deformation of nature and traditional order in relations between men. In returning attention to the significance of women in the play, Adelman deployed a similar intense attention to the deep structures of meaning revealed in the play's poetic imagery. However, where Knights located the deformation of nature in relations between men, she showed how the play's language responded to an interpretation based on Kleinian ideas about women's power of generation, the fantasy of male power which excludes the female, the triumph of authority over nurturance, and the desire of men to control and ultimately to replace that power.

It would be impossible in performance to reproduce the complexity of Knights's or Adelman's argument, but in however muted a form, *Macbeth on the Estate* signalled its Shakespearean seriousness by locating the critical conundrum of interpretation at its heart. In spite of the democratization of its setting, the sense that it allowed Shakespeare to be connected to working-class culture, this invocation of the play's universal human values had the effect of flattening out the complexity and tensions within the culture it claimed to represent. In the process, it completely, and comfortingly, marginalized any consideration of the social complex of cultural and economic forces which had brought the conditions of deprivation and violence into being. As Beatrice Campbell has analyzed (1993), women in deprived urban cultures fight a daily battle to sustain the social existence of family and community life. In this production, their powerful force could only be rendered in plangent images of maternal loss and female victimhood.

It is unlikely that *Macbeth on the Estate* will become a canonical production in theatre histories of popular Shakespeare. The limited localization of its time and place may have produced points of recognition for its target audience but they cannot be assimilated into the global consciousness that is required for the reproduction of "Shakespeare." The process of canonization requires multiple accounts of the performance, together with a sense that the production engaged both with a significant political issue and with the constantly reiterated tension between spectacle and language.

Orson Welles's production of *Macbeth* for the Negro Unit of the Federal Theatre Project in 1936 is one such event. Its significance among canonical productions of the play is assured in part because it was surrounded by a commentary that insisted on its novel opposition to establishment Shakespeare. *Macbeth* had, in fact, been performed by African-American actors before. The Astor Place Company of Colored Tragedians had put on the play at the Grand Central Theatre Astor Place New York in June 1878 and for 40 years of the nineteenth century it was played all over Europe and Russia by the African-American actor, Ira Aldridge (Hill 1984: 45). The Negro Unit production, however, crystallized the relationship between the interpretation of the play and the ways it could be used to focus questions of cultural value.

Welles consciously promoted a new style for Shakespeare, using the technologies of radio and film to reach a mass audience and to insist on the accessibility of Shakespeare's works (see Anderegg 1999). Richard France, whose edition of the script for the 1936 production has assured its currency, takes Welles's account of his own novelty at face value. He comments on Welles's "realisation that theatrical statement was not covered by rhetoric alone but by the totality of theatrical language. . . . all the elements of production collaborated not to convey a statement, but, of themselves, to be the statement" (1990: 3). In the case of the 1936 *Macbeth*, the process of creating theatre, rather than conveying a statement, involved adapting the Shakespeare text into a three-act play with a rich overlay, revealed in the transcript of stage directions, for sound and other special effects. What the audience heard and saw (assuming that the instructions in the script were followed) was a mix of theatrical tricks – rain noise created with cellophane, a witch speaking "through her teeth in the queer voice of her 'control'" (France 1990: 78) that may have created startling effects. All those who wrote about the production were excited by the central design idea of a "primitive" setting that used sound effects and lighting to create a total, consistent physical world for the play in ways that were closer to cinema than theatre (Davies 1988: 83–99). These technical effects, however, were given significance by the play's racial dimension. The commentaries and newspaper criticism reconstructed the performance in ideological terms. A theatre event thus became a cultural event located in the contested structures of contemporary meaning.

Welles's transformation of the witches into "voodoo" priestesses was seen partly as a simple solution to the problem of the supernatural. The witches' authenticity is assured by association with "real" witchcraft not in the historically distanced seventeenth century but in the geographically distant but globally accessible Haiti. The critic from the *New York Times* noted "ship the witches down to the rank and fever-stricken jungles of Haiti . . . and there you have a witches scene that is logical and stunning and a triumph of theatre art" (France 1990: 14). The confusion between localized theatrical effect and the authenticating analogy with an imagined Haiti (rank and fever-stricken jungles?) allows a slippage between the experience of theatre and its meaning.

The relationship between the theatre event and its cultural meaning was especially overdetermined by the racial politics of 1930s' America. In their desire to emphasize specifically African-American themes in the work of the Negro Units, the directors and managers of the FTP reached for signifiers of Africanness which sailed very close to racist stereotypes. The FTP had set itself a number of different and possibly contradictory objectives. They wished to provide work for unemployed African-

American performers; they wished to create a theatrical culture that would valorize and authenticate African-American culture; and they wanted to produce a genuinely popular theatre which would appeal to audiences that were being lost to the cinema and vaudeville (Frayden 1996: 104). Theatre was to provide a model for an idealized culture that would unite divided classes, races and peoples.

These requirements made impossible demands on a theatrical performance. They assumed that the content and style of the show could in some way substitute for the real social conditions in which both actors and audience existed. While the chance of paid work in the depths of the Depression for African-American actors was undoubtedly welcome, and "popular prices" may have made some difference to the composition of the audience, the deep racial and social divisions of 1930s' America could not be wished away by a theatre performance. They emerged in a variety of more or less sophisticated ways that reveal critical aspects of the relationship between performance and culture.

The "voodoo" setting of the production not only authenticated the witches, it also allowed reviewers to project onto the African-American actors their conceptions of a revived and regenerated Shakespeare. The *Vogue* review imagined the ghost of Shakespeare, bored by conventional productions of his plays, seeking a more exiting event at the Harlem theatre. There he found a mixed-race audience who had come to the Mercury Theatre: "Not to hear Shakespeare, who had bored most of them at school, but to get something different – that something at once innocent and richly seasoned, child-like and jungle-spiced, which is the gift of the Negro to a more tired, complicated and self conscious race" (Frayden 1996: 153). The authentic Shakespeare is distanced from conventional productions of his plays; he is used instead to endorse the fantasized exoticism of African-American culture. The racist condescension of the reviewer's remarks is all too evident but it shows how Shakespeare and theatre were used to fulfil the needs of a culture which longed, as he puts it, to "recapture briefly what once we were, or like to think we were, long centuries before our ancestors suffered the blights of thought, worry, and the printed word" (Frayden 1996: 153). Welles himself insisted on the populist dimension of Shakespeare which he thought would be immediately accessible to performers whose approach had not been deformed by the inappropriate and outdated performance styles of the nineteenth century. He enthused about his production in terms of its innovation, its freshness, its freedom from the shackles of older Shakespearean styles. He described his new audience as "people on a voyage of discovery in the theatre" and insisted that his actors were actually fortunate because they "never had the misfortune of hearing Elizabethan verse spouted by actors strongly flavoring of well-cured Smithfield. They read their lines as they would read any others" (Hill 1984: 108–11).

Welles's enthusiasm for working with the African-American actors of the Federal Theatre Project "Negro Unit" and his choice of a "voodoo" setting were informed by more specific resonances than a generalized connection between blackness and innocence. The American occupation of Haiti had ended in 1934 and in 1936, the Trinidadian historian C. L. R. James had published *The Black Jacobins*, an account of the 1790 Haitian revolution led by Toussaint L'Ouverture. Toussaint L'Ouverture was an important reference point in the alternative histories which informed the politics of African-American culture in the twentieth century. The reference to Haiti and to African culture more generally involved less "rank and fever-ridden jungles" than anti-colonial struggles in the Caribbean or popular protests against Mussolini's invasion of Ethiopia (Denning 1996: 396). Toussaint L'Ouverture had been defeated, not by a resurgence of white colonialism but by the black demagogue, King Christophe. Welles found in Christophe an image of fascism which he defined – with more passion than subtlety – as "the original sin of civilization, the celebration of power for its own sake"(Denning 1996: 376). Welles marshalled Shakespeare in support of his anti-fascist aesthetic, describing fascist showmanship (seen in the contemporary newsreels of the Nuremberg rallies) as "the old dumb-show of monarchy" (Denning 1996: 380) – surely a reference to an informing image for his conception of *Macbeth*.

Welles's use of a Shakespearean image for a political observation showed how deeply Shakespeare had become embedded in the twentieth-century cultural imagination. However, in subsequent accounts of the FTP *Macbeth*, Shakespeare is more often recalled than anti-fascist politics. In 1977 the Welles 1936 production was revived with an all-black cast at the Henry Street Settlement's New Federal Theatre in 1977. The New Federal Theatre was inspired by the earlier Federal Theatre project which had by the 1970s come to seem a heroic high point of cultural innovation. This exercise in cultural archeology disappointed the critic Robert Hapgood who disparagingly compared the bold effects of Welles's original production with the new production's "primitive" clichés of dancing and drumming:

> Hecate's twelve-foot bull whip, the onstage voodoo drummers, the giant mask of Banquo, the 18-foot drop of the cream-faced loon, whom Macbeth first shot and then kicked to the courtyard below. Sitting in the Library, I came to realize that I was finding there exactly the kind of theatrical excitement that I had missed in the theatre the night before. (Hapgood 1978: 232)

It is perhaps ironic that Hapgood found more excitement in the Library than in the theatre. His imaginative engagement with the earlier production gave it a reality which could not be reproduced in a performance constrained by the material circumstances of actors and setting. His description gives the Welles production a focus and purpose which may well have been dissipated by the actual experience at the Mercury and contributed to the creation of the production as one of the icons of the theatre history of the play.

The reproduction of Shakespeare in contemporary culture now seems unassailably assured. As Michael Bristol puts it, "there is ... a considerable market for a range of cultural goods that carry the Shakespeare trademark" (1996: 5) and both private and public cultural organizations across the world make a huge investment in Shakespeare as a staple of the classic repertory. The "Shakespeare" that they produce, however, carries with it a huge expectation of cultural meaning. The narrative of a murdered king and a tragic (or wicked) queen, the witches' prophecy and the final battle are as embedded in the common consciousness as any fairy story or founding myth. When that narrative is turned into performance, it raises instant expectations: how will they do the witches? Will Lady Macbeth be scary or sad? Will it be dull and wordy or spectacularly exciting? Those questions have been framed and formed partly by the old text but equally by the long history of performance that loses its particular localized meaning not long after the show is over and, if it is remembered at all, is subsumed by the shapes of interpretation. The long road from a twenty-first-century performance to a seventeenth-century play has to be taken every time one answers the student with whom we began.

References and Further Reading

Adelman, Janet (1992). "Escaping the Matrix: The Construction of Masculinity in *Macbeth* and *Coriolanus*." In *Suffocating Mothers: Fantasies of Maternal Origin in Shakespeare's Plays*. London: Routledge, pp. 130–64.

Anderegg, Michael (1999). *Orson Welles, Shakespeare and Popular Culture*. New York: Columbia University Press.

Berry, Ralph (1983). "Komisarjevsky at Stratford-upon-Avon." *Shakespeare Survey* 36: 73–84.

Bradley, A. C. (1969). *Shakespearean Tragedy*. London: Macmillan.

Bristol, Michael (1996). *Big-Time Shakespeare*. London: Routledge.

Brooks, Cleanth (1959). "The Naked Babe and the Cloak of Manliness." In *The Well Wrought Urn: Studies in the Structure of Poetry*. London: Dobson.

Butler, Martin (1984). *Theatre and Crisis 1632–1642*. Cambridge: Cambridge University Press.

Campbell, Beatrice (1993). *Goliath: Britain's Dangerous Places*. London: Methuen.

Cook, Ann Jennalie (1981). *The Privileged Playgoers of Shakespeare's London 1576–1642*. Princeton, NJ: Princeton University Press.

Davies, Anthony (1988). *Filming Shakespeare's Plays*. Cambridge: Cambridge University Press.

Dekker, Thomas (1955). *The Magnificent Entertainment*. In Fredson Bowers (ed.) *The Dramatic Works of Thomas Dekker*, vol. 2. Cambridge: Cambridge University Press, pp. 253–303.

Denning, Michael (1996). *The Cultural Front: The Labouring of American Culture in the Twentieth Century*. London: Verso.

Donohue, Joseph (1971). "Macbeth in the Eighteenth Century." *Theatre Quarterly* 1, 3: 20–4.

Downes, John ([1708] 1987). *Roscius Anglicanus*, ed. Judith Milhous & Robert D. Hume. London: Society for Theatre Research.

France, Richard (1974). "The Voodoo *Macbeth* of Orson Welles." *Yale Theatre* 5, 3.

France, Richard (1990). *Orson Welles on Shakespeare: The W.P.A. and Mercury Theatre Playscripts*. Westport, CT: Greenwood Press.

Fraden, Rena (1996). *Blueprints for a Black Federal Theatre 1935–1939*. Cambridge: Cambridge University Press.

Freud, Sigmund (1985). "Some Character Types Met with in Psychoanalytic Work." In James Strachey (ed.) *The Pelican Freud Library*, vol. 14. Harmondsworth: Penguin, pp. 291–320.

Furness, Horace Howard (1915). *A New Variorum Edition of Shakespeare*. Philadelphia, PA: Lippincott.

Hapgood, Robert (1978). "Shakespeare in New York and Boston." *Shakespeare Quarterly* 29: 230–2.

Heywood, Thomas (1637). *Londons Mirror*. London.

Hill, Errol (1984). *Shakespeare in Sable: A History of Black Shakespearean Actors*. Amherst, MA: University of Massachusetts Press.

Jonson, Ben (1972). *Everyman in His Humour*, ed. J. W. Lever. London: Edward Arnold.

Jonson, Ben (1995). *Bartholomew Fair*. In Gordon Campbell (ed.) *The Alchemist and Other Plays*. Oxford: Oxford University Press.

Kennedy, Dennis (1993). *Looking at Shakespeare: A Visual History of Twentieth Century Performance.* Cambridge: Cambridge University Press.

Knights, L. C. (1991). "How Many Children Had Lady Macbeth?" In Samuel Schoenbaum (ed.) *Macbeth Critical Essays.* New York: Garland, pp. 110–42.

Knutson, Roslyn L. (1991). *The Repertory of Shakespeare's Company 1594–1613.* Fayetteville, AK: University of Arkansas Press.

Marowitz, Charles (1991). *Recycling Shakespeare.* New York: Applause.

McLuskie, Kathleen E. (2003). "Macbeth, the Present and the Past." In Jean Howard & Richard Dutton (eds.) *Shakespeare, the Tragedies.* Oxford: Blackwell, pp. 393–410.

McLuskie, Kathleen E. (2004). "Humane Statute and the Gentle Weal: Historical Reading and Historical Allegory." *Shakespeare Survey* 57: 1–10.

O'Dair, Sharon (2000). *Class Critics and Shakespeare.* Ann Arbor, MI: University of Michigan Press.

Ristori, Adelaide ([1888] 1997). *Studies and Memoirs.* London: W.H. Allen. In Ann Thompson & Sasha Roberts (eds.) *Women Reading Shakespeare 1660–1900.* Manchester: Manchester University Press.

Rogers, Rebecca (2002). "Who Invested in the Early Modern Theatre?" *Research Opportunities in Renaissance Drama* 41: 29–61.

Rutter, Carol (1988). "Lady Macbeth's Barren Sceptre." In *Clamorous Voices: Shakespeare's Women Today.* London: The Women's Press.

Shakespeare, William (1997). *The Norton Shakespeare,* ed. Stephen Greenblatt et al. London: W. W. Norton.

Styan, J. L. (1977). *The Shakespeare Revolution: Criticism and Performance in the Twentieth Century.* Cambridge: Cambridge University Press.

Taylor, Gary (1991). *Reinventing Shakespeare: A Cultural History from the Restoration to the Present.* New York: Oxford University Press.

Trewin, J. C. (1971). "Macbeth in the Nineteenth Century." *Theatre Quarterly* 1, 3: 26–31.

Worthen, W. B. (1997). *Shakespeare and the Authority of Performance.* Cambridge: Cambridge University Press.

14

Stanislavski, *Othello*, and the Motives of Eloquence

John Gillies

Marvin Rosenberg is perhaps the first to have suggested that the performance culture of *Othello* has undergone a denaturing change this century relative to its previous performance history (Rosenberg, 1971: 142). Particularly in the eighteenth and nineteenth centuries – heyday of what W. B. Worthen has (non-pejoratively) called the "sentimental" tradition of English acting – *Othello* was a tremendous emotional experience in the theatre (Worthen 1987: 70–130). "Men wept," as Rosenberg quaintly puts it – indicating quite clearly their emotional investment – while for the actor, Othello was unquestionably the most demanding Shakespearean role (1971: 61). It is part of theatre legend that Edmund Kean collapsed onstage during a performance, dying some two months after. For Tommaso Salvini and Edwin Booth, the role was a career-length affair. The emotional demands on audience and actors alike can be directly related to the goals of "sentimental" tragic acting: to act with emotional intensity over the widest possible emotional range. Because Othello's part was regarded as unmatched in its combination of emotional intensity and range, it represented the highest histrionic challenge. Throughout the twentieth century, that challenge is either ignored or ignominiously ducked. Rosenberg tells of a prominent British actor-manager playing Othello to his best supporting actor's Iago (1971: 141). Unanimously, reviewers found the actor-manager overshadowed by his Iago, which led to his shamelessly substituting a series of progressively less talented actors in the part. All to no avail. Even when played by the prop-boy, Iago outshone the Moor. Finally taking the part of Iago himself, the lead actor basked in glowing reviews until the end of the run. The anecdote is, of course, from the earlier twentieth century, and Rosenberg's account was written before he could include Laurence Olivier's 1964 performance. Yet the same judgment – that late twentieth-century Othellos lack an essential dimension of the part – underlies Julie Hankey's more recent performance history. Thus, while she finds Ben Kingsley "intelligent, elaborate, moving when restrained but seldom convincingly beside himself," she prefers James Earl Jones's "big" Othello, which, though "old-fashioned" and psychologically crude, carries "a note of excitement which has not been heard for a long time in England" (Hankey 1987: 120–1). Her history ends with this reflection: "One is reminded of Henry James, slightly shocked at Salvini's lack of sophistication, and yet willing to concede that in the absence of an imaginary ideal, this general direction may offer the best hope" (1987: 121).

The future of Othello as a stage role, it would appear, lies in its past. Why have Othello the role – and *Othello* the play – so lost emotional power and theatrical authority? Three obvious critical or discursive explanations immediately present themselves. First, F. R. Leavis's attack on "the sentimentalists' Othello" remains effectively unanswered (1962: 136–59). If "sentimental" is a pejorative term, and Bradley's "noble moor" becomes Leavis's egotist – virtually the blowhard of Iago's account – then the traditional pathos becomes either overtly ironic or merely pathetic. Olivier was widely regarded as having enlisted his audience's sympathy despite playing Othello as a version of Leavis's egotist or, in the words of the director, John Dexter, "a pompous, word-spinning, arrogant black general" (Tynan 1966: 4). But Olivier has not managed to enlist the sympathy of later spectators of the film/video of his stage performance, who have tended to read it as racist. The twentieth-century politicizing of race represents a second complicating factor. It has become virtually impossible for a white actor in either the USA or the UK to play this famously or infamously black part for pathos. Yet the difficulty, though different, is scarcely less for black actors, for the problem is that pity tends to cancel out terror, and sympathy tends to translate into condescension. In playing Othello as an outsider and a representative of a downtrodden race, Paul Robeson was accused of diminishing the part's authority. James Agate found Robeson's "whole bearing, gait, and diction … full of humility and apology: the inferiority complex in a word"; Ashley Dukes remarked: "Robeson brings to his part the special … appeal of a Negro actor; he brings also a noble voice, a tremendous presence, and an infinite simplicity … He brings an infinite humility, too" (Vaughan 1994: 181–98, 188). Similar remarks might characterize John Kani in Janet Suzman's 1988 South African production, Willard White in Trevor Nunn's 1989–90 RSC production, or Sello Maake ka-Ncube in Gregory Doran's 2004 RSC production. Indeed, the *Guardian*'s Michael Billington wrote: "Othello requires not just nobility and temperament but the capacity to be 'perplexed in the extreme'; and it is the last of these that ka-Ncube lacks … You need to feel the character's nature is unraveling." Doran is taxed for losing "the sense that we are watching awesome, mythic events … largely because of an inequality in casting that makes this a study in villainy rather than the story of the Moor's madness" (February 4, 2003). These Othellos are simply too decent. And while Laurence Fishburne is a tougher, more street-wise figure in Kenneth Branagh's 1996 film, his jealousy (like Robeson's) seems insufficiently ugly. But it is perhaps a contradiction for black American actors to show Othello as too completely in the grip of ignoble passions, particularly if the perception is primarily of a black hero destroyed by a marginalized psyche, on the one hand, and white perfidy, on the other. This in turn bespeaks a third kind of difficulty experienced by recent Othellos: that of reconciling domestic violence with tragic dignity. As with Leavis, this has concerned critics, especially feminists, more than theatre practitioners. In the recent debate crystallizing feminist discontent with *Othello*, Richard Levin and his feminist antagonists would probably agree that a feminist reading of *Othello* focused on marginalizing women's experience in the play's tragic economy ("the male project of the play") necessarily amounts to a critique of Othello's tragic grandeur (Levin 1988, 1990; Sprengnether 1996).

The modern discourses of egotism, race and gender go far to explain the long-standing malaise of *Othello* in the theatre. In different ways, each assaults the moral and emotional consensus – what Worthen might call the performing "ethos" and "authority" supporting Othello's pathos in the "sentimental" tradition (Worthen 1987). All three deny Othello his traditional theatrical right to a high level of eloquence (verging on magniloquence), whether that is defined in emotional or in purely vocal terms. What I want to suggest, however, is that Othello's theatrical eloquence in both these senses – important not merely in the "sentimental" stage tradition, but in Renaissance rhetorical practice which above all sought to arouse *pathos* in the hearer – had begun to erode well before these discontents with the play. This began on the stage rather than the page, and specifically from the moment that the "sentimental" Othello of Worthen's began to metamorphose into the Stanislavskian Othello of histrionic naturalism. The moment of this transition is best exemplified in Stanislavski's own life-long engagement with the play, in the course of which *Othello* evolved from a nineteenth-century to a twentieth-century theatre script. Stanislavski's experience of the play began in 1882 when, as a teenager, he saw Tommaso Salvini play Othello in Moscow, indelibly described in his autobiography (Stanislavski 1982: 265–76). Thereafter, Stanislavski ranged from acting the lead himself in 1896 while still a young man (1982: 277–87), to directing the play for the Moscow Art Theatre in 1929–30 (1968), and then writing on the play in the 1930s in his pedagogical treatise, *Creating a Role* (1996: 107–210). While the experiences of 1882 and 1896 may be said to have occurred within the "sentimental" stage tradition, the later experiences – particularly those presupposed in the pedagogical writings – represent explicit attempts to realize *Othello* in terms of the acting system associated with his name, currently the dominant tradition in Shakespearean acting today (Benedetti 1982).

Briefly, I want to argue that Othello's loss of "eloquence" comes from a contradiction between Stanislavski's dramaturgical idea of the play and his acting system. The contradiction is that the driving force of Stanislavski's post-1882 encounters with the play – his love of Othello's verbal and emotional eloquence – is precisely what is not translated into the set of histrionic practices for which (it is claimed) Stanislavski saw *Othello* as an ideal vehicle. Elizabeth Hapgood Reynolds claims to have heard Stanislavski speak "of his idea of having all three of his books on acting technique centred on Shakespeare's *Othello*" (1996: ix), though Jean Benedetti is more guarded: "this appears to have been no more than the result of a passing enthusiasm" (1988: 294). Yet despite any lack of clarity, Stanislavski's enthusiasm for *Othello*'s "eloquence" is beyond question. Behind his failure to translate the value of "eloquence" into his evolving discourse on acting, there lurks, I will suggest, a deeper contradiction between, on the one hand, Stanislavski's revolutionary commitment to the rehearsal as a process of performative discovery and textual renewal and, on the other, his unrecognized addiction to archaic performance memories, mythologies, and practices. Further, I want to suggest that something like this contradiction has remained to bedevil the subsequent performance malaise surveyed by Rosenberg and Hankey. Thus, the loss of "eloquence" would be connected to a collective theatrical failure to accept, focus or otherwise negotiate the discursive assaults on, or reappraisals of, the play's traditional ethical substratum.

Othello after Salvini

Witnessing Salvini's Othello, Stanislavski was privileged to have experienced the very height of sentimental acting in the most challenging of sentimental roles. His account of the performance in *My Life in Art* is breathtaking. Up until Othello's address to the senate, however, the young Stanislavski had thought that Salvini was playing Iago. Othello's acting had been understated and his appearance slightly preposterous: "There were his large, pointed mustaches, his wig that looked too much like a wig, his figure, too large, too heavy, almost fat, great eastern daggers that dangled at his waist and made him look stouter than he was … All of this was not much typical of the soldier Othello" (1982: 265–6).

At the moment of the Senate speech, however, Stanislavski was left in no doubt as to who Salvini was:

> Salvini approached the platform of the doges, thought a little while, concentrated himself and, unnoticed by any of us, took the entire audience of the Great Theatre into his hands. It seemed that he did this with a single gesture – that he stretched his hand without looking into the public, grasped all of us in his palm, and held us there as if we were ants or flies. He closed his fist, and we felt the breath of death; he opened it, and we knew the warmth of bliss. We were in his power, and we will remain in it all our lives, forever. Now we understand who this genius was, what he was, and what we were to expect from him. (1982: 266)

Like generations of actors before him, Salvini had approached the part rhythmically, choosing certain key moments, long sanctified by the sentimental tradition, at which to put forth his histrionic power. The senate speech was such a "point," and though an actor was not obliged to rise to this occasion (Kean chose to bypass it), experienced spectators would have been expecting something special here. As well as power, Salvini was evidently communicating a certain emotional range ("breath of death," "warmth of bliss") but doing so in the quasi-oratorical way of the sentimental actor, speaking "through" his fellow actors to the audience itself. Then:

Having opened for a moment the gates of paradise in his monologue before the Senate, having showed for the duration of one second at his meeting with Desdemona what trustfulness and boyish love were possible for the courageous and no longer young soldier, Salvini closed for a time the sublime gates of his art, closed them intentionally. He had made sure of our trust in him at one stroke, and like trained dogs that sit on their hind legs and watch the eyes of their trainer we fell hungrily on those places and words of the role which Salvini commanded us to notice and remember. (1982: 268)

More, however, appears to have been at stake here than mere timing and eloquence. The great actor's charisma required something more like magniloquence: eloquence charged with a kind of mythical assurance of the speaker's grandeur. The difference would be that whereas "eloquence" might be found in weak or fallible characters (such as Richard II), "magniloquence" (as distinct from pompousness) will only be found in the magnificent. It was surely thus that Salvini "grasped all of us in his palm, and held us there as if we were ants or flies."

The impression that Salvini made seems to have been such that 14 years later Stanislavski himself attempted the role of Othello in an answerably high-flown mode. His autobiography – in which a chapter praising Salvini is succeeded by a rueful account of Stanislavski's own 1896 performance – invites comparing them in terms of the sublime and the unfortunate. In this connection, it is as well to remember that Stanislavski's breakthrough theatrical experiences – the Moscow Art Theatre, Chekhov, and the System itself – were still in the future and thus unavailable as histrionic alternatives. Whether it was quite so awful as he suggests, Stanislavski's 1896 performance seems to have failed out of his attempt to be "eloquent." While for some of the less demanding scenes, Stanislavski felt that he "had enough technique, voice, experience and ability," in the jealousy scenes, "I was able to reach nothing more than insane strain, spiritual and physical impotence, and the squeezing of tragic emotion out of myself" (1982: 282). Predictably perhaps, given that his valuable discoveries of "emotion memory" and "physical objectives" (whereby emotion was focused in terms of gesture and position) were yet to be made, the young Stanislavski appears to have fallen back upon "generalized emotions" and voice. The result was that Stanislavski's voice gave out after the first two acts (1982: 283). Even before this, however, his voice does not appear to have risen to the "point" of the Senate speech: "How did I say the famous speech to the senate? In no way. I simply told a story. At that time I did not recognize the importance either of the word or of speech. The outer image was more important to me" (1982: 279).

In all this woefulness, however, there was one genuine histrionic discovery, which may have owed something to Salvini. Stanislavski's costume had been copied directly from that of an Arab he had met in a Parisian restaurant. Dressed in this garment, he was able to find a whole new range of physical movement:

What is remarkable is that notwithstanding the fact that I was in a costume play, I did not fall victim to the enchantments of the opera baritone. The characteristics of the East built a wall between me and my former bad habits. I had made my own the suddenness of the Arab, his floating walk, his narrow palm, to such a degree that I was unable to control these movements even in my private life. (1982: 280)

The point about the costume, then, was not how it made him look but how it made him feel and move, thereby allowing escape from the twin banalities, "costume play" and "opera baritone," the latter phrase suggesting a caricature of the sentimental style he was trying to move beyond. Yet his earlier admission to "squeezing tragic emotion out of myself" suggests an equivalence with his own aesthetic goals in that, like the "opera baritone," he was confusing emotional expression with a blanket perception of tragedy as a genre (tragism). Costume, however, seems to have offered a way beyond this particular error. Whether Stanislavski was aware of it, Salvini had systematically used his costume in much this way. Indeed, Stanislavski tells of how Salvini would arrive at the theatre three hours before a performance and put on his costume and make-up layer by layer, while just as gradually trying on the voice, mannerisms and movements of Othello: "it seemed that Salvini not only made up his face and dressed his body, but also prepared his soul in a like manner, gradually establishing a perfect balance of character" (1982: 273).

Stanislavski's 1930 *Othello* for the Moscow Art Theatre

Stanislavski's next recorded encounters with *Othello* belong to 1928–33, when he first directed the play at a distance for the Moscow Art Theatre while recovering from an illness in France (1928–30), and then wrote an essay on how actors should approach the first act in rehearsal (1930–33). These are twentieth-century encounters both chronologically and theatrically, for they post-date the formation of the Moscow Art Theatre, Stanislavski's work with Chekhov, and his development of the System's first phase – that based on emotion memory. The long section on *Othello* in *Creating a Role* is particularly interesting, functioning as a kind of test case for evolving the system's second phase – that based on physical objectives (Benedetti 1988: 295). Taken together, they offer unparalleled insights into the strengths and weaknesses of Stanislavski's mature theatrical approach to Shakespeare – specifically, his attempt to translate eloquence from sentimental to psychological-realist theatrical value.

The direction-by-correspondence preceding the 1930 production now exists in the form of a published promptbook. Of prime concern here are Stanislavski's directions for the senate speech, the point of eloquence which Salvini's acting had once commanded him to "notice and remember." Against the first part of this speech – that beginning "Most potent, grave and reverend signiors" (Shakespeare 1989: 1.3.76) – Stanislavski wrote:

Othello's address: it is of extraordinary simplicity and full of consciousness of his own innocence. What would the actor require at this moment? I should feel very much inclined to remember there the lines Othello spoke in the preceding scene. ("I fetch my life and being / From men of royal siege ... "). In his heart, Othello despises all these nobles and in no way thinks himself inferior to them in dignity. (1968: 60)

Against the second part – "Her father loved me ... " – he wrote:

> The story now told by Othello always made me feel how very naive, besides being sincere and frank, was Othello's eastern mentality. Indeed, only a very naive person would thus open his soul and innermost feelings at such a moment of struggle and believe that he will earn sympathy. And yet, it was this naivety that conquered. Were I to act this moment, it would seem important to dwell in my mind on the thought that Desdemona is there, in my house, that I am on the verge of our wedding night, and I would be trembling all over with tenderness and happiness. (1968: 62)

There are two points of special interest here. The first is that Stanislavski should have so completely reduced the mysteries and challenges of eloquence to a question of character-motive. The second is that the character-motive adduced for the speech actually contradicts the subtextual dimension of Stanislavski's understanding of Othello's character in this situation. Thus, Stanislavski's insistence on Othello's "simplicity" and "naivety" is inconsistent with the idea that Othello "despises all these nobles" during the pomp and circumstance of addressing them. This latter idea emerges as an irresistible subtext of the constructed onstage situation.

Why should Othello despise the senators even as he flatters them? An easy answer advanced by Stanislavski is that Othello knows that he is "in no way ... inferior to them in dignity" (1968: 60). But a more interesting answer – implicit in the overall *mise en scène* – is that Othello, indignantly aware of their sense of superiority, of their distaste for his marriage with Desdemona, knows that their support of him is based on bad faith rather than principle. That attitude surfaces when the senators discover the concrete identity of the abstraction that Brabantio has been describing as Desdemona's "abuser." Stanislavski carefully crafts this as a subtextual point – a key moment of dramatic structure and theatrical power – that we may take as his own answer to the more obvious and rhetorically conceived points of the sentimental theatre. In one sense, this subtextual point arises out of Brabantio's political cunning in the text: withholding Othello's identity until he has first been successful in enlisting the indignant support of the senators and the Duke. But in a deeper sense, the point arises from Stanislavski's *mise en scène*. Unlike Salvini, who had begun the senate scene at Othello's entry, Stanislavski retained the lengthy council of war that precedes it. This was organized around several through-lines – the physical immediacy of the threat to Cyprus and Venice, a growing panic among the senators (expressed in group movements of Meininger-like precision and dynamism), and their increasingly urgent emotional need for a way out – which in turn were made to converge on Othello's entry.[1] It was the gap between the senators' emotional need for Othello and their unthinkingly tribal endorsement of Brabantio's lurid narrative of seduction and witchcraft that provided Stanislavski with his point:

> There must be a breaking point, a sudden change and transfer to a compromise. The senators look at Othello and at Brabantio ... At this moment every single senator nurses a grievance against Othello and casts evil glances at him, because in a few more minutes they will have willy-nilly to make up to him. This struggle between the innermost inclinations of pride and the duty of a ruler must be followed up to the end. (1968: 59)

The collective bad faith of this moment was also conceived as having an intimately personal edge. In a note "to help the actors performing ... the Duke and Brabantio," Stanislavski suggests that the Duke betrays a personal and political debt to Brabantio, who "ought to have been Duke himself but for various political and inner-party reasons, all of which have led him to decline in favour of the present Duke" (1968: 79–80). The present Duke, he suggests, has progressively been selling out Brabantio's "right wing" policy on colonies and aliens, which he had been bound to uphold as a condition of the deal, and had therefore (before his shameful back-down) jumped at the chance to repay Brabantio by punishing the seducer of his daughter.

This, then, was the subtext of Othello's address to the senate in Stanislavski's production. Murky already, it must have been murkier still given that the 1930 Othello must have been black rather than Arabic. Surprisingly, in view both of late twentieth-century sensitivities to race and his own earlier (and typically nineteenth-century) love affair with the 1896 Arabic Othello, Stanislavski says very little about this change in Othello's color. However, four details suggest that from 1930 on, Stanislavski's Othello was indeed black. First is a wonderful costume sketch by Golovin showing Othello as powerfully negroid rather than lithely Arab, and dressed in garments that are at once gaudily African and monstrously Renaissance, rather than in the flowing Arabian white of 1896 (see Figure 14.1). The second is an interesting variation of detail between Stanislavski's accounts of the scene's racial politics in the 1896 and 1930 productions. In his account of the 1896 production, Stanislavski asks the reader to "imagine that some Tartar or Persian stole a grand duchess from the palace of the grand duke" (1982: 279). But in the promptbook, he asks the actor to "reflect on how other haughty senators, or for that matter the aristocracy of St. Petersburg would have felt, if some Hottentot had carried off a Grand Duchess, daughter of the Czar" (1968: 58). The change from "Tartar or Persian" to "Hottentot" strongly suggests that Stanislavski was thinking of a black African figure. This suggestion is even stronger when read alongside another of Golovin's costume sketches, evidently resonating with his "Othello" sketch for two "natives" of Cyprus (Fedosova 1989, plate 110).[2] Both are strikingly Negroid: one sports an afro and wears a kaftan; the other wears an outsize fez with a carnivalesque uniform suggesting either a Moorish auxiliary or a Renaissance clown. A note of caution is perhaps warranted when making inferences about the production from Golovin's designs, for Stanislavski rejected his stage designs – larger than life, fluent and brilliantly stylized – for being too operatic and replaced them with designs by Simov (Onufrieva 1977: 120). The costume designs, however, appear to have remained. Moreover, the racial typing to which their style is keyed surely reflects Stanislavski's original,

FIGURE 14.1   "Othello's Costume," by Golovin, 1930
Museum of the Moscow Art Theatre

enduring intention. The last indication that Stanislavski's 1930 Othello was indeed black is found in the acting workshop on *Othello* described in *Creating a Role* and considered later in this chapter.

A similarly complex understanding of Othello's behavior at this moment (innocence and romance overlaid with contempt and flattery, against a background of explosive racial politics) also emerges from the pedagogical essay of 1930–33, where Stanislavski explains the circumlocution of "Most potent, grave and reverend signiors" by referring to the extreme delicacy of Othello's position as a despised foreigner who has stolen "the daughter of a high official" (1996: 158). In this essay, Tortsov explicitly urges his actors to find "the whole subtext, which underlies the words in the formal text" (1996: 160). In view, then, of this characteristically modern emphasis on subtext, and of the effort put into constructing a stage situation suggesting a non-transparent (non-naive) motive for Othello's eloquence, why should Stanislavski have so insisted to the struggling actor of the 1930 production that "naivety" is the key to the senate speech?

Before venturing an answer, I should add that Stanislavski's direction for Othello's senate speech is remarkably unhelpful by comparison with (for example) his direction to the actor of Brabantio regarding the "O thou foul thief . . ." passage (1.2.62–81) earlier in the promptbook:

> This is a strong monologue, and it is known that a strong monologue induces the actor to invest it with more temperament than he is capable of expending. In consequence, the correct line of acting is dislocated and turns into a wrong line of passion posing. Very clear and effective acting is needed to avoid this mistake. (1968: 45)

Here, Stanislavski gives a clear sense of the balance between emotional motive and rhetorical temptation. In *Creating a Role* he breaks the same "strong monologue" into a series of "coherent objectives" – moments of emotional, vocal, and physical focus – "each one flowing out of the previous one," thus enabling his Brabantio to envisage it as a lucid montage of histrionic elements (1996: 142).[3] Nothing Stanislavski says about Othello's senate speech, however, would have helped the actor out of "a wrong line of passion posing," which is to say out of Stanislavski's own prior investment in the speech as exemplifying the character's core identity as heroically naive and unselfconscious.

If it is granted, then, that "simplicity" is inadequate as a working direction, and moreover that it contradicts Stanislavski's own subtextual analysis of Othello's motive, then, one must ask again why he persists with it. One answer might be the siren call of what G. Wilson Knight would later call "the *Othello* music," nowhere more beguiling than here (Knight 1930). Looking at the larger context offers a further answer. Since simplicity and naivety were the keynotes of Salvini's characterization, I would suggest that Stanislavski had internalized this aspect of Salvini's performance so deeply that it remains to contradict his own more satisfyingly complex analysis of the senate scene. Salvini, of course, had not plucked these ideas out of the air. They were parts of the sentimental myth of the noble moor, indissolubly wedded to another part of that myth – the image of Othello as a spell-binding story-teller. This, as will become apparent, infiltrates Stanislavski's next engagement with the play in his pedagogical writing of 1930–33.

Othello in *Creating a Role* (1930)

The long essay on *Othello* in *Creating a Role* represents the most intimate and revealing record of Stanislavski's theatrical engagement with the play that we have. It is more revealing of Stanislavskian working practice than the 1930 promptbook in actually reconstituting the encounter between the director/dramaturg (in Stanislavski's persona, "Tortsov") and the actors, as a kind of drama in its own right. Here, we are given not just a list of directions as in the promptbook, but also the shifting and varied responses of the actors to those directions, the ebb and flow of dialogue, the trial and error of acting exercises as they unfold. Moreover, because this text is multivocal rather than univocal – we even hear interjections from beyond the charmed circle of director and actors – it allows contradictions within Stanislavski's vision of the play to emerge far more starkly than in either his autobiographical or purely directorial writing. For the most part, to be sure, these other voices are firmly under Stanislavskian control. Tortsov's actors tend to say what Stanislavski wants them to say. When they object, they tend to be soundly refuted. At crucial points, however, their doubts (and that of the assistant director) are such as to call into question the entire Stanislavskian vision of *Othello*, both as playtext and performance text – thereby uncovering its deeper ideological contexts and investments.

Tortsov's goal in this drama is to enable his actors to create authentic character performances from *Othello*'s first Act. For this he needs to break them of the nineteenth-century habit of imitation or repetition, in which a performance is cobbled together from a grab-bag of remembered histrionic tricks. Some of Tortsov's actors are more addicted to this vice than others. According to Tortsov, one way out of the habit is to imaginatively enter the world of the play. As a first step, the actors are encouraged to read the play far more carefully than they are accustomed to doing. This, however, is not enough. The actors must also expand the play's imaginative world by seizing on certain talismanic elements or effects and then actively extending or enlarging them in fantasy. Prime among such talismanic elements (for Tortsov) is Othello's eloquence as a story-teller. Thus, in one exercise, the actors are asked to invent a fantasy scene in which Othello arrives in Venice with crowds of onlookers dogging his heels. In this fantasy, Othello is already a great talker, entrancing his hearers with travelers' tales. It is in the midst of just such a performance that Desdemona first glimpses him (1996: 171–3). The point of these fantasies, Tortsov insists, is to inspire in the actors a vital investment in the characters they are to play. The fantasies should be freely rather than narrowly inspired, drawing not just on the text but also on "real" dream-stuff taken from the actor's own experience. Thus, relying heavily on his own emotion-memory, Kostya (Tortsov's favorite actor, and avatar of a younger Stanislavski) creates a love scene in Sevastopol, a city which is both romantically meaningful to him and the closest Russian equivalent of Venice (1996: 169–70).

However free-form these fantasies are, they should all – Tortsov insists – originate in the most "vivid" moments of the first Act. Such moments are established by introspection, discussion, and analysis. Increasingly, the senate speech itself comes to feature as the most important of these. Here, for example, is Kostya's response to Tortsov's request to recall the first vivid moment of the play:

> As for the beginning of the tragedy ... I have forgotten ... yet right now I have the feeling that there were interesting moods: an abduction, gatherings, a chase. No, that's not it. I am conscious of this through my mind rather than with my feelings. I have intimations concerning them but do not see them with my inner vision. Othello himself is not clear to me either in this part of the play. His appearance, his being

sent for by the Senate, his departure, the Senate itself – all this is clouded for me. The first vivid moment is Othello's speech to the Senate, but after that it is all dark again. (1996: 121)

Tortsov is predictably excited at this response and urges Kostya to "begin with these flashes of remembered light and emotion, and strengthen them" (1996: 121). The same question is put in different ways, until it virtually answers itself: "Without what thing, what circumstances, events, experiences, would there be no play?" (1996: 129). Various answers are given: "Othello's love for Desdemona, the cleavage between the two races, Iago's wicked intrigue, the trustfulness of the barbarian." But Tortsov prefers his own answer: "without the romantic ecstasy of a beautiful woman; without the Moor's fascinating, legendary stories" (1996: 129). In this way, the senate speech evolves into the dream-cave of the first Act.

As if haunted rather than inspired by the senate speech, Tortsov and his actors return again and again to it, until finally a revolt breaks out against Tortsov's utopian dream-vision of the text. This occurs in the course of a "seminar" on the play involving the whole company, when the assistant director Rakhmanov objects to their performing *Othello* at all. Why, he asks, are they bothering with so improbable a play? "Where," he wants to know, "do we see any negro generals?" How is it that "this nonexistent black general steals away the most beautiful, pure, naive, fairy princess?" (1996: 162). The seminar dissolves into uproar.

The interjection as such is of less moment than what happens when Tortsov and his actors reconvene the next day. Tortsov again tries to lure the actors back to the play's talismanic moments, its "flashes of remembered light and emotion." Again, the senate speech emerges as the brightest of these bright spots. Here, however, Tortsov over-reaches himself by asking Kostya whether the special quality of the senate speech is "auditory, visual or emotional" (1996: 165). The following exchange occurs:

– No, I do not hear the voice of Othello and the others … but I do feel and see something rather strongly, although it is indistinct.
– That's good. What is it you feel or see?
– It turns out to be very little, much less than I thought … I see the nobility of a generalized character.
– There is no real life in that kind of vision.

(1996: 165)

This "kind of vision," however, is all the actors now seem capable of. It is at this oddly self-deconstructive moment that the essay on *Othello* in *Creating A Role* begins to wind down. Tortsov talks about the potentialities of the play which they have not so far managed to engage: "such a clash of vivid, lifelike, human, social, national, psychological, and ethical excitements and passions" (1996: 166). But these are only words. There is no suggestion of their being transformed into the alchemy of performance. Tortsov likewise has something to say about the new method of "physical action," the method of cueing moments of text to specific physical actions. This, however, has been understood mainly as a method of retention rather than of invention, and it has been tested only on relatively minor passages (such as Brabantio's "O thou foul thief . . .").

The paradox, then, is that the attempt to reinvent the text in rehearsal – to evolve it through a kind of performative dialogue between the dream-work of the actors and the text's own glowing unconscious core – yields a banality on a par with the "opera baritone" of the sentimental tradition: "the nobility of a generalized character." To some degree, this banality seems to have been provoked by aesthetic hubris. Though superficially it seems related to the skeptical, no-nonsense assistant director Rakhmanov, in a deeper sense it is conjured forth by Tortsov's question to Kostya: "But what kind of bright spot is it? Auditory, visual or emotional?" What Tortsov wants is a phenomenological account of an ontological intuition. Roughly, the point of these questions is also: "Why did some places in the play excite feelings while others, which were logically bound up with them, did not; why did some spots vividly and instantly evoke emotions, affect our emotion memory, while others touched us only coldly, in a conscious, intellectual sort of way?" (1996: 123). The fault, one is tempted to surmise, lies not in the questions themselves but in the terms within which Tortsov expects the answers to be framed. Kostya's answer is very revealing, but not in a way that Tortsov wants it to be. Guided perhaps by his own newfound interest in physical objectives, Tortsov seems to want to fix what Goethe might have called the "elective affinity" between reader and text in a phenomenological key that will simultaneously preserve its aesthetic mystery and focus it as a precise performance value. What Kostya gives him instead is an image which, while apparently of unconscious provenance, seems to have irrupted from beyond the charmed circle of the rehearsal ritual and from beyond the special oneiric relationship that Tortsov has been cultivating between actors and text.

Where, then, has the "generalized character" image come from? My suggestion is that it comes from Stanislavski's own memories of the sentimental performance tradition. In his accounts of Salvini and of his own performance of Othello in 1896, the opera baritone figure exists as a kind of caricature, a histrionic Other against which both Salvini and Stanislavski strive to assert themselves, though with mixed success. Up until the senate speech, Salvini's appearance had struck the young Stanislavski as a caricature of what it should have been. The great actor was too stout, too obviously costumed, bewigged and made-up to be visually convincing as the heroic moor. In his own performance of 1896, Stanislavski felt that but for the physical expressiveness enabled by his costume, he would have fallen into the opera baritone caricature. What Kostya appears to have called to mind, then, is a version of this histrionic Other rather than the noble moor.

It remains to explain why the histrionic Other should have emerged at just this moment to undermine the rehearsal. No certain answer can be given, of course, beyond the speculations of psychoanalysis. My own is that the "generalized character" represents a form of self-mockery. Unconsciously no doubt, Kostya mocks both himself and the Tortsovian rehearsal project because Tortsov has been asking the impossible. In guiding his actors towards the glowing heart of *Othello*'s first Act, Tortsov has also been steering them towards the senate speech, the moment above all others at which the play is felt to achieve "eloquence." This is also, of course, the very moment at which Salvini himself chose to display his own histrionic eloquence, the moment that his brilliance commanded the young Stanislavski to "notice and re-member" above all others. What Stanislavski/Tortsov has been doing therefore (albeit unconsciously) is insisting that a treasured "sentimental" performance memory be resuscitated by actors of a later theatrical culture and with different histrionic values. Stanislavski himself, of course, had done much to create this very culture and value-set. But, like Tortsov, he seems to have forgotten that a Stanislavskian "rehearsal" is supposed to create a new performance text rather than simply duplicate a remembered one. The new performance text is to be created as a dialogue between the written text and the actors' own bodies, lives, and dream-work. Tortsov, however, has attempted to prescribe this dialogue rather than allow it to evolve on its own terms. In so doing, he has effectively inserted the memory of his enchantment by a sentimental performance 40 years earlier. "Eloquence" had been central to that enchantment, and so – insists Tortsov – should it be for his actors in 1930-33. Hence we find, against Stanislavski's own more sophisticated understanding of Othello's character, Tortsov insisting to Kostya that Othello is naive and simple on the one hand and spell-bindingly eloquent on the other. This is precisely the characterization played by Salvini, the Othello of nineteenth-century Romantic painting, and the "noble moor" of Bradley's eulogy (Bradley 1991). From the perspective of the 1930s, however, this figure might well have begun to blur, as it does for Kostya, into "the nobility of a generalized character," the caricature which Leavis would call by another name. But the image of Othello as spell-binding storyteller is a topos of the sentimental performance tradition, as also of a spin-off tradition of genre-painting exemplified by Henri Joseph Fradelle's depic-tion of Othello relating his travels to Desdemona and Brabantio (Figure 14.2) or by Carl Ludwig Friedrich Becker's "Othello relating his adventures to Desdemona" (1880), lavishly reproduced in nineteenth-century "trophy" Shakespeare editions.[4] It is suggestive that the rehearsal should have deconstructed at just the point at which Tortsov asks Kostya whether the special quality of the senate speech is "auditory, visual or emotional." For once the legend of Othello-the-storyteller had crossed over from the stage to painted canvas and book illustration, it could no longer be intuited from the text in a pure state. It was already contaminated by cultural tradition.

What is truly hubristic about Tortsov's project was not the Stanislavskian reinven-tion of the rehearsal. In its most rigorous form, this remains theatre's best hope of outflanking cultural repetition and ideological inscription. Nor was it the violence of Tortsov's attempt to derive a naturalistic performance from a single vivid master-image from the first Act – an approach more characteristic of *symboliste* dramaturgy than naturalism, associated with a radically counter-naturalistic performance style anchored in "vividness" as distinct from "clarity" (Deak 1993). Tortsov's real mistake

FIGURE 14.2 "Othello relating his adventures to Desdemona and Brabantio," Henri Joseph Fradelle c.1850
Image courtesy of the Archive of the Royal Shakepeare Company.

was to have lost faith in the rehearsal as an autonomous creative institution by foisting upon it the mythology of a bygone performance genre. The myth begets mischief here not because it is mythological, but because it is being foisted uncritically from a nineteenth-century cultural domain onto a twentieth-century rehearsal culture which quite literally refuses to entertain it. In the nineteenth century, the myth that Othello's spell-binding eloquence is co-extensive with his naivety seemed to work in the theatre and in the culture at large – which is all we can fairly ask of a theatrical myth. In the twentieth century, however, the idea no longer compels. The problem for Kostya was not eloquence as such but its supposed dependence on "the nobility of a generalized character." The problem for his heirs – particularly those of the "opera baritone" school such as Paul Robeson, Willard White, and even Lawrence Fishburne, whose voice takes on a strangely ululant quality in the senate scene – I would suggest, remains that of uncoupling the text from unhelpful cultural entailments, prime among which would be the unthinking equation of eloquence with magniloquence.

The paradox of Golovin's design

My analysis yields a final paradox. Stanislavski's attempt to derive a performance logic and style from a few vivid master images has struck me as a kind of cultural somnambulism, a repetition. But it has also struck me as a distinctively *symboliste* mode of approaching the text. These two explanations do not harmonize, particularly when we reflect that symbolism was not Stanislavski's theatrical idiom, but the modernist idiom through which Meyerhold (his most gifted student) had broken with Stanislavskian naturalism. My point is that for Stanislavski's musings to have savored of this heresy would suggest the very opposite of cultural repetition (whether in the sense of his repeating cultural stereotypes or in the sense of his repeating himself). In one way indeed, Stanislavski's 1930 production offers a tantalizing glimpse of what might have been: not the spiritless failure that history records, but the seed of a genuinely original performance text. In Golovin's costume design for Othello (see Figure 14.1), we see not the opera baritone of Kostya's dreams nor the statuesque Othellos of the story-teller tradition (the conventionally animated figures of Fradelle and Becker), but a vibrantly original dream image: dynamic and threatening, sublime and grotesque, heroic and brutalist. The image is thoroughly modern, unsentimental, and completely unbeholden to Stanislavski's treasured memories of Salvini. Where did it come from? How could Golovin have painted it while working to Stanislavski's direction? Part of the answer must be that Golovin was steeped in Russian theatrical symbolism and stylization, having designed for Vsevolod Meyerhold from roughly 1910 to 1917, exactly the period in which Meyerhold evolved through the stylized theatre of his revolt from Stanislavskianism to the grotesque and festive style of his maturity. Golovin's designs for Meyerhold were boldly impressionistic and stylized in the sense of gesturing toward a setting (or a period) rather than reproducing it, while also theatricalizing it, carnivalizing it. Their collaboration is said to have reached its height in Meyerhold's 1917 production of Lermontov's *The Masquerade*: "The arrangement of sets and costumes was based on the principles of an operatic score, providing the leading characters with a colour and rhythmical characteristics similar to musical themes used in operas" (Fedosova 1989: 56). Such was the spirit of Stanislavski's first collaboration with Golovin, a 1929 Arts Theatre production of *Figaro* that would represent the "people" in the person of Figaro and in terms of a self-consciously "people's" performance style emphasizing folk music and dance (Onufrieva 1977: 119). Flushed with this success, they embarked on *Othello* in the following year. Golovin's Venetian settings, both exterior and interior, were warm and colorful (Onufrieva, 1977: 120). "Othello's Room (Act 3)" is strikingly art nouveau, a beautifully textured interior, overlaid in stylized patterns and oddly suggestive of a Frank Lloyd Wright interior (Fedosova 1989, plate 109). One imagines the gaudy Othello of Golovin's design moving against this background somewhat like a butterfly against woodland. But where Stanislavski had found Golovin's festive visual style right for *Figaro*, he hated it in *Othello*, branding it as "operatic." A replacement set was botched up by Simov. Golovin was in despair. The senate chamber in particular struck him as hackneyed, tasteless and dull. "One could not," he said, "approach this scene in terms of photographic realism." By this time Golovin was quite ill and died before the premiere. A correspondent commented to Stanislavski on the difference between Golovin's sketches and the completed scenery, remarking that the latter was as bad as the *Figaro* scenery had been good (Onufrieva 1977: 121). Stanislavski appears to have been guilty of a category error as well as of a simple error of taste: the carnivalesque quality of Golovin's designs was deemed appropriate to opera (*Figaro*) but not for tragedy (*Othello*). As with the image of Othello the storyteller or the opera baritone, the generic intruded upon the genuinely original. Again it would appear to have been the case of fixed ideas (the dignity of tragedy as distinct from opera) intruding upon the rehearsal process and killing off the festive response that Stanislavski's own enthusiasm for *Othello* had inspired in Golovin. In the wake of the more recent paradigm of "festive tragedy," Golovin's take on *Othello* would not seem at all strange (Laroque 1991, Liebler 1995). That approach to Shakespeare was of course unknown in 1930, and I am not suggesting that Golovin had somehow foreseen it but merely that this unpredictable mix of Meyerholdian grotesquerie with Stanislavskian naturalism might well have led to a performance text that was "eloquent" in unexpected ways rather than the ways that Stanislavski remembered and insisted upon. The problem, it seems fair to say, was not so much with Stanislavski's "method" (which had invited this effervescent encounter between the naturalistic and carnivalesque idioms) as with the conservatism that put the lid down on their ferment.

NOTES

1 The Meininger Company, founded by George II, Duke of Saxe-Meiningen (1826–1914) "revitalised the handling of crowd scenes"(Hartnoll 1975: 630, DeHart 1981).

2 During September, 1929, Stanislavski, reportedly speaking to Leonidov, the actor of Othello, worried over Golovin's "native" costumes: "They are to pass in the scene of his reunion (with Desdemona) on Cyprus. But can they be seen in the dark?" (Onufrieva, 1977: 122 ff.) Translation by Angela Livingstone.

3 On the difference between the approach via emotion memory and that through physical objectives, see Benedetti (1988: 295).

4 This painting can be viewed by googling "Carl Ludwig Friedrich Becker," see www. artrenewal.org. See also Shakespeare (1906: 1168–69, 1200–1).

REFERENCES AND FURTHER READING

Benedetti, Jean (1982). *Stanislavski: An Introduction.* London: Methuen.

Benedetti, Jean (1988). *Stanislavski: A Biography.* London: Methuen.

Bradley, A. C. (1991). "Othello." In *Shakespearean Tragedy.* London: Penguin, pp. 167–94.

Deak, Frantisek (1993). *Symbolist Theater: The Formation of an Avant-Garde.* Baltimore, MD: Johns Hopkins University Press.

DeHart, Steven (1981). *The Meininger Theater: 1776–1926.* Ann Arbor: University of Michigan Research Press.

Fedosova, Yelena (1989). *Alexander Golovin*, ed. John Crowfoot. Leningrad: Aurora Art Publishers.

Hankey, Julie (ed.) (1987). *Othello: William Shakespeare*. Bristol: Classical Press.

Hartnoll, Phyllis (ed.) (1975). *The Oxford Companion to the Theatre*, 3rd edn. London: Oxford University Press.

Knight, G. Wilson (1930). "The *Othello* Music." In *The Wheel of Fire: Interpretations of Shakespearean Tragedy*. London: Methuen, pp. 97–119.

Laroque, François (1991). *Shakespeare's Festive World*. Cambridge: Cambridge University Press.

Leavis, F. R. (1962). "Diabolic Intellect and the Noble Hero: Or the Sentimentalist's *Othello*." In *The Common Pursuit*. London: Chatto and Windus, pp. 136–59.

Levin, Richard (1988). "Feminist Thematics and Shakespearean Tragedy." *PMLA* 103: 125–38.

Levin, Richard (1990). "The Poetics and Politics of Bardicide." *PMLA* 105: 491–504.

Liebler, Naomi Conn (1995). *Shakespeare's Festive Tragedy: The Ritual Foundations of Genre*. London: Routledge.

Onufrieva, Svetlana (1977). *Golovin*. Leningrad: Iskusstvo.

Rosenberg, Marvin (1971). *The Masks of Othello*. Berkeley, CA: University of California Press.

Shakespeare, William (1906). *The Complete Works of William Shakespeare with an Essay … by Sir Henry Irving*. Glasgow: Collins.

Shakespeare, William (1989). *Othello*, ed. Norman Sanders. Cambridge: Cambridge University Press.

Sprengnether, Madelon (1996). "Introduction: The Gendered Subject of Shakespearean Tragedy." In Shirley Nelson Garner & Madelon Sprengnether (eds.) *Shakespearean Tragedy and Gender*. Bloomington, IN: Indiana University Press.

Stanislavski, Constantin (1968). *Stanislavski Produces Othello*, trans. Helen Nowak. New York: Theatre Art Books.

Stanislavski, Constantin (1996). "Part 2: Shakespeare's *Othello*." In *Creating a Role*, trans. Elizabeth Hapgood Reynolds. London: Methuen, pp. 107–210.

Stanislavski, Constantin (1982). *My Life in Art*, trans. J. J. Robbins. London: Methuen.

Stanislavski, Constantin (1981). *Building a Character*, trans. Elizabeth Hapgood Reynolds. London: Methuen.

Tynan, Kenneth (ed.) (1966). *Othello: William Shakespeare, the National Theatre Production*. London: Rupert Hart-Davis.

Vaughan, Virginia Mason (1994). "The Ethiopian Moor": Paul Robeson's Othello." In *Othello: A Contextual History*. Cambridge: Cambridge University Press, pp. 181–98.

Worthen, W. B. (1987). *The Idea of the Actor: Drama and the Ethics of Performance*. Princeton, NJ: Princeton University Press.

15

Shakespeare, *Henry VI* and the Festival of Britain

Stuart Hampton-Reeves

Fire and Slaughter

April 1951 was unseasonably wet, so audiences stayed away from the Birmingham Rep's landmark production of *2 Henry VI*. If the start of the first ever repertory run of the *Henry VI* plays was, as producer Sir Barry Jackson claimed, a major piece of theatre history, no one in Birmingham appeared to bother much about it; they preferred to stay dry, and to let *Henry VI* remain undiscovered. But Jackson was doubly unfortunate, because the rain also delayed the other big event of 1951, which might have created an audience for the staging of Shakespearean history: this was the start of the Festival of Britain.

1951 was, after all, Festival Year, when the government attempted to draw a line under a decade of war and austerity with a national celebration of British history and the British character. The main attraction was a large exhibition center erected on the South Bank; but the Festival also included a funfair in Battersea, special museum events across the country and "celestial omnibuses" decked out with exhibits from British history. Meanwhile, nearly every town and village in the country celebrated the Festival in their own way with local history pageants and shows. And the theatre also celebrated Festival year: Laurence Olivier and Vivien Leigh performed a double bill of *Antony and Cleopatra* and *Caesar and Cleopatra* at St. James's Theatre; Glen Byam Shaw staged *Henry V* at the Old Vic with Alec Clunes and Dorothy Tutin; the Shakespeare Memorial Theatre produced Shakespeare's second tetralogy; York staged a mystery play cycle; London churches played a series of morality plays; and the Birmingham Rep offered the first part of what would eventually be a full run of the *Henry VI* plays. According to the *Theatre World Annual*, "never before had such a galaxy of stars been assembled" and there was no doubt that it was the Festival which was the main impetus for this theatrical *annus mirabilis*. For many who fondly remember that year, the Festival was a splash of colour which "blazed its sparkling star across the grey heavens of Britain in the aftermath of the Second World War"

(Banham & Hillier 1976: 6). But it was also a moment of history: or rather, a moment when (for the first time since 1945) history was revisited and renegotiated in the light of recent events.

But, I contend, the Festival did more than simply celebrate Britain – it played a crucial role in the subsequent remapping of British culture in the post-war, post-imperial years. After the Festival, many of the dominant institutions of national culture in our time first emerged, including the National Theatre, the RSC, the Royal Festival Hall and BBC television (especially after the coronation in 1953). The Festival was an opening salvo in this reconstruction; by analysing the Festival's ambitions, its sense of history, and its conception of Britain, we can get a clearer sense of the pressures that gave rise to these institutions, particularly in regard to Shakespeare's place as the poet of the new national culture.

The Festival looked back to (and in some respects rehearsed) the Great Exhibition of 1851, when Britain (then at the height of its Empire) had confidently displayed its achievements. In May 1951, King George VI opened the Festival by drawing a somber distinction between that thriving, powerful empire and the present, when much of Britain's wealth and power had been "dissipated in fire and slaughter." He went on to emphasize the painful difference between the "calm and security of the Victorian age" and the "hard experience of our own" (a video of the speech can be downloaded from www.britishpathe.com). The confrontation with the past, then, was a confrontation with a century of decline, war and trauma: many cities were still in ruins, the British Empire was severely eroded, and Britain's dominance of the world had given way to the rising superpowers of America and the Soviet Union. King George's take on the Festival was unexpectedly despondent for an occasion which was meant to be a celebration (even if he did temper his remarks with optimism about the future). But the King was only a player on this particular stage of history, which was rather directed by the government, whose minister Herbert Morrison insisted on a more upbeat tone to the year that the British people would "show themselves to themselves."

Jackson's provincial *2 Henry VI* did exactly that, it showed the British people a theatrical representation of themselves in the past. But Jackson was more inclined to King George's gloomy nostalgia than to Morrison's positive mood, and Jackson's choice of play for his Festival production reflects this. It is true that the *Henry VI* plays, at first sight, fit well with the major themes of the period: like England after Henry V, Britain in 1951 was facing the loss of Empire (India seceded from the British Empire in 1948, effectively heralding the decline of Britain's international supremacy) following a bruising international war. The plays go on to tell the story of the "fire and slaughter" which transforms the England of Henry V to the unstable celebrations of Edward IV's court – King George's speech could even be a good ending to *Part 3*, when Edward calls for "stately triumphs, mirthful comic shows" and cries "Farewell, sour annoy!". Yet this is exactly the story which the Festival of Britain did not want to tell. In the exhibitions on the South Bank, British history was presented without any memory of "sour annoy": there were no references to war, to Empire or to class difference. Instead, history was remembered in terms of cultural achievement, as, according to the Souvenir programme, the Festival told "the story of British contributions to world civilisation in the arts of peace." In this amnesiac context, the Rep's *Henry VI* plays, and King George's opening speech, were actually atypical: they were downbeat reflections on the "fire and slaughter" which ruined the legacy of the past, whereas the Festival sought to establish a positive vision of the modern national self.

Situating the *Henry VI* plays within the context of Festival year is thus fraught with difficulties. Jackson's productions were not radical: after all, each performance ended with the national anthem, as was the custom then. But the subject material rubbed against the grain by inviting an introspection that was not festive, but which opened up a theatrical exploration of some of the thornier issues confronting Britain at the dawn of the 1950s. It is helpful here to think about the distinctions which Nietzsche (1997) (in a similar cultural moment) drew between what he called monumental history and critical history. Monumental history includes the kind of national event we experience periodically: the coronations, military parades, state funerals, swearing-in ceremonies and national anthems which texture and continually re-create the nation state. Any act of historiography which is little more than an unquestioning homage to tradition can be called monumental and this, of course, includes much Shakespearean performance. But there is also critical history, in which the story of the past is told in order to achieve an "ironic self-awareness": critical history is as much about moving forward to the future as it is about dealing with the problems of the past. The Rep's *Henry VI* plays misjudged the mood of the times: they offered critical history at a time when the past was not being confronted, but actively, festively, forgotten.

The Birmingham Rep produced *2 Henry VI* in 1951, *3 Henry VI* in 1952 and all three plays in 1953 – all years which were dominated by public events and monumental histories which followed in the slipstream of the Festival's re-energizing of national consciousness. In 1951, following the Festival of Britain, Churchill was returned to power (having been booted out in 1945, he had become in the intervening years a figure of nostalgia). In 1952, the King died but his funeral, a somber antidote to the previous year's celebrations, was nonetheless a monumentalizing ceremony of national bonding; in 1953, the streets of provincial England were deserted, as families and their neighbors gathered around new television sets to watch the coronation of Elizabeth II (the birth of British television broadcast culture is often dated to this moment, when thousands of television sets were sold). Following the unscripted, unpredictable and dangerous war years, such monumentalizing ceremonies offered a series of ritualized closures – similar to Henry's doomed attempt to end his French wars with a marriage in *2 Henry VI*. But memorial acts are also a kind of collective forgetting, a wiping away of the horror and austerity of war – as Nietzsche points out, their invocation of history is curiously unhistorical.

A production of the *2 Henry VI* plays at least creates the conditions for "ironic self-awareness" because its opening scene, when Suffolk presents the new Queen to Henry, is a monumentalizing ceremony, marking the end of the French wars and the start of the peace, which soon splits into the factions of a civil war. Even during the opening scene, cracks appear in the monument, as what should be a ceremony of restoration, an incorporation of Margaret into the monumental history of England, is interrupted by Gloucester's inability to continue to play his part. Gloucester's role is to read out the marriage treaty, but as the political reality becomes clear to him, the King's uncle stops; he cannot carry on, he drops the treaty onto the stage. From this initial moment of disruption, *2 Henry VI* turns away from monumental history: the ceremonies and performances of the court no longer reflect political reality. In fact, they act as a way of avoiding it.

The scene began the Rep's cycle, and it established an uneasy relationship with the narratives of nation promulgated by the Festival. That the question of national politics would be foregrounded was signaled in that opening moment when Gloucester dropped the articles of marriage on the Rep's small, crowded, ordered stage. From this point, the production committed itself to a different kind of history, which was not going to be, like the SMT's histories, a commemoration of national identity, a theatrical equivalent to the Festival of Britain. Rather, the production traded on the unresolved, incomplete and fractured nature of a country traumatized by power politics. The Festival set out to show the Britons "to themselves" in a celebratory mood: the Rep offered, as a contrast, another level of introspection, in which self-awareness was, like Gloucester's sudden moment of awareness, critical and ironic. It performed the nation through, as *The Times* put it, a "cumulative disorder" in which the violence of the recent past was not elided, but revived.

The company surprised reviewers by not continuing (and concluding) the cycle with *Richard III*. Instead, in what was perhaps an echo of the VE day celebrations six years earlier, bells rang onstage and crowds cheered as Edward seemingly closed the trilogy with his call for "lasting joy." But then Richard added an ending of his own, stepping forward to speak the first lines of his famous opening soliloquy to *Richard III*, "Now is the winter of our discontent ... " Ironically, the most festive moment in the whole cycle was, then, thrown into critical doubt by this telling reminder of what is yet to come. Richard's voice was gradually drowned out by the sound of the celebrations, as if monumentalizing history had captured and silenced the dynamic which would eventually drive history forward to its ruin. In his recent edition of the play, Randall Martin criticizes the Rep's false ending, arguing that the reminder of *Richard III* weakened the plays' overall dramatic integrity by reducing them to the status of a prequel to a more well-known play (Martin 2002: 48). But the important point is that *Richard III* was not played – there was no final resolution, no final justice.

The production of *Part Two* began, as Trewin memorably describes it, with an "angry surge." There would be no "angry young men" for another five years, but Trewin's description nevertheless seems now to be a premonition of what was to come. The cast was young and the energy of the first scene was sustained through all three productions – many reviewers noted the pace, clarity and energy of the acting. York, Somerset, Suffolk and even Gloucester were prototype Jimmy Porters, railing at the betrayals of history, and the effect was explosive – a startling, dynamic, "in-your-face," angry representation of history which was ill at ease with the Festival's emphasis on achievement and forgetting.

The Experiment

The driving force behind the *Henry VIs* was Sir Barry Jackson, who was already in his seventies, and thus old enough to be a Victorian (he was 22 when Victoria died). He had lived through the Boer War, the two world wars, a general strike, the suffragette movement, and six monarchs (together with five royal funerals and five coronations). But Jackson was an innovator: his theatre, the Birmingham Rep (which he founded in 1913) was one of the first regional repertory theatres to develop a repertoire without regard for the box office. Jackson is one of the neglected visionaries of the twentieth century, but his role was vital in establishing the landscape of modern British theatre: he broke new ground by performing Shakespeare in modern dress, he premiered several of Shaw's plays and he was the first person to bring one of his most famous protégés, Peter Brook, to Stratford-upon-Avon. Jackson was briefly artistic director of the Shakespeare Memorial Theatre after the war, where he produced Brook's legendary, "Watteau-esque" *Love's Labour's Lost*, but financial disaster forced Jackson back to the Rep (Beauman 1982: 166–95). Jackson's approach to the role of artistic director (at the Rep and at the SMT) focused on young ensembles, driven by new, emerging talent rather than star names, who performed a repertoire which mixed classics with modern drama and rarely performed plays such as *Gammer Gurton's Needle*. In all these respects, Jackson anticipated the policies of the post-war subsidized theatres, including the RSC.

Jackson insisted that the *Henry VI* plays are "eminently actable" and the "experiment" (Jackson kept calling it an experimental, as he was well aware of the novelty of playing the plays in rep over three years) was to test this theory. Issues of authorship and questions of legitimacy were brushed aside: these were great works of theatre which had only been off the stage for so long because a myopic Victorian theatrical culture failed to see beyond the absence of any obvious star role. Jackson was very conscious of the ways in which the plays' themes could have contemporary relevance, in one case drawing suggestive parallels between the "father who has killed his son" scene and the Holocaust. His privileging of this scene ran against the grain of contemporary critical opinion: Tillyard had called it "dull, primitive, and ingenuous" and mocked "the utter artlessness of the language" (Tillyard 1944: 195). But for Jackson, the scene is a powerful and moving piece of theatre which "threw more light on the horror of civil war than all the scenes of wasteful bloodshed." For him, "the still figures of the father and son speaking quietly and unemotionally, as though voicing the thoughts that strike the saintly, sad King's conscience, presented a moment of calm and terrible reflection" (Jackson 1953: 51). For a generation that had lived through a war, reflection could be both terrible and calm: indeed, for a 1950s' audience, the twin nature of "reflection" was potentially problematic: the Festival's insistence on a certain kind of reflection, in which the British "show themselves to themselves" also, at the same time, elided any form of reflection on the events of the war. The father/son scene was one of the few moments in Jackson's production when the pace slowed. King Henry slept on the stage, surrounded by corpses: as he awoke, so did they. The effect was dreamlike, as the stage was transformed from a battlefield into an interior space, and the "still figures" of the father and son spoke not only to the audience but to other corpses, animated by Henry's dream: this was not a man's (or a King's) vision, but that of a whole generation of slaughtered soldiers, hearing their pain voiced. This "voicing" of a reflection was, Jackson discovered, not only a theatrical *coup*, but the very heart of the play's contradictory representation of war and victory. The family cleavage was, Jackson noted, a contemporary scene that prompted memories of, for example, Germany in the 1940s. The King, "saintly, sad," was an image of innocence and despair, like an Edwardian summer confronting the storm of war, or like Walter Benjamin's "angel of history" who stands gaping at the wreckage of history piling up before it, its wings turned against the future.

Jackson has sometimes been associated with the mock-Elizabethanism of William Poel, but this is to miss the point. Jackson did respect the need to reassess Shakespeare in the light of what was then known about the context of their original production and, like Poel, he saw this as a way of resisting the theatrical contamination of centuries of performance tradition. But unlike Poel, Jackson saw the need to constantly move between respecting the text and confronting the present. The script he prepared was, as a consequence, a practical response to the demands of playing the *Henry VI* plays which preserved the trilogy structure and made very few alterations to the Folio texts – though two of them were significant, for as well as adding lines from *Richard III* to the end, he also began *1 Henry VI* with lines from *Henry V*. When the productions were played as a trilogy in 1953, Jackson made a number of small alterations to their original productions, including casting changes, which reinforced the unity of the trilogy. Jackson's scripts thus took full advantage of the theatrical opportunities offered by the trilogy, with many characters moving from callow youth to disillusioned old age over the course of the nine-hour cycle. Yet Jackson's carefully judged cuts and interpolations did nothing to erode the episodic quality of the plays' narrative, preserving their "troubling inconclusiveness."

Jackson was the visionary behind the productions, but he did not direct them himself: instead, he gave this job to Douglas Seale, a young director (in his early thirties) who would later go on to be a character actor in Hollywood. Seale's vision for the plays was influenced by popular cinematic representations of history, so there was a pageant-like, Technicolor feel to his work which called to mind the medieval worlds of Errol Flynn's *The Adventures of Robin Hood* and Olivier's *Henry V*. In Seale's *Henry VI*, villains were clearly villains – they wore dark colors, their expressions were thick-set and their beards were either sinister or elegantly styled. Women, on the other hand, were slender and graceful and wore long, medieval dresses, hoods and crucifixes; the good guys were stern and grim and wore armor gilded with fleur-de-lis. Only Jack May's Henry, dressed in a simple black habit, went against type. Olivier's *Richard III* (not yet filmed but already well known in the theatre) also haunted this *Henry VI: The Times* immediately recognized that Paul Daneman's Richard was influenced by "Richard's most famous recent impersonator" (*The Times*, April 2, 1952).

The stage was set in the same way in all three productions, and its design concept was to create an uncluttered and open playing space. Three brightly painted arches set at the rear – almost the only "decoration" on the stage – established a cartoonish interpretative frame for the performance. The central arch was where the throne was often set, but more often than not this central space was used to represent disempowerment: for example, Talbot's death was staged here, the old soldier cradling his son while York and Somerset stood in the arches either side of him. The generals' stubborn refusal to send aid was played in tandem, a juxtaposition of scenes which brought home the bitter ironies of war. Here, the arches functioned in a similar way to stained-glass windows, which make "history" simultaneously present and which contrast the individual frames with the whole picture. The arches also served as exits and entrances but they could, at times, serve a more sinister function: a portcullis could be lowered over the arch, enclosing and imprisoning the characters onstage. In *Part Three*, the repeated use of the portcullis was a *leitmotif* for the production's constant movement between dark and light, passion and betrayal, liberation and imprisonment. Open, it represented freedom and victory; closed, it represented imprisonment and defeat. At the end of *Part Three*, Henry was butchered with his body pressed against the portcullis, his arms spread out in a helpless image of the crucifixion.

The Lion and the Unicorn

During the Festival of Britain, a 1623 Folio of Shakespeare's works was put on display as part of an exhibition dedicated to the "British character" called "The Lion and the Unicorn." This title, which was also the title of Orwell's wartime book on the need to rediscover a British national identity, was interpreted by a large sign at the entrance of the exhibition, which defined the lion as "action" and the unicorn as "imagination." The Lion and the Unicorn device has been a part of the symbology of Great Britain ever since James I combined the heraldic symbols of England and Scotland following his accession in 1603. In its 1951 appropriation, the symbols lost their original English and Scottish meanings and were instead used to define the essential characteristics of Britishness. But the Lion and the Unicorn has always been a curious trope for national identity, as it is also, famously, the title of an ancient nursery rhyme about civil war: "The Lion and the Unicorn / Were fighting for the crown."

In the Rep's productions, this question of national identity was revisited in the same way: against the harmonious visions of the Festival, the productions offered a vision of Lions tearing the country apart over the crown. Jack May played Henry straight off the page as a weak and pious King unable to comprehend either the political or sexual games played around him. He was often accompanied by monks and nuns, desexualized representations of gender that indicated Henry's own nostalgia for the moral certainties of religion, but he was out-of-place in the post-war, post-imperial world of *Part Two*. By staging Henry's murder as a form of sacrifice, the harmonious union of "imagination" and "action" suggested by the Festival of Britain programme was re-voiced in a different and more problematic vein. Edward's Victory in England celebrations were then tainted by this radicalized opposition between innocence and violence.

Against Henry's passive, docile unicorn, Suffolk and York were lions, fighting over the crown. The action was driven by two power-house performances from Richard Pascoe as Suffolk and John Arnett as York. Both were villains, but in some ways they were the most modern characters onstage: Pascoe smouldered his way through most of his scenes as a romantic anti-hero, a Rhett Butler in medieval dress. Arnett, Russian by birth, looked the part of a dissident outsider, an existential anti-hero who has no place in the dominant order of things. The main theme remained that of post-war politics, but Pascoe and Arnett voiced potential instabilities in the new national order. Both characters were brought into the opening pageants of *Part One*, anachronistically mourning Henry V, but it was the opening of *Part Two* which really defined their relationship: Suffolk was at the center of things, not only a substitute groom in the proxy wedding but a substitute king as well, already dominating politics through his presentation of Margaret to the ineffectual King. York, on the other hand, skulked on the margins of the stage, eyeing up the ceremonies that should be his, a self-excluded figure, biding his time.

An audience unfamiliar with the plays might have thought, at the outset of *Part Two*, that Richard Pascoe was the king: he was fierce, handsome and swarthy, and he commanded the stage in a way that Jack May's shy Henry never could. Suffolk's public subservience to the King was coded and ironic: at St. Alban's he obediently knelt to Henry, and then lounged on the stage with Margaret, openly flirting with her – only Henry was unable to read the signs. Suffolk's love scenes with Margaret were pure Hollywood romance: Margaret putting her head against his manly chest, digging her nails into his arms, Suffolk gazing into the distance with an impassive expression on his chiselled face ... Such scenes mined the clichés of films like *Gone with the Wind* and even had a smack of wartime weepies like *Brief Encounter*, but Suffolk was clearly the villain as well. As Margaret berated the petitioners, Suffolk nodded to Hume, who had lingered onstage after his scene with Eleanor: there were no words, but the complicity was clear enough.

After Gloucester's death, there was a rare moment when Henry broke out of the political frame which trapped him. Suffolk bowed down once more to Henry, but the King said, distantly, "lay not thy hands on me." It was a decisive moment: Suffolk's hold on the king was broken, the game was no longer going according to plan. Suffolk stood and backed away into the darkness (the stage was only lit above the center arch): once the center of a spectacle of national unity, Suffolk was now powerless in the face of the mob outside. His final scene with Margaret was naturally histrionic: but, rather than have Suffolk leave the stage, as he does in the play-text, Seale kept him onstage, watching Margaret go. For a moment, the man who had commanded the stage, and the woman, was alone: but only for a moment, as four pirates were waiting for him.

The real Lion, though, was York, who moved from being an outsider in *Part One*, to a brooding Machiavel in *Part Two*, and a tragic father in *Part Three*. Even in *Part One*, when York is not one of the main characters, Jackson's adaptation made it clear how important the character was by placing intervals (each of the *Parts* had two intervals) after York's key scenes: the curtain was brought down on York unfolding his claim to Warwick in the Temple Garden; later, the second interval curtain came down on York picking up a white rose discarded by Henry. When played by Alan Bridges in 1951/2, York was a clear-cut, even cartoonish villain whose "mad flaw" made him a proto-Richard III. Bridges (who would later abandon acting for a career as a director) was only in his early twenties and had to be heavily made-up to play the older York of *Part Three* (in fact, he was younger than Paul Daneman, who played his son Richard). But in 1953, Jackson and Seale gave the part to a tall, slender actor called John Arnett who could play both a young and a mature York. Known for his golden voice, Arnett recreated York as a man who is ambitious but "nobly graced": in *Part One* and *Part Two* he skillfully navigated the politics of Henry's court, often watching in grim horror at the ruin of the kingdom he claimed. But it was in his death scene in *Part Three* that Arnett's interpretation came into its own. Where Bridges had intoned and declaimed his final speeches, Arnett spoke them softly, with a "quiet realism" which belied the interior tragedy of a man with no ambition left. This transformed the scene: in the earlier version, Margaret had put the paper crown on York's head while he was held down by sneering soldiers. In Arnett's performance, York tried to pull away from Margaret as she came near him but, after he had said his final words, he stood up, quiet and resigned, and contemplated the stained hand-kerchief. Then, crying, he removed the paper crown from his head and held it out to Margaret, transforming Bridges' simplistic bombastic defiance into tragic pathos. But, as York held out the crown, which Margaret did not take, it was also an acknowledgment of the shared link between the two: York who has lost his son, Margaret who would lose her son.

The scene was haunted by the cycle's own roots in the Festival year: as written, the scene both recalls and travesties the tradition of the player-king. Some of the audience may have been player-kings themselves in the history pageants which were staged locally across the country: certainly, most would have seen such an event. Whether or not audiences did relate the performance of nation in the theatre with the celebration of the nation beyond the theatre, the recirculation of these images from triumphal communities to the lonely and wasted scene on the molehill made such a conjunction possible. But, perhaps to reinforce the point, Jackson and Seale made sure that York was the second player-king to wear the crown. The first was a boy, dressed as a jester, who was slaughtered alongside Rutland by the "pent-up lion" Clifford. This boy – a curious and unexplained double of Rutland – was first seen playing in the back-ground, wearing the paper crown, as Richard tried to persuade his father to break his oath. Even here, the paper crown was an ironic counter-point to York's own failed desires. Later, held silently between York and Margaret, the paper crown brought together History and festival in one ruined image.

Thou Hast Hit It!

But what of the British people, in Festival Britain? Where were they in the *Henry VIs*? A visual clue is offered by the posters for the 1951 *Part Two*, which tried to sell the show on the strength of "the wry humour of Saunders Simpcox." Simpcox, whose miraculous cure Gloucester exposes as a fraud in Act III, only has one scene in the play – he is a poor-man's Falstaff whose only role in the play is to be the foil for a brief comic interlude which anticipates Gloucester's fall from power. Yet Jackson made Simpcox one of the definitive aspects of the production's appeal, which suggests a certain kind of play and a certain kind of audience: the play is a history play with gags, the audience is one which looks for reflections of itself. The maneuver was both populist and popular: it brought the story of the ordinary people of Britain into view, and it promised a crowd-pleasing comic turn. The commoners' story was literally the center of Jackson's script for *Part Two* as the whole of the middle act was devoted to them, from Simpcox to Cade.

Hence the hitherto unsuspected "wry humour" of Saunders Simpcox became a central selling point, a way to bring in audiences. In effect, this was added: Jackson and Seale built on the banter between Gloucester and Simpcox to make a comic routine out of the charade. Gloucester and Simpcox were a double act, with Simpcox as the clown to Gloucester's straight-man. The vaudeville pastiches continued with the Cade scenes and, when *Part Two* was revived in 1953, Seale cast a rising comedian called Kenneth Williams as Smith the Weaver. Williams would later make a name for himself as a master of comic voices and *double entendres* in shows such as *Round the Horne* and the *Carry On* films – in *Henry VI*, he stole the show as Smith (and later played Rutland). Jackson and Seale developed Smith as one of the comic turns of the Cade scenes by giving him extra lines and routines, some of which were borrowed from other parts in the riot. Much of the humor was slapstick and involved Smith hitting various people with a wooden sword and shouting "Thou hast hit it!" But the comedy quickly developed into more familiar ground for Williams: at one point, Smith carried a peasant girl offstage, with the men shouting "Tumble her, Smith, tumble her!" and the other women screaming after him to put her down.

The humor was, nevertheless, ambivalent. The carnival banter of Smith and Cade soon turned violent, with decapitated heads forming the banners of the uprising. And who should an audience identify with, in Festival Year? The patriarch Gloucester, who sends up the lower classes? Or Smith the Weaver, whose seaside postcard humor is soon transformed into anarchic violence? Neither Shakespeare nor the Birmingham Rep left much room for a Festival-centric vision of British history stripped of class difference. On the contrary, the wry humor of Simpcox, Gloucester and Smith was a comedy based on class difference and its eventual ambivalence, its complex circulation of comedy, and violence, rehearsed potential instabilities in the new national order inaugurated by the Festival. By making the center of *Part Two* comic, Jackson and Seale may have been trying to diffuse the more difficult issues raised about national culture and civil war: but the ambivalence of the comedy created an ironic self-awareness of the problems of staging history in 1951.

Despite the initial adverts, then, the British people were imperfectly represented in the Birmingham Rep's contribution to Festival Year. The productions went against the grain of the Festival by flagging up difference as inherent instability within the identity of the British character: they floated potentially divisive images of nation against the harmonious tapestries offered by the Festival. For Roy Strong, the Festival's main contribution to British national culture was one of style: it gave a mythos and a history to the new urban spaces, plazas and espresso bars of the concrete new towns that were being built in the wake of the war. Birmingham, Britain's second city, had been badly damaged during the Blitz and so its rebuilding placed it firmly within the paradigm that the Festival was celebrating. Yet its civic theatre offered a vision of history which was unafraid to confront the memory of war, and which was willing to pit a vision of national disunity against the prevailing, festive images of nation.

The Festival's role in shaping the modern institutional context for Shakespeare has not been fully acknowledged; yet, in at least one sense, the Festival has left its mark on British Shakespeare in the form of the buildings that now stand on the industrial land used for the main attractions, among them the National Theatre (RNT). One of the final ceremonies of Festival Year was the laying of the first stone of what was to become the National Theatre, with an inscription, unveiled by the Queen, which dedicated the theatre to: "the Living Memory of William Shakespeare on a site provided by the London County Council, in conformity with the National Theatre Act MCMXLIX and in the year of the Festival of Britain" (Elsom & Tomalin 1978: 1). Shakespeare, the National Theatre, and the Festival of Britain were lumped together in a not-yet realized institution that would be civic (London City Council), national (the National Theatre Act), royal, and commemorative. By gesturing to Shakespeare's "living memory," the dedication not only invoked the oxymoron of the theatre, where past plays can be made present performances, but also of the Festival itself. As Roy Strong argues: "the Festival of Britain offered neither a mirror nor a window but rather an enchanted glass in which somehow the organizers, shorn of the magic of Empire, attempted to reconstitute a future based on a new secular mythology" (Banham & Hillier 1976: 8).

As the past was scoured for elements which could constitute a new de-imperialized history to drive Britain into the future, Shakespeare presented an unarguable figure of achievement, recognized nationally and internationally and, in the trope of the theatre, a true "living memory" in which the past could be translated into the currents of the future. In effect, the inscription recycled the ideologies of Festival Year as Shakespeare's festive memorial, making the South Bank a palimpsest, a physical and ideological location upon which the current institutions of British national culture today stand.

REFERENCES AND FURTHER READING

Banham, Mary & Hillier, Bevis (eds.) (1976). *A Tonic to the Nation: The Festival of Britain 1951*. London: Thames & Hudson.

Beauman, Sally (1982). *The Royal Shakespeare Company: A History of Ten Decades*. Oxford: Oxford University Press.

Elsom, John & Tomalin, Nicholas (1978). *The History of the National Theatre*. London: Jonathan Cape.

Greenblatt, Stephen et al. (eds.) (1977). *The Norton Shakespeare*. New York: W. W. Norton.

Jackson, Barry (1953). "On Producing *Henry VI*." *Shakespeare Survey* 6: 49–52.

Jackson, Barry, with Seale, Douglas (1951–3). Promptbooks for the *Henry VI* plays (archived by Birmingham City Library).

Martin, Randall (ed.) (2002). *King Henry VI, Part III*. Oxford: Oxford University Press.

Nietzsche, Friedrich (1997). "On the Uses and Abuses of History for Life." In *Untimely Meditations*, ed. Daniel Breazeale, trans. R. J. Hollingdale. Cambridge: Cambridge University Press, pp. 57–124.

Tillyard, E. M. W. (1944). *Shakespeare's History Plays*. London: Chatto and Windus.

16

Encoding/Decoding Shakespeare: *Richard III* at the 2002 Stratford Festival

Ric Knowles

The mid-season opening of *Richard III* at the Stratford Festival in 2002, in Ontario, Canada, was met with mixed reviews. In fact, reviewers often seemed to have seen different productions entirely. Kate Taylor, in *The Globe and Mail* (Canada's self-styled national newspaper), saw it as a failed *"comedy"* (emphasis added), "juxtaposing a clumsy, guffawing villain, more disruptive than seductive, with a Yorkish court of fancy dress and thinly disguised scheming," with court and villain sharing "an overblown style ... that can become so grotesque it obliterates the point." "What's missing throughout is the stark horror that would offset the comedy, underline its blackness," she argued (2002: R3). For Robert Reid, seasoned Stratford critic for the nearby Kitchener-Waterloo *Record*, on the other hand, the production was "a dark *tragedy*" (emphasis added), "perfect and brilliant," "riveting from beginning to end," as director Martha Henry "ma[d]e sure the tragedy maintain[ed] enough dramatic drive to make Richard's descent into existential hell inexorable and inevitable" (2002: B6). For Gary Smith, of *The Hamilton Spectator*, the production was an "imperfect end" to the cycle of Shakespeare's *history* plays, staged over three seasons at the festival (2002).

Similarly, reviewers found McCamus's performance to be everything from "mercurial" and "childlike in its selfishness" (Smith) through "richly comedic" (Reid) to "not especially charming" (Cushman 2002: D8), and his Richard everything from "entirely detached from history" to "malevolen[t] and menac[ing]," with veteran nationally-syndicated columnist Jamie Portman summing up an apparently quite different character as "the quintessential psychotic thug" (2002). Reviewers even seemed to see different set designs: what for one was "stultifying," "tritely metaphoric [and] mostly claustrophobic" (Smith), for another was "nothing less than brilliant," and "powerfully evocative" (Reid). What, apart from individual sensibilities and local journalistic contexts leads reviewers to such radically different readings of the same production viewed on the same night?

Theory

In developing a mode of performance analysis for contemporary theatre in English – what I call a "materialist semiotics" that attempts to answer this sort of question, takes into account the ways meanings are encoded and decoded in specific cultural and theatrical contexts, and takes into account the politics of location – I am attempting to bring some established theoretical approaches of the 1980s and 1990s productively to bear on one another. On the one hand, the reading practices loosely gathered together under the name "cultural materialism" (see Brannigan 1998, Ryan 1996, Wilson 1995) provide a model for locating cultural production within its historical, cultural, and material contexts, and for the politically engaged analysis of how meaning is produced within what Gramsci as early as 1917 called "the theatre industry" (1985: 56–8, 59–61, 63–5). Following cultural-materialist principles, I try to look at what performance studies scholars have called the performativity, and W. B. Worthen (2003) has recently called the *"force* of modern performance," including the ways in which versions of society, history, nationality, ethnicity, class, race, gender, sexuality, ability, or other social identities can be both instantiated and contested, to different degrees, through a given cultural production. In the larger project in which this chapter participates I look at the degrees to which the transgressive or transformative potential of a production functions on a continuum from radical intervention and social transformation to radical containment. Which end of this continuum each production tends towards depends, in part, on the material conditions, both theatrical and cultural, within and through which it is produced and received, conditions which function as its "political unconscious"(Jameson 1981) speaking *through* the performance text whatever its manifest intent or content. Cultural materialists, however, have only rarely focused on the specific practices and conditions of production in the contemporary theatre, and, as Keirnan Ryan points out, have rarely managed anywhere to model practices of "really close reading" of particular theatrical productions in particular places (Ryan 1996: viii).

Theatre semiotics (see Elam 1980, Pavis 1982, Carlson 1989, 1990, Aston & Savona 1991, de Marinis 1993, Ubersfeld 1999), on the other hand, has productively investigated the various intersecting (sign) systems of meaning production in the theatre, including, crucially, the reliance on convention in the culturally normative policing of the conventional relationships between signifiers and signifieds, signs and sign systems, in the communication of meaning. Semiotics has largely fallen into disfavor because of its increasingly taxonomic focus on the interaction of different signifying systems in the theatre: in its increasing concern with the systematic identification of intersecting signifying categories, it, too, failed to provide a practical model for the close reading of specific culturally located performances. But in its insistence on the arbitrary, culturally determined nature of meaning, production theatre semiotics usefully opened the way for the discursive (including ideological) analysis of the various meaning-producing technologies of theatrical production.

Theatre semiotics in the 1980s and 1990s was also criticized on the grounds that performance resists reduction to mere textuality. It was argued that the immanence of the theatrical event as event, as performance, or as phenomenon, and as received by audiences, exceeds the sum of its sign value as text. The title of my book, *Reading the Material Theatre* (2004a), in which "materialist semiotics" is expounded more thoroughly, establishes a tension between an insistence on the materiality (as opposed to textuality) of theatre, and the act of reading, which is usually understood to constitute what is read *as* text (and is often associated with the interpretation of published play scripts). It signals at once the non-textual, physical materiality, the ephemerality of the raw theatrical event, and the necessary instability of the relationships among each of the corners of the hermeneutic triangle with which I started my thinking:

Performance Text

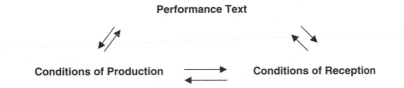

Conditions of Production   **Conditions of Reception**

Raw event – the performance – and the material conditions that produce it and shape its reception, can only endure and become available for analysis once they are together translated into the realm of discourse, where they come into being for critics and audiences alike as "theoretical objects" (de Marinis 1993: 48). Finally, theatre semiotics in its 1980s' and 1990s' manifestations came under criticism for its tendency to treat the theatrical event as contained within the discourses of the producers and the architectures of the stage, and for failing to consider three crucial factors: (1) the larger social and theatrical contexts within which performances occur; (2) the semiology of audience response; (3) and the iconic relationship between theatre and the life (or material world) it represents. These last three failures were addressed by Marvin Carlson in two books that, in attempting to shore up the field of theatre semiotics, moved it into productive relationship with other approaches, most notably phenomenology and cultural materialism (Carlson 1989, 1990). Carlson's work is particularly important to the development of a materialist semiotics insofar as he argued that such things as "[t]he physical appearance of the auditorium, the displays in the lobby, the information in the program, and countless other parts of the event as a whole are also part of its semiotic" (1990: viii) – that these things, as well as the events on stage, shape audience reception, which is by no means passive. Taken together, then, informed by work done in cultural studies on the reception of media and other productions (see Hall 1980, 1993; Morley 1980, 1992; Radway 1984, 1988; Ang 1985, 1991, 1996; Fiske 1993; Nightingale 1996; Bennett 1997; Tulloch 1999), and applied to specific shows thickly described, cultural materialism and semiology can usefully illuminate the cultural work those shows perform. Through a combination of theoretical rigor and located reading, these approaches can provide a model for performance analysis that takes into account the specifics and politics of location.

Precisely *how* audiences produce meaning in negotiation with the particular, local theatrical event, fully contextualized – what Carlson calls "Local Semiosis and Theatrical Interpretation," in a section of *Theatre Semiotics* called "Audience Impro-visation" (1990: 110) – has only rarely been analyzed or modeled in any detail. Considerable effort has been made in *literary* studies to theorize reader response, in work that has been analyzed, adapted, and applied to theatrical performance by Susan Bennett (1997). And models of the materialist analysis of audience "use" of popular cultural productions emerged from Cultural Studies, also in the 1980s and 1990s, in applied studies of audience response undertaken by David Morley, Janice Radway, Ien Ang, and others. The shared assumption underlying all of this work is that cultural productions neither *contain* meaning nor uni-dimensionally shape behavior and belief; rather, they *produce* meaning through the discursive work of an interpretative com-munity and through the lived, everyday relationships of people with texts and performances. Crucially for the purpose of forging an alliance between cultural materialism and semiology, these projects pursued the political objective of identify-ing ways in which, and degrees to which, popular audiences "answer back," activating meaning in their own interests rather than functioning simply as media dupes.

This cultural studies work on audience response was theorized by Stuart Hall in two influential articles first published in 1980, "Encoding/Decoding" and "Cultural Stud-ies: Two Paradigms." Hall's essays concerned themselves directly with the politics of the sign and the politics of reception, making connections and observing disjunctions between the ideologically coded material conditions for the production of signs and the similarly coded material conditions in and through which those signs are received. He outlined a model of production, circulation, use, and reproduction for the analysis of televisual significations in which power relations at the point of production loosely fit, but do not strictly reproduce, those at the point of "consumption," reproducing-with-a-difference societally dominant hierarchies (Hall 1993: 94).

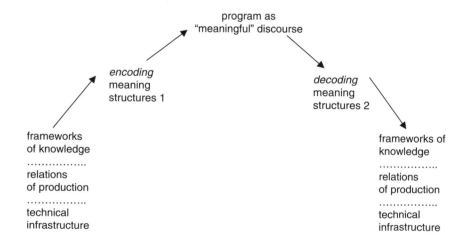

Crucially for Hall, that difference necessarily allows some space, however constrained, for reading against the grain. In "Encoding/decoding" he outlines three hypothetical decoding positions for televisual reception. The first is the *dominant-hegemonic position*, in which the viewer basically "gets the message," decoding it within the terms of reference in which it was encoded, *"operating inside the dominant code{s}"* (1993: 101), and in the process naturalizing those codes. The second is the *negotiated* position, which incorporates adaptive and oppositional elements, operates generally at a situational, situated, or localist level, and "makes its own groundrules" (1993: 102). This position resonates, for me, with Carlson's concept of audience improvisation and Michel de Certeau's account of user "tactics" (de Certeau 1984: 34–9). Finally, Hall cites a third, *oppositional* position, in which a viewer perfectly understands the literal and connotative inflection given by the dominant encoded discourse, but chooses to decode it in a globally contrary way (1993: 103).

Hall's work is useful as an analytical model for bringing together the cultural and theatrical relations of the production of signs with the technologies of reception that frame what Carlson calls "the entire theatre experience" (1990: 8). Indeed, it is possible to extrapolate from Hall's work, in conjunction with that of Carlson, a model of performance analysis that fleshes out the triangular one with which I began, and considers a formation in which conditions of production, the performance text "itself," and the conditions for its reception, operate (in distinction from Hall's model) as mutually constitutive poles:

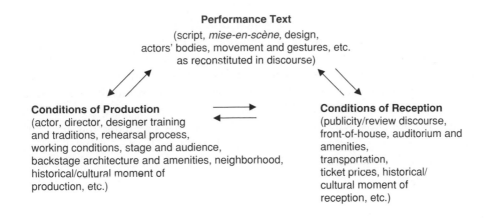

Performance Text
(script, *mise-en-scène*, design,
actors' bodies, movement and gestures, etc.
as reconstituted in discourse)

Conditions of Production
(actor, director, designer training
and traditions, rehearsal process,
working conditions, stage and audience,
backstage architecture and amenities, neighborhood,
historical/cultural moment of
production, etc.)

Conditions of Reception
(publicity/review discourse,
front-of-house, auditorium and
amenities,
transportation,
ticket prices, historical/
cultural moment of
reception, etc.)

As is clear from this expanded model, each pole of the triangle is constituted by multiple and multiply coded systems of production, communication, and reception, all working in concert or in tension both within their own "corner," and along the axes that hold the corners together and in tension with one another. "Meaning" in a given performance situation – the social and cultural work done by the performance, its performativity and its force – is the effect of all of these systems and each pole of the interpretive triangle working dynamically and relationally together. The degree to which reception is determined by culturally dominant contexts and mechanisms of production, and the degree to which resistant meanings are available, depend upon the amount of productive tension and slippage within and among the corners, as the discourses of design, acting, or directing, for example, rub up against those of marketing, mandate, location, or architecture.

Most performance analysis has concentrated its attention primarily on one corner of this triangle, the performance text, with a nod to a few conscious processes of production, mostly having to do with authorial or directorial intention. It has most often ignored both the taken-for-granted (and purportedly value-free) technologies of theatrical production – particularly training and tradition – and crucial local specificities of reception. But when the Stratford production of *Richard III* was "read" differently by different reviewers, fissures became apparent, and the divergences in meaning might most obviously be attributed to unacknowledged or unconscious differences in the technologies of production – among others, actor training and the public discourses of the Festival – and different conditions and cultures of reception. My project, then, is designed to undertake precise ideological analyses of the conditions, conscious and unconscious, of both production, within and through which performance texts come into being and make themselves available to be "read," and of reception, spatial and discursive, within and through which audiences perform those readings and negotiate what the works mean for them.

But the methodologies that might be expected to accompany such an approach are more problematic in practice than in principle, particularly when it comes to providing evidence of the ways in which productions have been read, and the specific ways in which the material conditions of production and reception have shaped those readings. My work concerns itself with these questions in four ways. First, I limit the range, not only of productions, but of actual located performances under discussion, almost exclusively to ones that I have seen myself, as a culturally positioned spectator, where possible, moving from site to site to see and analyze different performances both within their local contexts of production and within various contexts of reception. Second, I draw heavily on local reviews of the same productions, where possible in different places, contextualizing and locating the reviewers themselves within their cultural and journalistic settings, and considering them neither as consumer reporters nor aesthetic judges, but as providers of evidence of readings that were enabled by particular local stagings for specific audiences. Third, I try to cite my own, reviewers', and others' interpretations and responses, not as evidence of what audiences-in-general felt and understood – and therefore what the performance "really meant" – but as evidence of meanings and responses that specific performances in particular locations made available. And, finally, as an essential part of the overall project, I consider audiences themselves to be constructed and "performed," particularly in terms of class, race, gender, sexuality, ability, and other social positions, by the mutually constitutive technologies of production, performance, and reception that I am studying, rather than situating them, as most social science-based methodologies do, as independent agents operating somehow outside the loop.

My work, then, and the materialist semiotics it articulates and practices, employs a theoretical method of self-conscious and invested analysis, but it does not attempt to create a template that can be applied in any context; rather it articulates and demonstrates an open-ended practice in which theoretical approach, "object of study," and theatrical and cultural context are all both shifting and mutually constitutive. In *Reading the Material Theatre*, what follows the theoretical introduction – on which the "Theory" section of this article is directly based – isolates, articulates, and interrogates the most common practices and conditions that obtain in the English-language theatre and draws examples of the specific ways in which particular practices, traditions, and conditions have shaped meaning from a range of productions emerging from different national locations. The book then moves on to a series of case studies in order to deal in more thickly described detail with some of the ways in which these theatrical and cultural determinants have worked together (or against one another) in specific instances. I've focused there on productions and companies in which contextual circumstances are highlighted in localized readings either because of unique material conditions of production, such as repertory staging, or the opportunity for controlled comparative analysis of shifting conditions for reception provided by touring, festival performances, co-productions, remounts, or transfers – where the conditions for production remain essentially unchanged, but where the shows are read, received, and interpreted in and through different material, cultural and theatrical contexts. In this chapter I have chosen a case study involving the staging of a major Shakespeare play at a large repertory company invoking a range of competing material and discursive contexts of production and reception.

The Reception

When the opening lines of *Richard III* were spoken by Tom McCamus on July 13, 2002, curled, invisible at first, in the branches of an upstage tree at the Avon Theatre, he used a wireless microphone, and the lines echoed, disembodied, throughout the theatre. But the building was alive with echoes – different echoes for different audience members. For some in attendance, aided by various ceremonials, the lines were most clearly evocative of the opening of the same play, "50 years ago on the same date" as the inaugural production of the Stratford Festival (O'Connor 2002), when they were spoken by Alec Guinness under the direction of Tyrone Guthrie. For others, these opening lines directly echoed the same lines spoken down the street at the Tom Patterson theatre just weeks, days, or even hours earlier, by Haysam Kadri's Richard, as the interpolated ending of the two-part production of the *Henry VI* plays, to which *Richard III* served as sequel. For some, indeed, the lines most notably launched Richard as the final play in the complete cycle of Shakespeare's English History plays staged at the Festival over three seasons (and three theatres). For others, the lines evoked Tom McCamus's other "evil yet charming" role (*Beacon Herald*, 2002: 57) at Stratford in the 2002 season, MacHeath in Brecht's *Threepenny Opera*, or indeed any of the popular actor's previous roles. Others still may have recalled director Martha Henry's illustrious history as an actor and director, in particular her performance as Lady Anne in the star-studded *Richard III* staged by Robin Phillips to celebrate Stratford's twenty-fifth anniversary season, when she shared the stage with Brian Bedford, Maggie Smith, and Margaret Tyzak. Still others may have recalled the lines' delivery by McCamus's friend Stephen Ouimette when he performed the role in the festival's last production of the play in 1997. And the press and public responded to each of these echoes and many others.

The Company

The overriding context through which all productions at Stratford must be read is "the company." At Stratford, "the company" refers to two things: (1) the repertory acting company and the rest of the 3,511 employees – directors, designers, stage managers, craftspeople, technicians, administrators, marketing personnel and staff assembled in 2002 to mount a season of 20 productions, plus ancillary activities, running in repertory in four theatres; and (2) the company in its corporate sense, including donors, investors, members, a corporate board, and an incorporated "cultural industry" with a total budget in 2002 of $41,538,000 Canadian (Stratford Festival 2002b: 56).

Repertory staging and the Byzantine complexities of scheduling productions and rehearsals always condition what happens at Stratford, in positive and negative ways, in terms of everything from lighting to casting to the rhythms of rehearsal (see Knowles 2004b: 56–9). In 2002 they contributed, among other things, a frame that allowed Tom McCamus's Richard to be rehearsed and read against his MacHeath in *Threepenny Opera* in the same theatre in the same season, and the conjuncture no doubt contributed something to this Richard's charming swagger, as well as to the ways audiences read the performance. But the imperatives of repertory directly shaped, for example, one of the oddest moments of fissure in this *Richard*, which did not otherwise employ prominent doubling, in which we saw Scott Wentworth die horribly of an apparent stroke as Edward IV only moments after we had seen the same actor die horribly in a malmsey butt as Clarence: Stephen Ouimette, the actor intended for the role of Clarence by director Martha Henry, proved to be unavailable for rehearsals because he was busy directing *Threepenny Opera* across the hall. This circumstance was the occasion for an oddly alienating and destabilizing fissure in a production in which actor and character were otherwise to be read as merged.

But the overarching discursive context at Stratford, and one that shapes the meaning of all of its productions, is that of the corporate festival (see Knowles 2004b: 52–6). In this context Stratford audiences are constructed either as consumers or "patrons" (see Stratford Festival 2002a: 29–39, 2002b: 52–9). The shows themselves are similarly constructed as products for investment, purchase, or consumption, and the actors as "objects of the gaze" (Mulvey 1989). Ticket prices, audience amenities, and the advertising featured in Stratford programs all discursively align Stratford audiences with the "better sort" of people, capable (at least for the evening) of appreciating and paying for fine wine, fine crystal, fine dining, and the fine arts. Stratford programs are quite explicit in their construction of economic categories that closely mimic class stratification, at least at the upper end of the spectrum. While providing the requisite cast lists, they more than equally provide parallel but much more extensive and carefully ranked lists of the festival's financial supporters (flatteringly aligned with Shakespeare through the fundraising tag, "For All Time," echoing Ben Jonson's famous first Folio tribute to Shakespeare [Stratford 2002a: 29]). The listing of patrons is not unusual in a major Western theatre in the twenty-first century, but the extraordinary scale with which it is done at Stratford over no less than nine small-print program pages, and the care taken to precisely classifying, labeling, and publicizing no less than 17 different degrees of financial contribution, do seem excessive (Stratford 2002a: 29–39). Similarly, while programs provide portraits of the acting company, they more than equally provide portraits of the company's corporate sponsors, introduced by the Chair of the Festival's Board of Governors, and featuring statements about Stratford from each CEO – none of whom is a person of color, all of whom are middle-aged, and only one of whom, the last one pictured, is a woman (Stratford 2002a: 38–9). Not only, then, were audiences constructed (however these constructions were received) in terms of class, race, and economic position (at least for the evening or weekend) and thereby aligned with the interests of their medieval aristocratic equivalents in such moments as the "boardroom scene" in the Tower when the old boys met to plan the coronation (Figure 16.1), they were also constructed very much as middle-aged and male, well positioned to enjoy what in this production was Richard's very public and abusive "wooing" of Lady Anne – less seduction than bullying; well positioned to enjoy the caricatured sexuality of the interpolated appearance of Jane Shore in her nightgown as object of the gaze and of sexualized joking; and well positioned to dismiss as sentimental the potentially powerful chorus of more women than is usually seen on stage at Stratford. The tableau at the end of the first act featured eight women alone on stage gazing off towards the tower in a powerful but mute moment that didn't, however, compensate for the fact that the women's actual lines were among the most deeply cut in an otherwise lightly cut production (Figure 16.2).

The Anniversary

Most reviews of this *Richard* opened with a description of the ceremonies with which the 50th anniversary opening night performance was launched by Stratford's artistic director and executive director, flanking the founder of the festival, with Canada's Governor General in attendance. "The production ... proved special even before the curtain rose at the Avon Theatre," wrote Robert Reid:

FIGURE 16.1   The "tower" scene (3.4) of the 2002 Stratford Festival, Ontario's 50th anniversary production of *Richard III*, directed at the Avon Theatre by Martha Henry

Photograph courtesy the Stratford Festival Archives.

FIGURE 16.2   *Richard III* (2002) The play's women look toward the tower at the end of the production's first act

Photograph courtesy the Stratford Festival Archives.

A frail Tom Patterson – the son of Stratford whose dream of a Shakespearean theatre made glorious this very festival – was brought out on stage in a wheelchair. The applause was immediate, as people jumped to their feet and began shouting bravo.

The modest visionary raised a fragile hand, unsuccessfully beseeching people to sit down and cease fussing. Finally, people heeded the plea and Patterson bowed ever so slightly and whispered a simple thank you. (2002)

But these ceremonies were not alone in framing the event as a 50th birthday party, and audiences throughout the season were regularly reminded of the occasion. The Festival edition of the Stratford *Beacon Herald*, available throughout the city throughout the season, featured on its cover a collage that brought together a portrait of the young Tom Patterson with images juxtaposing the famous original tent and an exterior shot of the Festival Theatre as it exists today. Inside, the paper trumpeted "Festival pulls out all the stops for 50th season" (2002: 6) including no less than three glossy coffee table books to mark the occasion (the largest and glossiest of which was commissioned and paid for by the Festival). It featured articles on Patterson, "the festival's leading man" (*Beacon Herald*, 2002: 14–15); on the "supporting players" that brought the festival to life, with a photo featuring a dashing Alec Guinness in 1953 on the construction site for the Festival stage (2002: 3–4); on the supportive city that 50 years ago "issued a cheque to support [the] festival idea" (2002: 5); and on the late Irene Worth, Guinness's Lady Ann, to whom the 50th anniversary season was dedicated in every program throughout the season (2002: 62–3). The production of *Richard* was itself dedicated, through a prominent photograph and biography in the Avon Theatre lobby, to the memory of Timothy Findley, the Canadian novelist and playwright whose last play was produced at the Stratford Studio theatre in 2002, who died while the season was in rehearsal, and who had acted with Guinness in the fabled original tent in 1953. A display in the upstairs lobby included Guinness's acting script, sword and other paraphernalia from the first production. Within the show itself the musical motif played for Richard's coronation echoed Louis Applebaum's famous fanfare, played live at every Festival theatre performance to usher patrons to their seats, and the motif was reprised for the curtain call.

Clearly, part of what was encoded semiotically within and surrounding the 2002 *Richard III* was the Festival's own self-congratulatory discourse, aligning its present with its legendary past (a *Beacon Herald* article, for example, characterized Domini Blythe in the 2002 *All's Well* as "picking up the torch" from Irene Worth [2002: 25]), as well as with "new world" Shakespeare (Stratford 2002b: inside cover), capitalizing on the recent discovery in Canada of the so-called Sanders portrait of the playwright (without, of course, entirely losing sight of the more familiar image from the First Folio (Stratford 2002b: 1) (Figure 16.3). Indeed, the Droeshout portrait served as the basis for the souvenir program cover's self-portrait of the company *as* Shakespeare, characteristically appropriating his cultural authority) (Figure 16.4).

But fissures appeared in that discourse, partly because of competing imperatives at the encoding end. It may not have mattered much that this *Richard*, unlike its

FIGURE 16.3   The Stratford Festival's Artistic Director, Richard Monette, framed between two Shake-speares. This image appeared in all of the festival's programs in the 2002 season.

© Photograph by V. Tony Hauser, reproduced with permission.

predecessor, was not the season opener, the Stratford season having expanded expo-nentially since 1953. It may not have mattered that, in spite of the public discourse, the show didn't really open fifty years to the day after the original launching of the Festival, though it did have its first preview on the 50th anniversary, 49 years after the original opening night: for scheduling reasons, the press opening, including the celebratory appearance of Tom Patterson and the Governor General, occurred five days later. These slippages were perhaps inconsiderable, but it was hard to overlook

FIGURE 16.4 Many of the 2002 publicity materials, including the cover of the season program, used this composite portrait of the Festival company as Shakespeare (2002)

Reproduced by permission of the artist, Robert Silvers and photomosaic (www.photomosaic.com).

the fact that the production did not open on the famous Festival thrust stage that had hosted the Guthrie/Guinness premiere, and this was the result of conflicting impera-tives. Director Martha Henry had wanted to mount the show at the Festival stage (Henry 2002), but artistic director Richard Monette, anxious to involve the newly renovated Avon theatre complex in the 50th anniversary celebrations, determined that it would play the Avon, which instead of Tanya Moiseiwitch's famous stage featured a 6-meter-wide steel cartouche "inspired" by an earlier Moiseiwitch design (*Beacon Herald*, 2002: 12). It is not incidental, given these circumstances, that many were unhappy with Henry's old-fashioned proscenium stagecraft, static tableaux, and repetitive blocking patterns on a stage for which the director had not originally intended the production.

Perhaps a more serious question, at least as far as the encoding of Stratford's self-congratulatory discourse is concerned, is that of how celebratory any production of *Richard III* can actually be. *Richard* is, certainly, a play about success (for a time), but it is also a study of evil, a play about ruthless ambition, in which the pomp and ceremony associated with kings and Governors General (the crown's representative in Canada), not to mention CEOs, are at best suspect – the play has frequently been staged in this century as an unveiled allegorical critique of particular heads of state. And this fissure appeared graphically in the production. The second act opened with Richard's coronation, Shakespeare's Act 4 Scene 2. The new king stood crowned downstage centre when the lights came up after the interval (Figure 16.5). His back was to the audience masking his deformities, and his flowing robe echoed that of every previous Richard at the Festival. Louis Applebaum's heroic fanfare, used elsewhere to celebrate the Festival's achievements, played here to celebrate and accompany the demonized Richard's ascent to the throne. But as McCamus's Richard walked upstage between symmetrical columns of courtiers and aristocrats, he tripped and fell to the ground (Figure 16.6), scattering his orb and scepter about the stage, silencing the music, and brilliantly motivating his embarrassed line, "Stand all aside," to the horrified laughter of audiences onstage and off. Recovering his feet, his props and his dignity, he ascended the throne, turned to the audience, and grinned. The moment was, in the production's own terms, coherent and powerful, echoing earlier pratfalls, rhyming with a similar one in the play's opening speech, and underscoring the rebellion of Richard's body at the moment of his greatest success – a rebellion that ultimately led to his death when his Dr. Strangelove-like hand rebelled, refusing to stab Richmond when Richard otherwise had his enemy at his mercy. But within the larger discourses of the Festival, the moment threatened to undermine the celebratory message that the publicity department had worked so hard to encode.

And of course the very act of recalling a beloved moment lost in the overdetermined mists of time incurs significant risk: what contemporary production can compete with the soft focus of such nostalgia? That the Festival's risk in this case didn't entirely pay off is suggested by a number of reviews that set memories of Guinness's performance against that of his twenty-first-century successor, and others that went so far as to find the theatricality of even the frail Tom Patterson's pre-show appearance superior to that of the production that followed. Reviewer Donal O'Connor argued that:

> If the play commemorating the Festival's opening night 50 years ago on the same date did not provide the expected emotional charge, the surprise appearance on stage before the show of Tom Patterson, founder of the Stratford Festival, did. Welcomed by a sustained standing ovation and thanked by artistic director Richard Monette and executive director Antoni Cimolino, the ailing Mr. Patterson managed a "God bless you all" as he spoke with the help of his voice box amplifier. (2002)

"It was a theatrical moment to cherish," O'Connor remarks, in a review generally critical of the production itself.

FIGURES 16.5 and 16.6 *Richard III* (2002) The second act of the production opened in grand style with Richard's coronation, but before a line was spoken Richard stumbled and fell to the ground, scattering his orb and scepter about the stage

Photographs courtesy of the Stratford Festival archives.

The History Play

For Stratford patrons who didn't recognize or weren't interested in decoding intertexts with Stratford's illustrious history, other contexts were available through which to read the production, some of which seemed to be invoked with peculiar ambivalence within the discourses of the Festival. Chief among these was the obvious context of the larger arc of the plays of the first tetralogy – *Henry VI Parts 1–3* and *Richard III*, which have often been read or staged together (or together with the plays of the so-called second tetralogy, from *Richard II* to *Henry V*) as constituting a vast national epic comparable in scope and national significance to the *Oresteia* or *The Ring Cycle*. This *Richard* was staged in the same season as Leon Rubin's conflation of the *Henry VI* trilogy into two plays, entitled *Henry VI: Revenge in France* and *Henry VI: Revolt in England*; the three shows were scheduled in such a way that it was possible on occasion to see them in sequence in a single weekend, tickets for all three were offered at a 20 percent discount, and the opening of *Richard* represented the culmination of a three-season presentation of the full (originally) eight-play sweep of "Shakespeare's English Histories." This context was, moreover, consciously evoked, to some extent, in the framing and encoding of the *Richard*: the production was given the interpolated subtitle, *Reign of Terror* to parallel those of the adapted *Henries* that preceded it (*Revenge in France* and *Revolt in England*); the final image projected on the curtain at the show's end was the merging of white and red roses into one; and the show was identified as "The Wars of the Roses Part 3" in selected places in season publicity, including the informational "background book" to the season, on sale in the lobby (Stratford Festival 2002a).

But this identification was never prominent – the typesize used was consistently small – and the Festival's public discourse seemed almost apologetic about linking a main event in its anniversary celebrations with productions of non-canonical, "difficult" early plays mounted, not in the same theatre in order to provide continuity, but at its much smaller former "third stage" – now the Tom Patterson Theatre – employing a "B" company of mostly younger or less prominent actors. Within *Richard III* it is true that Michael Therrialt, the *Henries'* Henry VI, appeared on video to haunt McCamus's Richard on the eve of Bosworth (and to haunt the production itself as a ghost of the *Henries*), but the remainder of the casting was curiously disjunctive for those following the larger cycle. Unlike productions of the tetralogy at the Royal Shakespeare Company, the English Shakespeare Company, and elsewhere this sequence not only employed a different director/designer team for *Richard* than for the *Henries*, and not only eschewed the opportunity of continuous casting throughout the cycle to provide continuity and clarity for audiences – casting the same actors in each part of the tetralogy as Margaret, Clarence, Elizabeth, Edward, Richard, and so on – it positively confounded such continuity by casting many of the actors who were performing in the *Henries* in markedly different roles in *Richard*. Most prominently, the role of Margaret was split between the formidable

Diane D'Aquila in *Richard III* and the distinctive Seanna McKenna in *The Henries,* with McKenna cast, disconcertingly for many, as Elizabeth in *Richard*. Continuity was even neglected around such details as which hand the two actors playing Richard presented as deformed – left for one, right for the other. Finally, and perhaps most surprisingly, the cutting of the text of *Richard* seemed overwhelmingly to excise references to the action of the earlier plays in the tetralogy. Thus, in a relatively lightly cut production of one of Shakespeare's longest plays, a production that kept such moments as the rarely-staged citizen's scene (Act 2 Scene 3), Richard's references in Act 1 Scene 2 (lines 153–66 and 239–51) to the deaths of Rutland and York, and to his own killing of young Edward at Tewkesbury were cut, as were his references in Act 1 Scene 3 (lines 127–43) to the battle of St. Albans and to Clarence's shifting between the Yorkist and Lancastrian causes. Similarly the citizens' recollection of Henry VI's reign were excised from Act 2 Scene 3 (lines 12–26), Buckingham's recounting of Edward IV's broken marriage contract with Lady Bona was dropped from Act 3 Scene 7 (lines 178–90), and most of Margaret's litanies of past wrongs in Act 4 Scene 4 were left out. Indeed, even the structuring role of Margaret's curses and their fulfillment was played down, as most of the characters in this production failed to remember them when they met their demise. In many ways, then, the production replaced the play's history with that of the Festival itself, looking back less to the earlier plays in the cycle or to the historical events behind the action than to Stratford's own fabled history, which it routinely presents in its public discourse (including the season's "Background Book") as "The Stratford Story." But in fact, as is suggested by another small cut – the discussion between Buckingham and Prince Edward in Act 3 Scene 7 (lines 72–86) about the relationship between written history and cultural memory which has been the focus of Graham Holderness's suggestive analysis (2000: 97–100) – this production was not really interested in history, historiography, or historical difference.

The Tragedy

Tyrone Guthrie's selection of *Richard III* for the opening production of the Stratford Festival in 1953 had mainly to do with its qualities as a star vehicle and its long record of critical and popular success in the theatre. But it is a curious fact that neither the most celebrated productions of the play nor the most celebrated performances of its central character have been registered in productions of the whole tetralogy, or indeed when *Richard* has been treated as a history play. As notably successful as productions of the cycles have been – "canonical" productions such as the Barton–Hall, or Bogdanov–Pennington *Wars of the Roses*, or the Michael Boyd RSC production (2001) of the full tetralogy – rarely has *Richard* or its lead actor received the bulk of the good press in such shows, nor have these performances dominated stage histories of the play. What *have* dominated those histories have been one-off productions of the *tragedy* of *Richard III*, in which the roles of the women (the voices of history in the play) have been drastically reduced or entirely cut, and the dominance of the central character as individual tragic hero, isolated even from history, has been emphasized. This is also the type of production that has dominated at Stratford, where even the most popular of the history plays, though a necessary part of the mandate, have never fared very well, at least at the box office.

Nor was the creative team of *Richard III* in 2002 particularly disposed by training or taste to the staging of chronicle histories, invested as they were in the discourses of Method acting and psychological realism. The production was directed by Martha Henry, the first graduate of the National Theatre School of Canada, one of Canada's and Stratford's best and most celebrated naturalistic actors, who had made something of a specialty in the decade prior to the 2002 season of the great roles from the American naturalistic repertoire – including, in the 2001 season, Martha in Edward Albee's *Who's Afraid of Virginia Woolf*. Henry's Richard, Tom McCamus, is cut from the same mold; indeed, Henry and McCamus have worked together on a number of occasions as actors, often as mother and son, and most notably on the Festival's famous production of Eugene O'Neill's naturalist classic, *Long Day's Journey into Night*, which ran for two seasons at Stratford and was released as a feature film.

Both Henry and McCamus did their historical research for *Richard*, of course, but in both cases this was the character-based research of a Method-trained actor in search of psychological motivation. Henry admits when working as a director that she begins as an actor, and sees the play "through the eyes of the character" (*Beacon Herald*, 2002: 54). She talks about having done research into the treatment of deformed children in the Middle Ages, particularly the children of royalty (Henry). Some of the character work done by both Henry and McCamus had to do with finding Richard's body, and therefore revolved around the physical effects of cerebral palsy, from which they had decided he suffered. But much of this work was rooted in a reconstructed childhood for the character, in which he was understood to have been "kept" at the medieval court, treated like a kind of pet, similar to the way in which "fools" were produced and tolerated in the period (Henry 2002). This research informed much of the production's outrageous physical comedy, the character's lack of physical control converted into pratfalls and covered by a kind of grotesque laughter. It also motivated Richard's ambition, as a frustrated child who couldn't get his own way learned to envy his "two, big, handsome, sexy brothers," he learned to get what he wanted through deviousness, and "learned to lie" (Henry 2002). Finally, this reading led to the character's childishness: the drunken "rotten armour" scene was conceived as emerging from an adrenaline rush in the wake of Richard and Buckingham's first kill, the characters compared to "two kids who've stolen hubcaps" (Henry 2002); Richard crunched an apple while crossing items off the "to-do list" in his daytimer in Act 4 Scene 3 ("The son of Clarence have I pent up close [checks this item off], / His daughter meanly have I matched in marriage [checks this item off], The sons of Edward sleep in Abraham's bosom [checks], / And Ann my wife hath bid this world good night" [snaps the daytimer shut] [4.3:36–9]); and he exited Act 3 Scene 1, shortly after "chop off his head, man," trailing the hobby horse left behind by the young Duke of York. In the exchange with his mother in Act 4 Scene 4, in which she delivers her final curse to him and where in the script he drowns out the women with trumpet flourishes, he engaged in an outrageous slapstick routine with his henchmen, stopping, starting and bumping into one another, "showing off" as would a "cocky and headstrong" child (Henry 2002).

As Richard grew older, in this rehearsal-hall reconstructed childhood, he would, according to Henry's research, have been exercised as a warrior, and he was understood by the actor and director to have been more at home in the survival-of-the-fittest worlds of war and of nature than in the court – an interpretation that also fed Allan Wilbee's set design:

> The set design [said Wilbee] came from the question, "Where is Richard's comfort level?" Our answer was that Richard was a man who would rather sit in a tree than in a room at court. Richard is at home in nature, where the trees are gnarled, bent and grotesque but are still viewed as being majestic and beautiful in their own right; whereas in civilization, something that is disfigured or skewed is looked upon as being abnormal, something to be shunned. (Stratford 2002a: 9)

Thus, Richard was first seen perched in a gnarled upstage tree, and was finally returned to that tree at the end of the action, stripped and strung up by Richmond's soldiers where, according to Henry, McCamus discovered (sentimentally) that the weight of the body after death would finally let him straighten, and "he'd be like everyone else" (Henry 2002) (Figure 16.7). In terms of the background, training, and rehearsal process of the director and designer, then, this *Richard* participated less in the discourses of the corporate festival, the self-congratulatory discourses of its anniversary season, the discourses of chronicle history and the construction of English nationhood and subjectivity, or even the discourses of classical tragic inevitability in which Margaret's curses might have taken part; it participated in the psychologizing discourses of naturalistic tragedy.

The Tensions

But each of these discourses exerted its pull, and insofar as they worked together, they pulled the production away from any type of social or political analysis that might have made Stratford audiences sit differently or less comfortably in their seats. Taken together, their tendency was conservative and culturally reproductive, aligning as they did the corporate and consumerist with the self-satisfactorily celebratory, with the historical (both corporate and national) understood as pageantry, and with the psychological. But, of course, as I have suggested, the various encoded discourses that together framed the Festival's *Richard* in 2002 did not always work in consort with one another. In fact, their awkward intersection tended to denaturalize each of

FIGURE 16.7 *Richard III* (2002) The production's final image was of Richard, strung upside down in a tree by Richmond's soldiers, his body gradually straightening

Photograph courtesy the Stratford Festival Archives, with the permission of Tom McCamus and Canadian Actors' Equity.

the separate discourses or semioses, issued in a somewhat schizophrenic production, and opened various fissures for resistant readings. Perhaps the most interesting moment in the production for me, and one that resonated as the surfacing of tensions among the various encoded discourses that I have been analyzing, was the most clearly schizophrenic reading I have seen of Richard's speech on the morning of Bosworth, after he had been visited during the night by the ghosts of his victims. McCamus delivered his discordant lines in distinctly different voices, as if the character, the nation he represented, and the production itself were being pulled apart by the different discourses – psychological, historical, and corporate (the body of the king, country, and company) – that inhabited them. I quote them using different typefaces for the different vocal registers used by the actor:

> What do I fear? Myself?
> > **There's none else by.**
> Richard loves Richard: that is, I am I.
> Is there a murderer here?
> > **No.**
> > Yes, I am.

Then fly.
        What, from myself? Great reason why –
Lest I revenge.
        Myself upon myself?
Alack, I love myself.
        Wherefore? For any good
That I myself have done unto myself?
   . . .
Fool, of thyself speak well.
        Fool, do not flatter.
                      (5.3.183–9; 193)

He concludes:

My conscience hath a thousand several tongues,
And every tongue brings in a several tale ...
                  (5.3.194–5)

It was a remarkable embodiment of discursively fractured subjectivity, housed in a body, a nation, a Festival, a "company," and a production at odds with itself.

Acknowledgments

Research for this chapter was supported by a grant from the Social Sciences and Humanities Research Council of Canada, and was carried out in part through the assistance of the Stratford Festival archivist, Jane Edmonds and her staff. I am grateful to the students in my "Shakespeare in Performance" class in the summer of 2002, and to Christine Bold, Harry Lane, Paul Mulholland, and Skip Shand for their insights. The "Theory" section of this chapter is a light revision and extension of material that first appeared in my book *Reading the Material Theatre*. It appears with the permission of Cambridge University Press.

References and Further Reading

Ang, Ien (1985). *Watching Dallas: Soap Opera and the Melodramatic Imagination*. London: Methuen.

Ang, Ien (1991). *Desperately Seeking the Audience*. London: Routledge.

Ang, Ien (1996). *Livingroom Wars: Rethinking Media Audiences for a Postmodern World*. London: Routledge.

Aston, Elaine & Savona, George (1991). *Theatre as Sign-System: A Semiotics of Text and Performance*. London: Routledge.

Beacon Herald (2002). Stratford Festival edn.

Bennett, Susan (1997). *Theatre Audiences*, 2nd edn. London: Routledge.

Brannigan, John (1998). *New Historicism and Cultural Materialism*. New York: St Martin's Press.

Carlson, Marvin (1989). *Places of Performance: The Semiotics of Theatre Architecture*. Ithaca, NY: Cornell University Press.

Carlson, Marvin (1990). *Theatre Semiotics: Signs of Life*. Bloomington, IN: Indiana University Press.

Coulbourn, John (2002). "Richard's Return Triumphant." *London Free Press*, July 16: D8.

Cushman, Robert (2002). "All Dragon and No St. George." *National Post*, July 19: PM15.

de Certeau, Michel (1984). *The Practice of Everyday Life*, trans. Steven Randall. Berkeley, CA: University of California Press.

De Marinis, Marco (1993). *The Semiotics of Performance*, trans. Áine O'Healy. Bloomington, IN: Indiana University Press.

Elam, Keir (1980). *The Semiotics of Drama and Theatre*. London: Methuen.

Fiske, John (1993). *Power Plays, Power Works*. London: Verso.

Gramsci, Antonio (1985). *Antonio Gramsci: Selections from Cultural Writings*, ed. David Forgacs & Geoffrey Nowell-Smith, trans. William Boelhower. Cambridge, MA: Harvard University Press.

Hall, Stuart (1980). "Cultural Studies: Two Paradigms." *Media, Culture and Society* 2: 57–72.

Hall, Stuart (1993). "Encoding, Decoding." In Simon During (ed.) *The Cultural Studies Reader*. London: Routledge, pp. 90–103.

Henry, Martha (2002). Lecture to the "Academy at Stratford" class on "Shakespeare in Production," Stratford, August 12.

Holderness, Graham (2000). *Shakespeare: The Histories*. Houndsmills: Macmillan.

Jameson, Fredric (1981). *The Political Unconscious: Narrative as a Socially Symbolic Act*. Ithaca, NY: Cornell University Press.

Knowles, Ric (2004a). *Reading the Material Theatre*. Cambridge: Cambridge University Press.

Knowles, Ric (2004b). *Shakespeare and Canada: Essays on Production, Translation, and Adaptation*. Brussels: P.I.E. Peter Lang.

Morley, David (1980). *The "Nationwide" Audience: Structure and Decoding*. London: BFI.

Morley, David (1992). *Television, Audiences, and Cultural Studies*. London: Routledge.

Mulvey, Laura (1989). "Visual Pleasure and Narrative Cinema." In *Visual and Other Pleasures*. Bloomington, IN: Indiana University Press.

Nightingale, Virginia (1996). *Studying Audiences: The Shock of the Real*. London: Routledge.

O'Connor, Donal (2002). "Richard III Fascinating but Distant," clipping files, Stratford, ON: Stratford Festival archives.

Pavis, Patrice (1982). *Languages of the Stage: Essays in the Semiology of the Theatre*. New York: Performing Arts Journal.

Portman, Jamie (2002). "Stratford Festival Offers Compelling Portrait of Evil." *Ottawa Citizen*, July 18.

Radway, Janice (1984). *Reading the Romance: Women, Patriarchy and Popular Literature*. Chapel Hill, NC: University of North Carolina Press.

Radway, Janice (1988). "Reception Study: Ethnography and the Problems of Dispersed Audiences and Nomadic Subjects." *Cultural Studies* 2, 3: 358–76.

Reid, Robert (2002). "Stratford's Glorious Summer." *The Record* (Kitchener-Waterloo), July 16: B6.

Ryan, Kiernan (ed.) (1996). *New Historicism and Cultural Materialism: A Reader*. London: Arnold.

Shakespeare, William (1968). *Richard III*, ed. E. A. J. Honigman (new Penguin edn.). Harmondsworth: Penguin.

Smith, Gary (2002). "A Towering Performance in Richard III." *Hamilton Spectator*, July 16.

Stratford Festival (2002a). Program, *Richard III: Reign of Terror*, June 18–November 3.

Stratford Festival (2002b). *Visitors' Guide*.

Taylor, Kate (2002). "The King's His Own Jester," *Globe and Mail*, July 15: R3.

Tulloch, John (1999). *Performing Culture: Stories of Expertise and the Everyday*. London: Sage.

Ubersfeld, Ann (1999). *Reading Theatre*, ed. Paul Perron & Patrick Debbèche, trans. Frank Collins. Toronto: University of Toronto Press.

Wilson, Scott (1995). *Cultural Materialism: Theory and Practice*. Oxford: Blackwell.

Worthen, W. B. (2003). *Shakespeare and the Force of Modern Performance*. Cambridge: Cambridge University Press.

17

Performance as Deflection

Miriam Gilbert

Though directors and actors often insist that the performance of a play is just "telling the story," the history of performed Shakespeare suggests that performance can serve any number of purposes: social-political commentary, as in various productions of *Henry V* (most recently, Henry V in Nicholas Hytner's (2003) Royal National Theatre production besieged Harfleur with vicious threats until he noticed the "embedded" reporter, courtesy of the recently started war in Iraq, filming him); attempts to recreate the Elizabethan experience, particularly visible at London's Globe, with its emphasis on "authentic" costumes and on all-male casts; and, frequently, as Jonathan Miller points out in *Subsequent Performances*, "a desire to overthrow a tired interpretation" (Miller 1986: 109). This latter point is particularly relevant to productions by the Royal Shakespeare Company (RSC), where the same plays – which constitute the basic repertoire for the main house stage – turn up over and over again. Expanding on Miller's point, I want to consider performance not simply as a reaction against previous productions, although that too is a factor, but as deflection, a way to cope with plays that raise special problems as we view them in the late twentieth and early twenty-first centuries. I'm thinking particularly of plays with "hot-button issues," plays that are, by contemporary standards, politically incorrect and even, to some viewers, repulsive. After World War II, RSC stagings of *Merchant of Venice* have caused directors and actors so much discomfort that Clifford Williams, directing *Merchant* and *Jew of Malta* in 1965, felt compelled to write a program note expressing his dilemma: although he had agreed to direct the play, "in our racist-minded age, it would be better not to stage this play at all" (quoted in Gilbert 2002: 16). One could even argue that the increasingly harsh readings of the Venetian Christians, from Jonathan Miller's 1970 Old Vic staging, where Portia's jokes were clearly spoken with a sense of her cultural and ethnic superiority to her suitors, to Bill Alexander's 1987 RSC production, where both major and minor characters repeatedly spat on Shylock and even the hapless Tubal, to the 1930s setting for Trevor Nunn's 1999 Royal National Theatre production, in which Gobbo's monologue about leaving

Shylock became a cabaret turn for fascist viewers, represent a strategy of deflection. One must acknowledge, as Clifford Williams did, that Shylock is a "potential murderer" (Gilbert 2002: 16) as well as a Jew, but by making his opponents callous, insensitive, even nasty, production after production has raised the uncomfortable question of the justification for Shylock's murderous behavior.

A similarly difficult play these days is *The Taming of the Shrew* – like *Merchant*, a highly popular play and also one which raises problems for a contemporary audience. Even in 1978, the *Guardian*'s Michael Billington asked "whether there is any reason to revive a play that seems totally offensive to our age and society" – a view that echoes George Bernard Shaw's description in 1897 of the final scene as "altogether disgusting to modern sensibility". Indeed, the program for the RSC's 2003 *Shrew* featured two pages quoting these and similar remarks, arranged around a central panel with PROBLEM PLAY? stretched out across them. Looking back at 40-plus years of *Shrew* productions at the RSC, I see a series of performance strategies aimed at making the play not merely enjoyable but intellectually and emotionally satisfying. By looking at interpretative choices – elaborate program notes, the expansion and even the rewriting of the Induction, and striking interpretations by individual actors – we can map attempts to cope with the play's problems without sacrificing its obvious appeal.

While programs may seem merely a necessary source of information (actors', directors' and designers' names), they can also create expectation for the audience, even tell the audience what they should think. The RSC did not feature commentary in its programs before 1960, but even the cast list and the plot summary found in the 1939 Komisarjevsky production are notable for what they do include – and what they don't. The 1939 program lists characters in order of social rank, starting with the Induction's Lord, then Baptista, Vincentio and Lucentio; the three women appear last, and Katharina is identified – or, more accurately, labeled – as "Katharina, the Shrew." The brief plot summary focuses primarily on the intrigues connected with Bianca's wooing, while the last sentence reads simply: "Meanwhile Petruchio, greatly daring, has wooed and won – and tamed – Katharina." Though an audience may well need more help in straightening out the disguises and subterfuges associated with the wooing of Bianca than in following Petruchio's wooing of Katharina, the bland statement quoted above seems to gloss over any possible unpleasantness associated with the taming. Other programs in the 1940s and 1950s are similarly silent.

Not until 1960, when John Barton's production was accompanied by a general commentary from Ivor Brown about "the range, development and paradox of Shakespearean comedy," does a program note touch briefly on the subject of the taming. Brown describes the play as "farcical rather than comical" but mentions "a brusquely vigorous courtship and a honeymoon more harsh than honeyed." He immediately contextualizes that remark by pointing out that "the taming of shrews, whether by ducking, bridling, or other violence, has been widely common in folk-lore and folk-practice." In other words, things could have been much worse. He admits that "tastes and opinions about domestic discipline and the status of wives have radically altered" but then again uses the term "farce" ("a boisterous farce of its period") to explain the play's popularity.

Brown's strategy of dealing with the difficult question of Petruchio's treatment of Kate by simultaneously dismissing the play as "farce" while arguing that the violence is both "widely common" and "of its period" echoes in later program notes. The 1973 production, directed by Clifford Williams, featured a poster with a Renaissance woodcut of a woman on a ducking-stool about to be dropped in a river, while little ducks swim placidly by. The program opens with a letter commenting on the prohibition against professional acting in London during the plague, thus introducing the notion that the anonymous *Taming of a Shrew* was "a rough version of [Shakespeare's play] vamped-up from memory by actors and dramatists on tour in the provinces while plague closed London theatres." Such material implicitly categorizes the play as a document from the past, something "archaic." So too do the quotations referring to "the official, Church-approved doctrine ... that the wife should be obedient in all things to the husband, according to the teaching of Saint Paul." The program compiler's choice to foreground the Elizabethan context of the play, while admirable and informative, also tends to make the play seem "other" and "foreign." Indeed, Jonathan Miller's 1987 production quoted L. P. Hartley's opening line from *The Go-Between*: "The past is a foreign country; they do things differently there." The more a program quotes Elizabethan sources – on taming falcons, on Puritan marriage, on the power of the father, on acting conditions of the period – the more it implies that *Shrew* is a play from an earlier, less sophisticated period, and thus must be understood, and excused.

Another major strategy for dealing with the play's offensiveness is not to contextualize it but to skim past it, as the Komisarjevsky plot summary did. Clearly the program compiler/editor doesn't wish to reveal everything that happens, but it's startling to see the persistence of paragraphs such as the one used for Trevor Nunn's 1967 production and repeated almost without change up until 1995:

> Baptista, a gentleman of Padua, has two daughters. The younger one, Bianca, is much sought after; the other, Katharina, has no suitors. Baptista insists that Bianca may not marry before Kate does. Petruchio, an adventurer, undertakes to woo Kate; it will help his friend, Hortensio, one of Bianca's suitors, and besides, there is the dowry. Petruchio marries Kate and takes her to his country house. Meanwhile, Lucentio, in disguise like most of Bianca's suitors, outwits his rivals in Padua by posing as a schoolmaster. Hortensio consoles himself with a rich widow. In a wager on whose wife is most submissive, the winner is Petruchio.

Not until 1995, when Gale Edwards directed the play (thus becoming the first woman to direct a main-stage RSC production of *Shrew*), did the program note change substantially, as Edwards rewrote the description of Kate to explain her shrewishness: "The elder, Katherina, is considered shrewish and therefore undesirable because of her forthright and fiery nature, her scolding tongue and her intolerance of fools." More crucially, she used the program note to set out her interpretation of the play, describing it as Sly's dream: "As part of his dream, Sly will play the hero of his own fantasy, a cavalier fortune hunter called Petruchio." And, at the end of the plot summary, she added a major re-interpretation of Petruchio: "Petruchio slowly realizes what he has been attempting to do to Katherina in the name of love. By the end of the speech his dream has become a nightmare, and he is back asleep where he began. Christopher Sly awakes." While Gale Edwards can direct the play to present her interpretation of Petruchio/Sly's appalled moral awakening, her choice to put that reading into the part of the program called "plot summary" – a presumably neutral account of the play's events – was, for some critics, "demonstrably wrong-headed" (Benedict Nightingale, *The Times*, April 24, 1995) or made "at the expense of internal logic" (Michael Billington, *Guardian*, April 24, 1995). Though a number of critics used Edwards's summary to explain the production, it's difficult to escape the logic of John Peter's question: "What is the difference between interpreting a play and making it say what *you* want it to say?" (*The Sunday Times*, April 30, 1995).

Edwards's use of the Induction to frame a reading of the play is also part of a familiar RSC tradition. By combining Sly and Petruchio (as Michael Bogdanov did in 1978 or as Lindsay Posner did in the 1999–2000 touring production), Edwards connected the male–female confrontation of the Induction's opening lines, when Sly is thrown out of the tavern by the Hostess, explicitly to the Petruchio/Kate conflict. Both Edwards and Posner used, as Bogdanov did not, the ending of *A Shrew* to round off the story; in 1995, Michael Siberry's Petruchio turned back into Sly and begged forgiveness of his wife with whom he had been quarreling; in 2000, Stuart MacQuarrie's Sly, who had accessed *The Taming of the Shrew* on a computer, was once again thrown out on the street, and complained to two women (one of them played by Monica Dolan who had been Kate in his "fantasy") that he had just had the "best dream" of his life. Whether he learned anything, as did Siberry's Petruchio, was open to question.

The idea of the Induction as instruction, not for Sly, but for the Lord who so cavalierly decides to play a practical joke on Sly, seems to have been Bill Alexander's invention, first when he directed the 1990 RSC touring production and then in his 1992 mainstage production. Rewriting the Induction to set it in contemporary England, Alexander created not an anonymous lord and his servants, but Lord Simon and his upper-class friends who find the drunken Sly and think it would be fun to "mess with his mind" (promptbook, 1992). Sitting on overstuffed furniture in a gorgeously wood-paneled country house, the "hearties and Sloanes" (to borrow Benedict Nightingale's phrase, *The Times*, April 3, 1992) watched actors in Elizabethan costume performing *The Taming of the Shrew*. Gradually the watchers became drawn into the performance; scripts were thrust into their hands so that they could act as Petruchio's servants, and Ruth, one of the onstage watchers, eventually played the Widow who marries Hortensio (see Rutter, 1997, for a fine analysis of the revised Induction). Even though some reviewers criticized or argued with this rewriting, many seeming to miss the point, it was clear to Irving Wardle that Alexander's intent was "to pin the guilt [for the play's 'crude message of sexual dominance'] on the actors' ruling-class patrons whose crass behaviour they are merely reflecting" (*Independent on Sunday*, April 5, 1992).

Yet Alexander's 1992 production did more than merely rewrite the Induction; it suggested that assumptions of class privilege are central not only to the Induction but to the play itself. By offering a new view of Tranio, and especially of the Tranio/Bianca relationship, the production directly asked us to consider the change in power brought about by even a temporary change of clothes. In part, such a re-interpretation worked because of the actor playing Tranio, Richard McCabe. McCabe's first work at Stratford in 1987 was a memorable and frightening Chiron in *Titus Andronicus*; picking up the struggling Lavinia to carry her offstage, he thrust his hand up between her legs; re-entering after the rape, he crawled in on his elbows and knees, mocking Lavinia's painful movement; taunting his victim, he turned her over on her back and squatted over her as if to begin the rape all over again, but instead spat on her. He was also, more importantly for his reading of Tranio, Puck in the 1989 *A Midsummer Night's Dream*, given to repeating/echoing lines of Oberon's, handing over the magic flower by dropping it out of his mouth, muddy roots and all, and nonchalantly signing his name in the autograph book that the First Fairy proffered to him.

By 1992, McCabe had played not only Chiron and Puck, but also Wagner in *Dr. Faustus* and Truewit in *Epicoene*; moreover, on tour with Compass Theatre Company, he had played Mozart in a production of *Amadeus*, another role full of subversive moments. Bill Alexander lured him back to Stratford and the RSC with the leading role in a new play about Marlowe, Peter Whelan's *The School of Night*, but insisted that McCabe also had to play Tranio. McCabe's first view of Tranio was uncompromisingly negative: "I never liked the play or the character" (in conversation). But given that he had to play Tranio before he got to Marlowe (and, in between, Autolycus), he asked himself what he might make of the fact that Tranio is the second longest role in the play. He began thinking that it would be interesting if Tranio was not just playing a game, but playing for keeps. As McCabe saw it, Tranio and Lucentio had the same education; what else is the implication of Tranio's knowledge of Latin ("*Redime te captum quam queas minimo*," 1.1.153) and Vincentio's later comment, "I have brought him up ever since he was three years old" (5.1.63–4)? Tranio is clever enough to suggest the problem of Lucentio's planned disguise and the solution in a single speech, so why *shouldn't* he woo for himself? The possibility that marrying Bianca might work is, ironically, suggested by Lucentio himself. When Tranio declares that he will find a man to impersonate Vincentio to "make assurance here in Padua / Of greater sums than I have promised" (3.2.124–5), Lucentio thinks of a somewhat different strategy:

> 'Twere good methinks to steal our marriage,
> Which once performed, let all the world say no,
> I'll keep mine own despite of all the world.
>
> (3.2.130–2)

FIGURE 17.1   An already trouserless Tranio (Richard McCabe) pulls off Lucentio's (John McAndrew) boots in 1.1. of Bill Alexander's 1992 production of *The Taming of the Shrew* at the Royal Shakespeare Theatre

Photograph reprinted by permission of J. H. Bunting.

In this production, Tranio's face subtly reflected what he had heard: once married, Bianca would be his. And, on one level, Bianca, or at any rate, the actress playing Bianca, Rebecca Saire, already was, since she and McCabe had been in an offstage relationship for several years.

Tranio's possibilities for subversion became evident quite gradually. At first, the relationship between Lucentio and Tranio seemed the familiar one of the good-looking but somewhat vacant Lucentio advised by the street-smart and slightly cynical Tranio. Lucentio pretended to get an idea about how to woo Bianca, "I have it, Tranio" (1.1.180) but then asked "Tell me thine first" (1.1.182) in a tone implying that he didn't really have a good notion at all. The decision to change clothes almost stopped the show, as Tranio tried to put on Lucentio's trousers and encountered such difficulty that he had to lie down and wriggle his way into them, finally giving up on hooking the top button, and pulling out his shirt to cover the unbuttoned trousers (Figure 17.1). While I can't prove that this bit of business (stemming logically from the question which tends to pass through my mind whenever I see this scene, namely, do you have to cast people who wear the same size clothes as Lucentio and Tranio?) is McCabe's invention, it is exactly the kind of thing he would do. Or, as a friend reported who saw the production later in the fall, at a school matinee, it's also the kind of thing he might decide not to do. Evidently feeling that the laugh from a school audience might be too much, he took off his jacket, and when Lucentio offered the trousers, he just looked at him in surprise, shook his head, and made Lucentio put his own trousers back on!

But by the end of Act 2 Scene 1, the scene in which Tranio (as Lucentio) and Gremio bid for Bianca, Tranio was clearly more than just a comic servant. In an extra-textual choice, Bianca came onstage and sat down-center while the two men spoke of their wealth. Bianca's presence changed the dynamics of the scene, since Gremio's lavish offers were made directly to her, and she smiled as Gremio emphasized the luxury of "Costly apparel, tents, and canopies, / Fine linen, Turkey cushions bossed with pearl, / Valance of Venice gold in needlework" (2.1.341–3). But the looks of flirting approval that Bianca gave Gremio were nothing to the looks she bestowed on Tranio, resplendent in blue velvet, heavily trimmed with gold and pearls.

And certainly no one in the audience could miss the significance of the kiss Tranio and Bianca exchanged at the end of Act 3 Scene 2. After Grumio had carried off Kate while Petruchio was flourishing his sword in an excess of movement that would have delighted Errol Flynn, Baptista turned to Bianca and Tranio: "Lucentio, you shall supply the bridegroom's place, / And let Bianca take her sister's room" (3.2.238–9). Tranio's question to Bianca, "Shall sweet Bianca practise how to bride it?" (3.2.240) was followed by a very long and intimate kiss, one that implied that a good deal of offstage kissing had preceded the onstage one.

By suggesting that Tranio hoped to win Bianca for himself, McCabe's Tranio then turned what is usually a comic scene of pretence into something much darker. At the beginning of 4.2., Tranio asks Hortensio (still disguised as the music teacher), "Is't possible, friend Licio, that Mistress Bianca / Doth fancy any other but Lucentio? / I tell you, sir, she bears me fair in hand" (4.2.1–3), a question that has, in other productions, been part of Tranio's attempt to disillusion the disguised Hortensio and so get him out of Lucentio's way. But McCabe's Tranio, while seeming to play with Hortensio, was clearly bothered. His outburst, "O despiteful love, unconstant womankind" (4.2.14) was *actually* harsh, not merely pretence, as he watched Bianca kissing Lucentio. Similarly, his comment, "Fie on her! See how beastly she doth court him" (4.2.34) came with real feeling. Once Hortensio had left, Tranio expressed his bitterness toward what he regarded as Bianca's betrayal with an ironic tone on "Mistress Bianca, bless you with such grace / As 'longeth to a lover's blessed case!" (4.2.44–5) – the irony justified perhaps not only by his anger, but by the somewhat exaggerated language. The line, "Nay, I have ta'en you napping, gentle love," was accompanied by a rude gesture, as he grabbed at her crotch – and her surprise was really alarm, "Tranio, you jest – but have you both forsworn me?" (4.3.46–7, 48). And when Biondello interrupted with news that a "marcantant or a pedant" was just about to appear, we could see Tranio's mind ticking over with a new approach: "I'll make him glad to seem Vincentio, / And give assurance to Baptista Minola / As if he were the right Vincentio" (4.2.68–70). For what Tranio had planned, the real Lucentio might create problems, so his next line, "Take in your love, and then let me alone" (4.2.71), became necessary rather than just a way to move people offstage; indeed, "let me alone" was even a harsh rejoinder to Bianca's gesture implying that she would like to somehow explain things to him.

The more Tranio talked with the Pedant, the more clearly we could see his purpose: "My father is here looked for every day / To pass assurance of a dower in marriage / 'Twixt me and one Baptista's daughter here" (4.2.116–18). But the marriage, we realized, would be between Tranio and Bianca, rather than between Lucentio and Bianca. And in this production, that marriage might actually have taken place, were it not for Biondello. After Tranio introduces the false Vincentio to Baptista, he asks Cambio to bring Bianca to their lodging. Baptista repeats the order, ending with the phrase "how she's like to be Lucentio's wife" (4.4.66) and Biondello's reply, "I pray the gods she may, with all my heart" (4.4.67), may seem slightly overwrought if the scene is merely comic deception. But in this production, Biondello was clearly struggling with a huge problem; he had figured out what Tranio was doing and was torn between loyalty to a fellow servant and loyalty to his master Lucentio. Thus, his lines in Act 4 Scene 4 where he seems to be telling an exceptionally dense Lucentio to go off and marry Bianca grew out of his attempt to warn Lucentio without betraying Tranio's motives. The line, "Baptista is safe, talking with the deceiving father of a deceitful son" (4.4.80–1) was his first clue, meant to alert Lucentio to Tranio's deception. Lucentio's exasperated "And what of all this?" elicited Biondello's response, "I cannot tell" (4.4.88), which accurately described his dilemma of wanting to tell and yet not wanting to. His line "bid Bianca farewell forever and a day" (4.4.93) was not metaphorical but a warning, and the cryptic comment, "I knew a wench married in an afternoon as she went to the garden for parsley to stuff a rabbit" (4.4.95–6), seemed to imply that Tranio might steal the marriage. While it was never clear in the production that Lucentio picked up on the warning against Tranio, he did get the sense that if he wanted to marry Bianca, he had better hurry. Thus, at the beginning of 5.1, he rushed Bianca offstage while Biondello counselled "Softly and swiftly, sir" (5.1.1). What's noticeable about this reading is that none of the lines were changed, although, as McCabe admitted in conversation, the Biondello/Lucentio scene was the hardest one to fit into this interpretation.

Tranio's realization that he has lost the game gave added impetus to his attempts in 5.1 to swagger out his role before the real Vincentio. And the unmasking of the deception led to a reflective moment for Bianca who, until this point in the play, had seemed very much the winner in any game that was being played; she knew when to burst into tears to attract Baptista's attention, when to flash a smile, how to pretend that she was interested in Gremio, how to manipulate both Lucentio and Hortensio when they were disguised as tutors. But when Lucentio explained to the "right Vincentio" what had happened, Bianca stood center stage, fingering her new wedding ring. Lucentio's attempt to exonerate Tranio, "What Tranio did, myself enforced him to" (5.1.103) was painful for Bianca, her face silently asking "was Tranio just pretending to love me?" Her stricken look, alluded to, perhaps, in Lucentio's "Look not pale, Bianca" (5.1.112) showed us that Bianca had, on some level, fallen for Tranio, and that she was already regretting her marriage to Lucentio.

Thus, in the play's final scene, the Bianca/Tranio relationship continued to attract our attention. Bianca's sharp-tongued retort to Petruchio, and indeed to all the men who might try a "bitter jest or two," ties in with the play's repeated hunting metaphors: "Am I your bird? I mean to shift my bush / And then; pursue me as you draw your bow, / You are welcome all" (5.2.46–8). Petruchio admits that he has lost his prey, "She hath prevented me" and then says "Here, Signior Tranio, / This bird you aimed at, though you hit her not; / Therefore a health to all that shot and missed" (5.2.49–51). When I first saw the production and began to pick up on the hints of the Tranio/Bianca relationship, I thought that perhaps Petruchio had rewritten the line so that it would emphasize what McCabe was doing, but the line is in the text, making much more sense with a Tranio who was actually after Bianca. Tranio answers a bit sullenly, "O sir, Lucentio slipped me, like his greyhound, / Which runs himself and catches for his master" (5.2.52–3), acknowledging, at least in this production, that he has accepted his subsidiary role as servant. When Tranio follows up by implying that Petruchio has not been very successful either, "'Tis well, sir that you hunted for yourself; / 'Tis thought your deer holds you at a bay" (5.2.55–6), he got a little smile from Lucentio, "I thank thee for that gird, good Tranio" (5.2.58), and, to McCabe, the line implied the possibility of a reconciliation between the master and the servant.

I didn't see any such reconciliation, and the final moments of the "inside" play were bleak indeed if we consider Lucentio's future life. Kate shepherded the Widow and Bianca into the acting area, but Bianca refused to join the circle seated on the floor around the tablecloth, drinks and fruit. Instead, she planted herself on the sofa upstage, the sofa formerly occupied by the aristocratic watchers, but now Tranio's upstage perch. Looking longingly at Tranio, she stealthily sidled closer to him. After Kate's long speech, Bianca tried to take Tranio's hand, but he moved away and crossed his leg so that he faced away from her. As I read the moment, Tranio's body language was saying "You had your chance and you decided to marry Lucentio, so leave me alone." It could also be, as McCabe suggested, that his look of disapproval and his movement away from her meant "Don't be so insensitive as to make a play for me in front of your husband." However one read what was going on, it was clear that Bianca was still trying to get Tranio's attention, and thus wasn't focusing at all on Lucentio. The point was emphasized by Lucentio's position, alone, down left by the proscenium arch, about as far away as possible from Bianca and Tranio, visually together on the sofa up right. And in the play's last minutes, when Sly, stripped of his brocaded dressing gown, awoke on a bare stage to see the actors, now all in their modern clothes looking at him, the audience could see that the actors playing Tranio and Bianca were together.

On one level, this reading of Tranio merely supports what critics and audiences have noticed for years, namely that Bianca rather than Kate may be "the veriest shrew of all" (5.2.64) and that Lucentio's marriage, brought about through disguise and deception, leads not to Baptista's deception, but to Lucentio's. One could also argue that the challenge to the social status quo that the Sly scenes imply, namely that a drunken tinker might somehow become a lord, if only temporarily, finds an encouraging echo in Tranio's attempt to move beyond the social rank determined by his birth (his father was just a "sail-maker in Bergamo" [5.1.60]). The notion that Tranio represents or presents a challenge from one social class to another is not, of course, completely new. Other actors playing Tranio have brought the question of social class to the play, usually through a regional accent. Indeed, in 1928, when H. K. Ayliff directed a modern-dress version of *Shrew* at the Birmingham Repertory Company, Ralph Richardson played Tranio with a Cockney accent, anticipating more recent performances that have tried to remind the audience of Tranio's lower social status. One remembers the late Ian Charleson's strong (and native) Scots accent when he played Tranio for Michael Bogdanov in 1978, an accent which disappeared when he disguised himself as Lucentio but which would slip out from time to time. Or there was the Cockney accent of Nick Dunning's Tranio (RSC tour, 1985, directed by Di Trevis), which turned into an accent so refined when he disguised himself that one felt he was trying to speak a foreign language. All of these Tranios seem to have used the social class and the regional accent primarily for comic effect.

But McCabe's achievement, within the framework of the production, was to ask us to take the subplot not just as comedy or even as metatheatre, but as a serious challenge to the world of the play. Graham Holderness, writing about major twentieth-century performances of *Shrew* in *Shakespeare in Performance: The Taming of the Shrew*, emphasizes the usefulness of the subplot as "a thematic strategy which operates both at the narrative level of romance and comic courtship disguises, and at the psychological level of complicating an audience's perspective on Bianca" (Holderness 1989: 18). But not even Holderness suggests that we take Tranio seriously, as a character who might actually have his own story rather than merely serving as a cog in Lucentio's story or Bianca's story or even Sly's story. Richard McCabe's Tranio did have his own history, erected on the foundation of the text itself, inspired in part by Bill Alexander's choice to make the upper-class audience within the Induction a group of callous snobs who needed to learn a lesson. That reading, and, I suspect, Alexander's experience of directing *Volpone* in 1983, provided the environment in which McCabe's Tranio would flourish, Mosca-like.

Yet a further strategy for deflection through performance lies with the interpretation of the two main characters, Kate and Petruchio. Re-interpreting Kate as something other than "the shrew" is a familiar option. Jonathan Miller's 1987 production featured Fiona Shaw "gouging initials into the walls and hacking off handfuls of hair," a woman who is, in Shaw's words, "a misfit" and in Miller's mind, "a disturbed child" who needed therapy (Rutter 1988: 7, 6). The 2003 production at the Royal Shakespeare Theatre, directed by Gregory Doran, seemed to offer a similar reading, although Kate in this production clearly was a shrew, if by that we mean someone given to banging doors, throwing books, and generally expressing her bad temper (which might also have been her unhappiness). Her messy hair and drab blue dress gave her the look of a maid, while Bianca was elegant in a beige-gold dress, her long black hair carefully arranged. Baptista's favoritism for Bianca was clear, even to the extent of shutting the door in Kate's face as he exited with Bianca.

What's less usual than a rereading of Kate is the idea that Petruchio might, like Kate, also be "damaged goods," hurt in some way, insecure, and the real insight of Doran's production was to offer this possibility as well. Jasper Britton's Petruchio staggered onstage wearing a long red coat, clearly drunk, knocking at the wrong door as he called for Hortensio, stumbling over the Italian phrases, and occasionally taking a nip from his pocket flask. He also wore a black scarf around his arm, and his references to his father's death got special emphasis. In conversation, Britton pointed out that Petruchio mentions this event three times in this first scene (1.2.51, 1.2.98, 1.2.185). So his Petruchio not only wore the black scarf of mourning, but pointed to it ostentatiously. When he met Baptista, he again focused our attention on his father's death – "You knew my father well, and in him me" (2.1.112) – with another flourish of his armband. And although this Petruchio talked grandly of money, his attempt to find his purse ("Crowns in my purse I have," 1.2.54) was unsuccessful and his wide-eyed stare and silence when Baptista mentioned "twenty thousand crowns" (2.1.118) strongly implied that he didn't have a lot of money, and was now, for the first time in his life, having to find the means to live.

A later scene, in Petruchio's house, underlined the importance of Petruchio's father. As the servants arranged the table and strewed rushes on the floor, they also stood to ceremonious attention and then crossed themselves as a black-draped portrait of Petruchio's father was raised in the air. At the end of the scene, after Katharina had been pushed upstairs to the bedroom, Petruchio came downstairs, picked up the glass of wine that the servants had poured for him, lowered the portrait so that it rested by the stove, and brought a chair over so that he could "talk" to his father. "Thus have I politicly begun *my* reign" (4.1.159) he confided to the portrait, as if seeking reassurance, and the first reference to the falcon seemed to be the tactic he had learned from his father, namely keeping the falcon hungry; the portrait, not coincidentally, showed a man holding a falcon on his wrist. But then Petruchio seemed to get a slightly different idea as he talked – "Another way I have to man my haggard" (4.1.164) – and that approach made him feel increasingly confident. As he ended the soliloquy, without pausing after "'Tis charity to show" (4.1.182) – a pause that has sometimes seemed a challenge to the audience – he held the wine glass in his hand. But then he put it down in front of the portrait and padded up the stairs, without taking a drink at all. The taming of Katharina would, it seemed, also mean the reformation of Petruchio, and indeed at his next appearance, he had made an effort to slick down his unruly mop of curls and even to shave his stubble.

Not only did this Petruchio expose his own insecurities while also covering them up with clearly improbable bluster, but those same insecurities accompanied his wooing of Kate. Though he struck a "tough-guy" pose as he bragged, "I'll attend her here – / And woo her with some spirit when she comes!" (2.1.164–5), he didn't hold it for long, but shrank back into his normal posture. He brandished his whip for "and woo her with some spirit," then dropped it. He took off his jacket, as if getting ready for work, but looked nervous. Thinking of the strategy of complimenting her with the phrase, "as clear / As morning roses newly washed with dew" (2.1. 168–9), he smiled, pleased with himself, yet the smile became a nervous one when his mind shifted to a new possibility, "Say she be mute" (2.1.170), followed by another bad moment, the realization that she might "deny to wed" (2.1.175). This playing of the soliloquy made Petruchio likeable for the audience; the playing of the first encounter with Kate – or Kath-e-rine, as Alexandra Gilbreath insisted immediately – became an exercise in making himself likeable for Kate.

There seemed to be nothing Britton's Petruchio wouldn't try. He joked with her – hey, "dainties are all Kates" (2.1.185), isn't that a real knee-slapper? He didn't just invite Kate to "sit on" him but lay down on the floor. Finally, he got her to laugh on "What, with my tongue in your tail?" (2.1.212) as Kate cracked up with the dirty joke. In a reversal of the familiar chase pattern, where Kate tries to get away from Petruchio, this Petruchio kept trying to walk away from Kate. When she challenged him with "If you strike me you are no gentleman" (2.1.216), he picked up his stuff, as if to leave, but stayed, invited perhaps by her line, "No cock of mine" (2.1.221), as if he realized that she was still playing the word games. Then after "look not sour" (2.1.222), he started out again, and at last did exit on "Now, by Saint George, I am too young for you" (228), but returned. When he finally did grab her, "In sooth you scape not so" (2.1.230), he kept her at arm's length, then turned her to the floor, straddled her, but essentially was still playing with her. He took off one shoe, tickled her foot, and then played a keep-away game with the shoe, hiding it behind his back so that she had to guess where it was. Of course, it wasn't in either hand, but stuck into his belt, so in order to get it from him, she had to embrace him. Finally, after both Kate and Petruchio collapsed on the floor in laughter, they ended up sitting by side, feet out in front of them, like children resting from play.

Petruchio's announcement of their marriage also worked on several levels. At first, he seemed to mock Kate, imitating her carefully enunciated "Kath-e-rine" on "Marry, so I mean, sweet Katherine, in thy bed" (2.1.256). But then his tone changed, as he put his arm around her shoulder and gently touched her cheek: "For by this light, whereby I see thy beauty, / Thy beauty that does make me like thee well" (2.1.262-3) was heartfelt (Figure 17.2). Jasper Britton pointed out that the repetition of "thy beauty" seemed to him a cue that Petruchio was serious. But he was also still afraid to show his feelings, so there was a long stammer on "l---like" as if he couldn't yet bring himself to use the word "love." Katherine's reaction was stunned; as Alexandra Gilbreath said in conversation, "No one had ever called her beautiful before." Then Petruchio heard people coming, and indeed the stage direction, "Enter Baptista, etc." appears in the Folio just before the line "For I am he am born to tame thee, Kate" (2.1.265). For Britton, the entrance of the other men cued his move back to his previous "tough guy" pose. His voice and demeanor changed, and Kate, sitting next to him, looked at him in surprise. His explanation that Kate would be "curst" for "policy" (2.1.180) seemed to come from nowhere, as her expression made clear. She stared at him in bewilderment, through her tears,

Figure 17.2 Petruchio (Jasper Britton) and Katherine (Alexandra Gilbreath) share a moment of rapport in 2.1 of Gregory Doran's 2003 production of *The Taming of the Shrew* at the Royal Shakespeare Theatre

Photograph reprinted by permission of Metro Imaging.

although Petruchio's lines about how much Kate loves him sent her back to her more defiant crossed-arms pose. When Petruchio demanded "Give me thy hand" (2.1.303), she did so gently, wiping it off on her skirt first, as if trying to make sure that it was clean – or was that gesture another challenge? Petruchio held her hand, "I will be sure my Kath-e-rine shall be fine" (so he could mock right back) and then faltered as he tried to imagine what he should buy, "We will have rings," pause, "and things," pause, "and fine array" – implicitly, "something better than what you have on now" (2.1.312). He asked for a kiss and what he got instead was a bite on the hand, but Petruchio tried not to react in pain. His final challenge was to toss her shoe back to her, and Kate then exited, not stamping off, but quietly, even shutting the door with extreme care. After she passed through the door, one could see her doing a little jig of triumph – and happiness?

So appealing was this scene – and reviewer after reviewer praised its freshness and charm – that one might well wonder whether any taming would be necessary, given what seemed Kate's happiness and Petruchio's ability to make her laugh. The fact that Petruchio was late to the wedding seemed very strange, and the fact that he was, again, drunk, stranger still. Kate, decked out in a truly unbecoming pastel blue dress with little ornaments all over it and a tight-fitting hat (the kind of outfit that Bianca would have chosen, Alexandra Gilbreath felt – as if Kate somehow wanted to be Bianca on her wedding day), was appalled by his lateness and his behavior, and we were appalled with her, in large part because we thought he was in love with her. Perhaps, as Jasper Britton suggested in conversation, Petruchio was now getting cold feet, or just facing up to the reality that he actually was going to get married; perhaps he had spent his money on drink rather than on new clothes.

So the relationship had to work its way through the rest of the play as Petruchio struggled to figure out exactly what to do with his new wife (once he was sober) and Kate tried to maintain her sense of individuality. Costume choices were crucial here, with Kate appearing at Petruchio's first in a muddied version of the wedding dress, and then in a petticoat, with a long gray cardigan jumper as a kind of jacket. When Petruchio tore apart the dark red dress that the tailor had brought, just the kind of dress so often worn by actors playing Katharina, both at the beginning of the play and at the end, Kate was in tears, sitting on the floor, holding the remnants of the dress. Petruchio stooped down to talk with her gently, and the stage picture took us back to their intimate moments in 2.1. He tried to reassure her that "honour peereth in the meanest habit" (4.3.168), and she was almost convinced by his example of the jay and the lark. But then when he insisted on messing about with the time of day, she rebelled again. On the road, Kate added a long droopy blue-gray coat over her petticoat, plus trousers, socks and shoes; the total lack of glamour in the costume, plus the combination of trousers and petticoat, gave Kate the appearance of someone inventing her own style, rather than imitating Bianca's.

And, surprisingly, but utterly plausibly, Kate wore this unusual outfit, topped with the little red hat that had survived the tailor scene, for the wedding feast. The Widow was resplendent in brocade, Bianca had a new dress, but Kate didn't. Hortensio was visibly frightened of the Widow who disapprovingly took away his wine glass. Bianca had clearly had too much to drink, so that she was casting amorous looks at an embarrassed Tranio, and indulging in risqué remarks ("I mean to shift my bush,"

5.2.46); Kate promptly hustled her offstage before she could say anything else. When Kate returned at Petruchio's order, he tossed her his whip as he ordered her to "swinge" the other women out. She threw the cap to the floor, but Petruchio promptly picked it up and handed it to her. And as she began her final speech, she utterly controlled the stage, so much so that the mere mention of the husband as "king" made Hortensio sit up straighter. She used "true obedience" to turn Bianca's head so that Bianca looked at Lucentio rather than Tranio. And when she spoke of the subject and the prince, she crossed stage left to where Petruchio was sitting and sat across the table from him; he held her hand, in an image of unity rather than hierarchy. Their agreement, signaled earlier in her delighted realization that she could play the "sun and moon" game with him, as well as her ability to remain independent, evident in the "so-so" hand gesture that answered Petruchio's question, "Is not this well?" after the kiss in 5.1 seemed clear.

But the production offered one more surprise. Standing center stage, at the end of her long speech. Kate extended her hand to Petruchio, "My hand is ready, may it do him ease" (5.2.179) and waited. Petruchio seemed taken aback, pausing after "Why, there's a wench!" and then raised his foot, "Come on," and paused again. The ripple of sound from the audience suggested that they – that we – were as shocked as Kate, who hesitated but finally crossed over to him and knelt down. Before she could put her hand out, Petruchio fell to his knees and swept her into his arms for a big romantic kiss. As they left together, Kate blushing on the line "we'll to bed," Petruchio pouring the money he had just won onto the stage, they were clearly the happy couple, while everyone else stood around looking dumbfounded.

Petruchio's gesture with the foot came, I discovered, from a rehearsal in which Jasper Britton had momentarily blanked on the line "come on and kiss me, Kate" – after remembering "come on" he couldn't remember the rest, and so put out his foot. The look he got from Alexandra Gilbreath was enough to convince him that the moment was absolutely right, and it continued to play beautifully. The gesture reminded us of the Petruchio who had praised Kate's beauty but then turned back into the "tough guy" when her father arrived, and, followed by the big kiss, enabled the production to both question and affirm the couple's current – and future – rapport.

The production's strength lay in its willingness to play this duality, a willingness in part stemming from choices made by the actors and the director, but also in part from the unusual context of this production. For in 2003, Gregory Doran and most of the cast of *The Taming of the Shrew* were also rehearsing and performing John Fletcher's 1611 continuation of *Shrew, The Woman's Prize, or the Tamer Tamed*. Fletcher's play picks up the characters at some unspecified time after the events in *Shrew*, when Kate has died and Petruchio has just remarried, and the cast rehearsed both productions together, finally opening for the press on the same day, with *Shrew* in the afternoon and *Tamer* in the evening. Thus the actors had, as Alexandra Gilbreath (who played both Kate and Maria, Petruchio's new wife) put it, the luxury of being able to play *Shrew* on its own terms, without feeling that they had to invent a happy ending to make it palatable; if Kate didn't triumph in the afternoon, she would that evening when Maria, wearing a series of attractive dresses (in contrast to Kate), would speak the play's Epilogue, with its claim that the play meant "To teach both sexes due equality, / And, as they stand bound, to love mutually." For Jasper Britton, the combination may have seemed less appealing, since Fletcher's Petruchio is much less interesting than Shakespeare's, and is reduced to losing face time and time again as he is outwitted by Maria. Perhaps, though, playing Fletcher's Petruchio may have – paradoxically – contributed to Britton's choice not to play Shakespeare's Petruchio as the same loud-mouthed boorish character. Instead he showed Shakespeare's Petruchio as a man who slipped into such behavior to cover grief over his father's death, and insecurity with women. Just as Richard McCabe's Tranio forced audiences to rethink issues of class privilege and abuse within the play, so too did Jasper Britton's Petruchio create a multi-layered character who repeatedly surprised the audience into reconsidering Petruchio's behavior. Both performances and both productions offered, to my mind, intriguing new commentaries on this perpetually irritating and perpetually fascinating comedy.

Acknowledgments

All quotations from actors are taken from personal conversations and/or public question-and-answer sessions at the Shakespeare Centre in Stratford-upon-Avon. RSC programs and promptbooks are in the Shakespeare Centre Library, Stratford-upon-Avon, and are quoted by permission of the Royal Shakespeare Company and the Library. Quotations from newspaper reviews are taken from *Theatre Record*, or from RSC programs.

References and Further Reading

Gilbert, Miriam (2002). *Shakespeare at Stratford: The Merchant of Venice*, Arden edn. London: Thomson Learning.

Holderness, Graham (1989). *Shakespeare in Performance: The Taming of the Shrew*. Manchester: Manchester University Press.

Miller, Jonathan (1986). *Subsequent Performances*. London: Faber and Faber.

Rutter, Carol (1988). *Clamorous Voices: Shakespeare's Women Today*. London: The Women's Press.

Rutter, Carol (1997). "Kate, Bianca, Ruth, and Sarah: Playing the Woman's Part in *The Taming of the Shrew*." In Michael J. Collins (ed.) *Shakespeare's Sweet Thunder: Essays on the Early Comedies*. Newark: University of Delaware Press.

Shakespeare, William (1984). *The Taming of the Shrew*, ed. Ann Thompson. Cambridge: Cambridge University Press.

18

Maverick Shakespeare
Carol Chillington Rutter

Histories

London. Winter. 1978. The best of times – the worst of times. Off the Strand at the Aldwych Theatre, the Royal Shakespeare Company was playing what Michael Billington called "Shakespeare's dance to the broken music of time" (Beauman 1982: 341). An epic sweep of four plays hurtling through 50 years of English history took spectators across France and England, from Agincourt to Tewkesbury, from brilliant court splendor to mud and muddle, wars of conquest to the Wars of the Roses, the triumphs of *Henry V* to the disasters and death of *Henry VI* – a trajectory, did we but know it, predictive of a future coming soon to Britain. In Balham, around the corner from a tube stop once glamorized by London Transport as "the gateway to the south" (and to the south coast's naughty seaside playgrounds) but now signposting a slummy borough a long way down the grimly unreliable Northern Line on the wrong side of the Thames, I was living in a cold-water flat hatching plots to extend my student visa while spending most of my time hanging around theatres watching Shakespeare. Meanwhile, all over London the Winter of Discontent (as the tabloids dubbed it, making one of their oh-so-regular returns to Shakespeare to name the national mood and write the day's headlines) was beginning to bite. Balham looked more like a redoubt than a gateway. At the bottom of every road, piles of bulging bin liners were thrown together in heaps like barricades erected in an urban war zone. The rubbish men were on strike. So were health workers, lorry drivers – and gravediggers. Fleet Street, British Leyland, British Rail, the BBC followed. In November, *The Times* stopped printing. At Christmas, a TV blackout was threatened.

But the uncollected garbage on the streets was by far the nastiest visible sign of the ugly political reality. Across Britain working people had gone beyond grumbling mutiny into open rebellion against a Labour government that, after four years in power, had spectacularly failed to deliver its 1974 manifesto promise: a "fundamental and irreversible shift in the balance of power and wealth in favour of working people and their families" (see www.news.bbc.co.uk). There'd been a shift all right – but only to make things worse for workers. Unemployment, up from 500,000 in 1974 to 1.6 million in 1976, hit 3 million in 1979. For the first time in living memory, schoolteachers were among the unemployed. The cost of living doubled. National-ized industries hiked up electricity, gas, and rail prices; interest rates soared; inflation sky-rocketed; public services plummeted. While a government White Paper attempted to control inflation by capping wage rises at 5 percent, union after union put in demands for increases of 30 percent, 35 percent, even 50 percent. It was obvious that militants had infiltrated the unions and were calling the shots – in effect, holding the nation to ransom. Watching these unions adopt bully-boy tactics of intimidation, even dyed-in-the-red Labour supporters began rethinking their affiliations.

At the Aldwych, scenes from Shakespeare were looking very much like rehearsals for class action (from the left *and* right): Talbot on the frontlines wearily sandbagged his defenses against the inevitable defeat while back at Whitehall the politicians jawed and jawed and made no decisions; Jack Cade whipped his plebeian uprising into a frenzy – then fell victim to its mindless violence, betrayed by his own "machine" when his "gimme, gimme, gimme" aspirations rotted the revolution from within, allowing it to be co-opted by the ruling class who brought the "unwashed" to heel by cynically distributing some paltry "welfare."

Outside the theatre, hoardings went up as campaigning began for the election triggered when Labour lost a vote of "no confidence" in the Commons in March 1979. One Tory campaign poster said it all. Produced in shades of gray, it showed a vast queue of dead-eyed people winding across the otherwise empty frame and out of sight. Waiting for a bus, perhaps? Or Harrods' doors to open on the first day of the spring sales? No. The punning caption – "Labour Isn't Working" – made the queue a dole queue. The effect was devastating. Of course, the photo-image wasn't "real." But that was irrelevant. The political point was scored. In May, Margaret Thatcher became Prime Minister when the Conservatives won power – and immediately set about dismantling the welfare state, liquidating the nation's capital assets and privatizing everything from British Rail to British Telecom, a program that even an ageing former Conservative Prime Minister, Harold Macmillan, likened to selling the family silver. Public subsidy in the arts was replaced with private sponsorship; a new class hero, the Entrepreneur, was promoted, and a new household god, Acquisition, installed. In "Great Britain, plc" (where, said Thatcher, there "was no such thing as 'society' "), "socialism" became a dirty word and "united" an irrelevant one, particu-larly when attached to "kingdom," for Thatcher's policies worked effectively to divide the nation, culturally, economically, ideologically: north/south, haves/have-nots, them/us.

None of this was irrelevant to Shakespeare. On London's South Bank, an embattled Peter Hall (the same who, as Artistic Director from 1960–8, had invented the new-model Royal Shakespeare Company in Stratford-upon-Avon, fighting for its first public subsidy and a London shop-front at the Aldwych) was struggling to get the

National Theatre established in its new home. Frustrated by endless delays from go-slow construction workers, Hall finally moved the company into its building in March 1976 – before even the stages and foyers were complete. Immediately, props men demanded a 50 percent rise to move the two blocks from the Old Vic on the Waterloo Road to the new site on the South Bank; stage staff refused to work integrated rotas; a wildcat strike by militant NAATKE (National Association of Theatrical, Television and Kine Employees) closed the theatre in August. The following May, it happened again, stage staff walking out to protest a plumber being sacked. By summer – that of the Queen's Jubilee, celebrating 25 years of the "second" Elizabethan age – illegal NAATKE pickets ringed the National demanding a 35 percent rise and a four-day working week. Arbitration failed. Unofficial NAATKE action forced cancelation of a string of performances in November and February and put new productions in jeopardy; by March, strikes were a daily threat and pickets blockaded the theatre. As Hall wearily watched more performances canceled, it dawned on him that his theatre was actually small beer in the militants' much bigger project: the National was being targeted because the new building made the management vulnerable, but once it capitulated to the militants' demands, every other theatre from the RST to Covent Garden and the West End would be hit (Goodwin 1983: 296–315). Along with Pinter, Bond and Schaffer, Shakespeare would go out of business.

As it actually happened, over the Winter of Discontent, *Britain* went out of business. Strikes, "the blood sports of the seventies," finally bled Labour to death. The "resounding victory" Peter Hall (and many like him) helped achieve on 3 May by voting Tory for the first time in his life set in place a government that would survive for 17 years, busting the unions in ways that no doubt satisfied Hall-the-manager but simultaneously degrading the arts in ways Hall-the-theatre-director found monstrous (Goodwin 1983: 435). The new Thatcherite buzz words for arts policy were "private sponsorship," "accountability," "enterprise," and "brand recognition" in a "global market economy" where plays were "products" like Levis and where washing powder sold Shakespeare – and vice versa. As Peter Thomson has wryly observed, Thatcher and her Conservative Cabinet never officially made the case against state subsidy for the arts: "There was no need. Innuendo and the propaganda of accountability were sufficient to undermine confidence and deter experiment – because a threat to subsidy was always implicit" (2001: 161). In this nanny state where "bad" children were controlled by sending them hungry to bed, risk was out, self-promoting hype, in, and Shakespeare in Stratford learned to play safe. He had to – co-opted by a government, wrote Peter Holland, that believed "in the divine right of Toryism to appropriate Shakespeare for its version of English culture" (1997: 254). Worse, by the end of the 1980s when a new Artistic Director took over (one who would build his career commercializing Shakespeare and selling the company's brand name world-wide), the RSC knew it had "lost the right to fail." Perhaps it was just as well, then, that the "RSC logo rode into the nineties in tandem with that of Royal Insurance" (Trussler 1994: 364).

"Have You Heard the One about the Irishman?"

I recite these various Shakespeare histories to bring me to my real subject, a parallel (or counter) history that spans the same 25 years. I want to consider the work of three theatre directors whom British critics have both celebrated and slammed: they're the awkward brigade, scrappers, innovators, anarchists, the avant-garde, wreckers, visionaries, purists, vulgarians mindlessly courting controversy, geniuses. They are mavericks who, as much playing the system as bucking it, have achieved for Shakespeare in Britain over the past quarter century a radically alternative performance life to the "official" one on view at the NT and RSC. On paper, Michael Bogdanov (b. 1939), Declan Donnellan (b. 1953), and Barrie Rutter (b. 1946) look like cultural outsiders, a line-up for an ethnic joke, especially compared to the "Cambridge mafia" and "new university" men who've been running the Establishment British theatre since the 1960s. The first is a Welshman with a Russian father, educated in Ireland. He first caught Peter Hall's (horrified) attention in 1977 when Hall wandered into the Cottesloe where Bogdanov was directing the NT's first family Christmas show just in time to hear the community sing-song belting out "Bums and tits, bums and tits, Having it away" (Goodwin 1983: 326). The second is a London Irishman educated at Cambridge who, called to the Bar, spent only six months in a pupillage before leaving Town in the company of a cry of players, Becky Sharp-ing his law degree out the window of the touring van he'd bought on borrowed money. The last is a Yorkshireman raised alongside Hull's fish docks who went to drama school in Glasgow where he "bollocks-ed" all attempts to eradicate his regional (and class) accent when the Scots tried to teach him to speak English RP (Received Pronunciation).

Undoubtedly outsiders by habit, practice, politics and artistic vision, these three have all, significantly, spent plenty of time inside the theatre Establishment, regularly recruited to it by a mainstream anxious to annex their radical street cred. All three have worked at the National and the RSC; in regional theatres around Britain and in national theatres (or what doubles for them) world-wide (in France, Germany, Russia, Japan, Greece, India, Hungary, Brazil, Cyprus, Israel, the USA, to name some); in opera, film and television; all three have represented the UK on British Council tours – and you can't get more Establishment than that. But their permanent address is on the margins where alternative Shakespeare lives, sometimes "tragedians of the city," but more characteristically, leading their touring companies where metropolitan Shakespeare doesn't go: Cleethorpes, Buxton, Middleham, Oldham. At a time when "corporate image" was settling over Shakespeare like a death mask, Bogdanov's English Shakespeare Company (co-founded with the actor Michael Pennington), Donnellan's Cheek by Jowl (a partnership with designer, Nick Ormerod), and Rutter's Northern Broadsides broke the mold. Not everyone approved. It was, after all, the best *and* worst of times.

Towards Popular Shakespeare

Michael Bogdanov sees Shakespeare as a "writer of the people" whose work belongs among the "truly popular cultural activities – football, karaoke, pop, drag, strip, bingo": a "subversive" whose "texts must be made accessible not only by making the language understandable but also by restoring what Stephen Greenblatt calls 'invisible bullets' – those things consistently suppressed and misinterpreted that show Shakespeare the revolutionary throwing down the gauntlet of challenge." Bogdanov wants a Shakespeare who's alive and kicking in today's theatre. So he's happy to cut textual difficulty and modernize hard words. He habitually puts productions in modern dress to make them visually accessible, and invents stage images that connect with spectators, that speak to "right now." Bogdanov's politics offer a smack in the face to middle-class "niceness": he wants to "reclaim Shakespeare for the anarchists." And his target audience is adolescent: he wants "our young" to experience "the plays through live radical performance," to hear in Shakespeare "a contemporary voice used to articulate protest" (Bogdanov 2001). Three productions give a sense of Bogdanov's concerns.

1978. May 4. Opening night of *The Taming of the Shrew* at the Royal Shakespeare Theatre. The director, an unknown quantity at the RSC, trails the reputation of a Wunderkind. On stage, he's put a sight to gladden the eyes of Stratford's sixty-something theatre-going traditionalists who make up the numbers, year in, year out, at what is, after all, their "local" rep. For eight weary years, ever since Peter Brook's *A Midsummer Night's Dream* revolutionized what performance spaces looked like, they'd been subjected to whole seasons of Shakespeare set in white – or black – boxes that didn't pretend to be anything but stages and didn't even bother to mask their workings, leaving lighting in view and walls exposed. For Stratford's traditionalists, Brook's "empty space" was charmless, not a blank canvas open to imaginative free play but, well, *empty*. So first sights of Michael Bogdanov's *Shrew* cheered them up enormously. They were looking at a "proper" set, with curtains and pillars and balustrades and painted canvas, a delicious Italianate version of John Barton's "real" Elizabethan Padua from 1960. Scenic décor was back! Pictorial realism was restored! But just as grateful eyes were growing misty, they had to switch attention from the stage to an unseemly disturbance in the auditorium. A drunken lout was stumbling down the aisle, an usherette trying to restrain him – but no "bloody woman" was going to tell *him* what to do. He took a swing at her – then jumped onto the stage and began wrecking it. Lights exploded, pillars fell, all the pretty scenery came tumbling down – and "gullible patrons," wrote *The Guardian*'s Michael Billington (May 5, 1978), started "making for the exit to call the police."

Of course it was a trick, a stunning *coup de théâtre*. The drunk was Jonathan Pryce playing Christopher Sly, the usherette, Paola Dionisotti, who would return as Kate. And as the dust slowly settled on the ruined set (and, painfully, their ruined expectations), spectators were faced with yet another box, "the bare bones of the stage," and let in to the "real" scenic world of this altogether grimmer *Shrew*, "an elaborate structure of rusting iron arches" designed by Chris Dyer that suggested to Billington "a combination of the west wing of San Quentin and Paddington Station." So the pretty illusion was a ruse designed to *épater les bourgeois*, its destruction an act of violence that caught them out, mimicking, proleptically, the violence in the "taming" story to come and forcing them radically to readjust their sights on a play with which they thought themselves comfortable. For Peter Thomson, "Bogdanov's aim was to pitch the text into the present tension": culture was currently exchanging the opening salvos in the gender wars. But since audiences don't like being mocked, making fools of them in the opening five minutes meant that "a degree of hostility between audience and play" lingered (Thomson 2001: 165). Clearly, spectators weren't in for a replay of Barton's happy ending *Shrew*. Even more disturbing, Sly's original act of vandalism looked prophetic of this young director's future designs on Shakespeare.

Billington wondered about Bogdanov's iconoclasm. Was *it* a ruse? And where did it leave Shakespeare's play? "After all," he wrote, "if you start your production with what looks like the climactic scene from *A Night at the Opera*, you are in danger of making the delivery of the published text seem curiously redundant." But the "published text" was precisely what Bogdanov – no iconoclast *poseur* but a genuine wrecker of received readings – was putting up for grabs. He had Shakespeare's performance text also in mind, and directed scene after scene to interrogate the relationship between playtext and performance text – between, that is, words, actions, images, bodies, persons and politics. Greenblatt's "invisible bullets" ambushed spectators from every direction. Sly in the Induction was scrubbed up by the Lord's lackeys in a scallop shell bath – and bizarrely transformed into Botticelli's Venus. Later, listening to Gremio's complaints in the "comonty" (Induction 2. 132)[1] arranged for his entertainment that Kate was a shrew too tough for any man to handle, he made a loud exit – and returned as Petruchio, Mr Macho-man, straddling a motor bike and clearly geared up for a little recreational violence. Baptista, a hard-knuckled Mafioso sitting behind a massive CEO's desk calculating their competitive claims on an adding machine, made his younger daughter's suitors bidders in an auction, she the "commodity" (2.1.320) for sale. Kate stood under a black umbrella in the rain waiting for her groom. Even when he turned up looking like a tartan wino, mad on meths, "society" insisted the photographer record the "society" wedding. At the end, what Bogdanov called *Shrew*'s "wish-fulfilment dream of a male for revenge on a female" fulfilled itself in the triumph of the supremacist – which was also his defeat (Bogdanov 1988: 90). This Petruchio had beaten a wife who could have been an equal partner in marriage into a groveling submission he no longer wanted but had been duped into believing made him a real man.

All of these performance choices, beginning with the director's decision to put the play in modern dress, required spectators to re-think what "kind of history" (Induction 2.135) was at stake in Shakespeare's *Shrew*. Thomson certainly saw current debates argued out in an aggressively politicized text. For him, "The real villain" of Bogdanov's production was "an acquisitive society . . . governed by men who carve up first women and then each other." He heard Kate's final speech, set against heavy drinking and heavier gambling at a green baize table where the wedding party was sinking in a fug of expensive cigar smoke and even more costly male rivalry, articulating an indictment of what feminists were just then teaching the present to call "the patriarchy" (2001: 166). This was a *Shrew* that stunned Billington into seeing the "suppressed" play inside the "official" play that he'd been delightedly watching for 30 years, a play about male brutality and wife bashing, a play he found so hard to watch that he wanted *Taming of the Shrew* "put firmly back on the shelf" and left there. But turning a blind eye on controversy wasn't Bogdanov's practice.

Nine years later he returned to the RSC to direct *Romeo and Juliet*, re-working ideas from *Shrew* and intensifying them. Once again the play was made contemporary, set not in Zeffirelli's medieval walled town where fates were written in the stars, beauty taught torches to burn bright, and poetry rose naturally to adolescent lips but rather in a high-tech Verona of slick marble surfaces that had clearly caught the British disease, "Thatcherism": the whole world looked like one vast commercial district. Verona's children wheeled through town on roller-blades. They went to parties, got drunk, chatted up the host's wife, fell into his swimming pool, and later pissed from his balcony – a nicely irreverent piss-take on the play's most famous scene. The villains were the grown-ups: a brittle, vacuous Lady Capulet who wasn't ready to have a marriageable daughter and compensated by playing prick-tease with Tybalt; a deeply stupid Nurse whose chief moral guide was her hip flask; a drugs dealer (instead of Shakespeare's apothecary); a "swinger" Priest who rode a motor bike, identified with the "youth" (thereby demonstrating just how wide the generation gap was); and a vulgar, volatile, cigar-chomping big-business Capulet who sat behind a desk twice as big as Baptista's and clearly saw his daughter as an item in his investment portfolio (Figure 18.1). The lines that shouted out of this production were his, the "careful" father's, when Juliet refused to marry Paris: "God's bread, it makes me mad. Day, night; work, play; / Alone, in company, still my care hath been to have her matched." But this claim to paternal virtue was exposed as twisted hypocrisy by another adult hypocrite, the Priest, as they stood over Juliet's "corpse": "The most you sought was her promotion, / For 'twas your heaven she should be advanced" (3.5.176–8, 4.4.98–9). Twinning "heaven" with social "promotion," the Priest underscored that God, in this Verona, was gold, love was a matter of counting "the chinks" (2.1.114), and dehumanization was the end-product of lives dedicated to materialism. Puppets, not people, were pulling the strings – a trope literalized in the nightmare that overwhelmed Romeo as he trawled Mantua's alleys, looking for poison and finding it at the tail end of a carnival procession that paraded monster-sized figures, jigging on stilts, faces bloated, a weird dance of death: one of them, clearly Maggie Thatcher.

Laying the teenagers' deaths squarely at their parents' doors, Bogdanov refused to let the adults off the hook by playing the end as tragedy: there was no suffering into knowledge, no consolation registered in the wake of tragic recognition. Bogdanov cut straight from a black-out on Juliet's death to lights up on a media event. As the press jostled each other for the best photo op, the Duke delivered the Prologue in the past

FIGURE 18.1   Aggro between swaggering Capulets (Tybalt: Hugh Quarshie) and hung-over Montagues
(Benvolio: Martin Jacobs; Mercutio: Michael Kitchen) the morning after the night before in Michael
Bogdanov's RSC *Romeo and Juliet* (1986)

Photograph from Joe Cocks Studio Collection, copyright The Shakespeare Birthplace Trust.

tense. In ones and twos, the families stood in front of the hacks. The Nurse dabbed her
eyes. Flash-bulbs popped. Behind this PR performance, silently watching the status
quo smoothly reassert control over a Verona only temporarily disturbed by their
short-lived rebellion, the statues of the dead children were already raised – in gold.

Reviewers called the production "tabloid Shakespeare" (Irving Wardle, *The Times*,
April 16, 1987) and accused Bogdanov of "pandering to the groundlings with his
crude visual effects" (Eric Shorter, *Daily Telegraph*, April 16, 1987) – criticisms,
ironically, that went straight to the heart of Bogdanov's achievement and registered
his "invisible bullets" hitting home. Adults hated this show. Adolescents – Shorter's
"groundlings," who, of course, weren't groundlings at all, but packed the galleries,
unable to afford ticket prices in the RST's stalls – loved it.

Bogdanov has never ducked controversy. Even as *Romeo and Juliet* opened, his epic
seven-play history cycle, directed for the newly established English Shakespeare Company, a joint venture with Michael Pennington, was hitting the road – and *The Wars of
the Roses* pulled no punches in delivering a view of English history that some thought
bolshie and anti-establishment, others, reactionary and jingoistic, the wrong side of
"vulgar." The ESC counts among Bogdanov's best achievements.[2] Launched a year
earlier, in 1986, as a protest against government under-funding in the arts that was
starving regional theatres up and down the kingdom, the ESC had a mission to tour,
and Bogdanov left an eight-year stint as Associate Director at the National to lead the

new company from the front, to take his "popular playwright" Shakespeare to venues the national poet (and national theatres) seldom reached. Choosing the histories for openers was clearly a political choice: the *Henry IV*s and *Henry V* in the first year, *Richard II*, *Richard III* and the *Henry VI* trilogy (condensed into two parts) following in 1987. Reviewing the cycle, Macdonald P. Jackson saw Bogdanov ransacking the whole of the twentieth century – and most of the nineteenth – for materials: Bolingbroke and his council could have been "in Whitehall in Victorian times"; the traitors Harry exposed were "a trio of gangster-movie spivs" and the troops he rallied were "dressed for Ulster or the Falklands, but, sprawling behind sandbags," had "the exhausted air of First World War veterans of the trenches"; Cade's rabble belonged "to one of the nastier branches of the National Front," their faces daubed with swastikas and shirts with obscenities, while the *habitués* of the Boar's Head, both staff and customers, had "walked in off the streets of Thatcherland" – indeed, Margaret in *Henry VI* was dressed to bring "to mind a more recent iron lady also named Margaret" (Jackson 1989: 208). In this cycle, Bogdanov and his 30-strong company offered no analysis of the grand mechanism of history. Nor were his contemporary citations bids towards historical analogies. Rather, Bogdanov, perhaps the first post-modern director of Shakespeare, was working by pastiche, using Shakespeare's histories as Shakespeare himself used history, ana-chronistically, inconsistently, inaccurately, deconstructively, fictionally, subversively *to talk about the present* (see Hodgdon 1991: 88–9). So acts of brutality committed in the national interest weren't packaged in the wrapping paper of the past to allow spectators to believe them delivered to addresses the nation no longer occupied. Joan of Arc was necklaced Township-style: a rubber tire was thrown over her head and she was torched. "Jerusalem" swelling out over the sound system was drowned by lager louts chanting "'Ere we go, 'ere we go" as, shipping for France as if to a football match, they unfurled a banner reading "Fuck the Frogs." In the closing minutes of the 21-hour-long cycle, when the lights came up on Richmond, his slaughter of Richard already "history," he was sitting behind a presidential desk, facing the TV cameras. His last speech was a prepared newscast to the nation, his face in close-up projected onto three studio monitors. How did this final image read? Was he a hero or a hydra? Or did the multiple talking heads more chillingly register his transformation from soldier to politician?

Reviewing *The Wars of the Roses*, Stanley Wells complained, "I tend to feel got at by Bogdanov's productions" – but admitted he might "be the kind of person" Bogdanov wanted "got at" (Wells 1989: 162). Billington had "some doubts about the Bogda-novisation of the Bard" but "at least" felt he was "watching a company show rather than a piece of decadent star Shakespeare" (*Guardian*, February 13, 1989) – a dig at Adrian Noble's de-politicized Merchant–Ivory *Plantagenets* currently playing at the RSC. For Jackson, the cycle's bitter aftertaste expressed "a contemporary skepticism about all political action" and "a profound pessimism about Thatcher's Britain" (1989: 210).

The pessimism Jackson sensed was well founded. While Bogdanov never intended the ESC to survive forever, to grow institutionalized with age and wake up one morning to find itself no longer the fox but the gamekeeper, when the Arts Council cut its grant by £500,000 after only five years, then, two years later altered the conditions of that grant, effectively pulling the plug on long-term planning, Bogdanov raged: "not just at the cuts but at the way the arts world has let them happen ... at the way we've allowed TV companies to rob and pillage and rape the British theatre and its talent," and at "the Arts Council, who'd rather subsidise five marketing people than one artist" (*Guardian*, December 1, 1993). Touring was "a mug's game," said Bogdanov, throwing in the towel in 1994, disbanding the ESC.

The outspokenness was typical. Probably Britain's most politically committed director, Bogdanov is definitely her most combative. Back in 1973, he'd issued a socialist manifesto for the arts that "posited the arts as a service," "placed the artist at the center of society," "saw theatre as the natural debating platform" for the nation, and knew how to fund his proposals. In 1993, as the ESC was foundering, he revisited his agenda. How did things look 20 years on? "Appalling": the Arts Council had "degenerated into a bungling, bureaucratic ... government lackey"; theatre companies charged "from one hand-out to another in a desperate bid for survival"; "the once-proud repertory movement" was "on the brink of collapse"; and the RSC and National had perpetually to "tread in fear of offending." In other countries, "artists would riot." In Britain, they "retreated" (*The Sunday Times*, May 23, 1993).

In his fight for a living theatre Bogdanov takes no prisoners. His prime targets are politicians and bureaucrats, but he trains his sights on anyone who deadens Shakespeare. European directors. (They "get away with work that would be howled off the stage in Britain.") Academics. (They "swamp" the plays with "the glutinous blancmange of academia.") Exam boards. ("Candidates are forced to embrace a shared system of beliefs.") The ruling elite. ("Hijacked by the Establishment," Shakespeare serves "the purpose of shoring up the status quo.") Reviewers. ("A flock of Oxbridge chums"; "vicious, vituperative, vitriolic, objectionable, abusive, arrogant, excretory, disgruntled, cavilling, small-minded, arse-licking, toadying" [*New Statesman*, November 15, 1996].)

Bogdanov's diatribes would be insupportable if he didn't put himself in the firing line, as he certainly did when he accepted the assignment from BBC television's "Bard on the Box" project (1994), to take a camera crew onto one of Birmingham's most deprived housing estates, to film him knocking on doors, facing aggro and incomprehension, finding himself suddenly, uncomfortably the "bullshitting academic" surrounded by a jeering crowd, inviting the people of Ladywood – from kids to mothers with babies in pushchairs to loutish youths to retirees – to put "Shakespeare on the Estate." As Bogdanov said, "The object was to gather evidence as to the impact of Shakespeare on the lives of the greater part of our population" – but also to test whether "the myth of Shakespeare, the popular writer of and for the people" was "true" (Bogdanov 2001). The 50-minute film that came out of the project is a remarkable document of Ladywood "coming out" – and of the performances it records: a Jamaican "Nurse" remembering Juliet's childhood in patois; a jazz quartet stringing lines of poetry into the "Shakespeare Blues"; two flaming drag queens doing an outrageous take on Katherine, Alice, and the English lesson on ladies' night at the community center, making "de fingres" hilariously, unimaginably lewd (*Henry V*, 3.4.9); a dole-queue cowboy, overweight, too young for the scrap heap, propped against the wire fence cordoning off behind him a wasteland of estate dereliction, sipping a beer, speaking straight to camera, "This island's mine. By Sycorax, my mother" (*Tempest*, 1.2.334). Bogdanov thought he made "a patronising prat of myself" on the film (Bogdanov 2001). He was wrong. The film vindicated his life's work, proof that Shakespeare, the "popular writer," belongs among the "truly popular cultural activities" – and belongs certainly among the people of Ladywood. If anybody needed it, final proof came three years later when Penny Woolcock, the documentary filmmaker who'd shot "Shakespeare on the Estate," returned to Ladywood to film the most remarkable television Shakespeare of the decade, "*Macbeth* on the Estate."[3]

The Regeneration Game

You might expect a company called "Cheek by Jowl" to take Shakespeare deeper into the territory scouted by Bogdanov, the combat zone. After all, when Demetrius proposes going "cheek by jowl" with his rival Lysander in *A Midsummer Night's Dream* (3.2.338), he's intending grievous bodily harm. But that would be to miss the ironic force of Demetrius' trope: when Lysander challenges him to "follow," Demetrius roars, "Follow?" Then tops him: "Nay, I'll go *with* thee, cheek by jowl." Going "with thee" makes rivalry an odd form of collaboration – and fisticuffs a kind of bonding. Enemies work out in pairs, and theatre – *Twelfth Night*'s Feste provides its definitive epigram, "the competitors enter" (4.2.9) – puts together what *Dream*'s Hippolyta sees as "something of great constancy" (5.1.26) out of Peter Quince's "parts" (1.2). It's in these senses that the oxymoronic challenge to "go with thee cheek by jowl" has informed the 25-year collaboration between Declan Donnellan, director, and his partner, designer Nick Ormerod.

Seeing the cultural wasteland that under-funding was spreading across provincial Britain, and enough "Maggie's children" to respond to her government's infamous instruction to the unemployed to "get on your bike" to find work, Donnellan and Ormerod first made themselves unemployed, *then* got on their bike. (But they weren't *really* Maggie's children: after all, they were ditching careers as *barristers*.) And the metaphoric bike was a van, which launched Cheek by Jowl from the Edinburgh fringe in 1981 onto its inaugural regional tour, 49 performances of *The Country Wife* played by a company of 12, funded with a £6,000 Arts Council grant. (It would be another five years before Bogdanov would follow the lead and decide to fight the metropolitan hijack of Shakespeare by committing himself to the regions and touring.)

From the first, Donnellan and Ormerod made a virtue of their necessity. Owning almost nothing, attached to no theatre, having practically no production budget, Cheek by Jowl on tour was nevertheless instantly recognizable by the company's definitive house style – a style *sans* house – that had as much to do with ensemble playing as visual design. They cornered the market, which anyway no one was contesting, on European classics un-performed (and English classics under-performed) in England: Racine's *Andromache*, Corneille's *The Cid*, Ostrovsky's *A Family Affair*, Sophocles' *Philoctetes*, Calderon's *The Doctor of Honour*; Etherege's *The Man of Mode*, Webster's *The Duchess of Malfi*. From this repertoire base they fixed the reappraisal of classic texts as a company trademark, which in turn licensed them, when they came to Shakespeare, to treat his "classic texts" to the same appraising scrutiny – to make Shakespeare somehow wonderfully "foreign," and the plays, miraculously, British premieres.[4]

Not just the way they worked on texts but every mechanical aspect of the company's life on stage produced this quality of "new" Shakespeare. In the early years, Donnellan could rarely afford a company large enough to cover all of Shakespeare's parts. By necessity, actors had to double and re-double roles: Hamlet's ghost returned as the Player King, Polonius, a Gravedigger; Egeus as Bottom; Mrs. Overdone as Mariana; the Duke at Court, his brother in Arden; the fairies as mechanicals; Brabantio's kinsmen as senators, then hell-raising squaddies. Roles disappeared: the witches in *Macbeth* were voiced, chorus-like, by the company. Others were invented: in *The Tempest* two actors mimed baby Caliban, bawling bewildered by his mother's dead body. Regularly, roles swapped gender: Alonso was queen of Naples, the Porter at Glamis was a foul-mouthed harridan; Quince, the lady director of the local am dram society. Such de-familiarizing re-visions worked on the ears as much as the eyes, preparing audiences to listen to Shakespeare differently. Moreover, the return, by necessity, to what, after all, was standard Elizabethan playhouse practice, made doubling practical, not "knowing," but, by the very pleasures of its theatricality, informative. Importantly, it established actors as *players* and, on a stage like Cheek by Jowl's that is always a stage as well as a world, it understood "character" not as internalization but as personation, a sequence of role-plays directed *out*.

By necessity, Cheek by Jowl's casting policy had to be inventive, to think outside the box – not least because not every actor in Thatcher's Britain would leap at the offer to play Hamlet on Equity minimum wages. But their necessity produced radical results that reached far beyond the company to transform the whole culture of casting in Britain. For at a time when the RSC was dithering about the politics of color-blind casting, wondering whether in multi-racial 1980s' Britain they could do something so radical as casting a black actor to play Othello, Donnellan cut through all the nonsense, instituting fully integrated casting for all Shakespeare roles. The effect was not just to claim those parts (among them, Lear, Hero, Claudio, Mariana, Mrs. Overdone, Emilia, Rosalind, Jacques – but, quite deliberately, *not* Caliban) for black and Asian actors, but, by putting actors in those parts on view to multi-ethnic Britain, to claim Shakespeare for all comers. Willingness to cast creatively has made Cheek by Jowl a nursery to young talent and a "reform" school for some of the best of their elders: Saskia Reeves, Adrian Lester, Matthew Macfadyen, Amanda Harris, Sally Dexter, Paterson Joseph, Scott Handy, Anastasia Hille, Danny Sapani, Marianne Jean-Baptiste, and in the latest generation, Nonso Anozie, Matthew Douglas, Caroline Martin, Jaye Griffiths. For Donnellan, casting matters because "the art of the theatre is, first and last, the art of the actor," the "communication between the actor and the audience" that "should explore and wander over territories that obsess us at any time." Touring has suffered a bad press ever since the tragedians of the city arrived in Elsinore (did they ever get paid for *The Murder of Gonzago?*). But Donnellan thinks touring is good for actors. It intensifies their communication with their audiences since, on tour, actors "have no relationship with the building, with dressing rooms, the loos, the front of house staff. All they have is those people in the audience, so they're launched into this relationship of love and terror every night. It's nerve-shredding for the actors, but it keeps the thing alive" (*Birmingham Post*, February 27, 1988).

In terms of design, "keeping the thing alive" means stripping away everything that comes between the actor and the spectator. The consumerist 1980s was the decade that invented and marketed the "design concept" – both in British houses and on British stages – but while other designers, stylists of the acquisitive, fell in with the "greed is good" mind-set of the times, put more and more stuff on stage, and required Shakespeare to be read through "image," Nick Ormerod cleared the stage. He trades in expressive minimalism, his genius, a visual poetry of suggestion that mixes mischief with iconoclasm. In *As You Like It* the Forest of Arden was two strips of green silk that dropped from the flies – and "rustic" Phoebe (played by a man in this all-male production) flouncing on in twin-set and pearls, primly clutching a handbag. In *A Midsummer Night's Dream* Hermia arrived in the woods hugging her sleeping bag. The madhouse in *Twelfth Night* was a garden recliner where, blindfolded and strait-jacketed, Malvolio in plus-fours, yellow stockings and tasselled golf shoes lay stretched out, close prisoner glaringly exposed, while Feste, superfluously disguised as Groucho Marx in espadrilles and rolled-up trousers like T. S. Eliot's Prufrock ("I grow old, I grow old . . ."), hunched intently on a camp stool, psychiatrist's notepad in one hand, cigar in the other. The storm in *Lear* was a heavy silk curtain, dropped at mid-stage, that actors tugged and lashed into billows and blusters and cutting planes. *Measure for Measure*'s Vienna was a black stage, a massive desk positioned at its center for authority to seat itself, a scattering of chairs and a narrow banner of red silk that, by turns, signified the law or the red light district. *Othello*'s Venice was three long boxes draped in tapestry whose covers were whipped off when they were shoved together to make Desdemona's bed – where she and Emilia collapsed after the ghastly state dinner party, eased their high heels off aching feet and laughed about "these men, these men!" (4.3.58).

Ormerod's minimalism makes possible another Cheek by Jowl trademark, continuous play. There's no set to clear; indeed, actors frequently stand-in as parts of the set. So scenes play into each other, frequently overlapping. In *Measure for Measure* Claudio was on stage while Isabella and Angelo argued his future; in *The Winter's Tale*, directed in Russian for Theatre Maly, scenes froze, people became statues, anticipating Hermione in the final scene but also obliquely commenting on the terrors of a totalitarian regime that could petrify its people. Ormerod's habit of working on ideas throughout the rehearsal period means that what he produces as designs are active instructions from actors that translate their discoveries into visual meaning. In the cliché (see Welles, Parker, Nunn, Mendes, Doran on stage and film)[5] Othello "goes native" to kill Desdemona. A costume change "naturally" reveals the savage beneath that so far has been covered up by the military uniform that codes civilization. Not so Nonso Anozie. He killed Desdemona in the spotless white boiled shirt and dinner jacket he'd changed into from his uniform for the state banquet – the killer was white cultural sophistication personified. In the cliché, Bianca, the "house-wife" who, "by selling her desires / Buys herself bread and clothes" (4.1.94–5), is *Othello*'s "black" woman who proves misogyny's stereotype making all women presumptive whores – in Welles, she's the brunette set opposite the platinum blonde, in Nunn, a black gipsy Carmen, in Parker, a "high yellow" courtesan, in Doran, a Muslim Cypriot who's shed the burkah for Western clothes. Cheek by Jowl's Bianca reversed the exposure. She was a walking sado-masochistic fantasy, a *white man's* fantasy, straight out of *Pulp Fiction*, with black, black hair, red, red lips, pale, pale skin – and high, high heels. And enough metal strapped to her to open a hardware store. This Bianca said nothing about what women are – but everything about the tropes that crowd the desiring (white) male imaginary.

Such design doesn't decorate. It interprets, supporting the detailed actorly and directorly work of interpretation that constantly produces the fresh insights for which Cheek by Jowl is known. In *Macbeth* the little Macduff boy, a product of the disturbed times, played war-games at his mother's feet while she complained of the husband who'd left his "nest" unprotected; his grown-up incarnation was Edgar in *Lear*, who started out as a "retarded adolescent forever playing childish wargames with toy swords before learning to kill in earnest" (Dobson 2003: 284). Strangling Desdemona, Anozie's Othello lifted her, choking, by the throat and held her over his head. Saved, but not by his sister, Claudio pushed Isabella roughly away. Blinded, Gloucester's sightlessness plunged the whole theatre into darkness. In *The Winter's Tale*, Mamillius, whispering in his mother's ear, suddenly dragged her violently to the floor, as though infected with his father's disease. A silent hag-like babushka with a broom was constantly present – "one of those battered but dogged women always sweeping the debris after the killer tornadoes engineered by the murderous messiahs who have ruled Russia intermittently since Ivan the Terrible" (John Peter, *The Sunday Times*, May 16, 1999). But after the interval, she suddenly straightened, threw off her rags, and revealed herself as Time, now young, hopeful and healing. In the statue scene, which ended not as a miracle of warm life restored but as animation suspended, the family frozen, all of them statues hardened by loss, it was Time who passed through the court, leading the dead child Mamillius by the hand, allowing him to reach out – rebuking? forgiving? – to the father who'd squandered his life before moving on.

While Michael Bogdanov in the late 1980s staged modern dress productions of the histories as investigations of public life, yob culture, and the ugliness of "this England" – a trashy "precious stone" set in a polluted sea of despair (*Richard II*, 2.1.50, 46) – Donnellan and Ormerod used the comedies (and tragedies) to explore another branch of politics, sexual politics, in an England whose undisclosed private practices surfaced in disturbing, and wonderful, ways. Politics in ESC productions brayed. In Cheek by Jowl's productions, politics toyed and fumbled, grinned goofily and suffered. And perfected the arts of the double bluff and the double take. Clearly, like Bogdanov seeing popular culture everywhere in Shakespeare fighting to be put in view, Donnellan and Ormerod saw erotic culture offering up untold Shakespeare stories from a Shakespeare occupying pervasively and ambiguously charged sexual territory – and they didn't tiptoe through it.

In *Twelfth Night*, Feste was "a white-faced-and-gay Fool," not a "detached, witty observer" but "an active participant in the pursuit of love" for whom an "indiscreet episode with Aguecheek ('gracious fooling') was an embarrassing memory." But "he had great hopes of Cesario" – and went off trilling "I Feel Pretty" (Cochrane 1987: 89). All Illyria's relationships were sexually conflicted. Was it the boy, Cesario, Orsino longed to kiss, women he felt contempt for? Was it the woman Olivia desired, drawn against the "bias" of "nature" (5.1.252)? What was it that continually had to be "shh-ed" up between Antonio and Sebastian? At the end, Orsino nearly went off with Sebastian, Antonio looking on devastated, until Feste sidled up and introduced himself. In *Much Ado About Nothing* Messina was full of Hooray Henries in "dandyish Edwardian uniforms," wrote Benedict Nightingale, who lived as though life were one continuous "rowdy hunt ball, or a regimental thrash." Drink and horseplay: were they covers or cures for the men's sexual unease? Was the jokey homoeroticism actually homophobia dressed as camp? Duke Pedro, "clearly the sort of chap for whom towel-flicking in the locker-room" was "not just hearty fun," made desultory passes at Beatrice "probably only to reassure himself that his feelings for Claudio" were "weaker than they are" (*The Times*, June 8, 1998). It was only when Benedict burst into tears as the truth of Beatrice's love finally hit him that masculinity appeared able to break through the mask of stultifying child's play and take on women face to face. As Donnellan staged it, Messina was a disturbing, bitter-hearted place.

Not all of Cheek by Jowl's bright ideas come off. ("I have no taste," Donnellan cheerfully admits. "And my partner ... has less" [Donnellan 2003: 165]). But when the ideas do come off, they click into place like the optician's instrument that gives you 20/20 vision. In *Othello* when Ryan Kiggell's Cassio tried to pacify Kirsty Besterman's sadie/max Bianca with a promise of "convenient time" to "strike off this score of absence," he offered her the handkerchief; then, as she suspected the gift – "This is some token from a newer friend" – answered with a gesture, moving to the wall, bracing himself against it, buttocks thrust out as if inviting sodomizing, and flinching with shudders of pleasure as she slowly whipped him with the handkerchief while she laconically talked him through its provenance. He climaxed; wiped his groin; held the damp handkerchief out – "I'ld have it copied" (4.1.173–4, 176, 185). And in the later scene she furiously returned it to him, stuffing it into his protesting mouth – momentarily suffocating him. This scene was stunning not only in its radical reappraisal of the woman-idealizing Cassio and the "magic" in the handkerchief but in

FIGURE 18.2 Orlando (Scott Handy) and Rosalind (Adrian Lester) settle down to wooing games in Arden in Cheek by Jowl's *As You Like It* (1991)

Photogaph by John Haynes. Reproduced with permission of Cheek by Jowl.

its alert theatrical fashioning of a terrible parallel: this public schoolboy-fantasy Bianca flagellating the sexual-repressive Cassio was playing out, for kicks, a deeply clichéd jealousy/punishment scenario – that elsewhere was no cliché, offered no kicks, and would end not in sexual "dying" but the real thing.

One final example comes from Cheek by Jowl's most celebrated production, the all-male *As You Like It* (1991, revived 1994), with Adrian Lester playing Rosalind (Figure 18.2). No attempt was made at female impersonation. From the opening moment when, the full company on stage, Jacques began, "All the world's a stage / And all the *men* and *women* merely players" (2.7.138–9), it was clear that the ten who stepped left on cue were the "men," the two who stepped right, the "women": the clothes on top were markers, but maybe also red herrings. So Rosalind's disappoint-ment – then indignation – in Arden was palpable when, learning who the arboreal graffitist was, she *saw him coming*, placed her body to best female advantage inside Ganymede's trousers, batted her eyes, hallooed, "Do you hear, forester?" (3.2.272) – and watched Orlando turn *and see a boy*! In that shocked silence when he couldn't see through her clothes to the "real" Rosalind and so failed to recognize her, she made her decision: she'd *stay* cross-dressed! In the play's final moments, a reversal equally painful, equally comic occurred. A figure walked on in a dress, but when Orlando lifted the veil and Rosalind smiled, he recoiled, appalled – he saw Ganymede – *in skirts*! Turning away he was furious at the disastrously miscalculated joke, bewildered, bitterly disappointed that for him there would be no "hey nonny nonny" wedding. Only when the Duke embraced his *daughter* did Orlando's stunned face swivel around, his eyes registering a complete wipe of his gender memory as his arms reached out to the person he now saw as Rosalind.

At least, that's what *I* saw. Because, extraordinarily, at the end of *this* production, everybody saw something different: Peter Smith, a Rosalind "rejected" by an Orlando who "staggered back and shoved her from him," only recanting when, hearing her "submit herself to male authority figures," he crossed "downstage to claim his wife" – but "the damage had been done" (Smith 1992: 74). Nightingale, an Orlando fascin-ated equally by the wooing games with Ganymede and the flirtatious attentions of a would-be sugar-daddy Jacques. ("Homo, bi, trisexuality" was "all about" in this Arden.) So when he lifted the veil and twigged the truth, shied off "in conventional dismay," then returned, he was an Orlando who'd "had doubts all along" but now accepted "the scope and contradictions of his sexuality" (*The Times*, December 6, 1991). Paul Taylor saw in Orlando's "brief outbreak" a "little pang for the displaced 'Ganymede' " (*Independent*, December 6, 1991); Peter Holland, masculine pride taking a tumble: Orlando stalked upstage because he was "shocked at the trick and shamed at his failure to have recognized her" (1997: 94). "You've got to forget to know," says Donnellan of theatre. In this *As You Like It*, you did.

Profiling the company in 1991 Simon Reade wrote, "There's a spirit in Cheek by Jowl which is intimate but raucous, private yet public, cerebral yet celebratory. They play with a play, make theatre in a theatre, dramatise the dramatic … Never shy, never cynical, their productions celebrate both the play and the art of theatre itself. Theirs is the regeneration game" (1991: 11). A decade on, that's still true. But equally, as Donnellan and Ormerod have gone on to premiere plays such as Tony Kushner's *Angels in America* and *Homebody/Kabul* alongside Shakespeare, plays with exposed political nerve endings, they've found Shakespeare's sharper political edge. Their Shakespeare is not an establishment playwright. Quite the opposite. "You have to do a lot of really quite desperate things to make Shakespeare appear to support the status quo," says Donnellan drily (*Guardian*, June 15, 1994). And it certainly doesn't trouble them that he's occasionally an "offensive" playwright – because "the opposite of offensive is inoffensive … and there's nothing worse than a work of art that is inoffensive" (Donnellan 2003: 166).

Regional Returns

Bogdanov and Donnellan wanted a theatre that reclaimed Shakespeare for the popular audience. Barrie Rutter wanted more: a theatre that reclaimed Shakespeare for the kind of "popular" actor Shakespeare himself was when Robert Greene, *c*.1592, mocked him as the "upstart crow." For unlike Donnellan and Bogdanov, Rutter is first and foremost an actor. By 1992 most of the standard exclusions regulating who played what on Shakespeare's English stage – race, gender, age, body form – were under sustained attack and falling. Comments from reviewers like he's too "young to play Lear," "chubby to play Hamlet," "short to play Hal," "black to play Banquo" persisted, but sounded increasingly bizarre. One remained. Accent. Voices like Rutter's have never been cast as Shakespeare's kings – not at the RSC and National. Why not? Because he has a strong Northern accent, and, as every English schoolchild, thoroughly indoctrinated in the legacy of the late Victorian cultural hi-jack of "the Bard," used to know before Broadsides came along, Shakespeare is "posh" (see Chillington Rutter 2003). His kings "talk posh": they talk poetry; they talk "RP." *Clowns* talk prose, low "funny talk." So as poetry and RP mark the elite, the prose demotic and regional accent (which also, in England, is class accent) mark the plebeian comic. Plebs need not apply for elite Shakespeare roles, unless, of course, they're willing to erase their real voice or to become bilingual – and many are. Not Rutter. He'd acted at the RSC long enough in the 1970s to know that his voice would always ghettoize him, so when Bill Bryden recruited him to the National to work on the Leeds-born Tony Harrison's *Mysteries*, he went – and stayed when Peter Hall invited him to work on Harrison's Aeschylean trilogy. The *Oresteia* (1981) was written entirely in poetry – poetry for kings, captives, messengers, shepherds, gods alike. And it was written, quite specifically, *for the northern voice.* Rutter spent the 1980s collaborating on various projects with Harrison, who constantly raged against Thatcherite economic and artistic policies that effectively excluded the plebs from culture, thereby rendering culture "elite" – and legitimating that exclusion. With such a mentor, Rutter discovered the politics of his own voice. The result was Northern Broadsides, the actor-led company Rutter founded in 1992 whose mission was to deliver what the name promised, verbal attack: Shakespeare performed in a Northern voice pitched to do for him what Jimmy Porter had done for the rest of the British theatre back in 1956, to end the myth of mystification and to put Shakespeare acoustically into the equivalent of modern dress in front of audiences who heard him as one of "uz" not one of "them."

Northern Broadsides's inaugural production was *Richard III* – a canny choice, since the Richard of history, a Yorkshireman born and bred in the North, gave Rutter the one king in the canon that "naturally" talked Northern.[6] Reviewing *Richard*, Irving Wardle loved it. "Some extraordinary things," he wrote, "happen to the lines" as "Elizabethan English comes into Yorkshire close-up" (*Independent on Sunday*, July 25, 1992). But John Peter witheringly dismissed it as "karaoke theatre" (*The Sunday*

Times, December 13, 1992), and the *Evening Standard*'s Michael Arditti thought Rutter's efforts put "regional actors back where they began: as comic relief" (*Evening Standard*, December 11, 1992). Charles Spencer, however, first aligned himself with Peter, but then found he sided with Wardle: "I confess I thought it sounded dotty, but the weird thing is it works ... Shakespeare sounds terrific in authentic Northern voices. The flattened vowels, dropped aspirates, and use of words like owt and ee ... give the language a real immediacy and speed" (*Daily Telegraph*, December 14, 1992). And Aleks Sierz was delighted to hear "none of the plummy, tight-arsed home county accents normally associated with the bard" (*Tribune*, December 18, 1992). It's an interesting comment on cultural life in Britain in the 1990s that, writing about class accent, review discourse permitted itself language long banished from discussions of race.

Twelve years on, Northern Broadsides has normalized the Northern voice to Shakespeare the way Cheek by Jowl normalized cross-cultural casting and erotic mischief. The gains are palpable: Rutter's actors speak Shakespeare with "a real immediacy and speed," early modern English in "close-up" with the present, matching the presentational quality of the Northern voice to disciplined attention to the formal qualities of Shakespeare's verse. As Robert Butler has observed, on Broadsides's stage, "No one lingers": characters speak verse "because it's the fastest way to make themselves understood" in a story-driven theatre that allows "no room for displays of sensibility, which so often slide in, like double-glazing, between us and the play" (*Independent on Sunday*, October 15, 1995; *Independent*, June 20, 1993). Northern speech, shortening vowels, hitting consonants, produces a powerful travelling language that, collapsing pronouns and connectives, accelerates the verse line while punching out the nouns and verbs that drive the argument of the speech and the pace of the play. "With" becomes "w'," "him," "'em," "to do," "t'do." One consequence is that playing times shorten, and audiences, probably for the first time in their lives, hear Shakespeare at tempo, hurtling, with no time for second-guessing, through the poetry-packed obstacle courses of his plays, *A Midsummer Night's Dream* in 130 minutes, *King Lear*, 2 hours 25 minutes, *Antony and Cleopatra*, 2 hours 30 minutes. Play here is urgent, speech a parcel of argument, not a cue to pause for interpretation or internalization. As Broadsides played it, Lear's row with his daughters weighed in like a street brawl, and his curse of Cordelia, uttered, it seemed, on a single breath, hit her like the storm that later flattened him. Shylock, daffing aside mercy, released in Portia a tirade – no sweetness in the quality of *her* mercy – that pinned his ears back even if it didn't change his mind. The grieving queens in *Richard III* were not *Sound of Music* wailers but Aeschylean harpies – "From forth the kennel of thy womb ..." (4.4.47) – and next casting for the witches in *Macbeth*. The Merry Wives, comparing letters, plotting revenge on Falstaff with wicked relish, made each word a world of anticipation – "entertain him with hope, till the wicked fire of lust have melted him in his own grease" (2.1.68) – and frank-talking Anne was her mother's daughter. Marry a gormless git, and a Frenchman to boot? "I'd rather be set quick i'th'earth / And bowled to death with turnips" (3.4.83–4). The Northern voice is not a "polite" voice, and listening to it speak Shakespeare, audiences become aware how much rough-and-tumble, how much verbal warfare explodes in the plays: Antony v. Cleopatra, Macbeth v. his conscience, Beatrice v. Benedick, Capulet v. his daughter (and Egeus and Leonato v. theirs), Juliet v. the priest, the potion, and dead Romeo, hunchbacked Richard v. his ghosts and Henry V v. his father's legacy. It's a voice that produces sound from the bowels, not the throat, and shifts the center of gravity from the head to the gut: words like "hope," "womb," "blood," "body," "love" deepen in delivery, and lines like "my heart misgives me," "a lass unparalleled," "old men forget," "Take her or leave her," "Madam, you have bereft me of all words," "The barge she sat in" sound current.[7] And because of its cultural associations, this is a voice that gives as much power to women as men.

Visually, Northern Broadsides's signature is as instantly recognizable as Cheek by Jowl's – not least because both, to begin with, were too poor for flourishes. Broadsides's first designs restated in material terms the company's working-class roots and felt right at home in the working-class venues (derelict mill rooms, an empty boathouse, a former wool-combing shed, the sale ring in a cattle market) that served for performance spaces. Richard Gloucester wore a wooden clog on his gammy foot – the kind mill workers in the north of England wore on shop floors right up to the day those industries died, post-war. The Battle of Bosworth was staged as a clog dance, the armies – men and women alike in industrial boiler suits – lined up opposite each other, stomping their advance, retreat and rout in a deafening thunder of clog-on -stone, Richard riding a mill cart for a horse, swinging a wool hook. His abrupt death silenced the din. The actors unlaced their clogs, dumped them in a heap, and stood, silent, in peace. Clog dancing produced a physical – and acoustic – analogue to the percussiveness of the Northern voice: in *A Midsummer Night's Dream* the fairies at the end literally "rock[ed] the ground" (4.1.84); the masked ball in *Much Ado* and Capulet's "accustomed feast" (1.2.19) in *Romeo* clattered and banged instead of gliding and swooning, and the Witches in *Macbeth* beat out their waywardness in their footfall. This sort of expressive minimalism was used to brilliant effect in *Antony and Cleopatra*. Actium set both boiler-suited armies on stage, facing out, behind oil drums; the battle, all sound, building up from slow beating, then accelerating, army answering army: defectors abandoning Antony by crossing sides, amplifying Caesar's sound, Cleopatra dropping sticks to flee, Antony, missing a beat, then following. Faltering, the Egyptian drums tried to pick up the war rhythm again, lost it – and one by one fell silent. In *King John* war again was percussion: two massive kettle drums mounted on low trolleys stood in for the armies, wheeled and shoved into conflict like monstrous warhorses. Caught in the deafening cross-fire, little Arthur crouched center-stage, hands pressed against ears, wide-eyed. In *Lear*, the storm was heard a long way off, a rumble that finally crashed over Lear – and the audience – terrifyingly relentless, wave upon wave of sound.

On Broadsides's near-empty (but increasingly, visually sophisticated) stage, costumes and props signify much. In their original *Richard*, as the demon-king's victims died, their personal effects were hung up on the industrial fence that backed his claims

– the princes' school caps, the upstart Rivers's wide-boy jacket. The fur coat that made whoever wore it queen was finally slipped by Richard off Anne's back and hung carelessly over the throne, waiting its next wearer, as he shoved his redundant queen into oblivion. In *Dream*, the woods were a strip of green carpet unrolled by a tumbling fairy, the purple flower, a bunched silk handkerchief that magically divided as Oberon reached for it. Cleopatra's asp was a necklace clasped around her throat; Shylock's destruction, Antonio slowly sliding the yamulke off his head; Lear's madness, the king in a string vest, bowling an industrial-sized cotton reel as if it were a boy's top; Falstaff's come-uppance, discovery under Herne's oak, got up like a stag (or cuckold?), antlers made from bicycle handlebars (complete with bell) attached to a kitchen colander wedged onto his head (Figure 18.3); the witches' vanishing, a fall face down, invisible against the surface that, burnt orange like their costumes, absorbed them. In *Henry V* the stage was a wooden-O of honey-colored pine, set low enough for actors to step over, simultaneously a magic circle where a muse of fire could flame, the vasty fields of France where warriors preened, the loneliness wrapped round the king in his midnight meditation. In *Macbeth* the heath was a rough square patch of tangled carpet; surrounding it, a metal catwalk that groaned and clattered as men crossed it. A beautiful, stylized *Merchant of Venice* was set on a raised white platform, cut down the middle by a straight strip of blue, with miniature bridges – little Rialtos – set at either end.

When Declan Donnellan says that "Theatre is the actor's art, first and last. And what happens in the theatre is that the actor communicates with the audience through the imagination" (*Guardian*, December 10, 1988), he could be talking about Northern Broadsides. Like Donnellan's company, Rutter's is a tight ensemble that lets spectators get up close to actors, close enough to see Edmund's smile twitching as his father reads the (forged) letter he supposes tells Edgar's heart; close enough to see the beefy servants in the Page household, caught out by the contents of the last buck basket, exchange shrewd looks before attempting to shift this next one; to watch the tears silently slide down Octavia's face as she learns of her husband's return to his "Egyptian dish" (*Antony and Cleopatra*, 2.6.123); to notice Snug, the tongue-tied little joiner, at the second rehearsal of *Pyramus and Thisbe*, his eyes widening in silent terror, as Bottom invents prologue after prologue, transforming the Lion's part into a major speaking role. Up this close, spectators can observe Shakespeare building plays out of acting parts, seeing Fluellen, for example, as the spine and masculine "default position" of *Henry V*, a theatrical alter-ego not just to Pistol but to Harry.

Ten years ago, some reviewers still operating under outmoded drama school regimes that heard the actor's voice not as the sound of his selfhood but as something to correct, dismissed Northern-voiced Shakespeare as an affectation, a gimmick – or a defect that could be cured. They had little way of knowing that Northern Broadsides would have such staying power; indeed, would animate a new regionalism, securing a local audience who didn't think Shakespeare's voice as Broadsides spoke it needed curing, and a local base. In 1995 Sir Ernest Hall, owner of Dean Clough in Halifax, formerly the largest carpet mill in Europe but now housing everything from work-

FIGURE 18.3   Falstaff (Barrie Rutter) ambushed by fairies at Herne's Oak in Northern Broadsides's *The Merry Wives* (2001)

Photograph by Nobby Clark.

shops to an art gallery, offered Northern Broadsides a vaulted underground space in which to play. Not insignificantly, perhaps, it used to be a "space between" connecting two workhouses in the mill. The Viaduct Theatre is Broadsides's permanent home in the North. And from the Viaduct, the view across Britain's post-Thatcher landscape looks very different from what the metropolitan bias in the arts imagines. At the mill when Broadsides are in town there's little sense of the North being culturally deprived, of lives languishing on the wrong side of the Trent, of waiting hungrily for a London (or Stratford) Shakespeare company to appear. In among a Viaduct audience there's mostly a sense of "London? What London?" now that Shakespeare is recognized as a local lad.

Wrighting the Radical Future

Bogdanov, Donnellan, Ormerod and Rutter haven't spoken their last words on Shakespeare. The histories they started 25 years ago are still in the making. In their time, they've extended Shakespeare's playing field immeasurably, not just in the UK but world-wide, opening him up to new audiences, performers, venues, performance styles, and visual vocabularies, and seeing him as a playwright in urgent dialogue with the present. They've politicized Shakespeare, popularized Shakespeare, eroticized Shakespeare, de-class-ified Shakespeare, put color into him and given him new voices. But if they're radicals, they're also conservatives: their theatre, like Shakespeare's, is an actor's theatre; their companies, ensembles; their poet, a wrighter of theatre language that structures and sustains actors' performances while demanding from them discipline and craft. From the margins, these practitioners have re-sited the center. Today, anybody who wants to know what Shakespeare "means" in performance has to take account of them. They, of course, are less interested in chewing over the past than imagining the future: the play, the *next* production, is "the thing" (*Hamlet*, 2.2.581). So keep your eyes peeled and your ears cocked. The way the mavericks get around, they're quite possibly coming to a theatre near you soon – or to a space they'll transform into one. And it's a sure bet they'll be bringing Shakespeare with them.

NOTES

1   All citations of Shakespeare are from Stephen Greenblatt et al., *The Norton Shakespeare*.
2   For a full production listing for the English Shakespeare Company, see www.members.aol.com/engshakes.
3   Screened on BBC2, April 1997.
4   For a full production listing for Cheek by Jowl, see www.cheekbyjowl.com.
5   The productions I refer to are Orson Welles's film *Othello* (1952); Trevor Nunn's BBC Channel Four television film (1990) made in association with the Royal Shakespeare Company from his RSC theatre production (1989); Oliver Parker's film (1995); and Gregory Doran's RSC stage production (2004).
6   For a full production listing for Northern Broadsides, see www.broadsides.com.
7   *The Merry Wives of Windsor*, 5.5.192; *Antony and Cleopatra*, 5.2.305; *Henry V*, 4.3.49; *King Lear*, 1.1.206; *The Merchant of Venice*, 3.2.175; *Antony and Cleopatra*, 2.2.197.

REFERENCES AND FURTHER READING

Cites for reviews and directors' commentaries are taken from cuttings held in records volumes at The Shakespeare Centre Library.

Beauman, Sally (1982). *The Royal Shakespeare Company: A History of Ten Decades*. Oxford: Oxford University Press.

Bogdanov, Michael (1988). "Sexual Politics." In Graham Holderness (ed.) *The Shakespeare Myth*. Manchester: Manchester University Press.

Bogdanov, Michael (2001). "Playlist," BBC Radio 3 Shakespeare Lecture. Available at: www.bbc.co.uk/radio3/playlists/Bogdanov.shtml.

Bogdanov, Michael & Pennington, Michael (1990). *The English Shakespeare Company: The Story of "The Wars of the Roses" 1986–1989*. London. Nick Hern Books.

Cheek by Jowl: www.cheekbyjowl.com.

Cochrane, Claire (1987). "*Twelfth Night*." *Cahiers élisabéthains* 32: 88–90.

Dobson, Michael (2003). "Shakespeare Performances in England, 2002." *Shakespeare Survey* 56: 256–86.

Donnellan, Declan (2003). "Directing Shakespeare's Comedies." *Shakespeare Survey* 56: 161–6.

Elsom, John (ed.) (1989). *Is Shakespeare Still our Contemporary?* London: Routledge.

English Shakespeare Company: members.aol.com/engshakes.

Eyre, Richard & Wright, Nicholas (2001). *Changing Stages: A View of British Theatre in the Twentieth Century*. London: Bloomsbury.

Goodwin, John (ed.) (1983). *Peter Hall's Diaries*. London: Hamish Hamilton.

Greenblatt, Stephen et al. (eds.) (1997). *The Norton Shakespeare*. London: W. W. Norton.

Hodgdon, Barbara (1991). *The End Crowns All: Closure and Contradiction in Shakespeare's History Plays*. Princeton, NJ: Princeton University Press.

Holderness, Graham (ed.) (1988). *The Shakespeare Myth*. Manchester: Manchester University Press.

Holland, Peter (1997). *English Shakespeares*. Cambridge: Cambridge University Press.

Jackson, M. P. (1989). "*The Wars of the Roses*: The English Shakespeare Company on Tour." *Shakespeare Quarterly* 40: 208–12.

Northern Broadsides: www.northern-broadsides.co.uk.

Reade, Simon (1991). *Cheek by Jowl: Ten Years of Celebration*. Bath: Absolute Classics.

Rutter, Carol Chillington (2003). "Rough Magic: Northern Broadsides at Work at Play." *Shakespeare Survey* 56: 236–55.

Smith, Peter J. (1992). "*As You Like It*." *Cahiers élisabéthains* 42: 74–6.

Thomson, Peter (2001). "Shakespeare and the Public Purse." In Jonathan Bate & Russell Jackson *The Oxford Illustrated History of Shakespeare on Stage*. Oxford: Oxford University Press, pp. 160–75.

Trussler, Simon (1994). *The Cambridge Illustrated History of British Theatre*. Cambridge: Cambridge University Press.

Wells, Stanley (1989). "Shakespeare Performances in London and Stratford-upon-Avon, 1986–7." *Shakespeare Survey* 41: 159–82.

19

Inheriting the Globe: The Reception of Shakespearean Space and Audience in Contemporary Reviewing

Paul Prescott

In the mid-1990s the South Bank of London witnessed the most important innovation in British Shakespearean performance practice since the founding of the Royal Shakespeare Company in 1960–1. In order to distinguish it from the Globe Theatre on Shaftesbury Avenue, and to sell more tickets, the new theatre was rebranded with the (inauthentic) title "Shakespeare's Globe." The opening of this theatrical space within a few hundred yards of the site of the original(s) marked the climax of decades of campaigning and research, and the beginning of an ongoing experiment in "authentic" staging. For the optimistic, the project offered an authorially intended, unmediated access to the plays, an education in their original performance conditions commingled with the chance to inhabit a quasi-spiritual location. For the cynic or agnostic, the enterprise too closely resembled the recently opened EuroDisney for comfort, and threatened to descend into a commercial exercise in ersatz. From its inception, the Globe not only has provoked controversy but constitutes one of the key sites for the cultural contestation of Shakespeare. While it has long since proved its commercial value (regularly attracting audiences of 90 percent capacity upwards), the Globe's cultural capital remains a subject of debate, a debate that inevitably centers on the question of what constitutes Shakespearian authority and authenticity.

What follows analyzes this debate as it has taken place in the columns of national newspapers. The hundreds of reviews written in response to Globe productions in the seven years since its reopening offer insights into both the characteristics of an interpretative community and the cultural status of Shakespeare at the turn of the twentieth century. Newspaper theatre criticism is a key genre for the study of Shakespeare and performance. Since the age of Garrick, newspaper critics have played a key role in mediating and circulating performance in the public sphere. For most readers, the review-text stands in and substitutes for the experience of performance, thus blurring the boundaries between performance and criticism, production and reception. Marvin Carlson writes:

> Since theatre analysis in the past has emphasized the study of the text and of the performance over the study of reception, it has given almost no attention to those elements of the event structure aside from text and performance or of the larger social milieu, which may be as important to the formation of the reading of the experience as anything actually presented on the stage. (1989: 90)

Carlson cites such elements as publicity, programs, and reviews as vital in mediating between performance and spectator, "suggesting to the latter possible strategies and mechanisms to be employed in reading performance" (1989: 94). Since Carlson wrote that, many performance historians have indeed sought to move, in Barbara Hodgdon's words, "beyond text-centered analyses to situate spectators and their reading strategies as the primary objects of investigation" (1998:171). In her exploration of the London reception of Robert Lepage's *A Midsummer Night's Dream*, Hodgdon argues that it is possible to read the discourses of national newspaper critics as not only "a struggle over the meaning of theatrical signs but as symptomatic of current cultural anxieties about gender, race, and nationality" (1998: 173).[1] And in his discussion of Globe performativity, W. B. Worthen describes "the press's general condescension to (and ritual skewering of) the Globe's foreign, tourist audience" (2003: 102). Here, I want to look at this condescension and skewering, and the anxieties motivating it, in some detail. I am, therefore, not strictly concerned with onstage performance at Shakespeare's Globe; rather, my interest lies in considering how a community of professional interpreters have responded to and made meaning from the Globe's "garrulous and energetic performativity" (Worthen 2003: 101). In short, I am interested in how the most influential and widely read critics of Shakespearean performance have inherited the Globe.

Rather than offering a year-by-year survey of which productions and performances have been favorably or unfavorably reviewed, and why, I instead focus on the representation of space and audience in the review discourse, for it is in the rhetorical depiction of Globe audiences and the evaluation of Globe space that the critical anxiety about Shakespearean authenticity is most complexly registered. It is an anxiety provoked, I will argue, by unresolved tensions between national identity and global tourism, between high and low cultural forms, and between incommensurable constructions of "Shakespeare."

Michael D. Bristol argues for an awareness of the public playhouse as "a politically significant *mise-en-scène*," a communicative space which is not "an empty or uncluttered space in which a message is disseminated without interference"; on the contrary, the theatre is always and "already full of sound and of other socially significant semiotic material. In such a state of affairs, a serious dislocation of authority is not only possible but likely" (1985: 5, 111). In its emphasis on "the immediate social purposes of theater . . . over the specialized appreciation of durable literary values," the festive theatre offered an interlude from authorized activity, "an escape from supervision and from surveillance of attitude, feeling and expression." Such an escape enabled a subversive form of spectatorship, and with it the possibility of "vernacular misinterpretations of high culture" (Bristol 1985: 4, 112, 123). Similarly, Robert Weimann claims that the early modern theatre was characterized by the presence of multiple, often discordant authorities. "Contrary to the sanctioned modes of authorizing political, ecclesiastical, and juridical types of discourse, the theatre could not but acknowledge as authoritative the provision of pleasure." What was so potentially radical about this acknowledgment was its situating of power in the act of audience reception: "Authority in this theatre . . . needed to be validated by the audience and was unlikely to result without the cooperative effort of the audience's 'imaginary forces' " (Weimann 1988: 403, 405).

How can Bristol and Weimann's insights into early modern playgoing speak to our own historical moment? Shakespeare's Globe has been since its opening one of the most *popular* performance venues in London. Does its distinctively festive atmosphere, buoyed up by the presence of so many tourists and holidayers (late modern equivalents of Bristol's carnival spectator, enjoying an interlude between periods of the authorized activity of labor) lead to the same dismantling of authority Bristol diagnosed in the early modern popular theatre? Might that dismantling of authority be all the more violent and noteworthy given the now high cultural status of Shakespeare? Finally, if Bristol's theatregoers were free from the "surveillance of attitude, feeling and expression," can the same be said of contemporary Globe visitors, given the presence of theatre reviewers, the "uniformed members of the public" (Shuttleworth, in Stefanova 2000: 83) who mediate and evaluate the cultural worth of the theatrical event?

Damn Yankees: Reviewing the Shakespearean Audience

First, it is necessary to acknowledge that many reviewers have commented positively, in an uncomplicated fashion, on the aura and authenticity of the Globe. Particularly during the Globe's opening two seasons, a number of critics were attracted by the venue's perceived ability to bring the viewer "closer" to Shakespeare. In the first full season, Charles Spencer wrote that the staging of *Henry V* was "as close as we are likely to get to what watching a play in Shakespeare's day was like" (*TR* 17.12: 729);[2] the following season he reiterated that "there are moments at the Globe when one feels closer to the spirit and the sense of Shakespeare than anywhere else" (*TR* 18.11: 690). John Gross, in describing the "magical" atmosphere of the space, concurred that "every so often it makes you feel in touch with Shakespeare as no other theatre can —

with the Elizabethan Shakespeare, that is, the one whom his first audiences actually knew" (*TR* 18.11: 691). Shakespearean presence also underscored Robert Butler's verdict on *Julius Caesar*: "It's as if, inside this particular building and presented in a certain way, the cast lock into a forgotten radio frequency. When they hit on this waveband – as they do here – Shakespeare seems closer than ever" (*TR* 19.11: 671). The unmediated strains of Shakespeare FM were also audible to Roger Foss, for whom the cast of *Cymbeline*'s "communication with the audience resounds across the ages with digital clarity" (*TR* 21.14: 909). The Globe represents "Shakespeare as Shakespeare intended" (Holden, *TR* 19.11: 673), offers a glimpse into "Shakespeare's enigmatic heart" (Spencer, *TR* 19.11: 702), promises "a spine-tingling experience, listening 400 years later to the words of the poet in his own home, as it were" (Gore-Langton, *TR* 21.11: 670). What is surprising, however, is how infrequently this "closer to Shakespeare" motif surfaces in most Globe reception. With the exceptions of Charles Spencer (*Daily Telegraph*), Michael Coveney (*Daily Mail*) and Susannah Clapp (*Observer*), no critic returns with any consistency to the idea that the Globe affords unmediated access to its proprietor playwright. For the majority of reviewers, there is something irritatingly obstructing, both figuratively and literally, their access to the Shakespearean stage. That something is the Globe audience.

Much of the Globe's *raison d'être* rests on its offer of restored Shakespearean authenticity. An enormous amount of care and pride has been taken in the production of material facsimiles, from the first thatched roof built in London since the Great Fire, to the minutiae of musical instruments and costume. The Globe's niche in the economy of modern Shakespearean production largely depends on these markers of authenticity. We are even assured that beneath their costumes, the actors are sporting authentic early modern underwear, although, like the existence of newsreader's trousers, this must be taken on trust. Clearly the most obvious obstacle to authenticity is the irredeemably contemporary audience, which, no less than the roar of a 747's engine overhead, is a constant reminder of the impossibility of stepping back in time, of fully restoring the Shakespearean stage. How can early modern, if inevitably invisible, underwear hope to compete with the semiotic burden of a postmodern, highly visible audience?

The visible positioning of the standing audience between the critic and the stage, and the perspectival disruption this causes, are mentioned in a startling number of reviews. In the 1999 season, Michael Billington complained that "seated in the lower gallery you become unduly aware of the chatting, chaffing and canoodling going on in the yard in front of you" (*TR* 19.16: 1004); in 2003, Billington was again distracted by "the endless gropings of the groundlings" (*TR* 23:13: 817). Georgina Brown agreed in 2000 that "if you sit in the stalls, there's a lot of drama to take in before you come to the stage itself with the groundlings lolling in the pit, eating, drinking, chatting, snogging" (*TR* 20.11: 691). In these accounts, the piling up of verbs of consumption and concupiscence curiously recalls Philip Stubbes's description of an early modern audience in *The Anatomie of Abuses*: "such laughing and flearing, such kissing and bussing, such clipping and culling, such wincking and glauncing of wanton eies, and the like, is vsed, as is woonderfull to beholde" (Stubbes 2002: 203–4). The cumulative depiction of the Globe audience, and specifically the groundlings, that emerges from reading reviews may not be predicated on Stubbes's overheated anti-theatricalism, but nevertheless shares his critique of spectatorship and distrust of a carnivalesque crowd.

Notably, audience allusions are generally rare in theatre reviewing. That the audience has generated so much commentary in Globe reception is, of course, partly a direct consequence of its visibility in largely day-lit outdoor performances. The critical awareness of the Globe audience is also inevitable given both the theatre management's policy of encouraging an informal relationship between actor and audience as a marker of authenticity, and the simultaneous project to highlight the contrast between conventional theatrical architecture and etiquette and that at the Globe. However, the frequency with which critics comment on audience reaction or interaction in Globe reviews is striking, especially so given that the default option in theatre reviewing is to avoid all mention of the audience. With the possible exception of children's shows, unconventional physical theatre, or unscripted interventions, it is almost a matter of principle for many reviewers to ignore audiences altogether, as it is widely recognized that press night audiences can be crammed with claques of relatives and friends, and that their inevitably enthusiastic response should not be used as a guide to artistic or commercial quality. One might, of course, object that critics are more likely to comment on and evaluate audience behavior in *any* open-air Shakespeare event. The Globe, after all, is not unique in offering a season of outdoor performances. As a point of comparison, which will help tease out the unique rhetoric of Globe reviewing, let me briefly summarize the critical attitude to Shakespeare performances at The Open Air Theatre, Regent's Park.

Overall, what is striking about Regent's Park reviews in relation to those of Globe productions is the *absence* of the open-air audience. The audience is rarely mentioned or characterized in reviews, and it is never represented synecdochally by an individual audience member. Of all the critics, only Madelaine North and Fiona Mountford in *Time Out* convey the anti-populist strain that is so common in Globe receptions. Reviewing the 2000 production of *Dream*, North wrote that the lack of directorial innovation in the production would not "worry the Open Air's average audience member," and concluded "it's serviceable Shakespeare for the deck chair crowd" (*TR* 20.12: 762). Of the following year's *Love's Labour's Lost*, Mountford wrote of the temptation for directors to "stage an unimaginative Shakespeare-lite production, safe in the knowledge that the masses will flock to drink their alfresco Pimms anyway" (*TR* 21.12: 759). Although Pimms is hardly the opiate of choice for the masses, these comments are consonant with the strain of Globe criticism that accuses productions of pandering to a lowest-common-denominator, culturally impoverished audience.

North and Mountford, however, are exceptional among reviewers of Regent's Park productions in foregrounding the audience. Most reviews contain no mention of audience response. When Michael Billington does comment on the open-air audience, it is only to contrast it favorably with that of the Globe. Responding to the 1998

Troilus and Cressida, he approved of how "no one hisses Achilles or boos Diomedes as they might down at the Globe; the audience simply engages with the argument," adding that "there is none of that hideous faux-naiveté which in Southwark turns Shakespeare's plays into The Perils of Pauline" (*TR* 18.12-13: 784). In his review of the 2001 *Love's Labour's Lost*, Billington also praised Regent's Park Shakespeare for having "none of that fatal audience self-consciousness you find at other open-air venues" (*TR* 21.12: 758), which is another way of saying that the audience did not impinge on *his* consciousness. The Globe is also, unwittingly, invoked in Robert Hewison's response to the 2000 *Dream*: "[l]ed by Paul Bradley's am-dram aficionado Bottom, the groundlings stay solidly and entertainingly in the real world" (*TR* 20.12: 761). Hewison could only have meant "mechanicals" when he wrote "groundlings," but the subconscious association is intriguing. Is it that the pantomimic, misguided efforts of the amateur theatricals, not to mention their low social status, reminded Hewison of the Globe audience?

Many reviewers critique the Globe audience in an off-hand, but loaded way; they may talk of "groundling-pleasing excess" or criticize an actor for "playing to the gallery" – a metaphor, as the critic actually means playing to the yard. On other occasions, the reviewer composes a group portrait. Since the staging of authenticity is a social event, it is unsurprising that many critics are prompted to offer quasi-anthropological accounts of the neo-Elizabethans in the yard. Perhaps the least flattering portraits can be found in reviews of the 2000 season. On the press night for *The Tempest*, the heavens opened and many of the groundlings donned plastic Pacamacs, leading no fewer than three critics to compare them to condoms or "a convocation of contraceptives" (Nightingale, *TR* 20.11: 693). The condom, which affords short-term pleasure without long-term repercussions, is a fortuitously apt symbol for an audience critics depict as more interested in fun than profundity. Responding to the controversial *Merchant of Venice* in 1998, David Nathan worried that "when an audience is on its feet, it loses any sensitivity it might individually possess" (*TR* 18.11: 691), a phenomenon known to group psychologists as "risky shift." Critical anxiety about the Globe audience's lack of sensitivity registers in a number of reviews. Alastair Macaulay claimed that "the audience is never so happy as when it can boo, hiss, cheer, or roar with laughter" (*TR* 18.11: 689), while Stephen Fay corroborated the image of subnormal intelligence: "They respond well to music, especially if encouraged to clap" (*TR* 20.11: 692). In these two accounts, actual noise, whether of hissing or clapping, becomes symbolic noise, signifying cultural incompetence.

These constructions of a vulgar, lowest-common-denominator section of the audience set the tone for much of the critical coverage devoted to the groundlings in subsequent Globe seasons. By the third season, Roger Foss worried that "[m]aybe a Globe audience can't be expected to pay attention to a serious thought or a poetic allusion for much longer than a sound-bite" (*TR* 19.16: 998). Attention deficit disorder was also diagnosed by other critics. In its second season, both Rhoda Koenig and Billington rhetorically set the theatre management a stark choice: "when it must choose between customers who care about poetry and those who want souvenirs, it's clear which kind it wants to cultivate" (Koenig, *TR* 19.16: 1003); "is it an artistically ambitious organisation? Or is it content to go on churning out inexpressibly dreary productions, such as this *Julius Caesar*, to restless, inattentive, largely tourist audiences?" (Billington, *TR* 19.11: 673).

The presence of the audience in Globe reviews is at its most striking when the critic shifts focus from the general to the particular. Many reviews feature a vignette of an individual audience member (almost invariably a groundling) whose stupidity and restlessness are offered as a synecdoche of the problematic audience. These would-be representative anecdotes often involve direct quotation, and tend to specify the culprit's nationality. Thus, Macaulay was distracted by two men having a conversation in Spanish (*TR* 19.16: 1000), while Paul Taylor's concentration on *Henry V* was broken by "a young Japanese woman" sitting next to him, "who kept a camera trained on the production throughout as though it were some extended alternative to the Changing of the Guard" (*TR* 17.12: 726). Hannah Betts, in the process of despairing at some "idiot gag-milking" in *Cymbeline*, dropped her head into her hands, only to witness "a mulleted German youth, hitherto insufficiently impressed to raise his eyes from his Gameboy, [jump] up and down with glee" at the offending idiocy (*TR* 21.14: 912). For Robert Gore-Langton, *King Lear* "even survives the backchatting of Americans ('Hey, honey, he just got mad at Cordelia!') and confused Swedes" (*TR* 21.11: 670). This, it could be argued, is the heteroglossic condition of both carnival and contemporary, global theatre-going, and London's critical community is clearly uncomfortable with it.

As in Gore-Langton's anecdote, the foreign body foregrounded in reviews usually belongs to an American. On leaving his seat and descending among the groundlings at *Julius Caesar*, Billington found himself "surrounded by snickering American jocks who were so caught up in the play that they supplemented the wails that greeted Caesar's ghost with their own derisive groans" (*TR* 19.11: 673). The same critic's appreciation of "To be or not to be" likewise had a transatlantic nemesis: "some Yankee tourist...wrestling with his crinkly Pacamac" (*TR* 20.12: 755). Charles Spencer claimed that the same tourist should have been "tossed into the Thames" (*TR* 20.12: 756) by the ushers, and, appropriating the authority of Hamlet/Shakespeare, found comfort in the fact that "the Globe's audience got on Shakespeare's nerves too."

Frequently in these anecdotes, American characters function as culturally incompetent counterpoints to the critic. Carole Woddis began her *Herald* review of *Macbeth* with direct quotation: "'My heart sank,' said the American beside me; 'here I am at Shakespeare's Globe and they're all in tuxedos.' There you have it in a nutshell," Woddis asseverated, "Is the Globe part of the English Heritage tourist trail or a living, breathing, risk-taking, theatrical organism?" (*TR* 21.12: 750). As with Koenig's comment on the incompatibility of "souvenirs" with "poetry," Woddis presented tourism as inimical to theatrical health. The vocabulary of her Heritage-bashing betrays the intellectual genealogy of her position: "living, breathing...

organism" bears the unmistakable marks of New Left and New Wave rhetoric, and behind that, the socio-literary criticism of F. R. Leavis and T. S. Eliot. Fiona Mountford began her *Time Out* review of *Cymbeline* with a similar exposé of American cultural illiteracy: "'Is Cymbeline a tragedy or a comedy?' an American tourist asked me as I loitered outside the Globe" (*TR* 21.14: 909); Mountford omitted mentioning that few actors, directors, academics or other professional Shakespeareans would pretend to know the answer to that question. On his way into the Globe in the opening season, Robert Butler walked past "a dapper American TV presenter... talking to camera: 'For an audience,' he enthused, 'this is as close as you can get to an Elizabethan theatre-going experience.' It was a dismal endorsement," sighed Butler (*TR* 17.12: 724). In all three examples, the naivety of the American is contrasted with the artistic, generic, and cultural sophistication of the (British) critic.

Audience impropriety was similarly registered in a number of reviews of *King Lear*. Apparently, when Edmund asked the audience which of the sisters he should take, "Both, one, or neither?" a woman in the crowd had responded "Both!" Benedict Nightingale described the woman "as a cheery bimbo in row C... sounding as if she were at a Chippendales strip-tease" (*TR* 21.11: 668), but Charles Spencer went further, describing her as "the American lady" who behaved not only "as if watching a baseball game," but also, to compound her low cultural profile, "screamed like a member of the *Blind Date* audience." Spencer, who has already flexed his muscular attitude in wishing for a Yankee to be drowned in the Thames, now felt "like ramming her programme down her throat" (*TR* 21.11: 668). Maddy Costa in the *Guardian* at least had the honesty to admit that "there's nothing quite like it for making one reel with snobbery" (*TR* 21.11: 669).

I am not questioning whether the American audience members mentioned by Billington et al. actually were American; what I find interesting is that the reviewers chose to specify their nationality. Although these anecdotes illustrate a generalized carping about audience etiquette at the Globe, complaint could easily be made without reference to nationality. After all, the man wrestling with his Pacamac need not be identified and labeled as "some Yankee." It is, perhaps, an unconscious decision but nevertheless a decision on the parts of these critics to consider the nationality of audience members significant enough to flag. More particularly, the presence of a generic American tourist in these reviews could be understood in a number of ways. First, it reads as a submerged anxiety on the part of critics about the financial provenance of the Globe, its American-born founder Sam Wanamaker, and the importance of the dollar in establishing and maintaining the Globe – and global – economy. Britain's poor relation status has recently been reinforced in theatrical circles with, for example, the American bailing-out of the *Tantalus* project and the RSC's more general search for patronage from American universities.[3] A second, and contiguous, explanation of reviewers' anti-Americanism relates to a general resistance to the phenomenon of Shakespeare's international popularity: anyone expecting the kind of one-nation, microcosmic little-England-Globe offered by the opening of Laurence Olivier's film of *Henry V* would be jolted by the contemporary reality of the multinational and heterogeneous Globe audience. Either way, there is an overlap here between responses to the postmodern and the early modern spectator. Like their early modern counterparts in Puritan accounts, tourists at the present Globe are skipping work, having a good afternoon – or night – out between periods of authorized activity. The carnivalesque elements of popular theatre that caused Puritan writers so much angst – the holiday cocktail of food, drink, and sex – are also present in contemporary Globe reception.

It is clear that the singling out of incompetent audience members in Globe reviews can also be seen as part of a wider strategy of validating the critic's authority. As Barbara Herrnstein Smith points out in *Contingencies of Value*, normative evaluation and validation rely on standardizing a community's preferences while simultaneously "discounting or pathologizing" other people's tastes. "Thus," she continues:

> it is assumed or maintained . . . that the particular *subjects* who constitute the established and authorized members of the group are of sound mind and body, duly trained and informed, and generally competent, all other subjects being defective, deficient, or deprived: suffering from crudenesses of sensibility, diseases and distortions of perception, weaknesses of character, impoverishment of background-and-education, cultural or historical biases, ideological or personal prejudices and/or undeveloped, corrupted, or jaded tastes. (1988: 41)

The caricaturing of the Globe audience in newspaper reviews can be seen as part of a wider anti-heritage strain in contemporary journalism and cultural commentary, and one which seeks to pathologize the tastes of the tourist. "The charge of vulgarity," as Raphael Samuel writes, "is a leitmotif of heritage criticism, and may account for the frequency with which heritage is bracketed with theme parks, toytowns and Disneyland" (1994: 265). Samuel continues:

> For the aesthete, anyway for the alienated and the disaffected, heritage is a mechanism of cultural debasement. It leaves no space for the contemplative or solitary. It forbids discrimination and the exercise of good taste. Its pleasures are cheap and nasty, confounding high and low, originals and copies, the authentic and the pastiche. It brings "crowd pollution", in the form of mass tourism, to sacred spots. (1994: 268)

All this is entirely consonant with the fears of most reviewers when confronted with the Globe experience. Whether it is the crudeness of the mulleted German, the underdeveloped tastes of the simple-minded groundlings, the perceived cultural impoverishment of the American who doesn't know what type of play *Cymbeline* is, or the weakness of character and lack of *savoir faire* that allows the "cheery bimbo" to answer Edmund, Globe audience members function not only as implicit contrasts to the trained competence of the reviewer, but as a damning commentary on a project that confounds cultural hierarchies, originals and copies, and brings crowd pollution to the potentially most sacred spot in Shakespearean theatre.

"Arsenal/Tottenham": Reviewing the Shakespearean Space

The critique of the Globe audience, whether generalized or specific, is compounded by a series of analogies that run throughout the theatre's reception history. Comparing the heckler at *King Lear* and an audience member at *Blind Date* or a Chippendales show discursively transforms the Globe into a low cultural arena, no different from those that house tabloid television or soft porn. Similar critical maneuvers compare the Globe, on numerous occasions, with the music hall or pantomime – traditionally, working-class forms of theatre. Indeed, the term "pantomime" has a very high frequency in Globe reviews. In 1997, Macaulay complained of *Henry V* that "[t]hough Rylance & Co. could have invited audiences to behave with the high-spirited seriousness of Albert Hall promenaders, they have instead encouraged them to behave as if these plays were Christmas pantomimes" (*TR* 17.12: 730).[4] The Proms were also in John Gross's mind: "[o]ne wouldn't want to see the last-night-of-the-Proms treatment applied to *Hamlet* or *Lear*, but it doesn't seem unreasonable when it comes, say, to heckling the Dauphin" (*TR* 17.12: 731).

Popular sporting events are also invoked in the effort to describe the social atmosphere of the Globe. Jane Edwardes, in *Time Out*, wrote in the 1997 season that "the atmosphere is one of a football match and it demands its stars and their followers . . . If Rylance is a Ryan Giggs, the present company still needs a Shearer and a Seaman" (*TR* 17.12: 724).[5] It is now hard to imagine the theatrical equivalent of David Seaman – when Edwardes wrote that, Seaman connoted "a safe pair of hands," an association that has since lost its currency – but then Edwardes's analogy is hyperbolic in the first place. Behavior at football matches is governed, or sometimes fails to be governed, by very different codes than those pertaining at most theatres, no matter how much audience participation they encourage. Yet the comparison resurfaced in Patrick Marmion's verdict that "the Globe's volatile dynamics . . . encourage actors to play to the gallery [read "groundlings"], so reducing the intellectual atmosphere to the level of an Arsenal/Tottenham football derby" (*TR* 18.11: 691), a sentence designed to strike fear into the heart of any sophisticated urbanite.

The analogy between a football crowd and the Globe audience has been more positively circulated both in Globe conferences and in publications appearing under the theatre's auspices. At the International Shakespeare Globe Centre conference in April 1995, Franklin Hildy gave a paper on audience dynamics in which he "related the Elizabethan playgoers to latter-day 'fans' at sporting events or rock concerts and suggested that, given the right chemistry, future Globe audiences would react in a more fan-like manner at Globe performances than they would in a conventional theatre setting" (Nelsen 1995: 28). Six years previously, when the theatre was still in its embryonic phase, Andrew Gurr wrote that in Shakespeare's theatre "The conditions and the time of day were closer to those for a modern football match than a play" (1989: 53). And in *Shakespeare's Globe Rebuilt*, the post-opening sequel to Gurr's study, Mark Rylance illustrated the theatre's "Artistic Policy and Practice" with a footballing anecdote:

At a football match some time ago a perfect stranger turned to me during play and gave me his full opinion of the quality of the game and what should be done about it. I experienced the same easy communication between strangers while watching [Northern Broadside's 1995] *A Midsummer Night's Dream* at the Globe. (1997: 171)

Curiously absent from these reflections on theatre, sport, and social engineering is any mention of Bertolt Brecht. Indeed, Rylance's "stranger," in his ability to step outside the excitement of the event and offer a reasoned analysis, closely resembles the ideal spectator of Brecht's "smokers' theatre." In a fragmentary note, Brecht wrote that "I even think that in a Shakespearian production one man in the stalls with a cigar could bring about the downfall of Western art" (1964: 8). In the elision of sport and theatre lay a liberatory potential:

There seems to be nothing to stop the theatre having its own form of "sport." If only someone could take those buildings designed for theatrical purposes which are now standing eating their heads off in interest, and treat them as more or less empty spaces for the successful pursuit of "sport", then they would be used in such a way that might mean something to a contemporary public that earns real contemporary money and eats real contemporary beef. (1964: 6–7)

The Globe clearly does mean something to our contemporary public. But for critics accustomed to treating Shakespearean performances as interpretation rather than mere "play" or "sport," Globe productions tend to offer few interpretive, Shakespearean "discoveries." Michael Billington argues that reviewing Shakespeare involves the optimistic quest for insights: "one is always looking for new discovery, some new awareness, some moment in the text that you've never really discovered before. Discovery is what you are after" (personal interview, June 2000). Worthen describes a similar terminology (and its interpretive implications) in academic performance criticism: "Hapgood and others assign the Shakespearean text a more overtly theological function: the text determines a range of potential meanings which the performance works to discover" (1997: 164). In 2000, Billington felt that he had not "yet found any Shakespeare play coming alive in that space in the way that it does in a controlled environment," and that none of the productions had "enhanced my understanding of Shakespeare in any way" (personal interview, June 2000). Could this be because an "uncontrolled," playful environment such as the Globe is inimical to the presentation of "discovery," if discovery is conceived as directorial interpretation and insight into character or theme? As Rylance prophesized before the theatre's official opening: "It will be very difficult to 'present' a play there, to present a 'solution' to a play. An audience responds to the playing" (1997: 171). In this sporting environment, the critic, denied a modern "reading" of the play, in turn responds to the audience response.

In their concern with audience response, national newspaper critics are positioning themselves as critics of reception in addition to their more obvious function as critics of Shakespearean performance. Adapting the perspective of reader-response theory to the act of theatrical spectatorship illuminates a key dynamic of Globe reviewing. Hans Robert Jauss argues that reception involves "the carrying out of specific instructions in a process of directed perception, which can be comprehended according to its constitutive motivations and triggering signals" (1982: 23). Before encountering a work of art, the reader-spectator will have internalized a framework of ideas and values which form a horizon of expectations against which the new art work will be judged. As Susan Bennett writes, "[a]t its first publication/performance, a work is measured against the dominant horizon of expectations. The closer it correlates with this horizon, the more likely it is to be low, pulp, or 'culinary' art" (1997: 49). When the Globe's actors and audience are associated with indigenous forms of popular theatrical entertainment, such as the pantomime or the music hall, or with *Blind Date* and the Chippendales, or with football – *the* center of British popular culture – the theatre is being found guilty by association of correlating too closely with low cultural forms. Indeed, the idea of culinary art is strangely literalized in some Globe reviews when they comment on the food and drink available for purchase in the theatre. Alastair Macaulay's steady course of disenchantment with the theatre, for example, can be traced in his attitude to the culinary dimension of the Globe experience. Reviewing *The Winter's Tale* in 1997, he wrote: "[t]he atmosphere is relaxed, with drinks and food being quietly sold from time to time in the central promenade area. In the intervals, you can buy bagels and champagne and consume them by the Thames, looking over to St Pauls [*sic*]" (*TR* 17.12: 723). Four years later, however, in a review that begins with the bald verdict "[t]he worst Shakespeare in London is usually whatever's on at Shakespeare's Globe," the presence of the culinary is no longer so civilized. When Macbeth said "Come, seeling night," the "come" was apparently taken as a cue "for uniformed flunkies in the middle-tier audience boxes to start serving chipolata sausages and other buffet food to the toffs seated there" (*TR* 21.12: 748). In Macaulay's complaint we can see the results of optical chaos: the critic's gaze is torn between high and low cultures, and the meaning of Shakespearean performance must somehow reconcile Macbeth's soliloquy with an all-too conspicuous act of consumption.

The coordinates of many reviewers' lowest expectations of the Globe are made clear in reviews of seasons 1997–99. In 1997, Benedict Nightingale wrote approvingly that "[t]he thatched-and-timbered cylinder opposite St Paul's is not going to be a theme-park for trippers or a playpen for academics" (*TR* 17.12: 723; the phrase is recycled almost verbatim in Nightingale's review of *Hamlet*, *TR* 20.12: 756). These worst case scenarios also surfaced in Paul Taylor's review of the same production: "A tourist-trap-cum-playpen-for-cranky-academics? The Globe can be infinitely more" (*TR* 17.12: 726). Notably, both Nightingale's and Taylor's images infantilize academic spectators. Within two years, many critics had decided that the Globe had failed to steer a consistent course past the Scylla of tourism and the Charybdis of academia. For Michael Billington in 1999, the theatre was "[c]aught halfway between academic exercise and tourist totem," and needed to "urgently rethink its future" (*TR* 19.11: 673).

In the theatre's defense, Sheridan Morley wrote that "the Globe may well be at its best when filled not by theatregoers but by schoolchildren and scholars desperate to see Sam Wanamaker's impossible dream made timber" (*TR* 19.16: 1000). Despite differing attitudes to the value of the theatre, both Billington and Morley share the assumption that tourists, schoolchildren, and scholars are in a mutually exclusive category to that of "theatregoers." And this despite, or perhaps because of, the fact that the Shakespearean theatrical economy (whether in London, Stratford, North American festivals, or elsewhere) is heavily dependent on tourist and school group bookings.

In their anxiety about the low cultural atmosphere of the Globe, these reviews reveal a more general concern with what conditions of production and reception are most appropriate, even authentic, for Shakespeare's plays. The critique of the perceived pantomimic, sporting, Disneyfied and multinational Globe audience is motivated by the assumption that none of these conditions is appropriate to the perpetuation of what is valuable in Shakespeare. Subtlety, sub-text, psychology, thematic and linguistic complexity are the characteristically valorized concepts of twentieth-century Shakespearean criticism and reception. Since a majority of reviewers studied English as undergraduates at a time when New Criticism dominated English studies, it is therefore unsurprising that the values of that methodology inform their collective construction of Shakespeare. The Globe, seemingly led by its audience, is frequently found wanting in its ability to reproduce these values. In a bizarre trope, the would-be authentic space for Shakespeare, the facsimile of the theatre in which many of his plays premiered, is repeatedly critiqued as unworthy of his plays.

Writing about the Globe's second season, Macaulay opened his review of *The Merchant of Venice* with this injunction: "Go to Shakespeare's Globe and discover why, in Shakespeare's day, his plays seemed no greater than those of several other playwrights" (*TR* 18.11: 689). Macaulay's argument, in essence, was that the Globe space dumbs down all it contains, leveling Shakespeare to the reduced stature of his contemporaries. Implicitly, he suggests that Shakespeare's peerlessness, his supremacy over all other playwrights, only became apparent with the advent of naturalism and inhibited audiences. Indeed, surveying the reception of non-Shakespearean Globe productions throws a revealing sidelight on reviewers' Shakespeare. Take, for example, Kate Kellaway's verdict on Middleton's city comedy: "*A Chaste Maid in Cheapside*, directed by Malcolm McKay, is a play for groundlings and last Wednesday a responsive audience had a great time of it – spitting, hissing and cursing [really?] – just as Middleton would have liked" (*TR* 17.17: 1084). In addition to implying that there must also be plays that are *not* for the groundlings, that are so much caviar wasted on the general, Kellaway further invoked authorial sanction for the "spitting, hissing and cursing." Significantly, I have not found one example of a reviewer using Shakespeare in the way that Middleton is used here: as an authorizing presence for audience participation. On the contrary, in the Globe's first full season, Jane Edwardes commented that the open-air audience was so distracting that "for all we know

Shakespeare let out a sigh of relief when his plays were moved indoors" (*TR* 17.17: 1082). Robert Gore-Langton in a similar maneuver offered the hypothesis "that when the original Globe burnt down, Shakespeare himself torched it out of frustration at the awkward working conditions that have now been so lovingly recreated" (*TR* 19.11: 673). Hannah Betts, also speaking on behalf of Shakespeare's real feelings about the Globe, claimed that while the theatre may have captured Shakespeare's imagination when it first opened, "it wouldn't do much for him today" (*TR* 21.14: 912). The Lazarus Shakespeare also made an appearance a hundred years earlier in Max Beerbohm's verdict on William Poel's Elizabethan Stage Society: "if Shakespeare could come to life again he would give Mr Poel a wide berth, and would hurry to the nearest commercial theatre in which a play of his happened to be running" (Beerbohm 1969: 222).

"Bringing People Together": Global Differences

The staging of authenticity is a social event. In all theatre, as Anthony B. Dawson writes, a "habit is put into play, an institutional one specific to theatre in which we might say that social ritual is "remembered" and a temporary community nostalgic-ally configured" (1999: 62). That nostalgic configuration is the subject of intense scrutiny in the staging of Shakespearean authenticity. In the 1890s and early 1900s Max Beerbohm objected that Poel's attempts at historical reconstruction were doomed as "we, in the twentieth century, cannot project – or rather retroject – ourselves" into the original audience's "state of receptivity" (1953: 258). Beerbohm then devoted much of his review, not to the production, *Twelfth Night*, but to an analysis of the contemporary audience and the motivation of its desire for this nostalgic configur-ation. Beerbohm's epithet for the members of the Elizabethan Stage Society was "owlish," "implying a certain rather morbid and inhuman solemnity and a detach-ment from the light of day" (1953: 258). Almost a hundred years later, the reception of Shakespearean authenticity is once again permeated by audience analysis. But that audience is no longer the archeological, dusty and nocturnal Edwardians Beerbohm mocked; rather, the contemporary Globe audience is defined by its multinational, hedonistic, and day-lit characteristics.

In reading theatre reviews for evaluative patterns and ideological subtexts, I do not mean to conduct a witch-hunt of critics, outing some as xenophobic, others as conservative or elitist. Every theatregoer at some point has had the experience of being irritated or distracted by their fellow audience members. It could also be argued that much of the criticism of Globe productions has been justifiable. Freud, warning against over-interpretation, allegedly advised "Sometimes a cigar is just a cigar." Similarly, sometimes a bad review is just a bad review, a bad show just a bad show. As W. B. Worthen had to admit when discussing the antagonistic reception of a Peter Sellars production: "It is possible, of course, that the kind of acting that Sellars developed for *The Merchant of Venice* was just plain bad" (1997: 86). Arguably, many

Globe productions have been "just plain bad" – under-cast and unimaginatively directed. Yet much of what appears in Globe reviews seems to be energized by a response to something other than onstage blocking, diction, and characterization, or any other component of what is traditionally defined as "the performance." Rather, much of the hostility in Globe reviews stems from a number of deep-seated cultural presuppositions: (1) that audiences at Shakespeare, if they must be seen, should not be heard; (2) that the requisite atmosphere for Shakespearean reception is one of silence and reverence, like that of the naturalistic theatre, or indeed, the act of reading; (3) that Shakespeare – but *not* his contemporaries – had a low opinion of the groundlings and preferred the higher culture of indoor theatre; (4) that foreign audience members are liable to be disruptive and incompetent readers of drama, and are prone to come between the Englishman and his Shakespeare; and (5) that "Shakespeare" should exist in a discrete cultural sphere, uncontaminated by contact with popular cultural forms such as television, pantomime, or football. It would be quite possible, of course, to criticize Globe productions without holding any of these assumptions. Hannah Betts's verdict that "the Globe serves up a lowest common denominator *non speaka da lingo* farce that you wouldn't wish upon your least favourite au pair" (*TR* 21.14: 912) says more about the social situation and privileged day-care arrangements of the writer than it does about the theatrical merits, or otherwise, of Mike Alfred's *Cymbeline*.

In a 1988 interview, Graham Holderness asked Sam Wanamaker whether he thought that the Globe, when constructed and opened to the public, would "represent a genuine ground of international solidarity and friendship." Wanamaker responded: "If we are looking for forces to bring people together whatever their language, social status, culture, educational level; and if we seek within English culture a fitting representative figure manifesting the language and people, where else would we look but to Shakespeare and a few other great writers?" (Holderness 1988: 19). This is an attractive, idealistic image of the globally cohesive power of performance and of communal space. In much of the Globe's reception, however, we see the results of the implicit tensions of Wanamaker's utopian project. If Shakespeare manifests English culture, language, and people, *which* aspects of this culture does he embody? How is it possible to represent a distinct idea of Englishness (for Wanamaker this clearly is what is at stake) and simultaneously to include the foreign or the culturally incompetent without threatening the ideal self-conception of the privileged national culture? Pierre Bourdieu writes that "the sacred sphere of culture" is defined by its denial of "lower, coarse, vulgar, venal, servile – in a word, natural – enjoyment." That denial, he suggests, "implies an affirmation of the superiority of those who can be satisfied with the sublimated, refined . . . distinguished pleasures forever closed to the profane. That is why art and cultural consumption are predisposed, consciously and deliberately or not, to fulfill a social function of legitimating social differences" (Bourdieu 1986: 7).

In July 1993, Wanamaker was made a CBE in recognition of his work on the Globe and for the "remarkable contribution [he] has made to relations between Britain and the United States" ("Biography of Sam Wanamaker"). Although it could not have been predicted at the time, the next decade would prove that part of that remarkable contribution was to create a space in which the special relationships (or social differences) between the indigenous and the foreign, and between high and low national cultures would be provoked and brought to light through the apparently cohesive force of Shakespeare.

NOTES

1 Other interesting examples of reviewer-reception can be found in the works of Daileader, Osborne, Roberts, Rutter, and Werner listed in the further reading

2 For the sake of brevity and ease of consultation, all review quotations are sourced to their reprinted appearance in *Theatre Record* (*TR*) in the seven volumes between 1996 and 2003 (vols. 16–23). So, for example, (*TR* 20.12: 687) denotes that the review is reprinted in vol. 20, issue 12, and can be found on p. 687.

3 John Barton's epic treatment of Greek myth and history premiered in November 2000 at the Denver Center for the Performing Arts as a co-production between that institution and

the RSC, the latter having failed to raise sufficient funds to produce the event exclusively.

4 The Henry Wood Promenade Concerts, or Proms, is an annual two-month festival of mostly classical music held at the Royal Albert Hall, London. Those who "promenade" pay a small amount of money to stand, like the Globe's groundlings, in the center of the auditorium. Audience participation is more or less limited to the licensed raucousness of the Last Night.

5 Ryan Giggs is a mercurial winger, an exciting, crowd-pleasing individualist; Edwardes invokes the footballing careers of Alan Shearer and David Seaman as patterns of consistency and "team-player" professionalism.

REFERENCES AND FURTHER READING

Beerbohm, Max (1953). *Around Theatres*. London: Rupert Hart-Davis.

Beerbohm, Max (1969). *More Theatres: 1898–1903*. London: Rupert Hart-Davis.

Bennett, Susan (1997). *Theatre Audiences: A Theory of Production and Reception*. London: Routledge.

"Biography of Sam Wanamaker" (n.d.). Shakespeare's Globe website: www.shakespeares-globe.org/navigation/frameset.htm;   path: Reference; Online Reference Library; The Biography of Sam Wanamaker (accessed February 5, 2003).

Booth, John E. (1991). *The Critic, Power and the Performing Arts*. New York: Columbia University Press.

Bourdieu, Pierre ([1979] 1986). *Distinction: A Social Critique of the Judgement of Taste*, trans. Richard Nice. London: Routledge and Kegan Paul.

Brecht, Bertolt (1964). *Brecht on Theatre*, ed. and trans. John Willett. London: Methuen.

Bristol, Michael D. (1985). *Carnival and Theater: Plebeian Culture and the Structure of Authority in Renaissance England*. London: Methuen.

Carlson, Marvin (1989). "Theatre Audiences and the Reading of Performance." In Thomas Postlewait & Bruce A. McConachie (eds.) *Interpreting the Theatrical Past: Essays in the Historiography of Performance*. Iowa: University of Iowa Press, pp. 177–202.

Daileader, Celia R. (2000). "Casting Black Actors: Beyond Othellophilia." In Catherine M. S. Alexander & Stanley Wells (eds.) *Shakespeare and Race*. Cambridge: Cambridge University Press, pp.177–202.

Dawson, Anthony B. (1999). "The Arithmetic of Memory: Shakespeare's Theatre and the National Past." *Shakespeare Survey* 52: 54–67.

Gurr, Andrew, with Orrell, John (1989). *Rebuilding Shakespeare's Globe*. London: Weidenfeld and Nicolson.

Hodgdon, Barbara (1998). *The Shakespeare Trade: Performances and Appropriations*. Philadelphia, PA: University of Pennsylvania Press.

Holderness, Graham (ed.) (1988). *The Shakespeare Myth*. Manchester: Manchester University Press.

Jauss, Hans Robert (1982). *Toward an Aesthetic of Reception*, trans. Timothy Bahti. Brighton: Harvester.

Kiernan, Pauline (1999). *Staging Shakespeare at the New Globe*. Basingstoke: Macmillan.

Nelsen, Paul (1995). "Oaths and Oracles: Will the Globe Spin on an Axis of 'Authenticity'?" *Shakespeare Bulletin* 13, 3: 27–32.

Osborne, Laurie E (1996). "The Rhetoric of Evidence: The Narration and Display of Viola and Olivia in the Nineteenth Century." In Edward Pechter (ed.) *Textual and Theatrical Shakespeare: Questions of Evidence*. Iowa: University of Iowa Press, pp. 124–43.

Roberts, David (2002). "Shakespeare, Theater Criticism, and the Acting Tradition." *Shakespeare Quarterly* 53, 3: 341–61.

Rutter, Carol Chillington (2001). *Enter the Body: Women and Representation on Shakespeare's Stage*. London: Routledge.

Rylance, Mark (1997). "Playing the Globe: Artistic Policy and Practice." In J. R. Mulryne & Margaret Shewring (eds.) *Shakespeare's Globe Rebuilt*. Cambridge: Cambridge University Press, pp. 169–76.

Samuel, Raphael (1994). *Theatres of Memory*, vol. 1: *Past and Present in Contemporary Culture*. London: Verso.

Smith, Barbara Herrnstein (1988). *Contingencies of Value: Alternative Perspectives for Critical Theory*. Cambridge, MA: Harvard University Press.

Stefanova, Kalina (2000). *Who Keeps the Score on the London Stages?* Amsterdam: Harwood.

Stubbes, Philip (2002). *The Anatomie of Abuses*, ed. Margaret Jane Kidnie. Tempe, AZ: Renaissance English Text Society. Originally published 1583.

Weimann, Robert (1988). "Bifold Authority in Shakespeare's Theater." *Shakespeare Quarterly* 39, 4: 401–17.

Wells, Stanley (ed.) (1997). *Shakespeare in the Theatre: An Anthology of Criticism*. Oxford: Oxford University Press.

Werner, Sarah (2001). *Shakespeare and Feminist Performance: Ideology on Stage*. London: Routledge.

Worthen, W. B (1997). *Shakespeare and the Authority of Performance*. Cambridge: Cambridge University Press.

Worthen, W. B. (2003). *Shakespeare and the Force of Modern Performance*. Cambridge: Cambridge University Press.

20

Performing History: *Henry IV,* Money, and the Fashion of the Times

Diana E. Henderson

It is difficult, if not impossible, for most people to think otherwise than in the fashion of their own period.

George Bernard Shaw, Preface to *Saint Joan*

A living theatre that thinks it can stand aloof from anything as trivial as fashion will wilt.

Peter Brook, *The Empty Space*

What dimensions of Shakespeare's historical vision does fashion allow to be performed in this moment, and what role does criticism play in shaping and recording the theatrical fashion of our time? These would seem elementary questions for those concerned with Shakespeare's history plays and their performance. Yet often we take them for granted or consider them unanswerable, instead desperately seeking an ingenious new twist to make old matter our own – which might itself be regarded as symptomatic, a fashion of the time. With this in mind, I want to return to some basics of the Shakespeare trade as now practiced professionally in the United States, tracing their connections to and disconnections from a primary textual pattern within *Henry IV* (especially *Part Two*): the circulation and exchange of money, flesh, and names.

In her 2003 Presidential Address to the Modern Language Association, Mary Louise Pratt suggested the need for interdisciplinary discussions of two topics she considers fundamental to understanding present-day American culture: greed and pragmatism (2004: 427). Viewed thus, the United States could be considered a version of a Falstaff-nation, in which we manipulate any given occasion to indulge our insatiable appetites for consumption. Given Pratt's diagnosis, we should not then find it surprising that the publicity and reviews for the 2003–4 *Henry IV* at New

York's Lincoln Center focused primarily on the figure of Falstaff. The specific terms and mechanisms of that focus nevertheless bear looking into, for they illuminate one of the very few recent spaces of overt cultural convergence melding theatrical practice, literary study, and mass media coverage in American performances of Shakespeare.

Scott McMillin reports that *I Henry IV* in performance "came in the twentieth century to be seen as a study of political power with Prince Hal as the central character" (2003: 312); if so, then this first Broadway production of the twenty-first century signaled either a reactionary impulse worthy of Harold Bloom's return to nineteenth-century character-based Bardolatry or else some new spirit or configuration of forces in the theatre.[1] *The New York Times* abetted the former interpretation, both by repeatedly invoking Bloom's reading of Falstaff and, more generally, by publicizing *Shakespeare: The Invention of the Human.* Furthermore, in the *Lincoln Center Theater Review,* director Jack O'Brien invokes Bloom, and in the Washington, DC-based Shakespeare Theater's program guide during the same season, the first of several quotations about "Falstaff" came from Bloom (Pavlin 2003: 8; *Asides* 2003–4: 10). Even O'Brien's attempt to emphasize an edgier interpretation was framed as a reaction against Bloom. Whereas most professional literary scholars see little new – and a good deal of personal projection – in Bloom's sentimental reading of the fat knight, because print journalism has made Bloom's Shakespeare the dominant paradigm for the theater-going public, he must be acknowledged by those who make their living in theatre.

But this interest also may derive from the fact that, despite Bloom's anti-theatrical preference for reading, his attention to character makes more sense to actors than does most scholarship which academicians consider fresh and important. While finding critical distance and deep structures of significance has been central to humanities research, actors have to go out on a stage and bring a particular character (or several) to life: simultaneously brave and vulnerable as they stand before a paying crowd, they need to know who they are pretending to be. Scholars seek to impart an idea when they speak in public, but actors need to perform a role. All very well to invoke structural patterns, historical allusions, and textual indeterminacy in a classroom, but unless actors can see how those issues are reflected within the language they speak or how issues might be embodied through gesture and positioning, such scholarship will not help get the job done. Even if one grants that experimental and academic theatrical venues often challenge the realist assumptions underlying this modern character-driven form of acting, Actors' Equity performers trying to survive in mainstream theatre seldom get time, occasion, or support to think about doing anything other than making plausible "persons" from their parts. If they fail, they rejoin the vast majority of their colleagues in the unemployment line. And the director who knows the show (and his/her own career) depend upon the creative intelligence of those performers would be unwise to undermine their focus or confidence. It does not take all *that* much pragmatism to see why Bloom's focus on invented humans would be more appealing than, say, attention to early modern economics.

The New Yorker and PBS's *News Hour*, however, confirmed another reason for the renewed focus on Falstaff in the Lincoln Center production: the established star power of Kevin Kline in the role. And here again, late rather than early modern economics play their part. As Julliard graduate, former director of the Public Theater, acclaimed stage Hamlet, and (most crucially) bankable movie actor, Kline is one of the few successful crossover artists who can lure both theatrical veterans and newcomers – and get national media attention. Granted, this was a particularly "star-studded" production (as *Playbill* reinforced), mixing established theatrical headliners with those recognizable from screen performances (Ethan Hawke as Hotspur, Richard Easton as Henry IV, Dana Ivey as Mistress Quickly and Lady Northumberland, Audra MacDonald as Lady Percy), but it was all Kline in the national coverage. Despite Hawkes's presence, this adaptation's condensation of Shakespeare's *Part One* and *Part Two* into a single evening discouraged giving him "equal time" with Falstaff: Hotspur's death before the third and final act subordinated his structural centrality. Furthermore, the not-for-profit Lincoln Center Theater location – where, unlike typical Broadway productions, season subscriptions support most of the limited run – made it possible to market its stars selectively so as to enhance Mr. Kline's – and Falstaff's – comparative stature.

By contrast, the Washington, DC, Shakespeare Theater's 2004 production (of both parts, on separate evenings) emphasized Henry IV. But again the reason appears to have been linked with film – albeit for the arthouse crowd. Keith Baxter's having played Hal in Orson Welles's *Chimes at Midnight* (1966) added cachet to his self-begetting return as Hal's father. In this case – as in Kline's – one could argue that the theatrical companies had found an appropriate way to merge publicity for their show with a display of its artistic strength: Baxter's rendition of an often-thankless part was a highlight of this performance. And again the evidence qualifies McMillin's generalization about recent emphasis on Hal. While the specific character focus differed, in both these theatrical productions the publicity relied upon mass media associations with veteran actors rather than the distinctiveness of live performance. And as with the reiterated attention to Bloom in print, this way of marketing the performances exemplified the commercial angle of the phenomenon known in comparative media studies as "multimedia convergence."

In thinking about this fashion of the times, a paradox, if not a contradiction arises: those who care about keeping the professional theatre lively emphasize its "liveness" as an essential quality distinguishing the relationship between performer and audience – yet that very sense of immediacy is increasingly shaped or informed by more overtly commodified, indirect media encounters. And yet theatre reviewers still tend to express surprise when an actor familiar from the television set, rap music, or popular film can manage the particular demands of stage performance (and they barely suppress their glee when one fails). Unlike Britain, where traditions of state-backed television and radio drama combine with the geographical centralization of various entertainment forms, in the US it remains harder to achieve recognition as an equally adept actor across media. Furthermore, the coastal competition between New

York and Los Angeles aggravates the New York theatre community's (often valid) sense of threat and distinction from the large studio model of Hollywood – even as the success of Disney on Broadway blurs the boundaries. Increasing labor costs, reliance on tourist audiences, and the presence of large studio or multiple-producer shows all encourage safe(r) choices.

It is against this background, then, that the unusual Shakespeare production making it beyond the fringes of the New York Shakespeare Festival/Public Theater takes shape. Seldom do reviewers or even scholars attend to these market forces with anything like the scrutiny accorded them in studies of mass media. Nor do I propose to displace the kind of analysis of specific artistic choices and traditions that makes reading Shakespeare's performance history much more nuanced and enjoyable than are most (rather predictable) sociological analyses of popular culture. We might nonetheless better serve the theatrical performance of Shakespeare in the present moment by balancing knowledge drawn from a wider range of sources along with a pragmatic sense of practice and current possibilities. This includes not only an awareness of the economic conditions of theatre but also renewed attention to those very "literary" dimensions of performance that the past generation of scholarship has worked to displace. To be sure, such displacement was a necessary corrective – within both academia and theatrical practice. But now it seems timely, at least in the United States, to reconsider the interplay between words and theatrical performance – not as yet another reactionary impulse, but as a newly-informed, pragmatic next step. Let me then turn back to the texts of *Henry IV* before returning to these modern performances, and talk more pointedly about war, money, and words.

Economies of Exchange

At the dead center of the *Henry IV* plays stands the figure of Rumour, History's secret sharer. His arrival to open *Part Two* makes explicit the unreliability of report – especially war reporting – already evident in *Part One* (in the debate over Mortimer's behavior and the divergent accounts of Bolingbroke's rise). Storytelling easily shifts to telling stories in the "counterfeit" sense – to invoke a word echoing everywhere. But even more disturbing than the ability to spread particular lies is Rumour's power to destabilize the referentiality of all words:

> I speak of peace, while covert enmity
> Under the smile of safety wounds the world;
> And who but Rumour, who but only I,
> Make fearful musters, and prepar'd defense,
> Whiles the big year, swoll'n with some other grief,
> Is thought with child by the stern tyrant war,
> And no such matter?
>
> (Induction. 9–15)[2]

Amidst inversion, that "other grief" – like that in the womb of Richard II's Queen before her husband's fall – remains nameless, murkily undefined; as such, it creates the climate of fear that encourages unnecessary militarism. Rumour also sets the stage for *Part Two*'s disturbing military "climax" at Gaultree Forest when "peace" is reiterated with great intensity to cover (among other things) ambition, conquest, and treachery, and where Prince John (himself a subtle manipulator of language) accuses Archbishop Scroop of "Turning the word to sword, and life to death" (4.1.236) – before deceiving him to death. In these history plays, the always-only conventional and communally sustained assumption of stable correspondence between words and things has come unhinged, and the consequences are fatal.

Even "proper" names are unstable: when Hotspur faces Hal, "Harry is dead" can mean either a battle lost, or won. Directly after Rumour exits, Lord Bardolph enters – not the red-nosed Bardolph of the tavern scenes but a Lord with the "same" name. While the origin for this confusion has been plausibly explained away,[3] the verbal effect compounds and confirms Shakespeare's choice throughout the Lancastrian tetralogy to create doubles (and more) using the same names (Kate, Harry). As here, such doubling ultimately undermines both individuation and class distinction. Bardolph's name repeatedly enters the dialogue before the character familiar from *Part One* arrives, and tellingly it is associated with bargaining and trade – and with the thin line between those activities and fraud, lies, and robbery (see also 1.2.52–3). Encounters and identities echo like the reports of Rumour, enmeshed in a larger system of circulating commodities.

Aptly, then, it is (Lord) Bardolph who quickly establishes *Part Two*'s vocabulary of barter and exchange among the rebel forces even as he upholds a false report, telling Northumberland, "If my young lord your son have not the day, / Upon mine honour, for a silken point / I'll give my barony" (1.1.52–4). Although he invokes a fashionable luxury item dismissively, it will prove more durable than a rebel's barony or the speaker's "honour" – and in the emerging market economy, may prove more valuable too. It is not only in our contemporary world that those plotting war have difficulty listening to unexpected intelligence. In the face of counter-evidence, Lord Bardolph posits that the reporting "gentleman," who (as Northumberland notes) had no reason to lie, was a mere "hilding fellow that had stol'n / The horse he rode on, and, upon my life, / Spoke at a venture" (1.1.55, 57–9). Now wagering "his life" on his opinion, Bardolph discredits the messenger through association with risk, and by reminding us of the transferability of status symbols – in this case, the horse. For the Harry Hotspur whose fate is the subject under inquiry, a "roan" horse had signified chivalric honor (indeed, in a comical rhyme, the "throne" itself; *1*, 2.3.68); with his death, we are reminded that such signs can become devalued through exchange. When Morton gives his eyewitness account, Percy himself is recalled as the metallic substance of rebellion, "For from his metal was his party steeled" (1.1.116) – and without him, they revert into mere "dull and heavy lead" (1.1.118). Post-Hotspur, the coin of the realm has been debased.

Contemplating this military and material loss, Morton reminds the grieving Northumberland that "You cast th' event of war... / And summ'd the account of chance" (1.1.166–7), and Lord Bardolph elaborates:

> We all that are engagèd to this loss
> Knew that we ventured on such dangerous seas
> That if we wrought out life 'twas ten to one;
> And yet we ventur'd for the gain proposed,
> Choked the respect of likely peril feared,
> And since we are o'erset, venture again.
> Come, we will all put forth, body and goods.
>
> (1.1.180–6)

His metaphor comes close to exposing an alternative interpretation of the rebellion, conceived in the most concrete and mercantile of terms. It has nothing at all to do with Hotspur's love of honor yet better accounts for his father's behavior: this is all a gamble of "body and goods" on "the gain propos'd." Rumour has already warned us that the distinctions between wartime and peacetime can be murky; what becomes increasingly apparent, within the play and through subsequent centuries, is that they are all part of market time. Or as Thomas Pynchon would later put it, "Don't forget the real business of the War is buying and selling ... The true war is a celebration of markets. Organic markets, carefully styled 'black' by professionals, spring up everywhere" (2000: 05).

Enter the great corrupter of recruitment, Falstaff, and with him the signifier that binds this emergent system of exchange: money. While many have noted the tonal difference of *Part Two* from *Part One*, the most obvious source of its destabilizing effects is often overlooked or immediately transformed into a spiritual, sexual, national, or familial metaphor. But what happens if we redirect our attention back to the circulation of money itself, the "crowns" and "angels" that reconfigured inherited social and religious hierarchies as material means for exchange?

Falstaff's first scene, which immediately follows Lord Bardolph's exchange, makes explicit the involvement of trade and money in the play's human relations. Falstaff considers his page an object of exchange with the Prince, a jewel/juvenal whom he may send back to the face royal – playing on the coin dubbed the real, or royal. (When the page does follow Hal again, it will be to dishonored death among "the boys and the luggage" at Agincourt.) Mocking the absent Hal for his lack of a manly beard ("for a barber shall never earn sixpence out of it"; 1.2.24–5), Falstaff's words also call attention to his absorption with a system of trade in which, as the very embodiment of conspicuous consumption, he is in constant need (and lack) of money. Upping Lord Bardolph's extraneous "silken point" to fit his monstrous girth, Falstaff is attempting to buy 22 yards of satin for his own garments. But his negotiations with the merchant have hit a snag: the Page reports that Master Dommelton "said, sir, you should procure him better assurance than Bardolph. He would not take his bond and yours; he liked not the security" (1.2.30–2). This sets off Falstaff to rail upon security as knavish and unworthy of a "gentleman" like himself (1.2.35); as ever, he finds a rhetorical solution by exchanging one meaning for another, attacking the sexual rather than economic "security" of the merchant (the stereotype of the merchant's wife being sufficient to create a cuckold). But given Lord Bardolph's prior debasement of a gentleman's title, not to mention Sir John's general demeanor and social location, this resort to the same word holds (unlike Falstaff) no water.

These expository moments with Falstaff establish both the resemblance and difference of *Part Two* of *Henry IV*. Whereas the first, more popular play mocks aristocratic hypermasculinity in the energetic figure of Hotspur, after his death that rhetoric devolves to Falstaff and Pistol: indeed, Falstaff's anger at the merchant's demand mimics Hotspur's initial spleen over the King's unmanly emissary in prisoner exchange. But the violence these tavern roisterers produce results not in battlefield glory but swaggering offstage murder, with the Hostess and Doll Tearsheet likewise implicated (and hence carted away to prison in Act 5). If Hotspur at his worst produced too much hot air, Falstaff produces too much water (as the English Shakespeare Company's production made evident in a sustained auditory joke): both anatomically and verbally, *Part Two*'s "humor" is more base. With Falstaff's first line ("Sirrah, you giant, what says the doctor to my water?" [1.2.1–2]), we have moved away from the always-already outmoded attempt at a glorious feudal economy and into a world of waste products. The body that once bounced back from seeming death now is old and weighed down by mortality.

Falstaff, ever hopeful, may try to "turn diseases to commodity," but his economy is false: unlike a prostitute, he has nothing desirable to offer in exchange (1.2.243). As Doll says of the "huge full hogshead," "There's a whole merchant's venture of Bordeaux stuff in him" (2.4.62–4) – but the only way to tap it is as "water." When we continue to identify Falstaff as consumer of the good life, we overlook this dimension of his bodily experience, more vulnerable in itself and less appealing to witness. Falstaff can only offer witty words – but located within a social world not (yet) willing to disconnect language from material referents utterly, the great consumer will ultimately learn that he too is trading in airy nothing. This aspect of his character cannot be ignored in *Part Two*, and accounts for much of what is missing from Dakin Matthews's adaptation performed at Lincoln Center. Although Kevin Kline achieved a more melancholy note in Falstaff himself, there was little sense of how his wasteful circulation connected with anyone else onstage – much less with the larger thematic doublings, the multiple fathers and sons, and the "honour" of battle.

Yet Shakespeare scripted bodily signs of a more general descent from the symbolic realm of "honour" (repeatedly enacted throughout the Lancastrian tetralogy), even at Shrewsbury. Befitting Henry IV's topsy-turvy reign, it was the lean king rather than the fat beggar who signaled the change. In precisely the way his initial rise to power was accompanied by a parody of feudal ritual (the multiple gauntlet-throwing scene in *Richard II*, 4.1.25ff.), Henry's single represented battlefield triumph is undermined by multiplicity – and *his* multiplicity, in particular. Epitomizing Bolingbroke's craft as a political manipulator, the King's use of body doubles is perceived by the rebels as less than chivalric or manly.

Surrogation – what Joseph Roach has perceived to be the essence of dramatic embodiment – threatens to undo the mystical symbolism of royalty, that singularity and rarity in appearance of which Henry is so conscious when advising his son. My point is that it does so in precisely the form of the emergent money economy in which this dramatically-staged surrogation was being performed: through the circulated image of the king.[4] Aptly, this "counterfeiting" of the King especially frustrates the Douglas, of whom Hotspur affirms (using coinage metaphorically) that "not a soldier of this season's stamp / Should go so general current through the world" (*Henry IV, Part One*, 4.1.4–5). While coinage (like historical drama) was underwritten by representation of the monarch's special image, his stamp, it was repeatedly being devalued during the late sixteenth century. Such changes drove home to its users the potential arbitrariness of any correspondence between metal and mettle (its "buying power"), and increased their consciousness of the variable "substance" accorded value through a process that could also be "counterfeited." The upheavals conjured by what the poet John Donne dubbed the "king's real, or his stamped face," in other words, bring the battlefield strategies of Henry IV up to date and into the commodity culture in which Falstaff, Bardolph, the marketable Doll, and that stealing Spanish-style braggart soldier Pistol(e) seek "crowns, brave crowns" (*Henry V*, 4.4.38). As did Shakespeare's theatre-going audience.

Commodity Production

The economic fashions of the times were changing. Money and words had been perceived as homologous systems, Richard Waswo (1996) reminds us, since the days of Quintilian, being similarly reliant on custom, currency, and the "public stamp." But the specific shift in the usage of the word "commodity" – from a reference to the useful qualities of an object, to an object itself produced exclusively for sale – began during the fifteenth century (1996: 5–6). Aligned with the political shift from late feudalism to the early modern nation-state, this naming and the economic change in priorities that it epitomizes are part of the subject of history in Shakespeare's drama. "Money," Fernand Braudel observes, "is never an isolated reality; wherever it is, it influences all economic and social relationships" – and yet it "never ceases to surprise humanity. It seems to them mysterious and disturbing" (1973: 325). Moreover, "every society that is based on an ancient structure and opens its doors to money sooner or later loses its acquired equilibria and liberates forces thenceforth inadequately controlled. The new form of interchange jumbles things up, favours a few rare individuals and rejects the others." This was the case in Shakespeare's

England, as it faced the "recurring drama" of an extension of the European money economy (1973: 326).

The rapid growth of that economy in the late sixteenth century produced huge and fundamental changes at both the macro- and micro-economic levels, with the growth and increasing "placelessness" of markets, expanding international trade, and inflation (see Agnew 1986). The changes brought both excitement and fear as it was recognized how people's labor and language, indeed their bodies themselves, were part of the mercantile "traffic" in commodities:

> The Prince with his subjects, the Master with his servants, one friend and acquaintance with another, the Captain with his soldiers ... all the world choppeth and changeth, runneth and raveth after Marts, Markets and Merchandising, so that all things come into Commerce, and pass into traffic ... not only that, which nature bringeth forth ... but further also, this man maketh merchandise of the works of his own hands, this man of another man's labor, one selleth words, another maketh t[r]affic of the skins and blood of other men, yea there are some found so subtle and cunning merchants, that they persuade and induce men to suffer themselves to [be] bought and sold. (John Wheeler, *A Treatise of Commerce*, 1601, in Raman 2001: 220)

We certainly see the exchange of money for men in *Part Two*, when Bardolph accepts bribes from Mouldy and Bullcalf to gain exemption from military service. But it is the performative tension between this and an older system of valuation, perceived as ethically superior even if pragmatically stupid, that sustains the drama: the willingness of Feeble to serve his prince poignantly counters the cynicism otherwise encouraged by Shakespeare's representation of recruitment. This is still a world in which Feeble tellingly asserts (twice) that he will "bear no base mind" (3.2.228, 234). Yet doubts about the market in men are not thereby contained, nor confined to the "lowlife" characters and scenes.

Even on the "battlefield" at Gaultree Forest, echoes of this "base" commodification of flesh appear (as they will in *Henry V*'s parallel scene of Pistol and Monsieur Le Fer at Agincourt), in the terms of Falstaff's capture and exchange of one Coleville of the Dale. First, the rebel Coleville is moved to surrender because of Falstaff's (false) reputation – Rumour returning from Shrewsbury. This is Falstaff at his most effective: here his words do win him flesh. But then the two encounter the "victorious" Prince John, fresh from his verbal outmaneuvering of the rebel leaders. Defiantly, Coleville speaks out:

> Had they been ruled by me,
> You should have won them dearer than you have.
> FALSTAFF: I know not how they sold themselves, but thou like a kind fellow gavest thyself away gratis, and I thank thee for thee.
>
> (4.3.63–7)

The prince, however, treats this prisoner-of-war as badly as his elder brother will the French prisoners at Agincourt: he commands that the hapless Coleville be sent "with his confederates / To York, to present execution" (4.3.70–1). Thus Prince John outwits Sir John out of a captive also dubbed (in Holinshed) "Sir John," and deprives Falstaff of ransom. This decision, a chilling commentary on (il)legitimate power, also serves as a reminder of what can happen once words, bodies, and names begin to circulate like money. For, as Shankar Raman notes of Wheeler's passage above, "the qualitative distinctions among these sorts of relationships . . . are gradually dissolved by the market process, the fluid logic of money and commodity circulation" (2001: 221); moreover, "what disappears in the money-form is the uniqueness of the commodity" (Raman, forthcoming). The distinction between a rebel and his leaders, a surrendered prisoner and food for powder, one man and another, recedes. As Braudel remarks, the new "uneasiness" about money was also "the beginning of the awareness of a new language. For money is a language . . . ; it calls for and makes possible dialogues and conversations; it exists as a function of these conversations" (1973: 328). Money changes everything.

"What's aught but as 'tis valued?" Shakespeare's proto-monetarist Troilus famously argues in defense of retaining stolen goods (*Troilus and Cressida*, 2.2.52). Trying to sustain the kind of correspondence theory undergirding precious metal exchange, the ill-fated Hector retorts that "value dwells not in particular will, /It holds his estimate and dignity / As well wherein 'tis precious of itself" (2.2.53–5). Although value in "itself" becomes increasingly difficult to describe or maintain once the marketplace rules, Hector is accurate in thinking that the community creates and sustains that value, not the individual: radical subjectivity, in opinions or trade, is a losing proposition. Money requires partners in exchange. And thus Falstaff, for all his involvement and delight in the material world, falls prey to exactly the new demands for goods, and the confusion of words with commodities, that he has toyed with in self-defense and for self-advancement. Ultimately he cannot, and cannot make, change.

It is the fleshly commodity herself who challenges his verbal rate of exchange: when Falstaff accuses Doll Tearsheet of giving men the diseases he wishes to transform to commodity ("we catch of you; grant that, my poor virtue, grant that"), she retorts in his own rhythms, "Yea, joy, our chains and our jewels" (*Henry IV, Part Two*, 2.4.45–7). Giving more than she gets and aware of which commodities the market will bear, her exploited body contrasts with exploitative Falstaff's. We learn during *Part One* that Mistress Quickly purchased "a dozen of shirts" of "holland at eight shillings an ell" for him, covers his board, "and money lent you, four-and-twenty pound" (3.3.65, 67). By *Part Two*, she is seeking the law's intervention in her vain attempt to recover her expenses, for she has "put all my substance in that fat belly of his," and has been forced to "pawn both my plate and the tapestry" (2.1.73, 138). Though many have concentrated on his ethical lapses, the point here is that Falstaff has no place in the new *financial* order, the economy of crowns-supporting-Crowns that will underwrite Henry V's invasion of France. Laboring only in his own pleasure, Falstaff becomes a sinkhole of consumption and abortive trade, undoing the system that requires (the illusion of) equivalent exchange. He is thus as much a threat to the new mercantile order as he is to the old moral one; he cannot circulate quickly, and his expansive girth expands no markets.

In *The Comedy of Errors*, the plot eddies around the circulation of a 1000 marks; in *Henry IV*, it is, tellingly, a thousand pounds. If the "marking" of the body constitutes a comedy (see Raman, forthcoming), in Shakespeare's histories it is the weight of that synecdoche of rule, the crown, that enters the commodity trade. When this play was first performed, weight was a concern for all traders, involving more crowns of "golden care" than the king's alone (4.5.23). The fluctuating value and amounts of precious metals in coins led to uncertainty, distrust, and the hoarding that spurred the formulation of Gresham's Law: bad money drives out good. The received crown's weight is too much for the dying Bolingbroke, who rests his weary head by removing it, leading to its (limited but disturbing) circulation into another room of the palace, on his son's head. When the King awakes, he too makes the correlation between the crown and its metallic substance, and generalizes the conflict into a social crisis undoing familial loyalty and affecting all inheritance:

> See, sons, what things you are,
> How quickly nature falls into revolt
> When gold becomes her object!
> For this the foolish over-careful fathers
> Have broke their sleep with thoughts, their brains with care,
> Their bones with industry;
> For this they have engrossèd and piled up
> The cankered heaps of strange-achievèd gold . . .
>   (4.5.65–72)

Despite Henry's fears, he has of course created this economy: it is simply that Hal's timing is off. "Piling up" gold, after all, does no good for the nation reliant on marketplace exchange. By placing accumulation in the crown rather than in his own mortal body as Falstaff does, Henry succeeds in passing along the inheritance as he wishes. Ironically, though, the "price" is the devaluation or demystification of the Crown itself, in that only its circulation and commodification allow Henry's goal of succession once direct lineage has been usurped.

Hal takes up his father's mercantile vocabulary along with the crown. In his awkward self-defense for removing the object prematurely, he recalls his (fictitious?) apostrophe to that object:

> The care on thee depending
> Hath fed upon the body of my father;
> Therefore thou best of gold art worst of gold.
> Other, less fine in carat, is more precious,
> Preserving life in medicine potable;

> But thou, most fine, most honored, most renowned,
> Hast eat thy bearer up.
>
> (4.5.159–65)

The crown becomes part of a continuum of gold, comparable to less fine forms in circulation rather than different in kind. Its distinction lies in its greater destructive properties; the object itself becomes the feeder, a projection of human desire turned back upon itself. If Falstaff eats up money, here gold eats up the King. His only relief will come through the ultimate exchange, in which Hal takes on his care and Hal's "wild" ways accompany Henry's dead body to the grave (5.2.122).

This royal (real) movement is made more vivid through contrast with the shadowy (fraudulent) circulation of that large monetary sum – many crowns – from Prince Hal to Falstaff, and from Master Shallow to Falstaff – but *not*, crucially, from the Lord Chief Justice. Refusing Falstaff's request to "lend me a thousand pound" with his curt "Not a penny, not a penny," that figure of the Law provides the proleptic equivalent to Hal's *Part One* banishment warning, "I do, I will" (*2* 1.2.217, 219; *1* 2.4.383). When Henry V takes up his new name, he likewise refuses the further circulation of pounds upon which Falstaff has been banking ("Master Shallow, I owe you a thousand pound" [5.5.72]). Turning instead to the Law, Henry seems to redeem and stabilize the old order. But even if we are among the cold-blooded few, like Prince John, who enjoy this momentary fantasy of an absolute monarch's dream, the play recognizes that the commodity circulation of names, money, and desires has not been halted. And if the epilogue was indeed embodied by Will Kemp, trying to "dance out of your debt," the oscillation between hierarchical and mercantile logic was certainly not over (Epilogue. 19). As the Epilogue describes "the venture" (line 7): "I meant indeed to pay you with this [play]; which, if like an ill venture it come unluckily home, I break, and you, my gentle creditors, lose. Here I promised you I would be, and here I commit my body to your mercies. Bate me some, and I will pay you some, and, as most debtors do, promise you infinitely" (Epilogue. 9–15). Credit is indeed a system of promises for future fulfillment, and the play ends with preparations for a future military venture to France. As the newly crowned monarch asserts, "I will deeply put the fashion on" (5.2.52). But Falstaff, from first to last unable to "secure" credit in the world of finance, is left behind. While tears may be shed and new leaders celebrated, the lesson echoes from early to later modern times, and leads back to the battlefield: it's the economy, stupid.

Disappearing Acts

How did these Shakespearean economies inform what was performed onstage at Lincoln Center during a time of war deeply involved with international (oil) trade, overseas invasion, and (Iraqi) state legitimacy? At the most literal level, they quite simply did not. The figure of Rumour was gone, as were Lord Bardolph and Coleville of the Dale: the names and words that create a destabilizing "modern" market context for the leading characters' story were condensed or removed completely, as was the potentially scathing commentary on war reporting. Instead, the announced and performed emphasis remained on the familiar domestic themes of fathers and sons, and the question of personal honor. Everything edgy about the text in Shakespeare's day became an occasion for personal rather than political contemplation. Thus, Richard Easton, playing the role of King, says his situation is "the same as a commuter from New Jersey who is having trouble with his son. The history part is less interesting than the father who wishes Hotspur was his son because Hal is such an unsatisfactory one" (Rothstein 2003: 45). "All things come into commerce, and pass into traffic" indeed, in a way the early mercantilist could never have imagined. Director O'Brien likewise says the story is "painfully applicable to everyone who sees it. Because you don't see a historical pageant. You see your own life passing before your eyes...It's a play that almost every one of us, particularly men, have been through." He continues, "We all need mentors. And then, because you can't live your entire life with your father hanging over your head, you have to get rid of them. That's what this play is about" (Rothstein 2003: 44).

I doubt such remarks signify a lack of knowledge on the part of theatrical practitioners regarding changes in family and patronage structures over the past four hundred years. O'Brien and Easton surely know that Henry IV's relationship to his son could not possibly be "the same" as a New Jersey commuter's, and that this workplace model of male mentorship is as modern a concept as the nuclear family. They also know, however, that they must grab an audience viscerally and quickly where that audience believes it lives, addressing what it professes to value – which in 2004 America means the putatively private domestic space. In maintaining the text's setting of the action in a consistent (if stylized) medieval past, the producers had already confronted the challenge of connection; ours is, after all, an era when "history lessons" are presumed to be an immediate turnoff among theatre practitioners and critics alike. Considered thus, it may be less surprising that, as in Kenneth Branagh's *Henry V*, the visual setting is the only truly "historical" dimension of the performance (see Worthen 2003: 69): the wonder is that one still attempts the imitation of history at all.

Having chosen to try, however, they opened up a space for recognition of differences between kings and commuters – yet did little with that space. In condensing the two plays and reordering scenes to create a more unified evening, Matthews erased the sequence of debasement: the Falstaff who began the evening sitting in a drunken stupor, tankard dangling from his sword, was the same in Act 3, and the belligerent energy of Hotspur reappeared in Prince John at Gaultree. One could argue that the commuter as king constitutes a nice *reductio ad absurdum* of Henry IV's battlefield logic of surrogation (no longer a temporary strategy but the capitalist condition of male adulthood) – but if the audience were to discern this, it would not be because the performance choices encouraged it. The optimistic American interpretation would more likely assume that such a generalization indicated democracy, not a dog-eat-dog marketplace of destabilization. Although the distinction and relationship between these two conclusions would seem an urgent ethical issue to pose if performing *Henry IV* in 2004, the more concrete immediacy of this play's awareness about its "new world order" was not part of O'Brien's perceived connection. Instead, theatre announced itself as concerned with eternal verities, and as a result became enmeshed in a deeply conservative invocation of the past. Thus, too, although the movement away from standardized metal to an entirely free-floating economy took place only 33 years ago (see Waswo 1996: 9), and anxieties about investment markets and this newly immaterial system of exchange certainly preoccupy many heads in Lower Manhattan, the Upper West Side was having none of it.

Nor, to be fair, do most productions of *Henry IV*, conservative or radical, on stage or on screen (the oblique exception being Gus Van Sant's *My Own Private Idaho* [1991]). The most famously "political" of contemporary British performances, Bogdanov's ESC production, chose not to include the figures who establish *Part Two*'s particular preoccupation with rampant circulation, and much of Gaultree Forest's disturbing language about "peace" was cut: Rumour and Coleville of the Dale went missing and Lord Bardolph was re-dubbed, usurping Morton's name. Even when the "matter of Britain" and connections with political history were more pronounced, then, this drama of destabilization did not fully embrace the economic story. Those with an interest in the history and politics still consider it necessary to focus audience attention on the consequences for "individuals" and work exclusively through that model. Annmarie McDonald, interviewing the British director of the 2004 Washington production, observes:

> With precision, [Bill] Alexander has set up the [political] relevance of the *Henrys* like so many regiments of toy soldiers, but then with just the sweep of his hand knocks them out of his way, saying, "...but really the only way in which this can be relevant to a modern audience is if they are engrossed by the characters, follow the story and see that whatever form it takes, politics doesn't change. It's about individuals." (*Asides* 2003–4: 7)

Again, this is not a matter of knowledge but pragmatics. The theatrical productions of non-musical drama that currently "succeed" imitate the fashion of the times, and make it personal.

The Lincoln Center production's use of period setting discouraged modern political analogies as well as distinction; had O'Brien chosen modern dress, as did Nicholas Hytner directing the National Theatre *Henry V* (2003), he might have considered including, say, a war correspondent as Rumour. That was the analogy Hytner suggested to Penny Downie in rehearsing Chorus, before they decided it did not allow a sufficient "journey" through her part (not such a problem for the one-off appearance of Rumour). Downie's comments about her role reinforce the necessity of scholars finding a way into the realities of character acting if they wish to see their ideas performed: aware that she was "trying to find a character for the Chorus who doesn't essentially have a character," she still strove to create a compelling line of development for a recognizable modern woman in order to inhabit the part. (As Adrian Lester, the production's Henry, put it, "I can't play anything on stage unless it makes sense to me, a 35-year-old guy from Birmingham"; see the rich archive at www.stagework.org.uk). The Lincoln Center performance clearly shared this methodology but a different temporality, allowing no imaginative space for either the overt anachronism of a modern Rumour or the conventional representation from Shakespeare's time.

And why should it? More broadly, why should the circulation of commodities be part of this *Henry*? One might say mine is still too literal as well as literary a response to performance, looking for the exact patterning or emphases from Shakespeare's text. A generation of performance studies has taught us to see embodiment and presence rather than seek ghosts of an old script, so my willful search is itself open to accusations of conservatism. Moreover, the emphases on "fathers and sons" and personal "honour," dramatized in New York and Washington, are precisely those themes highlighted in *Cliff Notes* and other study guides, not to mention more widely respected scholarly editions, for more than a generation. Such themes, if not the academic fashion of these times, are certainly still part of our pedagogical vocabulary and our students' interests, which we who are teachers ignore at our peril.

A complacent approach to the relationship between the scholar's work and the theatre might simply presume a 40-year lag time, give or take a decade, between the textual circulation of new interpretive emphases and their stage effects: the application of insights drawn from economic historians and post-structural criticism through close reading might filter via the classroom into younger brains and eventually beyond. Perhaps – but the condescension of such a "trickle-down" theory in ignoring more challenging recent performance work and in presuming scholarship leads the way is only part of its problem. It also denudes criticism of all cultural urgency and political impact in the present and near future; for me, witnessing and then writing while soldiers fight and die under what I consider false pretenses, precisely because the naming and exploitation of markets and threats have not been adequately understood, this is an ethically inadequate conclusion. While cognizant of the old clichés regarding art's ability – much less scholarship's – to "change" anything, both must continue to try. And some do: Theater Complicite's (2004) *Measure for Measure* and Hytner's (2003) *Henry V*, for example, are contemporaneous examples showing more direct engagement with the moment and its shaping economic motives.

My emphasis on the absent economies of *Henry IV* is thus motivated less by love of "Shakespeare" or the text (a love I acknowledge, fraught though it be) than by a continuing interest in history as it bears upon our moment, the politics implied by our use of the vexing, tattered documents which constitute our remembered connection with the past. At the same time, in writing about this production I become another voice in performance history (that most suspect form of describing past events) and likewise confront the tension between fidelity to the past and current use, my role not being merely to criticize but to document. What I document cannot help but be shaped by immediate concerns. But from within this interested body, I can and should look harder to make sure I at least acknowledge any performance moments that hint at a common ground, or suggest grounds for a future connection upon the stage. This entails searching for signs of awareness and engagement with the text's economy of circulation and its specific potential within this sociohistorical moment, even if not directly expressed through the vocabulary of the marketplace. The work deserves this attention whether or not those engaged in professional theatre care after the fact, any more than they delight in "history lessons." (They have moved on to new projects, to the next always uncertain performance in the present.)

Widening one's gaze, for instance, might encourage a glance back at the scene in the ESC's *Part Two* in which Hal learns about a seemingly harmless rumor: indirectly, via Falstaff's letter borne by Bardolph, the Prince hears that his companion Poins has circulated word that Hal would marry Poins' sister. Michael Pennington conveys the wariness and pained disappointment the incident creates for Hal as he realizes (at least) one of his seeming friends is lying to him. By focusing the distrust on Poins despite the unreliable narrators, this scene sets the stage for both the traffic in women (including a compellingly streetwise Doll) and Hal's increasingly bitter isolation in – and perhaps as part of – an untrustworthy world. The actors' looks, gestures, and demeanors emphasized that even on a sofa in Hal's private apartment, no space could be "safe" or simply domestic for the heir apparent, nor ever would be.

Space took on even more symbolic importance in Lincoln Center's opening sequence, as music and quick spotlights faded in and out revealing various not-yet-identified, physically isolated characters. In these non-verbal tableaux, modern theatrical technology produced something like the playtext's sense of dislocation and circulation among bodies only later differentiated and defined. The competition and interchangeability among men that make Henry's claim to the throne and entire reign essentially unstable were forecast, gesturing towards a larger scale of consequences than the oedipal struggles of most New Jersey commuters. Later on, the stage-left scaffolding became a staircase up and down which Henry IV energetically ran, anxiously staving off rebellion on all sides. What struck me at the time as oddly energetic behavior for the beleaguered, putatively impassive king makes more sense in retrospect as a symbolic expression. Such an interpretation gains support from the ultimate ascent of the stairs by the newly crowned Henry V, from whence he looks down upon, and rejects, Falstaff. Hal would indeed be like his father, but with more emphasis on theatrical energy and placement than on strategic calculations. The production put a premium on vigorous movement throughout, not only with Hotspur in battle but among the entire royal family – contradicting Falstaff's lines about Prince John being a cold fish (he was attractive, almost swashbuckling at Gaultree), but establishing another essential form of theatrical circulation and "currency." This production refused to be many an American's idea of classical British Shakespeare – all words. But in addition, in Hal's final ascent, the echoing location allowed the perception that the position trumped the inhabitant, letting the darker overtones of *Part Two*'s commodity market creep into the dominantly lively mode. Perhaps some of those critics who were less enthusiastic (or even kind) about Michael Hayden's embodiment wanted Hal to be a more pronounced "personality," but this is precisely what the play's movement conspires against: instead, Hayden aptly adapted and adopted the positions of those among whom he circulated.

An even more compelling combination of spatial relations, Shakespearean text, and actors' moving bodies initiated the third and final segment of the evening: it substituted, in the sequence of conflated *Henrys*, for Rumour's entrance. This (for me) most impressive scene in the entire production had nothing overtly to do with Falstaff: rather, it involved Lady Percy's lamentation, moved up from Act 2 Scene 3 in *Part Two* and powerfully rendered by Audra MacDonald. Beginning where the second act left off – with the battle dead of Shrewsbury still strewn across the stage/field – MacDonald descended a mesh screen along the back wall in order to approach the body of her beloved Hotspur, grieving and reproaching old Northumberland as the latter stood upon a downstage scaffold, above and removed from the slaughter. Then, when she had successfully persuaded the lofty Earl not to dishonor her husband's sacrifice by honoring the pleas of others more diligently than those of his own son, the "dead" soldiers rose in silence and slowly marched away into ghostly darkness, leaving Lady Percy alone in her grief, her empty arms reaching after the receding figure of her husband. This silent interpellation of dead men walking was perhaps the only time when the production addressed its present-day historical moment with directness and intensity, honoring the pain felt by those losing their loved ones at war.

This was a wartime production: while the directorial concept may have originated in O'Brien's San Diego Old Globe production featuring John Goodman, neither the New York cast could perform nor the audience witness the show unaware that US soldiers (along with many other people) were dying at the time in Iraq (and in that parenthetically remembered battleground country, Afghanistan, as well). This sequence, highlighting the distance between leaders and those they sacrifice, more than compensated for the loss of Rumour and his many tongues. Nevertheless, what remained missing was the transmission of the other dimensions of war beyond the emotional cost, and how this scene linked with its wider surround. As a theatrical "moment," it stood in isolation (like Kline's Falstaff and its press coverage), rather than creating another strand in a larger web.

One reason for this lack of connection arguably resided in its tangential relationship to the themes articulated by the producers. Choosing to emphasize the palatable rather than provocative, the directorial approach marginalized concern with "war" in favor of (an individuated) Falstaff and family. And who can deny that family values are the fashion of the times? Which links with another reason directly involving money: who can (and will) afford to attend this kind of high-quality professional show when ticket prices approach $100/person? Simply getting inside the door of a theatre is becoming an increasingly rare experience for many young people – and they are often the audiences who want to see more provocative (or at least spectacular) work. Instead, older subscribers are the ones who consider theatre worth the price, and their desires must be taken seriously. In this instance, the subscribers were a particularly astute,

New Yorker review-reading group. Still, as well-heeled mainstream patrons, they did not appear likely to clap enthusiastically at startling satires about the corruption of "free" markets. Indeed, their warm reception for Kline's rendition of the fat knight, a star turn separable from rather than symbolic of all that swirled around him, confirmed that – like the reviewers – they sought and found their greatest pleasure in the "old style," reserving their accolades for the actors who created memorably individuated characters.

What can a scholar add to this performance landscape? Locally, it seems worth attending to the more complex moments of multimedia theatricality such as began the third act, recalling too those silent actors, designers, technicians, and musicians whose contributions too often disappear from our performance histories – and hence from collective memory – like the dead. Further, we should include the audience as part of the performance conditions when evaluating productions. And finally, we could reinvigorate the topic of language within performativity: not as a nostalgic burden or old idol, but as an "asset," a "currency," a powerful, underutilized – or underacknowledged – resource for a more politically engaged American theatre. This is language in exchange, not hoarded or merely displayed in the mellifluous set speech elegantly crafted, but a visceral action that prompts further effects on bodies, hearts, minds. And this is what I in fact carried away from my evening with *Henry IV*, in exchange for my time and money. For although the non-verbal tableaux such as those which opened the evening were invested with special power, it was not the silence alone that spoke in the scene that most moved me: when the dead soldiers exited, the drama took place in the chasm between MacDonald's eloquent reanimation of Shakespeare's verse and that heartbreaking silence. The actress herself compared her lines to the musical scores she has become famous re-sounding, in a wide range of genres. The barking of Ethan Hawkes's comically hyperbutch, utterly sincere Hotspur also haunted the moment, his aggressively American phrasing and energies gone. To talk about what reiterated attention to language might add, then, does not mean only attention to verbal patterns such as those I have highlighted (valuable though that could be), nor should it be disconnected from the other sign systems that constitute performance. But perhaps more analysis of words – the words of the makers of productions, as well as those edgier speeches that are or aren't spoken onstage – will prompt further thought about the immediate cultural contextualization of theatre, by practitioners and scholars alike. It might help us discern and confirm something more than the obvious contours of familiar themes and our own emotions.

Money Talks

What kind of commodity trading are we engaged in, and what kinds do we acknowledge in theatre and academia? When Falstaff is accused of lying about debts, he tries to transform the economic fact into a metaphor of affection:

PRINCE: Sirrah, do I owe you a thousand pound?
FALSTAFF: A thousand pound, Hal? A million. Thy love is worth a million, thou owest
　　　me thy love.

(*1* 3.3.135–7)

Shifting the conversation from money to love as a means to evade material reality may
be a practice too familiar for those who toil in theatre and humanities education to
recognize. Does this blindness make us the dupes of those who see that our economic
system is premised on money as the primary sign of value? We too may hope that our
(only comparative) poverty, as measured against the wages of business and other
professional careers, "shows my earnestness of affection" and "my devotion"
(*2* 5.5.15, 17). Yet if we are charmed by Falstaff, we may be more like Master Shallow
than like Hal. Or perhaps even more like the hoodwinked conspirators who believe
that Prince John's talk of "love and amity" (4.1.291) will advance their cause.

Works perceived as too "intellectual" or cold, even when magnificently performed
and advocated by critics, tend to fail on Broadway – witness the same season's revival
of Stoppard's *Jumpers* starring Simon Russell Beale, subsidized and successful in
London but closing at a loss in New York. Add to this the privilege of wealth and
power within a large country that both geographically and politically encourages
narcissism of the most flattering kind, and it hardly becomes surprising that the
public rhetoric of *Henry* productions emphasizes that audiences will see a mirror of
their (powerful male) selves. Obviously there is nothing wrong with an honest
attempt to render human relationships in their depth and complexity; there may
even be much of political "value" in encouraging powerful males to examine their
behaviors in situations where loyalties compete. But just as obviously, there is much
that such an emphasis leaves out: most notably, thought about the larger social
systems that shape and delimit personal agency and decision-making: the very kind
of consequential systemic thinking that distinguishes those who survive within the
Henry plays from those like Hotspur – and even, ultimately, Falstaff – who do not.

In academia, those who have time to write and reflect upon theatre are often those
most sheltered from the vagaries of the marketplace, with established careers and
predictable incomes. But even we are aware of our marginality within the economy
that Shakespeare discerned emerging, and we still return to older structures of value
for reassurance, perhaps now more than ever. While actors and directors struggle to
put on the next show, they have a much more immediate reason for trying to shelter
themselves from the reduction of all value to the market's appraisal, and much more
difficulty doing so: no wonder, then, that they might not wish to reflect upon these
limits within their created fictions. But if we wish to do more than provide the
circuses while Rome marches off to war, perhaps we need at least occasionally – and
Henry IV surely provides such an occasion – to reflect upon our uneasy role in this
larger economy. This is a play, after all, in which an Archbishop defines peace as the
ideal market transaction – "For then both parties nobly are subdued, / And neither
party loser" (4.1.316–17) – before he is tricked to his death by a bad deal. If we only

mourn the "fallen heroes" in battle's aftermath, with smoke machines and battle effects but no illumination of the logic of crowns and destabilized circulation that leads to these effects, then theatre may indeed seem unnecessary, a less realistic way of telling the same story as the mass media. This is why we should indeed turn back to *Part Two*'s Falstaff, whether we like him or not. For he is also our mascot, an oversized reminder of the ransom, the crassness, the system that creates "food for powder" less cynically – or less wittingly – than he himself can manage through overt corruption. In not thinking about those connections, we are doomed to that old cliché of repeating history – and finding ourselves surprised, yet again, and again, by the death of naive young men who thought they were going to war to rescue "drowned honour." Naming "greed" and "pragmatism" in itself isn't enough, nor are scholarly conferences that perform their own professional version of the status quo, no matter how challenging the talk. But if we could move beyond "business as usual" and bring those forces to theatrical life, using the resources of language and the brain as well as the heart and the body to confront the economies that surround our lives – and as a critical part of that process create appreciative yet astutely skeptical audiences who would attend such theatre: that would be a consummation of performance and criticism devoutly to be wished.

Notes

1   In Britain the political questions suggested by Prince Hal's coming of age have remained prominent in *Henry* stagings during the past 40 years (especially apparent in video presentations, including the ESC's "subversive" staging as well as more Tillyard-indebted cycles such as the BBC/Time-Life television production); for obvious reasons the "matter of Britain" speaks more urgently in that land.

2   All quotations from *Part Two* refer to the Oxford edition; quotations from *Part One* are drawn from the Bedford edition. All other plays are cited from the Riverside edition.

3   By analogy, scholars posit that re-naming Bardolph, like Falstaff, was a response to the distress of the Elizabethan descendents of Russell, like those of Oldcastle, at their name being used for an Eastcheap lowlife.

4   Kastan's "Proud Majesty" as well as other new historicist essays have called attention to the power struggles inherent in dramatizing royalty; I am less concerned with theatre's relationship to known human authorities than to the amorphous powers of the marketplace and its new monetary vocabulary.

References and Further Reading

Agnew, Jean-Christophe (1986). *Worlds Apart: The Market and the Theater in Anglo-American Thought, 1550–1750*. Cambridge: Cambridge University Press.

Asides (2003–4). *Henry IV Part 1*, Issue 3. Washington, DC: Shakespeare Theater.

Bloom, Harold (1998). *Shakespeare: The Invention of the Human*. New York: Riverhead Books.

Braudel, Fernand (1973). *Capitalism and Material Life 1400–1800*. New York: Harper and Row.

Kastan, David (1986). "Proud Majesty Made Subject: Shakespeare and the Spectacle of Rule." *Shakespeare Quarterly* 37, 4: 459–75.

McMillin, Scott (2003). "[Performing *I Henry IV*]." In Gordon McMullan (ed.) *1 Henry IV*. New York: Norton.

Orlin, Lena Cowen (ed.) (2000). *Material London, ca. 1600*. Philadelphia, PA: University of Pennsylvania Press.

Pavlin, Jordan (ed.) (2003). *Lincoln Center Theater Review*. New York: Lincoln Center.

Pratt, Mary Louise (2004). "Presidential Address 2003: Language, Liberties, Waves, and Webs – Engaging the Present." *PMLA* 119, 3: 417–28.

Pynchon, Thomas (2000). *Gravity's Rainbow*. London: Vintage.

Raman, Shankar (2001). *Framing "India": The Colonial Imaginary in Early Modern Culture*. Stanford, CA: Stanford University Press.

Raman, Shankar (forthcoming). "The Marks of Time: Memory and its Discontents in Shakespeare's *The Comedy of Errors*." *Shakespeare Quarterly*.

Rothstein, Mervyn (2003). "Fathers & Sons." *Playbill: Henry IV*. New York: Lincoln Center Theater at the Vivian Beaumont, pp. 44–5.

Shakespeare, William (1974). *The Riverside Shakespeare*, ed. G. Blakemore Evans. Boston: Houghton Mifflin.

Shakespeare, William (1997). *The First Part of King Henry the Fourth: Texts and Contexts*, ed. Barbara Hodgdon. Boston: Bedford.

Shakespeare, William (1998). *Henry IV, Part 2*, ed. René Weis. Oxford: Clarendon Press.

Waswo, Richard (1996). "Shakespeare and the Formation of the Modern Economy." *Surfaces* VI, 217: 1–32.

Worthen, William (2003). *Shakespeare and the Force of Modern Performance*. Cambridge: Cambridge University Press.

FILMOGRAPHY

Chimes at Midnight (1966). Directed by Orson Welles. Arthur Cantor Films.

Henry IV Part II (1990). Directed by Michael Bogdanov. English Shakespeare Company. Portman Classics Production.

PART IV
Performance Technologies, Cultural Technologies

21

"Are We Being Theatrical Yet?": Actors, Editors, and the Possibilities of Dialogue

Michael Cordner

Unlike their mid-twentieth-century predecessors, the major contemporary series of single-play Shakespeare editions advertise their alertness to the texts' origins as scripts for performance. General editorial statements promise close attention "to the realisation of the plays on stage" (New Cambridge Shakespeare) and exploration of "the conditions and possibilities of meaning that editors, critics and performers (on stage and screen) have discovered" in the plays (Arden 3). Such priorities signal a major shift from the characteristic practice of, for example, the Arden 2 series. In many of its volumes analysis of specifically theatrical issues consisted of dutiful recitals of selected performance dates and cast lists, and not all Arden 2s offered even that meager fare.

Publicity statements are one thing, detailed realization of new principles in the line-by-line preparation of editions quite another. How fundamental have the changes really been? The difficulty is that there has been little systematic discussion of how these promises can best be fulfilled. In effect, a revolution has been decreed without any consistent planning as to how to carry it out.

This willingness to trust in individual editors' improvisations is a recurrent motif in the history of Shakespeare editing. The establishment of the text itself generates energetic debate, but other aspects of preparing an edition, including the practice of annotation, remain largely undiscussed. As a result, contemporaneous editions frequently provide emphatically dissimilar patterns of annotation for the same play. Introduce a demand for a new responsiveness to a script's performance implications, *but* offer little guidance as to how the notes editors provide should be consequently redesigned, and you risk further confusing an already unsatisfactory state of affairs.[1]

Publicity quotes for current series feature tributes from actors like Kenneth Branagh and directors like Adrian Noble. If theatre professionals preparing productions are therefore now explicitly part of these editions' target readerships, how well do these newly-edited texts answer the needs of actors and directors during rehearsal? The latter face major challenges in finding performance solutions today for scripts originally written four centuries ago for performance circumstances radically unlike those which any modern company confronts. The more precise the map scholars can provide of a play in its moment of first creation, the richer the array of information on which actors and directors can call at need.

As a test-case of how far modern Shakespeare editing meets these challenges I propose to examine the editions of *Titus Andronicus* prepared for our three principal current series. Eugene M. Waith's edition (1984) was among the earliest to appear in the Oxford Shakespeare series, as was Jonathan Bate's for Arden 3 (1995). Alan Hughes's New Cambridge Shakespeare (1994) edition appeared almost simultaneously with Bate's and has often been reviewed in tandem with it. All have been praised by reviewers for their handling of the plays as performance-texts. MacDonald P. Jackson, for example, reviewing Bate and Hughes, reported that, "Each editor's critical approach to the play is deeply informed by consciousness of its stage history and its qualities in performance" (Jackson 1997: 947).

The major mid-twentieth-century predecessors against which Waith, Hughes and Bate measure themselves are John Dover Wilson's 1948 New Shakespeare edition and J. C. Maxwell's 1953 Arden 2 volume. When they were published, *Titus*'s critical reputation was low. Neither editor set out to alter that situation significantly. Dover Wilson, indeed, believed that the play "was probably by Greene and/or Peel, revised (with his tongue in his cheek) and much inflated by Shakespeare" (Dover Wilson 1969: 210). The script thus bears the imprint of a writer charged with revamping commercially attractive material, but "laughing behind his hand through most of the scenes" he reworked (Dover Wilson 1948: li).

The play was an extreme rarity in the theatre around the mid-century. The first time it had been staged without substantial alteration since the early Restoration was at the Old Vic in 1923. For the Old Vic's 1949 annalist, that production is only an entry on a score-card: with this show, he celebrates, the theatre completed in ten years "the whole cycle of the Shakespeare plays" (Williams 1949: 66). The Old Vic was at least braver than its Stratford-upon-Avon rival, whose plans to stage *Titus* in 1929 were aborted because of doubts about its stageworthiness (Dessen 1989: 14). As a result, its first appearance there was as recent as 1955, directed by Peter Brook and with Laurence Olivier as Titus. Nervous about its reputation, the first night audience was "embarrassed, even facetious ... before curtain-rise," fearful that the combined talents of Olivier and his brilliant young director could not redeem Shakespeare's early experiment from bathos (Trewin 1978: 44). The audience's transformed mood at curtain-fall, however, hailed the triumph of a production which Emrys Jones has recently celebrated, across half a century, as "an altogether exceptional event," adding that "a remarkably bold act of imagination" was needed "to bring this dead text, as it seemed then, back to life" (Jones 2001: 36).

In similar fashion, J. C. Maxwell acknowledged in 1957 that "Perhaps more significant than any written criticism the play has provoked in recent years is the

Stratford production of 1955" (1957: 3). Brook's achievement moved Dover Wilson to disown the premise on which his edition had been based. He had, he confessed, witnessed "a miracle of transformation" into "high tragedy" and was especially awed by the staging of the reunion of Titus and the mutilated Lavinia in 3.1 – a moment which "seemed to give us a human Pieta." The recollection prompted him to record his repeated indebtedness to "actors and producers" for enriching his understanding of Shakespeare's dramatic writing. As a further example of this he cites *Love's Labour's Lost*, which he had also edited, and "which cost me two years and more of wrestling with the text and attempting to understand its quips and quiddities." He then saw a production by Tyrone Guthrie, and "what had been flat-footed plodding on my part took wings." He reserves the right to be aptly "critical" of theatre professionals, but also never doubts that the imaginative deployment of their skills has much to teach the Shakespearean scholar (Dover Wilson 1969: 210–12).

Both *Titus* editors, therefore, confess the revelatory force of Brook's interpretation. Yet their editions, published before that revelation, continued to be reprinted long after 1955, and neither emended their work in its light. The 1961 revision of the Arden 2, for instance, reports Maxwell's reconsideration of several editorial decisions and summarizes selected post-1953 scholarship on *Titus*, but makes no reference to Brook and Olivier; while the continued availability of the unaltered Dover Wilson text inspired a 1986 Washington production, which accordingly treated the play as "a thoroughgoing parody" (Metz 1996: 207). It was thus left to the next generation of editors to remedy this inactivity. The latter also needed to respond to an extraordinary renaissance in the play's critical reputation in the interim. The post-1955 decades witnessed an eruption of deeply enthusiastic writing about *Titus*, partly enabled by Brook's demonstration of its theatrical potency. Even without the new performance imperatives to which their general editors committed them, post-1980 editions were bound to differ decisively from their predecessors.

In key ways, however, they are also their heirs – nowhere more palpably, one might anticipate, than in their explication of puzzling aspects of the dialogue. For an actor or director working on a production in the early twenty-first century this aspect of an edition is inevitably of fundamental importance. Without a precise and circumstantial grasp of the dialogue's moment-by-moment implications their work will be hamstrung from the start.

An idealistic notion of this aspect of the scholarly tradition might envisage a process by which each generation gratefully adopts the best aspects of its predecessors' commentaries and seeks to add to them. Examples of that paradigm at work can be glimpsed in our recent *Titus* editions. In Act 5 Scene 2, for instance, Titus greets the uninvited arrival in his house of Tamora and her sons, disguised as Revenge, Rape and Murder, with the question: "Is it your trick to make me ope the door, / That so my sad decrees may fly away, / And all my study be to no effect?" (10–12).[2] "Sad decrees" clearly invites annotation. Dover Wilson decodes it, via two entries in his edition's glossary, as "dismal resolves"; Maxwell offers "solemn resolutions." Among our modern editors, Waith stays in the same tradition with his "serious ordinances."

Hughes, bewilderingly, disregards "decrees" and glosses "sad" as "grave." None of these notes suggests why the "decrees ... *fly away.*" Bate improves significantly on this inheritance with his concise note: "grave resolutions, and more specifically his papers; the image as a whole perhaps echoes 4.1.105." In that earlier passage a despairing Titus imagines how "The angry northern wind / Will blow these sands [i.e. his words] like Sibyl's leaves abroad." Bate therefore enlarges the range of meanings in play and renders Titus's phrase more specific to the immediate situation, while also assisting us to think in larger structural terms and perceive how passages from different scenes can be brought into dialogue with one another.

Bate frequently enriches his inheritance in this way. Waith and Hughes lack his resourcefulness in detecting new possibilities of meaning and incisiveness in relating the dialogue's details to the unfolding dramatic action. At 5.3.43–4, when Titus says that Saturninus's moralization of the story of Virginius and his daughter is "A pattern, precedent, and lively warrant / For me, most wretched, to perform the like," neither Waith nor Hughes comments on "warrant," whereas Bate opens up an intricate array of possibilities with the following note: "Several senses are relevant: authoritative witness, conclusive proof, one whose command justifies an action, sanction, token of authorization, document or writ licensing execution." I will return to this moment from the play's climax later.

It might appear to be relatively easy for an editor to decide when the occurrence of words which are now archaic or which are used in meanings no longer current necessitates a note, though instances will inevitably occur where opinions legitimately differ. For instance, "sometime" (3.1.211) is used adverbially, where the modern form would be "sometimes"; but the nature of the context makes it unlikely to cause difficulty. Maxwell and Waith provide glosses; Dover Wilson, Hughes, and Bate do not. When, however, Titus instructs his family to "fall to" (3.2.34) – i.e., begin to eat – he is using a now unfamiliar idiom. Similarly, his imperative "Soft" (4.1.45) - "wait a moment, look, focus on this" – is not used in modern English in these senses. A few lines earlier, he encourages Lavinia to read and "so beguile thy sorrow" (4.1.35), where "beguile" invites explanation in terms of the meanings found in *OED* v. 5. These involve the idea of diverting attention from something (so perhaps by extension, here, dulling the pain of) and, in so doing, enabling time to pass. (The sentence goes on: "*till* the heavens / Reveal the damned contriver of this deed" (my emphasis).) When Titus with his hounds and horns proposes to "rouse the Prince" (2.2.5), the verb means more than "wake (from his amorous slumbers)," since as a hunting-term it also meant "startle (prey) from a lair." His apostrophe to "Rome, victorious in thy mourning weeds" (1.1.70) invites a note that "weeds" here means "garments" or "clothes." And when Marcus asserts, "That on mine honour here do I protest" (1.1.477), the verb signifies not its modern range of senses, but "affirm," "avow."

The problem is that none of our editors comments on any of these moments, and that the list of such omissions could be substantially extended. At numerous moments actor and reader alike, whatever their choice of edition, will be left without the information they have the right to expect.

The assumption that editions can be relied upon to build constructively on their predecessors' contributions also proves mistaken. At 4.1.39, for example, Marcus uses "fact" in the early modern meaning of "crime." Maxwell, Waith, and Hughes provide the apt gloss; Bate does not. Titus's bizarre image of Lavinia's tears "mashed upon her cheeks" (3.2.38) receives commentary – of varying degrees of helpfulness – from all our editors except Hughes. When Aaron images Lavinia as a "dainty doe" for Tamora's sons to hunt (2.1.118), Dover Wilson and Bate aptly explain that "dainty" carries meanings now archaic, but Maxwell, Waith, and Hughes remain silent. Marcus's horror at the "stern ungentle hands" which mutilated his niece (2.4.16) inspires Dover Wilson to report that "stern" means "cruel"; but the others ignore his precedent. His successors similarly disregard Dover Wilson's indication that "Buzz" (4.4.7) signifies "whisper." Tamora's resolution that her heart will not "know merry cheer" (2.3.188) until revenge is hers prompts Waith to gloss "cheer" as "frame of mind" (not ideally felicitous, but pointing in the right direction). Neither Hughes nor Bate follows his lead, although the word is being used in a sense no longer active. Dover Wilson and Waith note that, in Quintus's description of the forest pit as a "subtle hole" (2.3.198), "subtle" means "treacherous," while Maxwell, Hughes, and Bate pass by in silence. In urging Titus to bid farewell to "flatt'ry" (3.1.252), Dover Wilson explains, Marcus implies that his brother has been misled by "self-delusion" and must now purge himself of it – a helpful intervention, which only Bate emulates. Unlike his fellow editors, Hughes sees no need to observe that the frightening "urchins" (2.3.101) are in fact hedgehogs. Waith explains that the "languor" which burdens Titus (3.1.13) is "grief," while Dover Wilson and Hughes offer similar comments. Maxwell and Bate, however, see no need to act. And so on and on.

I can discern no principle or pattern at work in the ways in which our editors favor particular words and phrases for attention. Such unpredictability is, however, common practice in many contemporary Shakespeare editions. Reviewing the Hughes and Bate volumes, Jackson asserts that both contain "full and helpful commentaries" and then says nothing further about the annotation. This typifies current reviewing practice, which, by its inattention, in effect legitimizes these problematic practices. As a result, actors, seeking to master dialogue written four centuries ago and find persuasive ways of articulating it in performance, will often be left high-and-dry by the editor of the text they are relying upon, when the crucial nugget of information they need may well have been provided in one or more previous editions of the same play.

Even when all our editors single out the same passage for attention, problems may still arise. As the play's final scene begins, Marcus welcomes Saturninus and Tamora to Titus's house for a banquet:

> The feast is ready which the care-full Titus
> Hath ordained to an honourable end,
> For peace, for love, for league, and good to Rome.
>
> (5.3.21–3)

The hyphenation of "care-full" is Waith's way of emphasizing the sense in which he believes the word is being used – i.e. "sorrowful," or weighed down by cares. Maxwell, Bate, and Hughes essentially agree with him on this, though somewhat uneasily. Thus Maxwell: "Probably 'afflicted with cares' rather than 'taking trouble.' There might be an ironic pun, though it could only be Shakespeare's irony, not Marcus's, as he does not know the special kind of care that Titus has taken." Bate sings from the same hymn-sheet: "afflicted with care. Possible subliminal pun in that the audience (not Marcus) know that Titus is taking care of the arrangements." Maxwell and Bate are preferable to Waith in that they acknowledge the possibility of a pun here. "Careful" meaning "taking care" or "painstaking" is good early modern usage, and editors consistently so gloss the word when it appears earlier in *Titus* (4.3.28–30). Why then do they insist that "sorrowful" must be its sole or dominant meaning here? The answer partly lies in their conviction that Marcus is ignorant of what Titus has in store for his regal guests – i.e. human pie, baked from the butchered limbs of Tamora's sons. So their explication rests on presuppositions about narrative, which themselves rest on arguments, as it were, from silence. Marcus is not present when Chiron and Demetrius are trapped and killed, and no subsequent passage of dialogue records his being informed of their fate. Editors consequently assume that he enters the final scene still unaware of it. Dependent on this, for Bate in particular, is an image of Marcus as a figure rescued from complicity in the gory retribution Titus inflicts, and who can therefore convincingly emerge as the advocate of reconciliation and unity. Against that one might put another argument from silence. The dialogue records no surprised or horrified reaction from Marcus, as son-pie is served up and his niece is slain by her father, and his final speeches register no recoil from his brother's actions. It would be simple for an actor to indicate, by his bearing and tone, Marcus's knowledge of what is in store for Saturninus and Tamora – especially if he were allowed to exploit the double meaning in "careful," of which Bate and Maxwell seek to deny him knowledge.

In any case, why should we assume that "sorrowful" is the word's primary meaning here? In an extreme paraphrase, that might leave Marcus welcoming the new arrivals in the following style: "My brother is cracking up under the griefs and disasters you have inflicted upon him, but, despite all that, don't worry – he has prepared a great meal for you, and you can be sure he is totally determined to make friends with you." A parodic version, of course; but the performance problem it identifies is real. What if we entertain the possibility that the other range of meanings of "careful" might be predominant here? Then Marcus would be reassuring them that Titus will devote all his energies, as he does his preparation of this feast, to the cause of reconciliation between them. A supple command of tone by the player, if he so chose, could alert the audience to the word's darker meanings, of which Saturninus and Tamora remain oblivious. That generates, of course, a Marcus in league with his brother's plot. I can see no textual reason why that should be ruled out. Jacques Berthoud's concise note in the 2001 Penguin edition outdistances his competitors: "painstaking, but also full of grief." Unburdened by preconceptions, this gloss crisply indicates the two key senses active here and leaves the player free to generate his preferred performance meaning from the potentially rich interplay between them.

Another passage, this time in 1.1, which spurs recent editors into action is the burial of Mutius – the son whom Titus abruptly slays for daring to oppose his will. The patriarch first resolves that the rebel shall not be buried in the family tomb; but the pleas of his brother and other sons sway Titus into granting reluctant permission. As the body is interred, both Quartos and First Folio direct that *"all"* the Andronici *"kneele and say"* a formal couplet of praise: "No man shed tears for noble Mutius; / He lives in fame, that died in virtue's cause" (1.1.389–90). Dover Wilson and Maxwell followed the early printings without comment. Waith, however, demurs: "It seems probable that 'all' in this stage direction does not include Titus. He has told the others to bury Mutius and he would hardly say that Mutius 'died in virtue's cause.'" Accordingly, he adjusts the stage direction to exclude Titus from the unison.

Hughes reproduces the original stage direction unaltered, but adds this note: "It seems improbable that Titus would kneel here, or join in the eulogy (1.1.389–90), but this scene is not notable for probability." This is a bizarrely casual vote of no confidence in the quality of the plotting in the first act – especially given other scholars' recent arguments that this opening movement's ambitious and accomplished design is unprecedented in English drama. Its formulation is also unsatisfactorily curt. Why no mention of Waith's alternative? Why no speculation about other performance possibilities?

Bate shares Waith's worries, omits the Quarto and Folio stage direction, and adjusts the speech prefix for the offending couplet to "MARCUS & TITUS' SONS [*kneeling*]." An accompanying note, however, hints that he is not entirely satisfied: "I assume that Titus' command in line 391 means that he does not participate here; in the Warner production, however, he did, but he spoke a little more slowly than the others, so that 'in virtue's cause' emerged as his hollow echo after the others had completed the recitation." He is referring to Deborah Warner's magisterial 1987 Royal Shakespeare Company production, the second great peak in the play's recent British performance history, and one which deeply influenced Bate's work on the text. Elsewhere in his edition, he quotes details from Warner's production to clarify what he sees as the script's implicit demands. Here he cites one of her improvisations more cautiously. Her solution points up a weakness in Waith's position. The latter assumes that simultaneous delivery of lines entails identical expression of those lines; but this does not logically follow – in drama, any more than in an operatic ensemble. Warner's staging is one response to that fact; other productions could generate other variations from it. Once this possibility has been glimpsed, the original stage direction looks much more defensible. Bate's invocation of Warner is a move in the right direction; but a truly performance-friendly practice could afford to be bolder in its use of such evidence.

A few lines later a different kind of problem concerns editors. Marcus and Titus ponder the likely effects of the sudden elevation of Tamora, who entered the play as

Titus's humiliated prisoner, but who has now become Saturninus's wife and Empress of Rome. Titus asks:

> Is she not then beholding to the man
> That brought her for this high good turn so far?
> Yes, and will nobly him remunerate.
>
> (1.1.396–8)

The last line first appears in the 1623 First Folio and is absent from the numerous earlier Quarto printings of the play – a fact which has prompted much discussion, both about the line's authenticity and about who should speak it. It has been suggested that it would perform better as a reply by Marcus to his brother than as Titus's response to his own rhetorical question. Waith leaves it with Titus, on the grounds that its "naive confidence in Tamora's gratitude is more characteristic of Titus." Bate reassigns it because "the worldly-wise, ironic tone and the fact that it is a reply suggest that Marcus is intended." They implicitly agree that, if it *is* ironic in tone, it cannot be Titus's; but what Bate confidently hears as "worldly-wise" Waith perceives to be "naive." These contradictory *ex cathedra* pronouncements abuse editorial privilege. Neither scholar offers evidence in support of his preferred reading, and I cannot see how they could do so, since the six words in question are not imprinted with a rhetorical character so idiosyncratic as to prescribe only one mode of delivery. Both the versions proposed are possible; others are equally performable. Everything will depend, in a particular interpretation (in the study or on the stage), upon how the broader dramatic context is imagined, as also the moods of the two interlocutors. *Pace* Waith and Bate, the line can even be convincingly spoken with worried irony by Titus – as it is by David Troughton in the recent Arkangel recording of the play (ISBN 014180001-1). Troughton, while not overrating Titus's intelligence, credits him with sufficient wit to recognize – at least momentarily – how desperate the Andronici's plight may now be.

Academic commentary of this kind is not a good advertisement for the current series' claims to be freshly responsive to Shakespeare's plays as texts for performance. Open-minded exploration in rehearsal will swiftly expose as illegitimate the assumptions underpinning much of the annotation our editors provide on these two moments from the burial of Mutius. Narrowing the interpretative options down so severely is always likely to represent the taking of a wrong turning. In its absolutism, it also re-erects barriers between the world of scholarship and the world of performance practice.

The current generation of editions diverges most decisively from its predecessors in its professed willingness to explore staging issues with new thoroughness. Maxwell followed the predominant style of Arden 2 in his cavalier approach to such matters. His second note to 1.1, for instance, includes the inaccurate statement that "The staging of the play is throughout very simple and any standard account, e.g. the brief one by C. J. Sisson in *Companion to Shakespeare Studies*, ed. Granville-Barker and

Harrison, will give the necessary information." Thereafter, he offers only rare comments on staging, and his handling of such issues is problematic throughout (Wells 1984: 80–94).

Titus is, in fact, extremely adventurous in its exploitation of the acting and physical resources afforded by late Elizabethan playhouses and their companies. Decoding the details of its intended staging poses many, sometimes perhaps insuperable, problems for the commentator. Our recent editors provide sensible interventions here at points where their predecessors remain silent, as, for example, when Bate pinpoints the discovery of a weapon – an event indispensable, he argues, to motivate Saturninus's abrupt sentencing of the Clown to death (4.4.43). Similarly, Hughes sees the dangers of seeming to dictate, by an editorial stage direction's positioning, the one right moment for an indispensable action to be performed and provides notes to remind us, for example, that "The placing of these SDs should not be taken as prescriptive; alternative stagings are possible" (5.1.145–51).

Real gains have therefore been made; but editorial practice remains patchy. Waith's performance is especially faltering in this respect. When Aaron proclaims in his 2.1 soliloquy, "Away with slavish weeds and servile thoughts!" (18), Waith speculates that he "may discard some of the drab clothing ('weeds') he has worn as a prisoner and put on the 'bright' robe referred to in l. 19," without answering the obvious query: how does a recently released prisoner of war, who has not in the meantime left the stage, acquire these splendid new clothes? When Chiron and Demetrius enter quarreling at the end of Aaron's speech, Waith informs us that "During his soliloquy Aaron should probably move down-stage right or left so that he is at some distance from the door at which" they enter, since they remain unaware of his presence for some time (1984: 25). This depends on a tangle of unjustified assumptions – for instance, that Aaron will certainly have been positioned upstage center for his solo. What would justify that belief? Watching performances at the reconstructed Globe on London's Bankside suggests that, in this kind of open-air amphitheatre, that is not necessarily the most natural or commanding position from which to deliver such a display piece. Experience there has also demonstrated the ease with which actors, on entering, can reach the front-stage by moving rapidly forward on the outer side of the nearest stage-pillar. If that were to happen here, then a position for Aaron upstage centre might in fact be appropriate. But no purpose is served by editors miring themselves in this kind of speculation. Waith's note is, in any case, redundant, since readers can easily deduce from the dialogue itself that the angry Goths do not observe Aaron before he intervenes in their quarrel at l.45. Awkwardness of this kind afflicts many of his interventions on staging issues. His commentary also contains one of the most unfortunate moments of inattention in modern Shakespeare editing. At the close of 3.1 a moment of silent ceremony – "You heavy people, circle me about" (275) – unites the remnants of the Andronici family, including the handless Lavinia and Titus who has just been tricked by Aaron into cutting off his own left hand. At this point Waith proposes that "A simple ritual, *such as handshaking* or bowing to each of them in turn, is needed" (my emphasis).

Bate and Hughes also have their questionable moments. After her sons have killed Bassianus, Tamora demands, "Give me the poniard" (2.3.120), so that she can dispatch Lavinia. Bate puzzlingly identifies "the poniard" as "the dagger which Chiron has taken from Demetrius at 117." But lines 116–17 do not support this assumption:

DEMETRIUS: This is a witness that I am thy son.
CHIRON: And this for me, struck home to show my strength.

"This" in each line marks their sequential stabbings of their victim; but nothing in the exchange necessitates their sharing the same weapon, and in 2.1 both were armed. When Tamora demands "the poniard," the singular is presumably used because she is requesting the weapon held by whichever son is nearest to her. The likeliest candidate may be Demetrius, since he replies, "Stay, madam" (2.1.122). But this does not rule out Chiron: the request could be made to him, and he might be about to act on it, when Demetrius intervenes to stop him. Several options present themselves to actors performing this moment, or to readers attempting to imagine it in precise action. But Bate's would-be performance-friendly note misconstrues the real point at issue.

Hughes, too, often stumbles. Sometimes he can be unhelpfully evasive. At 5.2.121, both Quartos and First Folio arguably place a stage direction a line too early, so that Titus's "Marcus, my brother, 'tis sad Titus calls" follows Marcus's entry, thus obviating the need for Titus to summon him. Waith and Bate move the relevant stage direction back a line. Hughes, however, disagrees: "Marcus's entry in Q and F anticipates Titus's call; but there is no basis for emendation except a feeling that this should not be so. In performance, however, several plausible justifications could be found." This is unsatisfactory on two counts. The case for emendation is not based on a mere "feeling that this should not be so", but on the proposition that the sequence does not make sense as it stands. In addition, a mere assertion that performance would yield "several plausible justifications" is inadequate. For this claim to merit respect, we need examples of what those "justifications" might be.

At other points Hughes's notes become yet more confusing. For instance, he identifies the "abhorred pit" in 2.3 as being represented in the 1590s by an open stage-trap (1994: 198), and when Martius falls into the "pit," he observes: "Martius has fallen down the trap: now Quintus speaks down to him" (1994: 198). But he then offers this note when Chiron and Demetrius throw the dead Bassianus into the "pit": "Chiron and Demetrius probably throw Bassianus down the trap" (1994: 185–6). Why "probably"? The plot depends on Quintus and Martius sharing the "pit" with the murdered man; so, if the trap was used for the "pit," there can be no further doubt about the matter. This kind of uncertainty – and incipient self-contradiction – frequently recur in notes which are also, as here, arguably redundant. We need to be informed that the trap would almost certainly have been used for the "pit," but can then be trusted to work out for ourselves the consequences of that fact for later incidents.

The identification in the preceding paragraphs of passages where recent editors make unnecessary, and accident-prone, observations on staging issues is not intended to suggest that the project of generating a more performance-alert mode of commentary is itself flawed in conception. The fault lies in the execution, not in the ambition. While space is wasted on the kinds of note examined above, far more fundamental questions relating to the performance challenges of *Titus* receive scant, if any, attention from recent editors. I wish now to focus on one major example of this.

The play contains, at the start of 2.4, the most notorious of Shakespearean stage directions – "*Enter the Empresse sonnes with* Lauinia, *her handes cut off, and her tongue cut out, & rauisht.*"[3] Depriving Lavinia of speech in this way has drastic repercussions for both dramatist and player. It means that, for more than three acts, one of the tragedy's pivotal roles remains effectively unwritten. The primary vehicle of communication between early modern writers and actors was the distribution of cue-scripts, which recorded a character's speeches and the briefest of cues for each of them. For Lavinia, the possibility of such a cue-script ends with this horrifying entry. Thereafter, occasional stage directions sketch actions she must perform. Beyond that, in so far as the role has been scripted in a conventional sense at all, the evidence lies in the deductions which can be made about her behavior from the dialogue of others who share the stage with her. How such scenes were prepared for performance, given the dependence on cue scripts and the limited rehearsals customary in the 1590s, we will probably never know. But let us imagine that Shakespeare gave the player more detailed verbal instructions than usual. Those instructions were never recorded, and the forms in which the script survives consequently leave the Lavinia of the later acts doubly mute.

The youthful Shakespeare's eagerness to outdo his competitors – contemporary and classical – has often been remarked. Adapting Plautus's *Menaechmi* in *The Comedy of Errors*, he doubles the original pair of twins and adds a long-lost father and mother to enrich the brew and multiply the technical challenges he faced. In *Titus*, he similarly outbids the celebrated Roman analogues on which he drew for inspiration – "Not one rapist but two, not one murdered child but five, not one or two mutilated organs but six, not a one-course meal but a two" (Barkan 1986: 244). He was equally radical in the unprecedented demands he imposed upon his actors. The rhetorical intricacy and inventiveness of his dialogue presuppose extreme vocal dexterity and expressiveness in its performers. But Elizabethan acting was also rooted in gestural eloquence, to which the language of the hands was especially critical. Michael Neill has documented the complex "density of semiotic suggestiveness" with which early modern culture endowed the hand, as "not only a primary site of meaning," but also "the conduit of extraordinary energies." For students and teachers of rhetoric, gesture was "not a mere ornament of speech, but a vehicle of communication in its own right, a 'language' with its own rules." Thus, Montaigne praised gesture as "the proper and peculier speech of humane nature," since it was "common and publike to all" – a belief vindicated by those English actors who, performing in English in Frankfurt in 1592, won applause through "their gesture and action." "Acting" indeed "referred originally only to the player's art of gesture, and did not acquire its expanded meaning until the early seventeenth century" (Neill 1995: 23, 27, 30, 31, 34–5, 33). Given this context, a dramatist who deprives a key player of the ability to speak *and* to use his hands is setting him an exacting, potentially bewildering, challenge.

The events and characters depicted in *Titus*, unlike those in Shakespeare's other Roman plays, are unhistorical and may have been devised by Shakespeare himself. Various suggestions have been made about sources for aspects of the narrative and for characters' names. Neill invokes in this connection Livius Andronicus, a Greek who became a leading Roman actor in the third century BC, and who has been credited with being the first to adapt Greek plays for the Roman stage (Neill 1995: 39). Neill does not, however, mention the interesting information about him which Livy reports:

> the story goes that when his voice, owing to the frequent demands made upon it, had lost its freshness, he asked and obtained the indulgence to let a boy stand before the flautist to sing the monody, while he acted it himself, with a vivacity of gesture that gained considerably from his not having to use his voice. (Livy 1924: 363)

It is tempting to speculate about this story's impact upon Shakespeare, if he read it in Livy or heard of it from another source. Adopting Andronicus as the family name of a character to whom he assigned Lavinia's terrible fate might have seemed temptingly apt. Learning about an actor whose voice began to fail him, but who turned imminent disaster into triumph by correspondingly enriching his "vivacity of gesture," might have encouraged Shakespeare to devise a yet sterner test for the actor playing Lavinia – the demand that, deprived of both vocal and manual eloquence, he still devise ways of remaining in vivid communication with his audience. To the best of my knowledge, this possibility has not been previously noticed.

The ubiquity in *Titus* of references to hands, the deeds they perform, and the meanings their gestures communicate, as well as the ways in which these cross-resonate with the literal amputations its characters endure, has become a critical commonplace in recent years. But interest in it has tended to be thematic, rather than fully theatrical. In the 2003 Stratford-upon-Avon production, Titus's instruction to his brother to "unknit that sorrow-wreathen knot" (3.2.4) – i.e. unfold his arms – clearly puzzled some of the spectators with whom I saw it, partly because they were unaware that, for Shakespeare's contemporaries, folded arms were, in Bate's gloss, "a gesture denoting grief," and nothing in the performance rendered this fact apparent. But David Bradley, who played Titus, is an actor who carries to an extreme the modern disinclination to use arm and hand gestures ambitiously and who often holds his arms clamped tightly to his sides. Accordingly, his demand that Marcus restrict his gestures because Titus and Lavinia "want our hands, / And cannot passionate our tenfold grief / With folded arms" (3.2.5–6) made no sense. The passage only resonates as intended if a company's performance style generally deploys a sophisticated and extrovert gestural eloquence, and if Titus in particular earlier uses his hands with special authority and potency. Now cheated of one hand, character (and actor) are left to develop that novel and "lamentable Action of one Arme" which Middleton's mutilated soldier later celebrated as the distinguishing mark of "old Titus Andronicus" (Middleton 1604, sig.f2r) – an eloquent tribute to the impressive effect on spectators of Shakespeare's radical experiment with his performers' body language.

Space does not permit the more ample treatment this subject warrants; but we are broaching matters here of critical importance to the play in early modern and later performance. Despite their performance-friendly protestations, however, none of the recent editions engages seriously with such issues. It is symptomatic that Bate probes no further into that moment in 3.2 after explaining that folded arms signify grief. Of its performance ramifications, nothing is said. Titus's reprise of this theme – "how can I grace my talk, / Wanting a hand to give it action?" – in the penultimate scene (5.2.17–18) does prompt some belated comments; but, even then, in glossing "give it action," they all invoke the use of gesture in oratory, not in stage performance, and their comments remain unhelpfully generalized. All, therefore, remain disappointingly incurious about the performance styles for which, and by which, the play was originally shaped, and the ways in which its writing imposed unprecedented demands upon some of its players. Truly addressing its performance implications would entail making good these major deficiencies.

The mute nature of Lavinia's role after her rape and mutilation inspires Bate, but not Waith and Hughes, to listen carefully to other characters' words in order to discern their implications for the interpretation of Lavinia. Thus, at 4.1.39, he deduces the need for a specific indication of assent from Lavinia and suggests at 3.2.35 an innovative reading requiring a reaction from her to redirect Titus's thought, while at 3.1.250 he credibly proposes that Lavinia should kiss the decapitated heads of her two brothers, instead of, as other editors assume, kissing Titus. All this is invaluable. But a host of other staging issues concerning the character remain in the shadows. I will seek to illustrate what I mean by returning to the moments leading up to Lavinia's death in the final scene.

The dialogue here is often sparely enigmatic, as, for example, in the following exchanges:

TAMORA:	We are beholding to you, good Andronicus.
TITUS:	An if your highness knew my heart, you were.
	My lord the Emperor, resolve me this:
	Was it well done of rash Virginius
	To slay his daughter with his own right hand,
	Because she was enforced, stained, and deflowered?
SATURNINUS:	It was, Andronicus.
TITUS:	Your reason, mighty lord?
SATURNINUS:	Because the girl should not survive her shame,
	And by her presence still renew his sorrows.

TITUS: A reason mighty, strong, and effectual;
                     A pattern, precedent, and lively warrant
                     For me, most wretched, to perform the like.
                     Die, die, Lavinia, and thy shame with thee,
                     And with thy shame thy father's sorrow die.
                          He kills her

                                    (5.3.33–46)

Taken at face value, this passage suggests some striking conclusions. His acceptance of
Saturninus's moralization of the Virginius story could imply a Titus who intends to
survive this lethal encounter with his oppressors and live on unburdened by the
constant provocations to sorrow offered by his maimed daughter. This is not a tragic
hero who enters his story's last scene aware that death awaits him, and perhaps glad to
embrace the release it offers. Indeed, this Titus anticipates not the imminent tragic
concluding of his life's story, but a moment of liberation and new beginning. He will
accordingly be taken completely by surprise by the blow from Saturninus which fells
him. One might indeed detect a neat symmetry in the fact that it is the Emperor who
unexpectedly kills him, since it is to Saturninus that Titus implicitly boasts, via the
tale of Virginius, of how he intends his own story to continue.

But what if we do not read the exchange so literally? What if Titus is playing with
Saturninus in the expectation that the latter's verdict upon the Virginius narrative
will inevitably bear the imprint of his own shallowness and affectlessness? The
unlikelihood of the idea that Titus would seriously seek guidance from such an
enemy might encourage such a reading. If so, then the charade of asking his advice
dramatizes the gulf of values which, as Titus sees it, separates the Andronici from
those who preyed on them. His promise "to perform the like" will be inflected with
the knowledge of everything which divides his sorrowful act from Saturninus's glib
interpretation of Virginius's parallel deed as a neatly surgical way of opening an
optimistic new chapter in that other patriarch's life.

The situation is complicated by the fact that the dialogue here cannot, given her
plight, directly reveal Lavinia's state of mind, and no authorial stage directions
enlighten us about it. Does she come to the banquet assured that her revenge will
now be accomplished, and therefore ready to welcome her own fate at her father's
hands? Or is death dealt swiftly and unexpectedly to her by Titus's peremptory, self-
absorbed decree? Here too Shakespeare presumably had a clear intent in mind; but it
has not been written down, and the dialogue we seek to elucidate will accommodate
both these interpretations and others. As a result, radically divergent readings of the
dominant tonality of the tragedy's concluding moments can be generated with equal
plausibility from the play as it has come down to us.

Among our modern annotators only Bate concedes the possibility of such ques-
tions, and even he permits himself only one brief allusion to the subject in his notes.
At l.46 he reports that "In the Warner production, he crisply snapped her neck; at
Santa Cruz, she stepped towards him as he held out the knife, actively embracing both

her father and death." The implications of that contrast are massive, though Bate's non-emphatic way of reporting it calls no special attention to the fact. In one of these stagings, the revenging patriarch is totally in command, and we are given no indication whether the daughter consents to her fate or is even aware of its imminence. In the other, her death fulfills a pact between them, and she offers herself calmly and gratefully to the lure of oblivion. Both versions meet the script's demands comfortably, in that both make plausible sense of the words it provides to be spoken and the actions it explicitly or implicitly prescribes; but, in the process, they tell totally divergent stories. An editor of the play who seeks to absorb what *Titus*'s stage history can teach him/her needs to start from this truth about the text as it has come down to us. As far as the implications of all this for the annotation of the final scene of *Titus* are concerned, however, Bate's single note is the only concession to such priorities made by the recent editions. On this evidence, the promised dialogue between the world of scholarly editing and performance realities still seems to be in its early stages.

NOTES

1 I have explored related aspects of the problems encountered in rendering Shakespeare editions performance-friendly in three previous articles, details of which are provided in the References and further reading.

2 Quotations from *Titus Andronicus*, plus accompanying act/scene/line references, are taken from Waith's 1984 Oxford Shakespeare edition.

3 This is the First Quarto version. The First Folio differs in its spelling, punctuation, and use of italics and capitals.

REFERENCES AND FURTHER READING

Barkan, Leonard (1986). *The Gods Made Flesh: Metamorphosis and the Pursuit of Paganism*. New Haven, CT: Yale University Press.

Bate, Jonathan (ed.) (1995). *William Shakespeare, "Titus Andronicus."* London: Routledge.

Berthoud, Jacques & Massai, Sonia (eds.) (2001). *William Shakespeare, "Titus Andronicus."* London: Penguin.

Cordner, Michael (1996). "Annotation and Performance in Shakespeare." *Essays in Criticism* 46: 289–301.

Cordner, Michael (2002). "Actors, Editors, and the Annotation of Shakespearian Playscripts." *Shakespeare Survey* 55: 181–98.

Cordner, Michael (2003). "'To Show our Simple Skill': Scripts and Performances in Shakespearian Comedy." *Shakespeare Survey* 56: 167–83.

Dessen, Alan C. (1989). *Shakespeare in Performance: "Titus Andronicus."* Manchester: Manchester University Press.

Dover Wilson, John (1948). *William Shakespeare, "Titus Andronicus."* Cambridge: Cambridge University Press.

Dover Wilson, John (1969). *Milestones on the Dover Road*. London: Faber and Faber.

Hughes, Alan (ed.) (1994). *William Shakespeare, "Titus Andronicus."* Cambridge: Cambridge University Press.

Jackson, MacDonald P. (1997). Review of the New Cambridge Shakespeare and Arden 3 editions of *Titus Andronicus*. *Modern Language Review* 92: 946–8.

Jones, Emrys (2001). "Reclaiming Shakespeare." *Essays in Criticism* 51: 35–50.

Livy [Titus Livius] (1924). *Books V, VI, and VI*, trans. B. O. Foster. London: William Heinemann Ltd.

Maxwell, J. C. (1957). "Shakespeare's Roman Plays: 1900–1956." *Shakespeare Survey* 10: 1–11.

Maxwell, J. C. (1961). *William Shakespeare, "Titus Andronicus,"* 3rd edn. London: Methuen.

Metz, G. Harold (1996). *Shakespeare's Earliest Tragedy: Studies in "Titus Andronicus."* Madison, NJ: Fairleigh Dickinson University Press.

Middleton, Thomas (1604). *The Ant and the Nightingale*. London: Thomas Bushell.

Neill, Michael (1995). "'Amphitheaters in the Body': Playing with Hands on the Shakespearian Stage." *Shakespeare Survey* 48: 23–50.

Trewin, J. C. (1978). *Going to Shakespeare*. London: George Allen and Unwin.

Waith, Eugene M. (ed.) (1984). *William Shakespeare, "Titus Andronicus."* Oxford: Clarendon Press.

Wells, Stanley (1984). *Re-Editing Shakespeare for the Modern Reader*. Oxford: Clarendon Press.

Williams, Harcourt (1949). *Old Vic Saga*. London: Winchester Publications Limited.

22

Shakespeare on the Record

Douglas Lanier

On 25 June 1876 at the International Exposition in Philadelphia, Alexander Graham Bell made the first of several public debuts of his new invention, the telephone. To demonstrate the device for gathered dignitaries, Bell recited Hamlet's "to be or not to be" soliloquy which to the amazement of those gathered was at least partially intelligible (see Bruce 1973: 193–7). No doubt Bell chose this speech because it was familiar enough to be recognized easily over the primitive equipment. Perhaps, too, he wanted to show his audience the invention's capacity for transmitting messages more weighty than nursery rhymes, conventional speeches and popular songs. Yet Bell's choice of Hamlet's soliloquy, with its focus on bodily presence and absence and its concerns about the unpredictabilities of the hereafter, uncannily anticipates issues that haunt audio reproduction in general and the phonographic recording of Shakespearean performance in particular. For listeners, phonography eliminates the bodiliness of actors – they become pure sound – even as it gives a vivid impression of their physical and temporal presence. It alienates actors from their own voices, an effect conveyed by Sir Henry Irving's horror at hearing himself speaking from Edison's phonograph in 1888: "Is that my voice? My God!"[1] And because it preserves them for the future, audio recording deterritorializes Shakespearean performances, situating them in new contexts of time and space and opening them to uses unforeseen at the time of their commitment to the groove. The image of Nipper the dog, his ear cocked at the sound of his dead master's voice issuing from the Victrola's horn, turns these issues into phonography's signature icon: audio reproduction (re)creates performances that are delicately, movingly, uncannily poised between being and not-being.

During the past century phonography has become so thoroughly naturalized that its effects and their implications for Shakespearean performance have hardly seemed noteworthy. Despite more than 100 years of committing Shakespeare to record, the impressive body of audio recordings of his plays and poems, much of which remains active in the commercial catalog, has been largely ignored by scholars of mass media

Shakespeare, crowded out by the attention paid to performances on film and TV.[2]
Among the reasons for this are the predominantly visualist orientation of modern and
postmodern media culture, the pop cultural cachet attached to Shakespeare films, and
the coming of age of scholarship on mass media Shakespeare during the 1990s'
Shakespeare film boom. Most important, however, is the popular perception of
audio recording. It has been seen as film or theater *manqué*; as a dead medium,
superseded by film, videotape or DVD; or merely as a technological means for making
a record of a performance rather than as an art form with its own distinctive history
and aesthetic conventions. One strong assumption in critical commentary on phonographic Shakespeare is that the phonograph merely presents in aural form the
Shakespearean text in all its hermeneutic plenitude. Reviewing several recent recordings, one critic observes that "a special virtue of audio recordings ... is that they do
not close off the interpretation of character, relationship and theme in a way that
productions of stage and screen often do" (Jeffcoate 2001: 77). Simply put, audio
Shakespeare has been widely regarded as a form "between book and boards"[3] rather
than a distinctive medium for performance. By depending so heavily upon the
Shakespearean text, so the argument goes, audio recording minimizes the interpolations that characterize – and (for some) mar – modern (re)productions in other
media. Little wonder that performance critics might have so little to say about
phonographic Shakespeare: if indeed recordings merely present rather than interpret
the plays, attempting a critical reading of them seems futile. To confront these
premises, I want to reconsider Shakespeare for the record from two perspectives. I
will suggest how some specific qualities of audio recording have worked to recalibrate
the nature and social function of performed Shakespeare, in ways distinct from yet
intertwined with rival media. However, those qualities have not entirely predisposed
how in practice Shakespeare has been committed to recording. I also want to survey
how particular practitioners have conceptualized phonography as a medium for
Shakespeare performance at key moments in its history. My interest in interrogating
both the phenomenological nature of audio recording and its historical practices is less
to offer "readings" of specific Shakespeare recordings than to analyze phonography as a
significant, distinctive medium for Shakespearean performance.

A Phenomenology of Audio Shakespeare

Because it was among the first and most widely disseminated technologies of mass
reproduction, audio recording provides an apt example of "remediation" – adapting
content from an older medium to a newer one (see Bolter & Grusin 2000, esp. 44–50)
– that has been so central to Shakespeare's cultural longevity. Of course, transposing
Shakespeare from one medium to another began with the first print publications of
his plays, but the process has accelerated considerably with the twentieth-century
proliferation of mass media: film, phonography, radio, TV, and the Internet. This
process is not simply a matter of repackaging Shakespeare, for remediation funda-

mentally alters the meaning, experience and cultural purpose of Shakespeare's work. It entails, for example, readjusting the relative ratios of and interrelationships between elements of sensory experience – sight, sound, movement or fixity, sequencing of events, speed, venue, and the like. Considered in relationship to the stage, phonographic performance emphasizes the aural and downplays the visual, though, significantly, even on record elements of spatial placement – and thus of sight – can be implied by the particularities of recorded sound.[4] This shift in the ratio between sight and sound presents challenges for material crafted for a more visually oriented medium like live performance. How, for instance, to communicate aurally the characters' reactions to dialogue, the content of a dumb show, the action of silent eavesdropping or a swordfight's moment-by-moment progress? On the other hand, not seeing the onstage performers, costumes or set enables listeners' different sorts of imaginative participation than those prompted by stage performance. Most obviously, the physical bodies of stage actors stand in a different relationship to the characters they play than do those of phonographic performers. Remediation also involves striking new relationships of affiliation, hierarchy and legitimation as Shakespeare migrates between older and newer media. Since phonography bears a close family resemblance to radio, it is not surprising that several early Shakespeare recordings directly trace their pedigree to radio broadcasts – Barrymore's collection of speeches from his 1937 *Streamlined Shakespeare* (Audio Rarities LPA 2280 and 2281), and Gielgud's 1951 *Hamlet* for the Theatre Guild on the Air (RCA 6007-1, 2) prominent among them. Indeed, that relationship survives in recent British Shakespeare series such as "Shakespeare for the Millennium" and the Renaissance Theatre Company's recordings first broadcast on BBC Radio 3. Nevertheless, in the course of its history, phonographic Shakespeare has also been variously allied with and differentiated from theatrical performances and print editions, and the changing affiliations of Shakespearean phonography with these media illuminate how its practitioners understood the nature of recorded performance.

Among the many effects of transposing Shakespeare to the phonograph, four are particularly noteworthy: *textualization*, *interiorization*, *privatization*, and *commodification*. *Textualization* specifies several effects. From the start, audio recording sought to give sound a graphical, permanent form, as the various names of early apparatuses – *phonoautograph*, *gramophone*, *phonograph* – suggest. The exclusively aural nature of phonographic performances – like those on radio – tends to foreground Shakespeare's text, his poetry, wordplay, metaphorical density, and oratorical qualities rather than the dramatic narrative. This is particularly so given the contrast between Shakespearean language and the predominantly colloquial idiom of radio and recorded song. Moreover, committing a Shakespearean performance to record renders it fixed and permanent, in much the same way that printing gives definitive form to written drafts. In this, phonographic Shakespeare differs significantly from radio or early TV performances, which were typically live, ephemeral broadcasts shared by a communal audience (however atomized into thousands of separate rooms) in the present. Because recordings offer a fixed experience initiated by the individual listener rather than the performer or broadcaster, they encourage a more solitary form of listening akin to reading – even, Evan Eisenberg emphasizes, when that listening occurs in the company of others (1988: 46). "Where radio unites," he observes, "records fracture" (1988: 32). And although listening to a recorded performance is certainly an experiential event, once recorded a performance takes on the qualities of a stable "textual" object, allowing for much closer, analytic modes of listening made possible by repetition (1988: 72–3). In fact, because recording magnifies errors but also allows them to be edited out, it tends to encourage a performance aesthetic privileging technical precision over spontaneity and the felicitous accident.

Such effects, along with these recordings' place in the educational market, may explain why Shakespeare recording series have often been issued with accompanying texts or in coordination with established print editions, as if recording and print publication were analogous activities. In the late 1930s and early 1940s Orson Welles was the first to pair texts – his *Everybody's Shakespeare* editions – with recorded versions of *Twelfth Night*, *Merchant of Venice*, *Julius Caesar*, and *Macbeth*, the first continuity recordings of Shakespeare ever attempted (see Anderegg 1999: 39–56). The name of his never-completed series, the Mercury Text Records, underlines the project's hybrid nature and the type of listening experience it was designed to reward. Later series were also originally issued in conjunction with print texts. The Shakespeare Recording Society and Living Shakespeare series included printed scripts with their LP boxes; the Marlowe Society series from the same period proclaimed its fidelity to an "uncut" authoritative text, as have recent recordings in the Naxos and Arkangel series. The conjunction of text and record suggests that these recordings are designed, at least theoretically, to be heard with book in hand rather than experienced as independent performance events. Record and text legitimize each other: the performance establishes the stage-worthiness of the text and brushes away the air of academic mustiness, while the text elevates the performance to the status of an "audio edition," a "pure" realization of Shakespeare's words rather than a director's or an actor's interpretative concept. As if to hammer the point home, three "audio editions" – the Marlowe Society, Naxos and Arkangel – advertise "complete" texts, differentiating themselves from stage or film performances where, as a matter of practicality and interpretive license, scripts are routinely cut.

Equally crucial to the listener's experience is the disembodied nature of recorded performance, an encounter with "acousmatic" or "schizophonic" sound – that is, sound heard without seeing its source. Like radio, phonography requires the listener to supply imaginatively the dramatic *mise en scène*, creating mental images of the characters, setting and action from aural cues such as vocal tone, sound effects, music, acoustic resonance, and microphone placement. One advantage of this "theater of the mind" is that it allows for instantaneous changes in locale and doubling of characters impossible to stage. Because audio performance depends so heavily on the individual imagination, operating without the shared visual spectacle of stage or screen, this Shakespeare tends to be a more intimate, interiorized experience, one that not only differs from listener to listener but also changes the nature of the plays performed.[5] Because characters and settings of audio performances are partial projections of the listener's imagination, they move more readily towards abstraction and archetype than do performances rooted in the material particularity of actors' bodies and set designs. The dreamlike fluidity of fictional reality in audio, where speakers and settings have no existence apart from the sounds they make, also downplays the narrative world of material objects and actions and plays up the drama's psychological elements, the intimate revelation of character. Unlike film, which can establish points of view independent of the characters, the conditions of audibility favor proximity to its subjects – audio offers no equivalent of a long shot. First-person elements like soliloquies, where characters address the listener directly, are particularly effective; swordplay and physical farce are not. Put schematically, whereas the visual nature of film fastens on physical exteriorities, the auditory nature of radio and phonography emphasizes interiorities. In audio form Shakespeare's plays, especially the tragedies, tend to become psychological dramas focused on the protagonist's interior world, with other characters and events heard or imagined as functions of that world rather than existing independently. This effect is enhanced by the relatively close miking now preferred in most modern Shakespeare recordings, which creates the impression that the characters are intimate with the listener. Notably, the Shakespeare Recording Society's *Macbeth* (1960, Caedmon SRS-231) offers Lady Macbeth's sleepwalking speech in a near whisper punctuated with low sighs. Unlike the stage, where an auditor's distance may invite moral judgment, the intimacy made possible by phonography prompts a more empathetic response. In several ways, then, the aural medium recalibrates the relationship between interior states and external realities in Shakespearean theatre.

All forms of media technology resituate the performances they reproduce, but the phonograph and radio were the first mass media to relocate the performance of music and drama in private domestic space, a development which has had profound consequences for the social function of Shakespeare throughout the twentieth century. Although eighteenth- and nineteenth-century print editions had already made possible private study of the Shakespearean text and led to a growing distinction and competition between two modes of consuming Shakespeare's works, as text or in performance, the phonograph worked to collapse these two modes. In this regard phonography was distinct from live theatre, film and early radio, all of which shared various degrees of public "presence" that predisposed how their audiences watched or listened. Even though the audience make-up and the nature and economics of theatregoing were shaped by issues of cultural stratification, live performance served as a communal *public* ritual that (re)affirmed Shakespeare's value as common cultural property. Before videotape became widely available, showing a Shakespeare film had a somewhat similar function, since it too was a public event presented to an audience in a public space, with viewers in the company of one another if not in the company of the players. So too radio and early TV performances, which were typically live or aired only once. Even listeners in thousands of living rooms were aware of themselves as belonging to a larger group hearing the same broadcast simultaneously. American radio not only actively promoted the analogy between radio performances and theatre through the titles of its shows – Mercury Theatre on the Air, Great Plays, Theatre Guild on the Air – but in some cases it enhanced the illusion of liveness and communality by broadcasting before an audible studio audience.

Writing about the social effect of recording on music, Jacques Attali observes that "accessibility replaces the festival": "A work that the author perhaps did not hear more than once in his lifetime ... becomes accessible to a multitude of people, and becomes repeatable outside the spectacle of its performance. It gains availability. It loses its festive and religious character as a simulacrum of sacrifice" (1985: 100).

Unlike radio or early TV, the phonograph definitively converted Shakespearean performance into an experience for the individual listener, available at any time at home, with all sound traces of the audience and thus awareness of the potentially communal nature of the experience eliminated. Clive Brill, producer of the Arkangel Shakespeare series, sees this as the medium's advantage:

> If you go and see a great play in a great theater, with a great director and actors, you can't beat it ... But when do you ever see that? Almost never. At the theater you're battling air conditioning, coughing, you can't hear everything. The good thing about this is if you cast it well, you have very good actors, and you're not screwing it up, then you can hear every word. And you can hear it again and again if you want. (Gritten 2003)

Even as recording made Shakespearean performances widely accessible as never before, it also privatized the experience of those performances – in effect, the phonograph blazed the phenomenological trail for Shakespeare on home video in the past two decades.

Audio recording not only privatizes the experience of Shakespearean performance, it also makes possible its conversion into a marketable commodity. If admission charges involve live theatre and film screenings in networks of exchange, with the phonograph, Shakespearean performances first fully become mass-produced physical objects that can be bought, owned, collected, and used at will. Phonography, Attali observes, allows one to possess the performer's otherwise evanescent labor, making possible "the stockpiling of time"; moreover, collecting records "becomes a substitute, not a preliminary condition, for use." The impulse to collect, so Attali argues, especially feeds the value placed upon complete sets, recordings designated worth the effort of stockpiling (1985: 101; see also Eisenberg 1988: 17–24). Indeed, since the advent of the long-playing record, the audio recording of Shakespeare has tended to privilege "complete" series and "unabridged" recordings rather than notable performances of individual plays.[6] Particularly in the 1950s and 1960s, the albums were presented as high-art fetish objects, adorned with classical paintings and antique-style drawings and woodcuts; several Shakespeare Recording Society's releases featured photos of decorative *objets d'art* – a porcelain bust for *Merry Wives*, a bronze eagle for *Julius Caesar*, an ornate balcony for *Romeo and Juliet* – as if to reduce the plays to a single ornate object one might vicariously own. The Living Shakespeare series packaged its albums in boxed sets bound in faux maroon leather, as if they were books suitable for a country house library.

As is clear from these forms of packaging, commodification extends to the cultural capital that Shakespeare represents. Recordings allow the accoutrements of education, taste, heritage, and luxury associated with Shakespeare to be treated as private property; they become part of bourgeois regimes of cultural self-improvement and upward mobility. Caedmon's Shakespeare recordings were made available not only through stores but also through "membership" in the Shakespeare Recording Society, a subscription service modeled on the Book of the Month Club and classical music "societies," thereby providing the illusion of cultural sponsorship and quasi-exclusivity.[7] (The Shakespeare Recording Society was a commercial fiction created by Caedmon Records, its impressive name apparently imitating the prime mover in Argo's Shakespeare series, Cambridge University's Marlowe Society. In reality, this "Society" was nothing more than an *ad hoc* assemblage of actors who supported each recording's name stars.) Little wonder, then, that Shakespeare recordings were celebrated in the late 1950s and early 1960s in *House and Garden* and *House Beautiful* as emblems of middle-class cultural authority, a luxurious personal indulgence for the individual home listener: "Being read to by the world's most skillful voices would be judged a pleasure by anybody's scale of values. But when you can command these voices to read you the world's great literature while you are lolling at ease or doing some needed task with your hands, it is a deluxe delight of the first order" (Kinard 1961: 102).

Admittedly, these effects do not so readily pertain to that other principal consumer of phonographic Shakespeare, the educational market. Like videotape and DVDs in the 1990s, audio recording allowed teachers from mid-twentieth century on to include Shakespeare-in-performance in their classroom repertoire. It is indicative of the educational market's importance that Orson Welles and mentor Harry Hill touted the pedagogical potential of recordings in *English Journal* when Welles launched his Mercury Text Records series in 1939. Welles presents the phonograph as a means for (re)introducing into the classroom popular forms of aesthetic appreciation for Shakespearean performance – as opposed to the "scientific" philological analysis of the text that Welles found stultifying and elitist. If articles on the use of phonographic Shakespeare for teaching are any guide (see Weingarten 1939, Zahorski 1977, Rockas 1978), recording has tended to have the opposite effect: typically it not only puts performance all the more firmly in the service of textual analysis but also habituates students to experiencing Shakespearean theatre through protocols of reception specific to modern mass media. Welles confirms the importance of recording in circulating Shakespearean cultural capital by stressing his desire for students to have a visceral, sensory, unmediated encounter with Shakespeare, one which, he concludes, phonographic performance can supply. But when he turns to describing that moment of encounter – echoing Hamlet's "caviar to the general" – its proper enjoyment turns out to require what Welles dubs special pedagogical "cultivation": "Few exotic tastes are cultivated without some preliminary wry faces or some contemplative and questionate lip-smackings. But as caviar to the initiate is more thrilling than hamburger, so the exotic, zestful flavor of Elizabethan phraseology falls at first strangely on our dulled and jaded senses, but, cultivated, it can bring moments of ecstasy" (Welles and Hill 1939: 467). Properly "cultivated" by professionals, the ability to appreciate Shakespearean performance, like the predilection for Beluga over Burger King, becomes the distinguishing mark of cultural sophisticates, euphemized as "exotic" rather than elitist. What Welles's remarks reveal is the unacknowledged tension between his embrace of new media technology and his aversion to the kinds of popular taste the mass media propagated. I don't mean to disparage the motives behind Welles's pioneering project or to denigrate classroom use of recorded Shakespeare performances. Rather, I wish to stress that the classroom has become a crucial agent in spreading and legitimizing many of the effects I've been describing. To treat audio recording as merely a technological convenience – "the next best thing" to live or film performance – or as a tool for democratizing Shakespeare is to fail to recognize phonography as a powerful cultural force, with characteristics, predispositions, and social effects particular to it. That is, it is to fail to see how profoundly phonography has contributed (and continues to contribute) to the larger processes of mediatization that have so reshaped the nature of modern Shakespearean performance.

A Short History of Audio Shakespeare

And yet it would be a mistake to regard the phenomenology of Shakespeare on record as determined from the start by the predispositions of phonography. Discussing the early history of audio reproduction, Jonathan Sterne warns that we should not regard sound technologies as independent agents in cultural history, for they must be articulated into particular fields of combined physical, social, and artistic practices and institutions for them to function as *media*: "a technology is simply a machine that performs a function; a medium is a network of repeatable relations" (2003: 210). Phonography began its cultural life as a stenographic aid and a means for preserving the fleeting voices of loved ones and the powerful only to become by accidents of history and various forms of use a medium for musical and, to a lesser extent, spoken entertainment. The history of recorded Shakespeare suggests that how audio recording might be used as a vehicle for Shakespearean performance – indeed, whether it should be used at all – was anything but clear or natural to its practitioners. Here I want to survey some of the different ways in which phonographic performance of Shakespeare has been (re)conceived over time, attending particularly to how audio reproduction has allied itself with, borrowed from and competed against other media. Because non-musical uses of audio recording are so often perceived as purely documentary, I must reiterate an earlier point: sound recordings do not simply provide "mediated" versions of live Shakespeare performances, to be judged on the basis of fidelity – acoustic or interpretive – to some unmediated "source." The microphone does not simply capture a performance or reading that has some independent existence. Rather, phonographic Shakespeare has always been a *studio artform*. With very rare exceptions, recorded performances are produced expressly for the recording apparatus, shaped by its particular capabilities and the actors' awareness that they are making a record. Though the terms of that (re)production – and the conceptual investments driving them – are not entirely fixed by the technology, the paradox Walter Benjamin observes of film is also true of phonography: "The equipment-free aspect of reality here has become the height of artifice; the sight [here, sound] of immediate reality has become an orchid in the land of technology" (1968: 233).

This point bears repetition because so many early Shakespeare recordings trace their origins back to the theatre, particularly in the earliest days of the phonograph when the impetus to make Shakespearean recordings sprang primarily from its ability to preserve voices otherwise lost to time. Most of the earliest examples, dating as far back as 1890, feature established stars of the late Victorian and Edwardian stage – Edwin Booth, Ellen Terry, Henry Irving, J. Forbes-Robertson, Herbert Beerbohm-Tree. Many recorded at an advanced age, the disembodied nature of recording allowing them to return to roles which would have been preposterous for them to attempt onstage. And nearly all offer declamatory, to the modern ear mannered, performances, as if they were unable or unwilling to modify their accustomed stage delivery for the machine.[8] This quality of speechifying was exacerbated by the length of the single cylinder or Berliner's 78 rpm disc which limited Shakespeare recordings to single speeches, typically orations or soliloquies. Though the archival value of these recordings is indisputable, whether they offer an accurate glimpse of late Victorian theatrical practice is open to debate, for the orotund, deliberate manner of these performances was surely in part a response to the demands of the recording apparatus, which required high volumes and careful enunciation to create useable recordings. Although he lacked the articulatory command of his peers, Beerbohm-Tree's 1906 recordings demonstrate a developing if inconsistent understanding of how to perform for the phonograph. His delivery of Antony's "O pardon me, thou bleeding piece of earth" oration, ponderously rising line by line from public grief to indignation, is typical of the high declamatory mode, but his far more intimate approach to Falstaff's "Honor" soliloquy, with its finely timed "no"s, offers an early example of vocal characterization, by voice alone conveying Falstaff's bloated body and capacity for comic self-justification.

The advent of electric recording and the microphone in 1925 allowed for demonstrably clearer sound than earlier recording methods. John Gielgud's mellifluous tone and exquisite articulation especially benefited from the new technology, and he was to become one of recorded Shakespeare's earliest stars, though his preference for set speeches in his important 1930s Linguaphone discs maintained ties with the oratorical mode of earlier recordings. Electric recording also introduced the possibility of a director using studio techniques to actively shape the sounds listeners would hear. Having honed his skills on the radio, Orson Welles was among the first to exploit the technical resources of microphone and control room, as well as the conventions of radio drama, to explore its possibilities for recorded Shakespeare. The Mercury Text

Records aimed at dramatizations of plays, not the oration of isolated speeches, and though Welles issued his records in conjunction with texts, those texts are editions designed for performance rather than full texts for reading. The series has an experimental quality, for each of the recordings takes a slightly different approach to the challenge of phonographic performance. His *Twelfth Night* (re-released in 1998 on Pearl GEMS 0020), for example, oscillates between a straightforward radio dramatization, a reading edition (Welles speaks all the stage directions), and a historical documentary, with a prologue that imagines the play's theatrical genesis with Shakespeare and Burbage and an epilogue detailing its critical reception. Few, however, were willing to take up Welles's conception of a specifically phonographic Shakespeare after he abandoned the series in the early 1940s. The vast majority of Shakespeare recordings in the 1930s and 1940s followed the "highlights and excerpts" tradition and had their origins in theatre productions only minimally reconceived for the turntable. The most important of these, the groundbreaking production of *Othello* with Paul Robeson, José Ferrer, and Uta Hagen, issued in 1944 on eighteen 78s (Columbia Masterworks SL 153), is one of the first full-length recordings of a Shakespeare play and, critics universally acknowledge, a landmark in American theatre. Robeson's recording of *Othello* was to garner far less controversial reception than would his live performances of Othello's role, perhaps because audio recording amplified the power of his *basso profundo* while erasing the troubling presence of his black miscegenistic body. The liner notes by Goddard Lieberson, director of Columbia Masterworks and supervisor of the recording, stress not the historical importance of casting an African-American in the role, which is never mentioned, but rather "the vocal splendor of [Robeson's] delivery."[9] In fact, wittingly or not, the recording offers an oddly disembodied soundscape, noticeably sparing of those sound effects that might establish concrete details of physical action or setting.[10]

The 1950s saw three key technological innovations in rapid succession: the long-playing, "high-fidelity" record, made available commercially in 1948, which provided far longer sides and thus fuller-length performances; magnetic tape recording, first used in studio recording in 1949, which permitted new levels of technical control through mixing tracks and splicing together multiple takes; and stereo recording, first introduced in 1958, which added new spatial dimensions and analytic clarity to audio performances. The first Shakespeare series to exploit the long-playing record was the full-length recordings by the Old Vic Company, *Romeo and Juliet* (1952, RCA Victor LVT-3001), *Macbeth* (1953, RCA Victor LM-6010), *A Midsummer Night's Dream* (1954, RCA Victor LM-6110), and *Hamlet* (1957, RCA Victor LM-6404), all of which originated as stagings. Most striking about these productions is the tension between their dominant soundscapes, which recreate the resonant ambience of the theatre, maintaining the distance between performer and audience, and their movements towards a decidedly less orotund, more intimate style of speaking. A few of the recordings experiment with the possibilities of a more expressionistic sound, such as *Macbeth*'s opening scene with the weird sisters' voices aswirl in wind. By contrast, *Midsummer Night's Dream*, derived from a staging renowned for its neo-Victorian extravagances, finds no way to transpose the acting style appropriate to its lavish, large-scale sets into a more intimate medium, preferring instead to sandwich the rather formally staged scenes between liberal quotations of Mendelssohn, as if it were a concert with overly long readings. Like the company's North American tours, these recordings sought to broaden the audience for the Old Vic's more modern approach to spoken Shakespeare, with its emphasis on speed, variety and energy rather than elocution, much as Olivier had used the film medium to showcase Shakespeare's capacity for cinematic spectacle and his own virtuoso physical technique. By designating the Old Vic's productions worthy of preservation, these recordings also worked to establish the company's preeminence in Shakespearean performance over the Shakespeare Memorial Theatre in Stratford, from which it was facing competition as plans for a National Theatre were first coming into focus. The Stratford Festival Company itself had issued albums of season highlights during the late 1940s.

For several reasons, the late 1950s and early 1960s were to become the golden age of spoken word recording and of phonographic Shakespeare in particular. Certainly LPs made possible the recording of longer stretches of speech or dialogue without interruption, but other factors also contributed to the rise of the spoken word album. One was sheer economics: independent record label start-up costs were relatively low, and phonographic performances had a much lower break-even point than did live performances or print publication, making niche market productions profitable that were heretofore unsustainable, especially in the vastly expanded record market of the post-war period (see Hewes 1952: 26, Chanan 1995: 98–100). Other factors were cultural. Radio, and its successor television, established the private home as the epicenter of mediatized entertainment, and the phonograph emerged as an essential component in the bourgeois home's technological ensemble. Radio drama of the 1930s and 1940s had acclimated home audiences to the conventions of audio performance, and so its decline in the 1950s, particularly in America, created a space which spoken word recordings – literary works as well as a new subgenre, comedy albums – might occupy. Recordings of literature were part of a much larger middlebrow impulse to transpose traditional high culture – books, theatre, opera – into the media forms of modern pop culture, a trend exemplified, for example, by *Classics Illustrated* comic books, also at their zenith in the 1950s. While still using new mass media forms, these recordings had a more up-market veneer: they were literary (re)appropriations of a medium more closely associated with popular music, productions marketed like luxury books or classical music, set apart from the lowbrow fare of television and pulp publishing that so alarmed cultural critics of the 1950s. Several ambitious Shakespeare recording series were to trade upon the economic vitality of the spoken book genre, ratifying its cultural stature. Three of these – the Marlowe Dramatic Society series on Argo Records, the Shakespeare Recording Society series on Caedmon Records, and the Living Shakespeare series on the Odhams label, all of which appeared in coordination with the quatercentenary of Shakespeare's birth in 1964 – exemplify quite different conceptions of Shakespearean performance for the phonograph.

The first series to be begun (in 1958) and the first recording of the canon to be completed (in 1964), Argo's series came with formidable state and scholarly *bona fides*. Commissioned by the British Arts Council, the series was very much a Cambridge University production: George Rylands, Fellow of King's College, directed the performances by the Marlowe Society, a student company specializing in Renaissance drama (aided in the recording by a changing group of theatre veterans Rylands coyly dubbed The Professional Company), and the productions used Dover Wilson's New Cambridge text. Rylands conceived of the project as an aural presentation of an "authentic" Shakespeare, each level of the production rigorously faithful to textual details or Renaissance practice with few concessions to the modern phonographic medium. The Marlowe Society series offers not quite a reading but not quite an audio dramatization; it might best be understood as a phonographic recreation of a particular conception of period performance. Music, for example, consists largely of fanfares and song accompaniments on period instruments; sound effects are limited to those specified in Shakespeare's script, sometimes to the point of violating basic aural naturalism – the stylized storm sounds in *Macbeth* (1958) occur only where they are indicated in Folio, and clashes of swords in *Romeo and Juliet* (1960) and *Hamlet* (1961) have the quality of being mechanically inserted so as to preserve the integrity of the dialogue. Even the placement of microphones – at an unchanging middle distance from all the performers – seeks to evoke Rylands's conception of period stage practice, of the theatre as a space for formally declaiming Shakespeare's language, as if consciously pushing against the medium's penchant for auditory intimacy. Rylands's directorial emphasis falls principally on meticulous elocution, and so performers in major and minor roles alike tend to speak at a consistent mid-register volume, in a deliberate, even pace and Received Pronunciation, with vocal characterization minimized and largely confined to the low comic roles. Rylands's antipathy for highly individualized performances extends even to the cast list: there simply wasn't one, at least initially. Though the players' anonymity was apparently intended to emphasize the ensemble quality of the recording – subordinating individual actors' styles to serving the text and "democratically" leveling professional and amateur – it was also a way of asserting the series' resistance to crass marketing considerations or fleeting theatrical reputations, thus testifying to its putative timelessness and scholarly purity of purpose.[11]

In short, the Marlowe Society recordings seek to create the degree zero of Shakespearean performance, a phonographic (non)style so neutral and faithful to the text that it might allow the beauty and poetic sense of Shakespeare's language to stand transparently by itself. Of course, such a "philosophically neutral" style, as one critic put it, is a chimera. And, indeed, the Marlowe Society series offers the last gasp of the then waning declamatory mode with its emphasis on proper, class-coded accent and articulation, backed by gestures of "authenticity" and focused almost entirely on the aesthetic texture of the language, cleansed of any engagement with the contemporary world. Set within the controversies surrounding the formation of a National Theatre throughout the period, Rylands's "authentic" Shakespeare might be seen as rebuking the innovations made by the Old Vic and (especially) the Stratford Memorial Theatre, where Shakespearean directors' theatre had come of age and was establishing itself as England's "official" Shakespeare.

If the Marlowe Society series aspired to the condition of a scholarly print edition, Caedmon's Shakespeare Recording Society (SRS) series, recorded between 1960 and 1968 under the direction of Howard Sackler and later Peter Wood, was more closely affiliated with contemporary theatre and American-style radio drama. Unlike the Marlowe Society series, the SRS prominently featured established British theatre stars in their advertising – this was after all an unsubsidized commercial venture. Here, marketing materials proclaimed, is *Paul Scofield's* Hamlet, *Rex Harrison's* Benedick, *Claire Bloom's* Juliet, *Anthony Quayle's* Falstaff, *Richard Burton's* Coriolanus, an approach that provided the series as a whole with greater range – and less consistency – of conception. Equally important, and certainly more revolutionary, is director Howard Sackler's (re)imagining of Shakespearean performance in terms of the resources of phonography. Sackler, an American playwright with theatrically-honed skills for fast pacing, narrative clarity, and aural intensity, was the first phonographic director of Shakespeare to fully exploit stereophonic sound, sound mixing, and studio technique, and the first to conceive of the microphone as an active instrument in creating a Shakespearean performance. Sackler meticulously crafts his stereo soundscape to clarify the relationships between characters, control the levels of intimacy and distance between speakers and listener, and choreograph movement within the acoustic space. Using the microphone thematically, he consistently places the two twins of *Comedy of Errors* (1966) in separate stereo channels, dislocating (and thus disembodying) the witches within the soundspace for *Macbeth* (1960), or slowly brings up the sound of the storm as Paul Scofield's Lear progresses from "O reason not the need" to "I shall go mad." Sackler was also adept at judiciously using simple sound effects and musical cues, many of which he composed. He punctuates the final act of *Macbeth* with a continuous drumbeat that underlines the inexorable advance of Macbeth's fate; woodblock rhythms and breathy noises, used to separate scenes in *Antony and Cleopatra* (1963), give the production an exotic, ritualistic and small-scale quality while still allowing for a level of abstraction, scrupulously avoiding the association with sword-and-sandal epics then in cinematic vogue.

A typical example of Sackler's directorial technique occurs in his handling of the final scene of *Romeo and Juliet* (1961, Caedmon SR-228). Sackler distinguishes three spaces, each with its own distinct sound: the immediate area before the tomb, uncomfortably closely miked in a dry acoustic; the tomb itself, resonating with cavernous echo yet with the lovers miked intimately; and the churchyard, miked at middle distance to evoke a public space coterminous with the town. Before the tomb both Paris and Romeo offer equally tender and sincere, almost *sotto voce* professions of love, subtly suggesting their interchangeability as suitors. Sackler emphasizes the impression of a tight, small space by the quick lateral movements of Paris and Romeo and the fact that their servants seem unable to share the same space with them. Once established, this claustrophobic acoustic exacerbates the impulsive fight between the men, for it seems there's simply not room enough for both of them. Romeo's tender grief for Paris reestablishes the low-voiced intimacy that will dominate the scene's next section, begun when Romeo enters the tomb on the phrase "Oh no, a lantern." Its hollow acoustic provides grim counterpoint to Romeo's assertion that "Beauty's ensign yet / Is crimson in thy lips and in thy cheeks" (5.3.94–5); the ironic echoes deepen when Romeo, raising his voice to address Tybalt's corpse, ironically vows "with that hand that cut thy youth in twain / To sunder his that was thine enemy" (5.3.99–100). Indeed, throughout the scene the dark resonance of the tomb makes death an omnipresent destination and thus the lovers' passions seem all the more poignant. The emotional fulcrum of the passage is Juliet's anguished "thy lips are warm!" as she kisses Romeo. The scene's finale illustrates Sackler's skill at orchestrating crowd scenes, for though the pace is quite fast and sound image complex, the various individuals and groups remain easily distinguishable, each precisely situated in acoustic space, the Prince and watch in the center, Capulet and wife left center, Montague right center, the Friar right, Balthasar front left, the Page far left. Sackler adds a tolling bell to the mix, a leitmotif which sounds each time the Prince enters, but the effect takes on added significance when Capulet's wife observes to herself, "O me, this sight of death is as a bell / That warns my old age to a sepulchre" (5.3.205–6).

In contrast to Sackler's carefully choreographed sound image, typical of the thematic unity and narrative clarity of the Caedmon series, the Living Shakespeare series, 26 recordings produced between 1961 and 1963, experiments with an entirely different approach to sound design. Recorded quickly on the cheap and putatively directed toward an American market, the series was a collaborative effort between Morys Aberdare and Fiona Bentley who cut most of the texts for performance, Cyril Ornadel and Desmond Leslie who created the music and sound effects, and members of the Old Vic Company, supplemented by various prominently featured British theatre stars. Unlike the Marlowe Society or SRS, the Living Shakespeare series limited each audio adaptation to the confines of a single disc. A concession to the needs of the educational market, this choice also implicitly acknowledges that the single LP was becoming a standard compositional unit in youth culture, a length to which Shakespeare might be fruitfully adapted. The design, particularly for the tragedies, was a strange hybrid of concept album, "greatest hits" compilation, and stage dramatization. Aberdare and Bentley's adaptations preferred abridged key scenes rather than isolated speeches; narrative continuity was provided by refocusing the plays on the major protagonists and in some cases adding a narrator, as Welles had done for the Mercury Text Records. The productions consistently adopt the acoustic of a theatrical auditorium, sharp contrast between foreground and background marks their principal means of spatial design and sound effects are only sparingly used to establish the occasional realistic setting. Their most striking element, however, is the prominence of Desmond Leslie's *musique concrète*, which appears not only between scenes but sometimes also beneath the speeches and dialogue, giving some of the recordings the through-composed feeling of a film soundtrack. Modernistic and abstract, the aural equivalents of non-naturalistic set designs, these musical elements function expressionistically, drawing the listener into the unsettled psyches of the protagonists, especially at moments of self-doubt, madness or impending tragedy, repeatedly blurring the line between interior states and exterior reality. Recorded early in the series, the Living Shakespeare *Hamlet* (1961, Odhams SH-5A) offers the best example of this expressionistic approach: Hamlet's opening soliloquy is set against ebbing bass tones and metallic crashes which suggest the surfacing of unconscious sexual disgust; the Ghost's heavily processed voice emerges out of a bizarre mix of drips and screeches like a grotesque Oedipal projection, certain portentous words – "revenge," "murder," "foul," "unnatural" – reverberating as if echoing in Hamlet's brain; ethereal, wailing voices weaving in and out of Ophelia's speeches suggest the fragmentation of her mind. This attempt to portray psychological turmoil in audio form might be understood as the traditional theatre's response to the rapid ascent of method acting at mid-century, with its portrayal of volatile emotional subtexts at the expense of "proper" elocution. The Living Shakespeare tragedies offer both – elocution and subtext – in an uneasy mix that may for some listeners seem forced and for others have the tang of Brechtian alienation. Unfortunately, the association of *musique concrète* with horror and science fiction B-pictures of the period now tends to make the productions seem dated and melodramatic rather than psychologically rich. Even the producers seemed to recognize its limitations, for expressionistic music was used far more sparingly in the comedies and histories, one interesting exception being *Henry V*'s "touch of Harry in the night" scene. Even so, as a yoking of conventional Shakespeare performance with avant-garde elements in a mainstream production, this experiment offers an unusual example of how Shakespeare might be reshaped to exploit the potential of the phonographic medium.[12]

The final releases of the SRS series appeared in 1968, the year which brought an end to the first golden age of Shakespeare recording. (Perhaps not coincidentally, this was also the year of Zeffirelli's phenomenally successful *Romeo and Juliet*.) Though occasional isolated projects were to appear, no new Shakespeare recording series would be undertaken for 30 years as adaptational energies shifted decisively to television and film. Nonetheless, cassette tape, first introduced in 1963, revived audio books during the 1980s, prompting several re-releases of Marlowe Society and SRS recordings in the new format. Though the performances themselves were substantially the same, cassette tapes extended the process of privatization begun by records. Heard in the car or on a Walkman, Shakespearean performance became a private sphere of culture or entertainment actively deployed *against* public space rather than participating in it. Indeed, with the Walkman Shakespearean performance no longer need make contact with any material site at all; divorced from "real" space, it occupies an imaginary "stage" entirely between one's ears (see Hosokawa 1984, Bull 2000). One sign that tape has changed listening patterns for Shakespearean audio performances is that the packaging for these tapes tends to de-emphasize their relationship to the Shakespearean text. The expectation is, in other words, that one will not concentrate, book in hand, in one's study, but listen while pursuing another activity. The compact disc, a relatively new format for Shakespeare recordings, enables yet another form of privatization. Whereas the linear nature of cassettes tends to preserve the unity of the performance, with CDs (like record albums before them) listeners can move freely between segments of the performance, crafting their own personalized experiences of the work, sampling or repeating favorite passages or listening to them out of order. This penchant for private adaptation is magnified by the CD format, since, unlike 78s and LPs, Shakespeare on CD is less firmly tied to the Shakespearean text. Indeed, the technology allows for segments to be recycled in "unauthorized" ways, generating new works of art. Producer Richard Foos anticipates that his reissue of vintage Shakespeare recordings, *Be Thou Now Persuaded*, will be sampled by rappers, a development he welcomes presumably because it will boost sales beyond the collection's limited niche market (Bessman 1999: 55).

Shakespeare's newfound pop cachet in films of the 1990s and the continued strength of the audiobook market prompted several new Shakespeare recording series at the approach of the millennium: the Naxos Shakespeare series, in association with Cambridge University Press (at present nine full-length productions of New Cambridge texts, produced in association with Cambridge University Press); the CBC Radio series showcasing veterans of the Stratford, Ontario Shakespeare Festival, some performances abridged and others full-length; recordings by Kenneth Branagh's Renaissance Theatre Company from complete texts of *King Lear*, *Hamlet* and *Romeo and Juliet*, in association with BBC Radio 3; the BBC Radio "Shakespeare for the Millennium" series, as of this writing, 18 broadcast productions featuring different directors and casts; and most ambitiously, the Arkangel Shakespeare, a recording of the complete Shakespeare canon (in the new Penguin text) under the general direction of Clive Brill. Like the Caedmon series, the Renaissance Theatre's productions rely heavily on star power and imaginative microphone placement and audio design. In the opening scene of its *King Lear* (1993, Random House Audiobooks RC 155), for example, Cordelia's "Nothing, my lord" is placed very far right, from the start sonically isolated from her father and the obsequious court in the center channel. Lear's first storm scene (3.2) daringly juxtaposes two audio set-ups, subjective and objective: Lear is unnaturally close-miked and soft-spoken as he urges the winds to blow, his lines delivered against artificially lowered storm effects and ritualistic timpanis, an effect which signifies both the interior nature of the storm for Lear and his failure as yet to make contact with the physical realities of human suffering. By contrast, the other characters fully inhabit the raging natural world and must shout their lines from within the roaring maelstrom. Only with Lear's "My wits begin to turn" does he share the same windswept sound world as Kent and the Fool.

The Naxos, BBC and Arkangel series are rather more eclectic in their production techniques. The Naxos *Romeo and Juliet* (1997, Naxos NA 312512), for example, uses a speaker-and-backdrop approach, placing centrally-miked characters against realistic audio backgrounds, the sword-sound transitions and fades between passages supplying a structure akin to cinematic editing for many of the scenes. *Richard III* (2000, Naxos NA 321712) is a more "bare-stage" affair, preferring the spacious, largely neutral soundscape typical of the Old Vic and Marlowe Society recordings; the deep, resonating space – evoking both a stone castle and an empty theatre – is sharply contrasted with Richard's closely-miked soliloquies and asides. With its eerie, disquieting, often non-naturalistic soundscapes and Stephen Warbeck's moody bassoon- and cello-dominated score, the Naxos *Macbeth* (1998, Naxos NA316212) leans towards expressionism, though it focuses less on psychological subtext than on symbolism (note, for example, the prominence of water sounds and martial drumbeats, as well as suggestions of modern armaments).

Although, as these samplings suggest, recent series seem too varied in their phonographic styles to support easy generalizations, they do reveal two important trends in contemporary Shakespearean performance for the ear. First, these series display a much more thoroughgoing approach to audio design, blending sound effects, music, and actors' performances into the phonographic equivalent of high-concept production. Many of the BBC and Arkangel series use the now familiar stage and film technique of resituating the play's action in a new time frame: the BBC *Julius Caesar* (1999) is set in Fascist Italy (an homage perhaps to Welles's 1937 fascist staging), its *Othello* (2001) in the mid-century jazz scene, the Arkangel *Comedy of Errors* (1999) in the sound world of silent film slapstick. But most striking is the emphasis on sound effects and music rather than spatial placement within the audio image to dramatize the action. This suggests a fundamental shift in phonographic Shakespeare's affiliation with other media: once closely linked to the theatre, Shakespearean recording now takes its cues from a cinematic aesthetic. Music, often specially composed, is no longer largely confined to transitions and functions far more like a film soundtrack, playing underneath the delivery of lines, particularly soliloquies, to specify place, mood and listener response. Accompanying each of Macbeth's soliloquies in the Arkangel recording (1998) is a sour bagpipe drone, conveying his anxiety and isolation; in the Arkangel *Henry V* (1998) the king's exhortation to his troops at Harfleur is set against martial drumbeats and washes of electronic music, separating Henry from the battlefield until its sounds fade up at speech's end. Sound effects have become, writes Brill, "complete sound environments," aural backgrounds which are either fully representational and detailed (unlike the merely suggestive effects of classic radio drama) or highly stylized and patently artificial. Characters often speak not within a physical soundspace but rather against the backdrop of a hyper-real or sleekly designed symbolic "environment." Consequently many of these productions lack the secure sense of physical presence conveyed by Sackler's attention to microphone placement. As in Renaissance Theatre's *King Lear*, there are even non-spatial shifts of sound perspectives within scenes, an effect that resembles shot-to-shot cuts in film. Compared to earlier moments in recording history, contemporary phonographic Shakespeare tends to focus rather less on the text and actors and more on aural elements designed to direct the listener's emotions and imagination.

Second is the matter of accent. Whereas earlier recordings foregrounded the vocal refinement of the performers, enshrining Received Pronunciation as the accent "proper" to Shakespeare and reserving "regional" or "rustic" accents for lower-class or foreign characters, nearly all contemporary series offer a greater range and freer use of accents in all roles (with Renaissance Theatre productions a notable exception). This shift seeks to gesture towards a more multicultural, popular Shakespeare, less the exclusive property of an Oxbridge-educated elite, and it mirrors recent trends in RSC practice and British broadcasting. In a few cases accents evoke topical contexts – the BBC *Coriolanus* (2003) uses Irish and English accents to distinguish the warring Volscians and Romans; Othello's South African accent in the Arkangel recording (2000) conjures the ghost of apartheid; the subtle interplay between RP and working-class accents in the BBC *Merchant of Venice* (2000) suggests how class as well as religion underlies Shylock's ostracism. Even the Scots accents in the *Macbeth*s by Naxos (1998, Naxos NA 316212), Arkangel (1998), and BBC (2000) seem more interested in highlighting the play's relationship to Scottish national identity than, as is the case of the earlier Marlowe Society *Macbeth*, in parading historical or Shakespearean "authenticity." And accents also occasionally play against received performance traditions. In the Arkangel *Tempest* (1999), for example, Richard McCabe's odd, unplaceable accent for Caliban makes him into something other than the racialized or colonial figure familiar from recent productions; the mix of accents among the mechanicals in the BBC *Dream* (1999), director Susan Roberts notes, aims to avoid the cliché of aligning "regional" accents with working-class status. Yet though this diversity of accent intends to offer greater representation of regional, ethnic and class identities in Shakespearean performances, the relationship of those identities to Shakespearean roles or overarching production concepts is not always easy to specify. How, for example, might one understand the Caribbean accents of Titania and Oberon in the Arkangel *Dream* (1998)? Are they intended merely to reflect the range of voices in contemporary Britain? Are they signs of black exoticism and thus potentially racist? Or do they suggest a provocative reversal of Old World and New World? What of the Scottish burrs of Malvolio and Mercutio in the Arkangel productions of *Twelfth Night* (1998) and *Romeo and Juliet* (1998), or the strong Midlands accent of Iago in the Arkangel *Othello* (2000)? Why are "accented" characters so often antagonists or secondary characters rather than protagonists? Why no American, Australian or Indian accents in these series? As with color-blind casting in the theatre, the relationship between contemporary multicultural identities and the conventions and meaning of Shakespearean performance remains fundamentally unsettled, even contradictory.

This freer approach to accent points toward a fundamental change in what is most valued in phonographic Shakespeare. Earlier recorded performances stressed a certain "refined" articulation, as if savoring the sheer beauty and musicality of Shakespeare's language, though that "refinement" was signified through a narrow range of accents. Contemporary series, by contrast, place far greater emphasis on "full" dramatization of characters and narrative, a quality they trumpet in their advertising perhaps to differentiate themselves from audiobooks in which the text is simply read aloud. That is, whereas earlier recordings treated Shakespeare principally as a poet, recent recordings (re)conceive of him primarily as a dramatist. This distinction is not absolute: the Renaissance Theatre recordings, for example, clearly glance backward to the more "poetic" approach while aiming for a modern, conversational delivery of verse. And this change in emphasis sits rather uneasily with the impulse toward complete, uncut texts that dominates nearly all contemporary series.[13] As Brill observes, "with no cuts allowed, it is hard to have a consistent line" (in Neill 1998: 13). Although the *grande ligne* is often supplied by production design, this combination of full text and full dramatization depends heavily upon the performers' skill; notably, with the exception of Renaissance Theatre's recordings, these series stress dramatic ensemble rather than individual stars' idiosyncratic brilliance. To some extent, this simply reflects the repertory ethic that characterizes the RSC and the National Theatre, with which most actors heard on these recordings are associated. What emerges, then, from these full texts fully dramatized is an authoritative showcase for what has become "official" Shakespearean performance practice: glossy in its production values, ensemble-driven, fast, precise and thoroughly professional – but too often lacking individuality or political edge. One might even regard these series as a means to extend the hegemony of this mode of Shakespearean production beyond the "official" sites of the London and Stratford stage to the culture at large.

Some Conclusions

Audio recording, I have argued, is not merely a means for preserving performances that have or had an existence in some more complete or preferable form elsewhere. Rather, phonography is an artistic medium in its own right, with its own distinctive material and technological history, phenomenological dispositions, and changing aesthetic conventions which practitioners have chosen to develop in quite different ways. It has made possible experiences of Shakespearean performance which in form and significance cannot be duplicated in other media, and it has contributed in largely unrecognized ways to the mass mediatization of Shakespeare in the past 100 years. Most remarkably, it constitutes a body of material almost entirely neglected in the considerable critical literature on Shakespeare in performance. That neglect is revealing. The ascendancy of Shakespeare film and Shakespeare film criticism in the 1990s has had the unfortunate tendency to squeeze out consideration of other media forms and, sadly, it may have obscured the extent to which individual Shakespeare films participate in a larger historical process designed to make Shakespeare's ever-resilient cultural capital, still bound up with the stage, available to a modern, post-theatrical age. To understand this cultural process, we need to address its history in all its fullness, without replicating in our own criticism hierarchies of media and myths of technological progress purveyed by contemporary culture. And we need to attend not only to the cuts and high-concepts of particular productions but also more closely to the ways in which the phenomenological orientations of media forms shape – but never fully determine – the performance of Shakespeare for an age of mechanical, electronic – and now digital – reproduction.

NOTES

1   Quoted by Timson in his notes for *Great Historical Shakespeare Recordings and a Miscellany* (2000, Naxos NA 220012, 7).

2   Notable exceptions include Roach (1966: 106–35); Kliman (1988: 275–94); Behrens (1999); and Anderegg (1999: 39–56).

3   The phrase is from Lask (1959). For more examples of this assumption at work, see Wagenknecht (1963: 41) and Porter (1999: 18).

4   This ratio of sensory elements has influenced how different actors reacted to the phonograph. Laurence Olivier tended to eschew audio recording, for it robbed him of one of his most powerful tools, physical characterization. With the exception of his recording of the 1964 *Othello*, a recreation in the studio of his National Theatre production, nearly all authorized recordings of Olivier's Shakespeare performances are film soundtracks. By contrast, John Gielgud, an actor far more dependent upon his vocal skills and trademark tone, found phonography an especially genial medium and recorded often during his career, with recordings ranging from 1930 to 1999. Indeed, Gielgud is the twentieth-century's most frequently recorded audio performer of Shakespeare.

5   Sterne observes that crucial to the success of phonography was the promulgation of *audile technique*, practices of listening that were "more directional and directed, more oriented toward constructs of private space and private property," practices which "did not occur in the collective, communal space of oral discourse and tradition" but rather in "a highly segmented, isolated, individuated acoustic space" (2003: 24). "Even collective conceptions of listening," Sterne argues, come to "assume that collectivity is entered through this prior, private auditory space" (2003:93).

6   There are many important exceptions to this observation. For example, in the "golden age" of audio book recording, one might cite Olivier's *Othello* (1964), Gielgud and Burton's *Hamlet* (1964), and Zeffirelli's *Much Ado about Nothing* (1965), in addition to the soundtrack albums of Olivier's *Henry V*, *Hamlet* and *Richard III* and Castellani's and Zeffirelli's *Romeo and Juliet*s.

7   Selections from The Living Shakespeare recording series, published by the Classic Record Library, were in fact offered as a Book of the Month Club selection in the early 1960s.

8   These recordings have been collected and re-released on CD, *Great Shakespeareans* (1990, Pearl GEMM CD 9465) and *Great Historical Shakespeare Recordings and a Miscellany* (2000, Naxos NA 220012).

9   On voice and race in Shakespeare recordings, see Dethier (1965: 742).

10 The relative sparseness of the recording may be partly explained by the fact that it was made during a mid-1940s strike of Columbia Records by the American Federation of Musicians. The strike crippled Columbia's production of music recordings and forced it into alternate sources of revenue, including spoken word records; one can only speculate whether the recording would have ever been made without the catalyst of this labor dispute.

11 In 1964, conceding to economic necessity and growing competition from the star-driven Caedmon series, Argo made the names of actors and roles available to those who took the trouble to write in for a booklet.

12 Warranting brief mention are two other quatercentennial series, both associated with the Dublin Gate Theatre. The first, the Dublin Gate Players series, offered full-length performances of the Oxford text for Spoken

Word Records. The series first appeared in 1958, the same year that the Marlowe Society series began, but its stars-and-satellite approach was far closer to that of the Old Vic recordings of the 1950s. At first directed by Micheal MacLiammoir and Hilton Edwards, the company's general directors, later recordings were directed by other members of the company. Ten plays were completed before the series ran its course in 1962. A second series, on the Spoken Arts label (no relation to Spoken Word), offered one-disc recordings, at first "highlights" of single plays, later dramatic abridgements, all featuring members of the Dublin Gate Company (but later billed as the Folio Theatre Players).

13 Indeed, Arkangel has done all previous series one better in completism by recording Shakespeare's co-written *The Two Noble Kinsmen*.

References and Further Reading

Anderegg, M. (1999). *Orson Welles, Shakespeare and Popular Culture*. New York: Columbia University Press.

Attali, J. (1985). *Noise: The Political Economy of Music*, trans. Brian Massumi (*Theory and History of Literature* 16). Minneapolis: University of Minnesota Press.

Auslander, P. (1999). *Liveness: Performance in a Mediatized Culture*. New York: Routledge.

Behrens, F. A. (1999). "Meanwhile, Back at the Castle: Audio Recordings of the Shakespeare Plays." *Shakespeare Bulletin* 17, 2: 41–3.

Benjamin, W. (1968). "The Work of Art in the Age of Mechanical Reproduction." In *Illuminations*, trans. Harry Zohn. New York: Schocken, pp. 217–52.

Bessman, J. (1999). "Shakespeare's the Thing on Rhino Set." *Billboard* 111, 25 (June 19): 55.

Bolter, J. D. & Grusin, R. (2000). *Remediation: Understanding New Media*. Cambridge, MA: MIT Press.

Bruce, R. V. (1973). *Bell: Alexander Graham Bell and the Conquest of Solitude*. Boston: Little Brown.

Bull, M. (2000). *Sounding Out the City: Personal Stereos and the Management of Everyday Life*. Oxford: Berg.

Chanan, M. (1995). *Repeated Takes*. New York: Verso.

Dethier, J. (1965). "The Tragedie of Othello, the Moore of Venice." *American Record Guide* 31, August: 739, 742–5.

Eisenberg, E. (1988). *The Recording Angel: The Experience of Music from Aristotle to Zappa*. New York: Penguin.

Gritten, D. (2003). "To the Last Syllable." *Los Angeles Times* 3 August. Available at: www.calendarlive.com/stage/cl-ca-gritten3aug03.story

Hewes, H. (1952). "Masters' Voices." *Saturday Review* 35, August 16: 26–8.

Hosokawa, S. (1984). "The Walkman Effect." *Popular Music* 4: 165–80.

Jeffcoate, R. (2001). Review of the Arkangel Complete Shakespeare: *Love's Labour's Lost*, *The Merry Wives of Windsor*, *Troilus and Cressida*, *Othello*, *King Lear*, *Cymbeline*, *The Winter's Tale*, *Henry VIII*. *The Uses of English* 52, 3: 77.

Kerr, W. (1955). "Theatre in Your Home." *House and Garden* 108, October: 125–6.

Kinard, E. (1964). "Enjoy the Recorded Riches of Complete Shakespeare Plays." *House Beautiful* 106, March: 38, 40.

Kinard, E. (1961). "Talking Books: New Ways to Do Two Things at Once." *House Beautiful* 103, January: 102.

Kliman, B. (1988). *Hamlet: Film, Television, and Audio Performance*. Rutherford, NJ: Fairleigh Dickinson University Press.

Lask, T. (1959). "Between Book and Boards." *New York Times*, June 28: X11.

Lowry, M. (2003). "CD Project Brings Out the Poetry in Shakespeare." *Fort Worth Star-Telegram*, August 5.

Neill, H. (1998). "Bard on the Ears." *Times Educational Supplement* June 5 (Supplement Friday issue): 13.

Porter, P. (1999). "A Better Kind of Picture." *Around the Globe* Spring: 18–19.

Roach, H. P. (1966). *Spoken Records*, 2nd edn. Metuchen, NJ: Scarecrow Press.

Rockas, L. (1978). Reply to Kenneth Zahorski. *College English* 40, 1: 105–6.

Sterne, J. (2003). *The Audible Past: The Cultural Origins of Sound Reproduction*. Durham, NC: Duke University Press.

Wagenknecht, E. (1963). "Here's Richness!" *High Fidelity* 13: 40–3, 106–7.

Weingarten, S. (1939). "The Use of Phonograph Recordings in Teaching Shakespeare." *College English* 1, 1: 45–61.

Weinstein, C. (1993). "Olivier's Coriolanus: The Unknown Sound Recording." *Shakespeare Bulletin* 11, 4: 35–6.

Welles, O. & Hill, H. (1939). "On the Teaching of Shakespeare and Other Great Literature." *English Journal* 27: 464–8.

Zahorski, K. J. (1977). "The Next Best Thing . . . Shakespeare in Stereo." *College English* 39, 3: 290–3.

23
SShockspeare: (Nazi) Shakespeare Goes Heil-lywood
Richard Burt

Der Will(helm) zur Macht

In Steve Martin's 1991 romantic comedy *L.A. Story*, Shakespeare and Nazi Germany haunt Hollywood. Replacing the words "this England" at the conclusion of John of Gaunt's death-bed speech in *Richard II* with "this Los Angeles," Harris K. Telemacher (Steve Martin) later shows his Australian date, Sara McDowel (Victoria Tennant), Shakespeare's grave (Figure 23.1). A gravedigger (Rick Moranis) hands Telemacher

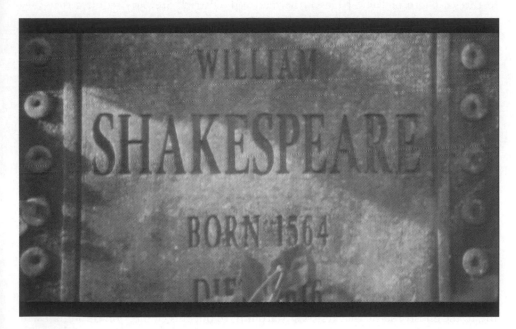

FIGURE 23.1   Calling up Shakespeare from the grave in LA; *L. A. Story* (1991)

FIGURE 23.2   Fourth Reich Bank of Hamburg; *L.A. Story* (1991)

the skull of a magician Telemacher had known as a child, and Sara begins reciting Hamlet's lines about Yorick.

When Telemacher wants to make a reservation at a trendy restaurant (its menu features a photo of Rudolf Hess), the maître d' (Patrick Stewart) requires that they first meet at the Fourth Reich Bank of Hamburg to review Telemacher's finances (Figure 23.2).

Commenting on the film's Shakespeare to Hollywood, via Germany, connection, Laurence Rickels writes, "no England to California connection without the phantom presence of Nazi Germany down in the displacement center of all bi-coastal transfers (vol. 3, 2003: 222–3). If Shakespeare has to hold the line for Nazi Germany when it places a call to Hollywood, might it also be said that Nazi Germany has to hold the line for Shakespeare before Hollywood can take the call? No Nazi Germany to California connection, as it were, without displacing the phantom presence of Shakespeare?

I want to consider this possibility by tracing the calls from Nazi Shakespeare to Hollywood and by examining a series of return calls, or films, that put the SShockspeare connection from Berlin to London to Hollywood in a more or less "live" theatrical frame. By SShockspeare, I mean the way a connection between the Nazis, Hollywood, and (English) Shakespeare theatre and performance is made through technology and film. Typically, in these films, actors either are putting on a Shakespeare play or characters are disguising themselves and citing Shakespeare. In attending to the ghostly static that resists any attempt to put this connection through, I will focus less on canonical film adaptations and citations that bear on Nazism – Olivier's

Henry V (1942), Ernest Lubitsch's *To Be Or Not to Be* (1942) as well as Mel Brooks's remake (1983), and Richard Loncraine's *Richard III* (1996) – and more on largely unknown (to Shakespeare film critics) films in which citations of Shakespeare are not thematized but are made on the boundaries of signification and insignificance. These include Roy William Neill's *Sherlock Holmes and the Secret Weapon* (1943), in which Sherlock Holmes (Basil Rathbone) masquerades as a rare bookseller in order to disguise his (false) identity as a Nazi agent and pretends to hawk the collected works of "Wilhelm Shakespeare"; Peter Godfrey's *Hotel Berlin* (1945), in which a Nazi actress is cast as Portia in the Nazi production of *The Merchant of Venice*; Leslie Howard's *Pimpernel Smith* (1941), an adventure comedy in which an archaeologist rescues anti-Nazi Germans and discusses Shakespeare's identity with a German general; Hans Jürgen Syberberg's *Hitler: Ein Film aus Deutschland* (1978), where Hitler cites *Hamlet* and *The Merchant of Venice*; and William Peter Blatty's *The Ninth Configuration* (1980), set in a psychiatric hospital near California's Camp Pendleton but shot in Germany and featuring a planned production of *Hamlet* with dogs as actors directed by possibly psychotic Vietnam vets while the guards and psychiatrist dress in Nazi uniforms.

In various ways, these films align mimicry of Shakespeare with mimicry of Hitler and Nazi Germany in order to resist and subvert Nazi politics and Nazi and anti-Nazi Hollywood cinema. The distance between original and copy is often considered the source of a debilitating anxiety (power can't perform itself confidently but fears it only mimics authentic power); contrarily, deconstructing original and copy into a series of always already mimicked performances is often regarded as enabling subversive, parodic resignifications of hegemonic norms (Butler 1990) or as critical alterity (Taussig 1993). Whereas performance studies has been most concerned, via the work of Jacques Derrida (1977) and Judith Butler (1993), to deconstruct J. L. Austin's distinction between serious and parasitic performative speech acts in order to recuperate theatrical speech acts as politically serious and efficacious, studies of performed Shakespeare tended to universalize the performative across live theatre and electronic media, treating films and theatrical productions indifferently, that is, as performances.

By framing theatrical citation and performance in cinema, these SShockspeare films call for a psychoanalytic and transmedia account of the performative scene and screen. These films screen a different (borderline) psychotic notion of mimicry framed as a specifically theatrical performance in which warfare and psychological warfare fail to be fully coordinated. Here, Shakespeare appears as an uncanny third term in a binary opposition (Nazis/Allies) or is cited as one term of a binary (English/German) in relation to a third; consistently, the performer mimicking Shakespeare takes on aspects both of a Shakespearean role and of his or her Nazi or anti-Nazi double. The result, in each case, works to allegorize the collapse of any distinction between psychotic breakdown and therapeutic working through, between theatrical success (taking on the role) and theatrical failure, between Nazi Shakespeare and anti-Nazi Shakespeare. Mimicry, then, not only involves parody but connects doubles, inner projections, hauntings, the occult, and the paranormal. The party line which the Nazi and English Hollywood film directors and actors picked up to call and to answer Shakespeare meant that lines between parties could not be disentangled: it was impossible for actors and directors on either side to toe a party line, telephonic or political.

Sshocktroupes: Shakespeare über Alles?

Philip Purser's novel, *Friedrich Harris: Shooting the Hero* (1991), tells the story of an ex-Nazi officer, Friedrich Harris, now teaching film in Los Angeles having been sent by Joseph Goebbels to meet Laurence Olivier in Ireland in 1943 when Olivier was filming the battle of Agincourt for *Henry V* (1944). The narrator's World War II mission is either to persuade Olivier to come to Germany to make pro-Nazi films, or failing that, to kill him. Deciding not to kill Olivier when he has the chance, Harris returns to Germany to find himself cast as an extra for Veit Harlan's propaganda epic *Kohlberg* (1945). The premise of Purser's novel is not entirely fanciful. Paul Virilio points out in *War and Cinema* that

> British defense secrets, protected by a censor's office that was to remain in place for more than thirty years, really did reside as much in Shakespearean theatre as in the head-quarters of the armed forces. For example, the plan for Montgomery's famous victory over Rommel at El-Alamein was drawn from *Macbeth* by a film director, Geoffrey Barkas, and a music hall magician, Maskeline, the two men reproducing Malcolm's action at Birnam Wood. Over the hard sand of the desert, virtually devoid of landmarks, the British army moved so slowly that the enemy's sharpest lookouts, equipped with the best field-glasses, could detect no real advance. (1989: 63)

Certainly the Nazi interest in Shakespeare has been well documented. Noting parallels between Olivier's *Henry V* and Veit Harlan's *Der Grosse König* (1942), Peter Drexler concludes: "it is highly improbable that a director of Olivier's astuteness and subtlety ... failed to take account of the kind of film the other side were using to bring home their propagandistic message" (1995: 127–32, 131); moreover, Ton Hoenselaars (2005) argues that similar parallels may be traced in Olivier's career and Purser's novel. Yet the symmetries are not as exact as Purser, Drexler, and Hoenselaars imply because mass media and theatre were not as fully coordinated in Nazi Germany as they were by the Allies when it came to Shakespeare (see Habicht 1985, 1989). In fact, Shakespeare double-faulted along Nazi party lines. After war was declared in 1939, Hitler directly intervened to allow Shakespeare to be read and performed, overruling Goebbels. Colonel Claus von Staufenberg, however, left "an open copy of *Julius Caesar* on his desk in which the relevant speeches were underlined" (Hortmann 1998: 143) before directing the coup against Hitler at his headquarters on July 20, 1944. While *Hamlet* is cited in an anti-authoritarian critique of German teaching methods in Joseph von Sternberg's talkie, *The Blue Angel* (1930), there is no

clear dividing line marking off Weimar Republic Shakespeares from Nazi Shakespeares. Willem Hortman notes, for example, that Werner Krauss's post-war defense
of his performance as Shylock in a 1943 *Merchant of Venice* has a degree of plausibility:
"there may even be some truth in his ... claim that his Viennese Shylock was no
different from his Shylock under [Max] Reinhardt in Berlin twenty years earlier"
(1998: 136). A similar doubling may also be found in the mutual citations of theorists
one might think would have had nothing to say to each other. Carl Schmitt devoted
an appendix of *Hamlet oder Hecuba: der Einbruch der Zeit in das Spiel* (*Hamlet or Hecuba:
The Interruption of Time in Play*), to Walter Benjamin's *Trauerspiel* (1929), in which
Benjamin had cited Schmitt. Yet, as Lawrence Guntner comments, almost no Nazi
film productions of Shakespeare were made (1998: 100). Given the numerous German
silent film adaptations of Shakespeare and the reference to *Hamlet* in *The Blue Angel*,
this absence seems quite striking.

We can begin to grasp more concretely how performing Shakespeare "live" in films
that (dis)connect Nazis and Shakespeare disturbs oppositions between Nazis and anti-
Nazis by turning to two British films and one American film made during World
War II, *Sherlock Holmes and the Secret Weapon*, *Pimpernel Smith*, and *Hotel Berlin*. Based
on Holmes's tale "The Dancing Men," *Sherlock Holmes and the Secret Weapon* begins and
ends with Shakespeare references and offers a relatively straightforward opposition
between fake German and authentic English Shakespeares. At the film's beginning,
two unidentified Gestapo officers show up at a restaurant in Switzerland, where they
recognize an old, white-haired, mustachioed man, masquerading as a bookseller in
order to avoid being seen as a Gestapo agent from Berlin. The bookseller is easily
identifiable as Sherlock Holmes (Basil Rathbone), disguised as a German spy disguised as a bookseller, as it were. Apparently intent on fooling the waitress and maître
d' into thinking he is a bookseller, Holmes actually means to dupe the two Nazi
agents into kidnapping Dr. Franz Tobel (William Post, Jr.), a Swiss scientist with a
new bomb design. In the process of maintaining this double deception, Holmes opens
his bag of books, picks one up, says with a German accent, "Now here are the
complete works of Wilhelm Shakespeare, an old German writer." "Heil Hitler,"
they respond, identifying themselves as Gestapo spies. In the film's last shot, after
footage of R.A.F. bombers in the sky, Holmes' friend Watson says to Holmes: "Things
are looking up, Holmes. This little island is still on the map." Citing lines from
Richard II, Holmes replies: "Yes, this fortress built by nature for herself, this blessed
plot, this earth, this realm, this England."

Yet even this relatively simplistic framing use of Shakespeare to differentiate
between German stupidity and English acumen within the context of an arms race
entails some static interference in its decoding. For one thing, there's a curious
asymmetry in the use of Shakespeare: although the film's opening names him, no
lines are cited, but when they finally are cited, neither Shakespeare nor *Richard II* is
named. The contrast between fake and authentic Shakespeare is undercut at the film's
end by a shot of bombers taken from military footage and cut gracelessly into studio

shots, complete with (bad) eyeline matches of Holmes and Watson supposedly looking up at them. The Swiss setting further complicates citationality by intruding a third agency. Though hardly neutral, Dr. Tobel does not fully cooperate with the English air force after he arrives in England. And the use of English actors speaking English throughout undercuts pointed differences: Holmes speaks with a German accent when posing as a German spy posing as an old bookseller, but the two Nazi agents in the restaurant speak with English accents. And after Holmes leaves the restaurant, one Nazi agent says to the other, "English. How I hate those languages." "Calm yourself my dear Braun," says the other, "In a short time there will be only one language." The joke depends on our taking "one language" for German, but their lack of German accents is at odds with a cinematic code through which the audience hears English as German.

Even more obviously contradictory, the American film *Hotel Berlin* (dir. Peter Godfrey, 1945), makes a joke about Shakespeare as German while also placing Shakespeare in Nazi hands. Blonde Nazi actress Lisa Dorn (Andrea King) is rehearsing a new production of *The Merchant of Venice* and mentions the play when she runs into General Dahnwitz (Raymond Massey). Dahnwitz has participated in the failed Claus von Stauffenberg plot to kill Hitler. They sit down for lunch in the restaurant, and when von Stetten (Henry Daniell) comes by, disguise their conversation by talking about the play. He asks to join them, and sits down and asks "What are you two conspiring about?" Dahnwitz replies: "We were talking about Fraulein Dorn's new production of *The Merchant of Venice*. Shakespeare." Von Stetten replies, "A writer of true Germanic sensibility." Oddly, however, the film revised the 1944 novel, *Hotel Berlin '43* by Vicki Baum, making the Shakespeare-citing heroine into a Nazi anti-heroine who betrays the anti-Nazi hero, thereby placing Shakespeare on the side of the Nazis and the anti-Hitler Nazi general.

More consciously produced as anti-German propaganda, *Pimpernel Smith* offers a more interesting and complicated example of how Shakespeare destabilizes Nazi and anti-Nazi oppositions. The film updates *The Scarlet Pimpernel* (dir. Harold Young, 1934) with the Gestapo as Reign of Terror and Leslie Howard reprising his role as secret agent in the earlier film which, incidentally, closes with Sir Percy Blakeney (Leslie Howard) reciting the last four lines of John of Gaunt's death-bed speech in *Richard II* to his French wife Lady Marguerite (Merle Oberon) as they return from France to England. *Pimpernel Smith* begins in 1939 just before the outbreak of war, and Shakespeare comes up several times in a quasi-theatrical context involving hidden and mistaken identity. Using his identity as a Cambridge don of archaeology as a cover to help Germans persecuted by the Nazis escape to England, Smith takes some of his students, including an American, on a trip to Germany to excavate a dig in the hope of discovering the existence of an Aryan race. At a British embassy party in Berlin, Smith meets General von Graum (Francis Sullivan), who is attempting to discover Pimpernel Smith's true identity. The two men have an exchange about Shakespeare's national identity:

GENERAL:	But we have one problem. "To be or not to be?" as our great German poet said.
SMITH:	German? But that's Shakespeare.
GENERAL:	But you don't know?
SMITH:	Why, I know it's Shakespeare. I thought Shakespeare was English.
GENERAL:	No, no, no. Shakespeare is a German. Professor Schluessbacher has proved it once and for all.
SMITH:	Yes, how very upsetting. Still you must admit that the English translations are most remarkable.
GENERAL:	Good night.
SMITH:	Good night. Good night. "Parting is such sweet sorrow."
GENERAL:	What is that?
SMITH:	That's one of the most famous lines in German literature.

The parody here is clearly aimed at an earlier Germanizing of Shakespeare, his appropriation by Hitler for the Nazi cause. Hitler himself cited *Hamlet* in *Mein Kampf*. "When the nations on this planet fight for existence – when the question of destiny, 'to be or not to be' – cries out for a solution – then all consideration of humanitarianism or aesthetics crumble into nothingness . . . " (1925; trans. 1943: 177). Hitler puts Shakespeare at the end of the line of German art, which the Nazis have now supposedly surpassed. "But after all," Hitler asks, "What are Schiller, Goethe, or Shakespeare compared to the heroes of the newer German poetic art?" (1925; trans 1943: 259–60). *Pimpernel Smith* broadly satirizes overweening Nazi attempts to annex Shakespeare, much as they had annexed Austria and the Sudetenland. Smith's use of Shakespeare also seems straightforward, and citing *Romeo and Juliet* floods out to encompass Howard's career as a Shakespearean actor: Howard starred as Romeo in George Cukor's 1936 film of *Romeo and Juliet*, performed Hamlet in a New York production that same year, competing with Sir John Gielgud's Hamlet, and played a Shakespearean actor opposite Bette Davis in *It's Love I'm After* (dir. Archie Mayo, 1937).

Yet *Pimpernel Smith* proves to be even more elusive than his *Scarlet* predecessor. In the scene at the embassy party, we know, unlike the general, that Shakespeare is English, not German, and, unlike the general, we know that Smith is the Pimpernel. Yet the question of Shakespeare's identity and authorship is not simply laid to rest. In a later scene, Smith shows the General a book that proves conclusively, Smith says, that Shakespeare wasn't Shakespeare but the Earl of Oxford:

SMITH:	Now you can't pretend that the Earl of Oxford was a German, can you? Now can you?
GENERAL:	No.
OTHER GERMAN OFFICER:	No.
SMITH:	Well, there you are.
OTHER GERMAN OFFICER:	I didn't come here to discuss Shakespeare. If you want me, you know where I am.
SMITH:	The Earl of Oxford was a very bright Elizabethan light.

We never see the title of the book nor the author, perhaps because if it were shown to be *Shakespeare Identified* (1920), the only book then in print arguing the Oxfordian case, the author's last name – Looney – would give away the joke. Moreover, Howard's status as *auteur* here is questionable: although he didn't write the script, he did direct and star in the film. Yet he does speak these lines more sincerely than those he clearly delivers mockingly.

Far from locking down Shakespeare's national identity, the Earl of Oxford becomes a third term which keeps it open. Howard's Smith makes his case in the negative: Shakespeare is not German, not positively, Shakespeare is English. (Interestingly, an English wartime film with a faux-Nazi sympathizer, *Yellow Canary* [dir. Herbert Wilcox, 1943], opens with a discussion between two air-raid wardens about the Bacon/Shakespeare authorship controversy. One quotes Caliban's "be not afear'd; the isle is full of noises . . .") And what initially seemed an opposition between English and German Shakespeare also appears in relation to another third term, *Alice in Wonderland*, one that the General, who doesn't understand English humor, can't make out. Von Graum's turn to *Hamlet* at the British embassy party follows from a discussion of British humor that includes Smith's citation of what the General assumes is a nonsensical line from Carroll. Smith, however, informs him that the line "makes perfect sense. It means whatever you want it to mean. As a matter of fact, you know, ever since I've been in Germany, I've felt exactly like Alice in Wonderland."

The way Shakespeare comes up in relation to a third term – whether *Alice in Wonderland* or the Earl of Oxford – is performed, as it were, by the film, when Shakespeare, Oxford, and national identity occur in a third, uncanny and final scene of deception. A large box with a false bottom that Smith is using to smuggle out anti-Nazi Germans appears to be full of dirt and the bones of a Teutonic warrior. When General von Graum eyes the box suspiciously, Smith offers to open it, then takes up the warrior's skull, and cites some of Hamlet's speech about Yorick.

> SMITH: Would you like to see it? There we are, you see. Buried with all his weapons, you see, presumably, in the belief that there might be a rearmament program in the hereafter. An ancient Teuton. "Alas poor Yorick, get thee to my lady's chamber, my dear general. Tell her that though she paint an inch thick, to this favor must she come, make her laugh at that." The Earl of Oxford wrote that, you know.

And in a subsequent scene (Figure 23.3), he holds up a skull, cites a line from *Hamlet* and repeats, "The Earl of Oxford wrote that."

Here, the Teutonic warrior's skull becomes the third term. It's hard to tell if we are meant to take Smith (and by extension Howard?) at his word, for the remark about Oxford is delivered in the same mocking tone with which Smith earlier spoke about the greatest lines in German literature. In other words, just as he was putting on the General by seeming to agree that Shakespeare was a German, so he here appears to

FIGURE 23.3   What lies beneath Hamlet; Leslie Howard in *Pimpernel Smith* (1941)

mock von Graum by appearing to believe that Shakespeare was really Oxford. Trying to decide is made all the more difficult, as the first scene looks, in retrospect, deceptively simple.

The ending of the film, set at the border of France and Germany, leaves the question even more unsettled, as a subplot's resolution about whether there was an Aryan civilization in Germany parallels the plot about Shakespeare's identity. Caught at the German border, Smith manages to escape by tricking the General into breaking an Aryan vase, but when von Graum turns his back to Smith to express irritation at his own staff, Smith disappears into the fog. Smith's assertion about the vase contradicts his discovery of a Teutonic warrior, offering evidence of an Aryan civilization in Germany, but, of course, that assertion may be simply a trick. If so, the film's last frames only make Smith's identity more elusive, as he effectively becomes a ghost. Von Graum calls to him to come back, and we hear Smith's voice-over, "Don't worry, I'll be back." Von Graum shoots into the darkness at Smith, who then says, now in an unlocatable voice-over which seems extra-diegetic, "We'll all be back." Has von Graum missed, and is Smith responding to him out of the darkness? Or does the disembodied voice-over suggest that Smith is now a spirit speaking from another worldly place to the film audience rather than to von Graum?

Smith's ghostly come-back was realized when Howard's airplane was shot down by Nazi anti-aircraft guns over Portugal. Josef Goebbels's propagandist newspaper, *Der Angriff* (*The Attack*), happily headlined the incident with "Pimpernel Howard has made his last trip." Almost immediately, theories sprang up that Howard was leading a double life as a spy for British intelligence and that his plane was shot down because Howard's manager was mistaken for Churchill, who was in Lisbon at the time (see

Ronald Howard, 1984: 118). Yet shortly after *Pimpernel Smith* was released, Howard was already dabbling in the occult, performing séances in attempts to communicate with his dead mistress, Suzanne Claire, who had played the shop-girl in *Pimpernel Smith*. Although Howard did not follow *Pimpernel Smith* with more Shakespeare, *Hamlet* continued to haunt him, despite (or because of) his failed 1936 New York production, which marked his last stage appearance.

After *Pimpernel Smith* was released, Howard planned to film *Hamlet*, setting it in contemporary Denmark. Hamlet was to be a national resistance fighter opposed to a Hitlerish young Fortinbras; military uniforms were to be worn and tanks and machine guns used (Ronald Howard 1984: 122). The British War Ministry rejected Howard's proposal on the grounds that it was "a loser" and bad propaganda material. Howard was able, however, to take *Pimpernel Smith* on a lecture tour of Lisbon: one lecture on filmmaking followed a screening of the film; a second was indebted to J. Dover Wilson's *What Happens in Hamlet* (1935), and, the next day, a third devoted to Hamlet's soliloquies, entitled *An Actor's Approach to Hamlet*. (Howard's posthumously published autobiography is entitled *Trivial Fond Records*.) If the *Hamlet* lectures were meant as part of the war effort, Howard's emphasis on the play's timelessness may have made it harder to decode as such. When his suitcase was searched and a copy of *Hamlet* was found in it, Howard was amused to think of Goebbels trying to decipher messages in the soliloquies. But Howard's son, Ronald Howard, regards his father's stress on "a patch of ground" in his soliloquies' lecture as a subtle form of propaganda that the Nazis may have perceived, perhaps accounting for why the lecture tour was cancelled the day after the second *Hamlet* lecture.

Shakespeare: Ein Film aus Deutschland

Problems with opposing Hitler as a performer are explored in relation to citations of Shakespeare and other writers and actors in Hans-Jürgen Syberberg's *Hitler: A Film from Germany* (1978). Shakespeare comes up twice in the seven-hour film, first when Hitler appears as Hamlet holding a skull and second when he paraphrases Shylock's line "Hath not a Jew eyes? Hath not a Jew hands? ... If you prick us, do we not bleed?" as "I am a human being with two eyes and ears, like you ... and if you prick me do I not bleed?"

Syberberg uses a highly theatrical, consciously Brechtian, *mise en scène*, often interchanging puppets and actors, to mount a critique of Hitler's afterlives in both Nazi and Hollywood fictional films, documentaries, images, and spectacles. Citation, in this film, is a mimetic performance. Yet by foregrounding Hitler as performance and performer, Syberberg makes it difficult to distinguish between miming the Führer and the Führer as mimic. In Syberberg's Hollywood to *Hamlet* connection, the appearance of Hitler as Hamlet comes at the end of a series of similar mimings that begins with a circus showman turning his back to the camera, changing his costume, and then turning back to the camera as Charlie Chaplin's tramp wearing a

Nazi armband. The film then cuts to him as a window washer, then to Hitler as mimicked by Chaplin in *The Great Dictator* (dir. Charlie Chaplin, 1940), then as Napoleon, then as Hitler biting a piece of carpet, then as Hitler posing as a knight (much as in some Nazi paintings), and then as Hamlet holding a skull. An Orthodox Jewish man wearing a yellow star caps this rapid, strobe-lit montage, during which speeches by Goebbels and Hitler are heard in voice-over but not lip-synched by the actor, Heinz Schubert, who had earlier appeared in a West German situation comedy television series playing an Archie Bunker-like character and sporting a moustache. Chaplin, Napoleon, and Hamlet all signal "themselves" with iconic gestures (the tramp twirling his cane, Napoleon placing his hand over his stomach, Hamlet holding the skull), as does Hitler, who holds up his arm, his hand back, and looks into the camera as he gives (or receives) the "Heil." On the one hand, the film suggests, in moving from a parody of Hitler (Chaplin) to his precursor (Napoleon) and to the painting, that Hitler has seemingly inexhaustible power to parody various kinds of actors and incorporate them. On the other hand, however, Syberberg deconstructs an apparent distinction between original and mime in which a series of vertiginous possibilities open up: Hitler is miming Hamlet who is miming Hitler who is miming Hamlet miming Hitler, and so on. It is, for example, hard to know at what point Chaplin leaves off and Hitler begins. Well before Chaplin mimicked Hitler as Adenoid Hynkel in *The Great Dictator*, Hitler was already being compared in the US – as early as 1933 – to Chaplin's tramp in order to minimize the Nazi leader's importance (Tift 1991).

Like Hitler, Chaplin also had ties to Shakespeare. Chaplin had appeared in a cartoon as Hamlet holding a skull with the caption "I am too tragic to play Hamlet" in a *New York Times* story entitled "The Hamlet-like nature of Charlie Chaplin" (1920). Indeed, a film even was planned, in which Chaplin would play Hamlet, with Shakespearean actor and Hollywood movie star John Barrymore as his stand-in. Chaplin came to Berlin in 1931 to express support for the Communist workers (Peterson et al. 2000: 64–6), and footage from Chaplin was inserted into *Jud Süss* (1933), whose star, Werner Krauss, also performed as Shylock and in *Twelfth Night*. And in his post-war film *A King in New York* (1957), made in England, Chaplin plays a broke, exiled Russian prince who cites Hamlet's "To be or not to be" soliloquy while becoming, first, an advertising huckster and, then, the target of McCarthy's Communist witch-hunts.

While I would not want to claim that Syberberg or his film is conscious of this dense network of links between Shakespeare, Hitler, and Chaplin, the Shakespeare citations serve as a third term that helps Syberberg shape Hitler and Chaplin into closely mirrored images of each other. Just as Chaplin's Nazi-armband-sporting tramp blurs the lines between Hitler as tramp and the tramp's Hitler, the Heil Hitler–Heil Hamlet connection is similarly complex. Hitler's later assimilation via citation of Shylock –"And if you do prick me, do I not bleed?"– stages citation as resurrection. Dressed in a Roman toga, Hitler arises from Richard Wagner's grave as the overture from Wagner's *Rienzi* plays on the soundtrack. Hitler defends himself by comparing himself to the Renaissance artists Leonardo da Vinci and Michelangelo and to classical music composers Beethoven and Wagner. But, in a humorous moment, he mentions Mozart as another example and then dismisses him, as he was not to Hitler's taste. While Hitler's citation of Shylock occurs in a rather comic context, making him seem bathetic, it also calls attention to the afterlife of citation. More significantly, the place from which Hitler gives the citation, a grave, suggests that Hitler's destructive, psychotic death drive and fantasies of immortality are inseparable from psychotic delusions (anti-Semitism and aggressor being transformed into philo-Semite and victim) in which citation might offer a means of evacuation and safety. Though Syberberg adopts a Brechtian strategy of foregrounding the theatrical apparatus to alienate, or more precisely in this case, to enervate if not bore the spectator, his film demonstrates the impossibility of adopting a critical position which would allow one to sort out Nazi and anti-Nazi aesthetics as two different fronts, with Shakespeare clearly positioned on one side against the other.

Good Mourning, Vietnam: SShocktreatmentspeares

William Peter Blatty's *The Ninth Configuration* (1980) brings further into relief issues already at work in films like *Pimpernel Smith* – that of the heroic/psycho leader and of the group – as Shakespeare moves toward ghostly static and noise. Smith's borderline identification as heroic leader ("I'll be back") and group member ("We'll be back) mirrors his "other" on the German side. Shakespeare is a key element in *The Ninth Configuration*, which focuses on a Vietnam vet and war criminal named "Killer Kane" (Stacey Keach). (Blatty had also written a novel entitled *I, Billy Shakespeare* [1965].) Kane thinks he is a psychiatrist whose mission is to decide if the vet inmates are faking or truly psychotic and to help a former astronaut who refuses to take any more space flights. But some of the staff and patients know that Kane is actually a patient and are hoping that he will work through his own repression of his violent past. Two of the vet inmates talk about doing *Richard III* with dogs, one of which is named Sir Laurence Olivier, and, after considering *Julius Caesar*, they settle on *Hamlet* (Figure 23.4). Although the idea of dogs acting Shakespeare may be explicitly nonsensical, a lengthy discussion about Hamlet's character mediates as a third term between a psycho/heroic patient/doctor soldier/killer and a failed astronaut, who, by the film's end, has gone back into space again.

Because of a bureaucratic mistake, the patient, Colonel Vincent Kane, is confused with his brother, Colonel Richard Fell (Ed Flanders), a real shrink, who is also at the asylum. Fell allows Kane to function as the head psychiatrist in the hope that Kane will recover his repressed memories of massacring Vietnamese civilians.

The asylum which provides the film's setting is located in a castle set up by the Army in Southern California near the end of the Vietnam War. Kane's use of "shock therapy" both for the prisoners and on himself takes a metaphorical detour through Shakespeare as a theory about *Hamlet* becomes a means of connecting to the Gestapo

FIGURE 23.4 Shakespeare goes to the dogs; *The Ninth Configuration* (1980)

via psychodrama and a theatrical miming of another film, *The Great Escape*. Lieutenant Frankie Reno (Jason Miller), who is adapting Shakespeare's plays for dogs, barges in on Kane and Fell one evening to discuss his ideas about *Hamlet*, apparently informed by Olivier's 1948 film, a film itself underpinned by Ernest Jones's Freudian interpretation of *Hamlet*. I quote the conversation in full:

RENO: I'd like to ask your opinion about a problem in *Hamlet*. See, if I cast a Great Dane in the role, they're going to accuse me of being so ... Some Shakespearean scholars – say that when Hamlet is pretending to be crazy he really is crazy.

KANE: That's right.

RENO: Other Shakespearean scholars say that when Hamlet is pretending to be nuts he really isn't nuts, it's an act. Please give me your opinion.

KANE: I would like to hear yours first.

RENO: Ah, terrific psychiatrist. That's class. Now, Colonel, considering how Hamlet is acting, is he really and truly crazy?

KANE: Yes.

FELL: No.

RENO: You're both wrong. Now, think what happens. First his father dies. Then his girl leaves him flat. Then there's an appearance by the father's ghost. It's bad enough. Then the ghost tells him he was murdered. And by whom? By Hamlet's uncle, who recently married Hamlet's mother. Now that is a hell of a hang-up. Because Hamlet liked his mother a lot.

KANE: But then we're agreed. Hamlet is insane.

RENO: No, we're not. He is pretending. If Hamlet hadn't pretended to be crazy, he really would have gone crazy. Hmmm? You see Hamlet isn't psycho. He's hanging on the brink. A little shove, a little tiny eentsy push and the kid's gone bananas, whacked out. So his unconscious mind makes him do what

FIGURE 23.5   Getting on the Nazi psychic hotline to Hamlet; Stacey Keach in *The Ninth Configuration* (1980)

keeps him sane, namely, acting like he's not. See, because acting crazy is a way of letting off steam, a way to get rid of your fucking aggressions, a way to get rid of your fears and your terrors. If I did what Hamlet does in this play, they'd lock me up, they'd put me in prison, they'd punish me, sure. But him? Royal prince and garbage mouth gets away with murder. And why? Because nuts are not responsible. Meantime, the crazier Hamlet acts, the more he indulges himself, the healthier he gets.

KANE: Yes. I think I agree with your theory.

RENO: From now on we do the scene my way. Come on, Sir Laurence ... Sir Laurence, you don't know shit.

Reno's (neo-Freudian) theory is actually aimed at Kane, who is supposed to read himself into Reno's Hamlet. But instead, Kane adopts it in order to help the patients.

The film takes a strange movement away from Hamlet, however, as Kane puts a call though to Nazi Germany. After Reno leaves, Kane tells his brother Ed that the *Hamlet* theory is correct and asks him to get the Quartermaster's office at Camp Pendleton on the phone: "We'll need some supplies ... We're going to indulge the men." Now wearing a Gestapo uniform (Figure 23.5), Kane then gets a return call from the office asking him if he would like "to comment on the frogman suit or the German Gestapo uniforms."

Hamlet is displaced as the Nazis come on the line. Kane explains that the inmates want to act out *The Great Escape*, casting themselves as prisoners of war and the doctors and staff as Nazis. The film's Shakespeare–Nazi–Southern California connection becomes stronger when a discussion of *Julius Caesar* occurs in relation to an

African-American inmate dressed as Superman and another as a rocket man out of a James Bond movie. He has a Nazi uniform folded over his left arm, as if to bring out a connection between Superman the action hero and the Nazi/Nietzschean *Ubermensch*. Addressing Kane, Reno asks:

> Colonel, do me a favor, please. Explain to this moron [the inmate dressed as Superman] that in none of the plays of Shakespeare can there be a part for Superman ... Jesus. You know what he wants? You want to hear? When the conspirators draw their knives, he wants to rescue Caesar, swoop down like a rocket, pick him up and then go hurdling mighty temples in one single bound. [Turning to the inmate dressed as Superman.] Jesus, man, are you crazy?

Like the inmate dressed as Superman, Kane has "crazy" fantasies of being an *Ubermensch* who can save Billy, an astronaut inmate. The Shakespeare connection is also lightly marked. After the rocket man crashes off screen, Reno jokingly compares him to Caesar: "Go talk to your brother. I think he has the falling sickness."

Instead of targeting a Superman or a Julius Caesar for assassination, Hamlet opens up a connection to Jesus – seen, in one of Billy's dreams, crucified on the moon next to astronauts. Before the film's climax, a Hamlet-cum-sacrificial lamb of God connection is made when Reno walks among sheep saying "To be or not to be." And in the climax itself, Kane becomes a sacrificial lamb and self-destructs as he saves Billy from a group of sadistic, neo-Nazi, gay bikers, all of whom Kane, in a rage resembling his barbaric act in Vietnam, savagely beats to death. Through a "to bleat or not bleat" messianic Hamlet, Kane is able to save the astronaut inmate, sublimate a male buddy bond of love through homophobic, anti-Nazi violence, and help get the ex-astronaut back his Air Force wings, which are clearly differentiated from a Nazi wing insignia seen in close-up on the jacket of a Nazi biker Kane kills when rescuing the astronaut at the local biker bar.

But Shakespeare won't get off the phone. Whether to let Kane be or not be the lamb of God was a question that gave the film's director pause: a melancholic Blatty was indecisive over how to shoot Kane's death (several very different cuts of the film have been released). Kane either dies from a mortal wound at the biker bar or kills himself with a knife (two different versions of his death were shot to decide the issue; both are on the DVD edition, along with Blatty's audiocommentary). Kane's double-version death registers the extent to which Kane's violence in the biker bar and his violence in Vietnam (violence done to him and by him) cannot save anyone or, more precisely, can save through ghostly means. Christianizing Kane as a redeemed and redemptive messianic Hamlet only works by displacing and ending war's violence and madness with putatively non-militaristic, sane space flight. The happy ending of *The Ninth Configuration* – Billy discovers a necklace Kane has left him, thereby proving that God does exist – requires a post-*Hamlet* paranormal connection between dead Kane's ghost and the living ex-astronaut.

From Desert Stuerm to SShock and Awe: To Be
or Not to Be All You Can Be

More SSshockspeare effects, ranging from the hermeneutic to the remote, even post-hermeneutic, may be found in a number of other films, including Kenneth Anger's *Scorpio Rising* (1964), which includes a clip of Mickey Rooney as Puck from Max Reinhardt and William Dieterle's *A Midsummer Night's Dream* (1935) as well as photos of Hitler and Nazi kitsch; Fred Zimmerman's *Julia* (1977), in which Lillian Hellman (Jane Fonda) telepathically witnesses Nazis murdering Julia (Vanessa Redgrave) while drifting off during the gravedigger scene of a Moscow production of *Hamlet*; Armin Müller-Stahl's *Conversation with the Beast* (1996) in which a man claiming, perhaps accurately, to be Hitler (Müller-Stahl) recites the "To be or not to be" soliloquy in tribute to Lubitsch's *To Be or Not to Be*; Russ Meyer's *Up!*, about the murder of a Hitler look-alike who lives in a German castle (supposedly) in northern California and a woman chorus (Kitten Natividad) who cites lines from *Macbeth*, *Hamlet*, and *Othello*; David Twohy's *Below* (2002), a submarine thriller set in WWII and spin-off of *Macbeth*; *Which Way to the Front?* (dir. Jerry Lewis, 1970); *Mephisto* (dir. Istvan Szabo, 1981); *Zelig* (dir. Woody Allen, 1983); *Tea with Mussolini* (dir. Franco Zeffirelli, 1996); *Schindler's List* (dir. Stephen Spielberg, 1993); *Enigma* (dir. Michael Apted, 2001); and *The Pianist* (dir. Roman Polanski, 2003); and a number of films about Nazis, the titles of which cite Shakespeare: *This Happy Breed* (dir. David Lean,1944); *The Demi-Paradise* (dir. Anthony Asquith, 1943); and *Ill Met by Moonlight* (dir. Michael Powell and E. Pressburger, 1957). Television SShockspeare episodes include *The Adventures of Charlie Chan* (dir. Don Chafeey, 1957) and *Combat!* (dir. Boris Sagal, 1962; dir. Bernard McVeety, 1964).

Although space does not permit pursuing these SShockspeare effects as well as those cataloged by Mitchell (2002), I would like to conclude by considering some of the ways in which the SShockspeare, or Nazi/English/American Shakespeare connection, continues to appear in various political theatres. George Schultz had said before the first Gulf War that the United States would not be "the Hamlet of Nations" (Boose & Burt, 1997) and Saddam Hussein was compared to Hitler, and Shakespeare and Hitler resurfaced in Gulf War II. *Henry V* was one of three classical texts issued to all soldiers deployed to Iraq (Burns 2003) debates over the analogy between George W. Bush and Henry V, construed positively or negatively, continue as I write in September 2004 (see Ferguson 2004, Huffington 2004, Kristof 2004, see also Newstrom 2003). On his summit trip to Ireland in June 2004, George W. Bush was met by some 500 protesters who blocked a road and invoked

> Macbeth, a ghost and a witch to cast a spell on the U.S. president and drive him, symbolically at least, from Irish soil … The protesters held up a banner adorned with a quote from Macbeth, Shakespeare's powerful drama of death, destruction and ambition in feudal Scotland. "There's the smell of blood still," read the banner, on which was

painted a gory hand. "All the perfumes of Arabia will not sweeten this little hand." (Reuters 2004)

A fundamentalist, an alcoholic convicted of a DUI, an AWOL National Guard member, and a former cocaine user turned US President was compared both to Henry V by numerous pundits and to Hitler in a controversial advertisement sponsored by MoveOn.org (retouched photos of Bush as Hitler appeared on numerous anti-Bush websites). And in October 2003, a Terminator-Hamlet movie star named Arnold Schwarzenegger, whose father was an SS officer, was elected Governor of California. Moreover, in June 2003, George Herbert Walker Bush's collaboration with Nazi banks in World War II was revealed shortly after his grandson prematurely declared the end of major hostilities in May 2003 (see the articles linked at the Bush Hitler Project www.btinternet.com/~nlpwessex/Documents/bushhitlerprojecthtm. htm). Two days before the US presidential election in 2004, an essayist (Giardina 2004) unfavorably compared Bush and his administration's foreign policy of finding a quarrel in a straw to Hamlet's admiration of young Fortinbras' military aggression.

The Hitler/Henry V comparisons to Bush proved to be politically reversible. Hitler was employed by the Bush re-election campaign in an internet ad entitled "Coalition of the Wild-Eyed" that ran on the BushCheney.com website in June and July 2004. The ad juxtaposed footage of Hitler giving a speech with footage of Kerry, Gephardt, Moore, and Gore giving speeches critical of Bush, none of whom mentions Hitler or sounds like Hitler. Perhaps in response, Ozzie Osborne opened a July 2004 Ozzfest concert with "War Pigs" while "the giant screens next to the stage showed pictures of President Bush juxtaposed with pictures of Hitler" (Ratliff 2004). *Henry V* was also pressed into service by the Democrats during the 2004 Presidential campaign. Ex-US Senator and Vietnam veteran Max Cleland began a "band of brothers" tour for US Presidential candidate John Kerry with a recitation of Henry's St. Crispin's Day speech (Moranis 2004).

When the Hitler card is played or Nazi Germany is mentioned, whether in politics or the academy, the issue is generally cast in terms of showing how someone or something has been tainted by the Nazis. Haunting turns into hunting. While Carl Schmitt's notions of sovereignty, the exception, and the state of emergency have received new interest and urgency, one critic has recently sought to rescue *Hamlet* from Schmitt's reading of the play in relation to *Hamlet oder Hecuba* (1951) and elsewhere, and the extent to which Ernst Kantorowicz, who arrived in Berkeley, California, after World War II, was a Nazi sympathizer even though a Jew, has been a topic of controversy among historians.

Nazi Shakespeare is something of an exception to the usual way cultural critics approach Nazi culture. Though many continue to discuss German actors and directors either in terms of their complicity with the Third Reich or their criticism of it, Shakespeare's plays, unlike Richard Wagner's *œuvre*, are not regarded as having been contaminated by the Third Reich. Shakespeare is apparently the one cultural icon that can circulate without being contaminated by Nazis but not identified as British either. He can't be arrested – both in the sense of being stopped and in the judicial sense of being charged with one specific allegiance or identity. Instead of getting stuck in different registers, Shakespeare can manage to pass – and to get a pass – everywhere. Even Hitler, as we have seen, was not going to blockade Shakespeare. The result of this passing is not, however, some transcendental triumph of Shakespeare's will but all kinds of weird crossovers, cross-currents, crossed wires, and cross-hairs in which opposite sides double up and mimic one another. In these phantom gatherings and connections, one can reasonably say that Shakespeare is indeed *über alles*.

REFERENCES AND FURTHER READING

Baum, Vicki (1944). *Hotel Berlin '43*. Garden City, NY: Doubleday, Doran and Company, Inc.

Blatty, William Peter (1965). *I, Billy Shakespeare*. New York: Doubleday.

Boose, Lynda E. & Burt, Richard (eds.) (1997). *Shakespeare the Movie: Popularizing the Plays on Film, TV, and Video*. London: Routledge.

Burns, Margie (2003). "Pentagon Censors the Classics, but Shakespeare Slips Through." Available at: www.warletters.com/book/asedition.html.

Butler, Judith (1990). *Gender Trouble*. New York and London: Routledge.

Butler, Judith (1993). *Bodies that Matter: On the Discursive Limits of "Sex."* New York: Routledge.

Derrida, Jacques (1977). "Limited Inc." *Glyph* 2: 162–254.

Dover Wilson, John (1935). *What Happens in Hamlet*. New York: Macmillan Co.

Drexler, Peter (1995). "Laurence Olivier's *Henry V* and Veit Harlan's *Der Grosse König*: Two Versions of the National Hero on Film." In *Negotiations with Hal: Multi-Media Perceptions of (Shakespeare's) Henry the Fifth*. Braunschweig: Seminar für Anglistik und Amerikanistik, Technische Universität Braunschweig, pp. 127–32.

Ferguson, Niall (2004). "The Monarchy of George W. Bush." *Vanity Fair* September: 382–9, 411–14.

Giardina, Anthony (2004). "A Page from Hamlet's Book: Prince Mused on Going to War over a 'Straw' of Cause." *San Francisco Chronicle* October 31: M3. Available at www.sfgate.com/cgi-bin/article.cgi?f=/chronicle/a/2004/10/31/RVG8G9DII11.DTL&type=books.

Guntner, J. Lawrence (1998). "Expressionist Shakespeare: The Gade/Nielsen *Hamlet* (1920) and the History of Shakespeare on Film." *Post Script*

17, 2 (special issue: "Shakespeare and Film: Derivatives and Variations," ed. Lisa S. Starks): 90–102.

Habicht, Werner (1985). "Shakespeare in the Third Reich." In Manfred Pfister (ed.) *Anglistentag*. Passau: Vorträge, pp. 194–204.

Habicht, Werner (1989). "Shakespeare and Theatre Politics in the Third Reich." In Hanna Scolnicov (ed. and introduction) & Peter Holland (ed.) *The Play out of Context: Transferring Plays from Culture to Culture*. New York: Cambridge University Press, pp. 110–20.

Hitler, Adolf ([1925] 1943). *Mein Kampf*, trans. Ralph Mannheim. Boston: Houghton Mifflin.

Hoenselaars, Ton (2005). "Shooting the Hero: The Cinematic Career of *Henry V* from Laurence Olivier to Philip Purser." In Sonia Massai (ed.) *World-Wide Shakespeares*. London: Routledge.

Hortmann, Wilhelm (1998). *Shakespeare on the German Stage: The Twentieth Century; with a Section on Shakespeare on Stage in the German Democratic Republic by Maik Hamburger*. Cambridge: Cambridge University Press.

Howard, Leslie (1985). *Trivial Fond Records*, ed. Ronald Howard. London: William Kimber.

Howard, Leslie Ruth (1960). *A Quite Remarkable Father*. London: Longmans Green.

Howard, Ronald (1984). *In Search of My Father: A Portrait of Leslie Howard*. London: Smith Publications.

Huffington, Ariana (2004). "Shakespeare Turns a Spotlight on Bush and Iraq." *Ariana Online* June 2. Available at: www.arianaonline.com/columns/column.php?id=714.

Kahn, Victoria (2003). "Hamlet or Hecuba: Carl Schmitt's Decision." *Representations* September 83, 1: 67–96.

Kittler, Friedrich A. ([1986] 1999). *Gramophone, Film, Typewriter*, trans. Geoffrey Winthrop-Young & Michael Wutz. Stanford, CA: Stanford University Press.

Kristof, Nicholas D. (2004). "Crowning Prince George." *New York Times* September 1. Available at: www.nytimes.com/2004/09/01/opinion/01kristof.html?ex=1095074642&ei=1&en=02d2b8144cfd0334.

Mitchell, Charles P. (2002). *The Hitler Filmography: Worldwide Feature Film and Television Miniseries Portrayals, 1940 through 2000*. Jefferson, NC: McFarland & Co., Inc.

Moranis, David (2004). "Band of Brothers: Kerry's Rise Lifts Fellow Vietnam Vets." *Washington Post* July 29: A01. Available at: www.washingtonpost.com/wp-dyn/articles/A22228-2004Jul28.html.

Newstrom, Scott (2003). "Step Aside, I'll Show Thee a President": George W. as Henry V?" *Poppolitics.com*. Available at: www.poppolitics.com/articles/2003-05-01-henryv.shtml.

Peterson, Wolfgang et al. (2000). *Film Museum Berlin*. Berlin: Nickolaïsche Verlag.

Purser, Philip (1991). *Friedrich Harris: Shooting the Hero*. London: Quartet Books.

Ratliff, Ben (2004). "Ozzfest Trudges on, Laden with Sponsors and Politics." *New York Times* July 16. Available at: query.nytimes.com/gst/fullpage.html?res=9A04E1DC143AF935A25735A257 54 C0A9629C8B63.

Reuters (2004). "Protesters 'Drive' Bush from Ireland." June 26. Available at: www.cnn.com/2004/WORLD/europe/06/26/us.eu.protests.reut/index.html.

Rickels, Laurence A. (1991). *The Case of California*. Baltimore, MD: Johns Hopkins University Press.

Rickels, Laurence A. (2003). *Nazi Psychoanalysis*, 3 vols. Minneapolis: University of Minnesota Press.

Ronell, Avital (1989). *The Telephone Book: Technology, Schizophrenia, Electric Speech*. Lincoln, NB: University of Nebraska Press.

Schmitt, Carl ([1951] 1999). *Hamlet oder Hekuba*. Berlin: J. G. Cotta'sche Buchhandlung.

Schmitt, Carl (1987). "The Source of the Tragic." *Telos* 72, Summer: 133–51.

Taussig, Michael T. (1993). *Mimesis and Alterity: A Particular History of the Senses*. New York: Routledge.

Thurmann, Imgard (1940). "Shakespeare im Film." *Shakespeare Jahrbuch*, vol. 76, ed. Wolfgang Keller. Weimar. Verlag Herman Boehlaus Nachfolger, pp. 189–98.

Tift, Stephen (1991). "Miming the Fuehrer: *To Be or Not to Be* and the Mechanisms of Outrage." *Yale Journal of Criticism* 5, 1: 1–40.

Vaget, Hans Rudolf (1984). "Die Auferstehung Richard Wagners: Wagnerismus und Verfremdung in Syberberg's *Hitler* Film." In Susan Cocalis & Henry A. Lea (eds.) *Film und Literatur: Literarische Texte und der neue deutsche Film*. Bern: Francke Verlag, pp. 124–55.

Virilio, Paul (1989). *War and Cinema: The Logistics of Perception*, trans. Patrick Camiller. London: Verso.

Virilio, Paul (2001). "My Kingdom for a Horse: The Revolutions of Speed." *Queen's Quarterly* 108, 3: 329–338.

Winthrop-Young, Geoffrey (2002). "Drill and Distraction in the Yellow Submarine: On the Dominance of War in Friedrich Kittler's Media Theory." *Critical Inquiry* 28, 4: 571–98. Available at: www.uchicago.edu/research/jnl-critinq/issues/v28/v28n4.winthropyoung.html.

Worthen, W. B. (2003). *Shakespeare and the Force of Modern Performance*. Cambridge: Cambridge University Press.

SELECTED FILMOGRAPHY

Der Grosse König (1942). Director Veit Harlan. UFA. Germany, B&W.

Henry V (1944). Director Laurence Olivier. UK. DVD edition.

Hitler: A Film from Germany (1978). Director Hans-Jürgen Syberberg. Germany and UK.

Hotel Berlin (1945). Director Peter Godfrey. USA. B&W.

Jew Süss (1940). Director Veit Harlan. UFA. Germany. B&W.

Kohlberg (1945). Directors Veit Harlan & Wolfgang Liebeneiner. Germany.

L.A. Story (1991). Director Steve Martin. USA.

Mephisto (1981). Director Istvan Szabo. Hungary. DVD edition with English subtitles.

Pimpernel Smith (1941). Director Leslie Howard. UK. B&W.

Richard III (1996). Director Richard Loncraine. UK. MGM.

Schindler's List (1993). Director Steven Spielberg. 2-disc DVD edition, 2003.

Sherlock Holmes and the Secret Weapon (1943). Director William Neill. UK. B&W. DVD edition.

The Great Dictator (1940). Director Charlie Chaplin. United Artists. B&W. 2-disc DVD.

The Great Escape (1963). Director John Sturges. USA.

The King of New York (1942). Director Charlie Chaplin. UK. B&W. DVD edition.

The Ninth Configuration (1980). Director William Peter Blatty. USA. DVD edition.

The Pianist (2002). Director Roman Polanski. France. DVD edition.

The Scarlet Pimpernel (1935). Director Alexander Korda. UK. B&W.

This Happy Breed (1944). Director David Lean. UK. B&W.

To Be or Not to Be (1942). Director Ernst Lubitsch. USA. B&W.

To Be or Not to Be (1983). Director Mel Brooks. USA.

Up! (1972). Director Russ Meyer. USA.

Which Way to the Front? (1970). Director Jerry Lewis. USA.

Yellow Canary (1943). Director Herbert Wilcox. UK. B&W.

TELEVISION PROGRAMS

Chaffey, Don (1957). "*Hamlet* in Flames." *The New Adventures of Charlie Chan*. TV series. Episode 17. B&W, 50 mins.

McEveety Bernard, dir. (1964). "A Silent Cry." *Combat!* TV series. Episode 55. First aired February 18.

Sagal, Boris, dir. (1962). "A Day in June." *Combat!* TV series. First aired December 18. *Combat! – Season 1 – Campaign 1*, DVD 2004.

24
Game Space/Tragic Space: Julie Taymor's *Titus*

Peter S. Donaldson

Julie Taymor's *Titus* begins in a familiar, even stereotyped contemporary setting, a modest apartment where a hyperactive, media-dependent child is abusing his toys on the kitchen table. The published screenplay suggests that "we could be in Brooklyn or Sarajevo" (Taymor 2000: 19), invoking the trope of Shakespearean universality while hinting at particular commonalities of violence linking the dominant world power to the regional wars and outbreaks of genocide that punctuated the emergence of a "new world order" in the 1990s. The setting shifts quickly to a realistic-looking Roman amphitheater, an arena for gladiatorial combat that also carries multiple traces and suggestions of other performance spaces, including Greek tragic theatre, the set of an over-the-top 1930s' film musical, an experimental theatrical space as imagined by Artaud in "The Theater and Its Double," a WWF professional wrestling ring, or one of the many stadiums that have been used as sites for political detention, interrogation and execution in the past decades. As the action of *Titus Andronicus* unfolds and Shakespeare's words are once again spoken in a tiered and circular auditorium open to the heavens, this arena also comes to stand for the Globe Playhouse of Elizabethan London or its postmodern successor, Shakespeare's Globe on the South Bank of the Thames. And because the child from the modern world is positioned at the center of the action, part observer, part actor, amid characters who often seem like larger versions of his toys and move with the rigid gait of the cruder forms of computer animation, this space also resembles such simulated environments as historical videogames or forms of interactive virtual cinema in which the spectator is immersed in the story world, assumes a role within it, and is able to make choices or intervene in ways that may alter the narrative's outcome.

In the pages that follow I want to track some of the implications of Taymor's overlay of game, virtual and historical performance spaces in greater detail, and suggest a placement for her work in the context of several shifts in cinema history occasioned by the convergence of media in the early digital age. One such shift is the trend toward regarding films not as isolated works but as part of a spectrum of media and marketing forms that extends to action figures, source and derivative print fiction, videogames, and fan activity. Though *Titus* was not a commercial success and spawned little fan activity beyond scholarly commentary, the film tropes the protocols of science fiction and fantasy blockbuster films and their "horizontal integration" with other products and practices in its attempt to create a *Titus* that crosses time and media. And, though it is not a work of interactive or virtual cinema, *Titus*, like such diverse contemporary films as *Strange Days* (1995), *The Cell* (1998), *Run, Lola, Run* (1998), *Being John Malkovich* (1999), *The Matrix* (1999), *Memento* (2000) and *Eternal Sunshine of the Spotless Mind* (2004), anticipates a cinematic future in which films will increasingly incorporate elements of immersive video games and virtual reality experiments (see Davenport 2000: 79–82). Several of these films will figure in the discussion that follows, especially *Run, Lola, Run*, in which the video game metaphor is perhaps most salient.

As a film that reflects on the passage from historical to contemporary media forms and performance modes, Taymor's *Titus* also belongs to what is by now a rich tradition of combining Shakespearean adaptation and media allegory. Just as Shakespeare's work foregrounds its own media of manuscript, printed book and stage, such films reflect on the media history of which they are a part. Though many earlier Shakespeare films include brief metacinematic moments, Olivier's *Henry V* (1944) is perhaps the first to interpret a Shakespeare play as a kind of allegory of media history. Moving from a model of the Globe Playhouse stage to the outdoor battles characteristic of epic cinema and back again to the stage, the film connects wartime Britain to a glorious moment in its history (Henry V's Agincourt victory) and its culture (the period of Shakespeare), suggesting an almost providential fulfillment of Shakespeare's intentions in the shift from stage to screen. Later Shakespeare films in which media history constitutes a second narrative include Godard's *King Lear* (1985), in which cinema has to be reinvented *ex nihilo* in a post-nuclear future and Shakespeare's text must be pieced together from remembered fragments; Peter Greenaway's *Prospero's Books* (1991), which experiments with multiple digital overlays as an analogue to the Renaissance magic book; Richard Loncraine's *Richard III* (1996), in which Clarence is an amateur photographer, Richard a Hitler-like master of amplified sound and a necrophiliac media voyeur, lovingly reviewing photographs of executed enemies and replaying key moments in home movies of his coronation; and Baz Luhrmann's *William Shakespeare's Romeo + Juliet* (1996), in which the ubiquitous presence of television and print news media sustains the violence of the family feud.

Media Effects: A Kitchen Table Massacre

Like these recent films, *Titus* offers a more nuanced and critical, if often more surreal account of media in transition than Olivier's celebratory *Henry V*. This account begins with the film's first moments, a scene of media reception that enacts the well-known dystopic stereotypes of the case against children's television watching. The first shot, before the credits, shows us bright, blinking eyes peering through holes cut in a brown paper mask illuminated by the flickering light of a television screen positioned behind the filming camera.

The mask is the simplest form of Halloween disguise (Rutter 2003), but in an eclectic and allusive work such as *Titus*, it may also be read as a reference to the film *Halloween* (1978) in which a masked child becomes a serial killer. *Halloween* begins with a long sequence filmed entirely from the point of view of the protagonist. We never see his face until, as the camera is reversed after the first brutal killing, we see this diminutive attacker, dwarfed in the frame, frozen in place clutching a huge kitchen knife, wearing a mask based on a space alien character. Unmasked by his father, he is revealed as a frightened grade school child who has just murdered his sister. When the mask is suddenly torn off in a key sequence later on, he cannot continue killing until it is replaced. In *Halloween* the mask is a ritualistic necessity, differentiating the human being from the psychopathic killing machine (called, in the film, "The Shape") he has become.

The child in *Titus*, frenzied by sugar and food additives, alone in front of the television, is a much milder version of the cinematic evil child. Blinking in hypnotic attention as he watches a noisy children's show, he doesn't take his eyes off the television even to bite into his hot dog. Then the camera pulls back, discovering a kitchen table covered, indeed crawling with dozens of toy soldiers, gladiators and robots, many of them squirming about, moving their arms or heads, accompanied by "action" sounds and simulated speech. The toy figures have a creepy, chaotic life, like worms in a bucket. They share the messy table with the boy's lunch, and elicit a division of attention: now multitasking – listening to and intermittently watching the screen, eating, playing with his food – the boy savagely attacks his toys like Sid, the bad kid in Pixar's *Toy Story* (1995), who dismembers and explodes his action figure victims. This boy, who will become Young Lucius within the *Titus* world, is a living example of the "media effects" argument against television watching, oscillating between intensely focused and fractured attention and incited to heedless acts of violence by television, though, so far, that violence is enacted only in play.

The boy's mask also works to align him with tragic theatre: if the kitchen table is a play space, play here is a form of cruel puppetry in which the boy takes the role of the unfeeling gods. Nearing frenzy as a jack-in-the-box version of "Pop Goes the Weasel" plays on the soundtrack, the boy decapitates a soldier with a table knife (just on the cue *"pop!"*), adding to the mask's associations that of executioner. Crash landing a plastic fighter jet into his huge slice of chocolate cake, he then douses the crawling GI Joes with ketchup and sugar and drowns them in milk, anticipating in the register of play the confounding of dining and slaughter at *Titus*'s conclusion. The child is the evil demiurge of this toy world, a role Titus suspects the gods have taken in Rome as tragedy descends upon him. "As flies to wanton boys are we to the gods: they kill us for their sport" says *King Lear*'s Gloucester, borrowing an image from the fly-killing scene in *Titus Andronicus* (3.2). Later in Taymor's film it will be this boy (now identified as Young Lucius), not Marcus Andronicus as in Shakespeare's text, who kills the fly, but by then he will have developed a more complex attitude toward violence.

The final toy left standing on the table is a robot whose head rotates wildly, 360 degrees, like a panning movie camera on a tripod, as the boy douses it in sugar from a shaker. This moment passes quickly but is echoed in the next sequence: the boy himself stands in the middle of a threatening space, turning his head to every quadrant in terror. In that sequence the boy is positioned as potential victim, and the panning camera is closely identified with his perspective. But in this initial scene we never see from the puppet victims' point of view. Taymor's *Titus Andronicus* begins as if it were *Toy Story* filmed from the point of view of evil Sid the toy destroyer.

The kitchen table sequence is brought to a close by an explosion and fire that recalls the frame story of *Time Bandits* (1981), where, as in Titus, a home invasion signals time travel, and a way out of the stultifying, television-saturated world of the middle class (in *Time Bandits* the final explosion destroys the child's parents as well as their bourgeois home). In *Titus*, the boy hides, at first, cringing under the table, as his derisive mock compassion for his victims suddenly turns to terror. A strongman in a tank top and old-fashioned military goggles – perhaps a paratrooper or a wrestler – emerges from the smoke, grabs the boy, unmasks him, and carries him off weeping down a narrow flight of stairs. Unmasked, the boy is vulnerable; slight and delicate, frightened, he evokes compassion: no trace of his former role as demiurge or mad puppeteer remains. The home invasion has turned the tables, turning him into a plaything in the hands of a terrifying warrior.

The sudden shattering of the boy's world parallels Richard of Gloucester's tank crashing through a wall to interrupt Prince Edward's quiet fireside supper in Loncraine's modern-dress *Richard III*. In Shakespeare films that cross period, the transition is sometimes orderly, as is the shift from 1600 to 1414 AD and back in Olivier's *Henry V*; sometimes abrupt as it is in Kenneth Branagh's *Henry V* (1989), which makes the transition from modern to medieval by having Chorus fling open heavy doors that lead from a brightly lit late twentieth-century sound stage to a dark chamber in a fifteenth-century palace where the Bishop of Ely and the Archbishop of Canterbury conspire in guarded whispers. In *Richard III*, an even more abrupt changing of the times suggests continuity, rather than disjunction, between the violence of the modern world and that of Shakespeare's plays. When Ian McKellen's Richard breaks through the wall of the royal encampment of a twentieth-century "Tewksbury," his execution of King Henry at prayer with an automatic pistol is synchronized with the appearance of Shakespeare's title on the screen in block capitals, as if the civilized life of the British ruling class in the 1930s is given the lie by the eruption within it of the medieval/Machiavellian cruelty of Shakespeare's history plays. In *Titus* as well, a Shakespeare play intrudes violently into the medium of cinema and into a twentieth-century setting. However, there are differences: McKellen's Richard is associated with modern weapons and with the ruthless *Realpolitik* that marks the shift, during World War I and its aftermath, from the class loyalties and limited warfare of Old Europe to the horrors of the twentieth century. When the gasmask is removed, we see

Richard's cruel impassivity beneath. In Taymor's *Titus*, however, the valence of the home invasion is more complex. Certainly it reminds us that the false securities of modern life can vanish in a moment. But the scene also suggests that the boy now begins a confrontation with violence that can lead to a new perspective. The destruction of his home is a reminder of the ambient uncertainties of contemporary life, but it also stands, in some measure, for the transforming violence of theatre.

The Coliseum/The Titus Doll

In *Titus*, the passageway into historical space opens instead onto a vast arena, where the camera again takes the point of view of the child, still held, now high overhead, by his abductor, to the cheers of an unseen crowd. The choice of a Roman amphitheater was central to the director's design: "To frame the narrative I chose an architectural structure to function in a symbolic manner: the Roman Coliseum; the archetypal theatre of cruelty, where violence as entertainment reached its apex" (Taymor 2000: 178). The location is not simply a historic setting in the manner of mainstream epic cinema, however: this Coliseum is layered with traces of other times and other spaces. A burning structure in one corner links it to the fire in the boy's twentieth-century home; it is empty at first, with no spectators in the tiers (though their cheers can be heard); and the sequence was shot not in Rome but in Pula, Croatia, in the best-preserved of all imperial Roman amphitheaters. Too complete to be the well-known ruins of the real Coliseum, too real to be a model, and tinted a surreal blue, this building, like other locations in the film, hovers between historical authenticity and obvious artifice. And if the Roman Coliseum typifies the ancient theatre of cruelty, this building's associations with the Balkan wars and ethnic massacres instance a modern and widespread practice in which amphitheaters and sports arenas are used for political detention and murder, as in such widely distant cases as Santiago, Chile (1968) and the public executions held in the soccer stadium in Kabul, Afghanistan, before the fall of the Taliban. Such associations are latent at this point in Taymor's narrative but will come closer to the surface at the end, when silent spectators in modern dress will take seats in the arena, witnesses to the savage climax of *Titus Andronicus*.

As the Coliseum sequence begins, the boy is held aloft at the center of the arena to the cries of an invisible crowd. The meaning is ambiguous. Is he an intended sacrifice (for human sacrifice takes place in *Titus*), or a gladiatorial or wrestling opponent whose life or death is to be decided by the crowd? Or does his elevation signify celebration rather than threat? He might be a future leader or savior, displayed for all to admire like the infant Simba, heir apparent to the kingdom of nature in the film of *The Lion King* (1994). In Shakespeare's *Titus*, Lucius becomes emperor at the end of the play and Young Lucius might succeed him. We cannot tell if the spectators are to be taken as real or imagined (no faces appear in the tiers of the amphitheater), and whether their cheers are for the boy or for his captor, or for both. Whatever their verdict, these unseen viewers identify the film audience with the life and death powers of an ancient Roman crowd at a gladiatorial contest, and therefore also with aspects of video game and interactive "reality" television. Media critics have speculated that the trend of reality television could lead, in an imagined future, to live executions, and, while this seems fanciful, a form of fictional life and death choice is imminent on NBC's *Law and Order: Criminal Intent*, in which audiences will soon be able to vote on the fate of Detective Goren's nemesis, child murderer Nicole Wallace. *The New York Times*'s account of the plan describes this form of interactivity as "anointing viewers as virtual Romans at the Coliseum who can snuff out life with a flick of the mouse" and cites Janet Murray's view that the device "[puts] the audience in the role of the virtual executioner" (Carr & Gross: 2004: A17).

In *Titus* the strongman turns at the center of the space, displaying the boy to all quadrants, and as he does so the camera moves in and down, circling slowly in the reverse direction around the pair so that, in this low-angle shot only the boy is seen, rotating in one direction while the amphitheater itself seems to move in another. Once the boy is set down, much of the next sequence follows his gaze, seeing what he sees and his reactions to what he sees, at close enough range so that he seems at times alone in an imagined spectacle: briefly the strongman disappears, and the audience is no longer present to us, even aurally.

Catching sight of a modern realistic toy in the sand – a caped Roman legionnaire, a double of one of his own toys – he stoops to pick it up. In contrast to his behavior just before his capture, he now handles the toy as if it were a thing of wonder, rotating it as he endows it with imagined life, valuing, perhaps for the first time, this remnant of his life at home. As the noise of the boots of Titus's approaching army startles him and he snaps his head to the left, the camera follows him with a rapid pan to frame a living Roman soldier, nearly identical in dress to the doll the boy holds, his features masked by the caked blue-grey dust of battle so that, like the boy himself in the preceding scene, the eyes and lips offer the only glint of color. Suddenly the boy's head turns to the right, where he sees the funeral procession for Titus's sons lost in battle approach, and then back again to see the Goth captives led into the arena in captivity, carried in anachronistically motorized vehicles, their captured armor and weapons conveyed in a plexiglass coffer or display case more appropriate to a Damien Hirst exhibit in a contemporary art gallery than to ancient Rome. The soldiers move with mechanical precision, underscoring the analogy between them and the boy's toy soldiers. At a signal from Titus, they present arms, and perform an elaborate 360-degree rotation with their weapons. Carol Rutter (2003) aptly suggests that this sequence evokes the grand production numbers of 1930s' Busby Berkeley musicals: these soldiers overplay their rigidly choreographed entrance to a degree that can be read as a campy parody of military exercises.

Titus, his features also masked by the dust of battle, removes his helmet in unison with his troops and addresses the crowd – "Hail Rome, victorious in thy mourning weeds!" The camera circles around Titus as it had around the boy, and again the tiers of the amphitheater seem to move behind him. At "Here Goths have given me leave to sheath my sword" we cut to a close-up and then to a two-shot of the boy and Titus. Moved by compassion or by a sudden recognition of kinship, the boy reaches out and touches Titus on the arm. The gesture turns Titus's public, formal declamation into a reflective, intimate communication, shot in alternating close-ups, as if only he and the boy were present, and as if they shared a close bond. This first step toward the boy's assumption of Young Lucius' role also is the first of many moments in which wordless contact between the two is a part both of Titus's recognition of his own losses and of the boy's growing moral depth. Here too, the shift in tone and camera distance mirror the textual shift from second to first person address, from heroic comparisons to self-reproach:

> Romans, of five-and-twenty valiant sons,
> Half of the number that King Priam had,
> Behold the poor remains alive and dead:
> These that survive, let Rome reward with love;
> These that I bring unto their latest home,
> With burial amongst their ancestors.
> Here Goths have given me leave to sheathe my sword.

At this point in the film, the boy touches Titus's shoulder:

> Titus unkind, and careless of thine own,
> Why suffer'st thou thy sons unburied yet,
> To hover on the dreadful shore of Styx?
> (1.1.82–91)

Formally, this Coliseum sequence introduces the signature set-ups and camera movements of the film as a whole: circular and arena-like locations with the focal character at the center, rotating shots from this central point of view, initial and/or concluding shots from directly overhead, and role reversals as characters shift from aggressor to victim, or from spectator to actor. In this design, repeated throughout the film in key scenes such as the confrontations that take place before the "loathsome pit" (Act 2 Scene 2) and at the conclusion (Act 5 Scene 3), rotations of point of view, snap pans and rapid turns of the head bring spectators into identification with the figure at the center who may be victim or tormentor (or who may occupy both roles successively) and who cannot see the whole. Taymor's shooting of much of the scene from the boy's point of view aligns the film with the reversals of spectator and spectacle of Artaud:

> We are eliminating the stage and the auditorium and replacing them with a kind of single site, without partition or barrier of any kind, which will itself become the theater of the action. A direct communication will be established between the spectator and the spectacle, between the actor and the spectator, because the spectator, by being placed in

the middle of the action, is enveloped by it and caught in its cross-fire. (Artaud 1988: 248)

The boy's participation in the spectacle, his ambiguous role within it, and the sense of uncertainty caused by being placed *in medias* also connect Taymor's *Titus* to contemporary media forms and practices: the "ancient Rome" the boy has entered is not so much a historical setting as a cinematic version of the interactive virtual story worlds that now ever more closely connect cinema and video games and extend to individual play with physical action figures. Taymor's *Titus* is the first attempt at Shakespearean tragedy in the new mixed medium that is taking shape through the convergence of these elements. There are a number of "Roman" video games on the market and in development including *Age of Empires: The Rise of Rome* (Microsoft, 1996), *Gladiator* (Acclaim, 2003), *Shadow of Rome* (CapCom, forthcoming, 2004), and *Rome, Total War* (Activision, Fall 2004), a real-time strategy (RTS) game in which the aim is to become emperor.

> Over the past decade, we've seen many a large battle scene in movies. Everything from Braveheart to Lord of the Rings has featured a people-heavy clash in which thousands run at thousands, arms flailing, soldiers screaming and dying by the handful. And, while we've seen several RTS games bring these grand battles to life in pre-rendered form, there's never really been a strategy game that made you believe you are in control of it all ... that you could rush with your pikemen or call in your heavy infantry whenever you wanted ... that you could mortar the main gates or try to bust it down with man-power. Not in the thousands, that is, until Rome: Total War. Check out screens of the game in our gallery. (UnderGroundOnline)

This game has already been used by the History Channel to recreate battles scenes in its 13-episode *Decisive Battles* series (Gaudiosi 2004).

Action Figure Cinema

The use of toy soldiers in *Titus* is on one level a narrative device, allowing for a transition from the twentieth-century frame to the Roman story space, from contemporary child's play and the roots of that play in ancient modes of war and performance. At the same time, the toy soldiers and the imperial legionnaires who resemble them allow Taymor to position her work in the context of two of the major redefinitions of cinema in the last quarter century: the emergence of the blockbuster whose subsidiary products are as or more lucrative than ticket sales, and which is conceived from the outset not merely as a film but as an array of "horizontally integrated" media, toy and print products; and the various forms and dreams of forms of virtual interactive surround cinema that now constitute, to use a term William Uricchio employs for television in the period between the 1870s and the 1930s, the "horizon of expectations" of the new medium (Uricchio 2003).

As noted above, *Star Wars* was a landmark film in the first category. Lucas took no initial salary, preferring a share of expected revenue from subsidiary sales; these materialized, making *Star Wars* the first film for which merchandise sales exceeded box office receipts. Although this marketing story is well known, what is perhaps less attended to is the shift in the nature of cinema itself implied by its location in a planned spectrum of art, game, and entertainment products. We have not yet fully learned to read the expanded, cross-media cultural texts of which many high-budget mainstream films are now merely the center. Critics, non-fans, adults and others still tend to think of films as bounded works, with the merchandise, toys, novels made from films, websites and the spectrum of fan reworkings as peripheral phenomena, usually irrelevant to appreciating or assessing the film. Yet for the creators and a large fraction of the audiences for such works, a film is but one element in a larger imaginative work. It is the *Star Wars* world, story and characters, as these cross media and lend themselves to a wide range of entry points and fan practices, that is the *work*; the film is only a part of that world, a telling of the story, a view of its characters. In time a film like *Star Wars* also spawns a range of unauthorized, piratical uses which lead, on the one hand, to new digital forms of amateur cinema and, on the other, are duly woven back into the official commercial structure. Hasbro's site, for instance, offers dozens of action figures for sale. So little do former distinctions between marketing and cultural value and authenticity hold that last year's figurines can now be proudly advertised as novelties, with sunburst icons announcing "New *packaging* (coming February 1)!!!." Some of the figures here can be rotated on screen using a mouse, in a simulation of actual play, lending a tactile dimension to their value as advertising: rolling the mouse over the three-dimensional model of Darth Moll, a child or fan can begin to feel the pleasure of controlling the figure, and perhaps begin to create a story for it (www.Hasbro.starwars.com; consulted December 7, 2001). By 2004, this feature of the Hasbro site had become more cinematic, less interactive: 38 different characters are now displayed in a rotating "action figure arena." Once selected, individual figures rotate to the front, take center stage, as it were, and perform a circular dance on their own, without further control by the user (www.starwars.Hasbro.com; accessed October 11, 2004). This feature, too, resonates with the visual design of *Titus*, but the earlier version of the Hasbro/Star Wars site is closer to Taymor's interest in action figures as a species of hand puppet. Now famous for the innovative puppetry of *Lion King*, Taymor has been preoccupied throughout her career by inanimate figures that can be endowed with imaginative life by artists and audiences. In *Titus* she pays tribute to the wonder of puppetry at the level of child's play, in a context that connects such play to the dreams of virtual immersive cinema.

If children's imaginative play with action figures is now in a sense "built in" to such films as *Star Wars* and *Toy Story* along with their prequels and sequels, the interactive penumbra of such films also includes re-imaginings by fans in several media, including print, re-edited and original video narrative, and what is known as "action figure cinema," in which commercially available figures are used as characters to create new animated video narratives loosely based on major films. Early on, fans began to create their own stories using these figures, and to record them on videotape (see Jenkins 2003: 281–312). The wide accessibility of low-end digital equipment has greatly increased the quantity of fan cinema, and sites such as Probot Productions offer on-line and for-purchase digital action figure films (www.probotproductions. com). Some action figure fan films, like Damon Wellner's *Prequel: The Return of Snaggletooth* (1999) re-stage the epic battles of the *Star Wars* series using the marketed action figures, swiping sound track and some footage from the original films to complement the toy animations. By the time of this writing, the forces of co-optation and the threat of the Millennium Copyright Act have limited public availability of some fan action figure remakes: Damon Wellner's films were taken off his own site in 2003, but *Snaggletooth* remained publicly available through a link to the Hasbro "Action Figure Theater" where it was next housed. Then the "Action Figure Theater" was succeeded by the "Action Figure Arena," with no amateur video at all.

But other fan sites have survived. Evan Mather's seven Star Wars titles from 1997–99 are still available, for example, at www.evanmather.com; accessed October 11, 2004. Mather experiments with eclectic and parodic forms – *Les Pantless Menace* (1999), perhaps the most notorious and critically successful of the fan films, mixes action figures from *The Phantom Menace* and vapidly menacing naked Barbie Dolls who glide through space like spaceships in *2001: A Space Odyssey* (1968) to the music of Shostakovich's *Jazz Waltz 2*, the theme music for *Eyes Wide Shut* (1999), thus embedding a spoof on Kubrick's dreamy science fiction romanticism (itself ironic) within a parody of the then latest *Star Wars*. In another action figure film, Mather crosses *Phantom Menace* (1999) and *The Truman Show* (1998) to create the hybrid *Qi-Gon Show* (1999), in which a Liam Neeson/Qi Gon action figure moves through an artificially constructed bland suburban life of the future ("What did you do at work today, honey?" "The usual," he says, ponderously bored, "practiced with the light saber; reached out with my feelings . . . "), half noting the imperfections in his world that might reveal it to be a movie set, as Jim Carrey's character does in *Truman*. "That was odd," Qi Gong says when a defective light bulb (standing for the second sun of Tatiana in this illusory world) burns out and pieces of it fall on the pavement with a glassy tinkle.

I know of no action figures marketed in concert with the release of a Shakespeare film, but last year an impressive Shakespeare action figure, complete with removable book and pen appeared under the Accoutrements trademark. The package text attempts to align Shakespeare with the "action" genre by listing the quill pen as his "weapon of choice . . . (mightier than the sword!)" This manufacturer also offers action figures of Einstein, Edgar Allan Poe (with removable raven), and Pope Innocent IIII (see www.accoutrements.com/actionfigures; accessed October 11, 2004). Whether or not this figure may soon star in an amateur remake of *Shakespeare in Love* in digital video that moves nomadically from fan sites to semi-official versions on the websites of Accoutrements and Miramax is beyond the scope of this chapter. My more modest suggestion is that the cycle of possible as well as actual ancillary media forms that any film might now take function as an important context for interpreting Julie Taymor's approach to *Titus*.

Videogame as Cinematic Protocol

If *Titus* is in a sense a form of action figure theater – or, in the term the amateur filmmakers themselves prefer, toy cinema – it is also related to videogame-inflected cinema. *Run, Lola, Run* (1998) is a good example of the emerging genre, with a 90-minute "game" at its center, a time clock to keep track, and an array of rotating perspectives, overhead shots, and choices at crossroads that parallel such formal elements in *Titus*. The premise is that Lola has 20 minutes to find 20,000 marks and save her drug-courier boyfriend's life. Her red hair and cartoon style make her a kind of game figure, as she selects strategies. Unlike life or its shadow, conventional cinema, the "game' is replayed three times during the film, each with a different strategy and a different ending, and with accidental occurrences as well as subtle moral choices affecting the timing and therefore the outcome.

Titus and *Lola* are among the growing number of contemporary films that draw on the example of video games, virtual reality and interactive cinema experiments to create a new set of formal codes for cinematic representation, usually highly protagonist-centered in contrast to the dialogic conventions of mainstream Hollywood cinema, or the so-called "Griffith codes" of the past. I would include among such films *The Matrix, Strange Days, The Cell, Memento* and *Being John Malkovich*, whose director, Spike Jonze, moved from the world of amateur skateboard video (in which the camera is attached to the skateboard itself) to create a style adequate to the first-person intimacies of a film whose characters and we, as audience, with them, inhabit John Malkovich's body and look at the world through his eyes. I would distinguish these films from others in which there is a game or virtual reality theme or subject, but in which the received conventions of cinematic representation are relatively unaltered, such as *eXistenZ* (1999) or *Lara Croft: Tomb Raider* (2001).

Action figure theatre, amateur digital forms like skateboard video, video games and virtual reality/interactive cinema all share the aesthetic of first-person agency and perspective in surround space. We are "in" the game – at least in the sense that our point of view is closely associated with one of the players – and the game world responds to moves made within it. But if close first-person point of view is characteristic of films influenced by these forms, so is the idea that the story world is or may be unreal, contingent, *ad hoc*, hallucinated, misremembered, implanted, or constructed. *The Matrix*, of course, names such a constructed world in its title, and contrasts it with the "desert of the real" inhabited by its liberated protagonists. Like these films, *Titus* draws on the representational styles of new media to move toward a set of cinematic conventions that share in the excitement of video games and virtual reality while permitting a critical perspective on current media culture.

The Loathsome Pit

Because Taymor's shooting style in the first Coliseum sequence is so striking, the associations of that space are in a sense portable: the combination of overhead shots, circular spaces, slow pans around the space, quick pans from a central character's point of view, and shifts at the center from victor to victim position established firmly in the amphitheater sequence are repeated to suggest an agonic "theatre of cruelty" in other places, including outdoor locations and even eventually cosmic settings. The hunting scene (Act 2 Scene 1) begins with overhead rotating shots of the chase, descending to ground-level presentation of the clearing in the forest, where Aaron the Moor digs a hole to bury his bag of gold. Here, a succession of characters will occupy the center as the "loathsome pit" in which Titus's sons are trapped replaces Aaron's hole. First, Aaron is surprised and in effect sexually assaulted by Tamora. Aaron and Tamora occupy the center as Bassianus and Lavinia, discovering their tryst, taunt and threaten them. Then Tamora's sons enter the clearing and turn the tables, finally killing Bassianus and dragging Lavinia off to a wasteland marsh where she will be raped, mutilated and set in mockery on a tree stump, as on a pedestal. Through point-of-view shots of conflict, uneasy hand-held partial pans around the periphery of the clearings and the marsh, Taymor emphasizes the centrality of the main characters on such "stages" as well as the potential of such settings to bewilder, confuse and threaten role reversals of victim and victor. In this way the forest itself becomes an arena, a "theatre of cruelty."

"O earth"/"I earth": Globe and Self in *Titus*

Though Taymor's cinematic constructions differ from what was possible on the stage of the Rose or the Globe, she follows Shakespeare's practice in making her represented world one that can move from intimate portrayals of subjective, imagined worlds within a character's thoughts to a space that mirrors the earth and also the heavens, imagined here, as in the text, as indifferent to suffering. In Act 3 Scene 1 "the action returns to Rome" (see Bate's note on Act 3 Scene 1 stage direction in the Arden 3 *Titus*), where Titus pleads with the tribunes to spare his sons' life as they are led to their execution. In Taymor's film the scene is set at some distance from the city, at the crossing of two roads, paved with immense stones set in earth. In the distance are ruined arches and other architectural remains of imperial Rome (real objects in the modern locations in which the sequence was filmed but anachronisms for the period in which *Titus* is set, when these authentic survivals of the Roman Empire would have been new). The sequence begins with an overhead shot of the road as the tribunes pass by Titus on either side, ignoring his lament. As the camera moves down, its field of view ranges from wide, even panoramic shots of the roads, the low skyline of a distant city, far off hills behind it, and the horizon to close shots of Titus in his grief. The tribunes pass, followed by a sacrificial bull and the horse-drawn cart in which Quintus and Martius are hung up in chains. As Titus speaks "For these two, tribunes, in the dust I write," he literally falls between the cart's wheels and the camera follows in tight close-up, the turning wheels becoming a passing blur about his face, pressed to the gravel in the dusty road as he addresses his lament to the stones. The camera returns briefly to a wide overhead shot, with Titus stretched out on the road, the procession moving away slowly toward the city, then to Titus's face, as he lifts his head in the opposite direction. Now follows one of several dreamlike sequences that Taymor uses to connect the secret or unconscious thoughts of her characters to broader patterns of symbol they share with others. The road has not changed, but is now lit with a golden light and appears as a highway in heaven, suspended in billowing copper-gold clouds. An angel, part fairy-tale waif with red hair and heavy shoes, appears with a long trumpet at the vanishing point, moving slowly toward Titus. As he turns his head in the opposite direction, toward "Rome," perhaps to see if the illusion persists, perhaps to avoid the angel's gaze, she swings around before his eyes and we now see – for there were no cues of scale in the previous shot – the angel as a tiny figure, dwarfed by Titus's face, which fills the image in an immense close-up as she floats before his eyes. Behind her, there is an altar and on it a lamb with a human head; a carved inscription on the altar's base identifies the figure as "Mutius," the son Titus killed for disobedience. A sword descends in front of, but not touching the sacrifice, and as it twists in the air the lamb's body twitches as if in pain or in the throes of death; suddenly the angel proliferates into many identical angels, swirling around the altar, each on a different path.

On the level of tragic narrative, the condemnation of Martius and Quintus thus is framed as divine retribution for the killing of Mutius. This sequence also associates the violence of *Titus Andronicus* with the *Akedah*, the binding of Isaac for sacrifice in Genesis 22, and also with Jacob's dream vision of angels ascending and descending from Heaven in Genesis 28. Bate suggests that the sacrifice of Alarbus, followed by Titus's murder of his own son Mutius, indicate Rome's reversion to barbarism. Shakespeare's anachronism – Rome having long abandoned human sacrifice at the time of the wars with the Goths – works to imply a return to the savage past. In Bate's reading, Shakespeare conflates Rome's early history with the late Empire precisely in order to question the relevance of Roman culture as an exemplum to Christian, Elizabethan England. By connecting these questions to the *Akedah*, however, Taymor's *Titus* implies not so much that ancient Rome is an unworthy model for Christendom, but that it remains an all-too relevant one: the taint of human sacrifice entailed by Titus's leading 21 of his sons to death in battle calls in question both Jewish and Christian claims to have transcended the savage past.

It is characteristic of Taymor's approach that at this point, as the film comes closest to sacred literature, it also evokes game style. The cosmic road at whose vanishing point Titus is greeted by an angel is also, seconds later, a subjective space in which the angel is reduced, like a fairy in *A Midsummer Night's Dream*, to a tiny figure, revolving around Titus's head, seen in close-up. Taymor called these oneiric sequences Penny

Arcade Nightmares or PANs, stressing both their subjective character and their links with the history of animated media. Looking in one direction, Titus sees the angel as in a divine vision, immense and powerful; looking in the other she is a toy, a Tinkerbell no larger than the bridge of his nose. In this latter view we also see the angel as a more rigid and simplified figure than she first appeared; she does not really fly under her own power but is moved about in a fixed posture as if by wind. This rigidity links her to videogame figures and to the "sprites" in such consumer animation programs as QuickTime 4 and later versions, simple figures who can be made to move, unchanged in shape, through a video image simply by specifying the coordinates of their path. Taymor is at pains here to make the artificial look of such 3D digital animation techniques apparent, foregrounding the medium at this crucial moment, and rendering the status of Titus's incongruously Biblical vision doubtful (see Manovich 2001: 137–41; also www.apple.com/quicktime/reources/qt4/us/help/ QuickTime%20Help/htm, accessed September 14, 2004).

Angel/sprites and echoes of the story of Isaac do provide a kind of anachronistic Judeo-Christian context for understanding Titus's suffering, however, for it is he and not the omnipotent god of the patriarchs or the Gospel who has sacrificed his son. Like the boy's compassionate touch in the Coliseum sequence, Titus's vision prompts a turn toward intimacy and quiet sorrow, a moment that becomes literally "reflective" as Lavinia and Marcus join Titus to kneel and affirm their bond to one another as they gaze into a rain pool that mirrors their faces and the heavens above. The boy, often the catalyst for recognition in the film, is absent, but a shot of him sorrowfully looking through a rain-streaked window in Titus's house makes him a part of the circle.

Part theodicy, part hallucinatory vision, part a reframing in cinematic terms of the 3D animation techniques of games and consumer video, this sequence is also a version of the Shakespearean trope of stage as world, adapted for the medium of digitally-enhanced cinema. Beginning in the forest sequence, the visible space of performance begins to expand outward – in part through wider fields of view, in part through visual and verbal metonymies that take their cue from the text – until it seems to encompass the world, rather than merely a small part of a fictionalized fifth-century forest near Rome. The loathsome pit itself, which would have been a below-stage space beneath a trap door in early performances, takes on layered and multiple significances in the play: a trap for animals as well as for Titus's sons, it brings the trope of man as beast into play; on the literal level, it is a kind of grave for Bassianus and a cue for Lavinia's vaguer wish to be thrown into "some loathsome pit"; in Tamora's lying account of Bassianus' and Lavinia's description it becomes a "hellish pit," filled with a hissing of fiends, snakes and toads capable of producing madness and suicide; speaking from within it, Martius and Quintus call it a "swallowing womb" whose "ragged entrails" are "a fell devouring receptacle / As hateful as Cocytus' misty mouth" (2.3.230, 235–6, 239–40), where "Lord Bassianus lies betrayed in blood / All in a heap, like to a slaughtered lamb. / In this detested, dark, blood-drinking pit" (222–4). From a human trap improvised by Aaron, the pit becomes a center of the earth, a hell-mouth into which the blood of innocents flows.

This movement outward through language continues in 3.1 where Titus writes in the dust, weeps upon the stones (in the film in wide shots that include the horizon alternating with the tightest of close-ups, as I note above) and apostrophizes the earth, promising to shower regenerative tears upon it on condition that, unlike the "loath-some pit," it will refuse to "receive my dear sons' blood." Later in this long scene, Titus's sorrow of course deepens, as he discovers Lavinia's mutilation, and allows Aaron to cut off his hand in the hope of redeeming his condemned sons. The metaphors reverse now – Lavinia's tears are troped as rain from the heavens, and Titus himself, both sea and earth, receives them:

> If there were reason for these miseries
> Then into limits could I bind my woes.
> When heaven doth weep, doth not the earth o'erflow?
> If the winds rage, doth not the sea wax mad,
> Threatening the welkin with his big-swollen face? . . .
> I am the sea. Hark how her sighs doth blow.
> She is the weeping welkin, I the earth . . .
>
> (3.1.227–34)

In this scene, Titus's suffering comes to outweigh his folly, and he assumes the god-interrogating attitude of a classical tragic protagonist or of the biblical Job:

> O, here I lift my one hand up to heaven
> And bow this feeble ruin to the earth.
> If any power pities wretched tears,
> To that I call.
>
> (3.1.207–10)

Taymor's bold alternations of camera distance and angle of view, and her Penny Arcade Nightmares, game-inspired innovations in subjective filmmaking that also relate the characters' thoughts to cosmic and mythic *motifs*, are analogous to and also versions of Shakespeare's theatrical ways of making his stage stand for the terrestrial globe, and of making the words spoken *in extremis* by his tragic characters seem universal in import.

The Workshop at Cinecittà

The recognition of deep suffering in *Titus* 2.2 and 3.1 brings a kind of peace, signaling a new *persona* for Titus, whose words now often oscillate between a kind of wisdom that had been absent in the play and an even more profound and comic folly. In the film, this change is seconded by a shift in the boy, who now begins to speak Young Lucius's lines and is no longer merely a visitor but a member of Titus's family and of the company of mourners and revengers that family has become. This perhaps is the most troubling aspect of both play and film, for the turn toward introspection, repair and resolution is inseparable from Titus's commitment to consciously planned revenge. Just as the boy's initial gesture of comfort at the start is quickly followed by his serving as assistant to Titus as the swords used to dismember Alarbus are heated in the fire and afterward wiped clean of blood, the boy now shares in both sides of Titus's increased capacity for wisdom and for violence.

He participates fully in the film's reparative movement – it is he who, apparently, has the idea, not in Shakespeare, of providing Lavinia with prosthetic wooden hands. Here he visits a workshop – an actual workshop at Rome's Cinecittà where wooden props are handcrafted, selects an appropriate one, and, in what is perhaps the central "rhyming shot" of the film, rotates it slightly in the soft light of the workshop window, like a craftsman, endowing it with imagined life and remembering, perhaps, his identical gesture on discovering the Titus action figure in the dust of the Coliseum.

This sequence "answers" the action figure sequence, transforming mindless violence to reparation and elevating mass media play to the status of art. Though not in Shakespeare's script, the restoration of Lavinia's hands parallels the turn toward art and artistry in the play text, as Titus transforms himself into chief actor, scriptwriter and stage manager to turn Tamora's masked pageant of revenge against her and play master chef and host at the Thyestian feast which climaxes the action.

The close association of art and hideous violence in *Titus Andronicus* has always raised questions. Taymor's overlay of antifascist allegory in her modernization raises more, many of which are explored brilliantly, if controversially, in Richard Burt's "Shakespeare and the Holocaust: Julie Taymor's *Titus* is Beautiful, or Shakesploi meets the Camp" (Burt 2002: 295–329). Locations, allusions and direct references to fascist Italy abound, and Taymor's remarks in interviews make clear that her intention was through them to evoke the Holocaust as a modern equivalent to the culture of violence represented in the play. Here, that web of allusions works in a particularly complex way, for, as we shift from the milieu of *Star Wars* action figure violence to props as works of art, Taymor shoots the scene in the workshop founded by Mussolini, and pays tribute to a now dying art whose history spans that of the studio, first an instrument of fascist propaganda, then a central institution in the emergence of neorealist and art cinema of Fellini and Visconti, and others.

The restoration of the hand in *Titus* parallels central *motifs* in the films and autobiography of Visconti's disciple, Zeffirelli, who uses the haptic memory of touch to structure the reparative movement of his *Romeo and Juliet* (1968). Zeffirelli uses the association of emotional memory and the touch of the hand to create a sense of fulfillment and completion even in the Capulet tomb and it resonates with a central story in his autobiography, in which, as an art student in 1939 at the outbreak of World War 2, he is troubled by the practice of drawing severed hands in his drawing class, and traces the hand used as a model to the morgue where it has been rejoined to the body of an indigent young girl, briefly joining the girl's grandmother in mourning. For Zeffirelli, this story comes to stand for his vocation as a popular artist, seeking reconnection to ordinary people and impatient of the boundaries that render art a high mystery; it also begins the story of his finding a relation to the events of the war which leads to his joining the resistance. Just after the war, these autobiographical strands come together when he happens to attend a screening of Olivier's *Henry V* (Donaldson 1990: 145–68). I resist the drift of Burt's argument that Taymor's work remains confusingly tainted by its evocation of the Fascist era and his formulation that Taymor presents Titus as "antifascist as serial killer." But, in contrast to Zeffirelli, for Taymor the intermingling of fascism and the roots and antecedents of her own art remain troubling, serving in *Titus* to suggest a kind of necessary complicity linking tragic art and the real-life violence it may once have been thought to refine or transcend. Perhaps her position is closest to Benjamin's dictum that there is no work of civilization that is not at the same time a work of barbarism (Benjamin 1968: 256).

Final Frame

At the film's conclusion, Taymor returns to the Coliseum in a *tour de force* sequence in which the revenge action that culminates in the deaths of Lavinia, Titus and Saturninus is relativized, reframed as theatre. The action takes place in Titus's house, and ends with the horrific choking of Saturninus with a spoon wielded by Marcus. At the culminating moment, the frame freezes and the entire tableau formed by Titus's dining table with the living and dead arranged around it is rotated as if the scene itself were a dish on a lazy susan, and the camera pulls back to discover, amid the tiers of the vast Pula Coliseum, bleachers where somberly dressed spectators, denizens of our own time, sit. This movement from spectacle to audience reverses the dynamics of the first sequence shot in this location, in which the boy from our time enters the action of *Titus*. Here the audience are not actors but silent witnesses, not participants but spectators experiencing, in their view of this rotating diorama, a digitally-enhanced version of what we have come to think of, since Steven Orgel's ground-breaking work (1975), as the royal position in the theatre. Hauntingly absent in the opening sequences, the audience has now appeared as verbally associated with "the sad faced men of Rome" who, at the close of Shakespeare's text, are asked to repair the mangled body of the state. Visibly modern, somber viewers (one has a baseball cap, many are dressed in dark sweaters), these spectators are part theatrical audience, part silent cinematic spectators, occupying an impossible intermediate space between the tiers of the theatre and the central ring. In real life they are Bosnians, witnesses, it is suggested, to the atrocities of our own times.

In the final moments, Young Lucius leaves his place within what, in a simpler film would be called the diegesis – in a sense an adopted young man of Rome, he takes action to partially resolve the questions concerning the fate of the child of Aaron and Tamora which the text does not answer, taking the child in his arms and walking through the gates of the amphitheatre (a walk that the design of Roman amphitheatres was intended to make as difficult as possible in order to prevent the escape of combatants or animals). The sun appears to rise as he reaches, but does not quite cross, the outer threshold. Yet it rises on the bleakest and emptiest of prospects, and if it is intended to invoke a hopeful view of the future, such hope is slender, for nothing in the action of the film or in Shakespeare's play suggests that the territory outside the walls is safe. This is where Tamora's body will be thrown to be eaten by dogs and birds.

Afterword: The Amphitheater of Curio (50 BC)

In *Historia naturalis*, Pliny the Elder tells the story of the construction of the first Roman amphitheater as a digression within a digression (Pliny 1962; vol. 36:24.113–20). In addition to being a treatise on the varieties of stones, their properties and their uses, Book 36 allows the author ample scope for disquisitions on the folly of mining and on greed and luxury generally, for, as he writes, even leaving aside precious gems, work in stone (he means marble in particular) gives rise to "the prime folly in our behavior" (*hoc est praecipua morum insania*). Mountains were "made by Nature to serve as a kind of framework, holding together the inner parts of the earth" and allowing it to withstand the force of rivers, seas and storms. In quarrying such stone as marble, we haul away vast portions of this vital structure, "often on a mere whim." In due course, this introduction to Pliny's treatise on stone leads to extensive description (and condemnation) of the building program of imperial Rome and to a short history of the roots of excess in the late Republic. The huge theatre of the aedile Scaurus, built in 50 BC which Pliny calls, sarcastically, "the greatest of all the works ever erected by man," comes in for special scorn. An immense structure with seating for 80,000 spectators, the theatre was sustained by 360 columns in three tiers: the bottom constructed of marble, the middle of glass, and the highest of gilded wood; between the columns were more than 3,000 statues and countless paintings and decorations. Pliny considers Scaurus's theater even more wasteful than Nero's *domus aurea*, yet he goes on to describe an "even more frenzied fantasy, in wood," constructed in the same period by Gaius Curio, who was later to die at Caesar's side in the Civil Wars.

Curio's structure, built for the funeral of his father, was a double theatre (hence the term amphitheatre). Curio could not hope to equal the costly embellishments of Scaurus, but tried to surpass him in technical flare:

> He built close to each other two very large wooden theatres, each poised and balanced on a revolving pivot. During the forenoon, a performance of a play was given in both of them and they faced in opposite directions so that the two casts should not drown out

each other's words. Then all of a sudden the theatres revolved (and it is agreed that after the first few days they did so with some of the spectators actually remaining in their seats), their corners met, and thus Curio provided an amphitheatre in which he produced fights between gladiators. (36.245.117)

This roughly circular enclosure was a better space for gladiatorial combat or animal hunting than the rectangular spaces previously used: when the circle was closed, there was no way out, the combatants or animals being surrounded by the tiered seats of the audience, and by gates in the later and much larger stone amphitheatres of the Empire.

Pliny comments ironically that the gladiators in Curio's amphitheatre may have been in less danger than the people of Rome who were whirled round in their seats. "Here we have the nation that has conquered the earth, that has subdued the whole world, that distributes tribes and kingdoms, that dispatches its dictates to foreign peoples, that is heaven's representative, so to speak, among mankind, swaying on a contraption and applauding its own danger! (*in machina pendens et ad periculum suum plaudens*)." Developing the motif of the reversal of roles of spectators and combatants, Pliny sees the rotating double theatre as evidence of reckless disregard for human life and as a judgment on the moral fiber of the community that participated: "For, if we must confess the truth, it was the whole Roman people that struggled for its life in the arena at the funeral games held at his father's tomb" (245.117). Later amphitheatres, including the Flavian amphitheatre or Coliseum, dedicated in 80 AD by the Emperor Titus (not Shakespeare's Titus) did not double as theatres; they did not rotate, and they were made of marble rather than of wood.

This chapter, like Pliny, yields to the temptation of a closing digression because so much of the visual and moral design of Julie Taymor's *Titus*, and so much of the force of her original take on Shakespeare's *Titus Andronicus*, seems anticipated by Curio's double theatre and Pliny's account of it. Since excerpts have occasionally made their way into standard source books for theatre history, e.g. Nagler (1959: 21–2), it may even be that Pliny on amphitheatres should be included, along with Artaud's rotating spaces, as one of the sources for the layered theatrical history imbedded in *Titus*.

Curio's amphitheatre was a structure in motion, as is Taymor's presentation of the Coliseum in which key sequences of the film take place, though the motion, for the most part, of *Titus* is a function of editing, shifts in point of view, and camera movement, rather than of the structure's actual movement in space. Curio's theatre is also a space in which the point of view of the audience undergoes a 180-degree shift, as does the cinematic presentation of the arena as the camera turns on its axis. It is a space not only of movement but of a transformation that moves from one set of historical forms (theatre for plays and athletic games, open rectangular spaces for gladiatorial combat and *venationes* or animal fights to a new form, the (non-rotating) amphitheatre, which would become the paradigmatic space for mortal combat, with the participants visible from all around the circle or oval and more easily confined within it than in a theatre of the semicircular design of each of Curio's theatres. And, if we read the amphitheatre through what Pliny makes of it in his prose, it is a space in which spectators and participants in the spectacle, victors and victims, exchange roles and status, even one in relation to which present times and manners can be seen to change places with those of the past. For one lesson Pliny draws from the folly of Curio is that "it is worth our while to be acquainted with his discovery, and so to be thankful for our modern code of morality and call ourselves 'elders and betters,' reversing the usual meaning of the term." Further, it is one that lends itself to expansive metonymy, the assembled spectators standing for "the whole Roman people," in their worldwide imperial role. The rotating of the theatre reaches outward in Pliny's prose, evoking the whole of the turning terrestrial globe. Thus, in a sense, Pliny describes the amphitheatre in terms that might have been borrowed from theatrical discourse, and especially from the Aristotelian theory of tragedy that counts sudden reversals of fortune and role as among the primary characteristics of the genre, and Renaissance tropes that make the theatre or arena a model of the world.

Though the Roman Coliseum is not mentioned or implied as a setting by Shakespeare, *Titus Andronicus* might make us think of the Coliseum without the help of Taymor's film. The building was constructed largely in the reign of Vespasian but was dedicated, as it happens, by the Emperor Titus (not Titus Andronicus) in 80 AD. The Roman Coliseum (named for a hilltop Temple of Isis in the environs, or, in its alternative spelling "colosseum," for the possibly legendary "colossus", a 100-foot statue of Nero that was said to have stood nearby) was, of course, a place for bloody games, the word "arena" used to denote such a place deriving from *harena*, the sand that caught the falling blood, a detail relevant to the *motif* of the earth as a receptacle for shed blood in *Titus* 2.2 and 3.1 as well as to the burial of Aaron in sand at the end of the film.

Pliny's prose version of Curio's amphitheatre is not only an account of a technological marvel that made it possible to move in real time from theatre to violent games, in anticipation of Taymor's central conceit: it is also a critique of the folly of a dominant imperial power, layering, in its retrospective scorn for Curio, commentary on the age of Nero, just past, as well as on the excesses, waste and violence of Pliny's own time, the time of the construction of the Roman Coliseum. Pliny's history is not itself a work of theatre, of course – yet its mingling of wonder and satire hints at something missing or imperfectly realized in Taymor's anti-imperial media allegory, a quality of outrage that might have altered the balance between art for art's sake and political engagement in this brilliant restaging of *Titus Andronicus*.

Note

Titus Andronicus cited is from the Arden Edition, 3rd series.

References and Further Reading

Artaud, Antonin (1988). "The Theater of Cruelty." *Antonin Artaud: Selected Writings*, ed. Susan Sontag. Berkeley, CA: University of California Press.

Benjamin, Walter (1968). *Illuminations*, ed. Hannah Arendt, trans. Harry Zohn. New York: Schocken.

Burt, Richard (2002). "Shakespeare and the Holocaust: Julie Taymor's *Titus* is Beautiful, or Shakesploi Meets (the) Camp." In *Shakespeare after Mass Media*. London: Palgrave, pp. 295–329.

Carr, David & Gross, Michael Joseph (2004). "She's a Killer and Her Life IS in Your Hands." *New York Times*, October 16, A17, A22.

Davenport, Glorianna (2000). "Your Own Virtual Storyworld." *Scientific American* 283, 5: 79–82.

Donaldson, Peter S. (1990). " 'Let Lips Do What Hands Do': Male Bonding, Eros and Loss in Zeffirelli's *Romeo and Juliet*." *Shakespearean Films/Shakespearean Directors*. Boston: Unwin Hyman, pp. 145–68.

Gaudiosi, John (2004). "Rome, First a Game, Now on TV." *Wired News Online*. May 17. Available at: www.wired.com/news/games/0,2101,63455,00.html (accessed September 4, 2004).

Jenkins, Henry (2003). "Quentin Tarantino's *Star Wars*? Digital Cinema, Media Convergence, and Participatory Culture." In David Thorburn & Henry Jenkins (eds.) *Rethinking Media Change: The Aesthetics of Transition*. Cambridge, MA: MIT Press, pp. 281–312.

Manovich, Lev (2001). *The Language of New Media*. Cambridge, MA: MIT Press.

Nagler, A. M ([1952] 1959). *Source Book in Theatrical History*. New York: Dover.

Orgel, Stephen (1975). *The Illusion of Power*. Berkeley, CA: University of California Press.

Pliny (1962). *Natural History*, vol. X: Books 36–7, ed. and trans. D. E. Eichholz (Loeb Classical Library). Cambridge, MA: Harvard University Press.

Rutter, Carol (2003). "Looking Like a Child, or *Titus* the Comedy." *Shakespeare Survey* 56, 1–26.

Shakespeare, William (1995). *Titus Andronicus*, ed. Jonathan Bate (Arden Shakespeare, 3rd series). London: Routledge.

Taymor, Julie (2000). *Titus: The Illustrated Screenplay*. New York: Newmarket.

UnderGroundOnline (n.d.). www.ugo.com/channels/games/gallery.asp?gallery = rometotal war_games (accessed September 14, 2004).

Uricchio, William (2003). "Technologies of Time." In J. Olson (ed.) *Allegories of Communication: Intermedial Concerns from Cinema to the Digital*. London: J. Libby/Bloomington, IN: Indiana University Press.

25

Shakespeare Stiles Style: Shakespeare, Julia Stiles, and American Girl Culture

Elizabeth A. Deitchman

Shakespeare Sister

In the Fall of 2001, Julia Stiles appeared on the inaugural issue of *Ellegirl* magazine. According to the editor's letter, Stiles was chosen as cover-girl because: "Julia is the ultimate ELLEgirl: She's confident, attractive, independent, and scary smart. In addition to being one of Hollywood's hottest young actresses, she's a sophomore at Columbia University, a self-described feminist, a monster on the soccer field, and someone who's not afraid to express herself" (Holley 2001: 26). In addition to her celebrated beauty and intelligence, Stiles has a well-documented reputation for being nice, with a "down-to-earth attitude" (Waterman 2004: 157) that makes her seem like the girl next door. Her status as the "ultimate ELLEgirl" and subsequent appearances as the cover-girl for magazines ranging from *Cosmopolitan* to *TeenVogue* mark Stiles's arrival as an icon of teen femininity, representing a clearly defined image of ideal American girlhood based on her appearance, achievements, and personality.

With central roles in *10 Things I Hate About You*, *Hamlet*, and *O*, Stiles could also be called a poster girl for teen Shakespeare movies. For though her acting career began in the theatre, her success has come primarily from cinema, especially with her first breakthrough role as Kat Stratford (Shakespeare's Kate) in 1999's *10 Things*. Her two subsequent Shakespearean roles – Ophelia and Desi (Desdemona) – also contributed significantly to her rising fame, her career and talent fostered by her appearance in Shakespeare movies: "[In *O*] Stiles' talent and savvy – enhanced by appearing in two other successful Shakespeare modernizations, '*Hamlet*' and '10 Things I Hate About You,' a '*Taming of the Shrew*' update – is every bit [Josh] Hartnett's equal, and sometimes more" (Carr 2001: D1). Stiles's connection to Shakespeare continues to play a significant role in shaping her image, figuring prominently in interviews and articles about the actress, as a recent interview titled "Shakespeare Sister" illustrates (Rimmer 2002: 12). Shakespeare's prominence in Stiles's press coverage and film career adds a significant layer to Stiles's representation of ideal teen girlhood, lending high cultural weight to Stiles's image and *œuvre*, a cultural weight generally absent from teen idols and lacking in the typical teen movie fare. Moreover, though Shakespeare makes substantial contributions to shaping Stiles's persona, theirs is a mutually supportive and reciprocal kinship: "The charismatic newcomer is appearing in two more Shakespeare-derived films this year, and she'll make them better" (Gershman 1999: 2B). And teen Shakespeare queen Stiles even seems to make Shakespeare particularly appealing to teen movie audiences: " '0' has been the movie I have been waiting for since I found [out] Julia Stiles was in it. Not even *American Pie 2* excited me as much" (angel_aims_135). Yet a close examination of their reciprocal relationship reveals that underneath its shiny, happy surface their kinship performs more pernicious ideological work. Together Stiles and Shakespeare sell a disturbing image of American teen girlhood, an image based on and perpetuating idealized representations of race, class, and gender.

Girl Power: Taming the Teenage Shrew

As a "scary smart" feminist and "monster on the soccer field," Stiles seems to embody Girl Power, a concept first introduced into early 1990s' popular culture by the third-wave feminist Riot Grrrls, emerging out of the alternative rock scene in America's Pacific Northwest. Their version of Girl Power fueled the movement as "riot grrrls [sought] to forge networks and communities of support to reject the forms of limitations on women's behavior" (Gottlieb & Wald 1994: 253). With the slogan "Revolution Girl Style," theirs was a vocal feminism with a punk rock beat as riot grrrls formed bands and taught themselves to play instruments, taking their fierce feminism to the stage:

> Riot Grrrls weren't pushing a rational feminism. They scrawled *slut* on their stomachs, screamed from stages and pages of fanzines about incest, rape, being queer, and being in love. They mixed a childish aesthetic with all that is most threatening in a female adult: rage, bitterness, and political acuity. In bands such as Bikini Kill, Bratmobile, Huggy Bear, and Heavens to Betsy, these Grrrls shot up like flames, influencing countless girls and showing them feminism before dissipating, seemingly, around the mid-nineties. (Baumgardner & Richards 2000: 133)

Unsurprisingly, however, authentic Riot Grrrl culture seemed to disappear more or less at the moment of its appearance in mainstream media. In many cases the media either oversimplified or misrepresented the movement or patronizingly belittled it. Even an ostensibly sympathetic view masks a patronizing attitude: "Riot Grrrls run the gamut from 14-year-olds who trade fanzines to keep up with their favorite bands to the truly – and sanctimoniously – committed" (Chideya 1992: 85). Faria Chideya's "sanctimoniously" enacts the typical mass-media attitude toward the Riot Grrrls by simultaneously undercutting and deriding the movement's commitment to feminist politics. Before long, mainstream popular culture had produced its own version of Girl Power, but instead of featuring screaming girl-groups in baby-doll dresses hammering instruments they taught themselves to play, the pop media gave us the Spice Girls and pop princesses, also dressed as little girls baring their navels, but cooing "Hit me baby one more time" (Britney Spears 1999) to music they never claimed to own.

Though no longer a visible presence in mainstream American culture, riot grrrls remain vocal with websites and blogs offering astute commentary on mainstream – especially corporate – appropriations of Riot Grrrl. As one riot grrrl writes "[corporate culture] has perverted the idea of 'girl power' and tried to [sell] it back to us as something 'cute' and 'sexy' that exists only to get boys off" (http://rgny.8m.com/about.html). Stripped of its rage and feminist politics, Riot Grrrl's impact on mainstream millennial teen culture nevertheless lingered in shopping malls and fashion magazines, leaving only naked belly-buttons, school-girl clothes, and even combat boots. Instead "girl power propels tween-teen culture, from *Clueless* to *Buffy* to *Legally Blonde* to the new *Charlie's Angels*, where cute guys are the reward for a greater, deeper self-realization and chick solidarity" (Wolcott 2003: 98). Girl Power fashion spreads, like the one featured in *Ellegirl*'s inaugural issue, provide prime examples of how mass media sells Girl Power to teenage and pre-teen ("tween") girls. With the headline "Girls Kick Butt!" the magazine introduces a Riot Grrrl-inspired fashion spread that also draws on the recent popularity of cinematic super-heroines: "Lara Croft and Charlie's Angels never had a bad fashion moment – why should you? Whether you're fighting evil like this dynamic duo or just battling through back-to-school, you've gotta look hot without losing your cool"(Van Cook 2001: 107). On the following pages, two models with carefully made-up, clean faces, perfect hair and "nary a pleat out of place" (2001: 109), well, kick butt superheroine-style. The text's emphasis on the girls' ability to maintain their looks as they fight crime prevents these action heroines from actually crossing the body-centered lines separating masculinity and femininity into sharp binary categories. Unlike male heroes, whose heroics leave them bloody, sweaty, dirty and – crucially – wearing torn clothes, these girls remain, above all, pretty to look at.

Like the Riot Grrrl movement, however, Girl Power does modestly challenge stereotypical girl behavior. As this cover of *Ellegirl* demonstrates, Girl Power cele-brates academic achievement, proclaiming "Smart Girls Rule!" Yet the cover also promises such hair and skin care advice as "28 ways to make the most of your locks" and "our guide to glowing skin" (*Ellegirl*, Fall 2001), weaving intelligence together with appearance and licensing teenage girls to be smart in the same way Girl Power licenses them to kick butt – as long as they still look good. The original cover-girl for *Ellegirl*, whose Botticellian beauty tempers her "scary" smartness and athletic prowess, Julia Stiles is the perfect icon of this de-fanged Girl Power femininity.

Whereas Riot Grrrl challenges the politics of licensed gender performance by pushing at its boundaries, Girl Power merely re-draws those boundaries by licensing a mildly transgressive performance while reaffirming the basic codes of conventional gender roles, ensuring that girls remain girls even when they seem to be acting like boys. Though sold to girls as strength and empowerment, mediatized Girl Power locates a young woman's strength in her ability to look good, be good, and get a boyfriend. As a pop culture phenomenon, Girl Power is really about preserving patriarchal values, and particularly about protecting heterosexual masculinity. More to the point, the teen romance – the principal genre of Girl Power fiction, a genre that suffuses and sustains the contemporary Shakespeare teen-film – provides the principal vehicle for Girl Power's consolidation of masculine, heteronormative identities.

Gil Junger's *10 Things I Hate About You*, a teen adaptation of *Taming of the Shrew* and the first of the Julia Stiles's Shakespeare trilogy, instantiates the rules of Girl Power and contributes substantially to Stiles's Girl Power iconicity, partially by replaying the course of mainstream media's appropriation of the Riot Grrrl. Though the story focuses mainly on taming Kat Stratford (Shakespeare's Kate) by moving her from Riot Grrrl politics to Girl Power behavior, almost all the film's characters are tamed into the rules of Girl Power, marrying Shakespeare's patriarchal world of sixteenth-century Verona to the corporate patriarchy of millennial mass media. By co-opting the Riot Grrrl movement to represent a teenage shrew, the film appropriates Shakespeare's cultural power to critique – or tame – the movement and to sanction its own de-fanged version of Girl Power – a power that benefits, rather than threatens, boys.

Junger moves Shakespeare's tale of taming a headstrong woman from sixteenth-century Padua to late twentieth-century Seattle, setting the action in the suburban Padua High School of the Stratford sisters, Bianca (Larisa Oleynik) and Katarina (Julia Stiles). Their single father, Walter (Larry Miller), is a harried obstetrician so obsessively worried that his daughters will get pregnant that he forbids them to date. When Walter changes his rule, proclaiming that Bianca can date when her older sister does, two rivals for Bianca's affection – sleazy Lothario Joey Donner (Andrew Keegan) and sweet guy Cameron James (Joseph Gordon-Levitt) – set out to find a date for Kat. They find a worthy suitor in Patrick Verona (Heath Ledger), a scary outsider (much like Kat) who takes shop and is rumored to have sold his liver to buy a set of stereo speakers. As in Shakespeare's play the shrew is eventually tamed, and according to the mutual conventions of teen romance and Shakespearean comedy, the teens all pair off into heterosexual couples.

Kat's distance from the kind of "chick solidarity" championed by Girl Power and represented by most of *10 Things*'s female cast establishes her as Padua High School's most feared shrew. From the film's opening moments Junger sets Kat against the other girls, juxtaposing her with a group of carefully made-up young women who listen to perky music and carpool to school in a cute blue convertible Volkswagen. Not only does Kat drive to school alone, Joan Jett pealing "I don't give a damn about my bad reputation" loudly from her car stereo, but she frequently objects to such "antiquated mating rituals" – and staple teen movie scenes – as big parties and the

Prom. Her bad reputation also stems from her overtly feminist politics: she calls Hemingway "an abusive alcoholic misogynist," and complains about "the oppressive patriarchal values that dictate [her] education" (*10 Things*). Her dedication to Sylvia Plath and her desire to go to Sarah Lawrence College supplement the film's portrait of Kat's feminism. Combining feminist politics – voiced through somewhat clichéd critiques of patriarchal society and her refusal to date – with musical taste ranging from Joan Jett to proto-Riot Grrrl band the Raincoats and full-fledged Riot Grrrl band Bikini Kill, in Kat *10 Things* conflates Riot Grrrl imagery with a simplified version of second-wave feminism, creating a shrew who closely resembles the stereotype of the angry, man-hating "femi-nazi," the cartoon icon of 1980s' antifeminist backlash. Though both Richard Burt and Michael Friedman find a sympathetic view of Riot Grrrl in the film (Burt 2002, Friedman 2004), its conflation of the man-hating second-wave feminist with the Riot Grrrl draws on the deep-seated cultural anxiety generated by feminism that contributed to the 1980s' backlash and later re-worked Riot Grrrl into its more mainstream acceptability as Girl Power.

The femi-nazi stereotype and the anxiety it engenders combine to sanction the film's portrayal of Kat's taming. Whereas Julia Stiles suggests that "Kat is definitely a positive role model for women ... She's opinionated and isn't afraid to express her thoughts. She's assertive, intelligent, very independent and strong-willed. The story says that it's okay for a woman to be like that" (qtd. Press Kit 1999: 8), both the film and its source play assert otherwise. Until Kate conforms her opinion to Petruchio's, she is denied food and sleep, and put in actual, physical danger. Whenever Kat expresses her opinion in class she gets sent to the office, even when she agrees with the teacher. The film further denies the acceptability of Kat's Riot Grrrl opinions by foregrounding her threat to the film's boys, making her frightening effect on masculinity central to her characterization as a riot grrrl/femi-nazi:

MS. PERKY: ... So I hear you were terrorizing Mr Morgan's class, again.
KAT: Expressing my opinion is not a terrorist action.
MS. PERKY: The way you expressed your opinion to Bobby Ridgeway? By the way, his
             testicle retrieval operation went quite well, in case you were interested.
KAT: I still maintain that he kicked himself in the balls.

(*10 Things*)

In this visit to the guidance counselor, Ms. Perky, the film offers its clearest articulation of riot grrrl Kat's threat to masculinity. The abrupt shift from discussing Kat's behavior in her English class to Ms. Perky's update about Bobby Ridgeway's surgery frames Kat's intellectual independence as an act approaching castration. Though we learn much later in the film that she kicked him because "he tried to grope [her] in the lunch line" (*10 Things*), the narrative distance between Bobby's injury and our knowledge of its cause invites us to equate feminism with a kind of mindless anti-male violence. Any momentary concerns that Kat's sexual orientation – made questionable by her lack of interest in dating – may also fuel her violence against boys are soon put to rest when her sister admits to having found a picture of Jared Leto in Kat's room, banishing the possibility that she was "harboring same-sex tendencies" (*10 Things*).

Kat's subsequent taming occurs primarily as an induction into the rites of hetero-sexual chick solidarity. She agrees to take her sister to a big party, goes to the Prom for Bianca's sake, and gets a boyfriend for her trouble. Despite Patrick's patronizing reference to Kat's favorite bands as "chicks who can't play their instruments" (*10 Things*), Junger paints her ostensible tamer with a sympathetic brush. In fact, Patrick seems to be the only character not trying to get Kat to conform to expected patterns of behavior, telling her "I say, do what you want to do" (*10 Things*). Moreover, not only does he take care of her when she gets drunk, but he also shows that he respects her by refusing to kiss her while she is drunk. He manages to get her favorite band to perform at the Prom, and even serenades her at soccer practice as a way to offset her humiliation. Although Patrick is an outsider like Kat, he is also cute, clearly a very desirable boyfriend, and a suitable reward for Kat's developing chick solidarity with Bianca, despite the fact that he has been paid, as Kat learns at the Prom, to date her. The sweetness of their relationship, like that with her sister, masks the film's ideological work of turning Kat from Riot Grrrl to Girl Power and making her perform according to the standards of proper girl-dom.

Of course, Shakespeare, as "ultimate authority on romantic love" (Burt 2002: 215), plays a significant role in Kat's taming. As Richard Burt observes, "the film fore-grounds Shakespeare's status as cultural authority" (2002: 215) most powerfully in Kat's easy acceptance of this authority. For not only does she not challenge her teacher's assignment to adapt Sonnet 141, but she also uses the assignment, drawing on Shakespeare – and the authority the film grants him concerning heterosexual love – to tell a boy that she likes him:

> I hate the way you talk to me and the way you cut your hair
> I hate the way you drive my car, I hate it when you stare.
> I hate your big dumb combat boots and the way you read my mind.
> I hate you so much it makes me sick; it even makes me rhyme.
> I hate the way you're always right, I hate it when you lie
> I hate it when you make me laugh, even worse when you make me cry
> I hate it when you're not around and the fact that you didn't call
> But mostly I hate the way I don't hate you, not even close
> Not even a little bit, not even at all.

> (*10 Things*)

Angrily reiterating "I hate," Kat's poem appears to be a Riot Grrrl anthem – even some of the lines fit into Riot Grrrl objections to women's treatment as objects: "the way you talk to me," "the way you stare." But her costume and performance belie this characterization. Instead of her usual cargo pants and t-shirt, Kat wears a skirt and a feminine blouse over a camisole, her hair pulled softly back into a loose braid, tendrils curling around her face, making her the picture of girlish femininity. Her quiet delivery of the poem also distances her from the usual fierceness associated with Riot Grrrl performance. As Barbara Hodgdon points out: "Stiles's extraordinary stillness, her ability to register feeling with a subtle look or gesture, astonishes both the class and Patrick" (2003b: 262). The scene creates a cinematographic intimacy between Kat and Patrick by cutting from medium shots of Kat reading her poem to reaction shots of Patrick as she finishes the poem, underlining the audience's understanding that she wrote this poem specifically for and about him. Her words may say Riot Grrrl, but the performance is all Girl Power.

The film closes with a final picture of this happy couple kissing next to Kat's car where she discovers the gift – a Fender Stratocaster – Patrick bought with the money Joey paid him to date her. Though, as several scholars have suggested, the guitar Patrick gives her gestures towards her potential to remain a Riot Grrrl by starting her own band (Burt 2002, Hodgdon 2003b, Friedman 2004), the film's happy ending coupled with 1980s' music threaded throughout the soundtrack suggests another possibility; Kat could start the kind of perky, chick-music girl band popular in the 1980s like the Bangles or the GoGos. For Kat has nothing left to make her angry: she gets to go to Sarah Lawrence, she and her sister are no longer at odds, she has a boyfriend, and a great guitar to boot. What more, the film seems to suggest, could a girl want?

But underneath this sweet ending, the soundtrack restates Kat's poem in blatantly Girl Power terms while the camera work finishes the job of integrating Kat (and Patrick) into the Girl Power world of teen romances where everyone has an appropriate mate. As the two stand kissing by her car, the camera pulls upward and they vanish into the crowd of Padua High students while, on the soundtrack, Letters to Cleo begins their cover version of Cheap Trick's "I Want You to Want Me." The female voice singing "I want you to want me / I need you to need me / I'd love you to love me / I'm begging you to beg me," erases any lingering traces of the Riot Grrrl politics squashed by the film's narrative. The music of the finale also bookends the film's opening tune, Bare Naked Ladies's "One Week." The film is framed by two parodies of Riot Grrrl bands, one an all-male group with a riot grrrl-worthy band name, the other a group fronted by a girl but backed by *boys* who *can* play their instruments. Just as Girl Power and fashion features proclaiming "Girls Kick Butt!" merely gesture toward a politics of equality for girls, these faux Riot Grrrl bands – indie in ethos but mainstream in commercial success – merely gesture towards a transgressive narrative space. The soundtrack maps that potentially transgressive space as safely patriarchal, a space, like that of *Shrew*, that firmly ostracizes a truly resistant, Riot Grrrl feminism, while letting us know how acceptable girls ought to speak – I want you to want me, I need you to need me.

In some respects, Stiles herself continues to articulate the film's compromised representation of feminism. Several years after playing Kat Stratford, Julia Stiles's public persona continues to be defined against that role. Despite assertions that her

"American-sweetheart status was sealed with *10 Things About You*" (Bardin 2002: 140), Stiles expresses concern over the film's lingering impact on her image: "Well, maybe it's just paranoia, but I always think, instead of being perceived as the girl next door, I'm more perceived as, like, the femi-nazi, man-hating lesbian. I mean, [guys] say, 'You were such a bitch in *10 Things I Hate About You*' – I thought I was just a strong, opinionated girl"(quoted in Bardin 2002: 140). Feminism is a frequent topic in her interviews, and the actress, as a responsible Girl Power icon who seems to give a damn about her reputation, repeatedly defines her feminism against the image of the man-hating femi-nazi. For example, speaking in a *Glamour* interview about presenting Catharine MacKinnon's *Toward a Feminist Theory of the State* to her philosophy class, Stiles explains: "I was careful not to alienate the men and to make them understand that a lot of feminists *love* men" (Kourlas 2003: 92, 155). Though characterized as "someone who is not afraid to express herself" (Holley 2001: 26), Stiles – at least occasionally – carefully regulates her self-expression. As Shakespeare's (and Hollywood's) tamed teenage shrew, Julia Stiles and her Girl Power iconicity sell the same brand of feminism (and femininity) as *10 Things*, a feminism and femininity focused, like so much of popular culture, on boys, leaving little room for any real female empowerment.

The Good Girl: Shakespeare's White Lady

Although *10 Things* established Stiles as a Girl Power icon, its narrative also contains another strand that contributes significantly to Stiles's public image, an image refined in her next two Shakespearean roles, Ophelia and Desi (Desdemona). As Richard Burt points out, "*10 Things*'s feminism, such as it is, comes at the price of harnessing it to a conservative idealization of the good girl" (2002: 214). The film works to retain Kat as a "good" (that is, not sexually active) girl, firmly assigning her bad reputation to her "feminist" behavior. Rather than condemning Kat for sleeping with Joey in the ninth grade (a surprising fact Kat confides in Bianca), the film applauds Kat's choice to say no after realizing she was not ready to be sexually active by informing the audience of this choice well after her taming has begun. By this point in the narrative we see a kinder, gentler Kat, encouraging us to sympathize with rather than criticize her actions and subsequent choices. The rest of the narrative also celebrates the good girl as virginal. Bianca chooses nice guy Cameron and punches Joey during the Prom when she learns about his original intent to "nail" her. Instead of judging Bianca harshly for her Kat-like behavior, the rest of the teens merely snicker at Joey, and even her father, Walter, admits to being impressed by Bianca's actions. Put simply, in *10 Things* good girls, much to their fathers' relief, wait to have sex. And Julia Stiles is a good, white, girl.

In fact, *10 Things I Hate About You* rides the cultural current which has seen the return of the Good Girl to prominence in American culture. Tracing the mainstream success of Good Girls such as Katie Couric, Helen Hunt, and Alicia Silverstone,

Sandra Tsing Loh asserts: "Good Girls are back in. Demure behavior is suddenly clever, fashionable, even attractive" (2000: 358). According to Loh, the Good Girl's current incarnation involves several characteristics:"She is (a) spunky; (b) virginal; (c) busy with purposeful activity. But not obsessively so. Her hormones are in balance. Brave chin up, she works within society's rules, finds much to celebrate in her immediate surroundings, makes the best of her lot. Good Girls don't challenge the status quo" (2000: 358–9). Not only does Loh's list of exemplary Good Girls suggest that Good Girls are, by and large, white women, her definition also matches the qualities inherent in the social construction of whiteness that Richard Dyer details in *White*. For though the Virgin Mary – Good Girl *par excellence* – is the model for white women (Dyer 1997: 29), whiteness does not hinge solely on the physical aspect of sexual purity. Achievements and behavior also aid in its construction: "It is not spirituality or soul that is held to distinguish whites, but what we might call 'spirit': get up and go, aspiration, awareness of the highest reaches of intellectual comprehension and aesthetic refinement" (Dyer 1997: 23).

Julia Stiles's Good Girl image – and the way her whiteness works as part of that image – depends in many ways on this intersection between the Good Girl and the social construction of whiteness. For unlike many of her famous contemporaries' publicly shifting romances, Stiles keeps her love life closely guarded. Her exploits do not land her on the cover of *US Weekly* or *People* alongside Britney or Jason or Janet. Though she discloses in interviews that she has a boyfriend, she does not reveal his identity. When her boyfriend is mentioned in articles about the actress, journalists stress both the nature and longevity of her current relationship: "She's in love (one year and counting)" (Rogers 2002: 266). Moreover, this discretion is keyed in the register of race: "A blush of crimson spreads across Stiles' china-white complexion as she relives the shock of learning that her love life had become public" (Givens 1999: 41).

Framing Stiles for consumption by the mass-market reading public, the press shapes her Good Girl image in ways that resonate with race and class. The press accounts of Stiles's achievements – both acting and academic – amply testify to her "spunk" or "get up and go." For example, articles frequently document the young actress's initiative in starting her career by writing a letter to a Manhattan-based theatre company offering to participate in their productions. They answered her letter; she got a small part in a production, became a member of the company, and subsequently developed a flourishing acting career. Now as "one of Hollywood's hottest young actresses" (Holley 2001: 26), Stiles earns millions of dollars for her film work, enabling her to move out of her Columbia dorm room and into a "fancy uptown pad" (Rimmer 2002: 12). In addition to chronicling the work ethic and initiative that aided in her acting success, articles about the actress also highlight her other achievements by focusing on her work as a student at Columbia and a volunteer for Habitat for Humanity. Of course, her affinity for Shakespeare figures prominently in many of these articles and interviews, revealing her "awareness of the highest reaches of intellectual comprehension and aesthetic refinement" (Dyer 1997: 23) through her appreciation of the Bard. Despite her spunky and monstrous energy on the soccer field, Stiles's discretion, her prim privacy, and even the good sense with which she chooses films that carry the cultural capital of Shakespeare, help to categorize her in slightly different terms: as a lady. And as Richard Dyer reminds us: "to be a lady is to be as white as it gets" (1997: 57).

Stiles's "white as it gets" whiteness registers on two levels, demonstrating the uniquely white mobility between visibility and invisibility. On the one hand, whiteness, especially in American culture, brings with it the power of invisibility: "because we are seen as white, we characteristically see ourselves and believe ourselves seen as unmarked, unspecific, universal" (Dyer 1997: 45). With magazine covers proclaiming "Julia Stiles: As Real as it Gets" (*Marie Claire*, August 2002) and "Why Everyone Loves Julia Stiles" (*Glamour*, January 2003), Stiles, despite her celebrity status, still maintains an everygirl image. Co-stars call her "a brave, grounded, normal person" (Kerry Washington, quoted in Kourlas 2003: 93), while Stiles reports that in an effort to deflect potential misconceptions about her as " 'a glamorous, stuck-up Hollywood girl,'" she "went to class [at Columbia] in [her] pajamas just like everyone else" (Stiles 2003: 76). Stiles's everygirl whiteness is invisible, registering as normal and unmarked. *10 Things I Hate About You* naturalizes race in this way by assuming the conventions of the teen-movie genre, in which the white, upper-middle-class suburb provides the setting of average American life. Among *10 Things*'s mostly white, upper-middle-class teen characters, Kat stands out *only* because of her shrewish behavior. Once tamed, she becomes simply one of many students dancing at the Prom and swarming through Padua High's parking lot. As Stiles's first big role and first Shakespearean part, her turn as Kat Stratford establishes Stiles's universal Good Girl appeal in direct relation to Shakespeare's cultural authority: like Shakespeare, Good Girls are universal. Just as Shakespeare seems to transcend time and nationality, being "not of an age, but for all time" (Jonson 1986: 1228), Julia Stiles as everygirl seems to transcend the very real boundaries that materialize identities in American culture.

On the other hand, because "[v]isual culture demands that whites can be seen to be white" (Dyer 1997: 44), Julia Stiles's whiteness has very specific dimensions. On the cover of *Elle Magazine*'s August 2002 issue, for instance, Stiles, clad in a ruffled black blouse, looks up at the reader, her blonde hair blending into a white background composed, it seems, primarily of light, the top of her head and the side of her face glowing in the brightness. Her alabaster skin, with just the hint of pink on her cheeks and lips, is luminescent and perfectly smooth. Inside the magazine, photographs continue this pattern of lighting as they follow the actress strolling through Venice. In one photo, as Stiles walks next to a canal, the sunlight reflecting off the water bathes her in a glow that seems to come from within, recalling Dyer's sense that "Idealised white women are bathed in and permeated by light. It streams through them and falls on to them from above. In short, they glow" (1997: 122). In the press, Stiles's staging provides a strikingly clear instance of the way hegemonic visual discourses (advertising, fashion, teen-magazines) naturalize whiteness: like light itself, whiteness is what makes everything else *visible*.

In Michael Almereyda's *Hamlet* lighting design and Stiles's white-as-it-gets white-ness combine to stage Ophelia as an ideally white Good Girl. In Shakespeare's *Hamlet* Ophelia is the linchpin of the play's discursive concern with chastity. Like *10 Things*'s Walter Stratford, Polonius and Laertes see only danger to a maid's chastity in Ophelia's suitor. Both her brother and father warn her away from Hamlet, Polonius claiming that what Ophelia sees as sincere declarations of Hamlet's love are really "springes to catch woodcocks" (1.3.115). Hamlet also (momentarily) obsesses about Ophelia's sexuality. When Ophelia returns Hamlet's love tokens, Hamlet turns on her, asking if she is "honest" and "fair" and telling her "Get thee to a nunnery" (3.1.105, 107, 122). After her death Laertes insists upon her purity, exclaiming to the priest who refuses her further funeral rites:

> Lay her i'th'earth
> And from her fair and unpolluted flesh
> May violets spring. I tell thee, churlish priest,
> A ministr'ing angel shall my sister be
> When thou liest howling.
>
> (5.1.221–5)

The play raises these concerns but never quite clarifies the extent of Hamlet's involvement with or commitment to Ophelia: this ambiguity is explored, for in-stance, in the interpolated sex scenes that Kenneth Branagh includes in his *Hamlet* film.

Like Branagh, Almereyda lends definition to Hamlet's relationship with Ophelia, and frames this relationship in sexual terms. Yet while Branagh stages a sex scene between Hamlet and Ophelia (played by voluptuously nude Kate Winslet), Almer-eyda shows us something else: Hamlet's digital camera records a presumably post-coital Ophelia, but Hamlet himself is behind the camera – in her bedroom but not in her bed. To put it simply, while Branagh's film frames an undeniably sexually-active Ophelia, Almereyda's film tempers Ophelia's sexuality, maintaining a physical dis-tance between the two and staging Ophelia as an arty nude rather than a woman caught in the act. For in Almereyda's film, Ophelia appears on Hamlet's computer, as he reviews his recordings – these are retrospective scenes, the digital echo of sexuality, caught from the perspective of the obsessively-visual Prince. As in the photos of Stiles in Venice, light plays an essential part in defining Ophelia's purity. As Hamlet ponders his mother's frailty in his "too, too solid flesh" speech (1.2.129–59), he watches Ophelia's face glow from his computer screen. He has shot Ophelia lying in bed reading against a background of white sheets. A close-up shot of her face reveals it to be barely discernible against the whiteness of the background with white bleeding into white as her blonde hair blends into the pillow. He freezes the frame on this whitest of white feminine beauty glowing from his computer screen as he finishes his speech. Against this discourse on female sexual frailty, Almereyda's Hamlet frames a portrait of ideal womanhood by setting and lighting Stiles in (and as) white.

In fact, in every scene in which Ophelia's sexuality is discussed, the lighting functions in the same way, bathing Stiles in light and creating the illusion of an inner illumination. Even when not seen through Hamlet's pixellated imagery, Ophelia appears to glow. When Laertes (Liev Schreiber) and Ophelia part and Laertes warns Ophelia to stay away from Hamlet, light from the windows of the Polonius family's apartment shines on her face, and seems almost to radiate from her; the light frames an implicit negative to Laertes's suspicions about Ophelia's sexuality. Yet while Almereyda's use of light primarily assures us of Ophelia's sexual purity, his staging and lighting of Ophelia's death introduce another significant element of Ophelia's radiant whiteness. At the scene's beginning, the camera looks down into the fountain pool where Ophelia frequently waits to meet Hamlet, showing her body floating in the water. Though spotlights cast some light toward her body, she remains mostly in shadow. After the guard removes her from the fountain, however, a shot of the pool features light rippling through the water before the scene fades to black. If, as Richard Dyer suggests, "To be seen as white is to have one's corporeality registered, yet true whiteness resides in the non-corporeal" (1997: 45), then the light dancing among Hamlet's love tokens on the water of the pool associated with Ophelia registers Ophelia's whiteness as true, left behind when her corpse is removed from the fountain. Combined with Julia Stiles's other radiant appearances in popular culture, her performance as Almereyda's Ophelia – her only Shakespearean role in which she speaks Shakespeare's text – underlines her ideally white image by linking it directly to Shakespeare through his words.

More than any other film in Stiles's Shakespearean *œuvre*, *O*, Tim Blake Nelson's high school version of *Othello*, illustrates how her status as a Good Girl, dependent upon her classed and gendered whiteness, allows her to be at once invisibly universal and visibly ideal. On the one hand, like *10 Things I Hate About You*, as a teen film *O* participates in the mostly-white-cast genre convention which makes Stiles's upper-middle-class whiteness merely the "natural" or "normal" state of being. Only one of many white girls in the film's private Palmetto Grove High School, Stiles's Desi (Desdemona) often blends into the crowds packed into the stadium cheering for high school basketball star Odin James (Mekhi Phifer). In the audience's first view of her, for instance, the camera pans across the students seated in the gym to watch Odin receive a Most Valuable Player award; here Desi blends into the crowd until a close-up shot on her singles her out.

The film, which closely follows *Othello*'s narrative, also draws on and contributes to the Stiles's Good Girl whiteness. While Almereyda keys Ophelia's whiteness as a register of sexual purity, Nelson – appropriately enough for *Othello* – frames Desi's whiteness as an index of racial as well as sexual purity. Like all narratives of miscegenation, Stiles and Phifer stage a familiar cultural anxiety:

> Inter-racial heterosexuality threatens the power of whiteness because it breaks the legitimation of whiteness with reference to the white body. For all the appeal to spirit, still, if white bodies are no longer indubitably white bodies, if they can no longer

guarantee their own reproduction as white, then the "natural" basis of their dominion is no longer credible. (Dyer 1997: 25)

For while the film seems to present a critique of the notion of miscegenation itself, in the film's use of light and shadow it maintains the boundaries between Desi's whiteness and Odin's blackness in ways that reinforce the notion that racial purity, particularly the purity of whiteness, must be maintained. For instance, when, during a party celebrating a basketball victory, Odin confides in Desi that he feels completely safe with her and suggests that the two might one day marry, the light falling on Desi illuminates her completely, leaving Odin's features barely discernible in shadow.

In *O* black and white skin also work to build a clear separation between black and white people. Nelson translates the black/white imagery running through *Othello*, especially in such lines as Iago's "old black ram tupping [Brabantio's] white ewe" (1.1.88–9), into human bodies, frequently contrasting Phifer's dark skin with Stiles's blonde whiteness. In our first extended view of the couple together, black and white skin set each other in relief as the two cuddle in Desi's bed. As Desi's white hand caresses Odin's black back, the two skin colors are seen in sharp contrast – each further defining the other. In a later scene these images are repeated as a "highly erotic sequence of near-abstract extreme close-ups of body parts" (Hodgdon 2003a: 103) as the couple go from light caressing to sexual intimacy. These close-ups locate race firmly in the body – framing it as essential and inseparable from the body through this imagery of bodies cut into separate parts – suggesting that if bodies cannot live in fragments, they also cannot live unraced. This imagery works against the film's disembodied, yet definitely racialized soundtrack juxtaposing "white" and "black" music. If, as Barbara Hodgdon suggests, "Here, too, race is sound, which operates in several ways, juxtaposing high to mass culture entertainment and white noise to black – even conflating the two" (2003a: 101), the sharp contrast between Phifer's and Stiles's bodies erases this conflation, removing the possibility of inter-racial "tainting" suggested in the film, for example, by their relationship and the other white students' interest in rap music and basketball.

Race is a crucial concern of *Othello*, but in *O* it seems to be Desi's sexual relationship with Odin – which degenerates from sex to rape during a night the two spend together off campus – that literalizes Richard Dyer's suggestion that "[d]ark desires are part of the story of whiteness, but as what the whiteness of whiteness has to struggle against" (1997: 28). At the scene's beginning, Desi tells Odin "I want you to have me however you want; don't hold back" (*O*), evoking the relationship between whiteness and dark desires posited by Dyer. As Hodgdon observes: "Desi's 'I want you to have me however you want' not only suggests that sexuality – and its transgressive potential – are wedded to blackness but figures her desire to be 'made black' by consuming O's body language" (2003a: 102). As Desi struggles against Odin's increasingly violent thrusts, their love-making performs in raw detail white America's racist fears of black masculine sexuality. The camera's focus on their faces also adds to this specter. Not only does Odin grimace, baring his teeth, but Desi also blushes a deep red as she struggles. At the scene's end the camera's focus on her pink face before shifting quickly to shots of white doves reaffirms the innocence of white womanhood by relying on the trope of the virginal blush – the same blush reportedly staining Stiles's complexion after details of her private life were made public. By staging the only actual sex scene between the two as a rape, the film removes the taint of sexual desire from Desi, externalizing Desi's darker desires by making them literal in Odin's black body. The image of the rape, with its focus on Desi's blushing face and Odin's black body, is echoed when Odin strangles Desi. Not only do his black hands stand out against her white skin, but also despite Odin's insistence that "she was a 'ho,'" the final shot of her, bathed in warm light, assures the audience otherwise, instead leaving us with a vision of innocent – and pure – white womanhood.

As Shakespeare's white lady, Stiles brings her well-established Good Girl sensibility to this role, demonstrating an acute sense of how this scene, and the dark desires it articulates, could affect an audience's sympathy for Desi:

> it matters so much if a girl is pure or slutty. That was something I was really worried about in relation to Desi. I didn't want the audience to think she was slutty. I felt so uncomfortable about that line where she tells Odin: I'll do anything for you. I kept saying to the director that's going to sound slutty. Couldn't I say: I love you? (Stiles, in O'Sullivan 2002: 11)

Echoing Desdemona's wifely chastity in her fidelity to Othello, Stiles astutely redefines the Virgin/Whore binary in Good Girl terms by framing Desi's purity in relation to her love for Odin rather than to her virginity. In her concern over the audience's perception of Desi, Stiles also voices her awareness of the fine line drawn between sexy and slutty when talking about how a young woman's sexuality registers in American culture. That awareness – and its important contribution to her Good Girl image – are exemplified by her recent appearance as the cover-girl for *TeenVogue*'s March 2004 issue, which features an editor's letter ushering in a return to the Good Girl in teen fashion:

> Hey, lady! Are you sick of watching nearly naked girls grinding next to fully dressed guys on MTV? Of movie stars and singers dressed as if they moonlight as strippers? ... Clearly it's high time for a cover-up and designers came out in complete support of a ladylike, feminine new way to dress for spring: full skirts, twinsets, trench coats, pearls and neckscarves, vintage-inspired jackets, pretty dresses, and tons of vibrant color and pattern ... The result? A look that oozes attitude – with not a thong in sight. (Astley 2004: 54)

Just like the feminism of Girl Power, the latest fashion of the Good Girl takes a nostalgic look back, invoking the values of a pre-1960s' America. With her address to ladies, *TeenVogue* editor Amy Astley also participates in another backward-looking trend of teen representations. For though, as historians Neil Howe and William

Strauss suggest, teens are currently "America's most racially and ethnically diverse, and least-Caucasian generation" (2000: 15), the teen face offered by popular culture is overwhelmingly white.

Shakespeare's contribution to Stiles's career and image also involves a nostalgic look back, creating an icon of teenage girlhood linked to Shakespeare's patriarchal world and supported by his cultural weight. Stiles's connection to Shakespeare, then, lends her iconicity a durability not generally associated with the ephemeral world of popular culture. As a result, unlike the purely pop culture depictions of American teen girlhood in movies, magazines, music, and television programs, Shakespeare Stiles Style merges the authority of high culture with the appeal of the popular to commodify a monolithic vision of teen girl culture that celebrates – in fact idolizes – upper-middle-class white girls who "dart not scornful glances from [their] eyes / To wound [their] lord[s], [their] king[s], [their] governor[s]" (*Shrew* 5.2.142–3) – in other words, little ladies don't kick butt.

References and Further Reading

Angel_aims_135 (2001). "Awsome [*sic*] Movie, Worth the Wait." *Internet Movie Database User Comments*. Available at: us.imdb.com/title/tt0184791/usercomments-27.

Astley, Amy (2004). Letter from the editor. *Teen-Vogue* March: 54.

Bardin, Brantley (2002). "Elements of Stiles." *Elle Magazine*. August: 136–45.

Baumgardner, Jennifer & Richards, Amy (2000). *Manifesta: Young Women, Feminism, and the Future*. New York: Farrar, Straus and Giroux.

Burt, Richard (2002). "Te(e)n Things I Hate about Girlene Shakesploitation Flicks in the Late 1990s, or Not-So-Fast-Times at Shakespeare High." In Courtney Lehmann & Lisa S. Starks (eds.) *Spectacular Shakespeare: Critical Theory and Popular Cinema*. Madison, NJ: Fairleigh Dickinson University Press, pp. 205–32.

Carr, Jay (2001). Review of *O. Boston Globe* August 31: D1.

Chideya, Faria (1992). "Revolution, Girl Style." *Time* November 23: 84–6.

Dyer, Richard (1997). *White*. London: Routledge.

Friedman, Michael (2004). "The Feminist as Shrew in *10 Things I Hate about You*." *Shakespeare Bulletin* 22, 2: 45–65.

Gershman, Rick (1999). "Teen Reworking of Shakespeare Classic Makes the Grade." *St Petersburg Times* March 31: 2B.

Givens, Ron (1999). "Things to Like about Julia: Actress Stiles is a Far Cry from her Shrewish 'Hate' character." *Daily News* April 12: 41.

Gottlieb, Joanne, & Wald, Gayle (1994). "Smells like Teen Spirit: Riot Grrrls, Revolution, and Women in Independent Rock." In Andrew Ross & Tricia Rose (eds.) *Microphone Fiends: Youth Music and Youth Culture*. New York: Routledge, pp. 250–74.

Hodgdon, Barbara (2003a). "Race-ing *Othello*, Re-Engendering White-Out, II." In Lynda Boose & Richard Burt (eds.) *Shakespeare the Movie II: Popularizing the Plays on Film, TV, Video, and DVD*. New York: Routledge, pp. 89–104.

Hodgdon, Barbara (2003b). "Wooing or Winning (or Not): Film/Shakespeare/Comedy and the Syntax of Genre." In Richard Dutton & Jean E. Howard (eds.) *A Companion to Shakespeare's Works*, vol. III: *The Comedies*. Oxford: Blackwell, pp. 243–65.

Holley, Brandon (2001). "Welcome to Ellegirl." *Ellegirl* Fall: 26.

Howe, Neil & Strauss, William (2000). *Millennials Rising*. New York: Vintage Books.

Jonson, Ben (1986). "To the Memory of my Beloved, the Author, Mr. William Shakespeare, and What He Hath Left Us." In M. H. Abrams (ed.) *The Norton Anthology of English Literature*, vol. 1. New York: W. W. Norton and Company, pp. 1227–8.

Kourlas, Gia (2003). "Julia Speaks her Mind." *Glamour Magazine* January: 92–3, 155.

Loh, Sandra Tsing (2000). "The Return of Doris Day." In Sonia Maasik & Jack Solomon (eds.) *Signs of Life in the USA: Readings on Popular Culture for Writers*. Boston: Bedford/St Martins, pp. 357–65.

O'Sullivan, Charlotte (2002). "Film: That Sound's Slutty." *The Independent*, September 13: 10–11.

Rimmer, Louise (2002). "Shakespeare Sister." *Scotland on Sunday*, September 15: 12.

Riot Grrrl NYC (2003). "Rgnyc Grrrl-ifesto." Available at: rgny.8m.com/about.html.

Rogers, Ray (2002). "Stiles and Substance." *Seventeen* September: 266–71.

Shakespeare, William (1997a). *The Tragedy of Hamlet, Prince of Denmark*. In Stephen Greenblatt et al. (eds.) *The Norton Shakespeare*. New York: W. W. Norton and Company, pp. 1668–759.

Shakespeare, William (1997b). *The Tragedy of Othello, the Moor of Venice*. In Stephen Greenblatt et al. (eds.) *The Norton Shakespeare*. New York: W. W. Norton and Company, pp. 2100–74.

Stiles, Julia (2003). "No One Can Shut Me Up." *YM* February: 74–7.

10 Things I Hate about You (2000). Press book. New York: Touchstone Pictures.

Van Cook, Marguerite (2001). "Girls Kick Butt." *Ellegirl* Fall: 106–11.

Waterman, Lauren (2004). "Crown Julia." *Teen Vogue* March: 156–9, 194.

Wolcott, James (2003). "Teen Engines: Riding with Kid Culture." *Vanity Fair* July: 96–109, 156–7.

FILMOGRAPHY

Hamlet (2000). Directed by Michael Almereyda. Double A Film. Videocassette.

O (2001). Directed by Tim Blake Nelson. Lion's Gate Films. DVD.

10 Things I Hate About You (1999). Directed by Gil Junger. Touchstone Pictures. DVD.

26

Shakespeare on Vacation

Susan Bennett

The question of audience for Shakespeare's plays has always been a compelling one for scholars, a consideration since, as Jean Howard suggests of the spectatorship for sixteenth-century public theatre, "the ideological consequences of playgoing might be quite different for different social groups" (1991: 70). This is a topic that continues to provoke a rich debate not only in the specifics of theatre spectatorship in Shakespeare's time, but also for any later historical moment up to and including the twenty-first century. It has become a cliché, after all, to describe Shakespeare as "our" most popular, oft-produced contemporary playwright. Every year very many theatre companies and the directors who work for them devise productions with interpretations that range from the dutiful rendition of Shakespeare's text to adaptations where the original play is little more than a token reference for the contemporary show. Nor is Shakespeare's currency restricted to the stage, with frequent film versions and other related spin-offs (for example, the extraordinary worldwide interest in the Sanders portrait, putatively of the playwright). This is the industry that now is Shakespeare and it is, patently, a business based on one certain fact: there is a ready, enthusiastic market for the product. My interest here is less in Shakespeare's place in the arts and culture economy broadly conceived, but more specifically in the relationship between England's most distinguished playwright and the ever increasingly pervasive and prosperous world tourism industry. What this relationship provokes, then, is a new configuration of audience composed not necessarily or perhaps even primarily of a group we would call theatregoers, certainly not an elite of Shakespeare mavens, but, instead, tourists.

The purchase of a ticket to a Shakespearean production is for the tourist but one transaction in a series that gives vitality and economic significance to the tourism industry and which offers the peripatetic consumer a return on that investment – as Briavel Holcomb notes of urban tourism, "visitors are disproportionately drawn by cultural, historical, architectural, and ethnic attractions in the creation of a city image, projecting an aura of high quality, civility, creativity, and sophistication and consequently conferring status on its visitors" (1999: 53–4). What approaches to this phenomenon should we take in thinking through the production and reception of Shakespeare's plays for contemporary audiences? How have the marketers of cultural product harnessed Shakespearean performance to tourism economies? Are the questions for a performance of a Shakespeare play designed specifically or significantly for a travel-in tourist audience the same ones as we would ask for the production and reception of any other contemporary performance, of any other contemporary performance of Shakespeare? It seems to me that where tourism overrides, or has the potential to override, a practice of theatregoing as the fundamental context for the performance event, then the conditions for and of reception are necessarily circumscribed somewhat differently. Yet, the discipline of theatre studies has generally not shown much interest in the tourist audiences that do much to sustain live theatre in major urban centers as well as in many other locations. If we are to understand the "who" and "why" of Shakespeare's audiences in the present-day marketplace, we must surely begin to rehearse these and other questions derived from a tourism economy.

More familiar to us, I suspect, is the anti-tourism attitude that tends to prevail in any discussion of the vast tourist audience for contemporary productions of Shakespeare's plays. That these audiences are not appropriately appreciative (positively or negatively) and, even more frequently, that they are easily pleased consumers, ignorant of what constitutes "good" or "bad" Shakespeare is, more or less, a commonplace. To take one example, in an otherwise interesting and engaging account of modern Shakespearean production, H. R. Coursen ends the Introduction to his recent book with this statement: "I look at the 1994 season in Great Britain and issue another indictment of what the big theaters are doing these days. In that the tourists seem to be pleased, no one is listening" (1996: xiv). How can we pursue a more nuanced understanding of practices and expectations brought to bear for the tourist spectator who selects a Shakespearean production as one marker or motivation in an overall tourist experience, and how would a better recognition of the tourist market impact our own critical practices as scholars interested in performance and/or the plays of William Shakespeare? There is, of course, already some important scholarship in this specific area and Dennis Kennedy's "Shakespeare and Cultural Tourism" provides a rich interrogation of the Globe Theatre in London and its particular interpellation of the tourist. Kennedy notes that "[t]heater historians and theorists have not paid much attention to this side of the spectator's condition" – that of cultural tourist (1998: 181) – and he issues a timely warning to the management of the Globe not to have the theatre become little more than a Disney theme park. Bill Worthen, too, draws a comparison with the theme park, suggesting that the Globe is "informed by the audience's familiarity with cognate performance forms: living-history sites, battlefield reenactments, theme parks, and themed performances in general" (2003: 84). Some half a dozen years after the publication of Kennedy's article, it is easy perhaps to argue that the Globe Theatre has fallen into many, if not all, of the traps Kennedy predicted, but rather than see this as a terrible thing, or even an inevitable process, I am more interested in thinking about the effect of tourist audiences on how we (performance scholars, theatre historians, cultural theorists among others) think about and record such theatregoing.

To begin to address these questions, I will look at two separate performance contexts where Shakespearean production is at the heart of the tourism experience. In the first of these performance contexts, the tourist audience is drawn to the Shakespearean performance by some semblance of authenticity or, at least, proximity to apparent historical fact. The tourist comes to performance in an explicit recognition of a Shakespearean heritage and history. The obvious examples here are those productions at the Globe Theatre in London as well as the annual production season of the Royal Shakespeare Company at Stratford-upon-Avon. In the second case, a Shakespeare festival may be the inspiration for tourists visiting a particular place or region. The tourist comes, here, to the Shakespearean performance in an explicit context of recreational travel. Well-known examples in this instance include the Stratford Festival in Ontario, Canada, and the Oregon Shakespeare Festival in Ashland, Oregon. In all these subject examples, the audience will be substantially comprised of people who have already committed to travel as a precondition to their attendance at the theatre, whether their actual ticket purchase was planned or impromptu. This suggests that theatre producers well understand Shakespeare's role in the creation of that (tourist) audience and that tourism economies recognize how Shakespeare mobilizes a variety of theatrical and other products for the consumer. How do we, then, account for the critical and cultural contexts in which this Shakespeare/audience relationship becomes an act of tourism?

As Lucy Lippard so trenchantly puts it, "[h]istory is the motherlode of tourism" (1999: 54), and it is not at all surprising that Stratford-upon-Avon has developed as such a successful destination for the cultural tourist since it provides the most exquisitely authentic context for William Shakespeare. What Stratford sells is the Shakespeare heritage with the Royal Shakespeare Company as its living history. In what is now a landmark article, Graham Holderness usefully described the role played by the Shakespeare Birthplace Trust in determining what buildings, places and artifacts are distinctively part of the official Shakespeare narrative and which are not; he suggests the Trust behaves as "the authentic clerisy of the Shakespeare religion" (1988: 5). However authoritative the Shakespeare Birthplace Trust imprimatur might appear to be, in 2000 new research revealed that the property long known as Mary Arden's House was, in fact, not the birthplace of Shakespeare's mother; instead, Mary Arden was found to have been born at Glebe Farm some 50 yards away. Now Glebe Farm is Mary Arden's House and the former Mary Arden's House is Palmer's Farm, a transformation whose impact was immediately felt since, as one report described it, "merchandise bearing images of the current Mary Arden's House ... will now have to be redesigned" (www.edition.cnn.com/2000/STYLE/arts/ 11/29/shakespeare.poet.ap/). Indeed, Barbara Hodgdon has elucidated the powerful place of the souvenir in the maintenance of "the narratives of identity and authorship that circulate in Stratford's commemorative spaces" (1998: 191), and commodity representation has an important role, of course, in apparently authenticating the tourist experience.

In any event, it is self-evident that the tourist is generally encouraged to see Stratford as thoroughly imbued by the Bard's heritage whether these buildings, places and artifacts are sanctioned as authentic or not – an experience that leads Holderness to conclude that the town has "an atmosphere of unscrupulous opportunism, commercial exploitation and gross imposture" (1988: 5). At the other end of the critical scale, and more reverently, Balz Engler argues that Stratford is better understood as a place of pilgrimage, that its connections to Shakespeare give it sacred status (1997: 355–6). Whatever the case, the motivation to be there in Stratford and the pleasure the tourist derives from the visit circulate around signs of Shakespeare, whether this is a production of one of his plays, a tour of credited authentic sites, the purchase of a Mary Arden House souvenir, or a visit to a restaurant or pub with a Shakespearean name (Will's Place and Othello's Bistro among them). From my own perspective, this is not at all a recognition of the tourist as a cultural dupe but instead the practice of a finely tuned market that understands the "unusually large role [of myth and fantasy] in the social construction of *all* travel and tourist sights" (Rojek 1997: 53, emphasis in original). As Chris Rojek insists: "It should not be assumed that either the factual or the fictional have priority in framing the sight. Rather, sight framing involves the interpenetration of factual and fictional elements to support tourist orientations. One should add that indexing operates on conscious and unconscious levels" (1997: 53).

This, it seems to me, has very real implications for how a tourist audience understands and enjoys, among other things, the experience of Shakespearean performance at Stratford. Unless, of course, the tourist lands at the Swan Theatre in 2004 where there is nary a Shakespeare play to be seen but rather a season of Spanish Golden Age theatre – and, provocatively, the promise of an "attempt to recreate the heady atmosphere of Spanish theatregoing for one day only by separating the audience by sex!" (promotional materials, punctuation in original).

Notwithstanding the Royal Shakespeare Company's newfound interest in a global-historical theatre-tourism, the town of Stratford understandably relies on the history and heritage derived from its dramatist icon. And this is, as Hodgdon has ably demonstrated, both a political and an economic resource for Stratford in particular and, more elaborately, for the country as a whole. Yet, as Kevin Meethan has suggested for heritage and authenticity in general, "the contingent and malleable nature of heritage also means that it is not one product, but many, and as such, is partly determined by the consumer at the point of consumption" (2001: 107). If heritage cannot afford to be singular, this is because its tourist audience is fully diverse: in its expectations, in its desire, in its pleasures, and thus, necessarily, in its social construction. It is precisely for this reason of difference within an overarching tourist category that the Shakespeare Birthplace Trust provides a range of heritage consumables for a market segmented by income as well as many other identifications.

For the discerning Shakespeare shopper, the Trust has a range of high-end products, embedded in other icons of an English cultural heritage. For example, there is a

Wedgwood Shakespeare bust, several limited edition Coalport figurines (Juliet, Titania, Ophelia – 2000 of each, certified and numbered; Ariel – only 1,000, certified and numbered), as well as a limited and authenticated edition Hamlet chalice made of English full lead crystal (only 200 made), produced to commemorate the four-hundredth anniversary of the play's publication. These items retail between £145 and £230 apiece. Hodgdon reminds us that although upscale items "offer tourists the opportunity to indulge their taste for British artistry, by far the largest volume of sales comes from tea towels featuring panoramic views of the Shakespeare properties: expressly commissioned by the Trust, four such designs are purchased in minimum lots of 240 dozen, testament to their popularity" (1998: 234). The £13.50 tea towel packs are among a variety of mass market souvenirs including an Anne Hathaway Sun Flower Sandwich Tray (£4.95) and a generic William Shakespeare bust – what Hodgdon would describe as a "down-market substitute" (1998: 234) for the Wedgwood traditional, but available at only £10 (a savings of some £135) and, according to the Trust's online shopping catalog, "suitable for home and office" (www.shakespeare. org.uk/homepage). The provision of online shopping by the Shakespeare Birthplace Trust signifies a willingness to serve a broad market that must surely include, among others, those who purchase on the internet what they wish they had thought to when in Stratford-upon-Avon and those who browse and/or buy as a vicarious and virtual Shakespeare vacation.

At the heart of the heritage/tourist interaction, however, is Stratford's most significant locus of consumption, the theatres of The Royal Shakespeare Company. Certainly, in the first instance, the theatres' function is no more than a substantial reminder of why Stratford is in the top tier of heritage/history tourism sites: the town's website opens with an animated art work depicting the Festival Theatre on the banks of the Avon against a background of vaguely Elizabethan music (www.stratford-upon-avon.co.uk). The availability of performances (matinees and evenings) allows for an extension of activity through most of the consumer's day – effective tourism economies must maximize the duration of spending potential. But, most significantly, the variety provided by the number of productions in any season, the changing repertory from one season to the next, and the predictability/surprise continuum that underpins any single RSC season – 2004 productions match the unexpected Spanish Golden Age emphasis with four of Shakespeare's tragedies: *Macbeth*, *Romeo and Juliet*, *King Lear*, and *Hamlet* – encourage tourists to visit more than once. It's the Shakespeare that keeps on giving to the tourist whose appetite for the authentic Bard is more than a passing one.

An appeal to authenticity underwrites performances of Shakespeare's plays at the Globe Theatre in London, too. This theatre, equally, makes a claim on Shakespeare's life and enjoys an even broader connection to heritage/history than the London city brand offers its tourism clients. It matters not that this is a replica theatre; what counts is the performance of authenticity available to the consumer. As Worthen puts it (and again in the context of the theme park experience):

Much as the entertainment at Disneyland and Disney World depends on a familiarity with "Disney" (you do not need to have seen the films, but you *do* have to know who Mickey and Donald and Bambi and Pocahontas are), performing at the Globe may depend on a similar acquaintance with "Shakespeare," not an intimate knowledge of his plays, theater, or society, but a sense that the bustling wooden O will generate a very different – more enjoyable, more involving, more historical, more authentic, more "Shakespearean" – experience than we usually have sitting in the dark through three hours of obsolescent versified drama. (2003: 99)

This makes the point wonderfully clear: the expectations of a Globe audience are rarely if ever the same as those for conventional theatre. Moreover, as with the Stratford-upon-Avon setting, the tourist may want to engage with Shakespeare in ways that go beyond the performance of the play or even, perhaps, without a performance at all. The locale of the Globe Theatre allows the claim to history (its proximity to the original building), and the full development of the site is determined to convince audiences of its validity. This requires not only the requisite gift shop, but also the provision of a permanent exhibition to allow tourists some expert insight into Shakespeare's theatre. As Diana Henderson states, "Here at ground zero of Shakespeare's professional career, simple tourism or reconstruction is not felt to be adequate. And so attempts are made to educate as well as amuse the visitor" (2002: 120). Not exactly an unwelcome strategy since, as David Brooks has noted, "[t]he code of utilitarian pleasure means we have to evaluate our vacation time by what we accomplished – what did we learn, what spiritual or emotional break-throughs were achieved, what new sensations were experienced?" (2000: 205).

In other words, the Globe Theatre has developed in response to patterns of tourism rather than patterns of theatregoing and this makes for quite a different performance-spectator contract. Of course it is tempting to point out the failures, the deceits, and the trivialities in the Globe's claim to its special place. But, nonetheless, it is the realization of the Globe Theatre project that accounts for an extraordinary regeneration of what had previously been a dilapidated neighborhood in central London, with zero (or perhaps a minus integer) in tourist appeal. Along with the new Tate Modern and a pedestrian bridge to the north bank of the Thames, the Globe Theatre has stimulated significant development both for tourists and for resident/worker populations: renovated and updated pubs, a range of restaurants and coffee houses, interior design shops, lofts in warehouse conversions, a new Holiday Inn, and other business activity. Ironically, it is the provision of the new that ensures a thriving tourism based on the old. As Peter Ackroyd optimistically puts it:

[T]he South Bank has been able triumphantly to reassert its past. The restored Bankside Power Station, with its upper storey resembling a box filled with light, is aligned with Cardinal's Wharf and the newly constructed Globe in a triune invocation of territorial spirit. This is surely a cause for wonder, when five centuries are embraced in a single and simple act of recognition. It is part of London's power. Where the past exists, the future may flourish. (2000: 697)

For tourists and, of course, for Shakespeare.

Without the anchor of heritage/history, however, performances of Shakespeare have flourished by accessing other experiences as equally attractive and/or impactful in tourist incentive. Both the Stratford Festival in Ontario and the Oregon Shakespeare Festival (OSF) in Ashland demonstrate this well. Here, Rojek's assertions have very real implications for how a tourist audience understands and enjoys the theatrical event in general and Shakespearean drama in particular: when the geographical context is Ashland rather than Stratford-upon-Avon, the balance between factual and fictional swings heavily to one side. Similarly, Stratford (Ontario) is pure fantasy in its place in the history of Shakespeare, even if it still manages to mobilize the practices and textures of its factual reference point of Stratford-upon-Avon (not simply its nomenclature but in details such as swans on the river) to allow for its own validity and, indeed, appeal. As well as its echoes of the "real" Shakespearean setting, Stratford has the advantage of location – a small and pleasant town within easy traveling distance of several major North American cities (Toronto and Detroit most obviously). Ric Knowles has noted a particular attention to the American market since "[t]hirty-four percent of the Festival's ticket revenue comes from direct sales to the United States" (1994: 212).

The Oregon Shakespeare Festival in Ashland is undeniably more remote both literally and figuratively. The town of Ashland is some 300 miles from the nearest major metropolitan center, but not too far beyond the reaches of Portland, San Francisco, Seattle, Vancouver, and even Los Angeles; the OSF has a history that owes more, in the end, to the American Chautauqua theatre than to the English stage. Notwithstanding a lack of obvious connection to England's Bard, in both Stratford (Ontario) and Ashland the success of Shakespeare as a tourist attraction has allowed for and relied upon other development (including in the realm of the performing arts – what Ashland has come to call "Off Bardway"!). The two towns have each, over time and with Shakespeare to thank, become what Lippard describes as a "sustainable destination area" (1999: 78).

That the theatre activity is necessarily located in this "destination area" framework is evidenced in the construction of each festival's website (www.stratford-festival.on.ca and www.orshakes.org). These websites provide not just information on the theatre season, but a wealth of other materials targeted at the visitor – accommodation, dining, shopping, and other ways to spend a few days in recognition that not all (or, even, most) visitors will commit to a full diet of theatre performances to keep themselves fully and appropriately occupied – and spending. While the average OSF visitor sees 3.5 productions (Berlin 2003: 531), it is entirely possible that some Ashland tourists limit their Shakespeare encounter to the free performances in the theatre courtyard and other venues, a theatre tour, or a visit to the OSF gift shop. These are all, in the end, activities that credit Shakespeare with value, and both the OSF and the Stratford Festival market these value-added contexts as well as those of their non-urban surroundings: the website for Stratford, Ontario, for instance, offers a section called "diversions" and that for the OSF "river trips, adventures & tours." In this regard, the Stratford website is extremely well developed, and the link to "Shopping" takes the user to a variety of sub-categories (antiques, books, fashions, for the kids, galleries, spas and treatments, and so on) where the OSF site relies on a selection of classified advertisements for various businesses in Ashland and environs. This kind of combination matches perfectly what Brooks has identified as a new "set of social regulations constructed to encourage pleasures that are physically, spiritually, and intellectually useful" (2000: 200). A day of river rafting followed by an evening of Shakespeare might be the epitome of such a value system. Of course, these festivals also encourage what Jennifer Craik calls "complementary commercialization" (1997: 122) and thus the tourist audience for a mainstream cultural product – Shakespeare – can impact the production of other local arts (off Bardway, certainly, but also in other domains such as visual arts and crafts galleries). It also allows for the development of restaurants, wine bars, and brew pubs that towns of the size of Stratford or Ashland could not support with only its permanent resident market.

It is, then, within this broad context for local and regional tourism (visit the theatre, visit the town, visit the area) that the festivals address their audiences. So this need to appeal as a tourism opportunity (rather than simply a theatre visit) permeates every level of their marketing and, for that matter, product. As Knowles has illustrated:

> The larger discursive context within which the 1993 season produced its meanings inhered in various brochures, press releases, and other written material; in the physical environments of the Festival itself, including audience amenities, gift shops, and ancillary spaces, as well as the performance venues; and of course in the individual productions of the season's repertoire. (1994: 213)

In short, the Stratford Festival put together a package intended to reward the tourist with exactly the kind of experience that the Festival believes that tourists will necessarily expect. It is patent that the horizon of expectations for such a constructed spectatorship involves significantly more (economic) activity than the mere act of theatregoing. Knowles continues:

> How do the productions *mean* for audience members who sit in plush seats that sport brass plaques acknowledging individual or corporate donors and who read programs full of upscale and globally "intercultural" (or multinational) advertisements for Parisian watches, Jamaican rums, Japanese electronics, Ralph Lauren clothing, and American luxury cars named after Spanish cities? How is meaning shaped by the ad that appeared in each program, inviting the theater's "patrons" to relocate to Stratford, where "the quality of life is unmatched in North America," particularly for those who may be "traveling by corporate jet" and are desirous of having " 'just-in-time' proximity to major Canadian and American markets"? In other words how does the discourse of the Festival construct its audiences? (1994: 214, emphasis in original)

Whether the subject is the Royal Shakespeare Company in Stratford-upon-Avon or the Stratford Festival in Ontario, it is important to recognize the interpellation of a particular construction of theatregoer in the imagination of the organization. As Knowles points out, the marketing of the Stratford Festival casts its ticket buyers as "well-to-do consumers" epitomized in "accompanying photographs of corporate sponsors as exclusively white, male, and middle-aged" (1994: 214–15); by contrast, but equally the product of imagination, the Audience Survey 2003 distributed by the RSC to its Stratford-upon-Avon audiences asks for data about age (eight categories ranging from Under 16 to 70+), annual income level (eight categories ranging from under £9,999 to £100,000+), and ethnic origin (white, Indian, Pakistani, Bangladeshi, African, Caribbean, Chinese, Mixed, Other), among others. But what relationship do these fantasies of audience have to the actual spectatorship each theatre attracts? To address what seems to me a significant difference in experience if not demographic, I want to focus on the emergence and development of the Oregon Shakespeare Festival since, of all my examples, it is the farthest removed from the all-important signifier Shakespeare. The OSF history is relevant here since this is a theatre practice that has always been dependent on audiences willing to travel and it has built up its season in recognition of the specificities of those tourists who make the journey to southern Oregon. It is in this case study, then, that this chapter's questions come into sharp relief.

The remarkable growth and sustained success of the OSF over the past 70 years have, quite simply, provided the *raison d'être* for regional tourism. When in the early 1930s, Angus Bowmer, a teacher from Southern Oregon Normal School (now Southern Oregon University), proposed to the city a festival of two Shakespeare plays as part of celebrations for the Fourth of July, he was inspired by a similarity between drawings of theatres in sixteenth-century London and the ruins of a Chautauqua theatre in Ashland itself. Townspeople in Ashland had first built their Chautauqua theatre in 1893, expanding it in 1905 to seat 1,500 (drawing its audiences, Ashland's earliest tourists, from across Northern California and Southern Oregon), and then replacing it with a new theatre building in 1917. After the theatre fell into disuse during the 1920s as the Chautauqua movement had declined, it was torn down in 1933 (although some of the exterior walls remained, the traces of local theatrical activity that inspired Bowmer and that were eventually incorporated into the OSF Elizabethan Stage). Bowmer's modest proposal – met with skepticism by the city that offered an advance not to exceed $400 and then added day-time boxing matches on the stage since they felt the plays would almost certainly lose money – became a stage reality in 1935 with productions of *Twelfth Night* and *The Merchant of Venice*. Box-office receipts from the play performances covered the costs of their production, but the boxing matches did not break even – a loss that the City of Ashland was required to cover.

Despite a fire that destroyed the first Elizabethan stage in 1940 and a subsequent closure of the festival during World War II, the history of the OSF is one of growth and expansion. It is, at the same time, as I've already suggested, a history that has had,

of necessity, to imagine a theatregoing public never solely or even primarily constituted by the local community. In 1953, the first full-time OSF employee was hired
(General Manager William Patton), and 1959 saw the debut of the new Elizabethan
Stage, modeled on London's Fortune Theatre of 1599 and thus, among other things,
an open-air amphitheatre design. The addition of an indoor auditorium, the 600-seat
Angus Bowmer Theatre, in 1970 brought the following season's attendance to more
than 150,000. In 1977, an intimate venue, the 140-seat Black Swan Theatre, was
opened; in 1992 the $7.6 million Allen Pavillion was added to the Elizabethan Stage,
and in 2001 the Black Swan closed and the New Theatre opened. The latter provides a
flexible space with seats for between 250 and 350, built at a cost of $21 million and
funded by a capital campaign. And OSF's overall growth in attendance figures is as
impressive as the building history: in 1963 annual attendance exceeded 50,000 for the
first time; in 1999, audience capacity ran at 93 percent for a total of 374,246; in
2001, at 95 percent for a total of 380,101; and in 2003, at 86 percent for a total of
381,340 (the second largest audience in OSF history, producing a record revenue of
more than $13 million) (www.osfashland.org/about/archives.asp). In 1987, OSF
registered its five-millionth visitor and in 2001, its ten millionth. How much these
attendance numbers rely on a travel-in audience is patent, read against Ashland's
current permanent resident population of around 20,000.

Theatre, then, is Ashland's business and it has functioned as a replacement to the
economy that has traditionally supported the city's inhabitants. As Sharon O'Dair
puts it:

> Thirty or even twenty years ago, Ashland's economy and built environment, like those
> of other towns in Jackson and Josephine counties, was dominated by those who lived off
> the extraction of natural resources from the surrounding heavily forested mountain
> areas: the families of millworkers and owners, of truck drivers and loggers. Today,
> Ashland is dominated by those who live off of William Shakespeare. (2000: 91)

As both the history outlined above and O'Dair's argument evince, the "transformation
– from (working-class) logging center to (upper-middle-class) cultural tourism center
did not occur overnight" (O'Dair 2000: 92), but Ashland's metamorphosis is not
likely to be reversed. The success and duration of the theatre season have provided for
significant urban development – hotels, restaurants, and shopping, in particular – and
this is where the city's prosperity is now anchored, no longer in natural resources but
within a matrix of cultural amenities. Thus, as the OSF sustains and, indeed, grows its
attendance figures, the local economy sees commensurate rises in its own size,
viability, and wealth. For all the cultural capital inherent in any performance attached
to the signifier Shakespeare, this is, then, theatre that is fundamentally commercial in
both its means and its ends.

Inevitably the explosive growth of tourism has presented some concerns for Ash-
landers themselves, but I want, here, to consider its effects in light of OSF's repertory
development. In an article entitled "Bigger Than Broadway!," Richard Zoglin wrote

in *Time* magazine that "challenging American theater is alive and well and nowhere near Broadway." In a discussion of David Edgar's two-part, six-hour epic *Continental Divide* (given its world premiere at the OSF in 2003), Zoglin (2003) argues that plays "that examine American history and the American experience, plays that attempt to engage the audience in social and political issues," are much more readily found in regional theatres than elsewhere and despite the fact that the OSF example leans on English history and the Shakespeare experience for its market appeal. With its 2003 production season running from February 23 to November 2, comprising 778 performances of 11 plays (only four of which were by Shakespeare), certainly the OSF in Ashland is a significant contributor to the country's regional theatre. But it should be noted in the context of Zoglin's argument that, since the OSF requires its region to be very widely drawn in order to sustain both box office and city tourism, I would argue that OSF's marketing cannot rely on regional geography alone – and certainly not only, as it once did, on southern Oregon. It has had to focus efforts on a range of much more detailed demographic data and on a much wider construct of playgoing appeal. The Shakespeare summoned in the Festival's name provides significant motivation, but the OSF has developed sophisticated approaches to audience – which is to say, tourist – development.

While Shakespeare may be the brand that justifies the destination, the actual repertoire of the OSF is, as noted above, much wider than its title would suggest. The ongoing popularity of the festival – or, more bluntly put, its ticket sales – seems just as dependent on other classical, contemporary, or commercial plays as it is on the works of the Bard himself. Shakespeare's *œuvre* is still the heart of the OSF repertory – it fulfills the role of sight framing, Rojek might say – but in the 2003 season, for example, the OSF also offered O'Keefe's *Wild Oats*, Ibsen's *Hedda Gabler*, August Wilson's *The Piano Lesson*, the newly commissioned two-part epic from David Edgar, *Continental Divide* (a co-production with the Berkeley Repertory Theatre), as well as Noel Coward's *Present Laughter* (a play that, incidentally, was also part of the Ontario Stratford Festival's 2003 season). In 2004, the OSF offered productions of Shakespeare plays along with Dürrenmatt's *The Visit*, Lorraine Hansberry's *A Raisin in the Sun*, Frank Galati's adaptation of *Oedipus Rex*, Suzan Lori-Parks's *Top Dog/Underdog*, Charlotte Jones's *Humble Boy* (a Best New Play award winner when it premiered at the Royal National Theatre in London in 2001), and the George Kaufman/Edna Ferber comedy, *The Royal Family* (which was also staged at the Ontario Stratford Festival in 2003). That a diverse repertoire of classic and modern plays, set on the pivot of Shakespearean production, generates such a significant box office over an eight-month season tells us something about American theatregoing in particular and theatre audiences in general. I agree with Zoglin that this asserts the contribution of regional theatre to the national stage, as it were, but it also contributes to an overarching sense of audience, both actual and desired.

Choices made for the OSF repertoire must be keenly linked to audience appeal because of that reliance upon travel-in theatregoers who must be persuaded to make Ashland a vacation destination. Ashland is, as previously noted, not particularly accessible: the nearest cities are San Francisco (350 miles to the south) and Portland (285 miles to the north) – neither an easy drive – and there is no large commercial airport, with the nearest facility served by major airlines some 15 miles away in Medford. The OSF website is structured to make its case for cultural tourism to apparently upper-middle-class urbanites who might link theatregoing, symbolically and practically, with some gourmet meals, the acquisition of arts, crafts, and/or antiques, and perhaps a side trip to one of Oregon's wineries. The tourist invoked by the website recalls the privileged elite of Noël Coward's salon as easily as it does that of Shakespeare's cultural authority since both playwrights, in rather different ways, access a sense of cultural comfort and class stability that festivals like the OSF and Ontario's Stratford Festival look for in bringing in a theatre audience. I do not mean that to apply monolithically to one socio-economic group, but to suggest more simply that the marketing strategy summons the quality and range of experience that might be available to a present-day version of Coward's characters with all their sophistication and wit (and money), even though the reality requires a much more diverse *actual* consumer of the cultural product.

I recognize, too, that the OSF experience might be substantively different for any of the groups that come into the festival in the context of "education," a byword, as Lippard has noted, "for goal-oriented tourism" (1999: 149). In fact, OSF attracts various goal-oriented constituencies: school, college, and university groups (locally through Southern Oregon University and area high schools, but also drawing much more widely from the Bay Area and from Portland), for whom a production is tied to curriculum, general ticket buyers who link their theatregoing to OSF institute classes, or even those who seek no more than the value-added of festival membership (with access to the Gertrude Bowmer Members' lounge, post-matinee discussions, and various ticket-buying privileges). Peter Parolin has written about the constituency for the summer seminar at the Stratford Festival in Ontario – a group of approximately 120 people annually, many attending year after year – that "their 'Stratford experience' satisfies a number of important needs, paramount among which is the need to participate actively in artistic processes" (2003). He notes that these spectators "can compare a current production to the different kinds of performances and production concepts that obtained in the past, producing a kind of insider feel." "Nor do I think," continues Parolin, "that this feeling is illusory – years of dedicated attendance at a theater company's productions can indeed ground an audience member's credible claim of having made a real contribution." This dedicated attendance may be inseparable from the spectator's tourism practice, but it poses particular questions about long-term relationships between audiences and theatres, about how production seasons evolve and change or, for that matter, stay consolingly the same. If the vast majority of the Shakespeare audience is middle-aged, middle-class, and white (which it is – whether this is Stratford-upon-Avon; Stratford, Ontario; or Ashland), then these various groups of goal-oriented tourists certainly provide an alternative constituency that complicates the plays' address.

Formally, "[t]he mission of the Oregon Shakespeare Festival is to create fresh and bold interpretations of classic and contemporary plays in repertory, shaped by the diversity of our American culture, using Shakespeare as our standard and inspiration" (www.orshakes.org/about/mission.html), and the annual play roster more than achieves this mission. The OSF has a harder task, as do most theatres, to match the range and diversity among regular audience members. The continuing growth of Ashland's attendance figures and the integrity of its education programs to the overall season – not to mention the overall buoyancy of tourism in the region – more than likely promise it a prosperous future. This is a reality that speaks, on the one hand, to the extraordinary achievement of the OSF within the parameters for serious theatre in general and regional theatre in particular, and, on the other hand, to the contrast with those audiences, a more diverse group, who attend commercial theatre in major urban centers.

One final example from the OSF repertoire demonstrates the very segmentation of the theatregoing marketplace to a range of cultural tourism expressions. A fusion of urban-inspired and history-inspired tourisms, of a nostalgia for the golden age of travel and an appetite for the entertainment-retail fusion of more contemporary vacationing, the Oregon Shakespeare Festival offered in 2003 its "OSF/QE2" package (www.orshakes.org/getinvolved/qe2.html). In this instance, elitist aspirations and connotations have been literalized and targeted at what one imagines must be a relatively narrow demographic, but one that was likely identified as a segment of the regular audience at the OSF who might be persuaded to take their Shakespeare tourism "to the next level." A combination cruise and city vacation scheduled from September 1 to 11, 2003, the OSF/QE2 tourist spent six nights at sea on the luxury Cunard ship, the *Queen Elizabeth II*, and four nights in London enjoying in both venues all kinds of Shakespearean and other cultural fare. Needless to say, this was not an inexpensive venture, for the ten-day trip came at a cost of between $5,089 and $6,859, based on New York departure and cabin selection. Prices were also quoted for add-on flights from all the major west coast American cities, the prime constituency for regular OSF audiences. A blend of Noël Coward's twentieth century and the contemporary tourist's twenty-first, such a trip also has much to say about how Shakespearean performance might mean in ways that far exceed the matter of the plays themselves. It also shows how stunningly mobile the sight framing has become for contemporary performance of Shakespeare as well as how refined marketing practice must be in order to attract the target audience to the cultural tourism product. The reach of a sales strategy that has both a Mary Arden kitchen towel and the QE2 at its disposal is awe-inspiring; it also humbles, I think, the authority of the theatrical event.

These different examples of audiences and Shakespeare indicate a necessity for comprehension of that specific context – tourism – if we are to fully appreciate how Shakespeare's plays work for the breadth of contemporary audiences. In some ways, we distract ourselves with a focus on a single production in light of other Shakespearean productions (though I do not mean to suggest this is an unimportant activity – far from it). We do, however, need to more thoroughly locate contemporary Shakespearean performance in the frame of other performances seen by the audiences for his plays. This can be other mainstream drama – and the repertoires at Stratford, Ontario, and Ashland can suggest the diversity of available product – but, in terms of tourist spectatorship, this is more likely to be popular, spectacular theatrical productions tied to particular tourist destinations. For example, the tourist population for the summer season in London are perhaps just as likely to be found at *The Lion King*, *Mamma Mia!*, or *Jerry Springer: The Opera* as at the Globe Theatre. Moreover, the Shakespearean performance must compete with other types of entertainment-retail products that jostle for the spectator's dollar (other cultural events, for sure, but also professional sports, heritage and theme park attractions, dining and drinking, shopping, and like activities). Worthen cites the complaint of a Globe Theatre actor about spectators who have "spent their five quid to have a quick look, and after ten minutes they feel they've done their Globe experience, and they go on to the Tate Modern" – a vexation that Worthen both acknowledges and explains: "It happens: the Globe makes it happen. The question, I think, is whether it is ever *not* happening. The performance onstage takes place in a deeply overdetermined venue, a place where a range of alternative performativities compete with, structure, and enable the precipitation of theater" (2003: 110, emphasis in original). And he is right – this is, precisely, the experience of taking a vacation with Shakespeare.

Cultural analyses of theatrical performances, whether of Shakespeare's plays or not, must now recognize that, in the context of predominantly tourist audiences that undoubtedly sustain particular venues, the fundamental premises for the production/reception contract are significantly rewritten. In short, all of this activity begs the question: is the play, in fact, the thing? Where the context is tourism, it would seem that the play is but one thing among many that produce, confirm, and encourage a register of experiences that cumulatively allow for the pleasure that underwrites the spectator's presence. This conclusion is not to serve the cause of wringing our collective scholarly hands over the fate of Shakespearean performance but to understand an economic and cultural reality – one that, rather surprisingly, assumes the viability of theatre in the twenty-first-century marketplace. The challenge for the fields of theatre studies and Shakespeare studies is to open up our assumptions and methodologies to a more comprehensive account of the very many people whose travels take in Shakespeare and, in this way, to recognize that Shakespeare's theatre – and perhaps all theatre – has found new conditions and engagements under which it most certainly thrives. Moreover, this fact of tourism-driven audiences should not inspire obsequies for serious theatre but instead insist upon critical approaches that, in contemplating the production-reception contract of theatregoing, take the task of inclusivity very much more to heart.

References and Further Reading

Ackroyd, Peter (2000). *London: The Biography*. London: Chatto and Windus.

Berlin, Normand (2003). "Traffic of Our Stage: Shakespeare in Oregon." *The Massachusetts Review* 44, 3: 531–45.

Brooks, David (2000). *Bobos in Paradise*. New York: Simon and Schuster.

Coursen, H. R. (1996). *Whose History?* Athens, OH: Ohio University Press.

Craik, Jennifer (1997). "The Culture of Tourism." In Chris Rojek & John Urry (eds.) *Touring Cultures: Transformations of Travel and Theory*. London: Routledge, pp. 113–36.

Engler, Balz (1997). "Stratford and the Canonization of Shakespeare." *European Journal of English Studies* 1, 3: 354–66.

Henderson, Diana (2002). "Shakespeare: The Theme Park." In Richard Burt (ed.) *Shakespeare after Mass Media*. London: Routledge, pp. 107–26.

Hodgdon, Barbara (1998). *The Shakespeare Trade: Performances and Appropriations*. Philadelphia, PA: University of Pennsylvania Press.

Holcomb, Briavel (1999). "Marketing Cities for Tourism." In Dennis R. Judd & Susan S. Fainstein (eds.) *The Tourist City*. New Haven, CT: Yale University Press, pp. 54–70.

Holderness, Graham (1988). "Bardolatry: or, The Cultural Materialist's Guide to Stratford-upon-Avon." In Graham Holderness (ed.) *The Shakespeare Myth*. Manchester: Manchester University Press, pp. 2–15.

Howard, Jean E. (1991). "Women as Spectators, Spectacles, and Paying Customers." In David Scott Kastan & Peter Stallybrass (eds.) *Staging the Renaissance: Reinterpretations of Elizabethan and Jacobean Drama*. London: Routledge, pp. 68–74.

Kennedy, Dennis (1998). "Shakespeare and Cultural Tourism." *Theatre Journal* 50, 2: 175–88.

Knowles, Richard Paul (1994). "Shakespeare, 1993, and the Discourses of the Stratford Festival, Ontario." *Shakespeare Quarterly* 45, 2: 211–25.

Lippard, Lucy (1999). *On the Beaten Track: Tourism, Art, Place*. New York: The New Press.

Meethan, Kevin (2001). *Tourism in a Global Society: Place, Culture, Consumption*. New York: Palgrave.

O'Dair, Sharon (2000). *Class, Critics, and Shakespeare: Bottom Lines on the Culture Wars*. Ann Arbor, MI: University of Michigan Press.

Parolin, Peter (2003). "Imaginary Forces: The Audience as Collaborator at the Stratford Festival." Paper presented at the Shakespeare Association of America annual conference, Victoria, Canada.

Rojek, Chris (1997). "Indexing, Dragging and the Social Construction of Tourist Sights." In Chris Rojek & John Urry (eds.) *Touring Cultures: Transformations of Travel and Theory*. London: Routledge, pp. 52–74.

Worthen, W. B. (2003). *Shakespeare and the Force of Modern Performance*. Cambridge: Cambridge University Press.

Zoglin, Richard (2003). "Bigger than Broadway." *Time* 161, 22 (June 2): 66–9.

PART V
Identities of Performance

27

Visions of Color: Spectacle, Spectators, and the Performance of Race

Margo Hendricks

In the beginning was the image, and the word was race.

"Authenticating" Race

Anthropologist Agnes Smedley has argued that "race as a mechanism of social stratification and as a form of human identity is a recent concept in human history. Historical records show that neither the idea nor ideologies associated with race existed before the seventeenth century" (1998: 690). Smedley's assertion about the origins or emergence of a concept of race is not unique; on the contrary, the idea that race is a modern or post-Enlightenment notion has nearly universal acceptance within and outside the academy. Yet, especially among Renaissance and early modern scholars, there are voices crying out in the wilderness against this presumed universality, voices that seek to challenge presentist assumptions about the concept of race and its relation to pre-modern and early modern Western societies and the belief that earlier societies did not deploy race as a "mechanism of social stratification and as a form of human identity." This scholarship increasingly demonstrates that the concept wallowed in ambiguity, purified itself in practice, and infused itself into the daily discourse in Western cultures even before race's first registered (i.e., dictionary) appearance in the languages of Europe. Finally, voices that argue that race has shown itself, conceptually and linguistically, to be very adept at assuming, chameleon-like, whatever appearance its natural surroundings require.

Without question, use of the term *race* with regard to pre-1700 cultures clearly reveals an implicit semiotic schizophrenia: in this context *race* signifies this meaning and in that context it registers that meaning yet, in neither context, are these two meanings really elided. In his intriguing, but flawed, study, *Race: The History of an Idea in the West*, Ivan Hannaford acknowledges this semantic mutability when he highlights the various significations that surfaced with the word's initial usage. According to Hannaford, for the most part, when first used, the word *race* signified a person's genealogy, and so the lexicon of "descent" was associated with its definition – lineage, stock, pedigree. The late sixteenth and seventeenth centuries were pivotal moments in the transition of *race*'s shift in meaning from "lineage or continuity of generations in families, especially royal or noble families to ethnicity or physiological characteristics." In Hannaford's view, "it was not until the late seventeenth century that the pre-idea began to have a specific connotation different from that of gens (Latin, clan) and to be used in conjunction with a new term – 'ethnic group' " (1996: 5–6). While Hanford rightly draws attention to some of race's earliest predicates, I cannot entirely agree with his general hypothesis that the modern predicate of race was absent in pre-seventeenth-century cultures, especially if one of those cultures is England. The problem with Hannaford's dating is that he overlooks important works such as Edmund Spenser's *The Present State of Ireland* where the Irish are frequently referred to as a "race" – as are the English. Even Hannaford's "evidence" to support this contention contradicts his supposition; his discussion (albeit brief) of Raphael Holinshed's *Chronicles* and its use of the word race belies the multiple signification of race in Holinshed's text, including the discussions on various "races" such as Celts, Romans, Trojans, and so on. Hannaford's aim is to argue that race as ethnicity was not a factor in pre- and early-modern cultures; unfortunately, the very texts he uses undermine his claims.

As Hannaford acknowledges, *race* could refer to any number of things – human beings, horses, lines or marks on a surface, wine, or motion. However, as Hannaford's argument unfolds it becomes clear, despite his argument against a concept of a pre-seventeenth-century notion of race, the idea of race was an integral part of the fabric of pre-modern cultural thought. In fact, race was defined based on now-familiar assumptions about exclusivity, authority, ethical, and moral character, and, most importantly, belonging. *Race* denoted a membership in an elite "club" – the noble family, the *gens*, the *polis* or the nation. Membership, however, was limited to those whose claims of affiliation could be substantiated, and substantiation was inextricably tied to birth; hence, race also denoted a concept dependent to some degree upon bio-physicality. By birth I mean both the literal act of being born and the ideological sense of inherited rank and/or social position inherited from parents. An individual's first psychic affiliation, however, is not to a place, a group, a color, or an idea but to his or her parents – and more specifically because she is the locus of nourishment, to the mother. Yet claiming a racial identity in Renaissance and early modern Western cultures was rarely articulated through a relationship to the mother. Patriarchal hegemony dictated that racial membership in terms of family, *gens*, *polis*, or nation was primarily (though not always) determined through patrilineal descent.

Janet Adelman contends that "patriarchal society depends on the principle of inheritance in which the father's identity – his property, his name, his authority is transmitted from father to son ... But this transmission from father to son can take place only insofar as both father and son pass through the body of a woman; and this passage radically alters them both" (1992: 106). In other words, children whose legitimacy can be called into question cannot make claims for the racial affiliation that would guarantee social status and/or financial success. These individuals have no privilege, under existing Renaissance codes of law, to a name, to political status (in some instances), to marriage, or to inheritance. Consequently, Marie-Hélène Huet posits, "in a political culture where the notions of inheritance, name, title, and lineage [were] reinforced by multiple rights (birthrights, rights to inheritance, entails, and so forth), the question of paternity [has] considerable urgency" (1993: 34). The concept of race was constituted to regulate human behavior, especially that of women, and as a corollary effect to avert the "confusion of blood" – a metaphor for race – that may occur as part of everyday gendered interactions (Abercrombie et al. 1989: 80).

By 1558 (the year of Elizabeth I's ascension to the English throne), the word *race* was firmly entrenched in the English language to aid in the construction of social and political hierarchy and differentiation. Elizabethans were quite likely to come across the word in a Shakespeare play, in a eulogy to a dead poet, in a history of Ireland, in a medical treatise, or in bi-lingual dictionaries – as well as in everyday speech. *Race* and its ancillary predicates ("a linage, a breed, issue of one's bodie, a progenie, a stocke, an offspring, a pedigree, stocke, or descent of kindred," nation, sex, tribe, and so on) were being used to categorize and differentiate among and between human beings, and such usage inevitably invited further distinctions (Percyvale 1591: n.p.). In using the word *race*, pre-1700 cultures clearly understood it to be an ordering principle to which predicates based on difference might be attached. The predicates for defining *race* were determined according to cultural or political need. For example, when *race* was used to differentiate within the human species, ideological predicates such as lineage, geographical locus, status or sex were created. If further differentiation was needed additional predicates might be conjoined with the initial ones; thus, in addition to lineage and locus, religion or physiognomy or social customs might be invoked to highlight racial difference.

Central to the arguments of Smedley, Hannaford, and others is that their intellectual and epistemological perception of race is not only dependent upon but also inevitably linked to an absolutist ontological belief that the primary predicate of race is skin color. Thus, the view that race was not a pre-seventeenth-century idea grows out of the presumption that there was extremely limited contact between Europeans and non-Europeans and that exploitative and oppressive elements that inform modern notions of race and its partner racism were absent from (or at least not documented in) these interactions. In other words, since evidence documenting deep and sustained social, political, and ideological interactions between these cultures does not exist, it is problematic to argue that pre-1700 cultures had a concept of race, especially one that includes color as a racial predicate.

What is not obvious in these arguments about the definition of race is the sense that race in pre- and early modern culture was also perceived as a performative act: that is, as a situational experience born not only of an individual's interpellation into a particular social formation but also as carried out or enacted by the individual. For example, when the term race was used to distinguish between social classes or to adumbrate social status, its visibility and definitiveness were manifested in the behavior of the designated individual. Hence, a person of "mean race" would never nor could ever exhibit the attributes associated with a noble race. No matter what the fabric of one's attire, the wealth in one's coffers, or the company one might keep, a "mean" person's racializing attributes would always reveal themselves to a "knowing" subject. Race in this context, in effect, always gestures towards the performative. When the word *race* is used to denote bio-physicality, and with all the assumptions about racial behavior it encodes, however, we rarely perceive this definition as performative, Yet, I would argue, it is precisely the perception of bio-physical stability that makes the performance of color – and blackness or whiteness in particular – a very real phenomenon that was as much a part of early modern society as it is today.

Performing Race

Recent theoretical and scholarly attention to "passing" has increased our awareness of the epistemological complexity of racial passing and its relationship to American literary and historical texts. Yet few social and cultural historians of Renaissance and early modern English culture, as part of the analysis of race, have explored the status and semiotics of color passing within the social and cultural fabric of sixteenth- and seventeenth-century England. In part, this reluctance derives from the ideological, political, and epistemological reasons I have outlined here: the persistent view that the modern predicates of race were not as important to sixteenth- and seventeenth-century English society; the overarching hold empiricism has on modern historiography and its methodologies; and a deeply-held sense that race is always visible. It is this final presumption, the infallibility of the eyes as the means to recognize and know a person's racial identity that we need to challenge if we are to grasp the significance of race as a performative act in Renaissance and early-modern culture.

Julia Thomas remarks that "our eyes are not simple recorders or receptacles of information: they do not simply mirror a world that exists unproblematically outside them" (2000: 4). In fact, she continues:

> perception involves not just the act of looking but decision-making too: the brain searches for the best possible interpretation of the available data. And this idea of "interpretation"

is of more than passing significance because in order for the brain to transform what is seen into something recognisable, to create meanings through sight, it relies on learnt assumptions about the characteristics of, and differences between, things. Such distinctions, however natural they seem, are not inherent in sight or even in the visualized world. But if these distinctions are not inherent to vision or the visual then where do they come from? Why do we see things differently and as separate entities?

For Thomas, linguistic and cultural knowledge is the tie that binds sight and its object.

Jonas F. Soltis makes a similar argument when he suggests that "seeing is neither simple nor plain but rather that our ordinary notions about seeing are complex, and though consistent, confusing" (1966: 140). Soltis offers a cogent reminder that seeing operates on multiple levels, some more successful than others. More important to me here, though, is Thomas's observation that

> it is more than biology that dictates how one sees. Seeing is bound up in value judgements (one assesses things by their appearance) and, because it is spatially and temporally limited (one cannot see everything simultaneously but only a certain amount and at any one moment), it involves an element of choice. (2000: 4)

Thomas's point is especially cogent when we consider race and the essentially unstable nature of its predicates. In the context of race as ontological biophysical differences, passing arises as the cultural and ideological interlocutor of a concept that insists upon sight as the infallible medium of recognition and knowledge. Generally, one person sees another, he or she puts into a play a systematized, if unrecognized, set of values, which enable the viewer to read the other's physical appearance and so to decide whether, and in what ways, race may be an important predicate of identity. Of course, this system works well if one can be certain that the interpretation of what one is seeing will be validated. For example, a man racially designated as "white" sees a woman whose skin color is "dark brown." The man racially designated "white" draws upon a received body of cultural and linguistic codes designed to aid his interpretation of what he sees: assumptions about color, physiognomy, culture, status, and hierarchy, as well as a cultural lexicon to name what he is about to interpret. As a result, the man "sees" the woman as a "Black" woman, and thus as racially different and possibly inferior. Conversely, if the woman "seen" has "white" skin, then our "white" man undergoes the same reasoning process but reaches a different conclusion.

The telling epistemological problem is, I would argue, dramatized by the second scenario. Here, we need to recognize that the "white" man may be "reading" the woman's body both correctly and incorrectly; that the woman in fact was born to black parents yet by virtue of her physical appearance must be viewed as "white." If there is no other sign to indicate the woman's lineal "blackness," the man does not question what he sees. Should the woman be joined by two "black" individuals and she acknowledges a kinship relation or if through some other means the man discovers his mis-reading, then this relationship between seeing and knowledge, and the belief system that constitutes such seeing and its interpretation are thrown into question. Moreover, should the man remain ignorant of the woman's genealogy *and* the woman is aware of his mis-reading *and* she does not correct his assumption about her racial identity, then her action constitutes color passing. Similarly, even if the woman is unaware that racially she might be labeled "Black" – because her parents did not inform her of her lineage or that she had been adopted, or even because her parents were themselves "passing" – she still is constitutively engaged in the act of color passing and thus enacts a problematic subjectivity.

Modes of "passing," whether race is defined as gender, class, ethnicity, or color, occur in a symbolic economy predicated upon a presumed violation of social, political, and juridical norms. As a result, racial passing is always understood as a self-conscious "performative enactment" of those very norms; "performative" here signifies both its theatrical connotation and the gestural threat that the performance makes to an essential notion of blackness and, by extension, race. Harryette Mullen rightly argues that for individuals who pass, "passing is not so much a willful deception or duplicity as it is an attempt to move from the margin to the center [of social] identity" (1994: 77) so as to participate in the political economy denied to them on the basis of sex, color or religion. In the end, " 'passing' is, after all passing oneself off as a human person with all the rights and privileges thereof" (Sollors 1997: 248). In fact, as most critics of "passing" literature have inferred, economic and social inequality is often the primary reason for most types of passing.

Color passing, then, evokes not only a sense of power and privilege but also, simultaneously, duplicity and denial. In the end, Sollors offers this cogent reminder:

> these social rules have sometimes sanctioned a moral condemnation of passing on the grounds that it is a form of deception, hence dishonest. Yet this only works as long as it is taken for granted that partial ancestry may have the power to become totally defining. This aspect of passing distinguishes it from true masquerades in which an identity choice need not at all connect with any part of the masked person's particular background. "Passing" can thus justly be described as a social invention, as a "fiction of law and custom" (Mark Twain) that makes one part of a person's ancestry real, essential, and defining, and other parts accidental, mask-like, and insignificant. (1997: 249)

The irony, of course, is that the belief in the inviolate visibility of color = race is what ultimately comes to undermine the power of the predicate itself.

William Shakespeare's tragedy *Titus Andronicus* stands as one of the earliest spectacles of what twenty-first-century spectators and readers would recognize as racial passing in the fullest sense of the word race as understood by Renaissance and early modern English theatre-goers. In the play, Shakespeare traces the political and social turbulence that ensues when the boundaries of racial identity are transgressed.

Shakespeare's handling of race, it should be noted, is not limited to the love affair between Aaron and Tamora. Rather, the concept of race encompasses the filial and paternal connections between Titus and his sons, the marriage of Lavinia to Bassanius (the dead Emperor's son), and especially the playwright's representation of the conflict between the Romans and the Goths. This racial spectacle, however, is masked by the Aaron/Tamora liaison. As Guy Debord writes:

> since the spectacle's job is to cause a world that is no longer directly perceptible to be *seen* via different specialized mediations, it is inevitable that it should elevate the human sense of sight to the special place once occupied by touch; the most abstract of the senses, and the most easily deceived, sight is naturally the most readily adaptable to ... generalized abstraction ... Whenever representation takes on an independent existence, the spectacle reestablishes its rule. (1995: 17)

Nowhere is this observation more aptly demonstrated than in Act 4 Scene 2 of *Titus Andronicus*. Tamora, Queen of the Goths, is brought to bed and gives birth to the son of Aaron the Moor, whereupon she immediately sends the child to Aaron with orders for its death. Aaron refuses to slay his own child and offers instead a solution that will protect both Tamora's honor and his son's life:

> And now be it known to you my full intent.
> Not far, one Muliteus my countryman
> His wife but yesternight was brought to bed.
> His child is like to her, fair as you are.
> Go pack with him, and give the mother gold,
> And tell them both the circumstance of all,
> And how by this their child shall be advanced
> And be received for the Emperor's heir.
>   (4.2.150–7)

With this advice, Aaron offers Tamora and her sons the means to further their political power and ambition and to save the life of his son.

Eldred Jones has argued in response to Aaron's inventive plan to save his child, that

> it is no diminution of Aaron's quickness of wit to suggest that Shakespeare intends this story of Muly and his white son to be taken as a complete fabrication. Indeed the speed with which Aaron devises the story is the supreme demonstration of his skill. The happy coincidence of the birth of a white child to a moor and a white woman with Aaron's desperate need for just such a child, would otherwise be the least credible of the chances which fortune presents to the villain in this play. That the child is white at all would have appeared nothing short of miraculous to an Elizabethan audience if they believed the popular idea that "in truth a blacke Moore never faileth to beget black children, of what colour soever the other be." (1965: 53)

Interestingly enough, the "fair" child of Muly receives no further attention from Shakespeare, thus seeming to affirm Jones's observation that the scene was invented to demarcate and highlight Aaron's "quickness of wit." In response, I want to suggest a different reading of the implications of Aaron's plan. To me Aaron's plan is less important as a signifier of character, as sign of innate wit or villainy, but as a sign of a larger cultural anxiety, an anxiety that is at once exposed by Aaron's scheme and elided by Jones's reading of it. I want to propose, then, a different representation of the play's articulation of itself as a racializing spectacle and what that represents to its spectators.

Very few critics have remarked on the performative gesture behind Aaron's proposed exchange, never asking why is it necessary for him to substitute one mixed child for another. Though Aaron offers a plan, in many ways (as Jones argues) he does not offer a rationale for the plan to exchange Muly's son for his own. Strictly in terms of the play's plot, Aaron would be better served if he were to exchange a Roman or Gothic child for his own. Francesca Royster has argued that Aaron's proposal is more than just a plan to save his child; it is also reflective of Aaron's "allegiance to his race, a commitment to establishing a foothold of power for Moors within the very heart of Rome" (2000: 453). Royster's point astutely captures the "politic" Aaron, yet it perhaps over-reads the motivation behind Aaron's proposal. More important for the character that Shakespeare has drawn is Aaron's ability to disrupt, disturb, define, and redefine how racial identity is to be understood. Muly's child "passing" among the Romans would become Aaron's "private joke" on the Romans. Aaron's attempt to "dispose" of his "treasure" among the Goths and to "bring up" his son "to be a warrior and command a camp" inevitably fails and the fate of the two mixed-race infants, linked as they are by their Moorish genealogy, appears to hang in the balance. Yet, only Aaron's son remains a dramatic force throughout the final scenes of the play. As spectators, we know the outcome of the infant's fate – his father having extracted a promise from Lucius that the newly crowned emperor would protect the child's life. No such promise exists for Muly's "fair" son. In fact, the infant ceases to be of import once Aaron and his son are captured by Lucius and his newfound allies, the Goths.

At the play's conclusion, all the various racial conflicts are resolved – Titus, Lavinia, Chiron, Demetrius, Tamora, and Aaron are dead, and Lucius becomes Rome's new emperor – except the one generated by Aaron's proposed substitution of Muly's son for his endangered "first-born son and heir" (4.2.94). Yet Muly's son exists textually and dramatically as an unresolved tension, an ideological reminder of the dangers of relying too heavily on an inflexible concept of race. The specter of Muly's son dramatizes a fundamental incoherence in the play's understanding of race, as though Shakespeare either does not know how to resolve the racial spectacle he creates or he does not consider it significant enough to warrant resolution. The *Oxford English Dictionary* defines the word *spectacle* as follows: a "person or thing exhibited to, or set before, the public gaze as an object either (*a*) of curiosity or contempt, or (*b*) of marvel or admiration"; "A thing seen or capable of being seen; something presented to the view, esp. of a striking or unusual character; a sight"; or "an illustrative instance or example." Whatever the reason, Muly's son cannot help but serve as a paradoxically marked and unmarked spectacle whose body unknowingly gestures towards the performative that is race in *Titus Andronicus*.

Unlike Muly's son, Queen Anne, wife of James I King of England, and 11 of her ladies-in-waiting clearly understood the performativity that is racial passing. In 1605, the Queen and her women blackened their skin to take part in Ben Jonson's *Masque of Blackness*. The plot of the masque concerns the desire of 12 nymphs, "daughters of Niger," to restore themselves to their originary complexion – which once was "as fair / As other dames, now black with black despair," as a result of Phaeton's tragic ride. The masque represents the nymphs' journey to the West and their eventual restoration to a pre-Phaetonic state of whiteness. The Queen's performance in the masque generated quite a bit of commentary about the "blackening" of her "fair" skin. The problem was, aesthetically and ideologically, rectified in the masque's companion piece, *The Masque of Beauty*, where the "black" daughters of Niger are "washed" white by the River Thames. Kim Hall argues that the use of this trope derives from "actual contact with Africans, Native Americans and other racially different foreigners," rather than being solely dependent on literary or visual imagery, and so also indicates a greater engagement with "outsiders" during the reign of James I than in the reign of Elizabeth I (1996: 5). Thus, "the Jacobean royal engagement with blackness and foreign difference created strategies in representation for articulating and thereby solving the problem of difference in this court through the manipulation of blackness and gender" (1996: 5). In other words, Jonson's masques, and the Queen's performance in them, are very much linked to a shifting notion of race inside and outside the geographic boundaries of the island-nation.

The Queen's performance in *The Masque of Blackness*, to say the least, can be described as a spectacle of "color passing," even if it is passing under the guise of theatrical performance. In many ways, theatrical performance is an ideal way to project and contain the idea of color passing since, to perform a character, an actor must convincingly pass as that character. In other words, the actor theoretically must conceal, suppress or reduce all visible traces of her "actual" self in order to "pass" as the person called for by the script. Blackening her skin, the Queen undoes herself as a recognizable subject (including erasing her whiteness) in order to make recognizable her performative "self" as Niger's daughter. The fact that Niger's daughters also prove to be only temporarily black (their whiteness known to them even if concealed by sunburn) even heightens the Queen's act of passing. The literal restoration of the Queen and her women to their original color in *The Masque of Beauty* dispels the disruptive and disturbing effect that their color passing – no matter how symbolic – engenders. As any number of contemporary examples witness, passing as "Black," even if only onstage, is a highly fraught performance, especially when "racial passing" is coordinated with gender. As Dudley Carleton observed of the Queen and her women, "their black faces, and hands which were painted and bare up to the elbows, was a very loathsome sight" (1972: 68).

For male actors, passing for black was a less complicated though still problematic issue. Dympna Callaghan explores the relationship between the use of blackface and our understanding of the issue of race and Othello in her essay, "Othello Was a White Man: Properties of Race on Shakespeare's Stage." Callaghan begins her discussion by claiming that "this essay will investigate the obvious but none the less curious fact that in Shakespeare's plays there are histrionic depictions of negritude, but there are, to use Coleridge's infamous phrase, no 'veritable negroes.' There are, indeed, no authentic 'others' – raced or gendered – of any kind, only their representations" (2000: 193). Callaghan also calls into question the belief that these representations function as a form of mimesis: "mimesis entails an imitation of otherness, and its dynamism is a result of the absence of the actual bodies of those it depicts … Theatrical mimesis, however, involves the active manipulation of the body of the actor in the process of representation" (2000: 194). The question is whether this representation, this performative gesture towards blackness, can do all that it claims to do.

Blackface functions, according to Callaghan, as a "constitutive … articulation of racial difference: the display of black people themselves (exhibition), on the one hand, and the simulation of negritude (mimesis), on the other. These are the poles of the representational spectrum of early modern England" (2000: 194). In the theatrical performance, when "black" characters are incorporated into the script, what occurs is not the performance of blacks but, as Callaghan astutely argues, the exhibition of blackness: "people are set forth as objects, passive and inert before the active scrutiny of the spectator, without any control over, or even necessarily consent to, the representational apparatus in which they are placed" (2000: 194). When blackface is deployed as part of the representation of blackness, "race, crucially, *both* black *and* white, is articulated as an opposition on stage principally by means of cosmetics: burnt cork negritude projects racial difference against white Pan-Cake" (2000: 195). Early modern theatrical practices presumed an ontological identification, however temporary, between blackface and racial identity yet even though this performance was circumscribed by the stage and its two hours' traffic, staging race nonetheless focused an anxiety about the instability of race as a categorical predicate.

Nowhere is the "problem" of performance and race more deeply mired than in the study of Renaissance English culture, especially Shakespeare's plays. *Othello, Titus Andronicus, Antony and Cleopatra*, and to a lesser degree *The Tempest* have allowed for the centering of "race" as a performative issue in recent scholarship. The explosion of recent film adaptations of Shakespeare plays (*True Identity, O*) as well as filmed Shakespeare plays (*Titus, Othello, William Shakespeare's Romeo + Juliet*) similarly have moved "Shakespeare and race" to the forefront of Shakespeare cultural and performance studies. Of the recent essays exploring race and filmed versions/adaptations/gestures towards Shakespeare's play-texts, Richard Burt's "Slammin' Shakespeare in Acc(id)ents Yet Unknown: Liveness, Cinem(edi)a, and Racial Dis-integration" provocatively touches on the problematics of performing race even if Burt's "ending" is unsatisfying as spectacle.

Burt begins "Slammin' Shakespeare" by drawing attention to what he describes as the "mutual blindness" that marks "interest in Shakespeare and race": Shakespeare critics "interested in race" who have "largely ignored the citation and appropriation of Shakespeare in black films and other mass media" and "critics writing on race, cinema, and popular culture" who "have completely ignored the history of black actors either in Shakespeare films or films and related mass media that cite Shakespeare in racially marked contexts" (2002: 201). In this richly nuanced and complex analysis of what he describes as "cinem(edi)a" defined as "the circulation of all kinds of mass media in film (and vice versa)", Burt argues that "racial signifiers in filmed Shakespeare and other mass media need to be examined in relation to mediatization, which Fredric Jameson defines as 'the process whereby the traditional fine arts ... come to consciousness of themselves as various media within a mediatic system' " (2002: 201). While Burt's essay does not explicitly articulate itself as a study in Shakespeare performance, this notion very much inflects the way in which Burt reads mass media Shakespeare.

Burt's essay raises a number of important questions about the role of "authenticity" and performance in the cultural discourse of race and in Shakespeare. Drawing upon Philip Auslander's notion of "liveness," the sense that "live performance and mass media are not ontologically distinct," Burt concludes that "race is now always a mediatized rather than a live performance." As Burt notes, Auslander's concept is indebted to "Baudrillard's theory of simulation as recreation of performances that never took place, representations without real referents" (2002: 203). In essence, "racial performances are no more 'unplugged' than Shakespeare performances are" (2002: 203). Burt's citation of "mediatized" examples of "black" engagements with Shakespeare (from Lauryn Hill's *The Miseducation of Lauryn Hill* to *The Cosby Show*) encourages critics to reflect on that often overlooked phenomenon the "black voice" or as Burt graphically reminds us in the essay's title "accent." For Burt, "sound" is as much a "racial signifier" as color. Ultimately, Burt contends:

> in my examples of Shakespeare cinemedia, the simulation of liveness requires the synchronization of visual and aural racial signifiers (in order to achieve cinematic or televisual realism) as well as their integration of Shakespeare in relation to high and low culture, center and margin. Yet in each case the mediatization of liveness disrupts this dream of integration: a multicultural Shakespeare and a multimedia Shakespeare never coincide. (2002: 208)

Assuming that the notion of a "dream of integration" is valid, one must ask "for whom?" – for "blacks," "whites," "Asians," "Latinos," "Shakespeare critics"?

Burt's discussion highlights what is both illuminating and frustrating about cultural criticism and race, especially with respect to performance: that what is racialized is always already a performance whether live or mediatized, and that any notion of assumed authenticity is lodged not in performance but in the performative act or the Shakespeare play-text. As W. B. Worthen writes: "dramatic performance is not determined by the text of the play: it strikes a much more interactive, performative relation between writing and the spaces, places, and behaviors that give it meaning, force, as theatrical action" or, I would add, "filmic action" (2003: 12). It is this "performative relation" between race and text that Burt cogently makes references to in his essay but does not completely dislodge. My critique of Burt's essay should not be mis-read. "Slammin' Shakespeare" rightly takes issue with the presumed ontological status of a biological notion of race. What is not so obvious is how this essay helps us to move beyond the search for the "authenticity" of race as it promises. Here, I want to take up Burt's challenge and reflect on what Burt's observation about "race as a form of passing" and "sound as a racial signifier" can mean for the critical study of performance, Shakespeare's plays and the political engagement with the concept of race.

"Witnessing" the Spectacle

In her essay, "Brave New Bard," Courtney Lehmann argues that:

> whether classified as mainstream or radical. Loyal or loose, the cinematic adaptation of Shakespeare will always be the product of complex negotiations between text and screenplay, early modern and postmodern, live action and framed simulation. Consequently, the reception of filmed Shakespeare has historically been preoccupied with what gets "lost in the translation", a critical sensibility articulated through an inky rhetorical cloak of mourning for some violated conception of textual fidelity, historical accuracy, or artistic integrity. (2000: 2)

The desire for some authentic Shakespeare, dramatic representations that are "real" to us, for language that speaks to some inherently human element, haunts spectators of Shakespeare's plays – whether theatrically or cinematically performed. The desire for authenticity in performing "race" is even more profoundly framed by this sense of mourning. Despite the intuitive understanding that a "black" Shakespeare referent can never be an accurate representation of people of African ancestry, regardless of when the referent is performed, Shakespeare scholars continue to write as if blackness is an ontological state of racial being for millions of human beings.

Denise Albanese writes about the performance of Patrick Stewart as Othello:

> to accept the undeniably pale Stewart as black demands that the power of the script's fiction – what I've already termed the authority of the Shakespeare text – override all the cues to the contrary that the actor playing Othello is *not* black, nor is he making any somatic attempt to impersonate blackness, vexed, indeed, as that possibility would be.

Albanese claims, just as Burt does, the idea of an authentic black "race" (2003: 240). Nowhere in Albanese's discussion is there space for the person of African ancestry whose color is not "black." Would she have made the same argument had Patrick Stewart claimed African ancestry through a "passing" ancestor? Would his "whiteness" register the performance of blackness, of "race," in the same way as, for example, James Earl Jones's darker skin? If not, why not? More than any other factor, color passing wreaks havoc on the illusionary stability of the concept of race. Visibly registering normative expectations about racialized identity, the "white Moor" proves the permeability and the fragility of the idea of skin color as a predicate of race. To assume that the performance of race in a Shakespeare play-text is static, and one-sided, is to ignore the fact that being black is always already a performative act. There is no such thing as verisimilitude in the representation of "blackness."

I want to return to Richard Burt's insistence that sound be viewed as a racial signifier. As a preface, Burt argues that "like critics working on race (or 'race') in early modern culture, critics of filmed Shakespeare have attended to color rather than voice, accent, pitch, noise, and music soundtracks" (2002: 207). Baz Lurhmann's *William Shakespeare's Romeo + Juliet*, for example, figures prominently in Burt's analysis. Despite the "visual" predicates of "racial identity," none of the characters can be wholly read as emblematic of a race: "Can Mercutio be read as wholly African American when, seen from the perspective of Romeo on ecstasy, he lip-synchs a female vocalist's disco hit and crossdresses in white, calling up Ru Paul or possibly even Marilyn Monroe?" (Burt 2002: 207). Burt answers his question, contending "by not consistently opposing Montagues and Capulets racially either by color or accent, Lurhmann unsettles the idea that racial difference and racism drive their conflict" (2002: 207). While it is true that Lurhmann's film does indeed "unsettle," I am not so certain that the film unsettles in the area of race. In fact, I would argue that the film more solidly locates unmediated racial performances than Burt grants.

It is in Peter Greenaway's *Prospero's Books* (1991) that Burt finds that "sound and skin color can be "dis-integrated racial signifiers, so that some films do not consistently link racial difference to exclusion" (2002: 208): "the dancer playing Caliban is white, but dance, sound, baldness, nudity, gay sexuality, and cosmetic covering from head to foot contribute more to his exclusion and marginalization than skin color, suggesting levels of difference beyond race" (2002: 208). The King of Tunis, on the other hand,

> is black, and we see him being washed by his servants after having deflowered Claribel, who is seen lying on a bed with blood on her abdomen. Here only the King's color defines his race (he has no lines), which is articulated by Ferdinand and Sebastian in (Prospero's) voiceover, who blame the shipwreck on Alonso's arrangement of the

marriage. How much this scene represents the two villains' racist fantasy or Greenaway's own complicity in such fantasies is debatable, but the more interesting point, I think, is that, though the king is clearly raced, he is a master, like Prospero, not an excluded or marginal slave like Caliban. (2002: 208)

Here Burt becomes entangled in the performativity that is race as he is unable to "dis-integrate" color from his notion of race to understand that the King of Tunis' "race" is not predicated upon his color but on his status.

It is this performative gesture that Burt's "Shakebites" occlude when color, and more specifically blackness, becomes the first-order predicate for race either as a manifestation of some textual referent by Shakespeare or as a matter of modern and post-modern ideologies. Yet this blackness cannot obscure the fact that all gestures and speech, identified as "black" are performative. And what Burt's essay does so eloquently is to remind us that in Shakespeare's plays sound functions as a racial signifier, even if at times the analysis engages in slippages that seem to construe black speech as *a priori* always already black. In other words, presumptions about the ontology of blackness as a racially marked predicate incorporate all aspects of phys-icality: skin color, hair, muscularity and body shape, and of course the speaking voice. The idea that one can always "tell" a black person by voice and speech assumes that there is a singularity in voice for all blacks. Variables in speech pattern, timbre, tone, and vocabulary are as great between "black" people as they are between "non-black" people. Among "non-black" speakers differences in speech are most commonly understood to signify class and education; so too with "black" speakers differences in speech patterns are predominantly the consequence of class rather than what we refer to as "race."

Like class, race as a performative act is founded upon behavior, bio-physicality, and spectacle. In this context, passing becomes a useful theoretical framework for reflec-tions on race, performance, and Shakespeare. Race in Shakespeare's plays is always located in the performative register: whether it is Prince Hal "passing" as an ordinary soldier or Portia "passing" as a man or Othello "passing" as a Venetian. To consider the performance of race in Shakespeare in this light is to recognize the instability of "whiteness" as a centrifugal force for racial identity, let alone "blackness" as a signifier for people of African ancestry. In an essay on black women's sexuality, Evelynn Hammonds frames her theoretical inquiry by asking a seemingly unrelated question: "how do you deduce the presence of a black hole? And, second, what is it like inside of a black hole?" The answer, she observes, is that "the existence of the black hole is inferred from the fact that the visible star is in orbit and its shape is distorted in some way or it is detected by the energy emanating from the region in space around the visible star that could not be produced by the visible star alone" (1994: 139).

The spectacle of "blackness" as a racial predicate in Shakespeare's plays is as much a product of critical discourse as it is a by-product of Shakespearean dramatic represen-tations. This does not mean that these representations do not have ideological, cultural, and political implications for how "blackness" becomes constituted as a symbol for all that is wrong; rather, I want to argue that a search for authentic performances of blackness in Shakespearean performance is an exercise in futility, whether that performance is in the extraordinary "black talent" of theatrical actors such as Ray Fearon or James Earl Jones or Lauryn Hill's invocation of *Romeo and Juliet* in her *Miseducation of Lauryn Hill*. It is because there "ain't no such thing as blackness" that I make this claim. We would do better to examine the class issues that hide behind the representation of skin color in Shakespeare's plays if we truly want to understand how race comes to be (dis)authenticated within the Shakespearean performance.

References and Further Reading

Abercrombie, Nicholas, Hill, Stephen, & Turner, Bryan S. (1989). *Sovereign Individuals of Capitalism*. London: Allen and Unwin.

Adelman, Janet (1992). *Suffocating Mothers: Fantasies of Maternal Origin in Shakespeare's Plays, Hamlet to The Tempest*. New York: Routledge.

Albanese, Denise (2003). "Black and White, and Dread All Over: The Shakespeare Theatre's 'Photonegative' *Othello* and the Body of Desdemona." In Lena Cowen Orlin (ed.) *Othello: Contemporary Critical Essays*. New York: Palgrave/Macmillan.

Burt, Richard (2002). "Slammin' Shakespeare in Acc(id)ents yet Unknown: Liveness, Cinem(edi)a, and Racial Dis-integration." *Shakespeare Quarterly* 53: 201–26.

Burt, Richard & Boose, Lynda E. (1997). *Shakespeare, the Movie*. London: Routledge.

Burt, Richard & Boose, Lynda E. (2003). *Shakespeare, the Movie II*. London: Routledge.

Butler, Judith (1993). *Gender Trouble: Feminism and the Subversion of Identity*. London: Routledge.

Callaghan, Dympna (2000). *Shakespeare without Women: Representing Gender and Race on the Renaissance Stage*. London: Routledge.

Carleton, Dudley (1972). *Dudley Carleton to John Chamberlain, 1603–1624: Jacobean Letters*, ed. Maurice Lee, Jr. New Brunswick, NJ: Rutgers University Press.

Debord, Guy (1995). *The Society of the Spectacle*, trans. Donald Nicholson-Smith. New York: Zone Books.

Hall, Kim F. (1996). *Things of Darkness: Economies of Race and Gender in Early Modern England*. Ithaca, NY: Cornell University Press.

Hammonds, Evelyn (1994). "Black (W)holes and the Geometry of Black Female Sexuality." *Differences* 6, 2–3: 126–45.

Hannaford, Ivan (1996). *Race: The History of an Idea in the West*. Washington, DC: The Woodrow Wilson Press Center Press/Baltimore, MD: Johns Hopkins University Press.

Hornback, Robert (2001). "Emblems of Folly in the First *Othello*: Renaissance Blackface, Moor's Coat, and 'Muckender.' " *Comparative Drama* 3: 69–99.

Huet, Marie-Hélène (1993). *Monstrous Imagination*. Cambridge, MA: Harvard University Press.

Jones, Eldred D. (1965). *Othello's Countrymen: A Study of African in the Elizabethan and Jacobean Drama*. Oxford: Oxford University Press.

Jonson, Ben (1969). *The Complete Masques*, ed. Stephen Orgel. New Haven, CT: Yale University Press.

Lehmann, Courtney (2000). "Brave New Bard." *Cineaste* 26, 1: 62–6.

Mullen, Harryette (1994). "Optic White: Blackness and the Production of Whiteness." *Diacritics* 24, 2: 71–89.

Percyvale, Richard (1591). *Bibliotheca hispanica. containing a grammar, with a dictionarie in Spanish, English and Latine, gathered out of divers good authors: very profitable for the studious of the Spanish toong. by Richard Percyvall gent. the dictionarie being inlarged with the Latine, by the advise and conference of Master Thomas Doyley doctor in physicke*. London.

Robinson, A. (1994). "It Takes One to Know One: Passing and Communities of Common Interest." *Critical Inquiry* 20: 715–36.

Royster, Francesca (2000). " 'White Limed Walls': Whiteness and Gothic Extremism in Shakespeare's *Titus Andronicus.*" *Shakespeare Quarterly* 51, 453: 433–54.

Shakespeare, William (1988). *Titus Andronicus.* In *The Complete Works,* ed. Stanley Wells & Gary Taylor. Oxford: Oxford University Press.

Smedley, Audrey (1998). " 'Race' and the Construction of Human Identity." *American Anthropologist* 100: 690–702.

Sollors, Werner (1997). *Neither Black Nor White Yet Both: Thematic Explorations of Interracial Literature.* New York: Oxford University Press.

Soltis, Jonas F. (1966). *Seeing, Knowing, and Believing: A Study of the Language of Perception.* London: George Allen and Unwin Ltd.

Thomas, Julia (ed.) (2000). *Reading Images.* London: Palgrave.

Worthen, W. B. (2003). *Shakespeare and the Force of Modern Performance.* Cambridge: Cambridge University Press.

28
Shakespeare and the Fiction
of the Intercultural
Yong Li Lan

An intercultural performance of Shakespeare usually is thought to be a reproduction of the play in non-Western performance conventions, a means of exploring another culture's relationship to the culture represented by the English (or Western) Shakespearean classic text and its authority. An account of the "intercultural" relationship enacted by the performance, then, proceeds to understand how non-Western performance conventions relate to those implied by Shakespeare's text. Yet such an account is inextricable from unconscious assumptions of how to look at and think about the cultural implications of performance forms, and so becomes caught up in the "intercultural" process it attempts to describe. While critical discussions of intercultural performance point out that disrupting an audience's frame of reference and expectation is part of the cultural transaction, and that reception varies enormously depending on a spectator's cultural disposition, it is precisely these factors that have proved problematic for defining the interculturality of one's own response. The problem goes beyond ignorance of either Shakespeare or non-Western performance forms, because knowing enough about the pertinent forms or texts is not equivalent to experiencing how another culture relates to Shakespeare but is, rather, a shadow of that experience. In fact, intercultural performance is not only predicated upon some degree of ignorance, unfamiliarity and incomprehension for every spectator but calls into question how our discourses of cultural entry or access are inseparable from discourses of mastery. Here, I want to explore how non-understanding and foreignness play a role in audiences' participation in the intercultural transactions between Shakespeare and East Asian theatres.

Everyone Understands Shakespeare

Two accounts of a recent English Shakespeare production in Hong Kong illustrate the significance of how an audience's presumed "understanding" of a Shakespeare performance plays in the East. These accounts of a familiar kind of English Shakespeare illuminate the politics of understanding at the inception of Shakespeare performance, demonstrating the tenacity of that beginning. The Hong Kong Players' *A Midsummer Night's Dream* was directed by an Englishman, David Booth, and performed in English at two venues in Hong Kong (1992) and one in Hanoi, Vietnam (1993). Booth and one of the actors describe a fairly conventional interpretation of *Dream*, which equated the courtly and fairy rulers and the mechanicals and the fairies to suggest that one world is the dream dimension of the other. Yet this "standard" Shakespeare performed entirely different cultural functions in different contexts and was radically altered by its playing spaces, occasions, and audiences. Mike Ingham, who played Flute, describes how, when first performed in the banqueting hall of Government House to Hong Kong's elite in a charity performance, "the associations of the colonial apparatus [of Theseus' court] with Government House's spirit of place were profoundly symbolic ... the venue itself became the production environment. It became, if you like, the sub-text of the performance" (2002: 32, 48). With an entry price of HK$600 a ticket (the proceeds given to charity), the venue was much more than a sub-text: it was the main text for the audience's performance as the court of Hong Kong celebrating Britishness, to which *Dream* was like a play-within-a-play. Played without Chinese translation, this performance presumed an English-speaking audience, including the Chinese spectators, as part of its reification of the dominance and exclusivity of British colonial culture just five years before the colony's handover back to China. Ingham notes that, since the population is officially bilingual, English-language productions generally do not provide translation into Hong Kong's predominant language: "Shakespeare's supposed 'universality' is often an excuse to neglect the needs of an audience" (2002: 30). Given that Hong Kong has seen a separate line of Cantonese Shakespeare productions since the 1960s, one can conclude that English Shakespeare performance, not unmindful of its audience, was intent on reproducing and maintaining an English-speaking elite who needed no translation.

By contrast, in Hanoi no full-length English Shakespeare had ever been seen before. According to Booth and Ingham, the production was most successful there because it was altogether unfamiliar to its audiences. Ingham felt that the defamiliarization of the actors, who lacked feedback during preparation and were uncertain of being understood, displaced the burden of Shakespeare's canonicity and cultural associations and prompted the actors instead to establish "communication afresh." A narrator's part which Booth had scripted to provide summaries of each scene in Vietnamese "produced a kind of alienation effect in reverse, preventing us from immersing ourselves in the tried and tested play text" (Ingham 2002: 35). These accounts locate the intercultural event not onstage, in the performance text, but in the alignment or misalignment between the culture of onstage signs and that of the spectators reading them. In this transaction the place and occasion of performance, the provisions (or lack thereof) for bridging language barriers and the effect of an audience's expectations on the producers and actors were all foregrounded. In principle, then, the production's meaningfulness as an exchange between cultures is constituted by what the cultural status of Shakespeare represents for different Asian audiences, with different histories. This is not to say that reception contexts do not always shape what a performance signifies as an act of cultural production. Rather, when Shakespeare is imported into a society where his language, dramatic forms and the dramatic action's cultural referents are alien (even, perhaps especially, a society where Shakespeare has long been a foreign resident), the choice of performing and adapting his plays is heavily loaded to foreground Shakespeare's cultural authority above the play's content. The political context informing that cultural exchange can be quite complicated where those histories are re-staged through performing Shakespeare. Ingham explains that the Hanoi performance came about through connections that one of the company who worked in a law firm had with Vietnam. A previous colleague had reputedly saved Ho Chi Minh's life in the 1930s by smuggling him across the border when the Hong Kong Government, under French diplomatic pressure to hand him over as an anti-colonial terrorist for summary execution, had been about to arrest him (2002: 34). This incident resulted in the irony of a colonial play being warmly received in North Vietnam in gratitude for an anti-colonial alliance with another Asian country.

Although Booth and Ingham record striking contrasts between their Government House and Hanoi performances of *Dream*, the two events are also similar in reflecting, albeit differently, the beginnings of Shakespeare in Asia. In Government House, where even if some spectators did not understand it linguistically, the play was perfectly understood in conventional cultural terms, Shakespeare's role in colonial culture appeared to be arrested in a time warp, and the residency of colonial government staged the play. In Hanoi, Booth points persistently to the backwardness of the Vietnamese theatrical context for receiving Shakespeare, where lighting design and unamplified speech (in a Western-style performance) were previously unknown, and where "classical" was understood to refer to Greco-Roman culture – an earlier *Othello* in Vietnamese had dressed the characters in Roman armor (2002: 49). For Booth and Ingham, this ignorance of Western theatre signified a condition of innocence for a first encounter with Shakespeare, and it is to this "innocence" that Ingham ascribes *Dream*'s – and Shakespeare's – greater success in Hanoi, a first meeting between Shakespeare and the native, supposedly unburdened by a colonial relationship. But is not that "innocence" a fantasy of the first colonial meeting, where the power of the colonizer's culture (read, Shakespeare's art) is naturalized by staging a native audience who "understands without understanding it"? Explaining the performance's effectiveness in terms of "the total theatricality and integrity of the play" (2002: 36), Ingham cites John Russell Brown's argument that a spectator to whom Shakespeare's language is unfamiliar may penetrate further into "the heart of the mystery" than native English speakers; instead of assuming that to listen to the words is to understand the play, the spectator confronted with foreign words "will have to observe all 'looks' and try to probe to the 'quick' of every reaction" (Brown 1993: 31). The idea of Shakespeare running through these comments is that the performed play transcends, and is transmissible outside of, verbal communication: its dramatic value and power are intrinsic, and come into their own when divorced from colonial "baggage" – including the English (colonial) language. This claim is fundamental to, and tested *in reverse* by, intercultural performance's effect upon its English-speaking audiences, especially those in the West. My concern is not to refute this view, since the issue of non-communication in intercultural theatre is precisely what needs to be examined more closely, but to point out that one cannot exert it as a belief about Shakespeare without implicitly re-measuring the play's greatness by a native reception that is universalized to meet the play's essence. The context of Vietnamese theatre in which this *Dream* took place, as well as the actual audiences' responses, is silent in Booth's and Ingham's accounts, because as Rey Chow writes, "Whether positive or negative, the construction of the native remains at the level of image-identification, a process in which 'our' own identity is measured in terms of the degrees to which we resemble her and to which she resembles us" (1993: 34). Instead, their preoccupation with the naïveté of their Hanoi audience writes Shakespeare's colonial language upon the native's necessarily blank slate. At both venues, what happened was the erasure of the native audience's foreignness through their "understanding" of the play. Despite their sensitivity to the inflection of different occasions and foreign language contexts upon performing English Shakespeare, these accounts cannot extricate Shakespeare from the colonial rationale that locates Shakespeare as a universal value which is not culture-specific – unavoidably, these accounts re-enact the reason why Shakespeare is in Asia in the first place.

Intercultural Performativity

As the first aspect of Shakespeare in Asia, English or generally Western-styled productions make visible the Western cultural imperialism and colonialism that inform Shakespeare's return in foreign form to Western audiences, and which thus also condition those audiences' reception of his return. Although it has been generally accepted that Shakespeare's plays will localize where they have taken root, the recent circulation of Far East productions back to the West re-mobilizes the history of how the plays went out in the first place, testing the proposition of Shakespeare's universality in reverse. What part of another culture's assimilation and transformation of his plays is transmissible back to the culture(s) from which Shakespeare comes? The internationalization of Asian Shakespeares has been growing since the 1980s. Some better-known instances are the *Kathakali King Lear* (1989); the Kunqu Opera Troupe's *Macbeth* (1987); the Nomura School's *kyogen* adaptations (*Hora Zamurai – A Kyogen Falstaff*, 1991; *Kyogen of Errors*, 2001); Ninagawa Yukio's productions (*Ninagawa Macbeth*, 1980; *The Tempest*, 1987; *A Midsummer Night's Dream*, 1994; *Hamlet*, 1995; *King Lear*, 1999; *Pericles*, 2003); Suzuki Tadashi's versions (*The Tale of Lear*, 1984; *The Chronicle of Macbeth*, 1992); Wu Hsing Kuo's Beijing Opera adaptations (*The Kingdom of Desire* (*Macbeth*), 1986; *Li Er Zai Ci* (*King Lear*), 2002); and the multi-cultural productions of Ong Keng Sen (*Lear*, 1997; *Desdemona*, 2000; *Search: Hamlet*, 2002).[1]

Toured rather extensively through Western and Asian capitals, such performances contributed to the recent growth of intercultural theatre, but explanations of what "intercultural" designates as a process, performance, or cultural exchange have not accounted for either their range of approaches or the double or multiple transactions occurring when Shakespeare, adapted in Asian theatre forms, also is designed to address Western(ized) global audiences. Instead of taking the formal and representational transactions as a starting-point, thereby focusing on the director's position as a kind of cultural broker of dubious legitimacy, I take theatrical reception as the primary cultural transaction entailed in intercultural performance: that cultural groups and their relative positions are invested, evoked, and reproduced in a performance. As Susan Bennett argues, and Phillip Zarrilli eloquently illustrates in his detailed explication of *Kathakali King Lear*'s production and reception, very little of the rigorous intercultural process of preparing the performance is accessible or appreciable to an audience (Zarrilli 1992, Bennett 1997). As a public rather than a practitioner's or specialist's event, the intercultural transaction must be situated in its reception. Yet the question of how to read that transaction resists authoritative answers because our reading procedures are themselves implicated by and invested in the performance, which necessarily situates that act of reading as party to a particular position in the transaction. As such, the issue of intercultural transactions between Shakespeare and East Asian theatres imposes a negative, or at least paradoxical, two-part formulation: what role does *not* understanding the stage presentation perform in the intercultural transaction; conversely, how can a spectator relate to what resists access as the foreign in a performance? In order to explore these questions, I shall examine three productions: Ong Ken Sen's *Desdemona* (2000), Ninagawa's *Tempest* (1987) and Wu Hsing Kuo's *Li Er Zai Ci (King Lear)*, 2002). First, however, I want to frame them in terms of a wider sense of intercultural performance.

Although the term "intercultural" refers in some instances to new theatrical practices, it also marks a changed attitude to old ones. As distinct from translation or adaptation, it postulates *performance* as an interaction between cultures: implying at once a principle and an effect of translating or adapting, it refers not to these actions but to an idea informing them. The production or reception of the intercultural posits the value and significance of linguistic translation, formal re-coding, or social re-contextualization on a relationship between cultures that these acts represent. In its simplest form, this cultural interaction directs attention to the originating force of a source text or performance style whose foreignness to a target audience is kept in view. The relation of performance elements from a foreign source to more familiar elements draws the spectator easily into an interaction with that alien culture; correspondingly, a spectator also experiences the familiar in terms of the foreign. This basic scenario becomes complicated when the foreign/familiar opposition is presented from more than one viewpoint: (1) when the production is designed and staged for audiences of both cultures and geographical locations (which are not the same thing); (2) when cosmopolitan audiences in these venues actually occupy or identify in some way with both "foreign" and "familiar" positionalities or are situated outside either; and

(3) when a plurality of texts or styles are used. As these interchangeable viewpoints make themselves felt, the interaction grows more complex, eventually eroding the fundamental dichotomy of "foreign" and "familiar" that it mobilizes.

It is not often recognized that "intercultural performance" depends precisely on a "performative" understanding of "culture" itself, in which culture is basically sustained *by and as performance*, in the overlapping senses of enactment, staging, and efficacy. Onstage, a culture is dramatized by a particular play, theatrical convention, or style with which it is – at least for the duration of the performance – identified. Writing about India, anthropologist Milton Singer calls this "cultural performance," referring to performative practices such as weddings, temple festivals, dances, plays, musical concerts. Summarizing Singer, Erika Fischer-Lichte writes: "a culture articulates its self-image and self-understanding in the cultural performance, which it then represents and exhibits to its members as well as to outsiders" (1997: 16). With media circulation, the tourist industry, and international arts festivals, "cultural performance" as theatre increasingly applies to easily digestible packagings of a culture framed for "outsider" consumers. The distinction needed here with regard to how a culture performs *interculturally* is that for both insiders and outsiders the third sense of culture as performance – its effectiveness, worth, usefulness – becomes dominant where it is measured and staked against another's.

An example occurs towards the end of Ong's *Lear* (1997), in which each major character was played in a different Asian performance style and the performer's own language (except for the Singaporean actors, who had non-speaking parts or performed in Malay). When the Old Man (Lear), played by the *noh* actor Naohiko Umewaka, was stabbed by his Older Daughter (a composite of Goneril and Regan), played by Beijing Opera actor Jiang Qihu, it was not the character's death that constituted the climax but Umewaka's astonishing, heart-stopping dead fall, his body falling straight, face forward onto the stage. This technique, called "falling pine," evoked gasps from the audience, enabling the actor to triumph through the moving power of *noh* performance at the very moment of his character's defeat by patricide. Such formal and dramaturgical choices thereby stage political relations in the global cultural economy. Several Singaporean reviewers read the conflict of the Chinese Older Daughter and Japanese king in *Lear* as a struggle for power between two East Asian super-powers, who dominated the South-east Asian Tigers: the passive Thai Younger Daughter and subservient Indonesian retainers. The ordering of theatrical elements and actors belonging to different cultures presents a metadrama of cultural relations, or, perhaps more appropriately, a dense, undecidable collection of different forms of "intercultural performance." This *Lear* could be seen as re-forming the historical relations between Asian languages and peoples and the Western mastertext represented by Shakespeare – our answer to Peter Brook's *Mahabharata*, as Ong candidly put it (personal communication). Simultaneously – conversely and ironically – the praise *Lear* received for combining disparate Asian theatre styles not only reaffirmed but enhanced Shakespeare's (colonial) status as a universal theatre of shared human experience. As an inter-*Asian* negotiation that required adjustments to all the performance forms adopted, the production framed and tested any one form's cultural and aesthetic values by its passage through multiple, non-binary terms of the foreign. Yet it also exposed Ong and the Japan Foundation, who had commissioned the project, to contestations of appropriating other Asians' cultural property.

The performativity of the intercultural – where elements drawn from different cultures are mutually transformed, contrasted, or hybridized – comes into view if we think of what those who identify with one culture have at stake when performance texts and forms from elsewhere are adopted in their theatres; or when "theirs" are adapted for use elsewhere. This here/there, ours/theirs dialectic has been a crucial performative act of the intercultural, a polarizing effect of contrasting theatres drawn from two cultures, whether West and East, native and foreign, or even near neighbors. One pole of argument is represented by synthesizing a utopian vision of world theatre, the other by contentions of cultural appropriation and inauthentic style (see Bharucha on Brook's *Mahabharata* 1990: 94–120). Yet surely this polemic is a function of the structure of intercultural performance which, even in a hybridized or harmonized relation of elements, achieves its dramatic effect through differentiation – even (perhaps more so) when it takes pains to smooth over differences. Clearly, the intercultural transaction reproduces cultures according to their relational positions and identities in the performance. My point is not that historical, economic, and political bases for cultural polarization do not exist. Rather, an intercultural production's metadrama is performative, not representative, of cultures and our belongings to/in them – that is, since the intercultural performative enacts its audiences' sense of cultural identity, the polemical or reactionary cultural positions that resist being produced in the image of the staged interaction are part of its performativity. Similarly, often it is the absence, modification, or mutation of features of a form or text that perform most powerfully for a spectator, as a lack or "wrongness" introduced by the other culture. The performance presents what can be thought of as the *fiction* of the intercultural: the fictionalization of cultural relations which draws upon the dramatic plot, characters, or subject to stage the metadrama of their means of performance. And the audience's reproduction of their cultural identities, heritage and interests is structural to that metadrama.

Not Understanding Asian Performance

This formulation of intercultural theatre as a performative, not representative, act allows one to recognize that a common problem of non-understanding, or partial understanding – a condition of audience (in)competence across cultures – is part of its performativity, not a problematic crux of its attraction and mobility. When the performance does not fully communicate what is happening, what it is *about*, or allow us to grasp its meaning, it thereby also communicates something else, facilitating another relation of meaning. A productive lack of understanding is not of course unique to this kind of theatre. Beckett's or Pinter's plays, for instance, depend precisely on withholding what a spectator is invited to want to know. Specific to intercultural spectatorship, however, is the experience of non-understanding as a relation not only to the pleasure and meaningfulness of another culture's art but also to the meaning that art makes of *us*. Indeed, a Western audience's fascination with Asian theatre forms depends on just such a lack of understanding. Commenting on Roland Barthes's response to Hopi dances and rituals – "Can we Westerners really consume a fragment of civilization totally isolated from its context?" (1985: 120–1) – Susan Bennett asks:

> How, in any event, do we "really consume"? It is that consuming another's "civiliza-tion," whether consciously or not, presents particular and often fraught concerns. The interest in this not-like-us theatre is apparently especially (only?) its otherness, its seeming inability to be understood (and, as such, to be "really consumed") by conven-tional receptive processes. (1997: 167)

As an assertion of its own performance aesthetic, a Shakespeare production in Asian theatre forms will intentionally obstruct habits of reception and de-coding in Western theatre; but by the same token it is likely – unconsciously, unwillingly, or deliberately – to play into the fascination that adheres to the foreign.

It is in this dilemma of an inability-to-be-understood, which is both necessary and yet prone to (self-)orientalization, that I wish to situate the Asianness that Ong's *Desdemona* (2000) performed in relation to Shakespeare. I watched this production on its home ground, in Singapore, where Ong is the artistic director of the leading local professional theatre company, TheatreWorks, and where it was politely but clearly disliked. *Desdemona* was the second in Ong's intercultural Shakespeare trilogy, all of which adopted a bold inter-Asian strategy of bringing several contrasting perform-ance styles to bear on Shakespeare's plays: *Lear* and *Desdemona* featured only Asian performers; *Search: Hamlet* (2002) shifted ground by including European and Ameri-can performers and staging *Hamlet* at its "origin" in Elsinore. Ong's intercultural style showcased the plurality of Asia through diverse Asian performing arts, traditions, languages, and cultures. *Desdemona* assembled traditional and contemporary practi-tioners from India, Korea, Myanmar, Indonesia, and Singapore, and was, in turn, performed in Adelaide, Munich, Singapore, Hamburg, and Fukuoka. Each of the performers used his or her own language, while supertitles translated the text into the predominant language of the audience at each venue.

Scripted by the Japanese playwright Rio Kishida, known for her feminist subjects, *Lear* and *Desdemona* reversed the dynamics of Shakespeare's plays to centralize the female character (the Older Daughter in *Lear*). Othello was split into two roles: a younger Othello married to Desdemona was played in *kudiyattam* (by Madhu Margi) on a raised main stage, and an ambiguously gendered older Othello alone with his dreams was played by an Indian actress (Maya Rao) in adapted *kathakali*, mostly on an auxiliary stage jutting out towards the audience. Desdemona (Claire Wong) spoke in English and shifted her acting style with each sequence, often in relation to other performers. She too was doubled, by a contemporary correlate, Mona, who was only seen in fragments on a projection screen: her e-mail correspondence was typed out on-screen; images of fruit ("Mona is on a diet" is one episode title) were shown shrinking after each bite; and her magnified, lipsticked mouth ate a long sequence of pills with labels like "dictate," "fabricate," "tolerate," and "hesitate." The first part of the performance focused on reversing what we know of the protagonists' marriage in Shakespeare: by making Othello the colonizer of Desdemona's people, the racial hierarchy was inverted; moreover, the two hated each other from beginning to end. Because their master–slave colonial relationship duplicated their master–slave gender roles, Desdemona was doubly subordinated. These reversals undermined the tragic import of Othello's murder: when he realized in horror, "I have killed my wife," he quickly recovered himself: "She was only a slave meant to bear my children." In the dominance of power relations over human, even sexual relationships, both protagonists were de-humanized, transformed into symbolic masculine or feminine principles. Othello had no memories of his mother, only a family name, "Othello": "my father and my father's father were also called Othello, and when I have a son, he will also be called Othello." Like all her people, Desdemona was not allowed a name, only a number, but she declares to the audience: "I will tell you a secret. My mother gave me a name, my name is Desdemona." The use of Shakespeare's names – an unending line of Othellos and a secret name (that audiences know) – resonated with the characters' self-reflexive projection of their Shakespearean lineage. Ong explains: "I wanted to move away from the . . . obsessive stereotyping of black machismo. What if Othello was played by a woman or by a slight slender boy?" (2001: 126–7). In keeping with this idea, the performance did not present a different racialization of identity – an Othello in whose two selves a spectator could re-identify (one's own) Asianness – but two ways of personifying race as a performance style: Margi's *kudiyattam* style, formalized, dressed in shiny organza, with an unfamiliar, melodic vocal pattern that rose to a high pitch at the end of repeated phrases, was set against Rao's mostly wordless, gestural performance of anger and frustration, erupting in snarls and grunts. Ong's objective was not to present a character, but to challenge the performance of race at its conjunctions with gender.

This metadrama of race and gender was suggestive precisely for the meanings which it obstructed. In general, the gender conflict between the protagonists invited associating Desdemona's position as the oppressed woman with a feminine Asia versus the masculine West of Shakespeare's text. But at every point a spectator's relationship to that opposition was troubled by deflecting engagements with the fictional protagonists onto the metadrama of the theatrical styles with which they were performed (seven performers called "Zero" in the program simply performed their own art or, at times, took minor roles). The central section took Desdemona's words to an absent Othello – "I want a conversation" – as a cue to expand their non-relationship in the narrative into a metadramatic meditation on forms of performance. This substitution was enacted mostly in images on two large upstage screens, projected by two video installation artists who worked either around the main stage's edges or by transforming the stage itself into an installation. Clips of videotaped interviews were screened: Rao spontaneously demonstrated the diverse cultures she belongs to by singing the ditty "Buttercup" followed by a Malayali folk song; a pen writing Sanskrit in close-up was overlaid by a translated interview in voiceover between unseen speakers, one of whom said, "You do not speak my language and I do not speak yours." Documentary clips alternated with installation images: a series of socks – carefully placed one over another on the visualizer, each larger than the one below – to project an image of the foot composed in rings, like a tree-trunk's cross-section. Onstage, the puppet–puppeteer theme was literalized by a Myanmarese puppeteer (U Zaw Min) with a colorful puppet: playful, gleeful interludes turned harsh when the actors, including the puppeteer, imitated the puppet. The overall effect resembled television surfing between Asian channels. A self-reflexive method of juxtaposing performing styles repeatedly enabled one sequence or plane of the performance to interrupt another, on-screen versus on-stage and main versus side stages, producing a fracturing of Asias rather than their interaction. In the final section, Othello, of course, killed Desdemona – who, however, returned as a spirit to take her revenge. This second climax apparently adapted shamanist rites whereby her spirit simultan-eously possessed Othello's body and that of a male slave, who represented Desdemo-na's sword. Desdemona's spirit transformed both the slave and Othello into women dreaming of their lovers; as they kissed, the slave's poisonous saliva flowed into Othello's mouth and killed him (according to Ong, 2001: 127). But it was next to impossible to read this complicated process in performance. Desdemona sat down-stage performing rites few spectators could have recognized as shamanist, while the actor acting as her sword was upstage, gently embracing Othello. For the most part, the climax was driven by the powerful rhythms of the Korean *ajaeng* (a zither played with a bow) and drums.

Ong explicitly states his intention, not to re-tell the story, but to use it as the occasion for re-staging Asian interculturality:

> Desdemona, in her loneliness, states that she wants to speak to Othello. At this moment, we rupture the narrative introducing into it a conversation between individual artists of the company, from different cultures with different histories, memories, and languages. Desdemona's imagination becomes the vehicle through which they reveal their frustrations in communicating, and the attempts to find a common ground for dialogue – the dilemmas of any intercultural enterprise ...
>
> Ultimately, *Desdemona* is a cultural study about a group of Asian artists looking at themselves and rethinking the ways in which Asia has been represented on the stage in the past. (2001: 128–9)

According to Ong, the production presented a self-conscious re-staging of Asia's performances. But by objectifying Asia, he implies that the representations of Asia revised were those made by and/or seen in Western theatres, rather than by other Asians. Especially since it was designed to circulate to the West, *Desdemona* raises a crucial question about staging an Asian intercultural relationship to Shakespeare: how can that re-performance situate or negotiate an Asianness that is always already under Western eyes? The problem of situating a point of view *of* or *within* Asia was accentuated rather than resolved by presenting multiple Asian performances; the many "Asias" questioned what part a spectator's sense of his or her own Asianness could take in a re-performance of Asia through Shakespeare. Instead of offering different Asians' views of *Othello*, the performance's plurality simultaneously fragmented a relationship to *Othello* and self-understandings of "being Asian." Unlike *Lear*'s performance forms, more familiar and readily identified as national traditions, *Desdemona* adopted forms that presented the sharpest possible juxtapositions of Asian cultures: the ancient art of *kudiyattam* against avant-garde installation; the most remote form of puppetry against the popular, hip images of Mona. Most Asians in *Desdemona*'s audiences inhabit Asias somewhere in between these opposite extremes. The performance did not enact an *intercultural* process in the sense of an interaction between Asians, but a radical rejection of the intercultural proposition, where different Asias were presented as dissonant and contradictory. *Desdemona* refused entry into a narrative or imaginary coherence of Asian identity by presenting fragments, and by obstructing an engagement through which one could write oneself into the story-performance of Asia. As a result of unfamiliarity on one hand, and the fracturing of the scene on the other, it staged – or imposed – a kind of non-understanding upon its Asian spectators that can be seen as an inverse reflection of the non-understanding that has constituted the appeal of Asian theatres – and the cultures represented therein – for Western spectators.

Desdemona failed to produce a sense of belonging to extreme and divided Asias for spectators split between their traditions and the present, separated from each other by gulfs between their cultures. Rather, those conflicts staged the spectator as a non-identity between poles that were either unfamiliar or estranging (as in the case of Mona), and hence the Asian spectator was dispossessed and alienated from both, with neither a position between to stitch them together nor an understanding of where to stand in relation to past, present, or other Asias. "Our" ability to relate to, to re-make, the colonial text was dramatized as a shattered mirror whose image-making could not form a coherent picture of ourselves as a version of Shakespeare. In *Lear*, the Older Daughter sang after killing her lover the Retainer (Edmund): "The mirror has been broken. It has shattered into many pieces" (The Japan Foundation: Scene 17:2). *Desdemona* performed the otherness of Asia to itself in two ways. It performed at once the shattering of our self-images as the beautiful, exoticizable other to the West, and at the same time, the loss of cultural identity and wholeness in origins to which there was no possibility of returning. And so *Desdemona* was nowhere met with such hostility as "at home." Reviewer Ong Sor Fern felt insulted and "dictated to":

> TheatreWorks' Desdemona is symptomatic of what I call the theatrical equivalent of the Emperor's New Clothes Syndrome. It is a postmodern con-job perpetuated by theatre-goers' unwillingness to look uncultured in the face of artistic flim-flamming. When an

artist goes for the jugular by remaking a text so drastically, I expect to be rewarded with at least a Frankenstein's monster, not a wan corpse drained of all signs of life. With Desdemona, I got a whole load of little body parts dressed up in pretty trimmings, but no monstrous whole to make me challenge the text or the themes that were served up so haphazardly. (2000)

The production disintegrated the spectacle, beauty, and ritual which Asian theatres are expected to offer in place of the understanding, interiority and psychological drama of Shakespeare's characters. *Desdemona* rejected all those attributes that marked the success of the earlier *Lear*, by which Asianized Shakespeare takes on and reflects its self-identity as other to the West. The range of performance styles here no longer signalled the common cultural traditions of "Asia"; instead of presenting an opacity which promises the organic wholeness of the other to the "outsider" or of the "self" to the "insider," Ong's stylistic mélange finally refused any entry into any Asia by the presentation of surfaces, skins, screened images, and close-ups of body parts and wooden puppet parts.

Viewed through its obstruction of an Asian understanding of Shakespeare, *Desdemona* has several implications for the fiction of the intercultural. Its re-imaging of an Asianness seen by Western eyes could not escape self-display and self-degradation in the objectifying view of itself as the oriental native – a passive, female image. So Desdemona's central struggle for emancipation – as woman, as Asia – was travestied by the present-day Mona, whose magnified diets and lipsticked mouth dramatized her self-objectification as an object of "beauty." *Desdemona* foregrounded the East–West binary wherein the staging of an Asian view of Shakespeare is undermined by historical subject–object positions, in which it is Asia that is to be re-performed and looked at, not Shakespeare. By obstructing how to look at oneself "as Asian," it challenged the fundamental notion that culture *can* be performed: neither language nor action, form nor aesthetics, enabled the spectator to participate in the spectacle by identifying with the enabling fiction of a comfortable cultural positionality. Yet at the same time, this inefficacy of the intercultural process in Asia was ironically effective as an intercultural strategy marketed along the global theatre festival trade route. Its avant-garde mixture of multi-media and traditional forms showcased the sophistication of Asian intercultural performance for European audiences. Nele-Marie Brudgam wrote in the *Hamburger Morgenpost*: "Only a person who was an absolute specialist in Asian cultures could 'understand' the show in the narrow sense of the word. All the others – that means the large majority of the audience – could only feel this Desdemona and let themselves be impressed by it. Whoever was open to the experience felt tragedy, dreams and beauty" (2000). The contrast between "global" and "local" receptions demonstrates how audiences are implicated differently in the performativity of Asianness, depending on what they have at stake. But different as they seem, both global and local receptions foreground the imperatives of the festival market where Asianness, stylistic eclecticism, and the drama of cultural projection are of more interest than what these features say about the societies from which they come. So for all the effects of orientalization that it reveals, the point of view from which *Desdemona*'s Asianness still performs efficaciously is located in the arena of its cosmopolitan, internationalized audiences.

Authenticating Foreignness

Anthony Tatlow writes: "Every engagement with a Shakespearean text is necessarily intercultural. The past really is another culture, its remoteness disguised by language that can occasionally appear as familiar as we seem to ourselves, whom we understand so imperfectly" (2001: 5). His statements call attention to the self-consciousness demanded of any group position – a *we* – for responding to intercultural Shakespeare. For not only are there audiences for whom that language is not a disguise but the hallmark of Shakespeare's remoteness, or a sign of their acculturation through a *colonial* past, the *we* to whom Shakespeare's language is intermittently familiar are evidently made up of several positions of reception, of disparate cultures that *each of us* partially occupies, and of affiliations that may be incommensurate with one another. Intercultural theatre may evoke the fantasy of essentialized cultural identities as separable terrains, with discrete ways of life named and placed by national or linguistic boundaries. But *a priori* its project of bridging cultures involves a spectator in intermingling, partial identifications and alienations that are porous to one another, dynamically related by the mobility of people and media. In short, the performance appeals to and re-stages one's belongings in – and estrangements from – a sense of cultural identity, ownership and authenticity. The question I wish to pose is: how does Shakespeare's relation to foreignness – the signature innovation and interest of intercultural strategies – animate the disparities of a spectator's partial, occasional attachments to cultures? The negotiations between "Shakespeare" and "Japanese culture" would be different for each spectator at a Ninagawa performance, yet each spectator is negotiating the same terrain. Overtly intercultural strategies invoke an awareness that the subjective response is not simply personal but is implicated in the relativity of the group – that is, in the cultural values that shape taste, expectation, and perceptions of meaningfulness. On one hand these strategies can impose a sense of the insufficiency of a system of meaning and appreciation by which one relates to Shakespeare, perhaps exposing a given point of view as culturally chauvinistic. On the other, the proliferation of Shakespeares now accessible in a metropolitan center through which intercultural productions tour, and where popular (as well as canonical and foreign) film versions are available in multiple formats, has familiarized a notion of the composite cultural identity of both Shakespearean drama and the Shakespearean spectator. Intercultural performance plays to two apparently contrasting ways of understanding – and even seeing – Shakespeare across cultures: as a plenitude centered in the text, which is taken as a stable entity that is refracted and enriched by the performance forms and perspectives of other cultures (whereby its universality is enlarged); and as a de-centering foreignness, a strategic disruption of

"Shakespearean" meanings, and of the cultural power they evoke, through the deployment of a performance system that challenges the integrity, identity and singularity of "Shakespeare." As *Desdemona* illustrates, intercultural theatre may re-perform the historical conflicts that inaugurated and continue to enable the co-habitation of Shakespeare and his audiences in different cultures. And yet, those conflicts are reproduced to cater to the cosmopolitanism and festivalization of performance arts for an internationalized audience "community," whose cultural belongings are several, intermittent, incomplete.

The point of contact that intercultural Shakespeare performance now offers between theatre cultures of the Far East and the West has a compelling historical motivation. It is a counteraction by Asian practitioners to theatre traditions in their countries that are based on imported Western dramatic models: *shingeki* in Japan, *huaju* in China, or English drama in the British colonies (see Mulryne 1988, Zhang 1996, Brandon 1997, Fischer-Lichte 1997, Minami 2001, Li 2004). It is thus a reply to Westernization and its prerogatives, such as the status of Western culture, or the representation of modern humanity and society. But it is also a re-formulation of the mutual implication of Shakespeare's universality and the foreign in each other: whereas Shakespeare's universal text is constructed by at once designating and erasing *its own foreignness* to Asian audiences (as in the Hong Kong Players' accounts of how *Dream* worked in that setting), in contrast, the foreign is an entailment of that universality when mobilized in the reverse direction, as the export of Asian Shakespeares to the West. Nakane Tadao, Ninagawa Yukio's producer, asserts:

> Even if a production of Shakespeare is created in an Asian culture, it can be a genuinely persuasive piece of theatre for Europeans. Ninagawa's *Tempest* can be set on Sado island in the Sea of Japan and still be real Shakespeare. When we brought our *Tempest* to England, it was seen as universal. I simply wanted to demonstrate the universality of his production. (Minami et al. 2001: 212)

Asian performance presents the legacy and return of Shakespeare's universality, and I place my reading of Ninagawa's *Tempest* (1987) as a moment in that return, witnessed along the international trade route of Shakespeare performance from a vantage point that is neither English nor Japanese, but between them, with an Asian postcolonial stake both in the Shakespeare inherited through British education and in how other Asians re-make his plays.

Although Ninagawa worked closely with the translated text of the play, his tactic for making the play look Japanese, unlike the Westernized styling conventional of *shingeki* Shakespeare, was to present it as a rehearsal on one of the derelict *noh* stages on Sado island (where the *noh* master Zeami was exiled in the fifteenth century):

> I thought [it] would reduce the incongruity of the play being done in Japanese. If we set it during a rehearsal, we would be signaling our pretence. We wouldn't need blond hair. Everything would overlap between play and rehearsal. We could remain Japanese but

suggest Miranda or Prospero in any style of clothing. It would be a sort of play within a play. (Minami et al. 2001: 213)

Regarding the framing: the performance opened with the house lights on, as the actors seated in front of a *noh* stage-within-a-stage preparing their performance and a stage-hand hammered nails into it. This *noh* platform set on the proscenium stage composed the scene in inner and outer layers, similar to the levels of dramatic power and knowledge in Prospero's play-within-a-play. Replicating the traditional *noh* stage as well as the imaginary setting on Sado island, it appeared exposed on three sides by opening onto a seascape painted on the backdrop, enabling musicians and actors who were not performing to sit watching at the sides of the main stage. The flow of dramatic action was punctuated by closing off this inner stage with panels carried on from the walkway in a revolving motion and slotted into place at its edges; the sequence was reversed for opening it again. This repeated ceremony of opening and closing the *noh* stage, combined with the actors' movements up onto and down from it, formed a rhythm of scene change and shifts between different levels of the action. The spatial and rhythmic ordering of the performance through the stage-within-a-stage prompted the audience to recognize an inner layer in the action that was simultaneously a foreign place (Sado island) and the traditional stage of Japanese theatre. The *noh* stage was used as the inner circle of Prospero's magic but also to showcase Caliban, Trinculo and Stephano's *kyogen*-style routine (3.1).

Ninagawa's intercultural strategy was to layer different theatrical styles, making elements of distinct Japanese theatre forms legible in relation to Shakespeare's translated text by intercalating scenography, acting styles and music. The courtiers wore brightly colored kimonos as loose robes over their business suits; synthesizer and guitar music were interwoven with traditional *noh* clappers and chanting (*utai*); Caliban had an amphibian's tail attached and Ariel wore a *noh* mask, which he removed at times, revealing his face. Although the acting generally adopted a heightened psychological mode, it shifted to a *noh*-like presentational formality when enacting the play's magic: when Prospero cast a webbing with his wand to freeze Ferdinand's sword or when Ariel hovered above the stage, making a drumming motion with his hands, rhythmically punctuating his intervention in the action below (1.2) while a musician at the side did the actual drumming. In a continuum of constantly changing mixtures and transitions, this layering had the effect of producing two or more theatrical dimensions – and thus cultural planes – within the same character or scene. Its intercultural performativity consisted in moving the spectator in and out between a more familiar relation to the event and a sense of its strangeness and remoteness, between identification and alienation. The *noh* stage was both a rustic picture on the proscenium stage – complete with thatch roof, plantings, and a tree on which Miranda and Ferdinand perched to watch their betrothal masque – and a formal inner stage for moments of *noh* performance. The space was simultaneously representational and presentational of a Japanese *Tempest*, just as Prospero was both character and director in the performance. Ariel shifted from a mysterious figure in white concealed beneath the *noh* head-covering to the familiar boyish sprite: when he removed his mask, his acting style changed accordingly. He altered again when he emerged with the mask, "flying" in measured slowness, unlike the quickness associated with Ariel (who does his tasks "Before you can say, 'come,' and 'go,'" (4.1.44). In such passages between foreign and familiar Shakespeare, the spectator crossed between responses to a range of Japanese theatrical styles, from the ceremonial to burlesque, the mysterious to the melodramatic, traversing not an opposition of East to West but elastic proximities and distances between them that folded familiar over foreign, articulating the span of one's cultural compass.

The blending of traditional and contemporary performance elements from Japanese and world cultures in this *Tempest* formed a dense *mise en scène* that acted like a second text to the translated text of the play, a performance text composed of music, spectacle and the shifting layers of its formal elements. The relationship of foreign performance to translated text rested on the ambivalent link provided by the *shingeki* style of acting. *Shingeki* is the tradition of "authentic" Shakespeare performance in Japan, in which staging and production values were founded on and authorized as "true copies" of English productions. Minami Ryuta argues that since the translated text in performance is much more unstable than it is in English, the burden of authentication was carried by the performance style in *shingeki* Shakespeare (2001: 11–12). The more successful productions were publicized as imitations of specific English performances staged in London at the Old Vic, or at the Gaiety Theatre in the foreign settlement of Yokohama by touring English companies. By using *shingeki*-style acting, Ninagawa's *Tempest* incorporated its own origins in the English performance history and colonial agency of Shakespeare, re-situating that earlier relationship to Shakespeare by deploying the other form of the authentic that has nourished so much intercultural theatre: the pre-modern performance forms of a foreign culture.

The Tempest typically invites an intercultural reading because its magic and island setting outside Europe seem to enact an encounter with the foreign. Ninagawa's production, however, turned postcolonial readings of the play inside out by presenting not the island or its natives as a non-Western terrain encountered by the European explorer, but the play itself in rehearsal, as a sophisticated production being made by non-Europeans. In a kind of prologue that took place while preparations for the performance proper were still in progress, three of the actors performed alternately as dancers and drummers on an enormous drum, wearing masks and voluminous white wigs, flicking their hair with small sticks when they danced. This wordless interlude was unrelated to the subsequent *Tempest* and framed it by creating a liminal performance space, between on- and off-stage of the *Tempest*, in another theatre and hence for another audience. The percussion's rhythms and the formalized costumes and dance movements resembled a foreign ritual, native somewhere else, obviously encoding the customs of an alien culture that could not be understood by an outsider here – so every venue outside Japan was rendered an elsewhere. Followed by a dance that was similar to the Chinese lion dance, the prologue was tribal but sophisticated. As a tactic that destabilized a Westernized viewpoint for watching Shakespeare, it preempted ques-

tions of natives and nature (as well as culture and nature) which *The Tempest* dramatizes by implying a mirroring of the play from the other side, where the natives were
not discovered by but introduced the action. The production utilized Japanese theatre
as foreign ritual not only to ironize the native's status within the play but to stage the
spells cast by Prospero's magic. The banquet offered to the courtiers by strange figures
(3.3) was a processional, dream-like ceremony in which *noh* performers brought trays
of food to the edge of the inner stage. Small vases of flowers were evenly spaced in two
parallel diagonal lines on the outer stage. As prolonged chords on the synthesizer
swelled, the figures descended the stairs, each taking a courtier by the hand in a
trance-like dance of welcome. In the ritualization of formal clothing, movement,
gesture, without words but with music, Prospero's magic – and by extension the art of
Shakespeare with whom Prospero is habitually associated – became the magic of
Japanese theatre. Thus, the feature of pre-modern Asian theatres that has most
fascinated Western audiences, the aura of another culture as a foreign ritual, appropriated and transposed Shakespeare's creative power and vision, the heart of his
universality.

Ninagawa's intercultural strategies have often been criticized as a Japanese styling
and exoticism targeted at Western or global festival consumption. Dennis Kennedy
quotes John Peter (*Sunday Times*, September 8, 1996) on Ninagawa's *Midsummer
Night's Dream* (1994): it is "Shakespeare in Japanese but it is not really Japanese
Shakespeare" (2001: 323). Rather than engaging the question of what would qualify –
to whom – as "really Japanese Shakespeare" (see Anzai 2001), the more significant
question to ask is how this reiterated call for Shakespeare's authentic foreign identity
is related to the rise of intercultural performance. More specifically, what does the
intercultural performative enact that prompts its spectators to make distinctions
between real and fake foreignness? For although we recognize that any theatre project
involving texts or forms drawn from more than one culture entails their modification,
intercultural practice and reception seem paradoxically unable to validate that modification, whether as hybridization, shared theatrical language, or cultural dialogue –
in short, to justify the liberal ideals of the term *intercultural*, which, contradictorily,
discloses or exacerbates an anxiety over authenticity and authentication. Of Ninagawa's *Tempest*, Kennedy writes:

> the components of noh, kyogen, and kabuki were inauthentic or significantly adapted.
> Ninagawa had created a synthetic or artificial Japan parallel to that Mnouchkine had
> created a few years earlier. For both directors, a predominantly visual approach was
> based on the freedom to mix and match: culture for them is a matter of aesthetic choice,
> not something ingrained or predetermined. (2001: 319)

Clearly, the anxiety is that of being turned into a tourist who is sold a replica for the
real thing: presumably, Shakespeare truly assimilated into a foreign country and its
performance traditions. But is not the desire to find the "authentic" foreign art in the
Shakespeare that returns in some way a re-statement of what the Hong Kong Players'

accounts mark as a desire for the unspoilt native's appreciation of the "true" Shakespeare? For Shakespeare still functions as the measure of authentic human experience, the universality of which enables transferring his genuineness, trueness, legitimacy onto an experience of foreign authenticity. Ninagawa's apparent fidelity to Shakespeare's text is emphasized by the fact that it is heard in Japanese, and so provides the reassurance as well as attraction of a foreign Shakespeare's genuine return.[2] Yet as Kennedy also reminds us,

> Shakespeare is foreign to all of us ... In English the language will always be important to our appreciation, yet our ability to reach the plays directly in their original language lessens year by year ... Reflecting on performances outside of English, we can see more clearly how Shakespeare is alien, as well as what we continue to find indigenous or domestic about him. What is it that endures when he is deprived of his tongue? It's a question that will haunt the future. (2001: 16–17)

Acting Foreign Shakespeare

If the performativity of the intercultural depends on the productive use of forms of non-understanding and foreignness exerted by formal and stylistic strategies, these necessarily make their effect through the tension with their opposite: the moments of familiarity and recognition, and the forms of self-identification, that are correspondingly animated in an audience, if as equally unfulfilled. Of the various roles that an audience's understanding and identification can play in Asian intercultural productions of Shakespeare, the recognition of performance elements that one has prior knowledge or experience of has often been enacted by identifying the inappropriate or jarring use of those elements, thereby directing attention to a production's misrepresentation of the culture it invokes. But such a preoccupation with the authentic – or, more accurately, inauthentic – performances of one's own and others' cultures has regularly taken for granted the most common identification shared by audiences of Shakespeare across different reception contexts: identifying with a character/actor through whom one experiences the play/performance. I want now to shift away from intercultural theatre styles in order to situate an audience's non-understanding and perceptions of foreignness at their conjunction with how an audience relates to an actor's realization of his or her role.

Created by English performance history, the idea of the great Shakespearean actor who embodies and carries Shakespeare's art, and its significance outside native English-speaking contexts, resembles and is simultaneously distinguished from its importance within them. For Asian audiences as for those elsewhere, how the play's roles are acted defines the immediacy, relevance and presence of the dramatic action. By realizing some part of the potential immanent in the scripted role, a "Shakespearean" actor is distinguished by so convincingly embodying his role(s) as to be identifiable, by extension, with Shakespeare. Yet the idea of this actor is predominantly of a quintessentially English one, and this Englishness marks the non-English actor's embodiment of Shakespeare's roles with the sign of difference. When the actor is not only non-English but non-Caucasian and thus physically implausible in a European role like Hamlet, the interculturality of enactment extends beyond textual translation, beyond the metatheatrical layer produced by a strategic casting of race and gender (see Goodman 1993: 206–26), to the translation of performance forms, codes and conventions through which the character and, in turn, the play may be transformed by a different performance culture. One extreme form of propriety towards the Englishness of Shakespeare was the imitation or mimicry of it in Japan and China, using doublet and hose, wigs and false noses, as well as acting styles to re-create and re-form English performance culture and actual productions (see Fischer-Lichte 1997, Minami 2001, Li 2004). Conversely, the counter-performance of Shake-speare's roles in non-Western acting styles now represents an explicit relation to being non-English and non-white, as in Ong's *Desdemona*, where styles incommensurable with Shakespeare's own intercultural characters are not concealed but foregrounded. Intercultural actors perform beyond the limits of translation, where the performer's body exerts an untranslatable presence through ethnic features, skin color, vocal patterns, "body language" and acting repertoire conditioned by non-Western theatre forms. What is a great Shakespearean actor in an intercultural context? Is that possible?

Of course. Consider Wu Hsing-Kuo's Beijing Opera solo performance of *King Lear* for Taipei's Contemporary Legend Theatre (of which he is artistic director and co-founder), titled *Li Er Cai Zi* (*Lear Is Here*, 2002) as an instance suggestive of bifurcations of intercultural embodiment in the relationship between the actor's foreign art and Shakespeare's play. Wu scripted, directed and acted Lear, his three daughters, the Fool, Kent, Edmund, Gloucester and Edgar. Dressed in a magnificent costume and with a long white beard, he opened *Li Er Cai Zi* as the mad Lear "in high rage" (3.1.296) in the storm scene, a performance translation that matched the intensity of Lear's drama with the full tilt of Beijing Opera's heightened physical expression, dance and athleticism. Here, Wu took the high road often expected of Shakespearean performance translation, using the power of a different classical per-formance tradition to restyle Shakespeare's character with an equal force of complexity and richness. Evoking a memory of Lear in Shakespeare's play and exhilarating as spectacle, the scene (lasting half an hour) was a *tour-de-force* display that expressed distracted fury and hurt, childish delirium and regal self-assertion. Performed almost wordlessly, its stylized vocabulary dramatized Lear's states of mind, with a rhythmic development structured by music and percussion in sequences of pauses, shifts, and climaxes – one, a backwards fall, a dangerous move that drew appreciative applause. While an audience unfamiliar with the opera form might not read the gestural codes clearly – and thus not recognize the extent to which he was changing them – Wu's performance clearly enough referred to scenes of *King Lear* to allow a spectator familiar with it to interpret Beijing Opera's vocabulary according to a remembered Lear, as in a sequence when he removed a shoe or another with imaginary flowers in his hair. In a highly subjective and variable process, then, a spectator's prior experience of cultural forms comes to bear on interpreting foreign ones. One way of explaining why Shakespeare has been a popular choice for intercultural productions is that the widely accepted shared humanity of his plays continues to offer terms in which another culture is able to translate itself, despite how the universality of such terms has been historically constructed.

Embodying *King Lear* in another performance form was only fully realized in this scene, after which Wu's strategies for separating the actor from his role disengaged his enactment of them as cultural performance. After a long, still pause lying on his back, he sat up, slowly removing his long white hair and beard to reveal his crew-cut head. He spoke quietly and reflectively while holding the hair-pieces at arm's length:

> I have come back – an act more difficult than becoming a monk and forsaking one's family.
>
> Who is he? (*addresses the beard*) Does anyone know him? (*to audience*) He is not Li Er. (*to beard*) Where is Li Er? Does Li Er walk? Does Li Er speak? (*standing*) Where are his eyes? (*rubbing make-up from his face*) His flesh is rotten, his sense is dull, is he still conscious? (*catches his throat in his hand*).

The moment, defined by the physical disparity of the Chinese actor to the essentialized image of Lear signified by the white beard, presents the split between the actor and the character he has embodied – as Lear he had earlier also asked the audience, "Who can tell me who I am? My name is Li Er." As Wu smeared his facial paint he looked at the white hair as if into a mirror, or at a puppet, held in his hand with increasing tension till he appeared to strangle himself in a struggle with the character. Yet his echo of *King Lear* 2.1 produced a startling metatheatrical circle of undoing and re-creating his performance in the previous scene. He now performed himself, Wu Hsing-Kuo the Beijing Opera actor, who is not Lear, *at the same time* re-enacting Lear's displacement from his royal identity as King. The two roles and selves acted in tandem as reflections of each other, built on distinct yet mutually informing histories of self-alienation. Prior to this production, Wu had closed Contemporary Legend Theatre for two years due to funding problems, and *Li Er Cai Zi* represented his return to take up the standard of Beijing Opera, whose survival in the face of dwindling audiences and funding remains uncertain. In returning to the artistic kingdom that is his lineage and identity, he paralleled Lear, but as he folded his costume his role was projected towards a fate different from Lear's:

> Who can tell me who I am? (*removes costume*) Who knows who I am? (*folds costume*) My country, my wisdom, and my power all forsake me. I have come back. I am who I was before, myself now, as well as my future self. I return to my own post, a breakthrough more noble than becoming a monk. I have come back.

Holding the costume in a pile on the last line, he bowed low to the audience he addressed, and Taiwanese audiences were reportedly moved to tears while they applauded. What was being performed here was at once a personal history and the legacy of Beijing Opera with which Wu identifies. Although this localized meaning was identified (with) by Taipei audiences, the production's international circulation was also predicated on audience identifications in widening concentric circles: with the difficult position and extraordinary art of the Beijing Opera actor, with the (foreign) actor's relationship to Shakespeare's great roles, and with the survival of two great performance traditions. In effect, a spectator was asked to relate to Lear and Wu at once through the displacement of each from their roles, whereby the human being outside both was implied.

In juxtaposing Lear and Wu, the performative fictions of the iconic universal character and the dazzling oriental actor were re-framed against each other. Yet the questions this double enactment posed were ultimately concerned less with cultural identity than with cultural authority. Wu's role-playing of nine characters demon-strated the sovereignty of his theatrical command of the repertoire and resources of Beijing Opera role types (actors are traditionally trained to specialize in one). His metamorphoses from one character to the next, with minimal costume changes that quickly suggested a new character and a marked shift of performance style, were highlighted performative moments that celebrated the power and pleasure of the opera form's theatrical role-play. If such moments invested the authority to play characters from another culture in the actor's theatrical eminence, they also divested the characters of the authorizing presence of cultural embodiment by repeatedly dissembling and dissolving character into role. I do not mean to suggest that Wu's transformations had the effect of disembodied cultural form and gesture reduced to role-play; rather, the performativity of Beijing Opera role-types deployed by Wu corresponded with *King Lear*'s representative value rather than its narrative force. The long second Act of *Li Er Cai Zi* graphically illustrated how Shakespeare's cultural value and authority tend to be reproduced in terms of iconic key moments that encapsulate his characters, which are expanded and foregrounded over the narrative as an invocation of cultural memory. The effects of Wu's playing of Beijing Opera role types emerge repeatedly in recent Asian intercultural productions of Shakespeare. First, embodying a character as a dynamic relation with the playing of that role in another theatrical convention often converged to re-create role-playing within the play: for instance, Wu's female impersonation of the *hua dan* (flower woman) role parodied the false femininity of Regan. Secondly, his performance emphasized the appreciation and value invoked for Shakespeare's characters or Beijing Opera role types in their roles in cultures. Finally, abstracting character into a corresponding role in another form enabled performative equivalences not only within that form but also in the personal and social spheres that motivate re-performances of Shakespeare. In the programme, Wu asks, "Why adapt *King Lear*?" – and then answers:

Because Lear threw a sudden bomb into the apparently peaceful society and harmonious family life... The bombshell is capable of exposing human hypocrisy, and is also capable of destroying the tombstone that has been prepared for traditional Chinese theatre. I believed that there were many like me who still believe that traditional Chinese Theatre still has a life of its own. (Wu 2003: 18)

The ready association by which Wu equates Lear's destructive division of his kingdom with the impact he hoped his re-creation of the play would have on the cultural drifts that are burying traditional Chinese theatre can be thought of as a homologic principle animating each of the intercultural productions of Shakespeare I have discussed. By displacing Shakespeare's text into cultural forms in which his work and status are implicated through the history of his introduction into Asian cultures, each of these productions mobilizes fictions of the intercultural as the terms through which a spectator re-authorizes his or her cultural identity. Shakespeare is now a trade route, an international stage on which the partialness of our cultural identities, and the history of their collocations, is dramatized. What survives of Shakespeare without his language is how he has come to represent our need to recover, at the same time as we reject, the original. And it is the loss of, and need for, an authentic cultural identity that, finding a stage in Shakespeare's universality, constitute the signature of his intercultural performance.

NOTES

1 Dates refer to the initial production; many have been subsequently revived.

2 In Ninagawa's recent *Pericles* (2003), Japanese dialogue is ironically authenticated by being translated back into the original in supertitles.

REFERENCES AND FURTHER READING

Anzai, Tetsuo (2001). "What Do We Mean by 'Japanese' Shakespeare?" In Minami Ryuta, Ian Carruthers, & John Gillies (eds.) *Performing Shakespeare in Japan*. Cambridge: Cambridge University Press, pp. 17–20.

Barthes, Roland (1985). "How to Spend a Week in Paris: 8–14 October 1979." In Marshall Blonsky (ed.) *In Signs*. Baltimore, MD: Johns Hopkins University Press.

Bennett, Susan (1997). *Theatre Audiences*, 2nd edn. London: Routledge.

Bharucha, Rustom (1990). "Peter Brook's 'Mahabharata': A View from India." In Rustom Bharucha *Theatre and the World*. New Delhi: Manohar Publications, pp. 94–120.

Booth, David (2002). "Preparing Shakespeare's Texts for the Stage." In Kwok-Kan Tam, Andrew Parkin, & Terry Siu-han Yip (eds.) *Shakespeare Global/Local: The Hong Kong Imaginary in Transcultural Production*. Frankfurt: Peter Lang, pp. 43–54.

Brandon, James (1997). "Some Shakespeare(s) in Some Asia(s)." *Asian Studies Review* 20, 3: 1–34.

Brown, John Russell (1993). "Foreign Shakespeare and English-Speaking Audiences." In Dennis Kennedy (ed.) *Foreign Shakespeare*. Cambridge: Cambridge University Press, pp. 21–35.

Brudgam, Nele-Marie (2000). *Hamburger Morgenpost*, July 14.

Chow, Rey (1993). "Where Have All the Natives Gone?" In Rey Chow *Writing Diaspora*. Bloomington, IN: Indiana University Press, pp. 27–54.

Fischer-Lichte, Erika (1997). *The Show and the Gaze of Theatre: A European Perspective*. Iowa City: University of Iowa Press.

Goodman, Lizbeth (1993). "Women's Alternative Shakespeares and Women's Alternatives to Shakespeare in Contemporary British Theater." In Marianne Novy (ed.) *Cross-Cultural Performances*. Urbana, IL: University of Illinois Press, pp. 206–26.

Ingham, Mike (2002). "Shakespeare in Asian English-Language Productions." In Kwok-Kan Tam, Andrew Parkin, & Terry Siu-han Yip (eds.) *Shakespeare Global/Local: The Hong Kong Imaginary in Transcultural Production*. Frankfurt: Peter Lang, pp. 29–42.

The Japan Foundation (1997). *Lear* (Japan production). Unpublished manuscript.

Kennedy, Dennis (1993). "Introduction: Shakespeare Without His Language." In Dennis Kennedy (ed.) *Foreign Shakespeare*. Cambridge: Cambridge University Press, pp. 1–18.

Kennedy, Dennis (2001). *Looking at Shakespeare*, 2nd edn. Cambridge: Cambridge University Press.

Li, Ruru (2004). *Shashibiya: Staging Shakespeare in China*. Hong Kong: Hong Kong University Press.

Minami, Ryuta (2001). "What Happened to Shingeki Shakespeare? The Replacement of an 'Authentic' Shakespeare on the Japanese Stage." In Harry Aveling & Ian Carruthers (eds.) *Performing Shakespeare in Asia* (*La Trobe Asian Studies Papers Research Series* 9). Bundoora, Victoria: La Trobe University, pp. 10–17.

Minami, Ryuta, Carruthers, Ian, & Gillies, John (eds.) (2001). Interview with Ninagawa Yukio. In *Performing Shakespeare in Japan*. Cambridge: Cambridge University Press, pp. 208–19.

Mulryne, J. R. (1988). "Introduction." In Sasayama Takashi, J. R. Mulryne, & Margaret Shewring (eds.) *Shakespeare and the Japanese Stage*. Cambridge: Cambridge University Press.

Ong, Keng Sen (2001). "Encounters." *TDR: The Drama Review* 45, 3: 126–33.

Ong, Sor Fern (2000). "Moaning Desdemona." *The Straits Times Interactive: Singapore Arts Festival 2000*, June 3.

Shakespeare, William (1997). *The Riverside Shakespeare*, ed. G. Blakemore Evans. Boston: Houghton Mifflin.

Singer, Milton (ed.) (1959). *Traditional India: Structure and Change*. Philadelphia, PA: American Folklore Society.

Tatlow, Anthony (2001). *Shakespeare, Brecht, and the Intercultural Sign*. Durham, NC: Duke University Press.

Wu, Hsing-Kuo (2003). "Here is Lear," trans. Lee Chee Keng. Program booklet for Singapore performance.

Zarrilli, Phillip (1992). "For Whom is the King a King? Issues of Intercultural Production, Perception, and Reception in a *Kathakali King Lear*." In Janelle G. Reinelt & Joseph G. Roach (eds.) *Critical Theory and Performance*. Ann Arbor, MI: University of Michigan Press, pp. 16–40.

Zhang, Xiao Yang (1996). *Shakespeare in China*. Newark, NJ: University of Delaware Press/London: Associated University Presses.

FILMOGRAPHY

Desdemona (2000). TheatreWorks Videorecording of Adelaide production.

Li Er Cai Zi (2003). Contemporary Legend Theatre. Videorecording of Singapore performance.

29

Guying the Guys and Girling The Shrew: (Post)Feminist Fun at Shakespeare's Globe

G. B. Shand

Induction

Pondering cross-dressed performance brings back long-suppressed sensations of a "Bathing Beauty Contest" performed by Skippy and his fellow Boy Scouts some 50 years ago for an annual Father and Son Banquet. I was perhaps 12. Somewhere in the family archives, there used to be a photograph of us, a row of cross-dressed conscripts in fetching rope wigs and lumpy girls' swimsuits, the tops all stuffed with socks and Kleenex, the bottoms quite obviously stuffed with us. We variously simpered and smirked and smiled and sulked. We all wore ribbon-sashes over our shoulders, sporting such mirth-inducing monikers as Miss Behavior, Miss Take, Miss Demeanor, Miss Conduct, Miss Adventure. As far as I can remember, there was no Miss Ogyny. We came onstage one by one, strutted for the dads and leaders, who were falling off their chairs at our funny names and our gawky girlishness, and then we lined up for the judging – bathed, I would guess, in the warmth of the male gaze. Much detail has faded into the Land of Forget, but I don't think I won. I do, however, remember a certain frisson of blushing confusion at being told later (but by *whom?*) that I was the most convincing girl in the show!

I never heard that the Girl Guides did anything comparable.

I also never noticed that the experience was empowering. Indeed, I have come to think that theatrical cross-dressing for empowerment is a one-way street. Lesley Ferris speaks of "the gross lack of symmetry between men-acting-women and women-acting-men, an imbalance where women seek freedom through male dress and men achieve aesthetic creativity through acting women" (1990: xiv).

This was probably my first innocent footstep on the slippery slope down which I have subsequently slid into an adult history that includes playing Pericles in a transparently all-male production (Marina/Thaisa retained a drooping red moustache,

Lychorida a full beard), directing an all-male *Doctor Faustus* (also transparent, although with a Bowie-like indeterminate Helen), working as text coach and dramaturg on cross-cast Elizabethan productions (transparent and otherwise) both in Toronto and at Shakespeare's Globe, and so on. Intrigued lately by *The Taming of the Shrew*, I had already planned to see the 2003 all-female production at Shakespeare's Globe when Jim Bulman's 2004 SAA seminar, "Cross-Dressing in Contemporary Performances of Shakespeare," came to hand, prompting me to bring two strands together and think about reading *Shrew* with a company of women.

The Actor's Freedom

Let me say, first, what it is that compels my attention when women play men in Shakespeare. My points, though not new, are worth rehearsing. Lorraine Helms speaks of the limitations, for contemporary women actors, inherent in the majority of early modern female roles. In general, she suggests, female performers do not enjoy "the transhistorical privileges and prerogatives that Michael Goldman calls 'the actor's freedom'" (Helms 1994: 103). And more particularly, she notes the female performer's inevitable "on-stage-ness," that inauthentic condition in which she is constructed by Shakespearean textual cues "as the object of the male spectator's gaze," and performs accordingly. Helms goes on:

> Since women now, as boys then, must play their parts in societies where women share children's disenfranchisement, physical difference continues to reflect the hierarchy of male and non-male in Shakespearean roles. Techniques originally designed to feminize the boy actor may infantilize or eroticize those who now play his roles. They may turn women, like boys, into female impersonators. (1994: 108)

Angela Carter's Nora (1992: 192), playing fast and loose with Wilde, finds the problem to be much more general, and not at all confined to the stage:

> "It's every woman's tragedy" [she says] "that after a certain age, she looks like a female impersonator." . . .
> "What's every man's tragedy, then?" I wanted to know.
> "That *he* doesn't, Oscar," she said.[1]

Moving her argument to a focus on soliloquy, Helms points to the limited scope of female solo performance in the plays:

> With some exceptions, Shakespeare's female characters play their roles in the illusionistic scenes of the *locus*. They enjoy few opportunities to express the interiority of the reflexive soliloquy and even fewer to address the audience from the interactive *platea*. (1994: 111)

This denial of the female actor's freedom changes, at least potentially, when a woman plays a man. What excites me, therefore, about witnessing women taking on the great – and even many of the not-so-great – male roles in Shakespeare is being in the presence of working actors who are newly enabled, actors whose craft is expanding before my eyes. I am acutely conscious of the patronizing irony inherent in this situation, where women, to be fully alive as players of early modern scripts, must (frequently, if not always) play male roles. But overriding that pained consciousness, again and again, is the joy of witnessing the liberated actor stepping out into new territory, and of sharing her aesthetic exuberance as she claims that territory for female performance.

Interestingly, it seems often to be this focus on the experience of the actor(s), rather than on any direct cultural message to an audience, that drives women-playing-men. A (limited) website survey of the published mandates of all-female Shakespeare companies – Chickspeare, Woman's Will, LAWSC, Sphinx – offers initial confirmation: such companies evidently form not for particular interpretive agendas but for the artistic and social opportunities they give their membership, including the chance to work in nurturing and supportive surroundings. And even Mark Rylance, writing in *The Guardian* about the imminent all-female shows at the Globe, occasionally sounded as much like an equal opportunity employer as a crusader for feminist reading: "[W]e will be helping to realise the enormous potential of actresses who face diminishing opportunities as their expertise and life experience grow to maturity" (2003).

Access, then, becomes one of the definitive liberatory terms at the heart of this discussion. Women playing men have, first of all, new access to roles that direct or affect the action, rather than being confined to roles that are simply acted upon. Toronto actor Maggie Huculak says, speaking of early modern staged women:

> The arena of their interest, the arena of their action, is in their relationship to men, and the arena of men's action is in relationship to themselves, their ambitions, ... their relationships to the world, or to other men. The arena of preoccupation, for women, is men (how they're feeling about their daddy, and how they're feeling about their boyfriend) – that's what motivates them, and that's what propels them through their action ... That's what's nice about playing a guy in Shakespeare – it's not just about your relationship to your romantic life.[2]

Alisa Solomon supports Huculak's point: "[U]nlike many female characters, male characters rarely exist on traditional stages for their gender alone – they are statesmen, soldiers, salesmen, not merely men. More important, as the presumed universal, maleness is more invisible in its artificiality" (1993: 145).

It follows that the woman playing a man may well find herself in the unfamiliar and exhilarating realms of early modern politics and state, wheeling and dealing, pursuing self-realization that expands far beyond the domestic and personal spheres. And where the sphere of action *is* domestic and personal, she may find herself, like

Petruchio, driving that action rather than being driven by it. Incidentally, when I wondered aloud to Huculak, who has not played Petruchio, how it would feel, as a woman, to inhabit and present this man whose whole project is the subjugation of another woman, she responded, "Oh, I think it'd be a gas!" Clearly, it doesn't matter what you're driving if it has power and you're in the driver's seat.

There's also an expansiveness in many of the male roles that is rarely available to the female performer. I mentioned soliloquy a moment ago, and with it access to the *platea* (literal or figurative), to that dynamic mediating and liminal space between illusion and actual, and to the heightened interactive relationship with an audience that can accompany it (Helms 1994: 111; Weimann 1987: 73–85 and *passim*). Hamlet, Richard II, and Prospero – all famously played by women at the top of their game – share their interior processes directly with audiences, from positions of theatrical force. Richard III (played in 2003 at the Globe by Kathryn Hunter, *Shrew*'s Katherina), and *Lear*'s Edmund (played twice in Toronto by Maggie Huculak), share their machinations, their villainy, with audiences whom, vice-like, they actively enlist as their co-conspirators. Few female roles offer comparable possibilities.[3]

Another rather obvious realm of actorly empowerment comes with the access to new physicality, particularly as regards violence or fight. Maggie Huculak speaks of how she loved the fight rehearsals for *Lear*, the opportunity to work with weapons hand-to-hand, what she calls the sexiness of physical combat, first with Maria Ricossa's Edgar in 1994, and then, much more excitingly – because the opposing actor was now a man – with Rick Roberts in the 1995 revision. (The two productions are discussed, though with very different emphasis, in McKinnie 2002.) Huculak speaks of the challenge and satisfaction involved in teaching her body "not to throw like a girl." And there's evidently a potential element of actorly release in taking on (masculine) violence: Susan Hogan, rehearsing Cornwall in the 1994 workshop of *Lear*, came in one afternoon wearing her husband's workboots, and what had been a restrained performance suddenly caught fire, and left the company seeking space in the budget to repair several new holes kicked in the wall of the rehearsal room. Huculak, referring to moments like this, compares playing a man with wearing a mask, in terms both of its emphasis on body and of its liberating effect on performance. (In this case, presumably, the boots were the mask.)

And, finally, the woman playing a man may also, perhaps especially at times when the role/performance is particularly opaque, find herself newly freed from the eroticizing male gaze and the compulsion toward inauthentic female impersonation that may accompany it – she may find herself in the liberty of the "deroticized" gaze. To me, the moment that clearly marked such freedom for Janet McTeer in 2003 came in *Shrew* 4.1[4] when her Petruchio stepped to the front of the platform, hip-checked a shivering Katherina to one side, turned his back to the audience, flipped up his coat-tails, and forcefully thrust his breeches-clad butt out at the house, luxuriously warming his behind at the pair of andirons that stood for a fireplace. In contrast to Barbara Hodgdon's enthusiastic enjoyment of Mel Gibson's *derrière* in Zeffirelli's *Hamlet* (Hodgdon 1994: 283), there was here, as far as I could sense, no erotic content triggered by Phyllida Lloyd's staging of Petruchio's hearty male butt. Indeed, the gesture read like a flourish, a moment where the actor, freed from the conventional eroticizing and objectifying gaze, confidently says, "You want to see how far I can go? Just watch me!"

These then are the actorly opportunities that draw me to witness cross-cast shows in which women play some or all of the men. I don't think, frankly, that men who play women normally experience quite the same access to theatrical force.[5] When a man plays an early modern woman, he ordinarily enters those constricted domestic arenas that Huculak and Solomon speak of. When a woman plays a man, she is frequently, perhaps even usually, dressing for power.

This may be the moment to say a word about "realism" where it concerns all-female performance of early modern scripts. Any production may seek to hide its theatrical mechanics within representational opacity or it may seek the metatheatrical transparency that triggers an audience's dual awareness of story and story-tellers. Beyond that, I don't think that "realism," in any simplistic sense of visual or vocal verisimilitude, need be an issue in all-female performance. Theatre, after all, is conventionalized story-telling, not photographic representation. We go there to experience stories, and to make believe quite naturally. As Val McDermid put it in a recent interview: "Human beings are hard-wired for story" (Levin 2004). Echoing Doctor Johnson, Juliet Dusinberre observes:

> [N]one of the shadows on Shakespeare's stage are there. There are no kings, queens, murderers, monsters, fairies, politicians, wise counselors, or even fools. There are only actors. Why should it matter that they are not biologically female [or male], any more than it should matter that they are not royal, Roman, Moors, Egyptian, or Italian? Why should the fact of the male body make it impossible to conceive of a woman on the stage [or vice versa], any more than the fact of the commoner's body might make it impossible to conceive of Richard II's body? Both are figments of the actor's art. (2000: 251; my interjections)

And she then goes on with admirable clarity to examine deliberate textual moments of gender transparency that unsettle the illusion. Precisely. The production sets the rules of the game, manipulates them on its own terms, and the spectator buys into those rules or forfeits the fun.

Our Lances ...

And now to get down to cases, to ask what happens when a company of women turns its actorly and critical attention to *The Taming of the Shrew*.

The summer of 2003 might well have been called the Summer of the Shrew, with at least three mainstage English-language productions on offer in Britain and Canada, along with less prominent productions in Salisbury, Edinburgh, and elsewhere. The mainstage productions were at the Royal Shakespeare Company (directed by Gregory Doran), at Shakespeare's Globe Theatre (directed by Phyllida Lloyd), and at Stratford Ontario (directed by Miles Potter). Arguably the most intriguing *Shrew* of the summer, in terms of the material conditions of its presentation, strode the thrust platform of London's Globe. Here, one thought in advance, came a *Shrew* that, even in a mainstage, showcase – and hence, typically, unadventurous – production, was supremely equipped for radical feminist critique, primed to engage head-on with all the familiar (and justified) feminist/new historicist reservations about a play that glorifies the abusive masculine browbeating of a woman, forcibly reconstructing her subjectivity until, thoroughly coerced, she assumes her "proper" subordinate, mild, and uncomplaining domestic place.[6] I went to Phyllida Lloyd's all-female production anticipating a firm, perhaps even scathing, indictment of masculine complacency, a sternly resistant critique both of the play and, more significantly, of the dominant patriarchal culture from which it was written, and into which it still plays today. This was, after all, the Globe's "Season of Regime Change." How could an all-female company (from which even the original male director had mysteriously departed just as rehearsals began) – how could such a company fail to lay bare the awful gender inequities at the heart of Shakespeare's *Shrew*?

On its surface, the production seemed conceived to satisfy exactly this expectation. Janet McTeer's Petruchio was a huge, striding, womanizing force, whose every careless gesture spoke of complacently oppressive male privilege. He arrived in Padua direct from his pregnant whore, and went straight back to her when he claimed to be going off to Venice to shop for wedding clothes. The cash he received from Baptista at the wedding was immediately handed over to his waiting "tart in a cart" (as the company privately called her), maybe to support her imminent child, maybe just to signal her complicity in this scheme to "wive it wealthily in Padua" (1.2.72).[7] By way of underlining – or preserving – the masculinity of some of the all-male scenes, other silent female servants (housekeepers, companions) had been added to the households of Hortensio and Baptista, women whom the visiting Petruchio freely admired, ogled, and patted in the worst macho manner. All of McTeer's physicality said, stereotypically, "man," from the broad stance and stride, to the constant prominence of chest and jaw, to the lower-register guffaws, to his repeated Sicilian hand-jive routines with Hortensio (ba da bing!), right down to the occasional preoccupied back-of-the-fingers stroking of the whiskered underchin, and the extravagant and much-reported *League of Their Own* piss against the down left pillar, complete with its finishing shake-and-button routine, and a casual wipe of the hand on the seat of the breeches.[8] At times, this fem-built Petruchio could almost have been at home with Benny Hill, or in the leering world of Frankie Howerd's *Up Pompeii*. In conversation, Carol Rutter observed that if a group of men had set out to stereotype the feminine with comparably broad and dismissive strokes (she actually put it less politely), the predictable and proper response would have been outrage. And yet ... well, I'll return later to the compelling – and problematic? – sexiness of McTeer's performance.

FIGURE 29.1   Petruchio's faithful spaniel Troilus (Rachel Sanders) makes a typically aggressive entry, scrambling onstage over a sleeping Grumio (Linda Bassett) in Act 4 Scene 3 of the Globe's *The Taming of the Shrew* (2003)

Photograph by John Tramper. Reproduced with permission of Shakespeare's Globe.

Set against McTeer's manly butch giant was Kathryn Hunter's birdlike yet vivacious Katherina, and the design of the action housed an apparent feminist critique that was to offer her not only brutal discomfort and coercion to play against, but also plentiful mockery of, and ultimately triumphant containment of, Petruchio's overblown masculine ways – a mocking assault, indeed, upon the very socializing process through which he imagined he was putting her. Central to this was the production's inclusion of Petruchio's dog Troilus – certainly no spaniel, which is what the text describes, but rather more of a boisterous sheepdog, played by Rachel Sanders, who both obeyed his master with great joy, and aggressively recognized in the terrified and tiny Katherina a troubling competitor for Petruchio's favor.

There is much to say about the tense comic competition – for both food and affection – between this woman and this tellingly cross-cast dog, but two things are pertinent to the production's strategy of critique through mockery. First, at the close of Petruchio's 4.1 soliloquy detailing his strategy for breaking and training Katherina (the "falconry" speech), McTeer's Petruchio, about to make his exit, signaled to the soundly sleeping Troilus, who awoke instantly, sprang to his paws (well, to his hands and his kneepads), and bounded obediently over to his master, eager for the next command. His point emblematically embodied in his enthusiastically compliant pet, McTeer's Petruchio looked to the audience as if to say, "Point taken? So what's the problem?" before master and dog went off together to complete the taming of the shrew. Occasionally, as Andrew Hartley reminds me, there was audible disapproval from the yard directed at Petruchio's unadorned description of his patriarchal taming project. Ever the loyal defender of his lord, his life, his keeper, the dutiful Troilus would rush instantly to the very edge of the platform and bark the hapless audience member into sheepish submission (Figure 29.1).[9]

And second, from this clownlike elaboration of the script's single passing reference to Troilus grew, quite directly, Kathryn Hunter's subsequent performance in 4.3. Petruchio tormented her with a plate of food, but she topped his teasing by ostentatiously begging for the plate on all fours, tongue lolling out as she sat up on her hind legs and panted hopefully at her master's knee. Finally, the food achieved, she crept like a doting spaniel into his lap. Both gestures, the begging and the doting, were explicit exaggerations of exactly where Petruchio's project was positioning her, and both gestures, in their explicit exaggeration, silently laid the groundwork for what she would do to Petruchio in the play's conclusion.[10]

For this production ultimately turned the tables on Petruchio's taming process, seeming to fulfil one's expectations of all-female feminist critique by transforming Katherina into a kind of over-the-top domestic monster of Petruchio's own inadvertent making, and in the process initiating Bianca and the Widow into complicit resistant sisterhood. Katherina's speech of submission was broken down into six beats, with each transition played as a false ending producing concomitant relief among the men onstage, followed by an unwelcome renewed beginning. Beat by beat, the speech grew increasingly hyperbolic and insincere. At first gratified and triumphant, Petruchio was reduced to humiliated and impotent exasperation by the final beats as, after an aggressively indecorous display of thigh on the table at "Why are our bodies soft?" (5.2.165) – a display unsuccessfully covered by the mortified Petruchio using Grumio's coat – Katherina led the other women down right with "Come, come, you froward and unable worms" (5.2.169) to prostrate themselves, giggling uncontrollably, at "place your hands below your husband's foot" (5.2.177). The mockery of Petruchio and his fellow patriarchs was fulsome and unmistakable. Then, on Petruchio's "Come on and kiss me, Kate" (5.2.180), Hunter's Katherina declined, and as Petruchio struggled to maintain his bluster before his friends, she exited, abruptly and unnoticed. Only at "Come, Kate, we'll to bed" (5.2.184), spoken to the empty air, did her complete absence register with him, and so Petruchio's usually triumphant exit became an ungainly and anticlimactic moment of public deflation, following which we were treated to an epilogue in Italian: Petruchio and Katherina on the upper level, in full Mediterranean domestic quarrel – a sort of *Punch and Judy Meet The Sopranos* – by way of demonstrating the unquiet marriage Petruchio has actually achieved (Figure 29.2).

Among the production's other gestures toward a conventionally oppositional feminist stance, I'll mention only the commodification of Bianca. The contrast with Greg Doran's simultaneous RSC production was striking. There the story was very much about Bianca's freedom of movement and of affection. She clearly preferred Tranio's Lucentio to Lucentio's, and she clearly married the real Lucentio out of a cool decision for money and status, while continuing to thumb her nose at caste via a (probable) on-going affair with Tranio. The Globe's Bianca had no such agency, no such liberty. Indeed, her most telling moment, for me, came in 2.1, when she was brought on as the silent object of the bargaining between Gremio and Tranio.[11] Lloyd's whole point was evidently to present her as an object of (economic?) desire. Toronto's Patricia Hamilton (Feste in Theatre Columbus's 1990 *Twelfth Night*, and

FIGURE 29.2   Katherina (Kathryn Hunter) insists on her new hat in futile defiance of Janet McTeer's Petruchio – futile for the moment, that is; Act 4, Scene 3 of the Globe's *The Taming of the Shrew* (2003). Photograph by John Tramper. Reproduced with permission of Shakespeare's Globe.

then Lear in Richard Rose's 1994 workshop) once told me that she stayed away from Shakespeare for close to three decades because she tired of playing roles where you enter in a big dress, to music. Well, the Globe's Bianca, Laura Rogers, came on in a big dress, to music, and was plopped on the stage floor down center, whereupon the bargaining got under way upstage center. Early in the run, she faced out to the audience, so that her facial reactions to the beats of the bidding contest were at least evident. Later in the run, though still placed downstage on the floor, she had been turned to face upstage, so that her back was to the house, no reactions were recorded, and she was even more objectified. Sympathy for her was further resisted by the fact that she was now led off at the end by an anonymous servingman, a stagehand clearing a prop – earlier in the run there had been a hint of masculine sympathy as her father had come to her, raised her up, and helped her off.

So there was clear "feminist" interpretive intention in the Globe's all-woman production, aimed at telling a story of the suppression and commodification of women, and of the possibility – in the case of Katherina's deployment of those hackneyed old feminine wiles – of at least a brief triumph over it.

... are but Straws

What then was the problem? Quite simply, the apparent proactive feminist agenda of the reading was rendered benign, genial, ultimately toothless, by a simultaneous aim of the production, articulated by various actors in the course of an all-company Q&A on August 20, and constantly apparent on the stage: namely their project to "take the piss out of the blokes," to guy the guys. This pervasive and general strategy of gender mockery, leading inevitably into the merrily topsy-turvy conclusion, depended not only on a resistant reading of the action, but on the strategies of farce, particularly on caricature that was not scathing or pointed, but instead was little more than comic and fictive exaggeration. Rather than being played, that is, against opaque and threatening representations of a real-world patriarchy whose oppressive potential was actual and dangerous, much of this *Shrew*'s resistance was aimed harmlessly at openly staged "men" who, with the partial exception of Petruchio, were often transparently women. This is perhaps an inevitable condition of the production's material nature, but it's a condition that was nowhere accounted for in the fiction. By contrast, Kate Lynch's wonderful Passe Muraille *Dream* in Toronto a few seasons ago (see Shand 2002), invented a fictional frame, conceiving the women who so transparently played the play as a company of Amazons entertaining themselves with an impromptu cross-cast performance. Because Lynch's actors *played* women-playing-men, they were able to exploit moments of vulnerability (tears in particular), foregrounding them as little extrusions of their male character's inner woman. The Globe's "men" had no such latitude. Yolanda Vazquez (Hortensio) observed in passing (Q & A, August 20, 2003) that one of the challenges facing the women-playing-men was to avoid any sign of vulnerability because of the danger that it might read as feminine and so contradict the masculinity of the image.

Despite such precautions, Lloyd's production seemed to reflect an overall metatheatrical strategy that was more about the women playing the play than about the patriarchy which might have been under attack – less a critique than a licensed carnivalesque celebration, more like the temporary and ultimately self-contained Feast of Fools, Lord of Misrule, Boy Bishop than any pointed and proactive outreach against the oppressors; it read as exuberant and harmless venting. Mocking masculinity, Hortensio dug deeply and amusingly in his crotch for what turned out to be his lost gamut, rather than his complicatedly maladjusted personal equipment. But context is everything. Mary Walsh's outrageously macho Dakey Dunn, lambasting his masculine political targets on the Canadian Broadcasting Corporation's *This Hour Has 22 Minutes*, and hiking up his considerable crotch as he does so, is scathingly on target. Roseanne Barr as herself, performing a comparable gesture while "singing" the US national anthem at the beginning of a 1990 San Diego baseball game, earned the outraged attention of a nation. Her action was threatening. Hortensio's gesture was benignly contained by farce; it cohered with neither character nor moment, and was merely silly.

Petruchio, in the final scene, responding to Lucentio's wonderment as to what Katherina's behavior might bode, said, "Marry, peace it bodes, and love, and quiet life" (5.2.108), and then he proposed his next line as a laddish toast, raising a glass to "An awful rule and right supremacy!" The whole up-left row of solemnly ridiculous masculine caricatures – Hortensio, Lucentio, Baptista and the rest – reverently saluted this sentiment, intoning Petruchio's words as a kind of dim-witted blokes' mantra. Harmlessly playful stuff, it seemed to me. *The Times*'s Benedict Nightingale echoed this reaction: "Speaking as one of the Lords of Creation under sly female attack," he observed, "I enjoyed myself" (2003). The effect was, very successfully, to amuse the audience without inspiring thoughtful discomfort, and thus, as Augusto Boal (1985) might suggest, to underpin what is rather than to undercut it and by such undercutting lead an audience to seek what is not yet but ought to be. The problem, in other words, was that, as far as I could determine, the production preached to the converted, and declined to challenge the patriarchy in the audience by inviting us to identify with powerful and oppressive men whose complacently brutal misogyny is laid bare. The production housed a relatively safe critique of the early modern playtext, but did not extend into acts of criticism that representatives of contemporary masculinity might actually feel palpably and take to heart.

All this raises questions. Is farce compatible with proactive critique when the tool is all-female and the target is male? Or is a more potent and directly pointed satirical genre called for? Or, to take the opposite position, might the laughter of farce be ultimately a kind of silent and subversive invader, worming its revolutionary way into the consciousness of both women and the dominant masculinist culture? Or, yet again, is its effect neutralized by the fact that the exaggerations are too broad to really connect with the target oppressors? When the dominant culture goes away unconcernedly amused, has battle even been joined?

More particularly, is *Shrew*, particularly when stripped of its distancing Christopher Sly frame, really a vehicle that can carry an anti-patriarchal argument voiced exclusively by women, or does it require a clearer line of tension between male and female, a more direct pointing of patriarchal complacency and female pain, in order for its gender critique to be realized? And is part of the problem with an oppositional *Shrew* today, in any case, to be found in the (new?) fact that, as several women spectators suggested to me, the story is just too farcically absurd, too wildly exaggerated and improbable, to bear serious weight as a mirror of real conditions for a postfeminist audience? For such spectators, it's all just a wonderfully absurd masculinist fantasy for a girls' night out, to which the female audience is ultimately responding "Yeah, you wish," or "In your dreams," or "As if."

And, in any event, was 2003 really the moment for proactively resistant feminist performance on the mainstage, all-fem or otherwise, or is this not more accurately – and whether we like it or not – a postfeminist moment, in which the appetite for stern oppositional stances has passed, and a vision more oriented to partnership and reintegration, rather than to resistance and critique, is in the air?[12] Certainly, the company at the Globe spoke as if they saw their world and that of their audience as postfeminist – McTeer used the term in the August 20 Q&A – and guyed the guys much more in geniality than in anger (as, also, did Kate Lynch's *Dream*). They sought to play generalized blokes, rather than to inhabit real humans whose story-function outweighed gender conventions, finding the latter goal more appropriate to their process with *Richard III* than to *Shrew*. McTeer, for instance, describing her approach to Petruchio's maleness, spoke stereotypically of a difference between male and female takes on the emotions. With women, she quipped, the distance between heart and head is an A-road. For men, it's a B-road ... via Wales.

Paradoxically, Petruchio's sexy performance may well have been complicit in commuting the production's critique, for despite my earlier observations regarding his behind at the fire he was undeniably attractive, and it's a critical commonplace that an attractive Petruchio clouds the play's abusiveness, encouraging a desire text that can work to forgive the excesses of the "taming." The *Evening Standard*'s Nicholas De Jongh found McTeer "a convincing sexy man, with the looks of a young Peter O'Toole" (2003). More to the point, perhaps, Kate Bassett said that "handsome, strapping Janet McTeer makes an amazingly sexy Petruchio ... That's the extraordinary triumph of this production" (2003). And, from Liz Hoggard: "In Janet McTeer's Petruchio we have one of the sexiest romantic heroes I've seen on the stage in a long time" (2003). Significantly, Maggie Huculak received comparable endorsements of her Edmund at Toronto's Necessary Angel, and she considers those desire-marked responses from women one of the best things to be achieved when playing a man like Petruchio – after all, she says, the female actor is in some measure playing the man she would like to have. True for Petruchio and Edmund, perhaps; but, to be fair, it's unlikely that Pippa Domville, playing Oswald in 1994's Necessary Angel *Lear*, would have shared Huculak's view of this objective.

There's a hard – or maybe just a revealing – critical inconsistency here. I've already suggested that McTeer's Petruchio was constructed in part from extremely stereotypical performance choices. And yet some (or even many) straight women found the product sexy. I'm led to wonder, as Jean Peterson did more than a decade ago when describing a production at Temple University, whether *Shrew*, to really tell an oppositional story, might best have a Petruchio (male or female) who is a deliberately unattractive and even repulsive figure, rather than something of a hunk (1990). And I'm still led to wonder what is gained, what lost, when a woman exuberantly gives persuasive body and voice to a tyrannically sexy man who systematically torments and oppresses another woman, particularly when the undeniable strength of her performance is a major contributor to making oppression palatable.

Acknowledgments

With thanks to the participants in Jim Bulman's 2004 Shakespeare Association of America seminar, "Cross-Dressing in Contemporary Performances of Shakespeare," especially Barbara Hodgdon and Carol Rutter; and to Toronto actor, Maggie Huculak, as well as the Research Department at Shakespeare's Globe Theatre.

Notes

1 Momentarily catching a fragment of a recent *Much More Music* TV feature on gay icons, I overheard an unidentified commentator characterize Cher as "a drag queen who happened to be a woman." It's in the air.

2 Here and elsewhere, I depend on tape of a lengthy conversation with Huculak, held on January 13, 2004.

3 The writing of Marlowe's Queen Catherine, in *The Massacre at Paris*, suggests that, had he lived, he might have begun to correct this situation.

4 Observations based on the August 13 and 14 performances, and on archival videotape of the September 2 performance.

5 I am borrowing (and diluting) W. B. Worthen's hugely suggestive term (2003).

6 Any number of critics have commented on, and historicized, this version of Katherina's subjugation. Lynda E. Boose's resonant 1991 piece in *Shakespeare Quarterly* may serve as representative; the bibliography contained in her Notes, especially Note 5, tellingly documents the tradition.

7 My text is Elizabeth Schafer's 2002 Cambridge edition.

8 There is always the question as to which gestures will most economically express your character, and in this case the gender of your character. Early in the rehearsal period for *A Chaste Maid in Cheapside* at Shakespeare's Globe (1997), director Malcolm McKay ran an exercise in which each man who played a woman was paired with a woman to learn and present a single telling feminine gesture. At show-and-tell time, by far the most uncannily effective feminine gesture came from Bill Stewart, who had simply been taught, by Katie McNicoll,

how to fold a cardigan. It was so effective precisely because it spoke specifically to character, and did not merely reflect gendered generality. Fittingly, the best stereotypically female gesture was tossed off in a playful moment by Toby Cockerell, the boy (as he then was) who played a miraculously opaque Katherine in that summer's *Henry V*. Stewart's gesture said woman; Cockerell's said female impersonator. (There's an old chestnut that says "Only a man can accurately play a woman." Oddly enough, one doesn't often hear its reverse.)

9 Toronto columnist Margaret Wente recently observed in a piece on the Ontario debate over spanking children, that "[i]n fact, the principles of training dogs and training children are more or less the same, and it strikes [*sic*] me that if parents were required to attend dog-training courses, we'd all be a whole lot better off" (Wente 2004). Petruchio *in loco parentis*.

10 One almost felt Katherina's performance concealing a scornful reference to Helena's disturbingly apt words of subservience in *A Midsummer Night's Dream*:

I am your spaniel; and, Demetrius,
The more you beat me, I will fawn on you.
Use me but as your spaniel; spurn me,
    strike me,
Neglect me, lose me; only give me
    leave,
Unworthy as I am, to follow you.
What worser place can I beg in your love
(And yet a place of high respect with me)
Than to be used as you use your dog?
                                    (2.1.203–10)

11 Bill Alexander had made a comparable move at the RSC in 1992, but with quite different results (Rutter 1997: 201).

12 See my forthcoming "Romancing *The Shrew*" (Bamford and Knowles).

REFERENCES AND FURTHER READING

Bassett, Kate (2003). "Janet McTeer in Long Riding Boots? That's the Way to Tame a Shrew." *Independent on Sunday*, August 31: 8.

Boal, Augusto (1985). *Theatre of the Oppressed*. New York: Theatre Communications Group.

Boose, Lynda E. (1991). "Scolding Brides and Bridling Scolds: Taming the Woman's Unruly Member." *Shakespeare Quarterly* 42, 2: 179–213.

Carter, Angela (1992). *Wise Children*. London: Vintage.

De Jongh, Nicholas (2003). "Female Shrew Vaults the Gender Gap but Has No Fresh Insight." *Evening Standard*, August 22: 18.

Dusinberre, Juliet (2000). "Women and Boys Playing Shakespeare." In Dympna Callaghan (ed.) *A Feminist Companion to Shakespeare*. Oxford: Blackwell, pp. 251–62.

Ferris, Lesley (1990). *Acting Women*. London: Macmillan.

Gamble, Sarah (1999). "Postfeminism." In Sarah Gamble (ed.) *The Icon Critical Dictionary of Feminism and Postfeminism*. Cambridge: Icon, pp. 43–54.

Goldman, Michael (1975). *The Actor's Freedom: Toward a Theory of Drama*. New York: Viking.

Helms, Lorraine (1994). "Acts of Resistance." In Dympna Callaghan, Lorraine Helms, & Jyotsna Singh (eds.) *The Weyward Sisters*. Oxford: Blackwell, pp. 102–56.

Hodgdon, Barbara (1994). "The Critic, the Poor Player, Prince Hamlet and the Lady in the Dark." In Russ McDonald (ed.) *Shakespeare Reread: The Texts in New Contexts*. Ithaca, NY: Cornell University Press, pp. 259–94.

Hoggard, Liz (2003). "Girls and Girls Come Out to Play." *Observer Review*, August 24: 3.

Levin, Martin (2004). "Grand Banks." Toronto *Globe and Mail*, February 21: D13.

Marlowe, Christopher (1969). *The Complete Plays*, ed. J. B. Steane. London: Penguin.

McKinnie, Michael (2002). "Liberal Shakespeare and Illiberal Critiques." In Diana Brydon & Irena R. Makaryk (eds.) *Shakespeare in Canada*. Toronto: University of Toronto, pp. 212–30.

Nightingale, Benedict (2003). "The Shrew Has a Sting in Her Tale." *The Times*, August 23.

Peterson, Jean (1990). "Straw Lances: Performance as Weapon, or Untaming the Shrew." Unpublished, MLA.

Rutter, Carol (1997). "Kate, Bianca, Ruth, and Sarah: Playing the Woman's Part in *The Taming of the Shrew*." In Michael Collins (ed.) *Shakespeare's Sweet Thunder: Essays on the Early Comedies*. Newark: University of Delaware Press, pp. 176–215.

Rylance, Mark (2003). "Unsex Me Here." *The Guardian* May 7. Available at: www.guardian.co.uk/arts/features/story/0,11710,950564,00.html.

Shakespeare, William (1979). *A Midsummer Night's Dream*. In G. Blakemore Evans et al. (eds.) *The Riverside Shakespeare*, 2nd edn. Boston: Houghton Mifflin, pp. 251–83.

Shakespeare, William (2002). *The Taming of the Shrew*, ed. Elizabeth Schafer. Cambridge: Cambridge University Press.

Shand, G. B. (1990). "Directing *Doctor Faustus*." *Elizabethan Theatre* XI: 205–14.

Shand, G. B. (forthcoming). "Romancing *The Shrew*: Recuperating a Comedy of Love." In Karen Bamford & Ric Knowles (eds.) *Shakespeare's Comedies of Love*. Toronto: University of Toronto Press.

Shand, Skip (2002). "*A Midsummer Night's Dream*." *Shakespeare Bulletin* 20, 2: 23–4.

Solomon, Alisa (1993). "It's Never Too Late to Switch." In Lesley Ferris (ed.) *Crossing the Stage: Controversies on Cross-Dressing*. New York: Routledge, pp. 144–54.

Weimann, Robert (1978; reprint 1987). *Shakespeare and the Popular Tradition in the Theater*, trans. Robert Schwartz. Baltimore, MD: Johns Hopkins University Press.

Wente, Margaret (2004). "Worse Things than Spanking." Toronto *Globe and Mail*, January 31: A23.

Worthen, W. B. (2003). *Shakespeare and the Force of Modern Performance*. Cambridge: Cambridge University Press.

30

Queering the Audience: All-Male Casts in Recent Productions of Shakespeare

James C. Bulman

When Shakespeare's Globe Theatre decided to cast a male as Cleopatra in 1999, it was taking a risk. The Globe, after all, was a popular tourist venue whose audiences could not be counted on to respond appreciatively to the archaic convention of casting men in women's roles, and the challenges of playing Cleopatra had recently defeated a number of the most talented actresses on the British stage, including Vanessa Redgrave, Helen Mirren, and, in Stratford earlier that same summer, Frances de la Tour. Surprisingly, the Globe's *Antony and Cleopatra* became both a popular and a critical success *because* of Mark Rylance's performance as Cleopatra. Garbed in a succession of low-cut dresses in fashions ranging from milkmaid to gypsy, sporting long black curls, barefoot and ankle-braceleted, Rylance skipped and flounced, preened, swooned and died with a "histrionic excess" that drew attention to the role's flamboyant theatricality (Billington, *The Guardian*, August 2, 1999). His transvestite Cleopatra, as Paul Taylor observed, enhanced one's sense of the queen "as a fluid and compulsive actress who has enjoyed playing drunken gender-bending games with her lover and who always, even as she goes into her final, glorious apotheosis, keeps you guessing about the exact degree of seriousness behind the role-play" (*Independent*, August 3, 1999). Rylance performed the queen in all her infinite variety, and his emphasis on *performance* is what critics and audiences applauded most. Where the exaggeratedly "feminine" role-play of recent female Cleopatras had sometimes come across as "a toughened drag-act" which "made the queen's capricious volte-faces look crashingly premeditated" (Taylor, *Independent* August 3, 1999), Rylance, because he was *not* a woman, was praised for the spontaneity with which he embodied the same exaggerated femininity. "By showing an actor shadowing, or paralleling, the role rather than identifying with it," wrote Robert Smallwood, he demonstrated "the extent to which Cleopatra is constantly performing ... never identifiable as herself" (2000: 246).

His success shouldn't have come as a surprise. By 1999, the idea that gender is performative rather than innate had circulated widely, and audiences were proving receptive to the argument that gender might be a cultural construct, and sexual desire dependent on forces other than biological difference. Judith Butler had argued there is no such thing as an essential or interior gender identity; rather, gender can be identified only by external codes of conduct and by citational behavior. As the most obvious form of gender performativity, transvestism, according to Butler, "reveals the imitative structure of gender itself ... Indeed, part of the giddiness of the performance is in the recognition of a radical contingency in the relation between sex and gender in the face of cultural configurations of causal unities that are regularly assumed to be natural and necessary" (1990: 137–8). Thus, as Abbey Zink suggests, spectators at the Globe approved of Rylance's performance of Cleopatra because they recognized in it the imitative quality of all gendered behavior. His biological maleness worked to his advantage by helping to foreground the fundamental performativity of his queen: "His performance appeared to be evaluated not on his lack of womanliness, but on his ability to exaggerate the womanly despite biological obstacles" (2000: 21). The production's insistence on the *maleness* of Rylance's Cleopatra was thus crucial to its success: in playing the queen, "he seem[ed] not to transform himself at all" (Hewison, *The Times*, August 8, 1999), and the production gained considerably "from the audience's double awareness of character and actor" (Potter 1999: 514).

Let me pause briefly to consider the importance of Butler and other queer theorists to the study of theatrical representation in the 1990s. Their effort to de-essentialize gender, to regard it as an unconscious adoption of culturally prescribed roles played for a public who tacitly set the rules of representation, provides a compelling lens through which to view early modern plays; for in them, and especially in Shakespeare's comedies, gender is often interrogated as a form of role-play, and the historical practice of boys performing women's roles would have challenged the comfortable certainties of how one comes to know a person's sex. Unsurprisingly, then, contemporary directors such as Giles Block, who directed the Globe's *Antony and Cleopatra*, have responded to this performative "queering" of gender identity by staging Shakespeare's plays with all-male casts, ostensibly recuperating an Elizabethan practice in order to explore the ways in which gender is *now* perceived to be radically contingent, easily elided, always in a state of play.[1]

Under the influence of queer theory, however, Shakespeare critics turned their gaze not on contemporary all-male performances, to see how such cross-dressing manifests their own culture's obsession with gender's playful contingency, but on the Elizabethan stage, to debate the extent to which casting boys in women's roles had the power to destabilize gender identity and denaturalize sexual desire. In other words, they applied contemporary hypotheses about gender and sexuality not to performances they had seen, but to historical performances they had only *imagined,* hoping that speculation about original all-male casting might help them to recover the Elizabethan cultural moment. In the view of some, the Elizabethan stage was "a site where there was considerable fluidity and multiplicity in the channeling of sexual energies" (Howard 1994: 111), and cross-dressing boy actors became both a source and a reflection of cultural anxieties about gender identity and homoeroticism. These boys, it is argued – like the women and pages they played, marginalized figures without power or social position – were invariably subjugated to the controlling desires of men. Stephen Orgel's "Nobody's Perfect, or Why Did the English Stage Take Boys for Women?" (1989) remains the most influential expression of this point of view. Positing that homosexuality was the dominant form of eroticism for Elizabethans, Orgel argues that the feminized bodies of cross-dressing boys stirred vivid imaginings and sexual longings among men in the audience; for in Elizabethan England's misogynist culture, boys, serving as female analogues or substitutes, were apparently less threatening than women as objects of male sexual desire.[2] Such speculation draws strength from the diatribes of Puritan moralists who inveighed against the sins of theatrical representation and warned that the display of adult male actors embracing cross-dressed boys on stage could provoke men in the audience to sodomitical thoughts and acts (Howard 1988, 1994; Garber 1992; Traub 1992a; Levine 1994; Senelick 2000).

The danger of such arguments, according to David Cressy, "lies in projecting present preoccupations onto the past, and in bringing our opinions to the evidence rather than deriving them from it" (2000: 114). Indeed, other critics have countered that acceptance of male actors as women was such a long-standing stage convention, dating back to the Greeks, that it would have passed unnoticed. Elizabethan spectators, they argue, didn't "take" boy actors as eroticized bodies at all, but understood that during the two hours' traffic on the stage, they were to read as female the character as played: the boy actor "himself" became invisible, immersed in the role he assumed, his sex occluded by spectators' tacit complicity in the fiction. Bruce Smith, for example, insists that despite the Puritan moralists' objections, "all the unpolemical witnesses we have from the seventeenth century ... register no erotic interest whatsoever in the characters they saw onstage, much less a specifically homoerotic interest in the boy actors"; and further, "the all-male composition" of the company would have made the boys' gender unexceptional and inconspicuous (1991: 129–30). Anthony Dawson writes that "the audience by convention simply ignored the gender of the actor, reading him as her" (1996: 32); John Astington concurs that Elizabethans "didn't think twice" about boys performing female roles (2001: 109); and Juliet Dusinberre asserts that "[t]he actual biological male body of the boy is erased by the performative energy of the theatrical experience" (1996: 57). These critics dismiss the application of Butler's ideas to historical performance as a distortion of the available evidence. In effect, they accuse those who view cross-dressing boy actors through the lens of queer theory of foisting their own cultural anxieties onto the Elizabethans. As Carol Rutter concludes, "cross-dressing was an unremarkable stage convention, no more sensational, anxious or trangressive when practised by the Chamberlain's Men in 1601 than by Cheek by Jowl in 1991" (2001: xiv).

Implicitly, such thinking assumes that audiences in 1991 not only regarded cross-dressed adult male actors in the same way that Elizabethan audiences would have perceived boy actors, as "an unremarkable stage convention," but willingly surrendered to the play's heterosexual fictions, ignoring the male bodies beneath the skirts. This curious cultural elision needs to be examined in light of the recent proliferation of all-male casting, for in Cressy's terms, one would expect queer theory and arguments about the fluidity of gender identity to be more pertinent to present-day than to Elizabethan performances. Yet critics have been strangely reluctant to apply queer theory to contemporary all-male productions of Shakespeare, and even those few who have used Butler to explore the deconstruction of gender in same-sex productions at the new Globe have been guided more by a historicizing impulse than by an attempt to view the productions in light of current debates over gender, cross-dressing and homosexuality.

Queering *As You Like It*

Cheek by Jowl's audacious 1991 *As You Like It* deserves to be revisited in light of queer theory because it was the first all-male production of Shakespeare to win international acclaim – revived in 1994, it again toured internationally – and to introduce the convention of the all-male cast to audiences primed by recent social movements to view as "queer" the sexual politics of cross-dressing. Not only did the original staging occur just as Butler's ideas were becoming known, but, like most revolutionary productions, it gave voice to culturally contested ideas even as they were being theorized by the academy, leading Alisa Solomon to comment on how "a sexist old stage practice" could unleash an erotic dynamics with the power to deconstruct gender itself (Solomon 1997: 27). By using *As You Like It* to explore vexed notions of gender formation and sexual desire, Cheek by Jowl's production served as a touchstone for all-male productions during the decade to follow.

Yet the reluctance of critics at the time to view theatrical cross-dressing through a queer lens was amply evident in their responses to this *As You Like It*, whose all-male cast was widely praised for the effectiveness with which it rendered *invisible*, or at least irrelevant, the sex of those actors who played women. "Donnellan's production reveals that *As You Like It* is not about sexuality hetero-, homo-, bi-, or trans- but about love," exulted John Peter (*The Sunday Times*, December 8, 1991). Michael Billington agreed that while the production "brings out the polymorphous perversity of Shakespearean comedy ... Donnellan's real emphasis is on the transforming potency of love" (*The Times*, October 14, 1991). Of the 1994 revival, the reviewer for *Shakespeare Bulletin* wrote approvingly, "Soon, one forgot transvestism and gender-bending entirely"; and even the reviewer for *Shakespeare Survey*, who was perceptive enough to note that the cross-dressed actors "enabled a subtle consideration [of] the play's homosexuality," asserted that "the tremendous erotic charge between Rosalind and Orlando had nothing glibly homoerotic about it" and that finally, "[t]he problem of love and desire was defined as lying beyond gender." More surprisingly, the reviewer for a special issue of *Theatre Journal* devoted to queer theory, even as she acknowledged "the virtues of gender play" in the production, concluded that "same-sex casting … makes explicit the point that gender is ultimately unimportant in human relationships."[3] Such accounts are tantamount to avoidance behavior: they betray a discomfort with the production's sexual politics and a refusal to grapple with the homophobic social attitudes and government policies which, I shall argue, formed the context through which the production should be viewed.

Deeply influenced by Brecht's conviction that theater should alienate its audience by making strange what has been comfortably familiar, director Declan Donnellan's staging made spectators immediately aware of gender at play. Onto a bare stage strode 14 men wearing white shirts and black pants, clearly marked as actors in modern dress. As they faced the audience, the actor who would play Jaques spoke the opening lines of his Seven Ages of Man speech transposed from Act 2 Scene 7: "All the world's a stage, / And all the *men*" – on men, those actors who would play male roles moved stage right – "and *women*" – on women, the actors playing Rosalind and Celia moved stage left – "[are] merely players" (2.7.139–40).[4] Asking spectators to take two of these male actors, in clothing indistinguishable from the others, as women at once signaled the performative nature of both the play they were about to watch and the gender identities within it. In Brechtian fashion, the performers were insisting that spectators maintain a double consciousness of the character and of the actor playing the role (see Shapiro 1994 and Dawson 1996). And while Peter Holland argued that "the production allowed character to exist dissociated from performer" so that "sexuality was placed within the control of character, not actor," as if the gender of the actor were inconsequential (1997: 91), Benedict Nightingale countered that the production never let us "forget the gender behind the gender" (*The Times*, December 5, 1991), and Dominic Cavendish, in an article titled "What kind of man do you take me for?," concurred that "however good the performances, you never forget you are watching men" (*Independent*, January 5, 1995).

This double consciousness was crucial to the early scenes in which Rosalind is banished by the Duke and Celia vows to join her in exile. Usually of little dramatic impact and paced to move speedily to the Forest of Arden, these scenes were informed by a sexual tension unparalleled in modern productions. The mature male actors playing Celia (attired in a red silk dress) and Rosalind (in blue) could clearly be seen beneath their female garments; and though they made some effort to lighten their voices, their intention was to gesture towards femaleness, not to efface the maleness of their own bodies, an effect which lent a particular erotic frisson to their playing. During their initial conversation (1.2), Rosalind lay on the stage while Celia hovered over her, fondling and kissing her playfully; then Rosalind knelt next to Celia and brushed her hair. Their intimacy read as girlish: the adult actors were playing "young." But when reinforced by Le Beau's observation that their "loves/ Are dearer than the natural bonds of sisters" (1.2.260–1), the potential for an erotic attraction between them became palpable, and it was fully realized after Rosalind fell in love with Orlando at the wrestling match. As Rosalind lay with her head on Celia's lap praising Orlando (1.3), Celia became jealous and eventually slapped her on the back in frustration. Intimations of an erotic relationship between them grew stronger when Celia defended Rosalind to her father: she grabbed Rosalind's hand defiantly on "We still have slept together" (1.3.71); and when she taunted her father further with "I cannot live out of her company" (1.3.85), the Duke hurled his daughter to the floor. The clear implication was that the Duke suspected Celia of being infatuated with Rosalind – perhaps of having a sexual relationship with her – and, not understanding the depth of their attachment, viewed Rosalind as an unhealthy sexual predator. Later, as Rosalind prepared to leave the court, Celia burst into tears and begged to be taken along, pawing Rosalind's body and holding her face between her hands as she sobbed, "Shall we be sundered? Shall we part, sweet girl?" (1.3.97). What ordinarily is played as a comic scene here became emotionally compelling. But what was the audience watching? Two women (for they clearly were too old to be called girls) involved in a lesbian relationship? (See Traub 1992b: 158.) Two male actors whose playing of homoerotic attraction informed, but was not fully submerged in, the relationship of the two women? Or both (Figure 30.1)? In Donnellan's staging, spectators were constantly made aware that their perception of gender was contingent and determined by performance. Such awareness helped them to maintain a distance from the fiction sufficient to allow them to grasp the elision of heterosexual and homosexual identities and thereby to understand how cross-dressing could subvert a heteronormative reading of the text.

This elision of identities became more pronounced when Rosalind disguised herself as Ganymede and swore to cure Orlando of his love for Rosalind. In these scenes, spectators observed two men playing at love – the actor cast as Orlando (Patrick Toomey in 1991, Scott Handy in 1994), and Adrian Lester as Ganymede, a 6′2″ actor whose maleness, in the viewer's eye, was not a disguise at all. In one dimension, Lester's Ganymede performed credibly as Rosalind trying valiantly to act like a boy in the presence of the man to whom she longs to expose herself, angry that he does not recognize her, frustrated by his lack of demonstrative feeling, yet sensible that she can trick him into making love to her by pretending to be his Rosalind as part of the "cure." In another dimension, however, Lester as Ganymede was blatantly male, playing a love scene with another male actor with an intensity charged with homo-erotic potential. In the famous wooing scene, Ganymede's passion for Orlando came through repeatedly. Finding it increasingly hard to maintain the game of make-believe, Ganymede confessed that he was "like enough to consent" (4.1.63) to be wooed by Orlando, and the scene was played unabashedly as two men pledging their love to one another. When Ganymede asked Celia to marry them, a disapproving Celia refused even to look at them – a reminder of her earlier jealousy; and when Orlando threatened to depart, Ganymede threw a tantrum and tore up his love poems so convincingly that Orlando applauded as a performance what Ganymede had played in earnest. For spectators like Solomon (1997: 45), the scene embodied the "trans-gressive reinscription" of gender and erotic codes that Jonathan Dollimore (1991)

FIGURE 30.1   Simon Coates as Celia and Adrian Lester as Rosalind in the 1994 revival of Cheek by Jowl's *As You Like It*

Photograph by John Haynes. Reproduced with permission of Cheek by Jowl.

thinks characterized Elizabethan performances; and in doing so, it helped to advance the more subversive sexual politics of Donnellan's production.

These sexual politics were revealed in the program, which quoted at length from John Boswell's book *Christianity, Social Tolerance and Homosexuality*:

> Like that of the modern West, the gay subculture of the High Middle Ages appears to have had its own slang, which gradually became diffused among the general population. The equivalent of "gay," for example, was "Ganymede." The similarity of this word to "gay" in its cultural setting is striking. In an age addicted to classical literature, the invocation of Greek mythology to describe homosexual relationships not only tacitly removed the stigma conveyed by the biblical "sodomita," the only word in common use before or after this period, but also evoked connotations of mythological sanctions, cultural superiority, and personal refinement which considerably diminished negative associations in regard to homosexuality. Although "Ganymede" was also used derisively,

it was basically devoid of moral context and could be used by gay people themselves without misgivings. (1980: 253)

This program note reads like pseudo-historical wishful thinking, for the idea of a homosexual identity as such was unknown in the Renaissance (in Boswell's text, the High Middle Ages), only sodomy as a sexual practice was condemned, and certainly the term Ganymede did not sanitize sodomites any more than the word "gay," among conservative circles today, erases the moral revulsion with which homophobia is tinged.[5] But Boswell's remarks reveal a will to invest Elizabethan culture with present-day attitudes towards identity politics, and, even if anachronistically, they address how issues of gender formation have entered the discourse of educated Western audiences. Any attempt to read homoerotics into *As You Like It* reveals the significance which contemporary audiences may attach to cross-dressing. Arguing that "Ganymede" signifies gayness as an identity, Boswell's history was invoked by Cheek by Jowl to validate Donellan's decision to use the gender elisions of *As You Like It* to foreground a queer political agenda.

Nowhere was that agenda revealed more clearly than in his decision to have Jaques played as a Noël Cowardesque queen. Where Lester's Ganymede was virile, devoid of camp, and invested in the maleness of his ostensibly cross-dressed body, the Jaques of Joe Dixon (1991; Michael Gardiner in 1994) was a flamboyant dandy, dressed in a white morning suit and a cashmere coat, heavily made up, a beauty spot on his cheek. Next to his effete gayness, the sexual ambiguities of the principals seemed more "natural." He was a character whose status as an outsider could be stereotypically explained by his homosexuality – his exclusion from the boys' club, his failure to find a mate in the Forest of Arden. Forever trying to pick up young men, he attempted to hook the hunky Silvius by offering him a cigarette; but his supercilious come-on, "I prithee, pretty youth, let me be better acquainted with thee" (4.1.1–2) – a line directed to Rosalind in Shakespeare's text, but here appropriated for the conclusion of the preceding scene – was apparently misunderstood by Silvius, who happily accepted the cigarette and ran off. The bumpkin had proved immune to the courtier's covert invitation for sex.

Jaques' next target was the more knowing Ganymede. When Ganymede inquired why Jaques was so melancholy, the older man broke down and wept in his lap. But Ganymede-as-Rosalind was not about to accept Jaques's attentions, even if Ganymede-as-pretty-youth (or male actor) might have. When Ganymede stood to bid him farewell, however, striking a masculine pose and extending his hand for a firm handshake, Jaques would not let go of it. In self-defense, Ganymede reverted to playing "Rosalind" and disabused him by putting Jaques' hand on her "breast" as she told him emphatically to "chide God for making you that countenance you are" (4.1.33). Jaques recoiled: he had been mistaken about Ganymede's sex; Ganymede was a female cross-dresser! The audience laughed at his confusion. But Ganymede-as-Rosalind put her fingers to her lips, swearing him to secrecy. A pact of homosexual kinship thus made Jaques complicit in maintaining Rosalind's disguise. But what disguise? In what was Jaques complicit? Although, in the fiction of the play, he had discovered that Ganymede was female – she had a breast and therefore was not a youth at all – the audience knew there *was* no breast (see Stallybrass 1992, reprinted in Jones and Stallybrass 2000; see also Mazer 2004). The actor of Rosalind was feigning femaleness, and while spectators on one level might have imagined the breast to be there and thus been willing to buy into the fiction, on another, they knew that Jaques had felt Adrian Lester's chest and found only a pectoral muscle. This confusion, in the doubleness of vision encouraged by the performance of gender, heightened their sense of homoerotics at play.

In the ensuing scene, the production's political agenda grew more overt: Jaques became the victim of a vicious gay-bashing. With the hunt for deer over, Jaques now was the hunted, surrounded by hunters who in this production's gay aesthetic were burly men, shirtless and sweaty. When he asked sardonically, "Which is he that killed the deer?" (4.2.1), they manhandled him; and when they burst into song about "the lusty horn" (4.2.18) – goading him with its obvious phallic references – they pushed him around the stage with derisive brutality. If the machismo of the scene was redolent of gay culture, the bashing of the "fem" smacked of conservative cultural backlash. Yet these uncomfortable moments had a specific topicality – at least in 1991. In an article tellingly titled "The Worst of Times," Colin Richardson writes:

> The violent homophobia inspired by the advent of AIDS in the early 80s, inflamed by the tabloids and indulged by Thatcherism, had fostered in gay Britain a siege mentality … In 1988 Section 28, the first anti-gay legislation in a hundred years, became law. The recriminalisation of male homosexuality was high on the Tory wishlist … arrests of gay men for "gross indecency" doubled … [and] violence against gay people was spiraling out of control. In September 1989 a gay barrister … was murdered in his west London home. He was stabbed more than 40 times … Three months later, in another part of London, a gay hotelier … was stabbed to death at home. The following month [a] gay hotel porter … was found unconscious on a roadside in Acton [and] died soon after from severe head injuries.

The list of atrocities grows more ominous, because apparently sanctioned by the government: "In 1990 police [were] staking out the [public] toilets, arresting gay men in unprecedented numbers," and in one infamous case, on April 29, 1990, a man was lured into a toilet, savagely beaten by a gang of half a dozen men, and died of internal bleeding. "The reaction of the gay community was angry and terrified"; and out of their protests grew the activist group OutRage which "campaigned for the police to stop arresting gay men and start protecting them." More extraordinarily, in September of 1990 "gay [police] officers met anxiously in private to set up the Lesbian and Gay Police Association (Lagpa)" (*The Guardian*, August 14, 2002). This inflammatory chain of events provides a crucial context for understanding why, in the deer hunting scene, Cheek by Jowl's agenda turned activist, going beyond merely dramatizing gender ambiguities and same-sex desire to warn explicitly of the violence against homosexuals to which Thatcherism had given rise.

The final scene of pairings brought this political agenda full circle, though in a gentler tone. Ganymede had promised Orlando, "I will satisfy you if ever I satisfy man" (5.2.109), and the audience had been encouraged to hear his promise as a wryly gay threat. Would Orlando, at Rosalind's unveiling, see anything more than the "boy" whom he had been taught to think of as Rosalind until he complained that he could no longer live by thinking? When Rosalind appeared in a wedding dress – "To you I give myself, for I am yours" (5.4.112) – she went to take his hand, but he refused it. Shocked, he moved away from her; and she, dismayed, threw down her bouquet and wept in her father's arms. What did spectators see here? Through the lens of the play's heterosexual fiction, an Orlando who was disturbed at having been tricked by a woman wiser than he, confused that the boy he had rejected as a poor substitute for Rosalind was in fact female (Holland 1997: 94)? Or, through the lens of the production's sexual politics, a man confronting the fact that the object of his desire had all along been a male, here simply cross-dressed in woman's attire – a man disturbed to discover "the scope and contradictions of his sexuality" (Nightingale, *The Times*, December 5, 1991)? Or more open-mindedly, a man who at first resists the lesson that one's gender is a matter of choice but eventually accepts the cross-dressed Rosalind "for what she chooses to be" (Katie Laris, *Theatre Journal* 47, May 1995: 301–2)? In this production, all of these were possibilities: each assumed spectators' unflagging awareness of the male actor beneath Rosalind's skirt. When at last Orlando embraced her, asking incredulously, "You *are* my Rosalind?" (5.4.118) – the text's declarative, "If there be truth in sight, you are my Rosalind," delivered here as a tentative question – they indulged in a passionate kiss. Spectators of course saw two male actors kissing; but even in suspending their disbelief they might have perceived, with Orlando, that this Rosalind was, or could be, a man. The moment was richly nuanced: it satisfied the heteronormative fiction of the play yet admitted of homosexual self-realization – the queering of Orlando and, in so far as spectators had been taught by the production to see sexuality as fluid and gender as contingent, the queering of the audience as well.

The indeterminacy of sexual identity was playfully preserved in the Epilogue as spoken by Adrian Lester, who removed the bandana that he had worn as Rosalind and, in his own person, told spectators that "If I were a woman, I would kiss as many of you as had beards that pleased me" (16–18), teasing them with the possibility of homoerotic contact. The statement's conditionality reinforced the conflation of gender and performance in which spectators had been complicit throughout the play and reminded them that the heterosexual couplings they had just seen sanctioned might be as deceptive as the disguise by which Lester-as-Rosalind-as-Ganymede had presumed, ultimately, to fool no one. Lester's speaking the lines in his own voice, as male actor, challenged spectators to consider that when Rosalind had donned the attire of Ganymede, "she was perhaps not adding a layer of disguise so much as stripping one away, revealing the homoerotic foundations of the play's marital structure" (DiGangi 1996: 286).

Cheek by Jowl's production has become a landmark in performance studies because it so brilliantly destabilized gender assumptions which had characterized productions of Shakespeare since the Restoration. Actresses playing cross-dressing women's roles create a different sexual dynamic; such casting does not encourage so playful an awareness of gender difference among spectators, and the homoerotic potentials of performance are buffered by safe assurances that the real attraction Orlando feels, albeit unconscious, is to the woman's body beneath Ganymede's male disguise. Yet to effect such a change in the audience's way of looking, Cheek by Jowl's *As You Like It* was suffused with a gay aesthetic which politicized the production in a manner consistent with queer advocacy in late 1980s' and early 1990s' Britain. The erotic play between Ganymede and Orlando was the most prominent way in which the staging foregrounded same-sex relations; but the lesbian force of Celia's jealousy of Rosalind, the flaunting of macho versus fem culture, and hunky foresters with bare chests taunting a queenly Jaques carrying a cigarette lighter, made explicit an identity politics which a production that played the cross-dressing "straight" would have left unexplored. Intriguingly, even with such explicit references to gay culture, many critics insisted on seeing the production's cross-dressing as uninflected by a political agenda, "an unremarkable stage convention," not at all transgressive or reflective of contemporary cultural anxieties over gender identity and sexual desire. In 1991, I would argue, when AIDS was still regarded as God's revenge on homosexuals and homophobic violence was commonplace, it would have been impossible for a production as daring as this *not* to ground itself in gay political discourse.

Queering *Twelfth Night*

In the decade since Cheek by Jowl's 1994 revival of *As You Like It*, same-sex performances of Shakespeare have steadily gained ground on both sides of the Atlantic, and nowhere more than at London's reconstructed Globe. What began as an experiment with two productions in the late 1990s – an all-male *Henry V* (1997) preceded *Antony and Cleopatra* – attracted enough attention that within a short time same-sex casting had become company policy, yielding at the extreme, in 2003, a division of the actors into two separate companies, one male, the other female. The Globe's use of all-male casts is consistent with its claims to strive for Elizabethan authenticity in staging, music, props, and costumes; as such, it has renewed speculation about how boy actors would have been "read" on the Elizabethan stage. The Globe's all-male productions have therefore become imbricated in critical debates over the sexually transgressive nature of cross-dressing: they are seen as potent laboratories for measuring the extent to which boys "taken for" women might have heightened the anxieties of Elizabethan audiences over the instability of gender roles.

As several perceptive critics have pointed out, however, such claims to authenticity are bogus, raising expectations of historical verisimilitude only to satisfy them with an amusement-park version of Elizabethan culture. How could one expect to replicate the experience of an Elizabethan audience when cultural contexts have changed so radically? (Worthen 1999 and 2003: 79–110; also Rutter 2001: 88–9). The material conditions of performance are not the same today as they were in 1600: the structure of the new Globe itself makes many concessions to modernity, actors are differently trained, and rehearsal processes are more subject to a director's vision. Furthermore, audiences bring vastly different assumptions with them about family, courtship, and social class as well as gender, erotic desire, and homosexuality. More to the point, adult male actors on the new Globe's stage are fundamentally different – in physical appearance, maturity, voice, professional training, and social empowerment – from the boy apprentices who performed at the original Globe, and their playing roles written for boys casts doubt upon any claim the new Globe might make to replicate the experience an Elizabethan audience would have had.

In response to such criticism, the Globe's artistic director Mark Rylance has attempted to clarify that authenticity, which he considers a "confusing and arrogant" term, was never a goal of his company. Rather, the company uses what he calls "original practices" to test whether Elizabethan methods of staging may still be theatrically viable and to help "recover the original way of making art," thereby unearthing "layers of meaning that modern practice obscures" (Rawson, *Pittsburgh Post Gazette*, November 2, 2003). This all sounds innocent enough. But I shall argue that calling the use of an all-male cast an "original practice" is in fact a tactical ruse by which Rylance coaxes audiences to divest themselves of essentialized notions of gender and sexuality and, if only for the duration of the play, to entertain queer thoughts. In other words, the Globe's "original practices" productions advance a culturally transgressive agenda rendered safe by the distancing device of historical recuperation. They offer up a subversive sexual politics which, under the conservative guise of archeological work, are made palatable as popular entertainment.

Indeed, the Globe's production of *Twelfth Night* in 2002 prided itself on being the most authentically Elizabethan of all, right down to the hand-sewn underwear worn by the actors. Zoe Gray's essay on clothing in the Globe's program begins, "This production is the most authentic that the Globe Theatre Company has staged to date, with specially arranged period music, an all-male cast and authentic Elizabethan dress" (*Twelfth Night* program 2002). And despite Rylance's protestations to the contrary, when director Tim Carroll was asked, "Do you feel constrained or liberated by an historically 'authentic' approach to the play?," he made no effort to challenge the premise: "Since I was trying to create a believable set of Elizabethans, accurate research was a simple necessity" (*Twelfth Night* program 2002). Given this brief for historical accuracy, the all-male cast made Carroll's production a provocative test case for "original practices," especially because the play has become the *locus classicus* of scholarly debate over the impact of cross-dressed boy actors on the Elizabethan stage (Jardine 1992, Crewe 1995, DiGangi 1996, Hutson 1996, Orgel 1996). *Twelfth Night* offers ample scope for sexual role-play and confusions of erotic attraction to bolster the argument that gender was performative on the Elizabethan stage; and given the play's susceptibility to queer theory, it is not surprising that such issues were resonant in the new Globe staging, which played 100 sold-out performances in 2002 and was revived briefly in 2003 before embarking on a successful American tour. It was the Globe's most popular production to date.

Rylance's strategy of using "original practices" to challenge spectators' belief in a stable system of gender began as one entered the theatre and saw, on the stage, the actors applying make-up and wigs, fastening their corsets, adjusting their skirts and farthingales, and practicing the prim gestures and gliding walks that would mark them as feminine. This privileged glimpse into the artifices of the tiring house laid bare the illusionary nature of theatre, provoking in the audience, according to John R. Ford, "a self-conscious awareness of the processes, both social and theatrical, through which clothing and language both measure and construct a self" (2003: 49). Spectators were encouraged to enter into the spirit of Butlerian performativity – to watch men in the process of *becoming* the women they would play, adopting citational codes of femininity, and discovering "the 'reality' of social performance" (Ford 2003: 54). Writing in less theoretical terms, Ben Brantley observed: "the cast members bring out the actor in each of the characters," who in turn "do not let you forget that these actorly creatures are being portrayed by actors" – a mutual reinforcement of theatrical and gender artifice that Brecht would have approved (*New York Times*, August 29, 2002). This manipulation of the audience into accepting as historically conventional a casting that foregrounds adult transvestism and otherwise challenges inviolable beliefs about gender and sexual desire came into sharpest focus during scenes between Viola and her protector Orsino.

Viola originally must have been played by an adolescent boy. Disguised as the page Cesario, she is described by Orsino as having a maiden's voice and no facial hair (1.4.30–4);[6] she herself wishes to be presented to him as a eunuch (1.2.53); and we learn that she and her twin brother Sebastian lost their father, presumably not many years earlier, on the day they turned 13 (5.1.239) – an age at which boy apprentices were hired to play women's roles. The Globe's casting of an adult male in that role, therefore, was neither historically accurate nor an "authentic practice," as Katherine Duncan-Jones recognized (*Times Literary Supplement*, June 7, 2002). Yet for audiences in 2002 it proved more acceptable than the alternative of casting a boy in the role, because while sexual desire between adult males has become increasingly tolerated in Western societies, the sexual desire of an adult male for an adolescent boy would have raised the distasteful specter of child abuse and pedophilia – topics of no great concern to Elizabethans, perhaps, but of grave concern to us. In the view of today's audiences, if Orsino and Olivia were to traffic in 13-year-old boys, they would land in jail.

Instead, the casting of an adult male as Viola/Cesario foregrounded the possibility of mutual homosexual desire. In Act 2 Scene 4, Orsino, who has employed Cesario to serve as an emissary to the countess Olivia, grills Cesario on his experience in love. It is clear from the text that Orsino is attracted to what is feminine in Cesario, just as Viola has developed a passion for Orsino which she cannot reveal. At the new Globe, Orsino was played by a virile Scottish actor (Liam Brennan), and Viola by a spindly maypole of a young man with long hair, a cape, a hat and a discernible beard (Michael Brown). Hardly the eunuch called for by the text, the actor lightened his voice to sound more boyish; but it was clear to spectators that the adult male actor, in the process of playing Viola playing a page boy, was in fact looking and sounding much like himself. Furthermore, apart from the second scene of the play in which she washes up on shore in her women's weeds, Viola dresses throughout in male attire, thus keeping the sex of the actor abundantly clear. Casting two grown men made the homoerotic tensions of the scene palpable: Orsino wrestled with a passion for Cesario that he was ashamed to acknowledge, and Cesario pined with an unrequited love for him. When Orsino asked whether Cesario's eye had ever "stayed upon some favour that it loves" (2.4.23), the ambiguity of the younger man's answer, "A little, by your favour" (2.4.24), registered as a sexual hint to Orsino rather than as a secret confession. And when the hints kept coming – Cesario tells Orsino that his love is "Of your complexion" (2.4.25) and "About your years, my lord" (2.4.27) – the body language between them revealed that the hints had been understood aright. The two men glanced at one another, turned away in embarrassed confusion, then glanced again. As the Fool sang about a lover being "slain by a fair cruel maid" (2.4.53), they slowly moved towards one another and held hands. For spectators, a tension arose between what the fiction of the play suggests – an explicitly heterosexual attraction on Viola's part, an unconscious heterosexual attraction on Orsino's to the woman inside the male disguise – and what the performance by the actors was urging them to perceive, a homoerotic longing on the part of both men. By his looks, Orsino tried to assure himself that he was not feeling sexual attraction to this boy; but as they sat together on a bench and he took Cesario's hand, he suddenly commanded that "all the rest give place" (2.4.78) so that he could be alone with him.

The contest between the competing energies of sexual desire and denial grew heated when Orsino instructed his young minion to go again with a suit to Olivia – an odd displacement of his erotic desire onto an absent object – and Cesario protested that the suit was pointless. Their ensuing debate over a hypothetical lady who might feel "as great a pang of heart" (2.4.89) for Orsino led Cesario to the brink of confession: "Ay, but I know –" (2.4.103). The risk of exposure passed only when Orsino challenged him, "What dost thou know?" (2.4.104) and Cesario completed his thought with a safely ambiguous sentiment, "Too well what love women to men may owe" (2.4.105). If Cesario is taken for a woman in disguise, her interrupted line ("Ay, but I know –") becomes almost an accidental revelation of her female identity, and the hypothetical condition ("were I a woman" [2.4.108]) a poignant confession of her scarcely hidden passion for the man whom she is addressing. If Cesario is taken for a man, however, then the condition and the confession – "it might be, perhaps, were I a woman / I should [love] your lordship" (2.4.108–9) – reveal something more unnerving for both of them: a love that dare not speak its name. Both interpretive options were in play at the new Globe: for spectators, according to Brantley, "different levels of perception swim in and out of focus. It is sexy, uncomfortable and highly disorienting" (*New York Times*, August 29, 2002).

Cesario's final, enigmatic admission that he is "all the daughters of my father's house, / And all the brothers too" (2.4.120–1) – both sexes in one – instilled Orsino with confidence enough to make his move. On the pretext of comforting Cesario, he put his arms around him; and in the words of Nicholas de Jongh, "their consoling embraces turn[ed] passionate, their faces almost touch[ed], eyes held, mouths loitering on the verge of a kiss" (*Evening Standard*, May 23, 2002) (Figure 30.2), until Cesario in confusion broke off with "Sir, shall I to this lady?" (2.4.122). At this point, sexual tension eased and the audience laughed; the kiss had passed unconsummated, the norms of heterosexual behavior threatened but not violated. What was significant about this moment is that the production had made spectators complicit in the subversion of such norms: they expected the kiss to happen, had been rooting not only for Orsino to give Viola what *she* wanted, but for him to give Cesario what *he* wanted. Something of this same effect was achieved in Trevor Nunn's 1996 film, when Orsino and Cesario came perilously close to kissing in a barn while the Fool, wide-eyed, looked on. The difference, however, was that a woman was cast as Viola and looked (as most actresses do) more feminine than masculine as Cesario. In so far as Viola's male disguise is unconvincing to the audience, Orsino's attraction to his page may be sanctioned as permissible in heteronormative terms, even though *he* may find it perplexing. Homosexual desire thus remains latent, and audience awareness of the layers of gender performance never need extend beyond what is demanded by the text's fiction. In the Globe performance, however, the all-male cast served as an alienating device to provoke spectators to grapple with the conditionality of gender identity and sexual desire; and it is telling that even in so popular a venue as the Globe, appealing heavily to tourists, families, and parties of school children, audiences were receptive to such provocation.

This *Twelfth Night* managed to eschew the gay identity politics that characterized Cheek by Jowl's *As You Like It* a decade earlier and to carry cross-dressing into the cultural mainstream, indicating an evolution in the public's sensitivity to gender issues and receptivity to same-sex relationships. De Jongh's blithe assertion, for example, that the "production vividly reflects Shakespeare's sense of the fluidity and arbitrary drive of an erotic desire that leaps the bounds of gender" (*Evening Standard*, May 23, 2002) assumes in readers an understanding of the contingencies of gender identity and sexual desire that it would have been unheard of for a reviewer to assume only a decade earlier. It is symptomatic of such an evolution that director Tim Carroll chose to play as "straight" the play's most obvious locus of homosexual longing, Antonio's for the young Sebastian – an interpretation which has become commonplace in contemporary *Twelfth Nights* (see Pequigney 1992) – in order to focus sexual confusion on the ostensibly heterosexual couplings. Unlike Cheek by Jowl, the Globe needed to provide no such key to the production's political agenda. A persistent awareness of the actors' maleness in scenes depicting sexual desire was sufficient to

FIGURE 30.2 Liam Brennan as Orsino and Michael Brown as Cesario in the Globe's *Twelfth Night* (2002) Photograph by John Tramper. Reproduced with permission of Shakespeare's Globe.

keep Globe spectators alert to the production's invitation to see gender at play, gender *as* play, and unthreatened by the sexual indeterminacy which cross-dressing signifies.

The production complicated the audience's perception of gender even further by employing different types of transvestism – that is, by allowing spectators to see that men may cross-dress with various levels of artifice (Senelick 2000, Drouin 2004). Where Viola's disguise had much to do with "passing" – the phenomenon wherein the actor creates a sufficiently credible performance, in the theatre as in life, to convince spectators that he is a woman – the actor playing Maria, Paul Chahidi, drew much of the humor of his performance from drag.[7] A stocky man whose Maria was middle-aged and matronly, he made no effort to disguise the rich timbre of his baritone voice nor, despite the white make-up which the Globe's program noted was authentically Elizabethan, to fully disguise his dark beard (Figure 30.3). (Peter Shorey, who played Maria in the 2003 revival, was thinner, lither, of lighter complexion, and more conventionally "feminine.") The comedy of Chahidi/Maria's interactions with Sirs Toby and Andrew derived in part from his scarcely concealed masculinity, reminiscent not so much of cross-dressers who try to "pass" for women today as of comedians such as Dame Edna who camp it up in women's clothing. Drag is a sly parody of femininity: at once exaggerated and conscious of its own theatricality, it does not expect to be taken seriously. The delight spectators took in Maria's performance sprang from the parodic nature of her disguise, which made little effort at mimetic

FIGURE 30.3   Paul Chahidi as Maria in the Globe's *Twelfth Night* (2002)
Photograph by John Tramper. Reproduced with permission of Shakespeare's Globe.

credibility. When, for instance, Maria told Andrew to "bring your hand to th' buttery-bar, and let it drink" (1.3.66), a line by which she referred bawdily to her own breasts, she grabbed his hand and placed it on her chest. Laughter erupted first because the action was so brazenly unfeminine, and second because the audience was aware that there was no breast there – an absence that worked differently here than in Ganymede's similar action with Jaques in the Cheek by Jowl *As You Like It*, because it was not a serious reminder of the artifice of gender construction. Chahidi's performance of Maria was so blatantly parodic that spectators needed no reminder; and Andrew, for his part, reinforced the absurdity by reacting with shock to the breast that he ostensibly felt.

Further comic benefits of drag accrued when Cesario entered for his first interview with Olivia. Olivia had placed Maria at the table, holding an account book as if she were mistress, not maid; so when Cesario spied Maria and asked incredulously "if *this* be the lady of the house" (1.5.163), the effect was ludicrous. How could such a heavy, squat figure be the object of Orsino's sexual desire? The effect was capped when Maria replied to Cesario's impertinence with "No, good swabber" (1.5.195), which in his baritone sounded like an aggressively male insult. But the comedy of such an obviously male Maria elicited most laughter when Sir Toby, in gratitude to Maria for her plot against Malvolio, kissed her on the lips – "Good night, Penthesilea" (2.3.165) – then did a double-take. The view of a soused Sir Toby kissing a drag Maria was funny enough; but his looking puzzled by the kiss – perhaps because he had felt the beard – won applause. Unlike the near-kiss between Orsino and Cesario, this one

FIGURE 30.4   Mark Rylance as Olivia in the Globe's *Twelfth Night* (2002)
Photograph by John Tramper. Reproduced with permission of Shakespeare's Globe.

did not problematize spectators' perception of gender or suggest homosexual desire. Indeed, it may have served as a safety valve for spectators to release any discomfort they may have felt over the growing affection between Orsino and Caesario, to laugh at a farcical bit of gender schtick when elsewhere the production had insisted that the performance of gender be taken more seriously. Toby's confusion was momentary and, because the credibility of the situation was stretched beyond belief, uncomplicated. He was not as knowing as spectators: they were privy to the source of his confusion, he was not.

The recognizably comic style of Maria's drag lent, by way of contrast, greater mimetic credibility to the cross-dressing performance of Olivia, with whom she frequently appeared onstage. In Olivia's costuming the Globe's brief for historical authenticity reaped its richest rewards. Olivia entered to the tolling of a clock, in a black gown of mourning set off by a white ruff, a veil, and, once the veil was removed, a short black curly wig topped by a crown (Figure 30.4). The iconic resemblance to Queen Elizabeth was unmistakable, especially as she wore an almost grotesque white make-up which resembled that in Elizabeth's portraits. Time was clearly catching up with this Olivia: her costume and make-up spoke to her advancing years and her lack of female attractiveness. Actor Mark Rylance delivered his lines in a pinched, feminized voice, stammering at key moments, and glided when he walked as if on casters (Michael Coveney, *Daily Mail*, May 23, 2002; Rhoda Koenig, *Independent*, May 23, 2002). Such idiosyncrasies called attention to themselves as clever characterization but never once let spectators forget the male actor beneath the dress. Furthermore, Olivia's vow to remain unmarried and to put off all wooers alluded historically to Elizabeth's treatment of her suitors, particularly the Duke of Alençon, and to her status as Virgin Queen (Mallin 1995). Just as Elizabeth fashioned herself politically as both king and queen, so did Rylance construct his Olivia androgynously, as both male and female, and the deliberate historical artifice was part of the character's appeal.

Looking regal as she signs papers, clearly mistress of all she surveys, Rylance's Olivia was nevertheless defensive about her decision not to marry. Her vulnerability was most poignantly dramatized when she stammered to Cesario "You might do much" (1.5.266) and begged him to "come ... again" (271). Here she was clearly flustered over feeling passion for a man half her age in spite of her vow, at risk of making a fool of herself; and in her soliloquy following his departure, one heard the pangs of lost opportunity, the pining of age for youth. The text, of course, asks us to believe that Olivia is smitten with a pretty page boy. In the Globe performance, however, the spectators' perceptions of the actors' bodies complicated matters. When two actresses play the scene, as is typically the case, spectators may at once surrender to the heterosexual fiction and yet sense that Olivia unconsciously perceives the female beneath Cesario's male disguise, a possibility which suggests that she loses her heart to a woman, a younger version of herself – a kind of narcissism, if not lesbianism, to which she has seemed prone (Traub 1992a). At the Globe, however, an ambiguously male Olivia made a play for an unambiguously male Cesario; and when she sent the ring after him, Cesario's soliloquy, which ostensibly laments Olivia's misperception of his sex, took on new and potentially homoerotic meanings: "Fortune forbid my outside have not charmed her. / She made good view of me ... She loves me sure ... I am the man" (2.2.18–25). That line, "I am the man," is no longer ironic if Viola is gendered male. Instead, it signifies a young man's refusal to give in to the blandishments of an older woman or, more provocatively, a cross-dressing queen.

The deliberate confusion of the actor with the roles he plays was most tellingly enforced by the entry of Sebastian, Viola's twin brother. Ordinarily productions must finesse the similitude: where the text requires Cesario to be repeatedly mistaken for Sebastian and vice versa, in modern performances it is always a stretch for the audience to imagine that the actress playing Cesario could possibly be mistaken for the actor playing her brother, who typically is taller, broader, his voice deeper, his musculature more developed. In the Elizabethan theater, Cesario and Sebastian would, as played by adolescent boys, presumably have been more easily mistaken for one another. In the Globe production, too, Sebastian was readily taken for Cesario's twin: the two actors were of nearly identical build, their faces and voices similar, their costumes the same (Figure 30.5). Their similitude kept gender identities in flux and the potential for same-sex mating deliberately in play. Such potential was reinforced at the conclusion, when neither Olivia nor Orsino – nor, for that matter, the audience – could keep their mates "straight."

Figure 30.5 Rhys Meredith as Sebastian and Michael Brown as Cesario in the Globe's *Twelfth Night* (2002)

Photograph by Mike Torrington. Reproduced with permission of Shakespeare's Globe.

Olivia's ejaculation "Most wonderful!" (5.1.219) when she saw identical twins standing before her – two objects of sexual desire, doubling the fun – expressed the spectators' delight too; and as if to emphasize her own and the production's susceptibility to same-sex pairings, when Cesario told her, "So comes it, lady, you have been mistook" (5.1.253), she threw up her hands as if to say, "So what?" The precariousness of gender identity in the theatre was dramatized most potently when Orsino began, "If this be so" (5.1.259) and eagerly signaled his readiness to be mated with Viola, who stood before him still as Cesario, the only form in which Orsino had known her (Jardine 1992). The sexual dynamic at this point was complex: Orsino's coupling with the boy who had served him as a page was sanctioned because, in the text, the boy is in fact a woman; but on the Globe's stage, Orsino's readiness could be taken as an expression of his desire for the male he had lusted after all along; and as if comically to underscore the possibility, he mistakenly grabbed Sebastian's hand, not Viola's, when he vowed, "Your master quits you" (5.1.312). His mistake made comically visible the uncertainty of Globe spectators, for like him, they could not distinguish the man from the woman, since in performance there was no distinction: they could not tell the man from the man. Their applause for this moment indicated that they were complicit in the sexual politics of the performance, reveling in the ambiguities of gender role-play and accepting with pleasure the homoerotic potential of the final couplings. As Dominic Cavendish's review confirmed, the all-male cast dramatized

Figure 30.6   The jig: Liam Brennan as Orsino, Rhys Meredith as Sebastian, Michael Brown as Cesario, and Mark Rylance as Olivia in the Globe's *Twelfth Night* (2002)

Photograph by John Tramper. Reproduced with permission of Shakespeare's Globe.

the idea that "we never really know ourselves or our desires. The play may ostensibly right its deviancies by establishing joint-sex rather than same-sex partnerships, but the gender distinctions remain purely in our minds" (*Telegraph*, May 24, 2002).

No other modern *Twelfth Night* has so explicitly questioned the play's heterosexual affirmations or so pervasively queered the audience, educating them to appreciate the comic value of gender as performance and to delight in the sexually transgressive unions towards which the play's confusions move. The jig danced at the final bow cunningly reinforced this point. For the first measures, it appeared as if the couples were appropriately paired – Orsino danced with Cesario, who was still in his male attire, and Olivia with Sebastian. But suddenly, the actor playing Sebastian revealed that he had been dancing with the wrong partner: he stepped away from Orsino, bowed, tapped Olivia on the shoulder, and the partners switched (Figure 30.6). No one in the audience seems to have been the wiser. Spectators proved to be as susceptible to the deceptions of gender performativity as Olivia and Orsino had been. The final trick had been played on *them*.

What the Globe does by using all-male casts is not a matter, as Rylance claims, of historical recuperation. How could it be when grown men are playing roles written for boys, and when contemporary understandings of sexuality and gender identity are so different now from what they were in 1600? By placing all-male casts under the rubric of "original practices," however, Rylance cleverly co-opts audiences into accepting as authentically Elizabethan – and as archeologically sanctioned – a theatrical cross-dressing which undermines the essential nature of gender identity and the biological determinism of sexual desire. Globe productions thus foreground our own contested ideas about gender and homosexuality, those very ideas which scholars during the past two decades have projected, perhaps anachronistically, onto the performance of plays in the Elizabethan theatre. Cross-dressing at the original Globe may indeed have reflected cultural anxieties about gender, sexuality and self-representation; but those issues are of even greater fascination to us today, and ironically, the use of cross-dressing in contemporary productions of Shakespeare may speak with a greater force to us than it ever did to Elizabethan audiences. It has allowed us to turn our gaze on our own spectatorship and to find there a willingness to entertain culturally transgressive notions of gender and sexuality that, rightly or wrongly, scholars have presumed to find among spectators 400 years ago.

NOTES

1   Clifford Williams's celebrated 1967 all-male production of *As You Like It* (National Theatre at the Old Vic) was an isolated experiment. It occurred when audiences were not yet ready seriously to entertain questions of gender construction and when representations of homosexuality were still banned, by order of the Lord Chamberlain, from the British stage. For a history of the censorship of homosexuality on stage, see de Jongh (1992).

2   Several years earlier than Orgel, Lisa Jardine (1983: 9–36) had argued that cross-dressing boys were especially exciting to male spectators: "'Playing the women's part' – male effeminacy – is an act for a male audience's appreciation" (1983: 31). Orgel and Jardine differ, however, on the extent to which male transvestism was a symptom of a pervasive cultural misogyny: for Orgel, the homoeroticism of the Elizabethan stage was not *inevitably* misogynist. See also Orgel's essay on "The performance of desire" in *Impersonations* (1996: 10–30).

3   See Margaret Loftus Ranald, *Shakespeare Bulletin* 12.4 (Fall 1994): 10; Peter Holland, *Shakespeare Survey* 45 (1992): 128; and Katie Laris, *Theatre Journal* 47 (May 1995): 300; and compare Ben Brantley's assertion in his review for *The New York Times* that "[t]he fact that men are portraying women here is less a statement about sexual role playing than about playing

roles in its broadest and most resonant sense" (October 6, 1994). Holland's analysis of the production's depiction of gender was unchanged in his collection *English Shakespeares* (1997: 91–4) which appeared in the same year as Solomon's more Butlerian account of the effect of all-male casting. This inclination to de-emphasize the production's sexual role play in the interest of universalizing its performativity – and a sentimental insistence on subsuming gender in the transcendent power of love – was perhaps the most common critical response to the all-male casting.

4   All citations are to the Oxford *As You Like It* (1993).

5   The most influential studies of the representation of homosexuality in the early modern period are Bray 1982, Smith 1991, Goldberg 1992, DiGangi 1997, and Masten 1997. These writers help to clarify cultural differences between how homosexuality is viewed today, as a form of sexual identity, and how it was viewed in Shakespeare's time, when identifying oneself by sexual preference was unheard of and the only term for same-sex relations was sodomy. The myth of Ganymede as a vehicle for expressing same-sex desire in the period has been the subject of books by Saslow (1986) and Barkan (1991), and shorter studies by Smith (1991: 199–223) and DiGangi (1996: 281–5).

6 All citations are to the Oxford *Twelfth Night* (1994).

7 Beginning with *Tootsie* in 1982 and continuing with *Mrs. Doubtfire* in 1993 and *Adventures of Priscilla, Queen of the Desert* in 1994, Hollywood has popularized cross-dressing by making it comic and thus acceptable to a wide audience. Such drag performances betray the reactionary nature of much popular culture, yet more serious questions of gender difference and "passing" were being explored in films as early as *The Crying Game* in 1991 – a surprising success at the box office – and later in *Boys Don't Cry* (1999). The success of such films signifies a greater willingness in audiences to grapple with volatile issues of gender formation, cross-dressing, and homosexuality; and while comic drag remains the safest way for audiences to dismiss such issues, edgier films about "passing" testify to a growth in audience receptivity to the representation of same-sex love.

REFERENCES AND FURTHER READING

Astington, John H. (2001). "Playhouses, Players, and Playgoers in Shakespeare's Time." In Margareta de Grazia & Stanley Wells (eds.) *The Cambridge Companion to Shakespeare*. Cambridge: Cambridge University Press.

Barkan, Leonard (1991). *Transuming Passion: Ganymede and the Erotics of Humanism*. Stanford, CA: Stanford University Press.

Boswell, John (1980). *Christianity, Social Tolerance, and Homosexuality: Gay People in Western Europe from the Beginning of the Christian Era to the Fourteenth Century*. Chicago: University of Chicago Press.

Bray, Alan (1982). *Homosexuality in Renaissance England*. London: Gay Men's Press.

Butler, Judith (1990). *Gender Trouble: Feminism and the Subversion of Identity*. New York: Routledge.

Butler, Judith (1993). *Bodies That Matter: On the Discursive Limits of "Sex."* New York: Routledge.

Callaghan, Dympna (2000). *Shakespeare Without Women: Representing Gender and Race on the Renaissance Stage*. London: Routledge.

Cressy, David (2000). *Travesties and Transgressions in Tudor and Stuart England*. Oxford: Oxford University Press.

Crewe, Jonathan (1995). "In the Field of Dreams: Transvestism in *Twelfth Night* and *The Crying Game*." *Representations* 50: 101–21.

Dawson, Anthony (1996). "Performance and Participation: Desdemona, Foucault, and the Actor's Body." In James C. Bulman (ed.) *Shakespeare, Theory, and Performance*. London: Routledge.

Dawson, Anthony, & Yachnin, Paul (2000). *The Culture of Playgoing in Shakespeare's England: A Collaborative Debate*. Cambridge: Cambridge University Press.

de Jongh, Nicholas (1992). *Not in Front of the Audience: Homosexuality on Stage*. London: Routledge.

DiGangi, Mario (1996). "Queering the Shakespearean Family." *Shakespeare Quarterly* 47: 269–90.

DiGangi, Mario (1997). *The Homoerotics of Early Modern Drama*. Cambridge: Cambridge University Press.

Dollimore, Jonathan (1991). *Sexual Dissidence: Augustine to Wilde, Freud to Foucault*. Oxford: Clarendon Press.

Drouin, Jennifer (2004). "Gender on the Stage, Gender on the Street: Cross-Dressing, Drag, and Passing." Unpublished paper written for a seminar on cross-dressing in contemporary performances of Shakespeare, Shakespeare Association of America, New Orleans.

Dusinberre, Juliet (1996). "Squeaking Cleopatras: Gender and Performance in *Antony and Cleopatra*." In James C. Bulman (ed.) *Shakespeare, Theory, and Performance*. London: Routledge.

Ford, John R. (2003). "Estimable Wonders and Hard Constructions: Recognizing *Twelfth Night* at the Globe." *Shakespeare Bulletin* 21, 3: 47–60.

Garber, Marjorie (1992). *Vested Interests: Cross-Dressing and Cultural Anxiety*. New York: Routledge.

Goldberg, Jonathan (1992). *Sodometries: Renaissance Texts, Modern Sexualities*. Stanford, CA: Stanford University Press.

Holland, Peter (1997). *English Shakespeares: Shakespeare on the English Stage in the 1990s*. Cambridge: Cambridge University Press.

Howard, Jean E. (1988). "Cross-Dressing, the Theater, and Gender Struggle in Early Modern England." *Shakespeare Quarterly* 39, 4: 418–40.

Howard, Jean E. (1994). *The Stage and Social Struggle in Early Modern England*. London: Routledge.

Hutson, Lorna (1996). "On Not Being Deceived: Rhetoric and the Body in *Twelfth Night*." *Texas Studies in Literature and Language* 38: 140–74.

Jardine, Lisa (1983). *Still Harping on Daughters: Women and Drama in the Age of Shakespeare*. Totowa: Barnes and Noble.

Jardine, Lisa (1992). "Twins and Travesties: Gender, Dependency and Sexual Availability in *Twelfth Night*." In Susan Zimmerman (ed.) *Erotic Politics: Desire on the Renaissance Stage*. London: Routledge.

Jones, Ann Rosalind & Stallybrass, Peter (2000). *Renaissance Clothing and the Materials of Memory*. Cambridge: Cambridge University Press.

Levine, Laura (1994). *Men in Women's Clothing: Anti-Theatricality and Effeminization, 1579–1642*. Cambridge: Cambridge University Press.

Mallin, Eric S. (1995). *Inscribing the Time: Shakespeare and the End of Elizabethan England*. Berkeley, CA: University of California Press.

Masten, Jeffrey (1997). *Textual Intercourse: Collaboration, Authorship, and Sexualities in Renaissance Drama*. Cambridge: Cambridge University Press.

Mazer, Cary M. (2004). "Rosalind's Breast." Unpublished paper written for a seminar on cross-dressing in contemporary performances of Shakespeare, Shakespeare Association of America, New Orleans.

Orgel, Stephen (1989). "Nobody's Perfect, or Why Did the English Stage Take Boys for Women?" In Ronald R. Butters, John M. Clum, & Michael Moon (eds.) *Displacing Homophobia: Gay Male Perspectives in Literature and Culture*. Durham, NC: Duke University Press, pp. 7–29.

Orgel, Stephen (1996). *Impersonations: The Performance of Gender in Shakespeare's England*. Cambridge: Cambridge University Press.

Pequigney, Joseph (1992). "The Two Antonios and Same-Sex Love in *Twelfth Night* and *The Merchant of Venice*." *ELR* 22: 201–21.

Potter, Lois (1999). *Shakespeare Quarterly* 50, 4: 514.

Rutter, Carol (2001). *Enter the Body: Women and Representation on Shakespeare's Stage*. London: Routledge.

Saslow, James M. (1986). *Ganymede in the Renaissance: Homosexuality in Art and Society*. New Haven, CT: Yale University Press.

Senelick, Laurence (2000). *The Changing Room: Sex, Drag and Theatre*. London: Routledge.

Shakespeare, William (1993). *As You Like It*, ed. Alan Brissenden. Oxford: Clarendon Press.

Shakespeare, William (1994). *Twelfth Night*, ed. Roger Warren & Stanley Wells. Oxford: Clarendon Press.

Shapiro, Michael (1994). *Gender in Play on the Shakespearean Stage: Boy Heroines and Female Pages*. Ann Arbor: University of Michigan Press.

Smallwood, Robert (2000). "Shakespeare Performances in England." *Shakespeare Survey* 53: 244–73.

Smith, Bruce R. (1991). *Homosexual Desire in Shakespeare's England: A Cultural Poetics*. Chicago: University of Chicago Press.

Smith, Bruce R. (1992). "Making a Difference: Male/Male 'Desire' in Tragedy, Comedy, and Tragic-Comedy." In Susan Zimmerman (ed.) *Erotic Politics: Desire on the Renaissance Stage*. London: Routledge.

Solomon, Alisa (1997). *Re-Dressing the Canon: Essays on Theater and Gender*. London: Routledge.

Stallybrass, Peter (1992). "Transvestism and the 'Body Beneath': Speculating on the Boy Actor." In Susan Zimmerman (ed.) *Erotic Politics: Desire on the Renaissance Stage*. London: Routledge.

Traub, Valerie (1992a). *Desire and Anxiety: Circulations of Sexuality in Shakespearean Drama*. London: Routledge.

Traub, Valerie (1992b). "The (In)significance of 'Lesbian' Desire in Early Modern England." In Susan Zimmerman (ed.) *Erotic Politics: Desire on the Renaissance Stage*. London: Routledge.

Worthen, W. B. (1999). "Reconstructing the Globe, Constructing Ourselves." *Shakespeare Survey* 52: 33–45.

Worthen, W. B. (2003). *Shakespeare and the Force of Modern Performance*. Cambridge: Cambridge University Press.

Zimmerman, Susan (ed.) (1992). *Erotic Politics: Desire on the Renaissance Stage*. London: Routledge.

Zink, Abbey (2000). "The Lady Was a Dame: Gender Performance and the Role of Cleopatra in the 1999 RSC and Globe Productions of *Antony and Cleopatra*." *Shakespeare Bulletin* 18, 1: 20–3.

31

A Thousand Shakespeares: From Cinematic Saga to Feminist Geography or, The Escape from Iceland

Courtney Lehmann

Introduction: The Winter of Our Discontent

If the Shakespeare-on-screen explosion of the past 15 years has generated an affirmative response to the question, will the Bard "play in Peoria," then women filmmakers might do better to consider whether or not their Shakespeare films will survive Iceland. Such was Jane Smiley's shocking implication in her essay "Shakespeare in Iceland," wherein she recounts her writing of *A Thousand Acres*, a feminist retelling of *King Lear* from the perspective of the oldest daughter, Ginny. Smiley's painstaking experience of writing this novel emerged from her actual sojourns in Iceland and her intellectual journey through the Icelandic sagas, a genre that features interpersonal cruelty as a condition of everyday life. But it was her inescapable feeling that the patriarchal horrors showcased in Shakespeare's play surpassed even the *Njáls* saga – as well as her own take on medieval doom and gloom, *The Greenlanders* (1988) – that led her to imagine her version of *Lear* "not in populous, voluble, green England, but in treeless, distant Iceland" (1993: 168).

For the women who were brought there as slaves during the Viking raids of the British Isles, Iceland was a point of no return. For Smiley, however, Iceland is a point of perennial return as a psychological landscape that embodies the alienating experience of engaging with Shakespeare – *without* whom, she claims, "English cannot be written" (1993: 165) – but *with* whom she found only a disturbing absence of connection. In fact, she was increasingly convinced that Shakespeare's Lear, if not Shakespeare himself, shared something of the Viking temperament, a disposition marked by "cold, irreducible self-interest, unashamed, unsoftened by any sense of connection with others or of any common humanity" (1993: 172). Yet what Smiley deemed "courageous" in the Icelandic sagas, namely, the conviction to forgo the prospect of redemption and "to fall at last into total darkness" (1993: 171), she condemned in Shakespeare – for he took her along for the ride – and the journey back from this raw psychological abyss became the most challenging writing experience of her life. Though Smiley ultimately relocated the setting of *A Thousand Acres* to a place not unlike Peoria – the fictional Zebulon County, Iowa – her imaginative returns to and invocations of "Iceland" as a metaphor for an authorial process inseparable from abjection are particularly apt, I shall argue, for women filmmakers.

In the cinema, women have had to contend with a climate far more forbidding than the one Smiley faced when she and Shakespeare "set sail for Iceland" (1993: 165). Cecil B. DeMille put it bluntly when he exclaimed: "A director must sway his actors just as an orator sways his audience. There have been a few great women orators. There will be a few women directors" (quoted in Dunning 1927: 33). The fact that there have been more than a few women directors, not to mention great ones, remains relatively unknown nearly a century after DeMille uttered his disparaging remarks. Indeed, beginning with Alice Guy-Blaché, who is credited with directing the first narrative film in 1896, women have been on the scene of the most important developments in the history of the medium, ranging from innovations in proprietorship and studio management to technological, aesthetic, and ideological breakthroughs. Yet the view that cinema is inherently patriarchal – born of the masculinist imperatives of the scopic drive and shored up by an all-male pantheon of *auteurs* – persists, and nowhere is this assertion more tenacious than in the context of women's Shakespeare films.

In 1914, Lois Weber directed the first feature-length Shakespearean comedy, *The Merchant of Venice*, initiating a series of important but forgotten Shakespeare films by women. Prior to the 1996 discovery – in a Portland, Oregon, basement – of a five-reel *Richard III* dating back to 1912, Weber's film was considered to be the first Shakespearean feature ever made; yet this director, writer, actor, studio owner, and producer of hundreds of films has been virtually ignored by film historians and feminist theorists alike. Weber's film does not appear in any film history or compendium, nor, for that matter, does the first Shakespearean musical film, a Soviet adaptation of *Much Ado About Nothing* directed by Tatyana Berezantseva, entitled *Lyubovyu za Lyubov*. But there are more surprising "firsts" that suddenly come into focus when Shakespearean film history is filtered through a feminist lens. The first Shakespearean "talkie," *The Taming of the Shrew*, emerged through Mary Pickford's financing, as well as through her shrewd efforts to appropriate the new sound technology as an extension of the political voice American women acquired in 1920. Much later, Liz White would capitalize on the libratory environment of the Civil Rights movement to generate the first-ever all-Black *Othello*, filmed between 1962 and 1966. Featuring a distinctly African Othello, White's film updates Shakespeare's play to convey the perils of racial assimilation in America, as well as to comment on the tragic exclusion of women from the masculinist rhetoric of Black

Power. Remarkably, Liz White never obtained distribution for her path-breaking motion picture, screening it instead at Howard University shortly before she died. In fact, with the exception of Jocelyn Moorhouse's 1997 adaptation of Jane Smiley's *A Thousand Acres*, women filmmakers since Pickford have produced, directed, and distributed their Shakespeare pictures *outside* the Hollywood system, suggesting the extent to which the glass ceiling is supported by a filmmaking climate that is forbidding, treacherous and, unmistakably, "Icelandic."

During the singular decade of the 1990s, in which more feature-length Shakespeare films were released than in all the previous decades combined, women directors took their chances with Shakespeare in media other than celluloid. Working at Soyuzmultifilm in Moscow in collaboration with Christmas Films in Wales, Natalya Orlova, Mariya Muat, and Aida Ziablikova directed several films in the critically acclaimed HBO series, *Shakespeare: The Animated Tales*, in the early to mid-1990s. Rather than relying on computers or traditional cel animation, Orlova and Muat chose to adapt Shakespeare's plays through the most labor-intensive techniques, literally creating their signature films of *Hamlet*, *Richard III*, *Twelfth Night*, and *The Taming of the Shrew* by (sleight of) hand (Osborne 1997). In 1997, Penny Woolcock represented Shakespeare through the lens of alienated labor, setting her made-for-TV film of *Macbeth* in Birmingham, England, on the Ladywood Housing projects, where the survivalist climate of medieval Scotland is translated into a contemporary tragedy about life "on the dole." As if imagining a sequel to this film, Allison LiCalsi followed suit in the US with a scathing satire of corporate greed called *Macbeth: The Comedy*; however, given the lack of venues for digital distribution, this award-winning film has been shown exclusively at festivals. Only Christine Edzard (*As You Like It* 1992; *The Children's Midsummer Night's Dream* 2001), Jocelyn Moorhouse (*A Thousand Acres* 1997), and Julie Taymor (*Titus* 2000) emerged from this decade, having braved the cost-prohibitive medium of celluloid and the often chilly waters of commercial release for their Shakespeare adaptations. Indeed, although Edzard's two-part Dickens epic, *Little Dorrit*, won her instant critical acclaim upon its release in 1988, her two Shakespeare films met with equally swift denunciation. Similarly, despite becoming something of a household name with her Broadway adaptation of *The Lion King* (itself a spin-off of *Hamlet*), Taymor suffered violent rebukes for her mixture of horror, pathos, and the absurd in *Titus*. Moorhouse has enjoyed only marginally better reception for her version of *A Thousand Acres*, but here, too, reviews have been quick to locate the film's strengths in its cast, which features Jessica Lang, Jason Robards, Michelle Pfeiffer, Jennifer Jason Leigh, and Colin Firth, while attributing its weaknesses to its director.

Among these films, Edzard's *As You Like It* and Moorhouse's *A Thousand Acres* resonate as distinctly "Icelandic" adaptations, focusing on the idea of "the land" as an uncanny signifier of the female body-in-pain and the profoundly unnatural social antagonisms that perpetuate the mutual degradation of both habitat and humanity. Significantly, contemporary Icelandic women writers, when asked why they eventually return to their "distant, treeless" homeland, unanimously conclude: "the land"

(Sigurdardottir, quoted in Hoben 2002: 14). What they don't talk about is why – and how – they came to leave Iceland in the first place. This is the point at which *As You Like It* and *A Thousand Acres* enter the picture as sagas that document what I will call the *escape* from Iceland. As a real geography imbued with an originary oppression of and interminable allure for women, "Iceland" functions in my argument as a powerful synecdoche for the treacherous cultural terrain that women directors traverse in the process of engaging with Shakespeare; it is, in other words, the *imaginative* geography that they must enter into, decolonize, and emerge from long before the very prospect of "playing in Peoria" can be broached. Hence, the geographical locations featured in both *As You Like It* and *A Thousand Acres* bear little resemblance to this tidy, bustling, Bible-belt town where films go to be born again. Rather, Edzard's dilapidated English dockyards and Moorhouse's agribusiness-or-bust Midwest are landscapes scarred with losses – ranging from the loss of occupation and identity to miscarriage and mastectomy – all of which underscore the perverse symbiotic relationship between the films' female protagonists and the devastated "natural" habitats they occupy. Resisting the empty compensations of victimization, however, these cinematic sagas more powerfully affirm Smiley's assertion that adapting Shakespeare is inseparable from *adapting to* Shakespeare, embarking upon a perilous, reverse middle-passage back to "Iceland" and, ultimately, forward to the unforeseen alliances that form the coordinates of a distinctly feminist geography.

From Western to Eastern

As films that are preoccupied with the idea of the landscape as protagonist and, more often than not, as antagonist, *As You Like It* and *A Thousand Acres* necessarily imply a revisionary approach to the film genre that is most intimately tied to land: the Western. Though often associated with a series of unassailable stylistic components and archetypal themes, the Western is arguably one of the most elastic film genres. As André Bazin, Alan Lovell, and others have contended, the flexibility of the Western stems from the fact that the status of "the land" is inherently ambiguous, dependent for its meaning upon the film's social context. Perhaps the only staple of the Western is the movement it tracks from east to west, conveyed in stories of covered wagon convoys, the building of the railroad, and the settling of the frontier. It should come as no surprise, then, that the Western should be home to so many variations on the theme of manifest destiny, from Akira Kurosawa's "wild West" vision of the premodern and simultaneously post-atomic East in *Throne of Blood* to Ridley Scott's revisionary tale of two women "on the lam" and westward-bound in *Thelma and Louise*.

Elsewhere I have argued that in the context of *fin de siècle* film culture, the Western has become the register of a sinister mutation in the nature and status of authority, documenting the shift away from traditional ideas of law and order to the corrupt paternalism of the *noir* universe (Lehmann 2003). What I have called the "*noir* western" represents this problem of authority as something that is endemic to space, that is, as a crisis that inheres in the land itself. No longer presented through the romantic lens of the great outdoors but, rather, through *film noir*'s prurient fascination with post-industrial scenes of urban squalor and seedy suburban misery, the land in the *noir* western becomes a metaphor for the faceless, rapacious, corporatization of authority in the age of global capitalism, as well as for the dark corners of the unexamined conscience that perpetuates it. Hence, unlike the Wyatt Earp-style heroes of the classic Western, whose movement into "wide open spaces" is directly correlated with their ever-expanding base of power, the ambiguous hero of the *noir* western has more in common with a figure like Shakespeare's Macbeth or Kurosawa's Washizu, who finds that every action he takes leads to a claustrophobic reaction, as the space around him – both geographical and psychological – steadily contracts. Similarly, in Ridley Scott's portrait of reluctant *femmes fatales*, this implosion of space and perversion of authority is depicted in the obscene geology of the American Southwest, where the massive monoliths that could afford Thelma and Louise protection instead loom menacingly over their tiny convoy, as if poised for an easy kill. Here, the chiaroscuro effects of sun and shadow that track Thelma and Louise's westward progress serve as a natural surveillance mechanism, silently parodying their flight from a criminal justice system that is predisposed to shoot them on sight for robbery while letting their rapists go free. Naturally, the film ends when the heroines run out of space, opting for a short ride over the rim of the Grand Canyon rather than the life-sentence that awaits them. Yet this final act of implosion, a heroic act in the tradition of *Butch Cassidy and the Sundance Kid*, permits the corruption that inheres in the system to carry on unperturbed. This, then, is the missed opportunity that *As You Like It* and *A Thousand Acres* seek to redress, by asking the question begged by the conclusion of *Thelma and Louise*: what would have happened if they had decided *not* to keep going but, rather, to head *east*, back to the scene of their own complicity in the quotidian crimes of everyday life? This Icelandic journey "into total darkness," to a place beyond the distraction of spectacle, the consolation of revenge, and the hope of redemption, is the point at which *As You Like It* and *A Thousand Acres* – as "easterns" – begin.

As in Shakespeare's play, in Edzard's film this journey is precipitated by a crisis of authority. Whereas Shakespeare represents this crisis as the product of aberrant individuals and, therefore, as an exception to the otherwise benign court of Duke Senior, Edzard situates the opening frames of her film firmly in the province of the *noir* Western, wherein corruption is a natural byproduct of space itself. Yet Edzard's representation of the "court" as a contemporary stockbrokers' firm does not reinforce the stereotypical vision of the city as a gritty, urban jungle; rather, this preferred breeding ground of late capitalism is hyper-sanitized, polished, and exceedingly orderly, a place where commodities spring eternal from immaculate conception – or at least from male parthenogenesis. That all of the employees of the unnamed firm are identically attired, meticulously groomed men is, therefore, not surprising. What *is* surprising is the disturbing sense of priority that this "land" of marble and mahogany assumes over its comparatively lifeless occupants, who spend their days filing robotically through revolving doors, hallways, and foyers like so many accessories briefly adorning the oppressive permanence of the building's architecture. Akin to the status of the land in the *noir* western, then, the court is infused with a distinctly claustrophobic quality that is accentuated not only by Edzard's reliance on close and medium shots but also by her decision to locate the court exclusively indoors. Even the scenes that we would expect to occur outside of the firm – Rosalind's private confession to Celia of her newfound love for Orlando, as well as Orlando's wrestling match with Charles – all take place conspicuously within its clutches. Celia's bed-chamber, for example, is represented as an extension of available office space, a place where the lone horizontality of a single red couch vies for prominence amidst the imposing verticality of the columns, reinforcing our creeping suspicion that *there is no place* outside of the firm. Like the totemic father who hoards all the women and imposes his perverse monopoly on pleasure, here, the corporation is represented as the Saturnalian maw poised to devour even its most loyal drones. Hence, the only characters who appear even remotely comfortable in the building, refusing to churn its machinery by pausing to lean, sit, or lounge within its intimidating fixtures – Adam, Orlando, Celia, and Rosalind – are precisely the characters who will be exiled from it.

With an extraordinary economy, this sleek urban landscape demonstrates the extent to which authority in the *noir* universe is no longer recognizable in the form of the prohibitions and protection once offered by the paternal metaphor, by the absent Other who insures the smooth functioning of society based on a common experience of lack. Quite the contrary, authority in the *noir* universe is obscenely *present* as the source of unrelenting entreaties *to enjoy* within the purchase-or-perish logic of late capitalism. Edzard underscores this ethos of excess by featuring a scene of sumptuous banqueting in the firm as a prelude to the wrestling match between Orlando and Charles. But it is the wrestling match itself, designed not only as the perfect nightcap for the partygoing elite but also as an opportunity to eliminate other potential claimants to the corporate coffers, that suggests the extent to which consumption has become a pathology within this corporation. Moreover, as a kind of cock-fight between "undesirables" – the disinherited Orlando and the Black newcomer Charles – the wrestling match suggests the entertainment value that inner-city violence holds for the privileged while parodying the *laissez-faire* system of law enforcement that looks the other way at the self-destruction of the urban underclass. This endgame, in which the function of authority has shifted from protective to fratricidal, is the defining feature of what Juliet Flower MacCannell calls the "regime of the Brother," a putatively "post-patriarchal" power structure wherein the singular authority of the Oedipal father is, in reality, merely displaced by so many simulacra, the "wretched clones" and impostors who struggle for hegemony at everyone else's expense (Mac-Cannell 1991). In *As You Like It*, Edzard's decision to double the parts of Oliver and Orlando De Boys, Duke Senior and Duke Frederick, Le Beau and Corin, literalizes this idea of the "regime of the Brother" as a social order that derives its values not from an externalized principal of difference aligned with the traditional Oedipal father but, rather, from a narcissistic assertion of the same, a false brotherhood wherein mass conformity is treachery's greatest ally. Yet as the *mise en scène* morphs from the slippery marble interiors to the muddy and derelict docklands, we find something lurking therein that is far more sinister still: the specter of women seeking to enter the fraternity as one of "De Boys," that is, as Thatcherites.

Post-Thatcher Pastoralism

Edzard's relocation of the pastoral sequence of *As You Like It* from the mythical forest of Arden to the barren Rotherhithe docklands – home, both within the film and without, to indigents, thieves, and other victims of Thatcherite neglect – signals the film's investigative turn toward the provenance of the eastern. As the site of the *Mayflower*'s storied departure to America, Rotherhithe is inscribed with a long history of leave-takings, bearing the imprint of throngs of pilgrims in search of better lives. Even in its later incarnation as a flourishing Victorian wharf and, only decades ago, as the home of a lucrative shipping industry, Rotherhithe has always been associated with the prospect of departure. Hence, the *return* to Rotherhithe staged by Edzard's film reverses the escapist trajectory of Shakespeare's pastoral play. For contrary to the romantic vision of Arden as a journey into the great outdoors and, indeed, the great unknown, Edzard's industrial graveyard forces an encounter with the all-too-familiar specter of gender and class abjection. In this "distant, treeless" place there are no stealthy lions or sprawling snakes to attract tourists in search of the exotic; rather, what looms before us is an uninviting vista peopled with abandoned demolition projects, oil drum fires, and the makeshift dwellings of the homeless and hungry, a brutal burlesque of Thatcher's vision of a leaner, fitter Britain. That Edzard doggedly retains Shakespeare's copious references to deer, flocks, trees, and streams in a film wherein the only remaining sign of nature is the lone sheep that follows Corin about on a leash is a brutal reminder that, in the land of the eastern, as in this contemporary Arden, "greener pastures" simply do not exist.

Critical to our understanding of the eastern flow of Edzard's film into the abject spaces of Rotherhithe is its relationship to the Technicolor *film noir* revival of the early 1990s. As Dean MacCannell observes of *Public Eye*, *The Two Jakes*, and *Barton Fink*, these neo-*noir* films burst onto the screen as "a fictional recuperation of the proletarian city just as the actual proletarian space [was] historically lost" (1993: 282). MacCannell refers here to the urban impact of the Reagan and Thatcher revolution, in which cities were given the equivalent of face-lifts, that is, subjected to systematic gentrification under the alias of revised building codes and taxation schemes, as well as rezoning imperatives that rendered low-income housing virtually extinct. The *noir* films that appeared in the immediate aftermath of this process thus document a loss which, for the evicted occupants of such spaces, is experienced as literal homelessness. Edzard's *As You Like It*, released in the thick of the *noir* revival, evinces this relationship between urban renovation and abjection in the shift to the Rotherhithe location. Here, the shades of black that dominate classic *film noir* are replaced not by Technicolor but by a ubiquitous brown pall cast by the polluted, sepia-toned water, dirt, and docks – suggesting the seamy residue of Thatcher's white-collar urban renewal scheme. The exiled Duke Senior and his band of merry men thus represent the human casualties of this process, standing in for the countless victims of industrial downsizing, monetarist efficiency, and the collapse of the British welfare state throughout the 1980s. Yet the suggestion that this urban wilderness is also a site of potential subversion is evident not only in the many temporary dwellings and communal living arrangements that defy the capitalist commandment of private ownership, but also in the treatment of other values associated with Thatcherism, such as hard work and fiscal rigor, which are refigured parodically. Quite unlike the prescribed, robotic movements of the firm occupants, the forest-dwellers sport relaxed poses while engaging in profoundly non-productive activities, such as pipe-smoking, singing, and harmonica playing; meanwhile, Corin and Silvius, who have but one sheep to tend between them, form their own kind of labor union, as if to mock Thatcher's notorious assault on organized labor following the "winter of discontent" that preceded her reign (Figure 31.1). But it is in the interface between the derelict docklands and the Thatcherite city center – forged by Rosalind and Celia's wanderings – that we begin to read *As You Like It* as something more than a tragi-comic, Dickensian tale of Rotherhithe past and present. For in this film, released less than one year after the Thatcher era officially ended, Edzard offers us a glimpse of a far more disturbing future, where women, following in Thatcher's – or Rosalind's – footsteps, perpetuate their own abjection under the auspices of escape from it.

Brotherhood of Women

> What I am desperately trying to do is to create one nation, with everyone being a man of property, or having the opportunity to be a man of property.
> Margaret Thatcher, in Jenkins, *Mrs Thatcher's Revolution*

The problem generated by the encounter between homelessness and *film noir*, as Dean MacCannell explains, is that too often it precipitates nostalgia rather than intervention, satisfying the bourgeois fantasy of a "gamey or 'real' subproletarian existence" while inoculating audiences to the real thing (1993: 282). In other words, within the depraved, dog-eat-dog cityscapes of *film noir*, viewers are allowed "to live passively within the order of capitalism while imagining themselves to be opposed to it" (1993: 284). Reading against the prevailing feminist interpretations of *As You Like It*, I will argue that this is precisely the role that Edzard assigns to Rosalind, as a character who resembles less the subversive figure of "blue-jeaned freedom" (Lennox 1993: 62) than the ambivalent protagonist of *film noir* – the detective who has the luxury of

FIGURE 31.1   *As You Like It*, directed by Christine Edzard, Sands Films (1992)

standing outside of the capitalist totality to investigate its filthy edges without ever compromising his privileged place in the social order. Initially, though, it is not Rosalind but Celia who is aligned with the conservative upshot of the film's neo-*noir* trajectory, a point that is suggested by the rather comic packing scene that precedes the young exiles' flight to Arden, wherein Edzard takes pains to represent Celia's naïve preparations for the journey as the product of her affluent and sheltered lifestyle. As a door is thrown open to reveal a walk-in closet teeming with clothes that have never been worn, we watch as Celia rifles frantically through countless sartorial combinations to arrive at last at what Amelia Mariette describes as "the characteristic garb of a middle-class urbanite planning a trip to the country" (2000: 75). Particularly when compared with Rosalind's unkempt, longshoreman look, Celia's high-heeled entry into Rotherhithe does, at first glance, appear to stem from a bourgeois fantasy of "slumming it." Hence, hours later, when we see Celia slogging and limping through the mud while Touchstone drags her suitcases behind him, we can't help but feel some degree of smug satisfaction with her pain. But this is also the point at which Rosalind's and Celia's paths diverge, for whereas Celia comes to embrace the challenge of *adaptation* to her surroundings, Rosalind takes the path of least resistance, clinging to her role as a woman of propriety by becoming a Thatcherite "man of property."

Edzard develops this dichotomy through a politics of place and movement that is specific to the film's presentation of *As You Like It*'s female characters. Much in the same way that Agnes Varda's brilliant restoration of Jacques Demy's *Umbrellas of Cherbourg* employs color-coded costumes and décor to distinguish characters whose class is inexorably tied to location from those who are socially mobile and, hence, free from obligations of place, Edzard develops a similar scheme for exploring the social implications of location on women's bodies. In Edzard's film, however, to be a "fixture" – such as Audrey and Phebe are in Arden – is to establish a relationship to space that becomes an "occupation" in its own right, despite the specter of universal unemployment that haunts Arden and defines its inhabitants as implicitly out of place. Unlike the other characters in the film, Phebe and Audrey literally resemble their surroundings, as figures whose accessories – in Phebe's case, her make-up and in Audrey's case, her colorful snack van – are made to match the bright tones of Orlando's graffiti, which is the only source of color in the otherwise drab dockyards. When viewed as an extension of their surroundings, Phebe and Audrey assume strengths not attributed to them in Shakespeare's play. Phebe, whom Patricia Lennox describes as a "drop out from the local poly-tech" and "probably on the dole" (1993: 60) is, nevertheless, the diva of the docks; despite Rosalind's brutal judgment that she is "not for all markets," Phebe consistently asserts a powerful sense of self-ownership in her spirited rejections of her dejected admirer, Silvius. That she is always filmed out of doors ties these refusals to a more profound rejection of the feminized space of domesticity, which her aimless wandering of the dockyard implicitly subverts. Similarly, Audrey, who also lacks a proper sense of place as an owner-occupier of a traveling snack van, is likewise invested with the capacity for converting abjection into an asset. For example, although the stacks of unbought sandwiches that crowd her already tight quarters make it painfully obvious – when coupled with her intimidating girth – that she is herself her only regular customer, Audrey's physical robustness proves critical in her thwarting of Touchstone's aggressive sexual advances, as he discovers that neither rhetorical subterfuge nor manhandling will make her a "slut." Hence, while Audrey and Phebe occupy space in a way that *pre*occupies others, they do so in a way that subverts traditional cinematic objectification. Indeed, in a film wherein place functions as a protagonist, Edzard implies that objectification might prove a critical balance to personification; for to be an object, that is, to be an accessory *within* one's surroundings, is to be an accessory *to* a more encompassing conception of subjectivity – not a typology but, rather, a topography – attuned to the geopolitics of gender.

Somewhat surprisingly, Rosalind is not associated with this feminist geography in Edzard's film, for she is represented as literally incapable of settling into her Arden surroundings. When she is not cavorting about the docks in all her newfound androgynous glory, she is shown coming to rest in ever-new locations; be it on a stoop, in the shepherd's cote, or on the ground, Rosalind never appears in the same place twice. Thus, space is never figured as an extension of her subjective territory as it is for Phebe, Audrey and, eventually, Celia. This aloof and flighty characterization of Rosalind is indicative of her upwardly mobile desire to become "one of the boys." Her personification of Ganymede, as Patricia Lennox observes, transforms Rosalind into someone "whose ideas are now of interest to her fellow 'men.' Everyone seems to want to talk with her as a young male, even the solitary Jaques" (1993: 62). Indeed, this Rosalind clearly savors her borrowed robes and, while wearing them, shows a contempt for women that is equally unique to Edzard's film. Unlike the profound friendship that Celia and Rosalind share in Shakespeare's play, Rosalind is more than just mildly impatient with Celia's professed skepticism about the sincerity of Orlando's love, becoming petulant, if not openly angry with Celia on more than one occasion. In this context, Celia's rebuke of Rosalind for "misus[ing] our sex" in the guise of Ganymede is particularly apt, for she draws attention to Rosalind's unsavory habit of making her fellow women feel strangely out of place in their own surroundings: "We must have your doublet and hose pluck'd over your head, and show the world what the bird hath done to her own nest." But nowhere is Rosalind's bizarre brand of misogyny more pronounced than in her disdain for Phebe, whom she condescendingly instructs to "know yourself, down on your knees, / And thank heaven, fasting, for a good man's love." In Edzard's film, Rosalind's objection to Phebe's infatuation with her drag routine smacks not of homophobia but of the fear of class miscegenation – a transgression that jeopardizes Rosalind's own aspirations of becoming a Thatcherite "man of property." Right through the film's conclusion, then, where Rosalind playfully punches Orlando as a prelude to their wedding, she is represented as someone who, when push comes to shove, is more inclined to join an oppressive social order than risk beating it. Worse, as the implied marriages of Touchstone and Audrey, Silvius and Phebe – both of which take place back at the firm – suggest, Rosalind goes one step further by taking prisoners, calling the bluff of Phebe and Audrey's independence by convincing them that marrying a man is the next best thing to becoming one.

Democracy's Turn

> There is no such thing as society.
> Margaret Thatcher, quoted in Keay, *Woman's Own*

> "Society" is not a valid object of discourse.
> Laclau and Mouffe, *Hegemony and Socialist Strategy*

Celia is the leftover of this tidying-up operation, the figure who betrays the ideological fantasy of "society" – and the ties of "brotherhood" that bind it – as a ruse of multinational capitalism. Building on Laclau and Mouffe's observations, Slavoj Žižek explains:

society is always traversed by an antagonistic split which cannot be integrated into the symbolic order. And the stake of social-ideological fantasy is to construct a vision of society which does exist, … in which the relation between parts is organic, complementary. The clearest case is, of course, the corporatist vision of society as an organic Whole, a social body in which the different classes are like extremities, members each contributing to the Whole according to its function. (1989: 126)

Edzard's vision of the climactic conclusion of Shakespeare's play takes particular pains to establish this fantasy of society as a corporate body, as all the characters that have been doubled in the forest meet their counterparts in the firm to celebrate the weddings. In Shakespeare's play, Rosalind's epilogue ruptures this fiction of inclusion when she exposes herself to the audience as a man and, hence, violates the vision of society as a corporate (heterosexual) body in which the parts cooperate with each other to beget the "whole." Quite peculiarly, Edzard eliminates this epilogue in a film that is otherwise remarkably faithful to the text and, I would argue, assigns this disruptive role to Celia, whose transformation to and from "Aliena" becomes a palimpsest of the geopolitical transformation that Dean MacCannell refers to as "democracy's turn," or, "the perverse accommodation of capitalism by democracy" (1993: 289).

While in Arden, Celia experiences the inequities of late capitalism first-hand and, like Phebe and Audrey, her process of adaptation is encoded in the ways she is made to resemble her surroundings. The sparseness of her hut, for example, is mirrored in the stripping away of all her personal accessories, which have been replaced by uncoordinated layers of clothing, clothes she wears to keep warm. Suddenly a transient tenant rather than an owner-occupant, Celia nevertheless attempts to infuse her tiny shelter with everyday acts of proprietorship, such as boiling an egg, making a flower arrangement, or curling up on the floor; in so doing, she confronts the crisis of unemployment that permeates Arden with alternative "occupations." Celia's conversion is so convincing that her sudden silencing and return to the firm upon looking at – and, apparently, loving – the reformed Oliver, is believable only in light of the false choice between female independence and escape from class abjection that Edzard poses as a late-capitalist variation on the democratic theme implied by the phrase "as you like it." As a privileged character who exercises her democratic freedom in successfully becoming poor, Celia more powerfully represents the failure of the counter-fantasy that maintains democracy's rapport with capitalism: the inverse "freedom" of the poor to become rich. What Celia's journey eastward into the abject spaces of Rotherhithe exposes, then, is a democracy which has been so hopelessly compromised that it has been reduced to a choice between freedom and comfort. And Celia's "turn" westward, reflected in her decision to follow Rosalind's cue by marrying in – and into – the firm, is a vision of democracy's turn writ small, whereby perpetuating the regime of the Brother becomes the ultimate expression of "sisterhood."

The singular contribution of this film to our understanding of the broader adaptation process with which I am concerned, then, lies in its attempt to lay bare the mechanism that permits such oppressive geopolitical and interpersonal partnerships to proceed unimpeded by the eruptions of resistance that characterize Edzard's Arden. This mechanism or, better put, social *manqué*, is nothing other than love. In the Lacanian sense of the term, "love" is the fundamental deception that enables lack to annul itself in an illusion of mutual completion. In both Edzard's film and Shakespeare's play, the compensatory triangulation toward "love" is represented as the answer to the irreconcilable friction between political autonomy and personal comfort proper to Arden and the court, respectively; only in Edzard's film, however, is this vision of love as a bridge between the democratic freedoms of an impoverished Arden and the spiritually-bankrupt comforts of the capitalistic firm exposed as a sham. Specifically, it is Edzard's unique approach to Celia's character, whose migration between these locations renders her a kind of cinematic "Figurenposition," which affords us the "dual perspective that ... penetrates the showy surface" of both places to uncover their shared "hypocrisies, ... shames and rewards" (Weimann 1978: 226). For in her patently unbelievable transformation back from "Aliena," as well as her instantaneous and permanent silencing upon her first enamored glimpse of Oliver, Celia exposes what the obscene father and his band of brothers have labored to conceal all along: that *alienation*, not love, is what defines our real conditions of existence within global capitalism, and this is the only fringe benefit that democracy unconditionally guarantees for everyone. But if love nevertheless prevails in the series of festive unions that conclude *As You Like It*, so does Edzard's assertion of its artificiality, for both the firm and the brides-to-be are, in this resolutely anticlimactic final scene, bizarrely draped in polyurethane, as if to accentuate the fact that Rosalind and Celia have officially entered the land of the man-made. Indeed, although they have safely returned from "Iceland," their winter of discontent has just begun at the firm, where they will soon discover that the glass slipper and the glass ceiling are made of the very same stuff.

Family Values

Although the abandonment of Rotherhithe is rendered official by the conclusion of *As You Like It*, this drab urban dockland remains the site of a deliberate return for Christine Edzard, as the place that she and partner Richard Goodwin chose for the creation of their production company, Sands Films, purchased with the money made from Goodwin's highly successful commercial productions of *Murder on the Orient Express* and *A Passage to India*. Rather than agreeing to produce the entire series of Agatha Christie murder mysteries slated for adaptation, Goodwin and Edzard opted to invest in Rotherhithe over and against the westward pull of Hollywood. It seems more than a little ironic, then, that by some bizarre stroke of cinematic bureaucracy, Disney should own the rights to *As You Like It* and has never released the film in the

United States, where its vision of postindustrial squalor might not play well in post-NAFTA Peoria. It is in this context that Jocelyn Moorhouse's *A Thousand Acres*, released five years after Edzard's film, resonates as a provocative sequel to *As You Like It*. Tracing the decline of the uniquely American myth of manifest destiny – a social-ideological fantasy that places women and the land on the same brutal axis of exploitation – *A Thousand Acres* exposes the seamy underbelly of America's founding "corporation," the family farm (Figure 31.2). Hence, whereas the *noir* sensibility in *As You Like It* is evinced by an all-consuming corporate machine and the specter of homelessness that is its residue, in *A Thousand Acres*, the *home itself* becomes the site of this pathological implosion. What distinguishes both Smiley's novel and Moorhouse's film as neo-*noir* narratives, then, is their decision to broach the domestic territory that traditional *noir* fiction considers to be off limits; for to violate these formerly private and secure spaces is to render the home at once *heimlich* and *unheimlich*, a place where a suddenly "desublimated oedipality" forces us "to own up to the *familiarity* of all that is *officially Other and strange*, that makes home-making a dislocating experience, from blue-sky beginning … to blue-sky end" (Pfeil 1993: 238, emphasis mine). Framed by deceptively clear blue skies, *A Thousand Acres* presents us with the authorized story of "family values" in the American heartland only to yield to an Icelandic homily about a place where the gratifications of a plundered landscape are inextricable from those offered by the violation of the oldest taboo: father–daughter incest.

FIGURE 31.2 *A Thousand Acres*, directed by Jocelyn Moorhouse (1997), produced by Buena Vista/Touchstone/Beacon/Propaganda/Via Rosa/Prairie

Photograph by Photofest

In considering locations for an adaptation of *King Lear* that would approximate her harrowing experience of Shakespeare's play, Jane Smiley settled on a place that she knew as well, if not better, than Iceland – Iowa – in the midst of the "iron season," when everything is "frozen and dead and unattractive" (1993: 169). But Smiley soon found that by setting Shakespeare in contemporary Iowa as opposed to the Iceland of the sagas, the brutal bluntness and transparency of intent that fueled her long engagement with the medieval mind completely dropped away from her characters. Not only was Shakespeare, she complained, filled with "too much talk," but worse, Iowans – with their typical middle American manners – judiciously avoided self-revealing sentiments (1993: 161–2). Amidst such proprieties, how was she to depict the cruelty which, in her view, rendered *King Lear* more "Icelandic" than the sagas themselves? Nevertheless, the more Smiley thought about what separated Iowa from Iceland, the more these tensions between decorum and abjection became the very basis of her adaptation, crystallizing in an insidious poisoning process through which women and the landscape become the locus of a shared degradation. Indeed, while living in Iowa, Smiley herself became fearful that she was being incrementally poisoned by DDT and other toxins from the well water she was drinking and, like the character Ginny in her novel, she grew concerned about the prospect of serial miscarriage. But alongside this trepidation about literal, environmental poisoning Smiley became conscious of a more subtle, social toxin dramatized by setting *King Lear* in the American Midwest: the myth of "proper daughterhood" which, in "patriarchal capitalist Western European society," subtly reinforces the cultural mentality that seeks "to possess other persons as objects and to call that 'love' " (1993: 173). The Iowa setting of *A Thousand Acres* thus evinces both of these man-made poisons in the form of a uniquely American agrarian idealism – a pathological "love" of the land that is experienced *not* "as something similar to, or merely comparable to [woman], but as the female principle of gratification itself" – hence comprising, as Annette Kolodny observes, "all the qualities that Mother, Mistress, and Virgin traditionally represent for men" (1975: 150). As if imagining an alternative ending to Christine Edzard's *As You Like It* which, albeit reluctantly, refigures the myth of good daughterhood as the judicious modulation of the Mother, Mistress, and Virgin roles, Jocelyn Moorhouse's film ventures eastward to confront this cycle of female complicity in search of a place beyond its seemingly inexorable "loop of poison" (Smiley 1991: 398).

As in Edzard's film, *A Thousand Acres* takes for its point of departure the establishment of a corporation, only in this case, the scale is reduced from firm to family, as the aging patriarch Larry Cook announces his plan to preempt inheritance taxes and sign his farm over to his daughters and their husbands. The title of this adaptation, which displaces Shakespeare's Lear with the land itself, prepares us to interpret Larry's redistribution of his authority in this scene as indicative of a shift away from the traditional paternalism of the Oedipal family. What this shift more subtly heralds, however, is a turn toward the far more sinister regime of the Brother. Recognizing how this signature feature of the *noir* universe permeates *A Thousand Acres* is imperative, for we are set up to view Larry – whom all three daughters still call "Daddy" – as a traditional father-figure rather than the more menacing clone who, as Juliette Flower MacCannell explains, retains "the 'name' of the father" but in reality "embodies a misnomer," acting as "a superego whose existence [he] denies" (1991: 12, 2). It is not long before we realize, however, that as a father who repeatedly rapes his own daughters, Larry Cook is *exemplary* of this neo-totemic order based not on prohibition but on enjoyment. That his perverse authority both mirrors and is reinforced by the only slightly less offensive "brotherhood" of Zebulon County, comprised of Harold, Ty, Pete, Henry Dodge, Ken LaSalle, Marv Carson, and even Jess – all of whom enjoy some portion of Larry's bounty (including his daughters) – reveals the extent to which this *noir* order is sustained by a false sense of community, wherein "ever smaller factions of people proclai[m] their duty-bound devotion to their own special brand of enjoyment" (Copjec 1993: 183). Such is the vision of "family" that flourishes in Zebulon County where, as Smiley writes, neighbors "had only the most tenuous links to one another. Each lived a distinct style, to divergent ends" (1991: 158). But unlike Smiley's novel, Moorhouse's film seeks to redefine the family – and the land that sustains it – in post-patriarchal terms.

Set in 1979 at the beginning of the global farm crisis and the end of feminism's second wave, Smiley's novel culminates in a vision of Icelandic nihilism when the youngest member of the Cook family, Rose's daughter Linda, takes a business degree with a future in vertical food conglomerates. Not only has the farm been lost, sold to the enterprising Heartland Corporation, but so, too, has the family; for although Ginny survives to raise Rose's daughters, she observes that "they don't have a great deal of faith in my guardianship" (1991: 397). No wonder, given that the final section of the novel is virtually devoted to Ginny's attempt to poison Rose with arsenic-laced canned sausages after Rose discloses her affair with Jess. But Ginny is punished for her homicidal jealousy when Rose dies a slower, more painful death following a second bout with breast cancer. Similarly, in her relationship with her youngest sister, Caroline, Ginny can do little more than second-guess her convictions; having missed her opportunity to reveal the horrors of her past as she and Caroline wade through their now-deceased father's estate, Ginny flatly concludes: "I should have told Caroline the truth" (1991: 392). Hence, at the end of the novel, Ginny is left alone to cope with the only legacy she has after losing her father's land: the traces of it that remain in her body – the "molecules of topsoil and atrazine and paraquat and anhydrous ammonia and diesel fuel and plant dust, and also molecules of memory" – all the things that comprise the daily funeral of her "young dead self" (1991: 397, 399). Unable to break the cycle of complicity and victimization, Ginny obsessively takes the eastern pass through Rose's horrifying revelation that their father didn't rape either one of them but, rather, seduced them, pricking herself to life with the "gleaming obsidian shard" of his memory (1991: 399) which, like the smiling stretches of their sadomasochistic heartland, punishes its proprietors without conferring wisdom on them.

This sinister relationship between the land and its occupants is accentuated in Moorhouse's 1997 film which, like Edzard's approach to Rotherhithe, evokes the plight of the director's native Australia. Once an untamed wilderness, the formerly isolated penal colony has been forced to enter the global agricultural market on its hyper-productionist terms; the ensuing pressure to increase output at all costs has led to the near-extinction of the family farm and severely degraded the natural resources, while simultaneously accelerating local demands for participatory democracy and coalition-based, ecological measures bent on tempering the imperatives of trans-national profit-making. Moorhouse's reliance on panoramic cinematography and a dramatically condensed version of Smiley's narrative brings these antagonisms into sharp focus by prompting the spectator to identify with the female characters based on their relationship, or lack thereof, to the land. Despite the film's blue-sky beginning, its voiceover narration – a staple of *film noir* – immediately prompts us to question appearances, as Ginny's romantic memory of her 8-year-old view of the farm as a place that was "as flat and as fertile, as black and exposed, as any piece of land on earth" gives way to the blunt statement: "the next year my mother died." Following establishing shots of Ginny preparing breakfast for her father, the scene shifts to Rose's kitchen, where her husband Pete sheepishly points to a missed button on her dress that threatens to reveal her prosthetic breast. "Is it that ugly?" Rose snaps. Though as "fertile" as the land itself, Rose is more powerfully aligned with its "flatness" following a radical mastectomy for the same cancer that killed her mother, while Ginny, cancer-free, has suffered five miscarriages from her exposure to farm toxins that migrated into the well water. Like the aloof Rosalind in Edzard's film, Caroline is the only female character who is not identified with any aspect of the land; she is the city girl who, quite literally, got away – from her father's midnight rounds as well as from the other perils associated with life on the farm – leaving for law school in Des Moines without any appreciation of the sacrifices her sisters made to get her there. In Moorhouse's adaptation, then, the primary obstacle to the democratic governance of Larry's estate proposed at the outset of the film stems less from the obscene father and his drones than it does from the *sister* who preserves their power in the name of her own private enjoyment – a vision of "democracy's turn" writ small.

Whereas Smiley's novel ends by reinscribing the regime of the Brother in Ginny's memories of Pete, Jess, Ty and above all her father, whose inescapable figure metas-tasizes into a vast fraternity of associations with remorse, resistance, darkness and, ultimately, "the whole wide expanse of mid-continental sky" (1991: 398), Moor-house's film investigates the broken promise of this putatively "post-patriarchal" regime from the perspective of its most insidious clone: postfeminism. With updated accessories and attitude – including a laptop computer and a cultivated disdain for all things rural – Jennifer Jason Leigh's Caroline reflects the late 1990s' setting of Moorhouse's film, which was released in the very same year that the vogue for postfeminist fiction peaked with the publication of *Bridget Jones's Diary* (1997). Falsely heralded as feminism's "third wave," the postfeminist mentality typified by Helen Fielding's novel is predicated on the notion that "women are simply no longer afraid to honestly assess and define themselves without having to live up to standards imposed by either a persistent patriarchal world or the old feminist insistence that female characters achieve self-empowerment" (Mazza 2000: 104–5). Often coupling a fiercely individual, "liberal" agenda with self-destructive behaviors such as alcohol and drug abuse or predatory sexuality, postfeminists imagine a world wherein *only* the personal matters – and in this context, the personal is almost *never* political. Jennifer Jason Leigh might be considered the poster girl of this pop-cultural phenomenon. From her portrayal of Hedra Carson in *Single White Female* to Selena Claiborne in the Stephen King thriller, *Dolores Claiborne* and, even, to Blondie O'Hara in *Kansas City*, Leigh's roles support a pathologically estranged vision of female identity that is based on the mimetic desire to be "absorbed into [the] general brotherhood" (Flower MacCannell 1991: 26). Hence, Moorhouse's approach to Caroline as a glib, thirty-something professional whose success is the product of her lifelong denial of difference – from her childhood desire to be a farmer rather than a farmwife to her self-serving, adult alliances with men like Ty, Ken La Salle, Larry, and the deceptively-named Heartland Corporation that ultimately subsumes them all – gives the lie to the post-patriarchal auspices of the regime of the Brother while simultaneously exposing postfeminism as a "collective" movement which, in fact, reifies the capitalist totality as "mere multiplications of a singular, private self" (Flower MacCannell 1991: 33).

By contrast, Moorhouse's Ginny rejects this conformist enterprise and gains, in the process of losing the farm, a version of the family that denaturalizes such inequities of "love," exchanging its conditional promises for coalitional practices. Rather than shoring up the neo-*noir* order implied by the massive, leveling machinery of the transnational Heartland Corporation, Ginny – unlike Caroline and, for that matter, Edzard's Celia – retreats from both the disavowal of and the demand for difference by taking a step toward the *differential*: "the 'abyss' " where decolonized meanings, contradictory codings, and unexpected alliances constitute what "is best thought of not as a typology but as a *topography* of consciousness in opposition" (Sandoval 2000: 53). Whereas Smiley's novel concludes with a devastating implosion of bodily and geographical space, as the victory of vertical conglomerates christens Ginny's fatalistic resignation of her body to the whims of jealousy and other socio-chemical toxins manufactured on the farm, Moorhouse's Ginny chooses a course tied less to corporatism than to a desire to reorient and, in effect, "reincorporate" her body in a way that bears the scars of capitalism's productivity fetish while challenging its exploitative, global relations with a profoundly local, distinctly differential vision of the family. But as Chela Sandoval warns, "[i]t is a painful crossing to this no place, this chiasmus, this crossroads, for here new kinds of powers imprecate the body as it is dissolved" (2000: 140). Indeed, Ginny dissolves the Icelandic memory of her father's crimes only by entering into painful chiasmatic exchange with her sister, supplying the nurturing breasts that Rose has lost by becoming the surrogate mother of Rose's children, just as Rose concedes to her sister the fertile womb Ginny never had. Hence, where Ginny is going or what the future holds for her as she drives away from the farm with Rose's children in tow is uncertain at best at the conclusion of Moorhouse's film. Nevertheless, it is not the direction but the movement itself that is significant, for having at last owned up to the brutal *familiarity* of "all that is officially Other and strange" (Pfeil 1993: 238), Ginny is prepared to embrace a revolutionary concept of love – that is, of "family" – as a "relation *without* a site" (Barthes 1978: 36, emphasis mine).

Conclusion: Iceland Revisited

This state of mind, located at the easternmost border of the possible, gives us a sense of what Jane Smiley had in mind when she applauded "the courage to fall at last into total darkness" featured in the Icelandic sagas (1993: 171). In the cinematic sagas I have examined here, this Icelandic state of mind materializes in the commitment to occupying space differentially – to free-falling into the "abyss" where, quite literally, there is no ground for (re)inscribing domination, only space for practicing adaptation. But the question remains: why choose Shakespeare as a sailing partner to this no-place in the first place? The unlikely kinship between women filmmakers and Shakespeare hinges on their precarious ontological status as "authors." For if, as Judith Mayne contends, "the articulation of female authorship threatens to upset the erasure of 'women' which is central to the articulation of 'woman' in the cinema" (1990: 97), then "Shakespeare" is emblematic of the double-bind whereby absence is the very signature of authorial presence, indeed, the archetypal "relation without a site." This profound absence of the authorial root-and-branch – what Deleuze and Guatarri characterize in *A Thousand Plateaus* (1987: 520) as an "arborif[ied]" and, therefore, totalizing genealogy – is precisely what makes Shakespeare so adaptable to the undulating horizons of feminist geography, particularly in the context of imaginative travel to and from "distant, treeless" Iceland. Indeed, by entering into a "rhizom[atic]" (1987: 516) relationship with Shakespeare, women filmmakers confront the authorial possibilities of their own abjection, embracing the differential movement that Smiley characterizes in "Shakespeare in Iceland" as the "paradox-of-otherness-simultaneous-with-kinship-or-affinity" (1993: 176).

Such an outcome is, of course, far easier imagined than performed, for as Mayne observes, women filmmakers are the site of conflicting authorial imperatives, charged with displacing the "patriarchal and proprietary implications" of "the noun authorship" *without* emptying "the adjective female" of its gender-specific meanings and political implications (1990: 95). Hence, women filmmakers often solve this dilemma in idiosyncratic, highly personal ways, frequently resorting to the use of their own bodies as sites for "the inscription of authorship in literal terms" by appearing in their films (1990: 94). What makes the work of Christine Edzard and Jocelyn Moorhouse particularly significant in this context is the fact that while both directors recognize that such inscriptions of the personal are, importantly, political, they deploy the body in more encompassing, distinctly geopolitical terms – without, remarkably, losing sight of the adjective "female." In so doing, their films reconfigure biology not as destiny but as geography, approaching "woman" as the locus of a uniquely *global* intimacy which, like the body itself, is "threaded through and through with the cilia of affiliation" (Angier 1999: 364). These "cilia" are the source of a differential movement which, in the hands of Edzard and Moorhouse, is profoundly Shakespearean and, indeed, uncannily "cinemato-graphic – a kinetic motion that maneuvers, poetically transfigures, and orchestrates while demanding alienation, perversion, and reformation in both spectators and practitioners" (Sandoval 2000: 43). Hence, though far removed from the box office success which determines all that is familiar and officially Other in southern Illinois, Christine Edzard's *As You Like It* and Jocelyn Moorhouse's *A Thousand Acres* tap into an adaptation process that suggests their enduring significance – and survival – as "films" that have been playing for some four hundred years in a far more fertile place: Shakespeoria.

REFERENCES AND FURTHER READING

Angier, Natalie (1999). *Woman: An Intimate Geography.* Boston: Houghton Mifflin.

Barthes, Roland (1978). *A Lover's Discourse: Fragments,* trans. Richard Howard. New York: Hill and Wang.

Bazin, André (1976). "The Evolution of the Western." In Bill Nichols (ed.) *Movies and Methods.* Berkeley, CA: University of California Press, pp. 150–7.

Copjec, Joan (1993). "The Phenomenal Nonphenomenal: Private Space in *Film Noir.*" In Joan Copjec (ed.) *Shades of Noir.* London: Verso, pp. 167–97.

Deleuze, Gilles & Guatarri, Félix (1987). *A Thousand Plateaus: Capitalism and Schizophrenia,* trans. Brian Massumi. Minneapolis: University of Minnesota Press.

Dunning, Charles S. (1927). "The Gate Women Don't Crash." *Liberty* 4, 2: 33.

Fielding, Helen (1997). *Bridget Jones's Diary.* New York: Viking Press.

Hoben, Mollie (2002). "Iceland's Hot Writers." *BookWomen* August–September: 14–17.

Jenkins, Peter (1988). *Mrs. Thatcher's Revolution: The Ending of the Socialist Era.* Cambridge, MA: Harvard University Press.

Kavanagh, Dennis (1987). *Thatcherism and British Politics: The End of Consensus?* Oxford: Oxford University Press.

Keay, Douglas (1987). "Aids, Education and the Year 2000." *Woman's Own* October 31: 8–10.

Kolodny, Annette (1975). *The Lay of the Land: Metaphor as Experience and History in American Life and Letters.* Chapel Hill, NC: University of North Carolina Press.

Laclau, Ernesto & Mouffe, Chantal (1985). *Hegemony and Socialist Strategy: Toward a Radical Democratic Politics.* London: Verso.

Lawrence, Geoffrey (1992). "Farm Structural Adjustment: The Imperative for the Nineties?" *Rural Society,* 2, 4. Available at: www.csu.edu.au/research/crsr/ruralsoc/v2n4p5.htm (accessed March 10, 2004).

Lehmann, Courtney (2003). "Out Damned Scot: Dislocating Shakespeare in Transnational Film and Media Culture." In Richard Burt & Lynda Boose (eds.) *Shakespeare, the Movie II: Popularizing the Plays on Film, TV, Video, and DVD.* London: Routledge, pp. 231 51.

Lennox, Patricia (1993). "A Girl's Got to Eat: Christine Edzard's Film of *As You Like It.*" In Marianne Novy (ed.) *Transforming Shakespeare: Contemporary Women's Re-Visions in Literature and Performance.* New York: St Martin's Press, pp. 51–65.

Lovell, Alan (1976). "The Western." In BillNichols (ed.) *Movies and Methods.* Berkeley, CA: University of California Press, pp. 164–79.

MacCannell, Dean (1993). "Democracy's Turn: On Homeless Noir." In Joan Copjec (ed.) *Shades of Noir.* London: Verso, pp. 279–97.

MacCannell, Juliet Flower (1991). *The Regime of the Brother: After the Patriarchy*. London: Routledge.

Mariette, Amelia (2000). "Urban Dystopias: Re-approaching Christine Edzard's *As You Like It*." In Mark Thornton Burnett & Ramona Wray (eds.) *Shakespeare, Film, Fin de Siècle*. London: Macmillan, pp. 73–88.

Mayne, Judith (1990). *The Woman at the Keyhole: Feminism and Women's Cinema*. Bloomington, IN: Indiana University Press.

Mazza, Cris (2000). "Editing Postfeminist Fiction: Finding the Chic in Lit." *Symploke* 8, 1: 101–12.

Osborne, Laurie (1997). "Poetry in Motion: Animating Shakespeare." In Richard Burt & Lynda Boose (eds.) *Shakespeare, the Movie: Popularizing the Plays on Film, TV, and Video*. London: Routledge, pp. 103–20.

Pfeil, Fred (1993). "Home Fires Burning: Family Noir in *Blue Velvet* and *Terminator 2*." In Joan Copjec (ed.) *Shades of Noir*. London: Verso, pp. 227–59.

Sandoval, Chela (2000). *Methodology of the Oppressed*. Minneapolis: University of Minnesota Press.

Smiley, Jane (1988). *The Greenlanders*. New York: Ballantine Books.

Smiley, Jane (1991). *A Thousand Acres*. New York: Ivy Books.

Smiley, Jane (1993). "Shakespeare in Iceland." In Marianne Novy (ed.) *Transforming Shakespeare: Contemporary Women's Re-Visions in Literature and Performance*. New York: St Martin's Press, pp. 159–79.

Weimann, Robert (1978). *Shakespeare and the Popular Tradition in the Theater: Studies in the Social Dimension of Dramatic Form and Function*. Baltimore, MD: Johns Hopkins University Press.

Žižek, Slavoj (1989). *The Sublime Object of Ideology*. London: Verso.

FILMOGRAPHY

As You Like It (1992). Director Christine Edzard. Richard Goodwin/Sands Films.

Barton Fink (1991). Directors Joel & Ethan Coen. Rank/Circle.

Butch Cassidy and the Sundance Kid (1969). Director George Roy Hill. TCF/Campanile.

The Children's Midsummer Night's Dream (2000). Director Christine Edzard. Richard Goodwin/Sands Films.

Dolores Claiborne (1995). Director Taylor Hackford Rank/Castle Rock.

Hamlet (1992). Director Natalya Orlova. Shakespeare Animated Films/Christmas Films/Soyuzmultifilm.

Kansas City (1996). Director Robert Altman. Electric/Sandcastle 5/CiBy 2000.

Kumonosu jo [*Throne of Blood*] (1957). Director Akira Kurosawa. Toho.

Little Dorrit (1988). Director Christine Edzard. Richard Goodwin/Sands Films.

Lyubovyu za Lyubov (1983). Director Tatyana Berezantseva. Mosfilm Studios.

Macbeth, the Comedy (2001). Director Allison LiCalsi. Tristan Films.

Macbeth on the Estate (1997). Director Penny Woolcock. BBC2.

The Merchant of Venice (1914). Director Lois Weber. Universal Studios.

Murder on the Orient Express (1974). Director Sidney Lumet. EMI/GW Films.

Othello (1980). Director Liz White. Produced by Liz White.

Les Parapluies de Cherbourg [*The Umbrellas of Cherbourg*] (1964; restoration, Agnes Varda 1992). Director Jacques Demy.

A Passage to India (1984). Director David Lean. EMI/John Brabourne-RichardGoodwin/BO/John Heyman/Edward Sands.

Public Eye (1992). Director Howard Franklin. UIP/Universal.

Richard III (1996). Director Natalya Orlova. Shakespeare Animated Films/Christmas Films/Soyuzmultifilm.

Single White Female (1992). Director Barbet Schroeder. Columbia TriStar.

The Taming of the Shrew (1929). Director Sam Taylor. United Artists.

The Taming of the Shrew (1996). Director Aida Ziablikova. Shakespeare Animated Films/Christmas Films/Soyuzmultifilm.

Thelma and Louise (1991). Director Ridley Scott. UIP/Pathé Entertainment.

A Thousand Acres (1997). Director Jocelyn Moorhouse. Touchstone Pictures.

Titus (2000). Director Julie Taymor. Clear Blue Sky Productions.

Twelfth Night (1992). Director Mariya Muat. Shakespeare Animated Films/Christmas Films/Soyuzmultifilm.

The Two Jakes (1990). Director Jack Nicholson. Blue Dolphin/Paramount.

32

Conflicting Fields of Vision: Performing Self and Other in Two Intercultural Shakespeare Productions

Joanne Tompkins

What can Kathakali negotiate, and what must it still be silent about?
Ania Loomba, *Post-Colonial Shakespeares*

In 1710, Etow Oh Koam, King of the River Nation (and also known as Nicholas) was taken from the "new world" to visit London, where he and his three companions met Queen Anne. "While attending a performance of *Macbeth* at the Queen's Theatre, in the Haymarket, they created such a stir among the audience that they were asked to sit on the stage" (Living Words 2001). This is just one example of how the cultural "other" has been co-opted to perform exoticism against a background of Shakespeare. It is impossible to determine what meaning the audience derived from the ensuing performance of *Macbeth* or from the now-competing spectacle of otherness on stage. One can only assume that Etow Oh Koam and his colleagues, removed from the contexts of their own culture and their theatre seats, were unfamiliar with the performance tradition into which they were suddenly thrown. This experience exemplifies Jacques Lacan's depiction of self–other relations (or subject–other, in his terms): in his intersecting circles – one called the "being" or the "subject" and one the "meaning" or the "other" – the overlapping segment is a site of "non-meaning" (1979: 211). One would hope that the depth of the cultural clash in this production of *Macbeth* is not reproduced in too many contemporary intercultural productions of Shakespeare's plays, but the example does reinforce the challenge of directing and managing intercultural performance. Even though globalization provides audiences and practitioners with at least a passing acquaintance with a myriad of cultures (although the accuracy of such acquaintance may sometimes be dubious), the level of engagement required of each participating culture in an intercultural project may compromise all good intentions regarding mutuality. This is particularly true when Shakespeare – whose work alone has arguably come to be laden with more institutional, cultural, and historical weight than any culture or cultural tradition that undertakes a production of one of his plays – is one of the partners in the intercultural endeavor.

Unlike the accidental intercultural performance described above, contemporary interculturalism generally tries – in theory – to balance each participant's contribution so that the outcome of the collaboration is a whole that is greater than the sum of its parts, and new possible interpretations of the constituent texts, cultures, and recombinations result. Intercultural productions that take Shakespeare's plays as their starting point have become commonplace in recent decades, many using Asian theatre traditions. There are accounts of Kabuki-influenced *Macbeth*s (Senda 1998: 24), a kunju *Macbeth* (Tatlow 2001: 213–14), Beijing Opera-style *Much Ado About Nothing*s (Yang 1993: 56), Kathakali *King Lear*s and *Othello*s, and a Noh Shakespeare company in Tokyo (Kahan 1996: 26), among many others. The sustained proliferation of such intercultural performances prompts this examination of how new interpretive possibilities might develop amid the reservation that a production may merely replicate the "non-meaning" that was the likely outcome of the 1710 *Macbeth*. This chapter examines two intercultural Shakespeare productions – Tadashi Suzuki's *The Chronicle of Macbeth* (1992) and Ong Keng Sen's *Lear* (1997) – through Lacan's perception of the eye and the gaze to explore the ways in which each locates its cultures of performance. Both productions were directed by well-known directors who have combined classic western (Shakespearean) texts with Asian performance techniques, largely for international markets.

Suresh Awasthi explains that "[t]rue intercultural experiment ought to depend upon a creative utilization and merger of two performance cultures" (1993: 178), but performing with another culture inevitably complicates basic perceptions of self and otherness. While Rustom Bharucha argues that intercultural tension is based on a local–global dynamic (2001: 107), the intercultural performative encounter could also be said to pivot on different ways of exploring the tension between self and other. When both Shakespeare and the performance culture(s) involved in intercultural Shakespeare work have long histories of performance and cultural authority in their home contexts, neither is going to be "othered" easily. Yet paradoxically, neither can entirely escape the influence of the position of "otherness." Performing Shakespeare with, among, and against other cultures (particularly non-Western cultures) directly confronts otherness and the anxiety it produces, since Shakespeare – used for centuries as a marker of "self" in the Western world – is not the only "self" on stage. As each ostensibly equal group or tradition brings its own culture to the rehearsal space (where there is some structural parity at least for the duration of the production), each culture views itself as the "self" or "subject" culture approaching an "other." The anxiety that such interactions generate is evident in reviews of intercultural Shakespeare productions (see Zarrilli 1992, Awasthi 1993, Bennett 1996, and Allain 2002 for responses to intercultural Shakespeare productions). The productive tension of the self–other position is perhaps best summed up by Ania Loomba's discussion of a Kathakali *Othello*: "And even as 'Shakespeare' remains central for my own analysis of this production, the Kathakali *Othello* obliges me to mark the ways in which it 'provincializes' Shakespeare" (1998: 163). Loomba's observation of this conflicted field of vision demonstrates how interculturalism – and specifically intercultural Shakespeare – can act as a forum for the study of a reconfigured interpretation of self and otherness.

Further, Loomba's observations also intersect with Lacan's eye/gaze relationship in which "the subject ... is caught, manipulated, captured, in the field of vision" (Lacan 1979: 92) in such a way as to shift assumptions about both the nature of the scopic regime and identity construction, in other words, what one sees and how one interprets subjectivity based on what one sees. Applied metaphorically to intercultural Shakespeare, Lacan's eye/gaze relationship permits a reconfiguration of both the possible interpretations of Shakespeare's plays (including the institutional authority invested in Shakespeare) and the contemporary contexts of a variety of cultures. In this relationship, the apparently dominant visual field determined by a subject is contextualized and completed by an equally significant visual field in which the subject plays only a small part; or, as Margaret Iversen recounts, "[w]hile I look at things, I am looked at. My activity, then, is equally a passivity" (1994: 456). For Lacan, she explains, "the necessary pre-existence of the Gaze ... shows the subject as constituted by the desire of the Other. The subject is thus decentred in relation to any originary point of sight" (1994: 456).

Briefly to summarize Lacan's theory, the subject's overall visual field is formed by a combination of the "eye" and the "gaze" (corresponding to the Imaginary and the Symbolic). Lacan figures the eye, the gaze, and their effects diagrammatically by superimposing two isosceles triangles – the tips of their long side overlapping and facing towards each other – into a dihedron. One isosceles triangle depicts the eye, while the other, in reverse format, depicts the "landscape" in which the subject exists (the gaze). The triangles thus combine to produce optical awareness. Martin Jay explains that "the eye is that of the specular, Cartesian subject desiring specular plenitude and phallic wholeness, and believing it can find it in a mirror image of itself, whereas the gaze is that of an objective other in a field of pure monstrance" (1993: 363–4), or, in other words, in a field of pure display. While the eye and the gaze can operate separately (for example, in *trompe l'œil* art, the gaze overrides the eye), they more commonly operate as "two chiasmically crossing dimensions of the scopic field [... that can never] be reconciled harmoniously" (Jay 1993: 364). The fraught scopic regime of the eye and gaze is further complicated by the presence of the "other." The inability of the eye and gaze to reconcile with each other entirely, and the significant presence of the other make this relationship an ideal one for intercultural work, itself predicated on the inevitable clash of cultures coming together, and on otherness. Even though the eye and the gaze are part of the subject, they nevertheless intersect with the construction of alterity, which resides – concealed to some extent – in the gaze. Lacan's eye/gaze relationship can act as a metaphor to capture two different interpretational dimensions, based not on a given culture and the oppositional "culture" of Shakespeare but on what is exposed and what is (unintentionally) concealed in the cultural clash. Antony Tatlow explains that "[e]fficacious intercultural performance ... is most noticeable by the distress it causes, by its ability to disrupt 'aesthetic' conventions that themselves mask ideological protected presuppositions" (2001: 74). Here, I want to apply the potentially conflicting fields of vision of Lacan's eye and gaze relationship to *The Chronicle of Macbeth* and *Lear* to investigate the cultural, personal, and performative complexities that derive from the staging of competing selves.

Tadashi Suzuki's *The Chronicle of Macbeth*

For Leonard Pronko, *The Chronicle of Macbeth* "concentrate[s] on the theatricality of the thane's predicament and the decay of the royal couple, a vertiginously rapid seventy-minute process" (1993: 112). In *The Chronicle*, the essence of Macbeth's experience is framed by the action of a doomsday sect called the Farewell Cult (and which has featured in two other Suzuki productions, *The Bacchae* and *Ivanov*); this frame helps to focus the audience's attention on the central character's conflicting field of vision. *The Chronicle of Macbeth* combines Shakespeare's play with Suzuki's own well-known performance method to pursue issues of self and otherness by means of, first, the destabilization of the self and, second, performance in a cultural world significantly influenced by globalization.

First performed (in English) at Melbourne's Playbox Theatre and the Adelaide Festival in 1992 (before touring nationally and to the Mitsui Festival, Tokyo), *The Chronicle* was directed by Suzuki; a cast of Australians was joined by the American Ellen Lauren, the only participant then to have had extensive training experience with Suzuki. In his Shakespeare adaptations, Suzuki typically concentrates on just a few characters, substantially trimming the texts. Ian Carruthers details the Shakespearean deletions and additions to *The Chronicle* (1996: 222–4, 235–6), stressing that "Suzuki's stripping down of Shakespeare's play is done largely in the interests of intensification. He starts *in media res* and allows no secondary themes to distract us from his single focus on the Macbeths" (1996: 227). Suzuki's method works on "revealing as vividly as possible the inner landscapes of [characters'] fears and desires – 'making the invisible visible' " (Carruthers 1996: 221). Akihiko Senda calls the Suzuki method "a modern counterpart of Noh acting," with the actor's body resembling "a sculptured body in motion" (1998: 28). The actors perform with remarkable physical control of their bodies, adopting tableau-type poses, and holding their energy in a manner that recalls the German expressionist performance tradition that influenced the development of the Japanese performance form, Butoh. The stark conviction communicated by the voice and the intensity of the facial expressions demonstrate an impressive span of emotions. The drawn-out presentation of these features as a principal focus of the performance also fractures the narrative, forcing the audience to respond to the performance differently than to other types of theatre that are primarily plot-driven. Paul Allain summarizes a typical production:

> First, Suzuki nearly always organises his company on stage with a chorus and central protagonist … Second, Suzuki uses the recurring metaphor of all the world as a mental hospital … Third is Suzuki's dramaturgical technique of collage and juxtaposition … A fourth recurring aspect is his use of pre-recorded music to create contrasts or shifts in mood. It affirms the simplicity of his staging, which is reliant on the performer, lighting and sound to create a sense of mood, place and time, rather than on complex scenography. (2002: 140–1)

The austere set of *The Chronicle of Macbeth* contrasts with the intense reactions of the actors' bodies to the events around them. Ten white, unmatched dining room chairs are staggered across the wide stage while a section of red flooring bisects the stage once Duncan is murdered. The chorus introduces further geometric action: "[t]he Chorus's criss-crossing of the stage (from side to side or from upstage to downstage and back) may be seen as choreographing the external and internal planes on which the actions of the play develops" (Carruthers 1996: 227). The Chorus wears either nuns' habits or equally drab costumes when they play the witches or the murderers. The main characters' costumes, mostly loose gowns that are vaguely reminiscent of Noh tradition, are colored in tones of mostly grey, black, white, and tarnished silver; the dominant colour of purple in Lady Macbeth's gown is the only prominent colour in the production, aside from the red floor. The production thus concentrates the audience's attention on the complicated performance of self to the exclusion of almost all other "distractions."

Against this spare background, the display of Macbeth's fractured subjectivity illustrates Lacan's eye/gaze relationship. Suzuki's cult plot draws on the Noh drama's use of frame narratives to isolate Macbeth's precarious psychological state. The Noh structure's focus on the psyche of Macbeth (and Lady Macbeth) articulates with comparable undercurrents in Shakespeare's theatre, although the effect likely seems more confrontational to audiences used to traditionalist Shakespeare than to audiences familiar with Noh, since the particularities of psychological trauma from the Noh tradition appear to dominate the action, while most of the rest of the emotions and subplots of Shakespeare's play are abandoned. The play opens with Macbeth sitting among the cult members, but resisting their somewhat contradictory mantra about the end of history and memory. The cult narrative appears to frame the Shakespearean experience, but part of the production's success is its construction of a more complex intercultural relationship than a mere dichotomy between "Japan" and "Shakespeare." The assistant to the Farewell Cult leader (played by the same actor who plays Lady Macbeth) dictates that the followers will read *Macbeth*, and thus introduces the next level of narrative, the foreshortened Shakespeare play in which Macbeth enacts his part (or reprises his role, or possibly remembers his past glories). By the end of the play, Macbeth has abandoned himself to the cult, reciting the mantra enthusiastically with the other members. The play's structure is circular, its resolution substantially different from Shakespeare's original in its articulation of the conflicting fields of the eye (Macbeth the individual) versus the gaze (the eventually overwhelming presence of the group-based cult) in Shakespeare's *Macbeth*.

The chorus's collectivity deliberately clashes with the focus on the relative individuality of Macbeth and Lady Macbeth's emotions. The apparent interference of the chorus in the action comes to haunt Macbeth, as the chorus surrounds him physically and psychically. The chorus pound the floor with staves, punctuating their dialogue with an intensity that reverberates through the theatre: it feels as if the chorus is about to overwhelm the audience as well as Macbeth. While the narrative that Macbeth enacts is framed by the cult's reading of *Macbeth*, the play comes to disrupt assumptions regarding which action is the core and which is the frame. As *The Chronicle*'s chorus take on some of the subsidiary roles from *Macbeth* (including the witches) they overtly link the cult narrative with *Macbeth*. Eventually it becomes clear that the structural disintegration of Macbeth (and *Macbeth*) is partly an opportunity for a madman to play out his fantasies, partly a clever staging of split subjectivity, and partly a way to dismantle the authority vested in both a stable self and in Shakespeare. A character called the "illusion of Macbeth" enters – played by the actor who plays the cult leader – while Macbeth sits and contemplates the action. Macbeth becomes unsettled by the sight of Banquo's ghost during the banquet, but Banquo does not actually appear to the audience until his tableau in a version of the Act 4 Scene 1 witches scene. When Banquo finally appears in an embodied form that the audience can also see, Macbeth's difficulty in distinguishing between "real" images and apparitions has already been established, and the audience is encouraged to question his mental stability. His inability to differentiate between his own past and the cult's present culminates in Lady Macbeth's sleep-walking scene, where Macbeth remains on stage, possibly contemplating past events, or possibly conjuring them up through vision or memory, oblivious to the comedy provided by the doctor and the attendant. The personal is absorbed into the collective in a more pronounced way, as the cult frame narrative intersects overtly with Shakespeare's action: the cult's cook intervenes in Macbeth's contemplations, providing Macbeth not just with his dinner but also, when asked, his armor and sword (a visual joke in the form of a bib and fork). The cook humors Macbeth who speaks also to his wife's attendants in this scene, as if he is occupying both "worlds" at the same time.

Once the cook announces – almost maniacally – that the queen has died, Macbeth recites the "Tomorrow and tomorrow" speech, which is more profoundly elegiac to his troubled subjectivity here than it is to Shakespeare's Macbeth. Whereas in Shakespeare's *Macbeth* the speech suggests a futility and brevity of life that befits both the end of Lady Macbeth's life and Macbeth's meditations on his own agency in the light of the witches' predictions, in *The Chronicle of Macbeth* the speech returns to the production's beginning: the cult began its reading of *Macbeth* with this speech as part of its mantra about the end of history. This moment also marks the point at which Macbeth no longer resists the cult. As the chorus regroups, Macbeth joins in with the cult as they all enthusiastically recite the leader's creed. *The Chronicle* moves well away from the physical death of Macbeth which, for Shakespeare, is part of the mechanism by which order is restored: in abandoning that conclusion, Suzuki also moves away from the literal narrative of Shakespeare's play. Macbeth can be seen to be giving in to the gaze, and completing the eye/gaze relationship, even to the point of turning his back on the eye: his individual subjectivity as Shakespeare's Macbeth is to some extent replaced with the anonymity of being a member of the Farewell Cult.

Macbeth's actions provide just one path of subjectivity for him, but the production as a whole points to a selection of possible other signifiers of self, appropriate for a variety of cultures and traditions. Suzuki's own summary of *The Chronicle* helps situate the question of subjectivity in a context beyond the personal: *The Chronicle* is

> the tale of a man who is afflicted with a spiritual ailment called "Macbeth." . . . Macbeth is not an actual person or even a literary character. Macbeth is a symbol for the state in which one loses touch with one's own identity, and slips into an alienated anthropophobic condition in which there is no awareness of "self" or "other." (quoted in Mulryne 1998: 90)

While Suzuki's Macbeth may not be a literary character, he takes his existence in the first instance at least from a literary character. Shakespeare's Macbeth has an inevitable – othered – presence in *The Chronicle*. The stripped-down portrait of Macbeth produces the most meaning when read against Shakespeare's *Macbeth* since the focus on the psyche of Suzuki's Macbeth produces a more profound reading of character in Shakespeare's play. Suzuki's Macbeth does not exist without Shakespeare's, just as the self can only understand "self" when it knows otherness.

If *The Chronicle* outlines the workings of the eye/gaze at the individual level of Macbeth, and the broader context of *Macbeth*, it also resonates further in its discussion of symbolic memory. "Shakespeare" replaces memory when the chorus's staves are substituted for the book of plays from which each of them has been reading. Even though the cult professes to abandon memory and history, the production itself evokes cultural memory: the cult's recitation of the "Tomorrow and tomorrow" speech is not, for instance, intended to elicit linguistic or theatrical meaning, since the monotone, unmetered method of group recitation imitates the leader's blind devotion to his mantra. Rather, the speech comes to represent *Macbeth* and the authority of Shakespeare, concepts which consciously clash with the history and memory that the cult appears to be trying to abolish.

Just as Suzuki's Macbeth appears forced to straddle two worlds, the production itself speaks to the problems with "Shakespeare" as cultural commodity and the possibilities for broadening the visual field in which Shakespeare or Macbeth might figure. While *The Chronicle*'s cult may believe that there is no distinction between self and other, the audience inevitably distinguishes between the intersecting cultural traditions on stage. Yet *The Chronicle*'s cultural clash is more complex than Japanese "culture" being communicated through an English text with western performers:

instead, Suzuki chooses elements from each tradition, inherently highlighting display and specularity, and forcing audiences to look on the actors – and therefore the action – in a very different way. The resulting performative display relies on energy and emotion to "take what we know and construct the unknown" (Suzuki, quoted in Mulryne 1998: 90). His work thus redefines "otherness" away from the markers of national identity, towards the situational self/other tension that characterizes his Macbeth.

Cultural otherness comes to be explored more through the performance style of Suzuki's method than a Shakespearean elucidation of "Japan." Suzuki attempts to combine different (Japanese) performance traditions with (western) bodies to tell (western) stories from a (Japanese) perspective, rather than to overlay a specific performance tradition on a narrative from a different tradition. Suzuki has a reputation as a maker of elegant stage imagery, and while this production is no exception, it does require active viewing in its pushing of the boundaries of the cultural authority of Shakespeare, not passive enjoyment of the visual stage. At the same time, it takes seriously the challenge of incorporating a Shakespearean vision with a Japanese performance tradition. *The Chronicle of Macbeth* offers a conflicted field of vision in order to permit a constructive negotiation of the performance of self and otherness. *The Chronicle* insists that Shakespeare, like the Japanese theatre of Noh and other traditions, must be read in/through a wider frame of (cultural) otherness. The Shakespeare text is stripped back, its narrative reconfigured to remove almost all agency from the lead characters, while the Suzuki method is likewise othered by having it taken on by bodies that, in this instance, were, for the most part, unfamiliar with the substantially different performance tradition. Both experiences chart critical attempts to try out different roles of selfhood. They thus redefine self, other, and Shakespeare in a performance tradition that can no longer be limited to a European model.

That this union isn't entirely achieved is one of its measures of its success: the impossibility of a completely smooth convergence between disparate cultural contexts is hardly surprising. The exploration of otherness in this production inevitably results in some concealments. For J. R. Mulryne, the performance style itself takes over from meaning (see 1998: 85). Further, Lauren's experience with the Suzuki method was much more extensive than other cast members' in this male-dominated production, yet the substantial presence of Lady Macbeth in *The Chronicle* could be read as a demonstration of Lauren's impressive grasp of the performance style (particularly her vocal range), rather than as a substantial contribution to illuminating Macbeth's dilemmas. Nevertheless, the play is substantially successful in its execution of the issues involved in performing cultural exchange. In this uneasy occupation of two worlds, contexts, and traditions (often at once), Suzuki's character called Macbeth brings the audience, the cult, the Suzuki method, the Japanese and Australian performers, and Shakespeare into a common contact. *The Chronicle of Macbeth* reinforces the importance of (re-)interpreting Shakespeare in a context that accommodates complex subjectivity and cultural (re-)combinations.

Ong Keng Sen's *Lear*

Whereas *The Chronicle of Macbeth* is a reconstitution of one performance tradition (albeit one that is to an extent an amalgamation of the different Japanese performance codes that form Suzuki's method) in dialogue with a single Shakespeare text, Ong Keng Sen's *Lear* merges several Asian cultures in a narrative that is only loosely based on Shakespeare's *King Lear*. *The Chronicle of Macbeth* avoids cultural essentialism as it merges two performance contexts, two cultures, and two interpretations of *Macbeth*, even as it acknowledges the conflicting visual field, whereas the clashes between the eye and the gaze in *Lear* present greater interpretive challenges for the production and for intercultural performance of Shakespeare generally.

Ong's TheatreWorks company has capitalized on the intercultural Shakespeare format "to present a new vision of Asia" (quoted in de Rueck 2000: 5) by means of a variety of Asian performance techniques; he typically uses a core troupe of actors from his Singapore-based company, augmented by well-known performers of various other traditions. The company's first production to use Shakespeare as a base/starting point was *Lear*, which incorporated traditional and contemporary performance traditions from Japan, China, Indonesia, and Thailand in a script written by Rio Kishida, a well-known Japanese playwright. *Lear* toured to Japan in 1997; to Perth, Singapore, Hong Kong, and Jakarta in 1998; and to Berlin and Copenhagen in 1999. *Desdemona* (2000) incorporated mostly less well-known theatre techniques from India, Korea, Myanmar, Indonesia, Thailand, and Malaysia. Workshops for *Julius Caesar*, the third in Ong's planned trilogy (with practitioners from China, Hong Kong, Taiwan, Tibet, Mongolia, Philippines, and Papua New Guinea), have taken place, although the production that emerged from this workshop was "a less ostensibly inter-Asian *Search: Hamlet* (staged in Denmark's Kronborg castle)" (Bharucha 2001: 9).

Lear's multiple performance styles blend seamlessly in an impressive spectacle. Yet for all its spectacular beauty, this cultural exchange between Shakespeare's *King Lear* and Asian performance traditions is based on the creation of an illusory "new Asia" (see Bharucha 2001: 3, 15). Behind that image, which can be likened to Lacan's eye, the gaze, hosting a variety of "others," threatens to compromise the eye's control over the visual field in two specific ways: through the play's performance of gender and through its depiction of the traditions of specific cultures. The experience of *Lear* asks how contemporary intercultural Shakespeare projects might better negotiate cultural otherness to avoid the production of "non-meaning."

Lear begins with the entrance of a Noh-style king who typically wanders the afterlife, wondering who he is; while *Lear*'s discussion of kingship differs somewhat from *King Lear*'s, the play's central character nonetheless resonates with Shakespeare's. Lear, played by Naohiko Umewaka, a famous Noh actor, returns to the world of the living, and is reminded that he is king by his elder daughter, played by a (male) Beijing Opera actor, Jiang Qihu. This king has two (unnamed) daughters, the elder roughly equivalent to Goneril and Regan, the younger resembling Cordelia. The play takes a loose Noh structure, the king's very slow movement and drawn-out speech deliberately contrasting with the gestural range of the high-pitched, singing, Beijing Opera-styled daughter. The actors speak or sing using their own language and delivery styles, and so retain the essence of each tradition; while the performance is subtitled in the dominant language of the local audience, from the beginning the assumption is that no spectator will likely understand everything happening onstage. The elder daughter promises to guard the vacant throne while the king goes on a trip. His apparently mute younger daughter, a (male) Thai Khon dancer, Peeramon Chomdhavat, is banished for not speaking her love, even though Khon, a traditional (male) Thai court dance which characteristically enacts well-known narrative events from the Ramakian, relies on singers who ventriloquize for the actors (Bowers 1956: 133). The elder daughter usurps the throne on the king's departure, and blinds the king's loyal attendant. The elder daughter's lover, the retainer, is the chief of the warriors (played by members of a Jakarta-based dance company, costumed and choreographed in a contemporary martial format that suited their role rather than a specific "traditional" technique). He kills the younger daughter, but the elder daughter then kills the overly-ambitious retainer for fear that his attention to her is only to fulfill his own plan of overthrowing her. She then also kills the king on his return, in order to be ruler in her own right. The stylized violence is at times stunning: the younger daughter is strangled with her own hair, while one of the elder sister's personified shadows simultaneously wrings water from a cloth as life is wrung from the younger sister.

The focus of the New Asian "eye" in *Lear* is clearly gender, and the program notes explain that the elder daughter is trapped in a patriarchal prison; in killing her father, she is said to be overthrowing the bonds of patriarchy, which Ong deems necessary in the New Asia. More significantly, while Rio Kishida's brief script (which totals only 2,200 words, but it is augmented by a substantial amount of mimed, sung, or danced action) cuts all subplot and many supporting characters, the principal addition to the narrative is Lear's wife, mother to both daughters. This one character focuses the narrative clearly on gender issues. The mother, played by the actor who also played Lear, is rejected by the elder daughter because of her low social status and her apparent madness. It is left unclear whether this Noh-influenced mother is a ghost or is "real" (see Bainbridge 1992). At the end, only the elder daughter remains alive, her tragedy being that she is alone, just vaguely aware of the intangible presence of her mother, but unable to gain access to any emotional assistance the mother may be able to offer. *Lear* thus shifts the locus of the tragedy from the disastrous decision about the division of the kingdom to the crisis of a female self that appears to break down patriarchy.

Yet the disruption of patriarchy (which is described only in general terms, mostly in the program notes and less successfully in the production itself) yields its own representational problems, and it is here that the field of the gaze begins to become apparent. The placement of women in a position of authority does not, of course, automatically ascribe equality to all women. While some particular women are foregrounded in the visual field, there are many "others" who become visible by means of the gaze. The effect of the conflicted field of vision here is a reinforcement of the partiality of the gender component of *Lear*'s New Asia (see also Bharucha 2001: 120–1, de Rueck 2000: 2, Grehan 2000: 4). The mother, one of the key figures charged with disrupting patriarchy, seems to be co-opted by that patriarchy in her unsuccessful attempts to reach her elder daughter. The mother's identity exists only through Lear – metaphorically and physically – since they are played by the same actor. More importantly, all the main roles are played by male actors, partly because this is customary in several of the performance traditions, partly because Shakespeare used an all-male cast, and, partly, the program notes explain, to play with gender. It is, however, difficult to flag the overthrow of patriarchy if the only women actors on the stage are the Fool (who is a marginal character at best) and the bit-part actors who shadow various principal characters, particularly since Beijing Opera, Noh, and Khon now accommodate women performers in their practice. Patriarchy, then, is merely discursive rather than a performed strategy; the female other emerges through the gaze to signal the implications of the discourse in performance, especially the limitations of the visual field rendered by the eye.

More substantially, the representational strategies for depicting culture in *Lear* reveal blind spots, as the cultural negotiations that typically take place in intercultural performance appear to be submerged in a harmonious spectacle of split subjectivity. Ong's *Lear* portrays the difficulties of articulating the self coherently: for instance, the king wonders who he is. Further, the younger daughter appears to have no voice, while the elder daughter has too many versions of "herself": she is shadowed by three alter egos whom she names Obedience, Purity, and Innocence (later revealed to be Ambition, Unpredictability, and Vanity). Dislocations in personal agency are an inevitable effect of the fundamental crisis in how to represent contemporary Asia, and this exploration of subject positions is one of the strengths of *Lear*: "Ong mobilizes his performance praxis to complicate the questions of positionality, location, and subjectivity" (Grehan 2001: 117). The blind spots become apparent in the exploration of the detail of these articulations of self. *Lear* attempts to contrast New Asia with Shakespeare, but it settles more on a confrontation between New and Old Asia. If the Elder Daughter represents the New Asia, the chaos resulting from her usurping the throne is unresolved, the precarious new order looking likely to crumble imminently. Further, *Lear* mimics Asian self–other dynamics in a more hierarchical way than may at first appear, as the other's presence again comes to be felt. Each performance tradition (or, as it were, "self") comes to be positioned not against a Shakespeare-driven "other" but against an Asian "other." Even then, the implications of these combinations are not always explored as thoroughly as they might be. For instance, the silencing of the younger daughter (in part, by removing the opportunity for the performer to operate according to tradition with his customary ventriloquial interpreter) is convenient to communicate the narrative detail of the exile of the "Cordelia"-like character in the *King Lear* story, but the presentation and performance of Khon are thus compromised. Further, *Lear* is framed by the loyal attendant, an

Indian servant who opens the play and sings his mournful song at various points throughout the play. Both he and the warriors whose Indonesian dance tradition is restyled to suit the needs of the performance are marginalized and/or reworked in the performance and in the promotional material in terms of costume, performance, proxemics, and narrative. This marginalization prompts Rustom Bharucha to argue that Ong's New Asia is as (problematically) hierarchical as the existing Asia, with Indians ranking at the bottom, a ranking which also reflects the existing – and troubling, if frequently overlooked – social structure of Singapore (2001: 123–4). Japan is situated at the top of this hierarchy, partly because *Lear* was funded by the Japan Foundation (see Bharucha 2001: 110).

The "eye" of the performance foregrounds the wealth of cultural variety as *Lear* presents a showcase of cultures, while at the same time attempting to avoid conflict between cultures and their proponents. The gaze prevents this somewhat utopian scenario from being completed. The eye/gaze relationship explicates a problem of spectacularity in intercultural performance: while display is implicitly part of the gaze, the pageant-like spectacle of *Lear* is presented with a harmony that appears artificial, and therefore forced. The spectacular aspects of each performance tradition are placed in juxtaposition in the same spatial frame; in the absence of politics and textual analysis, spectacle and exoticism take over. At its best, interculturalism takes an audience from spectacular moments to discursive conclusions that productively disrupt insular interpretations of culture/cultures. The presentation of a series of cultures in *Lear*, each with its moment of harmonious exhibition, fails to be inter-active. Yuji Odajima, a Japanese theatre critic, recorded having "expected more tension, more chaos" in *Lear* "[s]ince there were so many theatrical styles and languages on stage" (quoted in Peterson 2001: 216). William Peterson describes the effect in more detail:

> It was as if each [performance tradition] was contained within its own box, unable to reach out in any meaningful way to connect with artists of a different cultural orientation ... [T]hat which makes us feel something – however disorienting and inchoate – is preferable to the institutionalization of a pan-Asian intercultural style that merely arranges items into lovely pan-Asian *ikebana* displays while avoiding the more difficult path where we are forced to encounter blood, guts, passion, and yes, even politics. (2003: 93)

For Anthony Tatlow, intercultural performance ought to "disrupt 'aesthetic' conventions that themselves mask ideological protected presuppositions" (2001: 74). *Lear* is an amalgamation of aesthetic conventions that attempt to overlook anchored inter-pretations of cultural, gendered, or social ideology in favor of a cultural harmony that remains outside its grasp: the disruption can be read as unintended, as the gaze makes its presence felt in spite of the eye's pretence to control the visual field.

In *Lear*, the eye attempts, unsuccessfully, to override the gaze: *Lear* spectacularly portrays a variety of decontextualized performance traditions against an equally unanchored abstraction of a Shakespearean narrative. Ong asserts that he chose a Shakespeare text with which to foreground Asian performance traditions because of Shakespeare's " 'neutrality,' in the sense that no theater culture from Asia could 'claim' Shakespeare on their own grounds" (quoted in Bharucha 2001: 113). This Shakespeare operates as a narrative template of archetypal characters and themes (in addition to providing a saleable commodity at international arts festivals, making the choice a shrewd marketing strategy). The "Shakespeare" used to interrogate Asian identities is as ahistorical and apolitical as the performance traditions Ong deploys: this Shakespeare signifies a vague internationalism, partly by virtue of the international arts market to which *Lear* was pitched, and also implies an unspecified traditionalism perhaps arising from the conservative portrayal of Shakespeare in Singapore colonial education and performance contexts. Herein lies the intercultural difficulty with the performance of any tradition, including Shakespeare: "Ong neutralizes or fails to sufficiently inflect the text's specific references to the ruptures of the real world" (Bharucha 2001: 117). The traditions showcased are, in their absence of location, unable to entertain the idea of giving literal and figurative ground. The gaze returns to meet the eye in an optical field that is a confusion of best intentions with a reinscribed and exotic pan-Asianism, tossed together for sale on the festival market. *Lear*'s move away from textual implications (even from the narrative itself) towards display in only one part of the optical field ironically opens it up all the more to what it inadvertently conceals.

The Chronicle of Macbeth capitalizes on the cultural clash between the tradition of Shakespeare's *Macbeth* and Suzuki's own interpretation of the current location of that tradition in political, geographic, and theatrical terms. *The Chronicle* makes plain the implications of its alterations to Shakespeare's play and to each of the performance traditions involved, and the potential for enriching each component. *Lear*, on the other hand, attempts to be visually spectacular by, in effect, bypassing the intercultural clash, but concludes by reinscribing the exoticism, the patriarchy, and the Shakespearean authority it apparently tries to avoid. Further, *Lear* sidesteps the implications of the new narrative it has created: this re-reading of Shakespeare through the constituent cultures of Singapore that may be said to describe "New Asia" overlooks the effects of specific and local politics on its own representation. As the other's presence comes to disturb the visual field of the eye, *Lear* comes unconsciously to mimic the existing, hierarchical self–other dynamics characteristic of contemporary Singapore.

The imbalance that becomes perceptible through the eye/gaze relationship in *Lear* differs from the more conventional risks of intercultural performance: that some of the participating cultures will not have the opportunity for cultural and performative exchange, and instead merely be exhibited, producing clichéd representations that merely stage an exotic display of otherness – as in the 1710 Haymarket *Macbeth*. The difficulties in balancing cultures in performance notwithstanding, intercultural Shakespearean productions have the potential to generate different (new) interpretations, based not on a given culture and the oppositional "culture" of Shakespeare but on what is exposed and what is (unintentionally) concealed in this cultural clash. In such cases, there can be no definitive answer to Loomba's question: the negotiations regarding the possibilities for intercultural Shakespeare productions need to continue to take place in order to negotiate the crucial questions of otherness that captivate audiences and challenge what might otherwise be taken as cultural certainties.

Intercultural theatre work is always going to be dangerous when the cultures involved investigate each other's limits. Those projects that are based on the use of a Shakespearean play risk tapping into a heightened cultural anxiety that privileges the self at the expense of the shadowy other. Not every intercultural production will be successful of course, but each encounter grounded on an equitable cultural exchange has the potential to stage the complex interrelationships between self and other. *The Chronicle of Macbeth* and *Lear* stage competing versions of self and other that, to varying degrees, investigate the conflicting fields of vision that continue to require performative negotiation in cultural, personal, and textual contexts.

REFERENCES AND FURTHER READING

Allain, Paul (2002). *The Art of Stillness: The Theatre Practice of Tadashi Suzuki*. London: Methuen.

Awasthi, Suresh (1993). "The Intercultural Experience and the Kathakali 'King Lear'." *New Theatre Quarterly* 9: 172–8.

Bainbridge, Erika Ohara (1992). "The Madness of Mothers in Japanese Noh Drama." *U.S.–Japan Women's Journal*, 3: 84–110.

Bennett, Susan (1996). *Performing Nostalgia: Shifting Shakespeare and the Contemporary Past*. London: Routledge.

Bharucha, Rustom (2001). "Consumed in Singapore: The Intercultural Spectacle of *Lear*." *Theater* 31, 1: 107–27.

Bowers, Faubion (1956). *Theatre in the East: A Survey of Asian Dance and Drama*. New York: Grove.

Carruthers, Ian (1996). "The *Chronicle of Macbeth*: Suzuki Tadashi's Transformation of Shakespeare's *Macbeth*." In Heather Kerr, Robin Eaden, & Madge Mitton (eds.) *Shakespeare: World Views*. Newark: University of Delaware Press, pp. 215–36.

de Reuck, Jenny (2000). " 'The Mirror Shattered into Tiny Pieces': Reading Gender and Culture in the Japan Foundation Asia Centre's *Lear*." *Intersections* 3. Available at: intersections_c-drom/issue3/jenny3.html (accessed October 10, 2003).

Grehan, Helena (2000). "Performed Promiscuities: Interpreting Interculturalism in the Japan Foundation Asia Centre's *Lear*." *Intersections* 3. Available at: intersections_cdrom/issue3/grehan.html (accessed October 10, 2003).

Grehan, Helena (2001). "TheatreWorks' *Desdemona*: Fusing Technology and Tradition." *TDR: The Drama Review* 45, 3: 113–25.

Iversen, Margaret (1994). "What is a Photograph?" *Art History* 17: 450–64.

Jay, Martin (1993). *Downcast Eyes: The Denigration of Vision in Twentieth-Century French Thought*. Berkeley, CA: University of California Press.

Kahan, Jeffrey (1996). "Noh Shakespeare: An Interview with Kuniyoshi Munakata." *Shakespeare Bulletin* 14, 1: 26–8.

"Khon" (1998). *Thailand: Thai Language and Culture Learning Resource*. SEAsite and the Center for Southeast Asian Studies. Northern Illinois University. 22 April 22. Available at: www.seasite.niu.edu/Thai/literature/default.htm (accessed March 12, 2004).

Lacan, Jacques (1979). *The Four Fundamental Concepts of Psycho-analysis*, ed. Jacques-Alain Miller and trans. Alan Sheridan. Harmondsworth: Penguin.

Living Words (2001). Aboriginal Diplomats of the Eighteenth Century. Exhibition at the McCord Museum, Montreal, May 4–September 9.

Loomba, Ania (1998). " 'Local-Manufacture Made in India Othello Fellows': Issues of Race, Hybridity and Location in Post-Colonial Shakespeares." In Ania Loomba & Martin Orkin (eds.) *Post-Colonial Shakespeares*. London: Routledge, pp. 143–63.

Mulryne, J. R. (1998). "The Perils and Profits of Interculturalism and the Theatre Art of Tadashi Suzuki." In Takashi Sasayama, J. R. Mulryne, & Margaret Shewring (eds.) *Shakespeare and the Japanese Stage*. Cambridge: Cambridge University Press, pp. 71–93.

Peterson, William (2001). *Theater and the Politics of Culture in Contemporary Singapore*. Middletown, CT: Wesleyan University Press.

Peterson, William (2003). "Consuming the Asian Other in Singapore: Interculturalism in TheatreWorks' *Desdemona*." *Theatre Research International* 28: 79–95.

Pronko, Leonard C. (1993). Review of *The Chronicle of Macbeth*. *Theatre Journal* 45: 110–12.

Senda, Akihiko (1998). "The Rebirth of Shakespeare in Japan: From the 1960s to the 1990s," trans. Ryuta Minami. In Takashi Sasayama, J. R. Mulryne, & Margaret Shewring (eds.) *Shakespeare and the Japanese Stage*. Cambridge: Cambridge University Press.

Tatlow, Antony (2001). *Shakespeare, Brecht, and the Intercultural Sign*. Durham, NC: Duke University Press.

Yang, Lingui (1993). "New Chinese Approaches to Shakespeare in Twentieth-Century China." *Shakespeare Newsletter* 43, 3: 56.

Zarrilli, P. (1992). " 'For Whom Is the King a King?' Issues of Intercultural Production, Perception, and Reception in a *Kathakali King Lear*." In J. G. Reinelt & J. R. Roach (eds.) *Critical Theory and Performance*. Ann Arbor, MI: University of Michigan Press, pp. 16–40.

FILMOGRAPHY

The Chronicle of Macbeth (1992). Director Tadashi Suzuki. Produced by TOGA and Playbox. Playbox Theatre, Melbourne. (Video of *The Chronicle of Macbeth*, courtesy of Playbox Theatre.)

Lear (1997). By Rio Kishida. Director Ong Keng Sen. TheatreWorks (Prod.). Kallang Theatre, Singapore. (Video of *Lear*, courtesy of TheatreWorks.)

PART VI
Performing Pedagogies

33
Teaching Through Performance
James N. Loehlin

The increased attention to performance in academic Shakespeare studies has been particularly fruitful in one vital and often overlooked area: teaching. Since the 1970s, performance has been used more and more in the classroom, both at the undergraduate level and in secondary and even primary education. The forms performance takes in classroom practice vary widely, from students reading scenes aloud in class to staging complete plays. Teachers may use performance to acquaint students with Elizabethan stage conventions, or to make them aware of performance cues inscribed into the text, or to encourage them to try out different interpretive possibilities for scenes. Performance pedagogy may include the comparative study of video or film performances, or such instructional materials as the *Playing Shakespeare* video series of Royal Shakespeare Company director John Barton. Students may approach performance at the level of character, exploring given circumstances, intentions and subtext in the manner of Russian acting theorist Konstantin Stanislavsky. They may use performance exercises to heighten awareness of a play's language and imagery. Instructors may bring particular theoretical frameworks to their performance work, incorporating cultural materialist, feminist, or psychoanalytic perspectives. The range of methodologies is as broad as that of literary instruction in general; there are few approaches to Shakespeare to which performance cannot contribute.

The fact that Shakespeare wrote his plays for the stage, and that performance can bring them to life for students, is something few people would dispute. However, the increasing theoretical and political sophistication of Shakespeare studies generally, and of performance criticism in particular, has made the field of performance pedagogy somewhat more complicated in recent years. As Milla Riggio noted in her Introduction to the 1999 MLA collection *Teaching Shakespeare Through Performance*, the use of performance in the classroom "is no longer an easily romanticized option" (1999: 11). Nonetheless, performance remains a valuable teaching method, flexible enough to accommodate and profit by the advances of theory – and, when necessary, to ignore them.

This chapter will attempt to trace the history of performance pedagogy, and to enumerate some of its advantages for teaching Shakespeare. I will conclude by discussing a particularly thorough model for teaching through performance, the Shakespeare at Winedale program of the University of Texas. I won't try to disguise the fact that I am an advocate for the performance approach to Shakespeare, but I have no wish to be dogmatic about it. There are countless ways performance can inform pedagogy; I hope anyone reading this chapter will be inspired to develop new performance methodologies to meet the challenges of teaching Shakespeare in the twenty-first century.

History of Performance Pedagogy

Students have performed Shakespeare's works for as long as they have studied them – perhaps longer – but performance pedagogy as we know it grew out of the "Shakespeare revolution" of the 1960s and 1970s. The growth of "stage-centered" criticism by scholars like J. L. Styan and Bernard Beckerman, the dissemination of the RSC training methods of Cicely Berry and John Barton, and the creation of the touring performance/education group ACTER (now Actors From the London Stage), together with the educational experimentation of the period, all combined to give performance a place in the college English classroom. By the mid-1980s, it seemed that performance would dominate pedagogy for generations to come. Homer Swander, in a 1985 essay forecasting the future of Shakespeare teaching and scholarship, hailed the arrival of a new discipline:

> It is easy enough to point to the major areas of activity toward which the logic of the New Discipline (if for convenience I may continue to call it that) appears to lead any interested teacher: playgoing; using film, television, and video cassettes (though with great care for the differences among the media); bringing professional theatre people into class; doing scenes in class with the students as performers (what Styan calls the "direct method"); practicing the kind of reading demanded by scripts but not by literature; and probing (through demonstration, discussion, and assignments) the theoretical and specific differences between drama and literature. What is needed is fifty years of exploration and experiment in class, nourished by fifty years of investigation and dialogue by scholars committed to the discipline. (Swander 1985: 887)

Defining the subjects of inquiry of this new discipline as "scripted signals" and "performed signs," Swander proclaimed that "The future is going to tell us much about them – and thus much about Shakespeare's art – that, strangely and excitingly enough, we do not yet know" (1985: 887).

Swander had reason to be sanguine about the prospects for his new discipline. A special teaching issue of *Shakespeare Quarterly* the year before had focused overwhelmingly on performance. In the Introduction, editor John F. Andrews noted the trend with surprise and approval:

A decade ago "performance-oriented" pedagogy was relatively unfamiliar among Shake-speareans and was anything but universally accepted as the wave of the future. Now it is difficult to find a dissenting voice: virtually everybody acknowledges the need to approach Shakespeare's plays as dramatic rather than literary works. The only real question seems to be just how to put the consensus into practice. (1984: 515)

Swander himself issued a challenge to teachers "to accept the pedagogical conse-quences of recognizing the obvious: that Shakespeare's words, deliberately designed by a theatrical genius for a thrust stage with live actors and an immediately respond-ing audience, cannot be satisfactorily explored or experienced in any medium but his own" (1984: 540).

Within a few years, however, the situation had changed. The ongoing development of energetic and compelling sub-disciplines within Shakespeare studies, informed by contemporary theory and animated by political commitment, called the "stage-centered" approach into question. New historicism and cultural materialism, femi-nism, psychoanalytic criticism, and other postmodern theoretical approaches raised new questions that did not lend themselves to performance teaching, at least as it had been practiced up to that time. In the next *Shakespeare Quarterly* teaching issue in 1990, Ann Thompson commented critically on the performance approach that had dominated in 1984: "Rereading these essays in 1989, after having been invited to contribute to the present issue, I was immediately struck not only by the over-whelming consensus that the 'right way' to teach Shakespeare was through perform-ance and classroom workshops but also by the almost total absence of literary theory and cultural politics" (1990: 139).

In his Introduction to the edition, Ralph Alan Cohen noted with surprise that only two essays dealt directly with performance; the majority considered broader ideo-logical issues of pedagogy, centered on teaching a "problematized Shakespeare" and "de-authorizing" the instructor (1990: iii). Cohen suggested hopefully that the relative silence about performance indicated that it had become a widespread and accepted practice, no longer needing to be explained or justified. But his Introduction betrays a degree of uncertainty about "the upheaval in Shakespeare criticism – from deconstruction to the new historicism," and its implications for performance peda-gogy (1990: iii).

By the time Milla Cozart Riggio's *Teaching Shakespeare through Performance* volume came out in 1999, "the potentially smug assumption that plays are meaningful only when performed" had been cast aside, some teachers had given up classroom perform-ance, and the methodology behind much stage-centered work had been undermined (1999: 11). Furthermore, while performance was rejected by those pursuing work in other directions, it also underwent a rigorous scrutiny by performance critics themselves. James Bulman's anthology *Shakespeare, Theory and Performance* (1996) and W. B. Worthen's *Shakespeare and the Authority of Performance* (1997) questioned many of the tenets of the performance movement, including its approach to pedagogy. Worthen contended that much performance practice, criticism and pedagogy relied on a conservative notion of textual authority that actually reduced the creative potential of the performer. Worthen's critique included stage-centered scholars and teachers, directors, and instructional materials like the *Playing Shakespeare* videotapes, in which John Barton works with a group of RSC actors to find subtle textual cues to guide their performances. Worthen argued that such work "finally represents modern performance almost exclusively as a mode of interpretation, committed to replaying meanings already inscribed in the text" (1997: 160). In Bulman's book, Richard Paul Knowles attacked the approaches of voice teachers Cicely Berry, Kristin Linklater and Patsy Rodenburg, all of whom had had a significant impact on performance pedagogy through their books, workshops and exercises. For Knowles, these teachers' emphasis on a universal, "natural" voice tends "either to resist or comfortably contain any genuinely oppositional attempts to stage the plays" (1996: 107). Cary Mazer, in the same volume, questioned Alan Dessen's attempts to reconstruct Elizabethan stage conventions, a frequent subject of classroom performance teaching. Mazer argued that Dessen's reading of the "patterned action" of Shakespeare's plays derived not from a thorough understanding of playhouse practice, but from a conception of the performed play as "an organically unified work of art," a conception ultimately derived from twentieth-century formalist criticism (Mazer 1996: 165). These theoretically-informed questionings of performance critics and teachers challenged the very bases on which performance pedagogy had been established: the discovery of textual meaning through an exploration of the conditions of theatrical performance.

Some theory-influenced performance critics have recently attempted to find ways of accommodating postmodern views into classroom performance practice. Many of the contributors to Riggio's teaching anthology show an awareness of the imperatives of postmodernism, which she summarizes as "its focus on historical relativity, its emphasis on the culturally marginal, its awareness of issues of gender and racial identity, and its impulse to deconstruct textual authority" (1999: 7). David Kennedy Sauer and Evelyn Tribble point out that some of the tenets of postmodern performance theory, derived ultimately from the work of German Marxist playwright Bertolt Brecht, can help students break out of a unified view of character and engage more fully with the complex ways identity is constructed in the Shakespearean subject (1999: 37). Tribble's classroom exercise of giving student groups different props – flowers, a sword, a Bible – with which to explore the Polonius family scene (*Hamlet* 1.3) not only encourages students to construct markedly different characterizations, but makes them aware of their assumptions in doing so: "The exercise makes [Ophelia] an empty stage on which ideology, revealing the contradictions of our society, is enacted" (Sauer and Tribble 1999: 43). G. B. Shand describes how he has reconceived his Shakespeare-in-performance course with a shift "away from the authoritative maker of a fixed textual signifier and toward the interpretive processes of reading, both variable and contingent, as well as toward the multiple valid playing and signifying possibilities illuminated by such processes" (1999: 246). By adopting a more pluralist approach and encouraging students to take "earned possession of their interpretive responses to Elizabethan texts," Shand has had the pleasure and excitement of learning from his students, sharing in their investigations and discoveries and questioning some of his own assumptions (1999: 248). Shand gives vivid accounts of classroom stagings in which, for instance, a quick-witted Christopher Sly recognized and exploited the deception being attempted against him in the *Taming of the Shrew*, and an Amazonian Lady Anne sexually dominated a timidly grieving Richard Gloucester (1999: 253).

In the same volume, Cary Mazer acknowledges that "it used to be easier studying and teaching Shakespeare in performance" (1999: 155). He discusses how materialist criticism has destabilized the notion of the early modern subject, and with it the whole idea of Shakespearean "character." He comments that Worthen, Knowles, and others have made him suspicious of the Cicely Berry/John Barton approach to the Shakespearean text, with its ahistoricist assumptions, in spite of its obvious and continuing value. He indicates a degree of skepticism about Alan Dessen's work on recovering Elizabethan theatrical meanings, though he assigns "healthy chunks of Dessen" to his students (1999: 157, 161). But he devotes most of his essay to a demonstration of how some traditional performance techniques can have practical value for students even in a theorized classroom. Specifically, he discusses the use of the Stanislavskian idea of playing an action, working against obstacles to achieve a character objective, as a cornerstone of his approach to teaching Shakespearean performance:

> If we start with the actor, if we begin our exploration of the script with our own theatrical sensibilities – our own definitions of character, psychology, behavior, and action – and if we are particularly careful not to make undue claims for the transhistorical universality of theatrical practice or artistic meaning, then we can begin to understand how the scripts can be made to work for us, and perhaps even how they may have worked for the dramatist and his contemporary coworkers and audiences. (1999: 158)

Mazer ends the essay with a gracious acknowledgment of Bernard Beckerman's work on the dynamic patterns of action that can be discerned as the motivating energies of a Shakespeare play. Mazer recognizes that Beckerman's theatrical model does not "transcend time or sidestep twentieth-century paradigms of character or acting," but it has value nonetheless (1999: 167). Moreover, Mazer recognizes that his own work is equally contingent, and equally productive; that even if we are limited to approaching Shakespeare through the historically contingent practices of our own time, those practices can still provide vital access to the "vivid, profound and human stories" that the playscripts have to tell (1999: 167).

At any rate, it is clear that in spite of the many challenges and revisions that performance pedagogy has faced, it is still in widespread use. Numerous new books on teaching Shakespeare incorporate discussion of performance, including Salomone and Davis's *Teaching Shakespeare into the Twenty-First Century* (1997), Aers and Wheale's *Shakespeare in the Changing Curriculum* (1991), and Rex Gibson's *Teaching Shakespeare*

(1998). Many performance materials are available for instructors. The Folger Shakespeare Library has produced the *Shakespeare Set Free* series, with practical lesson plans for primary and secondary school teachers. Both the Oxford and Cambridge School Shakespeare series suggest many practical exercises, and encourage students reading the plays to imagine them, or realize them, through performance. The increasing availability and sophistication of these materials indicate how well performance has been able to adapt itself to changing institutional, ideological and methodological environments. While performance criticism continues to engage with the challenges of postmodern theory, the very vigor of these debates has given performance pedagogy a revitalized presence in the Shakespeare classroom.

Performance in the Classroom

For the next section of this chapter, I want to concentrate on what I believe to be some of the particular virtues of performance for teaching. My focus is on undergraduate courses, but much of this discussion applies to high-school students as well. I will not go into much detail about specific exercises or assignments, nor will I address the problems of class sizes, grading issues and so forth. I will try rather to catalogue the attributes that make performance an exciting approach to teaching Shakespeare, and to suggest some ways that current critical controversies may be engaged – though certainly not resolved – through performance pedagogy.

Attention to the Text

In spite of the widespread rejection of New Criticism over the past generation or so, most Shakespeare teachers would agree that giving detailed attention to the language is a useful practice for students to pursue. Annabel Patterson, in the 1994 collection *Teaching with Shakespeare*, cautions that in the highly theorized classroom, there is a danger of students merely imposing "prefabricated" readings on texts without going through the old-fashioned but still valuable process of close reading (1994: 258). And for promoting scrutiny of textual detail and nuance, performance is hard to beat. As Miriam Gilbert puts it, "the anxiety (even panic) created by actually having to speak the line works for both professional actor and student performer; there is a real *need* to know what these words mean, and so students take the trouble to find out" (1984: 603).

Students pay particular attention to their lines if they actually have to learn them. One can use performance effectively in a classroom setting without memorization, but fully internalizing the lines gives students a particular command of sentence structure, word order, meter, linguistic register, imagery, rhetorical devices – indeed, of the entire panoply of effects through which language becomes a register of human action and identity. In my own teaching I suggest that students approach learning lines from two different directions. On the one hand, it can be useful for them to try to improvise their way through a scene before they know it fully; to try to create a sub-textual mental process that will lead them to "need" the particular words the play gives them. I encourage them to balance this modern Method approach with the rather medieval discipline of copying out textual selections exactly longhand, line by line. This process can make students more aware of the interplay of meter and syntax in verse speeches, and the antitheses, repetitions and the other structuring devices that organize prose. A student playing Leontes, through the process of confronting and assimilating the metrical design of the verse, can become graphically aware of the violent dislocations incorporated into his language:

> Inch-thick, knee-deep, o'er head and ears a forked one!
> Go play, boy, play. Thy mother plays, and I
> Play too, but so disgraced a part, whose issue
> Will hiss me to my grave. Contempt and clamour
> Will be my knell. Go play, boy, play.
> *(The Winter's Tale*, 1.2.185–9)

A student wouldn't necessarily need to mark the line-endings in performance, with pauses after "I," "issue," and "clamour." Simply developing a consciousness of the disjunction between verse-rhythms and sense-rhythms in the speech will give the student greater expressive potential than learning lines simply for their meaning, as though they were prose.

I also encourage students to tape-record and listen to their own readings, to swap roles with their scene partners, to sing their lines aloud as hip-hop or opera, to have unShakespearean roommates read their speeches aloud to them, and so forth. All these exercises give them an awareness of the relationship of sound and sense. As noted above, contemporary criticism has undermined some of the claims of voice teachers like Cicely Berry and Kristin Linklater, so that we can, perhaps, no longer assert that we are freeing Shakespeare's natural voice, or that the sound of the words gives us unmediated access to some universal truth in the language. Indeed, this variety of possible approaches to line-learning serves not merely to create many alternative readings; in an important sense it takes the language away from a simplistic identi-fication with a univocal "character," or even a determined "Shakespearean" meaning. It nonetheless remains the case that the sound of Shakespeare's language plays some part in its meaning, and that an awareness of assonance, consonance, rhyme, rhythm, and the like can contribute to a student's knowledge of the text, and of the varied means – many of which are remote from contemporary acting, Method or otherwise – by which Shakespeare uses writing to suggest character. In the Leontes example above, for instance, the explosive and biting consonants and hissing sibilants are as much a part of Leontes' tortured mental world as are the fractured rhythms of the speech. The kind of detailed, practical analysis suggested by Berry's *The Actor and the Text* is valuable for any Shakespeare student, whether he or she is performing or not. Speaking and hearing the text can give the student a visceral understanding, a sense of chewing on and tasting the words of a speech, of truly embodying it. And, of course, embedding the language in the body enables student actors to engage with the different kinds of bodies we have: a significant issue in contemporary performance studies.

Consciousness of Interpretation

In fact, a primary virtue of any performance approach to Shakespeare is the insight it gives students into the process of interpretation. In this regard performance pedagogy accords well with the de-authorizing tendencies of postmodern criticism. Students working on a text in performance quickly discover that the meaning is not fixed in the language; that the process of performance will involve them in multiple interpretive decisions that will make them co-creators of the play's meaning, and that may in some cases challenge the authority of the text.

When they first get on their feet to read a scene, students will probably just approach it straightforwardly for a primary level of meaning: "Lady Macbeth persuades Macbeth to murder King Duncan." But as they work closer to the conditions of real performance, they will begin to recognize that even such an apparently transparent reading involves countless points of interpretation. When, exactly, does Macbeth give in, and what pushes him over the edge? Does Lady Macbeth confront him aggressively, or does she work by indirection? Does she already have the plan to drug the grooms when the scene begins, or does she make it up on the spot under the pressure of circumstances? And while this kind of question may seem merely to reaffirm the centrality of "the subject," the circumstances of theatrical performance necessarily locate the individual "character" as part of a complex social network. How near are the party guests, how much is the scene affected by the fear of others overhearing? Are there other characters visible on the stage at any point (servants, partygoers, guards?) – and if so, how do Macbeth and Lady Macbeth respond to them? The fact of embodiment also necessarily weighs on the actor's work. What is the physical relation between Macbeth and Lady Macbeth in the scene: are they close together, at a distance, standing, sitting, moving? What role does Lady Macbeth's physical presence – threatening, seducing, resisting – play in her persuasion? And what are the intention, tone and effect of her lines about dashing the baby's brains out? With apologies to L. C. Knights, at this point it becomes necessary to ask: how many children had Lady Macbeth?

The point here is not to get mired in the psychological speculation Knights feared, nor to indulge in the unified, Stanislavskian approach to character warned against by postmodern critics. Performance pedagogy is not trying to unlock the inner life of the character, but to understand the force of the text's rhetoric under different interpretive conditions. How does the line about the child play differently, based on different actor choices about the characters' histories? Which of these interpretations can the students successfully convey to an audience? How does the rhetoric of maternity and masculinity function differently if Lady Macbeth is played by a male actor? By an adolescent male actor? If both characters are played by women? If Lady Macbeth is visibly pregnant? The questions and options are considerable, and working through them will give the students a vivid awareness of the role of interpretation in creating the play's meaning through performance.

In performance, every moment of every play is conditioned by interpretive decisions: by the actors, directors and designers, and also by the audience, in observing and processing the choices that have been made. There are countless examples that can express this idea dramatically for students. How does the silent Isabella respond to the Duke's proposal at the end of *Measure for Measure*? Why is Antonio so sad at the beginning of *The Merchant of Venice*? In *King Lear*, do sympathetic servants tend to the blinded Gloucester, as in the 1608 Quarto, or not, as in the 1623 Folio? When Lear says "Look there, look there" over the body of Cordelia, where is he looking, what does he see, and what does his final attitude contribute to the overall meaning of the play?

Some of these are old questions, but in many cases they are new to the students. More to the point, performance pedagogy provides a valuable means for students really to experience them, to explore them as flesh-and-blood possibilities that they try out for themselves.

Sense of History

Another thing that a performance approach can give students is an awareness of the plays as situated in history: conditioned by the original circumstances of their performance, but also remade according to changing cultural conditions, down to the present. One of the objections to performance pedagogy has been its universalizing tendency, its collapsing of historical difference. But it seems to me that when effectively employed, it can have the opposite result. Not only does performance work afford a great opportunity to learn about how meaning was produced in the Elizabethan theatre, but it can also help to make students more aware of subsequent cultural changes, their impact on the plays' meanings, and the historically situated character of the students' own interpretations.

Classroom performance can reveal the workings of various conventions of Shakespeare's theatre: the dimensions of the stage, the absence of representative scenery, the fluidity of scene changes, the constant daylight, the possibility of direct address to the audience, and so forth. Critics like Alan Dessen and Ralph Alan Cohen have demonstrated a number of ways that an awareness of staging conventions can illuminate classroom teaching. In performing the first scene of *Hamlet*, for instance, students become aware of how the guards create the *illusion* of darkness through their difficulty in seeing and recognizing one another. When the Ghost appears, the convention changes – everyone sees it immediately and clearly – so that on a bare daylit stage, "Shakespeare has, in effect, made his Ghost glow in the dark" (Cohen 1999: 90). There is of course a danger in growing too confident about what the conventions were, and also in assuming that because something can be made to "work" in a modern classroom, that it worked in the same way in Shakespeare's theatre. But by exploring ideas about Elizabethan stagecraft, we can get our students thinking practically about theatrical possibilities, and the implications of choosing one mode of representation over another.

The subsequent performance history of the plays is also a significant part of performance pedagogy. Students can experience for themselves the difference between playing on a thrust stage or behind a proscenium arch. They can recognize the opportunities provided by the increasing representational sophistication of the English stage, and consider some of the effects on the plays of realistic scenery. University campuses generally provide examples of pseudo-historical architecture, as well as different sorts of playing spaces, where students can gauge varying aesthetic impacts. For instance, performing the Forum scene of *Julius Caesar* in makeshift togas, on the steps of a neoclassical administration building, can give students a fair sense of the effect Victorian directors were striving for when they introduced historical costumes and settings; an effect students could contrast with a modern-dress version of the scene as a violent campus political rally. An awareness of the historical contingency of such theatrical effects works against any complacent belief in the universal, unchanging, and ultimately conservative nature of Shakespearean drama.

The history of different acting editions of Shakespeare also provides material for practical explorations. Students could perform Garrick's revised ending to *Romeo and Juliet*, for instance, and consider the dramatic value of having Juliet wake before Romeo dies from the poison. After all, this version held the stage for nearly half of the play's history, and a variation on Garrick's ending concludes Baz Luhrmann's popular film. Tracing the performance history of a particular play can give students an opportunity to see how the cultural context of a production enables or precludes certain meanings. A review of the stage history of *The Merchant of Venice*, *Othello* or *The Taming of the Shrew* – inviting students to perform some of the significant scenes from that history – can show how profoundly these plays have been transformed through performance in changing historical moments, and the extent to which some of those transformations do and don't live with us today. Issues of casting are especially relevant in this regard. When students debate the effects of cross-gender or race-specific casting in modern productions, they can read nineteenth-century accounts of Ira Aldridge's Macbeth, or Madame Vestris' Oberon, or Charlotte Cushman's Romeo. And while these issues are potentially explosive in the classroom, performance provides exactly the kind of laboratory where the implications of gender, race, sexuality, and social empowerment – and their inheritance in the traditions of received "Shakespeare" – can become visible, and discussible.

Understanding of Expressive Choices

A further value in teaching with an emphasis on performance is the ability to open students up to the range of expressive factors available in contemporary production: to make the students more sophisticated and critical audience members. I am often disturbed to find how fully students' perceptions of a given Shakespeare play have been conditioned by their viewing of a particular movie or video version. While the new wave of Shakespeare films has been of great value in many respects, students often watch them too passively and accept their versions of the plays at face value; in an important respect, and perhaps as an unfortunate consequence of the popularity of performance pedagogy, the complete, "canned" performance sometimes comes to replace the generative options implied by the text. I have had students take for granted that the conflict between the Montagues and the Capulets is ethnically motivated, or that Ross is the Third Murderer in *Macbeth*, or that Hippolyta advises Theseus to overbear Egeus's will in *A Midsummer Night's Dream*, all because these things have happened in films of the plays. Students don't necessarily know how to take apart a performance, to unpack its many systems of signification, the codes they use and the assumptions on which they rest. By engaging in performance work themselves, students become more aware of the effects of casting, costume, make-up, lighting, vocal quality, and so forth, and of the kind of work these elements of performance do with and to the text. In the case of films, even without any great degree of technical knowledge, a student who has explored the plays in performance will be less easily seduced by Nino Rota's *Romeo and Juliet* score, or less mystified by the jump-cuts in Welles's *Othello*. He or she will recognize these things as aesthetic devices in the service of a particular interpretation, and be more prepared to be a critical, skeptical reader of performance.

An informed viewing of Shakespeare films, especially when students can compare one or more different versions, can help attune them to the expressive potential of different devices like camera movement, soundtrack music, or editing, which often go more or less unnoticed by passive viewers. But when students get to do the performance work themselves, to experiment with their own set of tools, they develop an even greater understanding of the complex range of artistic factors that go to make up a theatrical (or cinematic) performance. Students involved in a classroom workshop *Henry V*, for instance, will be able to confront the challenges and possibilities inherent in staging the battle of Agincourt. They will keenly feel the limitations of "four or five most vile and ragged foils, / right ill disposed in brawl ridiculous" (4. Chor. 50–1), but they will also confront the problems raised by the Chorus's rhetoric. What is the relationship between what the Chorus describes and what can be enacted on the stage? How much of the battle should be performed? How will what the audience sees match or contradict the text? How will their "imaginary forces" be engaged (Prol. 18)? The text explicitly raises many of these questions, but students may not fully apprehend them until they themselves are "ciphers to this great account" (Prol. 17).

Sense of Ownership

The most important thing that performance gives to students is a sense, perhaps illusory, but nonetheless truly earned, of mastery over the text. They feel that Shakespeare belongs to them, they have made his words their own, they have bodied forth his characters, given them a local habitation and a name. Performance gives students a uniquely personal stake in the work, whether it is a short scene for class, an interpretive approach to a play, a video clip, or a full-blown production. There are costs, of course. As Miriam Gilbert has dryly noted, "No one will argue that getting students to perform a scene in class, or even to work on an exercise related to a scene, is anything other than a very slow way to work" (1984: 601). Performance takes a lot of time and commitment, both inside and outside of class. On the other hand, the payoff is immediate and evident; students can see performance working. A student can't play Hamlet in Act 3 Scene 1 without making concrete decisions about Hamlet's mental state, his relationship with Ophelia, and whether or not he knows Polonius is behind the arras. By trying out different possibilities, the class can develop a nuanced understanding of the play *from the inside*. And while it's certainly possible to carp at a sense of "mastery," it can be argued that a student who engages with a text through performance can see it from more angles, and in more detail, than one who has merely developed a univocal "reading." More importantly, perhaps, the student has a real investment in the play; by standing up in front of the classroom or audience, the student has put not just ideas on the line, but him or herself also.

Performance beyond the Classroom: Shakespeare at Winedale

For the final part of this chapter I want to discuss a rather unusual and extreme example of performance pedagogy with which I have been connected, in one way or another, for several years. The Shakespeare at Winedale program at the University of Texas provides a kind of total-immersion model of studying Shakespeare through performance. While a program like this is very demanding, both in time and resources, much of what works at Winedale could be adapted to other circumstances. I offer this discussion not in order to prescribe this particular approach, but to encourage instructors to be creative with performance options, to think outside the classroom when they want to bring Shakespeare to life for their students.

Participants in the Winedale program spend an entire summer exploring three Shakespeare plays in a secluded environment in the Texas countryside. The course culminates with four weekends of productions in repertory, followed, in recent years, by a two-week trip to England to study and perform. But the program differs from traditional Shakespeare festivals in that the focus is on the learning experience, both for the students and their audiences. Many Winedale students have no previous theatre experience or training, and few aspire to careers in the theatre. Winedale is founded on the conviction that anyone can benefit from an intense engagement with Shakespeare's plays in the medium for which they were written.

Shakespeare at Winedale was founded in 1970 by James B. Ayres, of the University of Texas English Department. Ayres's approach to teaching was built on his belief in performance – or *play*, as he prefers to call it – as one of the essential activities of life. Influenced by the psychologist Erving Goffman (*The Presentation of Self in Everyday Life*, 1959), Ayres developed a method of teaching that brought art and life together, encouraging students to discover more about themselves through the quintessentially Shakespearean activity of role-playing. In an essay entitled "The Play and Self," Ayres defines some of the principles that led to the creation of Shakespeare at Winedale:

> Performance as a means of studying the play *and* the self is one way of reintroducing premises basic to dramatic art but often neglected in the literary classroom: that imitation is perhaps the most natural of human instincts; that plays are written to be performed, that *plays are entire only when recreated on a stage* (however defined), moving through human action, time and space; that plays require, indeed ofttimes demand and provoke in human beings (whether student, performer or audience) an understanding of self and others; and that plays are expression of the human spirit, mind, and body, always in more than language, their final effect depending on a synthesis of related arts. (1975: 15–16)

Ayres's teaching has had a transformative effect on generations of students, myself among them. I was his student at Winedale in 1983 and 1984, and since I succeeded him as director of the program in 2001, I have had the humbling but inspiring charge of trying to extend his legacy. Any remarkable qualities of the Winedale program derive from his original vision.

An important dimension of the Shakespeare at Winedale experience is the setting. The Winedale Historical Center is a 270-acre property in an isolated rural part of central Texas. It contains a number of historic structures built by the German immigrants who settled the area in the mid-nineteenth century. Among these is a large hay barn that bears structural and aesthetic similarities to an Elizabethan playhouse, with heavy timber beams, hayloft galleries, and rough-hewn construction. At the suggestion of Texas philanthropist Ima Hogg, who donated the property to the University, Ayres began bringing his students down from Austin to work on scenes from Shakespeare in the barn. Soon they began to stay for longer periods and to perform whole plays. Eventually Shakespeare at Winedale became a six-credit summer course taught in residence at the center. Away from the distractions of Austin, students could engage fully in the demanding work of interpreting and staging the plays. Ayres, inspired by the archetypal criticism of Northrop Frye and the theatrical experiments of Peter Brook, saw Winedale as a "green world" where students could engage in licensed misrule, and the barn as an empty space where they could create a theatre that was both rough and holy.

About 18 students are in the class each summer, and they do everything necessary to stage three Shakespeare plays. There are no directors, designers or technicians as such; everything is an ensemble effort. All of the students are in all of the plays; roles are distributed so that each student has an approximately equal number of lines over the three plays. The students also all make their own costumes, compose their own music, and create any props that are needed for the performances. The staging is roughly Elizabethan. There is a thrust stage (built by Ayres and his students) with a permanent façade approximating the structure of an Elizabethan playhouse, with a discovery space flanked by two entrance doors, and an upper level reached by side staircases. Little is attempted in the way of scenery or lighting, though there are stage lights for evening performances. The sides of the barn are open, but it does have a roof to keep off the brutal Texas sun and the occasional thunderstorm. The audience members do not stand, but sit in rows of chairs surrounding the stage on three sides, and in a balcony formed by the barn's hayloft.

The educational project of Winedale builds on the pedagogical principles discussed elsewhere in this chapter, but the residential aspect of the course allows an especially deep and thorough application of them. The students begin the course with four weeks of independent study, directed reading, and online discussion, before arriving at Winedale in early June. By this time they have been assigned roles and have learned their lines. The work on the plays then begins in earnest, seven days a week, 15 hours a day. Intensive scene work is supplemented by improvisations, sonnet workshops, movement exercises, fight training, and individual text work. The students scrutinize the language for sound and sense, staging clues, and interpretive options, combining scholarly study with practical experiment. They try out multiple possibilities for every scene. In keeping with the student-centered dimension of performance pedagogy, I don't direct the plays in a conventional sense, but try to encourage this communal investigation. Every scene, line, moment has to be tested, played with, made fresh each time. One of the basic philosophies of the Winedale method, established by Ayres, is that there are no rehearsals: each engagement with the text *is* a performance, as valid as any other, and demanding the same level of commitment. Accordingly, our work on the plays is not so much directed toward a finished "product" – though of course we are deeply concerned to *have* a play to put on for our audiences – but toward defining and exploring problems, both of text and performance. The productions continue to evolve and change even during the public run, and students will often find themselves acting on a new impulse or responding to a changed inflection up to the very last performance.

This openness of interpretation is very liberating for the students, and allows them to experience powerfully their own expressive potential. I will give a couple of examples from the time when I was first a student at Winedale in 1983. I remember my astonishment when our Hamlet, John Rando (now a Tony award-winning director), had a different response to the Ghost every night, each time taking his character in a new direction. Our Polonius, likewise, never knew what form Hamlet's baiting of him would take, so their scenes together were charged with an atmosphere of real mockery and danger. The autonomy of the students in the ensemble process can lead to inconsistency – some experiments work, others don't – but it allows meaning to be discovered, or created, in real time. We also staged *The Merchant of Venice* in 1983, a play that occasioned passionate arguments among the group. Each of us became attached to his or her own character; we all wanted to represent ourselves in the most favorable light. Rather than resolving the conflict through an imposed interpretation, Ayres encouraged us to play it out onstage, and, as it were, let the audience decide. I remember the intensely charged atmosphere of the trial scene (I played Bassanio), and the wild fluctuations of audience response. The relief at

Antonio's deliverance and the exhilaration at Shylock's defeat that were whipped up by Gratiano – the audience were often literally laughing and cheering – were invariably silenced by Shylock's response to his forced conversion. As he made a slow circle, looking into the faces of both those on stage and in the audience, the sense of shame in the barn was palpable. Neither the Venetian lords nor the Texan spectators were able to meet his gaze; characters and audience were alike confronted with the cruel stupidity of the court's decree.

While the audience very often plays a role in the creation of meaning at Winedale, as in the above instance, many of the most revealing moments occur during the day-to-day work on the plays. Discoveries can be valid, instructive, breathtakingly illuminating without necessarily being repeatable. One of my most memorable experiences at Winedale came in the summer of 2003, after I had returned to the English Department as a member of the faculty, and we were working on *Julius Caesar*. Because of essential construction work on the theatre barn, we found ourselves without a stage on what was supposed to be our final night of rehearsal before opening. With no time to prepare or consider, we decided to perform the play outdoors in an improvisational fashion, using the whole grounds of the Winedale Historical Center for our theatre. Every scene was charged with new discoveries. The tribunes in the opening scene had a much harder task than usual, having to rein in an unruly crowd of twenty (the entire class) instead of the five or six we usually had onstage. For their secret meeting with Brutus, the conspirators emerged from the purple gloom of a grove of flowering crepe-myrtles. The murder of Caesar was bathed in the red light of the sun setting across the lake. The killing of Cinna was a twilit scene of lynch-mob savagery, against the disturbing backdrop of Southern pecan trees. The battles took place in near total darkness, with soldiers running and shouting over a vast field. Brutus died in the glare of a lone street lamp near the highway. Throughout the play, the students made bold, original and effective choices. This was experiment of the most productive kind, in which training and study brought performance to the point where experiment could lead to new, unpredictable under-standing. Some few of these insights were eventually included in the public perform-ances; most were not. But it was a performance of *Julius Caesar* that all those who were present will remember for the rest of their lives. One student wrote to me later that it was "the most intensive play experience" he had ever had, because "everyone remained constantly committed to the play, 100% invested in what was going on, and everyone felt free to try anything and everything to feed the performers" (Shakespeare at Winedale student journals, 2003).

I want to let the students speak for themselves a little, to illustrate some of the kinds of thinking that intensive performance work encourages. The following comments come from students in the 2003 class, from various journal assignments I gave them over the course of the summer. A student who had struggled with the character of Benedick commented, "My breakthrough in *Much Ado* came right about the time I started working on and watching the parts of the play I wasn't in." Noting the alterations and shifts of tone from scene to scene, the student observed: "I've come to think that the best way to prepare for a scene is to watch, or at least listen to . . . the scene before, rather than trying to get all up in your head about your character." His practical experience of the play in performance led him to reject a Stanislavskian approach to character in favor of an attention to the dramaturgy of the play as a whole, to see Benedick as part of a texture of emerging social relations and theatrical dynamics (Shakespeare at Winedale journals, 2003). Similarly, another student observed:

> I love the idea of letting the words motivate each scene emotionally. I think I am getting better at realizing what I am saying as I'm saying it, not beforehand. Letting the words themselves draw out the emotion takes off me a lot of the pressure of conjuring up the emotion outside the confines of the scene. (Shakespeare at Winedale student journals, 2003)

Another student entertained, and then rejected, various psychologically-based approaches to the character of Moth in *Love's Labour's Lost*:

> I began the role searching for some long, extensive back-story and motivation for why Moth says what he does: Moth loves Armado's attention, wants to play when Armado wants to pine; Moth is inherently intolerant of ostentation, and, simply because he's precocious, mocks Armado; Moth is a pseudo-character, playing more for the audience than his fellow players . . . and so forth. The thing is, none of these are useful because subtleties are only clutter in scenes of dueling wit. (Shakespeare at Winedale student journals, 2003)

Students sometimes relate their individual acting problems to questions about Elizabethan theatrical convention. A female student who was cast as Don John and Casca became very interested in the performance of gender, both in the Shakespearean theatre and in contemporary life: "I wonder how those young boys fared as Juliet and Gertrude? Did they spend time watching women move and interact, studying how they were different? If nothing else, playing men has taught me how to be more aware of my own body and its movement, as well as others' physicality" (Shakespeare at Winedale student journals, 2003).

All these comments indicate a movement away from contemporary notions of character and psychology, and toward a recognition of the practical demands of the plays, of the mechanics of Shakespeare's stagecraft, and of the social and theatrical conventions embodied in Elizabethan plays. Their discoveries during the summer led these students deeply into the plays and themselves, and also out into the rapidly changing world that had delivered Shakespeare to them through four centuries of history. But whatever they learned in their summer at Winedale, these students felt they had earned it, that it was a part of them. And that, finally, is what is so exciting to me about performance pedagogy: it makes Shakespeare real for the students, a part of their bodies and not just a wisp of discourse. It works, it gives the students something they can live with and live through, and for that, a few essentialist assumptions may not be such a high price to pay.

REFERENCES AND FURTHER READING

Aers, Lesley, & Wheale, Nigel (eds.) (1991). *Shakespeare in the Changing Curriculum*. London: Routledge.

Andrews, John F. (1984). Introduction. *Shakespeare Quarterly* 35: 515–16.

Ayres, James B. (1975). "The Play and the Self." Unpublished essay.

Barton, John (1984). *Playing Shakespeare*. London: Methuen.

Berry, Cicely ([1987] 1992). *The Actor and the Text*. London: Harrap. (Reprint of *The Actor and His Text*.)

Bulman, James C. (ed.) (1996). *Shakespeare, Theory, and Performance*. London: Routledge.

Cohen, Ralph Alan (1990). "Introduction." *Shakespeare Quarterly* 41: iii–v.

Cohen, Ralph Alan (1999). "Original Staging and the Shakespeare Classroom." In Milla Cozart Riggio (ed.) *Teaching Shakespeare through Performance*. New York: Modern Language Association of America, pp. 78–101.

Gibson, Rex (1998). *Teaching Shakespeare: A Handbook for Teachers*. Cambridge: Cambridge University Press.

Gilbert, Miriam (1984). "Teaching Shakespeare through Performance." *Shakespeare Quarterly* 35: 601–8.

Goffman, Erving (1959). *The Presentation of Self in Everyday Life*. Garden City, NY: Doubleday.

Knowles, Richard Paul (1996). "Shakespeare, Voice, and Ideology: Interrogating the Natural Voice." In James Bulman (ed.) *Shakespeare, Theory, and Performance*. London: Routledge, pp. 92–112.

Mazer, Cary M. (1996). "Historicizing Alan Dessen." In James Bulman (ed.) *Shakespeare, Theory, and Performance*. London: Routledge, pp. 149–67.

Mazer, Cary M. (1999). "Playing the Action: Building an Interpretation from the Scene up." In Milla Cozart Riggio (ed.) *Teaching Shakespeare through Performance*. New York: Modern Language Association of America, pp. 155 68.

Patterson, Annabel (1994). "Palinode." In Bruce McIver & Ruth Stevenson (eds.) *Teaching with Shakespeare: Critics in the Classroom*. Newark: University of Delaware Press, pp. 254–9.

Riggio, Milla Cozart (ed.) (1999). *Teaching Shakespeare through Performance*. New York: Modern Language Association of America.

Salomone, Roland L., & Davis, James E. (eds.) (1997). *Teaching Shakespeare into the Twenty-First Century*. Athens, OH: Ohio University Press.

Sauer, David Kennedy, & Tribble, Evelyn (1999). "Shakespeare in Performance: Theory in Practice and Practice in Theory." In Milla Cozart Riggio (ed.) *Teaching Shakespeare through Performance*. New York: Modern Language Association of America, pp. 33 47.

Shakespeare at Winedale student journals (2003). Quoted by permission.

Shand, G. B. (1999). "Reading Power: Classroom Acting as Close Reading." In Milla Cozart Riggio (ed.) *Teaching Shakespeare through Performance*. New York: Modern Language Association of America, pp. 244–55.

Swander, Homer (1984). "In Our Time: Such Audiences as We Wish Him." *Shakespeare Quarterly* 35: 528–40.

Swander, Homer (1985). "Teaching Shakespeare: Tradition and the Future." In John F. Andrews (ed.) *William Shakespeare: His World, His Work, His Influence*, vol. 3. New York: Scribner, pp. 873–87.

Thompson, Ann (1990). "*King Lear* and the Politics of Teaching Shakespeare." *Shakespeare Quarterly* 41: 528–40.

Worthen, W. B. (1997). *Shakespeare and the Authority of Performance*. Cambridge: Cambridge University Press.

34
"The eye of man hath not heard, / The ear of man hath not seen": Teaching Tools for Speaking Shakespeare

Peter Lichtenfels

My primary experience in teaching acting has been in the conservatory system in England, although I have had several experiences teaching in university settings in North America, and currently teach in the Department of Theatre and Dance at the University of California, Davis; I am, then, familiar with a number of European training schools for actors. While I work constantly with actors as a director in professional theatre, and teach acting also at the graduate level, this chapter is mainly focused on techniques for teaching conservatory students.

In the UK conservatory system, there is only one school within a university setting offering acting as a course of study: Manchester Metropolitan University where I worked. What this means is that training cannot be afforded by many students because only the universities have government-controlled fees. Even conservatories that do have some scholarships to offer, such as the Royal Academy of Dramatic Art and the London Academy of Music and Dramatic Arts, only have a few scholarships and the fees are high. At Manchester Metropolitan, there was an evident hunger for actor training with over 1,700 applicants for 24 places, all of whom were auditioned. These potential students came from all parts of the UK: many were from the North, many from working-class backgrounds, and, as a group, applicants came from all strata of society, from a wide variety of ethnicities, and had a striking range of abilities as well. Yet some of these students already had a strong relationship with words, since they came from areas and cultures with developed oral traditions. But there were also many students more typical of the encroaching contemporary attitude toward language, a world where words are not recognized as powerful, and the spoken word is not respected as a communicator. This fact colored much of the teaching that I have developed for training students to act Shakespeare, and has proved invaluable in the North American setting in which I now find myself, and find a similar loss of a living, oral tradition.

It is important to remember that a conservatory system allows for teaching one group of students for 35 hours each week. Working so intensively over the course of three years, students have the opportunity to develop at their own pace; and, as in any group, one person will have trouble with one element but find another easy, and for another student it will be the other way around. In an important sense, the intensity and duration of the program turn out to produce a surprising flexibility; since the program progresses so methodically, each student not only develops at his or her own pace, but the students learn to measure themselves against their own inner judge. When I worked in the North American university teaching system, teaching acting four to six hours per week as part of a conventional ten-week course, I was struck by how difficult it is for the human body to *learn* in that time frame. This structure sets up a pressure to define a result at the end of the course, which students may not have the time to fully explore because of the needs and abilities they bring to the course in the first place. The first thing I have to do when teaching Shakespeare to students is to get them into a different time and space frame. They need the experience of slowing down, taking things apart, slowing down further, and allowing things to happen. If you slow down and allow your being time to experience where something sits in the body, the words will teach you rather than you imposing a result on them.

My sense of teaching actors in training is that, in the main, they are disenchanted by, bored with, and/or scared of Shakespeare. Sometimes it's from the high school introduction they have had, sometimes from seeing bad productions, but there's a definite sense of estrangement. They may have a grasp of some technical aspects such as iambic pentameter, but they are not taught how the language can be useful to their speaking; or how to own the language. It seems that they are usually taught Shakespeare from a literary point of view. They may read it aloud or act out scenes, but usually from the point of view of literature; even in literature classes that seem to use "performance" as a teaching technique, performance is deployed as a means of teaching themes, ideas, patterns somehow *in* the play's writing. Rather than teaching students what theatre should teach them – to *own* the language – such teaching sees acting, performing as a kind of subsidiary art, a way of learning something *about* the language without really inhabiting it. It doesn't leave students with a sense of owning the language as spoken word and maybe because of that they are scared of it.

When I work with actors, it takes a long time to get to the end of the line. The actor has to understand word for word where a line wants to go – not what it *means* in a semantic sense, but how it acquires a forward *energy*. As actors take the time to slow down and learn each successive word, they begin to understand how Shakespeare's words are helping them shape their pace, their breathing; as well as the transformation of energy between words. Shakespeare begins to teach you his language. When most people first begin to read Shakespeare, the language feels so foreign that it runs away from them, they have no control over it. Most of the time, they have only the most generalized idea of what the text is saying, what they might be able to make it say or do. As they work it from word to word to the end of the line, they begin to understand what the text is talking about: that's the moment when they realize that it's not obscure, that there is clarity, that it is accessible. And that's when they start to understand how to begin shaping the language through their breath. All of a sudden, they gain confidence.

In other words, I try to teach actors by showing them the sheer amount of information they can learn from the text before going into semantic meaning. Many of the people who come to acting schools are shy of ideas, although there is a hunger to express themselves through their bodies. So when I teach, one of my concerns is to take students through practical, concrete ways of accessing the language without going first for meaning, for themes or ideas. In other words, I try to take away their fear.

I usually begin by asking them to learn a Shakespearean sonnet, and for the next short while explore strategies to shake them out of their preconceptions, to move away from their conventional, or cultured selves. Once they have memorized the sonnet, I ask them to speak it out loud so they begin to get a sense of the language in their mouth, ands the rest of the class begins to hear what is or is not being said. Usually, when a person first says the sonnet, the performance has no sense of shape or forward movement. There is little dynamic and you tend to hear a received sense of what they think Shakespeare should be. The actor lacks a sense of a need and takes little responsibility for *saying it*. It is then I begin to explore distraction techniques with students.

Distraction Techniques

I create many exercises which ask the student to say the speech while I also give them something physical to work against. One example is to restrain a student while asking him or her to walk forward speaking the sonnet; then letting the student go at the point when the search for breath supplants the ability to speak. At that moment, before the student is able to recover the breath, I ask him or her to stand absolutely still and speak the sonnet. The actor often becomes electrifying because s/he is fighting for breath, and the shape and the needs of the words respond to and are structured by this need. Neither the actors nor the audience know where the next word is coming from, where it will go to, or even if it will make its way out; yet the need to speak it, to create it is visibly *there* in this dynamically still body. In other words, distracting students from the "conceptual" aspect of Shakespearean language, giving actors a physical obstacle to struggle against, tends to put the words *into* the body, tends to make the act of speaking articulate a *need* to speak, to be heard, to be understood. Distraction techniques are used by many theatre teachers, and some of those that I have developed are:

- The students line up back to back with knees slightly bent, and the instructor works to push them to one side of the room, while they speak the speech. When the instructor hears them struggling for breath they are asked to stand up straight and speak.
- The student is asked to sing the sonnet in a specific, "big" style, such as *opera buffo*, without imposing a melody or song onto the sonnet but letting the words carry them along. Try to get them to sing until they forget to be embarrassed, and then get them to just speak it.
- The students do charades of a given speech, one for every word, and once they have done that they speak it out.
- Asking the actors to polish the floor with every word: moving as they speak each word their feet always slide flat along the floor; once they have done that, really working at it, they stand still and speak the words, and there is contrast between heaviness and lightness, effort and release.
- Ripping up pieces of paper and scattering them on the floor; the student speaks out the next word in the sonnet as if it's just been picked up from the floor, and once finished, s/he then discovers the next word in the sonnet and eventually speaks out the whole sonnet.

You have to find the right technique for each student, but when you do and it works, when you judge that they have taken their concentration to a different place, the body will be charged from the physical task, and for a few moments there is no self-consciousness. Often the sonnet comes out in a centered or focused manner, the actor is present, and the words are present as if there is a need to say them. When you do these exercises in a roomful of students, the concentration becomes electrically charged because the sonnet has an authority and a simplicity that they have not seen before in their fellow actor.

Often when I ask the person who has just said the sonnet, "What happened?," s/he will reply "I don't know," "I can't remember what I did," "It felt like I didn't do anything." And sometimes the student asks me whether they are acting because it doesn't feel like they have "done" anything. There is no "effort" involved. What they are clear about is that they have gone to a different place, that they can feel a difference between the way they said it before and the way they said it after. Sometimes the student will suddenly become emotionally affected, and something will be released in their body; someone whose body is tightly controlled, holding the muscles taut, will suddenly relax. They open up. But because they have so much time and all their energy goes into being specific with the word, it feels that they are present with it and recognize it in the moment: they experience the concreteness of the word. They have time because the body has speeded up, and they are in the frame of the word's occurring, so they are not doing the work for the words but allowing the words to work on them. Occasionally they cry, as if the words become so powerful that something is unblocked within them. That is the moment when many students around them feel impelled to cuddle them, to hug them, to reassure them. But it is also the moment when the teacher has to ask them to stay with the words. This will give an extraordinary shape and focus to the rest of the sonnet. If they use their energy to cry instead of putting it into the words, the speaking becomes diffused.

I also tell students that they cannot work like this onstage, it is too physically exhausting. But it is important they remember the difference of before and after within themselves, and of seeing that difference in their fellows. It is when they realize the need to train for that freedom of speaking the words and finding positive ways of using the energy that the experience has released in them, that I start on a range of more detailed techniques.

Training Techniques for "Going Forward"

Students today have no daily connection with Shakespeare's English, in part, because there is less familiarity with the King James Bible, so they have to be taught how to gain access to this English. And language within society has changed. Many students no longer feel words are powerful. Their habits include stringing a whole series of words together, gliding over words, eliding words all into one tone. There is a tendency not to finish the word, they begin and then trail it off, so the thinking or energy do not even carry to the end of the word. At the same time, while the emphasis on important words and phrases trails off, student actors continually hit the personal pronouns: I, me, my, and mine. They have to discover that words are an important part of the means to change a character-part on stage, either your own or someone else's. This takes time.

When an actor is preparing for a role, it's important to take the time to go through the experience of each word and allow the particularity of the sound of that word to become a presence. The individuality of a word, or its uniqueness, lies in the combination of resonances it has in the body, and through the body, in the voice. Working on consonants and vowels, or on punctuation, trains the student actor to go from word to word in the moment.

Consonants and vowels

The consonant-and-vowel exercise was introduced into acting training in the 1960s, largely through the efforts of Cicely Berry (1987: 151–2), and it is the smallest unit of performance I've yet worked on (Lichtenfels & Hunter 1999: 55–7). When you are doing it, the sounds resonate in different parts of the body, and depending on their combination, they slide, or grate, or jostle. What you feel about the ease, or slowness, or difficulty of saying a sound, teaches you the cost and effort of speaking it – not only about its energy, but how quickly you can say it, its duration in the body, and where specifically any particular sound resonates in the body. You will probably find that when you do the consonant/vowel exercise, you use your breath in a way more than in everyday life. Your use of language becomes heightened and bigger, so the quality of the sounds in the combinations hits the ear more. Eventually this is where the music in the language comes in, through that heightened combination of resonant places with the time of speaking the sound.

If the student takes a sonnet or speech by Shakespeare and reads it in everyday time, it may take, say, two minutes. But when you break it apart, something that long will easily take four to five minutes for the consonants, and another four to five for the vowels. You end up with eight to ten minutes of work for lines that are usually glided over in two. Students are always surprised by the sheer hard work there is in speaking a word. The consonants and vowels take such a long time to speak that the exercise is a concrete way of showing the students the text by way of their bodies, so that the energy costs, and thus the joy, are in saying, rather than indicating, the word. Although actors can never speak that way on stage, the exercise provides a way of preparing the body, as by following the shape of the word, they explore the text without necessarily going toward meaning. Consonants can be thought of as the "doing" part of the word, they expel breath by contracting muscles, while vowels, the "feeling" part of the word, extend them, using energy and breath in quite a different way. What you explore in that combination of consonants and vowels teaches you the rigor with which the word requires itself to be spoken. If a student now reads the sonnet, having done the exercise, it is remarkable how accessible Shakespeare's language begins to feel.

Through the process of this exercise, the student starts to develop concentration. Going from consonantal sound to consonantal sound requires the students to be in the present. For example, they may ask, "What sound does a *ct* make?" In order to keep up the pace of the line and do that combination of letters, and to maintain the shape of the word, they have to focus on where the consonants are going to occur and how to adjust their bodies in preparation for the next one. This has ramifications later on when the actors go into rehearsal and production because they learn to read the words literally, one by one, simply because they are there. They know the individual word from the exercise. They have a body memory of its unique combination of resonance, breath and energy. But when they have finished that set of sounds they have to let go and move on to the next. Then words become transforming, because their different energies are allowed to clash.

As student actors go through the exercise with a Shakespearean text, they visually notice patterns of repeated sounds and where they resonate. They begin to feel "This character-part is concerned with these sounds, and they live in that particular part of the body." So there is something happening in that part of the body that they need to deal with, or that particular sedimentation of body memory is where they want to be. If we look at the vowels of Sonnet 129: up to about line 10 the vowels are hard to speak, they take their time, yet after that line, they become effortless. The experience of saying them indicates that there's a shift going on. So when you go through the exercise, the work is sometimes about the effort, but it also tells you where the character wants to reside. When you eventually look at meaning, it's a preparation and a countercheck. Whatever the words do in the actor's body is what the character-part becomes.

Punctuation

Punctuation can also tell you things about the character-part. There is of course no standardized punctuation or spelling for Shakespearean texts, and a whole world of explanation has to go into explaining the implications to students. But when you start working on a character-part, you begin by accepting the punctuation of your edition because you have to begin somewhere, and that somewhere is usually the printed text (see Berry 1987: 104–8). A lot of what an actor does is based on the text s/he is using, and an editor's role is fundamental to interpretation. Only when actors become much more experienced do they embrace that it is a shifting structure, and there has to be flexibility in what they do.

There are several exercises a student can do to use the punctuation they find in front of them to help them understand more about their character. For example, if a line represents a given distance from A to B, every time there is an internal punctuation mark in the line, the student has to move in that space. If the first piece of punctuation comes at around 20 percent of the line, you move through 20 percent of the space. And if there is no punctuation, you move at the end of the line. The process is tiring but teaches you in a physical or schematic way that there are shifts in the language and a periodicity to those shifts – in other words, a spatial and temporal body syntax.

If you take Sonnet 129 and start with the comma, there are five or six lines with four or five commas, making you stop and stop and stop within the line. On the other hand, in Sonnet 29, it's rare to have the comma as punctuation internal to the line, so you move only at the ends of lines. The punctuation may lead the reader or actor to understand a particular rhythm in the character-part, whether the character is going through something that interrupts their actions or is settled. If there is a lot of comma punctuation internal to the line, then the body is riled up, or struggling, or moving in different directions, or embracing different energies that haven't yet coalesced. This contrasts with the more even rhythm that Sonnet 29 acquires with no commas, a rhythm which may be dynamic but may also be a more reasoned and controlled way of being. The commas become pointers toward something that is happening, even if the actor doesn't know what that is. Working on the exercise takes time and releases many possibilities. Often actors in training say, "Oh, why didn't I see that?" But it is just taking the time to allow the meaning to happen, rather than trying to will it.

This physical exercise with space and punctuation works in a similar way to that of the consonant/vowel exercise. Once the particular piece of punctuation has been dealt with, the actor leaves it behind and goes on to the new concern, staying always in the present moment. The next step is to go to a partially completed thought in the syntax, often indicated by a semi-colon, dash or colon. While still recognizing internal shifts within the larger unit, commas are now left behind. For example, Sonnets 129 and 29 have almost as many larger units of thought as each other, despite the different comma pattern. If you do the exercise and move between A and B, you still find you are walking on the punctuation but you find out where the movement stops mid-line or at the end of two or three lines. You move less, but the commas are still making internal movements in your body memory even if you do not mark them out on the floor.

It's possible to build on this further by moving on the larger syntactical units of period, question mark or exclamation mark, working from unit to unit. And the last element is to go from complete thought to complete thought, to the end of the speech, so you move only to the end of the speech when you have internalized the other movement. When I teach younger actors, this exercise seems to help them get their mouth and head around the words and eventually the thought, because language is broken down to understandable structures. They work through it and begin to trust that the way to get to the end of the line, or the end of the sentence, or the end of the speech, is to go from word to word, to phrase to thought. It gives them a physical way of understanding the grammar of the text. The movement tells them there has to be differentiation, and it begins to help them shape their breath.

Once actors learn this exercise, the way they treat punctuation changes and they begin to choose it or embrace it. An inexperienced person reading a Shakespearean text finds a piece of punctuation like a comma, and uses it to go on "vacation." When they get to a comma, they often drop their energy then allow themselves to think about what they will say next, gear up the energy again and go on to the next phrase, building a rise and fall between inertia and energy. Someone who has trained to work word-to-word forward, comes to punctuation as a possible natural moment for breathing, but understands breathing as a dynamic action, not a moment of resting but part of the line's movement forward. Almost always, the punctuation works like an intensifier, regulating the pitch of the phrase, or changing the register: the trained actor no longer hangs out as if on vacation. There are times in Shakespeare when it's absolutely appropriate to pause, but when that moment comes, it has to be a dynamic pause or charged silence, it takes the story forward. Once the actor has earned the words, the moment or spontaneity takes over, the scene can be played in different ways and the punctuation and other layout guides can be left behind.

Body movement and the energy of words

The joy of speaking out loud is not that words share the same quality, but that in their juxtapositions with each other they have their particular clarity, and there is the possibility of a clash that sparks. For the actor, there might also be an embedded world of sound in those words that the character-part needs to come back to again and again. What is exciting about using individual words is that it allows the individual actor to keep transforming, to go from A to B by embracing, by speaking each word, rather than indicating, describing or showing what you think it means through adopting a "tone."

One of the other habits that student actors bring to speaking Shakespeare is a tendency to emphasize or enunciate the beginning of a word and then trail off. This happens especially with -*ing* or -*ly* at the end of words, but there are many more examples. Their job is to take responsibility for the whole word, which means that their imagination, thinking, breath, and enunciation have to drive through right to the end of the word, because that is where the word is going. For example, take the word *laughing*: it needs to go to the end of -*ing*; or take *sickly*, which needs to go through to the end -*ly*. It is the actor's responsibility to take the word there. When I point these elisions out to students, they are usually surprised to find that they are not pronouncing the full word. A young actor will then say the word, but bounce on top of words so they become *laugh-ing*, or *sick-ly*; rather than going through the word when they become "laughing," "sickly." Physically, while they speak, they often have a neutral body stance and may well be sitting in their hips or standing collapsed. Their body is not engaged, so you'll hear many actors whose body is ahead of the word – their body arrives first and the word comes second. Or they say it and their body follows. What you want is for the body and the word to arrive together.

One exercise I use to break down the distinction between voice and body is to get students to say the word, for example, *laughing*, at the same time as pushing the hand forward, so that they push the word forward as they extend their arm and get to the end of the -*ing* just before they have reached the limit of their reach. In this way, they have the measure of the word, and it doesn't get away from them. The converse of this movement of energy is that the actor doesn't complete the word. The word tails off as the breath tails off, and your imagination tails off. The audience follows that and then, as the actor cranks up to the next word, they come with you. And as you say the next word, they follow you, and as you tail off, they tail off. Very quickly they will learn that the movement goes toward a collapsed energy, almost an imaginative inertia.

When an actor allows the words to work through the body, then the habitual rhythm is broken up because of the need of the moment. The color and shape of the word are dictated by the breath. But to provide such color and shape requires preparation, and the preparation requires learning and training. You cannot speak using the exercise techniques when you are on stage, but unless you do the preparation, you will not be at the place where your body can be spontaneous. The actor has to prepare the conditions for spontaneity to arise.

With Shakespeare the words always go forward, and one way of talking about that is for the actor to say, "OK, I've said this word. I'll let it go. Make room for the next word. Then let it go." The temptation, and this is why it is extraordinarily difficult work, is to hang on to what they have, so they bring the energy of the last word into the new word, rather than letting that energy go and embracing the new word. But if the actor does let go and go forward, that's when it becomes exciting for the audience. As the actors go to the next word, and the next word, the audience begins to sit on the edge of their seats because there's always something new happening, the energy, rhythm and dynamic in the production are going forward. The production ends up thinking faster than the audience, so the audience is always still being affected by the last word, while the actor has gone on to the next word, and a new energy. This does not mean that the production has to race quickly, but it means that the audience is playing catch-up in thinking, because the energy of the speaking builds a time frame that keeps going forward and the audience has to move with it.

Like a soufflé, if the actor is using energy, and keeping it up there, going from the energy of one word to the energy of the next, the energy becomes virtuous. The kinds of energy may be different and engaged, and easier to draw on them. But if you do not pick up the particularity of the next word, the energy of the one bleeds into the next, you cease going forward, and the movement collapses. One exercise that helps students to work on this forward movement involves using the traditional Chinese "dragon" stance, where the weight is over the front leg and there's a sense of impelling forward. The stance also requires the body to be light in the hips, rather than sunk into them, and to understand that there is a strong connection with the floor so that when you push forward, you are completely rooted at the same time. The exercise helps actors in training to understand that the energy needs physically to impel forward, yet not get away from them. If you speak while standing in dragon, there's a cost involved in saying the word. The student usually feels lighter in the body, and the words feel as if they take less effort, as if they are not fighting so much against the body. If the actor is not sitting in their hips, the possibility for movement becomes easier, and you get the feeling that the text is going forward.

If an actor doesn't finish the words at the end of the verse line, it's because s/he hasn't completed the thoughts. Going through to the end of the verse line and taking the energy to the next line and to the end of the sentence, teaches actors the need to get to the end of the thought. It also teaches them the highways and byways that the character-part takes to get to the end of that thought. If the character has a long speech, then it graduates from thought to thought until it comes to the end of the speech. And just as the character says the second word because the first one does not complete what it is s/he has to say, and needs the third, because the first and the second are not yet sufficient, so finally nothing is sufficient and the character has to keep going forward to the last word of their speech. A complete thought is again a temptation to take a holiday, but within the terms of a speech, it represents a partial completion, a signpost on the way, and a need to keep going.

Techniques for Empowerment

Meter

Once students begin to understand about moving forward word for word, or if they come in already with some command of Shakespearean verse, that's when I like to introduce more technical instruction. When I begin with taking them through the iambic pentameter on the line, I think of it as another empowering means of connecting the verse to the body. The iambic pentameter of Shakespeare's line is like blood pressure of the pulse in the actor's body. The regular iambic has sometimes been compared to our heartbeat, or the way we think about our heartbeat in English-speaking countries, so it goes ba–bump, ba–bump, short–long. That's the underlying rhythm that you come back to all the time, and sometimes it's foregrounded. The pulse of the language, which in our daily life changes depending on our activity, speeding up or slowing down, is determined by varying the meter. I think of the spondee, pyrrhic, or trochee, as those moments when Shakespeare leaves the iambic, taking our body or ear to a new place so we come back to the iambic refreshed (on meter, see Wright 1988).

When actors come to speak the words in front of an audience, they cannot give all the words equal emphasis because the audience would not be able to hear any syntax or structure, any grammar or rhetoric, and so would not be able to make any meaning. So once you have worked with exercises like the consonant/vowel technique, you have to choose to shape the words and one way of doing this is to use meter as a check on emerging rhythms. Meter can also help point up what the audience will hear or not hear. For example, actors find that the most difficult words to keep alive are *a*, *an*, *the*, *and*, and *but*. If the actor understands the meter that this kind of word is part of, it can guide them toward giving their energy in an appropriate way. Another example: long polysyllabic words are likely to be the ones that the audience hears because it takes the actor longer to say them, but the meter they are in may have three strong stresses, or two strong and one weak, or three weak stresses. Following the metric pattern may help to address whether your audience will hear what you want them to hear, whether the word is foregrounded or not, through changing what the ear has to hear in a different way. In Shakespearean verse, the blood pressure tends to be simple one or two syllable words, often nouns or verbs, while the pulse is polysyllabic.

Etymology

Words are powerful. They change you, and they change and affect others. Part of the power of words arising in performance comes from the fact that while Shakespeare has written them, the actor has to *choose* them. The actor needs to work to the point that, of all the possible words the English language could offer to express a particular thought, s/he would want to choose the words that Shakespeare wrote. This kind of training teaches you about using words. It broadens your respect for them, and makes you think about how you choose to express yourself rather than using words habitually.

Etymological excavation can help with this process (on etymology and interpretation, see Parker 1996). Like most people, actors get so many words thrown at them in daily life, often words that are cynically misused. Students frequently end up not being curious about words, with no desire to find out what they might signify. They also usually assume that they understand what the word means. But going back to the root of the word, and to the meanings of the word in Shakespeare's era, usually releases a moment of wonder. What I do is try to get the student to get a few moments of wonder together so that they feel there is a pattern. The technique is there to get them to a place where they become curious, and work out why Shakespeare used that particular word rather than any other.

Size of language

The point of empowering exercises is to get the brain out of the conscious self by giving it tasks that the actors do so that language can come forth. The actor starts to need language more. At the same time the exercises teach students how much size a word is able to take, how to absorb or how to release it, how to float with the word and how to bring it into their bodies. In combination with discovering the words as you say them, or saying them as you choose them, you realize that their size empowers people. It helps to know that in Shakespeare's London, spoken, public language – onstage and elsewhere – lived on a much larger scale than it does today. To recognize this is not to say that Shakespeare's language is over the top, but that its home is on a different level, a level we no longer use in today's society, but a level we need to become acquainted with or need to embrace as an actor (see Barton 1984: Chapter 2). Students I teach who have come from middle-class families in Western English-language speaking countries, do not have the same engagement with language. But when actors learn to taste and smell that size, it becomes satisfying and nourishing in ways that language does not, on the whole, nourish people in social settings today.

Addressing the audience

In one production I directed that included students, I used a technique in rehearsal to sensitize the actor to the audience: whenever anyone in the audience coughed, fidgeted, moved, made loud noises, it was the actor's job to look at the person, deal with him or her, ask some questions, while carrying on with their scene. The exercise was not there to quiet everyone down, but to help the actor understand that to work with Shakespeare's words means that you should be open, you acknowledge the audience. This openness is one of the ways the modern theatre has recovered something of early modern theatre practice: I first began to learn about the relationship of Shakespeare's text to the audience while working with *commedia dell' arte* techniques that I later developed in a production of *Romeo and Juliet* as Granada Artist-in-Residence at the University of California at Davis in 1998; I had the chance to explore this relationship again in the context of Shakespeare's Globe Theatre in London with the Winter Players of Globe Education (1999–2003). What I learned from this work is that openness to the audience creates energy, because the audience quickly understands that their presence is recognized, and that they are part of the action in the room. They feel that if they give, they will receive, sometimes the more they give, the more they will get back. The interaction builds that virtuous circle or spiral of energy that is important to bring the text to life/keep the text alive.

The exercise is particularly useful if you are working with students on a proscenium arch stage where there are such strong conventions about the fourth wall, which actors play to the exclusion of the observing audience. One way to break down that barrier is to give the actor the license (even the responsibility) to react to noises from the audience, to respond to them rather than to override them. It may not always be appropriate to acknowledge the noise-maker, but often it is. The audience is a character in Shakespeare's plays, if not the major character, because at the end of the day it has all the information and any one character on stage only has part of it. If the production makes room for the audience as a character in the play, it brings the production out beyond the fourth wall because at times the audience has to be addressed directly, not be treated merely as a voyeur. Making room for the audience begins to create different kinds of possibilities for staging, because you can potentially look at the audience, but talk to another character on stage – it may not be naturalistic, but it's clear to the audience what is happening.

Acknowledging the audience is also helpful in terms of soliloquies, which are usually either direct address or problem-solving speeches. When the actor gets to a soliloquy, if the audience is involved, the character-part can work it out publicly rather than experiencing a private moment inside the brain. The actor can develop the performance openly, with vulnerability, acknowledging the audience while working the soliloquy out, rather than working it out inside an isolated bubble. When the soliloquy is done inside the bubble, an audience has to go to the actor rather than the actor coming to them. The experience is not being shared and the audience has no right to be carried along with the action: it's private to the character-part. The private bubble also signals that the actor is not committing, that the characterization has already been fixed, that the character is not undergoing the process of change *here and now, with us*; it also often means that there's an inner world of modern psychology going on that often does not work well for Shakespeare. But openness that includes the audience in whatever struggling, grappling and shifting of position the character-part is going through, leaves the audience more persuaded that the new course of action has emerged alive onstage.

There are many other tools for empowering the actor's use of language, and these last four are only sketched in to suggest where I would start with more experienced actors. Beyond these there are innumerable other training practices, including those involving gesture, poetic device, rhetoric, as well as different kinds of sound and movement, but they lie outside the scope of this chapter.

Discussion

Shakespeare's spoken language presents new challenges for teaching. Ways of life are changing, and many people are growing up in cities where they rarely leave their buildings, their interactions are less direct and more mediated, not least by the tools of digital culture – email, instant messaging, cell-phone texting, and so on. Of course there are many places where speaking to others is still vital – in sports, for example, or in school hallways – but even in the small sphere of actor training, it seems to me that there's plenty of evidence that the way young people use their jaws and mouths has radically changed in the past ten years at least. Voice trainers say that the tongue is simply not as strong a muscle as it used to be, and one of the basic exercises they have had to do is get people to read out loud just to strengthen the tongue. Another issue faced by voice trainers is that living in densely urban cities, people begin to minimize the range of sounds they can hear, and it tends to be the lower registers they favor. The result is that people have to be trained for longer to hear the higher ranges of expressive speech. If you cannot hear the note, you will not be able to speak it, and unless you can hear a greater range of sounds, you are not able to access the full range of color of your vocal instrument – or, finally, of Shakespeare's human instruments, his characters.

There is another factor limiting the range of voice that students can acquire, and that is the cultural attitude toward accent and dialect. On television, in particular, but also in film and radio, there has been an evening out of differences in intonation and stress that define local and regional ways of speaking. There are some teachers who even think that Shakespeare should only be spoken in a specific version of "received pronunciation," the BBC norm in the UK that has proved useful in countering class discrimination by making it possible to hide one's social background; the "nonregional speech" of network-television news anchors is the cognate accent in the US (though Peter Jennings's Canadian vowels, or Dan Rather's Texas twang are occasionally just audible). The danger is that these standardized pronunciations tend to disconnect actors from their life experience in expressing the full range of English; while modern actors need to learn to develop their expressive means technically, they should also understand that staying connected to dialect, to the color and rhythm and weight and historical particularity of a local accent is the most immediate, though not the only, way of connecting Shakespeare's language to the breathing, speaking body.

My experience in teaching semi-professionals at MFA level, and working with actors on productions of Shakespeare's plays, is that these issues have had an impact throughout the professional theatre. Even with professional actors working in internationally recognized theatres, you can tell if the actor has been trained outside the conservatory system. In the UK, theatres depend on conservatories to teach the actors how to speak Shakespearean language because there is no knowledge passed down from generation to generation of actors, there are no companies where older members teach younger ones, no apprenticeships when you learn from the experienced actors and from your peers. Nor are you given sufficient rehearsal time in most repertory theatres to explore and learn the craft as you do it. This seems to be true in the United States and Canada as well, except in places such as Ashland and Stratford where there are enough resources to teach the actors how to speak while rehearsing.

This is a surprising situation, arising as it does in spite of the fact that Shakespeare is the most-produced playwright in the world, and despite the widely held sense that if you can deal with Shakespearean language, you can respond creatively to other people's language in all walks of life. When you work on Shakespearean language it teaches you and teaches you and teaches you. Most actors, when they learn how to inhabit Shakespeare's language say it's such an intensely satisfying experience that they get hooked on it: the text asks you a question and the language is there for you, there's always an answer. You can simply take those tools and apply them to any life situation; they offer a way of understanding and empowering yourself within language as a whole.

REFERENCES AND FURTHER READING

Barton, John (1984). *Playing Shakespeare*. London: Methuen.

Berry, Cicely (1987). *The Actor and His Text*. London: Virgin.

Lichtenfels, Peter & Hunter, Lynette (1999). "From Stage to Page: Character through Theatre Practices in *Romeo and Juliet*." In S. Chew & A. Stead (eds.) *Translating Life: Studies in Trans-positional Aesthetics*. Liverpool: Liverpool University Press, pp. 53–74.

Parker, Patricia (1996). *Shakespeare from the Margins: Language, Culture, Context*. Chicago, IL: University of Chicago Press.

Wright, George (1988). *Shakespeare's Metrical Art*. Berkeley: University of California Press.

Index

Works by Shakespeare are entered under title; productions are entered under the name of the director or company. Page numbers in *italics* signify illustrations.